WESTERN EUROPEAN
POLITICAL PARTIES
A COMPREHENSIVE GUIDE

WESTERN EUROPEAN POLITICAL PARTIES

A COMPREHENSIVE GUIDE

LONGMAN INTERNATIONAL REFERENCE

Edited and compiled by
FRANCIS JACOBS

with contributions by the following:

John Fitzmaurice, Doosie Foldal, David Lowe,
Maria Mendrinou, James Spence and Dr Roland Sturm

WESTERN EUROPEAN POLITICAL PARTIES
A COMPREHENSIVE GUIDE

Published by Longman Group UK Limited, Westgate House,
The High, Harlow, Essex, CM20 1YR, United Kingdom.
Telephone (0279) 442601
Telex 81491 Padlog
Facsimile (0279) 444501

Distributed exclusively in the United States
and Canada by Gale Research Company
Book Tower, Detroit, Michigan 48226, USA

ISBN 0-582-00113-7 (Longman)

0-8103-7482-X (Gale)

British Library Cataloguing in Publication Data
Jacobs, Francis B. (Francis Brendan), 1951–
   Western European political parties: A comprehensive guide —
   (Longman International Reference)
   1. Western Europe. Political parties
   I. Title   II. Series
   324.24

   ISBN 0-582-00113-7

Printed in Great Britain by
Richard Clay Ltd, Bungay, Suffolk

To my parents
David and Mariagrazia Jacobs

Contents

CONTENTS

III WESTERN EUROPEAN POLITICAL GROUPINGS   *Francis Jacobs*

Introduction

The objective of this book is to provide up-to-date information on individual political parties within their national, regional and European contexts. The book is thus divided into three sections, the political parties of the countries of the European Community, those of other Western European democracies (with all countries having been included apart from those, such as Monaco and Andorra, which do not have a party political system) and finally Western European political groupings (including party groups within the European Parliament, Nordic Council, Council of Europe and Western European Union; international groupings, such as the Socialist, Liberal and Christian Democratic Internationals, have not been included as separate entries).

For each country, there is first a general section, comprising a brief introduction to the country, its political institutions (electoral system, type of government, etc.), recent political history (usually in short summary form) and main features of its political system (structure, cleavages, topical policy issues and unusual characteristics). The emphasis in all these sections is on providing those background facts which enable the reader to place the sections on the individual parties within their proper perspective. Where appropriate, these introductions are also accompanied by a map of the country (showing its main regions and cities, and, where possible, electoral boundaries) and a table (or tables) of recent electoral results, generally going back to 1945.

The individual parties are then examined under a number of headings. After a brief factual introduction there are sections on party history, support (the regional and social implantation of the party), organization, policies (beginning, where appropriate, with a discussion of the party's current place in the national political spectrum), and personalities (the main leadership figures within the party).

Where parties take part in elections under wider umbrella organizations (e.g. Izquierda Unida in Spain) these have also been described, with an outline of their structures and methods of co-ordination.

The emphasis has been primarily on parties which are currently represented in national parliaments. The major parties are described first and the smaller parties are covered in less detail at the end. Extraparliamentary parties and movements are given little emphasis, with the limited exception of historically important parties which have lost parliamentary representation, of new parties which show significant potential for growth, and of parties strongly represented at regional or local level.

Regional parties are covered in the main text, unless the regional political system differs so considerably from the national one (e.g. where there is a high degree of autonomy, or where regional rather than national parties are politically dominant) that a separate sub-section is needed. These begin with a general introduction to the region and its political institutions and characteristics, and then cover the major and minor parties which are active within the region; regional branches of national parties are only covered when they have a distinctive identity of their own.

Although each chapter has a similar structure to facilitate easy reference, the length of each section has inevitably had to vary from country to country. Certain countries, for example, with unusual constitutional features (e.g. Belgium) or where most of the political parties in their current form are only of recent formation (e.g. Turkey and France), have required longer introductions and shorter sections on the individual parties.

INTRODUCTION

The editor has put considerable emphasis on some of the smaller European countries, whose political systems and parties are often less familiar. Regional and green parties have also developed considerably in recent years and yet are often given scant treatment in political literature. The editor has tried to cover these parties to a greater extent, although information on them is not always easy to obtain.

Much of the background information on which the book is based has been supplied by the parties themselves. The editor has also conducted extensive interviews with national and European Parliament politicians and party secretariats, and he wishes to thank them all for their time and help. Strenuous attempts have been made to ensure that the book contains the most recent information possible (up to early 1989), but the subject matter of this book is peculiarly vulnerable to sudden changes, such as turnover in leadership, mergers or disbanding of parties, or major alterations in a country's political landscape after new elections. It would be greatly appreciated if any errors or major alterations in a party's status could be brought to the editor's attention. More general suggestions and comments are also welcomed, so that any subsequent edition may constitute a more complete source of reference.

The editor would like to thank warmly the six people who have contributed chapters in this book: John Fitzmaurice (Belgium), David Lowe (France), Maria Mendrinou (Greece), Dr Roland Sturm (Federal Republic of Germany), James Spence (Malta) and Doosie Foldal (Sweden).

He would also like to thank all those friends and colleagues who have offered comments on individual parties or countries. Particular thanks to Katherine Meenan, who helped to launch the project on a rainy day in Bantry.

Also special thanks to Anne Gray (and her assistant, Jan Brady) and Marion Cheshire, who with great patience and skill succeeded in deciphering the editor's hieroglyphics, and to Susan, who provided the greatest of support in the course of what turned out to be a marathon project.

Francis Jacobs   *May 1989*

The publishers wish to thank staff at various embassies and government departments who have supplied information used in some of the maps in this book. The maps of Austria, France, West Germany and the Netherlands were supplied by Carpress International Press Agency, Brussels, Belgium. Thanks are also due to the Economist Publications Ltd. for permission to adapt the maps of Cyprus, Denmark, Finland, Greece, Iceland, Ireland, Italy, Luxembourg, Norway, Portugal, Spain, Sweden and Switzerland from the *World Atlas of Elections* (1986). Copyright for these maps remains with the artist, Richard Natkiel. In addition, the publishers are grateful to the *Turkish Daily News*, Ankara, for the use of an adaption of the map of Turkey which appeared in the November 27th, 1987, edition. Finally, thanks are due to *Le Monde* for permission to reproduce the table on p 105 from the issue dated April 3, 1987, and to authors/publishers of various publications for the reproduction of tables in the section on the Federal Republic of Germany, as cited in full in the captions.

I   EC COUNTRIES

Belgium

John Fitzmaurice

The country

Belgium is a country of 11,779 square miles, with a population of 9.9 million. Sixty per cent of its land area is in French-speaking Wallonia and 40 per cent in Dutch-speaking Flanders (the form of Dutch spoken in Flanders is called Flemish). The capital, Brussels, has a French-speaking majority but is surrounded by Flemish-speaking districts. Of the Belgian population 58 per cent live in more densely populated Flanders, 32 per cent in Wallonia and 10 per cent in Brussels. The language frontier between Flemish and French-speaking areas is not a tidy one. Besides the anomaly of Brussels (complicated by the fact that French-speaking commuters into Brussels are settling in Flemish-speaking communes in the suburbs) a particular problem is posed by the district of Voeren (Fourons), which is a French-speaking majority enclave between Francophone Liège and the Dutch border, but in the Flemish-speaking province of Limburg.

There is also a small German-speaking minority of around 70,000 in the eastern cantons of Wallonia. There is a large immigrant population of around 850,000. Many of the earlier immi-

Map of Belgium showing provincial and language boundaries.

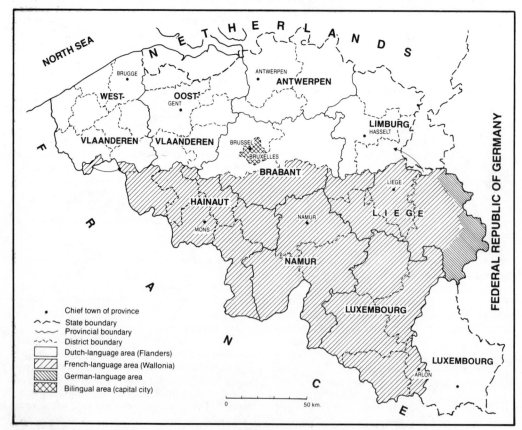

Source: Institut Belge d'information et de documentation.

grants come from other European countries (notably Italians working in the traditional industrial areas of Wallonia), but there are now increasing numbers of non-Europeans as well, including considerable numbers of North Africans, especially in inner Brussels.

In religious terms Belgium is predominantly Catholic.

Political institutions

Until 1980 Belgium was a unitary state, but as a result of political developments since then it has become less unitary without becoming fully federalist. Besides the central government there are three regions, Flanders, Wallonia and Brussels, and three cultural communities, the Flemish, French and German communities.

The central government is responsible for foreign policy (except in those areas devolved to the communities), defence and internal security, macro-economic policy, those aspects of industrial and social policy (such as the level of pensions and benefits) which remain national, those aspects of education where national uniformity is retained, and transport.

Belgium is a constitutional monarchy. The King is a titular head of state only, though assuming some importance in the formation of governments when election results point to no clear government majority. The executive consists of a Cabinet of about 15 ministers, headed by the Prime Minister (and several deputy prime ministers, to balance coalition parties), appointed by the King and responsible to the legislature. According to the Constitution, the Cabinet must include an equal number of French and Dutch speakers (the Prime Minister is an exception, but he is now in practice normally Flemish).

The Parliament is bicameral. The House of Representatives consists of 212 members elected for four years (although early dissolution is possible) in multi-member constituencies (each electoral district, or *arrondissement* is accorded a number of seats proportional to its population revealed in each census, with the number ranging from two to 34) by the d'Hondt list system of proportional representation.

The Senate currently consists of 183 members. There are three categories of senators, 106 directly elected in multi-member constituencies by proportional representation, 51 elected by the provincial councils, and 26 co-opted by the elected senators. The process is, in practice, in the hands of the political parties and produces a very similar result to that from the House of Representatives, though some variations may occur. (However, the Senate may be reformed. The proposal is that it should consist of 212 members elected for a fixed term of four years, not subject to prior dissolution.)

In theory both Houses of the legislature have equal powers, with some minor exceptions, but political practice gives primacy to the House of Representatives.

The unique feature of devolved government in Belgium is that it is not based merely on territorial units (as it would be in a classic federal structure), but on a mix of territorial regions and overlapping linguistic and cultural communities. The main reason for this complexity is to try to overcome the special problems posed by Brussels in particular.

The Flemish region consists of the four Flemish provinces of Antwerp, East Flanders, West Flanders and Limburg and the Flemish area of Brabant (Leuven and Hal-Vilvoorde). The Walloon region consists of the four traditional Walloon provinces of Hainaut, Liège, Namur and Luxembourg, as well as a small part of Brabant. The Brussels region consists of the 19 communes making up Greater Brussels. The Flemish community is made up of the population of the Flemish region, plus the Dutch speakers in Brussels. The French community of Belgium is made up of the population of the Walloon region, plus French speakers in Brussels. The German community consists of some 70,000 German speakers who live in the Eupen-Malmédy area close to the German border.

The regions have more important powers than those of the communities, covering a large range of matters in the social and economic fields, such as employment, energy (but not nuclear energy), planning, housing, water and environmental matters. The communities are responsible for cultural matters (such as language and media policy, sport and tourism, training and scientific research), so-called "personalized matters" (e.g. certain aspects of health and welfare policy) and also certain education matters.

In theory each region and each community is meant to have both a council (a parliamentary assembly consisting not of separately elected members, but of the nationally elected representatives and senators from the appropriate regions and language groups) and an executive.

The current practice is more complex.

In Flanders the regional and community institutions have been combined, with a common 186-member council and nine-member executive. Flemish-speaking representatives and senators elected in Brussels (thus wearing a community council "hat" only) may not vote in Flemish "regional" matters.

In Wallonia there are separate councils and

executives for the Walloon regions and for the French community.

Brussels was excluded until 1989 from the regionalization process, although French and Flemish-speaking parliamentarians from Brussels have participated in their respective community councils. For some Brussels regional matters there was a "preparatory" regional structure, including an "executive" within the national government (rather unrepresentative of the capital's electorate, and called the "ministerial committee for the Brussels region"). Regional council elections were held on June 18, 1989, to elect 75 regional councillors for a five-year term of office (63 were Francophones and 12 Flemish speakers). There is an executive of five ministers (the president and two others being Francophones and two being Flemish speakers). The Flemish minority on the council is able to block a project for a 30-day period. These bodies also exercise by delegation some of the powers of the two communities in the capital.

The reforms of the 1980s both created a political dynamic for greater reform and showed many structural weaknesses (overlapping powers, inadequate financial and administrative infrastructure). Thus the legislature elected in 1988 was *"constituant"* and the Martens VIII Cabinet has embarked on an ambitious programme of further reforms. The first phase, devolving education and some other areas to the regions and communities is complete. The second phase (dealing with Brussels and the financial arrangements) is now being initiated and a third phase (restructuring the Senate and the national level) is well in the future. Overall, some 40 per cent of state expenditure will be devolved and when the third phase is completed, the regional/community assemblies will be directly elected. The Brussels regional council has been directly elected from its initiation.

Finally, in the German-speaking cantons (too small to have their own regional structure) there is a directly elected 25-member German community council (some matters within the competence of the Walloon region may be delegated to it by mutual agreement) and a community executive. Otherwise this area is part of the wider Walloon region.

Below the regions and communities are the four Walloon provinces (Hainaut, Namur, Liège and Luxembourg), the four Flemish provinces (West Vlaanderen, Oost Vlaanderen, Antwerpen and Limburg) and bilingual Brabant (which includes Brussels). Each province has a provincial council (elected for four years within cantons — the numbers within the provincial councils range from 50 to 90) and a

rather weak six-member permanent committee (the executive) elected by each council. The committee is presided over by the powerful provincial governor, who is appointed by the Crown.

The lowest tier of government in Belgium incorporates its 589 communes (308 in Flanders, 262 in Wallonia and 19 in Brussels), with their communal councils and local executives (consisting of a mayor and a college of *'echevins'* or the "executive"). The communal councils are elected for six-year terms. Mayors are appointed by the King (i.e. by the Minister of the Interior) who does not have to respect local political majorities, although he usually does in practice.

Brief political history

1830   Belgian Independence and promulgation of new Liberal Constitution.

1830–47 Period of "Unionist" dominance (national coalition of Catholics and Liberals, declining after 1840).

1847–84 Period of Liberal dominance (with two short interludes of "Unionist" and Catholic rule), culminating in a radical Liberal government after 1878.

1884– Uninterrupted Catholic rule (Liberals
1914   gradually lose their position as the major opposition party to the Socialists, especially after the extension of the suffrage and the introduction of proportional representation in the 1890s).

1914–18 Occupation of most of Belgium by the Germans (Belgian government in exile in France incorporates Socialist ministers for the first time, occupation of Belgium also gives great stimulus to radical Flemish nationalism).

1919   Introduction of universal suffrage for men.

1918–39 Series of short-lived governments (mainly Catholic-Liberal coalitions or grand coalitions of Catholics, Liberals and Socialists, but also one Catholic-Socialist left-of-centre coalition lasting a year from 1925–26).

1940–44 Belgium occupied by Nazi Germany.

1945– Further sequence of mainly short-lived
present governments, of different permutations of the Christian Democrats, Socialists and Liberals (although there have only been Christian Democratic and Socialist prime ministers).

1948   Women get the vote.

1949   Belgium becomes a founder-member of NATO.

1950	Referendum on the future of Leopold III (overall majority of 57.6 per cent in favour of King's return, with big majority in Flanders, but minority votes in Brussels and Wallonia), but King later forced to abdicate in favour of his son after referendum result not accepted in Wallonia.
1952	Belgium joins European Coal and Steel Community.
1957	Belgium joins EC.
1960	Granting of independence to the Belgian Congo.
1970	Packet of constitutional reforms providing for a semi-federal Belgian political structure, recognizing three cultural communities and three regions (1970 reform only established general principles and procedures, opening up lengthy period of parliamentary debate over how to implement the principles).
1977	Egmont Pact to develop 1970 constitutional reforms is itself not implemented.
1980	New constitutional settlement extends scope of 1970 reforms. New regional and community institutions are established, but there is still no agreement over the regional status of Brussels.

Main features of the current political system

There are six broad groupings in Belgian political life, of varied size and importance and mostly subdivided into two parties, one for each linguistic community. These groupings are: Socialists (PS and SP), Christian parties (CVP and PSC), Liberals (PVV and PRL), Regional parties (FDF, VU and Vlaams Blok), Greens (AGALEV and ECOLO) and the Far Left (PCB/KPB and PVDA).

Coalition-making is always complicated by the unequal strength of the Christian Democrats and the Socialists in each region. When the reform of the state has been at the centre of the political stage, a further complication for coalition-building has been the fact that the Constitution imposes special majorities for certain laws. Thus revision of the Constitution requires one Parliament to adopt a statement of intention to revise specified articles, and for amendments to pass both Houses in the next Parliament by a two-thirds majority. Other special laws on the structure of the state or language laws require a majority in each language grouping in each House. These requirements mean that coalitions at these moments need a wider basis than a simple parliamentary majority.

Apart from a period of one-party Catholic rule (1950–54) Belgian governments since universal suffrage have always been coalitions. The main permutations have been Christian Democrat-Socialist (the most popular), Christian Democrat-Liberal (1974–77, 1981–88) and Liberal-Socialist (1954–58, now unlikely). Some or all of the federalist parties (RW, FDF, VU) have been added to coalitions when, as in the 1970s or now, the reform of the state is the main issue. Otherwise, when broader majorities are needed, as in periods of crisis, a tripartite coalition of the three traditional parties is preferred.

Belgian politics have had a number of major divisions, notably between left and right, and between clerical and lay parties (anti-clericalism has been a marked feature of Belgian politics, and differences have been particularly sharp over the education question).

The central division, however, especially in recent years, has been between Flemish and Walloons.

Belgium was an artificial creation of the great powers, established as a state in 1830 to meet their interests and without any real cement for national unity. From 1830 to 1980 Belgium remained a unitary state. For much of this time, however, there was a considerable imbalance in power between the two language groups. Wallonia was the centre of Belgian heavy industry and the institutions of the Belgian state were dominated by a Francophone bourgeoisie, who ensured that it was practically a unilingual as well as unitary state. The Flemish remained in a subordinate position, and Flanders remained a relatively poor peasant society.

The situation gradually evolved. Flemish rights were asserted ever more vigorously, and Flemish people gained increasing political powers. Wallonia's traditional industry entered into crisis, whereby Flanders began to develop new and more dynamic industries and services. Moreover Flanders had a higher birth rate. Eventually the changing balance of political and economic power led to a developing Walloon counterpart to Flemish nationalism, and to increasing pressure for greater separation of the two communities.

Disputes over the extent and form of devolution have thus been a dominating feature of Belgian politics. Major disputes have arisen in two areas. One is the periphery of Brussels, where an increase of French-speaking commuters in originally Dutch-speaking villages has led to demands for transfers of these communes to Brussels (resisted by the Flemish) and for

Belgian elections (Percentages of vote and seats won in House of Representatives 1945–present)

	1946	1949	1950	1954	1958	1961	1965	1968	1971	1974	1977	1978	1981	1985	1987
Christian Democrats PSC	42.5% (92)	43.6% (105)	47.7% (108)	41.1% (95)	46.5% (104)	41.5% (96)	34.4% (77)	31.8% (69)	30.1% (67)	32.3% (72)	36.0% (80)	36.3% (82)	7.1% (18)	7.6% (20)	8.0% (19)
CVP													19.3% (43)	19.8% (49)	19.5% (43)
Socialists PS	31.6% (69)	29.8% (66)	34.5% (77)	37.3% (86)	35.8% (84)	36.7% (84)	28.8% (64)	28.0% (59)	26.4% (61)	26.7% (59)	27.1% (62)	25.4% (58)	12.7% (35)	13.3% (35)	15.7% (40)
SP													12.4% (26)	17.1% (32)	14.9% (32)
Liberals PRL	8.9% (17)	15.2% (29)	11.2% (20)	12.1% (25)	11.1% (21)	12.3% (20)	21.6% (48)	20.9% (47)	15.9% (34)	15.2% (30)	15.5% (33)	16.4% (37)	8.6% (24)	10.2% (24)	9.4% (23)
PVV													12.9% (28)	10.7% (22)	11.5% (25)
FDF/RW							2.3% (5)	5.9% (12)	11.2% (24)	10.9% (25)	7.1% (15)	7.1% (15)	4.2% (8)	1.2% (3)	1.2% (3)
Volksunie		2.1% (0)		2.2% (1)	1.9% (1)	3.5% (5)	6.7% (12)	9.8% (20)	11.1% (21)	10.2% (22)	10.0% (20)	7.0% (14)	9.7% (20)	8.5% (16)	8.0% (16)
Vlaams Blok											—	1.4% (1)	1.1% (1)	1.4% (1)	1.9% (2)
Communists	12.7% (23)	7.5% (12)	4.7% (7)	3.6% (4)	1.9% (2)	3.1% (5)	4.6% (6)	3.3% (5)	3.1% (5)	3.2% (4)	2.1% (2)	3.2% (4)	2.3% (2)	1.2% (1)	0.8% (0)
Ecologists ECOLO												—	2.1% (2)	2.5% (5)	2.6% (3)
AGALEV													2.3% (2)	3.7% (4)	4.5% (6)
Anti-tax (UDRT/RAD)												0.9% (1)	2.7% (3)	1.2% (1)	0.1% (0)
Others	2.2% (1)					2.9% (2)	2.1% (0)						2.4% (0)	2.3% (0)	1.7% (0)

requests for special facilities (such as French-language schools) for Francophones (largely accepted by the Flemish). The other flashpoint has been the dispute over Voeren (Fourons), and over its controversial Francophone mayor José Happart, who refused to use Dutch as required for official duties as mayor in an officially Dutch-speaking province, or even to take a test to prove that he could use it. Happart's adoption by a major political party, the Walloon Socialists, and his election as member of the European Parliament have helped to intensify divisions over this issue, and incidentally to widen the gap between the Walloon and Flemish Socialists.

Since the first reform of the state in 1970, which resulted in the enactment of the new devolution articles of the Constitution, the basis of two distinct political systems in Flanders and Wallonia have been laid, with an awkward overlap in Brussels. Between 1968 and 1978 each of the three main Belgian political families, the Christian Democrats, the Socialists and the Liberals, each split into independent Walloon and Flemish parties. Over time the divergencies between the two branches of each family has extended beyond language and community issues, to the point where one can talk of quite distinctive parties which are evolving in different directions. Political trends and voting patterns have followed different paths in Wallonia and Flanders.

Thus, in the 1985 election, the four parties of the coalition fared differently. The CVP gained in Flanders and Brussels, but the PSC only gained in Wallonia, losing in Brussels. The PRL gained support, but the Flemish Liberals saw a notable fall in their share of the vote in Flanders, but a small increase in Brussels. Both the PS and SP gained in both Wallonia and Brussels. The *Front des Francophones* (FDF), which only stands in Brussels, lost heavily, to the point where its continued existence could be called into question (a drop from 22.6 per cent to 10.9 per cent). In 1987, the CVP continued to lose support, whereas the PSC gained in Wallonia, but lost in Brussels. The Liberal "couple" saw the reverse phenomenon: PRL losses and PVV gains. Overall, there was a net shift to the left in Wallonia and a shift to the right in Flanders. The outgoing PRL/PSC coalition lost its majority, which had always been razor-edged in Wallonia and the French community, whereas the CVP/PVV majority was maintained in Flanders. The "green" sensitivity of the regions has also varied. ECOLO obtained only 2.8 per cent of the total national vote, a gain of a mere 0.1 per cent, whereas AGALEV obtained 4.9 per cent (+ 1.1 per cent) in 1987. Indeed, ECOLO actually lost seats in the Chamber, in Brussels it showed no gains and in Wallonia advanced from 6.2 per cent to 6.5 per cent.

The balance of political power is thus also quite different with a different one of the traditional parties dominating each region. For all these reasons there are separate sections on the Walloon and Flemish political systems below.

Nevertheless these differences should not be exaggerated either. Belgium is a small country in which some centralization is inevitable. Brussels is easily accessible from anywhere in Flanders and Wallonia, and is still the main political centre of the country, especially as the Flemish regional and community institutions and administration, and those of the Francophone community, are all located in the city.

Belgium is still some way from becoming a full federal state, and despite far-reaching structural changes it is not clear to what extent there has been a real change in political mentality. The central government is still more prestigious than the devolved executives. It is unclear to what extent this will be changed by further reforms, and, in particular, by direct election of the devolved assemblies. National developments still tend to take priority over regional politics and predetermine regional coalition alliances.

The Flemish political system

The Flemish movement has developed in three distinct phases. Before World War I the emphasis was on ensuring greater equality for the Flemish language (in the 19th century Flemish could not be used in Parliament or in the courts, and was not used in the school system, and its disadvantages were only slowly removed).

World War I gave a significant stimulus to the Flemish movement, which profited from the new circumstances created by the German occupation (such as a German decree pronouncing the university of Ghent a Flemish institution). Between the wars considerable steps were taken towards clearer linguistic divisions in Belgium on the basis of the territorial principle, with bilingualism gradually fading.

During World War II a number of radical Flemish nationalists (such as the *Vlaams Nationaal Verbond* and the group *De Vlag*) openly collaborated with the Germans, and this set back the Flemish movement for the first decade after the war.

From the 1950s onwards radical federalism again developed, and intensified over such issues as the school war in the mid 1950s, the language census of 1960, Brussels and its language boundaries, and the division of Leuven (Louvain) University into separate French and Flemish Universities in the 1960s. In 1954 an explicitly Flemish (but not right-wing extremist) nationalist party, the *Volksunie*, had again been created.

Flemish nationalism thus has a much longer history than Walloon regionalism, and there is a greater state consciousness in Flanders. The Flemish political system is thus further developed, and more use has been made of regional powers.

In Flanders the regional and community institutions set up after 1980 have been amalgamated into one. As the size of the councils is related to population and the Flemish population has risen faster than that of Wallonia the Flemish council has risen in number from 182 in 1981 to 186 in 1987. The 12-member executive must include one member from Brussels.

From 1981–85 the executive was composed in proportion to the parties represented in the Flemish council. After 1985 the executive was run by a coalition of the Flemish Christian Democrats (the CVP) and the Flemish Liberals (the PVV), and these two parties initially sought to prolong this coalition after the 1987 elections as they would still have had an overall (if reduced) majority. Because of the new developments at national level, however, with the return of the Socialists into government, a proportionally-based coalition was again re-established in Flanders, with the CVP, PVV, Flemish Socialists (SP) and the *Volksunie* all participating in the executive. This was despite PVV objections to this change, which led to them refusing to participate in the negotiations for a new government programme, which was therefore agreed without them. Compared to Wallonia there has been greater stability at the head of the executive with Gaston Geens of the CVP as its leader since 1981.

The dominant party within the Flemish political system is the Flemish Christian Democratic Party, the CVP, which is the largest political party in the whole of Belgium, and has generally provided the Belgian Prime Minister in recent years.

The second-largest Flemish party has generally been the Socialist Party, and the third the Liberals or PVV (although in 1981 this had more seats than the Socialists).

The most striking feature, therefore, of the Flemish political system, has been the persisting centre-right dominance within the region, unlike the situation in Wallonia.

A second feature has been a sharp division between Catholic and lay parties. This has been somewhat attenuated in recent years, and both

the Liberals and the Socialists have attempted to open up their ranks to Catholic support (the so-called *doorbraak* or "breakthrough") with somewhat more success in the case of the Liberals than in that of the Socialists. Shared lay values, however, have not made it easy for the Liberals and Socialists (who differ greatly on economic policy) to join forces against the dominant CVP, except occasionally in local government. For instance, there is now a Socialist-Liberal coalition for the first time in the city of Ghent, and it will be interesting to see if this is an isolated occurrence, or is an indication of possible future developments.

A third feature of the Flemish political system has been that the regionalist parties, especially the *Volksunie*, appear to be a more permanent feature of the political landscape than their Walloon equivalents.

There is also a more extreme separatist wing than in Wallonia, as exemplified by the *Vlaams Blok*.

Composition of Flemish council			
	1987	*1985*	*1981*
CVP	65	74	65
SP	49	48	39
PVV	36	33	42
VU	24	23	30
AGALEV	9	6	3
Vlaams Blok	3	1	1
UDRT-RAD	—	—	1
Total	186	185	181

The Walloon political system

Of the two distinct political systems in Belgium, the Walloon system is the least developed. Walloon political consciousness initially developed as a defensive response to the rising tide of Flemish nationalism and the resulting recognition that Wallonia too had its own distinct political culture, whose main characteristics were more lay and progressive than the more Catholic, conservative and nationalist tendencies of the Flemish political culture. It was for these reasons that the *Parti Socialiste* (PS) became converted to federalism by the early 1980s.

The Walloon system has its own structure, which is not symmetrical with the Flemish system, and its own distinct institutions, party system and media circuit — all vital elements of a political system.

Unlike Flanders, where the regional and community institutions have been amalgamated into one, there are two distinct sets of institutions in Wallonia with overlapping membership in the councils (parliamentary assemblies). As in Flanders, the members of these councils are not specially elected, but are formed from the representatives and directly-elected senators of the Walloon Provinces and the Arrondissement of Nivelles for the regional council, plus the French-speaking deputies and senators elected in Brussels for the community council only. The German community council is specially elected.

The size of the councils (except the German community council) is variable, both for demographic and linguistic reasons. The Walloon and Brussels electorates are falling, at least relative to the total electorate. The Walloon electorate only rose by under 10,000 between 1985 and 1987, against a rise of 40,000 in Flanders. Indeed, the number of people actually voting in Wallonia fell by 1,000 between 1981 and 1987. Thus, the Walloon regional council has 104 members, as against 106 in 1981. The size of the community council is also affected by demographic change, but a second factor also comes into play. In Brussels electors can vote for either Flemish or French or bilingual lists. As a result, the number of members in each language group can vary. The share of the vote going to French-speaking lists has risen from 64.9 per cent in 1981 to 72 per cent in 1987 and the share of Flemish lists has also risen from 22 per cent to 24 per cent and bilingual lists have virtually disappeared. Thus, the community council in 1987 had 132 members, as against 133 in 1985, and 137 in 1981.

During the first legislature (1981–1985) following the implementation of the first reform of the state, all the executives were proportionately composed. The Walloon and French community executives were tripartite executives (PS/PRL/PSC), with a PS president in both cases. From 1985, the normal parliamentary

principle has applied and hence the executives are now negotiated coalitions unlike in Flanders, where there is again a proportionally–based executive. The Walloon region executive has six members and the community executive has three members. The executives are elected by the councils and remain responsible to them, but can only be removed by the so-called "constructive" motion of no-confidence, based on the German model. A motion of no-confidence must at the same time elect a new executive.

The political profiles of the Walloon region and Brussels are quite different from Flanders and indeed from each other. Wallonia is dominated by the PS, which comes close to an absolute majority in the Walloon council and is by far the strongest party in the community council. In 1987, the PS registered 43.9 per cent of the vote in Wallonia. Even in a poor election such as 1981, it held 36.3 per cent, which makes it the regionally dominant party. In Brussels, the PRL is the leading party, but in linguistically and politically fragmented Brussels, it only obtained 25.3 per cent of the vote and the Liberal family (including the 5.8 per cent of the PVV) 31.1 per cent. Apart from the 1985–87 legislature there has been a progressive majority in the Walloon region and to a lesser extent in the community council. Thus, the PS could count on the support of small progressive parties such as the ECOLO, RW, FDF, PCB to provide the additional votes to reach a majority.

The PRL and PSC made a coalition deal at regional and community level for two terms (eight years) in 1985. As the table shows, this was an uncharacteristically narrow base for a Belgian government. This was in the heyday of anti-Socialist confrontation politics. Consensus was not in vogue. The deal in a certain sense negated the idea of regional devolution, in that it deliberately presupposed the same coalition at regional and community level as at the national

Composition of Walloon council and community council

	Regional council seats			Community council seats		
	1987	*1985*	*1981*	*1987*	*1985*	*1981*
PS	51	47	47	60	53	53
PRL	25	26	28	35	37	35
PSC	25	26	22	28	33	26
ECOLO	2	4	3	5	7	5
FDF	1	—	—	4	4	12
PCB	—	—	3	—	—	2
UDRT	—	—	—	—	1	3
RW	—	—	2	—	—	—
VU	—	1	—	—	1	—
Total	104	104	106	132	133	137

level. It was only possible by the illegal exclusion of a VU senator who had been elected in Brabant by a quirk of the electoral system (now blocked). He was however legally elected, absurd though his presence may have been. Without him, the coalition had 52 seats out of 103 in the region and 67 out of 132 in the community. After the 1987 elections, this coalition lost its majority. Matters were made more complex by the national situation. The PS had begun separate talks with the FDF and ECOLO, but extended these to include the PSC when the national five-party talks got under way (PS/SP/CVP/PSC/VU). At this point, ECOLO, with whom an initial agreement had been reached, left the talks. A pact between the PS/PSC/FDF was reached in the region and the community. There are three PS (including the president) and one PSC minister in the community executive. The FDF got the chair of the community council for its former president, Mme Spaak. This illustrates several points about the Walloon political system: there is a progressive majority, but the PS prefers to subordinate this card to the national situation; ECOLO are *koalitionsfähig*, as a very moderate green party; national concerns still largely predetermine the shape of coalitions at the regional and community levels.

1. The Socialists

The first Socialist Party, the *Parti Ouvrier Belge*, was founded in 1885, avoiding the term "Socialist", which was even then considered a threat to the party's essentially pragmatic outlook. Its basic doctrinal charter, the *Charte de Quaregnon* (1894), remained in force long after its quasi-revolutionary rhetoric had in the pre-1914 period been superseded by more specific pragmatic demands, to the point where the reformist current in the party forced through an anti-clerical cartel with the Liberals in 1912.

The party first entered the Chamber in 1894 with 28 seats and first entered the government in 1916. Apart from a short Catholic Socialist government in 1925–6, the party only participated in *Union Sacrée* governments in the early postwar period, and in the crisis years in the 1930s. However, it soon surpassed the Liberals as the second party, and even became the largest party in 1925–9 and 1936–9.

After the end of the *Union Sacrée* period in 1921, it moved to the left, but in the 1930s espoused the non-Marxist and nationalist theses of Hendrick De Man in his quasi-Keynesian *Plan du Travail*. De Man became President in 1939, succeeding the "grand old man" of Belgian Socialism, Emile Vandervelde on his

death. De Man dissolved the party in 1940, and entered into open collaboration.

A new party, the PSB (without collective union affiliations) was born clandestinely and from the activity of P. H. Spaak in exile in London; it was less clearly a "workers' party". Since 1946, it has always been the second largest "family", with a high of 36.7 per cent in 1961 and a low of 25.1 per cent in 1981. Before the ravages of the "community parties", its low was 29.7 per cent in 1949. It has often been in government since 1945; in the period 1944–7 in "national" or "left" coalitions; in 1954–8 with the Liberals; in 1961–5, 1968–73, and 1981 in coalitions with the CVP/PCS; and in 1973–4 and 1977–81 in broader "tripartite" or "community coalitions". It has only twice provided the Prime Minister since the late 1940s (Van Acker 1954–8 and Leburton 1973–4).

The PSB/BSP long resisted the inevitable in the matter of regionalization. The holding of separate and simultaneous congresses of the Walloon and Flemish organizations in 1967 did not wreck national party unity. A number of expedients, such as linguistic parity in all governing bodies and a system of co-presidents (since 1971), were tried until the collapse of the Egmont Pact and the resulting radicalization of positions made separation inevitable. The party split in 1978 into the SP in Flanders, more pragmatic and open to Christians (its manifesto entitled *Doorbraak* or "breakthrough", of 1979), and the Walloon PS with diametrically opposed views on "community questions". Initially PS and SP doctrine on other issues was very close. Over time the two have moved apart in cultural, economic and, above all, defence policy issues, but they may well be converging again in government.

Parti Socialiste — PS
(Socialist Party)

Headquarters	: Bvd. de l'Empereur (Keizerslaan) 13, B–1000 Brussels (tel: 02-513 82 70)
Chairman	: Guy Spitaels
National secretary	: Roger Gaillez

History

After the Socialist Party of Belgium split into two separate parties in 1978 the PS participated in government until 1981. In the 1979 European Parliament elections it obtained four seats out of 11 on 30 per cent of the vote.

In the 1981 elections the PS obtained 36.3 per

cent of the vote in Wallonia and 12.3 per cent in Brussels. It subsequently went into opposition to the Christian Democratic-Liberal coalition formed by Martens.

In the 1984 European Parliament elections it fielded the controversial (and previously non-party) José Happart, the mayor of the Fourons as one of its candidates. This brought the party additional electoral success (the PS obtained five seats on 38.5 per cent of the vote), but also brought problems with the Socialist Party in Flanders, for whom Happart was a symbol of Walloon intransigence.

After the 1985 elections when the PS obtained 39.4 per cent of the vote in Wallonia and 14.8 per cent in Brussels it remained in opposition. In the 1987 elections the PS further progressed in both Wallonia (to 43.9 per cent) and in Brussels (to 20.6 per cent), and it subsequently re-entered government with six ministers and three state secretaries in a coalition with the Flemish Socialist Party, with the Christian Democrats in Wallonia and Flanders, and with the *Volksunie*.

The PS is the dominant force in Walloon politics. It heads the Walloon and French community executives. The PS currently has 60 out of the 132 seats in the council of the French community and 51 out of 104 seats in the Walloon regional council.

Support

The PS has the largest electoral support of any party in Wallonia, and has strengthened its position in successive elections in 1981, 1985 and 1987. In the fragmented political system of Brussels it has also improved its position between 1981 and 1987, and is the second largest party behind the PRL.

Past surveys of PS voters have shown that they are older, almost equally male and female, working-class and non-practising Catholic. In the past, workers accounted for well over 60 per cent of its electorate. The party was weaker among white-collar employees, and especially weak among farmers (only 1.8 per cent of PS voters in the early 1980s).

The party has been strong among people over 60. In the early 1980s only 16.5 per cent of practising Catholics voted PS compared to 56.1 per cent of the non-practising.

In 1987 the PS had its highest vote in Wallonia since 1965 and it was over 20 per cent ahead of the next party. The PS won over 50 per cent of the vote in 21 cantons, and over 60 per cent in four (Grâce Hallagne 67.1 per cent, Boussu 61.9 per cent, Seraing 61.3 per cent, Dison 60.8 per cent). In the wider electoral districts its highest votes were in Mons (54.5 per cent),

Huy-Waremne 51.2 per cent and Liège 50.2 per cent.

The PS is the majority party in three of the four provinces of Wallonia, Hainaut (47.9 per cent in 1987, 43.5 per cent in 1985), Liège (46.3 per cent in 1987, 42 per cent in 1985) and Namur (42.1 per cent in 1987, 36.3 per cent in 1985).

In the province of Luxembourg the PS was in second place to the PSC in 1987 with 29.6 per cent, but this represented a considerable improvement over its 1985 vote of 24.7 per cent, when it was also behind the PRL, and was in third place. The lowest vote for the PS in the province of Luxembourg in 1987 was its 13.9 per cent in the canton of Bastogne.

The PS was also especially weak in the German-speaking cantons in the province of Liège, such as Eupen (17 per cent in 1987) and particularly St Vith, where it only obtained 10.4 per cent, and was in fourth place.

Within the Brussels area the PS was particularly strong in St Gilles, where it obtained 46.9 per cent in 1987, which represented a huge increase over the 28.3 per cent that the party had won in 1985.

Organization

The PS has a more hierarchical structure than the Flemish Socialist Party. The basic unit of organization is a local section in each *commune* which holds periodic general meetings and elects a committee to run its affairs. Organizations may affiliate to the PS, but they have no voting rights. These bodies may set up joint committees with the party at various levels for common action. The section has a model statute laid down by the *bureau*.

In each *arrondissement*, there is a *fédération d'arrondissement* (FA) with a model statute. It holds periodic congresses, which elect a committee and national congress delegates. The secretaries of the FA form a college, which the *bureau* may consult on administrative matters. In each *canton* (provincial electoral unit), there is a *cantonal* committee for campaign work. In the four Walloon provinces there is a provincial committee composed of not less than two delegates per FA, which holds a provincial congress at least once a year; this nominates the Socialist candidates for the *députation permanente* and as provincial senators. The *fédérations* of Brussels and Brabant also co-ordinate their activities. At the request of the *bureau* of one FA, the provincial committee must call a meeting of the FA (congresses or committees). The *bureau* attends these congresses.

The *fédération de Bruxelles* and the four Walloon provinces have a regional committee and congress, which is responsible for taking decisions on regionalized (107 *quater*) matters. The Walloon congress meets no less often than once a year or when it is called by the regional committee or by at least three Walloon FAs. Representation (in addition to the *bureau* and the regional committees which attend as of right) is on the basis of delegates from the appropriate FA.

At the national level, there is the party congress, which meets at least annually and always before the opening of the parliamentary session. Congresses may be called by the *bureau* or by a minimum of three FAs representing at least one-fifth of all members; they are also held to endorse PS participation in governments. The congress defines party policy, elects the president, receives a report from the *bureau*, which it may censure, and elects the *bureau* for two years. If an FA so demands, voting takes place by *fédération* block vote. Each *fédération* has one delegate per 250 members. *Bureau* members, deputies and *députés permanents* may attend and speak, but may not vote. The congress is run by a *bureau* and a *commission des resolutions* (compositing committee).

Between congresses, the supreme body is the *conseil général* (CG) which appoints party officials, editors of party papers, candidates as co-opted senators, and discusses urgent policy issues which the *bureau* may submit to it. Three FAs can demand a meeting of the *conseil général*. The voting members are delegates of the FA (one per 750 members) elected by their congress for three years, deputies and the *bureau*. Representatives of various Socialist organizations may attend. In the *bureau*, there are 25 voting members; the president, the two vice-presidents (the president of the Walloon regional committee and the president of the Brussels *fédération*), the general secretary, and 21 members elected by the congress. The parliamentary group chairman and representatives of various Socialist organizations, ministers, representatives of the *Action Commune* (which includes the FGTB) are non-voting members.

The *bureau* appoints the deputy general secretary, and takes day-to-day political decisions, consulting if necessary the *conseil général*. The executive, consisting of the president, vice presidents, secretary-general and the latter's deputy, are responsible for day-to-day administration and finance.

A wide range of bodies surround the party: its youth, women's, educational and cultural organizations, as well as the unions (FGTB), co-operatives and *mutualités*, which form the *Action Commune*. These make up the "*monde socialiste*". The party used to share the *Institut*

Emile Vandervelde with the SP as a party research institute. The PS now have their own smaller centre Fernande Dehousse.

The statutes of the party provide for the statutes of the parliamentary groups to be submitted to the *conseil général* for approval, and lay down that all parliamentary initiatives must be concerted within the group, and for matters not in the party programme must obtain a favourable opinion from the party *bureau*. The PS is one party which still holds polls to designate parliamentary candidates, especially in Wallonia (not in Brussels), although this practice is declining since the congresses of the *arrondissements* usually decide against a poll. However, in 1978 polls were organized in the *arrondissements* of Charleroi (9,800 voters), Mons (8,170) and the Walloon part of Brabant (2,500). No other *arrondissements* held any polls.

Policies

When Guy Spitaels won the party chairmanship, which was quite close-run (Spitaels gained 53 per cent, as against 47 for the left-wing MEP Ernest Glinne), it led to a number of changes in the PS. He sought to turn it into a more modern party with a clearer doctrine. This was the aim of the 1981 congress, which had been planned since 1979, but only the energy of Spitaels enabled the doctrinal and administrative congresses entitled "*Renover et Agir*" to be held in March and October 1982. There was also the opening to Federalists and Catholics such as Yves de Wasseige, Jean Mottard and Marie Caprasse, who were elected on PS lists. This was strongly contested in Charleroi and by more traditional party members, but on the whole the more autonomist *démarche* of the party was easily accepted. There was also a clear "presidentialization" of the PS, with the considerable use of the personality of Guy Spitaels.

The mainspring of recent PS electoral programmes has been the need to find a coherent response to the economic crisis, without accepting the logic of the market economy as inevitable. The basis of the PS response was to give absolute priority to employment and measures to create and conserve employment, especially for the most disadvantaged groups, using an interventionist approach to industrial and taxation policy. The PS accepts the need to control production costs, but refuses to see salaries as the sole element involved.

The party accepts the need to limit public spending, but to do so only in a moderate way covering all areas (including defence) and safeguarding acquired social rights, with a greater effort of national solidarity being required from those with higher incomes, in the framework of a more equitable tax system. Above all the state — both in the form of intervention and of public enterprise — is seen as having a positive role in reviving the Walloon industrial infrastructure in a socially acceptable manner.

The PS has moved to a rigorously autonomist position, espousing a federalist viewpoint for the first time. Not only does the PS fully assume the reforms of 1980 and urge their completion, but it proposes to regionalize five key industrial sectors: steel, textiles, energy production, glass and shipbuilding. The powers of the regions should be extended to other areas such as applied research, agricultural policy, major public works and nuclear materials policy under public (regional) control.

The PS is not influenced by the economic crisis to abandon its ambitious objectives in the social field, for youth, for equal opportunities for women, in environmental protection which should be increased by better planning and land use legislation, in health care, housing (a major effort needed) and consumer protection (the PS is also less opposed to civil nuclear energy than its Flemish sister party, and has generally been less influenced by "green issues").

Measures are favoured to improve the situation of immigrants. The party remains fully committed to the NATO alliance, but wishes to see reductions in military expenditure and measures to reduce tension. It is opposed to the Neutron bomb and favours the so-called "zero option" on TNF-dismantling of Soviet SS-20s in exchange for non-deployment of Pershing and Cruise. It has generally been to the right of its Flemish sister party on defence issues. The party remains strongly in favour of the EC, but seeks a more dynamic community with genuine social and regional policies. It seeks to maintain public development aid at the present 0.55 per cent of GDP at least, and to extend the North-South dialogue.

The programmes have been pragmatic rather than ideological, although they proposed some important structural reforms. The "Renover et Agir" congress sought to give the party a clearer ideological basis, anchored in a coherent analysis of the crisis, a resolutely federalist démarche, and support for the new phenomenon of an active "Vie Associative" (lit. "associational life") involved in environmental, consumer and labour battles at the grassroots, which has hitherto by-passed traditional party structures.

The 1982 communal elections saw some practical attempts to put these concepts of "Ouverture" into practice in the form of progressive alliances before or after the elections, of which the most spectacular executive was the RW/PS/ECOLO alliance in Liège under which two ECOLO members became echevins. The results of these experiments were rather inconclusive.

In recent years the Happart issue has pushed the PS in a more Walloon federalist direction and caused severe internal tension, to the point where the pro-Happart and anti-leadership federations such as Charleroi opposed the 1988 coalition agreement.

Personalities

The party's dominating personality has been Guy Spitaels, who controls the centralized and disciplined PS with a strong hand. He is both the party president, and the mayor of Ath in the province of Hainaut.

Philippe Moureaux is one of the Deputy Prime Ministers in the current Martens government, and was president of the community executive.

Guy Coême was the head of the Walloon regional executive before leaving to become Defence Minister in the present government.

José Happart, from the Fourons, has been an intensely controversial member of the party.

Socialistische Partij — SP
Flemish Socialist Party

Headquarters	: Keizerslaan (Bvd. de l'Empereur) 13, B-1000 Brussels (tel: 02-513 28 78)
Chairman	: Frank Van den Broucke
National secretary	: Carla Galle
Membership	: 103,000

History

The Flemish Socialist Party (SP), which became a separate entity in October 1978 after the division of the Belgian Socialist Party, took part in government coalitions until 1981. In the 1979 European Parliament elections it obtained 21.6 per cent of the Flemish vote and three seats. In the 1981 national elections it obtained under 21 per cent and went into opposition for a period of seven years.

In the 1984 European Parliament elections it did outstandingly well, obtaining 28 per cent and four seats. In the 1985 national elections it obtained 23.7 per cent and in 1987 it improved its position slightly to 24.2 per cent, although it did not have the same success as its Walloon sister party. It subsequently entered into a coalition government with the PS, the two Christian Democratic parties and the *Volksunie*. The SP has three ministers in the government, and four state secretaries.

In January 1989 Frank Van den Broucke succeeded the party's long-standing chairman, Karel Van Miert.

The SP has 49 out of the 186 seats in the Flemish council. After being in an all-party Flemish executive from 1981–85 it was in opposition to a Christian Democratic-Liberal coalition from 1985–88. After its return to national government, however, it insisted on a parallel return to a wider-based government in Flanders. It now has two seats on the Flemish executive.

Support

With the exception of the 1981 elections the SP has been the second largest party in Flanders, but far behind the dominant CVP, although the gap between the two parties has narrowed. The highest ever Socialist vote in Flanders was 29.7 per cent in 1961, but there was then a steady decline until the late 1970s, when the party's support in Flanders was only just a little over 20 per cent. The party's vote then stabilized, and has since increased to a considerable extent.

The SP does not benefit to the same extent from the traditional industrial working-class vote which is the bedrock of support for its Walloon sister party. On the other hand, under Van Miert's leadership the party has been relatively successful in attracting new support, especially from younger people in the ecology and peace movements. The SP now has a younger and more middle-class membership than it used to have in the past, and than the PS in Wallonia.

The SP has also made an attempt to open itself up to Catholic voters, (*doorbraak*), but this has not proved very successful. It now has substantial support from middle and upper grade management, but very little from farmers.

While the SP is much weaker in Flanders than the PS in Wallonia, the much higher population of Flanders means that the two parties have rather similar shares of the national vote (14.9 per cent for the SP compared to 15.7 per cent for the PS).

The SP has a relatively even spread of support from province to province. In 1987 it was second in every province, with a high of 27.3 per cent in Limburg and a low of 23 per cent in Antwerp. In West Flanders it polled 25.6 per cent and in East Flanders 23.4 per cent. It does not have the electoral bastions of its Walloon sister party, and its highest vote in any Flanders canton is only 37.6 per cent (*Landen*). It tends to be strongest in urban areas. It was the largest

party in 1987, for instance in the town of Hasselt (32 per cent), Mechelen (31.2 per cent), Ostend (28.4 per cent) and the city of Antwerp (27.3 per cent), whose mayor has been Socialist since the 1920s. Its lowest 1987 vote in Flanders was 10.2 per cent in the canton of Bree.

In the bilingual province of Brabant, the SP obtained 11.6 per cent in 1987. Its highest votes in the Brussels conurbation were in the communes of Anderlecht (8.3 per cent) and Schaerbeek (7.2 per cent). Its lowest votes were in Ixelles (3.3 per cent) and Saint-Gilles (1.6 per cent).

Organization

The organization of the SP is very similar to that of the PS, although it has a less tight central discipline. On the lowest tier are the *sections* at the *communal* level, with a general assembly and committee. The general meeting must meet to prepare for *arrondissement* and national congresses and to appoint delegates. The committee must include at least 25 per cent women and 25 per cent members under 35.

Above these are the *arrondissement organizations (AF)*. The AF holds a congress which elects its executive. This must include 25 per cent women and 25 per cent of members must be under 35; up to half its membership may be elected officials (deputies *et al*). *Sections* within an electoral *canton* co-operate in an ad hoc structure, as do the AFs within the same province, particularly for the nomination of candidates for the *Bestendige Deputatie* and as provincial senators.

At national level the congress is the highest body, meeting at least once a year; it gives its approval to the political report of the *bureau*. It elects, every two years, the party president, the *bureau* and the administrative commission. The congress delegates are appointed by their *fédérations* on the proposal of the *sections*, on the basis of one delegate per 300 members. Members of the *Algemene Raad* (general council), *bureau* and administrative commission, deputies, provincial councillors may also participate, but not vote. The party also has an *Algemene Raad* which meets to appoint the general secretary and co-opted senators, and to discuss major political issues. Voting members are deputies, MEPs, members of the *Bestendige Deputaties* and delegates of the AFs (one per 500 members elected for two years).

More day-to-day work is split between an administrative commission (responsible for administration, finance and audit, and information) and the *bureau*, which deals with political questions. However, since the administrative commission (20 members) includes the president and four representatives of the *bureau*, there is a close overlap and co-ordination.

The *bureau* deals with political matters, but must present a report and a political resolution on future policy to the congress. It has 19 members, 16 of them elected by the congress on proposals from the AFs, and the president, the secretary-general (more powerful than the equivalent post in the PS) and the latter's deputy. The party has a retirement age of 65 for elected office-holders and rules against *cumul*, which became stricter with effect from 1983. The party now rarely organizes polls to select parliamentary candidates. Indeed, in 1978 there were none, and in the *arrondissement* of Antwerp the federal congress specifically voted down a proposal for a poll. The SP has introduced a 30 per cent quota for women within the party, but this has not been very successful, and not enough women have come forward.

The party's research institute, the Emil Van der Velde Institute, has grown rapidly from five to 50 researchers. It is larger than its Walloon Socialist equivalent, and has played an important role within the SP.

There is a co-ordination committee between the SP and its Walloon sister party, composed of the two bureaux which rarely meets. The two parties' headquarters are still, nevertheless, within the same building (unlike the two Christian Democratic parties which have moved into adjacent buildings).

Like the PS, the SP's members in the European Parliament sit within its Socialist group. The SP is also active in the Confederation of European Socialist parties, and in the Socialist International.

Policies

As a permanent minority in Catholic and nationalist Flanders, where it is the only significant left-of-centre party, the SP has lived in a completely different environment from the PS. It has been forced much earlier than the PS to become a strongly Flemish party, and its style, rhetoric and policy have had to be more pragmatic and more nationalist in order to survive in a more hostile environment, which it could do little to control or shape. It has pursued a *doorbraak* strategy of opening up the party to Catholics (in the 1984 European election it even put a Catholic priest, Jef Ulburghs, on its list), but this has not been very successful in attracting new support.

Under Karel Van Miert, the party has been modernized and also become more open to new ideas, and to the new activist environmental and other grassroots groups. At the same time, it

has lost the national Belgian viewpoint which characterized it as a junior partner of the PSB in the old unitary PSB/BSP, and has fully adopted Flemish positions on the reform of the state and cultural matters.

The PS' espousal of Happart as a candidate has widened the gap between the two parties. The SP has moved back to the middle ground, however, enabling it to participate in government without any major difficulties.

The SP has sought to develop specific Flemish socialist policies in a number of fields, such as housing and education. It has remained more influenced by an environmental perspective than its Walloon sister party. The SP has opposed, for example, civil nuclear energy (it rejected new nuclear reactor number 8) and has made much more of an issue of the dumping of nuclear waste.

It has also distanced itself from the PS on defence and foreign policy matters, strongly opposing — even when in government in the early 1980s — the use of Belgian territory for Pershing and Cruise TNFs, considering these weapons unnecessary and provocative and emphasizing instead the need for negotiations. The SP, however, is not anti-NATO, nor is it unilateralist or neutralist. The SP also puts a strong emphasis on third-world development, and human rights issues. In its economic policy it is no longer very different from the PS.

Personalities

The SP has had a more collective leadership than the more centralized PS leadership of Guy Spitaels.

Karel Van Miert led the party from its inception until 1988. From 1976 to 1978 he had been co-president of the Belgian Socialist Party. He is still only in his mid-40s, and has helped to widen the appeal of the party to young and "green" voters. In 1988 he was appointed the Belgian member of the European Commission.

His successor is the 33-year-old Frank Van den Broucke. Another key leadership figure is Louis Tobback. He is the current Interior Minister, and is the party's defence specialist. He has been head of the party's research institute, the Emile Van der Velde Institute.

Another influential leader is Willy Claes, who is slightly older than Van Miert and Tobback, and has had extensive government experience. He is currently a Belgian Deputy Prime Minister, and the Minister of Economic Affairs. He has been the Chairman of the active Economic Affairs Committee of the Confederation of European Socialist Parties.

Another figure within the party is Freddy

Willockx, the former PTT Minister, and now mayor of St Niklaas.

The party's secretary-general is Carla Galle, the first woman to hold the post.

2. The Christian social parties (CVP/PSC)

Long the dominant political family in Belgium and despite the recent decline in its vote, especially in Flanders, it still occupies a strategic position in the political spectrum. It can choose its allies (Liberals or Socialists) and is virtually indispensable to any coalition. It has been in power since 1958, without interruption, and before 1954 it was in power continuously since 1844, apart from a short postwar period. It has provided all but three of Belgium's prime ministers in this century and has held that office for all but five years of the century.

It began in Flanders, where its dominance has always lain. Catholic political doctrine was formed in a series of conferences held in Mechelen (Maline) between 1863–67. The hitherto localized and fragmented Catholic organizations based in the *Unions Conservatrices et Constitutionelles*, federated in 1864. The more conservative Catholic forces organized themselves in the *Cercles Catholiques*, which also set up a national body in 1855. At the same time the more progressive Catholics established the *Fédération des Sociétés Ouvrières Catholiques* to propagate Catholic social teaching. These three organizations formed the Catholic Party under Beernaert in 1888, following the Catholic victory at the polls in 1884.

The party then retained an absolute majority until universal suffrage was introduced in 1919. This factor and the growth of union power forced the party to diversify its appeal on a broader basis. As a result, the party was reorganized on *standen* (literally estates) principles in 1921. Four special interests were recognized as the pillars of party organization: the political pillar (the UCCs); the Catholic Workers (the *Ligue Nationale des Travailleurs*); the *Boerenbond* (farmers); the *Fédération des Classes Moyennes*. In 1936, the party was renamed the *Bloc Catholique*, as a first recognition of regional realities, as two wings were formed. After World War II the *standen* system was officially abandoned as archaic, but in the reality of party life a very real degree of proportionality between these various interests has remained. The party was then reformed as a unitary party, the *Christelijke Volkspartij/Parti Social Chrétien* (CVP/PSC), whose regional wings moved apart

after 1965 and finally split into two independent parties after 1968.

Christelijke Volkspartij — CVP
Christian People's Party

Headquarters	: Tweekerkenstraat 41, 1040 Brussels (tel: 02–238 38 11)
President	: Herman Van Rompuy
Membership	: 140,000
Vote	: 19.5 per cent

History

The CVP is the pillar of the Belgian political system. It has changed less than most and more gradually under the pressure of the increasing community emphasis of political life. The basic characteristics of the party in Flanders were merely reinforced; pragmatism, moderation and a strong sense of Flemish cultural identity, within whatever Belgian framework was considered appropriate. As the dominant wing of the dominant political family, the CVP has been dominant in the state, extending its patronage network in the interests of its clientelist support. Hence the term *"CVP-staat"*. The party has managed to keep the levers in its hands and with the key prize of the premiership, which it has now held for most of the 1970s and '80s (Tindemans, Eyskens and Martens) at the head of a variety of coalitions.

Support

Despite its electoral decline, it has remained the leading party in Flanders and hence an indispensable partner in any coalition. In 1961 it still held an absolute majority in Flanders (50.9 per cent). With periodic recoveries, it has been on a steady downward trend, to reach a low of 32 per cent in 1981 and a new low of 31.4 per cent in 1987, but still seven percentage points above the SP. Thus there has been some levelling in the Flemish political scene, but still no politically meaningful majority can exist in Flanders, and hence at the national level, without the CVP. In Brussels, the CVP's position has remained relatively stable. In 1987, it registered 8 per cent, as in 1985. Its best results have been in rural areas and semi-urban areas and smaller towns. Its poorest results have been in Oostende. At the 1987 election, its best result was 42.3 per cent in Turnhout and in Brussels 12.7 per cent (in Anderlecht).

The CVP electorate is more strongly female than the PSC electorate and it is younger. It contains a larger proportion of workers and fewer farmers. Fifty-seven per cent identify with the working class and 37 per cent with the middle class; 90 per cent identify themselves as practising Catholics, but, and this is new, some 20 per cent are non-believers. CVP voting is determined by religious practice coupled with working class identification and a strong appeal to certain target interests: Catholic workers, farmers and the *indépendants*. Brussels CVP voters are more likely to be *indépendants*, older, middle-class or classless identifiers and less Catholic than their Flemish counterparts. Until the very recent rise of the SP, the CVP led in all social categories, including workers, and thus is a genuine *"volkspartij"* and certainly more so than the PSC.

Organization

The formal party structure is fairly classic and simple. It is described in some detail here because the structure of the other non-socialist parties is very similar. However, the real structure retains much of the old *standen* with consideration being given to forms of proportionality between regions and interests linked to the party such as the Catholic Trade Unions (ACW), *Boerenbond* and *Middenstandsorganisaties*. Yet, the interest-based factions are less ideological than the internal tendencies in the PSC and co-operate more harmoniously.

The CVP has also been able to assume the mantle of Flemishness and project, through figures like Eric van Rompuy (former *CVP-Jongeren* chairman), Luc van den Brande and Ferdinand de Bondt, following as intransigent a Flemish line as the VU. It has worked closely with all the other mainstream Flemish parties in a broad front to defend Flemish interests to a degree that the Francophone parties have never achieved. Thus, the CVP is deeply embedded in Flemish society and culture.

Party structure has been greatly streamlined in 1979. A parallel structure of congresses, *besturen*, bureaux and presidents exists at each level from section through *arrondissement*, province and national level. Each organization sets its own rules, based on national model rules. Sections are based on communes, with sub-division into more local branches possible. A section must be recognized by the *arrondissement bestuur* and must have membership equivalent to 7 per cent of CVP voters in the area or 3 per cent of all voters. The congress, which all members may attend, meets annually to approve rule changes and policy manifestos and to elect its president, *bestuur* and delegates to the *arrondissement* and national congresses for three years. The *bestuur* is responsible for medium-term policy decisions and control of

the *bureau* that it elects, as well as approving alliances and candidates' lists. There is a similar structure at *arrondissement* level, which is responsible for parliamentary candidates' lists and campaigns. The provincial organization is less complete. The provincial *bestuur* is padded out with more ex-officio members. Its task is nomination of lists for provincial elections and decisions on alliances in the deputations (provincial executives).

The national congress, composed of section delegates, all *bestuur* members and the members of the national executive, meets annually and whenever it is called upon to approve CVP participation in government. It elects some *bestuur* members, and there are numerous ex-officio members such as CVP ministers, the executives of the parliamentary groups and co-opted members who often come from interest groups close to the CVP. The *bestuur* controls the work of the *bureau*, approves rule changes and manifestos, as well as electing the president. It elects the *bureau* (executive), which meets weekly to deal with ongoing party business. The party has its youth and women's organizations and an organization for local councillors. It has a broadcasting committee and a research institute (CEPESS) which it shares with the PSC.

Policies

The CVP is par excellence a government party. It has been in coalition with almost all other parties. It is therefore pragmatic and flexible. It is a moderate classless party, with a degree of hard-nosed defence of Flemish interests. It has pursued a centre-left or a centre-right course, depending on circumstances. It is the arbiter of the course of Belgian politics.

In the 1980s it has moved to a less centrist position, arguing for a rigorous austerity programme under a strong government, in alliance with the Liberals. With the PVV, it steered the toughest course in seeking to resolve the problems raised by the public sector deficit, low competitivity of Belgian industry and high wages, especially in the public and semi-public sector. In the 1981–88 period, the party's right wing, under such figures as Leo Tindemans, was in the saddle. Yet, the CVP has found little difficulty in returning to a more centrist course and an alliance with the PS/SP that it earlier forswore, with figures such as Jean-Luc Dehaene in the ascendancy.

The party believes in the social market economy and maintains close links with the unions. It is a strong supporter of NATO, but some CVP MPs opposed the installation of Pershing missiles in 1982.

It is also a strong supporter of a federal

Europe. Its views on the reform of the state, like those of the dominant Walloon PS party, have evolved in a more federalist direction. The CVP now supports only minimal national solidarity and maximum devolution, but with each community financially responsible.

Personalities

Its leading figure is Wilfried Martens, the Prime Minister for ten years. He is a compromise figure in party terms, who has credibility with the other parties and an ability to deliver the CVP, often a problem in the past.

Other figures are Leo Tindemans, the long-serving Foreign Minister and himself Prime Minister (1974–77 and 1977–78); Mark Eyskens, son of the long-serving Prime Minister in the 1960s; and Jean-Luc Dehaene, who is on the left of the party and led the negotiations for the formation of the present government, before handing over to Martens.

Gaston Geens has been the president of the Flemish executive since 1981. Herman Van Rompuy is the new party chairman.

Parti Social Chrétien — PSC
Christian Social Party

Headquarters	: rue des Deux Eglises 41, 1040 Brussels (tel: 02–230 10 73)
President	: Gérard Deprez
Membership	: 55,000
Vote	: 7.8 per cent

History

The PSC has become very much the junior partner in the Christian Social family. However, its position over the Happart case, its refusal to accept communitarization of education in 1985 and its acceptance in 1987 only after solid guarantees for the Catholic education network had been obtained, and above all its effective imposition of a change of alliance on the CVP in 1988, show that it is a factor that cannot be ignored and that its independence of the CVP is real.

Until the election of Gérard Deprez as president in 1982, the PSC was driven by organized factions: the Christian Democrats (centre-left pro-trade union wing) and the *Centre Politique des Indépendants et les Cadres* (CEPIC) established in 1972 (conservative), identified with Van den Boeynants and a third group of "sans familles", outside these tendencies.

The *Démocracie Chrétienne* and the CEPIC were well organized parties within the PSC. The

CEPIC even organized its first national congress in 1977, with its main strength in Brussels and Liège. Its members are managers, *indépendants*, businessman and professionals. The *Démocracie Chrétienne* was strong in the industrial areas, such as Charleroi, and was identified with figures such as Philippe Maystadt and Deprez himself. The CEPIC was critical of the dominance of the *Démocracie Chrétienne* tendency in the parliamentary party and its lock on party strategy in the 1970s.

Power has been the cement between these factions and has made for considerable pragmatism. Yet, divisions have been serious. The PSC found it very difficult to agree to the *Wende* of 1981, which took it into a centre-right coalition. Deprez maintained party unity by abolishing the right of tendencies to organize, at least in theory. He was helped here by the rightward drift of the CEPIC, which had sailed close to the extreme right and the ephemeral *poujadists* such as the UDRT, with whom an unsuccessful alliance was made in Brussels in 1987.

Support

The PSC has been on a downward trend since the 1960s. In 1978 it still had 26.9 per cent of the Walloon vote, but fell back to 19.6 per cent in 1981 and recovered to 22.6 per cent in 1985 and 23.2 per cent in 1987. This corresponds to the levels of the mid-1960s. However, in 1961, the PSC still held 31.2 per cent. It has been the second party in Wallonia, except in 1971, 1981 and 1985. Its vote in Brussels was 8.5 per cent (even with its UDRT allies), down from 9.2 per cent in 1985. Its strongest positions have been in the southern Sambre-Meuse and Luxembourg (close to 45 per cent) and its weakest 15 per cent in Hainaut.

The PSC electorate is strongly female (57 per cent). Only 20 per cent is under 40. Twenty-nine per cent are workers; 13 per cent are *indépendants* and 9 per cent are *cadres*; 83 per cent are practising Catholics. Among practising Catholic men, 53.4 per cent vote PSC, whereas only 7 per cent of all men did so. Fifty-four per cent of farmers vote PSC. Determinants of PSC are, in order, religious practice, the occupation of farming, older age, and sex (women).

Organization

Organization is fairly classic. The basic unit is the section in each commune. These link up in associations for provincial elections on a district basis. In each *arrondissement*, the level at which parliamentary candidates are selected, there is a congress, a *conseil permanent* between congresses, made up of delegates from the sections and ex-officio delegates, such as deputies and senators and a *comité directeur* (executive).

At the national level, there is a congress, which meets annually and as required, though special congresses are rarer in the PSC than other parties. In 1988 a congress was held to approve the coalition and an unusually high 33.6 per cent of delegates did not support the agreement. The *conseil permanent*, with some 150 members from sections, elected by the congress (and ex-officio) often decides on coalitions.

The *comité directeur* meets weekly to deal with day-to-day business. Two interesting features of PSC organization are the use of preparatory congresses to prepare decisions on issues or themes and more importantly the fact that the president is elected by postal ballot of all party members.

Policies

The PSC has sought to avoid political isolation in Wallonia and has now aligned itself on federalist positions, against its earlier Belgicist tendencies. It has sought to avoid sharp conflict over economic and social policies and represented a moderating influence in the Christian Social/Liberal coalition 1981–88. It has distinct policies, in the Walloon context, on education, abortion and broadcasting policy. It is in favour of a strong defence posture and was less reluctant to support deployment of Cruise missiles than the CVP. As a minority party in more left and lay Wallonia, it has been forced to adapt its positions to avoid isolation.

Personalities

The key figures in the PSC are former Prime Minister Paul Van den Boeynants, active in Brussels (who survived a kidnapping), Charles Ferdinand Nothomb, Speaker of the Chamber and Interior Minister at the time of the Heysel Stadium tragedy, and president Gérard Deprez. Philippe Maystadt is another leading personality.

3. The Liberals (PRL/PVV)

The Liberals were the first to form an organized political party in Belgium, but their subsequent history has been one of splits and remergers. At the same time, the Liberals have moved from the progressive to the conservative end of the political spectrum and have reluctantly become organized along linguistic lines.

Brussels was always the centre of liberalism. Thus the Brussels *Alliance Libérale* organized the first Congress in 1846, leading to the

foundation of the *Parti Libéral* (PL). The PL dominated political life until 1884, from which time it remained in opposition until 1919. There were always two wings — the Conservatives who were Liberals only due to their anti–clericalism and the Progressives (called Radicals) who supported universal suffrage and social measures. The Radicals split off in 1887 and only reintegrated in 1900. During this long opposition period, the PL often worked with the Socialists who had supplanted them as the country's second largest party.

In the 1920s, the party was torn. Its economic doctrine led it towards conservative coalitions with the Catholic Party, whereas anti–clericalism remained a sufficiently live force to make coalitions with the Socialists a real possibility (even as late as 1954–58). It also served in tripartite governments, but had become a third "junior" political force. Indeed, the last Liberal Prime Minister was Frère Orban in 1878–84.

In the 1960s, the party lost its anti–clerical image. As it moved to the right in response to the series of *travailliste* Christian/Socialist governments, it actively sought to attract conservative Catholics as well as non-Catholics in defence of the free market, individual freedom and Belgian national unity. The new formula, under a new name, the *Parti de la Liberté et du Progrès* (PLP/PVV), was very successful, doubling its vote to 21.6 per cent in 1965 and holding this gain in 1968 (20.9 per cent).

Like the other traditional formations the Liberals were unable to resist the rising tide of community-based politics and the community parties. The PLP fell into linguistic and sectarian splits, especially in Brussels, over co-operation across the linguistic divide and over co-operation with the FDF. By 1961, the Flemish Liberals had split away and the Francophones had split into three competing lists, which even together were very weak. Meanwhile, quite autonomous Flemish and Francophone wings had evolved out of the old unitary PLP. By 1979, two separate parties had been established.

Partij voor Vrijheid en Vooruitgang — PVV
Freedom and Progress Party

Headquarters	: Regentlaan 47/48, 1000 Brussels (tel: 02–512 78 70)
President	: Guy Verhofstadt
Membership	: 55,000
Vote	: 11.3 per cent

History

The PVV was first organized as an independent party at its 1972 congress, with Willy De Clerq as its president. It declared itself open to all who shared Liberal ideals, irrespective of religious or philosophical beliefs. The PVV has been the most consistently ideological and the least concerned about community questions of the major Belgian parties. The party took on its present strongly free-market aspect with the *Handvest van het moderne Liberalisme* (1979), the Kortrijk Manifesto.

The PVV took part in several broad-based coalitions between 1974 and 1980 that sought to resolve the community problem and indeed belonged to the tripartite government of 1980 that carried through the reform of the state. Yet, its real aim, achieved between 1981–88, was to establish a strong centre-right coalition, with a heavy dominance of Liberal policy.

Thus, it was active in promoting the CVP/PSC/PVV/PRL coalition of 1981, its regional and community counterparts and its maintenance in 1985. It was strongly committed to saving Martens VI in 1987 and sought to prevent the CVP from reversing alliances, as it eventually did in 1988. It sought stable, coherent governments, able to last out the legislature and wanted to put community issues onto a back-burner. It deliberately polarized debate with the Socialists.

Support

The PVV has seen the trend line of its electoral position improve, despite some setbacks. It began with 17.3 per cent in 1974, fell to 14.4 per cent in 1977, behind the VU, the CVP and SP. It climbed back to 17.2 per cent in 1978 and reached a high of 21.1 per cent in 1981, becoming the second party in Flanders, ahead of the SP and only 10 points behind the CVP. It fell back to 17.3 per cent in 1985 and rose to 18.5 per cent in 1987. It would seem that its "natural position" is that of third Flemish party with about 18 per cent of the vote. Its score in Brussels has risen from 3.7 per cent in 1918 to 5.8 per cent in 1987. Its best results have been about 35 per cent in Oudenaarde and its worst about 15 per cent in Antwerp.

In 1968 the majority of the Flemish electorate was female, but by the 1980s the reverse was true. Its electorate has the lowest share of workers of any party (22.5 per cent) and a high share of *indépendants* (23 per cent). Some 21 per cent are managers. Few (38 per cent) are working-class identifiers. Of all workers, only 8.5 per cent vote PVV, yet more *indépendants* vote CVP than PVV, but the gap has narrowed. Some 35 per cent of PVV voters are practising Catholics.

Organization

The PVV's structure is classic. The basic unit is the section in each commune. Each *arrondissement* has a *federatie*, linking up sections. Each *federatie* has its own congress and executive. At national level, there is a *politieke kommittee*, which takes major decisions between congresses. The *uitvoerende bureau* (executive) runs the party's day-to-day affairs. The PVV has its youth (*PVV-Jongeren*) and women's (*PVV-Vrouwen*) organizations and numerous social and cultural organizations for *indépendants*, for pensioners, for sports, for work in developing countries. It also has a shared Research Institute (Paul Hymans Instituut) with the PRL, and a party training institute.

Policies

As indicated, the party is now markedly more right-wing on defence, international relations and economic issues. On social issues such as abortion, it retains its free-thinking stance. Its young leader Guy Verhofstadt is an admirer of the ideology of Hayek and Friedman and the Thatcherite revolution.

The PVV oppose traditional Belgian corporatism and seeks privatization and competition. It seeks to reduce the role of the state and cut public expenditure and taxation. Its central aim is the restoration of individual economic and social freedom and private initiative. In social policy it seeks greater selectivity and self-help. It has sought to reduce the power of the various clientelist groups in Belgian society: unions, state industries, the civil service. It has strongly supported NATO and the Twin Track decision of 1979. It has also supported free-market European integration.

The party has been ideologically single-minded and in the first centre-right coalition (1981–85) imposed a strong and coherent Liberal perspective in government. However, its power was not adequate to overcome the inevitable need for compromise imposed in a coalition and in a fragmented state. In the end, the community perspective and the interest groups in the PSC and CVP prevented it from carrying out a neo-Liberal revolution. It was unable to prevent the community perspective from dominating the ideological perspective.

Personalities

Its leading ideologue has been its young president (1982–85 and again from 1988) and Vice-Premier and expenditure-cutting Budget Minister (1985–88), Guy Verhofstadt.

Other personalities are Herman De Croo, a long-serving Minister, Willy De Clerq, first PVV president, Vice-Premier and European Commissioner for External Relations (1985–89). Annemarie Neyts has been PVV chairman.

Parti Réformateur Libéral — PRL
Liberal Reform Party

Headquarters	: Centre International 1 Rogier (26ième boite 570), 1000 Brussels (tel: 02–219 43 00)
President	: Louis Michel
Membership	: 45,000
Vote	: 9.3 per cent

History

The PRL was formed out of the defunct old Liberal Party and the RW, which both collapsed in the mid-1970s. The Centrist wing of the RW, with leaders such as Jean Gol (a former young socialist), Etienne Knoops and François Perin linked up with the Walloon part of the old PLP led by André Damseaux, in the *Parti des Réformes et de la Liberté Wallone*, in November 1976.

At its first Congress, the PRLW declared itself to be "pluralist, reformist and federalist". It was thus an open, rather than anti-clerical and federalist Walloon party. In 1979, it absorbed the parlous remains of Brussels Liberalism in the form of the *Parti Libéral*. Out of this fusion came the PRL, which elected the ex-RW Jean Gol as president against Michel Toussaint, a more traditional Liberal, André Damseaux having retired from the field.

Gol created a strong and at times authoritarian presidential style of leadership, using his small ex-RW groups as a kind of praetorian guard, but without wholly alienating the old guard. Even when he left the presidency in 1981 to become first Vice-Premier in the centre-right CVP/PSC/PVV/PRL in government, Gol still almost totally dominated the party. In the public mind, he was the PRL.

Support

The Liberals are usually the third party in Wallonia, but fell into fourth position in 1971 and 1974. However, after 1978, the party began to recover, reaching 21.8 per cent of the Walloon vote in 1981, 24.2 per cent in 1985, close to the peak of 26.7 per cent in 1968. In 1987, the PRL, which had led the PSC in both 1981 and 1985, fell behind it with 22.2 per cent. Its natural position in the electoral spectrum must be close competition with the PSC for second place, at about 22–23 per cent of the vote and barely half the PS share. Its high point in Brussels was 33.4 per cent in 1965, a dominant first place. By the early 1970s, it had almost ceased to exist. Its recovery has taken the PRL back to first party in the capital, with 15.8 per cent in 1981, 26 per cent in 1985 and 25.3 per cent in 1987. Its best Walloon results have been Nivelles, the province of Luxembourg and its poorest results have been in Hainaut and Liège. Its best result in 1987 was in Nivelles with 34.6 per cent and in Brussels in Uccle with 31 per cent.

PRL voters are *indépendants* and *cadres* (managers) and middle-class or even bourgeois identifiers (70 per cent); 32 per cent of voters under 40 vote PRL (double the PSC share of the age group). Only 24 per cent of Catholics vote PRL. Of PRL voters, 40.9 per cent are practising Catholics, but only 25 per cent in Brussels. It is in Brussels that the old traditional Liberalism has most clearly survived at the base. PRL voters are on the whole equally male and female, young, middle-class identifying *indépendants* or professionals and not strongly Catholic.

Organization

Again, the structure of the PRL is classic: sections, where all members can attend and vote to elect the executive. At the next level stands the *arrondissement* federations, also with a congress, a *bureau* and a president. At the national level the same institutional structure is replicated. As already noted the structure of the PRL is very new and presidential.

Policies

The modern PRL has moved well to the right of the PSC as the "school war" lost relevance. The PRL is now a pluralist conservative party, but with some indications remaining of the diverse origins of the component parts of the party. There are still elements of the traditional Liberalism; the ex-RW contingent are radical individualists and federalists. The PRL under Gol is less federalist than the PRLW or of course the RW.

The electoral strategy has been "no enemies on the right", holding ground in Wallonia and taking votes from the PSC and FDF in Brussels. This has led the party into a form of "*neolibéralisme musclé*" emphasizing individualism, law and order and the family. Jean Gol, as Minister of Justice, was well placed to lead this drive. The aim was to overtake the PSC and constitute the strong conservative pole in Wallonia and Brussels, to which more PSC voters would then be attracted. In this scenario, the PRL would have become the opposition to the PS and the PSC would have been forced into a position of permanent junior partnership with the PRL, such as the eight-year coalition pact concluded in 1985. In line with this "tough image" the PRL has emphasized strong defence and has attracted military figures from outside politics, such as General Close. Yet, the strategy has failed. The PSC was able to extricate itself from the coalition and overtake the PRL and reverse alliances, putting the PRL in opposition in 1988. It failed more because of the ability of the PSC to remain a centrist party than because of the inherent weakness of the approach.

Personalities

The key personalities in the PRL have been Jean Gol, new figures like Robert Henrion, an economist, brought in from outside day-to-day politics. Louis Michel Defraigne, André Damseaux and Henri Simonet, the former PS Foreign Minister and European Commissioner, who left the PS over defence policy and joined the PRL. Roger Nols, the right-wing populist ex-FDF mayor of Schaerbeek, who once invited Jean-Marie Le Pen to speak in Schaerbeek, has also joined the PRL.

4. The regional parties

There are now three regional parties: traditional Flemish nationalist *Volksunie* (VU) and the right-wing nationalist *Vlaams Blok* (VLB), which in part broke away from the VU. In Brussels there is the broad-based, but now declining *Front Démocratique des Francophones Bruxellois* (FDF). In the 1960s and 1970s there was also a left-of-centre Walloon federalist party, the *Rassemblement Walloon* (RW), which was able to attain 20.9 per cent of the Walloon vote at its height in 1971 and took part in the Tindemans I government (1974–77). It subsequently split and disappeared from the political map and its former adherents spread out among the three main political families and ECOLO. Its controversial former president, Paul-Henry Gendebien, is now a PSC deputy. The regional parties' support peaked in 1971 with 22.3 per cent.

Volksunie — VU
People's Union

Headquarters	:	Barrikadenplein 12, 1000 Brussels (tel: 02–219 49 30)
President	:	Jaak Gabriëls
Membership	:	60,000
Vote	:	8.1 per cent

History

The *Volksunie* was founded in 1954 out of the *Vlaamse Concentratie*, a breakaway from the CVP. It won 3.9 per cent of the Flemish vote and one seat in the Chamber. It was in part a successor to the old right-wing interwar Flemish parties such as the *Frontpartij* and the fascist and later collaborationist *Vlaams Nationaal Verbond* (VNV), but it also attracted a younger, modernizing wing, with little in common with the nostalgic right. The party has been an uneasy amalgam of linguistic fanatics with links with Flemish language movements; the old nostalgic right, linking with collaboration and with movements such as the annual IJser Pilgrimage; pure cultural nationalism and a more pragmatic and even leftist modernizing democratic political nationalism.

The VU has twice been in government, as a Flemish guarantor for the CVP during periods of reform of the state: in the Tindemans III (1977–78) government and the present Martens VIII (1988–) government. Its 1977–78 period in government led to a severe loss of votes and self-confidence and the formation of the break-away right-wing *Vlaams Blok*.

Support

The VU vote is spread fairly evenly. Its peak was 18.8 per cent in 1971 and its low was 3.4 per cent in 1958. In 1987, it obtained 12.9 per cent of the Flemish vote and 3.7 per cent in Brussels, where its best result was 7.3 per cent in Anderlecht. Its overall best result was 22.4 per cent in Tongres-Maaseik. Of the VU vote 50.5 per cent are female and 34 per cent under 35. Workers made up 37.1 per cent of VU voters. Fifty-four per cent are practising Catholics. The main determinants of VU voting are youth and middle-class identification among workers.

Organization

VU organization is typical of Belgian parties, but is rather complicated. There may be several sections in each commune. Each section elects its executive for two years, which itself elects the chair and secretary as well as its members of the next level, the *arrondissementsraad*. Elected officials (*mandataires*) may attend such party bodies, but may not be in the majority.

The *raad* elects its executive of seven members, plus a chair and secretary who must receive a two-thirds majority. These bodies run local elections and fix lists of local candidates. The national *partijbestuur* (executive) appoints a provincial chair and co–ordination bodies.

At the national level, the party is run by

the congress, *Partijraad (arrondissement* chairs, deputies, senators, MEPs, ministers if any, representatives of the *arrondissements*) on the basis of one per thousand members and some other ex-officio members and up to ten co–opted members. It elects the *partijbestuur* (executive), which runs the party on a day-to-day basis and proposes lists of candidates for approval by the *partijraad*. The *bestuur* elects a smaller political committee and an administrative committee.

Policies

The VU claims to be a social and federal party. It espouses radical political and cultural nationalism. It seeks a Flemish state, not the Grootnederlands (Greater Netherlands) concept. It bases its political conception on its analysis of the failure of the Belgian state and the national parties. It rejects financial solidarity with Wallonia and argues for political autonomy for a Flemish state in a federal system. It favours integral federalism. For the VU, federalism rather then separatism is necessary to retain links with Brussels which it regards as a Flemish city.

In the 1978–88 period, its message became radicalized. Its political ideology is based on a form of social federalism, which rejects individualism and Marxism. It seeks to promote Flemish consciousness and culture. Its economic policy leans to Liberalism, but with a strong nationalist and social component. Thus for some key economic sectors, it has favoured considerable state control and even state ownership.

Peace and disarmament are important strands in party policy. The VU was active in the peace movement at its height and it opposed the installation of Cruise missiles in Belgium and seeks to increase development aid. Yet it has at times sought links with South Africa and opposes votes for immigrants.

This mix of policies and traditions makes the VU hard to place on the political spectrum. At "gut level" it probably leans to the right, but on some issues it appears closer to the SP than to the CVP or PVV. At the 1988 election, the party sought to widen its image and appeal beyond the traditional Flemish nationals by putting forward so-called "*verruimingskandidaten*", taken from outside the party's ranks, as the SP had already done earlier.

The VU has a youth organization (*Volksuniejongeren*), a women's section (*Federatie van Vlaamse Vrouwen*), a research institute and a broadcasting committee.

Personalities

The key personalities in the party are Vice-Premier and Budget Minister and former party president, Hugo Schiltz, and Vic Anciaux, party president 1979–86. He was a compromise president between right and left wings.

Vlaams Blok — VlB
Flemish Bloc

Headquarters	:	Schipperijkaai 17, 1210 Brussels (tel: 02–219 60 09)
President	:	Karel Dillen
Membership	:	2,000
Vote	:	2.0 per cent

History

The *Vlaams Blok* was formed in 1978 by the fusion of two small right-wing nationalist parties led by Lode Claes and Karel Dillen, who had both been VU members of Parliament. They opposed the Schiltz line in the VU and in particular the reform of the state package enshrined in the 1977 Egmont Pact.

Support

The main support for the VlB comes from Antwerp. The Party obtained 2.1 per cent of the Flemish vote in 1978 and 3 per cent in 1987. It obtained 10.1 per cent of the vote in Antwerp.

Organization

The *Vlaams Blok* has a youth organization (*Vlaams Blok Jongeren*), a research institute and a broadcasting committee (*Nationalistische Omroep*).

Policies

The *Vlaams Blok* is radically nationalist and potentially separatist. It is on the extreme right, emphasizing law and order and moral issues. It opposes abortion. It is strongly anti-Communist and supports closer links with South Africa. It supports economic Liberalism and a reduction of the role of the state. It is now also anti-immigrant.

Front Démocratique des Francophones Bruxellois — FDF

Headquarters	:	Chaussée de Charleroi 127, 1060 Brussels (tel: 02–538 83 20)
President	:	Georges Clerfayt
Membership	:	7,500
Vote	:	1.3 per cent

History

The FDF is a pluralist party formed for the defence of the interests of the French-speaking majority in Brussels and the French-speaking minorities of the Dutch-speaking communes of the periphery. It was formed in 1965, as the linguistic quarrel hotted up. It immediately obtained 10 per cent of the vote in Brussels and three seats in the Chamber. Its rise and fall have been spectacular. It then won 18.6 per cent of the Brussels vote in 1968 and 34.5 per cent in 1971, when with smaller allies it also captured an absolute majority in the Greater Brussels Council (a second-tier council covering all 19 Brussels communes). It peaked with 35.1 per cent in 1978.

Evidently, the party's participation in the Egmont Pact Tindemans III government did not hurt it. However, it failed to obtain any real concessions on its main aim, which was to achieve full regional status for Brussels and was forced out of the government in January 1980. The other Francophone parties adopted a solution without Brussels in the summer of 1980.

Attempts by the party to link up with the RW led nowhere and with the voters more concerned about economic issues and a degree of regional devolution achieved in the 1980 reform package, the decline of the FDF set in. Its share of the Brussels vote fell steadily to 20.3 per cent in 1981 and 10.8 per cent in 1987, more or less the same as in 1985. It now has only three deputies. Since 1981, it has lost its position as the premier Brussels party. It is now in third position. Its best vote was 15.6 per cent in St. Josse. It has also lost control of most of the Brussels communes that it controlled in the 1970s.

Support

The FDF electorate is predominantly female. Middle-class identifiers make up 59.3 per cent and 17.8 per cent are upper middle-class identifiers. Only 20 per cent are practising Catholics, the lowest figure for a non-socialist party. White-collar workers make up 39 per cent and 12.7 per cent are "indépendants" (self-employed/professionals).

Organization

Given its limited territorial field, the FDF organization is simpler than for other parties. At the local level, the basic units are the sections, which elect a president and executive and nominate commune candidates. The sections are grouped into commissions de district, covering electoral areas, which nominate candidates for the Brabant provincial council and propose nominees for provincial senators. At the central level, the supreme body is the congress, held every two years. All members may attend and vote. It elects the president and general secretary for a two-year term and approves party policy positions.

Between congresses, the conseil général is the supreme body. It can even amend the statutes by a two-thirds majority. It is composed of delegates from the sections (one per section plus an additional seven delegates up to 1,000 members and thereafter one per 300 members); delegates from FDF; communal councillors (176 elected in 1982); all provincial councillors; Greater Brussels councillors; mayors; échevins; FDF RTBF board members, representatives of the youth (10) and women's (20) organizations; all deputies, senators and MEPs if any. It is a large body of party notables.

The conseil général meets at least four times a year. Its executive arm is the comité directeur, elected from the conseil général. Day-to-day party management is in the hands of the bureau permanent (all deputies, the president, general secretary, representatives of the Jeunes-FDF and FDF-Femmes). It is still quite large and unwieldy, with up to 45 members, but decisions may be delegated to permanent officers. The party has its own research institute (Centre d'Etudes Jacques Georgin) and several cultural organizations. The commission électorale makes proposals to the comité directeur for candidates' lists.

Policies

The party is pluralist, with members coming from Liberal, Socialist and Catholic origins. Indeed, since the party began to decline several leading figures such as Roger Nols or Pierre Havelange have returned to the Liberal fold, feeling that the party had moved to the left. At the same time others have joined the PS, such as Serge Moureaux and Léon Defosset. Despite some left-of-centre positions, such as on development aid, energy policy and workers' participation, it is to a large extent the defender of the indépendants. Its main concerns are the institutional problems of the Brussels region and the rights of French speakers. It seeks genuine federalism and strongly supports European integration.

The party demands the extension of Brussels beyond the 19 communes. It seeks to improve employment opportunities for French speakers in Brussels and believes that greater regional autonomy is the best guarantee of job creation. It has proclaimed itself to be an ecological party and is active in the defence of the urban environment and quality of life. It emphasizes equal pensions for all, especially *indépendants*. It believes in pluralist education and strongly opposes racial and sexual discrimination. It is a centrist party.

Personalities

The veteran Belgian socialist Paul-Henri Spaak joined the FDF in his old age (1972). His daughter, Antoinette Spaak, has been the party's leading figure and Belgium's first woman party president (1977–1982).

5. The Greens

Anders Gaan Leven — AGALEV

Headquarters	: Tweedkerkenstraat 78, 1040 Brussels (tel: 02–23 66 66)
President	: Léo Cox
Membership	: not known (< 1000)
Vote	: 4.9 per cent (1987)

History

AGALEV (meaning *Anders gaan Leven* or "alternative living") began as an alternative movement in the early 1970s. It opposed society's emphasis on consumerism and competition, and put forward a number of counter-values, such as sobriety, harmony and silence. It was heavily influenced by radical Christianity, and a leading figure was Luc Versteylen, a Jesuit. A number of alternative and environmental groups, of which Inter-Environment, ARAU and Friends of the Earth were the most important, became associated with it.

Initially, there was some divergence of view as to the desirability of forming a political movement, and many of its original members have not become active in the political organization of AGALEV. Since 1982, the movement and the party have been formally separated, although they still have close links.

Political activities first began in the 1977 and 1978 elections, when candidates were put up in the Antwerp region with limited success. In the 1979 European elections AGALEV candidates obtained 2.3 per cent in the Flemish-speaking college, and in the 1981 national elections won 3.4 per cent of the vote, obtaining two seats in the Chamber and one in the Senate. In the 1984 European elections AGALEV obtained 7.1 per cent of the Flemish vote and one seat, that of Paul Staes.

Its vote has since continued to rise, and it obtained four seats in the Chamber in the 1985 and national elections and six in 1987.

AGALEV has also put recently naturalized immigrants on its lists for local elections.

Support

The party's electoral support comes mainly from young (under 30), urbanized, well-educated and alienated voters. It is more moderate and more ideologically broad-based than the electorate of the German Greens. Electoral support has grown from almost nothing in 1978, when there were other competing green lists, to 6.1 per cent of the Flemish vote in 1985 and 7.3 per cent in 1987. Its best result in 1987 was in Antwerp, with 10.1 per cent of the vote.

Organization

The organization is very loose and membership is not a strict concept. AGALEV has a political secretariat and holds congresses. It publishes a monthly magazine (*Maandblad De Groenen*). Like all the other parties, it has its own research and training institute which is subsidized by the state (*VZW Ploeg Vorming* and *Animatie*). It is a member of the European Greens.

Policies

It is perhaps slightly further to the left than ECOLO, but has retained the quality of a "green movement" rather than a party. Like ECOLO, it is not greatly concerned with community conflict. It has proposed inter-community co-operation and linguistic courtesy, and worked out a joint platform on Brussels with ECOLO. It seeks to offer a real political alternative and several concrete, different policies. It emphasizes protection of the environment, opposes nuclear energy and supports the concept of a "green economy". It supports the referendum, and votes for immigrants with five-years' residence. It opposes compulsory voting. It is cautious on the abortion issue. It proposes more decentralization to smaller communes. AGALEV proposes a 32-hour week and a system of social wages to replace social security.

Personalities

The leading personality of AGALEV is Antwerp senator Ludo Dierckx.

Parti Ecologiste — ECOLO
Ecologist Party

Headquarters	: Rue de la Sablonnière 9, 1000 Brussels (tel: 02–218 30 35)
Spokesmen	: Paul Lannoye, J. Morael, P. Jonckheer

Membership   : unknown
Vote   : 2.6 per cent (1987)

History

Like AGALEV, the ECOLO party grew out of the Green movement. Paul Lannoye, a former member of the *Rassemblement Wallon*, was one of its early leading figures. It too first entered the electoral arena in 1978, obtaining 1.26 per cent in Wallonia and a respectable 5.1 per cent in Namur. In Brussels there were several competing more moderate or localized green lists, but these were eliminated or marginalized by 1981. In 1982, ECOLO obtained 6.3 per cent of the Walloon vote and 5.5 per cent of the Brussels vote, two deputies and two senators, becoming with AGALEV, the first European Green party to enter Parliament. The rate of growth has slowed and AGALEV has overtaken it. In 1987 it obtained 6.5 per cent of the Walloon vote and an unchanged 5.5 per cent in Brussels. This was a very modest gain, when it is born in mind that it ran in alliance with the party *Solidarité et Participation* (SeP), a left-wing offshoot of the PSC, that had obtained 1.4 per cent of the Walloon vote in 1985. Namur was its best result with 8.9 per cent. The 1984 local elections saw ECOLO elected to several city councils and become part of the governing coalition with the PS, in Liège.

Support

Its electorate is young, educated and perhaps less urban than the AGALEV electorate. It has stagnated in Brussels and gained ground in rural areas. Its activists are well to the left and there have been splits, with the formation of a leftist group (VEGA — *Verts pour une Gauche Alternative*). The same has happened in AGALEV in 1985–86. Both groups suffer internal tensions between Green radicals and pure environmentalists.

Each year, the general assembly elects five federal secretaries, who appoint three party spokesmen. ECOLO is a member of the European Greens.

Policies

The party remains pragmatic by Green standards and has been ready to take part in coalitions (Liège, the Walloon Region). Its policy stance is similar to AGALEV, with greater emphasis on support for small enterprises, tax reform and regional policy.

Personalities

ECOLO's leading figure is José Daras, a deputy from Liège, founder member of ECOLO and president of the ECOLO AGALEV group in the Chamber.

6.   The Far Left

Parti Communiste de Belgique/ Kommunistische Partij van België
Communist Party of Belgium

Headquarters   : Bd. de Stalingrad 18–20, 1000 Brussels (tel: 02–512 90 15)
President   : Louis van Geyt
Membership   : 10,000
Vote   : 0.8 per cent

History

The PCB/KPB lost its last parliamentary seats in 1985 and has been reduced to little more than one among the several small groups on the far left. It has flirted with Eurocommunism and various forms of broad progressive alliances, as for example at the 1988 local elections in many Walloon communes.

The party was born in 1921 as a result of a forced marriage imposed by the Communist International on two antagonistic groups: the *Parti Communiste de Belgique*, the *Ancien Parti* led by Van Overstraeten, which was anti-parliamentary; and the more reformist *Parti Communiste* led by Jacquemotte. From an initial 500 members, the party grew to a high point of 8,500 members. In 1935, the PCB espoused a popular front concept of *uni à la base* and in 1937 a Flemish section (the KPB) was established. In the war, the PCB played a major and active role in the resistance, especially in the pluralist co-ordinating body the *Front de l'Indépendance*.

After the war, the party saw a surge of support, with 12.7 per cent of the vote and 23 seats in 1946. It participated in several coalition cabinets in the pre-cold war period 1944–47. From then on it was in a political ghetto. The postwar reorganization of the trade unions was carried out in such a manner as to reduce Communist influence, which had been considerable in some unions before the war.

Support

The peak voting strength in Wallonia reached 21.7 per cent in 1946, 12.7 per cent in 1949 and 9.8 per cent in 1968. In 1981, it still obtained a respectable 6.3 per cent in Hainaut. In 1987, its best result in Wallonia was 3 per cent in Hainaut. In Flanders, it fell to 0.5 per cent of the vote and was overtaken by the far left *Partij van de Arbeid*. Its electorate is overwhelmingly male, and over 50 or under 25. Eighty one per cent of its voters are working-class identifiers.

Organization

The basic organization is the cell, grouped into sections and then *fédérations*, that do not always correspond to the electoral *arron-dissements*. Each *fédération* holds a congress and elects a committee. The national congress meets every three years and takes decisions by "double majority" of each language group. The president is elected by the same double major-ity. The congress elects the central committee which in turn elects the *bureau politique* for one year. Regional congresses have been held since 1980. Candidates are nominated by the central committee.

The party has a youth section (*Jeunesse Communiste de Belgique*) and a *Commission Féminine*. It publishes a daily newspaper (*Drapeau Rouge*). It has a research institute.

The PCB/KPB has become less unitary, but still retains a national president.

Policies

Since 1973 it has sought to promote the concept of a "*union des progressistes*", with the PS, left-wing Catholics and remnants of the feder-alist RW. It has played down its Marxist and lay ideology, emphasizing its socio-economic programme for job creation, shorter working hours, control of banks and monopolies by state intervention and some state ownership. It does not oppose NATO or the EC as such but attacks their policies. Despite internal conflicts the par-ty has maintained its generally Eurocommunist line and its strategy of broad alliances, although this approach has caused opposition within the party.

Personalities

The only important personality is the long-serving president and former deputy, Louis Van Geyt.

Partij van de Arbeid/Parti du Travail — PvdA/PTB
Belgian Labour Party

Headquarters	:	Lemoinnierlaan 171 (bte 2), 1000 Brussels (tel: 02–513 66 26)
President	:	Ludo Martens
Membership	:	2,000
Vote	:	0.7 per cent (no seats)

History

The PvdA/PTB is the largest of the "Trotsky-ite" far-left parties. It obtained 1 per cent of the vote in Flanders, 0.4 per cent in Wallonia and 0.5 per cent in Brussels. It was formed in 1973 at the time of the Antwerp dock strike, in which it played a major role. At that time it was called AMADA (*Alle Macht aan de Arbeiders*). It has polled over 4 per cent in Antwerp and hopes to elect city councillors there.

German-speaking Belgium

The 70,000 or so German speakers in the eastern cantons of Wallonia (in the nine communes of Kelmis, Raeren, Lontzen, Eupen, Büllingen, Bütgenbach, Amel, St. Vith and Burg-Reuland) have had their own cultural community since 1973.

Elections for the cultural community coun-cil took place in 1981. The community has since been given more extensive powers. The 24-member German community council is now directly elected (the first devolved assembly in Belgium to be so elected) for fixed four-year terms, with the first such election taking place in 1986. There is also a two-member executive.

Elections within German-speaking Belgium are dominated by the traditional national politi-cal families, especially by the Christian Demo-crats (PSC), which has retained 37–39 per cent of the vote in the three most recent elections. The executive is currently a coalition of the PSC and PRL. There is also, however, a purely regional party, the PDB (see below), with a significant minority vote in the area.

Partei der Deutschsprachigen Belgier — PDB
Party of German-speaking Belgians

Headquarters	:	Simarkstrasse 36, B–4700 Eupen (tel: 087–74 42 11)
Chairman	:	Alfred Keutgen
Founded	:	1971

History and Support

The PDB has been the third-largest party in the area in the last two national elections in 1985 and 1987, and the second-largest party in the 1986 community council elections. In 1985 it obtained 14.4 per cent of the vote. In the 1986 community council elections it obtained 20.4 per cent, and five of the 25 seats on the council. In 1987, it obtained 15.8 per cent in the national elections. It has never had a member of the Belgian Chamber or Senate, and is not participating in the German community executive.

It is strongest in the canton of St. Vith, where it had 21.5 per cent of the vote in 1987 and was the second party, and weaker in Eupen at 11.2 per cent where it was the fourth party.

Policies

The PDB is a regionalist party in the Christian Social tradition. Its main objective is the defence of the identity of German-speakers in Belgium, as part of the wider German-speaking cultural world but remaining within the Belgian state as a separate community from the Flemings and Walloons. The PDB wants to have a separate province for the nine German-speaking communes, and to have a single German-speaking electoral constituency, so as to ensure German representation in the Parliament.

The PDB wants to have enhanced cross-border co-operation through a strong Rhein-Maas Euro-Region. It seeks a United Europe of the peoples, regions and communities, and believes that there should be a common European Parliament electoral system, and a Second Chamber of the Regions.

The PDB supports federalism, and the principle of subsidiarity, whereby decisions are taken at the lowest possible level. It calls for application of Christian and humanist principles, and for social solidarity. There should be a shorter working week, a decentralized energy policy, and strong measures of environmental protection. Emphasis is also put on aid to developing countries.

The PDB has also called for special measures (such as early pensions) for those forcibly enrolled in the army in World War II.

Personalities

The party's chairman is Alfred Keutgen. Its top candidate in the 1986 community council elections was Lorenz Paasch.

Denmark

Francis Jacobs

The country

Denmark is a country with slightly over 5 million inhabitants, of whom almost 1,400,000 live in Copenhagen and its suburbs.

Denmark is a homogeneous country. The only national minority in Denmark proper consists of a small number of German speakers in North Slesvig. The country is also overwhelmingly Lutheran. Denmark is a unitary state with no regional tier (with the exception of the Faroe Islands and Greenland, which have home rule and are described in separate sections below), although there are of course regional differences, especially between populated and urbanized East Zealand (Sjælland) and the more rural and agricultural peninsula of Jutland (Jylland).

Denmark has little heavy industry, and the role of the agricultural sector is still of the greatest importance.

Political institutions

Denmark is a constitutional monarchy, but the monarch's only significant part in the government process is in the course of cabinet formation, and even then her role is more limited, for example, than in Belgium or the Netherlands.

The national legislature is the unicameral 179-member *Folketing*. The Prime Minister can dissolve Parliament at will, but there is a maximum term of four years. In practice Danish elections are held more frequently (on average every two years), and there have been 18 elections since 1945.

Denmark is divided into three electoral regions (Greater Copenhagen, Islands and Jutland) and 17 multi-member constituencies. Of the 179 *Folketing* seats 135 are chosen by the Sainte-Lagué system of proportional representation within the constituencies, two seats are allocated for the Faroes and two for Greenland, and the remaining 40 seats are supplementary seats, to give extra seats to parties which have not won seats in the constituency allocation proportional to their strength in the country as a whole. Some of the smaller parties typically have no constituency seats at all, and win all their seats in this second allocation. To qualify for this second-round allocation, parties have to meet at least one of the three criteria, of which the most important is to win 2 per cent of the national poll. Fifteen of the seats are allocated to the Greater Copenhagen constituency, 56 to the Islands constituency (which, in practice, includes many outer Copenhagen suburbs) and 64 to Jutland constituencies.

Preferential voting is permitted and plays a significant role. Parties may take advantage of local political circumstances by deciding which of three different types of list they wish to present in each constituency: local lists (putting a premium on concentrated local popularity), party lists (giving maximum control to the central party machine), or so-called "simultaneous lists", (where party votes are distributed equally between candidates and the decisive factor is the amount of personal votes for each candidate).

Since 1969 there has been a scheme for allocating public funds to parliamentary parties based on the number of their seats in the *Folketing*. The sums involved have been small, but in 1987 a more ambitious scheme was introduced.

The Danish Constitution also contains elements of direct democracy, introduced in 1953 at the time of abolition of the Upper Chamber as a check on a narrow *Folketing* majority enacting radical changes. Referenda are automatic on changes in the voting age and on Treaties ceding sovereignty unless a five-sixth *Folketing* majority ratifies the Treaty. One-third of *Folketing* members can require a referendum on bills other than financial bills. There have also been two referenda on EC matters (on entry in 1972, and on the Single European Act in 1986).

Denmark has 15 members within the European Parliament, chosen by proportional representation within one single national constituency.

Brief political history

Denmark was an absolute monarchy until 1849, when a new Constitution was drawn up which was one of the most liberal in Europe at the

Map of Denmark showing 3 electoral regions — Jutland (Jylland), Islands and Greater Copenhagen (København) — as well as 17 multi-member constituencies, and the number of seats per constituency. Also shows number of seats in Faroes and Greenland.

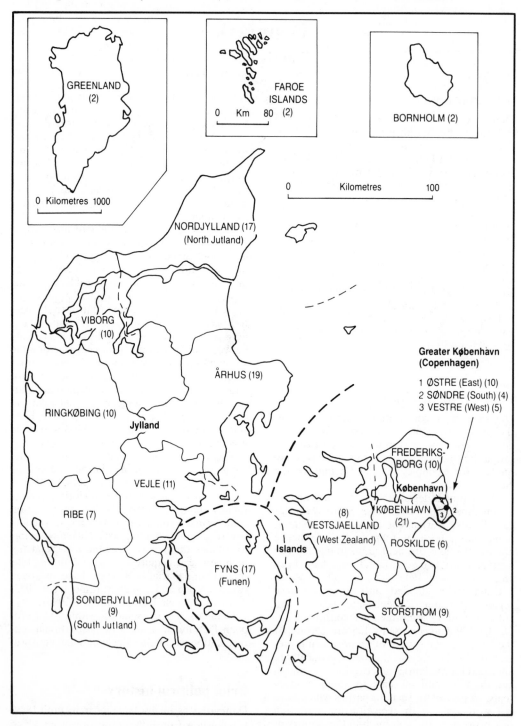

GREENLAND (2)

0 Kilometres 1000

FAROE ISLANDS (2)

0 Km 80

BORNHOLM (2)

0 Kilometres 100

NORDJYLLAND (17) (North Jutland)

VIBORG (10)

ÅRHUS (19)

RINGKØBING (10)

Jylland

Greater København (Copenhagen)

1 ØSTRE (East) (10)
2 SØNDRE (South) (4)
3 VESTRE (West) (5)

FREDERIKS-BORG (10)

København

KØBENHAVN (21)

VEJLE (11)

RIBE (7)

VESTSJAELLAND (8) (West Zealand)

ROSKILDE (6)

Islands

FYNS (17) (Funen)

SONDERJYLLAND (9) (South Jutland)

STORSTROM (9)

Source: adapted from *World Atlas of Elections*.

time, providing for a far-reaching system of male suffrage and for a bicameral legislature (with a Lower House called the *Folketing* and an Upper House called the *Landsting*).

In 1855 a limited form of proportional representation was introduced for elections to the Upper House, making Denmark the first country with such a system.

In 1866 conservative forces won the upper hand within Denmark, and a more restrictive constitution was introduced, which provided for indirect election to the Upper House, and even for a number of Royal nominees to that chamber.

From 1870 to 1906 there was a long constitutional battle between the dominant Upper House which provided the government and had a built-in conservative majority, and the directly elected Lower House, where the reformists had the majority and which sought a government responsible to itself. This was the origin of the historic division between the right (*Høyre*) and the left (*Venstre*).

1901 saw the introduction of a fully fledged parliamentary system, with the arrival of the first ever liberal reform government, provided by a majority in the Lower House. The Reformist Liberals (*Venstre*) remained the largest party until after World War I, in spite of enduring a schism in 1905 when a new Radical Liberal Party was founded. The Social Democrats also gradually built up their parliamentary strength.

In 1915 a new and more liberal constitution was introduced. It ensured the pre-eminence of the Lower House, and reformed the Upper House. It gave women the vote, and replaced majority voting by proportional representation for all elections (used for the first time in 1918 in Copenhagen and in 1920 in the rest of the country).

In the interwar years the old Right reorganized itself into a new conservative People's Party. The once pre-eminent *Venstre* suffered a continuing erosion of support and the Social Democrats became by far the largest party, rising to a high of 46 per cent in 1935, but never gaining an absolute majority in their own right. Instead they depended for parliamentary support on the Radical Liberals, whose vote declined dramatically after 1919 but who retained a vital role. From 1929 until World War II the two parties were in power under the leadership of the Social Democrat Thorvald Stauning.

After World War II the Social Democrats remained the largest party, and provided the Prime Minister on all but five occasions (1945–47, 1950–53, 1968–71, 1973–75 and 1982 to the present), but their share of the total vote gradually declined.

In 1949 Denmark entered NATO, thus formally ending its long-standing neutrality. In 1953 it revised its constitution yet again, abolishing the Upper House or *Landsting*, and increasing the number of seats in the *Folketing*.

In 1959 a new left-wing party, the Socialist People's Party, was founded and enjoyed considerable success, especially in the 1966 general election. The Social Democrats then remained in power with the Socialist People's Party's parliamentary support, a new formula in Danish politics, and one which later provoked a schism within the Socialist People's Party and brought down the government. It also drove the Social Democrats' former allies, the Radical Liberals, (they had renewed their pre-war coalition from 1957 to 1964) to go into coalition with the so-called "bourgeois" parties to their right. In 1973 Denmark joined the European Community, confirmed by a 63 to 37 per cent majority in a referendum.

1973 was an earthquake year in Danish politics, when the traditional parties lost support (some dramatically), the Justice Party and Communist Party returned to Parliament after long absences and three new parties — the Centre Democrats, the Christian People's Party and the Progress Party — all entered Parliament, the latter with a staggering 16 per cent of the national vote. The dramatic nature of the 1973 election was shown by the fact that half the Danish electorate changed their vote between the 1971 and 1973 elections — and 45 per cent of the new Parliament in 1973 were first–timers.

Since 1973 there has been considerable volatility among the electorate. While the old patterns of government formation have resumed there have continued to be more parties represented in Parliament than before 1973 (eight in 1988).

In 1982 a "bourgeois" coalition government was created with Poul Schlüter as Prime Minister, the first time that the Conservatives have provided a Prime Minister since before World War I. It included the Conservatives, *Venstre*, Centre Democrats and Christian People's Party ("four-leaf clover" government) and was renewed in 1987. A new Schlüter-led minority coalition government of Conservatives, *Venstre* and *Radikale Venstre* (Radical Liberals) was formed in 1988.

Main features of the current Danish political system

Denmark is a country with a large number of political parties (eight currently represented in the *Folketing* and often more) and yet without any ethnic or religious divisions, with only a weak core-periphery cleavage, and with weakening class differences as well.

Until the rise of the Socialist People's Party in the 1960s, politics in Denmark was dominated by the four traditional parties, with the Social Democrats winning most of the working-class vote in the town and cities, *Venstre* (the Agrarian Liberals) winning most of the farmers' vote, the Conservatives doing well among businessmen and professionals in the cities and suburbs, and the Radical Liberals getting support from a combination of urban intellectuals and rural smallholders. The Social Democrats dominated most governments, often in partnership with the Radical Liberals and the only other possible government was a "bourgeois" coalition.

Since the 1960s, and especially since the 1973 elections, the political spectrum has become more complex with the position of the traditional parties weakening considerably and with the emergence of new parties on the left, centre and right of the political spectrum. Consensus positions on foreign policy makers have been increasingly challenged by the new parties of the left, on cultural matters by the Christian People's Party and the framework of the welfare state and the tax structure by the Progress party of Mogens Glistrup. These new parties do not represent clear-cut interest groups, and parties like the Progress Party and the Socialist People's Party have won support from all classes. The identification of particular interest groups with the traditional parties has also weakened. Membership of political parties has dropped considerably, and voter volatility has increased.

Nevertheless, in spite of frequent elections, the increasing number of parties and rapid changes of government, Danish politics have continued to be characterized by co-operation and consensus. The main parties continuously negotiate with each other over contentious issues. As a result, in the 1964–65 period, almost 60 per cent of all bills were passed unanimously in the *Folketing*. Not only are there formal coalitions, which are a regular feature of Danish political life, but, more unusually, support is also given to numerous governments by parties which are not directly participating in the government. Moreover, Social Democratic governments have been supported by Conservatives and even gone into coalition with *Venstre* (1978–79). Minority single-party governments have been able to survive for some time, such as the *Venstre* government of Poul Hartling in 1973–75 which only had 12.6 per cent of the seats in the *Folketing*. Governments have thus not

needed positive majorities, as long as they have been able to prevent a negative majority being mustered against them. Votes of confidence are not taken when a government is formed. Related to this has been the comparatively powerful position of the *Folketing* and of its main committees. The Market Relations Committee, for example, which deals with European Community matters, and before which Denmark's EC negotiators have to present their mandate, is one of European's most powerful parliamentary committees.

The homogeneity of Danish society has also helped in forging broad agreement on the general direction of economic and social policy, and in reducing the attraction of the political extremes. The Social Democrats have generally adopted a moderate reformist line, and the Conservatives have not been very conservative either. Differences between urban/industrial and the powerful agricultural interests have caused divergences but not major ones. The main sets of issues which have caused considerable divisions in recent years have been over defence and EC membership, and the burgeoning welfare state.

Denmark's former neutrality was ended when it joined NATO in 1949, a choice which has been subsequently challenged primarily by the political left. This has led not merely to calls to leave NATO (an important element in the programme of the large Socialist People's Party), but also to lengthy debates on the size of Danish military expenditure, and its contribution to NATO.

From 1982 to 1988 the Schlüter-led governments enjoyed a parliamentary majority on economic issues but not on defence and security issues, largely because *Radikale Venstre* were closer to the Social Democrats on these questions. The Social Democrats have also moved to the left on these issues. This severity constrained the government's freedom of manoeuvre, leading to so-called "footnote diplomacy". In 1988 a new election was called over the controversial issue of NATO warships visiting Danish ports, possibly with nuclear weapons on board. A compromise was reached over a circular letter that would be sent out with a reminder of Denmark's non-nuclear policy.

The other key postwar decision has been to join the European Community in 1972, a decision taken mainly on practical economic grounds. In spite of the two referenda in favour of joining the European Community, and of ratifying the Single European Act, there has been strong opposition to the Community and its development. The People's Movement against the EC won 20 per cent of the vote both in 1979 and 1984, and in the 1986 referendum the

Danish election results (percentage of vote and seats won, 1953–88)

	Sept. 1953	1957	1960	1964	1966	1968	1971	1973	1975	1977	1979	1981	1984	1987	1988
Socialdemokratiet (Social Democrats)	41.3% (74)	39.4% (70)	42.1% (76)	41.9% (76)	38.2% (69)	34.2% (62)	37.3% (70)	25.6% (46)	29.9% (53)	37.0% (65)	38.3% (68)	32.9% (59)	31.6% (56)	29.3% (54)	29.8% (54)
Det Konservative Folkeparti (Conservatives)	16.8% (30)	16.6% (30)	17.9% (32)	20.1% (36)	18.7% (34)	20.4% (37)	16.7% (31)	9.2% (16)	5.5% (10)	8.5% (15)	12.5% (22)	14.5% (26)	23.4% (42)	20.8% (38)	19.3% (34)
Venstre	23.1% (42)	25.1% (45)	21.1% (38)	20.8% (38)	19.3% (35)	18.6% (34)	15.6% (30)	12.3% (22)	23.3% (42)	12.0% (21)	12.5% (22)	11.3% (20)	12.1% (22)	10.5% (19)	11.8% (21)
Det Radikale Venstre	7.8% (14)	7.8% (14)	5.8% (11)	5.3% (10)	7.3% (13)	15.0% (27)	14.4% (27)	11.2% (20)	7.1% (13)	3.6% (16)	5.4% (10)	5.1% (9)	5.5% (10)	6.2% (11)	5.6% (10)
Danmarks Kommunistiske Parti (Communists)	4.3% (8)	3.1% (6)	1.1% (0)	1.2% (0)	0.8% (0)	1.0% (0)	1.4% (0)	3.6% (6)	4.2% (7)	3.7% (7)	1.9% (0)	1.1% (0)	0.2% (0)	0.9% (0)	0.8% (0)
Denmarks Retsforbund (Justice Party)	3.5% (6)	5.3% (9)	2.2% (0)	1.3% (0)	0.7% (0)	0.7% (0)	1.7% (0)	2.9% (5)	1.8% (0)	3.3% (6)	2.6% (5)	1.4% (0)	1.5% (0)	0.5% (0)	—
Socialistisk Folkeparti (Socialist People's Party)	—	—	6.1% (11)	5.8% (10)	10.9% (20)	6.1% (11)	9.1% (17)	6.0% (11)	5.0% (9)	3.9% (7)	5.9% (11)	11.3% (21)	11.5% (21)	14.6% (27)	13.0% (23)
Venstresocialisterne (Left Socialist)	—	—	—	—	—	2.0% (4)	1.6% (0)	1.5% (0)	2.1% (4)	2.7% (5)	3.7% (6)	2.7% (5)	2.7% (5)	1.4% (0)	0.6% (0)
Kristeligt Folkeparti (Christian People's Party)	—	—	—	—	—	—	2.0% (0)	4.0% (7)	5.3% (9)	3.4% (6)	2.6% (5)	2.3% (4)	2.7% (5)	2.4% (4)	2.0% (4)
Fremskridtspartiet (Progress Party)	—	—	—	—	—	—	—	15.9% (28)	13.6% (24)	14.6% (26)	11.0% (20)	8.9% (16)	3.6% (6)	4.8% (9)	9.0% (16)
Centrum Demokraterne (Centre Democrats)	—	—	—	—	—	—	—	7.8% (14)	2.2% (4)	6.4% (11)	3.2% (6)	8.3% (15)	4.6% (8)	4.8% (9)	4.7% (9)
Fælles Kurs (Common Cause)	—	—	—	—	—	—	—	—	—	—	—	—	—	2.2% (4)	1.9% (0)
Others	3.2% (1)	2.7% (1)	3.7% (7)	3.7% (5)	4.1% (4)	2.2% (0)	0.2% (0)	—	—	0.9% (0)	0.4% (0)	0.2% (0)	0.1% (0)	1.5% (0)	1.3% (0)

urban areas (notably inner Copenhagen) voted against ratifying the Single European Act, being outvoted largely because of the heavy majorities in favour of those areas benefiting most from the Common Agricultural Policy. Even the majority of the pro-EC parties have been very cautious about further European political integration and the loss of the national veto. An important contributory factor has been that Denmark has been torn between its formal links with the European Community and those with its fellow Scandinavian countries.

The other issue which has been particularly contentious in recent years has been economic policy, with Denmark having a very big budget deficit. Unemployment has been much higher than in neighbouring Sweden. There has been a parliamentary majority in recent years for the present government's attempts to impose greater economic austerity. Some of the sharpest criticism, however, has come from the right-of-centre Progress Party, in particular, which is continuing to strike a responsive chord with many voters with its attacks on bloated bureaucracy, unnecessary government expenditure and high levels of taxation. These themes have been taken up by some of the government parties, but they still feel unable to make major cuts in taxation in existing economic circumstances. The Progress Party has thus continued to revive.

Another controversial economic issue has been economic democracy to which most of the parties subscribe as an objective but on which they are polarized over the means, especially over the proposals for centralized wage earner funds.

Socialdemokratiet
(Social Democratic Party)

Headquarters	:	Thorvaldsensvej 2, 1998 Frederiksberg C, Copenhagen (tel: 01–39 15 22)
Party chairman	:	Svend Auken
Chairman of the parliamentary group	:	Ritt Bjerregaard
General secretary	:	Steen Christensen
Youth movement	:	*DSU*
Members	:	100,000 (1988)
Founded	:	1878

History

A Danish section of the First International was founded in 1871, by Louis Pio, Harald Brix and Paul Geleff. In 1876 the first party congress was held, and a radical party programme (the *Gimle* programme) was adopted. In 1878 the party changed its name, and made a clear separation between its trade union and political activities. In 1882 P. Knudsen became chairman. *Det Socialdemokratiske Forbund* (The Social Democratic Association) made its entry into the *Folketing* in 1884 with two seats on 4.9 per cent of the vote. It supported the liberal opposition to the ruling conservative government.

In 1909 it won more votes (28.7 per cent) than any other party, but was far behind the Liberals in terms of seats. It lent its support, however, to a Radical Liberal-led government under Zahle. In 1913 the Social Democrats revised their 1876 programme, confirming their evolution into a moderate party seeking a parliamentary route to socialism.

During World War I the party's leader, Thorvald Stauning (who had taken over from P. Knudsen in 1910), joined a coalition government (in 1916), and became the first Social Democratic minister.

In 1924 Stauning formed the first Social Democratic government, on a minority basis, but with support from the Radical Liberals. This followed the 1924 elections in which the Social Democratic Party won 55 seats on 36.6 per cent of the vote and overtook *Venstre* to become the largest party in terms of both votes and seats.

In 1929 the Social Democrats won over 40 per cent of the vote, and formed a coalition government with the Radical Liberals. Stauning again became Prime Minister, and the coalition lasted until 1940. Its greatest achievement was to lay the basis for the Danish welfare state, which was confirmed by a broad inter-party agreement in 1933 on a package of social and other measures (the *Kanslergade Forlig*).

From 1918 until 1935 the Social Democrats gained more votes in each successive election, rising to their best ever performance of 46.1 per cent in 1935. Party membership also rose steadily, from 78,000 in 1917 to over 200,000 at the onset of World War II.

In 1939 Hans Hedtoft took over from Stauning as the new Party chairman. After the war proposals that the Party should merge with the Communists came to nothing. The Social Democrats' support fell sharply away to 32.8 per cent and 48 seats in the first postwar election, largely as a result of the Communists new-found strength. Although the party had formed the first postwar government (under Buhl) it now went into opposition until 1947.

The Social Democrats, however, made a strong recovery. From 1947 to 1968 the Social Democrats provided all the Prime Ministers, apart from a short period in 1950–1953 when they were in opposition. Hans Hedtoft led Social Democratic minority administrations in

1947–50 and 1953–1955, as did H. C. Hansen in 1955–1957. In 1957 a period of formal coalition governments was initiated, under Hansen (1957–1960) and Viggo Kampmann (1960) with the Radical Liberals and the Justice Party, two more under Kampmann again (1960–62) and then Jens Otto Krag (1962–64) with the Radical Liberals only.

In 1961 the party revised its programme. The new programme "The Road Forward" downplayed the importance of nationalization.

The party's electoral support remained steady for the whole period from 1947 to the mid 1960s, fluctuating around the 40 per cent figure. Party membership, however, drifted slowly downwards. In 1965 the party's name was changed to *Socialdemokratiet — Danmark*.

From 1964 to 1966 Krag led a minority Social Democratic administration but in 1966 the Social Democrats and the Socialist People's Party (SF) won an overall left-wing majority for the first time. While no formal coalition was possible because of SF's objections on foreign policy issues such as NATO, it provided parliamentary support to a Krag government, and a contact committee ("Red Cabinet") was set up to liaise between the two parties. In December 1967, however, the government was brought down as a result of a schism within the SF, in particular over the government's devaluation of the Danish Krone and accompanying wage freeze. In the ensuing elections in 1968 the Social Democrats lost substantial support and went into opposition for the first time for 15 years. In opposition the party revised its internal structures and made a marked shift to the left.

In 1971 Krag returned to power. His new administration was dominated by the issue of Danish entry into the EC, which the leadership supported but which divided the party. In the decisive vote in the *Folketing* 12 Social Democrats voted against adhesion and one abstained. Krag later stood down for personal reasons, and was replaced as Prime Minister by the trade unionist Anker Jørgenson.

In 1973 Jørgenson also became party chairman. In the run-up to the 1973 election the party was also damaged by the resignation of one of its most popular vote-getters, Erhard Jacobsen, who objected to the party's leftward drift and founded a new Centre Democratic Party. The 1973 elections saw a major setback for the Social Democrats, with the party vote dropping from 37.3 per cent in 1971 to only 25.6 per cent.

Since 1973 the Social Democrats have had fluctuating success, but generally with much lower support than before. Anker Jørgenson succeeded, nevertheless, in forming five more governments from 1976 to 1982, mainly on a minority basis but including one, from 1978–79 in coalition with its traditional adversary *Venstre*, which provoked unrest within the labour movement.

The European issue also caused difficulties for the party, with strong opposition within it to the concept of direct election to the European Parliament. When the first direct elections were held in 1979 the party lost much support to the new People's Movement against the EC, a setback which was repeated in 1984 when the Social Democrats were dislodged for the first time since 1924 from their position as Denmark's largest party in all elections.

In 1977 the party re-wrote its basic programme. In 1982 it again went into opposition. After the 1987 elections, Anker Jørgenson stood down as leader after 15 years and was replaced by Svend Auken.

In 1988 the Social Democrats helped to bring down the government over the issue of visiting NATO warships to Danish ports. In the subsequent election they rose slightly to 29.8 per cent of the vote, but with the same number of seats (54) as in 1987. They again remained in opposition, extending their longest period of opposition since the 1920s.

The Social Democrats are also the strongest Danish party at local level. In 1985 they provided the mayor in 99 out of Denmark's 275 communes (in 27 of which they had an absolute majority), and won control of seven of the 14 *Amts* or County Councils.

Support

In spite of the loss of support from the 40 per cent level they generally enjoyed from the late 1920s until the late 1960s, to the the present level of around 30 per cent (31.6 per cent in 1984, 29.3 per cent in 1987, 29.8 per cent in 1988), the Social Democrats are still Denmark's largest party in national elections, with broad-based support in cities and small towns. They are considerably stronger in local elections (35.2 per cent of the vote in the last communal election in 1985, and 36.2 per cent in the 1985 county council election). Only in European Parliament elections have they been much weaker (21.9 per cent in 1979, 19.5 per cent in 1984).

They are still strong among industrial and white-collar workers. Trade union members, pensioners and the less well educated have given higher than average support to the party.

In the 1988 election the Social Democrats had a very even distribution of support between the three major electoral regions of Denmark, 29.4 per cent in Greater Copenhagen, 29.9 per cent in the Islands and 29.8 per cent in Jutland.

The Social Democrats used to have a higher than average vote in inner Copenhagen, but their vote fell by between 7 and 8 per cent in each of the three Greater Copenhagen constituencies between 1984 and 1987. Although it recovered by between 1.5 and 2 per cent between 1987 and 1988 it is still lower than the national average in the two of the three constituencies (28.6 per cent in 1988 in South Copenhagen, 28.8 per cent in West Copenhagen and 30.3 per cent in East Copenhagen). It has lost ground in particular to the Socialist People's Party, and is behind them in seven out of the 19 inner Copenhagen electoral districts. The Social Democrats are strongest in the electoral districts of Bispebjerg, Valby, Husum and Enghave, but nowhere does it now get over 40 per cent of the vote. It is weakest in Frederiksberg Commune and in the city centre (Radhus Kredsen).

The Social Democrats are somewhat weaker in the outer Copenhagen suburbs (27.8 per cent in Copenhagen county in 1988), with pockets of considerable strength and also districts with its lowest vote in the whole country (e.g. the affluent commuter zone of Hellerup where it is the third party with only 10.5 per cent in 1988). The party is also particularly weak in the prosperous *Amt* (county) of Frederiksborg in Northern Zealand (24.7 per cent in 1988, its second-weakest county in Denmark).

On the other hand the party's strongest county in Denmark is the *Amt* of Storstrøm (Southern Zealand, Lolland and Falster), where it won 38 per cent in 1988, and 46.1 per cent in the last county council elections in 1985. Its greatest stronghold is the shipbuilding town of Nakskov (49.7 per cent in 1988), which has had very high unemployment.

In Funen (31.9 per cent support throughout the *Amt* in 1988) the Social Democrats are strongest in parts of its largest town, Odense.

The Social Democrats have uneven support in Jutland, ranging from a high of 34.7 per cent in 1988 in North Jutland *Amt* (their second-best county in Denmark) and 31.6 per cent in Århus *Amt* to a low of 26 per cent in Ribe *Amt* and only 22.8 per cent in Ringkøbing *Amt*, its weakest county in the whole of Denmark. In individual Jutland communes the Social Democrats are particularly strong in parts of Ålborg and Randers, where they regularly obtain over 40 per cent of the vote. Unlike the rest of the country the party's 1988 vote in Jutland actually fell slightly compared to 1987.

The Social Democrats are also strong on the Island of Bornholm, where their vote has been rather stable and where they won 34.6 per cent in 1988.

Organization

The Social Democrats have more members than any other Danish party. They do not yet have a central membership register (now proposed) but this is currently estimated at around 100,000, down from around 307,000 in 1949, although relatively stable over the last 10 years. Basic party membership dues are currently 120 crowns a year.

The lowest tier of the party organization is its local branches, currently around 685. Above these are the 103 electoral district organizations and the 15 *Amt* or county organizations.

At national level a congress is held, generally on a four-year basis. It consists of around 900–1000 delegates. One of its main tasks is to elect the party's national chairman (effectively its political leader), vice-chairman and also secretary-general. A smaller annual conference (*Arsmøde*) is also held, and discusses broad political questions.

The party has a national board (*Hovedbestyrelse*) of around 80–100 members, of whom 56 have voting rights. Besides the top party officers (and only one representative of the *Folketing* group) and representatives from associated organizations, it generally includes the chairman of the *Amt* (county) organizations, and further representatives from each *Amt* according to their size. The national board generally meets every second month.

The executive committee (*Forretningsudvalg*) has 15 members, including the party's top national officers, the chairman of the *Folketing* group, representatives from associated organizations, as well as six other representatives from the national board. It generally meets every four days.

The Party's *Folketing* candidates are chosen by ballot or meetings within the electoral districts. The party now generally opts for the system according to which its elected candidates are those who receive the most personal votes within the constituency rather than on their place on a party list. Individual parliamentarians are closely accountable to their local organizations.

The party has a youth organization, the DSU, which currently has around 17,000 members. It is a totally separate organization, and its members do not have to be members of the main Party. It has two representatives on the main party's national board, and one in its executive committee. There are also student branches (*Frit Forum*).

The Social Democrats have another youth and sports organization *DUI-leg og Virke*, which has two representatives on the national board, and also a high-school organization.

There is no separate Party women's organization, but there must be at least 40 per cent representation of either sex on local branch executives, as well as a certain percentage of either sex on the party's lists for communal elections. The party is currently examining a proposal for a certain percentage of women candidates within a multi-member constituency for *Folketing* elections (less easy to impose because of candidates being chosen in individual electoral districts).

The trade union federation, LO, is not organically linked to the party but relations are very close. The Social Democrats and LO are represented in each other's top management bodies, with LO having two representatives on the party's national board and two on its executive committee (including LO's chairman) while the chairman and vice-chairman of the party are themselves on the LO executive. Moreover all chairmen of individual trade unions who are Social Democrats attend the party congress. At lower level relations are more informal.

The non-agricultural co-operative movement also has close relations with the party and has a representative on both the party's national board and its executive committee.

The Social Democrats have the largest further education association of any of those linked to Danish political parties. It is called the AOF.

The party currently has no newspaper going out to its membership. It used to have one, but it was wound up in the early 1980s. It does, however, produce a magazine to which members can subscribe, *Ny Politik*, of which there are six to eight editions a year.

Under the auspices of the so-called *A Pressen*, which is owned by the labour movement, there is a national newspaper *Det Fri Aktuelt*, which supports the Social Democrats. There are also two much smaller local newspapers owned by the labour movement, one in Bornholm (*Bornholmeren*) and one in Nakskov (*Ny Dag*).

The Social Democrats are members of the Socialist International. Their three members in the European Parliament sit in the Socialist Group, and are also non-voting members of the party's national board within Denmark.

The party is in the Social Democratic group within the Nordic Council, and also represented within SAMAK, the Nordic Co-operation of Labour Movements. It is also active within SCANDILUX, the disarmament and defence policy group of Social Democratic parties in small northern European NATO lands.

Policies

Socialdemokratiet is a pragmatic party in the Scandinavian Social Democratic tradition. During the current and unfamiliar period of opposition, its policies on economic and social issues have not changed greatly, and mainly differ in emphasis and tone from the present government, whereas its policies on defence and security issues have tended to move to the left.

Socialdemokratiet is still a not very ideological party in terms of its economic policy. It calls for a public sector with a more active role in co-operation with the private sector, but it does not call for major nationalizations in the conventional sense. It has opposed some suggested privatizations, but this has not been a major plank of its policy. It supports planning, but opposes a rigidly planned economy. It has put a major emphasis on the need for a stronger industrial policy, and for more investment in industry.

Its most distinctive policies concern the spreading of economic democracy and industrial ownership to wider numbers of people. Wage earners would come to jointly own capital in companies through collective ownership based on common central funds.

The Social Democrats do not believe that the Danish economy can afford any cuts in taxation at present. There should, however, be tax reform, tough action against tax evasion, and lowering of VAT rates for some goods. They strongly defend the Danish Welfare State of which they were the most prominent architects. They believe that social services should be maintained and strengthened, but that their administration should be streamlined.

The Social Democrats put an increasingly high emphasis on environmental policy. The party has become increasingly opposed to civil nuclear energy, and is now working towards its eventual abandonment at wider European level.

As regards refugees into Denmark, the party calls for a more coherent policy for their integration into Danish society.

In the course of its history the party has had several shifts on defence policy. Before World War II they supported Danish neutrality, but in 1949 it was a Social Democratic government under Hedtoft that brought Denmark into NATO. As late as 1979 the government under the leadership of the Social Democrat, Jørgenson, supported NATO's dual track strategy. In opposition however, the Social Democrats have changed emphasis, while still not opposing NATO. Their opposition has had considerable effect as the Schlüter government has not enjoyed the same parliamentary majority on these issues or on economic questions. In December 1982 the Social Democrats successfully sponsored a resolution in the *Folketing* that Denmark should not accept NATO missiles on Danish soil whilst the Geneva talks were in progress. They later pushed for a Nordic nuclear-free zone and for the development of a more "defensive" Danish defence. They sought a NATO commitment to no first use of nuclear weapons, a nuclear test ban and nuclear weapon freeze and also a phased reduction in conventional weapons. In 1988 they effectively brought down the Schlüter government over the issue of strengthening Danish policy over the visits of NATO warships, which might be carrying nuclear weapons, to Danish ports.

An issue which has been highly divisive within the party has been the question of Danish membership of European Community. The party took a decision in favour of entry, but the trade union movement was split and a significant minority within the party were actively hostile. Some (including the present party leader) were active in a Social Democratic movement against the EC, and some subsequently joined the People's Movement Against the EC.

The party now fully accepts Danish membership of the European Community. It supports enhanced European co-operation, reflating the European economy, providing a concerted response to environmental pollution, and asserting greater European independence from the two superpowers. It is still opposed, however, to a political union. It does not want to change the existing institutional balance and supports the retention of the national veto. It believes that the European Parliament should not be turned into a fully fledged legislature, and it was opposed also to the ratification of the Single European Act. It supports European Political Co-operation as long as national sovereignty is properly maintained, and is hostile to any transfer of powers to the Community institutions in the fields of defence policy.

The Social Democrats support the development of a full European internal market, although this should be complemented by measures to help Europe's peripheral regions. European standards should be the highest possible minimum standards, and should not stop individual member states adopting even higher standards if they so desire. The Social Democrats are opposed to full monetary union. They support the development of European industrial policy, European merger policy and enhanced research and development. They call for reform of the Common Agricultural Policy.

The Social Democrats also emphasize that European co-operation should be seen in wider terms than just the EC. They are strong advocates of enhanced Nordic Co-operation and would support Norwegian entry into the EC. They also call for stronger links with Eastern European countries.

They advocate an increase in aid to developing countries. They have been leading advocates of sanctions against South Africa.

Personalities

The party's current leader is Svend Auken, born in 1943. He had been chairman of the party student group *Frit Forum* and was elected to the *Folketing* in 1971. In 1971–72 he was a leading member of "Social Democrats against the EC". From 1977 to 1982 he was Denmark's Labour Minister. He took over from Anker Jørgensen as party chairman in 1987.

The chair of the party's *Folketing* group is Ritt Bjerregaard and its two vice-chairmen are Birte Weiss and Paul Nyrup Rasmussen.

Socialistisk Folkeparti — SF
(Socialist People's Party)

Headquarters	: Christiansborg, DK 1240 Copenhagen K (tel: 01–12 70 11)
Chairman	: Gert Petersen
Chair of parliamentary group	: Ebba Strange
General secretary	: Lillian Ubbesen
Youth movement	: *Socialistisk Folkepartis Ungdom*
Newspaper	: *Folkesocialisten*
Members	: 9,300 (1988)
Founded	: February 1959

History

The *Socialistisk Folkeparti* (SF) was founded in 1959 as a result of a split within the Danish Communist Party, which had been severely shaken in 1956 by Kruschev's revelations about Stalin, and later by the events in Hungary. Its charismatic chairman, Aksel Larsen, was at the forefront of efforts to open up and liberalize the Danish Party, which met with intense resistance from the old guard. Larsen was expelled and then formed SF, of which he became the first chairman. The new party put itself forward as a Marxist party that was critical and independent of the Soviet Union, that accepted a peaceful and democratic transition to socialism within Denmark, and that was democratic in its own internal functioning.

In its first election in 1960 SF proved to be a successful new challenger to the traditional

Danish parties, winning 6.1 per cent of the vote and 11 seats, and forcing the Communist Party's vote to fall to only 1.1 per cent of the vote and to lose its last seats in the *Folketing*.

In the 1964 election SF's vote remained stable, but in 1966 it rose to 10.9 per cent and 20 seats in the *Folketing*, giving the left-of-centre parties a parliamentary majority for the first time. There were significant policy differences between SF and the Social Democrats, notably on foreign policy and defence, but SF decided to lend parliamentary support to a Social Democratic minority government under J. O. Krag. A liaison committee was established between the two parties, that became known as the "Red Cabinet". SF was forced to make compromises, accepting, for example, a budget including defence expenditure, whereas they had previously abstained on such votes. There was increasing tension within SF over this co-operation with the Social Democrats, and eventually there was a split within the party , which led to six of its *Folketing* members voting against the government, and helping to bring it down. The immediate cause was disagreement over government economic austerity measures, but personal factors, involving clashes with Larsen's strong personality, also played a role. The dissident members subsequently formed a new party *Venstresocialisterne* (Left Socialists — see separate entry).

In the 1968 election SF was punished by the electorate, and its vote dropped to 6.1 per cent and 11 seats, with the new Left Socialists winning 2 per cent and four seats. Larsen stood down as SF chairman in 1968 and was replaced by Sigurd Ømann.

In the 1971 elections the party's vote again rose to 9.1 per cent and 17 seats, and it later co-operated with Krag's new minority Social Democratic government from 1971–72. SF adopted a hostile position to the European Community, and a number of its members became closely involved with the People's Movement Against the EC.

In the three subsequent elections SF's vote dropped sharply. In 1974 Gert Petersen became the new party chairman, a post he has retained to the present day. In 1976–78 the party was troubled by more internal controversy, between former Larsen supporters ("Larsenists") and other members, and between members of the parliamentary party and the party activists. Before the 1977 election, five of its *Folketing* members were pushed out. A number of the "Larsenists" left the party, and several joined the Social Democrats. All this contributed to the party's worst ever election result in 1977, at only 3.9 per cent and seven seats.

In 1979 the party's vote went up to 5.9 per cent and 11 seats. In the European Parliament elections it had a lower vote, at 4.7 per cent and one seat, and was clearly damaged by the success of the People's Movement against the EC. In 1980 SF adopted a new party programme.

In the 1981 and 1984 elections it won over 11 per cent of the vote and 21 seats, and its vote went up sharply compared to 1979 in the 1984 European election, where it won 9.2 per cent, with two seats in the Parliament. In 1987 SF was able to take advantage of left wing disillusionment with the Social Democrats, especially within Copenhagen and other Danish cities, and its vote rose to its highest ever level of 14.6 per cent and 27 seats in the *Folketing*. In 1988 its vote fell back again to 13 per cent and it obtained 23 seats.

Support

SF's highest support base is among left-wing intellectuals. It also had strong working-class support when it was first founded, but this later dropped, although it has again recovered to a considerable extent in the 1980s. SF is strong among young people, women, workers in the public sector, and among teachers, nurses and social workers. Its support is concentrated in the inner cities and to a much lesser extent the suburbs. It is weak in rural areas.

Its strongest political base is inner Copenhagen, where it won 23.9 per cent of the vote in the 1988 elections (25.3 per cent in 1987), and where its strength is not far short of the Social Democrats. It has a higher vote than the Social Democrats in seven out of the 19 electoral districts in the city, and is the largest party in five (Blågård, Nørrebro, Vesterbro, Østbane and Østerbro). In Nørrebro and Vesterbro it won over 30 per cent of the vote in 1988.

It is weaker in outer Copenhagen (15.8 per cent in 1988), although even here it has pockets of support such as "academic" Albertslund (28.2 per cent in 1988). It has over 10 per cent of the vote in the rest of Zealand (significantly winning a higher vote in 1988 in affluent Frederiksborg *Amt* at 12.9 per cent than in less privileged and more Social Democratic Storstrøm *Amt* at 10.7 per cent), in Funen *Amt* (12.9 per cent in 1988, with its highest vote in east Odense) and in East Jutland (14.5 per cent in Århus *Amt* and 10.9 per cent in Vejle *Amt*). Its strongest base outside Copenhagen is Denmark's second city of Århus where it has won almost 25 per cent in its eastern electoral district, and won almost as many votes as the Social Democrats in 1988.

SF is weakest of all in southern and western Jutland (6.5 per cent in Ringkøbing *Amt* in 1988,

6.9 per cent in South Jutland *Amt*, 7.6 per cent in Viborg *Amt*, 8.5 per cent in Ribe *Amt*). It won under 5 per cent of the vote in some of the small towns in western Jutland (e.g. Skjern in Ringkøbing *Amt*, where it won 4.3 per cent in 1987). It is slightly stronger in Bornholm *Amt* (9.5 per cent in 1988).

Organization

SF's organization is particularly characterized by the tighter accountability of its parliamentary group to the national party organization than in most other Danish parties. The parliamentary group has to follow the guidelines laid down in the annual conference and has an obligation to report to the party's central committee or executive committee before voting on important political matters. There can be no more than three *Folketing* members on the executive committee. The party organization also has a greater say over the order in which the party's *Folketing* candidates are elected. At times this has seriously limited the room for manoeuvre of the parliamentary leadership.

SF currently has over 9,300 members, with a slowly increasing membership. It has 200 branches around the country, each with between 10 and 400 members. It has no organizational tier within the electoral districts, and the next level of organization is its *Amt* (county) organizations.

SF's annual national conference (*Landsmøde*) has greater significance every second year when it elects the party chairman (who is the party's national leader) and the nationally elected members of the central committee. Each party branch is eligible for one voting representative for every 40 members, and each *Amt* organization sends an observer.

The party's central committee or national executive (*Hovedbestyrelse*), which has a very powerful role within the party, consists of 39 members, the party chairman, 23 members elected at national conference and 15 by the *Amt* and Greater Copenhagen organizations. The central committee chooses the party's general secretary. It meets around 10 times a year.

SF has an executive committee (*Forretningsudvalg*) of nine members, the chairman, the chairman of the *Folketing* group and one more member from the group, and six members chosen by the central committee. It meets every two weeks. There is a smaller executive committee secretariat of four, including the chairman and the chairman of the *Folketing* group which meets every Wednesday. There are also 20 party committees, which prepare the party's policies in specific fields, such as taxation and agriculture.

The party's *Folketing* candidates are generally chosen by secret ballot of all SF members within an *Amt*. Three of the *Amt* organizations have opted to let their *Folketing* candidates be chosen by the number of preference votes that they have received. The others have chosen the party list system, whereby the order of election is determined by a candidate's position on the list, with the order also being decided in the secret ballot of members.

The party's youth movement is called the *Socialistisk Folkepartis Ungdom* (Socialist People's Party Youth, SFU) and is an independent organization, with its own structure and programme. It has two representatives on SF's central committee and one on its executive committee. This is also the case within the party's women's groups, the *Kvindegrupperne i SF*. The party also has a rule whereby either sex has a right (but no duty) to constitute 40 per cent of the party's office-holders. Recently new rules have been put forward to ensure more even balance between the sexes (although SF already has a good record in this respect) in the lists of *Folketing* candidates. European Parliament candidates are chosen by members throughout the whole country.

SF also has its own labour organization, *Fagligt Landsudvalg* (FLU), a local government organization, KPLU, and a party further education association, the *Socialistisk Folkeoplysningsforbund* (SFOF).

The party has a newspaper, *Folkesocialisten*, which goes out to all party members. There is a theoretical magazine, *Praksis*, of which there are around five editions a year, and another weekly periodical *Socialistisk Weekend*. The SF also has its own publishing house *Socialistisk Perspektiv*, SP-forlag.

Membership dues are based on members' gross incomes, from 45 crowns for a three-month period up to 135 crowns. Seventy per cent of membership dues go to the central party organization, and 30 per cent to the branches.

SF's closest international affiliations are with the other Scandinavian left Socialist parties who sit in the Left Group within the Nordic Council.

Within the European Parliament its two MEPs are in the Communist and Allies group. the MEPs have speaking but not voting rights on SF's own central committee.

Policies

The Socialist People's Party is a left-wing socialist party which seeks to occupy what is seen as a wide political space between a communist party too closely linked to Moscow, and a Social Democratic party which has been too much a part of the existing system. SF has emphasized its own internal democracy, and the party's independent defence of Danish interests outside the framework of superpower block politics. It has developed close links with the women's, environmental, anti-nuclear and peace movements.

While SF seeks major changes in the Danish capitalist system it recognizes that these cannot be carried out overnight. It has, therefore, emphasized a gradualist approach aiming at the election of a left-wing reformist Danish government, which would make a few breaches in the existing system. Its immediate objective is achievement of a parliamentary majority for the left-of-centre or "workers'" parties, primarily itself and the Social Democrats (the two parties were only seven seats short of such a majority in 1987). It has thus sought closer co-operation with the Social Democrats before elections. SF would then be in a better position to decide whether to enter a formal government coalition, which would give it greater influence but lessen the party's independence, or else to support a minority government from outside on the basis of a co-operation agreement.

SF's economic policy calls for economic decisions to be taken on a wider basis than just profits, such as the need for full employment and environmental protection. It seeks radical redistribution between the public and private sectors, stronger public support for industry, and more public investment. There should be more selective state management of trade policy.

The party does not call for extensive further nationalizations, as it believes that these could lead to more bureaucracy and inefficiency. Even in the sensitive field of provision of credit SF believes that public objectives can be achieved in other ways than outright nationalization of banks and credit institutions, such as through more state appointees on their management boards. It also wants public administrations as a whole to become more efficient.

SF does not believe that there is currently scope for generalized wage increases, but wants these to be concentrated on those with lower incomes. It does not believe that the existing tax burden can be cut in the current economic circumstances. The emphasis should be on redistributing the burden of taxation and on imposing, for example, a special tax on the wealthy. SF also calls for a reduction in the working week to 35 hours.

SF puts a particularly heavy emphasis on the need for greatly increased economic and industrial democracy. Workers should have much more influence in their workplace, and

there should be a Central Economic Democracy fund based on distributed profits.

SF strongly defends the welfare state. It supports central state pensions rather than firm-based pension schemes. It strongly opposes the use of civil nuclear energy, and emphasizes support for conservation and for renewable sources of energy.

SF calls for foreign refugees to be better integrated within Danish society. It recognizes that there have to be some limits to the numbers entering, but that this has not yet been reached.

SF has always had strong links with the peace movement. It campaigned strongly against US involvement in Vietnam in the 1960s. It has constantly advocated Danish departure from NATO and has strongly supported the idea of a Nordic nuclear-free zone. It believes that the recent circular letter compromise on the issue of visits of NATO warships to Denmark is too weak.

SF calls for Danish departure from the European Community on the grounds that it makes it more difficult to carry out Socialist policies, and undercuts Danish sovereignty. While Denmark is still a member, however, SF is prepared to take an active role within the Community institutions in order to defend Danish interests as well as possible. SF seeks the highest possible European environmental and safety standards which under no account should prevent Denmark from applying even higher standards.

SF strongly opposes any moves towards further European integration. It defends the continuation of the national veto, and opposed the Single European Act. It believes that the European Parliament can be a useful forum for developing wider international contacts, but that its powers should not be increased. At present, SF seems prepared not to make these longer-term foreign policy positions (especially on NATO and the EC) such obstacles to co-operation as they were in the past.

SF is a strong advocate of enhanced solidarity with developing countries. It is opposed to sophisticated hand-outs to these countries, and to tied development aid. On other foreign policy issues SF has attempted to be even-handed in its criticism of human rights violations and foreign policy intervention, whether committed by capitalist or socialist countries. It has called for tough sanctions on South Africa.

Personalities

SF's chairman since 1974 has been Gert Petersen, who was born in 1927. He was in the German resistance movement, and was in a German prison camp in 1944–45. He has been a *Folketing* member since 1966, and was in the European Parliament in 1977–79. The chair of SF's parliamentary group is Ebba Strange, who has been in the *Folketing* since 1973, and has chaired the SF group since 1977.

Det Konservative Folkeparti
(Conservative People's Party)

Headquarters	:	Tordenskjoldgade 21, 1055 Copenhagen (tel: 01–13 41 40)
Party chairman	:	Poul Schlüter
Chairman of the parliamentary party	:	Hans Engell
Youth movement	:	*Konservativ Ungdom*
Party newspaper	:	*Vor Tid*
Membership	:	45,000
Founded	:	1915 (under present name)

History

In the late 19th century the main political struggle in Denmark was between the "right" (*Høyre*) who dominated the Upper House and ran the Danish government, and the left (*Venstre*), the primarily liberal opposition in the Lower House, who sought the introduction of true parliamentary government. Once the latter was achieved in 1901 *Høyre* lost power. While they continued to win between 18 and 24 per cent of the vote they had a much lower proportion of actual seats, and were well behind both the Liberals and the Social Democrats.

In 1915 a number of members of the old "right" adopted a more reformist stance, and re-named themselves the Conservative People's Party. In the interwar years the new party had a relatively stable level of support at between 16.5 and 20.5 per cent of the national vote, and generally remained the third-largest party after the Social Democrats and *Venstre*. In the 1920s it provided parliamentary support for three *Venstre* governments but from 1929 onwards the conservatives and *Venstre* were constantly in the opposition, although they continued to hold a powerful position in the Upper House.

Apart from one poor election result in 1947 (when the party only won 12.4 per cent of the vote) the Conservatives continued at their pre-war level of support (16–20 per cent) from 1945 until the mid-1960s. They remained in opposition for the entire period apart from in 1950 to 1953, when they held Cabinet posts in a coalition government under the *Venstre* Prime

Minister, Erik Eriksen, and with their leader Ole Bjørn Kraft, as Foreign Minister.

Closer co-operation with *Venstre* culminated in the adoption of a joint programme on economic policy at a meeting of the two parliamentary groups in 1959. During the 1960s there was persistent speculation about merger, although this did not materialise.

In 1966 party membership was at a peak of around 142,000. In 1968 the Conservatives entered into a new coalition government with *Venstre* and *Radikale Venstre*, with the latter's leader, Hilmar Baunsgaard as Prime Minister. While it had a number of successes, the coalition was perceived to be unsuccessful in reversing the growth of the welfare state and of taxation. Conservative ministers, in particular, become associated with a number of controversial measures, such as legalising pornography, and abortion law reform.

In 1971 the Party's vote fell sharply from 20.4 per cent to 16.7 per cent, but a far more severe drop occurred in 1973, when it only won 9.2 per cent and 16 seats. The party was especially hurt by the arrival of three new parties, tapping different elements of the Conservative support base. In the 1975 election the Conservatives fared even worse, obtaining only 5.5 per cent of the vote and 10 seats in the *Folketing*, by far their lowest level of support since their foundation.

From 1975 onwards, however, the Conservatives made a strong recovery, benefiting from an image of constructive opposition, from a fall in Progress Party and *Venstre* support, and also from becoming the main opposition party on the right when *Venstre* went into government coalition with the Social Democrats in 1978–79. Moreover Poul Schlüter, who became chairman of the *Folketing* group and of the party in 1976, proved to be a successful party leader. In successive elections the Conservatives improved their vote to 8.5 per cent and 15 seats in 1977, 12.5 per cent and 22 seats in 1979 and 14.5 per cent and 26 seats in 1981.

In the 1979 European elections they won 14 per cent and two seats in the Parliament. In September 1982 Poul Schlüter became the first Conservative Prime Minister since 1901, at the head of a four-party coalition between the Conservatives, *Venstre*, Centre Democrats and Christian People's Party (the so-called "four-leaf clover government"). An austerity economic programme was launched which, while not exactly popular, was regarded as constituting the firm action necessary by many in the Danish electorate. In the January 1984 election the Conservatives won their highest ever level of support with 23.4 per cent of the vote and 42 seats. In the European election of that year they won 20.8 per cent of the vote (and four seats in the European Parliament).

In 1986 the government called a successful referendum on the Single European Act. By the 1987 elections, however, the government had lost some popularity and the Conservatives slipped back. Schlüter, however, was able to re-form a minority four-party coalition.

In 1988 a dispute over how to react to possible visits of nuclear warships to Danish ports led to a wider dispute concerning Denmark's NATO and security policy. The government could not count on the support of *Radikale Venstre* on these issues and in May 1988 new elections were called, in which the Conservative vote again dropped to 19.3 per cent and a further four seats were lost, leaving the party with 34 seats. Nevertheless Poul Schlüter was again able to form a new government, this time with *Venstre* and *Radikale Venstre* as his coalition partners.

Support

The Conservative Party has traditionally been seen as the party of employers and industrialists, stronger in the urban and suburban areas, and weaker in the countryside. Even within the cities its appeal has been to the self-employed and those on higher salaries and managerial staff. It has had very little support among manual workers (less than the Progress Party, for example). Its voters have generally had higher incomes and higher levels of education than those of other Danish parties.

The party's recovery in the later 1970s led to a considerable extension in its electoral support among all social classes (although less among blue collar workers) and it became more of a national party, second only to the Social Democrats in terms of overall votes and in terms of winning support in all regions of the country. Its electoral support has again begun to fall, however, and it is clear that its electoral base is a volatile one, with a relatively low number of core voters, and subject to considerable variation from election to election.

In regional terms the party's strongest electoral base is North Zealand and the outer Copenhagen suburbs. In the 1988 election it won 25.6 per cent of the vote in Frederiksborg *Amt* (county), 23.9 per cent in Copenhagen county and 22 per cent in Roskilde *Amt*. Its highest votes of all are in the affluent suburbs and commuter towns just to the north of Copenhagen, such as Hellerup (at 41.9 per cent the highest vote that it won in any Danish electoral district in 1988).

It has much lower support in inner Copenhagen, where it only won 17.9 per cent in 1988. Some of the working-class areas in the city record some of the party's lowest votes in the whole country (such as the electoral districts of Versterbro, Nørrebro, Enghave and Bispeeng, where the party's strength is only around 10 per cent). Nevertheless even within inner Copenhagen there are areas where the party does better, such as the centre of town and the commune of Frederiksberg. Another feature of the party's 1988 vote in inner Copenhagen was that, unlike anywhere else in Denmark, it actually rose slightly compared to 1987 (17.7 per cent to 17.9 per cent). In the rest of Zealand and in Funen its support is rather even at between 18 and 18.5 per cent, although falling by between 1.5 per cent and 2 per cent as compared to 1987.

In Jutland there is a steady drop in support from South to North Jutland. In the South Jutland *Amt* the Conservatives won 21.1 per cent in 1988 (but around 24 per cent in 1987 and 28 per cent in the 1984 national elections), and they won 19.1 per cent in Vejle *Amt* and 18.3 per cent in Ribe *Amt*. On the other hand they only won 16.5 per cent in North Jutland *Amt*, and just over 17 per cent in Ringkøbing, Viborg and Århus *Amts*. Jutland saw some of the sharpest falls in Conservative support between 1987 and 1988, with a 2.9 per cent drop in Viborg *Amt* and one of 2.8 per cent in South Jutland.

In both the Islands and Jutland regions the Conservatives get their highest support in the provincial towns, and especially in the more affluent parts of the larger cities (such as the Odense South and Ålborg West electoral districts). The Conservative's lowest support in the whole of Denmark is on the Island of Bornholm, where it only won 10.8 per cent in 1988.

Organization

The Conservative Party has around 45,000 members in 1988 (compared to 142,000 in 1966). The party has a broad geographical coverage, however, being organised in 325 local branches, with membership ranging from 50 to 2000. The party is also organized within the 103 electoral districts and at *Amt* level. Above this it also has a regional tier of organization, with three large regional associations (*landsdelssamenslutningerne*), in Jutland, the Islands, and the Copenhagen area. The chairmen of these regional associations are automatically vice-chairmen of the national party.

At national level there is an annual national congress (*landsrådet*), in which around 1500 delegates take part. Its resolutions are not binding on the Conservative parliamentary group, which enjoys great freedom of manoeuvre.

There is also a smaller national representatives assembly (*Repræsantskabet*), with around 300 to 400 members which meets at least once a year, and which has major responsibility in the field of organization. It also meets when a general election is called. Its members include representatives of the local branches, of the party's local councillors and of the parliamentary group and youth movement.

The national executive board (*Hovedbestyrelsen*) consists of around 80 people and meets around three or four times a year. There is a smaller executive committee of seven, which includes the party's chairman (its political leader) and the three vice-chairmen.

The party's *Folketing* candidates are chosen by local ballots or at party meetings. The number of preference votes won by each candidate is the preferred system of election. European Parliament candidates are chosen by a special meeting of the national representatives' assembly on the basis of candidates put forward by the *Amts* and subsequent recommendations from the party leadership.

The Conservative Youth organization is called *Konservativ Ungdom* (Conservative Youth). At times it has had a different policy emphasis (e.g. it is currently more liberal on economic policy matters) than the parent party, from which it is organizationally separate but linked (thus it has representatives in the main party bodies, such as the representative assembly. There is also a women's committee, *Konservative Kvindeudvalg*. Its members must also be full members of the parent party.

The Conservatives have their own local government association, the *Kommunaludvalg*, and their own further education association, the FOF (*Folkeligt Oplysnings Forbund*). There are traditional informal links, with the Danish Employers' Confederation, Federation of Danish Industry and Federation of Small Industry.

The Conservatives have their own party newspaper *Vor Tid* ("Our Time") which goes out to members and sympathizers around 10 times a year. There are also three small local newspapers linked to the party, but these are of little importance and do not have the significance of the local press still linked to *Venstre*. Among larger papers, the *Berlingske Tidende* is sympathetic, but does not have any formal links with the party. Membership dues are fixed by local branches, and normally range from between 150 to 200 crowns per member per year.

The Conservatives are members of the European Democratic Union and of the International Democratic Union. Within the European Parliament their members (currently four) sit in the European Democratic Group with the British

Conservatives and with the Spanish *Partido Popular*. They participate in the Conservative Group in the Nordic Council.

Policies

The Danish Conservative Party is a pragmatic party on the right-of-centre of the Danish political spectrum, willing to cooperate with other parties, including the Social Democrats. It tempers its belief in the freedom of the individual and of the private sector, with a recognition of the key role of the public sector and of the need to maintain a strong welfare state.

In the past it was seen as the party of the Danish establishment. Since 1970 it has had to compete for a far more volatile electorate, and has lost some support among Christian and cultural conservatives to the Christian People's Party and Centre Democrats respectively.

Its main loss of support, however, both in the early 1970s and now again in the late 1980s, has been to the Progress Party, which has put forward a much more populist message of drastic cuts in direct taxation and in the size of bureaucracy and the public sector. As a party of government the Conservatives have been seen by many to be a party of caution and compromise.

The Danish Conservatives have never campaigned against the public sector or against the idea of a strong state. They now consider, however, that there needs to be a different balance between the powers of the state and of individual citizens, one which is more weighted towards the latter; with lower levels of taxation and less bureaucracy.

When they first came to power in 1982 they took part in developing an austerity programme, including incomes and fiscal policies, and more efficient management of the public sector. They have since worked to cut spending on certain public services and to cut down on the number of civil servants. They consider that the desirable goal of reducing levels of taxation will have to be postponed until a more appropriate moment. They are also opposed to the Social Democratic plan for company profits to be channelled into central wage earner funds.

The Conservative Party has been strongly in favour of Danish membership of the European Community, supporting the Single European Act and the internal market by 1992. On the other hand they have a cautious attitude towards further European integration, considering that the EC member countries should fully explore present possibilities of co-operation within the existing Treaty framework before making bold new steps into the unknown. They believe that the national veto must be maintained. They are opposed, however, to the development of a two-speed Europe.

The Conservatives have been strong supporters of NATO, and consider that they have been severely handicapped by not being able to command a majority in the *Folketing* on defence and security issues over the last few years. They have accepted a compromise solution to the issue of visiting warships by agreeing to send a circular letter reiterating Denmark's policy of not accepting nuclear arms on Danish territory in peacetime. In return they have accepted a standstill defence budget growing only with inflation.

The Conservatives have been highly sceptical of the creation of Nordic nuclear-free zones, which they believe cannot be created on the basis of an isolated agreement, and without adequate safeguards, between the Nordic countries and the Soviet Union.

Personalities

The party chairman and current Prime Minister is Poul Schlüter, born in 1929 and first elected to Parliament in 1964. He has been chairman of the Conservative party from 1974 to 1977 and from 1981 to the present. He was chairman of the Conservative *Folketing* group from 1974 to 1982, when he became the first Conservative Prime Minister since 1901.

The second most influential figure within the party is Palle Simonsen, Social Minister in 1982, and the Minister of Finance from 1984 until the present. Erik Ninn Hansen, born in 1922, has been the Justice Minister since 1982. He was Defence Minister from 1968 to 1971, and Finance Minister for a brief period in 1971. Knud Østergaard has been the chairman of the Conservative parliamentary group since 1982. He was Minister of Defence for a short time in 1971.

Venstre
(Liberal Party)

Headquarters	: Søllerødvej 30, DK 2840 Holte (tel: 2–802 233)
Chairman	: Uffe Ellemann-Jensen
Chairman of *Folketing* group	: Ivar Hansen
General secretary	: Claus Hjort Frederiksen
Youth group	: *Venstres Ungdom*
Newspaper	: *Venstre Her og Nu*
Members	: 85,000 (early 1987)
Founded	: June 30, 1870

History

Venstre was founded in June 1870 as a new grouping of liberal forces, and became the first formally organized Danish political party. It included large numbers of farmers and other groups in the Danish countryside (such as the co-operatives and the folk high-school movement) as well as many from the liberal middle classes. It was called *Venstre* ("the Left") as it campaigned for constitutional and social reforms, and to distinguish itself from the conservative landed aristocracy, civil service and industrial establishment that governed Denmark, and that later became known as *Højre* ("the Right").

Venstre remained in opposition in the 1880s and 1890s; due to its weakness in the Upper House, although it became increasingly dominant in the Lower House. It remained stronger in the countryside than in the towns. It was not a very cohesive group, however, and divided into factions and competing groups. In 1895 a *Venstre* Reform Party was founded.

In 1901, with the introduction of the fully fledged parliamentary system that *Venstre* had been fighting to achieve, a *Venstre* Reform government finally came to power with an overwhelming majority in the Lower House. The *Venstre* Reform Party had 76 out of the 114 seats in the Chamber (on 42.9 per cent of the vote) and a second liberal party, the Moderate *Venstre*, had 12 seats on 8.1 per cent of the vote.

The dominance of the *Venstre* Reform Party was severely undermined by the breakaway in 1905 of a large number of its reformist members to form a new party called *Radikale Venstre*. Largely as a result of this split the *Venstre* Reform vote dropped from 47.9 per cent in 1903 to only 31.6 per cent in 1906. This was only partially compensated for by the subsequent reunification of the *Venstre* Reform Party and the Moderate *Venstre* Party in 1910, under the simple name *Venstre*.

Venstre remained the largest Danish party until the 1924 elections, although it was in opposition from 1909–10 and 1913–20. From 1920–24 it formed a new government with Conservative party support. In the 1924 elections its vote had fallen to 28 per cent, and it was overtaken by the Social Democrats in votes and seats. Its vote remained constant for the rest of the 1920s and it formed a second government with Conservative support from 1926–29. In the 1930s, however, *Venstre* began a further electoral decline, which took the party to only 17.8 per cent in 1935. It remained at the same 18 per cent level of electoral support until the war and was in opposition for the whole of the 1930s.

After the war *Venstre* had an electoral revival, which brought it to 23.4 per cent of the vote in 1945. A minority Liberal government was formed from 1945 to 1947, and in 1947 *Venstre's* vote rose further to 27.6 per cent. In 1950 its vote dropped sharply, but it was able to head a Liberal–Conservative coalition government (with Erik Eriksen as Prime Minister and with six other Venstre ministers), which lasted until 1953.

Some of *Venstre's* more conservative members, under the leadership of Knud Kristensen (a former *Venstre* leader and Prime Minister) broke away in 1953 to form a new independent party (*De Unafhængige*), which contested elections until the late 1960s, and won *Folketing* representation from 1960 to 1966.

In 1957 *Venstre's* vote rose, but it then began a steady decline which saw it lose votes and seats in six successive elections. It remained, however, the second-largest party, if only by a generally narrow margin from the Conservatives until 1968. In 1965 it suffered another schism when members from its left wing (including two of its *Folketing* representatives who were opposed to what they saw as the party's drift to the right departed to form a new party, the Liberal Centre (*Liberalt Centrum*). This won 2.5 per cent of the vote and four seats in the *Folketing* in 1966, but lost its seats in 1968, and did not contest further elections.

In 1968 *Venstre's* vote, at 18.6 per cent, fell below that of the Conservatives, but it subsequently entered a coalition government with *Radikale Venstre* and the Conservatives, with Hilmar Baunsgaard of *Radikale Venstre* as Prime Minister, and which lasted until 1971.

Unlike some other Danish parties, *Venstre* supported EC membership. In the 1973 election its vote fell for the sixth successive occasion to a new low of 1.3 per cent. In spite of this its leader, Poul Hartling, managed to form a minority *Venstre* government with only 22 out of the 175 seats in the *Folketing*, which endured from December 1973 to February 1975. In the 1975 elections *Venstre* had a massive increase in its vote to 23.3 per cent and 42 seats, but returned to opposition. In 1977 its vote again collapsed to only 12 per cent and 21 seats. Since then its vote has stabilized at between 10.5 and 12.5 per cent in all subsequent national elections.

In August 1978 it entered into a coalition with the Social Democrats, with the latter's Anker Jørgensen as Prime Minister, which lasted until October 1979. In the first European elections in 1979 *Venstre* won 14.5 per cent and three seats.

Venstre was in opposition from 1979 to 1982, but in September 1982 it entered into a new four-party coalition led by Poul Schlüter of the Conservatives, in which *Venstre* had six ministries (including Agriculture, which *Venstre* has held in every government in which it has participated since the war). *Venstre* has since remained in government. In the 1984 European elections its vote dropped to 12.4 per cent, and it only obtained two seats. In 1984 Henning Christophersen became an EC Commissioner and Uffe Ellemann-Jensen became the new chairman of the party.

Venstre has seven ministers in the renewed four-party government formed by Poul Schlüter after the 1987 elections, in which it won only 10.5 per cent, the lowest percentage this century. In the 1988 elections its vote rose to 11.8 per cent and it won 21 seats in the *Folketing*. It is now a member of the new three-party government (Conservatives, *Venstre* and *Radikale Venstre*) formed by Poul Schlüter, in which Uffe Ellemann-Jensen is still Foreign Minister, and *Venstre* has six other ministers.

Venstre is traditionally stronger at local than at national election level. In the last municipal election in 1985 it obtained 1,306 representatives in Denmark's municipal councils, and provides almost half of all Denmark's mayors.

Support

Venstre has traditionally been associated as the party of Denmark's farmers, especially of those with middle-sized and larger holdings. This is less true than it was, but *Venstre* still gets its strongest support in rural areas of Denmark. It does well in many small towns, and also has a significant following among liberal voters in the suburban areas. It is much weaker among working-class voters.

In regional terms this has meant very sharp variations in support with very low votes in inner cities, especially in Copenhagen, and high votes in West Jutland in particular, where it is the largest party in a number of communes. In 1988 these variations were from 3.9 per cent in inner Copenhagen to 21.8 per cent in Ringkøbing *Amt*.

Copenhagen is the area of greatest weakness for *Venstre*. Its 1988 figures of 3.9 per cent in inner Copenhagen actually represented a significant increase from only 2.5 per cent in 1987, when it was only the eighth party in terms of popular support. *Venstre* was particularly weak in the working-class electoral districts such as Vesterbro, Enghave, Bispepjerg and Bispeeng. Its highest Inner Copenhagen votes were in the central city electoral district (Radhuskredsen) and in parts of Frederiksberg. *Venstre* has a slightly stronger vote in outer Copenhagen. It won 5.5 per cent in Copenhagen *Amt* in 1988 (a sharp rise from only 3.5 per cent in 1987), doing best in affluent suburban areas like Hellerup.

Venstre's weakness in the Copenhagen area is shown by the fact that in 1987 it had only 572 members in inner Copenhagen, and 1132 in Copenhagen *Amt* and only 40 branches in both areas. In comparison *Venstre* had 3,400 members and 45 branches in the small Jutland town of Ringkøbing. *Venstre* has moderate levels of support in the rest of Zealand (ranging in 1988 from 9.2 per cent in Roskilde *Amt* to 11.4 per cent in West Zealand) and in Funen (9.4 per cent in 1988), where it is particularly weak in Odense.

Venstre's stronghold is Jutland, which in 1987 had 56,000 of the party's 85,000 members, and 708 of its 956 branches. *Venstre* is strongest in rural western Jutland, especially Ringkøbing *Amt* (21.8 per cent in 1988), Ribe *Amt* (20.9 per cent), Viborg *Amt* (19.3 per cent) and South Jutland *Amt* (16.6 per cent). It is the largest party in such communes as Varde (28.7 per cent in 1988), Ribe Town (25.2 per cent), Give (24.4 per cent) and Skjern (26.3 per cent).

Venstre is weaker in more urbanized East Jutland, although still winning votes above its national average. It polled 12.6 per cent in Århus *Amt*, 14.1 per cent in Vejle *Amt* and 14.4 per cent in North Jutland (in which *Amt*, however, it has its highest membership). Its lowest votes were in parts of the cities of Århus and Ålborg, and in the town of Randers, Vejle, Fredericia and Kolding. *Venstre* is also strong on the Island of Bornholm (19.8 per cent in 1988).

Organization

Venstre did not develop a proper central organization until 1929, but it has very strong local roots. It has the largest number of local branches (957) of any Danish party, and its 1987 membership of 85,000 makes it the second largest Danish party in terms of members, not far short of the electorally much stronger Social Democrats, and far ahead of its government partners, the Conservatives. It has a very high membership relative to its voters, 20 per cent in the country as a whole and rising to well over 30 per cent in some communes.

Above its 957 local branches *Venstre* is organized in the 103 electoral districts and in all the *Amts*. Its annual national conference has 700 to 800 representatives with voting rights. The conference directly elects the party chairman (its national leader) and deputy chairman.

The national executive (*Hovedbestyrelsen*) has between 50 and 60 members, of whom seven are directly elected by the national conference. Among its other members are the chairman and vice-chairman of the party's *Amt* organizations, as well as extra representatives for the *Amts* with the highest number of *Venstre* members. The national board meets around three times a year. The party's executive committee (*Forretningsudvalg*) meets rather more frequently, and consists of 11 members, including the party chairman, vice-chairman, treasurer and the chairman of the *Folketing* group.

Venstre's Folketing candidates can be chosen within individual electoral districts or else at overall *Amt* level. Chosen candidates are either listed in alphabetical order (meaning that the decisive factor is the number of preference votes that they receive) or else placed at the head of a list in an individual district.

Venstre's youth movement is called *Venstres Ungdom* and has a current membership of around 3,000 (it used to be much greater). Its chairman and vice-chairman have voting rights on the main party's national board.

There used to be a women's organization *Venstres Kvinder* but this no longer exists. *Venstre* also has a further education association *Liberalt Oplysnings Forbund* (LOF), whose chairman and vice-chairman have voting rights on the national board.

Venstre has no formal links with farmers' organizations, although there is a good deal of overlapping membership.

The party has its own newspaper *Venstre Her og Nu* ("*Venstre* Here and Now"), which goes out to its members a few times a year. A striking feature of *Venstre's* organization is that it has managed to retain stronger links with the local press than any other Danish party. There are still a large number of liberal-leaning local newspapers, with a high overall circulation. There is even an organization for *Venstre* newspaper editors, *Venstre Redaktørsforening*, which has two voting representatives on the *Venstre* national executive. The party's membership dues vary from area to area, with the usual range being around 100 to 500 crowns a year.

Venstre is a member of the Liberal International, and is also a member of the ELD. It has two members in the European Parliament, who have a right to one voting representative on the *Venstre* national board. *Venstre* is a member of the Centre group in the Nordic Council. It has links with the *Sambandspartiet* in the Faroes and with *Atassut* in Greenland.

Policies

Although it still has strong support among farmers, *Venstre* has evolved from being a more distinctively farmers' party into a more general party of the centre-right. It emphasizes economic liberalism, and the need for more personal freedom.

In its economic policy *Venstre* puts more emphasis on the need to strengthen market forces than its Conservative government partners; although differences in outlook are more ones of degree than of real substance. *Venstre* believes that too many restrictions are imposed on the individual, and that a more decentralized economy is needed; tax levels are too high; public expenditure should be held back, and where possible tasks should be switched from the public to the private sector. Tax-financed transfer payments could be complemented in some areas by insurance based schemes, and unemployment benefits, for example, could be based more on contributions by employers and employees, and less on those of the state.

On the important issue of economic democracy *Venstre* opposes what it describes as "fund socialism". It is prepared to support arrangements giving wage earners joint ownership of their enterprise, on condition that these are voluntary. There should be no state-imposed solution and centrally governed trust funds. As with most other Danish parties, *Venstre* does not carry its belief in the market to extremes, and it has advocated income policies for example. *Venstre* has also called for more decentralized government, and for more power to be given to the regions.

While relatively close to its current government partner, *Radikale Venstre*, on economic policy questions, it differs sharply from it on defence and EC policy. *Venstre* is a strong supporter of Danish NATO membership, and has felt constrained by the lack of a parliamentary majority for the government on defence and security questions.

As a party with a strong base in agricultural districts, *Venstre* was a strong advocate of EC membership for Denmark. It is prepared to support more far-reaching European integration than the large majority of Danish political parties, although it is still cautious on this matter. It is in favour of abolishing the veto in the longer term, and of restricting its use in the shorter term. One of its three representatives in the European Parliament voted in favour of the Spinelli Draft treaty on European Union, and the two others abstained. *Venstre* was in favour of ratification of the Single European Act.

Personalities

The party chairman is Uffe Ellemann-Jensen, born in 1941. He is a journalist by background (chief editor of *Dagbladet Børsen* in 1975–76) and entered the *Folketing* in 1977. He has been Denmark's Foreign Minister since 1982 and has been party chairman since 1984.

The party's deputy chairman since 1985 has been Anders Fogh Rasmussen. The chairman of the *Venstre* parliamentary group is Ivar Hansen, born in 1938. Denmark's current member of the European Commission is a former *Venstre* leader, Henning Christophersen.

Radikale Venstre
(Radical-Liberal Party)

Headquarters	: Christiansborg, DK–1240 Copenhagen K (tel: 01–11 66 00 or 01–12 72 51)
Political leader	: Niels Helveg Petersen
Chairman of parliamentary group	: Marianne Jelved
Chairman of national organization	: Thorkild Møller
Secretary-general	: Jens Clausager
Youth movement	: *Radikale Ungdom*
Party organ	: *Radikal Politik*
Membership	: 10,000 (1988)
Founded	: 1905

History

Radikale Venstre was founded in 1905, mainly by members of the reformist wing of the *Venstre* Party, whose leading spirit has been Viggo Hørup, and who felt that *Venstre* was becoming too closely associated with conservative forces, and was not proceeding rapidly enough with constitutional reforms. They also included a number of Pacifists. While much of the new party's support came from the urban and intellectual wings of *Venstre*, it also attracted a number of smallholders who believed that the new income tax system was favouring larger over small farmers. The party's founders derived considerable inspiration from the French Radical Social Party.

Radikale Venstre's first programme advocated Danish neutrality, abolition of the privileged franchise for the Upper House, universal suffrage for men and women over 21, democratic local elections and provisions for popular referenda. The party also sought land reform and a wide range of social and economic reforms, including progressive taxation, unemployment insurance and reduction of working hours. It also supported the temperance movement.

In its first national election, in 1906, *Radikale Venstre* obtained 14 per cent of the vote and 11 seats, and in 1909 it formed a government with Social Democratic support. The first Radical Cabinet, with C.Th. Zahle (1866–1946) as Prime Minister, only lasted one year, but Zahle again became Prime Minister in 1913 for a further period of seven years.

In successive elections until 1918 *Radikale Venstre* gained an increasing number of seats, and in 1918 it achieved its best ever result with 20.7 per cent of the vote, and 32 seats in the *Folketing*. In 1920, however, the party's support collapsed to under 12 per cent and 17 seats. Its vote then stabilized but in the late 1920s and 1930s it dropped gradually to just over 9 per cent.

Radikale Venstre continued to play a role as a coalition partner of the increasingly dominant Social Democrats. A Social Democratic Radical government under Thorvald Stauning was in power from 1929 to 1940, and the Radical leader, Dr Peter Munch (1870–1948) was Foreign Minister for the whole of that period.

After World War II the party's support remained at around 7.8 per cent until 1960, when it fell below 6 per cent in successive elections. For the whole of this period it was led by Bertel Dahlgaard (1887–1972) and Jørgen Jørgensen (1888–1974). As a pivotal party in the centre of the Danish political spectrum it generally continued to support the Social Democrats rather than the "bourgeois" parties.

It had already lent parliamentary support to the Social Democratic government of Hedtoft from 1947 to 1950, but from 1957 to 1964 *Radikale Venstre* took part as one of the coalition partners in a succession of Social Democratic led governments (the Hansen government of 1957–60, and the Kampmann governments of 1960–62 and the Krag government of 1962–64). One of its leaders, Karl Skytte, remained as Agricultural Minister for the whole period 1957–64, and *Radikale Venstre* had a number of other important portfolios, such as Economics, Finance, Commerce and Education.

In the 1968 elections *Radikale Venstre* had its greatest postwar victory, more than doubling its vote from 7.4 per cent to 15 per cent, and its number of seats from 13 to 27. It reversed its former alliances, and formed a new government with the Conservatives and with *Venstre*. The *Radikale Venstre* leader, Hilmar Baunsgaard, became Prime Minister and his government lasted until 1971. It passed a number of controversial measures, such as

liberalizing abortion and abolishing censorship and controls on pornography, that upset many conservatives.

In the 1971 elections the *Radikale Venstre* vote held up well at 14.4 per cent and the coalition retained a wafer-thin majority in Denmark proper, but lost power because of the opposition of members from Greenland and the Faroe Islands. In the 1973 elections the party's vote dropped to 11.2 per cent (20 seats in the *Folketing*), and in subsequent elections continued to fall to 7.1 per cent (13 seats) in 1975 and to 3.6 per cent (six seats) in its disastrous election year of 1977. In the first European Parliament elections in 1979 it only won 3.3 per cent, and failed to win representation.

It subsequently made a limited recovery, winning 5.4 per cent and 10 seats in the October 1979 election, and remaining over 5 per cent in 1981 and 1984. When the four-party government led by Poul Schlüter was formed in 1982, *Radikale Venstre* did not directly participate in the coalition, but supported the government in Parliament on its economic policies, in particular, although disagreeing with it on certain energy, security and foreign policy issues. In the European Parliament election of 1984 it again polled poorly, winning only 3.1 per cent of the vote (again with no seats).

In the 1987 national election the vote rose to 6.2 per cent and 11 seats. It remained outside the 1987–88 Schlüter government, but there was increasing dissatisfaction within the party over its so-called "free position" and its lack of influence in the discussions on the 1987 budget. In the 1988 national election the party's vote slipped slightly to 5.6 per cent and 10 seats in the *Folketing*, but it entered formally into a new three-party coalition government with *Venstre* and the Conservatives under Poul Schlüter's leadership. Five of *Radikale Venstre's* 10 members of Parliament became ministers.

Support

Radikale Venstre's traditional support came from an unusual mix of urban intellectuals and smallholders from the country areas. Pacifists were an important element of support. These support patterns were long enduring although they have gradually weakened, most markedly that of smallholders in rural Denmark. *Radikale Venstre* has also won support from those who have appreciated its non-ideological stand on economic issues, and its independence from organized interests. In 1968, in particular, it benefited from a strong protest vote against other parties. It now does best among professionals, those in the education sector, and also within the public sector. It is less strong among working-class voters.

Its strongest area of support is in outer Copenhagen and in northern and western Zealand. In the *Amt* (county) of West Zealand it won 6.9 per cent of the vote in 1988 and a similar percentage in Roskilde *Amt*. In Copenhagen *Amt* (the outer part of the Copenhagen conurbation) it won 6.8 per cent, and in Frederiksborg *Amt* 6.3 per cent. It won high support both in the prosperous suburban areas (e.g. Værløse where it won 10.5 per cent), and in farming areas of Zealand such as its traditionally strong base of Holbæk in West Zealand (where it won 10.7 per cent in 1987, and where it has polled well over 20 per cent in the past). In Central Copenhagen *Radikale Venstre* has a lower vote (5.8 per cent in the inner Copenhagen constituencies in 1988), but a much higher one than *Venstre* or the Centre Democrats. *Radikale Venstre* is weaker, however, in southern Zealand, Lolland and Falster (4.7 per cent in Storstrøm *Amt* in 1988).

In the rest of Denmark *Radikale Venstre* has variable support, with pockets of particular strength. Its strongest *Amt* is Funen, where it won 6 per cent in 1988, and where it is traditionally strong in the area around Middelfart and on the Island of Langeland. It is also strong in the southern Odense constituency.

In Jutland *Radikale Venstre* is strongest (5.9 per cent in 1988) in the *Amts* of Viborg (in which Skive, where it polled 9.2 per cent in 1988, is one of its traditional strongholds) and in Århus where it polled 5.3 per cent in the *Amt* as a whole, and considerably higher in the city of Århus itself. In other parts of Jutland *Radikale Venstre's* 1988 vote ranged from between 4–5 per cent, with a low of 4 per cent in the Ringkøbing *Amt* in which the Centre and Christian Democrats are particularly strong. The lowest *Radikale Venstre* vote of all is on the Island of Bornholm (3.2 per cent in 1988).

Radikale Venstre's low share of the vote in the European elections of 1979 and 1984 is partly explicable as a result of the loss of many of its normal voters to more pro- and anti-community parties, in the latter case to the People's Movement Against the EC in particular.

Organization

Radikale Venstre has a current membership of around 10,000 (like most other Danish parties this has declined, and was 35,000 in 1961). It is organized in local branches, in the various electoral districts and at *Amt* (county)

level. At national level the national conference (*Landsmøde*) is held annually, and consists of delegates from the constituency organizations. The national council (*Hovedbestyrelse*) consists of 112 members, the most prestigious of which are the 15 members elected directly by the national conference. The other members include representatives of the *Amt* organizations in a proportion corresponding to the votes that they won in the last general election. There is also a much smaller executive committee (*Forretningsudvalg*), which includes the chairman of the party (directly elected at the national conference), two deputy chairman, four members from the party council, two from the parliamentary group, and the chairmen of certain key parliamentary committees.

The party's candidates for the *Folketing* are put at the head of the party list within their own electoral district, but are listed in alphabetical order in the rest of the constituency, with the order of election being decided by the number of preference votes won by each candidate.

The party's parliamentary group chooses its own chairman, who is normally the political leader of the party (unless its political leader is a government minister). The *Radikale Venstre* parliamentary group is given great freedom of manoeuvre by the national party organization, which cannot bind its decisions in any way.

The party's youth movement is called *Radikale Ungdom* (Radical Youth). It can send representatives to both the national council and executive committee of the parent party, but without voting rights. The party has no women's organization. It co-operates with the small farmers' movement (*Husmandforening*) but has no formal links with it or any other pressure group. The party has its own further education association, the *Frit Oplysningsforbund*.

Radikale Venstre has an internal party newspaper, *Radikal Politik*, sent out to its own members every two weeks. There used to be a strong party press throughout the country (in the 1930s almost 30 newspapers), but these have now almost vanished. There are still two *Radikale Venstre*-leaning local newspapers in the two traditional party strongholds of Holbæk and Skive, the *Holbæks Amts Venstreblad* and the *Skive Folkeblad*. They are independent of the party, but their editors are represented on the top party bodies as observers without voting rights. There is also another local paper *Middelfart Venstreblad* which is part of a larger paper on Funen which is itself not close to the party.

Membership dues are decided upon by the local branches, who then contribute to the national party. The normal range is 250–300 crowns per year. *Radikale Venstre* supported the recent bill for state subsidies to political parties to increase independence from pressure groups.

Radikale Venstre is a full member of the Liberal International, and has played a considerable role within it. It is not a member, however, of ELDR, as it believes the European Liberals are too conservative and too much in favour of European Union. In the 1984 European elections it co-operated closely with D66 and the French *Mouvement des Radicaux de Gauche* (MRG) and if it won representation in the European Parliament would try to form a new group of Social Liberal, Radical and Green parties. *Radikale Venstre* is a member of the Centre Group in the Nordic Council, and also has considerable links with Eastern European agrarian parties.

Policies

Radikale Venstre is a pivotal party in the centre of the Danish political system, currently closer to the parties of the right of centre on economic policy questions, and more to the left on foreign policy and defence issues. Often holding the balance of power within the *Folketing* it has been sought after as a coalition partner or for its parliamentary support on a more ad hoc basis. It has been proud of being linked to no-vested-interest groups, and of being free to co-operate with other parties of both the left and right. Until 1966 its favoured partner was the Social Democrats. This has now changed, but it still prefers a broad-based coalition "across the middle".

From 1982 to 1988 *Radikale Venstre* co-operated closely with the government on economic issues, but did not enter into the government. It also emphasized its reluctance to enter into any sort of agreement involving the Progress Party. In 1988, however, it came to believe that it needed to be within the government to exert more influence upon the course of policy.

Radikale Venstre has been a leading advocate of tough and restrictive economic policies in order to restore the Danish economy, and reduce its huge foreign debt. It has advocated strict income policies. It considers that current Danish taxes are a heavy burden, but that raising consumption by cutting taxes should have a lower priority at present than raising investment. It strongly defends the welfare state and social security in qualitative rather than quantitative terms. It has advocated a publicly financed minimum income for every citizen, but believes that individuals should then pay more for public services in consequence. *Radikale Venstre* has called for compulsory employer profit sharing

and decision-sharing. It believes that shared profits should be put into the firms concerned, not large funds.

The party has put a high emphasis on opposing civil nuclear energy. It has also called for a change in direction in Danish agricultural policy, criticizing over-emphasis on agro-industrial development and defending family farms.

The party has strongly defended the rights of refugees and asylum seekers in Denmark. It wants to improve their situation through joint European and Nordic action, but does not want more restrictive legislation in Denmark.

One constitutional reform that it would like to see introduced is to make it more difficult for the Prime Minister to call new elections at any time. On the European Community *Radikale Venstre* has had mixed views. It was under a *Radikale Venstre*-led government that Denmark applied to join the Community, but four of its *Folketing* members subsequently voted against EC entry, and there was considerable hostility to the EC within the party. More recently the party opposed ratification of the Single European Act, but two of its parliamentarians were in favour.

Radikale Venstre does not advocate Denmark leaving the European Community, but believes that it should concentrate on economic co-operation, and not get involved in cultural, foreign policy and security areas. It thus supports the achievement of the internal market by 1992, but opposes European union and believes that the national veto should be retained.

On defence issues *Radikale Venstre* has a long anti-militarist tradition, and a strong pacifist wing. It originally opposed NATO membership in 1948, and advocated Scandinavian defence co-operation instead. It now accepts NATO membership as a necessary evil, but has long sought restrictions on military expenditure. It believes that Denmark should support every step towards disarmament, and has taken a strongly anti-nuclear position, calling for the creation of a nuclear weapon-free zone in Scandinavia. In the recent controversy over visits of possible nuclear warships to Danish ports *Radikale Venstre* supported the Social Democratic position. It later agreed to the circular letter compromise on the warships issue, but the government has had to agree to a standstill defence budget that will only increase in line with inflation.

Radikale Venstre have put a particularly strong emphasis on development aid policy, and on the need for aid to reach 1 per cent of GNP as soon as possible.

Personalities

The party's political leader is Niels Helveg

Petersen, born in 1939. His father, Kristen Helveg Petersen, was a *Radikale Venstre* Culture Minister in two coalition governments of the early 1960s. Niels Helveg Pedersen was a member of the *Folketing* from 1966–74 and again from 1977 to the present. In 1978 he became the chairman of the *Folketing* group. In the present government he is now the Minister of Economic Affairs. The chair of the parliamentary group is Marianne Jelved, and the chair of the national organization is Thorkild Møller.

Centrum Demokraterne
(Centre Democrats)

Headquarters	:	Vesterbrogade 62–3, DK–1620 Copenhagen (tel: 01–23 71 15)
Leader	:	Erhard Jakobsen
Chairman	:	Arne Andersen
Youth movement	:	*Centrum Demokraternes Ungdom*
Party organ	:	*Centrum – Avisen*
Membership	:	2,500 (October 1987)
Founded	:	7 November 1973

History

The Centre Democrats were founded by Erhard Jakobsen, a Social Democratic member of parliament, the popular mayor of Gladsaxe. Jakobsen had become increasingly disturbed by what he saw as the take-over of the Social Democrats by left-wing intellectuals. He was critical of 1960s permissiveness, concerned about left-wing bias in eduction and in the media, and sought a return to traditional social democratic values. The specific reason for his resignation from the Social Democrats was their proposal to raise taxes on home-ownership. Jakobsen left the Social Democrats and on Nov. 7 1973, founded the Centre Democrats. The day afterwards the government called new elections.

New parties in Denmark need around 17,000 signatures to be allowed to contest elections, but the Centre Democrats deposited 51,400 signatures at the Interior Ministry within one-and-a-half weeks of their founding, having collected over 200,000 in all. On election day on Dec. 4, 1973, the Centre Democrats polled 7.8 per cent of the vote and won 14 seats in the *Folketing*. Only then did the party hold an official foundation meeting in January 1974, and a proper organizational structure began to be established.

In the course of 1974 the newly elected Centre Democrats helped to prop up the minority Liberal government of Poul Hartling on several occasions. The reasons for which the party had been founded appeared to be neglected, and a number of disillusioned members left the party. In the next election in January 1975 the party's support fell to only 2.2 per cent and four seats in the *Folketing*. They now entered into a pattern of rising and falling support as what one of their leaders has described as an "elevator party". In the 1977 elections their vote swung back to 6.4 per cent with 11 seats in the *Folketing*. In the first European elections in 1979 they won one seat, also with 6.2 per cent, but in the national elections later that year they were again down to 3.2 per cent and six seats. In 1981 they rose again to 8.3 per cent and 15 seats, their best ever performance.

In 1982 Erhard Jakobsen was one of the key architects of the new four-party government led by Poul Schlüter and in which the Centre Democrats, Conservatives, Liberals and Christian People's Party all took part. The Centre Democrats had four ministers in the government. In the 1984 national election the Centre Democrats dropped to 4.6 per cent and eight seats in the *Folketing*. Since then their vote has stabilized as they won 4.8 per cent and nine seats in the 1987 elections, and 4.7 per cent and nine seats in 1988. Only in the European Parliament election in 1984 did they obtain a higher vote, winning one seat with 6.6 per cent of the vote.

In the restructured four-party government again formed by Poul Schlüter in September 1987 the Centre Democrats had three ministers, with Erhard Jakobsen himself participating for the first time. However the Centre Democrats were excluded from the new three-party government formed by Poul Schlüter in the summer of 1988.

Support

The Centre Democrats are strong among white-collar workers, and among those in administrative jobs. They are weak among students and among elderly voters. They have higher than average support in the suburban areas of the larger cities and in middle sized towns of between 5,000 and 30,000 people. They are weakest in the countryside and in the central and working-class areas of the larger cities.

In regional terms they are particularly strong in the Copenhagen suburbs and northern Zealand. In the Copenhagen *Amt* (county) constituency they won 6.7 per cent of the vote in 1988 and in Frederiksborg *Amt* they won 6.6 per cent. In certain communes within these areas they polled between 8 and 10 per cent, notably Erhard Jakobsen's old stronghold of Gladsaxe (9.7 per cent in 1988). They also have pockets of particular strength in Jutland, notably Ringkøbing *Amt* (also the stronghold of the Christian People's Party) where the Centre Democrats won 7 per cent of the vote in 1988 (8.9 per cent in the European elections in 1984). In the town of Holstebrø within this *Amt* they won 8.6 per cent in 1988. Their second best *Amt* in Jutland is Vejle, where they won 4.7 per cent in 1988. Elsewhere in Denmark their vote was fairly evenly spread, ranging from 3.7 per cent (Funen *Amt*) to 4.3 per cent (Ribe *Amt*). There were two exceptions. In the inner part of the Copenhagen conurbation (the misleadingly named Greater Copenhagen) the Centre Democrats only polled 3 per cent in 1988, including working-class areas where they polled under 2 per cent. The other area where the party was particularly weak was the Island of Bornholm, where they polled 2.8 per cent in 1988.

Organization

The party's organization reflects its leaders belief that political power should be left with the voters and the elected parliamentarians rather than with the party activists. The Centre Democrats have a fairly stable (although slowly rising) membership of a little over 2,500. There are around 137 local branches. Where the party is stronger it is organized in individual communes and where weaker in the wider electoral constituencies, but in either case there is only one tier of local organization to avoid unnecessary bureaucracy. Above the local tier are the 17 *Amt* or county organizations.

The party's national congress is held once a year. The national congress cannot pass binding resolutions on matters of policy. The party's national council (*Landsråd*) meets four or five times a year, and consists of 31 members, including the party's top office-holders, three representatives of the parliamentary group, the 17 chairmen of the county organizations and six members elected by the national congress (including three from Western, and three from Eastern Denmark). Above this is the national executive (*Landsstyrelse*), which meets once a month and has a membership of nine, including the party leader and national chairman, and a number of others chosen by the national council.

The party's candidates for the *Folketing* are chosen by postal ballot among the party's members in each *Amt*, in order to avoid giving too much power to the local branch activists. Once the candidates have been selected the order of their election is left not to a party listing but according to the number of personal votes that they receive. The party also has a rule that any elected *Folketing* member has the right to be a candidate in the subsequent election, even if not chosen by party members in the postal ballot. This is to allow voters and not the party organization to judge. In practice this rule has never had to be applied. European Parliament candidates are chosen by a vote of members throughout the country. Each member has three votes, the first worth five, the second three and the third one, which must be cast for separate candidates.

A youth group has only recently been established, called *Centrum – Demokraternes Ungdom* (Centre Democratic Youth) with 200–300 members. All members of this group have also to be full members of the party. There is no separate women's organization within the party, nor are there any quotas for women as regards candidacies or party offices. The party has a monthly newspaper for its membership and other interested members of the public. It is called *Centrum – Avisen*, and has a normal print run of 7–8,000 copies.

The Centre Democrats have been represented by one member within the European Parliament (mainly Erhard Jakobsen). When the party was formed Jakobsen sat in the Socialist Group but was forced to leave the group at the insistence of the Danish Social Democrats. He then joined the Conservatives, but in 1980 crossed the floor to join the Christian Democrats. The Centre Democrats still sit with the Christian Democrats in the European Parliament, and attend meetings of the parliamentary group, but they are not full members of the European People's Party. In 1979 and 1984 they joined in an electoral agreement for the European elections with the Danish Christian People's Party.

Policies

The Centre Democrats see themselves as conservative on cultural and security questions, and closer to the Social Democrats on economic and welfare state questions. They claim to take decisions on a pragmatic case-by-case basis. They emphasize their moderation and common sense, and their role as "craftsmen" of agreements between the other political parties, and between the "left" and "right" political blocks. One of their main tenets is trust in the average voter rather than in elite and self-appointed mass movements.

The central set of issues on which they were founded were cultural issues, and the need to return to traditional values in such fields as education, which should not be the subject of social experiments or be based on the latest trends. The media too should become fairer and more objective. To help ensure this Erhard Jakobsen was a co-founder of a society called "Active Listeners and Viewers".

On economic issues they claim to be traditionally Social Democratic and to be further away from the more economically liberal parties such as *Venstre*. They are critical of excessive individualism, and believe that this should be tempered by collective responsibility. They support a strong welfare state, have no ideological prejudices against the public sector, which they believe should be modernized rather than cut back, and they are generally opposed to privatizations. They accept that the state of the Danish economy has necessitated restraint in public expenditure, but they do not believe in retrenchment for its own sake. In the longer term they wish to see a shift from direct towards indirect taxation. They believe strongly that managers should be allowed to manage. They are against a system of economic democracy which allows centralized funds. They support distribution of profits in compensation for wage restraint, but these should then be tied up in the enterprise itself.

They support vigorous environmental measures, but believe that industrial development should not be blocked as a result of purely emotive issues. They are opposed to the Social Democrats on security policy questions. The Centre Democrats oppose the idea of a more neutral Denmark, and are strong supporters of NATO. They are prepared to accept a rise in Denmark's defence expenditure. They are also strongly in favour of the European Community, and support the objective of European Union. They supported the Parliament's Draft Treaty of European Union, and also the Single European Act.

Personalities

The leading figure within the Centre Democrats since their foundation has been Erhard Jakobsen, born in 1917, who has been a member of the *Folketing* since 1953. He was a social Democratic member of the *Folketing* from 1953 to 1973, and mayor of Gladsaxe from 1958 to 1974. He was also chairman of the European Movement in Denmark. More recently, however, he has begun to move more into an advisory and less of a direct leadership role.

An increasingly important role is now being played by Jakobsen's daughter, Mimi Stilling Jakobsen. She became a member of the *Folketing* in 1977, was Minister of Cultural Affairs from 1982 to 1986 and Minister of Social Affairs from 1986 to 1988.

The chairman of the parliamentary group is again Arne Melchior, who previously had this task in 1973–75 and in 1980–82. Arne Melchior, born in 1924, was a member of the *Folketing* in 1973–75 and again from 1977 to the present. He was Minister of Public Works from 1982 to 1986. Peter Duetoft was the chairman of the party's national organization from 1978 to 1987. He briefly had a dual mandate as a member of both the *Folketing* and the European Parliament, the only Danish member in this position. The present chairman of the party's national organization is Arne Andersen.

Fremskridtspartiet
(The Progress Party)

Headquarters	: Christianborg 1240, Copenhagen K (tel: 01–11–66 007, ext. 1448-49-50)
Political leader	: Pia Kjærsgaard
Chairman of parliamentary group	: Helge Dohrman
Chairman	: Johannes Sørensen
Youth group	: *Fremskridtspartiets Ungdom* (FPU)
Newspaper	: *Fremskridt*
Membership	: 10,000
Founded	: 1972

History

The Progress Party was founded in 1972 by Mogens Glistrup, a tax lawyer who had been disillusioned by the failure of the right-of-centre government of Hilmar Baunsgaard to cut the bureaucracy and high levels of taxation that it had inherited from previous Social Democratic administrations. In early 1971 Glistrup had appeared briefly on television and had made an immediate impact by attacking taxation levels and their inequities, pointing out how easy taxes were to avoid, and recommending this as a perfectly legal course of action. He later decided to form first his own movement against taxation, and then a fully fledged political party.

By early 1973 it began to make an impact and by April was obtaining 25 per cent in the opinion polls. In the 1973 elections it was still able to obtain 15.9 per cent and 28 seats, and to become the second-largest party in the *Folketing*, taking votes not merely from the right of centre parties, but from the left as well.

The Progress Party was treated as an outcast. In the 1975 elections the Progress Party maintained itself fairly successfully with 13.6 per cent of the vote (24 seats) and in 1977 its vote again rose slightly to 14.6 per cent and 26 seats. In the 1979 European elections, however, it only obtained 5.8 per cent of the vote, and one seat. In the national elections of the same year its vote dropped considerably to 11 per cent and 20 seats, and in 1981 to 8.9 per cent and 16 seats.

Glistrup had long been in trouble with the authorities over his tax avoidance schemes, and in 1983 he was convicted of tax fraud and jailed for three years. In the 1984 national elections the party's vote dropped to only 3.6 per cent and six seats in the *Folketing*. Glistrup himself was elected, but was not permitted by Parliament to take up his seat. In the 1984 European elections the party obtained 3.5 per cent, and lost its only seat.

While Glistrup was in prison the party pursued the same policies but with a less uncompromising image under the new leadership of Pia Kjærsgaard. In early 1985 Glistrup was pardoned. By 1987 popular disillusionment had again grown with another right-of-centre government that was seen to have failed to reduce the burden of the state and of high taxation. Resentment at immigration from third-world countries, especially from the Islamic world, had also grown. Skilfully exploiting these themes in the 1987 and 1988 elections the new-look Progress Party made a limited recovery in 1987 to 4.8 per cent and nine seats, and a much more marked one in 1988 to 9 per cent and 16 seats in the *Folketing*. It had since risen higher in the opinion polls.

Support

For a protest party, the Progress Party has had a remarkably enduring level of support, broken only in the early 1980s. It has won support in all parts of Denmark (though more in the country than in the cities), and among all social classes. It had been more successful, for example, than the Conservatives or *Venstre* in winning working-class support. It has taken votes from left, as well as right-of-centre parties. Its greatest weakness, unsurprisingly, has been among state employees. When it first contested elections it was also weaker than average among the old, and among female voters.

Its highest level of support is currently in rural South and West Jutland. Its strongest *Amt* (county) in 1988 was Viborg at 12.4 per cent. On the Island of Morsø within this county it won 20.2 per cent. In South Jutland *Amt* (which had been its strongest *Amt* in 1987 with 7.3 per cent) it obtained 12.3 per cent. It also had good support in Ringkøbing *Amt* (11.7 per cent), Ribe *Amt* (11.1 per cent), Vejle *Amt* (10.2 per cent) and North Jutland *Amt* (10.0 per cent). Its only weak *Amt* in Jutland was Århus (7.8 per cent in 1988, only 4.1 per cent in 1987), where its lowest vote was in the city of Århus. The Progress Party also won over 10 per cent in 1988 in the *Amts* of Funen (10.4 per cent) and Bornholm (10.5 per cent). It was weaker in Zealand (between 7.7 per cent and 8.6 per cent in 1988 in the four *Amts* of West Jutland, Storstrøm, Roskilde and Frederiksborg). Its lowest vote of all was in the Copenhagen area, where it only won 7 per cent in outer Copenhagen (Copenhagen *Amt*) and 5.8 per cent in inner Copenhagen. Relative to its low 1987 starting point, however (3.8 per cent in outer Copenhagen, 3.3 per cent in inner Copenhagen), its vote in Copenhagen rose almost as much in 1988 as it did in the rest of Denmark. Moreover, even in its weakest area of inner Copenhagen, it was the fourth-largest party in 1988.

Organization

The Progress Party's founder, Mogens Glistrup, always professed to take little interest in organizational matters. The party only developed a formal organizational structure in September 1974, two years after its foundation. It had never been a mass membership party — although it now claims to have around 10,000 members.

The Progress Party has local and electoral district branches, and 18 regional organizations (14 in the *Amts* or counties, and four in the Copenhagen area). Its annual national conference includes 54 delegates from *Amt* executives and 350 representatives from local branches, as well as youth representatives, the party's top office-holders and representatives of the party's *Folketing* and local government groups. The party's national board has five elected members, partly renewed each year by a vote at the national conference, which also elects the party chairman.

The party chairman heads its national organization, but is not its political leader. For most of the party's history this has been Mogens Glistrup, although he has never been the chairman. He has, however, been granted permanent membership (as sixth member alongside the five elected members) of the party's national board. The current political leader of the party, Pia Kjærsgaard, is its political spokesman in the *Folketing*.

The party's youth movement is called *Fremskridtspartiets Ungdom* (Progress Party Youth) and has a right to 28 representatives at the national conference. The party's newspaper for its membership is called *Fremskridt*.

From 1979 to 1984 the Progress Party had one member of the European Parliament who sat with the French Gaullists, Fianna Fáil from Ireland and the Scottish Nationalist Party in the Group of European Progressive Democrats. The Progress Party has had links with its sister party in Norway, to whose founding Mogens Glistrup was invited and which has had a similar pattern of success, decline and recent revival.

Policies

The Progress Party is a populist protest movement, which has had three main planks in its programme, cutting taxes, cutting red tape and bureaucracy, and thinning out the "jungle" of Danish laws. In its 1987 and 1988 campaign it has added a new theme, the need to restrict immigration into Denmark, especially from Islamic countries.

Its initial programme was worked out mainly by Glistrup himself, and had a direct appeal to many. By the same token it was rejected as simplistic by the other parties in the *Folketing* who kept the Progress Party in isolation. Nevertheless, the other parties have taken up some of the Progress Party's themes, notably the need to cut taxation and roll back government. Moreover, the Progress party has now expressed its willingness to co-operate with other parties on measures that will move Danish society at least a few steps in the direction that it wants.

The central demand of the Progress Party has been to reduce taxation. Its most radical proposal is the complete abolition of income tax, to be achieved over a five year period. On the other hand it accepts the single Danish rate of VAT of 22 per cent, which it recognizes can be cut only marginally. Other tax targets have included capital gains tax and motor vehicle tax by weight. It believes there should be no new taxes, with the possible exception of pollution levies. The Progress Party has advocated the use of the compensation principle, with any rise being compensated by a matching decline somewhere else. The Progress Party does not, however, put its faith in supply-side boosts alone, and calls for drastic reduction in public expenditure as well.

Among its prime targets are development aid (which should be purely a matter of individual charity), public money used for cultural purposes, and all subsidies for business. There should also be a great reduction in the size of the civil service. At least 35,000 persons should be transferred from the least necessary jobs and redeployed in the productive sector. All sorts of unnecessary quangos such as consumer councils should be abolished, or receive no public support. The government should change its whole function and cease being a "prohibition machine". The number of existing laws should be drastically cut. Economic democracy is rejected if it leads to more bureaucracy. The agricultural sector should be freed from all restrictions.

The Progress Party does not completely reject public expenditure and the welfare state, and in a number of areas actually proposes increases in expenditure. The highest of such priorities would be expenditure on the health sector, and on old people. Other possible areas are environmental protection measures, and the fight against crime.

The Progress Party also advocates reforms in the Danish structure of government. In the past it has called for the *Folketing* to be reduced from 175 to only 40 members and for cabinets to consist of only eight ministers, including a Minister for the Abolition of Public Activities. Intermediate tiers of government (regions and counties) should be abolished. There should be no public support for political parties, and much greater use of public referenda.

A recent emphasis of the Progress Party has been on the dangers of immigration into Denmark, especially from Moslem countries. If possible they should be sent out of Denmark, but at the very least there should be a total stop to new immigration.

Defence was the subject of one of Glistrup's more celebrated original policies, when he advocated the reduction of defence expenditure to spending on only one item, a tape recorded message in Russian saying "we surrender". Glistrup himself continues to believe that defence expenditure is a waste of money, but his is only a minority opinion within the party. Since 1973 the Progress Party has been a pro-NATO party.

The party takes a pragmatic view of EC membership. It considers that there is no alternative to Denmark being within the EC, and it supported Danish entry, and also ratification of the Single European Act. European Union is a very long term objective. On the other hand the internal market is strongly supported as it will force Danish firms to be more competitive, and will lead to more goods and lower prices within Denmark. The liberalisation of capital movements is strongly supported. EC bureaucracy is opposed.

Personalities

The political leader of the Progress Party is now Pia Kjærsgaard, its political spokesman in the *Folketing*. She was born in 1947, and has been a member of the *Folketing* since 1984. She emerged as a party's effective leader when Glistrup was in gaol, and has contributed considerably to the party's revival, giving it a more conciliatory and less extremist sounding tone while maintaining its essential objectives. In the 1988 election she had almost three times more preference votes than Glistrup himself.

Mogens Glistrup still plays a considerable role, and received the second-largest number of personal preferences among Progress Party candidates in 1988. He was born in 1926 and a tax lawyer by profession. He was elected to the *Folketing* from 1973–83, and after his spell in prison during 1983 to 1985, was re-elected in 1987.

The chairman of the parliamentary group is Helge Dohrman, born in 1939. He was elected to the *Folketing* in 1973 and has been group chairman since 1983. Johannes Sørenson is the present national chairman of the party's organization.

Kristeligt Folkeparti — KRF
(Christian People's Party)

Headquarters	:	Skindergade 24, DK-1159 Copenhagen (tel: 01–11 31 60)
Chairman	:	Flemming Kofod-Svendsen
Party secretary	:	Niels Christian Andersen
Youth movement	:	*Kristeligt Folkepartis Ungdom* (KFU)
Party organ	:	*IdePolitik*
Membership	:	9,700 (End 1987)
Founded	:	April 1970

History

The Christian People's Party (KRF) was founded in April 1970 in reaction against what they saw as growing permissiveness in Danish society. More specific catalysts were the then government's proposals on abortion and pornography. Assistance was given by the Norwegian Christian People's Party. The new party's first chairman was Jacob Christensen.

In its first election in 1971 the KRF was only 625 votes short of meeting the 2 per cent limit for representation in the *Folketing*. In 1973 Jens Møller became the new chairman of the party, and in the election of that year the KRF won 4 per cent of the votes and seven seats

in the *Folketing*. Christian Christensen became the parliamentary group chairman.

In the 1975 election the KRF won 5.3 and nine seats, its highest total. The party's vote then slipped back in three successive elections. In the first European Parliament election in 1979 it only won 1.8 per cent and no seats. In 1979 Flemming Kofod-Svendsen took over as chairman of the party, a position he has retained until the present day. In 1982 the KRF joined the four-party ("four-leaf clover") coalition government led by Poul Schlüter of the Conservatives. The KRF only had one minister in the government. In 1984 the KRF made a limited electoral recovery, winning 2.7 pre cent and five seats in the national elections and 2.8 per cent (but no seats) in the European election. In 1987 it slipped back again to 2.4 per cent (four seats) but in the new Schlüter four-party government the KRF increased their number of ministers to two.

In the 1988 election the KRF won 2 per cent of the vote and four seats, only narrowly remaining above the national barrier for representation in the *Folketing*. The KRF did not participate in the new government formed by Poul Schlüter, and returned into opposition.

Support

The KRF is strongest in areas with higher levels of church attendance and membership of religious organizations. Two-thirds of its voters are women, and many are elderly. It is stronger in the country than in the towns. The party organization and parliamentary group includes a considerable proportion of teachers.

In regional terms the party is strongest in Jutland which has over 80 per cent of the membership, and where the party won three per cent of the vote in the 1988 election (3.5 per cent in 1987). The two *Amts* (counties) of Nordjylland (North Jutland) and Ringkøbing (in western Jutland) account for over 3,400 of the party's total of 9,700 members. Electorally, the strongest *Amt* by far is that of Ringkøbing, where it won 6.5 per cent of the vote in 1988 (7.4 per cent in 1987, and 8.5 per cent in the European Parliament elections in 1984). Within Ringkøbing its highest vote was in the municipality of Skjern (9.8 per cent in 1988). Its second-strongest *Amt* was Viborg (in Central Jutland) where it won 3.7 per cent in 1988 (4.3 per cent in 1987). Its vote in North Jutland (2.8 per cent) did not reflect the party's organizational strength in that *Amt*. The KRF's weakest *Amt* in Jutland is that of Århus (1.7 per cent in 1988).

Outside Jutland the only pocket of KRF

support is the Island of Bornholm, (5.2 per cent in 1988, 5.4 per cent in 1987). The KRF is weak elsewhere in the islands and in the Copenhagen area. In 1988 it averaged little over 1 per cent in the various Copenhagen constituencies, in central and southern Zealand and in Funen.

Organization

The KRF's 9,700 members are organized in 150 municipal branches (out of 275 municipalities in the whole of Denmark), with particular strength in Jutland. Above these are the 17 *Amt* organizations. At national level the annual national conference (*Landsmøde*) includes between 300 and 400 delegates, mainly chosen in the *Amts* on a mixed basis of the number of votes won in the last elections and of local membership.

The party has a national council (*Hovedbestyrelsen*) of 50 members, which meets around five times a year. Thirty-two of its members (plus the party chairman) are elected by the national conference (16 each year), and the other 17 members consist of the chairmen of the *Amt* organizations. There is also a smaller executive committee (*Forretningsudvalget*) of nine members, of whom one is the party chairman. The other eight are elected by the national council. The executive committee meets around eight times a year.

The party's youth organization is called the *Kristeligt Folkepartis Ungdom* (Christian People's Party Youth) and has around 1,600 members. The KRF's weekly subscription newspaper is called *Ide Politik*. Membership fees of the party were 140 Danish crowns in 1988.

The KRF is not a member of the European People's party, nor of the European or International Christian Democratic Movements. It cooperates closely with the other Nordic Christian Democratic parties in the Nordic Council.

Policies

The KRF is an ecumenical party with a Christian outlook. Its strongest emphasis is on moral and ethical questions, and one reason for its current electoral weakness may be that there are currently fewer specific controversies on these issues than when the party was founded. It is unclear whether the party will revive now that it is no longer a member of the government coalition, and has the greater freedom of an opposition role.

The KRF believes that the state has a

vital part to play in society, but that there should not be over-reliance upon it. A greater role should be played by small self-governing units, schools, local workplaces and local communities, where individuals can assume greater personal responsibility. Particular emphasis is placed on the welfare of the family, and public housing, labour and fiscal policies should all be structured with this objective in mind.

The KRF lost its battle to prevent a liberal abortion law and recognized that this is now highly unlikely to be repealed. It now puts its emphasis on social measures to encourage women to continue with their pregnancies. The KRF has a particular current concern with ethical questions linked with the new technologies, such as the issue of *in vitro* fertilization. The KRF considers that its major success on ethical questions has been to help pass a law to prevent scientific research on embryos.

The KRF's economic policy has not been strongly ideological. It seeks a smaller public sector and a more competitive private sector. It would be desirable to push down taxes, but in present economic circumstances this can only be a longer term objective. Environmental policy has received a high emphasis, and the KRF held the Environment portfolio in government for the whole period between 1982 and 1988.

The KRF is in favour of active Danish participation in the European Community, although it is not as enthusiastic a federalist party as other Christian Democratic parties within the Community. In 1985 it supported Danish ratification of the Single European Act. The KRF firmly supports Danish membership of NATO and has supported an increase in Danish defence expenditure.

The KRF puts a very strong emphasis on development aid for the third world, and supports the one per cent of GNP target set by the United Nations. One distinctive feature of its foreign policy is that the KRF has a stronger pro-Israel position than other Danish parties.

Personalities

The Party chairman is Flemming Kofod-Svendsen. He is a pastor, originally from the Island of Bornholm. He was general secretary of the Christian Association of Students and Pupils from 1970 to 1977, and editor of the periodical *Pro Fide* from 1971 to 1979. He was elected national chairman of the party in 1979, and became a member of the *Folketing* in 1984. In 1987–88 he was the Danish Minister of Housing. He was born in 1944.

Danmarks Kommunistiske Parti — DKP
(Danish Communist Party)

Headquarters	:	Dronningens Tværgrade 3, DK 1302 Copenhagen K (tel: 01–14 01 14)
Chairman	:	Ole Sohn
Secretary	:	Paul Emanuel
Newspaper	:	*Land og Folk*
Membership	:	10,000
Founded	:	1919

History

The party was founded in 1919 as the result of a merger of various left-wing groups. It was first called the Danish Left Socialist Party. In 1920 it joined the Comintern and fought its first national election, obtaining 0.4 per cent of the vote and no seats. In 1922 it changed its name to the Danish Communist Party (DKP). In 1932 Aksel Larsen became its leader, and the party won its first representation in the *Folketing*, with two seats on 1.1 per cent of the vote. By 1939 this had risen to three seats on 2.4 per cent of the vote.

The Communist Party's role in the Resistance during World War II gave it a new prestige. Larsen himself played a prominent role, and in 1945 took part in the new Danish government as a Resistance representative rather than in his party capacity. Also in 1945 the DKP won its greatest ever election victory, with 18 seats on 12.5 per cent of the vote. This had already dropped to 6.8 per cent and only nine seats by 1947. Nevertheless the DKP were represented in the *Folketing* right through the 1950s, and by 1957 they still had six seats (although only 3.1 per cent of the vote), but they exercised no real political influence.

The events of 1956 led Aksel Larsen to assert greater independence from Moscow and a Danish and more democratic road to Socialism. In 1958 he was expelled from the party, and founded the Socialist People's Party in 1959 (see separate entry). Knud Jespersen became the new chairman of the DKP. In the 1960 election the DKP's vote dropped to only 1.1 per cent and it lost its seats in the *Folketing* for the first time since 1932. The DKP remained out of the *Folketing* throughout the 1960s, polling only between 0.8 and 1.2 per cent of the vote. In the early 1970s it campaigned strongly against EC membership. In 1973, when many of the existing parties in the *Folketing* were chastised by the electorate, the DKP won 3.6 per cent and returned to the *Folketing* with six seats.

It retained its place in the 1975 and 1977 elections, with seven seats on both occasions. In 1977 Jorgen Jensen became party chairman. In the 1979 European election the DKP played an important role in the People's Movement against the EC, and a party member was elected to the European Parliament. In the 1979 national election, however, the DKP's vote dropped to 1.9 per cent, and it again lost its seats. Its vote dropped further to 1.1 per cent in 1981 and to 0.7 per cent in 1984. In 1987 the 32-year-old Ole Sohn took over as the new chairman, and began trying to modernize the party. In the 1988 election, however, the DKP still only won 0.8 per cent of the national vote.

Support

The DKP still has some residual support in individual trade unions, and among groups such as the metal workers and electricians. What little electoral support it has is mainly concentrated in urban areas, and notably inner Copenhagen where it won 2 per cent of the vote in both 1987 and 1988. Its highest vote has been in the inner Copenhagen electoral district of Blågård where it has won over 4 per cent. In outer Copenhagen it won 1 per cent. Elsewhere in Denmark its highest votes have been in the cities of Århus and of Odense. It is weak in all rural areas and especially in Jutland. In 1988 it won only 0.3 per cent in the *Amts* (countries) of South Jutland, Viborg and Ringkøbing.

Organization

The DKP has been traditionally organized on the basis of democratic centralism. Its national congress is convened every three years, and elects a central committee, central commission and auditors. The central committee then elects an executive committee and a secretariat. The DKP claims a membership of 10,000.

The DKP produces a daily newspaper called *Land og Folk* (Nation and People), with a circulation of 13,000 and a theoretical journal called *Tiden-Verden Rundt*, with a circulation of 3,200. The DKP has reportedly received extensive finance from the Soviet Union. DKP members have sat as People's Movement representatives in the European Parliament, within the Rainbow Group.

Policies

The DKP has been an orthodox Marxist party with a pro-Moscow line. It has called for extensive nationalization. It wants Denmark to leave NATO and for an end to military blocs. It supports Nordic and Baltic nuclear-free zones. It wants cuts in defence expenditure, and supports initiatives for detente. It has opposed Danish membership of the EC.

Under the new leadership of Ole Sohn the DKP is now trying to change direction, and to become less rigidly orthodox.

Arbejderpartiet Fælles Kurs
(Common Cause Workers' Party)

Headquarters   : Herluf Trolles
                          Gade 5,
                          1052 Copenhagen
                          (tel: 01–14 44 18)
Party leader and
  chairman   : Preben Møller
                          Hansen
Party secretary   : Ib Jakobsen
Party newspaper   : *AB-Weekend*
Founded   : April 1986

History

Fælles Kurs started as a club in 1979. On April 19, 1986, it became a fully fledged political party. It was closely associated with the Seamen's Trade Union, of whom its leader. Preben Møller Hansen was the longstanding national chairman.

In the *Folketing* election in September 1987 it reaped the benefits of a successful left-wing populist campaign, and won 2.2 per cent of the national vote and four seats. In the 1988 election, however, its vote fell, and, at 1.9 per cent was narrowly under the 2 per cent threshold for representation in the *Folketing*.

Support

Fælles Kurs has won its highest support in inner Copenhagen, especially in its port and working-class areas. In 1988 it won 3 per cent in inner Copenhagen (3.3 per cent in 1987). Its best areas have been Amagerbro, Vesterbro, Enghave, Ishøj, Tarnby and Bispeeng, where it has won over 4 per cent. Outside Copenhagen it polled over 2 per cent in 1988 in East Zealand (2.6 per cent), Storstrøm (2.2 per cent) and Funen (2.1 per cent). It was weakest in Jutland, only winning between 1.2 per cent and 1.5 per cent in 1988, with the exception of North Jutland (1.9 per cent). Outside Copenhagen its highest votes have tended to be in ports (e.g. Nykøbing and Frederikshavn).

Organization

Fælles Kurs has a number of local branches throughout Denmark, which can be organized on a territorial or workplace basis. It has an annual conference, at which all its members can participate, and which elects 20 persons to its national executive. It has a smaller daily executive of seven people. It has a newspaper *Arbejderbladet (AB)-Weekend*.

Policies

Fælles Kurs is a populist party of the left. It describes itself as a workers' party and believes that work can and must be found for everybody. It seeks a raised tax threshold below which no taxes are to be paid, and more progressive taxation for those above the threshold, with higher taxes also to be paid by multinationals, pension funds and banks. It supports more nationalization, especially in the oil and gas industry. It is totally opposed to civil nuclear energy. It advocates stronger social security measures, with emphasis on helping pensioners, improving health services and free day-care for children. One of its most popular policies in its successful 1987 campaign was opposition to further influx of immigrants into Denmark.

It is opposed to block politics, and seeks Danish departure from NATO. Denmark should be neutral and disarmed. The Nordic countries should be nuclear free. *Fælles Kurs* is also opposed to the European Community, and seeks Danish departure.

Personalities

The dominant figure within *Fælles Kurs* is its chairman, Preben Møller Hansen, born in 1929. He has been chairman of the Seamen's Union since 1968. He was formerly active in the Communist Party, for which he was a *Folketing* candidate, and member of its central committee and party executive. He became a vice-chairman of the *Fælles Kurs* club in 1979, and its chairman in 1982. He was elected chairman of the new party in 1986, and was a member of the *Folketing* from 1987–88.

Danmarks Retsforbund
(Danish Justice Party)

Headquarters   : Lyngbyvej 42,
                          2100 Copenhagen 0
                          (tel: 01–20 44 88)
National chairman   : Poul Gerhard
                          Kristiansen
National secretary   : Herluf Munkholm
Newspaper   : *Ret og Frihed*
Membership   : 1,300
Founded   : 1919

History

The Justice Party is the oldest of the smaller Danish parties, being founded in 1919 by supporters of the economic idea of the American Henry George, who advocated a single tax based on land values. In its first election in 1924 it only won 1 per cent and no seats, but in 1926 it obtained 1.3 per cent and its first two seats in the *Folketing*. From then until after World War II it fluctuated at between 1.6 per cent and 2.7 per cent of the vote, and between three or four seats in the *Folketing*. In 1947 its vote rose to 4.5 per cent and six seats, and in 1950 it reached its highest-ever level of support at 8.2 per cent and 12 seats. It declined again in 1953, but again rose to 5.3 per cent and nine seats in the 1957 election.

It now entered government for the first and only time in its history, in coalitions led by the Social Democratic leader H. C. Hansen from 1957 to 1960 and Viggo Kampmann in 1960. The Justice Party's leader, Viggo Starcke, was minister without portfolio, and the party also had the Ministries of the Interior and of Fisheries. The party's participation in government, however, was counterproductive electorally. Its vote dropped in the 1960 elections to only 2.2 per cent and it lost its representation in the *Folketing* for the first time since 1926.

In the 1960s its vote dropped further to only 0.7 per cent by the two elections of 1966 and 1968. The new period of volatility in Danish elections led to a limited recovery in the party's fortunes and it regained representation in the *Folketing* in the 1973 elections with 2.9 per cent and five seats. It lost it again in 1975 with only 1.8 per cent, but returned again in 1977 with 3.3 per cent and six seats and in 1979 with 2.6 per cent and five seats. In 1981 it again left Parliament with only 1.4 per cent. By the 1987 election it was only polling 0.5 per cent, the lowest figure in its history. It did not contest the 1988 election, the first time this had happened since the party's foundation, as it considered it impossible to collect the necessary signatures within the time available.

Support

The party's very low level of support of 0.5 per cent in 1987 was evenly spread around the whole country, with the same percentage in inner Copenhagen, the Islands and Jutland.

Organization

The Justice Party has a little over 1,300 members. It is organized in the 103 electoral districts around the country, in 14 *Amts* (counties) and in the three Greater Copenhagen constituencies.

At national level there is an annual conference, which elects the Party chairman and the party's nine-member executive council (*Forbundsråd*). There is also a smaller executive committee of four.

There is a youth organization, DRU, and a women's organization. The party's newspaper is called *Ret og Frihed* ("Justice and Freedom"). The majority of members pay 180 crowns a year in membership dues.

Many members of the party have been active in the People's Movement Against the EC, and one of its leaders, Ib Christensen (who had previously been a member of the European Parliament for the Justice Party before direct elections) is currently a member of the European Parliament for the People's Movement.

Policies

The Justice Party is a libertarian party, which emphasizes individual freedom above all other values. The party prides itself on its independence from special interests, and claims to decide on individual policy matters on their merits rather than automatically aligning itself with the left or right "blocks".

Its most distinctive policy is its call for a universal three per cent land value tax, which it believes would be the fairest and most justifiable form of taxation. It considers that the present Danish tax system does not allow people to enjoy the fruits of their work and has consequently advocated the abolition of income tax, of taxes of energy and VAT on housing. It believes that Danish public expenditure is too great, and that there should be a move away from subsidies to industry and commerce. Bureaucracy and paperwork should be drastically reduced. There should be completely free trade, and no interference with the results of free collective bargaining. The Justice Party is opposed to the centralized profit sharing funds that have been proposed by the Social Democrats. There should be a great increase in old-age pensions. There should be no money to political parties from special interest groups or from public funds. All party finances should be public.

The freedom of the individual should be strengthened in other ways, such as enabling a free choice of schools, with financial equality between public and private schools. Individuals should be allowed to consult and control their personal files. Environmental policy is highly emphasized.

The Justice Party wants Denmark to leave the EC, on the grounds of the EC's bureaucracy, interference with free trade and with national sovereignty. Denmark should have greater free-dom to develop relations with all countries and especially developing countries. The Justice Par-ty now accepts Danish membership of NATO, but it wants firm ground rules established for the operation of US bases at a time of crisis. There should be no nuclear weapons in Denmark at a time of war or peace, and there should be a nuclear-free zone in Scandinavia. It is opposed to obligatory military service, and seeks a com-pletely volunteer army.

Personalities

The party's chairman is Paul Gerhard Kristian-sen. Ib Christensen has been a member of the European Parliament both for the Justice Party (before 1979) and for the People's Movement Against the EC, and he is still a member of the Justice Party executive.

De Grønne
(Green Party)

National secretariat : Bryggerivej 10,
DK-5450 Otterup
(tel: 09–82 44 09)
National secretary : Per Christiansen
Founded : October 1983

History

The Greens were founded in October 1983 as the political arm of a much wider Green movement. They participated in the local and regional elections of November 1985, running candidates in 12 of the country's 16 regions, and averaging 2.8 per cent of the total number of votes. In both the national elections of 1987 and 1988 they obtained 1.3 per cent of the vote, and no seats in the *Folketing*.

Support

The Greens have won their highest level of support in Greater Copenhagen, in whose three constituencies they averaged 2.3 per cent in 1988. They have won over 3 per cent in the electoral districts of Rådhuskredsen (in the city centre) and Blågård. Their next best area was outer Copenhagen (they won 1.7 per cent in Copenhagen *Amt* in 1988) and North Zealand (1.8 per cent in Frederiksborg *Amt* in 1988). Elsewhere in Zealand they won 1.5 per cent in Roskilde, 1.4 per cent in West Zealand, and only 1.1 per cent in Storstrøm. They obtained 1.5 per cent in Funen. The Greens were weakest in Jutland, with a high of 1.1 per cent in Århus *Amt* (where the city of Århus is their strongest area) and lows of only 0.7 per cent in Viborg and

Ringkøbing. They were also weak in Bornholm (1.2 per cent).

Organization

The Greens have consciously rejected the organizational structures of other parties. They are organized instead in autonomous local groups, which send representatives to quarterly national meetings. These latter constitute the supreme authority within the party. The Greens became official observers within the European Green Movement in March 1985, and became a full member in January 1986.

Policies

The Greens call for the building of an ecologic-ally-based economy, taking into account the real costs of production and transportation. They support a system of cheap loans for ecological farming, and an end to mistreatment of animals. They are highly critical of genetic engineering, support use of alternative and renewable sources of energy and seek an international ban on the use of nuclear power.

In their economic policy they defend the right to work for all those who wish to work, and call for better working conditions and shorter work-ing hours. They seek a simplified social security system and a guaranteed minimum income for everybody. They call for a more decentralized system of government, and an increase in direct democracy.

The Greens are opposed to the European Community, and to European Union. They emphasize the need for peace and disarma-ment, and want to stop money going to NATO. The United Nations should be strengthened. Development aid should be changed so as to lead to greater self-sufficiency and sovereignty for developing countries.

Venstresocialisterne — VS
(Left Socialists)

Headquarters : Rosenørns Allé
44, DK-1970
Frederiksberg C,
Copenhagen,
(tel: 01–35 60 99)
Founded : December 1967

History

Venstresocialisterne (VS) was founded by mem-bers of the left wing of the Socialist People's Par-ty (SF), who opposed the compromises that were involved in SF's parliamentary support for the 1966–68 Social Democratic government of Jens

Otto Krag and felt that SF was too dominated by the personality of Aksel Larsen. In December 1967 six members of the SF *Folketing* group left SF, and formed VS. In the January 1968 national election, the new party narrowly crossed the 2 per cent threshold for parliamentary representation, winning four seats. The party won most of its support in Copenhagen, among young people, students, academics and teachers. By its first congress in 1968 it had 3,500 members.

The new party was immediately torn by conflicts between centralizers and decentralizers, and between the old SF left and the 1968 "flower children", alternatives and anarchists who had been attracted into the new party. Its first congress was chaotic. Already by the summer of 1968 VS had lost two of its parliamentarians, who felt that it was becoming too detached from working-class concerns. A number of Maoists also left. By 1971 membership had dwindled to only 1,000 and VS only won 1.6 per cent in the parliamentary election of that year, losing its parliamentary representation.

The party campaigned strongly against US involvement in Vietnam and against Danish entry into the EC. There was a further internal party struggle between Leninists who wished to impose democratic centralism and other members who opposed this line. The Leninists lost, but this led to a further split within the party in late 1972. In 1973 VS only won 1.5 per cent of the vote. In 1975, however, VS recovered and obtained 2.1 per cent of the national vote and four members of the *Folketing*. It retained *Folketing* representation in the 1977, 1979, 1981 and 1984 elections, with a highest vote of 3.7 per cent (and six *Folketing* members) in 1979. In the 1979 European elections it won 3.5 per cent of the vote, although with no seats. In the 1984 European election, however, the party's vote dropped to only 1.3 per cent. In the 1987 national election it obtained 1.4 per cent, and lost its *Folketing* representation. In the 1988 elections it only polled 0.6 per cent. A number of its activists left the party.

Support

VS has been strongest among academics and young people. The main base of support for VS has been inner Copenhagen, where it polled 2 per cent in 1988, but 4.3 per cent in 1987. In the southern Copenhagen constituency it had previously polled 8.7 per cent in the 1979 European Parliament elections. The party's main stronghold within Copenhagen has been the electoral district of Blågård, where it polled 7.1 per cent in its first election in 1968 and 9.5 per cent as recently as 1987. Other areas of strength have

included Vesterbro (7.8 per cent in 1987) and Østbane (7.1 per cent in 1987). Its 1988 vote fell sharply in all these areas. In outer Copenhagen its strongest base has been Albertslund (4.6 per cent in 1987, but only 2 per cent in 1988).

In the rest of Denmark the party's highest vote has been in the city of Århus (4.9 per cent in the East Århus electoral district in 1987). It also had some support in Odense (1.7 per cent in south Odense in 1987). VS has been extremely weak in rural Denmark, especially in Jutland, where it only polled 0.4 per cent in 1988. In the *Amts* of South Jutland, Ribe, Vejle, Ringkøbing and Viborg it only polled 0.2 per cent, the same percentage that it won on the Island of Bornholm.

Organization

VS has a number of territorial branches, as well as sectoral groups (for example among health workers and teachers). The party's national congress consists of delegates elected by branches from among their active members. The congress elects a national board of 21 members, which elects a smaller executive committee. The party's former *Folketing* group was subject to strict control from party activists. The principle of rotation was also established.

VS has a youth movement *Venstresocialisterner Ungdom* (Left Socialist Youth). It has had a party newspaper *VS Bulletin* and a subscription journal *Solidaritet*. It has had very high membership dues and also with progressive levies based on members' gross incomes. It has had links with various small parties of the Marxist and revolutionary left in other countries.

Policies

VS is on the far left of the Danish political spectrum. It has had representation in Parliament for 15 of its 20 years of existence (1968–87), but has also emphasized extra-parliamentary activities, and links with popular movements, such as the women's rights and anti-nuclear movements. It is currently in a critical state, and has explored possibilities of co-operation with other parties of the far left, and some of its members are returning to the Socialist People's party.

VS calls for a Socialist Democracy, where the people themselves decide how society is to be organized. It seeks a radical redistribution of wealth within Danish society. There should be a shorter working week, and the means of production should be jointly owned by all the people. There should be self government at work, and in local communities. Danish investment policy should support ecologically-based growth. VS emphasizes the struggle against racism, and defends the right of refugees and immigrant workers within Denmark.

VS wants Denmark to leave NATO, and for NATO and the Warsaw pact to be dissolved. There should be a Nordic nuclear-free zone. There should be general disarmament. VS is strongly opposed to the EC and to any transfer of political power to the European Community institutions. It campaigned against the Single European Act, and believes that the 1992 internal market will merely strengthen capitalism, and weaken the Danish working class.

VS is extremely critical of US imperialism, but has also criticized the Soviet Union. It believes that there is no true Socialism in the Soviet Union and Eastern Europe. VS has called for recognition of the PLO, and for a United Ireland.

Folkebevaegelsen Mod EF
(People's Movement Against the EC)

The People's Movement against the EC is not a political party, but an electoral alliance of anti-marketeers that contests European parliament elections only. In 1979 it won 20.9 per cent of the Danish vote and four seats in the European Parliament, in spite of other left wing anti-EC parties (the Socialist People's Party and the Left Socialists) putting up their own lists. The People's Movement was backed mainly by the Left (especially by the Danish Communist party, which did not put up its own list) but also by others, such as the Justice Party. Its elected members in the Parliament included Communists, a Social Democrat and a Radical. Its electoral support severely undercut that of certain other lists, notably those of the Social Democrats and *Radikale Venstre*. In 1984 it again won high support, with 20.8 per cent of the vote and four seats, and was only several hundred votes short of being the best supported list in Denmark.

The People's Movement has unsurprisingly received its highest support in those areas which had the highest level of opposition to Denmark joining the EC in the 1972 referendum (and subsequently also to ratifying the Single European Act in the 1986 referendum). Its highest support, therefore, has been in inner Copenhagen (where it won over 30 per cent in all three inner Copenhagen constituencies in both 1979 and 1984), and to a lesser extent in other large towns. In both 1979 and 1984 it received over 25 per cent in outer Copenhagen and over 20 per cent in Frederiksberg and Roskilde *Amts* close to Copenhagen and also in Århus *Amt* in

Jutland. It was weaker in rural Denmark, and especially in West Jutland, where its lowest votes have been in Ringkøbing *Amt* (11.8 per cent in 1979, 11.4 per cent in 1984) and in Viborg *Amt* (12.9 per cent in 1979, and 12.5 per cent in 1984).

The People's Movement has a loosely structured organization, with around 300 local branches and a decision-making annual congress. It has an executive committee of 21 members. Although its members come from many different political backgrounds its loose structure gives very considerable influence to better organized groups within it, notably the Communist Party and even the Justice Party, who have both elected party members on People's Movement lists. Ironically its electoral success means that it has received considerable funds from the European Parliament, which have helped the People's Movement to finance its own office in Denmark, and a weekly newspaper, *Notat*.

Its four MEPs sit in the Rainbow Group within the European parliament. At first they sought to have nothing to do with the Parliament's proceedings, but they are now increasingly taking decisions on a case-by-case basis.

Faroe Islands

The Faroe Islands (*Færøerne* in Danish, *Føroyar* in Faroese — the name means "Sheep Islands") are a group of islands located between the Shetlands and Iceland, and over 800 miles from the Danish mainland. They have a total area of 540 square miles, and a population of over 45,000. The capital and largest town in Torshavn. The Faroese language is closest to Icelandic, and then to the Norwegian Landsmål. Danish is also learnt at school.

Political institutions

The Faroes are part of Denmark, but enjoy extensive Home Rule. They have never joined the European Community. The islands' Parliament, which dates from Viking times, is called the *Løgting*. It has 27 members elected directly in seven multi-member constituencies, and a variable number of up to five additional members allocated to the parties to ensure a more proportional final result. There is currently the full potential total of 32 members. The seven constituencies are Sudurstreymoyar (currently with 11 seats), Eysturoyar (six seats), Suduroyar (four seats), Nordoya (four seats), Nordurstreymoyar (three seats), Vaga (two seats) and Sandoyar (two seats). Elections are normally held every four years, although the *Løgting* (but not the Faroese Prime Minister or his government) can call for Parliament to be dissolved before the end of this period. In practice this has only happened once since World War II, in 1980. The *Løgting* has 13 standing committees, and has legislative responsibility on all Home Rule matters.

The Faroese government is called the *Føroyra Landstyri* (Faroes National Executive) and must command a majority in the *Løgting*. It currently has six members, of whom one is the *Løgmandur* (Prime Minister) and another the *Varaløgmadur* (Deputy Prime Minister). Ministers in the *Landstyri* (*landsstyrismenn*) do not have to be in the *Løgting*. They all have seats in the *Løgting* but cannot speak unless they are also *Løgting* members. Faroese governments are invariably coalitions, normally of three or four parties.

The Faroes also have 51 municipalities or *Kommunes*. Denmark is still responsible for a number of policy areas (in particular defence and foreign policy are outside the scope of Home Rule) and the Faroes continue to elect two members to the Danish *Folketing*. There are also two Faroese representatives in the Nordic Council.

Brief political history

The Faroes were first settled by the Vikings in around 800, and their representative assembly (first the *Alting*, and later the *Løgting*) dates from shortly after that time. The islands were a province of Norway until 1380, when they came under the Danish crown, and they remained with Denmark after 1814. The main political events since that date include the following:

1816   *Løgting* abolished by the Danish government. The Faroes are reduced to the status of a Danish *Amt* (or county).

1851   Faroes gain representation in the Danish Parliament (one member in the *Folketing*, and one in the *Landsting*).

1852   *Løgting* is reconstituted (with 18 members), but only with consultative powers.

1856   End of Danish trade monopoly.

1906   Beginning of competitive party politics in the Faroes with the foundation of a party advocating Home Rule (*Sjalvstyrisflokkurin*), and of a rival Unionist Party calling for the maintenance of much closer links with Denmark (*Sambandsflokkurin*).

1907   Prohibition is introduced.

1918   Home Rule Party wins majority of *Løgting* seats for first time (Faroese flag subsequently introduced, and various measures taken to preserve Faroese language).

1923   *Løgting* is reformed. Four-year instead of two-year terms are introduced. All members are now to be elected (previously some had been appointed), and there are to be 20 members and up to 10 supplementary members.

1925   Faroese Social Democratic Party (*Javnadarflokkur*) founded, and development of three-party system.

1940   People's Party (*Folkaflokkurin*) founded.

1940–45 Faroes cut off from metropolitan Denmark, and demand for Home Rule is greatly intensified. British refuse request for independence from Denmark, and leave decision to Danish government.

1946   Plebiscite, in which 48.7 per cent of Faroese opt for independence and 47.2 per cent for limited form of Home Rule (other votes spoilt). Danish government considers result to be inconclusive, and does not grant independence. *Løgting* dissolved, and new elections called. Republican Party founded.

1948   Home Rule Act of March 23, 1948, grants extensive self-government to the Faroes, and provides mechanisms for further transfers of power in the future. *Landstyri* (Faroese national government) established.

1948–58 Coalition governments with Unionist Party (*Sambandsflokkurin*) Prime Minister.

1958–62 Social Democratic-led coalition government.

1962–66 People's Party-led coalition government.

1966–68 Social Democratic-led coalition government.

1968–70 Unionist party-led coalition government.

1970–80 Social Democratic-led coalition government.

    1970: Faroes obtain separate representation in Nordic Council.

    1973: Faroes given three years to decide whether they wish to join EC.

    1974: Faroes decide not to join EC.

    1978: Change in electoral law, with

27 members elected in constituencies and up to five supplementary members.

1980–84 Unionist Party led coalition government, with Pauli Ellefsen as Prime Minister.

1984–88 Social Democratic led coalition government, with Republicans, Home Rule Party and Christian People's Party. Atli Dam as Prime Minister.

1989– Coalition government of People's Party, Republicans, Home Rule Party and Christian People's Party. Jogvan Sundstein (People's Party) as Prime Minister.

Main features of the current Faroese political system

Faroese politics are characterized by two main divisions between left and right, and between those who seek the greatest possible self-government for the Faroes or even full independence, and those who wish to maintain closer ties with Denmark. There are thus left-of-centre parties seeking greater autonomy or independence (e.g. Republican Party), as well as right-of-centre parties (e.g. People's Party). Conversely there are both left-of-centre and right-of-centre parties which wish to maintain existing ties with Denmark (e.g. Social Democratic Party and Unionist Party respectively).

This has led to the development since Home Rule of a highly competitive multi-party system, with four larger parties of relatively equal strength and two or more smaller parties. There have thus often been six parties represented in the *Løgting*, and governments have invariably been three or even four party coalitions. In such a small community politics are also extremely personalized, and election campaigns are often more between strong personalities than between ideologies.

Sjalvstyrisflokkurin
(Home Rule Party)

Headquarters	: Løgtingid, Aarvegi, DK-3800, Torshavn
Leader	: Hilmar Kass
Newspaper	: *Tingakrossur* (weekly, 1,600)
Founded	: 1906

History

The Home Rule Party was founded by poet and farmer Joannes Patursson (1866–1946) in 1906, with a programme of giving more power to the *Løgting*, and preservation of the Faroese language. In its first election in 1906 (where its only rival was the Unionist Party) it won 37.6 per cent and eight seats in the *Løgting*, with its highest votes in the islands of Vagar (90.8 per cent) and Sandoy (76.8 per cent). In the two subsequent elections it declined in votes, but it was more successful from 1912 onwards. In 1916 it obtained 51.7 per cent of the vote, although a minority of the seats, and in 1918 it won 49.8 per cent and 11 out of the 20 seats, obtaining a *Løgting* majority for the first and only time.

Although its vote again dropped, it remained strong throughout the 1920s and 1930s, even after the creation of the Social Democratic Party. It was also represented in the Danish Parliament, where it had some links with *Radikale Venstre*. In 1940, however, it was severely damaged when a large proportion of its members joined up with the Small Commerce Party (*Vinnuflokkur*) to create a new People's Party, which also advocated greater autonomy for the Faroes. Whereas in the 1936 election the Home Rule Party had won 34.2 and eight seats, by the 1940 election it was down to only 16.7 per cent and four seats. In 1943 and 1945 it only won 10.3 per cent and 9.4 per cent respectively, and between 1943 and 1946 it had no seat in the *Løgting* for the only time in its history. In 1946 it returned to the *Løgting* with two seats as a result of an electoral pact with the Social Democrats.

In the first *Løgting* elections after Home Rule (1950) it won 8.3 per cent of the vote and two seats. After 1950 its vote declined to only 4.9 per cent and one seat by the 1966 elections, but has since slowly recovered to 8.5 per cent and two seats by the 1984 elections.

In spite of its electoral weakness since the achievement of Home Rule the party has often had a pivotal role in the competitive Faroese political system. It has thus taken part in coalition governments in 1948–50, uninterruptedly from 1954 to 1975, and again from 1981 to the present. It has thus participated in governments led by the Unionists, the Social Democrats and the People's Party. The Home Rule Party has not provided a Faroese Prime Minister since the introduction of Faroese autonomous government in 1948, and has not succeeded in electing a representative to the Danish *Folketing*. In 1987 it won 5 per cent in the *Folketing* elections. It won two seats, and has one minister in the current government.

Support

After being one of the two major Faroese parties from 1906 to World War II, the

Faroese election results, 1945–present (percentages of vote and seats won)

	1946	1950	1954	1958	1962	1966	1970	1974	1978	1980	1984	1988
Folkaflokkurin (People's Party)	40.9% (8)	32.2% (8)	20.9% (6)	17.8% (5)	20.2% (6)	21.6% (6)	20.0% (5)	20.5% (5)	17.9% (6)	18.9% (6)	21.7% (7)	23.2% (8)
Sambandsflokkurin (Unionist Party)	28.7% (6)	27.2% (7)	26.0% (7)	23.7% (7)	20.5% (6)	23.7% (6)	21.7% (6)	19.1% (5)	26.3% (8)	23.9% (8)	21.2% (7)	21.2% (7)
Føroya Jaunadarflokkur (Faroese-Social Democratic Party)	28.1% (4) (with Social Democrats)	22.4% (6)	19.7% (5)	25.8% (8)	27.6% (8)	27.0% (7)	27.1% (7)	25.8% (7)	22.3% (8)	21.7% (7)	23.4% (8)	21.7% (7)
Sjalvstyrisflokkurin (Home Rule Party)	(2)	8.3% (2)	7.1% (2)	5.8% (2)	5.9% (2)	4.9% (1)	5.6% (1)	7.2% (2)	7.2% (2)	8.4% (3)	8.5% (2)	7.1% (2)
Tjodveldisflokkur (Republican Party)	—	9.9% (2)	23.8% (6)	24.0% (7)	21.3% (6)	20.0% (5)	21.9% (6)	22.5% (6)	20.3% (6)	19.0% (6)	19.5% (6)	19.2% (6)
KFFF[1] (Christian People's Party—Progress and Fishing Industry Party)	—	—	2.5% (1)	2.9% (1)	4.5% (1)	2.8% (1)	3.7% (1)	2.5% (1)	6.1% (2)	8.2% (2)	5.8% (2)	5.5% (2)
Others	2.3% (0)	—	—	—	—	—	—	2.5% (0)	—	—	—	2.0% (0)

[1]KFFF: Kristeligt Folkeparti Framburds—Og Fiskivinnuflokkurin

Home Rule Party has been only the fifth-largest Faroese party since 1948, far behind the four major parties. In the last two sections in 1980 and 1984 (in which it won 8.4 per cent and 8.5 per cent respectively), its highest votes were in the constituencies of Nordoya (over 14 per cent), Eysturoyar (11.5–12.5 per cent) and Sudurstreymoyar (9 per cent). It was weakest in Suduroyar and Vaga at only around 3 per cent of the votes.

Policies

The Home Rule Party continues to call for greater Faroese autonomy. It has advocated establishment of a Faroese representation office in Copenhagen, and the consequent abolition of *Folketing* representation for the Faroes. It has also sought direct popular election of the Faroese Prime Minister.

Personalities

Hilmar Kass is the party leader. Lasse Klein was the party's minister in the 1984–88 Faroese government, where he has been responsible for transport and cultural affairs.

Sambandsflokkurin
(Union Party)

Headquarters	: Løgtingid, Aarvegi, DG-3800 Torshavn
Leader	: Pauli Ellefsen
Newspaper	: *Dimmalæting* ("Dawn", three times weekly, 11,600)
Founded	: 1906

History

The Union Party was founded in 1906 in opposition to the newly founded Home Rule party. The Union Party advocated the maintenance of closer ties with Denmark, and put less emphasis on the Faroese language. In its first election in 1906 it obtained 62.4 per cent of the vote, and won 12 of the 20 seats in the *Løgting*. From 1906 to 1916 it was always the largest party in votes (winning up to 73.3 per cent in 1910) and in seats. In 1916 it won fewer votes than the Home Rule Party for the first time (but more seats), and in 1918 fewer seats. Until 1936 it only polled less than 50 per cent on two occasions, but in 1936 its vote dropped sharply to 33.6 per cent, and since 1943 it has never again polled above 30 per cent.

After Home Rule was introduced in 1948 the Union Party provided the Faroese Prime Minister from 1948 to 1958, with Andreas Samuelsen heading a coalition with the Social Democrats and Home Rule Party from 1948–50, and Kristian Djurhuus a coalition with the People's Party from 1950–54, and with the People's Party and Home Rule Party from 1954–58. The Union Party took part in a further coalition from 1958–62, but was in opposition from 1962–66. From 1966–74 it was back in government (providing the Prime Minister from 1968–70), and from 1974–80 again in opposition. From 1980–84 it again provided the Prime Minister (Pauli Ellefsen) in a coalition with the People's Party and Home Rule Party. Since 1984, when its vote dropped from 23.9 per cent to 21.2 per cent (and it won seven instead of eight seats) it has again been in opposition. It has never been out of the *Løgting* since its foundation in 1906. In 1988 it won seven seats on 21.2 per cent of the vote.

It has had a representative in the *Folketing* from 1950 to 1964, and again from 1977 to 1987. In the 1987 *Folketing* election it won 24 per cent of the vote. In the *Folketing* it has worked closely with *Venstre*. It is in the Centre Group in the Nordic Council.

Support

Since Home Rule was introduced, the Union Party has no longer been a dominant party, but it has always remained one of the big four parties, and has been the largest party in votes in the 1954, 1978 and 1980 elections. Its highest percentages have been 27.2 per cent in 1950 and 26.3 per cent in 1978, and its lowest 19.1 per cent in 1974. Its 1984 vote of 21.2 per cent is its third-lowest since the beginning of Home Rule.

The strongest constituencies for the Union Party are Vaga (34 per cent in 1984) and Eysturoyar (28 per cent in 1984), where it is the largest party. Its weakest are Sandoyar (11 per cent in 1984) and Nordoya (12 per cent). In Nordoya it is only the fifth party.

Policies

The Union Party continues to call for the preservation of close links with Denmark. In Faroese politics it has a conservative orientation, and believes that private enterprise is the driving force of the economy.

Personalities

The party chairman is Pauli Ellefsen, who was Faroese Prime Minister from 1980 to 1984, and who was also a member of the *Folketing* for 10 years.

Kristeligt Folkeparti Framburds — Og Fiskivinnuflokkurin — KFFF
(Christian People's Party — Progress and Fishing Industry Party)

Headquarters : Løgtingid, Aarvegi,
DK-3800 Torshavn
Newspaper : *Sjon Fyri Søgn*
("See for Yourself")

History

The party was established before the 1978 elections as a coalition between the *Framburdsflokkurin* (Progressive Party), which had obtained one seat in the *Løgting* in every election since 1954 (with a high of 4.5 per cent of the vote), and also centre-oriented circles in the fishing industry. It obtained two seats in both the 1978 and 1980 elections, with 6.1 per cent and 8.2 per cent of the vote respectively. Having expanded its name as shown above, it again obtained two seats in the 1984 *Løgting* elections (with 5.8 per cent of the vote) and subsequently took part in a four-party centre-left government headed by the Social Democrats. The party had one of the six members in the government.

There was subsequently a schism within the party, with one of its two members in the *Løgting* breaking away to join a newly established Progressive Party. This latter contested the 1987 *Folketing* election (unlike the parent party), but won only 2 per cent of the vote. Only one, therefore, of the two members elected by the KFFF in 1984 supported the 1984–88 coalition. In the 1988 elections the mainstream party won two seats and subsequently re-entered government with one member, whereas the breakaway party was eliminated.

Support

In the elections that it has contested, the KFFF has been the smallest of the six Faroese parties. In the 1984 *Løgting* elections its vote was under 8 per cent in its two strongest constituencies of Nordoya and Eysturoyar. It won around 6 per cent in the most populous constituency of Sudurstreymoyar. It was especially weak in the constituencies of Nordurstreymoyar (under 2.5 per cent) and Sandoyar (around 1.5 per cent).

Policies

The KFFF is a centre party which has sought to establish links with the Christian Democratic parties of Scandinavia, and to a lesser extent those of the rest of Europe. It seeks increased internal self-government for the Faroes.

It is also in favour of increased popular democracy and decentralization. It has a non-socialist anti-Communist orientation. It has continuing links with the Fishermen's Association.

Personalities

The party's one minister in the 1984–88 Faroese government was Niels Pauli Danielsen, who was responsible for home affairs, social affairs and family affairs. Its one minister in the government set up in January 1989 is Tordur Niclasen.

Tjodveldisflokkurin
(Republican Party)

Headquarters : Løgtingid, Aarvegi,
DK-3800 Torshavn
(tel: 1–24 95)
Leader : Erlendur Patursson
Newspaper : *"14 September"*
(twice weekly,
3,600)
Founded : 1948

History

The Republican Party was founded in 1948, claiming that the logical result of the 1946 plebiscite should be Faroese independence from Denmark. In its first election in 1950 it obtained 4.9 per cent and two seats in the *Løgting*. It made a remarkable advance in 1954 to 23.8 per cent and six seats, and became the second-largest party in the *Løgting*. Since then it has remained one of the four major parties in the Faroes, with support fluctuating between a high of 24 per cent (1958) and a low of 19 per cent (1980) and with between five and seven seats in the *Løgting*.

It first entered government in a coalition with the People's and Home Rule parties between 1962 and 1966, and was again in government between 1974 and 1980. After the 1984 election, in which it obtained 19.5 per cent and six seats, it entered into a coalition government (with two ministers) with three other parties. In 1988 it won six seats in the elections on 19.2 per cent of the vote. In 1989 it entered the new coalition government with two ministers. It has never yet provided a Faroese Prime Minister.

It has only had representation in the Danish *Folketing* between 1973 and 1977. It is linked to the Left Socialist Group within the Nordic Council framework.

Support

The Republican Party is currently only the fourth Faroese party in terms of popular support, but not far behind the first three. In the 1984 elections its support was remarkably evenly spread at between 19 per cent and 27 per cent in five of the seven constituencies. It was stronger in the constituency of Sandoyar (27 per cent) and weaker in Vaga (10 per cent).

Policies

The Republican Party is a left-wing party calling for the establishment of an independent Faroese Republic. It has been anti-EC and anti-NATO. It has a socialist orientation in economic and social policy, and advocates a strong role for the public sector.

Personalities

Jogvan Durhuus was the Deputy Prime Minister in the 1984–88 coalition government, responsible for the portfolios of education, agriculture, health services and energy policy.

The other leading personalities in the party include Erlendur Patursson and Hergeir Neilsen, who has been President of the *Løgting*.

Føroya Javnadarflokkur
(Faroese Social Democratic Party)

Headquarters	: Løgtingid, Aarvegi, DK-3800 Torshavn (tel: 1–24 93)
Leader	: Atli Dam
Newspaper	: *Sosialurin* (three times weekly, 6,000)
Membership	: 1,000
Founded	: 1925

History

The party was founded in 1925. Its name literally means "equality party", but it has become known as the Social Democratic Party in Danish. It first entered the *Løgting* (with two seats) in 1928, when it obtained 10.6 per cent of the vote and became the first party to challenge the dominance of the two traditional parties, the Home Rule and the Unionist parties. It made a considerable electoral breakthrough in 1936, when it obtained 24 per cent of the vote and six seats.

In 1948 it entered the first Faroese Home Rule Government in a coalition with the Unionist and Home Rule parties, in which it had one minister (J. P. Davidsen). In 1950 it returned to opposition. In the 1958 elections it obtained 25.8 per cent and eight seats, and became the largest Faroese party for the first time, a primacy it retained until 1978 although never winning more than 27.5 per cent of the vote.

After its 1958 advance the Social Democrats provided the Faroese Prime Minister for the first time, with Peter Mohr Dam heading a coalition with the Unionist and Home Rule parties, which lasted until 1962.

The party was again in opposition from 1962 to 1966, but was continuously in government from 1966 to 1980, providing the Prime Minister from 1966 to 1968, and from 1970 to 1980.

In the 1978 and 1980 elections the Social Democratic Party became only the second party to the Unionist Party, and after 1980 remained in opposition until 1984. In the 1984 elections its vote increased to 23.4 per cent (eight seats), and it again became the largest party. It subsequently headed a new four-party coalition government, with its leader, Atli Dam, as Prime Minister. After the 1988 elections, when it obtained only seven seats on 21.7 per cent of the vote, it again returned to opposition.

The Social Democrats have had the longest *Folketing* representation of any Faroese party, with a member in the *Folketing* from 1948 to 1957, from 1960 to 1984 and again from 1987. They have co-operated with the Danish Social Democrats.

Support

The Social Democrats have been the largest Faroese party in six out of the last eight elections, if only by slender margins.

From the beginning the party's strongest base of support was the southernmost constituency of Suduroyar, where on some occasions it has won over 50 per cent of the vote. In 1984 it won over 42 per cent in Suduroyar, well over double the vote of the second party on the island.

In 1984 the Social Democrats were also the largest party in the constituency of Nordurstreymoyar (28 per cent), and were second in three other constituencies. They were weakest in the constituency of Eysturoyar, where they obtained little over 13 per cent and were only the fourth party.

Policies

The Social Democrats are a left-of-centre party but, unlike the Republicans, have emphasized the need to maintain links with Denmark, although they want adequate self-determination within that framework. They seek the creation of a Democratic Socialist society within the Faroes, and believe that the public sector should continue to play a major role in economic development. They are anti-militarist.

Personalities

Atli Dam is the party leader, and was the Faroese Prime Minister from 1984–1988. He also had the portfolios of constitutional affairs, foreign affairs, fisheries and wage policy. He has represented his party in the Danish *Folketing*.

The party's other minister in the 1984–88 government was Vilhelm Johannesen, responsible for industry, fish farming, judicial affairs, housing and shipping.

Jakup Lindenskov has been chairman of the *Løgting*. Another prominent party member has been Jørgen Thomsen.

Folkaflokkurin
(The People's Party)

Headquarters	: Løgtingid, Aarvegi, DK-3800 Torshavn (tel: 1–24 91)
Leader	: Jogvan Sundstein
Newspaper	: *Dagbladid* (three times a week, 5,500)
Founded	: 1940

History

The *Folkaflokkurin* (People's Party) was founded in 1940 as a merger between the right-of-centre majority of the Home Rule Party and a small party called the *Vinnuflokkur* (the Commerce Party), which has contested the 1936 elections and obtained two seats on 8.2 per cent of the vote. The new People's Party called for the cutting of ties with Denmark. In its first election in 1940 it obtained six seats on 25.5 per cent of the vote, with more votes than the parent Home Rule Party and also the Social Democrats, and second only to the Unionist Party.

In 1943 it obtained 41.5 per cent, becoming easily the largest Faroese Party with 12 out of the 25 seats in the *Løgting*. It retained this position in 1945 (11 out of 23 seats on 43.4 per cent of the vote), 1946 (40.9 per cent) and 1950, although its vote then dropped sharply to 32.3 per cent.

In 1950 it entered a coalition government with the Unionist party which lasted until 1954. From 1954 to 1958 it was in coalition with the Unionist and Home Rule parties. Its vote continued to fall, and in the 1958 elections it won 17.8 per cent and five seats, and was only the fourth-largest party. It then returned into opposition until 1962.

From 1962 to 1966 it took part in a coalition government with the Republican and Home Rule parties, and for the first time it provided the Faroese Prime Minister, Hakun Djurjuus.

The People's Party was again in opposition from 1966 to 1974. From 1974 to 1984 it participated in government. In 1984 its vote increased considerably to 21.7 per cent (seven seats), but it went into opposition. In 1988 it obtained eight seats in the elections on 23.2 per cent of the vote (making it the largest party), and Jogvan Sundstein became Faroese Prime Minister in the new coalition established in 1989, in which the party also had one other minister.

The People's Party has had representation in the Danish *Folketing* from 1948 to 1950, 1957 to 1960, 1964 to 1973, and again from 1984. In the *Folketing* it has moved towards co-operation with the current right-of-centre government, although it had not previously become closely involved in Danish internal politics.

Support

After its period as the largest Faroese party from 1943 to 1954, the People's party has only been the third or fourth party in all subsequent *Løgting* elections until 1984. Instead of the 40 per cent or more that it was winning for much of the 1940s, its vote since 1954 has fluctuated between a high of 21.7 per cent and a low of 17.8 per cent. In 1984, however, it again became the second-largest Faroese party, although only narrowly.

In 1984 it was the strongest party in three out of the seven Faroese constituencies, Sandoyar (28.5 per cent), Nordoya (25 per cent) and the most populous constituency of Sudurstreymoyar (25.5 per cent) which includes the capital Torshavn.

The People's Party was weakest in Eysturoyar (17 per cent) and especially Suduroyar, where it won little over 12 per cent, and was only the fourth party.

Policies

The People's Party is on the right wing of Faroese politics but, unlike the other main party of the right-of-centre, the Unionists, it has strongly emphasized the need for increased Faroese autonomy. It has called for the Faroes to move gradually towards complete legislative autonomy in all areas.

In economic policy it supports private enterprise and free trade.

Personalities

The party's chairman is Jogvan Sundstein, who became Faroese Prime Minister in 1989. Oli Breckmann has represented the party in the Danish *Folketing*.

Greenland

Greenland (*Grønland* in Danish, *Kalaallit Nunaat* in the Eskimo language) is an island of 840,000 square miles. It has a population of only a little over 50,000, with most of its population concentrated in a few settlements on the west and south-west coasts. The capital and largest town is Nuuk (formerly Godthaab).

Greenland has a native population of Eskimos (Inuit) and also a considerable Danish population. Both Danish and the Eskimo or Greenlandic language are in use.

Political institutions

Greenland is still part of Denmark, but enjoys extensive Home Rule. It is no longer part of the European Community. It has a representative assembly called the *Landsting* of 27 members, elected for a four-year period, although earlier elections can be called. There are three multi-member constituencies (the South constituency of five seats, the Central constituency of eight seats and the Disko constituency of five seats), and there are also five single-member constituencies for the more remote settlements of north-west and eastern Greenland. There are also four additional members.

The Home Rule Government of Greenland is called the *Landstyre*, and consists of a chairman and six other cabinet members. It must have majority parliamentary support within the *Landsting*, and *Landstyre* members do not necessarily have to be drawn from the *Landsting*.

There are 18 municipalities in Greenland, 15 in West Greenland, one in North Greenland and two in East Greenland. Municipal executives contain between three and 17 members, and are elected every four years.

Greenland continues to have two members in the Danish *Folketing* (in 1971, Greenland members were able to hold the balance of power, and to help bring down the Baunsgaard government). In recent years and since Home Rule was established, one Greenland member has always come from the *Siumut* party, and the other from *Atassut*.

Brief political history

1729   Danish political control asserted. Greenland becomes a colony of Denmark.

1931   Norwegian fishermen occupy part of East Greenland coast.

Greenland election results to the *Landsting*, 1979–87

	1979 votes	1979 %	1979 seats	1983 votes	1983 %	1983 seats	1984 votes	1984 %	1984 seats	1987 votes	1987 %	1987 seats
Siumut	8,505	46.1	13	10,371	42.3	11	9,992	44.1	11	9,980	39.8	11
Atassut	7,688	41.7	8	11,443	46.6	11	9,863	43.8	11	10,043	40.1	11
Inuit Ataqatigiit	1,813	4.4	—	2,612	10.6	2	2,737	12.2	3	3,823	15.3	4
Sulissatut	1,041	5.6	—	—	—	—	—	—	—	—	—	—
Issitrup Partii	—	—	—	—	—	—	—	—	—	1,119	4.5	1

Greenland elections to *Folketing*, 1987 and 1988

1987	Siumut	(40.5%) — 1 seat
	Atassut	(38.8%) — 1 seat
	Inuit Ataqatigiit	(11.7%) —
1988	Siumut	(37.9%) — 1 seat
	Atassut	(36.6%) — 1 seat
	Inuit Ataqatigiit	(16.3%) —

1933   The International Court of Justice rejects Norwegian claim to East Greenland, and judgement is accepted by Norway.

1941   With Denmark proper occupied by Germans, United States troops establish bases in Greenland. US presence is confirmed by Danish *Folketing* in 1945.

1951   Permanent formal agreement of US bases, with US allowed to maintain three such bases in Greenland.

1953   End of colonial period in which Greenland enjoyed no political rights. Greenland becomes a Danish *Amt* (county), with its own *Landsråd* (provincial council), with 21 members elected for four-year terms (16 in single-member election districts, five as additional members). Greenland sends two members to Danish *Folketing*.

1964   Advisory Greenland Council established.

1971   Knud Hertling (founder of *Suqaq*, early attempt at indigenous Greenlandic party) becomes first Greenlandic Minister for Greenland.

1973   Greenland becomes part of European Community, in spite of large "no" vote to EC membership in Greenland in Danish EC referendum.

1973–75 Greenland Home Rule Committee examines ways in which this could be implemented.

1975–78 Commission of Home Rule in Greenland (with five members of *Landsråd*, two Greenland members of *Folketing*, seven other *Folketing* members and chairman appointed by Minister for Greenland) put forward proposals for Home Rule, which are accepted in 1978.

1978   Alcohol referendum. Greenland voters reject prohibition with 7,327 "no" votes to 6,163 "yes" votes, but accept rationing by 6,701 "yes" votes to 4,630 "no" votes.

1979   Home Rule comes into operation on May 1, after plebiscite on Home Rule finds 12,756 Greenlandic voters in favour (70.1 per cent) and 4,703 against. Home Rule Assembly (*Landsting*) established, with first elections won by *Siumut* party, which then runs first Home Rule Executive (*Landstyre*), with Jonathan Motzfeldt as chairman.

1979–83 Majority *Siumut* government under Jonathan Motzfeldt (on Feb. 23, 1982, Greenland voters narrowly support Greenland's departure from the EC, with 11,174 "yes" votes to remaining in the EC, and 12,624 "no" votes).

1983   *Landsting* elections, in which *Siumut* loses its overall majority (and *Atassut* wins more votes).

1983–84 Minority *Siumut* government under Jonathan Motzfeldt, with *Landsting* support.

1984   Minority *Siumut* government loses vote of no confidence supported by both *Atassut* and *Inuit Ataqatigiit*. New *Landsting* elections are called, in which *Siumut* and *Atassut* have same number of seats and balance is held by *Inuit Ataqatigiit*.

1984–87 Coalition government under Jonathan Motzfeldt between *Siumut* and *Inuit Ataqatigiit* (Greenland leaves EC in 1985, new agreement over US bases at Thule and Söndre Strömfjord in 1986).

1987   Coalition government falls on March 11, 1987, over issue of whether new radar system at US base in Thule contravenes 1972 Antiballistic Missile (ABM) Treaty. New *Landsting* elections held on 26 May, 1987, in which *Siumut* and *Atassut* again win 11 seats each, *Inuit Ataqatigiit* wins extra seat and again holds balance of power, and new *Issitrup Partii* enters the *Landsting* with one seat. Negotiations between *Siumut* and *Atassut* break down, and new coalition government is formed between *Siumut* and *Inuit Ataquatigiit*.

1987–88 Coalition government under Jonathan Motzfeldt.

1988   Coalition government collapses. *Inuit Ataquatigiit* goes into opposition, and Jonathan Motzfeldt forms new *Siumut* minority administration while seeking *Landsting* support from *Atassut*.

Main features of the political system in Greenland

Greenland political parties were slow to develop, and Greenland's widely scattered and isolated communities tended to favour a highly personalized system of localized politics, and parties operating only in individual settlements. *Suqak* was one of the few parties to attempt to organize on a wider basis, but the first fully fledged Greenlandic party was *Siumut*, which developed its organization through the 1970s. Since Home Rule, however, Greenland has had its own competitive party system.

Greenlandic politics is now characterized by two evenly matched parties, *Siumut* on the moderate left-of-centre and *Atassut* on the moderate right-of-centre, with neither able to establish an overall majority since 1983. The balance of power has thus been held by the much smaller but growing left socialist and nationalist party, *Inuit Ataquatigiit*.

A new party on the right-of-centre, the *Issitrup Partii*, was founded in 1986.

The main issues in Greenlandic politics are the following:

- The ways in which Home Rule should be further developed.
- The degree of Greenlandic control over its extensive natural resources.
- The respective roles of the Greenlandic public administration and of the private sector in its economic development (e.g. whether the trawler fleet should be privatized).
- The way in which Greenlandic culture and language can be protected and developed.
- The best ways of combating Greenland's alcohol and drugs problems.
- The future status of the United States' bases, and the uses to which they can be put.

Siumut
(Forward)

Headquarters	: P.O. Box 357, 3900 Nuuk tel:2–20 77)
Leader	: Jonathan Motzfeldt
Chairman	: Lars Emil Johansen
Party secretary	: Peter Grønvold Samuelsen
Newspaper	: *Siumut* (also *Niviarsing*, review, 1,500)
Membership	: 3,000

History

The *Siumut* movement began to emerge in the early 1970s, inspired by a number of young Greenlandic politicians (of whom the most prominent were Jonathan Motzfeldt, Lars Emil Johansen and Moses Olsen), who sought much greater autonomy for Greenland. The first local branch was set up in 1975, and in 1977 *Siumut* became a fully fledged political party. It soon developed a strong organizational structure, with branches established throughout Greenland. Its party programme was Socialist in orientation.

In the 1977 Danish elections it won the most votes, and elected one of its members to the *Folketing*. In 1978 Motzfeldt made a successful comeback to the leadership after having been temporarily removed because he was perceived as being too pro-EC. In 1979 *Siumut* suffered a schism, when a new party, *Sulissatut*, was established to look more explicitly after workers' interests (the new party survived until 1982).

In the first Greenland elections in 1979, *Siumut* became the largest party with 46.1 per cent of the vote, and its 13 seats gave it an absolute majority in the *Landsting*. Jonathan Motzfeldt then became Prime Minister of Greenland at the head of a single-party *Siumut* government. *Siumut* also elected one of its members, Finn Lynge, to the European Parliament, where he sat in the Socialist Group. In the 1982 referendum on EC membership *Siumut* campaigned successfully for Greenland's withdrawal.

In the 1983 elections, however, *Siumut* obtained less votes than *Atassut*, and lost their absolute majority in the *Landsting*. Motzfeldt remained in government at the head of a minority *Siumut* administration with external support from the *Inuit Ataqatigiit* party. In the 1983 communal elections *Siumut* won 95 seats, 20 more than *Atassut*.

After the government was brought down in a no confidence vote in 1984, new elections were called, in which *Siumut* obtained slightly more votes than *Atassut*, but still had no clear majority. It then entered into a coalition government with *Inuit Ataqatigiit*. This new Motzfeldt-led government survived until 1987, when it fell primarily over the issue of the US airbase at Thule, with *Siumut's* more radical coalition partners claiming that it was being too passive in complaining about new radar equipment which might contravene the ABM Treaty.

In the subsequent elections *Siumut* obtained 39.8 per cent of the vote (with a handful of votes less than *Atassut*) and 11 seats. Motzfeldt's attempts to negotiate a grand coalition with *Atassut* led to him being temporarily deposed as leader, but he managed to re-assert himself and to forge a new coalition government with *Inuit Ataqatigiit*. This served until 1988, when differences between the two parties (for example over NATO and control of natural resources)became too great, and the coalition again fell. Motzfeldt then formed a new *Siumut* minority government, and sought support from *Atassut*.

Within the *Folketing, Siumut* has co-operated with the Social Democrats and it is a consultative member of the Socialist International.

Support

Siumut is one of the two major Greenland parties, and is remarkably evenly matched with *Atassut*, with almost exactly the same total of votes in the last two *Landsting* elections. There is, however, a considerable difference in their regional distribution of support. Of the three multi-member constituencies, *Siumut* is strongest in the South constituency, where it won 44 per cent of the vote in 1987 compared to 33 per cent for *Atassut*. It is particularly strong in Qaqortoq (Julianehåb), where it has had almost 50 per cent of the vote and in Nanortalik (over 46 per cent in 1987). It is weaker in the community of Narsaq.

Siumut is also the largest party in four out of the five single-member constituencies in the outlying communities of North and East Greenland. It is strongest of all in Lars Emil Johansen's home community of Uummannaq, where it received almost 60 per cent of the vote in 1987.

Siumut is generally less strong than *Atassut* in the two multi-member constituencies of Central Greenland and Disko. In the centre constituency it polled 35 per cent of the vote in 1987, and was particularly weak in the capital of Nuuk (Godthåb), where it obtained around 30 per cent. In the Disko constituency *Siumut* polled around 33 per cent in 1987, and was weakest in Aasiat, where it only received around 23 per cent of the vote and was the third party.

Policies

Siumut is a left-of-centre party with a generally socialist orientation. Its initial prestige stemmed from its central role in helping to achieve Home Rule.

Its actions, however, have generally been pragmatic. In the run-up to Home Rule it accepted a compromise on the issue of control of Greenland's natural resources. It has not adopted a maximalist approach as regards eventual achievement of independence of Greenland, and emphasis is put, instead, on the achievement of the maximum degree of autonomy within the Home Rule framework, with Greenland continuing to be part, with no specified time limit, of the Kingdom of Denmark. *Siumut* has also been much less militant than *Inuit Ataqatigiit* on the issue of the US bases in Greenland. It has not sought to have them removed as a priority objective, and Motzfeldt accepted that the new US radar at Thule was of a defensive nature. *Siumut* considers, however, that the actual terms governing the US bases (size, etc.) are a matter for further negotiation.

Siumut was in favour of Greenland's withdrawal from the EC. It has also supported moves to extend Greenland's exclusive fishing zone. It seeks co-operation with other Eskimo communities, and pushed for the establishment of the Inuit Circumpolar Conference.

Within Greenland its policies have emphasized the need to free the country from its previous state of dependence, and to reduce inequalities. It believes that public investment must play a major role. Use of the Greenlandic language is strongly promoted.

Personalities

Jonathan Motzfeldt has been the Prime Minister of Greenland since 1979, and has twice survived attempts to dislodge him as leader of *Siumut*.

Lars Emil Johansen is the party chairman, and one of its leading figures since its foundation, as is Moses Olsen.

Hans-Pavia Rosing has been *Siumut's* member in the *Folketing* since 1987. From 1980 to 1986 he was president of the Inuit Circumpolar Conference, and he is also a former minister in the Greenland Home Rule government.

Atassut
(Spirit of Community Party)

Headquarters	: Kongevejen 1, Blok P, Box 399, Nuuk (tel: 2–33 66)
Party chairman	: Otto Steenholdt
Party secretary	: Julian Egede Hennings
Newspaper	: *Atassut*
Membership	: 3,000

History

Atassut was founded at the beginning of 1977, although this was not finally formalized until 1981. Its first leader was Lars Chemnitz (who had occupied an important position as chairman of the pre-autonomy council), and other leading figures include Ole Berglund, Otto Steenholdt, and Niels Carlo Heilmann, the then chairman of the Whalers and Fishermen Association.

In the 1977 *Folketing* elections *Atassut* obtained almost as many votes as the better implanted *Siumut*, and Otto Steenholdt became one of Greenland's two members in Copenhagen; a position he has retained until the present day.

In the first *Landsting* elections in 1979, *Atassut* won 41.7 per cent of the vote and eight of the 21 seats, and went into opposition to the new majority *Siumut* administration.

In the 1982 referendum on Greenland's membership of the EC *Atassut* supported continuing membership.

In the 1983 *Landsting* elections *Atassut* obtained 46.6 per cent of the vote, a higher percentage than *Siumut*, but the party remained in opposition, as *Siumut* was able to form a minority government with support from the third party, *Inuit Ataqatigiit*.

In the 1984 communal elections *Atassut* obtained 75 seats, 20 less than *Siumut*. *Atassut* helped to bring down the government in 1984, and in new elections it obtained 43.8 per cent with the same number of seats as *Siumut* (11). *Atassut* was again kept out of power as *Siumut* and *Inuit Ataqatigiit* combined to form a coalition government. Also in 1984 Otto Steenholdt became the new chairman of *Atassut*.

After the coalition government fell in 1987, *Atassut* won 40.1 per cent in the new *Landsting* elections, again with the same total of 11 seats as *Siumut*. It remained in opposition as a new coalition was formed between *Siumut* and *Inuit Ataqatigiit* after Jonathan Motzfeldt had almost lost his leadership of *Siumut* after exploring the idea of a grand coalition between *Siumut* and *Atassut*.

The government fell in 1988 and *Siumut* sought *Atassut* support for its new minority administration.

In the 1988 *Folketing* elections Otto Steenholdt was easily re-elected. Within the *Folketing* he has co-operated with the present Danish government, and with the *Venstre* Party in particular. *Atassut* works with the Group of Centre parties in the Nordic Council.

Support

Atassut is one of the two major political parties in Greenland, and is well implanted throughout Greenland's scattered settlements, with a proportionally high membership. In all elections it has been extremely competitive with the main government party *Siumut*, and in two of the four *Landsting* elections has had more votes than *Siumut*; in 1987, by only 63 votes.

Atassut has had particular support among the employers and the trawler-owners, as well as among the Danish community in Greenland.

In the three multi-member constituencies *Atassut* obtained its highest 1987 vote in the Centre constituency, where it won around 42 per cent, and polled considerably more votes than *Siumut*. It was by a considerable margin the largest party in the capital, Nuuk (Godthåb), where it polled 43 per cent compared to 30 per cent for *Siumut*.

Atassut is also the largest party in the Disko constituency, where it polled around 41 per cent in 1987. A major contributory factor to its strength in this constituency is that the region of Aasimat (the former Egedesminde) is the political base of its leader, Otto Steenholdt.

Atassut is considerably weaker than *Siumut* in the South constituency, where it obtained 33 per cent in 1987. It had under 30 per cent support in 1987 in the communities of Nanortalik and Qaqortoq (the former Julianehåb), but was stronger in Narsaq.

Atassut is weaker than *Siumut* in four of the five isolated single-member constituencies, especially in Uummannaq, where it obtained under 24 per cent of the vote in 1987. The only exception has been Tasiilaq (the former Angmagssalik) in East Greenland, where *Atassut* was the largest party in 1987, with 43 per cent of the vote.

Policies

Atassut is a moderate non-socialist party to the right of *Siumut*, although both parties are more pragmatic than ideological. *Atassut* has sought to avoid confrontations with Denmark, and while it seeks the further extension of Greenland's autonomy, emphasizes the need to maintain strong links with Denmark.

It originally campaigned for Greenland to remain within the EC (although even it had members like Niels Carlo Heilmann who were opposed), but accepts the result of the 1982 referendum.

Personalities

Atassut's leader is Otto Steenholdt, born in 1936, who has been the party chairman since 1984. He has been a member of the *Folketing* since 1977, and a member of the Nordic Council since 1979.

Issitrup Partii
(Polar Party)

Headquarters : c/o Landsting, Nuuk
Leader : Nikolaj Heinrich

History

The *Issitrup Partii* was founded in 1986. A driving force behind its creation was Nikolaj Heinrich, the president of Greenland's Federation of Fishermen and Trawlermen. It was supported by members of the business community and fishing industry who maintained that private enterprise interests were being neglected by the left-wing coalition government in power since 1984. In the 1987 elections the party's manifesto called for the privatization of the state-owned trawler fleet.

The *Issitrup Partii* obtained 4.5 per cent in the 1987 election, and obtained one seat in the *Landsting*. It obtained 4 per cent in the South constituency and around 5 per cent in each of the Centre and Disko constituencies. In the capital city of Nuuk (Godthåb) it obtained over 6 per cent. In the single-member constituency of Tasiilaq (Angmagssalik) in East Greenland it obtained almost 8 per cent.

In the 1988 *Folketing* elections its unsuccessful candidate was Arne Ib Nielsen, who obtained 815 votes.

Inuit Ataqatigiit
(Eskimo Community)

Headquarters   : P.O. Box 321,
                     DK-3900 Nuuk
                     (tel: 2–37 02)
Leader   : Aqqaluk Lynge

History

Inuit Ataqatigiit was founded in 1978 (although local branches had already been created) by a group of radical Greenlanders, who had formerly been active in the Young Greenland Council — KIA — in Copenhagen. They were opposed to the compromises that had been accepted by *Siumut* and other Greenlandic representatives in the negotiations over Home Rule, and were particularly concerned about the lack of full Greenlandic control over natural resources. In the 1979 referendum the party was opposed to Home Rule, and called for a "no" vote.

In the first *Landsting* elections in 1979 they only came fourth, obtaining 4.4 per cent of the vote and winning no seats. They initially wished to make no compromises with the political system by co-operating with other parties. In 1979 they did not stand in the elections for the Danish *Folketing*.

In 1981, however, they made an electoral alliance with the *Sulissartut* Party (which became defunct in 1982) for the purposes of the *Folketing* elections of that year. In the 1983 Greenland elections *Inuit Ataqatigiit's* vote went up to 10.6 per cent, and it won two seats in the *Landsting*, subsequently leading parliamentary support to the minority *Siumut* administration. In the 1984 *Folketing* elections the party stood for election in its own right.

In the 1984 Greenland elections its vote rose to 12.2 per cent, and it won three seats in the *Landsting*. It then entered a formal coalition with *Siumut* with two ministers, Aqqaluk Lynge at building and social affairs, and Josef Motzfeldt at commerce.

In March 1987 the coalition fell, largely over the issue of the instalment of new radar equipment at the US airbase at Thule, on which Aqqaluk Lynge sought an investigation as to whether this violated the 1972 Treaty on the Limitation of Anti-Ballistic Missiles. In the subsequent elections the party's vote rose further to 15.3 per cent, and it obtained four seats in the *Landsting*. A new coalition government was formed with *Siumut*, in which the party again had two ministers, Aqqaluk Lynge at social affairs, housing and environmental affairs, and Josef Motzfeldt at trade, traffic and youth affairs.

In 1988 the coalition again broke down, primarily over the issues of NATO and control of natural resources, and *Inuit Ataqatigiit* returned into opposition. In the 1988 *Folketing* elections the party's vote rose to 16.3 per cent.

Support

Inuit Ataqatigiit is the third party in Greenland politics, far behind the dominant *Siumut* and *Atassut*, but its vote has, nevertheless, been slowly increasing from the 4.5 per cent it won in 1979 to the 15–16 per cent level it now enjoys.

Within the three multi-member constituencies it has been strongest in the Disko constituency, where it obtained around 18 per cent in the 1987 *Landsting* elections. It was particularly strong in Aasiaat (the former Egedersminde), where it obtained almost 30 per cent of the vote and came second, winning considerably more votes than *Siumut*.

In the South constituency the party won over 15 per cent of the vote in 1987, with almost 18 per cent in Qaqortoq (Julianehåb). In the Centre constituency it obtained just under 15 per cent, but with around 17 per cent in the capital, Nuuk (Godthåb).

The party was especially weak in the two single-member constituencies in East Greenland, winning under 5 per cent, for example, in Tasiilaq (Angmagssalik).

Policies

Inuit Ataqatigiit is the most radical of Greenland's parties, with a left socialist or Marxist ideology, and advocating full independence for Greenland. It opposed Home Rule as inadequate, and has put particular emphasis on the need for full Greenlandic control of Greenland's natural resources. It has called for Greenland citizenship to be restricted to those with an Eskimo mother or father. It strongly opposed Greenland's membership of the EC and emphasized instead the need for closer links with the Eskimos of Canada and Alaska by means of an Inuit Federation. It is more radical than *Siumut* on the issue of NATO, and has called for the closure of US bases in Greenland. It is anti-capitalist in its economic policies.

Personalities

The party's chairman, Aqqaluk Lynge, has twice been a minister in the 1984–87 and 1987–88 coalitions with *Siumut*. Josef Motzfeldt has also been a minister in both coalitions, and was the party's candidate in the 1988 *Folketing* elections.

France

David Lowe

The country

France is a country of 212,736 square miles, with a population of over 55 million. Its capital is Paris. The large majority of the population are (at least nominally) Catholic, although there are Protestant and Jewish minorities and an increasing number of Moslems (possibly three million including naturalized French citizens as well as immigrants). There are also a number of ethnic, cultural and linguistic minorities — Bretons (of whom an increasingly small number speak Breton, a member of the Celtic family of languages), Basques (three of the seven historic provinces of the Basque country are located in France, although they do not have their own *département*), Alsatians (who speak a Germanic dialect), and Corsicans (who speak a language closer to Italian than to French). There are also a number of Catalan speakers in Roussillon, and Flemish speakers near the Belgian border. In a larger area of southern France Occitan dialects, based on the *Langue d'Óc* have long persisted.

Besides metropolitan France there are a number of overseas regions, which have been considered integral parts of France. There are four overseas departments (DOM — Départements d'Outre-Mer) — Guyane, Guadeloupe, Martinique and La Réunion. Besides these, there are three overseas territories (TOM — French Polynesia, New Caledonia, whose status has been the subject of intense recent controversy) and Wallis and Futuna. There are two "territorial collectivities" — Mayotte (an island which decided not to be part of the independent Comoro Islands) and St. Pierre and Miquelon. As they are not in Europe, their political systems have not been covered in this book.

France has had a long tradition of immigration and has assimilated, for example, many immigrants from Southern Europe (e.g. Italy and Spain). After Algeria became independent there was also a large influx (around one million) of returning French *colons*, or *pieds noirs*, who settled above all in Mediterranean France. Of the other immigrants a large proportion are from the Maghreb countries of Northern Africa.

Political institutions

France is now governed by the Constitution of the Fifth Republic that was introduced by de Gaulle and adopted by referendum in 1958. Its main features were its reinforcement of the powers of the presidency, and its introduction of a majority rather than proportional system for parliamentary elections.

The President of the Republic is elected for a seven-year term of office by direct popular vote. If no candidate wins an absolute majority in the first round of elections, the two leading candidates have a runoff election two weeks later.

The French presidency is now one of the most powerful in Europe. Article 8 of the Constitution grants the President the responsibility of appointing the Prime Minister and of terminating his office. Among the President's other powers are the ability to call referenda, to dissolve parliament and to take on special powers at times of crisis.

For most of the time since the creation of the Fifth Republic the Prime Minister has been *subordinate* to the President. Nevertheless there was always a potential contradiction between the above cited Article 8 of the Constitution and Article 20, which gives the government the responsibility of deciding and directing the policy of the nation, making it also responsible to Parliament. The ambiguity of these two articles made for much constitutional theorising, but their juxtaposition was never tested until the Constitution was well into its third decade, as the problem did not arise as long as the majority of Parliament owed its political allegiance to the President as well as Prime Minister. Between 1986 and 1988, however, there was "cohabitation" between the left-wing President, François Mitterrand and the right-wing government of Jacques Chirac. Cohabitation managed to function while respecting the constitutional rights and prerogatives of both the President and his Prime Minister, but in practice the post of Prime Minister became more prominent than before.

Map of France showing the departments.

Source: Carpress.

The Prime Minister must be supported by a majority in the National Assembly and presents his or her government to the Assembly for a vote of confidence upon being appointed. The government can also be brought down by adoption of a censure motion in the Assembly, although an absolute majority of all members (not just of those voting) must vote in favour of the motion for it to be carried.

The powers of the parliament are less than those in the Third or Fourth Republics. Besides the powerful presidency, the government is also in a strong position vis-à-vis the Parliament, notably through such devices as the passage of legislation by decree (Article 38) and making votes on legislation matters of confidence (Article 49–3), thus ensuring that they are automatically passed, unless a vote of censure is adopted by the Assembly.

The National Assembly consists of 575 seats, of which 553 are in metropolitan France and 22 overseas (Guadeloupe four, Martinique four, Réunion five, Guyane two, Polynesia two, New Caledonia two, Wallis and Futuna one, Mayotte one and St. Pierre and Miquelon one). Its members are elected for five–year terms (but with the possibility of earlier dissolution).

In 1985 the socialist-led government introduced a system of departmental proportional representation to replace the majority system which had been used since the beginning of the Fifth Republic. In 1986 the incoming government of the right reintroduced a majority system in single-member constituencies, and this was used in the 1988 legislative elections. If a candidate has an absolute majority in the first round of voting he or she is elected providing they have received the support of more than 25 per cent of the registered electorate. Otherwise there is a second ballot a week later, in which a relative majority is sufficient. The runoff is normally between the two leading candidates from the first round, but any candidate who received a vote higher than 12.5 per cent of the registered electorate in the first round may participate in the second round. Each candidate has a designated substitute (suppléant) who takes the elected member's place if the latter accepts a government office (when he or she must leave the Parliament), resigns the seat or dies. If a suppléant resigns, a by-election is held.

There is also a 321 member Senate, a third of the seats in which are renewed every three years (309 in indirect elections from departmental electoral colleges consisting of the national and local elected representatives of the particular department, and 12 by the National Council of French Citizens Abroad).

France is entitled to 81 members in the European Parliament, who are elected by a system of proportional representation that was introduced in 1977. The whole country is treated as a single electoral constituency. There is a five per cent threshold below which lists are not entitled to representation.

France has traditionally been a highly centralized country, whose main unit of local government has been the department introduced after the French Revolution to undercut the autonomy of the historic provinces of France. These departments have been administered by powerful government-appointed prefects.

Twenty-two larger regions, however, were created in 1964 and were given regional assemblies in 1972. Although they are still not very powerful, they are now more so than before as a result of devolution measures introduced by the socialist government in 1982. The regional assemblies are now directly elected, the first such set of elections having taken place in 1986.

Below these are the historic departments (95 plus Paris), each with their own elected General Assembly (*Conseil Général*). The departments are subdivided into *arrondissements* and *cantons*. In the *Conseil Général* there is one elected member per canton. Half its members are elected every three years (most recently in 1988). The president of the *Conseil Général* has considerable political authority.

The lowest tier is that of the *communes*, of which there are more than 36,000 throughout France. Municipal elections take place every six years (most recently in 1989). The mayors of the larger cities have a high public profile, as do mayors of many smaller towns. It is not unusual to combine the roles of member of parliament and mayor.

There is now a new system of public financing of political parties.

Brief political history before the Fifth Republic

1789	Fall of the *ancien régime*. French Revolution.
1792	First Republic (Consulate of Napoleon, 1799–1804).
1804–15	First Empire (Napoleon Bonaparte).
1815-30	Bourbon restoration (Louis XVIII and Charles X).
1830	Rule of Louis Philippe.
1848	Year of Revolution.
1848-52	Second Republic.
1852-70	Second Empire of Louis Napoleon.

1870	French defeat in Franco-Prussian War (loss of Alsace-Lorraine); collapse of regime.
1870–1940	Third Republic (Paris Commune 1871, new constitutional law 1875, Dreyfus affair 1894–99, return of Alsace–Lorraine after World War I, victory of Popular Front of Léon Blum 1936).
1940	Petain given full powers, fall of France, German occupation in North, Vichy regime in South. De Gaulle forms government in exile, Resistance develops in France.
1946–58	Fourth Republic (women given the right to vote for the first time, de Gaulle's first period in power ends in 1946, France joins NATO 1949, French defeat at Dien Bien Phu 1954, anti-colonial struggle in Algeria).
1958–present	Fifth Republic. De Gaulle as President 1958–69 (introduces Presidential regime and restores two ballot-based electoral system.

Political history — the Fifth Republic

Party realignment in the early years of the Fifth Republic

One of the most immediate and significant effects of the electoral law of 1958, which re-established the two-ballot majoritarian electoral system, was to encourage the formation of electoral alliances. Whereas each individual party was of course able to present its candidate for the first ballot, it rapidly became apparent that the best way to ensure election was for the weaker parties to desist in favour of the best placed candidate in the second round.

Particularly in the legislative elections in the early years of the Fifth Republic, those parties who supported the President and his government became known as the parties of the "governing majority". At this time the opposition parties had no such pole of attraction and it took them longer to come to terms with this basic electoral necessity.

This constituency-based electoral system also allowed candidates to be elected on the first ballot if they succeeded in obtaining an absolute majority of votes cast, and more than a quarter of registered votes. It completely changed the political establishment's way of thinking as elections in the Fourth Republic (1946–58) had been by proportional representation — a

fact which encouraged a multiplicity of parties and a shifting and weak majority.

Although the division between parties of the Left and those of the Right has been a constant feature of French political history, dating back to the opposition between monarchists and republicans in the 19th century if not before, in the immediate postwar years it was the parties of the centre which held the balance of power. The advent of the Fifth Republic forced them over time to make a choice, and a majority of centrists opted to join the Gaullist "conservative" camp against the parties of the Left.

De Gaulle himself, to begin with, paid only a secondary interest to the formation of a party which was to rapidly emerge as the dominant electoral force. The carefully constructed ambivalence of his own political stance enabled the *Union pour la Nouvelle République* (UNR) to capture a broad spectrum of support, which was not based on any ideological principle. It was based, however, on the need to have a party which would be organized to support the government and defend its record. Its electoral success belied the fact that it was a relatively loosely organized party by modern standards; heterogeneous both in its membership and in its policies. This was true at least until 1967 when at its congress in Lille it began to adopt a more structured and better disciplined organization. This change was engineered primarily by Georges Pompidou and a group of close associates, including a young and dynamic political adviser named Jacques Chirac.

During this period, the UNR was not the only party in the governing majority coalition. It was allied with the main centrist Christian Democratic party — the MRP — and the non-Gaullist conservative CNIP. By 1962 the CNIP had been reduced to a rump and it split, leading to the formation of the CNI and the *Républicains Indépendants* (RI). The latter was led by Valery Giscard d'Estaing. Although the DNI gradually withered to only marginal significance, the RI continued to form a crucial ally for the Gaullists and provided the government with several key ministers.

The MRP, on the other hand, gradually became smothered by the Gaullist tide after being the major force of Fourth Republic politics. More than any other party at this time it espoused European supranationalism linked to Christian ethnics. It was unable, however, to consolidate its position on the bipolar stage.

From 1962 other smaller centrist forces began to ally themselves in a vain attempt to ensure the survival of a wider political grouping in the centre of French politics. This was the case of the *Rassemblement Démocratique* of Maurice Faure, the *Centre Républicain* and the *Centre National des Indépendants* (CNI). This new alliance was called *Centre Démocrate*, and its leader was Jean Lecanuet. It was not joined by the Radical Party. These political parties relied on the Gaullists for their electoral survival at local level, even if, for some time, they refused to support the government.

The parties of the Left — the Communists (PCF) the Socialists (SFIO) and the Radical Party — have a history which had always been characterized by division. Since the Congress of Tours in 1920, which led to the creation of the PCF, resulting from a split in the SFIO, the socialists and communists were suspicious and very occasional allies. The radicals, so powerful in the Third Republic, were on the verge of collapse as the Fifth Republic was founded. Their years in office during the Fourth Republic, when, led by Pierre Mendes-France, they could still rely on 15 per cent of the vote, were over.

The Left in France, during the Fifth Republic, has nevertheless waged a long struggle for unity. (For a detailed analysis see N. Nugent and D. Lowe, *The Left in France*, Macmillan 1982.) The 1958 elections showed the communists as being the dominant force, in terms of popular support, followed by the socialists and the Radical Party. Yet their electoral isolation meant that they retained only 10 seats. (See table 1.)

The Communist Party was the only major French political force to oppose the new Constitution in 1958. The SFIO was divided on the issue, whereas the Radical Party supported it. Outside these major parties, the UDSR of François Mitterrand also opposed the new Constitution, as did the newly formed PSA

(which included Pierre Mendes-France in its ranks).

It took the parties of the Left a long time to come to terms with the new Constitution and their poor electoral results demonstrated this quite clearly. The first years of the Fifth Republic were largely taken up, as far as they were concerned, with a tactical quest for electoral survival. The SFIO, led by Guy Mollet, and encouraged by Gaston Deferre, first sought alliances with the radicals and moved towards the centre. The international environment, including the building of the Berlin wall, led them to seek such a non-communist alternative. At local level such a move actually brought about positive results as old alliances were maintained..

For the communists, however, political options were rather more limited. Their secretary-general, Maurice Thorez, in spite of the party's persistent pro-Soviet allegiance, was obliged to make tactical concessions in order to shore-up their parliamentary representation following the disastrous effects which the two-ballot system had created for them. Both in terms of membership, however, and in terms of overall votes in national and local elections, they remained a force which could not be ignored by the non-communist left parties. Thus emerged the first steps of the left-wing road towards electoral alliances and programmatic unity.

During this period another typically French phenomenon began to re-emerge. This was the creation of political "clubs", particularly, but not exclusively, amongst the non-communist left. These clubs were to prove to be most significant as catalysers of opinion outside formal party machines, and as promoters of individual political ambitions. They also bore witness to the fact that the older established

Table 1: legislative election results 1958–1968
(1st ballot %)

	Nov. 1958	*Nov. 1962*	*March 1967*	*June 1968*
Extreme Left	—	0.04	0.1	1.2
PCF	18.9	21.9	22.5	20.0
SFIO	15.4	12.4		
	—	—	18.9	16.5
Radicals	9.7	7.4		
Other Left	1.2	2.0	2.1	3.9
UNR/UDR	20.6	33.7	33.0	38.0
RI	—	2.3	5.5	8.4
MRP	11.1	7.9		
			16.0	11.6
CNI/Centrist	20.0	11.5		
Extreme Right	2.6	0.7	0.6	0.08

political parties, with the notable exception of the PCF, were unable to provide an adequate framework for the development of an alternative approach, both towards the new regime and towards the rapid social, economic and cultural changes which were taking place in French society. The most significant of such clubs was the *Convention des Institutions Républicains* of François Mitterrand.

The influence exercised by the clubs on the left contributed greatly to the development of the non-communist umbrella organization, involving both the SFIO and the radicals, which emerged as the FGDS (*Fédération de la Gauche Démocrate et Socialiste*) for the 1967 legislative elections.

The reinforced powers of the presidency in the Fifth Republic and the constitutional reform of 1962, which led to the election of the President by universal suffrage, changed the nature of the regime. It also changed the function of political parties to a certain extent.

In addition to providing support for a government in the National Assembly, political parties were also forced to produce a potential presidential candidate. Having begun, so to speak, with "their" president in place, the parties of the right naturally and speedily adapted themselves (or established themselves) around this phenomenon. For the left, which believes it has stronger parliamentary traditions, the change was not so easy to accommodate in the early years.

The first presidential election by direct universal suffrage took place in 1965. From 1962 the political evolution of the parties of the Left was entirely geared to this perspective. For the parties of the governing majority, the same sorts of questions were not raised because, although his declaration of candidacy was made very late, few would have ventured to allow their names to go forward as long as de Gaulle himself had not spoken. Outside the governing majority, in the centrists camp, discussions had taken place for some time with a view to finding a common candidate with the SFIO. This

"third force" option was strongly promoted by Gaston Deferre (leader of the Socialist Group in the National Assembly) without, it must be added, the full support of the SFIO. It proved to be a failure and the centrists proposed their own candidate, Jean Lecanuet, as early as April 1964.

This left the SFIO in something of a dilemma. The PCF was not in a position to propose its own candidate and preferred a candidate acceptable to broad left opinion. This allowed François Mitterrand to step into the political vacuum on the left and emerge as the candidate of the united left, with the support of the new Secretary-General of the PCF, Waldeck Rochet, and of the SFIO leadership.

The extreme Right was also present in the 1965 election, through the candidature of Tixier-Vignancour from the *Rassemblement National*. His support was derived from the proponents of *Algérie-Française* and the remnants of the Poujadist movement of small shopkeepers and artisans, which had obtained electoral recognition in the 1950s.

Even though de Gaulle emerged victorious from the elections, a number of lessons were learnt, firstly that, though elected, de Gaulle was clearly losing support — this led ultimately to a broadening of the government majority to take in most of the remaining centrists. Secondly, François Mitterrand, having confronted de Gaulle in the second ballot, came out of the elections as the natural leader of an embryonic united Left. (See table 2.)

Alliances and bi-polarization 1968–1974

The civil unrest of May 1968 marked a profound turning-point for almost all of France's political parties. The nation's youth, supported by whole sectors of organized labour, disturbed the way politicians had traditionally viewed their own role. The extent of the disorder accelerated evolution in the political culture,

Table 2: presidential election results 1965				
	1st ballot millions votes %		2nd ballot millions votes %	
De Gaulle	10.83	44.64	13.08	55.19
Mitterrand	7.69	31.72	10.62	44.80
Lecanuet	3.77	15.57		
Tixier-Vignancourt	1.26	5.19		
Marcilhacy	0.42	1.71		
Barbu	0.28	1.15		

which otherwise would have taken much longer to materialize.

In the short term France appeared to be returning to order as the Gaullist UDR (*Union pour la Défense de la République*) swept to a landslide electoral victory in the June 1968 elections, which had been called by de Gaulle in the wake of the chaos. Yet there is no doubt that de Gaulle himself was shaken by the upheaval and few, if any, of the political leaders of the Right or Left understood what had taken them all by surprise. Strangely, only the small, and electorally marginal PSU led by Michel Rocard, appeared to be able to come to terms with the phenomenon. Apart from the PSU, the mainly Trotskyist alternative left parties, who had in no small way engineered much of the student movement, lived through a brief period of euphoria.

In the course of the next few years, with the exception of the French Communist Party, all of the political parties changed their internal structure and organization in an attempt to be more responsive to the demands of a nation which was experiencing the benefits of unprecedented economic growth, along with an accompanying social transformation accentuated by the postwar "baby boom".

For the parties of the governing majority, and in particular for the UDR, change was brought about by two significant "political earth tremors". After the June 1968 elections de Gaulle replaced Pompidou, his Prime Minister who was widely perceived as having been the architect of the electoral victory, by the obedient Couve de Murville who had been his Foreign Minister since 1959. Shortly after, de Gaulle announced a referendum on the reform of the Senate and the establishment of regional authorities. This policy was certainly in line with a generally held view of the need to decentralize French administration; it also coincided entirely with de Gaulle's conviction of the need to increase "participation". But it had many powerful opponents, not the least of whom were within the governing majority coalition. The referendum was also, not surprisingly, seen as a plebiscite for de Gaulle himself, who made no secret of his intention of resigning if his project were to be defeated. When this happened, de Gaulle vacated the presidency.

The 1969 presidential election could not have been called at a worse time for the parties of the Left. The SFIO was represented by Gaston Deferre, the PCF by Jacques Duclos and the PSU by Michel Rocard. None of these candidates obtained enough votes to qualify for the second ballot. The runoff between Georges Pompidou and Alain Poher — a "centrist" and president of the Senate — elicited a relatively low turnout which nevertheless secured Pompidou's election as the designated successor of de Gaulle within the Gaullist movement. (See table 3.)

The result showed, nevertheless, that (a) it was still possible for a centrist figure to gain considerable popular support; (b) the Communist Party could still lay claim to a sizeable portion of left-wing opinion; (c) that the socialists were in danger of losing heavily in the future if their plans for a new and more dynamic party were not rapidly put into effect.

The presidency of Georges Pompidou saw the gradual conversion of "Gaullism" from being a populist movement into a more structured political force. Consolidation of the Gaullist party was a political necessity, if the individuals and interests which had grown up "in the shadow of the general" were to survive him and to continue to govern France. However, the modernization of the UDR proved to be only partly successful as the older party barons were reluctant to give up such prestigious positions and the democratization of the movement took place only episodically. A number of "historic" Gaullist sympathizers were also lost on the way.

In parallel with such developments, the UDR was also establishing its members and supporters in many of the key administrative posts of the state, including the media. Not surprisingly, crit-

Table 3: presidential election results 1969

	1st ballot millions votes	%	2nd ballot millions votes	%
Pompidou	10.05	44.46	11.06	58.21
Poher	5.25	23.30	7.94	41.78
Duclos	4.81	21.27		
Deferre	1.13	5.01		
Rocard	0.82	3.61		
Ducatel	0.28	1.26		
Krivine	0.23	1.05		

ics of the UDR, including some from within the majority coalition, began to point to the growth of the UDR-state. Banks, insurance companies, and much of the French nationalized industrial infrastructure (nationalized, that is, by de Gaulle in 1946) were also led by prominent Gaullist businessmen.

Paradoxically, this evolution took place at the same time as the governing majority was being extended towards the centre, under the premiership of Jacques Chaban-Delmas with his "new society" programme.

Pompidou sought *rapprochement* with the Giscardian *Républicains Indépendants* in spite of the latter's opposition to de Gaulle in the 1969 referendum, and towards other centrists even though many had supported Alain Poher in the presidential elections.

With the passing of General de Gaulle from the political scene — he died in 1971 — not only the UDR, but also the other mainstream political parties appeared to emerge more in their own right. The stature of the founder of the Fifth Republic was such that even today his legacy is still eagerly disputed.

This was most clearly seen in the period prior to the parliamentary elections of 1973, as the parties of the governing majority jostled for positions and the UDR appeared increasingly cut off from its electorate. The Giscardian party began to gain in power. A series of political scandals also undermined the government's authority. The opposition parties were now able to exploit these changes.

After their catastrophic showing in the 1969 presidential elections, the socialists had been rebuilding a more united political movement. First of all, the "new" Socialist Party was formed, led by Alain Savary, at the congress of Alfortville in July 1969. It was composed of the old SFIO membership plus many of the left-wing clubs, such as the UCRG and CERES (which since 1964 had chosen to work within the SFIO). It was not, however, until the historic Epinay congress in 1971 that the present day *Parti Socialiste* was founded. The impetus for the Epinay congress was provided by the affiliation of the *Convention des Institutions Républicains* of François Mitterrand. As a result of skilful negotiations between the different tendencies of the party, François Mitterrand was elected as the new First Secretary of the Party. The old guard largely remained as a minority within the party. Epinay was also significant in that it brought many new members into the party, who had had no previous political affiliation.

The 1960s had demonstrated to many in the new Socialist Party that attempts to create a "Third Force", or to unite the centre-left, were not electorally attractive, nor politically promising, On the other hand, unity of the Left, when it had been attempted at local level in the 1971 municipal elections, provided clearer political advantages and was more coherent ideologically. Mitterrand's own experience in the 1965 presidential election was of fundamental significance in this context, given the persistent willingness of the communists to continue to move in this direction, under the leadership of Georges Marchais.

The attempt by President Pompidou to torpedo the socialist-communist alliance, by calling a referendum in April 1972 on the enlargement of the European Community (on which the two parties had differing views) did not have the desired effect. The results, however, showed not only a high abstention rate, but also failed to provide Pompidou with the political impetus he had been seeking. It was the last occasion on which a referendum was to be used until November 1988. The results were as follows: yes: 36.12 per cent; no: 17.22 per cent; abstention: 39.52 per cent.

The PS (*Parti Socialiste*) and the PCF then negotiated a Common Programme of Government, which was signed in June 1972. They were also joined by the *Mouvement des Radicaux de Gauche*, led by Robert Fabré, who had quit the old Radical Party as it moved steadily into the governmental orbit. The alliance strategy for the forthcoming elections called for "republican discipline" to be respected by all candidates of the Left. First ballot agreements between the PS and MRG (*Mouvement des Radicaux de Gauche*) notwithstanding, the candidate receiving the highest number of votes on the first ballot would thus expect the support of his alliance partners on the second ballot in order to stand the best chance of defeating "the Right".

Such left-wing unity was not without its problems at leadership level as both Mitterrand and Marchais made it clear that their own commitment to a programmatic alliance also required their own respective parties to dominate the alliance.

The 1973 election results showed that for the Left, at least, unity was beginning to pay political dividends — particularly for the socialists, even though they were still the junior partner in electoral terms. Allied with the MRG in the *Union de la Gauche Démocrate et Socialiste*, the socialists made considerable advances; the rebalancing of the Left was under way. (See table 4.)

For the government of Pierre Messmer, whom Pompidou had appointed Prime Minister following the "resignation" of Chaban Delmas in 1972, the results, although disappointing, were somewhat better than many had feared.

For those who remained in the opposition centre, now grouped in the *Mouvement Reformateur*, their showing gave them some satisfaction. Though most of their candidates had been elected on the second ballot with the tacit support of the governing majority, they were able to form their own political group in the new National Assembly. They were, however, losing ground compared to their 1967 results.

The sudden death of Georges Pompidou a year later caused further substantial changes in the fortunes of France's political parties.

The presidency of Giscard d'Estaing

Giscard d'Estaing won the 1974 presidential election, yet he never managed to control his governmental majority. He was rarely in the enviable position of his predecessor, who could call upon the almost unquestioning support of the dominant party in the governing majority.

The Gaullist UDR at the time of Pompidou's death was still hampered by the relative strength of the barons of Gaullism compared to the development and consolidation of a younger, more populist element incarnated by Jacques

Chirac and supported by two prominent advisers of Pompidou — Marie-France Garaud and Pierre Juillet. The interplay between these two different groups led on the one hand to the precipitate declaration by Jacques Chaban-Delmas concerning his candidature for the presidency and the subsequent declaration by Jacques Chirac and 43 members of the UDR in the National Assembly in favour of Valery Giscard d'Estaing — already supported by his own RI as well as the centrists. Chirac's support for Giscard d'Estaing had the effect of deliberately sabotaging Chaban-Delmas' election campaign while at the same time staking a claim for the undisputed leadership of the Gaullist movement were Giscard d'Estaing to win the presidency.

For the Left in 1974, electorally united by the 1972 Common Programme, the choice of a presidential candidate was made without great difficulty. Mitterrand became the "common candidate" of the parties of the Left. He did not, however base his electoral platform on the Common Programme but on a broader set of principles. Significantly, his election campaign headquarters was situated away from the Socialist Party offices and his campaign team contained certain prominent individuals such as

Table 4: election results, 1973 legislative elections

	1st ballot	seats
PCF	21.4%	73
PS & MRG (UGSD)	20.8%	101
PSU	3.3%	1
Radical & centre-democrate	13.1%	34
RI & UDR (URP)	36.0%	55 & 183
Other right	5.1%	12

Table 5: presidential election results 1974

	1st ballot millions votes	%	2nd ballot millions votes	%
Mitterrand	11.04	43.24	12.97	49.19
Giscard d'Estaing	8.32	32.60	13.39	50.80
Chaban Delmas	3.85	15.10		
Royer	0.81	3.17		
Laguiller	0.59	2.33		
Dumont	0.34	1.32		
Le Pen	0.19	0.74		
Muller	0.17	0.69		
Krivine	0.09	0.36		
Renouvin	0.04	0.17		
Sebag	0.04	0.16		
Heraud	0.02	0.07		

Michel Rocard and Jacques Delors who had yet to formally join the PS.

Apart from the major candidates, the elections attracted flag bearers of various minor parties such as Laguiller for the Trotskyist *Lutte Ouvrière*, Krivine for the *Ligue Communiste Révolutionnaire*, Le Pen for the extreme right-wing *Front National*, Dumont for the ecologists and Renouvin for a monarchist fringe element. Jean Royer, Mayor of Tours, basing his campaign on conservative traditional principles, made inroads into the Chaban-Delmas candidature and undercut his position prior to the elections, where opinion polls showed Giscard d'Estaing with an even clearer lead over his closest rival from his own camp. (See table 5.)

The election of Giscard d'Estaing, and the nomination of Jacques Chirac as his Prime Minister in a government which managed to include all the "republican right", heralded further changes in the strategies of the political parties.

The new President chose not to dissolve the National Assembly, partly in order to give his own movement the time to expand and take on board new allies, and partly to give the Gaullists the time to — as he hoped — become weaker in relation to his own party. Moreover, as Mitterrand had scored so well in the election, the threat of a left-wing electoral victory in parliamentary elections could not be excluded.

The main element of Giscard d'Estaing's strategy was the establishment of a broader non-Gaullist element within the governing majority. He set about the reorganization of the *Républicain Indépendant* into a more popular liberal orientated party, which in 1977 became the *Parti Républicain*, which was to serve as the key element in the formation of the large "umbrella" federation, the *Union pour la Démocratie Française* — the UDF. The objective of a federation rather than a united broadly-based liberal party was, in a sense, forced upon him by the reluctance of the other elements in the federation to give up their own political identity.

The *Centre Démocrate* of Jean Lecanuet, and the Radical Party of Jean-Jacques Servan-Schreiber both sought to retain their independence, while recognizing the necessity of closer co-ordination with the PR. The UDF also brought in the *Mouvement Démocrate et Socialiste Français* and the pro-Giscardian *Club Perspective et Réalités*, led by his Finance Minister Jean-Pierre Fourcade. The UDF was formed in time for the 1978 legislative elections, yet it failed to give an image of unity, as the diversity

of its constituent parties and the rivalry between its leaders was so strong. They all agreed, however, that the UDF had become a tactical necessity as well as a strategic imperative, in support of Giscard d'Estaing's presidency and its objectives.

The need to create such a force, which was to be a counterweight to Gaullist influence within the governing majority, was accentuated by the fact that the Gaullist party was itself undergoing yet another transformation.

Having failed to be given the responsibility to lead the parties of the governing majority, Jacques Chirac resigned as Prime Minister in 1976. He was replaced by Raymond Barre, who had no clear political affiliation, and was a more technocratic type of prime minister.

Chirac consolidated his hold over the UDR in December 1974, much to the chagrin of the President, who nevertheless succeeded in forcing Chirac to give up his post as Gaullist party leader a year later. Chirac persisted with his objective of remodelling the movement and, once freed of his governmental obligations, he launched the new Gaullist party, the *Rassemblement pour la République* (RPR) in December 1976 at a mass rally in Paris. Among its main objectives were to secure the election of Jacques Chirac as President of the Republic and to defeat the "socialist-communist" alliance.

The creation of a new party was also a political necessity for the Gaullist movement as the UDF, in spite of its diverse elements, was proving attractive to many Gaullist sympathizers. It was not long before the RPR reversed this trend. Jacques Chirac himself (who gained a new political power base when elected as Mayor of Paris in 1977) was widely perceived by the conservative electorate as being the most able politician to defeat the mounting threat of a victory of the Left at the 1978 legislative elections.

Neither Giscard d'Estaing nor Jacques Chirac had envisaged that the *Union de la Gauche* would itself deliver them from this threat.

The alliance between the parties of the Left had enjoyed considerable success in by-elections, particularly since the 1974 election, fielding successful candidates in the 1976 cantonal elections as well as in the 1977 municipal elections. This, however, was at the increasing expense of the communists, who were now very much the junior partner to the socialists.

In September 1977 the PCF quit the alliance, accusing the PS and their MRG allies of swinging to the Right. For such a split to have occurred at such a time, when more than 90 per cent of the left-wing electorate appeared to support *Union de la Gauche*, seemed remarkable. In addition, opinion polls had indicated a victory for the left-wing alliance in the March 1978 legislative elections. In such circumstances their defeat appeared more than anything else to be self-inflicted.

In spite of its loss of credibility, for the first time the PS emerged as the largest party of the Left in the National Assembly. The parties of the Left then remained in opposition.

Within the governing majority, following a campaign in which the President was himself very much engaged (contrary to normal practice in the Fifth Republic for legislative elections) the RPR managed to maintain its position as the leading conservative political force. However, its lead over the UDF had been considerably reduced. (See table 6.)

Alliances were no longer so important in the subsequent European Parliament election campaign in 1979 in which proportional representation was to be used for the first time in the Fifth Republic. The socialists, in spite of the demise of their left-wing strategy, were able to salvage a respectable though less than satisfactory result. The Gaullists suffered a humiliating loss of votes to the UDF. This latter, which also had the additional advantage of occupying the key decision-making centres of power, was seen as more favourable and constructive in relation

to European policy in general, and was able to become, for the first time, the largest electoral force on the Right, and in the country. (See table 7.)

The government of Raymond Barre subsequently continued to pursue its economic strategy of austerity, which was not an easy policy on which to fight an election. Jacques Chirac was able to portray himself as being much closer to the real needs of the electorate than the President, who was becoming widely criticized by the press and the opposition parties for appearing aloof, almost monarchic in his style and character. From the Giscardian camp, however, Chirac was widely criticized for having aggravated the nation's economic difficulties during the course of his premiership.

In spite of the collapse of the unitary strategy, and the Communist Party's intransigence, the PS provided the electorate with a realistic alternative. Opinion polls suggested that "republican discipline" was a spirit which still survived in the left-wing electorate. In addition, having moved away from such a close association with the PCF leadership, the socialists, and François Mitterrand in particular, aroused less apprehension among centrist or floating voters.

The logical consequence of the Communist party's strategy was for them to present

---

Table 6:   legislative election results, 1978

	1st ballot %	seats
PS-MRG	24.98	112
PCF	20.61	86
Ecologists	2.18	—
RPR	22.52	145
UDF	21.37	120
Other major parties	5.01	11

Table 7:   results of the 1979 European elections

	% votes	seats
Extreme left	3.1	—
PSF	20.6	19
PS-MRG	23.8	22
RPR[1]	16.3	15
UDF[2]	27.5	25
Ecologists	4.4	—
Others	4.5	—

[1]Presented as *Défense des Intérêts de la France en Europe*.
[2]Presented as *Union pour la France en Europe*.

their own candidate in the 1981 presidential election. Internal disputes among Communists led to many leaving the party. The PCF effort to consolidate its position at electoral level necessitated an early start to their campaign and their candidate, Georges Marchais, was duly adopted by a national conference in October 1980. All efforts were henceforth concentrated on securing as high a first ballot result as possible. The attacks on the socialists had the effect of reassuring many hesitant voters that, in voting for the Socialist candidate, they would not be associating themselves with the Communist Party.

After the socialist congress of Metz in 1979, it was not at all certain that Mitterrand himself would be its candidate for the presidency. Michel Rocard announced that in the event that Mitterrand decided not to stand, he would then seek to become the socialist candidate. Opinion polls indeed gave Rocard a lead over Mitterrand in terms of popularity. Mitterrand, for clearly tactical reasons in order to shield himself from concentrated attacks from the RPR and the UDF, only announced his candidature in November 1980, and Rocard Immediately withdrew and pledged Miterrand his support.

The MRG, while assuring their diminishing electorate that they would support Mitterrand on the second ballot, finally decided to present their party leader Michel Crépeau, mayor of La Rochelle. The minor candidates in the campaign included not only an ecology candidate, Brice Lalonde, but also two dissident Gaullists, — Michel Debré, ex-Prime Minister under de Gaulle, and Marie-France Garaud, who had fallen out of favour with Jacques Chirac. The PSU presented their national secretary, Huguette Bouchardeau. The Trotskyist *Lutte Ouvrière*, as in 1974, presented Arlette Laguiller. (See table 8.)

The socialist victory of 1981

The election victory of François Mitterrand clearly marked a dramatic turning point in French political history, as the first time that the Left had come to power in the Fifth Republic. In addition to sociological changes in the French electorate and the apparent greater willingness to accept change, Mitterrand's victory may be attributed to the solid backing of the left-wing electorate on the second ballot, to the less than full support given by Chirac to Giscard d'Estaing (only 73 per cent of first ballot Chirac votes went to Giscard d'Estaing; in the second ballot 16 per cent went to Mitterrand) and to the fact that more than half of ecologist voters supported the candidate of the Left.

The dissolution of the National Assembly was one of the first acts of the Mitterrand presidency. Pierre Mauroy was appointed Prime Minister and led a government drawn from all the various tendencies of the socialist party. His MRG allies also entered the government. The exception was Michel Jobert, a former Foreign Minister under President Pompidou who had publicly expressed his support for Mitterrand in the election campaign and therefore represented symbolic reassurance for the moderate voter.

In the election campaign for the new National Assembly, the socialists and the MRG renewed their alliance for the first ballot under the banner *avec François Mitterrand*. The communists affirmed that they were willing to co-operate with the PS and a joint declaration was published, including an agreement for second ballot withdrawals for the best placed candidate of the Left. The PCF fought the campaign on the basis of a slogan *pour la nouvelle majorité présidentielle*. The PCF received no commitment concerning their participation in a new government, which they had been claiming throughout the presidential election campaign.

Table 8: presidential electional results, May 10, 1981		
	1st ballot %	*2nd ballot %*
Giscard d'Estaing	28.8	48.2
Mitterrand	25.8	51.8
Chirac	18.0	
Marchais	15.3	
Lalonde	3.9	
Laguiller	2.3	
Crepeau	2.2	
Debré	1.7	
Garaud	1.3	
Bouchardeau	1.1	

For the parties of the previous majority coalition, a decision to present joint candidates for the first ballot in more than three-quarters of the 491 constituencies proved not too difficult to reach. They fought the election in such cases under the slogan *Union pour la nouvelle majorité*. Disputes occurred in many of the remaining constituencies between the RPR and the UDF.

The results of the elections confirmed the ascendancy of the non-communist Left and showed the PS-MRG candidates reaching historic levels. They captured almost 12 per cent more of the electorate on the first ballot than Mitterrand had himself obtained in the first ballot of the presidential election. The communist vote confirmed their decline and was 20 per cent less than that of the socialists.

The RPR once again emerged as the largest grouping in the liberal-conservative camp, its more disciplined and orchestrated campaign at local level having reaped an advance over the dispirited Giscardian UDF.

In the second ballot the socialists managed to obtain an absolute majority in the National Assembly, which meant that they need rely on no other party for support. The Communist Party lost almost half of its parliamentary group compared to the previous legislature, as did the RPR and the UDF. (See table 9.)

Only ten years after their constituent congress at Epinay, the socialists had thus taken over the centres of political decision-making in France. The Communist Party, in spite of the fact that it was granted four ministerial posts in the government of Pierre Mauroy that was formed after the legislative elections, faced a long period of severe internal crisis and electoral decline. The parties of the alternative Left were more marginalized than ever.

The conservative camp appeared stunned by such a heavy defeat. The only political power base which they held on to was the traditionally more conservative Senate, which had not had to face an election. They used the Senate in the next few years as a means of obstructing and delaying government legislation. Their divisions remained apparent, particularly at leadership level where many in the UDF felt they had been betrayed by the lack of loyalty displayed by the RPR leadership. It was not long before another factor entered into consideration; the re-emergence of the extreme Right in the form of the *Front National* of Jean-Marie Le Pen.

Government of the Left, 1981–86

The fact that the Left had not been in government at any level for a quarter of a century, and that, with few exceptions, no-one in the Socialist Party had any governmental experience (though many, including the Prime Minister were experienced mayors of large towns or cities), did not help the new government as it set about implementing its (over)ambitious programme of reforms.

The Left had been arguing for many years that the country was in need of substantial modernization and democratization. It correspondingly set about nationalizing the banking sector, nationalizing five major industrial holdings to make them more competitive, giving new rights to workers and establishing stronger regional authorities — which de Gaulle had failed to do in 1969. It abolished the death penalty and established a shorter working week and a fifth week of paid leave; it modified the electoral laws for local elections and took the audio-visual and communications sector away from governmental monopoly; it increased government spending on education and research, and on culture. The government increased the minimum wage and set about relaunching economic growth and increasing family, child and pension allowances.

The international economic climate was hardly conducive to such economic stimulation and the government was forced into three successive devaluations of the franc as the trade deficit and inflation began to get out of hand. Forced into an

---

Table 9: legislative election results, June 1981

	1st ballot %	seats
PS/MRG	37.5	285
PCF	16.2	44
Extreme left	1.3	—
Other left	0.7	5
RPR	20.8	88
UDF	19.2	62
Other right	3.2	7
Ecologists	1.1	—

austerity policy by 1983, the communist parties in the alliance began to look for ways out. The reduction in public expenditure and the fight against inflation became priorities which the government (PS-MRG-PCF) found difficult to manage. The reshuffle of March 1983 failed to resolve the political issues underlying the malaise between the coalition parties.

The change of direction in governmental strategy also, not surprisingly, led to dissent within the Socialist Party as well, though it was generally limited as a result of discreet but persistent pressure from the President.

Faced with such a situation, the UDF-RPR opposition responded with vigour, promoting the liberal free market alternative, which was being marketed with apparent success in the United States and in the United Kingdom.

The government began to promote alternative economic policies of the social-market type. Although the economy began to stabilize in response to the change of policy, the electorate of the Left began to desert, in spite of socialist government explanations that the international economic constraints on an expansionist economic policy were more powerful than had been anticipated. More openly than ever before, the government espoused a pro-European strategy, based on Franco-German co-operation, believing that the only path to economic growth and social enhancement lay in concerted economic development at European Community level.

The European elections of June 1984 confirmed the loss of confidence of the French electorate in the government led by Pierre Mauroy. The opposition list led by Simone Veil outdistanced the combined votes of the parties of the Left, and a major electoral breakthrough by the *Front National* surprised everyone. A high abstention rate demonstrated the lack of mobilization of much of the Left's electorate in a campaign which concentrated largely on national issues. The most burning of these were the government's plans to limit financial support to Catholic private schools which led to massive public demonstrations in Paris and throughout France (See table 10.)

François Mitterrand accepted the resignation of Pierre Mauroy in July 1984 and nominated Laurent Fabius to replace him to lead a government of the Left without the communists.

Since the change of government strategy in the summer of 1983, the PCF had become increasingly restless, though the four communist ministers maintained governmental solidarity at all times. The nomination of Laurent Fabius symbolized a complete change in style. With a more technocratic image, and very closely associated with the President of the Republic, Fabius

was to bring increased efficiency and authority to the Matignon, and give more credibility to the government's economic policy.

At the subsequent congress of the PS at Bourg en Bresse, the Socialist Party in its resolution voted unanimously (after some negotiation) to give its support for the Fabius government's new policy of *rigueur*.

The opposition parties, comforted by the European election results, reopened the debate on *cohabitation*. In the following months two distinct lines of argument emerged. Edouard Balladur, a close associate of Jacques Chirac, openly and publicly supported the constitutional right of the Prime Minister to govern, even when the President of the Republic was of a different political persuasion. Raymond Barre, on the other hand, considered that it would diminish the authority of the President and thus of France, internationally, and would lead to a crisis where the President might be forced to resign.

The announced change in the electoral law and the introduction of proportional representation made the debate on *cohabitation* more pertinent. Opposed to the change in the electoral law, Michel Rocard resigned as Agriculture Minister in April 1985.

The growth in support for the *Front National* during this period destabilized much of the political establishment. The increase in terrorist activity, which led to greater public insecurity, and a greater propensity to envisage extreme solutions to the problem, proved particularly damaging to the government.

In such circumstances, and in spite of the fact that the new economic policies of the government appeared to be working (inflation reduced dramatically, the franc in a strong position), the legislative elections of March 1986 led to the expected victory of the RPR-UDF coalition. The *Front National* made its entry into the National Assembly, having won 35 seats. The socialists however, paradoxically, increased their proportion of the vote and remained the largest political group. (See table 11.)

On the same day, new regional councils were directly elected by universal suffrage, in application of the government's law on decentralization.

Cohabitation, 1986–88

The period of *cohabitation* between a socialist President in the Elysée and a Gaullist Prime Minister in the Matignon tested the Constitution and led to a continued period of tension between the head of state and the head of government. For both men, and the parties which supported

Table 10: European election results, June 1984

	%	seats
PS-MRG	20.75	20
PCF	11.20	10
UDF-RPR	43.02	41
FN	10.95	10
Ecologists	3.36	—
Others	10.2	—

Table 11: legislative election results, March 1986

	%	seats
PS	31.6	206
PCF	9.8	35
MRG	0.4	2
Other left	2.5	7
RPR	11.21	76
UDF	8.31	53
RPR-UDF (Joint list)	21.46	147
FN	9.8	35
Other right	3.9	14
(MRG and other left elected on PS list)		

them, the battle lines were drawn for the next presidential election. It was also not long before the parties of the governing majority were forced into a position where they were obliged to pay increasing attention to the electoral threat posed by the *Front National*. A major change made by the new Chirac government was to eliminate proportional representation, and to reintroduce the previous two-ballot electoral system.

The parties of the Left maintained pressure on the government not only in opposition to its extensive and controversial privatization programme, its confrontational approach to the problem of New Caledonia, and its hard-line tactics in the fight against terrorism, but also to its proposed reforms of the Nationality Act which would restrict the rights of immigrants and limit eligibility for naturalization. Educational reform yet again provoked massive demonstrations, culminting in December with the death of a second generation immigrant student. Eventually, the government was forced to back down.

The government was forced to slow down its ambitious laissez-faire economic programme which had been criticized from within the UDF, in particular by Raymond Barre.

For the RPR, the period of *cohabitation* was a necessary exercise of governmental authority which would allow Jacques Chirac to fight and win the next presidential election. The UDF, on the other hand, was drawn between the longer-term ambitions of François Léotard, leader of the *Parti Républicain*, and the well-known intentions of Raymond Barre to stand for the presidency. Barre was strongly supported by the CDS and by part of the UDF, including Simone Veil. Yet, the ambivalence of the UDF as a whole led to complications, particularly as Raymond Barre had no party as such on which he could rely for support. He made plain, however, that he saw this as an advantage as it clearly set him in an "above party" mould.

The Communist Party nominated André Lajoinie as their candidate. The leader of the Communist Group in the National Assembly was considered to be more appropriate than the secretary-general, Georges Marchais, who had been candidate in 1981. Many saw this as indicating imminent changes in the Communist party's contested leadership.

The Socialist Party had to content itself with playing a waiting game in order to discover whether François Mitterrand would stand again. Mitterrand's stature had grown considerably during the period of *cohabitation*, yet he insisted that he would only make his mind up at a later stage. Mitterrand, drawing a parallel with de Gaulle, explained that this was necessary in order that, internationally, he be seen to maintain his full presidential authority without being seen as a more partisan candidate. This had the other advantage of placing all the other candidates in uncertainty. Meanwhile, Mitterrand allowed support committees to be established throughout France in order to create a public demand for his candidature. This proved most successful as the committees *avec François Mitterrand* managed to mobilize support beyond the confines of the Socialist Party itself.

The election campaign itself was noteworthy for two reasons. Firstly, the place taken up by discussions on the future of Europe predominated over almost all other issues, although the previous European election campaign in 1984 had concentrated on national issues. Secondly, the personality and competence of the candidates was considered by the media, at least, to be much more important than the respective electoral programmes, which received very little comment or debate.

The *Lettre à tous les Français* published by François Mitterrand and mailed to every household in France, constituted an innovation in both style and content. Whereas other programmes detailed proposals for economic, social and foreign policy, Mitterrand contented himself with tracing broad lines of action.

The campaign of Raymond Barre was exceptional in that he did not have the complete support of any party apart from the CDS. His personal integrity and clear message proved insufficient faced with the competition from Jacques Chirac within the Centre-right camp. The campaign network set in place by Raymond Barre lacked the efficiency and the finance which the RPR provided for Jacques Chirac.

In addition to the three principal candidates, the candidatures of Jean-Marie Le Pen for the *Front National*, and André Lajoinie for the PCF

were frequently contrasted with each other, not in relation to Mitterrand, Chirac and Barre. The other candidates were Antoine Waechter for the ecologists, Pierre Juquin for the alternative Left, Arlette Laguiller for the Trotskyist *Lutte Ouvrière*, and Pierre Boussel for the *Mouvement pour un Parti des Travailleurs*, better known under the name of Lambert, and founder of the "Lambertist" tendency in the Trotskyist world. (See table 12.)

1988–present

François Mitterrand eventually won re-election by a majority over Jacques Chirac, leading Chirac on the second ballot in 407 out of 555 metropolitan constituencies. In 101 constituencies he obtained scores in excess of 60 per cent.

The dissolution of the National Assembly and the campaign for the legislative elections which followed in June 1988 were, as in 1981, considered as a formality, though many in the UDF opposed the idea of dissolution. With Michel Rocard nominated Prime Minister, several independent centrist personalities accepted ministerial posts as part of the new governments opening to the centre. The grand *ouverture* never occurred, however, as the parties of the centre — notably the Radical Party and the CDS — confirmed their allegiance (for the time being at least) with their UDF partners and the RPR. (See table 13.)

The strategy of the President of the Republic was to obtain a socialist majority in the National Assembly to which others from the Left or the Centre could, in time, rally, but not so great a majority as to be uncontrollable. The campaign was virtually non-existent as attention focused on the new government and speculation was rife about the size of the Socialist Party victory.

With the record abstention rate of over 34 per cent, the new National Assembly ended up

---

Table 12: presidential election results, April–May 1988

	1st ballot		2nd ballot	
	votes	*%*	*votes*	*%*
François Mitterrand	10,367,220	34.09	16,704,279	54.01
Jacques Chirac	6,063,514	19.94	14,218,970	45.98
Raymond Barre	5,031,849	16.54		
Jean-Marie Le Pen	4,375,849	14.39		
André Lajoinie	2,055,995	6.76		
Antoine Wächter	1,149,642	3.78		
Pierre Juquin	639,084	2.10		
Arlette Laguiller	606,017	1.99		
Pierre Boussel	116,823	0.38		

Table 13:   legislative election results, June 1988

	1st ballot %	seats
PS-MRG	35.87	276
PCF	11.32	27
Extreme left	0.36	—
Other left	1.65	—
RPF	19.18	128
UDF	18.49	130
FN	9.65	1
Other right	2.85	13
Ecologists	0.35	—

without a majority for the first time in the Fifth Republic. The Socialists had gained 62 seats but were 12 seats short of an absolute majority. For the outgoing governmental coalition, the results were better than expected, while the National Front, with a single member, paid the price of the Chirac government's re-establishment of the two-ballot electoral system. The communists increased their vote compared to the presidential elections but lost eight seats.

The government of Michel Rocard had, nevertheless, obtained the minimum it needed to govern and this allowed it, paradoxically, to carry out its policy of broadening its support beyond the socialists to either the Left or the Right, as it appeared difficult to envisage the PCF voting with the RPR and the UDF to overturn the government.

Features of the French political system

Two hundred years after the French Revolution, France is experiencing a period of constitutional consensus unknown in its history. This is not to say that traditional cleavages in French society have disappeared, nor does it imply that political calm and inertia have taken over from confrontational politics. However, the establishment of the Fifth Republic in 1958, although inspired and initiated by Charles de Gaulle in the midst of the Algerian war, has proved to be far from an expedient gesture, but the foundation on which modern French politics are based.

Until 1986, the French National Assembly was able to provide the President of the Republic with a relatively stable political majority. This in turn led to a reinforcement of presidential power and authority. The inherent duality in the Fifth Republic's Constitution was never put to the test during the periods of office of de Gaulle (1958–1969), Pompidou (1969–74) and Giscard

d'Estaing (1974–1981), and even during the first five years of the new socialist president Mitterrand.

The period of *cohabitation*, however, between 1986 and 1988 showed that the Fifth Republic's Constitution was able to survive this test as well.

This constitutional stability has gone hand in hand with political bipolarization as the diaspora of political parties of the defunct Fourth Republic became consolidated in two major political alliances on the Left and Right of the political spectrum. The Centre, forced to make the choice, opted to conciliate with the republican Right against the communist-dominated Left. Yet, on both the Left and the Right, radical transformations later took place.

The Socialist Party has now completely displaced the Communist Party as the largest party on the Left, and has also gradually come to be seen as a natural party of government. The communists, on the other hand, have become increasingly marginal.

On the Right the once dominant Gaullist movement has dispersed and its most obvious heir, the RPR, is a very different sort of party. The RPR, however, has been the most tightly organized party on the Right and its main rival, the UDF, initially organized to support President Giscard, has remained a disparate coalition of centre and right parties. On the far right the National Front has come to play a significant role in the 1980s.

There now appears to be further change in the offing. The results of the 1988 elections indicate that no single party is in a position to govern alone. Alliance strategies will continue to be an essential element of French political life. This has placed the politicians of the Centre in a position of some strength, for the first time since the beginning of the Fifth Republic. No-one in France is seeking a return to the feeble arrangements which formed governments in the Fourth

Republic, so the involvement of centre ground politicians will have to be based on more than mere tactical considerations. A restructuring of the Centre, influenced by Mitterrand's global view of the direction to be taken by France towards the year 2,000 must now be considered probable. This will imply a division in the existing Centre-right alliance, which is already becoming manifest as preparations are made for the European elections of 1989. For all that, it is unlikely that the centre ground in France will capture the proportion of the electorate, which has for many decades identified itself with the Left or the Right, as old political allegiances remain strong, even 200 years after the Revolution.

One old tradition that was revived in 1985 and in 1986 was change in the electoral system, with the return of proportional representation in 1985 and its renewed abolition in 1986. There have been 10 changes in the French electoral system since 1871. There are several other distinctive characteristics of French political life. One is the impermanence and fluidity of French political parties as opposed to its political traditions. Apart from the Communist Party, none of the major French political parties in their present form predate 1971. Parties have easily changed their names or the labels under which they have contested elections. Political clubs and ginger groups have also played a role in France, greater than that in any other European country. A presidential candidate like Raymond Barre in 1988 was able to have a substantial support network that was linked to a national party structure but not directly part of it.

Another feature is the dominance of the national parties throughout French territory, and the weakness of regional parties even in distinctive areas like Corsica and Brittany.

Rassemblement pour la République — RPR

Headquarters	:	123 rue de Lille, F-75007 Paris (tel. 45 50 32 19)
President	:	Jacques Chirac (1976–present)
Secretary-general	:	Alain Juppé (since 1988)
Founded	:	Porte de Versaille, Paris, December 1976
Membership	:	450,000

History

The RPR is the successor to other parties in the Gaullist political tradition, notably the

Union pour la Nouvelle République (UNR) from1958–67, and the *Union de Démocrates pour la République* from 1967 to 1976. Jacques Chaban Delmas, the UDR's presidential candidate in 1974, lost to Giscard d'Estaing, who was supported by Jacques Chirac of the UDR. Chirac subsequently became Prime Minister under Giscard, and also took control of the UDR. In 1976 the UDR was transformed into the RPR.

The RPR contested the first round of the 1978 National Assembly elections independent of other parties. In the first round of the 1981 presidential elections Chirac came third with 18 per cent of the vote.

After the 1981 National Assembly elections (in which the RPR fought the elections as part of a wider centre-right alliance, the *Union pour la Majorité Nouvelle*) the RPR was reduced to 88 seats. In the 1986 elections the RPR won 155 seats and confirmed its position as the largest party of the centre-right.

Chirac was Prime Minister from 1986 to 1988, but was defeated in his bid to become President in 1988. In the subsequent National Assembly elections the RPR only obtained 128 seats, two less than the UDF.

Support

The RPR, in spite of its organizational strength, is a political force which has yet to dominate fully the centre and conservative electorate. In 1978, at the legislative elections it obtained 22.4 per cent of the vote. In 1981 it scored 20.9 per cent, in 1988 it combined its efforts with the UDF to form the URC (*Union Republicain et du Centre*) and was accredited with 19.2 per cent of the vote. At the last two presidential elections with Jacques Chirac as candidate, the RPR scored 18 per cent in 1981 and 19.1 per cent in 1988. Its main strength has remained the cohesion of the party compared to the more diverse and heterogeneous UDF.

The traditional RPR/Gaullist strongholds are in central France, in Alsace, the south-east and in Brittany, as well as in Paris and the Ile de France region. The RPR voter is likely to be more than 50 years old, either a farmer or a member of a liberal profession, often with his own small company.

The basis for successive Gaullist election gains, in the 1960s in particular, was an ability to appeal to a broad cross-section of French society, and the RPR in the 1980s has seen this broad support diminish to a considerable extent, so that its electorate is now closer to that of traditional conservatism. To begin to reconquer the lost ground may not be possible for the RPR without a change of strategy which, in turn, may mean a radical transformation, not only of the RPR but also of the other parties of the conservative opposition within the UDF.

Organization

The RPR has a strong and active local party organization, and mass membership. At the lowest level, the party is organized on a constituency basis with the constituency subdivided into wards (sections). Within the constituency organization the party members elect their secretary and influence the choice of parliamentary candidates. The main organizational arm of the RPR lies however at "federation" level. Each federation of the RPR has a department secretary who is appointed by and directly responsible to the national leadership. A federation, geographically, covers a département. The RPR is also organized at regional level, which allows the party to channel communications from the leadership through the regional co-ordinating structures to the federations and constituency parties. All regional heads are nominated from Paris, but have strong regional identities. In this way Conn Guy Guermeur in Brittany and the late Jean-Pierre Cassabel in Languedoc-Roussillon contributed greatly to renovating and regenerating the Gaullist movement. The federations meet when the leadership so decides at a congress or assise; mass rally of the party's delegates.

Some observers believe that the RPR reflects certain characteristics of the RPF, founded after the war in 1947 to support de Gaulle, but which was dissolved in 1954, when the General lost confidence in the organization. In spite of this, the RPR remains a highly centralized political organization. The local organization of the RPR has enabled it, even in times of difficulty, to maintain a solid local presence which is reflected in the fact that it controls 24 departmental councils. It has the majority, and therefore holds the mairie, in 47 towns with over 30,000 inhabitants including Paris (where Jacques Chirac has been mayor since 1977), Bordeaux and Grenoble. Moreover, it holds the presidency in six regional councils.

It is nevertheless very firmly led from the top, in particular by Jacques Chirac and his group of personal advisers in the executive committee. The parliamentary group is, certainly, influential even though the leader takes all the key political decisions on strategy and tactics. Its central committee, composed of the secretaries of each federation, MPs, MEPs and national and regional delegates, has a policy formulation role

which is not in any real sense sovereign, although the statutes give it nominally great authority.

The conseil politique is a political institution, broader than the executive committee, which meets periodically "to prepare" political strategy. It contains — apart from the president, Jacques Chirac, elected directly by the Assises — the secretary-general appointed by Chirac (now Alain Juppé, formerly Jerome Monod, Alain Devaquet, Bernard Pons and Jacques Toubon), ex-Prime Ministers, the presidents of the parliamentary group in the National Assembly and the Senate, and 15 members elected by the central committee.

In many ways, the RPR is a reflection of the presidential regime and its leader has considerable authority and decisive control over the movement at all levels. However, the rank-and-file can express itself openly and the membership of the party is numerous enough to make a strong media impact, particularly when the Assises take place. Yet the relative lack of democratic expression, particularly following defeat in the 1988 elections after the "experiment" of cohabitation, makes the RPR more fragile and sets it more on the defensive. The monolithic structure is showing the strains as various factions begin to emerge. Within the factions pressure to democratize the movement further has become strong, and reform of the statutes to permit more democratic accountability within the party is being implemented (new statutes were adopted in January 1989).

The RPR is a member of the International and European Democratic Unions and is part of the European Democratic Alliance group in the European Parliament, whose presidency it has held since the outset.

Policies

The latest incarnation of the Gaullist movement has already survived for longer than any of its predecessors. As a party, it is a very different organization compared to the UNR (1958–67) or the UDR (1967–76), being more populist, yet more tightly controlled. Before the RPR, Gaullism was an expression of fidelity to a certain idea of France, which although "Bonapartist" in many ways, was also "interventionist" and "legitimist" — respecting the state and its institutions.

The Gaullist movement was able to point to the fact that it drew its support from across the geographic and socioeconomic spectrum, including areas with no conservative traditions and including areas (such as Bordeaux) where radical traditions remained powerful. To be a Gaullist, for many, was to be patriotic; paying homage to the man who had inspired French resistance and established France as one of the great powers.

Today in France, Gaullist sympathies extend beyond the frontiers of the political organization which has persisted in claiming to be the inheritor of de Gaulle and his vision. Today in France, one does not have to be "RPR" to be Gaullist.

For as long as the Gaullist movement was able to survive in the shadow of de Gaulle — as the UNR, as the UDR, and before them the RPF — so its leadership derived its legitimacy from its identification with the General. Jacques Chaban-Demas, Michel Debré, Olivier Guichard, Pierre Messmer, Maurice Couve-de-Murville and Alexandre Sanguinetti, are all considered "barons" of Gaullism, yet they have never derived their authority from being elected within the Gaullist movement. Georges Pompidou was viewed with suspicion by the barons for many years, as he had not been present "at the beginning".

In 1967, Georges Pompidou began the task of organizing the Gaullist movement into a more efficient and structured electoral organization. Opposition from many barons prevented him from reaching his objectives in organizational terms. From that date, dissent increased within the Gaullist ranks and the pamphleteers began voicing their condemnation of the "treason" being perpetrated by the successors of the General. Those who cried "treason" were often themselves considered to be *Gaullistes de gauche* — René Capitant, Leo Hamon, and for the younger generation Olivier Germain-Thomas. Gaullism also gradually became more conservative, and was abandoned by a number of those on its left wing.

The current leadership obviously feels the need to maintain, at a symbolic level, the word Gaullist. The *croix de Lorraine* and giant portraits of de Gaulle and Pompidou provided the backdrop at the mass meeting where the party was launched in order to emphasize continuity. Yet, since its foundation, the RPR has gradually espoused new philosophies and new dogma as French society itself has evolved and advanced.

Beyond the fading attraction of Gaullism, the RPR has based its principles on support for the political institutions of the Fifth Republic, support for a strong state in areas of collective interest, a belief in a strong nuclear defence policy and a profound aversion to the parties of the Left, in particular to the communists. The social conscience of the movement, is still maintained, with social solidarity still receiving wide support from within the party, even if this view is contested by more vociferous conservative and liberal wings. Party conservatives also emphasize law and order and do not stand back from criticizing the multi-racial society and the supposed negative influence of the country's many immigrant communities.

At a time when the extreme-right National Front was making many RPR elected representatives vulnerable, Charles Pasqua mentioned the "shared values", which the RPR shared with the electorate of the National Front. This was quickly contested, however, from within the ranks of the RPR, notably by Michel Noir and Michèle Barzach.

Like other parties of the Centre-right in France the majority of those in the RPR have supported the reintroduction of the death penalty.

The RPR has also changed its emphasis on economic policy. Gaullism had traditionally been prepared to be interventionist, and de Gaulle himself, in the immediate postwar years had nationalized the country's five major banks and insurance companies. The RPR has now become more economically liberal and more closely associated with business and financial interests. The 1986–88 Chirac government privatized several public companies during the period when it was in power. It also sought an extension in public-share ownership.

Another major change has been on foreign policy in general, and on European policy in particular. De Gaulle always emphasized the autonomy of France and its separate identity as a nation state. His conception of Europe was that of the *Europe des Patries*. He withdrew France from NATO's military structure. The modern RPR is a more conventional party in its foreign and defence policy, and more supportive of closer European co-operation.

Personalities

Jacques Chirac has added his own dynamism and personality to the movement, and been supported in that by a younger generation of political leaders such as Alain Juppé, Jacques Toubon, Philippe Seguin and Michel Noir. Even though the barons are still present, their contribution to the organization of the RPR and to the mobilization of its electorate is no longer great. Yet as mayor of Bordeaux, for example, Jacques Chaban-Delmas still stands out as a man from a different political mould from the more conservative younger leadership. Other prominent figures who have contributed considerably to the RPR style of leadership are Edouard Balladur (Minister of Finance 1986–88 and adviser to Georges Pompidou during his presidency) and Charles Pasqua (Minister of the Interior 1986–88 and close associate of Jacques Chirac, also responsible for electoral strategy).

Union pour la Démocratie Française — UDF

Headquarters	:	12, rue François 1er, F-75008 Paris (tel. 43 59 79 59)
Chairman	:	V. Giscard d'Estaing, 1988–present
Delegate-general	:	Jean-Philippe Lachenaud
Membership	:	28,000
Founded	:	1978

History

More of a federation of parties than a party in its own right, the UDF nevertheless provides broad organizational support, particularly in the National Assembly, for its constituent parties. It defines itself in such a way that it can be seen to be a liberal/conservative formation. It was created primarily to support and promote the presidency of Giscard d'Estaing (1974–81). Since 1981 it has continued to work for the greater unity of the Centre-right in France. Its main components are the *Parti Republicain, Parti Radical, Centre des Démocrates Sociaux*, and the *Parti Social Démocrate* (see separate entries). It also has direct members (see below). The UDF is also organized at local level, but its significance at this level is marginal compared to the organization of its constituent parties.

It is governed by a National Council, composed of the presidents of each of its component parties, plus other leaders from these parties depending on their size. Eighteen national delegates cover the different sectors of activity of the organization.

The UDF (in its widest sense of all its component parties) is the "leading force in local politics", holding 12 presidencies of regional councils, 46 presidencies of *conseils généraux*, and with 1,080 local councillors. It is presided over by Valery Giscard d'Estaing. The four vice-presidents are François Leotard, Pierre Mehaignerie, Yves Galland and Georges Donnez.

It also has seven main committees (elections, education, Europe, defence, economics, institutions and decentralization, social affairs). The political bureau of the UDF meets at least once every month.

UDF
(direct members)

Delegate-general	:	Paul Girod
Membership	:	28,000

The UDF also allows members to join directly without belonging to any of the parties mentioned above. It has 17 seats in the National Assembly, 11 senators, and four members of the European Parliament.

Politically it is more significant and influential than any other composant of the UDF federation, except for the *Parti Républicain*. Raymond Barre has drawn more staunch support amongst direct UDF members than from any of the constituent parties. However, the recent evolution of the centre ground in France and the formation by Raymond Barre of a new political club with clear ambitions for the future — the *Convention Libéral Européenne et Sociale* (CLES) — could undermine the organization of the UDF's direct members.

The members of the UDF from each federation send delegates to the national convention, which meets every two years. The convention elects a bureau of 27 members including Michel Pinton, the secretary-general.

The members who belong directly to the UDF tend to attach great significance to the "union" of the various components of the umbrella organization, and therefore to the consolidation of the movement. However, since the 1988 elections, indications are that there is an increasing centrifugal tendency, particularly emanating from the CDS and from some of the UDF direct members. This, were it to bring about a split, would in all likelihood also bring about the end of UDF direct membership.

Four members representing UDF direct members sit on the National Council of the UDF.

Among prominent direct members of the UDF have been Raymond Barre, Simone Veil (former Minister of Health, and first president of the directly elected European Parliament) and Philippe Mestre.

Club Perspectives et Réalité

Though not a political party, the "club" is a useful instrument of the UDF leadership and in particular of Giscard d'Estaing. It sends two members to the National Council of the UDF. It is managed by Alain Lamassoure, a member of the National Assembly (PR).

Parti Républicain — PR

Headquarters	:	3 rue de Constantine, F-75007 Paris (tel. 45 44 44 20)
President	:	François Léotard (1988–present)

Secretary-general : Jean Pierre
Soisson (1977–78),
Jacques Blanc
(1978–82,
François Léotard
(1982–88),
Alain Madelin
(1988–present)
Membership : 150,000
Founded : Congress of
Fréjus, 1977

History

The *Parti Républicain* is the successor party to the *Républicain Indépendant* (RI) founded in 1966 by Giscard d'Estaing and Michel Poniatowski, which was in turn created from a split within the parliamentary group of the *Centre National des Indépendants et Paysans* (CNIP).

The current in French politics which has evolved under the leadership of Giscard d'Estaing was originally based on an independent liberal tradition, strongly republican at local level where, to begin with, its strength lay. It has, over the years, proved difficult to organize, as the conservative local "notables" were not at ease within a movement which at national level espoused many more liberal and social ideals. What brought the apparently contradictory elements together was opposition to the hegemonic brand of Gaullism of the late 60s and early 70s, and belief that the party's leader, Giscard d'Estaing, was a potential President of France.

The foundation of the RI coincided with the departure of Giscard d'Estaing from the government of Georges Pompidou — then de Gaulle's Prime Minister. Giscard d'Estaing remained outside government and the governing majority (supporting a "no" vote in the 1969 referendum which led to de Gaulle's resignation) until the election of Georges Pompidou to the presidency in 1969. Giscard d'Estaing then joined the government of Jacques Chaban Delmas as Finance Minister — a post he was to keep under the Messmer government until Pompidou died in 1974.

The election of Giscard d'Estaing to the presidency in 1974 raised the profile of the RI considerably. His close associate, Michel Poniatowski, became Minister of the Interior, a position of considerable importance, for the Interior Minister is responsible for the administration of each *département* of France via the system of *Préfets*. In addition he has responsibility for managing elections and is in charge of the police.

The RI gradually emerged as a more organ-

ized electoral machine during this early period of Giscard d'Estaing's presidency. Yet it lacked a dynamic image, particularly compared to the organized Gaullist movement and thus in 1977 the *Parti Républicain* emerged in order to try to create a more outward looking liberal, yet socially aware political movement.

As a party, the PR has above all significance at parliamentary level and at local authority level. Its membership and organization is not structured in such a way that the party as such directly influences decision making by the leadership.

It holds the presidency of six regional councils, and 13 "departmental" councils (*conseil général*), has 45 senators, 58 members of the National Assembly and four members of the European Parliament.

Organization

The leadership structure of the *Parti Républicain* combines directly elected representatives from the federations of the party with a number of co-opted members, elected members of the National Assembly and Senate and local authorities.

As president of the PR, François Léotard is the party's main spokesman and decision-maker. He is directly assisted by two close collaborators, Alain Madelin (secretary-general) and Gérard Longuet (delegate-general). The former is more of a political function, while the latter is more directly concerned with internal organization of the party.

The *bureau politique* of the PR consists of 30 members elected by the *conseil national* on a list proposed by the party leader, who heads the list. Additional members of the *bureau politique* include past secretaries-general and ex-ministers, plus the chairmen of the parliamentary group in the National Assembly and Senate. There are also 10 associate members, specializing in particular policy fields.

The *comité directeur* is a more broadly-based executive organ, which may propose policy between the twice-yearly meetings of the *conseil national*. It is composed of the presidents of 30 departmental federations of the party, 10 senators and members of the National Assembly plus members from the *Conseil National*.

The *Conseil National* itself is composed of elected representatives (MPs, mayors, senators, local councillors) which make up 40 per cent of the delegates, and delegates of the federations, elected in proportion to the size of the sovereign body of the party, electing the president and its executive organs.

The *Parti Républicain* is a member of the

Liberal International, and of the Federation of Liberal, Democratic and Reform parties of the European Community.

Personalities

One of the key personalities within the *Parti Républicain* is François Léotard. He has put a strong emphasis on economic liberalism, and has made no secret of his presidential ambitions. In 1988, however, an attempt by Léotard on the presidency was considered premature, and the *Parti Républicain* gave its less than full support to Raymond Barre. Among Léotard's supporters within the party are Alain Madelin and Gérard Longuet.

Jean-Pierre Soisson and Roger Chinaud were largely responsible for the successful beginnings of the PR and, with Jean Lecanuet from the CDS, and also the Radicals, they contributed to the formation of the UDF. Chinaud became president of the UDF group in the National Assembly.

Parti Radical — Valoisien

Headquarters	: 1 place de Valois, F-75001 Paris (tel: 42 61 56 32)
President	: Jean-Jacques Servan Scheiber (1972–83), André Rossinot (1983–88), Yves Galland (1988–present)
Membership	: 20,000
Founded	: 1901

History

For decades, the Radical Party was a major republican anti-clerical party which voted for the separation of Church and State in the early 20th century. It shared office with the SFIO at the time of the Popular Front in 1936 and was the focal attraction for other parties even in the Fourth Republic when Edgar Faure and Pierre Mendes-France both became *Président du Conseil* (Prime Minister). Other leading personalities from the party were Edouard Herriot and Edouard Daladier.

Between 1969 and 1972 growing divisions within the party came to the fore and the left of the party split and formed the *Mouvement des Radicaux de Gauche* (MRG — see below). In the 1970s, the remaining Radical Party situated itself firmly in the Giscardian camp, and its leaders were among the first to support the candidature of Giscard d'Estaing for the presidency in 1974. Servan-Scheiber was sacked from Giscard d'Estaing's first government, under Jacques Chirac's premiership, after only 15 days in office, due to his protests over French nuclear testing in the Pacific.

Following the 1988 elections, the Radical Party was left with only three members in the National Assembly, including André Rossinot (mayor of Nancy), and 17 senators. It is very much a party of the small town "notable" and holds the presidency of 13 *conseils régionaux*, and has nine mayors of towns with over 30,000 inhabitants.

Organization

For what has become a relatively small party, its structures are quite open and complete. The president of the party is elected for two years by the annual congress; he may only serve a maximum of two terms of office. The congress also elects an executive committee which, in practice, is a large and unwieldy institution which meets every two months. The executive committee consists of all the party's members of the National Assembly, the Senate and the European Parliament, all ex-presidents of the party, ex-Prime Ministers, presidents of each *département* federation and regional federations and presidents of the 16 standing committees of the party, plus 100 delegates appointed from the regional federations. All members of the party's *bureau* are also members of the executive committee.

The *bureau* is the senior administrative and political organ of the Radical Party. It consists of the president, the secretary-general (elected by the executive committee) and 30 party members elected by the executive committee on the basis of competing lists.

The congress itself meets every year, and is composed of all the elected representatives of the party (both local and national) plus all party candidates (who were not elected) for national elective office, plus one delegate per 50 members from each federation. The executive committee members are of course delegates at the congress as are the secretaries-general and treasurer of each federation of the party.

At local level, the party is organized most often on a parliamentary constituency basis, though smaller units may be created where the need arises. The party is a member of the Liberal International and of the Federation of Liberal, Democratic and Reform Parties of the European Community.

Centre des Démocrates-Sociaux — CDS

Headquarters	:	205, blvd Saint-Germain, F-75007 Paris (tel. 45 44 72 50)
President	:	Jean Lecanuet (1976–82), Pierre Mehaignerie (1982–present)
Secretary-general	:	Jacques Barrot (1982–present)
Founded	:	Congress of Rennes, 1976
Membership	:	51,000

History

The CDS has emerged as the inheritor of the *Mouvement Républicain Populaire*, the social-christian movement which dominated the French Fourth Republic. Its best known figure, Jean Lecanuet (mayor of Rouen) was a presidential candidate in the 1965 presidential election. The CDS was born as a result of the fusion of *Centre Démocratie et Progrès* led by Jacques Duhamel and the *Centre Démocrate* led by Jean Lecanuet. Both parties had actively supported the candidature of Valery Giscard d'Estaing in the 1974 presidential elections.

Organization

The congress of the CDS meets every two years and elects the president and the secretary-general and the other organs of the party. The party has two vice-presidents (B. Stasi and R. Monory) and several national secretaries responsible for specific policy areas.

The *bureau politique*, with 60 members, is the key executive organ of the CDS. Eight deputies, eight senators and the party's two members of the European Parliament are joined by representatives of the federations to make up this body.

A broader deliberating organ, the *conseil politique* meets every few months to discuss key political issues and party strategy. Composed of 600 members, largely directly elected from each federation, but also including parliamentarians and local officials, the *conseil politique* is a strong sounding board of party opinion between congresses of the party.

The CDS is a member of the Christian Democratic International, the European Christian Democratic Union and the European People's Party.

Policies

The CDS is a party of Christian Democratic orientation. It is a strong moderating influence on the UDF and fiercely hostile to any electoral relations with the *Front National*. The CDS has traditionally been pro-European, even when it was not fashionable to be so, and has been constructive within the UFD particularly as regards its social concerns.

The CDS was the only party within the UDF to strongly support the candidate of Raymond Barre in the 1988 presidential elections. It remains opposed to the unitary strategy between the UDF and the RPR which has been promoted by certain other components of the UDF, notably the *Parti Républicain*, believing that it is most important to maintain the pluralist relations which exist between the UDF and the RPR.

Parti Social Démocrate — PSD

Headquarters	:	191, rue de l'Université, F-75007 Paris (tel. 47 53 84 28 or 47 53 84 41)
President	:	Max Lejeune
Secretary-general	:	André Santini
Founded	:	1973
Membership	:	4,000

History

The party was founded in 1973 as the *Mouvement Démocrate Socialiste de France* (MSDF) by former socialists who were hostile to the Socialist party's common programme and alliance with the Communist Party. It later shortened its name to *Mouvement Démocrate Socialiste* (MDS).

In 1974 the party put forward Emile Muller as its presidential candidate, but he only obtained 0.7 per cent of the vote. It also adhered to the *Fédération des Réformateurs* in 1975, and Max Lejeune became the president of its group in the National Assembly.

In 1978 MDS became a member of the UDF. It won 4 deputies in the 1978 National Assembly elections, but lost these in 1981. In October 1982 it adopted its present name of *Parti Social Démocrate*. In 1986 it regained parliamentary representation and later obtained one post in the Chirac government.

Support

The PSD is a small party with localized support. It claims to be best implantd in Picardy (the home base of its president and first vice-president), the Nord, Normandy, Alsace, Provence, Rhones-Alpes, Languedoc-Roussillon, Aquitaine, Limousin and the Paris region.

Organization

The PSD has been organized on the basis of local sections within the departmental federations. Each federation sends a number of delegates to the party congress in proportion to its size. The party's national convention elects its political bureau, which has over 30 members, and meets at least once a month.

Since 1986 it has been linked with the Movement of Young Social Liberals.

The PSD's two members in the European Parliament sit in the ELDR group.

Policies

The PSD claims to represent humanist, reformist socialism within the liberal UDF. It has been anti-communist and has put a strong emphasis on human rights issues. It has supported a united Europe.

Personalities

Max Lejeune, the party's president, is a leading political figure in Picardy where he has been mayor of Abbeville and president of the General Council of the department of the Somme. He is a senator and a former minister. Charles Baur has been the president of the Picardy Regional Council and one of the PSD's two members in the European Parliament.

Georges Donnez is its other member in the European Parliament, and has become the Parliament's specialist on parliamentary immunity cases.

Parti Socialiste — PS

Headquarters	: 10, rue de Solferino, F-75333 Paris (tel. 45 50 34 35)
First secretary	: François Mitterrand (1971–1981), Lionel Jospin (1981–1988), Pierre Mauroy (1988–present)
Membership	: 210,000
Founded	: Congress of Epinay-sur-Seine, 1971

History

The Socialist Party is the successor party to the *Section Française de l'Internationale Ouvrière*, (SFIO), founded by Jean Jaurès in 1905. At the same time it includes elements who had systematically refused to join the SFIO in the postwar period, or, having been members of the SFIO, had subsequently resigned for political reasons.

Under Leon Blum, the SFIO governed in 1936 as the major partner, with the Radical Party, in the *Front Populaire*. Guy Mollet succeeded Daniel Mayer as secretary-general in 1946 (under Petain, the SFIO was declared illegal — Blum was imprisoned in 1940) and served until the dissolution of the SFIO in 1969. From 1969 to 1971 the *Nouveau Parti Socialiste* laid the foundation, under the leadership of Alain Savary, for the *Parti Socialiste* that was created in Epinay.

With François Mitterrand as leader (he was first secretary from 1971 to 81), the PS espoused democratic socialist principles linked to a modernist approach, which enabled the party to gradually capture an increasing portion of the traditional left-wing electorate, while appealing also to the more moderate young middle-class voters.

From 1972 to 1977 it entered into the *Union de la Gauche* (Left Unity), an alliance with the Communist Party and the *Mouvement des Radicaux de Gauche*, based on the Common Programme of Government, signed in June 1972. During this period the party expanded its membership, and many prominent personalities of the Left joined at the *Assises du Socialisme* in 1974 (notably Michel Rocard and Jacques Delors). The *Assises* were held in the wake of the defeat of François Mitterrand by Valery Giscard d'Estaing in the 1974 presidential elections.

At the same time, the PS continued to gain strength and influence at local — cantonal and municipal — elections. Although it had held important cities such as Marseilles and Lille for decades, it gained many footholds in new areas during the 1970s and 1980s.

Ten years after it was founded, François Mitterrand was elected President of the Republic and the Socialist Party won a landslide electoral victory at the legislative elections which followed (285 seats out of 491).

Although the Socialist Party remained the largest of the French political parties, the 1986 elections were a defeat for the socialist-led government of Laurent Fabius. The period of *cohabitation* between a socialist president and a conservative coalition government (RPR-UDF) under Jacques Chirac lasted only until May 1988, when François Mitterrand was re-elected President of the Republic. The Socialists returned to form a minority government, following the legislative elections of June 1988, led by Michel

Rocard and including many personalities from outside the Socialist Party — representatives of the "civil society" and some independent centrist politicians.

Besides their 176 seats in the National Assembly, the Socialists also hold the presidency of 23 departmental councils. They also hold 60 cities of more than 30,000 inhabitants.

Support

The electorate of the PS — ranging from 20.8 per cent in 1973 to 37.5 per cent in 1981 and 35 per cent in 1988 — has gradually evolved to become more homogeneous and more evenly dispersed throughout the country than any of its rivals. In 1980, the PS maintained its traditional areas of influence in the south-west and the Nord-Pas de Calais and confirmed its more recent establishment in the west and Brittany. It lost votes in the south of France and in the Marseilles region,where the extreme Right has made inroads.

The PS is now the largest single political party in France. It also has more than 80 per cent of the left-wing support in more than half of France's *départements*. It has gained support amongst salaried staff and members of the liberal professions in recent years as well as amongst the retired and elderly. At the same time it has increased its support from voters in the 18–24 age group. Unusually for a party of the Left, it managed in 1988 to do better among female than among male voters (51–49 per cent). In 1973, its support was more predominantly male (55–45 per cent). It is particularly strong among blue-collar workers and technicians, middle-level executives and the teaching profession.

Organization

Since its creation at Epinay, where the various political clubs (such as the CIR of François Mitterrand and the UGCS of Jean Poperen) joined with the other components of the old SFIO, the PS has been organized in such a way that "pluralism" within the party has been its main feature. On occasions this has led to criticism that the various leaders within the party have appeared more in competition with each other than with their opponents in other parties. Yet the principle of one member one vote has, nevertheless, been safeguarded and proportional representation is used to elect the various "federation" and "national" officers of the party.

The party's basic unit is the section (with a minimum of five members) and above these are the federations, which are organized in each department. At national level, a congress ordinarily takes place every two years. The party's top leadership consists of a Directing Committee (*comité directeur*) and an Executive Committee (*comité exécutif*), which are both elected by the congress, along with the party's first secretary. The party secretariat, its real organizational arm, is elected by the *comité exécutif*.

Attached to each motion presented at the national congress is a list of its subscribers, who are elected in proportion to their strength of support. Since 1971, motions have normally been identified with a particular "tendency" within the party. The leaders of each "tendency" are consequently elected on the basis of their motion, for they lead the list of names attached.

The Socialist Party is a member of the Socialist International, the Confederation of Socialist parties of the European Community and the Socialist Group in the European Parliament.

Policies

Throughout the 1970s, there were five main tendencies within the party — those led by Mitterrand himself (succeeded by Lionel Jospin in 1981), by Michel Rocard, by Pierre Mauroy (representing the stronghold of Lille–Nord-Pas de Calais),by Gaston Deferre (representing Marseilles and the Bouches du Rhone) and by Jean-Pierre Chevenement (leader of the former CERES — the "left-wing" tendency since 1974). Mitterrand's followers have always been considered the mainstream of the party. Since 1971 all alliances have been formed around the central kernel of Mitterrand's supporters, which even in a "bad" year (such as 1979) could still rely on over 40 per cent of the vote at congress.

From 1981 to 1988 Lionel Jospin had the task not only of leading the Socialist Party as first secretary, but also of ensuring the co-ordination between the party and the presidency and the party and the government. This was a new situation for the PS, which had spent all its life in opposition. With many of the party's leaders in government, the membership of the different party organs needed modification while ensuring continuity. From 1986 to 1988, when the Socialist Party returned to an opposition role in Parliament, prominent ministers had difficulty in fitting themselves into mere "party" positions.

The changing nature of the party can be clearly witnessed by briefly mentioning the different party congresses of the 1980s. The first congress of the PS after its 1981 successes was held in Valence. This had a triumphal tone and many had difficulty in adapting their discourse to the demands of government. By 1983, the Bourg en Bresse, the Socialists were facing up to the difficulties of a run on the franc and the need to establish more rigorous budgetary discipline — with all which that implied for cuts in public expenditure. The party began to learn a new language and to become less ideological and more pragmatically reformist. Having fared badly in the 1984 European elections, where they obtained only 22 seats out of 81 (with their MRG allies) the Toulouse congress of 1985 was remarkably calm. Opinion polls looked ominous for the forthcoming legislative elections and yet the debates were organized in a way which covered over much of the underlying tension and allowed the PS to go into the election campaign looking united and confident. The synthesis which emerged from the Toulouse congress has, in practice, been maintained since then, although there are still underlying differences of opinion. Table 14 shows the ideological attitudes of the main tendencies indicative of the party at the Toulouse congress.

Prior to the Lille congress in April 1987, the different tendencies had already reached agreement on a common motion for a resolution to be presented to the congress entitled *Rassembler pour Gagner*.

The Lille congress was also significant in that the PS began to look more closely at its basic principles with a view to their adaptation in order to take into account the lessons learned in government. Also of significance was the appeal for the creation of an anti-socialist coalition to replace, in effect, *Union de la Gauche* by expanding left-unity to moderate Gaullists. centrists and other progressive currents of opinion. Attempts were thus made to appeal to the political Centre before the presidential election began, whilst simultaneously maintaining *ouvertures* to the communist Left and its developing factions.

In attempts to redefine basic principles, the dogma of the "socialization of the means of production" is being questioned by the party as a result of its experiences in government. More emphasis is now placed on the acceptance of the market economy, without denying the state a regulatory role. Mitterrand's election campaign in 1988, based on the theme *La France Unie*, itself emphasizes the determination to bring together the different social categories and even ethnic groups faced with an aggravation of xenophobic and racist tendencies within French society.

The PS has generally been in favour of further European integration, with the exception of parts of its left wing (the former CERES group). It was also cautious on the issue of Spanish entry into the Community.

A distinctive feature of the socialist left wing in the European socialist context has been its support for a strong French defence posture and also of civil nuclear energy.

Table 14: tendencies in the PS and ideological attitudes (%)

	All	Jospin	Mauroy	Rocard	Ceres
The best regulator of the economy is ...					
the state	60	70	46	36	86
the market	32	19	46	60	9
Agree with the following:					
Class struggle is important characteristic of French society	51	60	54	25	74
Left-Right divisions are increasingly out-of-date	19	13	21	32	11
Justice must be more strict	21	23	39	16	20
Need to increase size of police force	37	40	54	33	36
Autogestion/self-management is a way to resolve social tensions	66	57	61	79	73
Consider the following references as being "very important"					
Marxism	33	35	39	20	52
Socialism of the SFIO	45	50	57	33	49
Mendesism	7	23	32	47	10

Source: *Le Parti Socialiste a-t-il change?* R. Cayrol and C. Ysmal. Extracts from *Le Monde*, April 3, 1987.

Personalities

François Mitterrand has been President of the Republic since 1981, and was re-elected in 1988. He was a minister on 10 occasions during the Fourth Republic, and an unsuccessful presidential candidate against de Gaulle in 1965 and Giscard d'Estaing in 1974, before defeating Giscard in 1981.

Michel Rocard is the current French Prime Minister. He was the former leader of the *Parti Socialiste Unifié* and was closely identified with the students and autonomists movement in the aftermath of 1968. He entered the main Socialist Party in 1975 and has since come to epitomise the moderate social democratic reformist wing of the party. At one stage he seemed a strong rival to Mitterrand, but was defeated at the party's Metz congress in 1979. He has consistently enjoyed a high level of popularity with the general public, but been regarded with suspicion by many of the party leadership.

Pierre Mauroy has been the party's first secretary since 1988. His political base is Lille, and he was Mitterrand's first Prime Minister in the period from 1981 to 1984.

Lionel Jospin was the party's first secretary from 1981 to 1988 and is currently the Minister of Education, ranking second in the government of Michel Rocard. Other leading party figures have included Jean-Pierre Chevenement (a long-standing leader of the party Left), Pierre Joxe, Louis Mermaz and Jean Poperen. Laurent Fabius was Mitterrand's second Prime Minister from 1984 to 1986. Jacques Delors is the current President of the European Commission, and is now in his second term of office. He is a former Minister of Finance. He was originally in the Cabinet of the Gaullist Prime Minister Jacques Chaban-Delmas, and only took the decision to join the Socialist Party in late 1974.

Parti Communiste Français — PCF

Headquarters	:	2 place du Colonel Fabien, F-75019 Paris (tel. 42 38 66 55)
Secretary-general	:	Georges Marchais (1970–present)
Membership	:	700,000
Founded	:	Congress of Tours, 1920

History

The French Communist Party was born out of a division of the SFIO at the congress of Tours in December 1920. It split from the SFIO and departed with a majority of delegates to join Lenin's Third International, which had been founded after the Bolshevik Revolution in 1917. Since then, it has maintained largely the same structure and ideology. At least until the 1960s it owed its ideological allegiance as much to the Soviet Union as it did to France, although this did not prevent tens of thousands of French communists from fighting and dying in the Resistance, nor did ideological allegiance to communist doctrines diminish a strong sense of French patriotism for the vast majority of the members of the party.

At the end of the war (having been members of the National Council of the Resistance), the PCF voted in favour of General de Gaulle as President of the provisional government. In return they obtained five ministerial posts, including the Armaments Ministry, and Maurice Thorez (the party's leader from 1930 to 1964) became one of the government's senior ministers with the rank of *Ministre d'État*, responsible for the civil service. With de Gaulle's departure from office in January 1946, the PCF obtained three more posts in the short-lived government of Felix Gouin. At the same time the Communist Party acted to prevent workers' unrest from destabilizing the government and many political strikes were averted. However, the relationship between the three major parties which formed the government (the PCF, the SFIO and the MRP) deteriorated considerably after almost three years in office. The beginnings of the Cold War led the other parties to exclude the PCF from power. This situation led the PCF into a political ghetto. Its well disciplined membership and its strong electoral support throughout this period enabled the PCF to pursue its opposition to the changing government coalitions while encouraging the existence of a strong counter-culture amongst the industrial working class. As the major party of the Left, the only party in France with a mass membership, and a strongly influential voice in the trade union movement (in particular with the CGT, whose secretary-general is traditionally a member of the PCF Politburo), the Communist Party maintained its distinctive role in the political system. By 1947 it had almost a million members.

On leaving the government, the Communist Party no longer considered it had the political responsibility of restraining the CGT and the other unions from strike action, which was to paralyse the country for much of 1947. Under pressure at the parliamentary level from the sister party in the Soviet Union and from the trade union movement and also influenced by the course of events of the Cold War, the PCF chose opposition and a return to more "orthodox" behaviour.

Having left office, the PCF concentrated all its efforts in the fight against "American imperialism" associated with the Marshall Plan, the creation of the Atlantic Alliance and the establishment of NATO. From 1952 to 1954 it fiercely opposed the proposals for a European Defence Community.

At the same time, and in parallel with the purges which were ruthlessly taking place in the East-bloc, the PCF set about expelling several prominent members while consolidating the control of Maurice Thorez over the entire party machine. The PCF was, nevertheless, severely shaken by the repression of the Hungarian uprising and by the revelations contained in Kruschev's report to the 20th Congress of the Soviet Communist Party in 1956, which condemned Stalin's purges and "crimes".

Its opposition to the establishment of the Fifth Republic in 1958 singled out the PCF from the other major political formations. Thorez came under increasing challenge within the party, notably from Servin and Casanova, the latter with the implicit support of Kruschev in Moscow. The fall of Kruschev, however, led in turn to the expulsion of both Servin and Casanova, and the PCF was once again exposed for its Stalinist and anti-democratic methods.

Under the leadership of Waldeck Rochet, from 1964, the PCF embarked on a more unitary strategy, envisaging for the first time at its 18th congress in 1967 a "peaceful path to socialism" and electoral alliances with the other parties of the French Left.

The events of May 1968 undermined the authority of Waldeck Rochet, who was finally pushed aside following his condemnation of the entry of Soviet tanks into Prague in August 1968. His authority was, to all intents and purposes, non-existent when the PCF designated Jacques Duclos as its presidential candidate in the 1969 elections. In Moscow, at the Third International Communist Conference, the PCF was the only major "non-satellite" Communist Party to align itself fully with the Soviet Communist Party on the issue of the "normalisation process" in Czechoslovakia. Ailing health was the reason finally invoked to replace Waldeck Rochet by Georges Marchais at the 19th PCF congress in 1970, a decision which was confirmed two years later at the 20th congress, where Georges Marchais officially became the party's fourth secretary-general.

Throughout Georges Marchais' period as secretary-general, the PCF has continued to maintain a rigorous internal control of the party organization, which is still based on the Leninist concept of democratic centralism, while advancing towards and then retreating from a form of *rapprochement* with the non-communist Left. It has, as a party, always continued to present itself as the party of the working class and therefore the most able to defend their interests. Following the signature of the Common Programme of Government with the PS and the MRG in June 1972 it appeared for a while to follow the ideological path traced by other "Eurocommunist" parties. At the height of the period of *Union de la Gauche*, the PCF abandoned the concept of the dictatorship of the proletariat, which was officially removed from the party's principles at its 22nd congress in February 1976. This particular congress marked the furthest that the PCF was prepared to go on the path to what many saw as "revisionism", which included a considerable renewal of the party hierarchy.

The abandonment of the left-wing unitary strategy with the PS and MRG following the failure to bring the Common Programme up-to-date in 1977, saw the PCF once again turn, albeit with some reservations, towards the Soviet Union and towards traditional orthodoxy. This led, amongst other things, to the PCF approving the Soviet intervention in Afghanistan in January 1980.

There was also increasing internal dissent within the party, which began to flourish after a series of powerfully critical articles by Louis Althusser appeared in *Le Monde* in 1978 and the subsequent publication of several further opposition articles by members of the PCF. The fundamental reproach made was that the party leadership had turned its back on the *Union de la Gauche* unilaterally and without consulting the membership of the party. The 23rd congress in 1979 managed to contain but not stop such criticism, which also undermined the candidature of Georges Marchais in the 1981 presidential election. Mobilization within the party for the campaign proved extremely difficult and several public figures formerly known for their sympathies with, or membership of, the PCF signed articles and pamphlets supporting an alliance with the Socialist Party, and also the candidature of François Mitterrand.

With 15.3 per cent at the first ballot, Marchais brought the PCF back to its electoral level of 1936. Marchais then, in a sharp about-turn, promised full support for Mitterrand on the 2nd ballot. Later it was revealed that many in the party leadership had in fact given instructions to party officials throughout the country to either abstain or spoil their ballot papers.

After the Left's victory at the presidential and legislative elections, the socialists introduced four PCF ministers into the Pierre Mauroy government on the basis of a solemn agreement which provided them with certain guarantees. This allowed the PCF to reaffirm its belief in democracy while limiting the damage caused by the persisting internal dissent. The party continually refused, however, to carry out an in-depth assessment of the causes of its electoral decline, which at the European Elections of June 1984 saw it obtain a mere 11.3 per cent of the vote. In July 1984, it refused to further associate itself with economic austerity policies and declined to enter the new government formed by the socialists under Laurent Fabius.

This provoked intensified internal criticism, led by Pierre Juquin, one of the more prominent of the Central Committee Secretariat. Further electoral decline in the 1986 elections, when it found itself on an equal footing with the extreme-right National Front with less than 10 per cent of the vote, indicated that the party was even losing its traditional bases of support.

The conservative government of Jacques Chirac from 1986 to 1988 should have allowed the Communist Party an opportunity to revive its strong opposition role, yet the rank-and-file of the party appeared more disillusioned than ever with the leadership of Georges Marchais and party membership continued to decline. When in 1987 Marchais announced that he would not stand in the forthcoming presidential elections, this was widely seen as a sign of his imminent departure from the party leadership.

With Andre Lajoinie as their candidate, the PCF obtained their lowest electoral score in their long history — a mere 6.9 per cent, in spite of Lajoinie's tireless campaigning, which led to him visiting almost every PCF federation. During this period too, changes in the statutes of the Party permitted the introduction of the secret ballot, and in the weeks prior to the party congress the party newspaper *L'Humanité* opened its columns to critical comment. Purges, not infrequent in the past have since given way to alternative forms of control. This has not, of course, prevented certain critics such as Henry Fiszbin and Pierre Juquin from "placing" themselves "outside of the party".

Support

For many years, in fact for almost its entire history, the PCF has been the opposition force in French politics. As such it has been able to attract electoral support even from people who have no particular knowledge of communist doctrine or ideology. By promoting the interests of the low paid industrial workers and the unemployed, the Communist Party has been able to maintain a considerable presence both in local and national politics.

Socioeconomic changes within French society and the emergence of a new class of salaried staff have recently reduced traditional areas of PCF influence. Structural changes in the productive sector now mean that there are fewer manual workers in traditional industries. Also, at the political level, other forces of "opposition" have succeeded in making inroads into the traditional areas of support.

The electorate of the PCF appears to be growing older and remaining relatively stable in the white-collar category while declining considerably in the working-class sector and the farming sector which were its traditional areas of support.

Geographically, the Communist Party areas of support are changing and its influence is weakening, notably in the old "red belt" areas around Paris as well as in the Nord-Pas de Calais, and the Bouches du Rhone.

In the last elections in June 1988, the PCF was only able to maintain a candidate in the second ballot (having gained more than the necessary 12.5 per cent of the vote) in 72 of the 575 constituencies. In most of these cases, the PCF arrived behind the socialist candidate and therefore withdrew. Emerging from the second ballot with only 27 seats, compared to 35 in 1986, the rules of the National Assembly had to be changed in order to allow the PCF to form a political group in parliament. It is now represented by members from 13 departments, compared to 24 in 1986. The communist vote held up best where it had a good record in local government, notably in cities where it held the *mairie* as part of a left-wing alliance with the PS and MRG. Eleven out of its 27 members of parliament are mayors in 1988 (prior to the 1989 municipal elections) compared to seven out of 44 in 1981. Its 14 senators will be vulnerable if its score further diminishes nationally.

The poor results of the presidential election were reflected in the ensuing legislative elections, and even though the party's overall percentage increased to 11.3 per cent, its total number of voters was only half that of 1967, which, given the increasing size of the French electorate and the lowering of the voting age, means that the PCF is now in greater danger of being reduced to a permanent marginal role in electoral terms.

Organization

The principles of democratic centralism dictate the structure of the French Communist Party and directly influence its pattern of behaviour. Discussions in party cells, or in federations has always been subordinate to decisions taken by the leadership and in particular by the secretary-general. Discussion and debate is therefore channelled and monitored by the Politburo and its various organs.

Posts of responsibility within the party are allocated by the leadership before being put to the vote of the members. When, as has happened recently, federations have been critical of leadership decisions or nominations and have chosen to elect alternative local party officers, the central party hierarchy has always imposed an official of its own choosing to supervise the party and oversee its activities — as was the case in Meurthe et Moselle and the Haute Vienne, two federations where dissent was most strongly felt in the post-1986 period. The structure of the party is thus of a vertical nature, and the organization of specific currents of opinion on a horizontal level actively suppressed. When dissent is voiced, it is rarely through party channels, and more often through the national press.

Party congresses, held on average every three years, elect the central committee (145 members) which in turn elects the politburo (28 members) and the secretariat (seven members) which is in practice the executive organ of the party. Federations, representing every one of the French *départements* send congress delegates chosen by a cell or by a workplace section of the party.

The central commissions are of some significance in the functioning of the PCF and are composed of several central committee members in addition to advisers, trade union officials or specialists in the work for which the commission is responsible. Central sections have a similar task, are more closely linked to the secretariat and are presided over by a member of the politburo. They are the organs which, amongst other things, have a key role in finance and administration, party ideology, candidate vetting and nomination, internal organization and careers of the party's permanent officials.

The French Communist Party therefore remains a rigidly structured, centrally controlled political organization. It is not, however, in any real sense a monolithic bloc as may have been the situation in the past. In fact, since the seventies in particular, differences of opinion have clearly existed within the highest echelons of the party.

Policies

The PCF has been a generally orthodox communist party in its policy stands. Besides traditional themes, such as the need for an increase in the minimum wage and job creation, the PCF has also taken up the issues of peace and disarmament, women's rights and third world development, as well as anti-racism, although its record on immigration questions at local level has sometimes left it open to criticism. The PCF is very critical of the European Community in its present form and voted against the Single European Act.

The PCF has appeared on several occasions to be much more of a pragmatic follower of left-wing opinion than the vanguard of the proletariat, contenting itself, for example, to support strike action by the railway workers when the latter had voted to strike over bad working conditions and poor career prospects in 1987. Its participation in government may have further undermined its "opposition" role in French society, and frequent changes of direction in terms of electoral tactics have led to confusion in the electorate and therefore to an increased marginalization.

Mouvement des Radicaux de Gauche — MRG

Headquarters	: 3, rue de la Boetie, F-75008 Paris
President	: Yvon Collin
Honorary presidents	: René Billeres, Michel Crépeau, Maurice Fauré, R-G Schwartzenberg, J-M Baylet
Membership	: 20,000
Founded	: 1972

History

Founded as a result of a division in the Radical Party, the MRG was a signatory in June 1972 of the Common Programme of Government along with the PS and the PCF.

For much of its history, the Radical Party had formed electoral alliances with the Socialist Party. However, in the Fifth Republic, the Radical Party, found itself torn in two directions — those who wished to join the government of the Centre-right and those who wished to maintain progressive, anti-clerical and pro-left orientations. To consolidate this latter tendency, Robert Fabre and Maurice Fauré organized the *Groupe d'Études et d'Action Radicale Socialiste*, first of all within the Radical Party. After they had then left the party, the *Groupe* formed the basis of what was to become the MRG.

Political necessity also motivated the change, as the leaders of the MRG were all, to a greater or lesser extent, dependent on the socialists for their election at local and national level. By forming an integral and essential part of the

Union de la Gauche, the MRG considered that it was following in the truest of radical traditions, first promoted by Gambetta, Ferry and Combes at the turn of the century.

The MRG has, since its foundation, supported François Mitterrand in the 1974, 1981 and 1988 presidential majority. This did not prevent Michel Crépeau, mayor of La Rochelle and a prominent leader of the MRG, from standing in 1981 for the presidency. He was never under any illusion as to the score he would obtain, but considered it necessary that the MRG clearly made its separate mark before committing itself solidly in support of François Mitterrand. In the first ballot, Crépeau obtained 2.2 per cent of the vote and, throughout its short history, the party has rarely managed a score in excess of this.

In the period of Mitterrand's first term of office, Michel Crépeau, Maurice Fauré and R-G Schwartzenberg all held ministerial office. in the same period, the party, in alliance with the socialists, held the presidency of five *conseils généraux* and boasted 10,000 municipal councillors and 1,041 mayors.

The 1986 legislative elections which saw a return of the RPR-UDF alliance to government created tensions within the MRG as certain members began to become restless within the left-wing alliance and sought to make *ouvertures* to the "other" Radical Party, the one allied with the Right. This unrest, which was manifest at the Avignon congress in 1986, has continued and caused severe divisions within an already small political party. At Avignon, François Doubin was re-elected president, with 60 per cent of the vote. The minority motion presented by Michel Crépeau was nevertheless supported by most of the party's MPs and prominent figures.

The defeat of Michel Crépeau in Avignon led him to create a new political club, *Libertés pour Demain*, with the objective of opening up the MRG to more "left-wing humanists" but not with the objective of dividing the party. However, in 1987, when the MRG met in Montpellier, the situation had not improved and with the number of delegates in decline, many envisaged leaving the MRG with the intention of creating yet another new structure to which dissident MRG members and others could belong.

In the new political context, resulting from the re-election of François Mitterrand to the presidency in 1988, the MRG has become a more significant element in providing an opening from the Left to the Centre in support of the government of Michel Rocard. Meeting in Versailles in November 1988, the MRG congress welcomed the participation of several nonpartisan members in the Rocard government, and there was much discussion about the possible participation of the MRG in a nonsocialist centre-left list in the 1989 European elections. The reunification of the Radical Party was yet again postponed at this congress, which proceeded to elect Yvon Collin as the movement's new president, to be succeeded by Emile Zuccarelli in a sort of revolving presidency.

Support

Like the Radical Party, the MRG has essentially failed to become much more than a collection of local notables, centred in its traditional areas of strength in the south west of France, in Aquitaine, the Dordogne and Poitou Charentes. Corsica is another stronghold.

Organization

The president of the MRG is elected by the annual party congress. All former presidents become honorary presidents and participate in meetings of the *bureau national* which, with 31 members, is also elected by the congress. The *comité directeur* in effect acts as the "parliament" of the MRG. In addition to the president and four vice-presidents, it is composed of all the members of Parliament from the MRG, the members of the *bureau national* and one representative from each federation representing a *département*. In addition six members of the MRG Youth Movement (the MJRG) are designated to the *comité directeur*. It meets at approximately monthly intervals in theory; in practice less frequently. In effect, the party structures reflect the decentralized nature of the movement and its philosophy.

The MRG is one of the few constituency based parties in France, even though small units may be created. The federation in effect, does little more than co-ordinate constituency parties as much as possible. Declining membership means that, election campaigns aside, local party organizations (apart from such key areas as La Rochelle, Cahors, Grenoble, Toulouse and Paris) remain fairly inactive. Most of the local party work is undertaken by the elected departmental or municipal councillors, who in any event make up half the party's membership!

Policies

The left-of-centre orientation of the MRG, strongly related to a humanist philosophy, has not surprisingly attracted many freemasons into the MRG. The party favours social market-style economy and decentralized planning. Fervently pro-European, it strongly encourages the initiatives of François Mitterrand for a European social dimension in the context of the 1992 single market.

Nouvelle Gauche — NG

Principal spokesman : Pierre Juquin
Founded : 1988

History

The *Nouvelle Gauche* is not yet a political party in the traditional sense; it does not have the ambition of becoming a traditional party. It is the expression, nevertheless, of a political current of opinion which has been a permanent feature of French politics and which may be classified as the alternative Left.

The *Nouvelle Gauche* was born out of the 1988 presidential election campaign and the local campaign committees of Pierre Juquin. Excluded from the PCF in October 1987, though earlier marginalized because of his role as the leader of the *renovateurs* within the PCF, Pierre Juquin was a member of the PCF central committee for 20 years, and from 1982 to 1985 a member of the PCF politburo. His appeal for greater freedom of expression within the PCF made him a national figure and (reluctantly at first), support came from other organizations of the alternative Left, from the ecology movement and from the student movement which had been mobilized in the 1986–87 period against the Chirac government's proposed educational reforms.

In the course of the presidential election campaign Juquin commanded considerable attention. This was partly because of the anti-racist, youth-oriented content of his campaign, paying attention to environmental issues, third world development and disarmament, but more especially because the media concentrated on his own self-criticism and criticism of the PCF (though he never attacked any individual member of the PCF, nor their presidential candidate). The primary objective of his campaign was, in the immediate sense, not electoral at all but more aimed at regrouping the disparate elements of the alternative Left. The 2.2 per cent he received in the election was, however, a disappointment, since certain opinion polls had credited him with 5 per cent. At the first national meeting of his support committees in January 1988, 15,000 members were claimed. Later in the campaign, between 24,000 and 26,000 members were recorded, 53 per cent of whom had never belonged previously to a political party.

The creation of the *Nouvelle Gauche* in December 1988 was the first sign of the regrouped alternative Left and the 400 delegates from 64 *départements* voted to elect a co-ordinating committee and an executive committee and to nominate Pierre Juquin as spokesman of the executive committee. A constituent congress is due to be held in 1989 to adopt the official policy statement and the party statutes.

Those represented at the meeting to launch the *Nouvelle Gauche* included delegates from the *Parti Socialiste Unifié* (which had voted its own dissolution to join forces within the NG), from the *Fédération de la Gauche Alternative* from the *Ligue Communiste Révolutionnaire*, and many "non-party" delegates. The majority came out in support of a motion presented by Pierre Juquin, which won 63 per cent of the vote. An opposing motion, supported by part of the LCR, obtained 18 per cent, with 19 per cent favouring a "federalist" approach. The final charter setting up the NG was adopted by 286 votes in favour, two against and nine abstentions. Sixty-two delegates did not vote.

An alliance with ecologist groups led by Antoine Waechter is to be sought for the European election of 1989 in order to enable the ecologists and the NG to obtain more than the 5 per cent threshold necessary for election to the European Parliament. In addition, great efforts are being made to make contact and gain support from the major trade union organizations.

One of the main organized components of the *Nouvelle Gauche* has been the former *Parti Socialiste Unifié* (PSU), following its decision to dissolve itself finally almost 30 years after its foundation. The PSU is itself a phenomenon of the Fifth Republic, never having attracted great electoral support but having nevertheless been a repository of ideas and a party within which many leading left politicians have been active. Michel Rocard was secretary-general of the PSU and their presidential candidate in 1969, when he obtained 3.61 per cent of the votes. One of the early members of the PSU when it was formed in 1960 was Pierre Mendes-France — one of France's most respected politicians of the century. However, the PSU drew its support largely from intellectual circles on the Left and was subject to persistent and damaging divisions between its various competing tendencies. There were those in the PSU, such as Rocard and Pierre Beregovoy, who saw it as an innovative force destined eventually to integrate with the established Left at the appropriate moment. Others in the party were for maintaining the PSU outside conventional political activity.

The departure of Michel Rocard in 1974, along with half of the party's membership, to join the *Parti Socialiste*, dealt the PSU a blow from which it never recovered. Thereafter the party found it almost impossible to carve out a distinctive role at the time when the moves towards the *Union de la Gauche* were bearing fruit. It sought agreements with the other parties of the Left in the 1977 municipal elections and by 1977 had moved towards a direct alliance as part of the *Front Autogestionnaire*, of which it formed the largest component. It was related in the FA to pacifist groups and women's rights organizations. Fielding 218 candidates in the 1978 elections, it obtained just over one per cent of the vote.

Its most recent national secretary to join forces with the PS was Huguette Buchardeau, who went on to become a minister in the government of Laurent Fabius. The PSU, however, remained on the fringes of the established Left until its recent adherence to the *Nouvelle Gauche*.

Lutte Ouvrière — LO

Headquarters	:	BP 233, Cédex 18, F-75865 Paris
Leader	:	Arlette Laguiller
Membership	:	5,000
Founded	:	1968

History

As a Trotskyist party, *Lutte Ouvrière* concentrates its activity in working-class areas, largely the old industrial sectors, and in the automobile industry. The party favours the expropriation of all capital not reinvested in job creation and industrial production and immediate and dramatic increases in salaries for the low paid. Critical of the Right and the established Left, the LO has been able to maintain a small but significant level of support within the trade union movement. Less intellectual as a party than the *Ligue Communiste Révolutionnaire*, it concentrates very much on the daily problems of low-paid workers.

Arlette Laguiller has been a candidate in every presidential election since 1974; her vote has, in percentage terms, remained stable at 2.3 per cent in 1974 and 1981, dropping to 1.99 per cent in 1988. In alliance with the *Ligue Communiste Révolutionnaire*, the LO obtained 3.08 per cent in the 1979 European elections; in 1984, LO obtained 2.06 per cent. The highest score obtained by LO was in the municipal elections of 1977 when in Orléans and two other industrial cities it scored more than 10 per cent on the first ballot.

Ligue Communiste Révolutionnaire — LCR

Headquarters	:	2 Richard Lenoir, F-93108 Montreuil tel: 859 23 00)
Leader	:	Alain Krivine
Membership	:	6,000
Founded	:	1966

Formed as a result of a division in the Communist Party's youth movement, the LCR played a "distinguished" role in the May events of 1968. It was banned by the government in 1973 for its "revolutionary activity", resulting from violent street clashes with extreme-right student groups. It has always had a Parisian intellectual image and its former strategy of working through the student movement to reach the working class was never really very effective. It has been prominent whenever student unrest has occurred since 1968, notably in 1976 and 1986.

Electorally, it has never been particularly concerned with winning votes, but always used election campaigns for propaganda purposes for the cause. In 1978 its 170 candidates obtained 0.33 per cent of the vote.

Continually subject to division, in spite of the longevity of its leadership, the decision of a large proportion of the LCR to join the *Nouvelle Gauche* will inevitably reduce its presence further as an organized Trotskyist group.

Front National — FN

Headquarters	:	8 rue du Général Clergerie, F-75116 Paris
Leader	:	Jean-Marie Le Pen
Secretary-general	:	Carl Lang
Founded	:	1972

History

In recent years the *Front National* has been the strongest European party of the extreme Right. The phenomenon of the *Front National* has had an extremely powerful impact on the whole of the French political spectrum from Right to Left and has forced some of France's major political parties to come to terms with it.

The extreme Right has come to the fore on several occasions in French political history. It has its origins in the anti-republicanism of the 19th century, and also in the anti-semitism which culminated in the famous Dreyfus affair of the 1890s. It was also a significant feature during the depression and the rise of Nazi Germany in the 1930s, when the *Croix du Feu, Action Française, Parti Social Français* and the *Parti Populaire* were all part of the anti-democratic extreme Right.

In the 1950s it had a short-lived but powerful revival in the form of the right-wing populist movement led by Pierre Poujade, which made a particular impact among small shopkeepers and artisans. A further reservoir of support for the far right was the war in Algeria and the subsequent return to France of a large number of French *colons*, who settled in southern France and around Paris in particular. Some of these had been active in the OAS, and many became bitterly hostile to North African immigrants in France.

For much of the Fifth Republic, however, the far Right remained weak in electoral terms. The *Front National* was founded in 1972, but initially made little impact. Its dominant leader, Jean-Marie le Pen was himself candidate for the first time in a presidential election in 1974 when he obtained 0.7 per cent of the vote. In 1981 he was not even able to obtain the support of the 500 elected representatives which is necessary to become a candidate in a presidential election.

The *Front National* first made a major impact at a by-election in Dreux in the autumn of 1983, when a list led by Stirbois, one of the leading figures within the party won 16.72 per cent of the vote in the first round thus forcing an alliance with the more orthodox Right. The *Front National* also obtained 9.3 per cent in an election at Aulnay-sous-Bois in traditional communist territory near Paris, and later Le Pen himself won 12 per cent in a by-election in the Morbihan in Brittany (Le Pen's birthplace, but where there were very few foreign immigrants).

Le Pen subsequently made a major impact on national television. The *Front National* obtained 10.95 per cent in the 1984 European elections and 10 seats in the European Parliament (helped by proportional representation). In the 1985 cantonal elections it won 10 per cent in those cantons where it put up candidates. In the 1986 legislative elections, which were also fought under a system of proportional representation, it obtained 9.8 per cent of the vote and was able to form a parliamentary group in the National Assembly with 35 seats.

Its best result of all was in the first round of the presidential elections in 1988, when Le Pen obtained 14.4 per cent of the vote in the first round. In the legislative elections a month later, however, its vote fell to 9.65 per cent. Due to the reintroduction of the majority system of voting, it only obtained one seat, that of Mme Yann Piat, in the Var. She subsequently left the party, leaving it currently without a seat in the

National Assembly. The *Front National* later suffered another severe blow with the death of its secretary-general and chief organizer, Jean-Pierre Stirbois.

Support

The *Front National* has won a consistent level of support at around ten per cent in recent elections (apart from its even higher score in the first round of the 1988 presidential elections). This is well beyond the level of support for the classical extreme Right, and the *Front National* has successfully managed to tap a wider protest vote, including a considerable number of former communist voters. It has been relatively weak in some traditionally right regions (in the west of France, for example) and been particularly strong in those areas with high concentrations of North African immigrants (although its performance has nevertheless been uneven in these areas). It has also had particularly strong implementation among the *pied noir* community.

In regional terms, the *Front National* has been strongest in Marseille and on the Côte d'Azur, although it has also won high votes in many other regions of France.

There has also been an evolution in the sociological composition of its electorate. Comparing its 1986 and 1988 election results, one discovers a significant increase in support from the agricultural sector, from shopkeepers and small scale independent businessmen and from blue-collar workers, particularly in the private sector. The *Front National* has also increased its support amongst the younger male electorate and amongst non-practising Catholics.

Organization

As leader of the *Front National*, Jean-Marie Le Pen operates both as main spokesman for the party and as final arbiter of all political decision-making. Until his death in 1988, Jean-Pierre Stirbois, as secretary-general, acted with full and uncontested authority over the movement as a whole and was primarily responsible for the well structured local and regional implantation of the *Front National*.

The FN congress meets on average every two years to elect the party's central committee on the basis of the candidates proposed by the secretary-general and the leader of the party. The central committee is composed of 100 members. In turn the central committee appoints a *bureau politique* which is composed of 20 members and, in principle, has executive authority.

Every six months, or more frequently if

the situation warrants, the national council of the *Front National* may be convened by the party leader. Composed of all central committee members, plus regional secretaries and internal committee secretaries, it provides a willing and enthusiastic audience for major political statements by Jean-Marie Le Pen.

Although organized tightly in each of the French *départements*, the FN has established an intermediate political authority at regional level by the appointment of a regional secretary in each of the 22 regions.

In the European Parliament the FN is the dominant component within the Group of the European Right that was formed in 1984.

Policies

The *Front National* is a populist party of the far Right, which has appealed to those sectors of the population worried about immigration, insecurity in the inner city areas (which the *Front National* has closely linked with immigration), unemployment and more general uncertainty about the future. It has succeeded in occupying the political terrain vacated by the republican Right as far as nationalism is concerned, and by the Communist Party as far as unemployment is concerned.

The *Front National's* clear-cut positions on these issues has enabled it to contrast itself sharply with the caution of other French political parties of both the Right and the Left (even including the communists to a certain extent) which have had to come to terms with the responsibilities of office. The *Front National* has thus been able to claim that it speaks the language of direct common sense rather than the coded language of other politicians, and dares to say out loud what others only whisper.

The *Front National* has not been left in complete political isolation, however, and the other parties of the Right, in particular, have had to respond to it. Alliances between the *Front National* and other right-wing parties were forged as early as 1983 in the commune of Dreux. Moreover, in the areas of Marseille and the Côte d'Azur, in eastern France and in the areas around Lyon, as well as in the Paris suburbs, the Gaullist and Giscardian parties have sometimes, in practice, had to form local or regional alliances with the *Front National*, in spite of opposition to such alliances by both the RPR and the UDF on a national level. In the second round of the 1988 legislative elections, nine RPR-UDF candidates in the Marseille region withdrew in favour of the better placed candidates of the *Front National*. In return, the FN actively supported RPR-UDF candidates in other constituencies.

This has led to certain divisions within the other parties of the Right as to whether they should have anything to do with the *Front National*. Opposition to the *Front National* has also been a mobilizing force for political parties on the Left, and for other groups, such as trade unions and explicit anti-racist groups, for example *SOS Racisme*.

Le Pen, himself, has sharply attacked both the Left and the Right, although he has left open the possibility of a certain co-operation with the latter. In 1988, for example, Le Pen announced that he preferred the bad choice of Jacques Chirac to the worse choice of François Mitterrand in the second ballot of the presidential elections, thus distancing himself from the political establishment while indicating a minimal allegiance to the orthodox Right in order to preserve the interests of the *Front National* at local level, and facilitate alliances for legislative and municipal elections.

In policy terms, the *Front National* has emphasized a number of clear themes. One is nationalism, and the need for France to maintain its pride, identity and traditions. The French state should regain its authority. A second theme is immigration, where the party points out the dangers of large concentrations of foreigners (especially from North Africa) for France's cultural identity, as well as increasing unemployment and crime levels. The *Front National* wants immigrants to adapt or leave, illegal immigrants and delinquents to be expelled, and multicultural education to be stopped. A third and related theme is law and order, where the FN calls for an increase in the size of the police force and the restoration of the death penalty.

The *Front National* has also made a major theme of France's moral decadence. The family should be restored to its proper role, and measures taken to increase the French birth rate. On the issue of AIDS (*SIDA* in French) Le Pen has called for the creation of *sidatoriums*.

The FN's economic policy is also populist. The economy should be liberalized and there should be deregulation and lower taxes. Ownership should be diffused among millions of small capitalists and small family farmers. On the other hand there should be French and European preference in foreign trade.

The FN is not opposed to the European Community, but strongly defends the concept of the Europe of the nation states. It abstained on the Single European Act. It calls, however, for a stronger European identity in the world (with Eastern Europe included) and for a common European defence. It is strongly anti-communist.

Le Pen's rhetorical flourishes have occasionally caused great controversy. He has associated the *Front National* with Joan of Arc, for example, and sees himself as the saviour of France. At times he has been violently critical of individual politicians of Jewish origin and described the Holocaust as a mere "detail" as well as attacking many public figures — musicians and writers — because of the colour of their skin. More recently such attacks have led to the resignation of several prominent members of the *Front National*, notably of its only member elected to the National Assembly in 1988, and earlier of a member of the European Parliament, Olivier d'Ormesson, elected on the FN list in 1984.

Personalities

The party's dominant figure is Jean-Marie Le Pen, a former paratrooper who served in the Algerian war and was first elected to the French National Assembly on the Poujadist list in 1956. After 1958 Le Pen was long relegated to the sidelines, although he supported the extreme right candidate, Tixier Vignancour, in the 1965 presidential election. He has only been a prominent figure again since 1983.

Les Verts
(Confédération Ecologiste — Parti Ecologiste)

Headquarters	: 9 rue Vergniaud, F-75013 Paris
Founded	: 1984

History

The French Greens were among the first ecologists to make an electoral impact in Europe, and have maintained a certain level of support. They have not consolidated their early gains, however, partly because of the French electoral system, but partly because of their own electoral divisions.

Green candidates were standing as early as 1973, when one such candidate polled 2.9 per cent in Mulhouse in Alsace. In 1974 René Dumont stood as an ecologist candidate in the presidential elections, and polled 1.32 per cent of the vote.

After ecologist candidates polled well in the 1977 local elections, 200 candidates were put forward under the banner *Ecologie '78* in the 1978 legislative elections, obtaining 2.1 per cent of the vote.

Profiting from proportional representation in the 1979 European elections, the list *Europe Ecologie* that was headed by Mme Solange Fernex won 4.4 per cent of the vote, only narrowly below the five per cent threshold for representation in the European Parliament. In 1980 a *Mouvement d'Ecologie Politique* was formally constituted.

In the 1981 presidential elections Brice Lalonde, the president of the French Friends of the Earth obtained 3.9 per cent but ecologists subsequently only polled 1.1 per cent in the legislative elections.

In 1982 *Les Verts — Parti Ecologiste* was formally constituted as a political party and in 1984 merged with a confederation of other ecologist movements to establish the *Confédération Ecologiste–Parti Ecologiste*.

In the 1984 European elections they stood under the label *Les Verts — Europe Ecologie* (a list headed by Didier Anger), but only polled 3.4 per cent, worse than in 1979. Their position was undercut by a rival list, *Entente Radicale Ecologiste* (ERE), which was a broader centre-left grouping, but in which Brice Lalonde was a prominent member. ERE obtained 3.3 per cent.

In the 1986 legislative elections *Les Verts* only polled 1.2 per cent. In 1986 *Les Verts* also won a case that they had brought before the European Court of Justice on the system of European Parliament financing of political parties for the 1984 election campaign. In the 1988 presidential elections, however, their candidate, Antoine Waechter obtained 3.8 per cent of the vote. They took practically no part in the subsequent legislative elections.

Support

Les Verts have only been able to make an electoral impact at local level, in those national elections where proportional representation has been used at national level (e.g. European elections) or in other nationwide rather than constituency-based elections (e.g. French presidential elections). They have primarily drawn votes from the Centre and Centre-left, and have been more successful among young voters.

Alsace has been easily their strongest area, because of local environmental issues (e.g. pollution of the Rhine), proximity to environmentally conscious Germany and because of the presence of Alsace-based politicians at the head of ecologist lists (e.g. Mme Fernex in 1979, Antoine Waechter in 1988). The ecologists won 10.6 per cent in the Haut-Rhin in the 1979 European elections and 6.5 per cent in Alsace as a whole in 1984. Antoine Waechter's presidential bid in 1988 obtained 9.4 per cent support in the Bas-Rhin and 9.24 per cent in the Haut-Rhin. Elsewhere *Les Verts* have been strongest in eastern France (Territory of Belfort, Jura) and in mountain regions (Savoy, Haute Alpes), in all of which Waechter obtained around 5 per cent support in 1988.

Organization

The party is organized in sections and groups which send representatives to an annual general assembly. This elects the movement's spokesmen (there is no single leader) and national secretary.

Les Verts are members of the European Greens.

Policies

The French Greens have concentrated on ecology issues, and have not forged a wider alliance with left alternative groups, as have *Die Grünen* in Germany. Although their voters have more sympathy with the Left, the French Greens have always emphasized that they do not fit into the old schemas of Left, Centre and Right. They have had severe internal divisions, and have been uncertain in the past as to whether to function as a fully-fledged political party and whether they should co-operate with other political groupings. The arrival of Pierre Juquin and the New Left poses this latter question in fresh form.

Les Verts are highly critical of civil nuclear energy, and campaigned, for example, against the construction of the proposed Plogoff plant in 1979. They seek a freeze on the construction of new nuclear power stations and a gradual disengagement from nuclear energy. The widespread support, even on the French Left, for nuclear energy has undercut their support on this issue.

Les Verts support decentralization and emphasize the fight against rural depopulation. They would like to see the French Senate replaced by a Council of the Regions, and have strongly defended minority cultures and languages within France. They support a Europe of the Regions.

They have also called for flexible working time, and the introduction of a 35-hour week (without salary compensation apart for those on low salaries). They seek the introduction of referenda by popular initiative and generalized proportional representation.

They call for progressive disarmament and the halting of nuclear tests such as those carried out by France in the Pacific. They have also called for a halt to the pillaging of the third world.

Regional parties

Regionally-based parties have had only very limited electoral success in France, with its high degree of centralization and electoral systems, which have penalized smaller parties.

The least weak regional parties have been in Brittany and Corsica, but there have also been small groups in the French Basque country and in French Flanders, as well as Occitan movements.

(i)   Brittany

Breton nationalism has had a lengthy history, with a large number of groups and parties having been created to defend the Breton language and Brittany's ethnic and cultural identity. A more recent persistent theme has been the need to attach the *département* of *Loire Atlantique* to the Breton Administrative Region, from which it is currently excluded.

An even smaller minority has called for full independence for Brittany. A party with such an objective, *Party National Breton*, was first founded in 1911. In 1927 a *Parti Autonomiste Breton* was also founded. Breton nationalism lost ground, however, after some of its adherents collaborated with the Germans during the Second World War. After 1945 Breton causes were revived however by the broad based *Comité d'étude et de liaison des intérêts Brétons* (CELIB). More recently, new movements and parties have developed, such as the *Mouvement pour l'organization de la Bretagne* (MOB), the *Strollad Ar Vro* (Party of the People), the *Parti pour l'organisation d'une Bretagne libre* (POBL) and for a while in the 1960s and 1970s even a violent movement, the *Front de la libération de la Brétagne*, although this latter has died down. The most significant Breton party, however, has been the *Union Démocratique Bretonne* (UDB).

Union Démocratique Bretonne — UDB

Headquarters   : B.P. 215, 44007
                         Nantes

The UDB (*Unvaniezh Demokratel Breizh*) was founded in 1963–64. It has taken part in elections since 1971, and has done particularly well in cantonal elections. In 1977 when it took part in lists of the Union of the Left it won a considerable number of seats on local communes, and even succeeded in electing a regional councillor, Ronon Leprohon, from the city of Brest. In the 1981 legislative elections its candidates averaged 2.2 per cent of the vote. In recent elections, however, its vote has dropped. It has become more critical of its former allies on the Left, and it has suffered from internal divisions and lost a number of its more prominent leaders.

The UDB has local cells and sections organized in federations, and has a political bureau, consisting of 12 members elected by a party congress every two years and also representatives of the federations. It has had up to 2,000 members in the past. It has also had a federation in Paris. Its organization has been characterized by democratic centralism. The UDB is linked with the European Free Alliance.

The UDB also produces a monthly newspaper, *Le Peuple Breton*, which has had a past circulation of up to 10,000 (currently 6,000), and a Breton supplement, *Pobl Breizh*.

The UDB has been on the Left of the political spectrum, and has condemned Brittany's colonial status. It has defended the Breton language and culture, and has called for Loire Atlantique to be added to a reunified Brittany. It has also emphasized environmental protection and strongly opposed the construction of the proposed Plogoff nuclear power station. The UDB has opposed violence.

(ii) Corsica

Corsican individuality has been recognized by the French government through its granting of a special statute for the island in 1987. (Corsica received a directly elected regional assembly before other regions of France, with more extensive powers). There have been two main autonomist movements, Dr Simeoni's *Union du Peuple Corse* and Pierre Poggioli's *Mouvement Corse pour l'Autodétermination*. There has also been a more extremist group espousing violence and fuller independence, the FLNC (the Corsican National Liberation Front).

Unione di u Populu Corsu — UPC

Headquarters	: c/o Assemblée Territoriale Bastia, Corsica
Leader	: Dr Edmond Siméoni
Secretary-general	: Xavier Belgodere

A group called *Action pour la Renaissance de la Corse* (ARC), led by Dr Edmond Simeoni was involved in a battle against the police in

1975. Simeoni was arrested, and the ARC was subsequently banned.

The new UPC was founded in July 1977. In the first elections to the new directly elected regional assembly in 1982 (the first such elections held in France), the UPC obtained 10.6 per cent of the vote and seven out of 61 seats.

In the Corsican Assembly elections of 1984 the UPC slipped to three seats. It contested the 1986 elections in an alliance with the *Mouvement Corse pour l'Autodétermination* (MCA), winning six seats. Following the banning of the MCA in January 1987, the UPC joined with its successor, the *Cuncolta Nazionalista* (CN) to contest repeat elections in Haute Corse. Its vote declined, and the UPC later withdrew from its alliance with the CN.

The UPC has a 21 member political bureau, and has claimed a membership of 10,000. It has been active in the European Free Alliance.

The UPC has called for more autonomy for Corsica to be achieved without violence. Its leading figure is still Dr Edmond Simeoni.

(iii) Basque Country

The Fench Basque country consists of three historic Basque provinces, which do not form a French *département* in their own right, being part of the wider *département* of Pyrénées-Atlantique. Compared to the part of the Basque country in Spain, there has been little violence, separatism has been weak, and there have been no significant Basque regional parties. The main demand has been for a separate Basque *département*. A political movement called *Enbata* was formed which won a few votes in elections in the 1960s but was banned in 1974.

In 1986 an EMA list (Basque patriots of the Left) was put up for the regional council elections, winning 6 per cent of the votes within the Basque country. Its main support was in the interior regions, where the French left-wing parties have made little impact. EMA called for closer links with the Spanish Basque country (south *Euskadi*), the development of Basque schools (*ekastolas*) and more general defence of Basque language and culture.

(iv) Flanders

A *Vlaams Federalistische Partij* (Flemish Federalist Party) has been established among the small Flemish speaking community in northern

France, and has taken part in the activities of the European Free Alliance. Flemish regionalization and European federalism have been its twin themes.

(v) Occitania

There have been a number of Occitan regional movements, such as the *Parti Nationaliste Occitan*, the *Mouvement Socialiste Occitan*, *Lutte Occitane* and *Poble d'Oc*. *Volem Viure al Pais* (We want to live in this land) is another such group, and has been active in the European Free Alliance.

Occitan movements have had more impact on the cultural than political levels, and have defended Occitan language (close to Provencal) and traditional culture.

Regional separatism has had little support, mainly because the wider Occitan region composes a very wide and heterogeneous part of southern France.

Greece

Maria Mendrinou

The country

Greece has a population of almost 10 million, of whom over 3 million live in its capital city of Athens. In comparison with most other European countries, Greece still has a large agricultural sector, but there has been rapid urbanization in recent years, primarily in the Athens region, but also in Thessaloniki, Patras, Volos and other cities.

In ethnic, linguistic and religious terms Greece is a generally homogeneous country. The vast majority of the people are of Greek mother tongue, although there is a small Turkish minority in Thrace, and also tiny Vlach, Slav and Albanian minorities. Greece is overwhelmingly Greek Orthodox in religious affiliation.

Political institutions

As a result of the plebiscite of Dec. 8, 1974, in which 70 per cent of the Greek electorate opted for a republic rather than a monarchy, and of the subsequent new Constitution of June 1975, Greece became a "presidential parliamentary democracy".

The Constitution provides for a unicameral Parliament of between 200 and 300 members, although in practice it is fixed at the latter figure. The 300 members are elected for a maximum four-year period (with the possibility of early dissolution). The minimum voting age is 18, and voting is compulsory, with certain exemptions, but penalties for not voting are not heavy. 288 of the 300 members are elected in the 56 electoral districts while the remaining 12 are allocated to "state deputies" elected not within individual constituencies, but "at large" within the whole country as one electoral district.

The electoral system is based on the Hagenbach-Bischoff system of proportional representation. Pure proportional representation is modified in national elections by a system of reinforced proportional representation. The electoral system mirrors the political structure and the dynamics of the Greek political system.

The 1985 electoral law with the amendments of 1989 defines two distributions of the seats. The first distribution takes place on the basis of the 56 electoral districts while the second one, using the remaining votes, takes place on the basis of the 13 larger electoral districts. Unallocated seats are then distributed to the parties or coalitions with the larger remaining number of votes. The 1989 amendments also provide that parties or coalitions present in at least three-quarters of the electoral districts of the country and with 2% of the vote in the whole country gain at least three seats, while parties or coalitions with more than 1% of the vote gain at least one seat. The 1989 amendments also reintroduced the preference vote. In general the new electoral law is more proportional and supports the minor parties.

The Government is the major agent of the political system which directs the general policy of the country. Along with the President of the Republic, it occupies the leading position in the executive function. The executive power was strengthened by the Constitution in order to provide greater governmental stability.

The presidency of the Republic is one of the most debated and ambiguous institutions established by the Constitution of 1975. This latter created a strong presidency with far reaching reserve powers which have been lessened as a result of the constitutional revision of 1986, which was occupied with restricting the scope of the President's actions by making him interdependent with other agents. The President is elected by open ballot of the Parliament for a five-year term under the complex procedures set out in the Constitution. Constitutionally, the President functions as a figure above party politics.

The Prime Minister is now more powerful than the President in theory as well as in practice. He is the leader of the majority party.

Greece joined the European Community in 1981, and has 24 seats in the European Parliament. Unlike the national elections pure proportional representation is used, with the whole of Greece forming one national electoral district.

Brief political history

1821   Revolution brings Greece independence from Ottoman Empire.

1830   Greek state formally recognized by Protocol of London.

1832   At behest of England, France and Russia absolute monarchy established in Greece, under Otto of Bavaria, contrary to the Greek will for a Republic as expressed during the years of the Revolution when three National Assemblies were convoked. Factions with a highly personalized and local character gradually develop, of which the most important are named the "English", "French" and "Russian" parties, after their respective links with the Great Powers.

1843   Uprising of Sept. 3 leads to Otto conceding a new Constitution in 1844, which provides for a bicameral assembly, and a constitutional monarchy (parties now develop a stronger organizational focus within Parliament but essentially remain personal factions without specific ideologies, and functioning on a patron-client basis).

Map of Greece showing the 56 electoral districts (corresponding to the 51 *Nomoi* or prefectures, with the exception of Athens and Thessaloniki), and number of seats in each district.

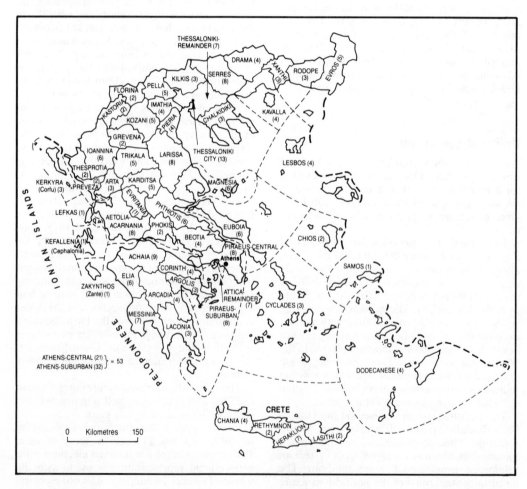

Source: adapted from *World Atlas of Elections*.

1862   Military revolt leads to expulsion of Wittelsbach dynasty, and to their replacement by a Danish Prince of the Glucksberg dynasty in March of 1863, who becomes George I (1863-1913).

1864   New Constitution, which defines political system as parliamentary monarchy.

1875   As a result of campaign led by Charilaos Trikoupis, George I accepts fundamental principle that the governing party should have a declared majority in the Parliament.

1880s– 90s   Two party system, with alternation of Liberals and Conservatives (not formally organized as such) in government under respective leadership of Trikoupis and Deliyannis.

1893   Economic crisis.

1897   Greece defeated in war with Turkey. Leads to reparations and new period of crisis.

1909   Military coup by Goudi brings Eleftherios Venizelos to power, a charismatic politician from Crete who dominates the Greek political scene up to 1936. Venizelos becomes champion of the so-called "Great Idea", whose objective is the unification of all lands inhabited by Greeks.

1910   Venizelos founds Liberal Party, which wins broad support, especially from emerging entrepreneurial middle class, and workers and peasants (and later also from inhabitants of New Greece, and refugees from Asia Minor).

1912–13   First and Second Balkan Wars are crowned by Greek success, and lead to massive expansion of Greek territory, with annexation of Macedonia and part of Epirus as well as Crete.

1913   King George I assassinated and replaced by King Constantine I.

1914   Outbreak of World War I leads to intense controversy as to whether Greece should participate on the side of the Entente powers (as favoured by Venizelos) or remain neutral (as advocated by King Constantine, who, along with the People's Party, favoured the Central powers). In 1915 this leads to the so-called "National Schism between Venizelists and Conservative Royalists". Venizelos twice forced to resign.

1917   King Constantine is forced to leave Greece under pressure from the Entente powers. Venizelos, Prime Minister of re-unified Greece.

1919   Greek troops in Smyrna region of Asia Minor.

1920   Venizelos defeated in elections by anti-Venizelist People's Party, King restored.

1922   Disastrous defeat for Greece in Asia Minor at great political, psychological and economic cost for Greece, and with arrival of 1.3 million refugees into Greece. Military coup, King abdicates and is replaced by his son, George II.

1922–36   Period of great political instability with dominant issue the so-called "regime question" as to whether Greece should be a republic or a parliamentary monarchy (monarchy abolished in 1924 plebiscite, dictatorship of General Pangalos from 1925–6, periods of deadlock between Venizelist Liberal Party and Conservative People's Party. Venizelist attempted coups in 1933 and 1935. Venizelos goes into exile, monarchy restored by plebiscite of November 1935 with return of George II).

1936   Metaxas imposes dictatorship (political parties repressed).

1940   Italian invasion of Greece.

1941   German invasion of Greece succeeded by Axis occupation of the country (Communist Party emerges as a central element of the Resistance, through domination of National Liberation Front — EAM and National Popular Liberation Army — ELAS).

1944   Liberation of Greece, Georgios Papandreou government in exile returns to Greece, Communist revolt.

1945   Varkiza agreement fails to achieve long term solution to Greek Constitutional crisis, left-right polarization worsens.

1946   Right-wing alliance wins elections with Communists abstaining from participation, plebiscite supports return of King from wartime exile.

1946–49 Civil War between Greek government and Communists ends with Communist defeat in 1949, but leads to schism in Greek political and social life which is to survive into the 1970s.

1949–63 Governments of the right monopolize power. Two largest political families are centre and right, which at first are split into a number of small parties or personalized factions, taking part in shifting electoral coalitions. 1952 new Constitution. 1952–55 government of Marshal Papagos, the founder of the Greek Rally Party, (ES — *Hellinikas Synagermos*), 1955–63 government of Konstantinos Karamanlis, founder of the National Radical Union, ERE — *Ethnike Rizospastike Enosis* (the successor party to the Greek Rally). Electoral system alternates between majority system and reinforced proportional representation, continued restrictions on left. Communist Party illegal, and left participating in elections through EDA — United Democratic Left.

1963 Centre finally manages to achieve unity under Georgios Papandreou, and new Centre Union (EK — *Enosis Kentrou*) wins power in elections.

1963–67 Centre Union government of Papandreou ends with Papandreou's forced resignation after confrontation with King Constantine in July 1965. Unsuccessful attempts for a Centre Union government, first with Athanasiadis-Noras and second with Tsirimokos. Finally defection (apostasia) of 45 members of the Centre Union under Stefanos Stefanopoulos, and government with the support of ERE and the Progressives. Elections are planned for May 28, 1967.

April 21 1967 Military coup by colonels.

1967–74 Dictatorship of military junta led by Papadopoulos (1968, King forced into exile after failed counter-coup, authoritarian Constitution introduced with civil liberties restricted; 1973, Presidential Parliamentary Republic established, and Papadopoulos subsequently elected President; Papadopoulos overthrown from within military, and Gizikis becomes President, with Ioannidis as regime strongman; 1974, Cyprus crisis and Turkish invasion leads to the collapse of the dictatorship).

July 23, 1974 Gizikis invites Konstantinos Karamanlis to return from exile and become Prime Minister in government of national unity; 1968 Constitution repealed and 1952 Constitution restored; Communist Party finally legalized.

November 1974 Karamanlis' new party, *Nea Demokratia*—New Democracy, wins elections, defeating Centre Alliance, new Panhellenic Socialist Movement (PASOK) of Andreas Papandreou and United Left (two Communist parties and the EDA). Karamanlis becomes Prime Minister.

Dec. 8, 1974 69 per cent of Greek electorate opt for a republic and under 31 per cent for a constitutional monarchy.

1974–81 New Democracy governments, with Konstantinos Karamanlis as Prime Minister from 1974–80 (with Konstantinos Tsatsos as President) and Georgios Rallis from 1980–1 (with Karamanlis as President).
(1975, new Constitution introduced; 1977, New Democracy wins elections with reduced majority, PASOK becomes main opposition party and centre fragments; 1981, Greece becomes full member of European Community; 1981, PASOK wins elections and Andreas Papandreou becomes Prime Minister.)

1981–present PASOK governments, with Andreas Papandreou as Prime Minister (Karamanlis, President until 1985 and then Christos Sartzetakis).
(1985 crisis over Sartzetakis nomination and manner of victory; electoral system modified; PASOK re-elected; President's powers subsequently reduced in constitutional revision. 1988 Koskotas's scandal shakes PASOK's government. 1989 changes in electoral law, elections planned for June 18, 1989.)

Main features of the current political system

The basic characteristics of the political system can be grouped into four categories. The first and the broadest is the domination of the political system by three major political families, the

Right, the Centre, and the Left, which had their roots in the two conflicts of the 20th century; the first two in the National Schism and the third in the Civil War. This tripartite structure was dominant in the pre-1967 political system but only after 1981 did it clearly re-emerge with the Right being expressed by New Democracy (ND), the Centre by PASOK and the Left by KKE. These three parties are supported by 95% of the electorate and have almost all the seats in Parliament. Although they are based on the pre-1967 political system, notable changes have taken place. Greece is now a Republic and there is little or no interest in the restoration of the monarchy. New Democracy is clearly linked to the old Right family but monarchy and even anti-Communism are no longer strong mobilizing factors. Moreover the far Right was discredited by the junta and New Democracy has generally kept its distance from it, while it has made a direct appeal to voters (and politicians) from the former Centre tradition. On the other hand in the Centre the revived centre parties lost their republicanism as a mobilizing factor while, as a result of low-key leadership and subsequent new polarization of the political system, the old-style centre parties fragmented and almost disappeared.

PASOK can now more accurately be seen as the main inheritor of the old centre tradition but with left-of-centre style and rhetoric to suit the changed post-1974 political mood. The Left is mostly dominated by the Communist party (KKE). The other Communist Party, the KKE party of the interior, split in 1987 into two parties; the Greek Left (EAR — Hellinike Aristera) and the KKE Interior — Renewed Left (KKE interior — Ananeotike Aristera), while the United Democratic Left (EDA — Eniaia Democratike Aristera) is still present. In 1988 the vigorous competition among the main Communist parties decreased.

However the three-party system has not weakened the existence of vigorous competition between the two big political parties, PASOK and ND, which is the second characteristic of the political system. This bipolar competition is due to the special position of the Centre as it was formed in the post-war period, which made it the only possible alternative to the Right. PASOK and ND gained about 96% of the parliamentary seats and in the elections of 1981 the elements characteristic of a development of a two-party system appeared. Here the function of the electoral system — reinforced proportional representation — whose objective is the reinforcement of the two largest political parties and the formation of a sufficient parliamentary majority for the existence of one-party govern-ment, is obvious. This is the third characteristic of the Greek political system. In each of the four elections since 1974 the absolute majority of the parliamentary seats was given to one of the two main parties. Even though the basic reason for this is the electoral system, the governments were characterized by stability and a broad and disciplined majority.

The reinforcing function of the electoral system also makes voters aware of the wasted vote, turning them to one of the two big parties, and reinforcing in this way bipolar competition in decisive elections. The confirmation of its function is obvious in other elections such as those for the European Parliament, where the percentage of the smaller parties is perceptibly higher than in that of parliamentary elections. The limited opportunity for the entry of the smaller parties into Parliament thus forms the fourth characteristic of the political system, the extra-parliamentary multiparty framework.

The Greek political system is characterized by a variety of modern and traditional features. The most striking element of modernization has been the development of more modern party organizational structures.

In the past, Greek political parties have been dominated by local clientelism, with strong local and regional party "notables", little mass organization and poor co-ordination at national level; only the Communists have had a longer organizational tradition. Since 1974 PASOK, in particular, has developed a much more tightly structured organization, with proper local branches, a mass membership and with local and regional parties much more clearly subordinate to a strong national party organization.

Other elements of modernization have included a greater measure of ideology in party political programmes (socialism in the case of PASOK, more recently economic liberalism in the case of New Democracy), and greater use of political campaigning and marketing techniques.

On the other hand a number of traditional elements remain. The Greek political system is still highly fluid. New parties are constantly being created, new alliances being forged and schisms taking place within existing parties. The strength of individual personalities is still the major determinant of Greek political success. Karamanlis and Papandreou have personified New Democracy and PASOK respectively. New Democracy entered into difficulties after Karamanlis ceased to be its leader, and the future of PASOK after Papandreou is also uncertain. Finally a strong tradition of clientelism and party patronage still remains,

Seats and percentage vote won in general elections 1946–85

	1946	1950	1951	1952	1956	1958	1961	1963	1964	1974	1977	1981	1985
Enosis Ethnikofronon (Union of Nationalists)	9	—	—	—	—	—	—	—	—	—	—	—	—
	2.49%												
Enomene Parataxe Ethnikofronon (United Party of Nationalists)	206	—	—	—	—	—	—	—	—	—	—	—	—
	55.12%												
Ethniko Komma Hellados (National Party of Greece)	20	7	—	—	—	—	—	—	—	—	—	—	—
	5.96%	3.65%											
Komma Fileleftheron (Liberal Party)	48	56	57	—	—	36	—	—	—	—	2	—	—
	14.39%	17.24%	19.04%			20.68%					1.09%		
Ethnike Politike Enosis (National Political Union)	68	—	—	—	—	—	—	—	—	—	—	—	—
	19.28%												
Enosis Agrotikon Kommaton (Union of Agrarian Parties)	1	—	—	—	—	—	—	—	—	—	—	—	—
	0.67%												
Laiko Party (Populist Party)	—	62	2	—	—	—	—	—	—	—	—	—	—
		18.80%	6.66%										
Politike Anexartetos Parataxis (Political Independent Party)	—	16	—	—	—	—	—	—	—	—	—	—	—
		8.15%											
Neo Komma (New Party)	—	1	—	—	—	—	—	—	—	—	—	—	—
		2.50%											
Metopon Ethnikes Anademiourgias (Front of National Recreation)	—	7	—	—	—	—	—	—	—	—	—	—	—
		5.27%											
Komma Georgiou Papandreou (George Papandreou's Party)	—	35	—	—	—	—	—	—	—	—	—	—	—
		10.67%											
Ethnike Prodeftike Enosis Kendrou (National Progressive Centre Party)	—	45	74	—	—	—	—	—	—	—	—	—	—
		16.44%	23.49%										
Parataxis Agroton kai Ergazomenon (Party of Agrarians and Labourers)	—	3	1	—	—	—	—	—	—	—	—	—	—
		2.62%	1.23%										
Demokratike Parataxe (Democratic Party)	—	18	—	—	—	—	—	—	—	—	—	—	—
		9.70%											
Hellinikos Synagermos (Greek Rally)	—	—	114	247	—	—	—	—	—	—	—	—	—
			36.53%	49.22%									
Eniaia Demokratike Aristera (United Democratic Left, EDA)	—	—	10	—	—	79	—	28	22	—	—	—	—
			10.57%			24.43%		14.34%	11.80%				
Enosis Kommaton (Union of Parties)	—	—	—	51	—	—	—	—	—	—	—	—	—
				34.22%									
Ethnike Rizospastike Enosis (National Radical Union), ERE	—	—	—	—	165	171	176	132	—	—	—	—	—
					47.38%	47.17%	50.81%	39.37%					

Cont'd

	1946	1950	1951	1952	1956	1958	1961	1963	1964	1974	1977	1981	1985
Demokratike Enosis (Democratic Union)	—	—	—	—	132 / 48.15%	—	—	—	—	—	—	—	—
Enosis Laikou Kommatos (Union of Populist Party)	—	—	—	—	—	4 / 2.94%	—	—	—	—	—	—	—
Proodeftike Agrotike Demokratike Enosis (Progressive Agrarian Democratic Union)	—	—	—	—	—	10 / 10.62%	—	—	—	—	—	—	—
Eklogikos Synaspismos (Electoral Coalition)	—	—	—	—	—	—	100 / 33.66%	—	—	—	—	—	—
Pandemokratiko Agrotiko Metopo Helladas (Pandemocratic Agrarian Front of Greece)	—	—	—	—	—	—	24 / 14.63%	—	—	—	—	—	—
Kommo Proodeftikon (Progressive Party)	—	—	—	—	—	—	—	2 / 3.73%	—	—	—	—	—
Enosis Kentrou (Centre Union), EK	—	—	—	—	—	—	—	138 / 42.04%	171 / 52.72%	—	—	—	—
Synaspismos ERE kai Kommatos Prodeftikon (Coalition of ERE and Progressive Party)	—	—	—	—	—	—	—	—	107 / 35.26%	—	—	—	—
Nea Demokratia (New Democracy), ND	—	—	—	—	—	—	—	—	—	220 / 54.37%	172 / 41.85%	115 / 35.86%	126[1] / 40.84%
Enosis Kentrou—Nees Dynameis (Centre Union—New Forces), EK—ND	—	—	—	—	—	—	—	—	—	60 / 20.42%	—	—	—
Panhellinio Sosialistiko Kinema (Panhellinic Socialist Movement), PASOK.	—	—	—	—	—	—	—	—	—	12 / 13.58%	93 / 25.32%	172 / 48.06%	161 / 45.82%
Enomene Aristera (United Left)	—	—	—	—	—	—	—	—	—	8 / 9.47%	—	—	—
Ethnike Parataxis (National Front)	—	—	—	—	—	—	—	—	—	—	5 / 6.07%	—	—
Enosis Demokratikou Kentrou (Union of the Democratic Centre), EDEK	—	—	—	—	—	—	—	—	—	—	15 / 11.88%	—	—
Kommounistiko Komma Hellados (Communist Party of Greece), KKE	—	—	—	—	—	—	—	—	—	—	11 / 9.31%	13 / 10.92%	12 / 9.89%
Kommounistiko Komma Hellados—Esoterikou (Communist Party of Greece—Interior), KKE—Interior	—	—	—	—	—	—	—	—	—	—	2[2] / 2.70%	—	1[3] / 1.84%
Others	2 / 1.64%	—	—	2 / 7.01%	3 / 4.47%	—	—	—	—	—	—	—	—

[1] In September 1985 10 ND deputies withdrew and formed DEANA, later one more deputy was added, but in 1987 three of them returned to ND.

[2] Coalition of KKE—Interior and EDA.

[3] In spring 1987 KKE—Interior split into EAR and KKE—Interior—Renewed Left.

although now more centralized and more subject to national party control.

Among the themes and issues in Greek political life are the following:

- The clash of modern and traditional attitudes on moral and social issues;
- The stance that Greece should adopt on basic foreign policy issues (there has been a division between those advocating a more Western orientation for Greece, and those preferring a more non-aligned position. PASOK, in particular, has benefited greatly in electoral terms by playing on resentment of past Greek dependency on the United States, in particular, and advocating a more independent and strongly nationalistic foreign policy);
- Differences in Greek attitudes on the EC (PASOK was originally opposed to Greek entry, and although it has changed its stance it still emphasizes Greek sovereignty and is unenthusiastic about far-going European integration, whereas New Democracy has always been in favour of Greek entry, and is more supportive of European integration);
- Relations with the United States (after the junta anti-Americanism had grown significantly, and the future of US-Greek relations and of American military installations in Greece have remained important issues);
- The Greek position within NATO (even the right-of-centre Karamanlis withdrew Greece from the military wing of the Alliance. On the other hand, PASOK in power has been much more pragmatic on this question than its 1970s policy positions appeared to indicate);
- The future status of Cyprus;
- Future relations with Turkey (relations which have always been bad have been further threatened by new issues such as over mineral rights on the Aegean continental shelf. At the end of January 1988, however, Papandreou and the Turkish Prime Minister Özal met in Switzerland. It is uncertain how, and whether, this limited "détente" will be pursued);
- The role of the state (should the role of the Greek state be cut back, and should there be a greater measure of economic liberalism?).

Panhellinio Socialistiko Kinema — PASOK
(Panhellenic Socialist Movement)

Headquarters : Charilaou Trikoupe 50, Athens (tel: 360–9831–5)

Leader : Andreas Papandreou
Publication : *Exormese*
Youth organization : *Panhellenia Agonistike Socialistike Parataxe* (PASP)
Estimated membership: 80,000 in 1984
Founded : 1974

History

PASOK grew out of the left-wing of the Centre Union, and was strengthened as a result of its role in the struggle against the seven-year dictatorship from 1967–74. The party sees itself as the fusion of three historical traditions: first, the Resistance, especially the National Liberation Front (EAM — *Ethnike Apeleftheriko Metopo*), against the Axis Occupation; second, the Centre Union and notably the centre-left experience of 1965–1967; and third, the resistance against the military dictatorship of 1967–74.

The resistance against the dictatorship was the main source from which the founding cadres of PASOK were drawn. They had been mobilized in resistance organizations like Democratic Defence (*Demokratike Amyna*) and especially the Panhellenic Liberation Movement (PAK — *Panhellinio Apeleftheriko Kinema*).

PAK was formed in May, 1968, by the present leader of PASOK and former member of the Centre Union, Andreas Papandreou. It constituted one of the most powerful resistance organizations, with a great number of members not only within Greece, but also abroad. Its goals were not limited, however, to its activities against the Junta but it also developed a political programme which could be implemented when the country was liberated. PAK thus functioned as the basis for the creation of PASOK, offering organizational experience and the charismatic personality of Andreas Papandreou, who had withdrawn from the Centre Union in 1971. It also constituted a pole of attraction for the centre-left and other resistance organizations.

The return of Andreas Papandreou from exile after the demise of the dictatorship created a dilemma: whether it would be better to revive the old Centre Union or to create a truly new political party based on the centre-left, PAK, and other resistance organizations. Finally the latter solution was chosen and as a result of the Declaration of Sept. 3, 1974, PASOK was created. It was different from both the old Centre and the Communist left. PASOK was the first self-styled socialist party in Greek politics, except the Socialist Labour Party of Greece (SEKE — *Sosialistiko Ergatiko*

Komma Hellados), which was formed in 1918. National independence, popular sovereignty, and social justice and equality formed the basis of PASOK's programme.

In the elections of November 1974, PASOK's programme appeared to be too radical for an electorate more concerned with the preservation of a tenuous democracy. In what was nevertheless a considerable achievement, the New Socialist party gained 13.58 per cent of the votes, to become the third party in the Parliament.

In the next elections of 1977, PASOK gained 25.32 per cent of the votes doubling its electorate to become the second party. It had thus attained its goal of becoming the only credible alternative to New Democracy, thrusting aside the Centre Union.

PASOK adopted a catch-all political strategy and programme, which looked for support to the "non-privileged" Greeks and attacked foreign and domestic monopolies, and put forward the promise of a non-aligned foreign policy. Above all, it promised "change". PASOK managed to cultivate the image of a pragmatic, moderate and responsible political party, capable of being the "ruling party" of Greece.

In the elections of October, 1981, PASOK secured 48.06 per cent of the votes and became the party with the most radical programmes ever to win an election in Greece. Papandreou became Prime Minister. PASOK again won the elections of June, 1985, for another four-year term of office, with 45.8 per cent of the vote.

In September 1988 Papandreou underwent heart surgery in London, while at the same time a major financial scandal broke out in Athens with the financial collapse of Koskotas. The impact of the latter for PASOK will become apparent in the elections of June 1989.

Support

The social base of PASOK is a broad one. It has been the most successful party in inheriting the centre tradition in Greek politics, and has strong lower-middle-class support in particular. It has also appealed to those who consider themselves less privileged within Greek society.

Its electoral rise from its foundation in 1974 has been a remarkable one. It won 13.58 per cent in 1974, 25.32 per cent in 1977 and 48.06 per cent in 1981. Its 1985 results saw a falling off in the level of its support (notably in some urban areas), but it still won an impressive total of 45.8 per cent of the vote.

A remarkable feature of PASOK's support is its relative homogeneity in the different regions of Greece, without significant differ-ences between urban and rural areas. The majority of electoral districts registered between 39 per cent and 53 per cent support in the 1985 elections, and the party averaged 46.9 per cent in urban areas, 41 per cent in rural areas and 46.4 per cent in mixed areas.

PASOK was strongest in Crete, where it won its highest 1985 vote in all of Greece in the Heraklion constituency with 64.3 per cent. Among other constituencies where it won over 50 per cent in 1985 were the Dodecanese islands (56.7 per cent), the island of Chios (52.3 per cent) and the district of Achaia (52.5 per cent).

Its weakest areas include parts of Thrace (notably Xanthi at 32.3 per cent) and above all Rhodopi, where it obtained its lowest vote of 30.4 per cent in 1985. In Laconia, in the traditionally royalist heartland of the Peloponnese it only obtained 34.9 per cent. Another constituency with lower than average support was central Athens, where PASOK obtained 39.8 per cent and was considerably weaker than New Democracy in 1985.

Organization

The organizational structure of PASOK marks a change in the Greek political party system, which has traditionally been characterized by a clientelist system, based on local party patrons. The strong organization of the party does not allow leeway for its members to develop their own client network, but substitutes the individual party member with the party itself as the "patron", converting the old networks into machine politics.

In practice, however, PASOK is dominated by its leadership and especially by the strong charismatic personality of its leader which weakens in many respects its organizational structure as embodied in the party's statute. A rigid discipline exists at all levels, and dissenters have been expelled from the party.

The membership of PASOK has risen remarkably from about 20,000 in 1977 to 80,000 members as estimated at the Congress of May, 1984. These members participate in a great number of local organizations throughout the country, establishing the first really extensive party organization except for that of the Communist party.

The basic organizational unit, the local organization (TO — *Topike Organose*) is formed mostly on the basis of the place of residence, so that each TO will not exceed 80 members. On the same organizational level is the professional Organization (KO — *Kladike Organose*) which consists of members grouped by profession.

There are also the organizational cells (OP — *Organotikoi Pyrenes*).

On the departmental level, the departmental assembly (NS — *Nomarchiake Synelefse*) is elected from the party organizations within each department. Every 18 months the NS is obliged to come together and to elect the departmental committee (NE — *Nomarchiake Epitrope*) and the departmental disciplinary office (NPG — *Nomarchiako Peitharchiko Grafeio*), pursuant to the decision of the executive office of the central committee, which fixes the number of the members for both the departmental committee — which can fluctuate from 11 to 17 members — and the departmental disciplinary office — from five to seven members.

The supreme organ of the party is the congress. It consists of representatives from all the departmental organizations of the country, and from abroad; from members of the outgoing central committee and disciplinary office; from the MPs and the president of the party. It has two main responsibilities: first, it gives its decision on matters put forward by the central committee and the disciplinary office, as well as on ideological, political, and organizational issues of the party; second, it elects the party leader and the members of the central committee and the disciplinary office. It is convoked every four years, although the central committee may decide to postpone this for up to one year or, by two-thirds majority, decide on an extraordinary general congress. The departmental committees may also, by two-thirds majority, convoke the congress, in emergencies.

The president represents the party in Greece and abroad. He heads the executive office of the central committee and the congress. He is responsible for decisions on pressing issues when the executive office of the central committee cannot be convened. He has a unique position in the party, for he is a member of neither the central committee nor the executive office.

The central committee is the supreme organ of the party in between congresses. It shares the governmental policy of PASOK on the basis of the principles of the Declaration of the 3rd of September 1974, (the party's initial declaration of principle). It consists of 140 members and the president. It elects the executive office and the seven-member committee of financial control, and nominates the candidates for parliamentary elections.

One of the most powerful executive organs is the executive office of the central committee, which is charged with controlling the implementation of the decisions of the central committee. It also deals with current party political and organizational questions. In addition to the president, 13 persons make up the executive office, of whom three are substitute members.

PASOK's parliamentary group has three collective organs: the parliamentary work sections, the committee for analysis and programming, and the commission for parliamentary control and documentation.

A large number of parliamentary group members also belong to the central committee. The director of the parliamentary group office, who is responsible for the activities of MPs, functions as the link between the parliamentary group and the central committee. The MPs are further restricted vis-à-vis the leadership, because they do not elect the president of the party.

A great majority of the MPs first worked in the local organizations of the party and were first elected under PASOK. A significant number of them had been active before 1967 in the Centre Union and particularly in the Centre Union's youth organization.

The selection of candidates is conducted by the central committee on the basis of nomination lists drawn up by the departmental committees, the president and the executive office.

Although PASOK advocates decentralization and democracy, policy-making within the party is highly centralized and is carried out mostly by the president and the executive office. Policy-making is facilitated by an excellent communications network between the local organizations and the executive office, which enables the latter to be well informed about issues throughout the country.

The party is financed from various sources: individual membership dues; contributions from fund-raising drives, donations and above all from state subsidies.

A special committee, which is set up by the executive office of the central committee, is in charge of the party's finances. It has the right to ask for a financial statement from every organization and agent of the party. The financial control committee is responsible for the management of the party's finances.

PASOK sits in the Socialist Group in the European Parliament, but is not yet a member of the Socialist International. There are 10 PASOK MEPs.

Policies

PASOK calls itself a socialist party. In the past, however, there has been no socialist tradition in Greece and PASOK's character differentiates it clearly from other European Socialist parties. On the other hand, it has advocated a "third road" to Socialism, and been critical of many European Social Democratic parties (and of the Socialist International, which in the past it has refused to join) as being too cautious and reformist and not radical enough. On the other hand, the political tradition from which it stems is primarily that of the former parties of the centre.

In practice, however, PASOK is now clearly a party of the centre-left, and on Oct. 6, 1986, Papandreou announced the party's intention to join the Socialist International, although no progress has yet been made on this matter. PASOK has also turned out to be much more pragmatic, for example, on the EC and NATO, than its early rhetoric appeared to warrant.

PASOK has a strong populist character, with a general and eclectic ideology. This, and its charismatic leader has helped to account for its nationwide appeal.

Although during the first years of its existence it tended to disavow any such links, PASOK later claimed itself as the successor of the old centre. The great majority of its supporters also see it as the new centre, while a significant number of its members and MPs have come from the Centre Union and especially its youth organization, EDIN.

The experience of the dictatorship of 1967–74 had a great influence on PASOK, which is clear in the emphasis that it has given to the safeguarding of national independence, popular sovereignty, social liberation and democratic structures as defined in its Declaration of the 3rd of September 1974. This helps to explain PASOK's original opposition to NATO, as well as its views that US policy was responsible for the seven-year dictatorship, the Cyprus invasion, the situation in the Aegean Sea and the general underdevelopment of the country.

In its early period PASOK adopted a Marxist (but non-Leninist) ideology. It made use of the Marxist method of analysis, although its ideas and policies were more linked to neo-Marxist dependency theory; it viewed Greece as a peripheral country in the global capitalist system, a position which condemned it to the scourge of underdevelopment and dependency, a view which underpinned PASOK's initial opposition to Greek adhesion to the EC. Andreas Papandreou had often referred to the gap between the wealthy nations of Northern Europe and their poorer neighbours to the South. He declared that it would be better for Greece not to adhere to the EC, but to conclude a special agreement. His foreign policy subsequently became more flexible, and he changed his policy vis-à-vis the EC, on the assumption that if the EC provided aid for the countries of the South it would be positive for the development of Greece.

A significant aspect of PASOK's foreign policy is its attempt to assert an independent position for Greece in European foreign policy-making (as in Papandreou's more critical attitude towards Polish Solidarity, and his failure to condemn the Soviet shooting down of a Korean airliner). It seeks to develop good relations with the Arab countries, the other Mediterranean countries and the Balkans. Papandreou has often argued for the creation of a nuclear-free zone in the Balkans. His activities in the field of nuclear disarmament are also manifest in his work with the Initiative of the Six Leaders for Peace and Disarmament.

PASOK's domestic policy has brought changes in the economic, institutional and social spheres. It has made changes in important sectors of production — shipyards, the Aspropyrgos refiners, etc. — by supporting participation of workers in the decision-making process, and decentralization in economic planning and management. An austerity policy was imposed in 1986 with the aim of stabilizing the economy and curbing the rising rate of inflation.

In the institutional and social spheres PASOK has established legal equality between men and women, revised the Family Law, introduced civil marriage, legalized abortions, etc. It also lowered the voting age to 18. It has also tried to make the civil service more democratic and implemented a variety of social welfare policies, such as the establishment of a national health-care system, and legislation to protect the environment. One of the most significant achievements of PASOK's governmental policy has been its efforts to heal the rifts caused by the Civil War. Although the first step took place under Karamanlis with the legalization of the KKE in 1974, it was PASOK that finally recognized the Resistance movement against the Axis Occupation and arranged for the repatriation of political refugees.

Personalities

The most prominent figure of PASOK is its leader, Andreas Papandreou, who has been Prime Minister of Greece from 1981.

He is a former member and deputy of the Centre Union, and founder of both PAK and PASOK. He is considered a charismatic personality and the main asset of the party, although he and his party have recently run into major difficulties.

One of the founding members of PASOK, who continues to play a significant role in the party is Giannes Alevras, President of the Parliament. He has been an MP of PASOK from 1974. He was an MP of the Centre Union in 1963 and

1964 and he was imprisoned by the Junta. He is on the moderate wing of the party.

Giannes Charalampopoulos has been an MP since 1974. He is Minister of Defence and Minister of the Presidency of the Government. Charalampopoulos was also an MP of the Centre Union in 1963 and 1964. He had been imprisoned and exiled by the Junta. He is a leading moderate within the party.

Georgios Gennematas is the Minister of Labour. He has also been Minister of Health and Welfare and Minister of the Interior. He had been a member of the Youth Organization of the Liberal Party and of the Centre Union. He is on the more Socialist wing of the party, and is one of its more popular members among the party rank and file.

Georgios Papandreou is the son of the Prime Minister. He has been the Minister for Youth Affairs, and is currently the Minister for Education.

Simites, who applied an austerity programme when at the Ministry of Finance, has close links with Brussels, and is within the European Social-Democratic tradition.

The actress Amalia-Maria Melina Merkoure is one of the founding members of PASOK and an MP from 1977. She has been Minister of Culture from 1981.

Kostas Laliotis is also one of the young and active personalities in PASOK.

Nea Demokratia — ND
(New Democracy)

Headquarters	:	18 Regilles, Athens (tel: 729–0072–9)
Leader	:	Konstantinos Mitsotakis
Youth organization	:	*Organose Neon Neas Demokratias* (Youth Organization of New Democracy) ONNED
Students' organization	:	*Demokratike Agonistike Parataxe — Neas Demokratias-Foitetike Kinese* (Democratic Fighting Party — New Democracy-Students' Movement) DAP-NDFK
Estimated membership	:	50,000 in 1986
Founded	:	1974

History

ND is the post-1974 representative of the Conservative tradition in Greek politics. In the interwar period the Conservative movement in Greece was represented by the People's Party (*Laiko Komma*), championed the monarchy and expressed the interests of the "old Greece" and of its notables. It strongly opposed Eleftherios Venizelos — charismatic leader of the Liberal Party — and his policy of territorial expansion. The party was one of the two protagonists in the National Schism of 1916.

The People's Party, like all the other Greek political parties, with the exception of the Communists, was characterized by a lack both of a specific ideology and of a strong organization. It functioned on the basis of clientelist networks at the local level, where the major figures of the party played a more important role than the organization.

The imposition of the Metaxas dictatorship in 1936 resulted in the collapse of the interwar party system and the rise of an anti-Conservative wave which was reinforced by the Resistance movement during the German Occupation.

In the first elections after the liberation of the country, People's Party support shrank to that of the old Monarchical Group, although the "threat" of Communism which was perceived in the rise of the Left during the Axis Occupation led to the formation of a new Conservative party, the United Nationalistic Front (*Enomeme Parataxe Ethnikofronon — EPE*), a constellation of various small right-wing groups. In 1946 the left and the majority of the centre-left decided to boycott the elections, a decision which allowed the EPE to become the leading party with 55.12 per cent of the votes. Its victory opened the way for the return of the King. The Union of the Nationalistic Front was succeeded in 1950 by the Greek Rally (*Hellinikos Synagermos*) which was formed by General Alexandros Papagos, the winner of the Civil War in 1949. It received 36.53 per cent of the votes in the elections of 1951, while a year later, its electoral percentage rose to 49.2 per cent. The Greek Rally further diminished whatever had been left of the old People's Party. The political cleavage of the National Schism (Conservative v. Liberal) was replaced by the new cleavage from the Civil War (Conservative/Liberal v. Communist).

The death of Alexandros Papagos in 1955 brought Konstantinos Karamanlis to the leadership of the Greek Rally. He was not elected by the party but was imposed on the party leadership by the King. In an effort to legitimize his succession to the party's leadership, Karamanlis formed the National Radical Union (*Ethnike Rizospastike Enosis* — ERE). Although it had more radical attitudes on socio-economic issues, there was generally little change from the policy stance of the Greek Rally, most of whose major figures had transferred to the National Radical Union. This latter continued to be a party with a loosely defined ideology, which stressed anti-Communism and had a loose organizational structure, grounded on the clientelist networks of the party "bosses". It governed Greece from 1955 up to 1963 when it lost the elections to the Centre Union (*Enosis Kentrou*), which in the next elections, a year later, reinforced its victory with 52.72 per cent of the votes. The defeat of the National Radical Union in 1963 was followed by a disagreement between the King and Karamanlis, who resigned from the party's leadership and was succeeded by Panagiotes Kanellopoulos. The intervention of the King and the later crisis of the parliamentary regime helped to lead to the dictatorship of 1967. The main repercussion for the Conservatives was the final separation of the right from the extreme right-wing.

After the fall of the dictatorship the Conservatives came to power as a result of three factors: the first was the charismatic personality of Konstantinos Karamanlis, who was considered the politician best able to restore parliamentary democracy; secondly the Conservatives had successfully distanced themselves from the Junta during the seven-year dictatorship, and thirdly the new party, established by Karamanlis (*Nea Demokratia* — New Democracy) could be presented as a completely new political party, quite distinct from the former National Radical Union.

Although still based on the old right (ERE) tradition, it also won broader support because of the collapse of the old centre.

ND won the 1974 elections with 54.4 per cent of the vote and 220 out of the 300 seats in the Parliament, and Karamanlis became Prime Minister. He took a neutral stand in the 1974 Plebiscite on the monarchy. In 1977 ND won re-election, but with a reduced majority of 171 seats on 41.9 per cent of the vote.

Despite Karamanlis's effort to form a party with a strong organization, the clientelist networks remained. The party preserved its personalized character and he experienced great difficulties in creating a mass organization. It is indicative that the temporary statutes of ND were signed by one person, Konstantinos Karamanlis. His charismatic personality so dominated ND, that a crisis of leadership arose as soon as he became President of the Republic in 1980 and the party then had three leaders with-

in a short period. Firstly Georgios Rallis became leader of ND and Prime Minister of Greece. The withdrawal of Karamanlis, combined with a party platform in the 1981 electoral campaign which dealt more with the achievements of the past rather than programmes for the future, led to public disillusionment with an ND which seemed to promise "more of the same". This contributed to the defeat of the party, which only won 115 seats on 35.9 per cent of the vote and lost power to PASOK. Evangelos Averoff then succeeded Georgios Rallis to the party's leadership, but after a further setback in the elections for the European Parliament he was succeeded by Konstantinos Mitsotakis.

The parliamentary elections of 1985 left ND still in the opposition, despite the fact that its electoral support had increased to 40.8 per cent (126 seats). In the municipal elections of 1986, Communist abstention in the second round allowed ND to elect mayors in major cities such as Athens, Piraeus and Thessaloniki. ND also has nine seats in the European Parliament.

Support

ND has benefited from the collapse of the centre parties (although to a lesser extent than PASOK) winning support from them, as well as from traditional Conservatives. The polarization of Greek politics under the reinforced proportional system has also caused it to be the main focus of support for all anti-PASOK voters of the right and centre.

ND is stronger among women than men, and also among older voters, whereas its electoral support from younger age groups has been weak. It is strong in the upper and middle class.

ND has generally been stronger in rural than urban districts, although a key element in its increased vote in 1985 was its improved vote in many urban districts.

Its highest vote in 1985 was its 56.9 per cent in the constituency of Laconia in the Southern Peloponnese, which at almost 60 per cent had previously had by far the highest pro-royalty vote in the 1974 plebiscite. In the constituency with the second highest pro-monarchy vote, Rhodopi in Thrace, ND obtained almost 50 per cent of the vote in 1985.

ND was generally strongest in the Southern Peloponnese, in much of Macedonia (e.g. Kastoria at over 52 per cent in 1985) and Thrace. In central Athens it outpolled PASOK, winning 44 per cent in 1985.

ND was weakest in the Greek islands. Only in the Cyclades did it win over 40 per cent in 1985. It was weakest of all in the anti-Conservative island of Crete where it only won 26 per cent in the Heraklion constituency and 31 per cent in Lasithi and Chania. In the left-wing Lesbos constituency it only won 30 per cent, and it was also weak in the Ionian Islands and the Dodecanese. On the mainland it was weakest in central Piraeus at under 30 per cent and in suburban Athens at under 35 per cent. It was also under 40 per cent in much of Epirus, in Northern Thessaly and in Achaia.

Organization

Although the number of ND's members is smaller than that of PASOK, its position as the leading opposition party and its catch-all strategy have led to an increase in its membership. Nevertheless ND has not yet developed a mass organization. The estimated number of members in 1986 was about 50,000.

ND is divided administratively into central and peripheral organizations. The major organs of the central organization are the congress, the central committee, the executive committee, the parliamentary group and the president.

The congress is the supreme organ of the party and has a wide variety of responsibilities. These include definition of the party's ideological principles and the party's general political line, approval of the party's platform, approval and modification of the party's statutes, and review and audit of the work of the central committee. The congress consists of the president, the ex-presidents of the party, the members of the parliamentary group and the central committee, the ex-MPs, the parliamentary candidates who were not elected in the last elections, representatives of the regional organizations, 36 representatives from the external party's organizations, 70 representatives of the special party organizations, 120 elected representatives of the youth organization of the party, ONNED (the youth organization), and one woman from each district administrative committee. The congress is convoked every three years but this can be delayed for up to one year, by decision of the central committee or it can be convoked earlier if there is any special reason, by decision of the president or by two to three of the members of the central committee.

The central committee is the supreme organ in the period between congresses. It consists of the president, the parliamentary representative, the secretary of the parliamentary group, the leader of the executive committee of ONNED and 75 members of the party who are elected by the congress. It deals with the political and ideological issues faced by the party and meets every two months.

The executive committee is the major organ between meetings of the central committee. It deals with all issues outside the jurisdiction of other party organs. It consists of the president, the parliamentary representatives, the secretary of the parliamentary group, the leader of the executive committee of ONNED and eleven members of the central committee.

The parliamentary group consists not only of the members of the Parliament, but also of members of the European Parliament. Since the MPs of ND are the ones who, for the most part, make decisions and shape the policy of the party, they constitute a very strong group in its organization, even though they do not hold administrative positions in the peripheral organizations and do not participate in other central organs except the congress. They do, however, maintain a close relationship with the president of the party, who is also president of the MPs.

The president has a key role in the party. He represents the party in Greece and abroad. He is the leader of the party's organization and the president of the central committee, the executive committee and the parliamentary group. He is able to convoke special congresses and the national conference, and is responsible for the carrying out of the decisions of the congress, the central and the executive committees and the parliamentary group. He is the key actor in the party's decision-making process, in conjunction with the members of the Parliamentary party. He appoints the general secretary of the parliamentary group and the general director of the party and also nominates candidates for parliamentary elections. The president up to now has always been elected by the parliamentary group.

The peripheral structure of the party is developed at three levels. At the base there are the local branches whose function is to put across the party's ideology and mobilize mass support in their districts. Above these are provincial and regional organizations.

Although ND has a complex organizational structure at the central and local levels, traditional patterns of clientelism are still strong within the party.

The procedure for selecting candidates shows the centralist character of ND, and the lack of influence exerted from the party's base. The list of candidates is first drawn up on the basis of nominations by the departmental assembly. The lists submitted from every electoral district are compiled in a master table of candidates, which is then submitted to the executive committee. The executive committee examines the table, adding or deleting nominations as it sees fit and then prepares a revised table which is presented to the president who makes the final choice and determines the list of party's candidates for the elections.

Nominations for the candidates at-large and for those of the European Parliament are directly selected by the party's leader.

The activities of ND are financed by state subsidies, the membership dues of the party's members, fund-raising drives and donations.

ND is a member of the European People's Party in the European Parliament, and of the European and International Christian Democratic Movements.

Policies

Ever since the fall of the dictatorship, ND has striven to distance itself from the extreme right. Even though it began to take on more conservative features after 1977, it implemented various social reforms when it was in power. After losing to PASOK in 1981, it tried to attract the centre-right electorate, thus losing a part of the right-wing vote which has been taken up by EPEN. ND is still characterized by two opposing tendencies, one right-wing and the other more to the centre and which seeks to distinguish itself sharply from the old right. This conflict has led to uncertainty about the party's true identity, and not always permitted it to appear as a convincing exponent of the Liberal tradition to which it has laid claim.

Although ND maintains to a large extent the traditional party organizational structure (the clientelist networks) it is, in fact, the first Conservative party in Greece which has sought to develop a specific modern ideology, including defence of the cultural identity of the Greeks, and of national independence. Another factor is free-market liberalism in the socio-economic sphere which has received a higher emphasis in recent years.

One of the major tenets of ND is that Greece is a European country. It cites the Greek adhesion to the EC as one of its outstanding accomplishments in this field. Its foreign policy is particularly geared towards the countries of the West. A well-known electoral slogan of ND states: "Greece belongs to the West".

Personalities

ND was dominated by the personality of Konstantinos Karamanlis, the founder of ND and former President of Greece.

From 1984 the president of ND has been Konstantinos Mitsotakis, a former member of the old Centre Union who took part in the defection of 1965, which led to the fall of Georgios Papandreou's Centre Union gov-

ernment. He took over the leadership from Evangelos Averoff, an influential member of ND's old guard, who has strongly defended Mitsotakis since his election.

Another personality who plays a significant role in ND is Miltiades Evert, who comes from a prominent political family and is the present mayor of Athens. He is of neo-liberal orientation, and is considered as a possible party leader of the future.

The withdrawal of Kostis Stefanopoulos in 1985, who formed a new party, DEANA, and Georgios Rallis in 1987, ex-president of ND and former Prime Minister of Greece, deprived the party of two well-known politicians.

Parties of the left

History

The development of a socialist and labour movement was slow in coming to Greece. The first socialist political party was the Socialist Labour Party of Greece (SEKE — *Socialistiko Ergatiko Komma Hellados*), which had been formed less than a week after the Panhellenic Socialist Congress, in November 1918, when the creation of the General Confederation of Greek Workers (GSEE — *Genike Synomospondia Ergaton Hellados*) took place.

The various left-wing forces rallied round SEKE whose programme was based on the Erfurt Declaration of the German SPD. The party developed a loose relation with the Second International in 1919, but in 1924 it joined the Communist International and changed its name to the Communist Party of Greece (KKE — *Kommounistiko Komma Hellados*).

In the elections of 1926 the KKE managed for the first time to enter the Parliament with 10 deputies. The party's relationship with the Comintern, however, and its support for an independent Macedonia tended to cultivate a negative image for the Left among the majority of Greeks, who considered the party a traitor to Hellenism and Greek national sovereignty. Thus, in the elections of 1928 it managed to elect only one MP. Soon after the party abandoned this stance, and in the elections of 1932 its parliamentary force increased to 10 seats. In the next elections of 1936 the number of KKE MPs rose to 16. The electoral success of the Communists was used, however, by Metaxas to justify his military coup as the only solution for the salvation of Greece from the Communist "threat". With the establishment of the dictatorship, the KKE was immediately outlawed but the coming of World War II in 1940 and the ensuing

German occupation of Greece soon led the KKE to reorganize itself and to become the leading force within the Greek resistance movement. In September, 1941, it drew together other, non-Communist groups of the left to create the National Liberation Front (EAM — *Ethniko Apeleftherotiko Metopo*) with a military branch, the National Populist Liberation Army (ELAS — *Ethnikos Laikos Apeleftherotikos Stratos*), which soon became a powerful army. Although various left and non-left groups and individuals joined it, it was in reality dominated by the KKE leadership.

By the end of the German occupation a power struggle began between EAM and the other resistance groups. The British, fearing the possible dominance of the Communists, sought to re-establish a constitutional monarchy as a guarantor of British interests in the area, and intervened to support the Greek government in exile. The Civil War soon started. The abstention of the Left from the elections of 1946 led to the establishment of a constitutional government with no representatives from the Left in the Parliament. In September of the same year the referendum for the monarchy was held, and the King, George II, returned to Greece. About a year later, in December 1947, the KKE was again outlawed and a total schism occurred. In 1949 the National Army began to prevail over the KKE and the great majority of the Democratic Army troops crossed the borders to the North. In October 1949, the KKE announced a "temporary" end of hostilities which turned out, nonetheless, to be permanent. With the end of the war a new rift in Greek political life was added to existing ones.

The presence of the Left in Greece was seriously weakened. The Communist Party had been banned, and most of its members, who had fled to Albania, Yugoslavia and elsewhere in the Balkans, found themselves suddenly in exile when the government refused their re-entry to Greece. Those Communists who remained in Greece rallied round the Democratic Party (DP — *Democratike Parataxe*), which, in the elections of 1950 polled 9.7 per cent of the votes and gained 18 seats in the Parliament. In the next elections of 1951 the same group formed the United Democratic Left (EDA — *Eniaia Demokratike Aristera*) which gained 10.57 per cent of the votes and 10 seats. EDA became a well unified and organized party, which, for the period 1958–61, was the main opposition party in the Parliament with 24.43 per cent of the votes and 79 seats. EDA, with its own ideological principles and its own political programme, had amassed a membership of nearly 70,000, with party offices throughout the country. The later decline in EDA's electoral strength — to 14.34 per cent and 28 seats and 11.80 per cent and 22 seats respectively — in the elections of 1963 and 1964, must be seen in connection with the rise of the Centre Union.

The question of what stance the Left should take in response to the military coup of 1967 and the persecution which the Junta unleashed against the Left soon led to bitter recrimination between the main factions of the party. In February 1968 the "interior" faction and its supporters in the top party echelons split apart. This split at the top spread throughout the Communist structure both in Greece and abroad. Furthermore, the invasion of Czechoslovakia in August 1968, the suppression of the "Prague Spring" and the rise of Eurocommunism widened the gap between the two factions.

With the demise of the dictatorship, the Communist parties were legalized. In the first election after the dictatorship, in 1974, the two Communist parties and EDA concluded an electoral alliance, called the United Left, which polled 9.47 per cent of the votes. The Alliance collapsed before the next elections in 1977, when the KKE chose to run on its own.

Kommounistiko Komma Hellados — KKE (Communist Party of Greece)

Headquarters	: 145 Leoforos Erakleiou (tel: 252–3635, 252–5621)
General secretary	: Charilaos Florakis
Youth organization	: *Kommounistike Neolaia Hellados* (Communist Youth of Greece) — KNE
Students' organization	: *Panspoudastike Kinese* — PSK
Publication	: *Rizospastis* (Radical)
Founded	: 1924

History

In exile the party was led by Nikos Zarachariades until 1956, and then by Kostas Koliyannis until 1972. Charilaos Florakis was elected leader in 1973. In the elections of 1977 the pro-Moscow Communist Party ran alone but still polled 9.35 per cent of the votes, electing 11 MPs. It thus managed to draw together the overwhelming majority of communist voters. The KKE became the only orthodox Marxist-Leninist party of Greece. In the elections of 1981 and 1985, it polled 10.92 per cent and 9.89 per cent of the votes with 13 and 12 MPs respectively. It failed, however, to attract the voters of the centre-left, who preferred to vote for PASOK.

Support

The party's membership is mainly drawn from the working class, although a significant number of the middle and lower-middle class is represented in it. Its membership is estimated at about 100,000.

Support for the KKE is disproportionately higher in the urban areas. The distribution of its electoral strength in the last elections range from a minimum of 2 per cent to a maximum of 22 per cent with the bulk of districts registering between 4 per cent and 15 per cent.

Its highest vote in 1985 was in some of the island constituencies, notably Lesbos (22.6 per cent), Samos (19.3 per cent) and Lefkos (19.1 per cent) as well as Kefallonia (15.6 per cent) and Zante (15 per cent). In central Piraeus it polled 17.1 per cent and in suburban Athens 15.5 per cent. Elsewhere it only won over 10 per cent in Epirus (e.g. Ioannina 14 per cent), North Central Greece (Larissa 14 per cent) and Central Thessaloniki. It was weakest of all in Thrace (e.g. Xanthe 2.4 per cent and Rhodopi 2.9 per cent), in Kavalla (4.3 per cent) and in the eastern Peloponnese. It was weak in the Cyclades (4.3 per cent) and the Dodecanese (5.1 per cent). In Crete it was strongest in Chania (around 10 per cent) but weaker elsewhere.

Organization

The basic principle determining the structure and functioning of the party is that of democratic centralism which is based on rigid guidance and iron discipline.

The main organ of the party is the congress, which is convoked every four years by the central committee. The number and election of its members are arranged by the central committee. The members of both the central committee and the central control committee, who are not elected as representatives to the congress, have a consultative vote at the congress. The main responsibilities of the congress are: to oversee the central committee, to determine the party's line, to forge the party's political platform and charter and to elect the members of both the central committee and the central control committee.

The guiding organ between two congresses is the central committee, which is responsible for the political, ideological and organizational work of the party. It overseas the activities of the political bureau and nominates the party's press representative. It can also create specific issue work groups in the central committee and is responsible for party finances. The central committee elects the political bureau, the general secretary, the secretariat and the central control committee. It also has the ability to convoke the party's Panhellenic congress.

The political bureau is elected by the central committee and guides the party during the period between the meetings of the central committee which are convoked every six to eight months.

The political bureau and the central committee play the leading role in the tightly controlled party structure.

The KKE also has a great number of smaller locally and professionally-based organizations. These are the district prefectural and workplace organizations of the party.

The party's youth organization (KNE — *Kommounistike Neolaia Hellados*) has about 30,000 members between 15 and 26 years old.

The majority of the party MPs belong either to the political bureau or the central committee.

The financial resources of the party come from membership subscriptions, new enrolments, and profits from various other sources, including a major publishing and printing company *Typoekdotiki*. The amount of both enrolment and subscription is defined by the party's charter as about 1 per cent of the member's income. The party's finances are administered by the central committee and the central control committee.

The KKE has three members of the European Parliament, who sit in the Communist Group, and are closest to the French and Portuguese members.

Policies

The KKE is situated further left on the Greek political spectrum than the other political parties represented in Parliament. With its particular emphasis on the class struggle and with its language and ideology derived from Marxist-Leninist theory, it is one of the most orthodox Communist parties in Europe. It seeks to establish a communist society and proclaims the spirit of proletarian internationalism. It is opposed to Greek membership of the EC and of NATO, and seeks the removal of American military installation in Greece. It is critical of PASOK's failure to carry out its pre-electoral promises.

The KKE is the third largest political party on the Greek political scene. Like other minority parties, it has attacked the bipolarism of the last few years. In the municipal elections of 1987 the KKE showed its power by urging its supporters to abstain from the second round of the elections in the major cities, an abstention which assured the victory of the ND's candidates.

During the 12th congress of the party which was held in March 1988, a renewal took place within the central committee. A great number of the older members, known for their resistance activities in the past, were replaced by younger members. This could be a sign of progress in the party's leadership and an indication of future changes in KKE policy.

Personalities

The party's general secretary is Charilaos Florakis. He was a member of the resistance movement against the Axis occupation and an officer in EAM during the Civil War. During the Junta he went into exile. He was elected party leader in 1973, replacing Kostas Koliyannis.

C. Capos is also a well-known party figure. He is now a parliamentary representative of KKE, and was a member of the resistance during the Junta.

Maria Damanake is the vice-president of the Parliament. She is a chemical engineer with a special involvement in the resistance against the Junta and she is particularly known for her activities during the events at the Polytechnic School of Athens in November 1973.

Farrakos belongs to the old guard of KKE. He participated in the resistance movement against the Axis occupation and in the Civil War. He was imprisoned by the Junta. Since 1974 he has been a KKE MP.

Androulakes belongs to the generation of the Polytechnic School. He is one of the renovators of the party. He is a member of the political bureau.

Gondikas belonged to the Lambrakides. He has been a KKE MP from 1974 and a member of the political bureau. He is also responsible for one of the most powerful local organizations of the party, the party organization of Athens.

The party's three members of the European Parliament are Demetrios Adamou, Alexios Alevanos and Vasileios Efremedes.

Kommounistiko Komma Hellados — Esoterikou — Ananeotike Aristera
(Communist Party of the Interior — Renewed Left)

Headquarters	:	9 Chalkokondyle, 10677 (tel: 361–9274)
General secretary	:	Giannes Banias
Youth organization	:	*Regas Ferraios*

Students' organization	:	*Demokratikos Agonas* (Democratic Struggle)

Hellenike Aristera — EAR
(Greek Left)

Headquarters	:	1 Plateia Eleftherias, Plateia Koumoundourou, 10553 (tel: 3217064)
General secretary	:	Leonidas Kyrkos
Youth organization	:	*Youth of Greek Left*
Students' organization	:	*Demokratikos Agonas* — EAR (Democratic Struggle)
Publication	:	*Avge* (Dawn)

Communist Party of Greece — Interior (KKE — Interior)/Communist Party of the Interior — Renewed Left/Greek Left — EAR

The KKE — Interior stemmed from a split within the mainstream Communist Party in 1968. The dissident minority were expelled, and formed an interior bureau, which subsequently became the basis for the new party.

In 1974 KKE — Interior formed an electoral alliance with the mainstream KKE and with the legal pre-junta party of the far left, the EDA. This coalition, the *Enomeni Aristera* (United Left) only won 9.5 per cent of the vote and eight seats.

In 1976 Babi Drakopoulos was elected general secretary of the KKE — Interior. In 1976 the party was excluded from the Berlin Conference of European Communist parties. In the 1977 elections it fought separately from the KKE, and only won 2.7 per cent of the vote and two seats fighting in a coalition with the EDA and a number of small left-wing parties.

The KKE — Interior advocated a much more moderate gradualist approach than the KKE. It supported Greek membership of the EC, and while advocating withdrawal from NATO in the longer term, did not put emphasis on this as an immediate short-term objective. It was much more internally democratic than the KKE, without unanimous decision-making and with statutory publication of minority opinions. It was not recognized by the Soviet Union, but enjoyed good relations with Eurocommunist parties such as the Italians. It had little industrial working-class support, but was primarily a party of left-wing intellectuals.

In the 1981 national elections it was reduced to only 1.37 per cent of the vote, and no seats in the Parliament. At the same time it won 5.2 per cent in the European Parliament elections, largely as a result of its higher profile on European issues. It elected one member of the European Parliament, Leonidas Kyrkos, who was accepted in the Communist and Allies Group in parallel with the KKE representatives. Unlike them his position was closer to the Italian Communists.

In 1982 Giannes Banias became the general secretary of the KKE — Interior. In the 1984 European elections the party won 3.4 per cent and held on to its one seat in the European Parliament. In the 1985 national elections it only won 1.8 per cent, but this slight improvement in its 1984 vote was enough to give it a seat in the National Parliament. This was taken by Kyrkos, who was replaced in the European Parliament by Konstantinos Filinis.

During the 4th congress of the party in May 1986 there was a serious split between a faction under Kyrkos which sought the creation of a new party, which would no longer be explicitly called Communist and would constitute a rallying point for the left, and a second faction under Giannes Banias, which sought a renewed party but still within a Communist framework. The former faction narrowly prevailed (with 53 per cent of the vote) and Kyrkos became the new general secretary. The old party label of KKE — Interior was kept for one more year until a founding congress could take place.

In April 1987 this congress was held, and the KKE — Interior finally split into two separate parties, the Communist Party of the Interior — Renewed Left under Giannes Banias and the Greek Left under Leonidas Kyrkos. The Greek Left has retained the party's only member of Parliament, and its member of the European Parliament.

Eniaia Democratike Aristera — EDA
(United Democratic Left)

Headquarters	: 62, Akademias, Athens (tel: 362–88 60)
Leader	: Manoles Glezos

After the fall of the Junta in 1974, the EDA (the main legal party of the far left before 1967) was revived under the leadership of Elias Eliou.

Like that of the KKE-Interior, the support for the EDA shrank after the split within the KKE to a very small percentage of left voters. In the elections of 1977 it ran along with the KKE-Interior. In the elections of 1981, when it ran alone, it polled a very small percentage of the total vote. In the elections of 1985 EDA chose to make an electoral coalition with one of the two major parties — PASOK — and thus managed to elect its leader, Manoles Glezos, as an MP.

Parties of the centre

History

The Liberal tradition in the early 20th century was represented by the Party of the Liberals (KF — Komma Fileleftheron), which was formed by Eleftherios Venizelos in September, 1910 and constituted one of the two major political organizations of this period. During the Balkan Wars, the Liberal leadership undertook internal reforms and also expanded the territory of Greece. This period of consensus ended with the National Schism in 1915–16, with the entry of Greece into World War I on the side of the Entente. The clash between the King and the Prime Minister led to a division of the Greek political scene into two competing blocks: the Venizelists, champions of republicanism, and the Anti-Venizelists. The schism ended with the victory of the Liberals and the consequent entry of Greece into World War I. The subsequent disaster in Asia Minor in 1922 rekindled divisions between the Liberals and their opponents.

Venizelism was a political constellation of several parties which arose during the interwar period, the dominant component of which was the Liberal Party.

The dictatorship of Metaxas and the following Axis occupation resulted in the Civil War, and this led to the rise of anticommunism which spread not only to the Conservative but also the Liberal parties. Consequently, the anticommunist stance of the Liberals, along with the rise of the Conservatives, shifted the former more to the centre of the political spectrum.

The centre during this period was divided into smaller political parties which ran in elections within varying coalitions. The dominant components were the National Progressive Union of the Centre (EPEK — *Ethnike Proodeftike Enosis Kentrou*) under the leadership of Nicolaos Plasteras, and the Liberal Party under Sofokles Venizelos.

In September 1961, a new party was formed under the leadership of Georgios Papandreou, the Centre Union (EK — *Enosis Kentrou*). This soon became the major party of the centre into which the smaller parties were incorporated. The fragmentation of the Greek centre was thus ended. EK was a true political party rather than a mere political coalition. In the elections of 1961, the Centre Union became the second political party in Greece, while in the following elections of 1963 it won a majority of the parliamentary seats and became the governing party of Greece. The majority was reconfirmed in the elections of 1964 when the Centre Union won 52.72 per cent of the votes. The success of the Centre Union was ended in July 1965 when the King intervened to force the resignation of Papandreou's government. Once again a struggle between a King and a Liberal Prime Minister led to a military coup, a central aim of which was to prevent a new victory of the Centre Union in the elections of 1967.

With the fall of the Junta, the Centre Union reappeared under the leadership of Georgios Mavros, on Sept. 21, 1974. A month later the Centre Union and the New Forces, a group of leading figures in Greek political and intellectual life who had participated in the resistance movement against the Junta, declared their intention to run as a coalition in the forthcoming elections. The coalition EK — ND went on to win 20.4 per cent of the votes in these elections. In February 1976, the Centre Union changed its name to the Union of the Democratic Centre (EDEK — *Enose Demokratikou Kentrou*), while the members of New Forces agreed to forfeit their right to be represented in the party's name. During the same year a number of its members started to withdraw from EDEK and after the 1977 elections, which proved disastrous for the Centre, it divided into two smaller parties.

As the centre has been relegated after 1977 to a peripheral position in Greek politics, the four minor groups that presently occupy the central ground in Greek politics are only dealt with briefly below.

Enose Demokratikou Kentrou — EDEK
(Union of Democratic Centre)

Local organization of
Kefissia   : 16 Evripidou,
                         Kefissia
                         (tel: 808–28 34)
Leader   : Giannes Zigdes

In February 1976 the Centre Union changed its name to the Union of the Democratic Centre, but soon afterwards a number of its members, (particularly those who came from the New Forces) started to withdraw. In July 1976, Demetrios Tsatsos was expelled after a clash with the leadership. Three months later he joined up with Anastasios Minis, George-Alexandros Mangakes and Protopapas who had also left EDEK, to form the Initiative for Democracy and Socialism.

As the main Centre party, EDEK was trapped by the developing bipolarism between ND on the right and PASOK on the left. Its platform did not attract the voters, while its leader, Georgios Mavros, although he was a well-known politician, did not have the charisma of Konstantinos Karamanlis of ND and Andreas Papandreou of PASOK. In the elections of 1977 EDEK saw its support shrink to 11.88 per cent of the votes, dropping to third place and yielding its position as the main opposition party to PASOK.

The ranks of EDEK continued to thin out in the years from 1978 to 1981. Soon after the elections Mavros, who had been replaced as party leader by Giannes Zigdis, declared himself an independent. He then formed his own centre party, PARKE, attracting other members of EDEK. However, when Mavros joined the electoral lists of PASOK in the elections of 1981, various PARKE members such as Venizelos, Bandouvas and Xyloures, attempted a revival of the Liberal Party. Other PARKE members like Papathemelis and Sergakes followed Mavros's example and joined PASOK.

EDEK was debilitated by withdrawals in other directions as well. In 1978, Kanallopoulos, Papachristou and others left to join ND, while a year later Pesmatzoglou, Tsouderou, Alavanos and Kardaras formed the Socialist Democratic Party, KODESO, as a modernized alternative to EDEK. Thus EDEK arrived at the 1981 elections deprived of almost all its leading political figures and deputies. Its support shrank to 0.4 per cent of the electoral vote. In 1985, it joined forces with PASOK.

Komma Demokratikou Socialismou — KODESO
(Party of Democratic Socialism)

Headquarters   : 9, Mavromichale,
                         Athens
                         (tel: 36 00 724–8)
Leader   : Charalambos
                         Protopappas

In 1979, in Thessaloniki, several former members of EDEK, Pesmatzoglou, Tsouderou, Alavanos and Kardaras, formed the Social Democratic Party KODESO, with the intention of creating an alternative to EDEK. It is a party with a strong European image that opposes the polarization of Greek politics. In the elections of 1981 KODESO joined forces with the revived Agrarian Labour Party (KAE) of A. Baltatzis, winning 0.70 per cent of the votes, though the results were better in urban areas: Athens I: 2.60 per cent, Athens II: 1.75 per cent, Pireius

I: 1.57 per cent, Thessaloniki I: 1.56 per cent, KODESO also polled significantly better in the elections for the European Parliament, obtaining 4.25 per cent of the votes, thus assuring its leader Pesmatzoglou of a seat in the European Parliament.

The polarization of the Greek political scene eventually forced KODESO, as it did other minor parties, to support one of the protagonists. Joining up with ND in the elections of 1985, it was able to elect some of its leading members as independent MPs in the Parliament in the lists of ND. KODESO's new leader Protopappas has recently declared that the party intends to pursue a "fourth road" to Socialism, a policy which may lead in their forthcoming congress to the formation of a new party — an alternative to PASOK — called the "Fourth Pole". This party, situated in the political spectrum between ND and KKE would theoretically draw off dissatisfied votes from both the centre-right and the centre-left.

Komma Fileleftheron
(Liberal Party)

Headquarters   : 1 Vessarionos,
                     Athens
                     (tel: 363–18 53)
Leader   : Niketas Venizelos

The Liberal Party, like other parties of the centre, had its origin in the Centre Union — New Forces of 1974 and EDEK, and took shape when Niketas Venizelos, Bandouvas, Xyloures and others withdrew from EDEK and PARKE, and made an attempt to revive the old Liberal Party. The LP is a highly personal party which relies more on the name of its leader — Venizelos (a grandson of former Prime Minister Eleftherios Venizelos) — than on its programme. In the elections of 1981 it won 0.36 per cent of the vote, although it made a strong showing in the Rethymno district in Crete with 17.38 per cent of the votes. In 1985 Venizelos was approached by both ND and PASOK, but decided to run on a separate ticket. The party only won 0.2 per cent of the vote.

It is a member of the Liberal International and of the Federation of European, Liberal, Democratic and Reform Parties (ELDR).

Christianike Demokratia
(Christian Democracy)

Headquarters   : 126 Solonos, Athens
                     (tel: 361–13 02)
Leader   : Nikos Psaroudakes

Christian Democracy is hard to classify within the Greek political context, since it has little similarity to European Christian Democracy. It is not a centre-right Christian bourgeois party but a centre-left populist party, with an ideology shaped by religious orthodoxy and with a platform opposed to both NATO and the EC.

Greek Christian Democracy is the creation of Nikos Psaroudakes, who started his political career in 1950 as a candidate of the Christian Labour Agricultural Order, a small Christian centre party. Four years after the elections of 1951, in which Psaroudakes ran with EPEK, he founded Christian Democracy. In the elections of 1974 the party joined EK-ND, and in the next elections of 1977 it was one of the parties which formed the "Alliance" (SPAD). Detached from the "Alliance", Psaroudakes and Christian Democracy ran alone in the elections of 1981, winning 0.15 per cent of the votes, as well as in the elections for the European Parliament where it gained 1.14 per cent of the votes. In the elections of 1985, Christian Democracy joined PASOK and Psaroudakes entered Parliament on PASOK's ticket.

Others

Demokratike Ananeose — DEANA
(Democratic Renewal)

Headquarters   : 30 3rd Septemvriou,
                     Athens
                     (tel: 65 33 533)
Leader   : Kostis Stefanopoulos

The second defeat of ND in the elections of 1985 caused turmoil in the party ranks, with disputes about the party's leadership and political platform. In September 1985 a well-known politician of ND, Kostis Stefanopoulos, who had been a candidate for ND's leadership in 1982 and 1984, withdrew from the party. He was followed by nine ND deputies. Stefanopoulos intended to form a centre-right party as an alternative to ND, although others in DEANA supported a shift to the extreme-right.

DEANA was dealt a hard blow in the municipal elections of October 1986 in which it polled a very limited percentage of the votes. In view of the forthcoming elections a dilemma has arisen concerning the position that DEANA should follow: to co-operate with another party — particularly ND — or to face the elections alone.

The number of DEANA's MPs decreased to seven after the departure of three members who returned to ND.

Ethniki Politiki Enosis — EPEN
(National Political Union)

Headquarters : 19 Voukourestiou,
Athens
(tel: 364–37 60)
Leader : Chrysanthos
Demetriades

The events of July 1965, which ended in the military coup of 1967 and the seven years of the Junta, led to a clash between the right and the extreme-right. With the demise of the dictatorship in 1974 the extreme right emerged as a discredited force, represented by its own party, the National Front (EP — *Ethnike Parataxe*), which, in the elections of 1974, amassed 1.10 per cent of the votes. The clash between the right and the extreme right was reinforced during this period when the ringleaders of the coup were convicted and imprisoned by the right which was in power under ND. In the elections of 1977 the National Front registered an increase in its support by polling 6.07 per cent of the votes and gaining five seats in Parliament, but soon afterwards the party divided into two factions, of which only one ran in the elections of 1981 under the name of the Progressive Party, receiving 1.69 per cent of the votes; MPs from the other faction joined the ND list.

In January 1984 a new party formed on the extreme-right: EPEN. In the elections of 1985 it garnered 0.60 per cent of the votes. EPEN's platform calls for the release from prison of military officers involved in the seven-year dictatorship, a referendum to restore the King, and the reassertion of the "patriotic right".

In the European Parliament elections of 1981 the then party of the far right, the *Komma Prondefdekon* (Progressive Party) of Markezinis won 2 per cent of the vote, and one seat in the Parliament.

In the 1984 European Parliament elections the new standard-bearer of the far right, EPEN, won 2.3 per cent of the vote and one seat for its current leader, Chrysanthos Demetriades, who sits in the Group of the European Right.

Eniaea Sosialistiki Parataxi Hellados — ESPE
(United Socialist Alliance of Greece)

ESPE, Stathis Panagoules' party, is another left socialist party. Panagoules is a former PASOK minister, who resigned and founded his own party. His brother was a hero of the resistance against the Junta, and subsequently died mysteriously in 1976.

Socialistiko Komma Hellados
(Socialist Party of Greece)

Headquarters : 2 Vilara Street,
Plateia Aghio
Konstantinou. 104,
37 Athens

The Socialist Party of Greece was formed by Gerasimos Arsenis, a former PASOK Economics Minister from 1982 to 1985, who disagreed with the party's leadership, after which he resigned to set up his own party in April 1987.

Apart from the better-known political parties there are a number of other minor political parties.

One of these is the **Revolutionary Communist Party of Greece** (EKKE — *Epanastatiko Kommounistiko Komma Hellados*). This is a group composed of various Marxist factions such as the Trotskyites, the Maoists, the Stalinists.

Another is the **Communist Party of Greece — Marxist-Leninist** (KKE — ml). At first a united party, it later split into the KKE ml — Major and the KKE ml — Minor.

Another party is the **Ecologists**; it has a limited appeal to Greek voters.

In 1989 a former MP and Minister of PASOK governments, Antonis Tritsis, after being expelled from PASOK, proclaimed his intention to form a new party whose name and platform has not yet been announced.

Ireland

Francis Jacobs

The country

Ireland is a country of 3 million inhabitants, one of the most sparsely populated countries in Western Europe, and yet with one of the youngest and fastest-growing populations. It is a homogenous country with no significant minorities and is overwhelmingly Catholic, with only a small number of Protestants. Dublin is the only large city, and with its 1 million inhabitants, has almost a third of the country's population.

Ireland is divided into four historic provinces, Leinster, Munster, Connaught and Ulster (whose nine counties are divided between six in Northern Ireland and three in the Republic). Ireland remains one of the most agricultural countries in Western Europe, and there is only a small industrial sector.

Political institutions

The head of state is the president, who is directly elected for a seven-year term, but who has only a few real powers which he has little discretion to use. Parliament (the *Oireachtas*) is divided into two houses, the 166-member *Dáil Éireann* and the 60-member *Seanad Éireann*.

Members of the former (known as *Teachtai Dala* or TDs) are elected by single transferable vote (STV), in 41 three- to five-member constituencies, a voting system in which the voter can vote for as many candidates as he or she wishes in an order of preference. The results are only partially proportional; in the 1979 European elections *Fine Gael* and Labour both won four seats with 33.1 per cent and 14.4 per cent of the poll respectively, but are much more proportional in five-member than in three-member constituencies. The balance between three-, four- and five- member constituencies is now decided by an independent commission rather than the incumbent government.

The *Seanad*, created in the corporatist climate of the late 1930s, is chosen by a complex system of indirect voting and nomination, with 43 members elected by members of Parliament and by county and county borough councillors from a list of candidates in five panels (education and culture, agriculture, industry and commerce, labour, public administration and social services), six members elected by the universities and 11 members nominated by the prime minister. The *Seanad* has only limited revising powers and is very much less important than the *Dáil*.

The government Cabinet can be drawn from either House but in practice most members come from the *Dáil*. The prime minister is called the *Taoiseach* and the deputy *Tanaiste*. The executive has a generally powerful position with regard to the legislature but it can be brought down by an adverse vote in the *Dáil*. The maximum term of a government is five years, but no recent government has lasted that long.

The Republic of Ireland has 15 members within the European Parliament, elected again by STV in four large constituencies (Dublin four, Leinster three, Munster five and Connaught-Ulster three).

Brief political history

The circumstances whereby Irish independence was achieved, have had a powerful influence on its subsequent political history. The treaty with Britain in 1921 was seen as "giving the freedom to achieve freedom" by its advocates, and as a sell-out by its adversaries. A brief civil war between the two in 1922 was won by the former, but the division within Irish society has lasted until the present day, with the pro-Treaty forces developing into the *Cumann na nGaedhael* party and subsequently into *Fine Gael* and the anti-Treaty forces into *Fianna Fáil*, and in their more extreme Republican form into the various manifestations of *Sinn Féin*. The continuing partition of Ireland has helped to ensure that this division, while much weaker than before, has not completely disappeared.

In the first few years of the Free State's existence (1922–32) the country was governed by the *Cumann na nGaedhael* party with W.T. Cosgrave as *Taoiseach*. In 1932 *Fianna Fáil* won power and its leader Éamon de Valera was to remain *Taoiseach* for 15 uninterrupted years (1933–1948), to win power on two subsequent occasions (1951–1954 and 1957–59), and finally

Map of Ireland showing the 4 historic provinces and the 41 multi-member constituencies for Dáil elections (showing the number of seats in each constituency).

Source: adapted from *World Atlas of Elections*.

to become President. He modified the terms of the Treaty with Britain and in 1937 introduced a new Constitution. From 1932 onwards *Fianna Fáil* has always been the largest Irish political party and the only one capable of government on its own. The only way, in which power has subsequently been wrested from *Fianna Fáil* has been through coalitions of rival parties. A multi-party coalition under John Costello of *Fine Gael* was formed in 1948 and lasted until 1951. Ironically it was under this government and not under *Fianna Fáil*, that Ireland finally became a republic outside the Commonwealth. Costello led a second multi-party coalition from 1954–57. Subsequent coalitions have all been *Fine Gael* coalitions with Labour, from 1973 to '77 under W.T. Cosgrave's son Liam Cosgrave, and from 1981 to '82 and again from the end of 1982 until early '87 under Garret Fitzgerald.

Interspersed between these periods of coalition government have been further periods of single-party *Fianna Fáil* rule. After de Valera's elevation to the presidency Sean Lemass became *Taoiseach* and presided over a period of rapid economic growth until 1966. Jack Lynch was *Taoiseach* from 1966 to '73, and again from 1977 to '79. Finally Charles Haughey was *Taoiseach* from 1979 to '81, again in 1982 and was re-elected to the office in early 1987.

On two occasions, in 1959 and again in 1968, *Fianna Fáil* has tried to get rid of the STV electoral system, and to replace it by majority voting on the British model, but on both occasions its propositions have been rejected by the Irish electorate, the first time narrowly, the second with greater ease.

The resurgence of the troubles in Northern Ireland in the early 1970s provoked a major crisis within *Fianna Fáil*. Subsequently other Irish political parties have had to re-examine how the 1937 Constitution's claim to sovereignty over the whole of Ireland can best be reconciled with the realities in the North. In late 1985 the Hillsborough Anglo-Irish agreement was signed, which gave the republic a much contested measure of involvement in political life in the North.

In 1972 Ireland's decision to join the EC was massively ratified in a referendum. In 1987 a substantial majority ratified the single European Act in a controversial referendum which touched the issues of neutrality and Irish sovereignty.

Main features of the current political system

Irish political life is distinctive in a number of ways. The central divisions in Irish politics are less on left-right lines than in almost any other country in Europe and the left, in general, is extraordinarily weak. There are a number of reasons for this.

The first is the persistence of Civil War divisions, which have gradually weakened, but not yet vanished. Family traditions and loyalties are still strong and the central divisions in Irish politics are still between *Fianna Fáil* and *Fine Gael*, in spite of their superficial similarities as right of centre political parties.

A second factor is that Ireland is still such a rural society. Significantly too, while many of the farmers are smallholders they do own their own land. Left-wing parties have had little appeal in this context. Most Labour Party deputies who have been elected in rural areas have owed their success to their personal qualities or local or family connections, and have been scarcely distinguishable in their policy positions from their *Fine Gael* or *Fianna Fáil* rivals.

A third factor has been the continued strength of the Catholic Church. Only perhaps in Poland among European countries has the Church retained so much prestige and influence on people's everyday attitudes, especially in the country. This has contributed to a deep-rooted social conservatism. A clear separation of the roles of church and state is still some distance away, as the recent *Fine Gael*-Labour coalition learned to its cost in its patchy attempts to implement what Fitzgerald had entitled his "constitutional crusade" to modernize Irish society and, inter alia, to make it more acceptable to Northern Protestants. While the government did succeed in liberalizing the provision of contraceptives it was forced into supporting a constitutional ban on abortion (although there was already a legislative ban) and was soundly defeated in its referendum to introduce divorce (1985). Only in the most prosperous parts of the Dublin conurbation was there majority support for the measure. Nevertheless, the major Irish political parties have hesitated to define themselves as conservative and have reserved that label for their opponents. They have prided themselves on their pragmatism, and indeed on such central economic issues as government involvement in the economy they have tended not to be very ideological. Economic liberalism in the continental sense has been a weak force.

Dividing lines on policy questions do of course exist, but they vary depending on whether economic or social questions are being considered. On economic issues *Fianna Fáil* (which is particularly strong in those poorer parts of Ireland — the rural west and the inner city slums — which are highly dependent on government expenditure) has been more

Irish elections 1948–present (share of first preference vote and seats won)

	1948	1951	1954	1957	1961	1965	1969	1973	1977	1981	Feb. 1982	Nov. 1982	1987
Fianna Fáil	41.9% (68)	46.3% (69)	43.4% (65)	48.3% (78)	43.8% (70)	47.7% (72)	45.7% (75)	46.2% (69)	50.6% (84)	45.3% (78)	47.3% (81)	45.2% (75)	44.1% (81)
Fine Gael	19.8% (31)	25.8% (40)	32.0% (50)	26.6% (40)	32.0% (47)	34.1% (47)	34.1% (50)	35.1% (54)	30.5% (43)	36.5% (65)	37.3% (63)	39.2% (70)	27.1% (51)
Labour	8.7% (14)	11.4% (16)	12.1% (19)	9.1% (12)	11.6% (16)	15.4% (22)	17.0% (18)	13.7% (19)	11.6% (17)	9.9% (15)	9.1% (15)	9.4% (16)	6.4% (12)
Clann na Talmhan	5.6% (7)	2.9% (6)	3.1% (5)	2.4% (3)	1.5% (2)	—	—	—	—	—	—	—	—
National Labour	2.6% (5)	—	—	—	—	—	—	—	—	—	—	—	—
Clann Na Poblachta	13.2% (10)	4.1% (2)	3.8% (3)	1.7% (1)	1.1% (1)	0.8% (1)	—	—	—	—	—	—	—
Sinn Féin	—	—	—	5.3% (4)	3.1% (0)	—	—	—	—	(H-Block) 2.5% (2)	1.0% (0)	—	1.9% (0)
Workers' Party	—	—	—	—	—	—	—	1.1% (0)	1.7% (0)	1.7% (1)	2.3% (3)	3.3% (2)	3.8% (4)
Progressive Democrats	—	—	—	—	—	—	—	—	—	—	—	—	11.8% (14)
Independents/others	8.3% (12)	9.6% (14)	5.7% (5)	6.6% (9)	6.8% (8)	2.1% (2)	3.2% (1)	3.8% (2)	5.6% (4)	4.2% (5)	3.0% (4)	3.0% (3)	4.8% (3)

favourable than *Fine Gael* to public sector investment in the economy. Ironically it has thus been closer on economic policy to *Fine Gael's* erstwhile allies in the Labour Party, and to the other parties of the left. On the other hand, *Fine Gael* has traditionally been more the party of government austerity and "hair-shirt" economics. The launching of the Progressive Democrats with their more conventional liberal emphasis on cutbacks in public expenditure and on lower taxation has put pressure on *Fine Gael* from this quarter.

On social questions in contrast it is *Fianna Fáil* which is relatively more conservative than *Fine Gael* or the Progressive Democrats or the parties of the left.

The dominant feature of Irish politics, however, is its intense localism. A deputy (TD) is expected to look after local constituency interests and to intercede directly on behalf of constituents in mundane administrative matters, rather than take a position on national issues. This is reinforced by the electoral system which forces TDs to compete at election time not just with the opposition but with members of their own party. "Quota sitting", whereby local party barons nurse their own personal vote, irrespective of the impact on party performance as a whole, is thus common. The level of activity within Parliament itself suffers as a consequence. A considerable number of politicians would now like to see reforms in the electoral system.

This localism also means that politics is more of a family concern in Ireland than almost anywhere else in Europe. In the 21st *Dáil* for instance, no less than 35 TDs (out of the then total of 148) were related in a direct way (sons, daughters, widows, etc.) to former deputies and there are a number of traditional family seats. On the other hand, this localism also means that it is extremely hard to impose candidates from outside, and "carpet-bagging" is rarely successful.

Finally, the system does also leave scope for independents to be elected, or for TDs to change parties, and still get elected. One TD, Noel Browne, was a member of no less than five parties during his career. All five of the defectors to the Progressive Democrats were re-elected in 1987 and four of the five topped their respective polls.

Fianna Fáil (FF) The Republican Party

Headquarters : Áras de Valera, 13 Upper Mount Street, Dublin 2 (tel: 76 15 51)
President and leader : Charles Haughey

General secretary : Frank Wall
Founded : 1926

History

Fianna Fáil is Ireland's largest party, and since it first came to power in 1932 has been in government for over 40 of the subsequent years. *Fianna Fáil* government has been single-party government: since 1932 it has been the only Irish party capable of forming a government on its own.

Fianna Fáil's origins lie within that element of *Sinn Féin* which refused to accept the Treaty with Britain, and after the Civil War took no part in Parliament for the first few years of *Cumann na nGaedhael* government. In 1926, however, a group led by Éamon de Valera decided that the time had come to participate in the institutions of the state. After the latter had narrowly lost a vote as to whether *Sinn Féin* representatives should take their seats in the *Dáil*, de Valera took his followers out of *Sinn Féin*, and on May 16, 1926 set up a new party *Fianna Fáil*, difficult to translate literally into English but loosely meaning "soldiers of destiny".

The first *Fianna Fáil* deputies took their seats in Parliament in August 1927, and the rump of *Sinn Féin* rapidly lost significance. In the years of opposition from 1927 until 1932 *Fianna Fáil* took the opportunity to build up a grass-roots organization which was far stronger than that of the governing party, *Cumann na nGaedhael*.

In 1932 it gained power and retained it for the next 16 years without interruption. Feared by many because of its republican and anti-establishment origins it rapidly became the establishment itself, and its leader Éamon de Valera became the undisputed dominant figure in Irish public life.

A man of De Gaulle-like stature, and generally known as "Dev" he aroused strong conflicting emotions of like and dislike. While he was associated with a particular set of ideals, notably the unity and independence of Ireland as a republic, the restoration of Irish language and culture, and economic self-sufficiency, in practice his rule was characterized by a series of pragmatic adjustments to reality. He got rid of the overt symbols of the erstwhile British dominance such as the oath of allegiance, but Ireland did not become a republic until after his opponents came to power in 1948. He got on with ruling the 26 counties rather than directly taking steps to end partition. Starting with a somewhat anti-clerical image and maintaining independence from the church on some issues (he remained neutral in the Spanish Civil War), he nevertheless gave a more privileged position to the Catholic Church in his new Constitution of 1936. Other professed goals of spreading the Irish language and promoting the ruralization of industries were not achieved.

His achievements were nevertheless considerable. By providing a peaceful alternation of government from his *Cumann na nGaedhael* predecessors he consolidated the institutional structures of the state. Above all he gave Ireland a stronger sense of identity and of real independence from Britain through such measures as the refusal to pay land annuities and through Irish neutrality in World War II.

In 1948, however, de Valera finally lost power, partly because a new republican party *Clann na Poblachta* took away some of *Fianna Fáil's* traditional support particularly in the west.

After three years in opposition de Valera returned to power for a further period of three years from 1951 to 1954. A second coalition government was then formed but after its fall in 1957 *Fianna Fáil* began a further uninterrupted period of government which lasted until 1973.

In 1959 de Valera finally stood down and was replaced by Sean Lemass, who remained *Taoiseach* until 1966. He provided a new image for *Fianna Fáil*, not that of the party of self-sufficiency and protectionism, but of the party of economic expansion, seeking to modernize the economy by dismantling numerous protectionist barriers and by attracting investment into Ireland. A new generation of *Fianna Fáil* leadership emerged, who were identified with the new businesslike ethos, the so-called "men in the mohair suits", like Brian Lenihan and Charles Haughey.

On the resignation of Lemass in 1966 the party had its first-ever contested election, which was won by Jack Lynch from Cork.

Lynch remained leader of the party from 1966–79, with two periods as *Taoiseach*, from 1966–73 and again from 1977–79. He was a quite different sort of leader from his predecessors (and his successor) in that his style of leadership was not charismatic, although he was personally very popular.

Nevertheless his period as leader saw the development of internal divisions within the party from which it has still not completely recovered. The catalytic event was the resurgence of violence in Northern Ireland and its effects in the South, in the form of the 1970 "Arms Crisis" in which prominent members of the government were accused of trying to smuggle arms to the North contrary to government policy. While the two senior ministers in trial, Blaney and Haughey, were acquitted, severe damage had been done. *Fianna Fáil* had been forced to re-examine its attitude towards partition as it had not had to do during the period when party policy concentrated on economic issues, and the party's professed republican faith was put to the test.

Blaney left the party to survive as an Independent *Fianna Fáil* TD in his Donegal bastion, and Boland, another implicated minister, created a new but completely unsuccessful party, *Aontacht Éireann* (Irish Unity Party). Haughey, however, subsequently reaffirmed his loyalty to the leadership and was reintroduced as a front bench spokesman within five years of his disgrace.

In the 1973 election *Fianna Fáil* finally lost power, but by a surprisingly narrow margin in view of the party turmoil in 1970. In opposition *Fianna Fáil* at first appeared unsuccessful but it took the opportunity under its young secretary-general Seamus Brennan, to greatly improve its organization.

The 1977 campaign was a novelty for *Fianna Fáil* in that it was based for the first time ever on a party manifesto. This had a strong populist and expansionary emphasis. *Fianna Fáil* went on to win its highest-ever number of seats.

In 1979 Lynch resigned, after a poor performance in the European elections and two disastrous by-elections which were accompanied by a considerable measure of discontent within the party. In the new leadership election, Charles Haughey, the choice of the majority of the backbenchers, narrowly defeated George Colley, who was supported by most of the members of the government.

Charles Haughey has continued as party leader since 1979, with three periods as *Taoiseach* from 1979–81, for a few turbulent months in 1982, and again from 1987. A strong but extremely controversial leader of the party, he has survived several attempts to remove him, on one occasion by only seven votes. In four general elections under his leadership *Fianna Fáil* has yet to win an overall majority, although it has always remained the largest party.

Support

Since it first came to power in 1932 *Fianna Fáil* has never had less than 40 per cent of the first preference votes, and has topped 50 per cent on two occasions. It is a catch-all party with the widest basis of support of any Irish political party, with at least one seat in every single Irish constituency. Its particular strength is not only that it appeals to traditional and small town voters (especially smaller farmers and tradesmen, and increasingly people in the west of Ireland in general), but it is also more successful among working-class voters in the towns than any of the parties of the left.

Generally (although not invariably) it is rather weaker in the more prosperous farming areas, and in the more upper–middle class areas in the cities.

These patterns were generally confirmed in the February 1987 elections. *Fianna Fáil* was very strong among small farmers and the less well-off self-employed, and was easily the strongest party among the working class. It made particular inroads into the already weaker *Fine Gael* working-class vote, and had almost double the support of *Fine Gael* among skilled working-class voters. It was weaker than *Fine Gael* among large farmers, and was probably only the third party among the more prosperous self-employed. With 44.1 per cent of first preference votes it was easily the first party, but its results in individual constituencies were highly uneven, and adversely affected by the successful retention of their seats by former *Fianna Fáil* deputies who had gone over to the Progressive Democrats.

The party remained strongest in much of the west of Ireland, and especially in Connaught-Ulster, where it had over 50 per cent of first preference votes in the region as a whole. Its highest percentage was the 58.2 per cent it achieved in Donegal South-West, and it also exceeded 50 per cent in other western constituencies, such as Sligo-Leitrim, Mayo East and West, Galway East, Limerick West, Clare and Kerry South.

It topped 50 per cent in six other constituencies around the country, mainly in the Midlands.

A region of relative weakness for the party, however, was Munster, where its vote dropped significantly from 1982 (from 46.1 per cent to 41.7 per cent).

Dublin was still the area where it had the lowest share of the first preference vote (40.5 per cent), but this represented an increase of more than 2 per cent from 1982. *Fianna Fáil* is again by far the largest party in Dublin after a brief period when *Fine Gael* had more votes. Its main strength is in more working-class North Dublin, and it remains weaker in more prosperous and middle-class South Dublin. In Dun Loaghaire it only received 26.2 per cent of first preference votes, and this was the only constituency in the country where it got a lower percentage of first preference than *Fine Gael*. The only other Irish constituency where it was outpolled in first preferences was Des O'Malley's Limerick East.

Organization

Fianna Fáil is by far the largest Irish party in terms of members, possibly as high as 70,000 or 80,000 although there is no precise central tally of its membership.

It has a powerful grass-roots organization. In rural Ireland, in particular, it has always had a strength-in-depth not shared by any of its rivals, and at election time has always had a formidable campaigning machine.

In addition it has always been a party which has prided itself on its discipline. It has a strong hierarchical structure with the powers of the party's national executive being greater than those of the *Fine Gael* equivalent and with a long tradition of strong control by the leader.

In keeping with its pragmatic character, however, *Fianna Fáil* is informally organized in many ways. It is an oft-repeated story that de Valera himself did not want the party constitution widely distributed so that it would not be waved around at meetings and disputes would thus be solved in a common-sense rather than legalistic way. Large numbers of matters are not regulated by the constitution. For example, the parliamentary party is not covered at all, although it has a vital role over the formulation of party policy, and chooses (or dismisses) the party's leader.

Several attempts have been made in recent years to modernize the party's structure. After the party's defeat in 1973 a number of changes were made, including the appointment of press and policy officers and the creation of the first youth wing of any Irish political party, *Ogra Fianna Fáil*. Attempts are now being made to have a more central record of membership as well as to rationalize and cut down on the number of party branches, although this is proving to be a slow and painstaking task.

Fianna Fáil's basic organizational unit is the local branch or *Cumann* (far more Irish terms are used in its constitution than in that of *Fine Gael*), centred on urban areas or wards in the towns and on church areas or polling station areas in the country. Each branch must have a minimum of 10 members. Each branch pays the same low party registration fee and has the same voting rights at selection conventions irrespective of size. There are no limits to the terms of office of branch chairmen and other officers.

In 1985 there were still over 2,500 branches. The highest concentration of branches is often in the west of Ireland (142 in Clare alone). Many branches are in fact inactive.

In each county electoral area there is a district executive or *Comhairli Ceantair*, and in each *Dáil* constituency a constituency executive or *Comhairli Dailcheantair*.

The party's supreme body is its annual congress or *Ard Fheis*, which up to 7,000 attend. In practice it ratifies rather than decides and motions selected for debate are generally supportive rather than critical of the party leadership, but it does act as an important sounding board of the party's mood.

The national executive (*Ard Chomhairle*) with over 40 members, including 15 members elected by the *Ard Fheis*, is given extensive discretionary powers and meets at least once a month. Much of its key work is done within committees. The national executive is served by a headquarters staff of 18.

The party leader is selected by the party's members in the *Dáil*. Although leadership challenges have recently been made, there is no provision for the party leader to be automatically selected to a reselection vote in the event of defeat at an election.

Selection of party candidates for *Dáil* elections is generally made at special constituency conventions. While in theory the national executive is given considerable reserve powers (such as choosing a candidate itself) it is wary of interfering too much with the prerogatives of constituency parties, and its power to add candidates is rarely used.

Party policy is largely made by the leader and by the *Fianna Fáil* members of the government, or by the party spokesmen when in opposition. The party's backbenchers and the party at large has only a limited role. The first general election manifesto was only produced in 1977, and most of the party's TDs only learnt of its contents at the last moment.

Fianna Fáil has an affiliated youth movement, *Ogra Fianna Fáil*, open to all members of the party under 25. There is also a special women's committee, with women's groups in individual constituencies. National *Fianna Fáil* women's conferences have been held since 1984.

There is no national membership fee for individual members of the party — and branches are free to collect their own funds in any way they wish. Each branch must pay £5 to the national party.

A main source of national party funding is the national collection, which takes place on particular dates each year (often at church gates) and which is the responsibility of each branch. Typically 40 per cent is refunded to the constituency executives and 60 per cent returned for use at national level. There have also been national members' lotteries. Besides these major sources of funds the party receives an annual Parliament grant, and receives considerable contributions from the private sector.

Within the European Parliament *Fianna Fáil's* eight MEPs sit in the RDE Group, along with the French Gaullists and the Scottish Nationalists.

Policies

Fianna Fáil has been consistently the stronger of the two traditional parties which stemmed from Ireland's Civil War divisions. Its appeal has been due to many causes: its vigorous assertion of Irish identity and independence; the force of Éamon de Valera's personality; the image that the party has provided of strength and discipline; its capacity (unique among Irish parties) to provide stable single–party government; and its ability as an electoral and patronage machine.

It has successfully sought to be a catch-all party, with an emphasis on social solidarity across class divides, rather than defence of individual class interests. It has also been generally successful in associating itself, especially since the time of Sean Lemass, with economic expansion rather than with economic austerity. It has been pragmatic and non-ideological in the policies that it has pursued in government, and this has enabled it to adjust to changing circumstances.

If the party has had an ideology it has been Republicanism. The party has continued to call for Irish reunification, and has consistently rejected partition. Suspicion of Britain, and even of "West British" attitudes within Ireland have remained strong within the party. Even here, however, as the party which originally opposed the Treaty, but then decided to participate in the Free State's institutions, its behaviour has been pragmatic in practice. It was this clash between Republican aspirations and practical realities (resolved in favour of the latter) which made the 1970 arms trial so traumatic for the party.

In the last few years the party has had to go through another crisis, largely stemming from controversy over the personality of its current leader, Charles Haughey, who has inspired intense loyalty in some and great dislike in others. Conflicts within *Fianna Fáil* over his leadership ultimately helped to lead to the creation of a new political party, the Progressive Democrats, and also damaged *Fianna Fáil's* image of discipline and unity. It was a sign of the party's enduring strength that it was, nevertheless, still able to form a single–party government after the 1987 elections.

In terms of its position on the Irish political spectrum, *Fianna Fáil* has presented a two-fold image in recent years. On economic policy, with its emphasis on economic growth and investment, resisting welfare cuts and promoting tripartite co-operation, it has sometimes appeared closer to the parties of the left and has historically had a close relationship with the trade union movement. On social and moral issues, however, it has appeared as the most uncompromisingly conservative of Irish parties, and the closest to the traditional teaching of the Catholic Church in Ireland.

Its economic policy has traditionally been the product of a variety of pressures. Apart from its general belief in the benefits of economic expansion, *Fianna Fáil* has also had to attempt to fulfil costly campaign promises (as, for example, after the 1977 election). It has not been afraid of direct state involvement where necessary, not least because of its strong support in those parts of Ireland, notably the west, which have been particularly dependent on state assistance. It has strongly emphasized expenditure on infrastructure. Its critics have thus accused it of financial profligacy.

In opposition to the last government *Fianna Fáil* was very critical of the high levels of unemployment, and of the economic trends that had led to a renewed flow of emigrants from Ireland. It also attacked government health cuts, and was critical of privatizations. In its 1987 election manifesto it called for the achievement of a much higher growth rate for the economy. It recognized, however, that expenditure should be contained at 1986 levels, and also called for tax reform. It put a strong emphasis on tripartite consultations between government, employers and unions, and social partnership.

Since it returned to power in 1987 it has again modified its image on economic policy by being more ruthless in carrying out cuts in public expenditure and in seeking to take control of public finances than the preceding coalition government. It has sought to streamline public administration and to achieve pay restraint, and also initiated tax reform, with the introduction of self-assessment for the self-employed and with the aim of substantial tax cuts.

Fianna Fáil has continued to call for the closure of Sellafield nuclear power station, and to underline the need for international control of civil nuclear energy.

On traditional moral issues it has been on the conservative side of the arguments in all the major controversies of recent years, such as contraception and the referendum on the inclusion of a ban on abortion in the Irish Constitution. It did not take a formal position in the divorce referendum but in practice gave a strong lead against divorce. *Fianna Fáil* has put less emphasis than other Irish parties on the need for a more pluralistic society in Ireland.

Since de Valera's day *Fianna Fáil* has always attached a particular priority to the defence of the Irish language. The party's own constitution still lays down that party selection conventions are expected to give priority to Irish-speaking candidates. The present government is seeking to implement a pilot Irish language television service, and a major Irish language centre in Galway.

Policy towards Northern Ireland remains a particularly sensitive subject for the party. When the Anglo-Irish Agreement was first promulgated, Haughey came out in strong opposition, claiming that it led to a recognition by Ireland of the legitimacy of partition, and an acceptance of British sovereignty over Northern Ireland, objectives rejected by *Fianna Fáil*. It has continued to insist on the goal of reunification of Ireland as being non-negotiable. In the face of popular support, however, for the Anglo-Irish Agreement, *Fianna Fáil* began to put less emphasis on its opposition.

From the start, moreover, the party has indicated that it would support any positive measures for the nationalist community in Northern Ireland that might emerge from the Anglo-Irish Agreement. It has called for progress, in particular, on reforming the British administration of justice and security in the province. In its 1987 election manifesto the whole subject received a relatively low priority. Since its return to power it has continued to emphasize these objectives, and has not sought to withdraw from the Agreement, although it still has difficulties with its grass-root supporters.

Fianna Fáil has consistently supported Irish membership of the European Community. It had initial reservations about the Single European Act, especially on the grounds of the possible threat to Irish sovereignty and to Irish neutrality. When in government, however, it supported the implementation of the Single European Act, and campaigned for its acceptance in the 1987 referendum on the subject. It supports the achievement of the internal market by 1992, but is concerned about the possible implications for Ireland of the harmonization of taxation. It also points out the risks of the internal market for countries on the periphery of the Community and thus calls for complementary regional and social measures to ensure greater cohesion.

Fianna Fáil strongly defends the maintenance of Irish military neutrality.

Personalities

Charles Haughey has led *Fianna Fáil* since 1979 (succeeding Lynch as *Taoiseach* in mid-term) and became *Taoiseach* for the third time in March 1987. He is a charismatic but controversial figure within and outside the party, and has survived a number of challenges to his leadership. Haughey entered the *Dáil* in 1957, and has had wide ministerial experience, having been Minister for Justice, Agriculture, Finance and Health and Social Welfare. He was previously *Taoiseach* in 1979–81 and from March to December 1982.

The current Minister for Foreign Affairs is Brian Lenihan, who is also the *Tanaiste*. He has previously been Minister of Justice, Education, Transport and Power, Forestry and Fisheries and also Minister for Agriculture. He has also had a previous stint as Minister for Foreign Affairs.

Another powerful figure within the party is Ray McSharry, Ireland's current EC Commissioner. He has previously been Minister for Agriculture, and was *Tanaiste* and Minister for Finance in 1982 and 1987–88.

Albert Reynolds is the new Minister of Finance, and is an influential figure within the party. He is a former Minister for Posts and Telegraphs, and for Transport, and was also once Minister for Industry and Energy, and Industry and Commerce.

Among the party's other experienced ministers are Gerry Collins, currently at Justice and Ray Burke at Energy. Michael O'Kennedy, a former member of the EC Commission is Minister for Agriculture.

A leading vote-getter within the party is Bertie Ahern, who was a successful Lord Mayor of Dublin and is now Minister of Labour.

The current Irish President, Patrick Hillery, another former EC Commissioner, also comes from *Fianna Fáil*.

Fine Gael — FG

Headquarters	: 51, Upper Mount Street, Dublin 2 (tel: 76 15 73)
President and leader of the parliamentary party	: Alan Dukes
General secretary	: Edward O'Reilly
Membership	: 40,000
Founded	: 1933

History

The origins of *Fine Gael* within *Cumann na nGaedhael*, the party set up in 1922–23 to represent those who supported the Treaty with Britain, which in their view, flawed though it was, still gave Ireland the "freedom to achieve freedom".

While it never won more than 40 per cent of the national vote *Cumann na nGaedhael* provided the first three Irish governments from 1923–33. Its greatest achievement was to provide a solid framework for the future governance of the country after the turmoil of the independence struggle and the Civil War. It was strong on law and order, and highly conservative on economic issues. It also supported free trade over protectionism. In the 1932 general election it came well behind the *Fianna Fáil* party of Éamon de Valera, and relinquished power on March 9 1932. In a new election in 1933 it fell further behind.

The second successive defeat led to a period of turmoil in the party and to a merger between *Cumann na nGaedhael* and the National Centre Party. The latter was a new party which won 11 seats in the 1933 elections and whose pattern of support was very similar to that of the earlier Farmers' Party. The third and most controversial partner in the political realignment of 1933 was the semi-fascist National Guard of Blueshirts of General Eoin O'Duffy, who became the leader of the new party, *Fine Gael*, when it was launched in September 1933. He was edged out a year later, when W.T. Cosgrave resumed the leadership.

Fine Gael was out of power for a first period of 16 years as *Fianna Fáil* consolidated its position as the governing party. At the 1937 election the merged party only won the number of seats (48) that *Cumann na nGaedhael* had won on its own in the disastrous elections of 1933, and in the 1938, 1943 and 1944 elections it won progressively less seats at each election, as well as a lower share of the total poll, so that by 1944 it was left with only 30 seats (down from 62 in 1927) and 20.5 per cent of the vote (down from 38.7 per cent in 1927). Few serious attempts were made to revitalize the party, and no new blood was being recruited. In early 1944 W.T. Cosgrave resigned and was replaced by Richard Mulcahy as president of the party. When Mulcahy returned to the *Dáil* in May 1944 he became parliamentary leader as well.

In 1948, however, *Fianna Fáil* was finally ousted from government. While *Fine Gael* itself had barely advanced, other parties had done well enough that an anti-*Fianna Fáil* coalition could be formed under *Fine Gael* leadership, but with J.A. Costello as *Taoiseach* rather than the less acceptable (because of his Civil War record) Richard Mulcahy.

Return to government helped to revive *Fine Gael*. Ironically in view of its origins as a pro-Treaty party (and one that was taunted as the West British party) it was the *Fine Gael*-led inter-party government which led Ireland out of the Commonwealth and declared the Republic. It was successful on a number of other fronts, notably the improvement of public health, but eventually one of its Ministers clashed with the church over the so-called "mother and child health scheme", and it fell in 1951. After the subsequent general election *Fianna Fáil* took power, although *Fine Gael* had gained nine seats and won a 6 per cent larger share of the poll than in 1948.

After three years of opposition a second inter-party government was constituted in 1954, after *Fine Gael* had made another strong advance in the general election of that year. J.A. Costello was again *Taoiseach*. The 1954–57 government is generally considered to have been less successful than the preceding inter-party government, and its tough deflationary economic policies lost it popular support. In 1957 it lost power to *Fianna Fáil* for a further 16-year period as the Irish economy entered a period of rapid growth.

In 1959 the joint leadership of Mulcahy and Costello ended with twin resignations and James Dillon defeated Liam Cosgrave. James Dillon had been the leading parliamentary dissident on Irish neutrality in World War II and had resigned from *Fine Gael* over the issue, only rejoining the party in 1952. As an Independent TD he had been a successful Minister for Agriculture in the first inter-party government and was also associated with opposition to the compulsory teaching of Irish in schools.

Dillon's leadership was a period of considerable stirrings within *Fine Gael*, as younger elements centred around Declan Costello, the son of the former *Taoiseach*, tried to change the conservative image of the party and provide it with a new set of economic and social policies. In 1965 this culminated in the preparation of a new *Fine Gael* programme entitled "The Just Society". The leadership and the parliamentary party's commitment to it was at best half-hearted, and a further electoral defeat led to the programme being sidelined. Its significance, nevertheless, was considerable in that new talent, such as Garret Fitzgerald, was attracted to the party.

After the 1965 defeat Dillion resigned and was replaced by his former rival Liam Cosgrave, son of Ireland's first *Taoiseach*. He was a cautious and conservative leader of the party. After seeing off a challenge to his leadership in 1972 Cosgrave finally became *Taoiseach* in 1973 in a coalition government between *Fine Gael* and Labour, on the basis of a joint election manifesto: the two parties had learnt their lesson from the 1969 election when they might well have been able to oust *Fianna Fáil* if they had come to a pre-election agreement.

The 1973–77 coalition started well but later lost the initiative. On social issues it took a generally conservative line and some of its eco-nomic measures, such as a wealth tax alienated many of its strongest supporters, such as large farmers. It failed to properly register the shift of public opinion against it and its severe defeat in the 1977 general election came as a complete surprise.

Liam Cosgrave immediately resigned and was replaced by Garret Fitzgerald.

In 1979 *Fine Gael* won four seats in the first European Parliament elections. In 1981 party reorganization paid off with the return of a *Fine Gael*-Labour coalition to power, with Fitzgerald as *Taoiseach*. This had only a precarious parliamentary majority and collapsed in early 1982 over its tough budget proposals. In the new general election in November 1982 *Fine Gael* won 70 seats and was only five seats short of *Fianna Fáil*, the party's best-ever performance in terms of votes and of seats. A *Fine Gael*-Labour coalition was again constituted with Fitzgerald as *Taoiseach*, but this time with an adequate parliamentary majority.

The government had an uneven record, with some marked successes (e.g. the signing of the Anglo-Irish Agreement in November 1985), and considerable failures (e.g. the government's decisive rebuff in the 1986 referendum on divorce). There was increasing dissatisfaction, however, with the government's record on the economy. The government was also affected by the rise of the Progressive Democrats. All this eventually caused increasing tensions between *Fine Gael* and its Labour coalition partners, especially in 1986–87. There were also problems with rebellious backbenchers within the party's own ranks. The government finally fell in January 1987. In the February 1987 election. *Fine Gael's* support dropped by over 12 per cent to only 27.1 per cent of national first preferences. Its total of seats fell from 70 to only 51. *Fine Gael* then went into opposition. In March 1987 Garret Fitzgerald stood down as leader of the party, and Alan Dukes defeated John Bruton and Peter Barry to become the party's new leader.

In the 1984 European Parliament elections *Fine Gael* had obtained six seats on 32.2 per cent of the vote. It has 16 members of the Irish Senate.

Support

Fine Gael is a party with broad-based support throughout Ireland, although with consistently lower overall support than its great rival *Fianna Fáil* . *Fine Gael's* strongest support base has been among the more prosperous people in Irish society, and, in particular middle-sized and large farmers, and professionals and the upper-middle classes in the cities. Its regional support has varied considerably according to the strengths of its local TDs, but in general it has had particular support in the southern part of Dublin county (the more middle-class part of the Dublin conurbation), in Cork city and in the wealthier agricultural areas of Munster. *Fine Gael* was traditionally weaker among smaller farmers, agricultural labourers, the smaller shopkeepers in the provincial towns and among the working class in the cities. It has also been losing support in much of the far west of Ireland.

In the late 1970s and early 1980s *Fine Gael* considerably extended its electoral support among all social classes. It took a strong lead over *Fianna Fáil* among the upper middle classes, and improved its position among both the skilled and unskilled working classes, although it was still well behind *Fianna Fáil* among these groups. It also did well among young people and women. In the November 1982 elections it even outpolled *Fianna Fáil* in Dublin by 41 per cent to 38 per cent.

In the February 1987 elections it suffered a severe electoral setback, and its recent gains were reversed. It appears to have lost sharply among middle-class and professional voters to the Progressive Democrats, in particular, and some of its working-class vote appears to have reverted to *Fianna Fáil*. Its highest support was among farmers with more than 50 acres, but it was a poor second to *Fianna Fáil* among smaller farmers. Elsewhere its strongest support was among the more prosperous self-employed and among professionals. Even among the skilled working-class voters it appears to have had only half *Fianna Fáil's* support, and it was weakest of all among unskilled working-class voters.

In regional terms it fared worst in Dublin where its vote dropped by 17.4 per cent to only 23.7 per cent in February 1987. The damage was most contained in Munster where the party lost 9.3 per cent of the vote, and polled 26.9 per cent. *Fine Gael* had a few setbacks even in this region, but held on to its seats in a number of potentially vulnerable constituencies (Clare, Cork North-West and South-West) and had one major success when it gained a seat in North Kerry. In Connaught-Ulster its vote fell by 9.9 per cent to 31.8 per cent, although this relatively high figure is more a reflection of third and fourth party weakness (the Progressive Democrats and Labour) in this region than of inherent *Fine Gael* strength.

Fine Gael obtained more first preferences than *Fianna Fáil* in only one constituency in the country, in its traditionally strongest constituency of Dun Laoghaire to the south of Dublin.

Organization

Fine Gael has had a traditionally weaker organization than *Fianna Fáil*, stemming originally from the failure of its predecessor, *Cumann na nGaedhael*, to build up a strong grass–roots structure when it was in government from 1923 to 1933. Total party membership was unknown, there was little central organization and the locally entrenched party barons sought the minimum of central interference. There were no major improvements until the late 1970s.

The severe and unexpected defeat of the *Fine Gael*-led government in 1977, caused partly by poor organization (the party had not even been commissioning private polls to gauge how the party was doing) led finally to a major restructuring under Garret Fitzgerald, the new party leader, and Peter Prendergast, the new general secretary. A new party constitution was prepared. A fully-fledged youth organization was set up. Tighter links were established between the central organization and individual constituencies (notably through the installation of constituency organizers and public relations officers) and the centre was given a greater say in candidate selection. Sitting TDs had to submit themselves for reselection. Proper membership registers were drawn up, and limits were established to the terms of office of local party officials. A "new model scheme" was also established for local branch representation, in order to make it more proportional to the number of electors within a branch's functional area, and thus to have fairer voting procedures within the party. *Fine Gael* now has a much more effective organizational structure than before.

It now has just under 2,000 branches around the country. Branches must have a minimum of nine members. Above these are the district executives. Constituency executives consist of delegates from each branch and the publicly-elected representatives from the area.

The party congress or *Ard Fheis* is held on an annual basis. It recommends policy for the party but does not decide it. It is generally less deferential to the party leadership than its equivalent in *Fianna Fáil*, but more so than that of the Labour Party.

The *Fine Gael* national executive consists of members elected at the *Ard Fheis*, party officers, elected parliamentarians and representatives of young *Fine Gael* and other organized groups within the party. The national executive is served by the party's central secretariat, with a staff of around 17.

The party's leader is elected by the *Fine Gael* parliamentary party. After each election in which *Fine Gael* does not subsequently form a part of a government, the parliamentary party must automatically vote on the leadership by secret ballot within a two-month period. The party president is elected at the *Ard Fheis*, and is almost invariably the same person as the parliamentary leader.

Party policy is largely decided by the parliamentary party. The party's parliamentary candidates are chosen at constituency selection conventions. The national executive instructs the constituency convention on the number of candidates to be selected, and has the right to confirm, delete or substitute as well as add candidates. It normally, however, ratifies the selection convention choices.

The party's youth movement is called "Young Fine Gael". It has been very successful, and has showed its independence from the parent party, as when it campaigned against the constitutional amendment on abortion in early 1983.

Party finance comes from the affiliation fees from the branch (£2 out of the £2.50 individual membership dues) a £1,500 levy per seat in each constituency (e.g. £4,500 from a three-seat constituency), a nationally organized constituency draw and contributions from business and elsewhere. The party also receives a special *Oireachtas* or parliament grant.

Fine Gael's six members are in the European People's Party in the European Parliament. The party is also a member of the European Christian Democratic Union, and the Christian Democratic International.

Policies

A central strategic problem for *Fine Gael* is that it has never been able to form a government on its own, and has always had to enter into coalitions. The severe reverse in the 1987 election left it far behind *Fianna Fáil*, and again having to face the issue of possible future coalition partners.

A complicating factor has been the rise of the Progressive Democrats. *Fine Gael* will probably either have to re-absorb Progressive Democrat support, or come to some form of arrangement with it. In the latter case, the Progressive Democrats are potentially a much more compatible coalition partner for *Fine Gael* than Labour proved in the 1982–87 government. On church-state relations, Northern Ireland and economic issues, *Fine Gael* and the Progressive Democrats are not too far apart.

Fine Gael and Labour, on the other hand, have been sharply divided on economic issues. In the past the two parties have needed each other to oust *Fianna Fáil*, but the experience of the last coalition, and the apparent determination of the Labour Party to try to rebuild in opposition, have made a coalition between them difficult to recreate in the near future.

A further difficulty for the new *Fine Gael* leadership has been the *Fianna Fáil* government's newfound emphasis on economic austerity, which has given *Fine Gael* a more difficult target to attack.

The party has been slowly changing in character. While both it and its main rival, *Fianna Fáil* have been essentially conservative parties in European political terms, *Fine Gael* has had the more conservative image of the two, because of the nature of its support, the lack of the populism that has often characterized *Fianna Fáil*, and *Fine Gael's* persistent emphasis on fiscal rectitude, and on a restrictive spending policy.

The "Just Society" initiative of 1965, while unsuccessful in the short term, clearly attracted new talent into the party, and marked a turning point for the party. In 1968 an attempt was even made to change the party's name to "*Fine Gael* — Social Democratic Party" but the proposed change was defeated after a postal ballot of party branches. With the arrival of Garret Fitzgerald to power the "Just Society" generation in the party finally came to the forefront.

The proposed name change was a misleading one. Garret Fitzgerald himself was the nearest person to a Social Democrat that the party possessed. The trend could more accurately be described as a reinforcement of the more liberal wing within the party on social and moral issues, and a new party emphasis on pluralism in Irish society. On issues such as divorce and contraception, for instance, *Fine Gael*, while still highly conservative by European standards, had generally been less so than *Fianna Fáil*. Originally closer to the church than was *Fianna Fáil*, it is now a stronger advocate of greater separation between church and state. *Fine Gael* has also been successful in electing younger and women candidates. Young technocrats of whom the current leader Alan Dukes is a good example, were attracted to the modern and less authoritarian structures of the party, and indeed the choice of Alan Dukes as leader after Fitzgerald was a confirmation of the changes within the party.

The modification in the party's character, however, is only relative, even on moral issues. *Fine Gael* never supported liberalization of the abortion law, for example, but merely felt that a referendum on a constitutional amendment should not have been necessary. Moreover not all of the party members have agreed with the change in emphasis and there remains a substantial conservative wing within the party. In the 1973–77 coalition government, the *Fine Gael Taoiseach*, Liam Cosgrave and his Minister for Education, Dick Burke, both voted against their own government's bill to allow the sale of contraceptives to married couples. Prominent members showed a marked lack of enthusiasm for the referendum on divorce. *Fine Gael's* 1982–87 parliamentary contingent included some of the most socially conservative members of the entire *Dáil*, such as Alice Glenn and Oliver J. Flanagan, although these became increasingly untypical of the party (and indeed Alice Glenn was not re-selected). In the 1987 election *Fine Gael* did not make a major issue of pluralism, but did call for reform of the laws on separation, marriage and family property. The party's less conservative course on social questions has had less of an equivalent in economic policy. Indeed its 1987 election manifesto saw a marked shift in the direction of economic liberalism. *Fine Gael* made a clear distinction between itself and the Labour Party, and emphasized the need to make large cuts in public spending, to reduce taxation and to liberalize the labour market. *Fine Gael* also advocated a substantial degree of privatization of state companies. *Fianna Fáil* was strongly attacked as a party of high borrowing and high spending.

Ideological liberalism is, however, still tempered. *Fine Gael* strongly defended its own record on social welfare, claiming that payments had been kept ahead of inflation, and that they would be maintained in the future.

An issue on which there has been considerable divergence with *Fine Gael* is Northern Ireland. In practice their respective policies when in government have not been very different, but *Fianna Fáil* has been the quicker to play the Republican card, and *Fine Gael* the more ready to concede the need for measures of rapprochement between the Nationalist and Unionist traditions within Northern Ireland. Both major Anglo-Irish initiatives in Northern Ireland in recent years, the failed Sunningdale agreement in 1973–74 and the more recent Hillsborough agreement of late 1985 have come when a *Fine Gael*–led coalition was in power. *Fine Gael* has continued to defend strongly the Anglo-Irish Agreement, where *Fianna Fáil* was initially very critical and still has internal party divisions on the issue. *Fine Gael* has also made a strong link, unlike *Fianna Fáil*, between its Northern Ireland policy and the need for a more pluralistic society within Ireland.

Fine Gael has strongly supported Irish membership of the European Community, and has supported further European integration, with its members in the European Parliament voting in favour of the Spinelli Draft Treaty on European Union. The inter-government committee which was subsequently set up to examine possible ways of strengthening the European Community was chaired by Senator Jim Dooge, a prominent member of *Fine Gael*.

The party also supported the ratification of the Single European Act, and campaigned in favour of it during the 1987 referendum. *Fine Gael* has called for increases in the Community structural funds, and defended the interests of Irish agriculture within the Common Agricultural Policy framework.

Fine Gael has committed itself to the retention of Irish political neutrality. Recent calls, however, for a debate on the issue have come far more from *Fine Gael* than from *Fianna Fáil*.

On the issue of civil nuclear energy *Fine Gael* has recently called for the creation of a European Community inspectorate.

Personalities

Alan Dukes was elected leader of *Fine Gael* in March 1987. He was born in 1945, and is a former chief economist of the Irish Farmers' Association and subsequently its first representative in Brussels. He was then in the cabinet of *Fine Gael's* EC Commissioner Richard Burke. He was first elected as a TD for Kildare in 1981 and became Minister for Agriculture on his first day in the *Dáil*. In the 1982–87 coalition he was first Minister for Finance and then Minister for Justice. He has a technocratic style of leadership.

The party's deputy leader is John Bruton, who is also its current spokesman on industry and commerce. He was one of the leadership contenders in 1987, and is a former Minister for Finance (on two occasions) and Minister for Industry and Energy, and for Industry and Commerce. He was born in 1947. He is the party's most forceful economic conservative, and a guardian of the traditional *Fine Gael* fiscal rectitude. He was one of those with most doubts about the coalition with Labour.

Peter Barry, the party's current spokesman on Foreign Affairs, was the third leadership contender in 1987. He is a successful businessman from Cork (based on his family's traditional tea business). Peter Barry has had extensive ministerial experience as Minister for Transport and Power, Minister for Education, Minister for the Environment, and then as Minister for Foreign Affairs during the 1982–87 coalition, during which he became responsible for implementation of the Anglo-Irish Agreement. Barry is more conservative than Fitzgerald or Dukes, and has been an important link between the old and the new *Fine Gael*. He was born in 1928.

Other *Fine Gael* front bench spokesmen include Michael Noonan at Finance and Public Service, Jim Mitchell at Social Welfare, Gemma Hussey at Education and Avril Doyle at Agriculture.

Garret Fitzgerald, who was a dominant figure in the party and in Irish politics for a considerable period, is still in parliament but is no longer playing a major role.

Peter Sutherland, the former EC Commissioner, is another *Fine Gael* member.

Progressive Democrats — PD

Headquarters	: 25 South Frederick Street, Dublin 2 (tel: 01–79 43 99)
Party leader	: Desmond O'Malley
Chairman	: Derry Healy
General secretary	: Patrick Cox
Founded	: 1985

History

The Progressive Democrats are the newest Irish political party, and have enjoyed considerable success since their foundation on Dec. 21, 1985.

The origins of the party lay originally with a schism within the *Fianna Fáil* party, essentially provoked by the controversial leadership of Charles Haughey. His most prominent critic within the party was Desmond O'Malley, TD for Limerick East and a *Fianna Fáil* minister on several occasions. After he failed to dislodge Haughey as leader, and after disagreeing with the party line on such issues as social policy and Northern Ireland, he left *Fianna Fáil*. In December 1985 he joined up with another dissident *Fianna Fáil* deputy, Mary Harney (who had just been expelled from the party for voting in favour of the Anglo–Irish Agreement), to form the Progressive Democrats.

The reaction to the party's launch showed that there was a considerable pool of opposition within Ireland to the existing party structure, and the public meetings held by the new party attracted unprecedented crowds of up to 2–3,000. Between 8,000 and 9,000 new members were recruited in the first week.

In mid-January 1986, two more *Fianna Fáil* TDs, Pearse Wyse from Cork, and Bobby Molloy from Galway West, joined the new party, followed by two Labour Party senators, Helen McAuliffe–Ennis and Tim Conway. Finally in April 1986 a *Fine Gael* TD, Michael Keating, also joined the Progressive Democrats.

Opinion polls showed a rapid rise in popularity for the new party, with one giving them 25 per cent support, 2 per cent higher than the then government party, *Fine Gael*. They later slipped in the polls, but in the general election of February 1987 they achieved an extremely creditable score in their first electoral outing, fielding candidates in 33 of the 41 constituencies and winning 11.8 per cent of the national first preference vote (almost double that of the Labour Party). Four of their five sitting deputies topped the polls in their constituencies, and the fifth was also re-elected. Nine new deputies were also elected, making the Progressive Democrats the third largest party in the *Dáil*.

Support

In the February 1987 general election the Progressive Democrats achieved respectable votes almost everywhere they stood, although their strongest area was the southern part of Dublin. They polled best in urban rather than rural constituencies. They did outstandingly well in certain constituencies where there were strong personal votes for sitting TDs like Pearse Wyse, Bobby Molloy and Mary Harney. The best result of all was in Des O'Malley's own fief of Limerick East, one of only two constituencies in Ireland where *Fianna Fáil* was outvoted on first preferences (the Progressive Democrats got 37.1 per cent, and where not only O'Malley but also his running mate, Peadar Clohessy, were elected.

It is difficult to distinguish personal from other reasons why people voted for the Progressive Democrats. Part of their vote was clearly a protest vote against the other parties. Nevertheless the pro-enterprise stance of the party on economic issues, and its liberal views on social issues, has given it a stronger basis of support among self-employed businessmen and young professionals and the middle class in general, than among other groups.

Although the party's founders come from *Fianna Fáil*, and they brought many of their local activists with them, surveys as early as February 1986 showed that its members included as many former members of *Fine Gael* as of *Fianna Fáil*. It is also evident that a considerable proportion of the 12 per cent drop in *Fine Gael* support in 1987 went straight to the Progressive Democrats, and that they have posed a particular threat to the *Fine Gael* support base. It is uncertain whether this initial support base can be further consolidated.

Organization

The Progressive Democrats have a membership list of around 10,000 names of whom 40–50 per cent are active members. The party is organized in 35 out of the 41 constituencies, and currently has around 250 branches. Each constituency group is controlled by a constituency council of local office-holders and branch representatives. The constituency organizer and public relations officer cannot stand as candidates in the subsequent general election. A register of members is maintained at constituency level.

A national conference is held annually, with constituency representation based on the size of their local membership. There is also a national council of over 50 members, including the parliamentary party, and one representative for each constituency group. The national council meets around once every six weeks, and acts as an important sounding board. There is also a smaller national executive of around 21–22 members, including 10 members of the national council and four representatives of the parliamentary group.

The party's president is elected by the national conference. The party's *Dáil* deputies elect their parliamentary leader (the effective leader of the party), who, as in the *Fine Gael* constitution, must submit himself or herself to a vote of confidence (within one month of each general election).

Dáil and local election candidates are chosen at constituency conventions with branches voting by single transferable vote. Each branch is entitled to one delegate per 10 members. The national executive may lay down geographical criteria for the choice of candidates, may add, delete or substitute a candidate, and must ratify all chosen candidates. Several candidates were added in the 1987 general election, including Geraldine Kennedy, the eventually successful candidate in Dun Laoghaire.

The party's constitution calls on the party's local units to have policy development officers. The parliamentary party and the national council are involved in policy development and review. There are provisions for issues which prove contentious at national council to be decided upon in a subsequent written ballot of members, although such a ballot has not yet taken place.

The party initially decided to have no special groups within the party. Although there has subsequently been some talk of creating a youth group, neither such a group nor a women's group has yet been established.

Each member pays a £5 registration fee to his or her branch. The branches send a total of £50 to the party's central organization. There is also an annual collection with a target or levy in each constituency, and the party also receives public funds in the form of a leader's allowance to the parliamentary party.

Donation from business played a certain role in the funding of the party's first general election campaign in February 1981, but not as much as had been hoped.

In May 1988 the Progressive Democrats were admitted as members of the European Liberal Democratic and Reformist Group (ELDR). They have no institutional linkage, however, with the Liberal International.

The leadership of the Progressive Democrats, the Alliance Party of Northern Ireland and the Social and Liberal Democrats in the rest of the United Kingdom have also met to discuss the possible establishment of common positions on certain policy issues.

Policies

It is still too early to say whether the Progressive Democrats will be a durable feature on the Irish political scene. They are currently in a difficult strategic position as the present *Fianna Fáil* government is putting into practice some of the rigorous economic policies which have been advocated by the Progressive Democrats in contrast to the previous expansionary policies of *Fianna Fáil*. Moreover support for the Progressive Democrats has also come from people disillusioned with the gap between the *Fine Gael*–Labour coalition's rhetoric and its actual practice in government. With the break-up of the coalition, and *Fine Gael's* current emphasis on economic austerity in opposition, the Progressive Democrats' distinctive stance has also been undercut.

At present the Progressive Democrats emphasize their independence, and their unwillingness to enter into any kind of pre-election pact with other Irish parties. They key to the party's future, however, may well lie in its relations with *Fine Gael*. In spite of their *Fianna Fáil* origins the Progressive Democrats appear closer in their social background and in their policy position to *Fine Gael*, although they are closer to its conservative wing on economic policy, and to the more social-democratic wing on traditional moral and church-state issues. Their vote may be absorbed by *Fine Gael* or the two parties may come to some future understanding. *Fine Gael* clearly sees them as a more promising coalition partner than its former Labour Allies.

In both economic and traditional moral policy terms the Progressive Democrats are liberal (in the continental sense) in orientation. They also make much of the fact that they are not beholden to any interest group, and that they represent a real escape route from the old Civil War division in Irish politics.

The party has carved out a distinctive position in economic policy issues, where it has been a leading advocate of cuts in both government expenditure, and in direct and indirect taxation. The party's strongest policy plank in the February 1987 general election was to reduce the standard rate of income tax to 25 per cent, and to maintain only one higher rate of income tax at 40 per cent.

The party advocates the closing off of certain corporate tax shelters and is also an advocate of privatization through selling shares in state companies. It wishes to overhaul the welfare system and to concentrate resources more selectively on the most needy. A key objective, however, is to encourage greater self-reliance on the part of the people, and a lesser role for the state.

While the party's liberalism has a conservative tinge on economic issues this is less so on traditional social and moral issues, where the party has advocated greater pluralism in Irish society, and independence between church and state. The party supported the implementation of divorce legislation, but in the light of the referendum result, put less emphasis on this issue in its 1987 manifesto. It recognizes that rapid progress cannot be made to what is still a desirable objective.

On environmental policy the Progressive Democrats advocate the closure of Sellafield nuclear power station in the United Kingdom. The Progressive Democrats emphasize the need for European–wide co-operation and monitoring of civil nuclear plants.

They also wish to see reforms of Parliament, including abolition of the Senate and a reduction in the number of *Dáil* deputies from 166 to 120. They wish to improve the role of backbenchers, and to strengthen *Dáil* committees. They advocate decentralization of government departments and administrations.

One of the main issues over which deputies like Des O'Malley and Mary Harney left *Fianna Fáil* was the latter's negative attitude towards the Anglo-Irish Agreement, for which the new party has given its strong support. The party's constitution calls for the advancements of unity among all Irish people, but by peaceful means and based on pluralist principles. The Progressive Democrats have also advocated a review of whether Articles 2 and 3 of the Irish Constitution should be re-phrased to show that Ireland only favours unity by consent. In this spirit they have also called for a wider constitutional review.

The Progressive Democrats are strong supporters of the European Community. They were in favour of the Single European Act and they support the fundamental aim of working for a closer union of the European peoples. They support progressive approximation of indirect taxation. In the ELDR draft programme they have called for Ireland's traditional neutrality to be noted and respected. The Progressive Democrats have indicated, however, that they are willing to debate the "sacred cow" of neutrality in the future especially in the context of enhanced European co-operation on security matters.

Personalities

Des O'Malley is the party's leader and clearly its dominant figure. The party's general election slogan in 1987 was "Dessie can do it". O'Malley's political base is Limerick City, where his uncle was his predecessor as TD. As a *Fianna Fáil* minister he was well respected, and at one point was seen as Haughey's leading rival for the leadership of the party.

The party's deputy leader is its main recruit from *Fine Gael*, Michael Keating, a Dublin TD who was also a former Lord Mayor of Dublin. The party's most popular speaker after O'Malley, however, is Mary Harney, a former *Fianna Fáil* TD who represents a Dublin constituency, and who is the party spokesperson on social welfare and institutional reform.

Bobby Molloy, the party's third recruit from *Fianna Fáil* was also a former minister. He has carved out a strong personal base for himself in Galway West, where he was easily re-elected in an area with a traditionally strong *Fianna Fáil* allegiance. Pearse Wyse, a fourth *Fianna Fáil* TD to join the new party also topped the poll in his constituency of Cork North Central.

The party has successfully recruited among the old *Fianna Fáil* political dynasties, and among its candidates in 1987 were an Aiken, a Gibbon and a Colley (the two latter elected). Further recruits to the Progressive Democrats' parliamentary ranks included Michael McDowell, the former party chairman and a former chairman of Garret Fitzgerald's own *Fine Gael* constituency, who is now the party's finance spokesman, and Geraldine Kennedy, a prominent journalist, who now speaks for the party on foreign affairs and on Northern Ireland.

Labour Party

Headquarters	:	16 Gardiner Place, Dublin 1 (tel: 78 84 11)
Party leader	:	Dick Spring
Chairman	:	Mervyn Taylor
General secretary	:	Ray Kavanagh
Estimated membership:		5,500

History

The Labour Party's date of foundation is usually claimed to be 1912, but its existence as a properly organized party dates more realistically from 1922, when it contested its first general election. Formal links with the Irish Trade Union Congress were maintained until 1930, when the party became a separate entity.

After the loss of its two most inspirational figures (James Connolly shot and James Larkin fleeing to the United States), the Labour movement lacked strong leadership and in 1918 took the decision not to contest the general election of that year. During the Civil War it remained neutral. During the first five years of the free state, Labour became the official parliamentary opposition to the *Cumann na nGaedhael* government. Its electoral performance fluctuated greatly, winning a percentage of votes in 1922 (over 25 per cent) which it has never since achieved, falling away badly in 1923, but again winning its largest ever number of seats in June 1927, after which it only narrowly failed to form a minority coalition government with the National League and with outside support from *Fianna Fáil*. This is the nearest that the Irish Labour Party has ever come to providing an Irish prime minister. Once de Valera had led *Fianna Fáil* back into Parliament, Labour slipped to a poor third. At successive elections in 1927 and 1932, the first two party leaders, Thomas Johnson and T.J. O'Connell lost their seats and in 1932 Labour was reduced to only seven deputies, its lowest ever figure. Nevertheless its seven votes turned out to be critical in bringing Éamon de Valera to power for the first time.

Fianna Fáil and Labour again worked closely together in the 1933 election and Labour again backed the return of a *Fianna Fáil* government in 1937, but for the last time. Since 1937 Labour has remained either independent on the backbenches or has joined a coalition with anti-*Fianna Fáil* parties.

The Labour Party was mainly conservative. Labour's deputies were generally well-known local personalities whose political survival depended more on local constituency service than on adherence to socialist ideology. Labour members were only too keen to declare their allegiance to Catholic principles.

Both the party and the trade union movement were greatly weakened by two schisms, one in the 1920s within the largest union — the Irish Transport and General Workers Union (ITGWU) — and one in the 1940s when the ITGWU disaffiliated from the Labour Party and five of the Labour members sponsored by the ITGWU formed the National Labour Party, which remained in competition with Labour from 1944 until 1950, when they again merged. The essential cause of these two schisms, which were particularly damaging to Labour in Dublin, was a bitter personal struggle between James Larkin (who had returned from the United States in 1923) and William O'Brien, the general secretary of ITGWU.

Labour had made a small-scale electoral recovery before the split but it again lost support. Nevertheless, in 1948 it participated in the first inter-party government under *Fine Gael* leadership. Such a coalition would not have been possible without the support of the five National Labour deputies, who defied a recommendation from the breakaway Union Congress to support de Valera's renomination.

Labour was then in government from 1948–51, and 1954–57. After Labour left office in 1957 it decided that it would try to win support on its own, and not enter future coalitions.

In 1960 its leader, William Norton, who had led the party since 1932, resigned and was replaced by Brendan Corish.

The 1960s saw the Labour Party in continuous opposition, but with rising electoral support and with the party belief (in the words of its own new slogan) that the "seventies will be Socialist", that the Civil War divisions were no longer relevant, and that there was at last real opening for a left-of-centre alternative. The party gradually became less conservative, became more prepared to call itself Socialist and attracted a large number of prominent intellectuals like Conor Cruise O'Brien. The party made particular advances in Dublin, where it had previously been weaker than in many rural areas.

The party's go-it-alone strategy had to be revised, however, after the 1969 general election when the party performed far worse than its ambitious expectations. Labour decided it would support a new coalition and in 1973 this paid off in electoral terms with Labour gaining one seat more than in 1969 on a lesser share of the vote and entering a new government with its leader, Brendan Corish as Deputy Prime Minister.

After the coalition lost power in 1977 Brendan Corish stood down, and was replaced as leader by Frank Cluskey. In 1979 Labour won four seats in the European Parliament elections, the same as *Fine Gael* although on a far lower share of the vote.

In the 1981 elections Frank Cluskey lost his seat, and Michael O'Leary became the new party leader. A new *Fine Gael*–Labour coalition government was formed, and Michael

O'Leary became *Tanaiste*. After the first 1982 election the Labour Party's anti-coalition wing came more to the fore. When he was defeated on this issue, Michael O'Leary, who remained strongly pro-coalition, resigned as leader. He later left the party and joined *Fine Gael*. His successor as Labour leader was Dick Spring. Ironically Spring was able to lead Labour back into another coalition with *Fine Gael* after the second 1982 elections, in which Labour won 9.4 per cent of the vote and 16 seats. Dick Spring became *Tanaiste* in the new government. In all Labour had four Cabinet ministers and three junior ministers.

In the 1984 European Parliament elections Labour only won 8.4 per cent of the vote, and lost its four seats.

In spite of certain popular successes (e.g. the Anglo-Irish Agreement) the coalition ran into increasing difficulties. In 1986 it lost the referendum on divorce. Relations between the two parties continued to worsen, especially over the issue of budgetary cuts. The anti-coalition wing of the party was again strengthened. In January 1987 the Labour ministers finally left the government, in order to avoid being associated with a further round of cuts (notably in the health sector), and to assert their independence before the anticipated election campaign.

In the February 1987 election Labour only won 6.4 per cent of the vote and 12 seats, a poor electoral performance, but less bad than many had feared. It is now again in opposition with the party strongly opposed to entering a new coalition.

Support

The Labour Party is the weakest Socialist party in any European Community country, and in the 1987 election, in which it won its second–lowest ever percentage it was only the fourth Irish party, far behind not only *Fianna Fáil* and *Fine Gael*, but even the newly founded Progressive Democrats.

Labour's weakness is partly due to the low level of Irish industrialization and lack of a large urban working class. More fundamental than this is that it has only been a minority party among the working class, and far weaker among this group than *Fianna Fáil*. Although Labour has been closely associated with the trade unions in a highly unionized country, it has only been able to win a minority of the vote among trade unionists. Labour's share of an already low left-wing vote has been further hurt by increasing competition from other parties and groups, notably the Workers' Party.

On the other hand Labour has enjoyed a certain degree of support in rural Ireland. Indeed its most consistent support has probably been among farm workers and white collar workers in rural Leinster, and, to a lesser extent, Munster (it has been much weaker among actual farmers).

These have also tended to be the areas where "Labour seats" have been created and handed down from father to son (as in the case of the Springs in Kerry North). From 1922 to 1982 Labour averaged 16.6 per cent of the first preference vote in rural Leinster and 13.4 per cent in Munster, compared to only 11.4 per cent nationally. In 1987, however, it only won 9.5 per cent in rural Leinster, and only 6.8 per cent in Munster. In Munster it lost five of its previous total of seven seats.

Labour has hardly a presence, however, in the west and north-west of the country. The party only averaged 2.9 per cent of the vote in Connaught-Ulster between 1922 and 1982. In 1987 it won only 1.2 per cent of the vote in the region.

Dublin is a special case and Labour's support has been far more inconsistent in the capital than in the rest of the country. In the 1960s Labour's share of Dublin first preferences went up from 8.4 per cent in 1961 to 28.3 per cent in 1969, with an increase from one to eight deputies. Labour's support has since dropped back again to only 7.1 per cent and four deputies by February 1987, coming fifth, and even being outpolled by the Workers' Party. Labour has no seats in the more working-class northern part of Dublin. All of its seats are on the south side, two of them in particularly prosperous middle-class areas of the conurbation.

In 1987 the ending of the coalition with *Fine Gael* was reflected in a much lower level of transfers to and from *Fine Gael*, although these were still significant in some constituencies.

Organization

Labour has had a far weaker organizational structure than *Fianna Fáil* or *Fine Gael*, being less strongly implanted around the whole country (with few branches, for example, in most of Connaught-Ulster), and with a much smaller and less well financed central organization.

The Labour Party currently has around 5,500 individual members. Unlike other Irish parties, trade unions, co-operatives and other associations can also affiliate to the party on a corporate basis. Unlike in the British Labour Party, however, these corporate affiliations are only at national level.

In 1986 Labour still had 436 local branches. Since 1980 branches must have at least 10 members in urban areas and five in rural areas. Above the branches are constituency and regional councils, but these are not very powerful organizational tiers within the party.

The Labour national conference meets on an annual basis, although special conferences can also be held (as on the issue of whether to go into coalition with *Fine Gael* after the November 1982 elections). There are representatives of the individual and corporate members, and other affiliated groups. Delegates to the conference can be mandated to vote in a particular way, and often are on important issues.

The national conference is far less deferential to the leadership and to the parliamentary party than its equivalent in *Fine Gael*, and especially in *Fianna Fáil*. The issue of whether Labour should participate in coalitions has attracted a particularly high number of critical motions.

An extremely important role within the party is played by its administrative council (popularly known as the AC), which consists of 20 members elected by the national conference (the three separately elected national officers and 17 others), six parliamentarians and a number of representatives of other associated groups (as well as two representatives from the party's weakest area, the west of Ireland). The AC is now felt by many to have become too large and cumbersome a group, and there are proposals to cut down its size.

Party leadership is much more clearly divided than in *Fianna Fáil* or *Fine Gael* between the party's parliamentary leader (who is elected by the parliamentary group) and the party chairman, who is elected by the national conference. In recent years there has been strong pressure to change the system of electing the leader, and a special commission is now examining ways of enlarging the franchise, so that the leader is elected by the national conference or even by the whole party membership.

Labour candidates for *Dáil* elections are chosen at constituency selection conferences at which each branch is entitled to four delegates irrespective of its membership. There are currently calls for this inequitable system to be changed, possibly to include the whole membership. Once selected, candidates must be ratified by the AC.

The party's youth movement, Labour Youth, was established in 1979. It is entitled to two representatives on the AC. From 1981 to 1988 it was in the hands of the Militant Tendency, but these have recently been ousted from the leadership. Labour Youth has around 1,200 members.

Labour now also has a National Women's Council, which is also entitled to two representatives on the AC. The AC has also approved their proposal that women should be reserved a minimum of one quarter of the positions available for Labour candidates on local election panels.

Labour retains strong links with the trade unions. There are still a considerable number of unions which are affiliated to the Labour Party (although there are constant threats of disaffiliation), and which are entitled to delegates to the national conference, although there is no union block vote as in the British Labour Party. The larger unions do not have the number of delegates that they would be entitled to, if a rule of strict proportionality were followed. The group of affiliated trade unions are also entitled to two places on the party's AC. The party does not make its own nominations for the Labour panel of the Irish Senate, but supports candidates nominated by the Irish Congress of Trade Unions.

The Labour party has been the most open of any Irish party in publishing its internal finances. Source of income includes individual membership fees (£6 per member, but with a reduced rate of £2 for the unemployed, young people and old age pensioners), the annual affiliation fee from each branch (currently £15) and revenue from a national collection.

The financial contribution of the affiliated trade unions (assessed in relation to a sliding scale of membership) is small in absolute terms, and is also far less significant in percentage terms than the contribution of the British trade unions to the Labour Party.

When the Labour Party had four members in the European Parliament, their contribution was double that of the affiliated unions. In 1984 the MEPs' contribution was 20 per cent of total party income, an indication both of the party's low income and the financial damage it suffered when it lost its MEPs in the 1984 elections.

In the past the Labour Party had only weak international links. It did not join the Socialist International until the late 1960s. It is now also a member of the Confederation of European Socialist Parties. In the 1979–84 European Parliament its members sat in the Socialist Group. After 1984 they had no members but were offered observer status.

Policies

The Labour Party is an electorally very weak but durable party which is hoping that its return to opposition after the 1987 elections will help to rebuild its strength.

It has never been a very left-wing party, although its policies became less conservative during its period of electoral revival in the 1960s, which brought a number of urban intellectuals into the party. It retained, however, a more traditionally conservative wing, based on some of its rural deputies, a few of whom were among the most conservative members of the *Dáil*. This group is now weaker, especially after the 1987 elections.

The party's small size has meant that it has never been able to aspire to power on its own and has always been faced with a basic choice of being a party of opposition or of entering into an agreement or formal coalition with another party. In the 1930s it supported *Fianna Fáil* but since the late 1940s its main coalition partner has always been *Fine Gael*. This has posed particular problems for the Labour Party on economic questions, where its policies have been most divergent from *Fine Gael* and often rather closer to *Fianna Fáil*. The Labour Party has been more in line with the recent *Fine Gael* leadership on issues of traditional morality and church-state relations. Moreover Labour's participation in coalitions as the minority partner has forced its ministers to accept measures which have created tension with the party activists on the national conference and elsewhere. The party has often been sharply divided between coalitionists and anti-coalitionists, and even lost one recent leader, Michael O'Leary, over the issue.

The experience of the 1982–87 coalition has helped to unite Labour in the anti-coalition stance that was recommended by its recent commission on electoral strategy. The party is now committed to retaining its electoral independence for the conceivable future. The party has been exploring the possibility of closer co-operation with the Workers' Party, the other main left-of-centre party in the *Dáil*, but there remain considerable differences in political culture between the two parties.

An area where the Labour Party has regained greater freedom is on economic policy. In the 1982–87 coalition Labour ministers were forced to back measures of economic austerity and cuts in public expenditure. The issue of health cuts was the formal breaking point for the coalition. Labour recognizes that there need to be some controls on public expenditure, but puts much more emphasis than *Fine Gael* on the need for more expansionary economic policies to tackle unemployment and to increase social justice. It also puts a greater emphasis on the need for state intervention and a strong public sector. It has long advocated the creation of a national development corporation to provide state-led investment, and now that it has been established, has called for it to be given more powers. Labour had also opposed privatization.

Labour has also called for tax reform, with groups such as farmers and the self-employed paying a bigger share than at present. In the 1987 election Labour called for the reintroduction of the wealth tax which it had helped to install in the 1973–77 coalition, but which had been dropped by *Fianna Fáil*. Labour also proposed a 25 per cent increase in corporate taxes.

Labour is also asserting its traditional emphasis on social welfare. In the 1987 election it sought an increase in welfare benefits, although it recognized that they might have to be more selective.

The Labour Party is at the opposite end of the political spectrum from *Fianna Fáil* on traditional Catholic moral issues, and on church-state relations, where Labour has pushed hard for a more pluralistic Ireland. It is closer to *Fine Gael* and the Progressive Democrats on these matters. Like *Fine Gael*, although to a much lesser extent, Labour has had its own conservative wing on these issues among its rural deputies. There was thus a voting division between its deputies during the debate on the proposed constitutional ban on abortion. Labour played a leading role, however, in the debates on contraception and more recently, during the campaign on divorce.

The Labour Party has not had an especially distinctive stance on Northern Ireland. It has called for a unified Socialist Ireland but in the past there has been a wide range of opinion within the party, ranging from traditional nationalism to the very different views of people like Conor Cruise O'Brien, who put more emphasis on the need to respect the two separate communities in Northern Ireland when he was Labour's spokesman on the issue. In more recent times, however, Labour was in government when the Anglo-Irish Agreement was negotiated. The Agreement has subsequently been supported by the party, which has called for reconciliation of the two traditions in the North.

For a long time the Labour party took relatively little interest in foreign policy questions. In 1972 it opposed Ireland's entry into the European Community, largely on the grounds of loss of sovereignty, and of Ireland's vulnerable economic position on the edge of the EC. After the referendum, however, it came to accept EC membership. The Labour Party has since called for co-ordinated European economic policies aimed at full employment, for stronger regional and social policies, and for greater democratic participation and control within the Community.

In the 1987 referendum on the Single European Act the Labour Party adopted a neutral posture. Some of its members joined in the opposition campaign, but the party leader made it clear that he was personally in favour of ratification. The party has since accepted the referendum results.

The party has strongly defended the maintenance of Irish military neutrality.

Personalities

The party's leader is Dick Spring, born in 1950 and the son of Dan Spring who served as TD for Kerry North from 1943 to 1981, and whose seat Dick Spring inherited in 1981. He was elected leader of the party in 1982 after only one year in parliament. He was *Tanaiste* (deputy prime minister) in the Fitzgerald coalition government from 1982 to 1987 as well as Minister for Energy. In 1987 Dick Spring won re-election by only four votes. He has been a moderate and non-ideological leader of the party.

The party's deputy leader is Barry Desmond, the Minister for Health and Welfare from 1982 to 1986, and for Health alone from 1986 to 1987.

The chairman of the party is now Mervyn Taylor, a TD from Dublin, and one of those with most reservations about coalition during the 1982–87 government. He is on the left-of-centre of the party.

The party's deputy chairman is Emmet Stagg, who was elected to the *Dáil* for the first time in 1987 and has had the highest profile of the younger leaders within the party. He helped to found the "Labour Left" ginger group in 1983, and was a fierce opponent of the coalition.

Another prominent leader of the party left and anti-coalitionist is Michael D. Higgins, who was chairman of the Labour Party for almost 10 years from 1978, and who is now again a TD from Galway West.

The party's other ministers in the 1982–87 coalition included Ruairi Quinn, Liam Kavanagh, and (briefly) Frank Cluskey, the party's leader from 1977 to 1981.

The leading member of the Militant Tendency within the Labour Party (Militant used to control Labour Youth, and still has a certain presence in the party) is Joe Higgins, who is on Labour's administrative council.

The Green Alliance
(Comhaoltás Glas)

Headquarters	: 5a Upper Fownes Street, Dublin 2 (tel: 77 14 36)
Founded	: 1981

History

The party was founded as the Ecology Party of Ireland in 1981, with support from the Ecology Party in the United Kingdom, and from members of anti-nuclear and environmental protection groups in Ireland. It had seven candidates in the second general elections in 1982. In 1985 Marcus Counihan became the Greens' first elected representative when he won a seat in Killarney in the 1985 local elections.

In February 1987 general election the Green Alliance put up candidates in nine constituencies, six of them in the Dublin area. Three of their Dublin candidates got over 1,000 first preference votes, and their best performance was 2.8 per cent of the vote in Dublin South. Half of their candidates were women.

Organization

The party consists of a network of semi-autonomous groups, with a national framework for the purposes of policy formulation. It has a collective leadership. The Green Alliance is affiliated to the European Greens.

Policies

Apart from its environmental demands the party advocates decentralization of power to local communities, the elimination of the existing system of social welfare and its replacement by a basic income scheme (tax-free and paid to all citizens as of right), the creation of jobs through a reduction in the working week and job-sharing, rescheduling of the national debt, and replacement of present taxes on income and goods with a tax on non-renewable sources and on land.

Communist Party of Ireland — CPI

Headquarters	: James Connolly House, 43 East Essex Street, Dublin 2 (tel: 71 19 43)
Chairman	: Andrew Barr
General Secretary	: James Stewart
Membership	: 500 (1985 est.)

History

The Communist Party of Ireland has had an on-off existence, and minimal electoral success. It was first founded in 1921 by Roddy Connolly (the son of the famous Labour leader James Connolly). It was subsequently succeeded as the Irish section of the Third International by the Irish Workers' League (IWL) of Jim Larkin. In 1927 Larkin became the only Communist to get elected to the *Dáil*, but he was then disqualified as a bankrupt. The League died out in the late 1920s and was followed first by the Revolutionary Workers' Groups led by Larkin's son Jim Junior (who was elected to Dublin City Council in 1930) and then by a re-established Communist Party in 1933.

It made little impact and suspended its activities in the Irish Republic in 1941, although remaining active in the North. It was reorganized under the IWL label in 1948, and as the Irish Workers Party in 1962. In 1970 it merged with the Communist Party in the North to again become the Communist Party of Ireland. In 1987 it only put up candidates in three constituencies, polling only 725 first preferences in all.

Organization

The CPI's triennial congress elects a national executive committee, but there are separate area committees for the Republic and the North. Associated organizations include the Connolly Youth Movement. It produces a number of publications including the *Irish Workers' Voice* (on a weekly basis), the *Irish Socialist* (monthly), *Unity* (monthly, in Belfast) and the *Irish Socialist Review* (quarterly).

Policies

The CPI has generally been an orthodox Communist Party. It opposed the Treaty, and has been firmly nationalist on the issue of Northern Ireland. It opposes terrorism, and supports Irish military neutrality.

Democratic Socialist Party — DSP

Headquarters	: P.O. Box 806, Dublin 8
President	: Alderman Jim Kemmy
Secretary	: Eoin O'Malley
Founded	: 1982

History

The DSP was founded by Jim Kemmy in March 1982. Kemmy was the independent Socialist member for the *Dáil* constituency of Limerick East, where he had been first elected in June 1981, and re-elected in February 1982. He had supported the first Fitzgerald coalition government but he rejected its austerity budget of January 1982 and helped to bring the government down in the ensuing confidence vote which it lost by a vote of 82 to 81.

The DSP put forward seven candidates in the November 1982 elections but Kemmy lost his seat, and the other six candidates lost their deposits. The only one who polled more than 1,000 votes was the candidate in Dun Laoghaire,

Dr John De Courcy Ireland, who also stood as the party's only candidate in the 1984 European Parliament elections, in which he polled 5,300 votes in the Dublin constituency.

In February 1987 Jim Kemmy won back his seat in Limerick East from Labour.

Support

The party's support is centred overwhelmingly on Limerick, which has also elected Ireland's only Trotskyist councillor, Joe Harrington. Before winning back his *Dáil* seat in February 1987, Kemmy topped the poll in his own area in the June 1985 local elections and the three DSP candidates who stood averaged 19 per cent of first preference.

The only other part of Ireland where the party has made even a small impact is Dublin, where it has been competing with the Labour Party and the Workers' Party for the left-wing vote, and where it averaged 4.7 per cent of first preferences in those few areas where it stood in the 1987 local elections. It did poorly, however, in the three Dublin seats where it stood in the 1987 general election.

Organization

Minimum membership for DSP branches is only four and branches of between four and seven paid-up members are entitled to two delegates at the party conference. They may choose by majority vote whether to mandate branch delegates on motions at party conferences.

The party conference is the principal governing and policy-making body of the party, and its decisions are binding on the executive committee and on the party as a whole. Conferences can be organized on either a delegate basis or on the basis that each paid-up party member may attend. The party conference elects the party's president and its executive committee.

The executive committee consists of the party president and not more than nine other members. It has far-reaching executive and administrative powers. Even if you want to become a member of the party you have to apply to the executive committee. The executive committee is also responsible for all party dealings with the media, but may delegate this if it wishes.

Policies

The DSP is a small party on the left of the political spectrum. The party sets itself the objective of building a Socialist society, the economic basis of which will be public ownership of the means of production, distribution and exchange.

This general objective is to be implemented by means of a seven-point party platform. Two are of particular interest. Point 4 calls for a clear separation of church from state, with religious beliefs not being enshrined in the Constitution or laws of the Republic.

To implement this, the party has called for the promotion of state non-denominational education, the speedy enactment of divorce legislation, a far more liberal contraceptive law, and for a health service in which the Church is no longer treated as a state within a state.

A further point emphasized by the party is complete equality in law and in practice for women. On the issue of abortion the party is opposed to indiscriminate abortion, but considers it to be a solution in certain circumstances such as when a women's life is at stake, or when pregnancy has resulted from rape or incest. This issue was probably one of the key factors in causing Jim Kemmy to lose his seat in November 1982.

Point 6 includes the most direct statement on Northern Ireland affairs of any party in the Republic: "the DSP rejects the constitutional claim by the Republic of Ireland to jurisdiction over Northern Ireland, and opposes any attempts to coerce the population of Northern Ireland into a United Ireland. The party accepts the right of the majority in Northern Ireland to live in the state of their own choosing . . .".

The party's platform is vague on economic policy issues, but the party is in favour of a wealth tax and higher capital taxation.

The Workers' Party — WP
(Pairtí na nOibrí)

Headquarters	: 30 Gardiner Place, Dublin 1 (tel: 74 07 16/ 74 10 45)
President	: Proinsias de Rossa
General secretary	: Sean Garland
Publication	: *The Irish People*

History

The Workers' party is a Marxist party, whose origins stem from a split within *Sinn Féin* in 1969–70, between a more left-wing group which sought to end the party's policy of abstention from elective politics, and a more traditional group of Republicans seeking to concentrate on the armed struggle in Northern Ireland. The former became known as Official *Sinn Féin* (or "*Sinn Féin*, Gardiner Place"), the latter as Provisional *Sinn Féin* (or "*Sinn Féin*, Kevin Street" —

see separate entry). Official *Sinn Féin* suffered a further split in 1974, when the Irish Republican Socialist Party was founded.

The party made a slow start electorally, saving only one out of its 10 deposits in the 1973 national elections, and only three out of 16 in 1977. During this period, however, it distanced itself from its IRA antecedents, with its central theme being the need to develop class politics throughout Ireland, North and South, rather than narrow Irish nationalism. Aiming at the working-class vote, it changed its name to "*Sinn Féin* — the Workers' Party" in 1977, and it finally dropped its *Sinn Féin* title completely in 1982.

The party's first electoral breakthrough, however, came not in Dublin or in the other larger towns, but in more rural East Cork, where Joe Sherlock was elected to the *Dáil* in 1981. In the first 1987 election, two more deputies were elected in the *Dáil*, Paddy Gallagher from Waterford, and Proinsias de Rossa from Dublin North-West. The three Workers' Party TDs had a pivotal role in the short-lived 1982 Haughey government, when they held the balance of power, and finally helped to bring the government down at the end of the year.

In the second 1982 election their overall vote went up, but they suffered a net loss of one seat, with the party president Tomás MacGiolla being elected in Dublin West, but with Sherlock and Gallagher losing their seats.

In the February 1987 election the Workers' Party doubled its representation in the *Dáil* from two to four, with its outgoing deputies re-elected, with Joe Sherlock making a comeback in Cork East, and with Pat MacCartan being elected in Dublin North-East. The party put up 29 candidates in 26 of the 41 constituencies, and achieved 3.8 per cent of the national vote.

In 1988 Tomás MacGiolla, its long-time president (26 years as President of the Workers' Party, and before that of *Sinn Féin*) stood down in that capacity (although remaining in the *Dáil*), and was replaced by one of the other TDs, Proinsias de Rossa.

Support

The party puts up candidates in both the Republic of Ireland and in Northern Ireland, but while it has won a few local council seats in the North (e.g. in Belfast and Downpatrick) it has had far greater electoral success in the South. Its support pattern is thus different from *Sinn Féin*.

The Workers' Party main support is among urban working-class voters, especially among unskilled workers. It has won local council seats in many of Ireland's towns, such as Cork, Galway, Wexford, Kilkenny and Waterford.

Its greatest strength, however, is in North Dublin, where it contests the working-class vote with *Fianna Fáil*, in particular, and where the Labour Party no longer holds any seats. The Workers' Party thus has three out of its four *Dáil* seats in North Dublin (a further seat is held by a left-wing independent, Tony Gregory, who is a former member of Official *Sinn Féin*). In South Dublin, on the other hand, the Labour Party still holds four seats, and the Workers' Party none, although it has considerable support in some areas, notably Dublin South-West. The Workers' Party has polled particularly well in some of the bleak outer city housing estates such as Ballymun.

In February 1987, the Workers' Party out-polled Labour in Dublin with 7.5 per cent of the vote to 7.1 per cent. Less meaningfully, because of the low support base for both parties, it also won more votes than Labour in Connaught–Ulster.

Organization

The Workers' Party had achieved much of its success on the basis of its internal discipline and tight organization in the constituencies on which it has decided to concentrate. It prefers a smaller but fully participating membership of party "cadres" to a mass membership on which few or no demands are put. It thus has around 2,000 members, with applicants having to go through a six-month apprenticeship before they are allowed to become full members, and having to pay very high annual dues. Branches are also kept small, with between five and 15 members.

Above the branches is a central executive council which is responsible for the party's decision-making in both Northern Ireland, and in the Republic. Decisions are taken on the basis of "democratic centralism" and are binding on members once adopted.

The party has a youth movement. There are no formal links with the trade unions, although some of its members hold senior positions within individual unions.

A considerable proportion of its funds comes from the high contributions of its members, and, in particular, of its elected representatives. Its *Dáil* deputies only retain the annual industrial average wage, and hand over the balance to the party. The party also makes money from its own publications, notably its own weekly newspaper, the *Irish People*, as well as the publications of other left-wing parties from outside Ireland (its party headquarters is above the party bookshop).

The Workers' party has established contacts with left Socialist and Communist parties in other European countries.

Policies

The Workers' Party is a left-wing Socialist party whose objective is to win state power for the working class and thereby establish a democratic secular, socialist, unitary state within the whole of Ireland. It is thus the most uncompromisingly Socialist party of any Irish party with more than a token electoral base. Its successes, however, have been within individual constituencies, especially in urban areas where its left-wing rivals have been less organized.

The Workers' Party's economic policies are expansionary in nature. It seeks a planned economy, believes that there has been too much reliance within Ireland on private enterprise, and that the state sector should play a larger role in the Irish economy. The party is totally opposed to privatization of state companies. It does not accept that overall Irish levels of taxation are too high, but calls for the redistribution of the tax burden away from employees in the PAYE sector, and towards employers, the self-employed and farmers.

The party is opposed to attempts to cut back on the welfare state, and seeks the introduction of a comprehensive free medical service, and of a minimum income for everyone. The Workers' Party advocates a major programme of urban renewal. It also calls for the closing of Sellafield.

The party seeks a clearer separation of church and state. On education it calls for a comprehensive state-funded education system, fully integrated from pre-school to third level. It wants full family planning, and the replacement of the constitutional prohibition on divorce by a non-sectarian divorce law. There should be an end to social and economic discrimination against women.

An issue of special sensitivity for the party is its policy towards Northern Ireland, in view of the Official *Sinn Féin* origins of the party, and the fact that some of its leading members were once in the IRA. The party's analysis is that class differences should override other differences, and that Northern Ireland citizens should identify themselves as workers rather than as members of sectarian Nationalist or Unionist blocks. The party recognizes the legitimate rights of the Northern Protestant population, who should not be forced into a United Ireland by violence. It calls for the elimination of terrorism, and considers that the solutions to Northern Ireland's problems lie instead in greater economic investment.

There should also be enhanced cross-border co-operation and a Bill of Rights should be established. The party voted in favour of the Anglo-Irish Agreement, but is now critical of some of its consequences, in particular the increased alienation of the Unionist majority, and the continued failure to introduce devolved government in the province.

On international issues, the party puts particular emphasis on strengthening Irish neutrality. Ireland should join the movement of non-aligned states, and have neutrality enshrined in the Constitution.

The Workers' Party is not in favour of Irish withdrawal from European Community, believing that Ireland's economy is now too closely linked to that of the EC for it to pull out. It has been highly critical, however, of the Single European Act, primarily on the grounds that it might undercut Irish neutrality, but partly because increased use of qualified majority within the council might work to Ireland's disadvantage, and partly because more emphasis is put on achieving the internal market than on strengthening Community regional, social and industrial policy. On the other hand party members have expressed the view that insufficient powers have been given to the European parliament.

On other international issues the party is firmly on the left, and highly critical, in particular, of American foreign policies in Latin America and elsewhere.

Personalities

The party's new president is Proinsias de Rossa, born in 1940. He is a former fruit and vegetable merchant. He was elected to the *Dáil* in 1982 and has been highly active there. He is also on Dublin Corporation. Besides the other three TDs, Tomás MacGiolla, Pat MacCartan and Joe Sherlock, the most prominent personalities within the party have been Sean Garland, its long-serving and powerful general secretary, and Pat Rabbitte, who has been an articulate media spokesman for the party.

Sinn Féin

Headquarters	: 44 Parnell Square, Dublin 1 (tel: 72 69 32)
Party president	: Gerry Adams
General secretary	: Joe Reilly

History

Sinn Féin, whose name means "ourselves", has had several manifestations in Irish politics after it was first founded as a national party in

1907: notably between 1918 and 1922 when it was the leading Irish party; from 1922 to 1926, when it was the leading anti-Treaty party; and from 1926 onwards when it has formed the extreme Republican fringe of Irish politics. Its permanent dilemma has been whether and under what terms to participate in elections within a system which it does not accept. Moreover it has had a fluctuating relationship with the Irish Republican Army (IRA), for which it has often constituted, notably since 1950, the civilian arm.

In 1958 *Sinn Féin* contested 19 constituencies after a long absence from the polls, and succeeded in winning four seats, which it again lost in the 1961 election.

In 1969–70 the movement again split over the issue of abstention between the "Officials" (see section on "Workers' Party"), who decided to follow the electoral road, and the "Provisionals", who concentrated on the armed struggle.

Provisional *Sinn Féin* again got involved in national politics in the 1981 elections as a result of the H-Block hunger strike in Northern Ireland. Nine H-Block candidates stood in the election, and two were elected to the *Dáil*. Standing instead under its own name in February 1982 *Sinn Féin* won no seats, and it did not put up any candidates in November 1982. From 1982 onwards the party could again appropriate to itself the name *Sinn Féin* as the former official wing finally dropped the title in favour of the name "The Workers' Party".

In 1986, and in the face of strong opposition from the traditionalists, *Sinn Féin* changed its policy of abstention from the *Dáil*, and decided that it would take up its seats if elected. Candidates were thus put up in 24 constituencies in the 1987 general elections, although they met with very limited success, gaining only 1.9 per cent of the Irish vote.

Support

In the North of Ireland *Sinn Féin* has achieved considerable electoral success, but it has had only patchy success in the Republic, and then only at times of high profile nationalist campaigns.

The main support base for *Sinn Féin* has been in areas close to the Northern Ireland border like county Monaghan, where the party has two county councillors and five urban councillors. In February 1987 its highest first preference votes were in Donegal North-East (8 per cent), Cavan-Monaghan (7.3 per cent), Sligo-Leitrim (5.7 per cent) and Louth (5.6 per cent).

Sinn Féin has also had certain support in a few other areas with a particularly strong Republican tradition, such as parts of Kerry. It has also attempted to make inroads in some of the more run-down urban areas like Dublin Central, where it has used a community politics approach, but so far with relatively little electoral reward.

Organization

The party branches or *Cumainn* are grouped in district committees (*Comhairli Ceanntaire*), based on electoral boundaries. The annual conference (*Ard Fheis*) determines policy, and elects the 32–member national council (*Ard Comhairle*), including at least eight women.

The party produces a weekly publication *An Phoblacht* (Republican News), a quarterly Bulletin (*Iris*), and an Irish language paper *Saoirse* ("Freedom"), which appears irregularly. *Sinn Féin* is closely linked to the Irish Republican Army (IRA).

Policies

Sinn Féin's policies have gradually been moving to the left. The 1951 party constitution had a strongly clerical tone which was vetted by the clergy. After the 1970 split the Provisionals were clearly perceived as not only more committed to the armed struggle, but also less to the left in policy terms. On institutional questions they advocated a federal system for a united Ireland. In 1982, however, the federal policy was dropped in favour of a demand for a single unitary state. The party's policies also took on an increasingly left-wing character.

Sinn Féin describes itself as an open, democratic and revolutionary party, dedicated to the reunification of Ireland, and the establishment of a 32–county democratic Socialist republic. They are now committed to take any seats they might win in the 26–county parliament, which they refuse to refer to as the *Dáil* but only as "Leinster House".

While ending partition is the main policy, the party puts forward a number of other policies as short-term measures needed to alleviate the grave situation facing the people of the 26 counties. The main emphasis is on radical community politics.

Some of its specific policies are not dissimilar, although much less sketched out, to those of the Workers' Party. It thus calls for large-scale job creation through productive state investments and expansion of the public sector. It opposes privatization. It also calls for reform of the system so that PAYE employees pay less, and big business, big farmers and the self-employed pay more. *Sinn Féin* similarly believes that there should be an immediate halt to cut-backs in spending on health, education and social welfare, that Sellafield should be closed, and that there should be an Irish-language television channel.

Sinn Féin, however, puts less emphasis than the Workers' Party on social issues, such as equal treatment for women, greater separation of church and state, divorce legislation, and so on. *Sinn Féin* is also more anti-EC. It believes that the Single European Act should be rejected, and considers that membership of the EC should be renegotiated as a first step towards withdrawal.

The party also seeks repeal of section 31 of the Irish Broadcasting Act, which prevents *Sinn Féin* from being given a platform on radio and television.

Personalities

Sinn Féin's dominant public personality is its president, Gerry Adams, who is the MP for West Belfast in the UK Parliament at Westminster, but who does not take up his seat. Danny Morrison has been another leading figure.

Italy

Francis Jacobs

The country

Italy is a country of 116,000 square miles, with a population of 58 million. The population is generally homogeneous in ethnic and linguistic terms and is overwhelmingly Catholic. There are, however, a number of national and linguistic minority groups: the German speakers of the South Tyrol (there are also small German-speaking communities in Trento and elsewhere); the French and Franco-Provençal dialect speakers, mainly in the Val D'Aosta, but also elsewhere in Piedmont; the Sardinian and Catalan speakers in Sardinia; the Ladins in the South Tyrol; and the Friulians. Besides these there are also some Slavs (in Friuli and Molise); Greeks (mainly in Calabria and Apulia) and Albanians (in seven regions, but mainly in Sicily and Calabria). There are Protestant communities in the Alpine valleys of Piedmont (the Valdesi).

There is a significant economic (and to some extent cultural) division between northern and southern Italy. The south has pockets of increasing prosperity, but is still much poorer than the rest of the country. Moreover there have been major migrations of southern workers to the northern industrial towns, notably Turin and Milan. There are a large number of Italian emigrants outside Italy, retaining the right to vote in Italy. Immigrants into Italy, notably from North Africa, have been less numerous, but are increasing.

Political institutions

Italy's political institutions are based on the 1948 republican Constitution. There is a bicameral legislature, consisting of a 630-member Chamber of Deputies and a 315-member Senate (plus five nominated members, and former presidents who are members by right), with practically identical functions and powers, although the Chamber probably enjoys more prestige. An unusual feature of both, however, is the practice of delegating large quantities of legislation to the permanent committees (14 in Chamber, 12 in Senate) with powers of final decision.

Elections to both houses are held simultaneously, with a maximum five-year term, but with the possibility of earlier dissolution. Members of the Chamber of Deputies are elected in a two-stage process in 31 multi-member constituencies, ranging from Trieste with two to Roma-Viterbo-Latina-Frosinone with 53 seats. In the first stage seats are allocated to parties on a proportional basis to their results in each constituency, using the Imperiali Quota (a modified version of the D'Hondt system). In the second stage remaining seats and votes (just over 90 of the 630 seats in the 1988 elections) are transferred to a national pool, and allocated to the parties in proportion to their total national vote, provided that the parties have polled at least 300,000 votes nationally, and won a seat in at least one constituency. (In 1972 this latter condition eliminated the PSIUP party from representation in Parliament, although it had polled 649,000 votes nationally.) The only exception to the above system is the Val D'Aosta, which has only one seat, filled on a plurality basis.

In the Senate, on the other hand, all 315 members are elected directly in the 20 Italian regions, which form the electoral constituencies, by the d'Hondt system. The constituencies range in size from 48 seats in Lombardy to one in the Val D'Aosta, and two in Molise. The Senate system, without a national top-up, is much harsher to the smaller parties. There is only one Green member, and one of *Democrazia Proletaria* in the Senate, compared to 13 and eight members, respectively, in the Chamber of Deputies. There is thus a greater incentive for parties to form electoral pacts.

Italy's 81 members of the European Parliament are elected in five vast constituencies, north-west Italy with 23 seats, north-east Italy with 15, central Italy with 17, southern Italy with 18 and the islands with eight.

In all the above elections preferential voting is allowed, with voters being able to strike out candidates or express a preference for a certain number of candidates. This option is used to a greater extent in southern Italy and has been criticized as helping to encourage clientelism, and the spread of party factions.

The Prime Minister (whose formal title is President of the Council) is chosen by negotiations by the parties, and need not

Map of Italy showing the 20 regions and 32 chamber constituencies (with number of seats per constituency).

Source: adapted from *World Atlas of Elections*.

come from the largest party, nor be the party leader. The Prime Minister's powers are heavily circumscribed, and he cannot directly choose or fire his Cabinet colleagues.

The Italian President is chosen indirectly by an electoral college of members of both houses of parliament and delegates from the regions, and has a seven-year term. The President nominates candidates for the premiership, but in practice has little effective power.

Five Italian regions (Trentino–Alto–Adige, Val D'Aosta, Friuli–Venezia–Giulia, Sardinia and Sicily) enjoy special statutes, with more extensive powers than the other 15 regions, which were established by the 1948 Constitution, but only implemented in the 1970s. Each region has a regional parliament of between 30 and 80 members, a regional executive and a regional president. Elections are generally held on a five-year schedule.

There are also the 94 traditional provinces, with their own parliament and executive. The relationship between their powers and those of the regions has not yet been satisfactorily defined. The political party "federations" based on the provincial tier of government are still generally more important than the regional organizations.

Below the provinces are the communes. The mayors of the larger communes, like Milan, Turin and Rome, often have a higher public profile than the regional presidents.

The 1948 Italian Constitution introduced the possibility of popular referenda, but again, this was only formally implemented in the 1970s. Such referenda may only repeal existing legislation rather than initiate new legislation. The first referendum was that over divorce in 1974.

Since 1974 there has been a system of public funding of the political parties, to cover both their electoral and general expenses. An attempt to repeal this law by referendum was unsuccessful.

Brief political history

1861–1918 Liberal parliamentary regime

Dominance of political system by "right" Liberals until 1876, "left" Liberals from then on. Radicals, Republicans and later Socialists in opposition. At insistence of Papacy, Catholic politicians not participating in national elections until after 1900.

1861	Italian independence under Piedmont royal family, with Count Cavour as first Prime Minister.
1870	Final unification of Italy.
1912	Constitutional extension of male suffrage under Giovanni Giolitti.
1914	Italy enters war on side of England and France. Socialists advocate neutrality.

1918–24 Collapse of Liberal regime

Fragmentation of Liberals, rise of Catholic *popolari* and Socialists; foundation of Communist Party; near civil war 1920–22; rise of Fascists, Mussolini consolidates hold on power 1922–24.

1918	Universal male suffrage.
1919	Proportional representation introduced.
1922	Mussolini becomes Prime Minister.
1923	New electoral system ensures majority for Fascists.
1924	Murder of Matteotti, Aventine secession, Parliament ceases to function.

1925–43 Fascist dictatorship under Mussolini

1929	Mussolini signs Lateran pacts with Church.
1935	Invasion of Ethiopia.
1936	Fascists and anti-Fascists participate in Spanish Civil War.
1940	Italian entry into war on side of Germany.

1943–45 Collapse of Fascist Regime

Allies invade Italy; Mussolini forms Salo Republic in northern Italy; partisans become more and more successful; war ends with settlement of old scores.

1943	Overthrow of Mussolini in Rome.
1945	Killing of Mussolini, formation of first postwar Italian government (a wide coalition of resistance parties, including Socialists and Communists, under Ferruccio Parri of Partito d'Azione.

1949–53 Era of De Gasperi

Italy became a republic, new Constitution enacted; Italy opts for Marshall Aid and Atlantic Alliance; Christian Democrats form "centre" coalition with lay parties of centre-right to centre-left; Socialists and Communists form Popular Front and go into opposition.

1945	De Gasperi replaces Parri as Prime Minister.
1946	Elections for constituent assembly, universal male and female suffrage. Italy narrowly chooses republic over monarchy in referendum.
1947	De Gasperi expels Socialists and Communists from his Government.
1948	De Gasperi election triumph.
1953	Enactment of so-called *"legge truffa"* (swindle law) which would have given a seats premium to allied parties winning over 50 per cent of vote. Christian Democrats and allies fail to gain over 50 per cent at 1953 election and new electoral law never put into practice.

1960   Reliance of Tambroni government on support of far-right MSI leads to riots and collapse of government. Helps to pave way for centre-left experiment.

1963–75 The Centre-left experiment

Christian Democrat-led government but with Socialist participation, carries out certain reforms but fails to live up to expectations; period of unrest in late 1960s; terrorism of right and left increases from 1969 onwards; centre-left gradually unravels.

1963   Moro forms first full centre-left government.
1968   Year of unrest.
1969   "Hot Autumn" of labour activism.
1970   Regional elections held for first time.
1974   Referendum on divorce.
1976   Major advance of Communists in national elections.

1976–79 Governments of National Solidarity

Christian Democratic-led governments supported by wide range of parties, including Communists.

1978   Communists enter parliamentary majority for first time. Aldo Moro kidnapped and killed by Red Brigade.
1979   Communists withdraw from majority and lose ground heavily in subsequent national elections.

1979–present The Centre-left revived

Christian Democrat domination of coalitions continues, but Christian Democrat Prime Ministers alternate with ones from other parties, coalition of five parties — Christian Democrats, Socialists, Social Democrats, Liberals and Republicans become dominant formula of government; Communists take up more active opposition stance; terrorism declines but is not entirely eradicated.

1981   Spadolini becomes first non-Christian Democrat Prime Minister since 1945.
1983   Craxi becomes first Socialist Prime Minister.
1984   Revision of Concordat with Church.

Main features of current political system

The main feature of the postwar Italian political system is its apparent instability, and its very real stability in practice.

The main indications of the apparent instability are the rapid turnover of governments (there have been 48 governments in 43 years), the high degree of fragmentation of the political system (there are 10 national parties represented in the two houses of the Italian Parliament), the presence of Western Europe's largest Communist party as well as a substantial party of the extreme right, the constant talk of a political "crisis", and the persistence of terrorism of the left and right.

In practice there have been only 19 different prime ministers, and all but three of these have come from the same party, the Christian Democrats, who have dominated all government coalitions since the war, and never been in opposition. Since 1947 only four other parties have formally shared power with them, and the main issue has been whether the government coalition should be of the centre, centre-right or centre-left. The same ministers have been re-appointed again and again. Moreover the degree of consensus between the political parties on many issues is quite striking, and even the main opposition party, the Communists, have often co-operated with the government and on one occasion even entered its parliamentary majority. The old Italian tradition of *trasformismo* has led to few sharp contrasts between government and opposition but instead to constant attempts to co-opt potential adversaries into a broad governing coalition. Much of the sound and fury of Italian politics is more apparent than real. The terrorism is very real, but has declined in the 1980s and its threat has tended to reinforce rather than undermine Italian democracy.

Dissatisfaction with the Italian political system is considerable. A central criticism is not of its instability, but of its rigidity, with the seemingly endless dominance of the Christian Democrats in unbalanced coalition with the Socialists and the smaller parties of the centre blocking the main opposition party, the Communists, from power.

A second central criticism is of the political system's inefficiency and low moral tone, with a weak executive and legislature, strong party barons and party factions (formalized to a degree unknown almost anywhere else in Europe), and widespread clientelism and corruption (a number of ministers and party leaders have been indicted). Government ministers are not chosen by the prime minister, but are chosen as a result of horse-trading between parties and factions, and patronage is then further exercised in the *Sottogoverno* of state and semi-state bodies under direct or indirect government influence.

While all Italian parties express criticism of this system a division between system and anti-system parties can be distinguished in Italian politics. The Communist Party has worked within the system, in practice, but has been perceived as wanting to make fundamental changes to it. The Italian Social Movement has always wanted to alter the 1948 Constitution which it did not help to draft. The Radical Party has been an anti-system movement in certain respects.

Differences in party support rest largely upon cultural and regional variations. Italy has long been divided into confessional and lay sub-cultures, with the latter subdivided into a socialist and much smaller, but still influential, liberal tradition. Confessional/lay differences are much less sharp than they were, especially since the divorce and abortion referenda, but still occasionally surface over such issues as the revision of the Concordat with the Church. Moreover, the sub-cultures flanking organizations have generally declined in membership. Nevertheless, there are whole regions of Italy where they still play a very important role, such as the "white" region of north-eastern Italy, where the Church and Christian Democratic Party have their greatest influence, and the "red" belt of Emilia-Romagna, Tuscany and Umbria, particularly, where first the Socialists and now the Communists have been the dominant political force.

Urban/rural divisions have been less important than class differences. The left has generally been stronger in the larger cities and the northern industrial regions, but in the "red belt" is strong in both cities and countryside.

A potentially important divide has been that between north and south Italy, with the persistence of much greater poverty in the south, and the massive presence of southern emigrants in the north. In fact, while some parties such as the Christian Democrats and the Italian Social Movement have tended to be stronger in the south, there have been no explicitly southern parties, and most parties have both southern and northern support. The monarchy/republic cleavage which divided north and south (the south voted heavily for the monarchy in the 1946 referendum and the Monarchist Party was largely southern-based) has now disappeared. The main distinctive political features of the south are its political volatility, and the exceptional extent of clientelism and party patronage.

To a limited extent, resentment of the south and of southerners, and also of Rome, has helped to spawn some of the smaller regional parties which have recently developed in the north, such as the *Lega Lombarda*.

Italy's ethnic and linguistic differences have had regional rather than national political impacts. The most important has been in the South Tyrol where the dominant party is the SVP. Other parties based on defence of linguistic and ethnic rights have included the *Union Valdotaine* in the Aosta Valley and the *Partito Sardo d'Azione* in Sardinia.

Another difference which was very significant, but is now much less so, has been international orientation. After the war the Socialists and Communists, in particular (although there were divisions in other parties as well) opposed Italy's firm adherence to the West and the Atlantic Alliance. Differences on these issues are now much more muted, and the Communists have even accepted Italian membership of NATO.

There is now a remarkable degree of inter-party consensus on what the main political problems are, and even on a number of possible solutions but very little agreement on how they should be implemented. The major areas of concern include:

Institutional reform. This is a central concern of policy-makers. Among the specific issues being examined are how to speed up Italy's system of public justice; strengthening the powers of the Prime Minister; direct election of the President; reform of Italy's electoral system; differentiating the functions of the two chambers of parliament or reducing them to one chamber; and providing for direct popular initiative through referenda, rather than having them merely for repealing existing laws.

Economic policy. All parties are concerned about Italy's high public budget deficit, the need to improve the functions of the public sector and to reduce fiscal evasion. There is disagreement over the precise mix of measures required, the balance between the public and private sectors, the degree of planning and public investment needed and the relative order of priorities in fighting inflation and unemployment. Policies followed, however, are pragmatic and ideological differences not very sharp.

Media regulation.

Environment. This is a more important theme than in the past, and the new alliance of Green parties has enjoyed considerable success.

Italian election results 1948–present (percentages and seats won)

	1948	1953	1958	1963	1968	1972	1976	1979	1983	1987
DC (Christian Democrats)	48.5% (305)	40.1% (263)	42.4% (273)	38.3% (260)	39.1% (266)	38.8% (267)	38.7% (262)	38.3% (262)	32.9% (225)	34.3% (234)
PCI (Communists)	31 % ⎫ joint	22.6% (143)	22.7% (140)	25.3% (166)	26.9% (177)	27.2% (179)	34.4% (228)	30.4% (201)	29.9% (198)	26.6% (177)
PSI (Socialists)	(183) ⎬	12.8% (75)	14.2% (84)	13.8% (87)	14.5%	9.6% (61)	9.6% (57)	9.8% (62)	11.4% (73)	14.3% (94)
				merged PSI/PSDI						
PSDI (Social Democrats)	7.1% (33)	4.5% (19)	4.5% (22)	6.1% (33)	(91)	5.1% (29)	3.4% (15)	3.8% (20)	4.1% (23)	3.0% (17)
PRI (Republicans)	2.5% (9)	1.6% (5)	1.4% (6)	1.4% (6)	2.0% (9)	2.9% (14)	3.1% (14)	3.0% (16)	5.1% (29)	3.7% (21)
PLI (Liberals)	3.8% (19)	3.0% (13)	3.5% (17)	7.0% (39)	5.8% (31)	3.9% (21)	1.3% (5)	1.9% (9)	2.9% (16)	2.1% (11)
PR (Radicals)	—	—	(with Republicans — see above)	—	—	—	1.1% (4)	3.5% (18)	2.2% (11)	2.6% (13)
MSI (Italian Social Movement)	2.0% (6)	5.8% (29)	4.8% (24)	5.1% (27)	4.4% (24)	8.7% (56)	6.1% (35)	5.3% (30)	6.8% (42)	5.9% (35)
Monarchists	2.8% (14)	6.9% (40)	4.8% (25)	1.7% (8)	1.3% (6)	—	—	—	—	—
DP (Proletarian Democracy)	—	—	—	—	—	—	1.6% (6)	0.8% (0)	1.5% (7)	1.7% (8)
Verdi (Green)	—	—	—	—	—	—	—	—	—	2.5% (13)
Others	2.5% (2)	2.7% (3)	1.7% (5)	1.3% (4)	6.0% (26)	4.0% (4)	0.8% (4)	4.1% (12)	2.7% (6)	3.2% (6)

Civil nuclear energy. Since Chernobyl the balance of Italian political opinion has moved against the further development of civil nuclear energy in Italy, although some parties still point to the economic costs of such a decision for energy-poor Italy.

European Community. Italian parties are among the most enthusiastic in all Europe for the creation of European political as well as economic union. This is not a controversial issue between the parties, although some put more emphasis than others on the need for Italy to put its own economic house in order before it is able to properly meet the challenge of a common market without frontiers.

NATO and defence. The major Italian parties support Italy's membership of the NATO Alliance, but would like to strengthen the European pillar within NATO. There has been disagreement over whether NATO missiles should be stationed in Italy.

Other foreign policy issues. The main differences are areas of emphasis only, over such issues as to Italy's role in the Mediterranean and the position it should take over Israel and the Palestine people.

Terrorism and organized crime. Both pose major challenges for the Italian state, but neither are partisan issues.

Democrazia Christiana — DC
(Christian Democrats)

Headquarters	: (i) 46 Piazza del Gesu, 00186 Rome (Political HQ — tel: 67751)
	(ii) 15 Piazza Don Luigi Sturzo, EUR 00144 Rome (Administrative HQ — tel: 5901)
Secretary	: Arnaldo Forlani
President of National Council	: Flaminio Piccoli
Chairman of DC group in Chamber	: Mino Martinazzoli
Chairman of DC group in Senate	: Nicola Mancino
Youth organization	: *Movimento Giovanile* (Delegate: Simone Guerrini)

Women's organization	: *Movimento Femminile*
Publication	: *Il Popolo*
Membership	: 1,445,000 (1985)
Founded	: 1942

History

The present Christian Democratic party was founded in November 1942 and has been the dominant party in every single government since the war, a period in which there have only been three non-Christian Democratic Prime Ministers. This uninterrupted hold on power contrasts sharply with Catholic political involvement before the war.

In the 19th century devout Catholics were forbidden by the Church to vote or to stand as candidates at parliamentary elections of the liberal Italian state which had deprived the papacy of its temporal possessions. A strong Catholic subculture developed, however, with Catholic workers' associations, banks, co-operatives, newspapers, schools and youth groups being created in large numbers, especially in Lombardy and in the Veneto. The 1890s, in particular, were characterized by periodic repression of this subculture by the Italian state, but the groups that had been broken up were quickly refounded. In 1905 the lay Catholic movements that had previously been grouped together in the *Opera dei Congressi e dei Comitati Cattolici* (founded in 1874) were re-organized under the name of *Azione Cattolica* (Catholic Action).

From 1900 onwards Catholic "intransigence" began to decline. The ban on electoral participation had never applied in local elections, and Catholic candidates had forged alliances in cities such as Milan as early as 1895. In 1904 Catholics were also permitted to vote in certain selected parliamentary constituencies, primarily to keep out Socialists. Three Catholic candidates were elected. By 1909 Catholics were standing in 150 constituencies, winning 4 per cent of the vote and 16 seats. Divisions also opened up between clerical conservatives and Catholic social reformers.

In 1913 the political weight of Catholicism was greatly reinforced by the so-called Gentiloni pact, whereby a large number of non-Catholic candidates were elected with Catholic support, in return for backing for Catholic political causes, such as religious education in schools, and opposition to any divorce law.

During World War I Catholics were divided between nationalists and pacifists, but the Church establishment generally gave support for Italian participation, and two Catholic ministers were included in government for the first time, Filippo Meda in 1916 and Cesare Nova in 1918.

Early in 1919 a new mass Catholic political party was founded, the *Partito Popolare Italiano*, with a Sicilian priest, Don Luigi Sturzo, as its most prominent leader. The *Partito Popolare* was conceived as a non-confessional party, with no direct link to the papacy and inspired by social Christian ideas. Its strength lay primarily in rural areas in central and especially northern Italy. In the 1919 elections it won 20.5 per cent of the national vote and 100 seats. From the start the *Partito Popolare* took part in government coalitions. In the 1921 elections the party retained 20.4 per cent of the vote, and gained 107 seats.

The rise of Fascism caused uncertainty among the *Popolari*, torn between suspicion of the new movement and dislike of the left. There were two *Popolari* ministers in Mussolini's 1922 government, but these were pushed out in 1923, and many leading *Popolari* turned against Fascism. By 1924 they were reduced to 9.1 per cent of the vote and 39 seats, and they were later dissolved by Mussolini.

In the meantime the Church, which had abandoned the *Popolari* at a relatively early date, came to an agreement with Mussolini with the 1929 Concordat.

During the Fascist period the Catholic sub-culture retained considerable strength, with over a million members of Catholic Action, and with future Christian Democratic leaders active in the Catholic youth movement, and in the Catholic student movement, FUCI. During World War II many Catholics were active in the anti-Fascist resistance.

The new Christian Democratic party (DC) was founded in November 1942. It included former leaders of the *Partito Popolare* as well as leaders of the Milanese *Movimento Guelfo*. The new party was to be inspired by Christian values but not to be explicitly confessional, and was to transcend class barriers. Alcide de Gasperi quickly became its dominant leader. Elected as party secretary in July 1944, he formed his first coalition government, including Socialists and Communists, in December 1945.

At the elections for the constituent assembly in 1946, the DC emerged as the largest Italian party, with 35.2 per cent of the votes and 203 seats. De Gasperi formed two new governments with Communist and Socialist participation but expelled them in May 1947, forming another government with the Social Democrats, Republicans and Liberals.

In the elections of April 18, 1948 the DC had its greatest ever triumph, winning 48.5 per cent of the national vote and 305 out of 572 seats in the Chamber, benefiting from fear of Communism as the Cold War intensified, and from strong support by both the Church and the Americans.

De Gasperi could have ruled on his own, but decided to maintain a "centre coalition" with the small lay parties. He remained Prime Minister until 1953.

In 1948 the united trade union movement finally split, and a Christian Democratic trade union was founded (LCGIL) which took its present name CISL in 1950.

De Gasperi led the party from the centre, with opposition from the clerical conservatives on the party right over such issues as agrarian reform, and with differences with the party left, led by trade unionists like Gronchi, and social Christian reformers, such as Dossetti and La Pira, over such issues as Italy's rejection of neutrality and adhesion to the Atlantic Alliance.

In 1952 the Church put pressure on the DC to accept a common list against the left in the Rome local elections, which would be headed by Don Sturzo (hence the name "Operation Sturzo"), and which would include extreme right candidates. This was successfully resisted by De Gasperi, a significant step in keeping the extreme right in isolation, and resisting direct clerical intervention in DC party affairs.

In 1953 the DC, with its allies in the small lay parties, passed a law (the so-called *legge truffa*) which would have enabled a group of parties winning over 50 per cent of the vote to automatically win two-thirds of the seats. In the 1953 elections, however, the DC failed to get over 50 per cent of the vote, its total falling from 48.5 per cent to 40 per cent. After one further short-lived government De Gasperi withdrew, and died in 1954.

His place as dominant figure in the party was taken by Amintore Fanfani, who was party secretary from 1954 to 1959, and whose main achievement was to build up a stronger party organization. Fanfani's period as secretary was also characterized by a massive development of the DC's network of patronage, and, in particular, its "colonization" of the public and semi-state sectors. Internal party factions also developed on a much wider scale.

A series of Christian Democratic Prime Ministers, Pella, Scelba, Segni, Zoli and Fanfani himself followed De Gasperi but there was no clear government formula to replace De Gasperi's centre coalition. As the Socialist Party became more independent of the Communists the DC began to consider an opening to the left, but at times was dependent on parliamentary support from the far right.

In 1955 the trade unionist, Giovanni Gronchi, was elected as the first Christian Democratic President.

In 1958–59 Fanfani combined being party secretary and Prime Minister, but internal party resentment against his accumulation of power, as well as opposition to his centre-left propensities, cost him both posts in 1959. He was replaced as secretary by Aldo Moro, who held the post until 1964.

In 1960 the disastrous Tambroni government, which came to power with explicit support from the far right and which was quickly brought down by popular protests, prepared the ground for an opening to the Socialists and to centre-left government.

Centre-left coalitions were formed first at local and regional level, while national governments led by Fanfani were not opposed by the Socialists. In December 1963 the first full centre-left government was created, with direct Socialist participation in a government led by Aldo Moro, who stood down as DC secretary and was replaced in this capacity by Mariano Rumor. Moro remained Prime Minister until 1968. In 1964 the centre-left was reinforced by the election of a Social Democratic President, Saragat, to replace Segni who resigned through ill health.

DC electoral support had previously risen in the 1958 elections (42.4 per cent) but fell sharply in 1963 to 38.3 per cent. There now began, however, a period of great electoral stability when the DC won between 38 and 39 per cent of the national vote in five successive elections until 1979.

From 1960 onwards internal party politics were dominated by the *Dorotei* faction which was a coalition of powerful party barons without any particular ideological stance. Left-wing factions (*Base* and *Forze Nuove*) on the trade union and Social Christian wings of the party continued to exist, but with a less sharp profile than before. The party "right" was even more amorphous.

The centre-left formula gradually became stale. Moro was replaced as Prime Minister by Leone, and then Rumor, whose job as party secretary was taken first by Flaminio Piccoli and then by Arnaldo Forlani. Some elements in the party began to look more openly towards closer links with the Communists, considering that they were in the "constitutional arc" of acceptable parties (unlike the far-right). Others began to advocate a revival of centrist formulas excluding the Socialists.

In 1970 the Christian Democrats overtook the Communist Party in total number of members. In 1971 Leone became President.

The last phase of the centre-left period was in some ways its most radical, with a far-reaching labour statute being passed, as well as a law on divorce. In 1972, however, a new centre-left government was created, with Andreotti as Prime Minister, and the Liberals and the Socialists excluded. This aroused strong internal opposition within the party, which brought down the government and replaced it by a new centre-left government under Rumor. Fanfani was brought back as party secretary.

The party now went through a period of turmoil. Fanfani put the weight of the party behind the 1974 attempt to repeal the divorce law, and the party was severely harmed by its massive repudiation in the referendum.

In the 1975 local elections DC support dropped sharply and Fanfani was replaced as secretary by Benigno Zaccagnini.

At the 1976 party congress Benigno Zaccagnini of the party's reformist left wing narrowly defeated Forlani to retain the secretaryship. This was the first time that the secretary had been directly chosen by congress delegates (although this reform was not finally confirmed until the 1980s). The party now opened up to further co-operation with the Communist Party. This was still very controversial within the DC, which had to steer a careful line between winning the support of the Communists for their parliamentary majority without associating them directly in the government. The main architects of the ensuing governments of "national solidarity" and of co-operation with the Communists were Aldo Moro and the Prime Minister, Giulio Andreotti. In March 1978 Moro was kidnapped by left-wing terrorists and subsequently killed.

In 1979–80 the DC rejected further co-operation with the Communists, and the centre-left formula of rule with the Socialists and the other lay parties was revived. Zaccagnini stood down as secretary.

The early 1980s were another difficult period for the DC. In 1981 it was damaged by the P2 scandal, and conceded the premiership to a non-Christian Democrat (Spadolini) for the first time since 1945.

In 1982 De Mita became party secretary, but only a year later the DC suffered its worst electoral defeat, slumping from 38 per cent to under 33 per cent, and losing 37 seats in the Chamber. A second non-Christian Democrat, Craxi, became Prime Minister, and held on for four years. In the 1984 European elections, the DC won fewer votes than the Communists.

In 1985 the Christian Democrats won back the Italian presidency through Francesco Cossiga. In 1986 De Mita was re-elected party secretary with over 75 per cent of delegates' votes. In the

1987 national elections the DC made a limited electoral recovery, winning 34.3 per cent of the votes and 234 seats in the Chamber (125 in the Senate). Subsequently a young Christian Democratic politician, Giovanni Goria, became Prime Minister at the head of a new five-party coalition.

Early in 1988 his government fell, and in April 1988 he was replaced by party secretary Ciriaco De Mita, as Prime Minister of a similar coalition.

In spite of their electoral decline, and weakened grip over the apparatus of government, the Christian Democrats are still the dominant Italian political party. Besides holding 17 of the 33 ministeries in the current De Mita government, the DC holds the presidency of over half the Italian regions, and almost half the provinces. In 1986 there were 4,400 Christian Democratic mayors in the 8,000 Italian communes, and over 70,000 Christian Democratic regional, provincial and local councillors.

Support

With around a third of the national vote the DC is still a mass party, with support in all areas and among all social groups. It has become more and more of a middle-class party, reflecting Italian social changes. The percentage of its members in the industrial sector declined from 18.4 per cent in 1977 to 15.4 per cent in 1979, whereas that in the tertiary sector increased from 7.7 per cent to 12.1 per cent.

The DC is strong among public sector workers who account for almost 15 per cent of its members (1985).

The DC has always relied heavily on women members and voters. Although the percentage of its members who are housewives declined from 25 per cent in 1959 to 17.6 per cent in 1985, 37 per cent of its total 1985 membership consisted of women, a higher than average figure for Italy. Moreover, it has been estimated that from 1947 to 1980 at least 60 per cent of the DC's electorate were female.

Not surprisingly the DC has been the dominant party among regular church attenders, although this is a declining asset, as can be seen from the lower church attendance of the younger DC members.

The DC has tended to be stronger in the rural areas, and in the smaller towns than in the big urban areas. There has been a striking decline in the percentage of its members in the agricultural sector, 24 per cent in 1969 and only 8.4 per cent in 1985. There has also been a considerable regional shift in its support from north to south, in terms both of members and votes.

The trend was reinforced in the 1987 elections, when the DC gained 2.8 per cent in the south and performed weakly in the north, actually losing votes compared to its already poor 1983 performance in certain constituencies. Another feature of the DC's 1987 result was that it won votes in certain traditionally weak areas, like central Italy and some of the northern cities, while doing particularly badly in the small and medium-sized northern towns, where it had previously polled well.

The stronghold area for the DC in northern Italy is that of the traditional Catholic or "white" sub-culture in Veneto and in eastern Lombardy, where church attendance (although falling) is at its highest, and where the Catholic lay associations are still strong. The DC's best northern constituency in 1987 was Verona–Padua–Vicenza–Rovigo (47.2 per cent) (where Vicenza is its greatest stronghold) and its second best, Brescia–Bergamo (44.1 per cent) where its vote fell since 1983. The vote fell elsewhere in northern Lombardy, southern Piedmont, Friuli (in all three it is now around 35 per cent) and in the Trentino.

In the northern cities the DC has polled poorly in recent years. Although there was a recovery in 1987, the figures are still low, 26.8 per cent in Venice, 24.4 per cent in Milan, 23.6 per cent in Genoa and 22.3 per cent in Turin.

The weakest areas for the DC are the "red regions" of Emilia–Romagna, Tuscany (e.g. Firenze–Pistoia 24.3 per cent, and with the limited exception of the traditionally "white" province of Lucca) and Umbria. The DC is stronger in the Marches (34.5 per cent) and in Latium (34.3 per cent in Roma–Viterbo–Latina–Frosinone, where it polled 32.2 per cent in the city of Rome).

The DC polls above its national average everywhere in the south. The largest number of DC members are in Sicily (200,000 or almost 14 per cent of the total in 1985) where it polled 38–39 per cent in 1987. Its second-largest number of members are in Campania (176,000 or over 12 per cent), where its vote rose particularly sharply in 1987 (from 43.4 per cent to 45.9 per cent in Benevento–Avellino–Salerno, and from 32 per cent to 40 per cent in Napoli–Caserta, 21.8 per cent to 31.2 per cent in the City of Naples itself). In Apulia the DC polled 38 per cent in 1987, in Calabria 37 per cent and in Sardinia over 34 per cent (rising from 26.7 per cent in 1983). The DC polls well in Abruzzi (42.3 per cent in 1987) and in Basilicata (46.1 per cent), but its strongest region in Italy is Molise where it holds both Senate seats, three out of the four Chamber seats, and where it polled 57.3 per cent in 1987.

Organization

Although the DC is Italy's largest party electorally, it is less tightly organized than the Communist Party. In the De Gasperi era, organizational weaknesses were successfully masked by the support that the party received from the Church and the powerful Catholic lay associations and unions. When Fanfani was party secretary in the 1950s he greatly strengthened the party organization and made it more autonomous. The party now has an extremely complex structure, with a huge network of committees and advisory groups as well as its territorial units.

The party's organization has been affected by two major trends, the decline of the Catholic subculture and the rise of internal party factions and clientelism.

The Catholic Church is now less directly involved with the party, Catholic lay associations like Catholic Action have declined, and Christian workers' associations and unions have either become more independent of the party, like CISL, or severed their links, like ACLI.

In recent years this has been only partly compensated for by the rise of new Catholic pressure groups within the party, of which the most significant is the *Movimento Popolare*, whose activists and organizational strength help to create almost a party within the party, especially in northern Italy.

The development of party factions has greatly undercut the power of the party secretary, and directed much of the party's energies into internal coalition-building between faction chiefs. At first factions developed on ideological lines, but distinctions between "left" and "right" factions have become increasingly blurred over time. Factions are largely based on allegiance to strong individuals within the party, and differences are, at best, more over strategic choices facing the party (relations with the DC's coalition parties, links with the Communists) than over policy. The factions have their own organizational structure and congresses and divide not only government ministries between them (originally on the basis of a manual drawn up by a DC official called Cencelli), but the whole range of party patronage posts in the state and semi-state sectors.

The territorial base of factions is evident in the area of Catholic subculture in the Veneto, but is particularly strong in southern Italy. Typically, southern party sections are much larger in size than in the north, and clientelist relationships help to explain the southward shift in the party membership and support.

De Mita has tried to reduce the role of the factions (for example, by entrenching the practice that party secretaries are directly elected by the party congress and not by its national council) but they are still alive and well.

In 1985 the DC had 1,445,000 members, organized in 12,541 territorial sections of which 6,597 were in northern Italy, 2,306 in the centre with only 3,638 in the south and islands. The party has also tried to organize *sezioni d'ambiente* in the workplace or in centres of cultural or social activity, but in 1985 there were only 308 such sections in the whole of Italy, of which over 100 were in Rome. The minimum size for any section is 15 members. Where appropriate, sections can group together in constituency or communal committees.

At provincial and regional levels, there are party committees and executives and biannual congresses. There are also sectoral committees dealing with cultural, industrial and labour issues, and others liaising with the trade unions.

At national level the national congress should be held every two years, but in practice it is often on a more irregular basis depending on internal party developments. Delegates are chosen in preparatory, sectional, provincial and regional congresses by a complicated key, based partly on population but mainly on votes won by the party at the preceding national elections. At the last party congress in 1986 there were 1,185 delegates, representing 11,854,865 congressional votes.

The national congress now directly elects the party secretary, and also elects 160 members of the national council, of whom half are parliamentarians.

The national council is supposed to meet at least once every three months. Besides the directly elected members it consists of the party's regional secretaries and the current and former party leadership. The presidency of the national council is one of the key party posts.

There are 36 full voting members of the national executive. Thirty are elected by the national council of whom a third must be non-parliamentarians.

The party secretary is assisted by a 7 to 11-member "political office", consisting of the top party office holders and selected members of the national executive. The party has a large central bureaucracy.

A national assembly can also be convoked, in order to discuss policy issues between national congresses. There are also possibilities for internal party referenda.

The party office-holders are elected by a

complicated set of rules providing primarily for election by proportional representation on a list basis with preferential voting. Party secretaries are elected on a majority basis, but with two or three ballots if no candidate has won an absolute majority. Party candidates for national elections are proposed by the party's provincial committees and approved by the regional committees. Special electoral committees are established for this purpose.

The DC has associated youth, women's and senior citizens movements, the *Movimento Giovanile, Movimento Femminile* and *Movimento dei Anziani* respectively. There are also several party foundations.

There are still privileged links with many Catholic organizations, such as FUCI (the Catholic University Students' Federation). There is a Christian Democratic trade union confederation, CISL, and an influential confederation of small farmers, *Coldiretti*.

The "shock troops" of the Catholic movement are now provided by the *Movimento Popolare*, the political arm of *Comunione e Liberazione*, an influential Catholic lay group.

The party's daily newspaper is called *Il Popolo*. Its readership is much less than it once was. There is also a weekly paper *La Discussione*. There are a number of other reviews (eg *Il Punto, Civitas*) and a rather reduced regional press. There is also a DC publishing house, Edizione Cinquelune.

Party membership dues are relatively low at 15,000 lire. Another useful source of party revenue are its popular festivals, *Feste dell'Amicizia*.

The party is linked internationally with the Christian Democratic International and the European Union of Christian Democrats. In the European Parliament it sits with the European People's party. Giulio Andreotti and Emilio Colombo are recent presidents of the European Union of Christian Democrats and Flaminio Piccoli is president of the Christian Democratic International. The chairman of the DC members in the European Parliament has a consultative vote in the DC's national council.

Policies

The DC is a difficult party to place in the ideological spectrum. As a catch-all governing party the party includes a wide spectrum of views within its ranks, and its "left" and "right" are not easy to define and are rapidly shifting.

The party's label is that of a Christian Democratic party, and yet it is non-confessional and has been almost permanently allied with lay political parties. It has had more explicitly Catholic groups within its ranks, such as the Social Christians of Dossetti and La Pira and more recently the *Movimento Popolare*, and the Catholic Church has often intervened directly in its favour, but the distance between the party and the Church ("the width of the Tiber") has gradually increased. The Catholic subculture has declined, and the papacy, more especially since John XXIII and the subsequent election of a non-Italian Pope, has been less directly involved. Moreover, the DC's last major involvement in an issue sponsored by the Church (the referendum on divorce) was a disaster for the party. It did not get directly involved in the subsequent referendum on abortion.

Nor can the party be accurately described as an ideologically Conservative party, although it is the party for which most Italian Conservatives vote in the absence of any major alternative to its right. The DC has always had considerable Social Christian and trade union wings, and its strong support in the poorest parts of southern Italy has also contributed to make it an advocate of state assistance, and of major state intervention in the economy (which has also helped to reinforce its powers of patronage). It has also participated in long periods of centre-left government, and taken part in such decisions as the nationalization of electricity, a radical statute for workers' protection, indexation, and tough rent controls.

Perhaps the greatest binding force for the DC has been anti-communism, and attacks on the Italian Communist Party and a pledge not to make a coalition with it feature even in the DC's 1987 election programme; yet even here the DC's leaders have been prepared to reach quiet agreement with the Communists, and even to associate them in their parliamentary majority in the years 1976–78.

In recent years the tide has shifted somewhat against the Communists, and the DC has had to respond instead to a reinforced Socialist party which is more difficult for it to attack.

The DC is not in an easy strategic position. It is still the largest party, but its electoral support has declined, and it has been harmed by its amorphous image, and too close association with abuses of patronage and the faults of the Italian state and institutions. The only untried formulas are direct alliance with the Communists, or for the DC to go into opposition. The most likely outlook is for a continuation of the present type of coalition, with the DC trying to prevent the Socialists from becoming too powerful.

No formal alliance is likely to be made with the Communists but they must, nevertheless, be kept in a relatively strong position, to maintain a strategic balance which keeps the DC in the centre of the governing spectrum.

On economic policy, DC governments have generally taken a pragmatic stand, at times expanding the role of the state and adopting an expansionist economic policy, at other times having to retrench. The current emphasis is on economic rigour, and on reducing inflation and the public deficit. De Mita's recent government programme put a particular emphasis on modernizing the Italian economy to meet the challenge of the 1992 European internal market. The DC supports privatization where appropriate and a more flexible labour market (including more part-time work) in order to help reduce unemployment.

The DC has not taken a strong position for or against civil nuclear energy, but was prepared to sacrifice the controversial Montalto power station in order to form a new government in April 1988.

Now that the divorce and abortion issues have been lost, the main moral issue in the DC's programme in 1987 was opposition to abuses of genetic manipulation.

Electoral reform is a sensitive issue for the party, as it would be the immediate beneficiary of any majority rather than proportionally-based system, and this is opposed by most of their allies. The 1987 DC electoral programme was thus more cautious, calling for a reduction in the number of Members of Parliament and for smaller electoral constituencies, as well as for restrictions (but not abolition), of preferential voting. The DC also supports greater differentiation in the functions of the two Houses of Parliament.

The DC does not adopt particularly distinctive positions on foreign policy or security questions. It is a strong supporter of the western alliance, and of European union. The DC recognizes the need for reform of the common agricultural policy and for fiscal approximation, and seeks to give the 1989 European Parliament a constituent mandate. The DC also supports moves towards collective European security.

Personalities

Ciriaco de Mita, a deputy from Avellino in Campania, who was party secretary from 1982 to 1989, became Italian Prime Minister in April 1988. De Mita is a member of the left-of-centre *Base* faction within the party, and has been a supporter of Christian Democratic co-operation with the Communist Party in appropriate circumstances.

The current Italian President is Francesco Cossiga (since 1985) who had previously been Prime Minister on two occasions in 1979 and 1980. Cossiga is a Sardinian, and a cousin of the late Communist leader, Enrico Berlinguer.

The leading party figures within the DC cannot be separated from the factions they represent which are constantly re-grouping and making new alliances.

The two largest power groupings within the DC in early 1988 were the so-called *Grande Centro* (Broad Centre) and the *Area Zac*.

Grande Centro is a new coalition between centre factions, the largest of which is known as the *Corrente del Golfo* (Gulf Stream), because its main leaders, Antonio Gava and Vincenzo Scotti, come from the Gulf of Naples. Gava is now one of the most powerful figures within the party and holds the post of Minister of the Interior in the De Mita government.

The other main group associated with the *Grande Centro* is that of the followers of Arnaldo Forlani, who was party secretary from 1969 to 1973, and Prime Minister in 1980–81. He has an electoral base in the Marches. Forlani was again elected as party secretary at the party congress in early 1989.

The other leading party barons associated with the *Grande Centro* are Emilio Colombo and Flaminio Piccoli. Emilio Colombo was Prime Minister in 1970–72 and was President of the European Parliament in 1977–1979. He has a powerful electoral base in Potenza in Basilicata, and is currently Minister of Finance in the De Mita government.

Flaminio Piccoli comes from Trento and has been party secretary on two occasions, in 1969 and from 1980 to 1982. He is currently president of the party's national council.

The *Grande Centro* currently has around 35–40 per cent of the party strength.

The second major grouping within the party is the *Area Zac*, with around 33 per cent of party strength, comprising a number of "left" factions within the party. It was named after another of the party's elder statesmen, Benigno Zaccagnini, a follower of Moro who was party president in the early 1970s and party secretary from 1975 to 1980. The *Area Zac* includes the *Base* faction, of which De Mita is a member. Among the other well-known figures of *Area Zac* are Mino Martinazzoli, (the head of the DC group in the Chamber of Deputies), Giovanni Galloni, Carlo Francanzani, Guido Bodrato, Guiseppe Zamberletti, Virgilio Rognoni and Nino Gullotti.

The third-highest party group, with around 18–20 per cent of party strength, is that centred around Giulio Andreotti, who was Prime Minister on five occasions, including the period of DC co-operation with the Communist Party. He has also been a long-serving and very independent Foreign Minister, a post which he still holds in the De Mita government.

His right-hand man is Franco Evangelisti from Latium. Other members of his faction include Paolo Cirino Pomicino, Nicola Signorello, the Mayor of Rome (and the only DC Mayor of a large city) and Antonio Drago.

Although Andreotti's faction is not associated with Catholic integralism, it has made a tactical alliance with the *Movimento Popolare*, whose most prominent leader is Roberto Formigoni, from Lombardy.

A further small faction on the left of the party is *Forze Nuove*, whose long-standing leader is Carlo Donat Cattin from Turin, a representative of the trade union, Social Christian wing of the party. He has been generally opposed to co-operation with the Communists. He is Health Minister in the De Mita government. Sandro Fontana is another prominent member of his faction. *Forze Nuove* currently represents 6–7 per cent of the party strength.

A similar faction, with only around 3 per cent of party strength, is that centred around Amintore Fanfani, now well into his 80s, party secretary from 1954 to 1959 and from 1973 to 1975 and Prime Minister on six occasions. Fanfani is the current Budget Minister.

Among the other well-known personalities within the DC are its commissioner, Pandolfi, from the Abruzzi, the economist Beniamino Andreatta, and Giovanni Goria, Prime Minister from 1987 to 1988.

Partito Comunista Italiana — PCI
(Italian Communist Party)

Headquarters	: Via Botteghe Oscure 4, 00186 Rome (tel: 67111)
Party secretary	: Achille Occhetto
Chairman of PCI Chamber Group	: Renato Zangheri
Chairman of PCI Senate Group	: Ugo Pecchioli
Youth organization	: *Federazione Giovanile Comunista Italiana* (FGCI) Secretary: Pietro Follena
Publication	: *L'Unità*
Membership	: 1,508,117 (1987)
Founded	: 1921

History

The Italian Communist party (PCI) was founded in January 1921, as a result of a split within the Socialist Party over whether to join the Third International. After the executive's decision to join had been overturned by the party congress, the minority then left to create the PCI. In the national elections in May 1921 the new party obtained 4.6 per cent of the votes and 15 seats in the Parliament.

A further schism within the Socialist Party in 1924 brought new recruits to the PCI, but it remained a small party of cadres. In 1924 Amedeo Bordiga, its first leader, was replaced as secretary by the 33-year-old Antonio Gramsci.

The PCI was persecuted under the Fascist regime, and Gramsci himself was imprisoned. His *Prison Notebooks* have since established him as one of the major Marxist philosophers, and were also used to justify the subsequent independent line of the Italian party.

In 1935 the party in exile concluded a pact with the Socialist Party. In 1943 this was renewed in "a unity of action" pact.

Its key role in the Italian Resistance brought the party immense prestige. In March 1944 its leader, Palmiro Togliatti, returned from exile in Russia and at the so-called *Svolta* or "turning point" of Salerno, announced a new strategy for the party to cease being one of elite cadres, and become one with a mass membership. It would co-operate with other democratic forces in Italy, and work within the system rather than trying to overthrow it by violent action. The party established a strong presence among the emerging trade union and co-operative movements.

The Communist Party took part as a full member of the Parri government in 1945, and of the first three De Gasperi governments from 1945 to 1947. It took a moderate line, and emphasized its acceptance of private property, and freedom of religious belief. It had originally even been prepared to accept the monarchy, and in 1947 it voted (unlike the Socialists) for incorporation of the 1929 Lateran pacts between Mussolini and the Church into the new Italian constitutional framework.

In the 1946 constituent elections the PCI won 18.9 per cent of the votes and 104 seats.

By 1947 the PCI had almost 2.25 million members. In May 1947 De Gasperi removed the Communist and Socialist ministers from his government, and the development of the Cold War split Italy into two opposing camps. The PCI opposed the Marshall plan, and Italy's alignment with the western powers.

In November 1947 a Popular Front with the Socialist Party was formally created, and a joint electoral list was drawn up for the decisive 1948 national elections. The united left was severely defeated with 31 per cent of the vote, but the greater discipline of Communist voters helped to ensure that no less than 132 of the left's 183 seats were won by Communist candidates. In 1949 the Vatican declared that anyone who joined the PCI or voted for it would be excommunicated.

In the 1953 national elections the left recovered considerable ground by successfully opposing the Christian Democrats' new electoral law. The PCI also clearly asserted its primacy on the left by winning 22.6 per cent of the vote and 143 seats, compared to the 12.8 per cent and 75 seats of the Socialist Party.

In 1956 Kruschev's denunciation of Stalinism enabled Togliatti to distance the PCI from the Soviet party, but later in the year it defended the Soviet invasion of Hungary. Over the next year party membership fell sharply and a number of prominent figures left the party. The PCI was also faced with an increasingly independent Socialist Party.

The creation of the centre-left government in the 1960s, with full Socialist participation, had mixed effects on the PCI. It made the party more isolated but reinforced its position as the only major opposition party. It had had a slight electoral setback in 1958 but in the 1963 and 1968 elections its vote rose significantly. By 1968 it was winning 26.9 per cent of the vote.

The party's independent line was gradually strengthened. It was opposed to the expulsion of the People's Republic of China from the International Communist movement, and began to drop its original opposition to the European Community. Togliatti died in 1964, but the PCI's new leadership under Luigi Longo, a prominent Spanish Civil War veteran and leader of the Italian Resistance, continued in his path.

The late 1960s, were another difficult period for the party. The PCI supported the "Prague Spring" and condemned the Soviet invasion of Czechoslovakia later in the year. In 1969 it finally sent a delegation to the European Parliament. Nevertheless the party was not at the forefront of the 1968 students' movement, nor of the "hot autumn" of trade union unrest in 1969. The PCI was seen, instead, as a conservative, restraining influence. In 1969 the Socialist "Manifesto" group of party dissidents, who criticized the lack of internal party democracy, and who sought an even tougher condemnation of the Soviet Union, were expelled from the party.

In 1972 Longo was replaced as PCI secretary by Enrico Berlinguer, an austere Sardinian aristocrat who subsequently brought the party to its highest level of success. When the regions were finally established the PCI won control of the three regional governments in the "red belt" of Emilia-Romagna, Tuscany and Umbria. With the waning of the "1968 spirit" new recruits were won by the PCI and party membership at last began to rise again after a long period of decline. In 1972 the majority of members of PSIUP, the left Socialist Party, joined the PCI.

The Chilean military coup against Allende in September 1973 led to a re-assessment of PCI strategy. Berlinguer now argued that achievement of a narrow left-wing majority was too risky and that the Communists should seek power instead in a wider coalition with the Christian Democrats. Such a "historic compromise" would win wider acceptance and give new respectability to the PCI.

In 1974 the PCI leadership accepted Italian membership of NATO. The PCI was also reinforced by the Christian Democratic defeat in the divorce referendum. In 1975 the PCI congress formally ratified the strategy of the "historic compromise".

The PCI also began to advocate a Eurocommunist alliance with the Spanish and French Communist parties to emphasize the differences between it and the Soviet party.

The PCI triumphed in the local and regional elections of 1975, obtaining 33.4 per cent of the national vote, and helping to win left-wing control of three more regional governments (Liguria, Latium and Piedmont) and most major Italian cities. In the 1976 national elections it won 34.4 per cent of the vote, and 228 seats.

There now began a period of attempted implementation of the "historic compromise" through close Communist co-operation with the Christian Democrats. The PCI abstained on the formation of the 1976 Andreotti government and adopted a "responsible" attitude towards it, being prepared to support it on a case-by-case basis. For the first time the PCI also obtained the presidency of the Chamber of Deputies, and the chairmanship of several parliamentary committees.

In March 1978 it voted in favour of Andreotti's new government, thus formally entering into the parliamentary majority for the first time.

The PCI was now in the difficult position of supporting the government without direct ministerial involvement. It began to pay the penalty in the 1978 local elections, and in 1979 it withdrew from the parliamentary majority, helping to force new elections in which it lost ground heavily, falling to 30.4 per cent of the national vote and losing 27 seats. In 1980 it finally abandoned the strategy of the "historic compromise", and began to advocate a "democratic alternative" of Communist coalition with the Socialists and other left-of-centre forces. At the same time Berlinguer strongly emphasized the distinctiveness of the PCI and criticized the Socialist Party.

Nevertheless the PCI became more and more distant from the positions of the Soviet party. It condemned the Vietnamese invasion of Cambodia and the Soviet invasion of Afghanistan in December 1979. In October 1981 the Ledda Report to the PCI central committee was openly critical of many Soviet actions and of the placing of SS 20 missiles. In December 1981 the situation in Poland provoked a final crisis in relations. The PCI supported Solidarity and condemned the imposition of martial law. Berlinguer spoke openly of the need to move on to a third phase of Socialism, in which the 1917 October Revolution was no longer the main inspiration.

In 1984 Berlinguer died suddenly during the run-up to the European Parliament elections, in which the PCI won 33.3 per cent of the votes and 27 seats, narrowly overtaking the Christian Democrats for the first time. This good result was largely a vote of sympathy for the popular Berlinguer, and helped to mask a steady erosion of party support in the 1980s, in terms of both members and votes.

Berlinguer's successor as party secretary was Alessandro Natta, a life–long party official. With the premiership being held by a Socialist from 1983 to 1987 the PCI adopted a more confrontational position, in Parliament and on the factory floor. In 1985 the PCI provoked a referendum in opposition to Craxi's attempt to reduce automatic indexation (*scala mobile*). It lost the referendum, and its populist stand cost it support and credibility.

In the national elections of June 1987 the PCI fell to 26.6 per cent of the vote, a loss of 3.3 per cent from 1983. It won 177 seats in the House and 100 in the Senate, with losses of 21 and seven seats respectively.

Shortly after the election Achille Occhetto was elected as deputy leader of the party. 41 members of the party's right wing voted against, and their opposition was expressed more openly than ever before in the party.

In 1988 Natta resigned as leader and was replaced by Achille Occhetto. The party polled poorly in the 1988 municipal elections, but despite its slippage in support the PCI is still firmly entrenched in regional, provincial and local governments.

In 1986 the PCI held the presidency of three regional governments and 16 provincial councils. It had 293 regional councillors, 881 provincial councillors, and over 15,000 municipal councillors in communes of over 5,000 inhabitants.

Support

The PCI is Italy's second largest party in terms of electoral support, and by far the largest party on the left. Industrial workers are still the largest component of its membership, 37.3 per cent in 1985 (compared to 45 per cent in 1947). On the other hand, there has been a dramatic decline in the percentage of its members who are farm labourers, from 17 per cent in 1947 to only 3.5 per cent in 1985. Farmers and share-croppers are also not well represented.

The urban middle classes play an ever-increasing role in the life of the party, representing 31.6 per cent of total party membership by 1985. White collar and technical workers and civil servants are increasingly well represented. There has been a particularly significant increase among teachers, who represented around 0.5 per cent of members until 1961 and have now risen to 3 per cent. Of the delegates at the 1986 party congress no less than 19 per cent were teachers and over 10 per cent came from other liberal professions.

There have also been steady rises in the percentage of party members who are craftsmen or commercial tradesmen.

Compared to the Christian Democrats the PCI has a much lower membership among housewives, and their percentage of total PCI membership has declined from 13.2 per cent in 1969 to 7.5 per cent in 1985. On the other hand, the PCI is particularly well represented among pensioners, and the percentage of PCI members in this category has almost doubled from 11.8 per cent in 1968 to 21.5 per cent in 1985.

In regional terms the PCI has been consistently the largest party in the "red belt" of central-northern Italy (Emilia–Romagna, Tuscany and Umbria). It has been particularly weak in the "white provinces" of north-east Italy and also in parts of the south where the PCI has a lower membership and has enjoyed a generally rising but also sharply fluctuating vote. In the 1970s the party also made a particularly large advance in the industrial cities of north-west Italy.

In the 1987 election it suffered its sharpest losses in the north-western industrial areas of Piedmont and Lombardy, substantial losses in its own strongholds in the "red belt", and its lowest decline in parts of the south.

In terms of party organization the PCI is strongest of all in Emilia-Romagna. It has been consistently in power in Bologna since 1945, and it has an absolute majority in many towns throughout the region. Even after the sharp drop in its vote in 1987 it still won 44.7 per cent of the vote in the constituency of Bologna–Ferrara–Ravenna–Forli and 43.2 per cent in the western Emilian constituency (where it is much stronger in the provinces of Modena and Reggio Emilia than in Piacenza and Parma).

The PCI has an even higher share of the vote in Tuscany, with 46 per cent in 1987 in the constituency of Florence–Pistoia and 45 per cent in Siena–Arezzo–Grosseto. Siena is its best province in all Italy. It is less strong in the third Tuscan constituency, especially in the "white" province of Lucca (40.2 per cent in 1987 in Perugia–Terni–Rieti).

Immediately across the Po from "red" Emilia–Romagna, the PCI is at its weakest in strongly Catholic north-eastern Italy, in Veneto, Friuli, and the Trentino. In the city of Venice the PCI won 27.9 per cent in 1987, but in the constituency of Verona–Padova–Vicenza–Rovigo, it obtained 16.5 per cent and in Trento–Bolzano 8.1 per cent.

In north-western Italy, where the PCI had such a sharp decline in 1987, the party is generally stronger in the cities (Turin 29 per cent) than in the surrounding country. The party is relatively weak in Milan (22.9 per cent in 1987), in north and east Lombardy (Como–Sondrio–Varese 18.2 per cent), Brescia–Bergamo (18.4 per cent) and in south Piedmont (Cuneo–Alessandria–Asti 20.2 per cent). It is stronger in Liguria (32.3 per cent in 1987).

The PCI has moderate strength in Latium (25.9 per cent) and in the city of Rome (25.8 per cent).

In the south of Italy the PCI is generally stronger in the country than in the cities. Whereas the party had over 23 per cent support in 1987 in Apulia, it won under 17 per cent (and was third) in its largest city of Bari. Similarly in Sicily where it won around 20 per cent support, it was in third place with only 14.2 per cent in Palermo. This pattern also prevailed in Calabria (20.9 per cent in Catanzaro compared to 25.3 per cent throughout the region); Basilicata (19.7 per cent in Potenza compared to 25.5 per cent); Abruzzi (L'Aquila 20.7 per cent compared to 27.4 per cent); and Sardinia. Only in Campania was the PCI stronger in Naples (26.7 per cent) than in the surrounding region (22.5 per cent) in Napoli–Caserta (and only 18.5 per cent in Benevento–Avellino–Salerno). The PCI's biggest losses in the south in 1987 were also in the cities. In two southern regions, Molise and Calabria, the party limited its losses in 1987 and in the former even advanced slightly from 1983 (19.7 per cent to 20.1 per cent).

Organization

At the end of World War II the PCI reorganized itself from being a party of cadres based on cells in the workplace, to being a party with a mass membership based on territorial sections. Since then the PCI has been the most tightly organized of any Italian party. It has had more members than other parties, and been more disciplined and unified. Democratic centralism has remained as a central party rule, and no open party factions have been allowed to develop.

In recent years there have been considerable changes. Party membership which declined in the late 1950s and '60s but rose again in the '70s has again declined considerably in the '80s to its present total of 1.5 million. Workplace groups have declined in number. Democratic centralism has been gradually modified, with more dissent being allowed.

The party is now attempting a new set of reforms. Party democracy is to be further strengthened, with more consultation of the "silent majority" of members and further protection of the rights of party minorities and dissenters. The party is aiming to have more, but smaller, sections with a maximum of 350 members per section (some sections, especially in the south, have over 1,000 members). The party is also trying to establish a more open structure, with a revival of sections in the workplace, with new sectoral and policy-based sections and new "centres of political and cultural initiative" working in harness with the new social movement and organizations. The party also wishes to tighten its links with the trade union movement, through less rigid rules of incompatibility of party and trade union office.

The lowest organizational level is the party cell, which must have a minimum of five members, and can be organized territorially or in the workplace. In practice, the basic party unit is now the section, which can have several hundred members. There are currently almost 13,000 such sections in the PCI, of which around 11,500 are territorial sections within Italy, 1,200 are workplace sections and 250 are party sections outside Italy. In the larger cities like Rome there are zonal committees.

The next tier is the party federation, of which there are 116. These are mainly based on individual provinces, but in large provinces there may be more than one (e.g. three in Rome). Above these are the 20 regional organizations.

The PCI national congress is now held every three years, and consists of delegates elected at the congresses of the federations. Just under 1,100 delegates attended the 1986 PCI congress. The national congress elects the PCI central committee of 184 members which meets every two months. It elects the 33–member party executive, and also the party's top official, the general-secretary, who is assisted by an eight-member secretariat. The party's central headquarters in Rome has a staff of around 200.

A new "programme office" has recently been established centrally to co-ordinate party policy-making. The party congress also elects the 55-member central control committee, which deals with disciplinary procedures, and disputes over the party statutes.

Candidates for national or European office are generally proposed by the federations, after consultation with the sections and the regions, and are then ratified by the central committee.

The party rules still permit extensive co-option to party posts. Length of party service is still formally more important than in other Italian parties. A member must be eight years in the party to be eligible for the central committee, and 10 years for the central control committee.

The PCI's youth group is called the *Federazione Giovanile Comunista Italiana* (FGCI). It is divided into leagues, such as the league for peace. There is also a PCI women's committee, and a women's conference.

The PCI does not have any directly associated trade union, but it still dominates Italy's largest union, the General Confederation of Labour (CGIL). The party is closely linked with the National League of Co-operatives, as well as with the National Peasants' Alliance (*Alianza Nazionale Contadini*), which is less powerful than its Christian Democratic equivalent, *Coldiretti*.

Other organizations in the Communist subculture include a sports association, UISP (*Unione Italiana Sport Popolare*) and a cultural association, ARCI (*Associazione Ricreativa Culturale Italiana*).

One of the party's most successful activities is to organize popular festivals (*Feste Del 'Unita*), of which there are up to 8,000 a year around Italy, culminating in a national festival in a selected city.

There are a number of party training institutes (the Instituto Palmiro Togliatti at Fratocchio near Rome, and other centres at Albinea in Emilia and Cascina in Tuscany) and four party institutes and foundations, the Study Centre for Economic Policy (CESPE), the Study Centre for International Policy (CESPI), the Gramsci Institute and the Centre for State Reforms.

The party's daily newspaper is called *L'Unità*, and has the largest circulation of any party journal in Italy. There is also a weekly newspaper *Rinascita*, and theoretical journals such as *Critica Marxista, Politica ed Economia* and *Studi Storici*. The PCI also has a publishing house, Editori Riunita.

Current party dues are 25,000 lire a year. A new objective is being set of 0.5 per cent of a party member's income. Elected politicians have to turn over their public salaries to the party, which then gives them a party wage.

The PCI is a member of the Communist and Allies Group in the European Parliament. The party is on good terms with the Spanish Communist party and the Greek Communist Party of the Interior, but has relatively few links and practically no common meetings with the French Communists, the Portuguese party and the Greek Party of the Exterior.

Policy

Throughout the postwar years the PCI has been in the position of being Italy's second largest party, and yet, since 1947, being blocked from participating in government. This has been partly due to external hostility from America and the governments of the Atlantic Alliance, but largely because of suspicion within Italy itself as to the PCI's real nature. The PCI claimed to accept the western democratic system, private property and freedom of religious belief, but many believed that this was a two-faced strategy aimed at reassuring the Italian people while masking the party's true goals. Moreover, the party's break with the Soviet Union came about only slowly, and many rank and file PCI members remained pro-Soviet hardliners.

The 1980s have been a time of difficult strategy choices for the PCI. It has failed to enter government, although this appeared possible in the late 1970s. The PCI made an even sharper break with the Soviet Union, notably over the Polish events in 1981, and the remaining PCI hardliners were isolated as never before. On the other hand, the Eurocommunist strategy of the 1970s collapsed, with the decline of the French and Spanish parties, and the reversion into hard-line policies by the former. Finally, the PCI itself, while remaining by far the strongest force in the Italian left, has itself suffered electoral reverses.

Although the party remained in agreement over the need for a "Democratic Alternative" to continuing Christian Democratic domination the PCI became increasingly uncertain as to its own identify. Before he died, Berlinguer was a prominent advocate of a *"Terza Via"* or "Third Way", in which a communist-led Italy would emulate neither the rigid and undemocratic path of the Soviet Union nor reformist social democracy. This was subsequently taken up by many on the left of the PCI.

On the other hand, the ambiguity of the *Terza Via* was criticized by many on the right, who indeed appeared to advocate the party's evolution in a social democratic direction.

Another problem faced by the PCI was how to appear as a respectable and responsible opposition party, without also being seen as too conservative.

In the 1980s it attempted to resolve this by adopting a sharper opposition stance than it had in the 1970s and by encouraging trade union militants. In this it only succeeded in losing support.

At the party's Florence congress in 1986, the strategy which gained new emphasis was that of co-operation between the combined forces of "the European lefts", defined in the widest sense to include all socialist and socialist democratic parties, and feminist, pacifist, ecological and "green" movements who had an alternative vision to the prevailing neo-conservative and neo-liberal consensus. The "democratic alternative" remained as a formula for the PCI coming to power in Italy, in conjunction with the socialist and progressive lay parties, the new social movements and with progressive Catholic forces as well.

The PCI emphasizes its commitment to political democracy as an irreversible and permanent feature of Italian political life. It recognizes that the "working class" in its old rigid definition is no longer a very meaningful concept and defends instead working people and the disadvantaged in the wider sense.

At the same time, the PCI continues to seek allies within the Christian Democratic Party. The PCI adopted a conciliatory approach to the De Mita government in April 1987. It would not form part of its parliamentary majority, but would co-operate with it constructively in any serious attempts at political reform.

The PCI is a defender of the mixed economy, in which the public sector, private sector and a strengthened co-operative sector all play a proper role. Nevertheless, it puts a greater emphasis on the role of the state than the present parties of the governmental majority, and is critical of their neo-liberal policies, which have put too much weight on measures of economic austerity. The free market must be complemented by incomes policies and increased state planning and investment to steer resources into strategic sectors.

Full employment should be the ultimate goal. There should be a reduced working week, and other measures to redistribute work in order to create new jobs. In the meantime, unemployment benefits should be increased.

The problems of the south of Italy and of declining urban areas should be vigorously tackled.

The Italian fiscal system should be reformed, in order to put less of a burden on salaried workers and on the self-employed. There should be a crack-down on fiscal evasion.

The PCI recognizes that the state needs major reform. Public administration should be made more efficient and effective. Public spending should be kept under control.

The PCI advocates the introduction of an Italian anti-trust law, and the development of industrial democracy, so that workers are both informed and consulted.

The PCI puts a greatly-increased emphasis on environmental protection. It has been divided over the future of civil nuclear energy. A majority within the party have gradually turned against it, particularly after Chernobyl, and the PCI was one of the main advocates of a referendum on Italy's nuclear power plants.

The PCI strongly defends the Italian welfare state, but calls for greater efficiency in the provision of services. The health services should be improved. There should be more public housing. Minimum pensions should be increased. The minimum school-leaving age should be raised to 16.

The PCI is a firm advocate of political reform. It denounces clientelism and corruption (it takes a harder line on the mafia than other political parties), and prides itself on being a "clean" party generally untouched by scandal.

It does not believe that the present Italian Constitution needs to be overhauled, but that its basic principles need to be better applied. It believes there should be only one chamber of Parliament, and there should be a reduced number of members. The PCI was in favour of retaining secret voting within the Parliament. The executive should be strengthened. Proportional representation should be retained, but within single, electoral colleges, and with preferential voting abolished. The rights of immigrants in Italy, Italian emigrants abroad, and linguistic and national minorities within Italy should be better protected. The powers of the Italian regions should be reinforced. The Italian system of justice should be radically reformed.

The PCI has evolved considerably in its stand on foreign policy and defence issues. Until the late 1960s it was opposed to the European Economic Community, and it was opposed to Italian membership of NATO until 1974.

The PCI now supports Italian membership of NATO (unlike, for example, the otherwise moderate Spanish party), to protect the strategic balance within Europe, on condition that

NATO only has a defensive role and does not involve itself in areas outside those foreseen by the original treaty. The PCI strongly advocates a reinforcement of the European pillar within NATO, with European countries standardizing their own military planning, and having a greater say in their own defence. The PCI emphasizes the need for progressive and agreed arms reductions in both east and west, concentrating initially on nuclear weapons, but also covering conventional weapons. The PCI supported the double zero option as regards Euromissiles, and opposed the installation of NATO missiles at Comiso in Sicily. It supports the establishment of nuclear-free zones, and opposes SDI.

If the PCI is an unenthusiastic supporter of NATO it is now an enthusiastic advocate of European unity, going beyond the creation of an area of full free trade to full political integration. Indeed, the prime mover of the European Parliament's draft treaty of European Union, Altiero Spinelli, although not a party member, was elected on the PCI list.

The PCI advocates strong European regional and social measures; the harmonization of social security schemes; and common energy policy; and an increase in community "own resources", accompanied by reform of the wasteful Common Agricultural policy. At one stage it was opposed to full Italian entry into the European Monetary System. It now supports the further development of the EMS and the introduction of a common European currency.

Relations with the Soviet Union have improved, but the PCI is still highly critical of many aspects of Soviet society and policy. In this context Gorbachev's reforms are welcomed in their own right, but also because they confirm so many of the PCI's own criticisms of the Soviet system.

The PCI recognizes that the United States is an ally of Italy, respects its democratic traditions and rejects anti-Americanism. It was highly critical, however, of the policies of the Reagan Administration.

The PCI has had good relations with the Chinese party.

It puts a strong emphasis on north-south relations, supporting the establishment of a new international economic order, and a moratorium on third world debt. It has good relations with many national liberation movements. It supports the PLO, and the establishment of a Palestinian state, but recognizes Israel's right to security.

Personalities

The party's new leader, Achille Occhetto, was elected in 1988 and is its former deputy secretary. He comes from Turin and is in his early 50s. He is a former head of the party's youth movement, and also a former secretary of the Sicilian party. He has a left-of-centre profile within the party, and his election as deputy secretary was opposed by some on the party right.

Among the other members of the party's central secretariat are Massimo d'Alema, who is responsible for party organization, Livia Turcho, who is responsible for the women's committee, Pietro Follena, who is the secretary of the youth movement, Gianni Pellicani and Claudio Pettruccioli. A key figure as regards policy-making is the head of the programme office, Alfredo Reichlin. The chairman of the PCI deputies in the chamber is Renato Zangheri, a former mayor of Bologna, and of the PCI senators, Ugo Pechioli. The leader of the PCI members in the European Parliament (and also the chairman of the whole communist group) was Gianni Cervetti.

Aldo Tortorella is the party member responsible for institutional problems. Liaison with the trade unions is ensured by Antonio Bassolino.

The PCI remains less affected by factionalism than any other Italian party. Nevertheless there have been divisions over policy and strategy, and these have become more visible as the party has become less secretive. For many years the leader of the party "left" was Pietro Ingrao and of the "right", Giovanni Amendola. Amendola advocated a more reformist strategy for the party, and yet was less anti-Soviet than Ingrao, who attacked the Soviet Union for having not lived up to socialist ideals. Upon Amendola's death, his role as leader of the party right fell onto the shoulders of Giorgio Napolitano, who is still the leading advocate of a social democratic path for the party, whereas Ingrao remains an advocate of the "third way". Napolitano is responsible for the party's international relations.

Another leading figure on the right of the party is the former secretary of the CGIL, Luciano Lama, who developed a reputation for blunt realism during his many years as leader of the union.

The pro-Soviet hard-liners within the party have become far weaker in the last few years. They were estimated as up to a quarter of the party's members in the 1970s, but in the showdown over the party's anti-Soviet line at the 1983 congress were only able to muster 5 per cent of the delegates, admittedly still probably an underestimate of their real strength.

Their most well-known leader has been Armando Cossutta, who was dropped from the party executive at the 1986 congress. Another is Guido Cappellani.

Among the other prominent figures in the party are Antonio Pizzinato, the new secretary of the CGIL, and Bruno Trentin, another leading figure within the CGIL, who has been more on the left of the party than Lama.

Among the party's historic leaders are Giancarlo Pajetta, for many years responsible for the party's international relations and now president of the party's central control committee, and Sergio Segre, now the chairman of the institutional Affairs Committee in the European Parliament. Nilde Jotti, the former companion of Togliatti, is the current president of the Italian Chamber of Deputies.

Partito Socialista Italiano — PSI
(Italian Socialist Party)

Headquarters   : Via del Corso 476,
                         00186 Roma
                         (tel: 67781)
Secretary   : Bettino Craxi
Youth Organization   : *Federazione
                         Giovanile Socialista*
Publication   : *Avanti*
Membership   : 620,000 (1988)
Founded   : 1892

History

Socialism began to spread in Italy in the 1880s, especially among the landless labourers of the Po Valley and the working class in the newly industrialized areas of Lombardy. In 1882 Andrea Costa, a former anarchist, became the first Socialist Member of Parliament, as a deputy for Ravenna for the newly-founded Italian Revolutionary Socialist Party. In 1885 the Workers' Party was founded and in 1889 a Milanese Socialist League, one of whose leaders was Filippo Turati, a lawyer who was to become the most prominent of the early Socialist leaders.

In 1892 these various strands came together at a conference in Genova, in a new Party of Italian Workers.

In 1892 six deputies were elected. In 1895 it changed its name to the Italian Socialist Party. The party was restructured on the basis of individual rather than collective membership, and a clear distinction was made between the party's political role and the parallel economic action to be carried out by the Chamber of Labour and other worker organizations.

The party was periodically persecuted but grew steadily. By 1897, when the party newspaper *Avanti* was founded, it already had over 27,000 members in 623 sections. By 1900 it had 13 per cent of the national vote, and 32 deputies.

A Socialist subculture was clearly established, with the party having an associated network of clubs, co-operatives and houses of the people. For a Socialist party it was unusually strong in rural areas. The Po Valley continued to be its main area of strength. Its leadership was primarily middle class.

In spite of the absence of anarchists the party became divided at an early date between pragmatic reformists, among them Turati and Bissolati, and more revolutionary "intransigents" and "syndicalists". In 1900 the party compromised by adopting both a "maximum programme" of longer-term revolutionary goals and a "minimum programme" of more immediate practical objectives, such as universal suffrage and a shorter working week.

In 1903 Giolitti invited the Socialists to join his government but Turati reluctantly refused. In 1904 the reformists lost power within the party to the intransigents, who quickly called a general strike. In 1907, however, the revolutionary syndicalists were forced out of the party, and in 1908 the reformists again took charge. In 1911 Giolitti offered Bissolati a place in his government, but this was again refused.

The Libyan war again changed the balance of power within the party. Those reformists who supported the war, like Bissolati and Bonomi, were expelled, and formed a short-lived Italian Reformist Socialist Party. Some of the reformists like Turati remained within the Socialist Party, but lost power to the maximalist wing, of whom Mussolini was a prominent member. With the extension of the suffrage in 1912 the Socialist Party became the largest single Italian party for the first time, with 53 seats in the Chamber.

During World War I the Socialists took a stand against Italian participation, although this was attenuated by some Socialist leaders. Mussolini, who came out openly in favour of Italian participation, was expelled from the party in November 1914.

After the war the Socialists became the largest political grouping in terms of votes and of seats, winning 32.4 per cent of the vote in 1919, and putting 156 deputies in Parliament. The party entered into a period of internal conflict, which divided it in three, and which prevented it from resisting the rise of Mussolini and Fascism.

In 1921 a group of dissidents left the Socialist Party to form the Communist Party. The revolutionary maximalists still had a majority within the Socialist Party and in 1922 the reformist wing was expelled and created a new group, the Unitary Socialist Party (PSU), under the leadership of Giacomo Matteotti. By 1924 the PSU was winning more votes (5.9 per cent) than the original Socialist Party (4.9 per cent).

In 1924 Matteotti was murdered by the Fascists. The two Socialist parties were reunited in 1930 under the leadership of Pietro Nenni in Paris.

In 1934 the Socialist Party and the Communist Party entered into a "pact of unity of action" against the Fascist government, and this was renewed in 1943, the year when the Socialist Party joined with another group under the leadership of Basso to form the Italian Socialist Party of Proletarian Unity (PSIUP).

In the first postwar elections, in 1946, the Socialists won the second largest number of votes at 20 per cent, while the Communists won 18.9 per cent. A narrow majority was later won by those, like Nenni and above all Rodolfo Morandi, who advocated unity of action with the Communists leading to a possible eventual merger. The dissidents, including both the moderate reformist wing of the party and "autonomists" from the left, went off to create a new party in January 1947 (see entry on Italian Social Democratic Party — PSDI). Around a third of the membership, and 40 per cent of the Socialist deputies, joined the new party.

The Socialists and Communists took part in government with De Gasperi until they were pushed out in 1947. In 1948 the Socialists decided to fight the national elections on a joint electoral list with the Communists. The combined list lost votes heavily, but the main victim was the Socialist Party, which was seen as subservient to the Communists and won a much lower share of the seats as a result of its lesser discipline and organization.

The autonomists briefly won back power after the 1948 election failure under Alberto Jacometti, but Nenni and Morandi recaptured the party in 1949. The Socialists remained closely associated with the now more powerful Communists. The party rejected Italy's choice to join the Atlantic Alliance, and organized itself internally on Leninist lines.

The cost to the party was considerable. It continued to lose members, and suffered two more internal schisms with the departure of members of its "autonomist" wing. It was not recognized by the Socialist International. It had only limited weight within the trade union movement. In the 1953 elections the Socialists again fought on their own, but won only 12.8 per cent of the vote and 35 seats compared to the 22.6 per cent and 143 seats won by the Communists.

The PSI slowly began to distance itself from the Communists, a process accelerated by the Russian invasion of Hungary, which was criticized by Nenni. At a meeting in Pralognan Nenni met Saragat to examine the possibilities of

Socialist re-unification, although no immediate progress was made. At the 1958 elections the party recovered slightly to 14.2 per cent and 84 seats. By 1959 the Socialist Party had accepted Italian membership of NATO — and from 1960 onwards began to forge centre-left coalitions with the Christian Democrats and the other lay parties at local level.

In 1962 it gave external support to Fanfani's fourth government, and in 1963 it entered government for the first time since 1947, with Nenni as Deputy Prime Minister, and with five other ministers.

The party's choice to go into coalition with the Christian Democrats was opposed by the party's left wing, which broke away in early 1964 to form a new Socialist Party of Proletarian Unity, costing the PSI around a third of the central committee and of its parliamentary representation, and an even higher percentage of its members. It also greatly weakened the party in the trade union movement.

The PSI continued to participate in successive centre-left governments, although it failed to carry out its full reform programme, and was perceived as increasingly subordinate to the Christian Democrats.

In 1966 the PSI merged with the Social Democrats, but the combined party involved cumbersome duplication of posts, and the merger was never fully carried out. At the 1968 elections the new party gained little more than the Socialists on their own in 1963, and in 1969 the merger collapsed, notably on the issue of possible links with the Communists.

The Socialist Party now slumped to its lowest levels of support since the war. Nenni's successors, Francesco de Martino and Giacomo Mancini, attempted to forge new political strategies for the party, but these were not successful. The so-called strategy of *equilibri piu avanzati* (literally "more advanced balances", a policy of maintaining the centre-left formula but making it more radical and more open to co-operation with the Communists) was unclear and difficult to realize, and the subsequent strategy of the "left alternative" (co-operation between Socialists and Communists) was made irrelevant by the Communists' own preference for a "historic compromise" with the Christian Democrats.

In 1972 the PSI only gained 9.6 per cent of the vote and 61 seats. In 1974 it withdrew from government and did not return until 1980. After the party won even fewer seats in the 1976 election De Martino was replaced as secretary by the 42-year-old Bettino Craxi who later forged an alliance with Claudio Signorile of the party's left-wing, which enabled him to fully gain control of the party at the 1978 congress.

In 1978 Sandro Pertini became the first Socialist President of the Republic.

Craxi played down the strategy of the "left alternative" and sharply differentiated the Socialist Party from the Communists. He emphasized the character of the Socialist Party as a pragmatic and modern party of government, downplaying Marxist rhetoric, replacing the hammer and sickle as the party symbol by a red carnation and altering the party's constitution to give him greater powers.

The left was gradually pushed out of leadership positions within the party, with Lombardi resigning as president in 1980, and with Craxi's former ally Signorile pushed aside in 1981. The party factions were gradually brought under control. The Socialist Party re-entered government.

In the 1983 elections the PSI won 11.4 per cent of the vote with 73 seats, and Craxi subsequently became Prime Minister. His two terms as Prime Minister were a period of exceptional political stability by Italian standards, and Craxi reinforced his reputation as a decisive leader. Although he was forced out of office before the 1987 elections the Socialist Party reaped the benefit of Craxi's premiership and advanced to 14.3 per cent with 94 seats in the Chamber and 36 seats in the Senate, their best performance since 1946.

In the current De Mita government the Socialist Gianni de Michelis is Deputy Prime Minister and there are six other Socialist ministers. The Socialist Party is represented in most regional governments, and the majority of provincial and larger communal administrations.

Support

It is too easy to say whether the increase in PSI support at the 1987 elections was merely a short term consequence of Craxi's premiership or part of a longer term trend. The PSI is still the weakest Socialist party in any major European country. Its membership and electorate are volatile, and it does not yet have the mass support enjoyed by the Christian Democrats or Communists. On the other hand, it has much wider support than the other lay parties and is the only major Italian party which is currently increasing its membership. Under Craxi's leadership it has widened its appeal among managers and professionals and clearly took substantial votes among these groups from the other lay parties in the 1987 elections.

Since the war the pattern of its support has changed considerably. The traditional area of Socialist strength was central and northern Italy, and particularly Emilia–Romagna. After the war the Communist Party largely supplanted the Socialists in these areas and among working class and trade union voters.

As the Socialist Party developed as a party of patronage from the centre-left period onwards, the basis of its electoral support shifted sharply towards the south. In the 1946 elections over 40 per cent of the Socialist vote came from the industrial north-west and 25 per cent from the "red belt". By 1983 these were down to 27 per cent and 18 per cent respectively. On the other hand, the party's vote in Latium and the south had risen from 19 per cent of its total vote in 1946 to over 44.5 per cent by 1983. This southern vote was often linked to the electoral bases of prominent Socialist personalities, such as De Martino in Campania and Giacomo Mancini in Calabria. A further distinctive feature of the Socialist vote was that it was considerably stronger in local and regional elections than in national elections. The Socialist vote also rose among pensioners and housewives.

In the 1987 elections the Socialists consolidated their steady gains in the south, but by far the biggest increases in Socialist support were in northern Italy.

The Socialist Party performed particularly well in Lombardy where its vote rose substantially. In the constituency of Como–Sondrio–Varese, for example, its vote rose from 12.8 per cent in 1983 to 17.6 per cent in 1987, and in both Sondrio and Como the Socialists overtook the Communists. In Craxi's base of Milan the Socialists rose even further from 11 per cent to 18.5 per cent. The increase was less marked, however in the constituency of Mantova–Cremona (14.3 per cent to 15.2 per cent), which has always been a Socialist stronghold. Lombardy also has the highest Socialist Party membership.

The other part of Italy where the Socialist vote rose sharply was in the north-east. In Udine–Belluno–Gorizia–Pordenone it rose from 12.3 per cent to 18.5 per cent. In Venezia–Treviso from 12.1 per cent to 15.9 per cent and in Trieste from 6.3 per cent to 18.5 per cent. Elsewhere in the north support fluctuated at between 12 per cent and 14 per cent, except in the Socialist weak spot of Trentino–Alto–Adige. Here, however, there was still a substantial increase (6.8 per cent to 9.6 per cent). The weakest city for the Socialists was Turin (11.3 per cent in 1987).

In central Italy support was relatively low in Rome (12.5 per cent) and highest in Umbria (14.3 per cent in Perugia–Terni–Rieti, 16.1 per cent in the city of Perugia).

In southern Italy the strongest Socialist region is Calabria (16.9 per cent). Apulia is another stronghold with over 15 per cent support (Bari, 19.2 per cent, more than the Communists), but there was little increase in the vote from 1983 to 1987. On the other hand, there were considerable increases in Campania (in Napoli–Caserta the vote has risen from 7.2 per cent in 1976 to 14.3 per cent, in Benevento–Avellino from 8.8 per cent to 16.2 per cent) and in western Sicily (15.5 per cent in 1987, but 16.4 per cent in Palermo, up from 9.8 per cent in 1983). The Socialists' weakest area in Italy is Molise, where it has only 8.3 per cent support.

Organization

The Socialist Party has gone through several major organizational changes. Until the rise of Fascism it had a broad-based structure, with strong trade union links, and with many other Socialist associations and clubs paralleling the party's territorial units. After the last war much of this structure has gone or fallen into the hands of the Communists and the party was rebuilt on centralized, almost Communist, lines with a strong central committee which then chose the party secretary. At a later stage, and especially from the mid 1950s to the late 1970s, the party became increasingly dominated by organized factions, which formed shifting coalitions and tied the hands of the party secretary.

Bettino Craxi has changed the party yet again, and has given the party secretary a much more presidential role. The factions have been severely curtailed. The secretary is now directly elected by the party congress giving him greater independence, and security of tenure between Congresses. The central committee and executive committee have been replaced by greatly enlarged bodies with less possibility to control the secretary's actions.

The party is trying to strengthen its still weak organizational structure, by cutting down on the number of inactive sections and by reinforcing the party in the workplace and in the community at large. Its membership has increased considerably in recent years and now stands at over 620,000.

The basic territorial units of the party are the sections, of which there are around 8,000, and which can subdivide into territorial nuclei or combine in communal co-ordinating committees or zonal committees. Parallel to the territorial structure are the Socialist groups in the workplace, known as NAS (*Nucleo Aziendale Socialista*). There are several thousand of these throughout Italy, but many more in the centre and north than in the south. The party is currently trying to strengthen their role.

At provincial level the party is organized in federations run by directorates of between 31 and 61 members. Provincial congresses are held every two years.

At regional level there are regional committees which are slowly gaining in importance. Regional directorates consist of between 31 and 81 members depending on the population of the region. Regional congresses are held every three years. At both provincial and regional levels the party secretaries are now elected directly by their respective congresses.

The national congress is held every three years and consists of delegates elected at provincial congresses. The 1987 congress at Rimini had 1,800 delegates. The congress now directly elects the party secretary by secret vote.

The national assembly is the parliament of the party, and consists of almost 500 members, with around a third of its members consisting of prominent Socialist sympathizers from wider economic and cultural circles. It meets two or three times a year.

The party's national executive (*Direzione*) consists of 54 members, 40 of whom are elected by the national assembly. It meets seven or eight times a year, and chooses the party's central administrative committee of three to five members.

PSI candidates for national elections are chosen initially by the provincial federations and approved by the national executive, which reserves itself the right to choose a certain number of candidates, especially the heads of the lists in the different constituencies.

The party's choice of national ministers and under-secretaries is by the executive and presidents of the parliamentary groups on the basis of names selected by secret vote by the parliamentary groups. There are analogous rules for the designation of Socialist mayors (even deputy mayors), and Socialist provincial and regional office-holders.

The PSI is trying to strengthen its ties with outside organizations and groups, with which it can draw up "national associative pacts". Among the organizations with which it is associated are AICS (Sporting Clubs), UCI (The Union of Italian Cultivators) and various "Green Leagues".

The Socialist Party has members in all national confederal trade unions, including the Christian Democratic dominated union (CISL). Its closest links are with the Communist dominated Trade Union (CGIL) and more especially with the UIL, which has a Socialist secretary-general, and a Socialist majority of members. The CGIL and the UIL each have seven members participating in a consultative capacity at the Socialist national assembly. There are no organic links with any one union and the party's workplace units (the NAS) are formally independent of the unions.

The party's youth organization is called the *Federazione Giovanile Socialista Italiana*. There is no parallel women's organization, although there is a women's co-ordinating committee. The party statute calls for 15 per cent of party executive posts at all levels to be reserved for women and there are proposals to strengthen this. The party sponsors two foundations, the *Fondazione Nenni*, which examines questions of party ideology and philosophy and the *Fondazione Giacomo Brodolini* which deals with labour and social problems. There is also a party centre for historical documentation.

The party newspaper is *Avanti*, first published in 1897, and once edited by Mussolini. There is also a monthly review *Mondo Operaio*.

The party's annual dues are 50,000 Lire, with a special rate of 15,000 Lire for the retired and unemployed. Party office-holders contribute at least 30 per cent of their net income.

The PSI is a member of the Socialist International. Both it and the Social Democrats are also members of the Socialist Group in the European Parliament and of the Confederation of European Socialist parties.

Policies

Since Craxi was elected to party secretary he has succeeded in changing the character of the Socialist Party to a significant extent.

The party has been split between those who sought the unity of the left above all (or at least closer relations with the Communists), and those who put more emphasis on the distinctive character and autonomy of the PSI as a non-Communist Socialist party, and who were also prepared to work in centre-left coalitions with the Christian Democrats and the other lay parties. Taking over at a period of particular confusion over strategy and objectives within the PSI Craxi has clearly asserted its character as a modern and pragmatic party of government. He has distanced himself from the Communists and sought to position the PSI as a reformist social democratic party. The Marxist left within the party has had its influence greatly reduced. The PSI has succeeded in strengthening itself among Italy's managers and technocrats. At the same time it is still a long way from Craxi's avowed objective to imitating the French example and overtaking the electoral strength of the Communist Party.

The economic policy of the PSI is no longer characterized by anti-capitalist rhetoric. The PSI puts a strong emphasis on its achievement during the Craxi Governments in reducing Italian inflation, in beginning to contain the budget deficit,

in promoting incomes policy, in successfully cutting back on the system of automatic wage indexation (the *scala mobile*) against Communist opposition, and in promoting greater fiscal equity. The party's 1987 programme considered that the Italian labour market was still too rigid and that greater flexibility and mobility was needed, along with enhanced measures for retraining. The party adopts a neutral position towards privatization, supporting it when there are no good reasons for keeping an enterprise in the public sector. On the other hand, the PSI strongly advocates the introduction of proper competition laws within Italy.

The PSI claims that the poverty of southern Italy is still the greatest Italian problem, but that measures which reinforce a southern welfare mentality should be avoided. The Italian social welfare system should be strengthened, and there should be no indiscriminate cuts, but clientelist abuses should be curbed. Corporatist pressures should be resisted. Working hours should be reduced. The existing laws on rent control (the *equo canone*) should be progressively liberalized, without creating problems for the weaker elements in society.

The Socialist Party has been to the forefront in opposition to civil nuclear power.

The PSI strongly promoted divorce and abortion liberalization. It has lost, however, most of its old anti-clerical image, and indeed it was the Craxi government which renewed, in a considerably modified form, the Concordat with the Catholic Church.

The PSI calls for the reform of public administration, and major changes in the Italian system of justice.

The PSI seeks the direct popular election of the Head of State, and greater power for the Prime Minister to choose his own ministers. The electoral law should be modified to reduce the value of preferential voting. There should be greater differentation between the functions of the two Houses of Parliament. The party pushed successfully for the abolition of secret voting in Parliament for the approval of laws.

The PSI strongly emphasizes the need for European union. It wants the European Parliament to have powers of legislative co-decision, and for the 1989 European Parliament to be given a constituent mandate. In the meantime, it supports new financial resources for the European Community, the radical restructuring of the Common Agricultural Policy, and a reinforcement of the European Monetary System, with the ECU becoming a real European currency.

The PSI supports a common European foreign policy. It strongly supports the NATO Alliance (and accepted the installation of Pershing missiles at Comiso) but seeks a strengthened European role in defence and security matters within the Alliance. European military forces should be more integrated.

Personalities

Bettino Craxi, a Milanese of Sicilian origin (born in 1934) has led the Socialist Party since July 1976, and has succeeded in imposing himself on the party to an unprecedented extent. He was a representative of the Nenni autonomist faction within the party, and has had the Milan federation as his power base. Craxi was Italian Prime Minister from 1983 to 1987. Respected for the stability he provided, and for his clear and decisive style of leadership, he has also made many enemies among those who feel that his style is too authoritarian.

Craxi's second in command is Claudio Martelli (45 years old in 1988), who is in charge of party organization. He has occasionally adopted a more populist tone than the party technocrats, and has taken a particularly strong stand, for example, against civil nuclear energy.

The Deputy Prime Minister in the current De Mita government is Gianni de Michelis, the former party leader in Venice, a former member of the party's left wing, but later a Craxi ally and man of government.

Of the other Socialist ministers within the government the most significant are probably Rino Formica and Giuliano Amato. Formica, whose political base is Bari in Apulia, is currently the Labour Minister. Amato, a political science professor, was Craxi's principal advisor on government affairs during his premiership, and is now the Treasury Minister. Another minister who is close to Craxi is Carlo Tognoli, a former popular mayor of Milan, and now the Urban Affairs Minister, Giorgio Ruffolo, the Minister for the Environment, is a well known economist, closely linked to the economic planning experiments during the earlier centre-left governments.

Among the PSI's main regional leaders are Paolo Pillitteri, Craxi's brother-in-law, and current mayor of Milan; Lelio Lagorio (a former Defence Minister and chairman of the party group in the Chamber) in Florence: Giusy la Ganga in Turin; Nicola Capria, Salvatore Lauricella and Salvo Ando in Sicily; and Giacomo Mancini, the last survivor among former party secretaries, in Calabria.

Mancini is one of the left critics of Craxi. The left represents around a quarter of the delegates in the party's national assembly. Among the leading figures on the left are Claudio Signorile,

Valdo Spini, Giulio Di Donato and Michele Achilli.

Other prominent personalities include Giorgio Benvenuto, the long standing secretary-general of the third Italian trade union confederation (the UIL); Carlo Ripa di Meana, former president of the *Venice Biennale* and now an EC commissioner; Enrico Manca, the president of RAI TV; and Francesco Forte, who is an influential voice on party policy matters.

Partito Socialista Democratico Italiano — PSDI
(Italian Social Democratic Party)

Headquarters	: Via S Maria in Via 12 00187 Rome (tel: 6797851)
Secretary Chairman of PSDI	: Antonio Cariglia
Chamber Group	: Filippo Caria
Youth Organization	: *Gioventu Socialista Democratica Italiano* (secretary: Paulo Russo)
Publication	: *L'Umanita*
Membership	: 180,000 (1987)
Founded	: 1947

History

A new Social Democratic party was founded in January 1947 as the result of a major schism within the Socialist Party over the extent to which the latter should be associated with the Communist Party in a popular workers' front.

After the war a large number of Socialists, notably on the moderate wing of the party, but also including Socialist autonomists who were further to the left, opposed the position of the pro-Communist party leadership. The dissidents called for the Socialist Party to be much more independent of the Communists and to put a greater emphasis on internal party democracy and freedom. They also believed that the working classes should ally with the progressive middle classes, and that Italy should be more independent of foreign influence, whether from America or from Russia.

The break finally came in early 1947. Forty-seven of the 115 Socialist deputies, and around 200,000 members (around a third of the party membership), including most of its youth movement, joined the new party. It took the name *Partito Socialista dei Lavoratori Italiani* (PSLI). The party's first secretary was Simonini, but its most prominent personality was Giuseppe Saragat.

The party also benefited from American funding. In May 1947 the PSLI took the fundamental decision to join with De Gasperi in his new government, on the grounds that this would prevent the government from slipping back to the right.

The PSLI supported Marshall Aid but still advocated an Italian and European "third force" outside American or Russian block politics. The party's executive narrowly voted against Italian membership of NATO in 1949 but the party congress subsequently decided to accept it as a "fait accompli". The party later abandoned its "third force" policy.

In its first national elections in 1948 the new party obtained 7.1 per cent of the vote and 33 seats in the Chamber, a result it has never since exceeded. It remained in successive De Gasperi governments until 1951. It also played a major role in the setting up of a new national trade union, the *Unione Italiana dei Lavoratori* (UIL).

In 1951 the PSLI merged with the *Partito Socialista Unitario* (itself a fusion between two groups of dissident Socialist Party members who wanted to abandon its popular front strategy in favour of socialist reunification).

In 1952, the merged party took the new name of *Partito Socialista Democratico Italiano* (PSDI).

Although the party had left government after the merger it supported the Christian Democrats' proposed new electoral law which was aimed at giving a reinforced majority to the coalition of centre parties (the so-called *legge truffa*). The PSDI was subsequently heavily penalized for this co-operation. A number of members of its left wing left the party and in the 1953 election its vote slumped sharply to 4.5 per cent and only 19 seats.

The PSDI continued to take part in several governments throughout the 1950s. After 1956 the Socialists began to distance themselves from the Communists and on Aug. 25, 1956 their leader, Nenni, met with Saragat at Pralognan in France to explore the possibilities for eventual Socialist reunification. This did not prove to be immediately possible, but the PSDI became firm advocates of an opening up of Italian government coalitions to the centre-left.

In 1962 the Social Democrats played an important role in the formation of the first centre-left government and they took part in all the full centre-left governments under Aldo Moro. Their membership rose steadily and in 1963 their vote rose sharply again to 6.1 per cent, with 33 seats in the Chamber. In December 1964 their leader Saragat was elected as Italian President.

Joint participation of the PSDI and the Socialists in the centre-left government gave a powerful spur to reunification of the two parties, and this was agreed upon at a constituent assembly on Oct. 30, 1966.

From the beginning the merged party suffered from severe internal difficulties. The merger came from the top, and the rank and file members were still suspicious of each other. There was duplication of posts throughout the party, with the former Social Democrats fearful of being swamped by the far more numerous Socialists. Most seriously there was no clear policy line for the merged party.

In the 1968 national elections the merged party fared disastrously, winning 14.5 per cent of the vote and 91 seats, 5.5 per cent less than the combined vote of the two parties in 1963. Disagreements as to whether the party should participate in government and on what terms, and over the closeness of its relations with the Communist Party gradually intensified. On July 4, 1969, former Social Democrats left the merged party and reformed their old party under the name *Partito Socialista Unitario*. A number of former Socialists, including Mauro Ferri, the secretary of the merged party, joined them as well. On Feb. 16, 1971, they reverted to their former name of PSDI.

In 1972, in the first national election since its reconstitution, the PSDI polled badly. Since then the PSDI has continued to participate in a large number of governments, but has failed to re-establish a clear identity for itself, especially since Craxi became Socialist secretary and took up many Social Democratic themes. The PSDI has also been severely harmed by a series of scandals involving its leadership. In 1975 its then secretary, Mario Tanassi, was indicted for having accepted bribes from Lockheed when Defence Minister. In the subsequent national elections in 1976 the party's vote fell away sharply to 3.4 per cent with only 15 seats.

In October 1978 Tanassi's successor as party secretary, Pier Luigi Romita, was replaced by Pietro Longo. A limited electoral revival led to the party gaining 3.8 per cent in the 1979 national elections (20 seats in the Chamber), 4.3 per cent in the European Parliament elections in 1979 (four seats) and 4.1 per cent in the 1983 national elections (23 seats). In 1984 Longo was implicated in the P2 Masonic scandal, and had to resign as Budget Minister. On Oct. 12, 1985 Franco Nicolazzi took over as party secretary.

The PSDI did well in the 1986 Sicilian regional elections, but lost many votes in the 1987 national elections, when it gained only 3 per cent of the vote (with 17 deputies and five senators), its lowest percentage since its foundation.

In early 1988 the party was placed in further difficulties by accusations of corruption against Nicolazzi in his former capacity as Minister of Public Works. In March 1988 Nicolazzi resigned as secretary, and was replaced by Antonio Cariglia.

In addition to its representation in Parliament, the PSDI has three members of the European Parliament. It has three ministers in the Italian government and participates in the large majority of Italian regional governments.

Support

The PSDI's electoral support comes largely from the lower middle classes and white collar workers among civil servants, pensioners, employees of banks and other institutions and among small tradesmen. Unlike the other Italian lay parties it is generally weaker in the large cities, apart from those in the south.

The main basis of party support is now in the south of Italy. Its vote in this area slipped less than in the rest of Italy in 1987, and in parts of Sicily even increased. In western Sicily the PSDI polled 5 per cent in 1987 (Palermo 5.5 per cent) and even in eastern Sicily, where its vote was lower, the party has strongholds such as Catania (6.3 per cent of the vote in the 1986 regional elections). The PSDI also polled well in Calabria (4.6 per cent in 1987), Basilicata (4.2 per cent), Puglia (Bari 5.9 per cent in 1987, 7.6 per cent in 1983) and in Campania (4.7 per cent in the Napoli–Caserta constituency).

With the exception of Latium (3.1 per cent in 1987) the party is very weak in central Italy, gaining between 1.2 per cent and 1.4 per cent, for example, in Tuscany and Umbria.

In the north of Italy PSDI support is very uneven. Its two best areas are Friuli Venezia–Giulia (4.7 per cent in 1987 and where it has been especially strong in the province of Belluno) and Piedmont (around 4 per cent). It polled between 1.5 per cent and 2 per cent in most of Liguria, Lombardy, and Emilia–Romagna, and in 1987 its vote was almost halved in some of these constituencies. In Trento it fell from 2.5 per cent in 1983 to only 1 per cent in 1987.

Organization

The PSDI has never really succeeded in developing a strong mass organization. It has more members than the Liberal and Republican parties, but only half those of the MSI.

The basic party unit is the "section", of which there are 4,300 around Italy. A section has a minimum of 10 members and a maximum of 500.

Above these are the federations, usually at provincial level, and the regional committees. At national level the national congress meets every two years. It elects 141 members of the party's central committee, as well as the party secretary and party president.

The committee meets three times a year, and chooses the president and secretary if the posts become vacant between congresses, as well as the party executive (*Direzione*). The executive consists of 21 members besides the president and secretary, and meets every week or ten days. The executive can intervene at any stage in the selection process, and gives the final approval to party lists. It also designates the party's candidates for ministerial posts, from a list chosen by secret ballot of the party's parliamentarians.

Besides the national executive there is also a small political secretariat, consisting of the president, secretary and one or two deputy secretaries.

The party's statute provides for strong protection of minority rights at all levels throughout the party (e.g. guaranteed representation for lists receiving more than 10 per cent of votes at the national congress).

One of the central principles since the party's foundation has been that party membership is individual and not collective. Nevertheless, the PSDI has tried to build strong links with the trade union movement. The *Unione Italiano del Lavoro* (UIL) has a member designated by its confederal secretary in the party executive. Moreover, in each workplace with more than five party members a party group (*Gruppo Aziendale Lavoratori Socialisti Democratici*) must be established. There are co–ordinating committees for these workplace groups at provincial and national levels.

A further feature of the PSDI is its strong organization outside Italy (in 1983 there were over 4,700 party members in Belgium, for example) and overseas sections are fully integrated into the party structure. There is also a party council on emigration matters.

In addition to the above, there are a number of other associated clubs and organizations, as well as national consultative committees on culture, science and economics, on civil rights, on regional affairs and on problems of administration.

In order to involve women more in the party a new national women's co-ordinating committee has recently been established. It consists of 70 women elected by a national women's conference to be held every two years, and elects a president and an executive committee of 10. The PSDI is also unusual among Italian political parties in providing for affirmative action for women in the party structure. No less than 10 per cent of the posts on the party's provincial committees must be occupied by women, as must 15 of the 141 elected posts on the party's central committee.

The PSDI's membership of the Socialist International dates from 1951 (when the Italian Socialist Party had been expelled from membership) and its three members of the European Parliament sit in the Socialist Group along with the members of the Italian Socialist Party. The PSDI is also a member of the Confederation of Socialist Parties of the EC.

Policies

The PSDI is currently in the difficult position of having had its Social Democratic identity taken up by larger parties, notably by the Socialist Party of Bettino Craxi, but even to a considerable degree by the Communists. It is neither a mass party nor a party of opinion in the Republican or Liberal sense. Its main remaining strength is its position as a pivotal party in both national and regional governments, and its implantation in many Italian institutions, but it has been undoubtedly harmed by the successive scandals involving the party leaders.

The PSDI portrays itself as a practical party without constraining dogmas, whose historic role has been to maintain centre-left governments and to separate Socialists from Communists. Although it has participated with Communists in regional governments (e.g. in Tuscany) its abiding theme remains one of anti-Communism and of hostility to Communist participation in national governments. In the longer term it puts forward what it calls a "democratic alternative", in which Communism will be overtaken by a coalition of Socialist and radical reforming parties, which will then permit a real alternative to continuing Christian Democratic hegemony. It thus seeks the closest co-operation with the Socialist Party, but it is still suspicious of merger, given the disparity in party size and tradition, and the memories of the failed merger in the 1960s.

On economic policy, the PSDI strongly emphasizes the role of the state in fixing the ground rules for economic activity. It advocates medium-term planning, notably to overcome ad hoc policies towards the development of southern Italy. It wants a higher priority placed on full employment, and new public investment in high technology areas and in infrastructure. On the other hand, it recognizes that the

state needs major reform, and that bureaucracy should be reduced. State holdings should be maintained in key areas, but privatization encouraged in other sectors.

The PSDI emphasizes its continuing defence of the welfare state and calls for greater social justice. It wants fiscal reform, to benefit salaried employees and the self-employed, and puts a strong emphasis on pensions policy. It supports investments in housing, schools and hospitals. The PSDI also calls for more rights for Italian emigrants, including fair social security treatment and the right to vote in local elections.

The PSDI has advocated a moratorium on the construction of new nuclear power stations, and the need for a common nuclear energy strategy at European level.

It does not advocate many major institutional reforms. It would like to strengthen the role of the Prime Minister and shorten the presidential term. It is prepared to see only minor changes to the electoral system. The PSDI also advocates greater financial autonomy for provinces and communes.

In foreign policy the PSDI is a strong advocate of the Atlantic Alliance and of the European Community, which should develop its political unity rather than being a mere free trade zone. The PSDI advocates a two-speed Europe where necessary. It has advocated the unilateral ratification of the European Parliament's draft Treaty of European Union by the Italian Parliament, and would like to see the 1989 European Parliament being given a constituent mandate.

Personalities

The party's current secretary is Antonio Cariglia, elected on the March 9th, 1988 after the resignation of Franco Nicolazzi. Cariglia, a former president of the PSDI group in the Senate, is close to Nicolazzi but has aroused strong opposition within the party. This came to a head after he chose two new PSDI ministers in the De Mita government without using formal party procedures, and without consulting some of the leading party barons.

His predecessor, Franco Nicolazzi, was party secretary from 1985 to 1988. A 63-year-old son of a Piedmontese carpenter, he was a strong advocate of the "democratic alternative" of Socialist alliance in order to break the present bipolar system of Italian politics. A former Minister of Public Works he was forced to stand down after adverse publicity during a parliamentary inquiry into his activities in that capacity.

The three PSDI ministers within the De Mita government are Enrico Ferri, a Milanese magistrate in charge of public works; Vincenza

Bona Parrino, the head of the PSDI senate group who is the Minister for Culture; and Antonio La Pergola who is in the PSDI "area" rather than a party activist and who has been responsible for European affairs in the last two governments.

Another significant figure is Pietro Longo, former party secretary (1978 to 1985), who is still only in his 40s. Longo originally supported Cariglia, but opposed his choice of ministers in April 1988.

Among the opponents of Cariglia within the party are another former leader and former Budget and Planning Minister, Pier Luigi Romita, and the two ministers dropped by Cariglia in April 1988, Emilio De Rose, the former Public Works Minister, and Carlo Vizzini, the former Culture Minister.

The current head of the Chamber Group is Filippo Caria.

The party's elder statesman, Giuseppe Saragat, the party founder and its secretary on several occasions, Deputy Prime Minister, and President of Italy from 1964 to 1971, died in 1988 aged 90.

Partito Répubblicano Italiano — PRI
(Italian Republican Party)

Headquarters	:	Piazza dei Caprettari 70, 00186 Rome (tel: 6544641/5)
Party secretary	:	Giorgio la Malfa (since September 1987)
President	:	Bruno Visentini
Chairman of Republican Group in the Chamber	:	Antonio del Pennino
Chairman of Republican Group in the Senate	:	Libero Gualtieri
Youth organization	:	*La Federazione Giovanile Repubblicano*
Women's organization	:	*Il Movimento Femminile Repubblicano*
Publication	:	*Voce Repubblicana*
Membership	:	120,000
Founded	:	April 1895

History
The father of the Italian Republican tradition was Giuseppe Mazzini, who gave it its high moral tone and austerity, its concern for social justice, and its emphasis on the solidarity of all social classes.

In the early years of unified Italy Republican sentiment remained strong in several regions of the country, but there was no organized Republican party. Republicans abstained from parliamentary activity, but concentrated on the creation of local workers associations. In 1871, 150 of these associations combined in a *patto di fratellanza* (brotherhood pact), which stimulated the development of co-operatives, mutual aid societies and popular schools. The Pact defended women's rights and called for wider suffrage and free lay education as well as for other social reforms.

The other major strand of Republicanism was that of Republican nationalism, seeking the unification of all Italian-speaking peoples, notably those living in Austrian territory in Trento and Trieste.

In the course of the 1870s the Republicans divided into those who came to accept the monarchy and to take part in parliamentary activity (the Radicals) and the intransigent Republicans who still followed an abstentionist policy, although individual Republicans, such as Napoleone Colajanni, began to enter Parliament in the 1880s.

In April 1895, an organized Republican Party was formally founded to contest elections but never became a real mass party. Even at its high point in 1900 it only obtained 33 deputies in the Italian Parliament on 6.2 per cent of the vote. By 1921 they were reduced to only six seats on 1.9 per cent of the vote.

The party was strongly anti-militarist and in 1911–12 opposed Italy's colonial war in Libya. On the other hand it supported Italy's entry into World War I on the side of England and France.

After World War I interventionist Republicans even co-operated at first with local Fascists against neutralist Socialists, but as Fascism became more powerful, the Republicans strongly opposed them.

When Fascism finally triumphed many Republican leaders went into exile, especially to France. Italian Republicans subsequently fought in the Spanish Civil War, with the Republican leader, Mario Angeloni, being killed. Other prominent Italian Republicans in Spain were Carlo Rosselli, and Randolfo Pacciardi, who later became a leader of the Resistance in which Republicans played an active role.

The Republican Party was severely divided in exile, with splits between left and right. On the re-establishment of democracy after 1945 the Republican Party was reconstituted, but many former Republicans joined the new *Partito d'Azione*. In the elections for the constituent assembly in 1946 the Republicans obtained 4.4 per cent, while the *Partito d'Azione* only obtained 1.3 per cent. The latter was subsequently dissolved, with some of its prominent personalities returning to the Republican Party.

The abolition of the monarchy led to a severe identity crisis for the Republicans. Its leaders now chose to ally themselves with the dominant Christian Democrats. They had already participated in the second De Gasperi government and after the Socialists and Communists left government in 1947 the Republicans justified their participation in the centrist alliance in terms of their being its "social conscience", pushing, for example, for the agrarian reform that was achieved in 1949 and for the establishment in 1950 of the *Cassa per il Mezzogiorno* on the lines of the Tennessee Valley Authority. Carlo Sforza, the Republican Foreign Minister, led Italy away from neutrality and into the Atlantic Alliance and the Council of Europe. Ugo la Malfa, as Minister for Foreign Commerce, opened up the Italian economy by removing many of its trade restrictions and quotas.

In the 1948 elections the party slipped from 25 to nine seats on 2.5 per cent of the national vote, and in 1953 fell further to five seats on 1.6 per cent of the vote, damaged even further by its support for the Christian Democrats' new electoral law (the *legge truffa*).

After 1953 the Republicans went into opposition until 1960. After the creation of the Radical Party the Republicans agreed with them on common lists for the 1958 elections but this was unsuccessful, and the Republican Party maintained a fragile toe-hold in Parliament with six seats on 1.4 per cent of the vote. The Republicans began to advocate an opening up to the centre-left with the Socialists, but this led to a split within the party, with a strong minority led by the Spanish Civil War veteran and Resistance leader, Randolfo Pacciardi, opposing the party's new line.

The Fanfani Government from 1960 to 1962 had the external support of the Republicans who then participated directly in the first explicitly centre-left government under Fanfani in 1962–63. The Republicans subsequently participated in the majority of centre-left governments, notably the first three governments of Aldo Moro. Oronzo Reale, who had been the Republicans' secretary from 1950 to 1963, was the Republican Minister in most of these governments. In 1965, Ugo la Malfa became Republican secretary, a post he was to retain until 1975. He was widely respected across the political spectrum and by the Italian public at large, who appreciated his critical comments on the state of Italian society. He was a strong advo-

cate of the centre-left government but he became increasingly disillusioned with its performance. The Republicans continued to participate, however, in several of the governments of the 1970s. In the fourth Moro government in 1974–76 La Malfa became Deputy Prime Minister. In 1975 he became party president and was replaced as secretary-general by Oddo Biasini.

The Republicans, made a slow electoral recovery in the 1960s and 70s. Until 1976 they had no international links but in that year they joined the European Liberal and Democratic Group.

The Republicans supported Christian Democratic co-operation with the Communists in the late 1970s, but became disillusioned with this as well.

In 1979 Ugo la Malfa became the first non-Christian Democrat to be asked to form a government since the war, although he did not succeed, and died shortly afterwards. Giovanni Spadolini became party secretary in 1979. In the European Parliament elections of that year the Republicans gained 2.6 per cent of the vote and two seats.

In June 1981 Giovanni Spadolini became the first non-Christian Democrat to be Italian Prime Minister since the war, heading a five-party coalition. His first government lasted until August 1982, when he formed a new four-party government which lasted until December. In the 1983 national elections this positive experience of government (the "Spadolini effect") led to the Republicans' best postwar electoral performance, with 29 seats in the Chamber, 10 senators and 5.1 per cent of the national vote.

The Republicans have participated in all succeeding coalition governments. In the 1984 European election they took part in a joint list with the Liberal Party, but the result was a disappointing 6.2 per cent and five seats for the combined parties. In the 1987 national elections the Republicans slipped back considerably to 21 seats in the Chamber, eight in the Senate and 3.7 per cent of the national vote.

In 1987 Giovanni Spadolini became president of the Senate and had to stand down as party secretary. In September 1987 he was replaced by Giorgio la Malfa, the son of Ugo.

Support

The Republican Party has never been a mass party. In much of Italy it has tended to be a party of "the enlightened bourgeoise" and a party of "the few but good". Only in a few areas of the country with long Republican traditions has the party enjoyed wider support across the social spectrum. In Romagna, in particular, the party has enjoyed strong support from small proprietors and small tradesmen and there is still a strong network of Republican co-operatives and clubs.

The policies of Ugo la Malfa, and the creation of the Spadolini governments in 1981–82 won the Republicans an influx of new support among technocrats and professionals, especially in the modern industrial areas. Many of these subsequently deserted the party in the 1987 elections (largely in favour of Craxi's Socialists), but the party still has considerable support among these groups. One of Italy's prominent industrialists, Bruno Visentini, is a party leader, and Gianni Agnelli of Fiat and Carlo de Benedetti of Olivetti have been party supporters. Among the other professional groups giving strong support to the party are journalists and secondary school teachers.

The Republicans with their lay image, have also been a party with strong support from Italy's religious minorities, such as the Protestants from Piedmont and the Jewish community.

Party membership almost doubled between 1964 and 1983, and is now at around 120,000. The rise in membership has been particularly marked in southern Italy, notably in Campania, Puglia and Sicily.

In the first postwar elections the Republican Party was strongest in central Italy, especially in the Marche (16.4 per cent in the 1946 constituent elections), Lazio (14.8 per cent in 1946), Umbria, as well as the Abruzzi, Emilia–Romagna and Tuscany. In much of this region the Republicans declined rapidly, although they have maintained above average strength in the Marche (especially Macerata), parts of Tuscany (e.g. around Massa–Carrara) and parts of Latium (e.g. in the Alban hills).

Their consistently strongest area has remained Romagna, and especially the triangle between Cesena, Forli and Ravenna where they still retain up to 30 per cent of the vote in some villages (e.g. San Pietro in Vincoli 31 per cent in 1987). The percentage of total party members from this region, however, has declined considerably (by 1983 only 13.8 per cent of Republican Party members were from Emilia–Romagna, compared to 33.5 per cent in 1964).

In the rest of northern Italy the Republicans were traditionally weak (e.g. Piedmont 0.4 per cent in 1948, Lombardy 0.9 per cent, Veneto 0.8 per cent) except in Liguria. It was in industrial north-western Italy, however, that the Republicans gained most new support in the 1970s and 80s. In the 1983 elections the Republicans polled 10.2 per cent in Turin and 12.3 per cent in Milan (20.8 per cent in the first Milan

electoral district). In 1987, the party fell away badly in most of north-western Italy, although it still had considerable support in many places (Turin 7.7 per cent, Milan 7.6 per cent). Among the pockets of particular Republican strength in this area are the Protestant mountain valleys behind Pinerolo and in Cuneo and Ivrea (all in Piedmont).

The Republicans are weaker in rural Lombardy, and in much of north-eastern Italy.

Sicily is a region with a long Republican tradition (among the progressive upper-middle classes in particular). The eastern Sicily constituency was one of only four in the country to give the Republicans over 5 per cent of the vote in 1987 (5.3 per cent). Catania, Syracuse and Trapani are among the places where the Republicans have polled particularly well. The Sicilian percentage of total Republican membership has risen from under 10 per cent in 1964 to 23.5 per cent in 1983.

Elsewhere in the south the Republicans have polled best in Puglia (over 4 per cent in 1987), the only region in Italy where there was a considerable increase in the Republican vote in 1987. On the other hand, the weakest region for the Republicans is Basilicata, where they polled 1.3 per cent in both the 1983 and 1987 elections.

Organization

The Republican Party has traditionally been a loosely organized party with the national leadership having considerable freedom of manoeuvre. The party has also been very unevenly spread, with regions where the party has hardly existed contrasting with regions with considerable organizational strength, such as Romagna with its network of Republican club-houses and associations.

The basic party units are the sections, of which there are currently 2,200. Each section must have a minimum of 10 members. New sections may be established when there are over 30 members.

Republican organizations, such as co-operatives or cultural groups, can be affiliated to the party on a collective basis — one of the organizational reforms of the 1960s aimed at providing a more "open" party.

On the next tier of the party organization are the Republican associations, which can be at provincial, sub-provincial or intercommunal level, deliberately left flexible in order to reflect differing local circumstances.

Above these are the regional federations. At national level the national congress meets every three years. An unusual feature of the

Republican Party is that the delegates to the congress are chosen directly by the sections, rather than by the intermediate provincial and regional organizations.

The number of delegates from each section is chosen on the basis of their total membership and also of votes won in the last two chamber elections and last regional election. This second criterion is aimed at minimizing the dominance of local party barons. There are also provisions to ensure the representation of minority lists. At the last national congress there were 2,400 delegates.

The congress elects 165 members of the national council, which meets every four to five months. One of its main tasks is to elect the national executive, which meets about twice a month and contains 33–45 members, as well as the party secretary (the party leader) and the party president.

The party secretary is helped by a secretarial committee, which provides the day-to-day leadership of the party.

Candidates for national office are put forward by electoral committees, consisting of representatives of the regional federations, the local associations and the communal unions, and are then ratified by the national executive.

There is the possibility of holding internal party referenda, among the federations, sections or the membership at large.

The party's youth movement is called the *Federazione Giovanile Repubblicana* and enjoys political and organizational autonomy. The women's movement is called the *Movimento Femminile Repubblicana*. It is organized in "circles" of at least 20 members. There are currently around 200 such circles and 5,000 members.

There are other organizations closely associated with the party, such as cultural and sporting groups. They are particularly active in Romagna. There are still special provisions for three Republican co-operators to participate in the national council.

The party newspaper is called *La Voce Repubblicana*. It was first founded in 1921, and relaunched in 1944 and 1982. The local sections are obliged to take out a subscription. There are other Republican periodicals, such as *Pensiero Mazziniano*, *I Ciompi* and *La Critica Politica*. Among the regional Republican journas dating from the 19th century are *Il Lucifero* (of the Marche association) and *Il Pensiero Romagnola*.

Party dues were fixed at 20,000 Lire for 1988, of which 10,000 Lire go to the section, 4,000 to the centre and 6,000 to the provincial and regional organizations. At least half the public finance received by the party goes to the periphery.

For a long time the Republicans had no international links and their representative in the nominated European Parliament sat as an independent in the Socialist Group. In 1976, however, they joined the European Federation of Liberal and Democratic Parties (having called for the additional label "Democratic"). They now sit along with the members of the Italian Liberal Party in the European Parliament.

Policies

The creation of the Italian Republic in 1946 left the Republican Party without its most obvious policy theme. Since then it has tried to fill the gap by portraying itself as the party of economic austerity and of reform of the Italian State, so as to permit the full political and economic incorporation of Italy among the most advanced western industrialized states. The Republican Party presents itself as a party of moral and intellectual rigour, opposed to clientelism and narrow party patronage, not linked to any class interests, preferring facts to ideologies, putting a high premium on managerial competence, and prepared to tell unpopular truths to the Italian people.

If this is the national image that the party has sought to portray (one which owes a great deal to Ugo La Malfa) there are still regional variations — such as the anti-clerical populism which has taken so long to decline in the Romagna and in a few other traditional Republican areas, and the more clientelist structure of the Sicilian Republicans, whose leader Aristide Gunnella has been accused of Mafia links in one of the Republican Party's extremely rare scandals.

A further issue which the Republican Party must now confront is whether it wishes to enter into further electoral alliance with the Liberals, as it did in the last European elections in 1984. Policy differences between the two parties are now much less than they were (in particular the Republicans have begun to accept the role of the state and of economic planning, are less hostile to the Socialists and Communists, and more prepared to define themselves as a left of centre party). Historical and cultural differences still play a role, with the Republicans still looking back on Mazzini as their founder and on his tradition of anti-establishment protest, but this has been greatly attenuated since the war, not least because the Republicans have taken part in more government coalitions than any party apart from the Christian Democrats.

On economic policy questions the Republicans put themselves forward as the party which faces up to hard economic realities. Ugo La Malfa was the great Italian advocate of long-term planning and of incomes policy. The party now puts its emphasis on attacking the public deficit which is weakening the Italian state. It believes that the state must continue to play an important role in the economy but supports privatization. The party also attacks sectoral and corporate interests. The former Republican Finance Minister, Bruno Visentini, passed a law to enforce more efficient tax collection (costing the Republicans dear among some of their small business supporters, especially in the Romagna).

The party also puts a strong emphasis on social policy and on reducing regional and social inequalities. It advocates the overhaul of public administration, in order to provide better public services.

The Republican Party claims that "the moral question" is one of Italy's main problems and that, along with the elimination of patronage and corruption, civic responsibility needs to be developed to a much greater extent.

Although the Republicans are still very much a lay party, campaigning, for example, in favour of the divorce and abortion laws, their former anti-clericalism is much reduced. The days are gone when some Republicans wore black on religious festival days and refused to give saints' names to their children. In 1984 the Republicans even accepted the new Concordat with the Catholic Church, although some members would have liked the party to leave the government in protest, and the party's stand damaged it among its Jewish and Protestant supporters.

On institutional matters the Republicans do not seek major changes to the existing Italian Constitution, but wish to have it properly applied. In particular, they have long been supporters of a strong regional tier of government in Italy, and wish to see the powers of the regions reinforced. They are opposed to any major change in the Italian electoral system, especially to any move towards majority rather than proportional voting.

They are opposed to what they see as the demagogic use of referenda. Not only did they advocate a "no" vote in the recent referenda on nuclear energy, but also in that on reform of the magistrature, on the grounds that the referendum question was poorly worded and obscure.

On foreign policy matters the Republicans are perhaps Italy's leading exponents of the country looking beyond the Alps rather than to the Mediterranean and of it having an Atlanticist and European vocation.

They advocate European union, but point out the structural problems which Italy will have to overcome if there is to be a true internal market by 1992. They wish to see the European pillar within NATO strengthened, and an improved military trade balance between Europe and the United States.

The Republicans are probably the most pro-Israel of any Italian political party.

Personalities

The party's current secretary is Giorgio La Malfa, son of the party's leading postwar politician, Ugo La Malfa. Giorgio La Malfa is an economist and a technocrat rather than a populist.

The party's president is Bruno Visentini, one of Italy's leading industrialists and a former Minister of Finance.

The party's most well-known personality is probably still Giovanni Spadolini, a professor of history who was secretary of the party from 1979 to 1987, and Italian Prime Minister from 1981 to 1982. He was Minister of Defence for a considerable period, and is currently president of the Italian Senate.

Of the party's three ministers in the De Mita government Adolfo Battaglia, the Industry Minister, was Giorgio La Malfa's main rival to become party leader in 1987, and showed that he had considerable support within the party before he stood down to prevent a potentially damaging formal vote.

The current PTT Minister is Oscar Mammi, the party's leader in Rome. The Minister for Regional Affairs and Institutional Reform is Antonio Maccanico, a former president of Italy's leading merchant bank, Mediabanca, who is also a former secretary-general of the Chamber of Deputies and of the President's office.

The Republican leader in the Chamber of Deputies is Antonio del Pennino, a lawyer who is the party leader in Milan. The chairman of the Republican senators is Libero Gualtieri from Romagna.

The party's boss in its stronghold of Romagna is Stello De Carolis. His predecessor in Romagna, Oddo Biasini, is now over 80 years old but is still a representative figure from the party's more populist past.

Another historical party figure is Randolfo Pacciardi, the former Spanish Civil War and Resistance leader and Republican Party secretary, who is now over 87 years old, and still active within the party.

Of the party's parliamentarians one of the more well-known is Susanna Agnelli, a sister of Gianni Agnelli and the mayor of the rich community of Argentario.

Partito Liberale Italiano — PLI
(Italian Liberal Party)

Headquarters	:	Via Frattina 89, 00187 Rome (tel: 6796951)
Secretary-General	:	Renato Altissimo
President of Liberal Group in Chamber	:	Paolo Battistuzzi
President of Liberal Group in Senate (and party President of Honour)	:	Giovanni Malagodi
Youth organization	:	*Gioventu Liberale Italiana* (national secretary: Paolo Sottili)
Publication	:	*L'Opinione*
Membership	:	50,000 (1986)

History

Under the system of restricted franchise, and in the absence of a major Catholic party, Liberalism remained the dominant political force within Italy from the unification of Italy under the Piedmontese Liberal, Camillo Cavour, until after World War I. There was no formally organized Liberal party as such, but Liberals were loosely divided into "right" and "left". The differences between them were not very clear–cut, but the "right" put more emphasis on fiscal rectitude, and the "left" on extending the franchise. The liberal "right" ran the country from 1860 until 1876, when the "left" took charge under Agostino Depretis and his successors. From 1901 onwards a more reforming brand of Liberalism came to power, first under Giuseppe Zanardelli, who restored full constitutional government after a brief conservative authoritarian interlude, and who even sought to introduce legislation on divorce, and then more lastingly under Giovanni Giolitti, who carried out extensive social reform and sought to respond to the rising Socialist challenge, even trying to incorporate them in government.

During World War I, Italy remained under the more conservative Liberal leadership of Salandra and Orlando. In the years immediately after the war Liberalism gradually lost its dominating position, under the combined pressures of an extended franchise and proportional representation, a strengthened Socialist party and a powerful new Catholic party. It was finally broken by the rise of Fascism, which divided Italian Liberalism between those who were clearly anti-fascist, like Amendola and Gobetti, and those who accepted it. In 1922 Luigi Facta was Italy's last Liberal Prime Minister.

Left Liberals participated in the Italian Resistance, and in the six–party transitional Government of Parri in 1945. Nevertheless Italian Liberalism emerged from World War II divided and electorally weak, although there were still a number of prominent Liberal personalities, such as Benedetto Croce, who was party president until 1947, Ivanoe Bonomi, Enrico De Nicola, the first Italian President, and Luigi Einaudi, who led Italian economic reconstruction after the war, and became Italy's second President.

In the 1946 constituent elections the main Liberal group took part in an electoral coalition called the *Unione Democrazia Nazionale*, which won 6.8 per cent of the vote and 41 members of parliament. After De Gasperi expelled the Socialists and Communists from his government in May 1947 the Liberals rejoined his coalition. In the 1948 national elections the Liberals took part in another electoral pact, the *Blocco Nazionale* which only obtained 3.5 per cent of the vote and 19 seats in the Chamber.

While thus further weakened the Liberals continued to take part in De Gasperi's fifth government, in which they had three ministers. In 1950 they left government, and abstained in the votes on De Gaspari's last three governments.

In 1951 the Liberals were finally reunited and Villabruna subsequently became the party secretary.

In the 1953 elections the Liberals slipped even further to 3 per cent of the national vote and only 13 seats. They gave external support to the Pella government in 1953 and in '54, and they participated directly in the Scelba government of 1954 to '55 and in the first Segni government of 1955 to '57, on both occasions with three ministers.

In 1954 Giovanni Malagodi became party secretary, a post which he was to hold until the 1970s. In 1955 a group of left-wing Liberals opposed to the party's conservative course broke away and formed the Radical Party (see separate entry).

From 1957 to 1962 the Liberals opposed some governments (including the conservative Tambroni government in 1960) but gave external support to others (Segni's second government in 1959–60, and Fanfani's third in 1969–62). With the opening of the Christian Democrats to the left, however, the Liberal Party went into outright opposition from 1962 to 1972. In 1963 its position as the "respectable" conservative opposition party led it to its greatest postwar electoral success of 7 per cent of the national vote, and 39 seats in the Chamber. Throughout the 1960s, however, its position gradually declined as the centre-left government became an accepted formula.

In 1972 the Liberals finally re-entered the government orbit by giving external support to the first Andreotti government, and they participated in his second government in 1972–1973 with four ministers, including Malagodi, who stood aside as party secretary in favour of Vignardi.

The Liberals' position continued to decline, and in 1976 they only won 1.3 per cent of the national vote and five seats in the Chamber.

Valerio Zanone then took over as the new party secretary, and gave the party a less uncompromisingly conservative image during his period as leader from 1976 to 1985. From 1973 to 1981 the Liberals were only once in government (the first Cossiga government from 1979 to 1980) but from 1981 onwards they have been members of every subsequent coalition, with either one or two ministers. This has thus been their longest period in government since the war.

Their electoral position has remained extremely fragile. From the low point of 1976 they made a gradual recovery until 1983, when they won 2.9 per cent of the vote and 16 seats, but they were again down to 2.1 per cent of the vote in 1987 with only 11 seats in the Chamber and three Senators. They stood on their own in the 1979 European elections, winning 3.6 per cent of the vote and three seats, but in the 1984 European elections they participated in a joint list with their old Republican rivals, which won 6.2 per cent of the vote and five seats.

In 1985 Zanone resigned as party secretary. His preferred successor was Renato Altissimo but he was defeated by his fellow minister Alfredo Biondi. Biondi remained as party secretary for only one year before being narrowly defeated by Altissimo, who won 52.7 per cent of the votes at the party congress in 1986.

In 1986 the Liberal Party was participating in seven regional governments.

Support

Since 1945 the Liberal Party has been a minor electoral force, with the limited exception of the 1963 and 1968 elections, when it won additional support from conservatives opposed to the Christian Democrats opening up to the left. Until 1972 it had more support than the Republican Party but in subsequent elections it has been the smaller of the two. It is a classic "party of opinion" rather than a mass party, winning support from intellectuals and top businessmen, as well as from large landlords and from the old aristocracy and "haute bourgeoisie". The party used to have pockets of strong support based on the electoral fiefs of some of its former leaders (such as that of Gaetano Martino in Messina, De Caro in Benevento and Grassi in Lecce), but these are now of less significance.

The party's strongest region is Piedmonte, especially the province of Cuneo. In the constituency of Cuneo–Alessandria–Asti the Liberals won 5.9 per cent in the 1987 elections (8.4 per cent in 1983) and in some of the smaller towns in Cuneo province wins much higher support (e.g. 54.7 per cent in the 1983 senate elections in Magliano Alpi and 34 per cent in Fraboso Soprana). In the city of Turin the Liberals won 3.9 per cent in 1987 (6.8 per cent in 1983).

In the rest of the north the Liberals have their highest votes in Liguria (3 per cent in 1987) and Lombardy (Milan 3.6 per cent in 1987, 6.2 per cent in 1983). In the 1987 election they also did well in Trieste with 5.6 per cent. They are weaker in the Veneto Emilia–Romagna and especially in Trento–Bolzano (only 1.1 per cent in 1987).

The Liberals are very weak in most of central Italy with around 1 per cent of the vote in 1987 in Tuscany, the Marche, Umbria and the Abruzzi. They are slightly stronger in Latium, especially along the Tirrenian coast and in Rome, where they obtained 2.3 per cent in 1987 (with 5.6 per cent in Rome's elegant second electoral district).

In the south the Liberals are strongest in Sicily, winning 3.4 per cent in the eastern Sicily constituency in 1987, and 2.5 per cent in western Sicily. Messina still has a higher than average Liberal vote (5.8 per cent in the 1986 regional elections, 7.2 per cent in the 1983 national elections). Catania voted 4.4 per cent for the Liberals in the regional elections in 1986 and Palermo 3.6 per cent (3.3 per cent in the 1987 national elections).

Elsewhere in the south the Liberals have over 2 per cent support in Puglia (Bari 2.9 per cent in 1987) and Campania, but are much weaker in Basilicata, Calabria and Sardinia, where they were at or below 1 per cent in 1987.

Organization

The party's basic territorial unit is the section which can be based on a commune (*sezione comunale*), part of a commune (*sezione circonscrizionale*) or several communes (*sezione comprensoriale*).

Minimum membership for a section is generally 10. All the sections within one commune can also get together to form a "communal union". At provincial level the sections are represented by delegates in a provincial assembly, which elects the provincial executive of between seven and 15 members. Above this there is a regional executive, with a regional executive committee. There is also a national regional consultative unit (*Consulta Nazionale delle Regioni*), which meets at least once a year to discuss regional problems.

At national level the national congress meets every two years. It consists of delegates elected in the provincial assemblies, on the basis of two delegates per province and with extra delegates depending on the votes won by the party in that province at the preceding national elections. Among the tasks of the congress is to elect 165 members of the national council, the parliament of the party, which meets every six months, and elects the party president and secretary-general, as well as 21 members of the central executive.

The secretary-general is the party leader, and is assisted by so-called "national delegates" and an executive committee as well as by a deputy secretary. The party president chairs the national council as well as the central executive. The party has a headquarters staff of 30.

Party candidates for national office are approved by the central executive (or a special electoral committee), and are based on lists originally proposed by provincial assemblies and approved by regional executives; 10 per cent of the posts are reserved for central allocation.

Besides the party's youth organization, *Gioventu Liberale Italiano*, the party has a number of other associated organizations, including a sporting centre, CSEN. There is also the *Fondazione Einaudi*, which carries out research into various economic themes.

Party membership dues are among the highest of any Italian party at 50,000 lire, with no exceptions made: 55 per cent of dues are allocated to the section; 15 per cent to the province; 15 per cent to the region; and 15 per cent to national headquarters.

The Liberal Party is an extremely active member of the Liberal International, of which Malagodi has been president on two occasions (1958 to 1960 and 1982 to the present) and of the Federation of European Liberal Parties. The Oxford Manifesto and Declaration, as well as the Appeal of Rome (see Liberal International entry) are annexed to the party's constitution. Within the European Parliament the Liberals have two members elected on a common list with the Republicans, and who sit in the Liberal Group.

Policies

The Liberal Party has been generally perceived as the most conservative of the lay parties in the Italian political spectrum, the party of big business interests, of elitism, of greater freedom from state control, and of opposition to the centre-left governments of the 1960s. It has been more often in opposition than the Socialists, Social Democrats and Republicans. In practice, however, the extent of its conservatism is limited. It is classically liberal on moral and civil liberties issues, and even on economic matters its policies are pragmatic ones. It is a party of opinion rather than of protest, and still retains considerable influence, in spite of its small size. Moreover, since 1981 it has been involved in all government coalitions.

A matter of particular importance for the Liberals is their future relationship with the Republicans. They have always sat together within the European Parliament's Liberal Group, and fought on a common list for the European elections in 1984. The result was disappointing, but this was probably due to a decline in the underlying strength of both parties rather than to the voters' disapproval of the alliance.

Policy differences between Liberals and Republicans do exist (for example, the Liberals have been less keen on economic planning and on state intervention and have been more anti-communist than the Republicans) but are much less important than differences of political culture between the two parties.

Nevertheless electoral realities may again force them to present a joint list for the next European elections in 1989, and perhaps in future Italian national elections as well.

The Liberal Party puts a strong emphasis on economic policy questions. It seeks a liberalization of the Italian economy in as many ways as possible. It attacks the excessive Italian public deficit, excessive taxation of Italian citizens without compensation, and the excessive bureaucracy and clientelism of the Italian state. It believes that the public deficit is better tackled by bringing public expenditure under control than by further rises in taxation. It supports privatization and deregulation, less price control and a liberalized and more flexible labour market. On industrial policy, it seeks selective state intervention in industry, concentrating on strategic sectors and based on fiscal rather than financial incentives. It supports the introduction of competition policy, and does not believe that the problems of southern Italy can be solved by having money thrown at it. On grounds of economic realism it also supports the continuance of Italy's programme of civil nuclear energy.

While the Liberal Party advocates "less state" in certain areas it calls for a more efficient state in others, notably in public administration, where it seeks simplifications of laws and a streamlining of bureaucracy. It advocates judicial reform, and faster and fairer civil procedures. Since 1968 it has also consistently called for the introduction of an Italian ombudsman. It advocates liberalization of the health sector, with a wider choice of public or private health care. It also seeks radical reform of Italy's rigid rent control law (*equo canone*).

It puts a strong emphasis on liberal policies on moral questions, campaigning in favour of the divorce and abortion laws, and calling for a strict separation of Church and state. It is opposed to compulsory religious instruction in schools, and criticizes the revised Concordat of 1984 between the Italian State and the Catholic Church.

The Liberal Party is opposed to major changes in the present constitutional structure, which it played such a considerable role in creating. It defends the present system of proportional representation, though it sees a case for introducing primary elections, and restricting preferential voting. It would also like to see a greater differentiation between the functions of the Chamber of Deputies and the Senate, with the former concentrating more on legislation (with less passed in parliamentary committees), and with the latter concentrating more on parliamentary control. The prime minister's role should also be strengthened.

On international policy the party is strongly Atlanticist and European. NATO should be reinforced (the Liberals supported the introduction of Euromissiles at Comiso in Sicily) but Europe should also play a greater role in its own defence.

On European integration the Liberals supported the European Parliament's draft Treaty on European Union and believe that the 1989 Parliament should be given constituent powers. They also put a strong emphasis on economic and monetary union and on removing remaining barriers to an internal market.

Personalities

The party's current secretary is Renato Altissimo, who defeated Alfredo Biondi in a 1986 leadership contest, after losing to him in 1985. Altissimo has a classic liberal background from the Piedmontese social elite, and has been Italian Industry Minister on numerous occasions.

Biondi, who was Liberal leader for only one year, is a former Environmental Minister. He is a penal lawyer from Genova.

The two most well-known Italian Liberals, however, are the former party leaders, Giovanni Malagodi and Valerio Zanone.

Malagodi, who is now over 80, was the dominant figure within the party for over 20 years, and is still the party's president of honour, and leader in the Senate. He is currently in his second term as president of the Liberal International. He has always been known as an uncompromising defender of Liberal economic principles and as a strong anti-communist.

Valerio Zanone led the party from 1976 to 1985. He is now the party's only minister, in his capacity as Minister of Defence. He has been a skilful party strategist and a successful minister.

The party's leader in the Chamber is Paolo Battistuzzi.

Partito Radicale — Partito Federalista Europeo
(Radical Party — European Federalist Party)

Headquarters	:	Via di Torre Argentina 18, 00186 Roma (tel: 654 7771) (Contact address in Belgium, Rue du Prince Royal 25, 1050 Bruxelles, tel: 230412)
First secretary	:	Sergio Stanzani
Treasurer	:	Paolo Vigevano
President	:	Bruno Zevi
Newspapers	:	*Notizie Radicali, Radio Radicale*
Members	:	10,100 (March 1987)
Founded	:	1955 (Refounded 1962)

History

The Radical Party (a party of the same name was active in the Italian Parliament in the late 19th century, but died out by World War I), was founded in December, 1955, primarily by left-wing Liberals and other reformists who advocated the creation of a powerful new lay bloc of the centre-left as a clear alternative to both clerical conservatism and totalitarian communism.

The Radical Party fought the 1958 national elections on a joint list with the Republican Party. This only obtained 1.4 per cent of the vote (less than the Republicans alone in 1958), and not a single Radical candidate was elected.

The party was subsequently divided over how close it should get to the Socialist Party (on whose lists a number of Radicals were elected in the 1960 local elections), and between its moderate reformist leadership, and its radical left minority.

In 1962 the Radical Party effectively collapsed, with most of its recognized leaders departing. By the end of 1962 the radical left were in control of what little was left of the party. They consisted of young activists, mainly based in Rome, and with Marco Pannella as their most prominent leader.

They decided not to fight elections in their own right, to concentrate on specific reform issues rather than putting forward sweeping ideological programmes, and to use new techniques of direct, non-violent action.

The party's emphasis was on civil rights and was anti-clerical, pacifist and anti-military, being clearly influenced by the example of CND in the United Kingdom. A Radical press agency was established to highlight specific Radical causes. Among the first such issues were attacks on clientelism in the state-run oil company, ENI, and in the system of social security and assistance.

The campaign which brought the Radical Party much more fully into the public eye was that over divorce, in which new direct action techniques were used. After Parliament finally adopted a divorce law in 1969 the Christian Democrats finally put forward a law to provide for abrogative, popular referenda (a provision contained in the postwar Italian constitution but never implemented), so they could overturn the divorce law by the supposedly conservative and traditional Italian electorate. The Radicals campaigned fiercely for its maintenance. The referendum victory in May 1974 was a considerable boost for their prestige. Use of national referenda subsequently became the party's main technique for the promotion of specific reforms.

Parallel to this the Radical Party helped to sponsor a number of other initiatives further developing the new techniques; non-party campaigns open to all interested parties using non-violent direct action, such as popular marches and demonstrations, sits-in, letter and telephone campaigns, hunger strikes, civil disobedience and self-denunciation to the authorities.

The party campaigned against the Italian state's Concordat with the Church and in favour of conscientious objection. It also launched a campaign on drugs reform and another in favour of an abortion law.

Marco Pannella became an increasingly national figure through such action as a seven-day hunger strike in 1974 to gain access to radio and television for groups not represented in the Parliament. When he did finally appear on television he sat silently bound and gagged throughout the transmission.

In 1976 the party decided that it would put up its own candidates in the national elections of the year: 50 per cent of the candidates were women, and women were at the head of each party list. The Radicals won 1.1 per cent of the national vote, and obtained four seats in the Chamber of Deputies.

In 1977 Adelaide Aglietta became the first woman to be the secretary of an Italian political party. In 1978 she was succeeded by a French conscientious objector, Jean Fabre.

In the 1979 national elections the Radicals polled 3.4 per cent, and won 18 seats in the Chamber and two in the Senate. In the European Parliament elections in 1979 they obtained three seats on 3.7 per cent of the vote. They then led a successful filibuster to prevent the raising of the threshold for political groups to be formed within the European Parliament which would have made it much more difficult for minority parties to create such a group.

In the 1983 national elections the Radicals called upon the electorate not to vote at all. Only if they did decide to vote should they vote Radical. Among their candidates was Toni Negri, an academic who had been in prison awaiting trial for four years on an accusation of master-minding left-wing terrorism, and whose candidacy was envisaged as highlighting the scandal of preventive detention. Negri himself was not a Radical, and his views were regarded as repellent by most Radicals.

The Radicals won 2.2 per cent of the vote, and 11 members in the Chamber, including Toni Negri. Negri was then released on the grounds of his new parliamentary immunity, and as his immunity was to be lifted by the Parliament he fled into exile in France.

In 1984 the party again won three seats in the European Parliament. One of their successful candidates was another who had been imprisoned before trial, the popular television presenter, Enzo Tortora, who had been accused of underworld connections. Unlike Negri, Tortora agreed to have his immunity lifted, and was subsequently acquitted. He later became the president of the Radical Party.

In 1986 the Radicals put forward a series of new referenda, including ones on reforming the Italian system of justice and on stopping the Italian civil nuclear programme, which won wider political support. In November 1986, the party congress decided that if the Radicals did not have 10,000 members by the end of the year (they had only 3,000 in October 1986) and if 9,000 of these had not renewed by the end of January 1987 the party would be wound up. Both challenges were successfully met, with many politicians from other parties taking double membership in the Radical Party.

In the national elections in June 1987 they slightly increased their vote polling 2.6 per cent, and gaining 13 seats in the Chamber and three in the Senate. Their most controversial winner was the Hungarian-born porno star Ilona Staller ("Cicciolina").

In January 1988 the Radical congress decided that the party would turn itself into a trans-national political party, and would no longer fight any national elections. The party also set itself the objective of winning 3,000 non-Italian members. An attempt by Pannella to make the party's survival conditional on winning 15,000 members was rejected by the congress, as well as his attempt to make a portrait of Gandhi the new party symbol.

Support

The Radical Party has been more concerned about the level of support for its causes than it has about the number of Radical members or its level of support in national elections (it does not fight local elections). When it has launched recruitment drives it has also enlisted members of other parties (mainly Socialists). Its true level of support is thus hard to gauge.

The party is mainly based in the cities. Rome and later Milan have been its main centres of activity, but the Radicals have considerable support in the other large cities, less in the smaller cities and least of all in the countryside. The party's membership is still youthful, but apparently much less so than in the past. (In 1976 60 per cent of its activists were under 30, compared to around 21 per cent of its members by 1987.) Radical Party members are also very well-educated, with an exceptionally high level of graduates. The upper middle classes and professional groups are strongly represented, and there are few members from working or lower middle-class backgrounds.

In 1987 no less than 15 per cent of its membership consisted of lawyers, doctors and other liberal professions; 8.5 per cent were teachers and 8 per cent were students. Over 18 per cent were office workers, with many working in banks, insurance and other service companies.

In regional terms Radical Party membership has been heavily biased towards northern and central Italy. This is also generally true in electoral terms.

In northern Italy the Radicals are particularly strong in Turin (5.8 per cent in 1987) and Trieste (5.7 per cent in 1987) and have also polled well in Venice (4.3 per cent in 1987) and Milan (4.1 per cent). They are stronger in north-western Italy and in the Catholic area of north-eastern Italy than they are in the "red belt" of Emilia–Romagna, Tuscany and Umbria (e.g. 1.4 per cent in 1987 in the western Emilia constituency, 1.5 per cent in south-eastern Tuscany and Umbria). Their only stronghold in central Italy is Latium and, in particular, Rome (4.4 per cent in 1987, a slight decline, however, from 1983).

The Radicals are weakest of all in southern mainland Italy, with the exception of the two largest cities, Naples (3.5 per cent in 1987) and Bari (3.8 per cent). In Bari, as in the rest of Apulia, their vote rose by 50 per cent over 1983, but starting from a low base. The Radicals' lowest votes were in the regions of Basilicata (0.9 per cent in 1987), Calabria (1.2 per cent) and Molise (1.2 per cent).

The Radicals won more support, however, in Sicily and Sardinia. In western Sicily the party's 1987 vote doubled to 2.8 per cent, and in Palermo reached 5.8 per cent. Its highest vote in all Italy was Cagliari, in Sardinia, with 6 per cent.

Organization

The Radicals have the most unconventional organizational structure of any Italian party. In many ways Radicals see themselves as a movement rather than as a party. There have been periodic attempts to tighten the party's structure but these have been followed by attempts to loosen it, in order to prevent a consolidation of the party's bureaucracy. The party's own continuing existence has often been brought into question, and made conditional upon the achievement of new party targets, such as a certain number of new members.

Party organizational theory and practice do not always coincide. The party has a "federative" decentralized structure, but the peripheral organization tends to be weak and the central leadership powerful, in particular the party's most charismatic figure, Marco Pannella, who has seldom held formal leadership posts within the party. There is no party discipline, but the party congress can take decisions binding on the party as long as a qualified majority is attained. The party is a stickler for the rules, but its own rule book is in rapid evolution.

The most recent change is the decision to become a transnational rather than purely Italian party.

Radical Party membership has fluctuated rapidly. Until 1986 it was seldom above 3,000 but by 1987 it has risen to over 10,000. However, several hundred of these are members of other parties. In 1986, 593 of the 732 *doppie tessere* (double members) were members of the Socialist Party. Anyone can become a Radical Party member, without any pre-conditions, and no one can be expelled or disciplined.

The party's basic structure is as a federation of Radical associations, as well as of non-Radical organizations which can affiliate to the party regionally or nationally for any length of time that they wish. The Radical association can be territorial or be based on particular policy concerns (e.g. a local consumers' group). No Radical association, however, can claim a monopoly over party representation within any given territorial area. As a result of recent rule changes the minimum size for a Radical association is 60 within Italy and 40 in other countries. The most active Radical groups outside Italy are in Spain, Portugal, France and Belgium.

The party's statute provides for regional Radical Parties, with rules for minimum size according to a region's population, but these have been of little practical significance.

The federal party congress has several unusual features. Unlike most Italian parties it meets annually or even more frequently if an extraordinary congress is convened. It is also unusually powerful, fixing the party's objectives for the next year. Any decisions it takes by a 75 per cent majority are binding on the party, and even those taken by simple majority if ratified by a two-thirds majority by the party's federal council. In theory the congress is comprised of delegates; in practice anyone can attend. In January 1988 1,250 members attended, of which 114 were non-Italian.

The permanent party consultative body at national level is the federal council. Its numbers and composition have fluctuated but at present 35 of its members are directly elected by the congress (18 of which are now non-Italian including six Spaniards, three Portuguese and three Belgians, as well as two French citizens, one Turk, one Israeli, one Yugoslav and one Greek). The other members are the representatives of the non-Radical organizations currently affiliated to the party. Acting by unanimity the federal council can overturn congress decisions. Other matters not treated by the congress but which are passed by two-thirds majority in the federal council must be taken up by the party executive.

The top executive position is that of the first secretary, who is elected by the party congress. There are no fixed rules as to how often the secretary can be re-elected. In practice the post is regularly rotated, and secretaries tend to remain in office for one or two, or more exceptionally, three years. Once elected the first secretary

chooses the members of the secretariat, who are then ratified by the congress. At present there are five deputy secretaries and 11 members of the secretariat, of whom four are non-Italians.

The second most powerful position in the party is that of treasurer, who is also directly elected by the congress and who has full autonomy over the party's budget, including the right of veto over certain expenditure. There is also a party president, without a clearly defined role.

The Radical parliamentarians are given wide autonomy, and cannot be bound by any party mandates. The Radical group in the chamber has re-named itself as the European Federalist Group. The Radical senators are in a mixed group with three other members elected on joint party lists (with the Socialists and Social Democrats in two cases, with the same parties plus the Greens in another). The senate mixed group is called the European Federalist and Ecologist Group.

The decisive roles over the choice of party candidates are played by the first secretary and by the federal council, with Marco Pannella also retaining great influence. Care is taken over the heads of its various lists, and over which candidates the party will promote, but subsequent candidates tend to be in alphabetical order. There is little or no control over who stands (e.g. the case of "Cicciolina" who could not be excluded once she wished to stand).

The Radical Party has no youth section (although it once had a national secretary who was under 21) nor any women's section.

The party newspaper is entitled *Notizie Radicali*. The most influential party organ however is Radio Radicale, which dates from the liberalization of private radio stations around 10 years ago. It provides direct coverage of Italian parliamentary activities, as well as of Radical party congresses and news of other party events, demonstrations etc.

The party campaigned against public funding of parties, and after it lost decided not to use the money it was owed for direct party purposes, but to channel it instead to public service activities such as those of Radio Radicale. The party aims to be completely self-financing, and has a fully transparent budget. Party dues are set at the highest level of any Italian party, with minimum expected contributions of 146,000 lire (100 ecu, £75, etc.).

A decision has recently been taken that the new transnational party should levy dues on the basis of 1 per cent of national per capita GDP. Fees in France, for example, would be 840 francs (182,000 lire) and in Spain 7,500 pesetas (81,000 lire). Members in authoritarian countries, where party membership puts them at risk, would be exempt from payment. Lists of members contributions are sometimes publicized in the party newspaper.

From 1979 to 1984 the three Radical members sat in the Technical Co-ordination Group in the European Parliament. After 1984 they were excluded from the new Rainbow Group largely on the grounds of the latter's suspicion of the highly personalized style of Marco Pannella. An attempt to combine with other independent members in a new technical group was short-lived, and the three Radical members are again sitting on their own as independents.

Policy

The Radical Party does not claim to have a dominating ideology, and permits its members to be members of other parties. It does not have an overall programme for government and does not, for example, get very involved in the details of economic policy-making. In many ways, it appears to function more as an umbrella organization for individual causes rather than as a broad movement, let alone as a party.

Nevertheless, the Radical Party is clearly bound together by a number of common beliefs, above all a commitment to libertarian values and to direct citizen action and to a lesser extent by other values, such as pacifism and anti-clericalism. The party's strategy has been generally consistent, concentration on specific reform objectives achieved by referenda or by other forms of direct non-violent action rather than by more conventional parliamentary activity. Even within Parliament direct techniques have been used, for example, through the tabling of large numbers of amendments and other filibustering techniques rather than the forging of parliamentary compromises. These tactics have often been successful and the Radicals have had an impact (as in the divorce and abortion issues) far beyond what their national strength would suggest.

Moreover, they have not always been as unconventional as they seem. While continually threatening to dissolve themselves as a party they have so far kept themselves in existence. While attacking the whole Italian political system they have attempted to make ad hoc alliances with other Italian parties of the left. In the past their main targets have been the two largest parties, the Christian Democrats for their links with the church and their role as lynchpin of the Italian political system, and the Communists because of their perceived illiberal ideology, lack of internal democracy and attempts to dominate the pacifist, women's liberation and other popular movements.

The Radicals appear to have two particular problems at present. The first is the continual public perception of the party as being dominated by Marco Pannella (and now to a much lesser extent by the image of Cicciolina). The second is over the implementation of the controversial decision to turn the Radical Party into a transnational party which will abandon domestic Italian parliamentary activities. The extent of the Radicals' appeal in countries with quite different political cultures to Italy is a completely uncertain factor. There is evidence of response in some of the Latin countries, but less elsewhere.

The party is still most closely identified with issues of civil rights. Besides its major reform campaigns (abortion, divorce, conscientious objection etc) it has championed the rights of ethnic, regional, sexual and other minorities. It has put a high emphasis on human rights in Eastern Europe. Its libertarian philosophy has also led it to sponsor unpopular causes. It has been the main Italian opponent of anti–terrorist legislation which it believes to go too far in curtailing human rights, and has defended the rights of free speech of Le Pen and others irrespective of the cause advocated. The Radicals have supported the liberalization of soft drugs, and controlled-availability of drugs for addicts, combined with tough action against traffic in hard drugs.

A recently strengthened emphasis has been on protection of animal rights. The Radicals now speak of defending the rights of "living beings" rather than just "human rights", and even refer to themselves as a "transpecies" as well as "transnational" party. They are opposed to vivisection and animal experimentation, as well as to hunting and to zoos. They are highly critical of genetic manipulation.

The Radicals have also taken a strong line against civil nuclear energy.

The other great Radical policy theme besides civil rights has been the need for reform of the Italian state and its malfunctioning institutions, and above all the Italian political parties and their clientelist links with an inefficient and corrupt public administration. The Radicals have taken a strong line against the public funding of political parties, and oppose public subsidies of all kinds. They have enjoyed the role of public subsidies of all kinds. They have enjoyed the role of "muckrakers" against the Mafia and other organized crime, and in putting the spotlight on the various political scandals that have bedevilled Italian political life.

Like other Italian parties, the Radicals have called for overhaul of the Italian system of justice. Their special emphasis has been on penal reform, and, in particular, in drawing attention to the delays before prisoners are brought to trial (hence the Toni Negri candidacy in 1983).

The Radicals are also strong advocates of a clear separation between Church and state. Their continuing anti-clerical streak is symbolized by their long-standing campaign against the state's Concordat with the Church, and against its recent revision by the Craxi government.

The Radicals do not want to make major changes to Italy's written Constitution, merely to the ways in which it has been applied in practice.

They do, however, seek to change Italy's electoral system by replacing proportional representation by a majority system in individual constituencies on the British model. They argue that this is the only way to break the existing Italian political stalemate. They agree that the small parties would all disappear, but claim either that a new left of centre lay party would be created or that the Christian Democrats and Communists would be forced to change their attitudes and policies.

The Radicals are strong European federalists. One of their main planks as a transnational party is for consultative referenda to be held in various European countries in support of the proposal that the European Parliament be vested with constituent powers to establish the United States of Europe. Europe is defined in the widest possible sense.

The Radicals have also put a high emphasis on development of the Third World. One of their most publicized initiatives in recent years has been that on combating hunger in the world. The fight against the international arms trade is another major theme.

Personalities

The overwhelmingly dominant figure within the party has been Marco Pannella who has only occasionally held formal party posts but has led many of the Radicals major campaigns as well as being its most charismatic spokesman in the Italian and European parliaments. The party is still highly dependent on him for leadership and for media profile but would also like to escape from his shadow. In 1979 he sought unsuccessfully to transfer the party congress from Italy to France and in 1988 he quarrelled with his own party congress, but there has never been a lasting breach. Even at the 1988 congress Pannella was elected top of the list for the party's new federal council.

The party leadership elected at the 1988 congress consists of Sergio Stanzani as party secretary, Paolo Vigevano as treasurer and Bruno Zevi as president. Stanzani is one of the longest-serving members of the party, having chaired the group which drafted its 1967 statute. Vigevano, who has been treasurer on several occasions, has led the development of Radio Radicale's network. Bruno Zevi is a distinguished architect who has only recently joined the party. The party also elected five deputy secretaries: Emma Bonino, one of the most well-known Radicals, stemming from her background as one of Italy's leading feminists and her role in the abortion campaign; Adelaide Aglietta the first-ever woman secretary of an Italian political party; Giovanni Negri, the party secretary before Stanzani; Guiseppe Calderisi, the party's specialist in organizing referenda; and Francesco Rutelli, also a former party secretary.

Roberto Cicciomessere made his reputation in the divorce and conscientious objection campaigns.

Adele Faccio is one of the more well-known of the party's campaigners, especially active in the feminist, abortion and now animals' rights campaigns. Angelo Pezzana is a leading gay rights campaigner.

The Radical party policy of permitting dual membership has contributed to numerous well-known public figures joining the party, such as the writer, Leopoldo Sciascia.

The most controversial party figure is the porno star, Ilona Staller ("Cicciolina") who was elected to the Italian Parliament in 1987, but who has been attacked by some within the party for giving it the wrong image. Pannella, however, has defended her.

Movimento Sociale Italiano — Destra Nazionale — MSI
(Italian Social Movement — National Right)

Headquarters	: 39 Via Dela Scrofa, 00186 Rome (tel: 654 51 26)
Secretary	: Gianfranco Fini
Youth organization	: *Fronte della Gioventu*
Publication	: *Secolo d'Italia*
Membership	: 380,000
Founded	: 1946

History

The Italian Social Movement (MSI) was founded in 1946 by former Fascists. Giorgio Almirante was elected as the first secretary of its executive committee. The new party supported the social principles of the Salo Republic, and a corporatist organization of society ("National

State of Labour") based neither on capitalism nor on the class struggle. It opposed many of the provisions of the new Italian Constitution, claiming, for example, that the president had been given too few powers, and that the proposed regions would undercut Italian territorial unity. The MSI was fiercely anti-communist, and saw itself as a particular defender of southern Italian interests.

In the Rome local elections in 1947 the new party polled 25,000 votes and obtained three councillors, with MSI votes subsequently being used to keep the left out of power. In its first national electoral test, in 1948, the MSI polled 2 per cent of the vote, and obtained six deputies and one senator.

In 1950 the party elected a new secretary, Augusto de Marsanich. The same year also saw the creation of an associated trade union, CISNAL. In 1951 the MSI decided to support Italian membership of NATO. In 1949 it had abstained in a vote on this issue.

The early 1950s saw a bitter struggle by the party against the enactment of the so-called Scelba law, which would have forbidden the party's existence, as a contradiction to the ban on a new Fascist party in the Constitution. The party's third national congress was banned by the Italian Government. The Scelba law was eventually passed, but subsequently never effectively enforced.

The MSI polled very well in the 1952 local elections in southern Italy. One of its main issues during this period was the return of Trieste to Italy.

In the 1953 national elections the MSI made a major advance, winning 5.8 per cent of the vote, with 29 deputies and nine senators. In 1954 De Marsanich was replaced as secretary by Arturo Michelini, who was to remain the leader until 1969.

After the loss of their majority in 1953 the Christian Democrats were occasionally forced to rely on external MSI support, for example for the composition of the Zoli government in 1957, and for the right-of-centre government of Fernando Tambroni in 1960. The riots that this caused led to the cancellation of the MSI's congress of that year, to the fall of the Tambroni government and subsequently to the Christian Democratic Party opening towards the centre-left. The MSI was left more isolated than ever. The MSI's opposition to the centre-left formula became one of its key policy planks in the 1960s. Another mobilizing issue later in the 1960s was that of the anti-italian terrorism in the Alto Adige (South Tyrol). Throughout the elections of the 1950s and '60s the MSI fluctuated between 4.4 per cent and 5.8 per cent of the national

vote and between 24 and 29 deputies in the Chamber.

After the death of Michelini in 1969, he was succeeded by the party's original secretary, Giorgio Almirante, who advocated a more aggressive opposition stance by the party. His return coincided with a period of severe social unrest in Italy, which won new recruits for the MSI, with its emphasis on law and order and on traditional moral values. It could not, however, completely disassociate itself from right-wing extremist groups like *Ordine Nuova*, which were responsible for street disorders and for a number of acts of random terrorist violence. The latter were strongly denounced by the MSI.

In the 1971 regional elections the MSI vote rose sharply. In the 1972 national elections it forged an electoral alliance with the monarchist party PDIUM (Italian Democratic Party of Monarchical Union) under the label of *Destra Nazionale* (National Right), which won 8.7 per cent of the vote for the Chamber of Deputies, and 56 seats. In January 1973 there came a formal merger, and the party has since been known as *MSI Destra Nazionale*.

In 1976 there was a serious split within the party, with a substantial minority group advocating the abandonment of Fascist slogans and symbols. In December 1976 MSI deputies and nine senators left the party and created a new party called *Democrazia Nazionale*. This won no seats in the 1979 elections and subsequently disappeared, but it did considerable harm to the MSI, with its vote and membership falling back sharply.

The MSI strongly opposed Christian Democratic co-operation with the Communists in the late 1970s; and put itself forward as the only real opposition party to the corrupt political system. In 1979 the MSI obtained four seats in the first elections for the European Parliament.

In the 1980s the party became rather less isolated in the Italian political spectrum, helped by the collapse of right-wing terrorism after the last and bloodiest outrage at Bologna Railway Station in 1980. It began to send delegates to the congresses of other Italian parties, Almirante went to Berlinguer's funeral and in 1986 the party was given a place on the RAI (Italian State Radio and Television) board of directors.

In the 1983 national elections its vote rose again, to 6.8 per cent (from 5.3 per cent in 1979) and it obtained 42 seats in the Chamber (12 more than in 1979). In the regional elections of 1983, 1985 and 1986 it averaged 6.6 per cent of the vote, and in the 1984 European Parliament elections it gained one seat, obtaining five in all. In the 1987 national elections, however, its vote slipped somewhat to 5.9 per cent obtaining 35 seats in the Chamber.

In late 1987 Almirante resigned as secretary, after 18 continuous years in the post and the party was severely divided in its choice of a successor, with four candidates standing in the first round. In the final round the party's youth secretary Gianfranco Fini defeated Pino Rauti, by the narrow vote of 727 to 608. Almirante subsequently became party president but died in 1988 as did another party leader, Pino Romualdi, leaving it bereft of its most well-known personalities.

Support

In spite of the fall in its vote in 1987, the MSI remains the fourth largest Italian party, as it has been since the 1972 national elections. Besides its 35 deputies and 17 senators, it has around 50 regional councillors. In 1984 it had 1,240 communal councillors. It also had 27 mayors, but only one in a commune of more than 5,000 inhabitants.

The MSI is particularly strong in the lower middle classes, among civil servants and clerks, and among shopkeepers. It also has a strong following in the armed forces and among the police.

It has traditionally been strongest in the south and on the islands, and in the provincial cities rather than in the countryside. Of its 380,000 members around 40 per cent are in the south and islands, 34 per cent in central Italy and only 26 per cent in the north. In the 1987 national elections it won 7.8 per cent of the vote in the islands, 7.2 per cent in the rest of the south, 6.4 per cent in central Italy and 4.7 per cent in the north.

This traditional pattern, however, is showing signs of change. In the 1987 elections the MSI vote remained relatively stable in the north (with major advances in Bolzano and Trieste) but fell sharply in many of its strongholds in the centre and south and especially in Naples, where its vote was almost halved. Nevertheless most of the party's strongest areas are still in the centre and south, and specially Latium (where it polled 8.6 per cent in Rome in 1987 but even higher in provinces such as Latina), Campania (in the city of Naples the MSI polled 11.2 per cent in 1987, down from 20 per cent in 1983), Puglia (Bari 9.7 per cent in 1987), Calabria and Sicily. The party polled 9.9 per cent in Palermo in 1987, but is even stronger in eastern Sicily, and notably Catania, where it polled 13 per cent in the 1986 regional elections. The MSI is less strong in western Sicily, in Sardinia, in Basilicata and in Molise.

In northern Italy the MSI's greatest strong-hold is now the city of Bolzano, where 40 per cent of Italian speakers voted for the party in the 1987 elections, in protest at their growing isolation within the South Tyrol. The other major stronghold is the city of Trieste, where the party won 11.3 per cent in 1987. Elsewhere in the north the MSI polls best in the cities with large populations of southern immigrants such as Turin (6 per cent in 1987) and Milan (6.8 per cent in 1987). It is generally weak in the provincial towns and countryside of Piedmont, Lombardy, in the Veneto, Emilia–Romagna (notably in Reggio Emilia, Modena and Ravenna) and in Tuscany.

Organization

The MSI's complex organizational structure reflects its position as a subculture within Italian society, with corporatist as well as territorial levels of organization, and with its own trade union and network of clubs and societies. It reflects the twin objectives of achieving a high degree of party discipline (elected members must adhere to the political line established by the national congress and other party bodies, and periodic attempts have been made to prevent organized factions within the party), and of ensuring internal party democracy (e.g. the MSI was the first Italian party to provide for direct election of its national secretary by the party congress).

The basic territorial unit of the party is the section, of which there were 3,180 throughout Italy in 1984. A communal section must have at least seven members, and a district section 21 members. Between the communal and provincial level zonal committees can be established (in 1984 there were 678 such committees throughout Italy). Much more significant, however, is the party's provincial tier of organization, based on federations (95 throughout Italy, with nine sub-federations). On the other hand the regional tier has relatively little power within the party.

In parallel to the territorial organization is the corporative organization, with local nuclei based on a particular profession, which band together in provincial groups (*Gruppi di Categoria* with *Consulte Corporative*) and at regional levels (*Consulte Corporative Regionali*). At national level all these groups are co-ordinated within a national council of labour, with up to 200 members nominated by the national political secretariat, and divided into 23 sections (public administration, the liberal professions, tourism, culture, etc).

At national level a national congress is held every two years. Among its tasks are to elect the party's national secretary. The delegates include those elected by the provincial federations on the basis both of votes won at the last national elections and of their total membership.

A curious feature is that all party members holding the Gold Medal for Military Valour have a statutory right to attend the congress.

The party's central committee consists of up to 280 members, and meets every three or four months. The central committee elects the national executive (*Direzione Nazionale*), a more powerful body of between 60 and 90 members, which meets every two months and has a vital say, for example, on electoral programmes.

The party's national secretary is its effective leader (the president has duties of a more honorific nature). The secretary cannot simultaneously be president of one of the parlimentary groups. He can be asked to resign by the central committee.

The secretary chooses the 24-member national political secretariat, who constitute his "ministers". Each member of the secretariat has a specific functional task.

The party's candidates for national and European office are proposed by the provincial federations. These proposals are then examined and ratified at national level.

One feature of the party's membership rules is that they explicitly exclude "traitors" to Italy, freemasons and members of any other secret society.

The party's youth organization is called the *Fronte della Gioventu*, and is open to 14–26 year-olds, although its leaders can be older.

There is no formal women's group within the MSI, but there are provincial and regional committees for women's problems, and a national women's conference and women's executive.

The MSI has an associated trade union, CISNAL (*Confederazione Italiano dei Sindacati Nazionali dei Lavoratori*), with around 500,000 members.

Among the other groups associated with the MSI are a sporting society, the *Centro Nazionale Sportivo Fiamma*, and a society for Italian expatriates, the *Comitato Tricolore per gli Italiani del Mondo* (CTIM).

The party's principal organ is its newspaper *Secolo d'Italia*. It also produces a daily press briefing *Nuove Prospettive*. The youth group provides its own monthly paper (*Dissenso*), as does the parliamentary group (*Destra Parlamento*). There are also numerous provincial papers, such as *Leonessa* ("Lioness") in Brescia and *Il Dito nell Occhio* ("The Thumb in the Eye") in Florence.

The party membership dues are currently 50,000 lire (10,000 lire for students), payable to the provincial federation, which retains half and remits the rest to the national party.

The party's elected representatives are meant to contribute 10 per cent of their salary to the party.

At international level the MSI is a member of the Eurodestra of European right-wing parties, including the National Front in France. In the European Parliament the MSI's five members sit in the Group of the European Right. the MSI emphasizes that this is not a Right International, and that right-wing policies must be pursued in a different way within each national context.

Policies

The *MSI-Destra Nazionale* is the only explicitly right-wing party represented in the Italian Parliament, and it retains enough popular support to be the fourth largest Italian party. Its continuing appeal has been due to a number of reasons. More obviously it has attracted former Fascists, and those who look back nostalgically to what they see as the positive features of the Fascist era, particularly corporatism and nationalism. Secondly, it has appealed to supporters of forthright conservative policies, especially in moments of social unrest, as in the early 1970s. Thirdly, it has had particular strength in the south as a defender of southern interests. Finally, its status as an anti-system party (having played no part in the creation of the Italian Republican Constitution, and only now beginning to emerge from its political "ghetto") has won it protest votes, from those disillusioned with the workings of the current Italian political system.

This diverse support base leaves the party with certain fundamental problems of identity. The first such issue is over the degree to which it is still a Fascist party. The leadership's general line is that the Fascist period has been a central part of Italian history, and cannot be ignored. Some of Fascism's ideological beliefs, in particular its corporatist philosophy, still have a vital role to play in modern society. On the other hand, the Fascist period should not simply be restored because history moves on, and the Fascist regime made many mistakes, e.g. severely curtailing personal liberty. The leadership thus still proclaims itself as heir to the Fascist tradition (those within the party who advocated a complete break with Fascism left the party in 1976, and had no electoral success as a conventional right-wing party), but downplays outright Fascist symbolism (such as black shirts and Roman salutes) and advocates the reconciliation of Fascism with personal liberty. It also distinguishes sharply between Fascism and Nazism.

The second issue has ironically been over the degree to which it is a party of the right. In certain respects, its corporatist philosophy, its defence of the public sector and of regional and social spending in the south of Italy are not those of a party of the economic right. At the recent social party congress a significant minority of the party advocated an opening up to the left, but the new leadership prefers to point to the reality of support on the right as opposed to hypothetical support further to the left.

Another problem for the MSI has been its attitude towards violence, which was idealized by traditional Fascist ideology and which became a major issue again during the troubled period of the 1970s. Certain of its leaders, like Pino Rauti, have been associated with street disorders in the past, but the party leadership has always denied any links with right-wing terrorism and has denounced violence. With the decline in violence in Italy in the 1980s this has become less of a problem for the MSI.

One problem of identity which is mainly resolved for the party is that of monarchism. In the early 1950s the Monarchist Party was a major rival of the MSI in the south and in the 1970s the MSI merged with the Monarchist Party (PDIUM). Demands for restoration of the monarchy play no part in the current party programme, which in fact calls explicitly for the replacement of the existing "First Republic" by a "Second Republic".

Finally, one theme which has been consistently emphasized by the party, and which still helps to define it more than any other policy, is that of anti-Communism, both within Italy and in the world at large.

As regards specific policies, the most distinctive feature of its economic policy is its continuing defence of corporatism, which it sees as an alternative economic system to that of Marxism and to capitalism. It is opposed both to a class-based analysis of society, and to unbridled pursuit of the profit motive, which leads to overconcentration of private economic power and dominance by multinationals. It believes that corporatism fits in with Christian Social philosophy, with ideas of industrial democracy and worker participation in management, and also with social trends in view of the decline of the traditional class system.

There should thus be maximum partnership between management and workers, and sectoral economic interests should be directly defended in parliament and elsewhere. On the role of the state, and in its support for state spending, the MSI distinguishes itself clearly from Liberal economic philosophies. It has campaigned against modifications to the system of indexation of wages and against attempts to crack down on the self-employed.

The MSI is critical of the new ecological movements which it sees as a Communist fifth column. The MSI also supports the continued use of existing civil nuclear energy capacity.

On moral issues, the MSI takes a strongly conservative stance. It campaigned against the introduction of divorce and of legal abortion, and has taken periodic initiatives to call for the reintroduction of the death penalty, notably for terrorists, drug traffickers and kidnappers who kill their victim.

On the other hand, whereas most parties of the European right (notably the *Front Nationale* in France) have immigration as their key issue, this is not an issue which is emphasized by the MSI. In contrast it has strongly defended the rights of Italian migrant workers, e.g. the right to vote within Italy.

The MSI has always argued against the provisions of the existing Italian Constitution. It is particularly opposed to the dominance of the parties within the present Italian political system, and their clientelism and corruption. It calls instead for the introduction of a more presidential system of government, with direct popular elections and greater powers for the national President. It calls for the numbers of parliamentarians to be reduced and for parliament to be reformed either to a unicameral system in which half the members would be elected on a corporatist basis, or else a system with a Senate elected on that basis. It supports the introduction of a minimum threshold of 5 per cent for a party to be represented in parliament. It also calls for the use of referenda to be increased.

The MSI is opposed to the Italian regions being given strong powers, since this undercuts Italian unity.

The MSI remains a strongly nationalist party, but accepts that the Italian "fatherland" cannot prosper in isolation, but only within a wider European entity. Like De Gaulle, the MSI speaks of "Europe of the fatherlands", but in practice goes much further in supporting a united Europe. The MSI supported the Spinelli Draft Treaty for European Union in the European Parliament. It advocates more powers for the European Parliament, and common European economic and foreign policies.

Its anti-Communism has led it to accept the necessity of Italian membership within NATO, but it advocates a much stronger European presence within NATO, true allies rather than mere subordinates of the Americans. The MSI is opposed to the treaty of nuclear non-proliferation, which it believes leaves Italy (and Germany) in a position of inferiority as regards France and the United Kingdom. It advocates a European army and a truly European nuclear deterrent. It also wants to see Italy move towards a professional army. It supports Euromissiles within Italy, and also the SDI Programme.

The MSI is suspicious of detente and of "Glasnost", which it believes has not changed the nature of the Soviet system, nor of Soviet imperialism.

The MSI emphasizes Italy's role in the Mediterranean. It supports security for Israel, but also the creation of a Palestinian homeland.

The MSI supports increased development co-operation with the poor countries of the third world.

The MSI is also a strong advocate of the rights of the Italian-speaking minority within the province of Bolzano, and remains highly critical of the 1975 Treaty of Osimo in which Italy renounced any claims to Trieste's hinterland.

Personalities

The MSI's new secretary, Gianfranco Fini, is 36 years old, and was the leader of the party's youth wing until his election at the special party congress in December 1987. He was the preferred successor of the party's long-time leader, Giorgio Almirante, who became the party president until his death in 1988.

Fini's defeated opponent was Pino Rauti, a controversial and turbulent figure in the 1970s, who is now an advocate of the MSI opening up to its left. The other defeated candidates for the leadership were Franco Servello and Domenico Mennitti.

The party's president in the Chamber is Alfredo Pazzaglia. The party's four deputy secretaries are Guiseppe Tatorella (organization), Raffaele Valensise (sectors), Mirko Tremaglia (international) and Guido lo Porto.

Federazione Liste Verdi
(The Federation of Green Lists)

Headquarters : (i) Via Magenta 5, 00185 Roma (tel: 06/4957383) (ii) Green Parliamentary Group: Via Ufficio del Vicario 21, 00186 Roma (tel: 06/67179837)

Chairman of Green Parliamentary Group in Chamber : Gianni Mattioli
Founded : 1986

History

Until the 1970s the Italian environmental movement was very weak, although there were a number of organizations concerned with the protection of Italy's natural and cultural heritage, such as *Italia Nostra*. The environmental movement was given a major boost by the disaster at Seveso in July, 1976 and by the development of a national energy plan (1975–77) which envisaged the opening of 20 new nuclear power stations. The 1970s also saw a rapid development of citizen action groups using methods of direct action, such as the Friends of the Earth and anti-vivesection and hunting leagues.

In 1980 the first ecology candidates began standing in a few local elections, in northern Italy. 1980 saw the creation of a *Lega per l'Ambiente* (Environmental League) which grew rapidly through the 1980s (15,000 members by 1983, 30,000 by 1986). A further loosely organized Green group, *Arcipelago Verde*, (Green Archipelago), was founded in 1981. In 1983 a large Green meeting was held in Milan. In 1984 a National Co-ordination of Green Lists was established.

The 1985 local elections saw the first substantial presence of Green candidates: 150 Green lists received 636,000 votes; 10 regional, 16 provincial and 115 communal councillors were elected.

The accident at Chernobyl provided a new wave of support for the anti-nuclear movement, and for Green causes in general. The Greens were active in the attempts to stop nuclear energy and to stop hunting.

At a meeting in Finale Ligure in 1986, the Federation of Green Lists was established to co-ordinate the action of the large number of individual green lists which had sprung up at regional, provincial and communal level, and which were themselves often alliances of single issue campaigners.

In the 1987 national elections lists were submitted all over Italy. Only 150 million lire was spent in the campaign, but the various Green lists with a smiling sun as their symbol, won 2.5 per cent of the votes in the Chamber (more than the Liberal Party) and 13 seats. In the Senate elections they won 2 per cent and had one Senator elected directly and another in alliance with Radicals and Socialists.

Green members are now also participating in

the government of the commune of Milan. The party won a considerable number of seats in the 1988 local elections.

Support

The Greens have a particular appeal to the better-educated and to those working in the professions and the new services. In the 1987 national elections they won particular support from young voters. They are stronger in the cities than in the countryside.

In regional terms they are strongest in northern Italy, have medium support in central Italy and are very weak in most of the south.

Their best results in 1987 were in the areas of Catholic subculture in north-eastern Italy. Their two best constituencies were Trentino Alto Adige where they polled 4.6 per cent (7.3 per cent in the city of Trento) and Venice–Treviso where they won 4.3 per cent (6.3 per cent in Venice). They also polled well in Liguria (4 per cent, Genova 4.4 per cent). In several constituencies in Lombardy and Piedmont they had around 3.5 per cent of the vote (4.4 per cent in the city of Milan, 3.9 per cent in Turin).

The Greens were weaker in the "red belt" of central northern Italy (e.g. 2.3 per cent in eastern Emilia and Romagna, under 2 per cent in Umbria). In Latium they won 3 per cent. They again polled best in the cities (Florence 3.9 per cent, Rome 3.8 per cent).

In most of the south the Greens polled poorly. Their best region was Puglia (where they won between 1.6 per cent and 1.7 per cent of the vote, their worst Calabria, 0.8 per cent, and the constituency of Naples–Caserta where they only won 0.7 per cent). Even in the city of Naples they only obtained 0.9 per cent of the vote, their worst result in any Italian city.

Organization

The Greens are in the dilemma of having to decide whether they are a movement or a political party. Their structure is still highly decentralized. The basic lists are the Green Lists, which are themselves local alliances of various environmental, animal welfare, pacifist and other organizations and leagues.

Green Lists can be formed at communal, provincial or regional level and then apply for affiliation to the National Federation of Green Lists.

The largest number of Green Lists is in Lombardy (around 30). There are very few in most regions in the south.

The sovereign body of the party at national level is the federal assembly, which must meet at least every six months. Five such assemblies have been held so far. Every regional Green List is entitled to three delegates, and every provincial lists to one delegate. The number of delegates from communal Green Lists depends on their population, one delegate for every commune under 100,000, two for communes between 100,000 and 300,000 and three for communes with populations larger than 300,000. Delegates may not be members of other political parties. The party's statute encourages decision-making by consensus and discourages attempts to take decisions on split votes.

Between assemblies the top decision-making body is the co-ordinating group (*Gruppo di co-ordinamento*). This consists of 11 members elected by the federal assembly for a one-year term of office. No more than two can come from any one region. None may be a member of another party, and none may hold any public elected post. The co-ordinating group elects the party treasurer from among its members. Two members of the Green parliamentary group can attend its meetings, but without voting rights.

The federal assembly also elects the guarantee committee (*Comitato di Garanzia*), consisting of 10 persons elected for two-year terms. The guarantee committee has a key role in accepting new Green Lists to the Federation. It also keeps a register of the issues on which unanimity was reached, those where there was broad convergence of views, and those where there were sharper divisions.

In the Chamber there is a Green parliamentary group. In the Senate the Greens participate (with the Radicals) in the European Federalist Ecologist Group. Besides these there is a co-ordinating group for all Greens elected to public office at different levels.

An important role in Green policy-making is taken by its *Forum Tematici* (literally "Thematic Forums"), which organize meetings and develop policy within their areas of competence. There are 10 such groups at present, each with two or more co-ordinators. One deals with animal welfare issues (*noi e gli altri animali* — "us and other animals"). Others deal with peace issues (*Ecopax*), agricultural and rural issues, urban and planning issues, health, techniques of artificial reproduction, citizen rights and institutional reforms, energy, environment and work, waste recycling and food and nutrition.

Rules regarding choice and rotation of candidates are not yet as formalized as in some other Green parties. In some cases candidates have been placed in alphabetical order to avoid favouritism. Some candidates who undertook to stand down at the half-way point of their mandates have not done so.

The Green parliamentary group produces a journal called *Raggi*.

Policy

The Federation of Green Lists consider themselves to be part of a wider "Green archipelago" fighting for much fuller application of ecological principles in the Italian economy and society. Among the other "islands" in the archipelago are the various ecological, animal welfare and pacifist organizations, as well as green politicians working in other parties. They believe in fighting for specific objectives, through parliamentary and also extraparliamentary direct action.

Their most prominent cause has been the struggle against civil nuclear energy. Now that a referendum has gone in their favour, they are campaigning for its full implementation. They are also opposed to coal-fired generation and seek a revised national energy plan putting its emphasis on energy conservation and on use of renewables.

Among their other areas of particular concern have been the need for tougher standards for air and water quality, and campaigns against toxic water and dangerous factories. They advocate full application of the "polluter pays" principle and of the EC "Seveso" directive on dangerous substances.

More waste should be recycled, and products which cannot be recycled should be eliminated. Agriculture should become less dependent on chemicals.

The Greens are prominent in the anti-hunting campaign (they seek an initial five-year moratorium on all hunting), and put a high emphasis on other animal rights issues.

They have led a number of campaigns against speculative building and are opposed to major new infrastructure projects, such as the proposed bridge over the Straits of Messina. They want much wider use of environmental impact statements. They would like to slow down the motorway construction programme and would like to see a reinforcement of public transport instead, as well as the transport of more goods by rail rather than road.

They want the Italian defence effort to move away from armed defence to what they describe as "civil non-armed defence". The Italian arms industry should be reconverted, and the export of Italian arms should be blocked.

Personalities

The chairman of the Green parliamentary group in the Chamber of Deputies is Gianni Mattioli, an anti-nuclear physicist who won an impressive number of personal preference votes in the 1987 national elections. Among the other prominent Green parliamentarians is Rosa Filippini. Anna Maria Procacci, another parliamentarian, is the national secretary of the abolition of hunting league. Gloria Grasso is active in the bird protection league.

Among the prominent Greens outside parliament are Gianfranco Amendola and Alexander Langer, the Green leader in the south Tyrol, who has had close contacts with the Austrian Greens.

Democrazia Proletaria — DP
(Proletarian Democracy)

Headquarters	: Via Farini 62, 00184 Roma (tel: 47 57 342)
Secretary	: Giovanni Russo-Spena
President of Group in Chamber	: Franco Russo
Women's organization	: *Co-ordinamento delle Donne DP*
Publication	: *Notiziario DO*
Membership	: 10,000
Founded	: 1978

History

Democrazia Proletaria is the only Italian party of the far left which currently has parliamentary representation, and is the main survivor of the numerous left-wing parties and groups which were set up in the late 1960s and early 1970s, such as the Manifesto, group of dissident Communists, *Lotta Continua, Potere Operaio, Vanguardia Operaia* and many others.

Several attempts were made to unify these groups. In 1974 a number of them, including Manifesto combined to form the *Partito di Unita Proletaria* (PDUP). In the 1976 national elections PDUP formed wider electoral alliance with other far left groups, including *Vanguardia Operaia*, under the label *Sinistra Democrazia Proletaria* (Proletarian Democratic Left). The final electoral result, however, was disappointing, with the alliance only gaining 1.5 per cent of the vote, and six seats in the Chamber of Deputies.

The alliance subsequently broke up. The majority of members of the PDUP, along with a minority from *Vanguardia Operaia*, formed a new party, *PDUP per il Comunismo*, which subsequently rejoined the Communist Party in the early 1980s. On the other hand the majority of members of *Vanguardia Operaia*, along with a minority from PDUP, set up *Democrazia Proletaria*, which was formally launched in 1978.

In the 1979 national elections, *Democrazia Proletaria* gained only 0.8 per cent of the vote and no seats. In the European elections, however, it managed to get its most prominent leader, Mario Capanna, elected to the European Parliament.

Democrazia Proletaria gradually built up its strength, winning new recruits from members of PDUP who were dissatisfied with the latter's merger with the Communist Party.

In the 1983 national elections, it gained 1.5 per cent of the national vote for the Chamber of Deputies and seven seats. In 1984 the party decided to create the post of secretary for the first time and Mario Capanna became its first occupant. The party also retained its seat in the European Parliament.

In the 1987 national elections *Democrazia Proletaria* made a further small advance, winning 1.7 per cent of the vote for the Chamber and eight seats, and also winning its first seat in the Senate. Mario Capanna subsequently stood down as secretary, and was replaced by Giovanni Russo-Spena.

Support

Democrazia Proletaria has had a high turnover of its membership. The majority of its current members are relatively recent recruits and the majority have not been active in other political parties, although a significant number come from the new left movements of the 1970s, especially *Autonomia Operaia* (around 10 per cent of the 1987 membership), PDUP (7.5 per cent) and *Lotta Continua*. There are also a considerable number of former Communists (over 9 per cent of the 1987 membership). A fair percentage have been active in various social movements, such as the ecological and peace movements. Few have been active in the feminist movement, reflecting the relatively low percentage of women in the party (currently around 21 per cent of membership).

Nearly half the membership are in the 25–35 age group. Over 27 per cent of members are manual workers and nearly 30 per cent clerical workers. Twelve per cent of the members are unemployed, and 12 per cent are from the teaching professions. Students are almost 10 per cent. The party is very weak among farmers, and professional and managerial groups. Only 40 per cent of members are in a trade union, of whom the vast majority are in the CGIL (72 per cent), and most of the rest in the CISL.

In terms of electoral support *Democrazia Proletaria* is much stronger in the cities than in the countryside. It is also generally stronger in the north of the country, though there are pockets of weakness such as western Emilia and Trieste. In the 1987 elections its highest vote in

any city was in Trento (3.6 per cent). Its strongest city, however, is Milan, where it won 3.4 per cent of the vote in 1987, and where it also has by far its largest group of members (over 1,500 in Milan province in 1987).

In 1987 *Democrazia Proletaria* had its highest increase in votes compared to 1983 in central Italy, especially in Rome (where it rose from 1.2 per cent to 1.9 per cent) and in Tuscany (where it polled 2.8 per cent in Florence).

The party is generally weakest in southern Italy, though it has pockets of greater support such as Palermo (2.4 per cent in 1987), Naples (1.8 per cent) and part of Calabria. It is especially weak in Puglia, Basilicata and eastern Sicily.

Organization

At the lowest level the party is organized both on a local territorial and sectoral basis in cells, sections and collectives at the place of residence or at the workplace. At provincial level there are federations with executive committees, and at regional level there are regional committees, elected by regional congresses, and which in their turn elect the regional executives and regional co-ordinators. The national congress takes place every two years. The congress elects a 65-person national executive which subsequently elects the party's secretary, and the central party secretariat, which staffs a number of sectoral departments. Between congresses the party's parliament is its permanent national assembly, consisting of delegates elected by the provincial federations, and which meets at least twice a year, and which is presided over by a bureau (*Ufficio di Presidenza*).

The party has developed very complex rules for internal party democracy. All party officials and delegates can be recalled at any time by those who elected them; no-one can hold more than two important offices at once, nor have more than two consecutive terms of elective office at the same level (the House, Senate and European Parliament are considered as one level; the Region, Province and Commune as another level, though provinces and communes with under 100,000 people are exempted). The party's constitution calls for women to be represented at all levels of the party and in all lists of candidates (but no quotas are established). The party's rules also try to strike a balance between internal party discipline (the party has a hierarchical structure, and no factions are permitted within the party), and the defence of minority rights.

Party candidates are designated by the permanent national assembly, on the basis of proposals from the national executive, and in agreement with the provincial federations and regional communities.

The basic party dues are 45,000 lire, or 20,000 lire for younger or retired members, or the unemployed, but the more ambitious objective is for members to pay dues in proportion to their income. Those holding elective office are meant to hand over their salaries to the party, and to receive a party wage instead.

The party believes in federalist principles, and in areas of Italy with regional or ethnic minorities the party has sought to enter into federal pacts with associated parties organized within these regions. At present the party has such a pact with DP of Trentino-Alto Adige, DP of Sardinia and DP of Friuli.

At European Parliament level the *Democrazia Proletaria* member sits within the Rainbow Group. The party has links with the German Grünen and the group around Pierre Juquin in France.

Policies

Democrazia Proletaria sees itself as a left-wing socialist party, fighting for the rights of the working class (in its "complex" modern form) and of other oppressed groups, ethnic and linguistic minorities, the handicapped, homosexuals and people in the third world. It seeks to reconcile Marxist with green themes, and the traditional working-class movement with the new social movements, such as the environmental, pacifist and feminist movements. It recognizes its debt to the new left of the early 1970s, but is critical of the latter's lack of organization and discipline. It believes that practical action is more important than theoretical purity. It considers that the Communist Party and the trade unions have been too bureaucratic, too conformist and too moderate. It is opposed to the current reactionary leadership of the Catholic Church (and would abolish the Italian state's Concordat with the Church) but pays tribute to left-wing Social Catholicism.

Democrazia Proletaria puts a particularly strong emphasis on decentralization, popular participation in decision-making through use of referenda and other forms of direct democracy, and worker self-management, and prior consultation on all decisions affecting them.

It is extremely critical of capitalism and the profit motive. Eastern European bureaucracy and centralism is also rejected. Economic development should be based on smaller and more self-sufficient units, and should be linked much more to environmental considerations. Employment must be defended at all costs, the working week should be reduced to 35 hours at the same rates of pay, there should be more flexible working hours, and retirement at 55. There should be a much more egalitarian fiscal policy, and the introduction of a wealth tax, tough action against tax evasion, and tax exemptions for incomes below 700,000 lire a month.

Social services should be expanded. There should be an equal base pension for all, with complete indexation.

Democrazia Proletaria claims to have collected the largest number of signatures for Italy's anti-nuclear referenda. It wants to eliminate Italian dependence upon nuclear energy, closing existing ones as well as blocking the construction of new plants. It is also opposed to large coal-fired power stations as well.

The party puts considerable emphasis on civil rights issues, within and outside Italy. On institutional issues it is opposed to the Christian Democratic proposals for electoral reform, and is a strong defender of integral proportional representation. It has a federalist concept of the Italian state, would like to see more power given to the regions, and defence of the rights of the Friulians, Sardinians and other national minorities.

Democrazia Proletaria emphasizes its character as a pacifist party. Italy should disarm unilaterally, leave NATO, and become neutral. Civil defence should have a higher emphasis. Production and export of arms should be stopped.

An alliance should be forged between the working class in developed countries and the poor in the third world.

Non-recognized nations, such as the Palestinians, Basques and Corsicans, are given strong support (DP's member in the European Parliament also defended Mohawk claims that the Lake Placid Winter Olympics were taking place on ancestral Mohawk rather than American territory).

Democrazia Proletaria is very critical of the current European Community, which it sees as centralist and imperialist, but it advocates its transformation rather than Italian withdrawal.

Personalities

The party's most well-known personality is its former secretary, Mario Capanna, an erstwhile student leader who is a member of the Italian Chamber of Deputies and was a member of the European Parliament from 1979 to 1984. He has a flair for dramatic gestures such as wearing Indian headdresses and waving Palestinian flags.

His successors in the European Parliament have been Molinari and Alberto Tridente.

The current party secretary is Giovanni Russo-Spena, and the president of the DP Group in the Chamber of Deputies is Franco Russo. *Democrazia Proletaria* also has one member of the Italian Senate, Guido Pollice.

South Tyrol

The present autonomous province of Bolzano is a predominantly German-speaking area south of the main Alpine watershed. Historically it has been an integral part of the wider region of the Tyrol; not only does the South Tyrol include the castle of Tyrol itself, after which the region was named, but also the birthplace of Andreas Hofer, the Tyrolean hero who fought to maintain the separate Tyrolean identity during the Napoleonic wars.

The autonomous province of Bolzano had a population in 1981 of 430,000 of which 280,000 were German-speaking, 124,000 Italian-speaking and 18,000 Ladin-speaking. This represents a massive change since 1900 when over 91 per cent of the population were German-speaking and there were more Ladin than Italian speakers and it reflects the Italianization campaign carried out both between the wars and after the last war. Nevertheless, in the last few years the percentage of Italian speakers has again declined somewhat from a peak of 34.3 per cent in 1981 to the present figure of 28.7 per cent. The language division has been an urban-rural one, with the Italian population concentration in the towns and the Germans in the country. Bolzano, the provincial capital, is almost 74 per cent Italian and Merano, the second town, around 50 per cent. Overall, out of the 116 communes in the province, only five have an Italian-speaking majority. Some of the country districts are over 95 per cent German-speaking.

The second feature of the South Tyrol is the Ladin-speaking minority (Ladin is related to Rhaeto-Romansch). While constituting only 4 per cent of the population as a whole, the Ladin speakers are heavily concentrated in eight communes in which they constitute between 84 per cent and 99 per cent of the population.

South Tyroleans have four representatives in the Chamber of Deputies in Rome, as well as two Senators. They also vote every five years for representatives to the 35-member provincial assembly, the *Landtag* (out of which the provincial executive is drawn). The provincial representatives sit jointly with the 35 elected representatives from Trento in the regional assembly of Trentino–Alto–Adige. Finally, there are also communal elections, often fought between local lists with colourful names such as Gentian, Deer Heads or Edelweiss.

History

Until World War I the South Tyrol was part of Austria as was the predominantly Italian-speaking province of Trento to the south; Alcide de Gasperi, the great postwar Italian leader, who came from the region, started his political career in the Austrian parliament.

In 1919 the South Tyrol was awarded to Italy. Italian speakers were encouraged to move into the area and under Fascist rule there was severe discrimination against the German-speaking majority.

In 1939, as a result of an agreement between Hitler and Mussolini, the people of South Tyrol were given a chance to opt for German citizenship if they moved to the Reich: over two-thirds of the South Tyroleans opted to transfer, but due to the outbreak of the war only a minority actually moved.

After the war, therefore, a number of problems had to be sorted out, not least the status of those South Tyroleans who had opted for German citizenship, but had not moved; and of those who had moved, but wished to return. Most of all, however, the South Tyroleans lobbied the Allies to be reunited with the rest of Tyrol and to become part of Austria.

This request was finally refused by the Allies, who decided that the South Tyrol should remain part of Italy. An agreement was reached between Italy and Austria (and included in the Paris Peace Treaty between the Allies and Austria) guaranteeing certain rights to the South Tyrolers, including provisions for and extensive regional autonomy.

The subsequent politics of the area have been dominated by disputes over the Treaty's implementation. The first major grievance was that the Italian government drew up an autonomous statute (which came into force in 1948) which provided not for an autonomous region of South Tyrol, but for a wider autonomous region of Trentino–Alto–Adige in which Italian speakers outnumbered German speakers. Moreover, this statute was drawn up without prior consultation with the German speakers. Nevertheless, certain powers were delegated to the province of Bolzano within the wider regional unit. Regular elections began for a provincial assembly, and a provincial executive was established.

In the 1950s protests against the non-implementation of the treaty gradually intensified. In 1956 the Austrian government again took up the case.

In 1957 an Italian government plan to build a new Italian quarter of Bolzano led to a mass protest of 35,000 South Tyrolers at Sigmundskron Castle, just outside the town. In 1959 an attempt to cut back on the province's privileges even further led to the withdrawal of the German-speaking representatives from the regional administration. Subsequently, the South Tyrol question was brought before the United Nations.

Matters came to a head in 1961 when a number of terrorist attacks took place, notably on the so-called *Feuernacht* on June 11 when a number of power lines were blown up. The Italian government finally set up a committee to examine ways of redressing South Tyrolean grievances and in 1964 this was superseded by an Italian/Austrian expert committee. A series of measures were drawn up which became known as "the packet" with an operational timetable for their implementation. Slowly this went through the various hurdles for approval, beginning with the South Tyrolean governing party (the SVP) and in December 1969 it was approved by the Italian and Austrian parliaments.

In 1972 the new autonomy statute came into operation, providing for a much wider range of powers to the German-speaking province of Bolzano within the wider region of Trentino–Alto–Adige.

Nevertheless, not all the measures provided for in the "packet" were immediately adopted, and the timetable for implementation of many of them fell behind schedule. In May 1988, however, a further set of measures were finally adopted by the Italian government. Citizens of the South Tyrol can now choose, for example, in which language they wish to present administrative documents, and there is equality of use of the German language in police and legal matters. There is also a clearer separation between German- and Italian-speaking schools.

The dominant political force within the province has been the *Südtirol Volkspartei* (SVP), which still has around 60 per cent of the total vote and is supported by the vast majority of the German-speaking electorate. In communal elections in the countryside it is almost completely dominant, and in many communes the competition is between different SVP lists. More extreme nationalist groups have also developed, pushing for a free state of South Tyrol. Of these the *Wahlverband des Heimatbundes* has contested recent elections. There have also been a number of other regional parties, such as the *Sozialdemokratische Partei Südtirols* and the *Partei der Unabhangigen* (now the *Freiheitliche Partei Südtirols*).

Recently parties in the Green Alternative tradition have also developed, such as the *Alternative Liste für das Andere Südtirol* (ALFAS). These regional parties have had little impact in national elections, but have won representation in provincial elections. Although the SVP won 59.4 per cent in the 1983 *Landtag* elections and 22 of the 35 seats, the other 13 seats were divided between eight parties, of which five were Italian parties and three were provincial parties.

An index of the increased polarization of voting patterns in the South Tyrol has been the great increase in strength of Italian nationalism, in the form of votes going to the Italian Social Movement (MSI). Until recently the Christian Democrats had been by far the largest of the Italian national parties, but in the 1985 communal elections, the MSI became the largest party in Bolzano with 22.6 per cent of the vote. In the 1987 national elections the MSI was the largest of the Italian parties with 10.2 per cent of the provincial vote and 27 per cent in the city of Bolzano. An MSI member from Bolzano, Dr Andrea Mitolo, was elected to the Chamber of Deputies. This trend was confirmed in the 1988 *Landtag* elections.

Main features of the political system

There has been continued tension in the South Tyrol with the German-speaking majority pushing for greater autonomy and full implementation first of the Paris Treaty and then the 1969 "packet", and with the Italian-speaking minority feeling themselves to be increasingly under-privileged, and second-class citizens within their own country.

While there has been no repetition of the substantial outbreak of terrorism of the late 1950s, there have been isolated violent incidents and threats up to the recent day. It is uncertain whether these will be reduced after the latest reforms.

Südtiroler Volkspartei — SVP
(South Tyrol People's Party)

Headquarters	:	Brennerstrasse 7/A 39100 Bozen (Bolzano) (tel: 0471/974484 or 974485)
Party Leader	:	Dr Silvius Magnago
General Secretary	:	Dr Bruno Hosp
Youth organization	:	*Junge Generation in de SVP* (founded 1979)

Women's organization : *Frauenbewegung*
(founded 1978)
Publication : *Volksbote*
Membership : 80,000
Founded : 1945

History

The party was founded on May 8, 1945. Its main purpose was to request self-determination for the South Tyrol from the Allied powers. Within four months of its foundation the party already had 50,000 members, around a quarter of the entire German-speaking population.

When the Allies refused to allow the South Tyrol to rejoin Austria the SVP helped to organize big popular demonstrations. The party also lobbied strongly against the Austrian government's decision to request border alterations so that part of South Tyrol only would rejoin Austria. This was eventually also rejected by the Allies.

During the negotiations which led to the Paris Treaty the Austrian delegation included top advisers from the SVP. While the final results clearly fell far short of their demands, they accepted them as the only solution in the circumstances.

The SVP could do nothing to change the Italian government's subsequent decision to include the South Tyrol within a wider Trentino region but obtained a few improvements to the statute. In the first provincial elections in late 1948 the SVP obtained 67.8 per cent of the votes and 13 out of 20 seats. Italian parties won all the seats in the parallel provincial elections in Trento so that Italian-speaking parties ended up with 32 of the 45 seats on the first regional council. The SVP members decided, however, to work in co-operation with the Christian Democratic members of the council.

After the departure of Erich Amonn as leader, the SVP changed leaders in rather quick succession with six leadership changes between 1948 and 1957. Dissatisfaction with the failure to implement the Treaty of Paris led to major changes at the party conference in 1957. No less than 11 of the candidates named by the executive committee for the new party leadership were defeated. Dr Silvius Magnago was elected as party chairman, a position he has now retained for 31 years. Three years later he became the provincial president as well, which he has also retained until 1984. Dr Magnago's role has been decisive in pushing consistently for greater autonomy, but within the bounds of the politically practicable.

The late 1950s and early 1960s were a period of great tension, with the SVP withdrawing its

representatives from the regional government and with the onset of terrorist attacks.

Finally, a compromise package was negotiated with Dr Magnago as its "father". A large minority within the SVP did not feel that the compromise went far enough — and the package and the timetable for its implementation were only adopted by the party's ruling committee by 41 votes in favour to 23 against with two abstentions. The vote was even closer at the party conference that was convened at Merano to ratify the compromise. Dr Magnago put his prestige behind the compromise, which was still only narrowly won by 583 votes to 492, with 15 abstentions.

Since the adoption of the new autonomy statute, the SVP has remained the overwhelmingly dominant party in South Tyrol politics. In the 1987 national elections it won 58.3 per cent of the vote and provides three of the five deputies from the province, two of the three senators and a member of the European Parliament.

Support

In the nine provincial elections that have been held since 1948 the SVP has only twice dropped below 60 per cent of the vote. Considering that the total German-speaking population in the province is not much above that figure (64.9 per cent in 1981) it is clear that the SVP has received the support of the vast majority of the German-speaking community.

Regional variations in the SVP's vote have thus primarily reflected the number of German speakers (and also Ladin speakers, since they have not had their own party and have generally supported the SVP). Thus, the SVP is at its weakest in Bolzano (Bozen) where it got only 20 per cent in the last communal election, less than the MSI, and gets almost 100 per cent support in many of the rural communes. A high percentage of its electorate has consisted of farmers, and the rural community is general.

Organization

The SVP is a mass party with around 80,000 members. Each member belongs to a local branch based on one of the 116 communes in the South Tyrol or on a smaller unit when these communes are themselves sub-divided into "*Fraktionen*": in the latter case a co-ordinating committee of all the local branches is set up at commune-wide level. There are seven district groups and each has a chairman, a district committee and a district executive.

At the provincial level, there is a party committee, a party executive and a party praesidium, consisting of the party chairman and deputy chairman, the provincial secretary and one representative of the district chairman. The provincial conference elects the chairman and the deputy chairman and also approves the party programme, which it must do with a two-thirds majority. Party officers have three-year terms.

The party can establish various advisory bodies at all levels in particular to represent the special interests of workers, the professions and farmers. The constitution now also provides for separate women's and youth organizations within the SVP, the *Südtiroler Frauenbewegung*, the South Tyrol Women's Movement, founded in 1975, and the *Junge Generation in der SVP*, founded in 1970.

One distinctive feature of the party's constitution is the special provision that it provides for the Ladin speakers, who, in spite of the greater similarity of the Ladin language to Italian than to German, have made political common cause with the German speakers and with the SVP. The Ladin-speaking area, which crosses the borders of two districts, has two area chairmen and two reserved places on the SVP party committee. In addition, one of the SVP's four deputy chairmen must be a Ladin speaker, as must one member of the provincial assembly.

The party's candidates for the Italian Chamber of Deputies and Senate, as well as for the provincial assembly, are chosen by the party committee from nominations submitted by the seven district committees. At provincial assembly level, two-thirds of the nominations submitted by the district committee are binding on the party committees.

The party's newspaper is called the *Volksbote*.

The SVP's representative in the European Parliament sits with the European People's Party. The SVP is also a permanent observer at the European Democratic Union. It has a sister party in the Trentino, the *Trentino Tiroler Volkspartei* (TTVP).

Policies

The party's original objective was the reunification of the North and South Tyrol. In this it has failed, although closer links between the Austrian and Italian Tyrol have been achieved through such means as joint sittings of the provincial assemblies. The party's guiding programme, adopted in 1972, now recognizes that the South Tyrol cannot achieve independence and sets out the party's main objectives as the protection of the rights of German and Ladin-speaking South Tyrolers within the Italian state.

On the other hand, the party's programme expresses strong support for a federal Europe as long as the individuality both of nations and of the minority peoples within those nations are properly safeguarded. It also seeks the establishment of a special Alpine region within a federal Europe. Within the Italian parliament the SVP has recently put forward a draft law for Italy to evolve into a federal state, with the present Italian Senate becoming a Senate of the regions.

The party's economic and social policies are of a conservative Christian Democratic nature with a strong family policy and the achievement of a social market economy as basic principles in the party programme.

The SVP is generally more conservative however, than the Italian Christian Democratic Party and looks less kindly, for example, on any co-operation with the Communist Party.

Personalities

The dominating personality within the party has been Dr Silvius Magnago, who has been its leader since 1957 and the provincial president from 1960 to 1989. His first deputy, Dr Alfons Benedikter, has also served in the role since 1960 and has been one of South Tyrol's representatives in all international talks on its status.

From 1989 the new provincial president is Dr Durnwalder, a party vice-chairman and former director of the South Tyrolean Farmers' League, who has been responsible for farming questions on the provincial council.

Since the European Parliament was first directly elected in 1979, Dr Joachim Dalsass has been the SVP's representative.

Wahlverband des Heimatbundes — WdH
(Electoral Association of the Fatherland Front)

This is the political wing of the *Südtiroler Heimatbund*, a pressure group representing the most uncompromising wing of German-speaking nationalism in the South Tyrol. It advocates a free state of South Tyrol.

In the 1983 national elections the *Wahlverband des Heimatbundes* stood in an electoral alliance with the PDU (see below under *Freiheitliche Partei Südtirols*) and obtained 4.2 per cent of the vote, not winning a seat on its own, but costing the SVP a fourth seat in the Chamber.

In the 1983 provincial elections the *Wahlverband* stood on its own, and obtained 2.5 per cent and one seat in the *Landtag*, that of Dr Eva Klotz.

In the 1987 national elections it again stood on its own, and polled 3.6 per cent of the vote.

Freiheitliche Partei Südtirols — FPS
(Freedom Party of South Tyrol)

In the 1972 national elections a former SVP member of parliament, Hans Dietl, stood under the label *Wahlverband der Unabhangigen* (Electoral Association of Independents), and only narrowly missed election to the Senate, winning over 20 per cent in the Brixen *Wahlverband* and formed the *Sozialdemokratische Partei Südtirols* (see separate entry) in October, 1972.

The *Wahlverband* then changed its name to the *Partei der Unabhangigen* (The Party of Independents) (PDU). It campaigned for the defence of the interests of German and Ladin speakers in the South Tyrol but above all it represented a protest against the performance and political dominance of the SVP in the South Tyrol.

In the 1973 provincial elections it obtained 1.1 per cent and no seat but in 1978 it won its first seat in the *Landtag*, with 1.3 per cent of the vote. In 1983 its vote rose to 2.4 per cent and it again gained one seat in the *Landtag*, that of Gerold Meraner, who was the party chairman from 1978 to 1983.

In the 1983 national elections it stood in an electoral alliance with the *Wahlverband der Heimatbundes*, an alliance which was not repeated in the 1987 national elections. In May 1987, the PDU renamed itself as the *Freiheitliche Partei Südtirols* (FPS)

Socialdemokratische Partei Südtirols — SPS
(Social Democratic Party of South Tyrol)

Headquarters : Nicolodistrasse 30,
39100 Bozen
(Bolzano)
Chairman : Albert Januth

This party was founded in 1972 by Hans Dietl, a former SVP member of parliament, who had then stood for the Senate under the label of the *Wahlverband der Unabhangigen*. In the provincial elections of 1973 it obtained 5.1 per cent and two seats in the *Landtag*. In the 1978 provincial elections its vote fell to 2.2 per cent and it only retained one seat. Its elected member subsequently joined the SVP provincial parliament group. In 1983, the SPS further declined, polling 1.35 per cent and winning no seats in the *Landtag*.

The South Tyrol alternative movements

Since the 1970s there has been a Green Alternative Movement in the South Tyrol which has sought to involve Germans, Italian and Ladin speakers in a common political cause, rejecting narrow ethnic nationalism and seeking to focus political attention on environmental, peace and other issues. Its most prominent personality has been Dr Alexander Langer.

In 1978 Langer helped to found the list *Neue Linke/Nuova Sinistra* (New Left), which won 3.65 per cent and one seat in the *Landtag* in the 1978 provincial elections.

In the 1983 provincial election, however, Langer stood under the new label ALFAS, *Alternative Liste für das Andere Südtirol* (Alternative List for Another South Tyrol), which obtained 4.5 per cent and two seats in the *Landtag*.

In the 1987 national elections ALFAS did not put up candidates. A *Lista Verde/Grune Liste* (Green List) stood instead in conjunction with other Green Lists throughout Italy. In an electoral alliance with Socialists, Social Democrats and Radicals, the *Grune Liste* managed to elect one of its members to the Italian Senate, Dr Gianni Lanzinger, an elected representative of ALFAS on the Bolzano Communal Council.

Trentino

Partito Popolare Trentino Tirolese/Trentine Tiroler Volkspartei — TTVP

Headquarters : Via Gazzoletti 15,
38100 Trento
General secretary : Dr Heinrich Pruner

This is the sister party of the SVP (see South Tyrol) among the German-speaking minority in the predominantly Italian-speaking province of Trento. It currently has two members in the Trento provincial parliament. It is a full member of the European Democratic Union (unlike the SVP, which is a permanent observer).

In the 1987 elections it made an electoral alliance with the UATT in Trento and with SVP.

Unione Autonomista Trentino-Tirolese/ Autonomistenunion — UATT

This group has three members of the Trento provincial parliament. In the 1987 elections it made an electoral alliance with the TTVP and with the SVP.

Sardinia

Sardinia is the second largest island in the Mediterranean after Sicily, and has a population of 1.6 million. It has a distinctive history and culture and its own language, Sard, which is closer to Latin than any other Romance language. There are also two linguistic minorities on the island, a group of Catalan speakers in the town of Alghero and a group of *Tabarchino* speakers (based on an old Genoese dialect) in the two communes of Carloforte and Calasetta.

Since 1948 Sardinia has had its own special statute of regional autonomy. Autonomist sentiments, strong in the immediate aftermath of World War I, have been rekindled in recent years, and there is substantial support on the island for greater autonomy from Italy, or even full independence.

Partito Sardo d'Azione — Partidu Sardu — PSd'A
(Sardinian Action Party)

Headquarters	: Via Roma 75, 09100 Cagliari
President of national council	: Michele Columbu
National secretary	: Carlo Sanna
Youth organization	: *Movimento Giovanile*
Publication	: *Il Solco*
Members	: 12,000
Founded	: 1921

History

The cause of Sardinian autonomy developed strongly among Sards fighting for Italy in World War I especially among those in the *Brigata Sassari* (Sassari Brigade). At the end of the war a veterans' association was established which took on a strong Sardinian autonomist character. The *Partito di Combattenti* won three deputies in elections in 1919. On April 16, 1921 the *Partito Sardo d'Azione* was formally established, calling for the creation of a federal Italy. In the 1921 elections it won four deputies.

In the 1924 elections it won 17 per cent of the Sardinian vote, polling particularly well in rural areas. In 1926, however, it was dissolved by the Fascist government, with its leaders having to operate clandestinely or in exile.

After the fall of Fascism the party played a central role in helping to obtain a special statute of regional autonomy for Sardinia. In the elections for the constituent assembly it polled 14.9 per cent, and became the second party in Sardinia.

In 1948, however, the party suffered a disastrous schism between those who put their emphasis on nationalism and others, including its most celebrated leader, Emilio Lussu, who emphasized socialism. Lussu then left the party and created a rival *Partito Sardo Socialista d'Azione* (Sardinian Socialist Action Party), which won 6.6 per cent and three seats at the 1948 regional elections compared to 10 per cent and seven seats for the parent party. Lussu's new party was short-lived and by 1949 had joined up with the Socialist Party, but lasting damage had been done to the Sardinian nationalist cause.

The PSd'A took part as a junior partner in a series of Sardinian regional government coalitions with the dominant Christian Democrats and with the Social Democrats. In 1967 there were further divisions within the party. In 1968 the party again began to call for stronger autonomy leading to independence. The party's long decline continued. From three seats in 1969 in the regional assembly, its vote dropped to its lowest ever figure of 3.1 per cent in the 1974 regional elections, and only one seat in the assembly. In 1975 there was yet another schism.

In the late 1970s the party began a slow recovery although it still only had 3.4 per cent and three regional councillors in the 1979 regional elections. At its 1981 congress the party formally put independence and federalism within its statutes. In the 1983 national elections, it won 9.5 per cent of the Sardinian vote in the Italian chamber elections and 9.1 per cent in the Italian Senate elections, winning one deputy and one senator respectively. In the 1984 European elections it forged an alliance with the *Union Valdôtaine* and other Italian national and regional minority parties. This list obtained 12.7 per cent of the Sardinian vote and respectable votes elsewhere in Italy, and Michele Columbu of the PSd'A was elected to the European Parliament. In the Sardinian regional elections a few weeks later the party obtained 13.8 per cent of the vote and 12 out of the 81 Sardinian regional councillors. It was subsequently able to form a coalition with the Communist Party with the external support of the Socialists, and Mario Melis became the first member of the party to head the Sardinian regional government. In January 1985 a separate Sardinian trade union confederation was established, the *Confederazione Sindicale Sarda* (CSS).

In the 1985 local elections the PSd'A continued its advance with 15.2 per cent of the vote. Mario Melis subsequently formed a second and broader-based Sardinian regional government with the help of four other parties. In the 1987 national elections the PSd'A polled 11.9

per cent of the Sardinian vote in the Chamber elections and 14.2 per cent in the Senate elections, obtaining two deputies and one senator respectively.

Besides the presidency, the PSd'A holds two other seats within the Sardinian regional government. It has 375 local councillors and 18 mayors.

Support

Within the four Sardinian provinces the PSd'A has generally been strongest in Cagliari and Oristano, and slightly weaker in Sassari and especially Nuoro. As a general rule it has been stronger in the larger towns and more industrialized communities, and along the coast, and weaker in the smaller towns and in the interior of the island. Among its strongest areas of support have been the districts of Montiferru (17.9 per cent in both the European and regional elections of 1984), Teulada, the mining area of Iglesiente and Oristano. It has also polled well in the city of Cagliari (15.8 per cent in the 1984 regional elections). The party points out that it has polled better in areas where Sardinian culture and traditions have been disrupted than where they have remained more intact.

Organization

The PSd'A currently has around 12,000 members. It has 286 local sections, each of which must have a minimum of 20 members. The sections are normally organized within individual communes, and can also be subdivided into nuclei with no less than 10 members or combined into inter-sectional co-ordinating groups.

Above these are the seven federations. Where there is more than one federation in a province a co-ordinating group can also be established.

At Sardinian level there is a national congress, which meets every three years and at which only delegates of the sections have voting rights. The national congress elects the national council of 71 members, by proportional representation on the basis of separate lists. The national council elects the party's national secretary, president, vice-president and also the 14 to 16 members of the party's national executive, which meets every two months. For everyday business there is also a smaller central secretariat (*Ufficio di Segreteria*) of five members.

The party has established a youth movement (*Movimento Giovanile*) open to 14–18 year olds. It also has close links with the new Sardinian trade union confederation, the *Confederazione Sindacale Sarda* (CSS).

The party's newspaper is called *Il Solco*. There is also a monthly publication produced by

the party's regional council group called *Forza Paris*.

The PSd'A is a member of the European Free Alliance. In the 1984 European elections its candidate was at the head of a list with other Italian national and regional minority parties, including the *Union Valdôtaine*, the *Movimento Autonomista Occitano*, and the *Unione Slovena*. He was elected and has been a member of the Rainbow Group in the European Parliament. The party is also active in the *Ufficio delle Communita Etniche e Nazionali dello Stato Italiano* (Bureau of Ethnic and National Communities within the Italian State).

Policies

The PSd'A calls for an independent Sardinia within the framework of a federal Europe of its peoples and not of the existing nation states. It would also like to see the establishment of a second European Chamber of the Regions.

The party seeks the attainment of independence through democratic and non-violent means. It recognizes that it will have to be achieved in stages, and its current main emphasis is on far-reaching revision of the existing Sardinian statute of regional autonomy. It has recently submitted a draft text to this effect which describes Sardinia as a nation, and calls for a federal Italy. It seeks more executive powers to be transferred to the region, and for voting rights within Sardinia to be confined to those who have either been born in Sardinia or resident for four years within it. The Sardinian language would have the same status as Italian, and there would also be protection for the linguistic rights of the Catalan-speaking minority in Alghero, and the Tabarchino (Genoese) minority in Carloforte and Calasetta. The region would have its own finances, and no new military installations could be constructed on the island without the region's consent. Any disputes between the region and Italian government should be submitted to a special section of the Italian Constitutional Court consisting of five Italian government nominees and five Regional nominees.

The PSd'A has been particularly critical of the neo-colonial status of the Sardinian economy, and the exploitation of Sardinian resources by outside speculators. The party has also long advocated the creation of a free zone within Sardinia for customs purposes. It seeks the reopening and redevelopment of Sardinian mines. It would like more preference to be given to Sards in exams for public posts and advocates the creation of a special Sard university. It is highly critical of the existing military presence in Sardinia, and seeks the dismantling of military bases. It has advocated the abolition of existing prefectures and provinces.

The PSd'A has strongly defended the rights of other Italian ethnic minorities, and its Senator in Rome, for example, has sponsored a bill for the protection of the rights of Slovenes within Italy.

Personalities

The party's national secretary is Carlo Sanna, who is also a member of the Italian Chamber of Deputies. The president of its national council and also member of the European Parliament has been Michele Columbu. Mario Melis has been regional president, and Francesco Puligheddu chairman of the regional assembly group. Giovanni Columbu is its other deputy and Giovanni Loi its senator.

Val D'Aosta

Val D'Aosta is the smallest Italian region, 3,262 square kms in area and with a population of around 110,000. It is traditionally French-speaking (a France-Provençal dialect) although waves of immigration from other parties of Italy, and periodic repression of the French language (notably under Mussolini) have now given it an Italian-speaking majority. Since 1948 it has been one of the five Italian regions enjoying a special statute of autonomy, although this was far less ambitious than the autonomy statute drafted the year before by the Aostans themselves in their valley council.

The Val D'Aosta has elections every five years for its regional parliament of 35 members, which then chooses the regional junta. The small German-speaking community (*Walser*) has its own limited local autonomy ("mountain community").

The largest political party in the Val D'Aosta is a purely regional party, the *Union Valdôtaine*. There is also a smaller regional party, the *Autonomistes-Democrates-Progressistes* (ADP).

Union Valdôtaine

Headquarters	:	29 Ave des Maquisards, 11100 Aosta, Valle D'Aosta (tel: 0165 41120 or 32532)
President	:	Alexis Betemps
Secretary-general	:	Leonard Tamone

Youth organization	:	*Jeunesse Valdôtaine* (secretary — Andre Vuillermaz)
Women's organization	:	*Entraide des Femmes Valdôtaines* (Josephine Gerard)
Publication	:	*Le Peuple Valdôtain*
Membership	:	4,000
Founded	:	1945

History

The predecessors of *Union Valdôtaine* in fighting for the French language and for defence of Aosta traditions and culture included the *Ligue Valdôtaine*, founded in 1909, and *Jeune Vallée d'Aosta*, founded in the 1920s. Prominent Resistance leaders came from these groups, such as Emile Chanoux, who advocated federalism on the Swiss model, and who died in a Fascist prison in 1944.

After the war a large number of Aostans sought a change in their political status, whether annexation by Switzerland or France or a much higher degree of autonomy within Italy. On Sept. 13, 1945, the *Union Valdôtaine* was founded, as a movement rather than a political party, and including personalities from the left, right and centre of the political spectrum.

In the 1946 communal elections it took control of 26 of the then 73 Aostan communes, and pushed hard for the development of an Aostan statute of autonomy.

In the 1948 national elections it did not put up its own candidates and supported Christian Democratic candidates, who then appeared to be most sympathetic to demands for greater autonomy. In 1949 the alliance between the *Union Valdôtaine* and the Christian Democrats was victorious in the first regional elections, and *Union Valdôtaine's* leading personality, Severin Caveri (who had been the second president of the valley council, and was to remain party president until 1973) became the first president of the regional *junta* or government.

In 1954 the *Union Valdôtaine*/Christian Democratic alliance broke up, and in the subsequent regional elections on a majority system *Union Valdôtaine* only won one of the 35 seats, although it gained 28 per cent of the vote. *Union Valdôtaine* was then completely marginalized until 1958, when it forged a new alliance with the Communists and Socialists, and its candidates were elected to the Chamber of Deputies and to the Senate. In 1959 the so-called "Lion" coalition between the *Union Valdôtaine*, Communists, Socialists and Social Democrats narrowly won the regional election, and the Christian Democratic government was replaced by one presided over by Marcoz of

Union Valdôtaine. In the first regional elections carried out by proportional representation in 1963, the coalition kept its hold on power.

In 1966, however, the coalition collapsed when the Socialists withdrew, and a new centre-left regional government was formed under Christian Democratic control.

Union Valdôtaine remained in opposition until 1974. Although it should have been helped by a split within the Christian Democrats which led to the creation in 1970 of a Christian Social party, the *Democrates Populaires*, it was itself harmed by a series of internal schisms.

In 1972 a number of members left the party to form the *Union Valdôtaine Progressiste* (UVP), and other small and more radical separatist groups were also founded. These latter were of no electoral consequence, but in the 1973 regional elections the autonomous vote was split three ways between the *Union Valdôtaine* (which only won 11.6 per cent of the vote and four of the 35 seats), the UVP (which won two seats) and a third party, the *Rassemblement Valdôtain*, which won one seat.

This poor result spurred attempts to reunify the autonomist parties. In 1974 a pact between the three parties brought Andrione of the *Union Valdôtaine* to the presidency of the regional government, with the support of the Christian Democrats and Socialists. The *Union Valdôtaine* has since held the presidency of the regional government until the present day.

In December 1976 the *Union Valdôtaine, Rassemblement Valdôtain* and the UVP were reunified into one party, although a minority within the UVP remained outside. *Union Valdôtaine* has since consolidated itself as the largest single political force within the Val D'Aosta, in spite of a crisis caused by the collapse of the Andrione government in 1983 over irregularities at the casino in St. Vincent. The presidency remained, however, in the hands of *Union Valdôtaine*, under Auguste Rollandin.

In the last regional elections in 1988, *Union Valdôtaine* won 12 out of the 35 seats and 34.2 per cent of the vote. It has also gained considerable votes in European elections. It failed to win a seat in the 1979 elections, but in the 1984 elections it forged an alliance with the *Partito Sardo d'Azione* and other small regional parties (the *Movimento Friuli*, the *Movimento Autonomista Occitano*, and the *Slovenska Skupnost*) which managed to get one member elected from the *Partito Sardo d'Azione*. He was supposed to stand down in 1987 in favour of a representative from *Union Valdôtaine*, but this was postponed.

In the 1987 Italian elections the *Union Valdôtaine* fought in an electoral alliance with the ADP and with the Italian Republican Party. The alliance won 55 per cent of the Aostan vote, and obtained a deputy and senator, who sit in the Mixed Group in the Parliament.

Support

Exact party support is difficult to calculate because of the shifting series of electoral coalitions which characterize Aostan politics, and because it stands in European elections as part of a coalition of regional parties throughout Italy. The best indication is in regional elections where *Union Valdôtaine* gained 27.3 per cent in 1983 and 34.2 per cent in 1988.

The *Union Valdôtaine* is stronger outside the city of Aosta.

Organization

The *Union Valdôtaine* still calls itself a movement rather than a party, although no-one belonging to another party or movement can become a member.

Its 4,000 members are organized into 71 sections (out of 74 communes in the Val D'Aosta). There are two sections within the City of Aosta. Subsections can also be formed. The national congress is held every five years (the first was only held in 1979). At the last national congress there were 341 delegates elected by the communes on the basis of the votes won by *Union Valdôtaine* at the last regional elections. The national congress elects the president and the secretary-general, by absolute majority on the first round or by simple majority thereafter.

The central committee meets at least every four months and includes parliamentarians, regional councillors and representatives of affiliated organizations as well as delegates chosen by the sections. Special provisions are made for two representatives of the German-speaking Walser community. The central committee has to ratify electoral lists for regional, Italian and European elections.

The executive committee consists of 20 members, and is chosen by the central committee. It is served by a headquarters staff which currently has five full-time staff (three administrators and two secretaries).

On special occasions there can also be national delegates conferences to examine particular policy matters.

Among the movement's affiliated organizations are a youth group, a women's group, and a liaison group of party administrators, *Conference des Administrateurs de l'Union Valdôtaine*. There is also a regional trade union, the

Syndicat Autonome des Travailleurs Valdôtains (SAVT).

The party newspaper was originally called *Union Valdôtaine*, but was closed after a conflict over its name in 1953, and relaunched under its present name *le Peuple Valdôtain*.

Union Valdôtaine puts strong emphasis on its links with other regional and ethnic minority parties in the rest of Italy and Europe. It is a member of the European Free Alliance, and participated in the last European elections in a common list with other Italian regional parties. Its links in the European Parliament are with the Rainbow Group.

Policies

The *Union Valdôtaine* sees as its primary tasks the defence of the ethnic character of the Val D'Aosta and of its regional, social and economic interests, promotion of the French language at all levels and the furthering of co-operation between ethnic communities throughout Europe. Its ultimate aim is full self-determination for the Val D'Aosta within a federal Europe. In the more immediate term it seeks full implementation of the 1948 statute of autonomy, especially the creation of a duty-free zone in the Val D'Aosta which was promised but never implemented. In 1984 the *Union Valdôtaine* collected 23,000 signatures in the valley in protest at this non-implementation of the duty-free zone. The *Union Valdôtaine* also proposed a modification of the statute to provide for full recognition of the rights of the small German-speaking minority. It also wants full rights to formulate regional electoral law, rights provided to other Italian regions with a special statute, but not the Val D'Aosta. Finally it seeks transformation of the Italian Senate into a Chamber of the Regions.

Union Valdôtaine is a strong advocate of administrative decentralization, and of enhanced popular participation in government through assemblies, referenda, etc. It seeks greater powers over regional planning and prides itself on having promoted a law providing for town planning and protection of the local environment, one of the first such laws in Italy when passed in 1962.

Union Valdôtaine is an extremely active member of the European Free Alliance, and defender of the rights of all European ethnic minorities. In 1983 *Jeunesse Valdôtaine* sponsored a demonstration in favour of the H-Block hunger strikers in Northern Ireland.

Personalities

The party's president is Alexis Betemps and its secretary-general is Leonard Tamone. Its deputy in the Italian Chamber is Luciano Caveri, a 30-year-old journalist who is a nephew of the former nationalist leader Severin Caveri.

Autonomistes–Democrates–Progressistes — ADP

(Progressive Democratic Autonomists)

This is a small Aostan regional party, which was allied with the Republicans and *Union Valdôtaine* in the 1987 national elections. In the 1988 regional elections it won four seats on 11 per cent of the vote.

Other Italian regionalist parties

Besides the larger regional parties in South Tyrol, Val d'Aosta and Sardinia, there are a number of other regionalist parties, some defending particular linguistic minorities (the *Movimento Autonomista Occitano*, the *Movimento Friuli*, etc.), and others defending regional identity in reaction against the central government in Rome, and against immigrants from Southern Italy. Parties in this latter category include the *Lega Lombarda* (currently the most successful), the *Liga Veneta* and *Piemônt*.

(i) Lombardy

Lega Lombarda
(Lombard League)

Secretary : Umberto Bossi

History

The *Lega Lombarda* was founded in 1986 by a former medical student, Umberto Bossi. In 1987 it stood on a Lombard nationalist platform in the national elections, winning 190,000 votes in Lombardy and obtaining one member in the Chamber of Deputies and one in the senate. In the 1988 local elections the *Lega Lombarda* consolidated its support, and won a considerable number of council seats in different parts of Lombardy.

Support

The *Lega Lombarda* now claims to have 10,000 members. In the 1987 national elections it performed best in the northern Lombard constituency of Como–Sondrio–Varese, where it obtained 6.7 per cent of the vote and its parliamentary seats. It was particularly strong in the city of Varese (over 7 per cent), in the city of Como, and in the region of the Brianza, north of Milan. It also did well around Bergamo. It was much weaker in Milan itself (only 0.75 per cent) and in most of south Lombardy.

In the 1988 local elections it continued to poll well in northern Lombardy where it was often the fourth party. In Lecco, for example, it polled 7.62 per cent. Its highest vote was in the commune of Gandino in the valleys behind Bergamo, where it polled 22 per cent. The party also had an unexpected success in parts of southern Lombardy, such as Pavia, where its vote rose sharply from around 1 per cent to 5.6 per cent.

Policy

The *Lega Lombarda* is a populist regionalist party which has won much of its support on a platform criticizing the colonization of northern Italy by southern Italian immigrants. It wants to see the number of immigrants halted, and seeks preference for Lombards over southerners in getting jobs and obtaining housing. It is also highly critical of the central government in Rome. It wants 90 per cent of the taxes paid in Lombardy to the central government to be reinvested within Lombardy, and Lombardy to be given a special statute of autonomy like the Val d'Aosta. It seeks a regional call-up for military service and regional management of the pension system. it defends Lombard distinctiveness and dialect.

Personalities

The dominating figure within the *Lega Lombarda* is its founder and secretary, Umberto Bossi, who is the party's representative in the Italian Senate. Giuseppe Leone is the party's sole representative in the Chamber of Deputies.

(ii) Venice

Liga Veneta

This regionalist party defends the identity and autonomy of the Veneto, and has been critical of the impacts of southern immigration into northern Italy. In the 1983 national elections it won substantial support (4.5 per cent in Venezia–Treviso, 4 per cent in Verona–Padova–Vicenza–Rovigo) and obtained one seat in the Chamber of Deputies, as well as one Senator. It has since been severely divided (six schisms in the last five years). Its vote has declined in successive elections, and it lost its seats in the Italian Parliament in the 1987 elections,

when it obtained 3.3 per cent of the Chamber vote in Venezia–Treviso, and 2.9 per cent in Verona–Padova–Vicenza–Rovigo. In the 1989 local elections it won 2 per cent in Belluno province. Its leader is Franco Rocchetta.

Unione del Popolo Veneto

This is a small regionalist party, which polled poorly in the 1988 local elections.

(iii) Friuli–Venezia–Giulia

Movimento Per Trieste

This movement (known familiarly as "melone" or "melon") was founded in protest against certain provisions of the 1975 Treaty of Osimo, in which Italy renounced its claims to Trieste's hinterland. It defends the separate interests of the city of Trieste within the Friuli region. In the 1979 parliamentary elections the movement (which included candidates from several parties) emerged as the strongest group in the city of Trieste with 27.4 per cent of the vote, and it gained one seat in the Chamber. The Trieste List gained 19.7 per cent in 1983, although its seat was lost. In the 1987 elections it did not put up its own candidates. It has also won seats in the Friuli–Venezia–Giulia regional council.

Movimento Friuli

Headquarters   : 33100 Udine
President   : Roberto Jacovissi

The *Movimento Friuli* (*Moviment Friul* in Friulian) first became active in the late 1960s. In 1968 it gained three seats on the regional council, where it has subsequently retained representation. It contested the European Parliament elections in 1984 as part of a regionalist alliance headed by the *Partito Sardo d'Azione*, and the *Union Valdôtaine*. In the 1987 national elections it polled 1.6 per cent in the Chamber constituency of Udine–Belluno–Gorizia–Pordenone, down from 3.3 per cent in 1983.

The *Movimento Friuli* calls for increased autonomy for Friuli, and defends the Friulian culture and language (which is related to Rhaeto–Romarsch).

Slovenska Skupnost

This group defends the interest of the Slovene minority, and fought the 1984 European elections as part of the regionalist alliance, headed by the *Partito Sardo d'Azione*.

(iv)   Piedmont

Piemônt

This is a similar party to the *Lega Lombarda* (with whom it has common electoral lists in some communes), but has been much less successful. It calls for defence of the Piedmont identity and dialect. It advocates preference for Piedmontese in public posts and is anti-Rome and anti-southerners. Its leader is Roberto Gemmo, a provincial councillor who only gives interviews in dialect.

Piemônt Autonomia Regionale

This is another small regionalist party, led by Gipo Farassino, a singer.

Movimento Autonomista Occitano — MAO
(Occitan Autonomist Movement)

This movement defends the Occitan (provençal) culture and language that is still maintained in some of the Alpine Valleys of Piedmont. It fought the 1984 European elections as part of the regionalist alliance headed by the *Partito Sardo d'Azione*.

Luxembourg

Francis Jacobs

The country

Luxembourg is a country of under 1,000 square miles (smaller than any of the states in the USA) with a population of approximately 365,000 (1983). Around 96 per cent of the population is Catholic. A quarter of the population live in the capital city, Luxembourg, and the main other centres of population are in the old industrial region in the south. The linguistic situation is complex. Legal and cultural matters tend to be written in French, and most others in German. The spoken language, however, is Lëtzebürgish, a West Middle German dialect with a few French words, whose use is becoming increasingly widespread as the main way in which Luxembourgish identity is expressed.

Map of Luxembourg showing 4 parliamentary constituencies and number of seats in each, and the cantons.

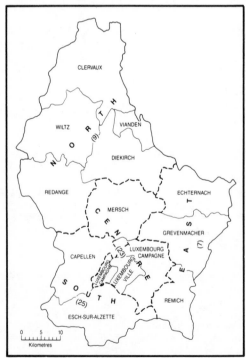

Source: adapted from *World Atlas of Elections*.

Some 26 per cent of the resident population are foreigners, with the two dominant groups being the Portuguese and the Italians.

Political institutions

Luxembourg is a constitutional monarchy. The head of state is the hereditary Grand Duke, whose powers are great in theory, but very limited in practice.

The Chamber of Deputies consists of 64 members, elected every five years, by proportional representation (Hagenbach-Bischoff) in four constituencies, the number of whose members are proportionate to their population (Centre: 23 deputies, South: 25, North: nine, East: seven). A peculiarity of the Luxembourgish political system is its powerful Council of State of 21 nominated members, which not only has extensive administrative and judicial powers, but in the absence of a second chamber of parliament, has a major legislative role as well: no law can be voted by the Chamber of Deputies before the Council of State has given its opinion. Deputies cannot be members of the government.

Luxembourg is divided administratively into three districts, 12 cantons and 118 communes. Municipal elections are held every six years, in the larger communes by proportional representation, elsewhere by majority vote.

A further distinctive feature of the Luxembourg institutional structure is the important role played not only by the tripartite Economic and Social Committee, but also by the six professional chambers (three employers' organizations and three of employees), which are consulted on all laws affecting them.

Finally Luxembourg has six members in the European Parliament, one member for around 60,000 people, the lowest percentage in the European Community.

Brief political history

1815   Luxembourg becomes autonomous Grand Duchy as part of the Germanic Confederation (with a Prussian garrison in the capital) but under the personal rule of William I of the Orange Nassau Dynasty of the Netherlands. Much of Eastern Luxembourg is ceded to the Prussians.

1839 French-speaking Western region of Luxembourg is annexed to the newly independent state of Belgium.

1841 William II grants Luxembourg its first Constitution, which gives it administrative autonomy. Progressive Liberals and Catholics begin to challenge "doctrinaire" Liberals in power.

1848 William II grants Luxembourg a more liberal constitution, guaranteeing many basic liberties and the separation of powers.

1856 More conservative Constitution introduced, which also creates the Council of State.

1867 Luxembourg almost sold to France. Compromise reached, whereby France renounces any claim to Luxembourg, Prussian garrison is withdrawn and Luxembourg becomes fully independent, demilitarized and neutral.

1868 More liberal Constitution again introduced, and is basis of current Luxembourg Constitution.

1890 Luxembourg gets its own independent dynasty when William III is succeeded in the Netherlands by Wilhelmina, and in Luxembourg by Adolf of Nassau.

1908 Anti-clerical bloc of the left between Socialists and certain Liberals. Period of *Kulturkampf* with Catholics, especially over 1912 education law.

1914 Occupation of Luxembourg by Germany. Grand Duchess Marie-Adelaide shows pro-German sympathies.

1919 Marie-Adelaide abdicates. Referendum held in which Luxembourg votes to remain a constitutional monarchy rather than become a republic and Marie-Adelaide's sister Charlotte is confirmed as Grand Duchess (reigning until 1964). Constitution revised, and universal suffrage and proportional representation are introduced. Luxembourg also leaves German *Zollverein*, votes to enter customs union with France but finally enters into an economic association with Belgium.

1919–37 Long period of Catholic Conservative dominance under Emile Reuter and Joseph Bech (at first on its own, and later in coalition with Liberals).

1937 Bech government narrowly defeated in referendum over *Maulkorbgesetz* ("muzzle law") that would have silenced

the far left, and was seen as a severe attack on civil liberties. Bech resigned and is replaced by another Catholic Conservative, Pierre Dupong. Socialists enter government coalition.

World Luxembourg occupied by Germans.
War II: Grand Duchess flees, and many Luxemburgers are forcibly conscripted into the German army.

1944 Political system again reconstituted but with two of the old parties (Catholics and Liberals) taking new forms.

1948 Constitutional revision ratifies Luxembourg's abandonment of its 80-year-old status of neutrality and its entry into the Western Alliance.

Main features of the current Luxembourg political system

Luxembourg is a small and homogeneous country, where there are no longer very sharp social differences among the native Luxembourg population. Both traditional cleavages, between left and right, and between lay and clerical values, are weaker than they used to be. There is also a long tradition of coalition governments (every government since 1925). In such a small country the impact of individual personalities has also been very great, and this has also been reflected in an electoral system in which there is a very high percentage of personal votes (in some cases exceeding the number of list votes for a party) and where *panachage* between different lists is also frequent.

There are, however, regional differences. The South constituency, with its steel plants and industrial working class has been the stronghold of the Socialist and of the much smaller Communist parties, and the Liberal Party has been very weak. The centre constituency, dominated by the capital city of Luxembourg, with its civil servants and service sector workers, has been competitive between all three main parties, and the Liberal Party has had its strongest implantation in this area. The North and East constituencies are the most rural areas of the country and although there are differences between them (the East has vineyards and is generally more fertile, the North has been the poorest and most isolated agricultural area), both have been dominated by the Christian Social People's Party, with the other two parties strong only in pockets. With modern communications and the decline of agriculture and of heavy industry these differences are being attenuated, but are

Luxembourg election results 1945–present (% of vote and number of seats)

Note 1: 1951 and 1954 elections not included because only partial—1948 in South and East constituencies only, 1951 in Centre and North.
Note 2: Percentages cited are not those of the gross vote. The latter would be misleading because a voter can cast between 7 and 25 votes according to the number of seats in a constituency.

	1945	1954	1959	1964	1968	1974	1979	1984
CSV/PCS	44.6%	45.2%	38.9%	35.6%	37.4%	29.9%	34.5%	34.8%
(Christian Democrats)	(25)	(26)	(21)	(22)	(21)	(18)	(24)	(25)
LSAP/POSL	23.3%	32.9%	33.0%	35.9%	30.9%	27.0%	24.3%	33.75%
(Socialists)	(11)	(17)	(17)	(21)	(18)	(17)	(14)	(21)
DP/PD	18.0%	12.2%	20.3%	12.2%	18.0%	23.3%	21.3%	18.5%
Democratic Party (Liberals)	(9)	(6)	(1)	(6)	(11)	(14)	(15)	(14)
KPL/PCL	11.1%	7.3%	7.2%	10.4%	13.1%	8.8%	5 %	5.1%
(Communists)	(5)	(3)	(3)	(5)	(6)	(5)	(2)	(2)
SDP/PSD	—	—	—	—	—	10.1%	6 %	—
(Social Democrats)						(5)	(2)	
Dei Greng Alternativ	—	—	—	—	—	—	—	5.2%
(Greens)								(2)
Others	3 %	2.3%	0.6%	5.9%	0.6%	0.9%	8.9%	2.6%
				(2)			(2)	(0)

still crucial in explaining Luxembourg political geography.

As a result of these factors Luxembourg has had a competitive three-party system, with the Communists as a significant fourth force only in the South. In the last three elections the three main parties have polled between 85 per cent and 90 per cent of the vote, and all government coalitions since the war have been between them. The lynchpin of the system has been the Christian Social People's Party, which has been the largest party, and which has provided the Prime Minister on all but one occasion since 1925 (the exception being 1974–79 when there was a Liberal-Socialist coalition). Each of the three main parties has had a distinctive policy emphasis; the Liberals on the need for a freer market, the Socialists on social measures, and the Christian Social People's Party on family policy and moral issues, but these have generally not impeded their co-operation on most core issues.

While these parties have dominated Luxembourg politics, it has also been relatively easy to start new political parties, although they have generally not been long-lasting. In recent years there has been a breakaway Social Democratic Party, which won seats in both 1974 and 1979, Independent Socialists who won a seat in 1979, and even a group *Les Enrolés de Force* to defend the interests of those forcibly conscripted into the German army in World War II, which also won a seat in 1979. In 1984 a Green party influenced by the German Greens, in particular,

won two seats in the Parliament, although it has since divided into two competing groups.

At local level the pattern is somewhat different. In some communes in the South there have even been Socialist-Communist coalitions. In most of the smaller communes, however, there is still a majority voting system in local elections, and independents rather than the national parties have played a much stronger role.

The current political issues in Luxembourg include the following:

Foreign immigration in Luxembourg: well over a quarter of the resident population in Luxembourg consists of foreign workers, and there are signs of a nationalist backlash against them. Particularly sensitive issues are adaptations of the country's educational system, to take account of immigrants, and voting rights for foreigners. All major parties were once agreed to concede such voting rights in local elections, but have since mainly withdrawn from their agreement. Luxembourg has been granted a temporary derogation from the proposed EC rules on this subject.

European issues: the major parties are all agreed in supporting further European integration leading to European Union. They are, however, very concerned about some of the implications for Luxembourg of the 1992 internal market, and, in particular, harmonization of excise duties which could have a very serious effect on the Luxembourg economy, which is highly dependent on cross-border shopping to take advantage of Luxembourg's very low duties.

Another issue is Luxembourg's future role as a centre for the European Community institutions. Luxembourg is lobbying hard to prevent the transfer of the European Parliament secretariat, and would also like to have other European institutions, such as the European Trademark Office or the possible European Central Bank.

Steel industry: the steel industry has in the past been Luxembourg's largest employer. As a result of co-operation between the major parties it has been relatively successfully restructured (although the Communists would still like to nationalise it), but its future development remains an issue in Luxembourg politics.

Financial services sector: for the first time this now employs more people than the steel industry. How this sector can be protected, and further stimulated, is an important issue.

Pensions: a highly topical issue is how best to reduce the discrepancies between the generous non-contributive pension system for public sector workers and the contributive pension system for private sector workers. Should there be a single system? How can any changes be financed?

"The third option": most areas of lay-clerical conflict have been greatly reduced (the last major conflict was over the liberalization of abortion in the 1970s). At present, however, there is a dispute over whether to maintain, restrict or abolish the so-called "third option", whereby children have been allowed to opt out of either religious instruction or an alternative course in lay ethics.

Media policy: an important issue because of the powerful position of RTL (Radio Luxembourg). Moreover there are no public radio and television stations in Luxembourg. Should they be created?

Civil nuclear energy: this is no longer a problem within Luxembourg (the 1970s attempt to build a nuclear power station at Remerschen in the Moselle Valley was eventually rejected), but the construction of the giant French nuclear power station at Cattenom a few miles away from the Luxembourg border has made this a subject of new sensitivity.

Defence policy: Luxembourg's membership of NATO is not at stake, but there is some dispute over the degree of its contribution. In particular should there be a third military camp in the North of Luxembourg?

Christlich-soziale Volkspartei (CSV)
Parti Chrétien Social Luxembourgeois (PCS)
(Luxembourg Christian Social People's Party)

Headquarters	: 38, rue du Curé, 1368 Luxembourg (tel: 2 57 31)
President	: Jean Spautz
Secretary general	: Guillaume Bourg
Chairman of parliamentary group	: François Colling
Youth group	: *Christlich Soziale Jugend* (CSJ)
Women's group	: *Christlich Soziale Frauen* (CSF)
Newspaper	: *Luxemburger Wort*
Membership	: 10,000
Founded	: 1914

History

Since World War I the Catholic political group has consistently been the largest in Luxembourg, and has provided the Prime Minister for 64 out of the last 69 years.

The first major Catholic political personality was Jean Theodore Laurent, apostolic vicar to Luxembourg in the years 1842 to 1848, who vigorously asserted the independence of the Church from the lay state, and also called for universal suffrage. He was withdrawn from Luxembourg in 1848 but in subsequent elections a Catholic Citizen's Association managed to win 10 out of the 51 seats in the Chamber. In the second half of the 19th century, however, Catholic Conservatives again became more dominant.

The first decade of the 20th century saw a rapid development of Catholic organizations. In 1903 a Catholic *Volksverein* was founded, and this soon had a mass membership. A Catholic teachers' association was founded in 1905, and Catholic workers' associations in 1906.

From 1908–1912 there was an intense period of *Kulturkampf* between lay and Catholic values, which culminated in the bitter debate over the new education law of 1912. Early in 1914 Catholic political forces finally managed to found their own political party, which took the name *Rechtspartei* or "Party of the Right" in order to attract wide support from Conservatives as well as from Catholic militants. In its first elections in 1914 it won 25 out of 52 seats.

In the turbulent period at the end of the war the Party of the Right strongly defended Luxembourg's independence and the retention of the existing Grand-Ducal dynasty, and its point of view prevailed in the 1919 referendum. In the subsequent national elections it won 52.8 per cent of the vote and 27 out of 48 seats in the Chamber. A single-party government was then formed by Emile Reuter. It was influenced by both Christian Social and corporatist ideas. In 1921 a Christian trade union, the *Letzebuerger Chreschtleche Gewerkschaftsbond* was formally founded. In 1924 a system of professional Chambers was introduced on corporatist principles.

In 1925 the Reuter government fell, and was replaced by a broad coalition of the opposition parties under Pierre Prum, but the Party of the Right again returned to power under Joseph Bech in 1926; this time in coalition with the Liberals. Bech remained as Prime Minister until 1937, when he was forced to resign after his narrow defeat in a popular referendum over his so-called "muzzle law" (*Maulkorbgesetz*), in which he had tried to clamp down on the far left.

Bech was replaced as Prime Minister by Pierre Dupong, from the Christian Social wing of the Party of the Right, whose new coalition partners were the Socialists. During World War II Dupong continued to lead the government in exile.

At the end of the war the party was rapidly re-established. The party itself first changed its name to the *Lëtzebuerger Chreschtlech-Sozial Volkspartei* and then in 1946 to its present name of *Christlich-Soziale Volkspartei* (CSV). In the 1945 elections the party won 25 out of 51 seats, and then participated in a short-lived National Unity government of all the main parties. From 1947 onwards the CSV was in power with the Liberals, and it was this government which brought Luxembourg into NATO. In 1951 the CSV switched coalition partners with the Socialists replacing the Liberals. In 1953 Pierre Dupong died after 16 years as Prime Minister, and Joseph Bech, who had played a key role as Luxembourg Foreign Minister (notably in procuring for Luxembourg the headquarters of the European Coal and Steel Community) again became Prime Minister, a post he was to retain until 1958. After the short-lived premiership of Pierre Frieden from 1958 to 1959 Pierre Werner then remained Prime Minister from 1959 to 1974, in coalition with the Liberals between 1959 and 1964, and from 1969 to 1974, and with the Socialists between 1964 and 1969. During this period Pierre Werner's name became associated with the Werner plan for European Economic and Monetary Union. In the 1976 elections the CSV had its worst election results since World War I, winning only 29.9 per cent of the vote and only 18 seats in the Chamber. It then went into opposition from 1974 to 1979, putting up

a particular struggle against the lay coalition's proposals to liberalize abortion.

In the 1979 national elections the CSV made a significant recovery to 34.5 per cent and 24 seats, and it won 36.2 per cent and three seats in the simultaneous European Parliament elections. Pierre Werner again became Prime Minister in coalition with the Liberals. In the 1984 national elections the CSV won 34.8 per cent and 25 seats, and 34.9 per cent and three seats in the European Parliament elections. Jacques Santer became the new Prime Minister, this time in a coalition between the CSV and the Socialists.

Support

Although less dominant than the Party of the Right was in the interwar years the CSV has continued to be the largest Luxembourg party in the years since 1945. It is absolutely dominant in two of the four constituencies, usually the largest in the third and consistently second only in the fourth. It has a broad social base, strongest of all in rural areas among agricultural workers, strong in middle-class areas in the towns and dormitory communities and with a significant, if lower, vote even in the industrial working-class communities of the South. Religious factors appear to play a less important role than in the past, but still have some significance. Personal rather than list voting plays a greater role for the CSV than it does for the Socialists.

The two strongest constituencies for the CSV have always been the East and the North. In the East the party's vote has slowly declined, from 75 per cent in 1919 to 58.2 per cent in 1945 to only 36.6 per cent in 1974. It has since recovered to 42.4 per cent (1984) — and the CSV remains easily the largest party in the constituency. Its strongest canton is Remich (46.1 per cent in 1984).

In the North constituency the party's vote also dropped from 61 per cent to 40.7 per cent in 1974. In 1984 it polled 45.5 per cent. Its strongest cantons in the North are Redange (50.1 per cent in 1984) and Clervaux (46.3 per cent), and its strongest commune is Eschweiler (66.8 per cent in 1984). In the 1984 national elections it had an absolute majority in 23 out of 45 communes in the constituency.

In the Centre constituency the CSV has been the largest party in national elections on all but a couple of occasions. Its vote has fluctuated between 27.6 per cent (1974) and 42.3 per cent (1954). In 1984 it polled 36.5 per cent. In the city of Luxembourg it obtained 35.7 per cent in 1984.

In the South constituency it is generally the second party to the Socialists, with its votes ranging from 25.7 per cent (1974) to 36.5 per cent (1954). In 1984 it polled 31.9 per cent. Even in the industrial towns it has a respectable vote, and nowhere in 1984 did it poll under 26.7 per cent (the figure it obtained in Differdange and Rumelange).

Organization

The CSV has not traditionally been a mass membership party, but its membership has increased, and is now at a figure of around 10,000. It now has easily the largest membership of any Luxembourg party. It has 150 sections, normally organized at communal level. At national constituency level there is a District Congress and a District Executive.

At national level the CSV holds an Annual Congress normally at the beginning of the year. The National Council consists of 80 members, and generally meets every trimester. The National Committee of 15 members meets every 15 days, and CSV government members also attend. Eight of the members of the National Committee are elected directly at the Annual Congress. The Party's president, secretary-general and treasurer are also elected by the Congress. Their terms of office are for three years, and they can only be re-elected on two occasions.

Responsibility for the choice of national candidates is divided between the districts and a special electoral committee, with final ratification at national level. Apart from the head of the list all the other candidates are in alphabetical order. The European Parliament list is chosen at national level.

The CSV has a number of associated organizations. Its youth movement is called the *Christlich-Soziale Jugend* (CSJ) and its women's organization the *Christlich Sozialen Frauen* (CSF). Both have their own statutes, and are represented at all levels within the party. There is also a local government association, the *Verband der Christlich-Sozialen Gemeinderäte* or FCCCS.

There is also a separate Christian trade union confederation, the *Letzebuerger Chreschtleche Gewerkschaftsbond* (LCGB), which is smaller than the rival OGBL, but which still has a substantial presence in certain areas, notably in commerce and in medium-sized firms. It was founded in 1921, and is formally independent from the CSV, with not all of its members also being members of the CSV.

The CSV has traditionally had strong links with the agricultural organizations, although after the schisms of recent years this support is now divided among rival associations.

The CSV has close ties with a daily newspaper, the *Luxemburger Wort*, founded in 1848. This has a circulation of around 80,000 and is easily the largest Luxembourg newspaper. It is formally independent of the party, but its support has nevertheless been an essential component of the party's success. It occasionally (notably at election time) produces a supplement, *CSV-Profil*, which is produced directly under the party's responsibility. The "friendly" press is also entitled to send a representative both to the CSV's National Council and to its National Committee.

The CSV currently has membership dues of 300 francs a year. A second member of the same family only pays half of the basic dues, and third and subsequent members nothing. Members of the LCGB trade union also pay a reduced rate.

The CSV is a member of the European People's Party, the European Union of Christian Democrats and the Christian Democratic International.

Policies

The CSV is the pivotal party in the Luxembourg political spectrum, and has thus provided the Luxembourg Prime Minister on all but one occasion since 1945. It probably also contains the widest range of opinion of the three major Luxembourg parties, from those with social Christian and trade union backgrounds (especially in the South of Luxembourg) to economic Liberals and agrarian Conservatives.

The CSV is not a confessional party. Its main policy differences with the other parties (otherwise not very great) have been over family and education policy. On economic policy there have been few sharp contrasts between the CSV and its current government partners, the Socialists. The CSV supports the concept of a social market economy, in order both to stimulate enterprise and to ensure social justice. The party's 1984 election manifesto put forward the pragmatic slogan "as little state as possible, as much state as necessary".

The CSV has opposed nationalization of Luxembourg's steel industry, but has played a major role in helping to restructure it. It has put a strong emphasis on social policy, and on family policy. It is concerned about the low birth rate in Luxembourg, and would like to see as many measures as possible to strengthen the family unit. When in opposition in 1974–79 it strongly opposed the Thorn government's law to liberalize abortion, but it has not made a major attempt to reverse this law after returning to office.

In the field of education the CSV has sponsored proposals to greatly restrict the so-called "third option", whereby children have been able to opt out of either religious instruction or an alternative course in ethics.

Like other parties the CSV is now adopting a stronger line on environmental policy. It considers that civil nuclear energy should be regarded only as a transitional source of energy, pending the development of new sources posing fewer problems. In the 1970s, however, it opposed the proposed Remerschen nuclear plant in Luxembourg, and has opposed the development of Cattenom in neighbouring France.

The CSV has had particular involvement in the details of agricultural policy (with the exception of 1974–79 the Agriculture Minister has invariably been a member of the CSV), and has strongly defended the individual family farm.

The CSV has called for greater integration of immigrants in Luxembourg society, but after a brief period of support now again opposes giving foreigners the right to vote in Luxembourg municipal elections.

On European Community matters the CSV strongly advocates the development of European Union. It supported the Single European Act, and has called for more powers to be given to the European Parliament. It also supports the objective of the 1992 internal market, whilst expressing concern about the impact of fiscal harmonisation, in particular, on the Luxembourg economy.

The CSV is a strong defender of NATO. One area of difference with its current government partners has been over the proposed development of a third military camp in the north of Luxembourg, which has been opposed by the Socialists but supported by the CSV.

Personalities

Jacques Santer has been the Prime Minister of Luxembourg since 1984. He is a former Finance Labour and Social Minister, and was the CSV party president from 1974 to 1982.

Jean Spautz has been party president since 1982, and has also been Interior and Family Minister. He has had a background on the trade union wing of the party.

François (Fränz) Colling is the Chairman of the CSV Parliamentary Group. Guillaume (Willy) Bourg is the Party's secretary-general.

Fernand Boden, the current Minister of Education, is the party's dominant personality in the East constituency, where he headed its list in the 1984 national elections.

A key figure from the North constituency is René Steichen, who has been mayor of Diekirch and Secretary of State for Agriculture.

An important younger leader in the party is Jean-Claude Juncker, the current Minister of Labour who is still only in his early thirties and has been head of the party's youth organization.

Luxemburger Sozialischtischen Arbeiterpartei (LSAP)
Parti Ouvrier Socialiste Luxembourgeois (POSL)
(Luxembourg Socialist Workers Party)

Headquarters	: 2, rue de la Boucherie, 1247 Luxembourg (tel: 20 557/28 791/ 47 11 75)
President	: Ben Fayot
Secretary general	: Raymond Becker
Youth group	: *Jeunesses Socialistes*
Women's group	: *Femmes Socialistes*
Newspaper	: *Tageblatt*
Members	: 5,800
Founded	: 1902

History

The first socialist-leaning deputies were elected in the 1890s. A Social Democratic Association was founded in 1902, which became the Social Democratic Party of Luxembourg in 1903. By 1905 it had five members of the Chamber of Deputies. Its initial leaders came from middle class intellectual backgrounds, with Dr Michel Welter being the most prominent figure. There were divisions within the party, and the first split occurred in 1904.

Local co-operation between Liberals and Socialists began in 1905, and in 1908 the two groups formed the so-called "Left Block", which governed Luxembourg for most of the next decade. The main unifying element in this otherwise disparate coalition was anti-clericalism, and opposition to the Catholic Party of the right, which came to the fore in the new education law of 1912.

The "Left Block" finally broke up during the years 1916–17, after disputes over mining concessions, social policy and universal suffrage.

The difficult conditions during World War I helped to strengthen the Labour movement. In 1915 the first working-class deputy was elected to the Chamber, and trade union leaders like Pierre and Antoine Krier and Nic Biever began to play a greater role in the Socialist Party. There were major strikes in 1917 and 1921, but the failure of the latter, in particular, helped to temper any revolutionary spirit. In 1921 a number of dissidents broke away to form the Luxembourg Communist Party.

The Socialist Party had seven or eight members of the Chamber for the first half of the 1920s. In 1924 it changed its name to *Arbeiterpartei* (Labour party).

After being in opposition from 1919 to 1924, it took part in a broad-based coalition from 1925 to 1926. From 1926 to 1937 it was again in the opposition and its support gradually grew. In 1936 it helped to secure proper recognition for the trade unions, and collective bargaining rights and in 1937 it gained new prestige from its successful referendum campaign against the so-called "Muzzle law" (*Maulkorbgesetz*) by which the ruling Conservative government sought to silence the far left. After the 1937 elections there were 17 Socialist members of the Chamber, and the Socialists subsequently entered government with Pierre Krier, who was both Socialist leader and Union leader, as Minister of Labour. The Socialists remained in a coalition government from 1937 to 1947, of which the years 1940–44 were spent in exile.

In 1945 the party suffered a severe electoral reverse, with a large drop in support even in its southern stronghold. A major contributory factor was the strong performance of the Communist Party. An attempt to change the party's name and character from being a narrowly anchored "Labour" party towards being a broader-based "Socialist Party" failed, largely because of Union opposition, but the party compromised by changing its name to the present title of "Luxembourg Socialist Workers' Party".

In spite of its 1945 defeat the party remained in government until 1947. It was then in opposition from 1947 to 1951. From 1951 to 1959 the Socialists were in a new coalition with the Christian Social Party, with the party president, Michel Rasquin, as Minister for Economic Affairs.

From 1959 to 1964 the Socialists were again in opposition. In 1964 they polled their highest ever percentage of 35.9 per cent, making them the largest Luxembourg Party in terms of votes but not seats. From 1964 to 1969 they were in a new coalition with the Christian Social Party.

After a sharp drop in the LSAP vote in 1969, the party returned to the opposition, during which severe divisions opened up between its right wing and its left and trade union wings, with one key issue being whether the Socialists should enter into coalition at individual communal level with the Communist party. In December 1970 a group of dissidents left the party, including six of the 18 Socialist deputies and the long serving party president Henri Cravatte, as well as a substantial proportion of the membership.

In January 1971 they formed a new Social Democratic Party, which won 10.1 per cent and five seats in its first election in 1974, 6 per cent and two seats in 1979 and was finally dissolved in 1984.

After the departure of the Social Democrats the Socialist Party moved initially to the left. In the 1974 elections its vote dropped but it re-entered government, this time in a coalition with the Democratic Party, which later tackled controversial issues such as school reform and liberalization of abortion.

In the 1979 elections the Socialists were subjected to a new if less serious schism led by Jean Gremling and his Socialist Independents, who won 6 per cent and one seat in the Centre constituency. The Socialist vote dropped to a new postwar low of 24.3 per cent and 14 seats. In the European Parliament elections of 1979 it only won 21.7 per cent and one seat.

The Socialists were in opposition from 1979 to 1984. In 1984, with the Social Democrats having collapsed and Jean Gremling also no longer a force, the Socialist Party's vote rose sharply to 33.6 per cent and 21 seats in the Chamber. In the European Parliament elections they won 29.9 per cent and two seats.

Since 1984 the Socialists have again been in a coalition government with the Christian Social Party and the Socialist Jacques Poos as Deputy Prime Minister and Minister of Foreign Affairs. Ben Fayot was elected as the new party president in January 1985. The Socialists have now shared power for 24 of the postwar years, but have still not provided a Luxembourg Prime Minister.

Support

Since World War I the Socialists have generally been the second largest political force in Luxembourg after the Christian Social Party. They have a broad electoral base, but are particularly strong among industrial workers and members of trade unions. They are weaker among the liberal professions, and among those working in smaller companies. An important feature of the LSAP vote within the Luxembourg context (where personal votes play an important role) is that it consistently receives a higher percentage of lists votes and fewer personal votes than either the Christian Social Party or the Democratic Party.

In 1984 the Socialists made a major electoral advance, and achieved their highest vote in a national election since 1964. In regional terms their stronghold is the South constituency, with its steel works and traditional industrial communities. The LSAP has consistently been the largest party in this constituency, and from

1948 to 1964 its vote never fell below 40 per cent. In 1984 its vote in the South was again over 40 per cent (41.3 per cent) with its highest votes in individual communes being in Dudelange (54.3 per cent) and Rumelange (52.8 per cent).

In the Centre constituency LSAP support has been very volatile, declining from 33.7 per cent in 1964 to only 17.9 per cent in 1979, but recovering to 25.4 per cent in 1984.

For most of the postwar period the LSAP has only been the third party in the East constituency, where it won 25.7 per cent in 1984. It is weakest in the canton of Remich (20.8 per cent in 1984). From 1948 to 1968 the LSAP was the second party in the North constituency (although far behind the dominant Christian Social Party), but since then it has only been third. Even here it has had pockets of strength, such as the communes of Wiltz and Vianden, which has had a popular Socialist mayor. The canton of Redange, however, is the LSAP's weakest area in the whole country (17.5 per cent in 1984 and with individual communes with only 10 per cent support).

Organization

The LSAP currently has around 5,800 members. At local level it has 67 sections, which must have a minimum of 10 members. The highest degree of party organization is in South Luxembourg. Above the sections are the four District Federations (South, Centre, East and North), with District Executives of between nine and 15 members and with District Congresses.

At national level the national congress is held annually, and includes delegates elected by the local sections in proportion to their membership.

The Party Executive (*Parteileitung*) consists of 17 members elected by the Congress for two year terms. No more than seven can be members of Parliament, and there are also special rules for ensuring adequate representation of each district.

The party executive elects the party president, who is the head of the party organization. After the departure of the Social Democrats in 1970 (whose leader Henri Cravatte had been LSAP president and member of the government at the same time), the LSAP adopted a new rule that the party president cannot be a member of the government, president of the chamber or president of the party's parliamentary group. There is no single post of Leader within the LSAP, and leadership responsibilities are currently shared, for example, between the party president, the Socialist deputy prime minister and the president of the parliamentary group.

Besides the party congress a general council (*Generalrat*) can also be convened to decide on such issues as disputes over candidatures or nominations of party members for government responsibilities. There are also working groups on specific themes.

In the past there has been a distinct socialist "family" of associated organizations within the Labour movement, and this still exists to a lesser extent. The OGBL, the Luxembourg trade union confederation has no formal links with the LSAP, and has emphasized its independence from any party. Nevertheless informal and personal links between the LSAP and the trade union movement are still strong.

The LSAP's Youth Movement, the *Jeunesses Socialistes Luxembourgeoises* has around a dozen local sections. It often takes an independent position from the party, as when it opposed Luxembourg's NATO membership in the early 1980s.

There is also a women's organization, the *Femmes Socialistes Luxembourgeoises*.

The LSAP has an associated communal organization, the *Fédération des conseillers communaux Socialistes* (FCCS).

There is a Socialist daily newspaper the *Tageblatt* which is not owned directly by the party (5 per cent of the capital) but by the Labour movement (which brought the then non-Socialist *Tageblatt* in 1927). *Tageblatt* has a circulation of around 25,000, far behind its Christian Social rival, the *Luxemburger Wort*.

The LSAP has membership dues of between 240 and 960 francs a year according to a member's income. A certain percentage of LSAP parliamentarians' or ministers' incomes are contributed to the party (e.g. 20 per cent of ministers' salaries).

The LSAP is a member of the Socialist International, the Confederation of Socialist Parties of the European Community and of the Socialist Group in the European Parliament. It also participates in *Scandilux*, the disarmament and defence policy group of Social Democratic parties in small Northern European NATO lands.

Policies

The LSAP is a pragmatic Social Democratic party, accustomed to coalition governments with parties of the centre, and right, and to the constraints imposed by Luxembourg's tiny size.

In the early 1970s the party's economic policies moved somewhat to the left, but this was a short-lived phase. The emphasis is now again on economic realism, and differences on economic policy with its Christian Social government partners are more ones of tone than of major substance. It calls for a mixed economy, with competition and the market playing a vital role, and also with the necessary measure of state planning and guidance, but without rigid economic dirigism. The state should not become too strong, and bureaucracy should be kept under careful control.

The LSAP played an important role in the 1974–79 government's response to the crisis in the steel industry, and the development of the "Luxembourg Model" of co-operation between employers, unions and the government, which helped to restructure Luxembourg's steel industry. The LSAP has also called for a shorter working week of 35 hours.

The LSAP has consistently put its major emphasis on the need for social reforms. It has advocated a minimum income guaranteed by the State. It now calls for better targeted social measures. It now puts a higher priority on environmental policy, with more environmental planning, and greater citizens' participation in planning decisions.

During the 1974–79 government, when a Luxembourg nuclear power station in the Moselle valley was a serious possibility, the party was divided over the issue, with its government ministers generally in favour but its ecologist wing and young Socialists strongly against. At the 1977 Party Congress, however, the idea of a nuclear energy plant was rejected by the delegates, if only by a narrow margin. Since then the party has swung much more strongly against civil nuclear energy. It has been very critical of the French nuclear plant at Cattenom near the Luxembourg border.

The LSAP has strongly emphasized the need for educational reform in Luxembourg. In the 1970s it called for comprehensive schools, but it now puts less accent on structural change and more on improved methods.

In media policy the party now advocates the development of a public radio station to meet cultural and information needs, and to counter the dominance of the private RTL.

The party's 1984 manifesto called for immigrants to be given the right to vote in local elections, although there is clearly now uncertainty within the party over this issue.

The LSAP has never been a strongly neutralist party, and did not oppose Luxembourg's abandonment of its former neutrality and entry into NATO in the late 1940s. It supported the idea of a European Defence Community in the 1950s. In the 1980s the party's Youth movement brought up the issue of Luxembourg's withdrawal from NATO, but this was rejected by an overwhelming majority (around 85 per cent) at the party congress in 1983.

On the other hand the LSAP has occasionally adopted a position distinct from the other major parties on certain defence questions. It was strongly opposed to compulsory military service (now abolished, but which was a persisting issue in the 1940s and 1950s). More recently the LSAP has opposed the establishment of a third American military camp in the north of the country, on the grounds that Luxembourg is already over-militarized and on wide economic and ecological grounds. On this issue it has taken a different stance to its Christian Social coalition partners.

When the European Coal and Steel Community was first mooted the LSAP had certain initial hesitations, but it swung strongly in favour, and is now one of the strongest advocates among European Socialist parties of further European integration. It believes that European economic and political unity are necessary if European countries are to play their full role in the World. It supported the Single European Act.

In the 1979 and 1984 European elections it campaigned on the manifesto of the Confederation of European Socialist Parties, but in 1989 it is likely to prepare its own complementary programme on account of the specific issues that will be raised (such as fiscal harmonization) with a direct effect on Luxembourg.

The Socialists put particular emphasis on the need to develop pan-European social and environmental measures.

Personalities

The three main leadership figures within the LSAP are Jacques Poos, who is the deputy Prime Minister and the first ever Socialist Minister of Foreign Affairs, Maurice Thoss, who is the President of the LSAP Parliamentary Group, and Ben Fayot, the leading historian of the party and its top candidate for the city of Luxembourg in the 1987 municipal elections, who has been the party president since 1985.

The party's secretary-general is Raymond Becker.

Demokratische Partei
Parti Democratique
(Democratic Party)

Headquarters	: 46, Grand Rue, 1660 Luxembourg (tel: 210 21)
President	: Colette Flesch
Secretary-general	: Henri Grethen
Youth movement	: *Jeunesse Démocratique*
Women's group	: Femmes Liberales

Newspaper	: Lëtzebuerger Journal
Members	: 6,500
Founded	: 1945

History

The Democratic Party was only founded in 1945, but it is the heir to a much older Liberal tradition in Luxembourg. In the mid-19th century there were already divisions between doctrinaire Liberals, who were anti-clerical but socially Conservative, and more progressive Liberals, who sought greater press and other freedoms and social reforms. Even the latter, however, were opposed to universal suffrage. During the last part of the 19th century there were many Liberals in Parliament, but there was still no organized Liberal Party. Only in 1904 did Robert Brasseur help to found a *Ligue Libérale* (Liberal League), but even this was only a loose electoral alliance rather than a structured party.

In 1908 the Liberals joined up with the Socialists to form the so-called "Left Block". The main point in common was anti-clericalism, and the Block clashed with the Catholic opposition over the issue of educational reform in particular. Later on, divisions between Liberals and Socialists over extension of the suffrage and economic policy became more marked, and the Block finally fell apart over the period from 1916 to 1917.

In the period of constitutional crisis from 1918 to 1919 the Liberals took a strongly pro-Belgian line. This, combined with the introduction of universal suffrage, which they had consistently opposed, led to their electoral decline in the 1919 elections. They then went into opposition to the majority government of the Party of the Right.

The Liberals remained extremely weak and divided during the remaining interwar years. In several elections there were two separate Liberal parties. Although there were few Liberal members of Parliament they held a pivotal position, and they participated in a long-lasting coalition with the Party of the Right from 1926 onwards. In 1937 the majority of Liberals supported the so-called "muzzle law" put forward by the Bech government to silence the Communists, but many Young Liberals opposed it.

After World War II a new *Groupement Patriotique et Démocratique* was founded in June 1945, in order to continue the spirit of wartime solidarity, and to break away from the old party divisions. It was based heavily on people who had been active in the wartime Resistance, but included prominent pre-war Liberal personalities. In the 1945 elections it came second in three of the four constituencies (Centre, East, North)

but only won 10 per cent and came fourth in the South constituency, where a separate Liberal list was also put forward.

The *Groupement* had two ministers in the 1945–47 Government of National Union, and after it collapsed remained in coalition with the Christian Social People's Party (CSV) from 1947 to 1951. Its Liberal character became more sharply defined.

After poor election results in 1951 the Party went into opposition where it remained until 1959. Its name was gradually shortened, first to *Groupement Démocratique* and then to *Parti Démocratique* in 1954. It continued to poll badly in elections and by 1954 its number of seats in the Parliament had declined from the nine of the 1940s to only six.

In the 1959 elections the party made a significant comeback, and won 11 seats. They re-entered government as junior coalition partners with the CSV, with three Ministers. In the 1964 elections they again lost five seats and went back into opposition. In December 1968 their vote went again up sharply to 18 per cent, and their number of seats in the Parliament returned to 11. The party went into a coalition government with the CSV as the junior partner with three ministers.

The Democratic Party enjoyed great success during the 1970s. In the 1974 elections its vote rose further to 23.3 per cent. It obtained 14 seats and was able to form a new coalition government with the Socialists, with its leader Gaston Thorn as the new Prime Minister.

In the 1979 national elections its vote dropped in percentage terms to 21.3 per cent but it gained an extra seat in Parliament. In the simultaneous European elections it benefited from the European prestige of Gaston Thorn and Colette Flesch to win 28.1 per cent and two seats in the European Parliament and the Democratic Party continued to participate in government, this time as the junior partner of the CSV.

In the 1984 elections the Democratic party was less successful, winning only 18.5 per cent of the vote and obtaining 14 seats in the Chamber. In the European elections it obtained 22.1 per cent and lost one of its two seats. It has since been the main party of the Luxembourg opposition.

Support

The Democratic Party has traditionally had its greatest support among senior executives, employers, the self-employed and the liberal professions. They have had strong support in small firms, in the services sector and in commerce. The growth of these sectors of the population clearly played an important role in the expansion of the party's electorate since the late 1960s. The Democratic Party has also had substantial support in agricultural areas, notably from larger farmers and from some of the wine-growers on the Moselle. Its greatest area of weakness has been among the industrial working class.

In regional terms its stronghold has been the Centre constituency, and in particular the capital city of Luxembourg and the rapidly growing commuter villages around it. Until 1974 the Democratic Party was only the third party in the Centre constituency, but in 1974 it won 33.3 per cent, and became the largest party. In subsequent elections it has only been second to the CSV, winning 26 per cent in 1984.

In the 1987 municipal elections it won 35.9 per cent in the capital and 10 out of 27 Council seats, making it the largest party. It was again able to provide the mayor of Luxembourg, a post it has held continuously (with only one five-year interlude from 1964 to 1969) since the 19th century.

A second area of strength for the party has been the East constituency, where it has normally been the second party, albeit far behind the CSV. Its highest vote in the constituency was 28.8 per cent in 1959, and in 1984 it won 27.4 per cent.

The Democratic Party was only the third party in the North constituency until 1974, but it has since been narrowly ahead of the Socialists, although still far behind the dominant CSV. Social change in what used to be a poor agricultural region has strengthened the party, and its 1984 vote of 26.2 per cent was its highest ever vote in the constituency. In some individual communes in the North it achieved its highest votes in the whole country (e.g. Bettborn 44.5 per cent).

The party has been weakest in the South constituency, where it was the fourth party behind the Communists until 1979, with votes as low as 4.8 per cent in 1954 and 5.3 per cent in 1964. It is now in a poor third place, with a high of 15.3 per cent in 1979, and with a 1984 vote of 11.7 per cent. It is weakest of all in the working class industrial communes, such as Rumelange (6 per cent in 1984).

Organization

The Democratic Party currently has around 6,500 members, organized in 53 local sections around the country. In each of the four constituencies the party has a regional organization, with a Regional Congress (held between mid February and mid-April), and a Regional Committee of between nine and 21 members.

At national level the party's national congress is held annually and is not a delegates' assembly, but open to all party members. It directly elects the party's national president, first vice-president and secretary-general, on separate votes for two year terms.

A large national council meets at least twice a year. In addition a 50-member directing committee (*Comité-Directeur*) meets at least every two months, and more often once a month. Besides the directly elected national officers it also includes 16 other members directly elected at the national congress (four per constituency). Among its main responsibilities are to debate the terms of the party's participation in any coalition.

A smaller executive committee (*Bureau Exécutif*) meets every 15 days. It has around 12 members, including all the top party officers, and must include representatives from each of the four constituencies.

The party's candidates for national elections are submitted by the regional committees for the final approval of the directing committee.

The party's youth movement *Jeunesse Démocratique* was founded in 1948, and currently has around 1,700 members. It is regarded at all levels within the party, including 12 delegates on the national council and three on the directing committee. In exchange the main party has three representatives on the central committee of *Jeunesse Démocratique*.

The party also has a women's organization, *Femmes Libérales*, which has been extremely active, and currently has around 1,000 members.

The party's official organ is the *Lëtzebuerger Journal*, founded in 1948. The party sometimes also produces a members bulletin on an ad hoc basis when a special problem arises.

The Democratic Party has low membership dues of only 250 francs a year, and has to rely considerably on other resources. It is a member both of the Liberal International and of the ELDR, of which Colette Flesch is the current president. The party's European Parliament members (as well as any party member of the European Commission) have the right to a place on its directing committee.

Policies

The Democratic Party is a centre-right party in the Liberal tradition, more free-market oriented than the other two major Luxembourg parties on economic issues and rather closer to the Socialist Party on moral and family policy issues.

On economic policy the Democratic Party calls for less State involvement and bureaucracy and more personal freedom and responsibility. Nevertheless it recognizes that the state must continue to play an important role and has defended the Luxembourg model of cooperation between the state, employers and unions, which has aided the restructuring of the steel industry, and which it helped to develop when in government.

The Democratic Party has put a particular emphasis on the need to reduce direct taxation.

The party is concerned about recent measures affecting the labour market which it sees as reinforcing existing rigidities. While it does not advocate hire and fire regimes it believes that greater flexibility is needed.

As regards social security measures it would like a greater degree of selectivity, so that more help is given to the neediest in society. On environmental policy the party supports the polluter-pays-principle. In the 1970s the Democratic Party was a strong advocate of a Luxembourg nuclear power station at Remerschen in the Moselle valley, and has not opposed the principle of civil nuclear energy. It now believes, however, that there should be limits to its use, and that alternatives should be sought. The party has been generally hostile to Cattenom.

The party's lay emphasis has caused it to adopt different policies from the Christian Social People's Party on a number of moral issues. It was the Liberal-led government of 1974–79 which liberalized abortion. Another contentious area has been education where the Democratic Party has always defended the state educational system. The party has defended the continued maintenance of the so-called "third option" (the right for children not to have to follow a course of either religious instruction or lay ethics), on the grounds of freedom of choice.

The Democratic Party has backed away from its previous support for immigrants to gain the right to vote in municipal elections.

The party has called for European economic and political union, and for a European defence policy. It supported the ratification of the Single European Act. While supportive of the 1992 internal market it points out the major adjustments that will be required for Luxembourg. It has been a strong supporter of NATO. It recognizes that Luxembourg has had to shoulder a very low burden of NATO expenditure, and considers that it is not unreasonable that Luxembourg should make a supplementary contribution. It has been in favour of the Third military camp in the North of Luxembourg. While in opposition it has supported one government partner, the CSV, over this issue against the other government party, the Socialists.

Personalities

Colette Flesch has been the President of the Democratic Party since 1980. From 1970 to 1980 she was the Mayor of Luxembourg, and from 1976 to 1980 secretary-general of the Democratic Party. From 1980 to 1984 she was Deputy Prime Minister, and Economics and Foreign Minister. From 1974 to 1980, and again from 1984 she was president of the party's parliamentary group. Since 1984 she has been president of the Federation of European Liberal Democratic and Reform Parties (ELDR).

Lydie Wurth-Polfer has been the Mayor of Luxembourg since 1982 when she succeeded her father, Camille Polfer. At 26 she was the youngest member of the Parliament when first elected in 1979.

A third influential woman within the party is Anne Brasseur, the president of the *Femmes Libérales*.

The party's secretary-general is Henri Grethen. Another powerful figure within the party is Paul Helminger. Gaston Thorn is a former Prime Minister (1974–79) and President of the European Commission (1980–84).

Kommunistesch Partei vu Lëtzeburg
(Luxembourg Communist Party)

President	:	16, rue Christophe Plantin, 2339 Luxembourg (tel: 49 20 95/ 49 20 97)
President	:	René Urbany
Youth movement	:	*Jeunesses Communistes Luxembourgeoises*
Newspaper	:	*Zeitung vum Lëtzebuerger Vollek*
Members	:	2,000 (1988)
Founded	:	1921

History

The Luxembourg Communist Party was founded in 1921 as a result of a schism within the Social Democratic Party over the issue of whether to join the Third International. In its early years it was not very successful. In 1928 it had only 200 members, of whom 149 were Italians and only 10 Luxembourgers. At the end of 1928 it was relaunched, with the objective of giving it stronger roots among the indigenous Luxembourg working class.

In 1934 Zenon Bernard became the first Communist to be elected to the Parliament, although his election was subsequently invalidated by the right of centre majority, and he was prevented from taking his seat.

In 1937 the Parliament passed the so-called *Maulkorbgesetz* ("muzzle law"), intended to give the government the power to ban revolutionary parties, and in particular the Communist Party. A wide coalition was forged to contest the law, and in subsequent popular referendum it was narrowly defeated, enabling the Communists to survive.

The Communists gained greatly in prestige during the Resistance and in 1945 they made a major electoral breakthrough, winning 11.1 per cent of the national votes and six seats in the Chamber. They also polled well in the municipal elections, becoming the largest party in Luxembourg's second largest town of Esch-sur-Alzette, where Arthur Useldinger became mayor in an unusual coalition between the Communists and Christian Social Party. In 1945 a separate Communist trade union organization was founded, the *Freie Letzeburger Arbechterverband* (FLA), which soon became very strong in Luxembourg's heavy industry.

The Communists participated in a Government of National Union from 1945 to 1947, when they left government, never since to return.

From the late 1940s to late 1950s the party declined electorally, and in the 1954 and 1959 elections only won three seats in the Parliament. The Russian invasion of Hungary made the party more unpopular, but did not cause major internal schisms within the party. In the 1960s, however, the party made an electoral recovery, again winning five seats in 1964. In 1966 the Communist trade union organization FLA merged with the Socialist LAV to disappear as a separate entity.

It came under severe attack in 1968 for having supported the Soviet invasion of Czechoslovakia, but in the 1968 elections it won its highest ever percentage of the vote and six seats in the Parliament.

After the next round of municipal elections talks began in certain communes concerning the creation of Socialist-Communist local coalitions, causing a split within the Socialist Party. In 1970 Arthur Useldinger again became mayor of Esch-sur-Alzette as a result of such a coalition.

In the 1970s the party began a new and steady electoral decline. In 1976 Dominique Urbany was replaced as president by his son René Urbany.

In the 1979 national elections the party suffered a major setback dropping to only 5 per cent of the vote and two seats in the Parliament. In the 1979 European elections it also won only 5 per cent and no seats.

In the 1984 national elections it won 5.1 per cent and retained its two seats, those of its President René Urbany and of Aloyse Bisdorff. In the European Parliament elections, however, it only won 4.1 per cent with no seats.

Support

The Communist Party's support has mainly come from working-class Luxembourgers, especially workers in the steel industry, with Arbed's steel plant at Belval as a particular stronghold.

Its strongest constituency by far is South Luxembourg where practically all of the heavy industry is located, and where it was the third party between 1945 and the late 1970s. In 1945 it won 20.7 per cent in the constituency. This fell to 15 per cent in the 1950s but again rose to 22 per cent in 1968. Since then it has fallen away, and the Communists now have a lower vote than the Liberals and have become the fourth party with only 7.3 per cent in 1984. Their strongest communes in the constituency are Sanem (12.2 per cent in 1984) and Esch-sur-Alzette (11 per cent in 1984). It still had almost 15 per cent in certain communes in the 1987 local elections, and been in local government coalitions with the Socialists in Esch, Kayl and Differdange.

The only other constituency where the Communists have won any support is Central Luxembourg. The party won 8.3 per cent in 1945, falling to 3.5 per cent in the 1950s but rising to 9.4 per cent in 1968. It is now back to 2.9 per cent. In the city of Luxembourg it won 3.4 per cent in 1984 (just under 5 per cent in the 1987 local elections).

The Communists have traditionally been weak in the East constituency (with a high of 5.1 per cent in 1968, but only 2.1 per cent in 1984) and the North (with a high of 4.1 per cent and only 1.5 per cent in 1984). In the canton of Clervaux in the North constituency it only won 0.8 per cent in 1984, and in one or two communes in the North it won no votes at all.

Organization

The Communist Party currently has around 2,000 members. It has 12 territorial sections and six workplace cells in the steel industry. The party's national congress is held roughly every three years — with around 300 delegates attending the most recent such congress. The central committee has 33–34 full members and six candidate members, who are elected at the party congress for three year terms of office. It meets at least four times a year. The central committee then chooses the party president (its effective leader), and the members of the executive committee. This latter has nine or ten members and meets on a weekly or fortnightly basis.

The party's youth movement is called *Jeunesse Communiste*, and claims to have several hundred members. There is no separate Communist women's organization.

The merger of the former Communist union, the FLA, with the Socialists' Union federation was a blow to the Communist party's position in the trade union movement. The Communists have no places on the merged Federation's (OGBL) Executive, although there are Communists on its National Committee. The party is much stronger, however, at individual plant level in the steel industry, especially in Arbed Belval.

The party's newspaper is called the *Zeitung vum Lëtzebuerger Vollek*. It was founded in 1946 and appears on a daily basis, with a current circulation of around 8,000.

The party has membership dues levied on a progressive basis, and ranging from 50 to 250 francs a month.

Policies

The Luxembourg Communist Party has been an orthodox pro-Moscow party, which has consistently supported the Soviet line on foreign policy matters, including those on Hungary, Czechoslovakia and Afghanistan. Moreover its pro-Soviet position in 1956 and 1968, did not lead to major internal divisions within the party. It has now expressed its sympathy for *glasnost*, believing that this can lead to greater economic and political efficiency. In domestic policy the party has generally taken a pragmatic line. It supports political pluralism and democracy, and co-operation between all parties on the European left, including the new peace, ecological, women's and other popular movements. Within Luxembourg it seeks closer co-operation with the Socialist Party. It also recognizes that the traditional definition of the working class is no longer satisfactory in the changed social circumstances, and now sees the salariat in the widest sense as its social base.

On economic policy matters the Communist Party calls for the nationalization of the Luxembourg steel industry, but it does not advocate nationalization in other sectors, such as banking. The party supports the maintenance of the private sector in the form of flourishing small and medium sized enterprises in particular. It also supports the development of Luxembourg as a financial centre. It is concerned, however, about Luxembourg becoming a vulnerable branch economy, with large foreign multinationals setting up subsidiaries in Luxembourg because of a favourable investment climate, but with no guarantee of a long-term presence in the country.

The Communist Party puts a strong emphasis on social measures. A leading current concern is pension reform, where the party seeks to improve the position of private pensions, but not at the expense of public sector pensions.

On the issue of immigration the party calls for greater integration of the foreign workers within Luxembourg society. It still supports giving them the right to vote in Luxembourg municipal elections, as long as certain minimum conditions are met.

The party has never taken a stand in principle against the use of civil nuclear energy. It originally supported the proposal for a nuclear power station in Luxembourg in the 1970s (which was at first linked to a possible contract with the Soviet Union), but later opposed it when the Soviet Union was no longer involved. It has opposed the Cattenom nuclear power station in the neighbouring region of France.

The Communist Party was originally opposed to the European Community, but has gradually come to accept it as irreversible, and is not in favour of Luxembourg's withdrawal. It supports enhanced European co-operation as long as individual national interests are taken fully into account. It opposes European Union, and voted against the Single European Act. It is suspicious of the 1992 internal market, believing that this is mainly in the interest of the multinationals, and is concerned that fiscal harmonisation will be of direct harm to Luxembourg.

In the 1940s the Communist Party strongly opposed Luxembourg's abandonment of neutrality and entry into NATO, but it does not now formally call for Luxembourg to leave NATO, believing this to be an unrealistic demand. If at all possible it would like a non-aligned Luxembourg in the longer term. In the shorter term it calls for Luxembourg to follow the American line less slavishly than at present, and to do all that it can to promote peace and disarmament from within NATO. It is opposed to what it sees as the current over-militarization of Luxembourg, and proposed new third military camp in the North of the country.

Personalities

The party's president is René Urbany, who has led the party since 1976, and who is the son of the previous party leader Dominique Urbany. Another relative, Serge Urbany, is on the executive committee and runs the party secretariat. Jacqueline Urbany is on the central committee. Another leading figure within the party is Aloyse Bisdorff.

Dei Greng Alternativ
(Green Alternative Party–GAP)

Headquarters : 72 Boulevard
de la Pétrusse,
PO Box 2711,
1027 Luxembourg
(tel: 49 00 49)
Secretariat contact
(1988–89) : Abbes Jacoby
Members : 130
Founded : June 1983

History

The environmental movement in Luxembourg was given considerable impetus by the successful campaign to block a nuclear power station at Remerschen on the Luxembourg Moselle. In 1979 a group of environmentalists and left-wingers contested the elections of that year under the title of *Alternativ Lëscht — Wiert Lesch*, only winning around 1 per cent of the vote.

On 23 June 1983 a diverse group of people, from ecological groups, from the green wing of the Socialist Party, and from the far left, who were inspired by the example of the German Greens, got together to form a new party, *Dei Greng Alternative* (GAP). In June 1984 the party enjoyed considerable success, winning two seats in the Chamber of Deputies. In the European elections it won 6.1 per cent but no seat. The two elected members in the Chamber of Deputies were supposed to stand down after one year and to give way to the next on the list. In all there were meant to be 10 Green deputies over the 1984–89 parliament.

Within a year there was a serious conflict between one of the deputies, Jup Weber, and the party organization over the principle of rotation, financial contributions, and over whether he was a mandated delegate or could make his own judgements. Weber subsequently left the party and became an independent member in the Parliament. He has now formed his own Green List (see separate entry).

Weber's departure upset the whole principle of rotation of parliamentarians. The other deputy, Jean Huss, did not leave until after the half-way point of the parliamentary term, but has now been replaced by Guy Bock.

In the 1987 municipal elections the GAP and the rival Weber group only competed directly in the city of Luxembourg. The GAP obtained 4.82 per cent in the city, and the Weber Green List 5.63 per cent, and each list obtained one seat on the city council. The GAP also won one seat in each of four other communes (Dudelange, Esch-sur-Alzette, Mondercange and Petange).

Discussions have since taken place between the two Green parties on a possible reconciliation, but serious political differences remain.

Support

Support for the GAP has been remarkably even. In the 1984 national elections the party polled 5.7 per cent in the South constituency and 5.9 per cent in the Centre (the only two constituencies that it contested), and 6.1 per cent in the 1984 European elections, winning similar support in all parts of the country. In the 1987 municipal elections the GAP polled between 8 per cent and 10.5 per cent in four of the five communes that it contested. Only in Luxembourg city did it get a lower vote of under 5 per cent, but the Green vote was split here between two parties, and the combined Green vote was over 10 per cent.

The Greens have appeared to poll as well in isolated rural communes as in the villages and suburbs nearer Luxembourg and in the industrial communities in the South. The highest Green vote in 1984 was 15.3 per cent in industrial Esch-sur-Alzette in the European Parliament elections (but only 5.9 per cent in the national elections) and 10.6 per cent in rural Vichten commune, also in the 1984 European elections. Its highest vote in the 1987 municipal elections was 10.5 per cent in Mondercange.

Organization

The GAP has an assembly-based organization, emphasizing the principle of rotation and control of the party's parliamentary deputies by the party at large. Its organizational structure is still only rudimentary. The party currently has 130 members and 350 sympathizers.

The GAP has a territorial structure based on a small number of local and regional sections. It also has an organization in the four electoral districts, whose main task is to choose the party's chamber candidates and to send representatives for one year terms (but with the possibility of revocation at any moment) to the party's co-ordinating council.

Besides the territorial structure there are also national working groups which discuss and put forward policy proposals in such fields as public transport, animal protection, third world and waste recycling. At national level there is a national plenary assembly (*Nationalvollversammlung*) which meets on an ordinary basis four times a year. Its meetings are open, and any member can participate. A quorum is attained if one-third of the party members are present, and its decisions are binding if there is a three-fifths majority. Decisions taken when there is no such quorum are then referred to the wider membership.

The party's executive is its co-ordinating council (*Koordinationsrat*) of nine members, consisting of district representatives and the party treasurer who is directly elected by the national assembly. There is no formal party leadership besides the council. The council elects the party's administrative secretary for an 18-month term.

The party's parliamentarians are not members of the co-ordinating Council, and can attend its meetings with a consultative vote only. The parliamentarians (all those who are to enter Parliament on the rotation principle) form the "parliamentary working group". They are obliged to follow the decision of the national assembly, and must discuss controversial issues with the co-ordinating council before casting their votes on these issues in the Chamber. If the parliamentarians and council cannot agree a special national assembly meeting is meant to be convened. The parliamentarians have to hand over their parliamentary salary to the party which pays them a standard wage.

The one-year rotation principle for parliamentarians is being replaced by a less frequent rotation, likely to be of two-and-a-half years. At communal level decisions on rotation are taken by each local branch; within the city of Luxembourg rotation takes place every two years.

There are no formal quotas for women's representation within the party, but 50 per cent of the party's candidates for the 1984 national elections and 1987 Luxembourg city elections were women.

The GAP has just helped to start a journal called *Grenge Spoun*, which is to come out initially on a monthly basis, and later on a 15-day basis. It has an autonomous editorial board.

The party's membership dues are of a highly progressive nature (100 francs a month if a members' net income is under 30,000 francs a month, rising to 1,000 francs a month for those with net incomes of over 80,000).

The GAP is a member of the Federation of European Greens.

Policies

The GAP emphasizes a mixture of Green and new left themes, considering that its task is not just to put forward policies on ecological issues but to promote wider changes in society. It believes in combining parliamentary and extra-parliamentary action through citizens initiatives and working through other popular movements.

The GAP believes that the thrust of economic policy-making must be altered to put less emphasis on economic growth alone and more on combining economic and environmental objectives. New investment should be more ecologically-based. The economy should become more decentralized. It has strongly opposed the Cattenom nuclear power station in France and believes that Luxembourg should not buy in any cheap electricity from this source. It seeks tougher energy conservation measures, energy recycling and more use of renewables. The need for much more extensive waste recycling is also heavily emphasized.

The GAP is highly critical of building speculation and the destruction of green spaces in Luxembourg, and calls for much stronger environmental planning. It is opposed to major new road projects and has called for a five-year moratorium on road construction. Funds should be placed to improve public transport instead.

Agriculture should become more ecological, with less fertilizers and pesticides, smaller farms, and simpler and more natural products.

The GAP calls for introduction of a 35-hour week with no loss of wages and for a higher minimum income. The GAP believes that the current inequalities in pensions should be eliminated, and that there should be a single state guaranteed system, with both minimum and maximum pensions.

The GAP strongly emphasizes the need for wider-based democracy within Luxembourg society. There should be more scope for direct democracy and greater equality for women. The party warns against rising nationalism in Luxembourg, and calls for immigrants to be given the right to vote. In its 1984 election programme the GAP also called for a referendum to remove the Grand Duke as the head of state and to have a republic instead.

The party calls for the withdrawal of Luxembourg from NATO, unilateral disarmament, and neutrality. It opposes both the proposed American military camp in northern Luxembourg, and the existing camps.

The GAP recognizes that Luxembourg must remain within the European Community, but is unhappy with the present development of the Community. It opposed the Single European Act, and believes that the 1992 internal market will only be the Europe of the special interests, putting its emphasis on economic growth and not enough on the environment or on social measures. The Common Agricultural Policy is described as scandalous. The GAP advocates a decentralized Europe of the Regions.

One of the highest priorities for the GAP is solidarity with the third world. Trade with the developing countries should be based much more on the latters' real needs. There should be more support for appropriate technology and appropriate production. Multinationals should be better controlled.

Personalities

The GAP opposes formal leadership structures. One of their leading personalities, however, has been Jean Huss, a former member of the Socialist Party's national executive who was a GAP member of Parliament from 1984 to 1987. He is responsible for much of the party's international contacts, and is now a secretary of the Federation of European Greens.

Greng Lescht-Ekologesch Initiativ
(Green List-Ecological Initiative)

Contact address : PO Box 1567,
1015 Luxembourg
(tel: 44 88 06)
President : Jup Weber
Founded : 1986

History

After the Green Alternative Party (see separate entry) had succeeded in electing two deputies to the Luxembourg Parliament in 1984 one of the two, Jup Weber, quickly came into conflict with the party organization over the degree to which he was able to take independent positions in the Parliament, over the principle of rotation (he was supposed to stand down after one year) and over financial remuneration. By early 1985 he had been forced out of the party, but continued to sit in the Parliament as an independent. He had taken a number of party activists with him and in 1986 formed a new political group, the "Ecological Initiative" which concentrated on environmental policy and not on the wider policy concerns of the Green Alternatives.

In the 1987 municipal elections the new group stood under the name *Greng Lëscht-Ecologesch Initiativ*, in two communes, the city of Luxembourg and Junglinster. In Luxembourg city it competed directly against the Green Alternatives, winning 5.6 per cent of the vote against 4.8 per cent for the rival Green Party and electing its President Jup Weber to the Luxembourg City Council. In Junglinster it won 12.8 per cent and one seat on the local council. It also has

five councillors in communes with a majority electoral system. It plans to put up candidates in all four constituencies in the 1989 national elections.

Organization

The Green List-Ecological Initiative has reacted strongly against the organizational principles of the Green Alternative Party. It does not support the principle of rotation of its parliamentarians, and believes that the latter must be allowed to make their own independent judgements without being forced to follow the party organization's line.

The group has only a small number of members and sympathizers, and has no formal territorial structure, but it has established a number of working groups at national level on such issues as waste management, energy and agriculture. At national level it has a general assembly, which generally meets once a year, but more often before elections. The general assembly elects the party board of seven members, including its president, two vice-presidents, and secretary.

The group has no quotas for women, but well over 50 per cent of its candidates in the city of Luxembourg in the 1987 municipal elections were women. It opposes the creation of a separate women's group.

It has a newspaper called *Zelleriszalot* ("celery salad"), which appears roughly once every one-and-a-half months.

Its members pay membership dues of 200 francs a year. It has no formal international links with the Federation of European Greens (which recognizes the Green Alternatives), but there have been informal links between its leadership and individual Green Parliamentarians from other countries.

Policies

The Green List-Ecological Initiative concentrates primarily on ecological issues. On all issues not linked to ecology, such as membership of NATO or abolition of the monarchy (issues raised by the Green Alternatives) the Green List does not get involved, and leaves a decision to the conscience of its individual members. On the issue, for example, of granting voting rights to immigrants its president has said he is in favour, while other members of the party are not. The Green List believes that the Green Alternatives are too influenced by the far left, and seeks to position itself as a group appealing to all voters with strong ecological concerns, including those from more conservative backgrounds. If it holds the balance of power within the Luxembourg Parliament it is prepared to come to an agreement with the government parties as long as they are prepared to accept a number of minimum demands on ecological issues, such as the introduction of subsidies to farmers willing to convert to biological methods. Energy, waste management and transport policies are all considered to constitute one interconnected ecological programme.

The Cattenom nuclear power station in France is strongly opposed, as is any use by Luxembourg of electricity from Cattendom. Renewable energies, energy conservation and cogeneration are strongly emphasized, as is improved waste management. Public transport should be improved, with a shift from road to rail transport.

The Green List has not taken a position on defence issues, but opposes the creation of a third military camp in north Luxembourg. It supports European integration only where it benefits the environment. It would like stronger powers for the European Parliament, and strongly opposes the Common Agricultural Policy.

Personalities

The leading figures within the Green List is its founder Jup Weber, who is its president as well as being a member of the Luxembourg Chamber of Deputies and of the Luxembourg City Council.

The Green List's secretary is Georgette Muller.

Nationalists of the Far Right

In the 1987 municipal elections an anti-immigrant group, *d'Lëscht fir de Lëtzebuerger* put up one candidate (Georges Dessouroux) in the city of Luxembourg. Since then a new and more extreme group, *d'National Bewegong* (National Movement) has been created.

D'National Bewegong
(National Movement)

Headquarters : PO Box 38,
3705 Tetange
(tel: 56 46 23)

This is a nationalist group, which calls for a Luxembourg of the Luxembourgers. It wants a stop to immigration into Luxembourg, and no voting rights for immigrants. It is concerned about the lowering of frontier barriers necessitated by the 1992 internal market within the European Community.

The Netherlands

Francis Jacobs

The country

The Netherlands is a country of almost 14 million population with the highest density in the three western provinces of North and South Holland and Utrecht. The only native minority language is Frisian – spoken mainly in the province of Friesland but also along the coast of the province of Groningen. There is also a significant immigrant population from the Netherlands' former colonies of Indonesia (e.g. the Moluccan Islands) and Surinam. Moreover in 1982 there were over 500,000 foreign nationals resident in the Netherlands of whom 147,000 were Turkish nationals.

Map of Netherlands showing 12 provinces and main towns.

Source: Carpress.

Political institutions

The national legislature, the *Staten-Generaal* or States General, consists of two chambers,

the *Eerste Kamer* (First Chamber), consisting of 75 members indirectly elected by members of the 12 provincial councils (with half retiring every three years) and the *Tweede Kamer* (Second Chamber), consisting of 150 directly elected members. Effective legislative power lies with the Second Chamber, although the First Chamber does have a general power of veto.

The Prime Minister and his Cabinet emerge after sometimes lengthy periods of negotiation after an election, 207 days in the case of the 1977 elections. The search for a viable coalition is carried out by *informateurs* and *formateurs* appointed by the monarch. Once appointed, Cabinet ministers cannot remain as members of the States General. A party leader in a coalition party, for instance, must decide whether to enter the government or to remain as the parliamentary leader.

Each of the Netherlands' 12 provinces has an elected Council, and an appointed Governor or "Queen's Commissioner". Each Dutch municipality also has an elected Council and an appointed Mayor or Burgomaster.

Elections to the Second Chamber and to the provincial and municipal Councils are held every four years, and have been by the d'Hondt system of proportional representation since 1917. The whole of the Netherlands is treated as one constituency for the purpose of elections to the Second Chamber, and there is only a very low threshold below which a party is not entitled to a seat, currently around 0.67 per cent of the national vote. There is thus a very strict correlation between votes gained and seats won, and a tendency towards considerable political fragmentation. Voting used to be compulsory, but this no longer the case (since 1970) although voter turnout has remained between 80 per cent and 90 per cent. In May 1985 a law was adopted giving the right to vote in local elections to foreign nationals who had resided in the Netherlands for five years. Dutchmen living abroad will also now have the vote for the first time. The Netherlands has 25 members within the European Parliament.

Brief political history

In 1815 the Kingdom of the north and south Netherlands was created, but the south seceded in 1831 to become the state of Belgium. For much of the 19th century there were no organized political parties but instead separate Liberal and Conservative associations and groups centred around particular individuals, of whom perhaps the most important was J. R. Thorbecke, the man primarily responsible for the new Dutch constitution of 1848. This provided in particular for a lessening in the powers of the monarchy through a directly elected Second Chamber, and Cabinet responsibility to Parliament.

Two great issues dominated Dutch political life in the late 19th and early 20th centuries and helped to stimulate not merely the development of organized political parties but also major divisions within them. One was the issue of whether religious as well as state schools should also receive state subsidies, and the other was the question as to how far voting rights should be extended. Other social questions, and the extension of workers' rights were important too, but to a lesser degree than in many other European countries, largely as a result of the very late industrialization of the Netherlands.

The first Dutch political party, the Anti-Revolutionary Party (the revolution in question was the French Revolution), was only created in 1878, in considerable measure as a reaction against the Liberal Education Bill of that year, which kept religious schools at a financial disadvantage. The first Liberal party, the *Liberale Unie*, was next to be created in 1885.

The Liberals' last great period of dominance in Dutch political life was the 1890s when they formed three successive cabinets. Although Liberal-led coalitions were formed later, their fortunes declined and the Socialists as well as the increasingly dominant Confessional parties overtook them as a political force.

A central event in Dutch political history was the constitutional settlement of 1917, when the different political forces in the country were finally able to agree on solutions to both the schools issue and extension of the suffrage. All elementary schools, whether public or private, were given an equal amount of government financial support proportionate to their size. Universal male suffrage was also introduced, as was proportional representation, universal female suffrage following in 1919.

Proportional representation with a very low national threshold led to a multiplication of parties within the already fragmented Dutch political landscape. Whereas seven parties had won seats in the Parliament in the 1913 election, no less than 16 did so in 1918.

The interwar years were also the period when the division of Dutch society into a number of cohesive blocs reached its highest stage of development, a process usually referred to as "pillarization". Each "pillar", Catholic, Protestant and Socialist, and to a lesser extent Liberal, provided everything from education and welfare to sports clubs, trade unions and associations, newspapers and radio stations as well as political parties for its own adherents. Of these blocs the largest was the Catholic one. The Confessional parties dominated the coalitions of the interwar years, and the Socialists only took part in a government for the first time in 1939.

After World War II a first determined effort was made to break down these pillars, the so-called *Doorbraak* or "breakthrough" initiative, which saw, for instance, the attempted establishment of a broadly-based Labour party consisting of former Socialist and Liberal supporters. The initiative failed, an important contributory factor being the earlier liberation of the Catholic southern Netherlands, and the consequent early re-establishment of the Catholic "pillar". The 1950s mainly saw Confessional party/Labour coalitions and 1960s Confessional party/Liberal coalitions.

In the late 1960s the existing political structure was challenged from different directions, with the creation of new political parties (one of which, D66, expressly advocated a change in the electoral system) and with considerable unrest within existing parties. During this period and since, the "pillarization" of Dutch society has continued to weaken, with church attendance beginning to decline, and with members of particular blocs voting much less monolithically for their own bloc's political party.

The three main Confessional parties have now merged but their combined total of votes is no more than the Catholic Party used to get on its own. But the Christian Democrats have remained the lynchpin of the Dutch political system. They have provided the majority of Prime Ministers and have been present in all recent coalitions. Increasingly Dutch politics has settled into one of two patterns, Confessional Party-Liberal coalitions (as in 1977–78, 1982–present) or Confessional Party-Socialist coalitions (as in 1973–77 and 1981).

Main features of the current Dutch political system

The Dutch political system has been characterized by fragmentation, with as many as

Elections in the Netherlands, 1945–present: percentage of vote and seats won by the political parties in the *Tweede Kamer* (Second Chamber)

	1946	1948	1952	1956	1959	1963	1967	1971	1972	1977	1981	1982	1986
Anti-Revolutionaire Partij (ARP) (Anti-revolutionary Party)	13 (12.9%)	13 (13.2%)	12 (11.3%)	15 (9.9%)	14 (9.4%)	13 (8.7%)	15 (9.9%)	13 (8.6%)	14 (8.8%)	13	—	—	—
Christelijk-Historische Unie (CHU) (Christian Historical Union)	8 (7.8%)	9 (9.2%)	9 (8.9%)	13 (8.4%)	12 (8.1%)	13 (8.6%)	12 (8.1%)	10 (6.3%)	7 (4.8%)	10	—	—	—
Katholieke Volkspartij (KVP) (Catholic People's Party)	32 (30.8%)	32 (31.0%)	30 (28.7%)	49 (31.7%)	49 (31.0%)	50 (31.9%)	42 (26.5%)	35 (21.8%)	27 (17.7%)	26	—	—	—
Christian Democratisch Appel (CDA) (Christian Democrats)	—	—	—	—	—	—	—	—	—	(31.9%)	48 (30.8%)	45 (29.3%)	54 (34.6%)
Partij van de Arbeid (PVDA) (Labour Party)	29 (28.3%)	27 (25.6%)	30 (29.0%)	50 (32.7%)	48 (30.4%)	43 (28.0%)	37 (23.6%)	39 (24.6%)	43 (27.3%)	53 (33.8%)	44 (28.3%)	47 (30.3%)	52 (33.3%)
Volkspartij voor Vrijheid en Democratie (VVD) (People's Party for Freedom and Democracy)	6 (6.4%)	8 (7.9%)	9 (8.8%)	13 (8.8%)	19 (12.2%)	16 (10.3%)	17 (10.7%)	16 (10.3%)	22 (14.4%)	28 (17.9%)	26 (17.3%)	36 (23.0%)	27 (17.4%)
Democraten 66 (D66)	—	—	—	—	—	—	7 (4.5%)	11 (6.8%)	6 (4.2%)	8 (5.4%)	17 (11.1%)	6 (4.3%)	9 (6.1%)
Communistische Partij Nederland (CPN) (Communist Party)	10 (10.6%)	8 (7.7%)	6 (6.2%)	7 (4.7%)	3 (2.4%)	4 (2.8%)	5 (3.6%)	6 (3.9%)	7 (4.5%)	2 (1.7%)	3 (2.1%)	3 (1.8%)	0 (0.6%)
Staatkundig Gereformeerde Partij (SGP) (Political Reformed Party)	2 (2.1%)	2 (2.4%)	2 (2.4%)	3 (2.3%)	3 (2.2%)	3 (2.3%)	3 (2.0%)	3 (2.3%)	3 (2.2%)	3 (2.1%)	3 (2.0%)	3 (1.9%)	3 (1.8%)
Reformatorische Politieke Federatie (RPF) (Reformed Political Federation)										(0.6%)	2 (2.0%)	2 (1.5%)	1 (0.9%)
Gereformeerd Politiek Verbond (GPV) (Reformed Political Union)	—	—	(0.7%)	0 (0.6%)	0 (0.7%)	1 (0.7%)	1 (0.9%)	2 (1.6%)	2 (1.8%)	1 (1.0%)	1 (0.8%)	1 (0.8%)	1 (1.0%)
Pacifistisch-Socialistische Partij (PSP) (Pacifist Socialist Party)	—	—	—	—	2 (1.8%)	4 (3.0%)	4 (2.9%)	2 (1.4%)	2 (1.5%)	1 (0.9%)	3 (2.1%)	3 (2.3%)	1 (1.2%)
Boerenpartij (Farmers' Party)					0 (0.7%)	3 (2.1%)	7 (4.9%)	1 (1.1%)	3 (1.9%)	1 (0.8%)			
Democratische Socialisten 70 (DS70) (Democratic Socialists 1970)								8 (5.3%)	6 (4.1%)	1 (0.7%)	0 (0.6%)		
Politieke Partij Radicalen (PPR) (Radical Political Party)								2 (1.8%)	7 (4.8%)	3 (1.7%)	3 (2.0%)	2 (1.6%)	2 (1.3%)
Centrum Partij (Centre Party)												1 (0.8%)	0 (0.4%)
Others	0 (1.0%)	0 (1.6%)	0 (1.4%)	0 (0.8%)	0 (0.6%)	0 (1.6%)	0 (2.6%)	2 (4.0%)	1 (1.9%)	0 (1.4%)	0 (1.4%)	1 (2.2%)	0 (1.4%)

14 parties being represented in Parliament in certain recent elections. While the electoral system has encouraged such a development there are obviously more deep-rooted reasons, including the division of Dutch society into the blocs or "pillars" referred to above, the tendency to have breakaway movements from within the blocs themselves and finally the tendency to create new anti-establishment parties on both the left and right of the political spectrum.

A further important characteristic has been the persistence of intense localism in voting patterns. In practically no other European country do very small parties get a majority of the vote in individual isolated villages as the fundamental Calvinists or extreme left parties do in certain places in the Netherlands.

In practice, however, the five largest political parties, the three Confessional parties, the Socialist Party and the Liberal Party have won the majority of votes and seats, and have dominated the political life of the country. This, combined with the development of certain "rules of the game" to mediate disputes between the blocs (see Lijphart's classic analysis in his *Politics of Accommodation*) has led to a much greater stability than the apparent fragmentation would lead one to believe.

A further feature of bloc or "pillar" politics has been to undercut traditional left-right divisions in that certain parties such as the Catholic Party have won support right across class lines, from working-class to wealthy Catholics. This is still true to a considerable extent for the merged Christian Democratic Party, although its electoral base has shrunk significantly with the decline of "pillarization".

Another distinctive aspect of Dutch politics is that there is often little direct correlation between the voting results in an election and the coalition that eventually emerges. In fact if a party is too successful and overplays its hand in the coalition negotiations, as the Socialists did in 1977, it may well provoke a coalition of the less successful parties. Such apparent thwarting of the democratic will has helped to provoke periodic protests against the system as a whole. When D66 was founded in 1966 it even called for the abandonment of proportional representation, and for the direct election of the Prime Minister.

One final set of qualifying comments must be made in evaluating the positions of Dutch parties in the political spectrum. The first is the importance with which moral questions are treated in Dutch life. This has been reflected in numerous ways in Dutch politics, such as an unusually strong commitment among most Dutch political parties to development aid, and

to intense political debates on subjects such as euthanasia, which is currently the centre of controversy to a degree unparalleled in other European countries.

Moreover the whole Dutch political spectrum is less conservative than that of most other European countries, including immediately adjacent states such as Belgium. Policies such as clamping down on drugs, reintroducing hanging, and getting tough on immigrants have not been the policy planks of any of the major parties; government secrecy is not an issue, the rights of minorities such as homosexuals are well protected, and so on. While there has been government austerity and a cutback in social security payments these have been cut from a much higher initial base than in many other countries. Discussion of Dutch parties as being more or less conservative must always be seen, therefore, within this perspective.

Christen Democratische Appel — CDA
(Christian Democratic Appeal)

Headquarters	: Dr Kuyperstraat 5, 2514 BA, The Hague (tel: 070 - 924461)
Party leader in Second Chamber	: Bert de Vries
Party leader in First Chamber	: Dr J H Christiaanse
Party Chairman	: Cees Bremmer
Youth organization	: *Christen Democratisch Jongeren Appel* (CDJA) (Chairman: Hans Huibers)
Women's organization	: *Vrouwenberaad* (Chair: Mevr van Aardenne)
Party institute	: *Wetenschappelijk Instituut voor het CDA* (Director: Arie Oostlander)
Party newspapers	: *CDA Actueel*; *CDA Krant*
Membership	: 130,000 (1987)

History

A unified Dutch Christian Democratic Party, incorporating Catholic and different Protestant denominations, only dates from 1980, when three separate parties, two Protestant and one Catholic, finally merged after 13 years of negotiations and slow rapprochement.

(i) Katholieke Volkspartij — KVP
(Catholic People's Party)

Dutch Catholics (fluctuating at around 35–40 per cent of the population, and especially concentrated in the southern provinces of Brabant and Limburg) were long disadvantaged within the Netherlands. Until 1795 they were barred from public office, and a properly structured Roman Catholic hierarchy was only re-established in 1853. In the 1840s and 1850s Catholics were in alliance with Liberals, but subsequently broke with them, primarily over the issue of state education, to which Catholics shared a common hostility with Protestant parliamentarians. The first prominent Catholic politician was a priest, Mgr. Schaepman, who in 1883 put forward a draft programme for a Catholic political party. This was not to come about until much later (Schaepman himself was opposed within the Catholic community over his support for extension of the franchise and for compulsory education) but in 1888 Catholic representatives took part in a coalition with the Calvinists for the first time (the Mackay government). In 1897 Catholic electoral organizations accepted a common programme, and in 1904 a General League of Roman Catholic electoral associations was set up. Catholics also began to organize among industrial workers and in 1889 a Roman Catholic workers' union was established at Enschede.

In the interwar period when Dutch society was most strongly "pillarized" the Roman Catholic "pillar" became the largest voting bloc in the country. The Catholic Ruys de Beerenbrouck was Prime Minister from 1918 to 1925, and again from 1929 to 1933, and even in other ministries Catholics always formed the largest component. While proportional representation led to a number of breakaway Catholic political movements to left and right, a well organized Catholic mainstream party, the Roman Catholic States Party (RKSP) was finally established in 1926. Catholic voters were highly disciplined, with over 80 per cent voting for Catholic candidates, and with over a third of Roman Catholic voters being party members.

After World War II a new Catholic party — the Catholic People's Party (KVP) — was formed, and retained the powerful position of its predecessor. The KVP had different coalition partners, but was present in every coalition from 1946 until the founding of the CDA, and had the largest number of ministers on all but three occasions. There were five KVP Prime Ministers, L. J. M. Beel (1946–48 and 1958–59), J. F. de Quay (1959–63), U. B. M. Marijnen (1963–65), J. M. L. TH. Cals (1965–66) and P. J. S. de Jong (1967–71). Moreover the two CDA Prime Ministers, Van Agt and Lubbers, have come from the KVP.

For the immediate postwar period its chairman was C. Romme, a strong and authoritarian party leader. While the KVP was the dominant Catholic political force there continued to be a number of schisms to left and right (e.g. the Catholic National Party, KNP, and the Dutch Roman Catholic party, RKPN, on the right, and the PPR on the left). The Roman Catholic "pillar" gradually became less monolithic. As the Dutch Roman Catholic Church became more independent of Rome and more ecumenical in spirit, support grew for the establishment of a wider Christian Democratic party.

In the 1960s a rapid decline in both KVP electoral support and in party membership helped to give a new urgency to the process of unity. Party membership had been as high as 430,000 in 1955 and was still around 385,000 in 1960. By 1970 however it was under 100,000 and at the time of full merger in 1980 was under 50,000. From winning 31.9 per cent of the Dutch vote in 1963 the KVP was only winning 17.7 per cent in 1972. In its fiefs of Limburg and Noord Brabant the party vote went down over the same period from 77.4 per cent to 43.9 per cent and from 71.9 per cent to 37.3 per cent respectively.

In spite of its decline the KVP was the biggest of the three religious parties at the time of merger. It was a party of government with no experience of opposition and with a pragmatic rather than ideological approach. It was still strongly regionally based in the south of the country. The role of the Catholic Church in the party's policies however had become much less direct.

(ii) Anti-Revolutionnaire Party — ARP
(Anti-Revolutionary Party)

The name Anti-Revolutionary Party refers to the 19th century reaction of devout Calvinists against the secular and materialist values of the Dutch governing elite, who were inspired by the Enlightenment and by the French Revolution. The movement's first major leader was Groen van Prinsterer, and the key mobilizing issue was the struggle against liberal school laws. In 1878 the first party programme in Dutch history was adopted, and in 1879 the first Dutch political party was established (also the world's first party of a Christian Democratic orientation).

Since the new movement could not take over the whole state apparatus its objective was to create a separate Calvinist "pillar" within Dutch society, the so-called concept of "sovereignty in one's own sphere". The movement thus led to the creation of a Christian Free University in 1880 as well as of a separate political party and of separate Catholic schools.

In 1888 the ARP formed a coalition with the Catholics under the ARP politician Mackay. This was the beginning of a long period of Calvinist/Catholic co-operation and even formal coalition.

The ARP was now led by the Rev. Abraham Kuyper, who was a philosopher as well as parliamentary leader and who championed the rights of the *Kleine Luyden* or "small people" within Dutch society. He also supported the extension of the suffrage.

In 1894 this led to a split within the anti-revolutionary movement, between the more radical wing led by Kuyper, and a conservative wing led by the aristocrat, De Savornin Lohman, which wanted to go less far in extending voting rights. This also mirrored a split within Calvinism as a whole, with those who had stayed with the mainstram Reformed Church (*Hervormde Kerk*) tending to support Lohman, and those who had joined the emergent Orthodox Churches (*Gereformeerde Kerke*) supporting Kuyper. Fourteen years after the original split and after a number of name changes Lohman's group helped to establish a new national party, the Christian Historical Union (see below).

The ARP provided two Prime Ministers in the years before World War I, Kuyper himself (1901–5) and Heemskerk (1908–13). In the latter's administration the most significant figure was the ARP minister Talma, who championed thorough social reform.

After 1918 the ARP actually lost in electoral strength but took part in all government coalitions, and had an influence out of proportion to its strength largely as a result of the prestige of its leader, Colijn, who was Prime Minister on five occasions. Colijn gave the ARP a much more conservative stamp than it had had under Kuyper, especially on economic issues.

This conservative position was initially maintained in the years after World War II under the leadership of Jan Schouten, who opposed decolonization, and also an increased role for the Dutch state in economic and social matters.

Although the ARP provided the first postwar Prime Minister (Gerbrandy) it was in opposition from 1946 to 1952. In the latter years however, it began a long period as a partner in government. It had already dropped its opposition to the concept of the welfare state.

The ARP provided two more Prime Ministers, Zijlstra (1966–67) and Biesheuvel (two administrations in 1971–73).

Throughout the 1950s ARP membership held steady at around 100,000 but in the 1960s and 1970s it began a gradual decline, which was much less dramatic than that in the Catholic Peoples's Party.

The party also moved somewhat to the left, putting more of an emphasis on third world development and becoming more sharply critical of nuclear weapons. Some of its more radical members joined the PPR. The merger debate led to further losses of members to the RPF on the right and to the EVP on the left. A minority of ARP members were highly critical of the Christian Democratic coalition with the Liberals (VVD) in 1977 and subsequently also to the installation of Cruise missiles in the Netherlands.

The ARP had the strongest organization of any of the Christian Democratic parties in the Netherlands. Its continuing association with orthodox Calvinism gave it a strong tradition of discipline but also led to considerable internal democracy, because of it members' belief that loyalty to the leadership was not unquestioned but had to be earned. Moreover church and political leadership were kept separate, since both had different responsibilities.

(iii) Christelijk - Historische Unie — CHU (Christian Historical Union)

As outlined above the CHU stemmed from the split between Dr Kuyper and De Savornin Lohman within the anti-revolutionary movement. The CHU was founded formally only in 1908. Its members came mainly from the mainstream Dutch Reformed Church rather than the Orthodox Reformed Churches. It tended to be more conservative than the ARP on social issues, and became the party of King, Country and established Church.

In the interwar years the policy differences between the two Protestant parties changed, with the CHU becoming if anything less conservative than the ARP under Colijn. One CHU leader, De Geer, became Prime Minister on two occasions (1926-29 and 1939–40).

After World War II a number of members on the left of the CHU took part in the foundation of the new Labour Party, the PVDA. The CHU survived, however, under the leadership of H. Tilanus, and took part in most postwar coalitions. It was by some way the smallest of the three Christian parties, and never had more than 50,000 members in the postwar years. Membership was down to 26,000 by the time of merger, and its support was declining more sharply than that of the ARP.

A key organizational difference between the CHU and the ARP was between their respective organizational structures, with the CHU being a looser electoral alliance than the tightly structured ARP.

The merger

The process leading to merger began as early as the late 1960s when the first contacts were made between the three parties with a view to the establishment of a unified Christian Democratic Party. It was a difficult process, with differences between the parties not just in terms of religious background or policy (although there was a wide ideological spread between left and right) but also in terms of political organization and culture. A particularly important catalytic role was played by Dr P. A. J. M. Steenkamp.

In 1971 a common programme was agreed upon and in 1975 the federation of the Christian Democratic Appeal (CDA) was established. A common list of candidates was offered for the 1977 parliamentary elections, and a single parliamentary group was subsequently established. In 1980 a unified party was finally achieved.

The CDA has been in government, and provided the Prime Minister, since its formation. After the collapse of the CDA - VVD coalition in 1981 there was a CDA - PVDA - D66 coalition again under Van Agt of the CDA from 1981 to 1982, followed by a caretaker CDA - D66 government after the departure of the Socialists.

Since 1982 the CDA has been in coalition with the VVD,, with Ruud Lubbers as Prime Minister. In the 1984 European elections the CDA obtained 30 per cent and eight seats in the European Parliament. In the 1986 national elections the CDA performed strongly with 34.6 per cent of the votes and 54 seats in the Second Chamber. It has 26 seats in the First Chamber.

Support

In the 1986 elections the CDA did outstandingly well and gained over 5 per cent more votes than in 1982 (29.3 per cent to 34.6 per cent). Nevertheless, that is little more than the Catholic Party used to get on its own (e.g. 31.9 per cent as recently as 1963) and far less than the combined total of the three parties which have gone to make up the CDA. From 1946 to 1963 the percentage of the electorate voting for the three main Confessional parties never fell lower than 48.5 per cent (1959) and rose as high as 53.4 per cent (1948). In the 1960s a precipitous decline began which reduced their combined vote from 49.2 per cent in 1963 to only 31.3 per cent in 1972, since when the decline has again been arrested.

The component parties of the CDA have had two main electoral strengths, the support of their own "pillars" (which meant that the Catholic Party, in particular, won the support of Catholics in all social classes) and their position in the middle of the Dutch political spectrum, which has made them a key element in most government coalitions, and given them the aura of power.

The former asset has clearly declined to a very considerable extent. The Catholic provinces, for example, no longer vote monolithically for the CDA, and both the VVD and the Labour Party have made major gains in those areas. "Pillarization" still has some impact and the CDA still appears to have the support of around half of Dutch Catholics and a considerably higher percentage of members of the Orthodox Reformed Churches. These percentages rise greatly when active church goers are taken into account. On the other hand relatively few non-church goers have voted for the CDA. A further feature of the CDA's support pattern has been that considerably more women than men have voted for the party.

If "pillarization" has declined, however, the CDA's 1986 election success appears to be more attributable to its aura as a governing party, and, in particular to the success of the Prime Minister, Ruud Lubbers. It is clear, for example, that a considerable proportion of its increased vote came from defecting VVD voters.

Interestingly enough the lowest increase in the CDA's vote in 1986 came in its strongest province (Limburg) and in it weakest (Groningen). The party's two strongest provinces are the predominantly Catholic Limburg and Noord Brabant where the CDA still has 46 per cent and 44.2 per cent of the vote respectively. The only other province where it still has over 40 per cent of the vote is Overijssel (41 per cent) with its heavily Protestant rural areas. Several of the party's greatest strongholds are in this province, notably the small town of Raalte where it obtained 66.6 per cent of the vote in 1986.

The CDA got between 30 per cent and 40 per cent of the vote in Gelderland (37.5 per cent), Friesland (34.8 per cent) Utrecht (33.7 per cent) and Zeeland (32.9 per cent). It is weaker in the heavily urbanized provinces of South (Zuid) Holland (29.4 per cent) and North (Noord) Holland (27.7 per cent). Even in these provinces it is much stronger in some rural areas and small towns where it gets over 50 per cent of the vote. It is also strong, although often as runner-up in the VVD, in the most prosperous commuter suburbs. It is weaker in the cities. Of the largest cities in the country, the CDA is the largest party only in Apeldoorn and Eindhoven. Even in The Hague (Den Haag) it only got 25.4 per cent of the vote in 1986, in Rotterdam 19.6 per cent and in Amsterdam only 15.8 per cent (where it was also in third place).

The CDA's two weakest provinces of all are in the north-east of the country in Drenthe (27 per cent) and in Groningen (27.9 per cent) with its strong left-wing tradition. The CDA got only 16 per cent in the main town of Groningen but fared even worse in some of the villages near the German border where it seldom gets much more than 5 per cent of the vote.

Organization

After a transitional period when members of its three component parties kept their original party membership the CDA is now a direct membership party in its own right. In organizational terms the CDA has taken most from the tightly organized ARP structure rather than the more regionally-based KVP and the very loosely organized CHU.

The CDA currently (1987) has 130,000 members. The basic unit is the communal branch of which there are 700: these may set up smaller units where necessary. The regional tier consists of district branches (*Kamerkringen*) which are based on national electoral districts and of "provincial branches", consisting of all the local branches within a province. In most parts of the country these two tiers are the same, but not in the more densely populated provinces of Noord and Zuid Holland, where there are several *Kamerkringen* within each province. In Gelderland and Noord Braant, where the CDA is particularly strong, there are separate organizational structures with sub-regional units as well. At national level there is a party executive of 40 members, consisting of representatives of the *Kamerkringen* (based on the number of party members within each district) and also of "freely chosen" experts, who are selected on a national basis. There is also a smaller daily executive with seven full voting members, and an even smaller party presidium.

The party council of around 300 voting members (mainly from the *Kamerkringen*) meets twice a year in the spring and autumn, and is very influential. The party congress only meets every two years and tends to be deferential to the leadership, more so, for example, than its equivalent in the Labour Party.

The CDA also has a separate campaign structure in election times. The party has a headquarters staff of around 50. Like most Dutch parties the CDA has no formal leadership structure. When the party is in power (as at the present time) the Prime Minister is the effective political leader. At other times this position would be taken by the leader of the parliamentary group in the Second Chamber. The party chairman also has a powerful role. There is a special procedure for electing the party's top candidate at national elections: a proposal is made by the party council, which is ratified at a special party congress.

Other candidates for national parliamentary elections are chosen by a lengthy and complex set of procedures involving initial proposals from the party executive (subsequently strengthened by the addition of district representatives), voting at the local branches and collating of the results at national level.

The CDA has a number of affiliated organizations. The youth organization of the CDJA has grown very rapidly in recent years (2,000 members in early 1987) and is generally on the left of the party on such issues as security policy and the future of civil nuclear energy. The women's organization is called the *Vrouwenberaad*. A third organization, the association of local and provincial representatives (*Vereniging van Gemeente en Provincie Bestuurders*) is a powerful force in a party so rooted in the smaller towns and communes.

The party has no formal link with the trade unions, but there are representatives of the Christian trade unions on the party executive. The party has an educational and training centre (*De Stichting Kader en Vormingswerk CDA* or KAVO) as well as a policy unit to examine Christian Democratic philosophy and policies (The *Wetenschappelijk Instituut*). This is relatively independent of the parent party and has its own board and has its own monthly publication, *CD Verkenningen*. Under its auspices an association for Christian Democratic Academics (*Platform Jonge Christen democratische Academici*) has also been established. Party policy formulation is assisted by a number of committees reporting to the party executive.

There are two Christian Democratic broadcasting associations (The NCRU or Dutch Christian Broadcasting Association and the KRO or Catholic Broadcasting Corporation) which are mainly supported by Christian Democratic sympathizers although they remain editorially independent.

Like other Dutch parties the CDA no longer has a tame party press. The former Calvinist paper *Trouw* is not longer associated with the party and the former Catholic paper the *Volksrant* is now a left of centre daily.

The CDA has its own internal party organs, a free bulletin distributed to members (*CD Krant*) and a subscription newspaper which appears every two or three weeks, *CDA Actueel*.

The CDA finance is largely based on membership subscriptions, for which there is a current minimum fee of 25 guilders but a target average of 50 guilders. Unlike the Labour Party the CDA does not impose levies on its office holders at national level, although this is done in some provinces (e.g. Limburg).

The CDA's international relations are overseen by a foreign affairs committee. The CDA is a member of the European and International Union of Christian Democrats as well as of the European People's Party within the European Parliament. The leader of its MEPs is an advisory member of the national executive.

Policies

The CDA is still the key pivot party at the centre of the Dutch political spectrum and the one most likely to participate in any government. The merger between three disparate parties seems to have been successfully accomplished, and the CDA is now a broadly-based party inspired by Christian principles but not linked to any one religious denomination. It contains a wide spectrum of political opinion from the centre-left to centre-right. With its emphasis on social issues and on third world development and its links to strong Christian trade unions it is still somewhat to the left of some other Christian Democratic parties elsewhere in Europe, and also puts less of an emphasis on family policy than, for example, the German and Belgian Christian Democrats. Nevertheless, the CDA has now been in coalition for 11 of the last 12 years with the right of centre VVD, and its own left wing is now much more muted, especially on defence questions. The success of the CDA in the 1986 elections was largely due to recognition of some of the tough economic measures carried out by the CDA Prime Minister Ruud Lubbers.

An important CDA principle is that of subsidiarity, with decisions being taken at their appropriate level, with responsibility dispersed and with centralization avoided where possible. The CDA emphasizes not just the important roles of government and of the private profit making sector but also of non-profit making collective organizations and volunteer groups, NGOs, citizen groups and trade unions.

In its economic policy the CDA has had to carry out a major exercise in retrenchment, and in limiting the growth of social security expenditure during its last few years of government. It has emphasized the need for sacrifices to be made, although there should be enhanced protection for the poorest. Social welfare payments should not perpetuate dependence but people should not be thrown back on individualism either. Solidarity is a key principle.

The CDA has advocated greater flexibility in the workplace. It agrees with the principle of shortening the working week, but considers that how this is implemented should best be left to the social partners. Co-determination and participation of employees in decision-making has been strongly supported. Multinationals should be subject to international legal rules.

Stewardship of resources is another repeated party theme. One of the key elements in this is environmental planning, which the CDA believes should not be conditioned by narrow economic reasoning. On the issue of civil nuclear energy the CDA believes that existing plants should stand, but that changes in the energy market have made it possible to be very cautious about any expansion of dependence upon nuclear energy. Where possible its use should be avoided.

On moral issues the CDA puts a major new emphasis on the potential risks of new scientific and technological developments, and the ethical and legal issues that are raised, for example, by biogenetics. The CDA is also very concerned about the issues raised by in vitro fertilization, surrogate motherhood and anonymous donors. The CDA is opposed to hired mothers and also believes that children should have a right to know their own fathers. The party believes that a law on euthanasia would be premature. It considers that so-called free decisions are not always really free.

The CDA advocates increased assistance for women with unwanted pregnancies. It also considers that durable relationships outside marriage, in which the participants accept responsibility for each other, are also entitled to recognition.

In education policy the CDA continues to defend denominational schools and institutes. It also considers that independent school boards should have a greater say than local authorities.

On the issue of asylum the CDA takes a middle position between the more expansive policy of the PVDA and the more restrictive policy of the VVO. The CDA also calls for greater integration of immigrants in the Netherlands. It even supported the subsidized building of mosques, but was opposed on the issue by other parties.

The CDA is in favour of stronger European integration leading to European Union. It voted in favour of the single European Act, and supports restrictions on the national veto. The powers of the European Parliament should be increased, and European political co-operation developed.

Defence policy has been a difficult subject,

as a minority within the CDA, especially some with ARP backgrounds, opposed the stationing of Cruise missiles in the Netherlands. In the end this opposition became isolated, and the CDA has now approved the deployment of the missiles (only six of its parliamentarians eventually voted against deployment).

The CDA strongly supports NATO, but points out the moral need for disarmament. There should be a steady reduction in dependence on nuclear arms. Any sudden or one-sided abolition of nuclear weapons, however, could itself endanger peace, and would be irresponsible. Defence policy should be restrained and non-aggressive, but effective and credible.

Third-world development is a very important area of policy for the CDA, and on two occasions in recent years was the first item on the party's action programme. There should be a new international economic order, more aid for developed countries and the latter should also be less protectionist.

Personalities

The dominant personality within the CDA is the current Dutch Prime Minister, Ruud Lubbers, to whose image as a strong leader a good measure of the party's 1986 electoral success can be attributed. The party chairman is Wim van Velzen, who (although he had been close to the former KVP) represents a new generation within the CDA in that he was never a member of any of its former component parties.

The chairman of the CDA parliamentary group in the Second Chamber is Bert de Vries and in the First Chamber Prof. Jan Christiaanse. The leader of the CDA delegation in the European Parliament is J. Penders.

Among the nine CDA members of the current government H. Van den Broek is the Minister of Foreign Affairs and Dr Onno Ruding Minister of Finance. Dr Piet Bukman, a former party chairman, is the Minister of Development. Frans Andriessen is a member of the European Commission, Lubbers' CDA predecessor as Prime Minister, Andreas van Agt, is now EEC Ambassador to Japan.

Partij van de Arbeid — PvdA
(Labour Party)

Headquarters : Nicolaas
Witsenkade 30,
1017 2T Amsterdam
(tel: 020 5512155)
Party leader in
Second Chamber : Wim Kok

Party leader in
First Chamber : Dr G. J. J. Schinck
Chair : Marjanne Sint
Party secretary : Wim van Velzen
Youth organization : *De Jonge Socialisten*
Women's organization : *Rooie Vrouwen*
Party institute : Wiardi Beckman
Stichting
Membership : 102,000 (1987)

History

The Dutch Labour Party was founded in 1946 but its roots go back to the 19th century. The first Dutch socialist party at national level was the *Social-Democratische Bond* (Social Democratic League) which was founded in 1882, and whose leader, F-Domela Nieuwenhuis was elected to the Second Chamber in 1888. It moved, however, in the direction of anarchism, and extra-parliamentary action, and in 1894 a new socialist party was founded, the *Social Democratische Arbeiderspartij* (Social Democratic Workers' Party), which decided to follow a parliamentary road to socialism. Heavily influenced by the German Social Democrats, its dominant personality was P. J. Troelstra.

The new party gradually gained in strength, and established close links with the new Dutch Federation of Trade Unions. In 1909 it expelled its radical wing, who went on to form the Dutch Communist Party (see separate entry). By 1913 it was sufficiently important to be offered places in the government, which it refused.

In the interwar period it consistently polled over 20 per cent of the vote. The rigid "pillarization" of Dutch society made it difficult for it to break out of its own support base, which it consolidated with its own newspapers, broadcasting organization (VARA), and other institutions. It increased its membership from 27,000 to over 82,000. It was, however, excluded from government.

In the late 1930s it moderated some of its policies, and dropped, for instance, its objections to the monarchy and to defence expenditure. Finally, in 1939 two socialists entered government for the first time in the Cabinet of De beer.

After the World War II, a determined attempt was made to break out of the socialists' pro-war ghetto. The so-called *doorbraak* or "breakthrough" was aimed at creating a much broader party of former Socialists, Liberals and Christians. The *Partij van de Arbeid* was founded in 1946, but soon proved to be the old Socialist Workers' Party a little larger. The most prominent liberal in the party, P. J. Oud, left and eventually helped form the new VVD.

Unlike the interwar years, however, the PvdA soon established itself as a party of government, being continually represented in the Cabinet from 1945 to 1958. In 1948 Willem Drees became the first Dutch Socialist Prime Minister, and went on to lead further coalition governments in 1951, 1952 and 1956. In the latter year it obtained a record total of 32.7 per cent of the vote, and 50 seats in the Second Chamber.

As a government party the PvdA took a more moderate line on economic as well as defence and foreign policy issues, although the question of East Indies decolonization proved to be highly divisive. By 1959, when its statement of basic principles was rewritten, it no longer paid even lip service to Marxism. Its rightward course caused dissent on its left wing. In 1956 some left-wingers formed the Pacifist Socialist Party (see separate entry), while others formed a left-wing "ginger" group, the *Sociaal Democratisch Centrum* within the party. In 1959 their activities within the party were curtailed.

The 1960s were a difficult time for the PvdA. It lost votes in successive elctions, its membership dropped from 140,000 to under 100,000, and it was excluded from government for all but one year (when it participated in the Cals government from 1965–66). The left wing had a much more successful revival than in the 1950s in the shape of *Nieuw Links* (New Left), which without being a formally organized group, managed to have a major influence within the party. *Nieuw Links* sought greater democracy and less elitism within the party, and more radical economic and foreign policies, with a greater emphasis on industrial co-determination, third world development, and so on. Above all it wanted the PvdA to become less of a cautious establishment party and more of an action party reflecting the new movements and ideas of the late 1960s. In 1967 and 1969 New Left managed to gain significant representation on the party executive and in 1971 one of its number, Van der Louw, became party chairman.

The increased influence of the left led to a schism on the party's more traditional right with a number of members breaking away and forming a new party, *Democratisch Socialisten '70* (Democratic Socialists 1970), under the leadership of Willem Drees junior, the son of the former PvdA Prime Minister. For a short time the new party did extremely well, and it had two ministers in the 1971–72 Biesheuvel government, but it eventually faded into insignificance. By 1983 it no longer existed.

An important development in 1971 was that the PvdA entered a pre-election agreement with D66 and the Radicals (PPR). In 1972 this was formalized in a detailed common programme between the three parties entitled *Keerpunt* or "turning point", which represented a significant shift in Dutch political practice.

In 1972 elections saw a recovery in PvdA votes (up from 24.7 per cent to 27.3 per cent since 1971), and in 1973 a coalition government was put together under the leadership of the Socialist Joop den Uyl. This included the other contributors to *Keerpunt*, D66 and the Radicals, but also two of the Christian parties, the KVP and ARP. This was the first government in Dutch history which had a left-of-centre majority.

In the next elections, in 1977, the PvdA obtained its best ever result, with 33.8 per cent of the vote, and 53 seats in the Second Chamber. In the negotiations that followed, however, the party overplayed its hand and an alternative coalition was formed between the Christian Democrats and the Liberals.

After the 1981 elections the PvdA briefly returned to government in a coalition with the CDA and D66 under the leadership of Van Agt of the CDA, but the coalition fell apart in 1982. The PvdA then went into opposition. In the 1984 European Parliament elections it was the best supported party, polling 33.7 per cent and obtaining nine seats.

In the 1986 national elections it increased its vote to 33.3 per cent, but remained in opposition. After the elections its long time leader, Joop den Uyl, stood down and was replaced as parliamentary leader by Wim Kok. The PvdA currently has 52 members in the Second Chamber and 26 in the First Chamber.

Support

When the party was re-established after the war it was hoped that it would attract wider and less class-based support than the pre-war Social Democratic Workers' Party. However, whilst it has had a generally higher level of support, it has only had limited success in breaking out of the old Socialist "pillar". Although its level of support has fluctuated considerably, with highs of 32.7 per cent (1956), 33.8 per cent (1977) and 33.3 per cent in 1986 (its second highest vote ever) and with lows of 25.6 per cent (1948), 23.6 per cent (1967) and 24.6 per cent (1971), it has never obtained more than a third of the total vote. Its good recent results have tended to be more at the expense of the small parties to its left than anyone else.

Successive surveys of its electorate have shown that its greatest strength has been among non-practising Protestants (many from the Dutch Reformed Church) and those with few religious convictions, although it has gradually won greater support among Catholics. Its potential to mobilize the working-class vote has been considerably undercut by the continuing strength of the Christian Democrats among all social classes. It is strongest in the cities with over 100,000 inhabitants in the overwhelmingly Protestant northern provinces and weakest in the southern Catholic provinces, and in the prosperous suburbs and Calvinist rural areas.

These patterns were confirmed but slightly modified in the 1986 national elections. It was the largest party, often by overwhelming margins, in all but two of the 17 largest Dutch cities, including cities as different as Rotterdam (49.6 per cent), Amsterdam (47.2 per cent) and even The Hague (36.4 per cent).

Its three strongest provinces were the northern provinces of Groningen (46.8 per cent), Drenthe (43.5 per cent) and Friesland (39.5 per cent). Its greatest bastions in the whole country are in some of the smaller towns in Groningen like Winschoten (58.9 per cent) and Veendam (56.8 per cent). Rural Groningen has always had a strong left-wing tradition.

In the densely populated Randstad region the party is also quite strong (Noord Holland 34.5 per cent, Zuid Holland 33.3 per cent), although Utrecht (26.6 per cent) is now the party's weakest province. The party did not, however, do well in the Rotterdam region where it has always been powerful in the past, and its vote slightly dropped between 1982 and 1986.

In contrast the party made major gains in the Catholic province of Noord Brabant and Limburg where it had always been weak. In Noord Brabant its vote went up from 24.6 per cent to 29.6 per cent and in Limburg from 26.2 per cent to 33.9 per cent. In several towns in Limburg the party's vote went up by over 10 per cent.

The Labour Party's weakest areas in Holland are in the most prosperous suburban areas, where they are usually third behind the Liberals and the Christian Democrats (e.g. Wassenaar where they have only 11.9 per cent to 43.8 per cent for the VVD) and in the fundamentalist Calvinist communities, such as Bunschoten (6.6 per cent) or Urk, where they only have 0.9 per cent of the vote.

Organization

The Labour Party currently has around 102,000 members (1987), organized in 750 local branches. There is also a regional tier of organization (known as a *Gewest* in the PvdA), generally based on individual provinces but on individual electoral districts in the more populated areas (Amsterdam, Rotterdam, The Hague; Noord Holland

and Noord Brabant are also divided). There are 17 such regional organizations.

At national level there is a party executive (*Partij Bestuur*) of 21 members, elected by the party congress, and generally meeting on a monthly basis. There is also a smaller "daily" executive (*Daagelijks Bestuur*) of eight members, which meets on a fortnightly basis.

The party council meets a few times a year, and tends to be the national sounding board for the party's activists. It was the party council which rejected the coalition terms that had been negotiated between the Labour Party and the Christian Democrats in 1977, and which had been accepted by the parliamentary party.

The party congress meets every two years. Largely as a result of the activism of the *Nieuw Links* period the congress has become more assertive towards the party leadership, although less so than the party council. The independence of the congress is underpinned by it having its own chairman, who is separate from the chairman of the party.

There is no formally elected leader of the party but in practice the political leader is the leader of the parliamentary group in the Second Chamber. This is generally the number one (*Lijstrekker*) on the Labour list in the preceding national elections, who is chosen by a separate procedure at the extraordinary party congress. While the leader of the parliamentary group is generally more powerful than the party chairman, the balance between the two depends to a considerable degree on their respective personalities. A strong party chairman (like Max van de Berg when elected to the post) can have a powerful position within the party.

The Labour Party has the largest headquarters staff of any Dutch party, with 85 full and part-time staff. Unlike the other main parties, the headquarters are located in Amsterdam rather than The Hague. It is felt that this gives it greater independence from day-to-day parliamentary pressures.

The candidate selection procedure for national elections has become much more decentralized since the *Nieuw Links* reforms. The national executive suggests a "profile" of the type of candidates required and an independent committee chosen by a party congress makes recommendations as to order of candidates but the final choice is made by the individual districts. Some within the party have felt that this has led to a premium being put on local activism rather than national experience and expertise. The party secretary led an attempt to modify this system at the 1987 party congress which would have given a greater say to the national party, but the proposal was narrowly defeated at the congress.

A further legacy of the *Nieuw Links* period are the tough party rules preventing cumulation of elected posts by one individual.

The most powerful policy-making body is the party executive, although a strong party leader like Den Uyl has had a decisive say. When the party is in government its council has a more powerful role, and can be ignored by the parliamentary party at its peril. There are also a number of party policy committees. At present a thorough review of policy is being carried out under Jan Pronk. The party's research foundation, the *Wiardi Beckman Stichting*, has relatively little influence, and tends to be on the right wing of the party.

Of the groups affiliated with the party, the most influential is probably its women's organization, *Rooie Vrouwen*, which has a major say, for example on the choice of candidates. The party's youth organization, *De Jonge Socialisten*, has a less influential role. Another significant organization within the party is *Abs*, a third world pressure group.

The pre-war "Red Family" of linked Socialist organizations of all types is much less closely knit than it was. After the war the party's links with the trade unions, for example, were established on a more distant basis. The unions have no special rights within the party, although they retain considerable influence, such as through the party's Labour work group.

The party's press has also fragmented and the former Socialist national paper, *Het Vrije Volk*, has been sold. There is still a Socialist broadcasting organization, the VARA.

Well over 80 per cent of party income comes from membership dues, which are levied on a sliding scale according to income, with a current minimum of around 25 guilders a year, and with an average levy of 60 guilders. Membership is organized centrally, and there is no direct financial link between a member and his or her branch. Another source of income is a special levy on political incomes, on those in the party holding paid offices such as mayors. This was extremely controversial when first introduced in the early 1970s, and it was alleged that it undercut office-holders' independence.

The Labour party is a member of the Socialist international and the Confederation of European Socialist Parties. In the European Parliament it sits in the Socialist Group. The PvdA is also a member of SCANDILUX.

Policies

From being a generally conservative social democratic party in the 1940s and 1950s, the PvdA became rather more radical in the late 1960s and 1970s. Its 1977 "platform of principles" proposed some very major changes in Dutch policy at home and abroad, and in the way society was organized. The influence of this period is still considerable although the party's attitude is generally a pragmatic and moderate one in everyday politics. It recognizes that it must maintain a broad appeal if it is to return to government, and that democratic Socialism can only be advanced by small steps. If it does re-enter government, it is highly unlikely to be able to lead a coalition with the other left-of-centre parties, and its most likely coalition partner is the CDA, which is somewhat closer to it on economic and defence issues than the VVD. A coalition with the VVD, with whom the only element in common is a lay perspective, would be much more difficult, although not impossible.

The PvdA has been highly critical of the austerity economic measures carried out by the Lubbers coalition government, believing that they have been carried out with insufficient consultation, delayed economic recovery, damaged economic cohesion and put too much emphasis on cuts in public expenditure. As a result unemployment has remained high, the purchasing power of lower income groups has been reduced, and the welfare state has been weakened.

The PvdA has called for work to be given a higher priority than income, and investment than consumption. It has called for higher economic growth, through measures to stimulate the economy at both national and joint European level. There should be major public investment in environmental technology, energy conservation, urban renewal, and other major infrastructure projects.

The organization of work should also become more flexible. There should be much shorter working hours. The 1986 manifesto called for any redeployment of labour to maintain the purchasing power of workers, but recognized that a high degree of co-operation on the part of the trade unions would also be required if labour costs were not to rise. The party has also called for measures to encourage part-time jobs, more generous paid leave for people to care after invalids, etc, and voluntary early retirement.

Its 1977 platform of principles called for more drastic measures to reduce inequalities, through establishment of a minimum basic income, special allowances for thos working in particularly unpleasant conditions and even establishment of maximum levels of private wealth or fair redistribution by means of taxes and levies on excess profits. The platform also called for all incomes to be a matter of public knowledge.

Defence of the welfare state and industrial

democracy have been important priorities for the party. It was a PvdA member of the European Commission, Henk Vredeling, who put forward the Commission's controversial proposals to strengthen information to, and consultation of employees in large companies. The party has also advocated measures to ensure much greater accountability on the part of multinationals.

The PvdA has also emphasized the need for economic development to be put in a much wider context of consumer protection, limits to natural resources and the need to fully protect the environment. Quantitative growth shuld be replaced by selective growth. Goods should become more durable, and there should be much more recycling and conservation. The PvdA has come out against any further expansion in the use of civil nuclear energy, and would like the existing Dutch nuclear plants to be closed.

The PvdA has put a high emphasis on measures to combat racism and discrimination against immigrants and minority groups. It supports a liberal asylum policy, and has strongly supported further female emancipation. In the past it has supported the abolition of legal penalties with respect to termination of pregnancies, and also the legislation of euthanasia at the request of the person concerned.

Protection of personal privacy and controls on the compilation and use of personal data have been given a high priority. In the past the party has also been very critical of coalition governments being created after elections, often with little direct link to the actual results. The PvdA thus called for potential coalition partners to present the main points of their joint programme before the elections, so that voters would know what they were getting. Moreover, there should be no changes of government in mid-term and a fall of government should lead to new elections. In its 1977 platform of principles the PvdA also called for the abolition of the First Chamber, and the election of Mayors and Queen's Commissioners by municipal councils and provincial assemblies respectively.

The PvdA has generally been strongly in favour of further European integration. It has had a supranationalist approach and does not fear the loss of national sovereignty. It has criticized the EC however, on the grounds that it has not been democratic enough, and has had the wrong policy emphasis.

The PvdA supports the ultimate creation of European Union. It voted in favour of the Single European Act and seven of its then eight members of the European Parliament voted in favour of the much more ambitious Spinelli Draft Treaty on European Union (the eighth member abstained). It calls for improved EC decision-making, with qualified majority voting in the Council and a reinforced European Parliament. European political co-operation should be reinforced.

There should be a general European economic recovery plan to increase employment, with concerted attempts to stimulate the economy, especially in countries with balance of payments surpluses. Reductions in working hours should also be concerted at European level. The internal market should be consolidated, but there should also be complimentary structural programmes to promote the development of the poorer regions. The European Monetary System should be strengthened. European-wide protectionism against third world countries, and in particular developing countries, should be resisted.

An area where the PvdA has been in sharp conflict with the present Dutch government is defence policy. The PvdA originally accepted Dutch abandonment of neutrality and entry into NATO, and in the 1940s and 1950s was a strong and unconditional supporter of the Atlantic Alliance. It began to adopt a more critical stance in the 1960s. It still accepts Dutch membership of NATO. It advocates the longer term dissolution of both military blocs, but recognizes that the NATO framework is needed at present. It has, however, had strong links with the peace movement, and has strongly opposed the deployment of Cruise missiles on Dutch soil.

The PvdA has called for a more defensive defence strategy. It supports nuclear free zones and the removal of battlefield nuclear weapons, and has opposed the strategic defence initiative. The PvdA has also advocated an independent European role on security matters with a stronger European voice in the disarmament process. There should be more co-operation between European countries with regard, for example, to standardization and rationalization of defence equipment, and there should be a joint Western European initiative to achieve a 5 per cent reduction in defence expenditure, to the benefit of the third world. The Western European Union should be the forum for debate on the military aspects of European security.

Development aid policy has had a particularly high priority for the PvdA, which emphasizes the achievements of its Development Minister, Jan Pronk, in the 1973–77 Den Uyl government. It has supported the development of a new international economic order, and has emphasized the need for solutions to the problems of third world debt, taking full account of the socio-economic situation of the debtor countries. Development aid should be increased, but directed to the poorest countries and poorest groups, and designed to help the recipient countries become more truly independent.

The PvdA has advocated increased powers for the United Nations, tough measures against South Africa, and support for the Contadora initiative in Central America. It recognizes Israel's right to exist within safe and recognized borders, but also the rights of the Palestinians to self-determination and to a Palestinian state,

Personalities

Wim Kok has been the party's parliamentary leader in the Second Chamber since July 1986, when he took over from Joop den Uyl. He is a former leader of the largest trade union federation, the FNV.

The first vice-chairman of the Second Chamber Group is Wim Meijer. Among the other influential parliamentarians in the Second Chamber is Thijs Wöltgens, its spokesman on financial matters. Jan Pronk, the former Development Minister, has also recently had an important role within the party in chairing its policy review panel.

The party's chairman in the First Chamber is Ger Schinck, and another prominent figure is Willem van de Zandschulp. The party's chairman is the 38-year-old Marjanne Sint. Wim van Velzen is the party secretary. Another leading party figure is Geke Faber of the women's organisation, *Rooie Vrouwen*.

Among the party's European parliamentarians, Piet Dankert is a former president of the Parliament (from 1982–84) and Hedy d'Ancona, a former junior minister, currently chairs the European Parliament's women's committee.

Volkspartj Voor Vrijheid en Democratie — VVD
(People's Party for Freedom and Democracy)

Headquarters	: Koninginnergracht 57, 2514 AE, The Hague (tel; 070-614121)
Party leader in Second Chamber	: J. J. C. Voorhoeve
Party leader in First Chamber	: D. Luteijn
Chairman of the VVD	: Dr L. Ginjaar
General secretary	: W. J. A. van den Berg
Liberal Research Foundation	: Prof. B. M. Telderstichting
Women's organization	: *Vrouwen in de VVD*
Youth organization	: *Jongeren Organisatie Vrijheid en Democratie* (JOVD)
Student's organization	: *Liberale Studenten Vereniging Nederland* (LSVN)
Party newspaper	: *Vrijheid en Democratie*
Estimated membership	: 85,000 (1986)

History

The first organized Liberal Party was established in 1885, the *Liberale Unie*. This was only a loose association, and within a few years it fragmented into three Liberal sub-groups. The first was the mainstream *Liberale Unie* which provided the nucleus for the three successive Liberal cabinets in the 1880s.

The second was a more radical group (the *Radicale Bond*, formed 1892) which was reinforced in 1902 when there was further schism within the *Liberale Unie* over the extension of voting rights. A new party was then formed, the *Vrijzinnig-Democratische Bond* (VDB), which lasted until World War II.

The third wing of the Dutch Liberalism was a more conservative one, consisting of Liberals who felt that the *Liberale Unie's* bills to extend voting rights and its proposed reform programme went too far. The so-called "Free Liberals" formed their own party structure, The *Bond van Vrije Liberalen* in 1906.

Of the three Liberal parties the mainstream *Liberale Unie* remained substantially the largest of the three, winning between 17 per cent and 20 per cent of the total vote in elections between 1901 and 1913, the radical Liberals between 7 per cent and 11 per cent, and the Free Liberals 4 per cent and 10 per cent. In 1913 the last pre-war election the Liberals still had around 30 per cent of the total vote, and 39 of the 100 seats in the Second Chamber. The final Liberal dominated government was that of Cort Van den Linden from 1913 to 1918 which was responsible for the great constitutional settlement of 1916.

The introduction of proportional representation of 1971 was followed by a severe decline in the Liberal vote, with the three pre-war Liberal parties going down from 39 seats to 15 between the 1913 and 1918 elections.

Shortly afterwards, however, dissidents within the radical Liberals got together with survivors from the *Liberale Unie* and the Free Liberals (as well as from some of the smaller parties which had won seats in 1918), to form a new Liberal Party, the *Vrijheidsbond*, later called the *Liberale Staatspartij* (the Liberal States Party). From 1921 until World War II there were thus only two main Liberal groupings, the Liberal States Party and the VDB. Their combined strength was low, with only 10 to 15 seats in each of the postwar elections, and with only one or two Liberal ministers in most interwar governments.

In a society dominated by "pillars" (see introduction to the Netherlands) Liberal "pillarization" was weaker than that of its rivals.

The differences between the two Liberal parties gradually lessened: one such difference, for instance, was removed in 1936 when the VDB abandoned their long-standing commitment to unilateral national disarmament. The 1933 to 1937 Colijn government included both Liberal States Party and VDB ministers.

The final period of major Liberal realignment took place just after World War II. The Liberal States Party changed its name once more to the *Partij Van de Vrijheid* (Freedom Party) in 1946, under the leadership of V. U. Stikker. The VDB or radical Liberal Party was dissolved and most of its members, including P. J. Oud who had been the Finance Minister in the 1933–37 coalition government, joined up with the Socialists to form the new *Partij Van de Arbeid* (PvdA — Labour Party).

Oud was not at home in the PvdA and in 1947 left it with some of his followers. In 1948 Oud joined up with the Freedom Party to form the present-day *Volkspartij Voor Vrijheid en Democratie* (VVD). The various Liberal currents in Dutch political life were again reunited.

From its foundation to the 1971 general election the VVD never got more than 12 per cent of the vote (in the exceptionally good year of 1959) and generally fluctuated from 8 per cent to 10 per cent.

However, whereas for most of the 1950s the VVD was in continuous opposition, for much of the 1960s the VVD remained in government, though as a junior partner to the Confessional parties and without ever once providing the Prime Minister (there were only two short breaks, one of which, in 1965, being provoked by a conflict between the VVD and its government partners over media policy, with the VVD in favour of the development of commercial television). The VVD more than doubled its vote from 1971 to 1983 and tripled its membership. It was in opposition during the PvdA-led coalition of Den Uyl from 1973 to 1977, and during the Christian Democratic-led coalitions of 1981 to 1982. From 1977 to 1981 and from 1982 to the present the VVD has been in government under Christian Democratic Prime Ministers, van Agt and now Lubbers. The Deputy Prime Minister (Dr R. W. de Korte) four

other Ministers and four state Secretaries are members of the VVD. Besides its 27 members in the Second Chamber the VVD has 12 members in the First Chamber.

Regional and social support

The current VVD, like its Liberal predecessors before the war, has had a relatively narrow basis of support, since it has primarily won its votes from the more prosperous middle-and upper middle-class segment of the secular bloc. From 1970 onwards, however, there was a steady expansion, from 10.3 per cent in 1971 to 17.9 per cent by 1977 and up to 23.07 per cent in the 1982 general election. In the 1984 European Parliament elections VVD support slipped back and this was accentuated in the 1986 election, when it only won 17.4 per cent of the vote, and in the 1987 provincial elections with 15.5 per cent.

As the old socio-religious blocs have become less monolithic, economic considerations came more to the fore. The VVD not only attracted economic conservatives from its old support base in the secular bloc, but also former Protestant voters and also, to a much greater extent than before, former Catholic voters. The party made considerable inroads into the Catholic bastions of the southern Netherlands, especially in North Brabant.

The party also made inroads into the youth vote, due to a considerable extent to its two successive young leaders, Hans Wiegel and Ed Nijpels, both chosen when in their early thirties.

The most striking element of continuity, however, in the VVD's vote has been its continuing support among the more prosperous elements in Dutch society, the self-made men, successful businessmen and professionals. A survey of the 1977 results showed only 16 per cent of its electorate describing themselves as working-class. In regional terms its highest scores in 1986 were in the three densely populated western provinces of North Holland (21.6 per cent, South Holland 19.8 per cent and Utrecht 21.7 per cent) and most particularly in the leafiest suburbs. Behind the western coast is a densely wooded commuter belt. Another such belt lies south-east of Amsterdam, and north and east of Utrecht. In these two areas, especially, the VVD got extremely high support, over 30 per cent in many communes and up to 43.8 per cent in Wassenaar, the prestige suburb north of The Hague.

The Hague, with its large community of lawyers and civil servants, was the major city where the VVD got the highest vote with 22.5 per cent, compared with only 14 per cent of the vote in more industrial and working-class Rotterdam. The VVD's weakest province was Catholic Limburg with 11.4 per cent where it lost particularly severely in 1986 (1982 18.6 per cent).

The VVD was also weak in Overijssel and in the two northernmost provinces of Friesland and Groningen, especially in some of the rural communes with a strong left-wing tradition. The VVD's lowest vote in the whole country was in the former island and highly traditional community of Urk where the VVD only won 1.9 per cent.

Organization (Membership and current structure)

From 1970 the VVD enjoyed a dramatic rise in membership from 30,000 to a peak of almost 110,000 in the early 1980s, the fastest growth of any major Dutch party and faster than the rise in its electoral support. Present membership, however, has declined to around 85,000–90,000.

The basic party units are the branches (*afdelingen*), based on local municipalities which must have a minimum of seven members and of which there are 604 in the whole of the Netherlands, groupings of four to ten branches called *ondercentrales*, and finally the *kamercentrales*, the main organs of the party in each province. The provinces with the largest population have several *kamercentrales*.

The *kamercentrales* send representatives to the main national bodies of the party, and play the main role in candidate selection for the Second Chamber of the national Parliament. The chairmen of the *kamercentrales* are thus the most powerful barons within the VVD.

At national level there is a national executive (*hoofdbestuur*) and an executive committee (*dagelijks bestuur*) of nine persons, responsible for the day-to-day business of the national party. There are currently plans to lower the number of members of the national executive, and to strengthen it with regard to the *kamercentrales*, in order to provide for clearer lines of responsibility within the party. The party is served by a general secretariat with about 20–25 staff of whom six are officers.

The supreme organ of the party is the national party congress, which must gather once a year, and to which all branches send representatives. Extraordinary party congresses are also occasionally held, for example to ratify the order of candidates for national office.

A party council also meets, up to three times a year, with representatives from each *kamercentrale*: the party council is essentially a platform for the party leader on policy matters, for example after the annual Queen's speech outlining the government's forthcoming programme.

The choice of candidates for national office is an extremely complicated process of nominations by branches, agreement on lists at *kamercentrale* level, the compositing of *kamercentrale* lists at national executive level, and final decisions by the national party congress.

In practice the national congress practically never overturns the order of candidates already arrived at, although there are signs that party members are getting more assertive.

Policy-making is primarily carried out by the parliamentary party (in the Second Chamber — the senators in the First Chamber have relatively little say) and to a much lesser extent by the national executive and the party council and congress. The party has a separate research foundation with a small staff which carries out reports on a number of subjects, but these appear to carry relatively little weight in the formulation of party policy. The party also has a number of standing committees whose members are appointed by the national executive.

The party's platform is decided on by the congress on the basis of a document put forward by a drafting committee. The VVD has five members at the European Parliament, who sit in the Liberal Group. The VVD MEPs' leader is on the national executive of the party. Each MEP is assigned in an advisory role to several *kamercentrales*; they are also added to most party committees, and take it in turns to attend the weekly meetings of the VVD parliamentary group in the Second Chamber, where they can take the floor and have influenced its decisions on issues such as preventing the reinstatement of border controls. Since 1984 the European dimension has been more integrated into party policy-making and organization.

Individual membership fees are the single most important component of party funds. The VVD has only three basic rates, for those under 27, those from 27 to 45 and those over 45. The standard rate is 75 guilders. The collection has become more centralized in recent years. This is a minimum contribution only: a very substantial portion of party funds, not far short of the basic membership contribution, comes from additional voluntary contributions. There are also substantial business contributions.

A certain percentage of income raised from the basic membership fee is set aside for the party newspaper *Vrijheid en Democratie* and the rest is divided between the centre (45 per cent) the *kamercentrales* (12 per cent), the *Ondercentrales* (3 per cent) and the local branches (40 per cent).

Policies

The VVD is seen as the most conservative of the major Dutch political parties although it should be recalled that the Dutch political spectrum is less conservative as a whole than many other European countries and secondly that the VVD's general conservatism on economic, defence and law and order issues has been partly offset by its position on certain social or "emancipation" issues (such as women's and homosexual rights).

Over the 1970s however, the party's character has changed. With its electoral success it has become less of a party of wealthy notables and more of a mass party attracting voters with conservative leanings from other political allegiances.

It is the party's position on economic issues which has had the widest appeal, where the party has been successful in winning the support of many of those who feel that the role of the state needs to be cut back, the growth of social security kept in check, fiscal policy kept tight, and so on. Some within the party would like to return to a more expansionary economic policy but they are in a clear minority.

On law and order issues too, the party has been the most conservative Dutch party, attracting support of those who want a much tougher law and order stance. There is no call of any significance, however, for a return to capital punishment, nor has the parliamentary group ever reflected some of the VVD electorate's wish for longer prison sentences.

Another field where the VVD has adopted a distinctive policy position is defence, where it has been the only Dutch party to support unambiguously the stationing of Cruise missiles on Dutch soil. Whereas opinion polls have shown that a significant minority (possibly 20 per cent to 30 per cent) of the VVD's electorate has been hostile to the stationing of Cruise missiles, this has been completely unreflected in the positions adopted by the leadership and by VVD activists in general.

This issue also led to problems with certain left-wing Christian Democrats at the time of the coalition formation in 1977. A Christian Democrat-VVD coalition was formed, nevertheless, and the Christian Democratic dissidents have since been marginalized within their party. This, combined with the Lubbers government's eventual acceptance of Cruise missiles, has led to this issue being removed, at least for the time being, as a source of division between the VVD and its coalition partners.

In the policy area where the VVD has traditionally been a socially liberal party in European terms, namely human rights or emancipation issues, there has been a trend toward somewhat greater conservatism. As the party has attracted many voters from a religious background (notably many Catholics in recent years), the party's position on issues such as abortion has become more nuanced than it was.

An important symbolic turning point was during the long-standing debate on abortion. A joint VVD/Socialist bill that had been adopted by the Second Chamber was voted down in the First Chamber, with VVD members split over the issue. The bill that did eventually pass was a greatly watered-down one sponsored by Christian Democrats and the VVD.

A current highly divisive issue within the VVD is the question of euthanasia. A D66 member of Parliament introduced a liberal bill, and the Christian Democrat/VVD government countered with a much more restrictive one, although the parliamentary party preferred the D66 bill. Here again, the position of the VVD is no longer clear-cut. This tendency to downplay civil liberty and moral issues has been reinforced in the current legislature, where the VVD has been more concerned to avoid public divisions with its Christian Democrat coalition partners. Division within the VVD, however, on any of the above issues, has not led to the development of major factions within the party, and critics prefer to stay within the party mainstream and try to change it from inside rather than become dissidents.

Personalities

The VVD has recently had a complete change of leadership, with the parliamentary leaders in the Second Chamber, and the First Chamber, as well as the party chairman, all being replaced. The period before the 1986 general election had been characterized by a considerable amount of argument within the party (over personalities rather than politics) and after the electoral setback it was felt that a new style of leadership was needed. The VVD has no formal post of party leader, but in practice this role is played by the leader of the parliamentary group in the Second Chamber.

For several years this was Ed Nijpels, like his predecessor Hans Wiegel, only in his early thirties when chosen as leader. After the 1986 election Ed Nijpels stood down and became a member of the new Lubbers Cabinet as the Minister responsible for environmental and planning matters.

His successor was J. J. C. Voorhoeve, a cautious technocrat with a less flamboyant public profile than his predecessors, and less inclined to emphasize differences with the VVD's Christian

Democratic coalition partners. The previous leader in the First Chamber, G. Zoutendijk was also replaced. His successor, David Luteijn, has a farming organization background.

Finally, the longstanding but youthful party chairman, Jan Kamminga, was replaced by the much older Dr L. Ginjaar, a former environment minister. Ginjaar is currently attempting to tighten the party's organizational structure by strengthening the authority of its national executive.

The VVD has five ministers in the present Lubbers government. The Deputy Prime Minister for Economic Affairs is R. W. de Korte who has been the party's economic spokesman for some years. A second important figure is the Justice Minister F. Korthals Altes, who has been secretary-general and party chairman. The Transport Minister is Nellie Smit-Kroes.

W. J. Geertsema who was leader in the 1960s is still a member of the First Chamber, and is one of those in the party less in agreement with the increased emphasis on economic conservatism and the downplaying of "emancipation" issues.

Hans Wiegel was a highly successful leader in the 1970s who has been in temporary exile as the Queen's Commissioner for Friesland – a powerful post but one not within the mainstream of national party life. He has recently been unsuccessful in reasserting himself within the party, but could again be influential in the future.

Democraten 66 (D66)

Headquarters	: Bezuidenhoutseweg 195, 2594 AJ S'Gravenhage (tel: 070 858303)
Party leader in Second Chamber	: Hans van Meerlo
Party leader in First Chamber	: J. Vis
Party chairman	: Saskia van der Loo-de Steenwinkel
Party foundation	: Stichting Wetenschappelijk Bureau D66 (Director: Dr van der Hoeven)
Youth organization	: *Vrijzinnig democratische jongeren organisatie Jonge Democraten* (Chair: E Hordijk)
Women's group	: *Politiek Emancipatie Activerings Centrum* (Chair: Irma Scheindel)
Party organs	: *Democraat;* *Voor de d'raad*
Membership	: 8,000 (1987)

History

D'66 was founded in 1966 by a group of reformers who wanted to develop a more open and accountable Dutch political system. In particular they sought direct election of the Dutch Prime Minister, and the replacement of proportional representation in one national constituency by a constituency-based system which would provide clearer government majorities, and more direct links between the electors and the elected.

In the 1967 national elections they surprised everybody by gaining 4.5 per cent of the vote and seven seats in the Second Chamber. Their first political leader was Hans van Mierlo. Party membership grew rapidly to 6,400 by 1970. In the early 1970s D'66 was forced to make the choice as to whether to remain an independent movement within the Dutch political spectrum, or to forge closer links with other reforming parties on the centre-left. It chose the latter option, and reached an electoral agreement with the Labour Party (PvdA) and the Radical party (PPR) for the 1971 national elections. It went up to 6.8 per cent and 11 seats, but this was well short of its expectations. Before the 1972 elections it entered into a much closer pre-election agreement with the same two parties, in which not just a shadow cabinet but also a draft government programme was agreed upon. The 1972 election saw a severe setback for the party, which fell back to 4.2 per cent of the vote and only six seats. Nevertheless D'66 then entered a coalition government under the PvdA's Joop den Uyl in which D'66 had one full minister, and three state secretaries.

In 1973 Van Mierlo, who had unsuccessfully advocated creation of a large people's party on the centre-left (D'66, PvdA and PPR) stood down as parliamentary leader and was replaced by Jan Terlouw. Membership of the party fell sharply and in 1974 the party almost disbanded. A majority to disband the party was actually achieved at the party congress, but it fell short of the percentage required in the party constitution.

Before the 1977 national elections, however, the party recovered through a clever publicity campaign led by its popular leader, Terlouw, and through distancing itself from its coalition partners, and emphasizing its character as an independent political force. The party did well in the 1977 elections (although subsequently being left out of government) and better in the 1979

European Parliament elections, when it won 8.9 per cent of the national vote and elected two members.

1981 was the year of its greatest success. Membership rose to almost 18,000, it won 11.1 per cent of the vote and 17 Second Chamber seats in the national elections, and re-entered a coalition government with the Labour Party (PvdA) and Christian Democrats. Its leader, Jan Terlouw, became Deputy Prime Minister, and D'66 had two other ministers and three state secretaries. After the PvdA left the coalition in 1982 D'66 remained in a transition government with the Christian Democrats, with no less than five ministers.

The 1982 elections saw a dramatic decline in the vote for D'66 from 11.1 per cent to 4.3 per cent from 17 to six seats. In the 1984 European elections it went down to 3 per cent and lost both of its seats. It was no longer in government. Membership again dropped to 8,500 by 1985.

The most recent development in its roller-coaster existence came when its original leader, Hans van Mierlo, returned to lead the party. D66 again recovered and in 1986 gained 6.1 pr cent of the vote and nine seats in the second chamber. D66 currently has 119 mayors. There are 164 D66 groups represented on municipal councils, as well as 25 others who fought local elections under other labels, but who are affiliated to D66. The party has five seats in the First Chamber. In 1985 D'66 dropped the apostrophe in its name and became D66.

Support

D66 has done best among upper middle-class voters, professionals and intellectuals, and also among those without religious affiliations. It has been stronger in the cities and in commuter towns and suburbs than in rural areas, and it has consistently done better among young voters than it has among the electorate at large. It has enjoyed little voter loyalty, and has had great swings in support. It has been a focal point for protest voters from larger parties.

Many of these trends were confirmed in the 1986 Second Chamber elections, when D66 received 6.1. per cent of the national vote. It won considerable new support from former Labour Party (PvdA) and Liberal (VVD) voters, and also did better among young voters than among the electorate at large.

Its best provinces were Flevoland (7.9 per cent), Noord Holland (7.7 per cent), Zuid Holland and Utrecht (7 per cent in each). Its best city was Amsterdam (8.4 per cent). It did well in university towns (Wageningen 9.3 per cent, Delft 8.8 per cent, Leiden 8.2 per cent) and also in new towns on recently drained polders such as Lelystad (9.7 per cent) and Almere (10.3 per cent) in Flevoland, where it got its highest vote in the country.

Two particular areas of strength have been the small community towns and villages north and east of Amsterdam, and south-west of Rotterdam, where it won between 9 per cent and 10 per cent of the vote in 1986 and where it won up to 18 per cent in its best year of 1981. D66 has done less well in the most prosperous wooded suburbs behind the coast, and east of Utrecht, where the Liberals (VVD) have had their strongest fiefs.

D66 has been less successful in rural areas, and away from the centre of the country. Its weakest provinces in 1986 were Overijssel (4.8 per cent) and Limburg (4.4 per cent), the only province where its vote actually fell from the previous national elections.

Organization

D66 was founded largely in reaction to back-room politics, and its organizational structure is thus characterized by a high degree of openness and internal party democracy. All major decision-making at every level (local, regional and national) is taken at general members' assemblies, at which all paying members can vote. Moreover, there are also strict rules preventing the cumulation of party offices so that no-one can hold more than one office.

There are currently around 8,000 party members, but also a considerable number of sympathizers who contribute to party funds. There are 350 local branches and 12 regional groups. The possibility of creating sub-branches and sub-regions is provided for in the constitution.

At national level there is a national executive (*Hoofdbestuur*) which includes regional representatives and generally meets on a monthly basis and a smaller executive committee (*Dagelijks Bestuur*), which is elected directly by the party congress, and which meets on a weekly basis. Members of the D66 parliamentary group are not allowed to sit on the executive. There is also an advisory council, a standing committee of regionally elected members convened to give the views of members between party congresses. The national party congress is open to all paid-up members and is convened once or twice a year. Typically about 900 members participate (almost one in nine of party members).

There are currently proposals to reform the party's national structure, to remove the regional element from existing national executive and to strengthen instead the regionally elected advisory council which, until now, has had little influence on decision-making.

Like most Dutch parties there is no formal post of party leader, but the political leader, when the party is in opposition, is, in practice, the leader of the parliamentary group in the Second Chamber, who was usually number one (*lijstrekker* or "list-puller") on the party's list at the preceding national elections. The *lijstrekker* is chosen separately at the party congress, and there is subsequently no need for the parliamentary group to formally elect him or her as leader. Candidate selection is the responsibility of all party members who vote on a list of all those who have put themselves forward as candidates. In 1986 this was done nationally, whereas in some previous elections there had been regional preselection. In 1986 19 candidates were put forward with a recommendation from the national party, and most, if not all of these, were accepted by party members.

Party policy draws heavily on the work of the programme committee and also of the party's foundation (*Wetenschappelijk Bureau*). The latter has a very small full-time staff (a director and vice-director) but also relies on volunteer helpers and outside experts working in study groups. The foundation has an influential advisory and policy-making role within the party.

D66 was long reluctant to set up separate organizations within the party, feeling that they were contrary to the party philosophy of direct participation in the party by all members. It was some time before a separate women's organization, the Political Emancipation Activities Centre, was established and the party's youth organization, the Young Democrats, was only founded in 1983. It has since grown rapidly, although only half of its members are also members of the parent party. Unusually, for a youth group, it is actually to the right of the parent party on some policy issues.

D66 has only a small headquarters staff, with four full-time staff, five part-timers and two volunteers. The party's membership dues are linked to members' incomes. They are steeply progressive and wealthier members pay up to several hundred guilders a year. There are currently plans to level out party dues to some extent. There are two party organs, *Democraat* and *Voor de d'raad*.

D66 is not formally a member of any wider international grouping, and the two members that it had in the 1979–84 European Parliament sat as independents. It has observer status, however, with the Liberal International.

Policies

D66 was founded as an anti-establishment party, and as a party of ideas rather than of ideology. It is a centre to centre-left party and has appealed particularly to left-wing liberal voters, and to protest voters from the VVD and also the PvdA. Its position in the centre of the political spectrum has sometimes given it a powerful strategic position but has also sometimes led to divisions as to which political option it should follow and has also increased its electoral vulnerability, as its up and down electoral performance has often shown.

D66's calls for a new style of politics in the Netherlands have made it devote particular attention to constitutional reforms. It has been particularly critical of what is sees as the undemocratic way in which cabinets are put together after elections, sometimes in seeming defiance of the popular will. It has thus long advocated direct election of the Dutch Prime Minister, if necessary in two separate rounds. D66 also believes that the link between MPs and their voters needs to be strenghtened, by basing the electoral system more on individual constituencies. It has called for the introduction of referenda at national, provincial and local levels. It seeks greater decentralization of government. It calls for open government in general.

In its economic policy D66 supports a market economy, but with corrections being made where necessary. In its 1986 election programme it called for the highest priority to be given to reducing unemployment. One key way of doing this should be through redistribution of work. Part-time work should be made more attractive, and more flexible retirement should be introduced. Over the years 1986–90 there should be an average 10 per cent reduction in working hours.

There should also be a social contract for more than one year between government and employers and employees' organizations, with broad national agreements on such issues as wage moderation and redistribution of work being implemented to the greatest possible extent on a decentralized basis within individual enterprises. Statutory measures should be imposed by government as a last resort. Training and retraining are also given a high emphasis.

D66 has called for government spending to be stabilized at its present level. The budget deficit should be decreased by an average of one half per cent of national income per year. The tax structure should also be simplified.

D66 puts a high priority on consumer protection measures, and on environmental policy, where it believes that there need be no conflict between economic and environmental objectives. D66 is hostile to the continued development of civil nuclear energy, and seeks a halt in the construction of new nuclear energy plants, and, when possible, the closing of old ones. The emancipation of women (and of men), and the protection of minority rights are also given a high priority.

D66 supports the creation of a united Europe. It voted in favour of the Single European Act, but would like to go much further in developing new Treaty Commitments in the economic, social and other fields. There should be streamlined decision-making in the EC institutions, with more use of majority voting. The powers and influence of the European Parliament should be increased. D66 has supported the concept of a two-speed Europe if some countries are reluctant to proceed down the road of integration. D66 seeks the removal of intra-community borders and barriers and also calls for the development of a proper European industrial policy. There should also be less EC protectionism, and a much more market-oriented Common Agricultural Policy.

On defence policy D66 has called for a stronger European identity within the NATO alliance, with reinforced European co-operation in the buying and selling of arms, both to reduce the imbalance in weapons purchases between the USA and Western Europe, and to control arms exports to countries outside NATO. D66 supports an active nuclear disarmament programme, and believes that there should be a nuclear freeze. On the other hand it rejects complete unilateral disarmament. It also recognizes that some increase in conventional defence expenditure could be necessary.

D66 calls for the development of stronger economic and cultural ties with Eastern Europe. It seeks active protection of human rights, and help for refugees. It wants a concentration of development aid on the poorest countries, especially in Africa.

Personalities

The party's leader is once again Hans van Meerlo, who was the first leader of D66 back in the 1960s. He is a former Minister of Defence, and is more conservative on defence issues, and less so on economic policy than his predecessor, Jan Terlouw, who has withdrawn from a leadership role within the party.

Jan Vis is the party's spokesman in the First Chamber. Saskia van der Loo is the party chairman.

The D66 group in Amsterdam has always played a key role in the party and the long-time Amsterdam chairman Kohnstamm is an important figure within the party. Other leading figures have included Martin Engwirda, the party's former floor leader in Parliament, and Laurens Brinkhorst, who is now outside active Dutch politics after being nominated first EC Ambassador to Japan and now EC Commission Director-General for the Environment.

Politieke Partij Radikalen — PPR

Headquarters	: le Weteringdwarstraat 4, NL-1017 TN Amsterdam (tel: 020-247570)
Party leader in Second Chamber	: Ria Beckers-de Bruijn
Chair	: Janneke van de Plaat
Youth group	: *PPR Jongeren*
Women's group	: *PPR Vrouwen*
Party institute	: *Studiestichting voor Radicale Politieke Vernieuwing*
Newsletter	: *Radikalenkrant*
Membership	: 6,300 (1985)
Founded	: 1968

History

Politieke Partij Radikalen (PPR) was founded on March 1, 1968, by left-wing Christians who were disillusioned with the existing Confessional parties. The majority (such as Jacques Aarden) came from the Catholic Party, the KVP, while a minority (such as another prominent leader, Bas de Gaay Fortman) came from the predominantly Calvinist Anti-Revolutionary Party. Fewer came from the third major Confessional party, the Christian Historical Union.

Quickly seeing the need for close co-operation with other left-of-centre parties, they formed alliances with the Labour Party and with the Pacifist Socialists in a number of provinces and communes in the 1970 local elections, when they gained 2.5 per cent of the vote. In their first national elections test, however, in 1971, they gained only 1.8 per cent of the vote, although they succeeded in electing two members (Aarden and de Gaay Fortman) to the Second Chamber.

In the 1972 national elections, however, which the PPR fought on a common programme with the Labour Party and D66, they made a major breakthrough and won 4.8 per cent of the vote and seven seats in the Second Chamber. In particular they made a big impression on younger voters. Over half their support came from 18–25 year-old voters and they won 18 per cent of all votes cast by 18–20 year-olds.

PPR subsequently participated in the 1973–77 government led by Labour's Joop den Uyl. They had two ministers within the Cabinet, Harry Doorn at Culture, Recreation and Social Work and Boy Trip at Science Policy and also one State Secretary for Transport.

In 1977 they suffered a severe reverse and were reduced to 1.7 per cent of the vote and only three seats. They retained three seats in the 1981 election but sank to two seats in both the 1982 and 1986 elections. In the latter selection they gained only 1.3 per cent of the vote, their lowest total since their foundation. Beside their two members in the Second Chamber (Ria Beckers and Peter Lankhorst) they have one member in the First Chamber (Bas de Gaay Fortman). In 1984 they also won a seat in the European Parliament as part of an electoral alliance with the Pacifist Socialists, the Communist Party, and the Green Party (the combined list known as *Groen Progressief Akkoord*). The PPR member has now been replaced by a member of the Communist party.

Support

In the 1986 national elections the PPR's strongest support was in the provinces of Utrecht (1.7 per cent) Groningen (1.6 per cent) and North Holland (1.5 per cent), all majority Protestant areas. Ironically, in view of the Catholic origins of many of its founders, it was weakest in the Catholic provinces of Southern Holland at only around 1 per cent. It was also generally stronger in the cities than in the country (Nijmegen 3 per cent, Groningen 2.9 per cent, Utrecht 2.7 per cent). Its best performance was in the town of Wageningen (with a large student population at the agricultural college) where it gained 5.1 per cent of the vote.

Organization

The PPR has 8,000 members organized in 250 local groups or "Action Centres" with a minimum membership of five. There are now proposals to set up rather larger branches as well, with a minimum membership of 25. Local leadership is provided by so-called "core-groups". At national level, there is a national executive and party congress as well as a women's group and youth group. Another feature of the party is its working groups on particular policy subjects.

The PPR member in the European Parliament sat as a member of the Rainbow Group.

Policies

The PPR policies show that it is very much a party of the alternative left with a mixture of Socialist, Pacifist and *Groen* policy themes. In spite of its origins it can no longer be classified as a Confessional party.

PPR is strongly in favour of decentralization, with decisions taken at the lowest possible level. Rather than nationalization, it prefers workers' self-management, with encouragement of small companies and co-operatives and with curbs on the power of multinationals.

The party supports selective economic growth, with imports reduced, with less use of energy and raw materials, and with greater respect for the environment. It also seeks greater flexibility in the workplace with shorter working days and weeks, more part-time jobs and unpaid leave and earlier and gradual retirement. It wants more job rotation and job enrichment. The existing statutory works councils should develop into central management bodies, with a key say in investment and innovation decisions. The PPR supports a guaranteed basic income for all, income levelling, and special income allowances for those in unpleasant jobs. It seeks integration of taxation and national insurance contributions and wants the surplus profits of enterprises to be turned to social purposes.

In energy policy the PPR is strongly anti-nuclear and advocates the immediate closure of Holland's two nuclear power stations. It also wants tough standards for energy conservation. It seeks environmental accounting for firms and bans on phosphates in detergents and on aerosols. Public transport fares should be cut, and eventually abolished. As far as housing is concerned PPR believes that squatting is justified and supports a ban on owning two or more homes for private use. It seeks production controls on agriculture and compensatory measures — including deficiency payments to help small farmers.

The PPR puts a strong emphasis on libertarian and civil rights. The privacy of the individual should be safeguarded and there should no longer be a national census. Abortion should be left to a woman's discretion and euthanasia should be permitted at the patient's own request. There should be research into reliable but less harmful contraceptives. The age limits for sexual contact should be removed from the penal code. Criminal justice should focus more on violations of economic, social and environmental laws by the powerful in society. The right to civil disobedience should be recognized.

There should be a considerable increase in development aid. There should be no Dutch nuclear role, and existing missiles should be removed from the country, which should also disengage from NATO. The Netherlands should push the other European countries to make a declaration renouncing the idea of a federal European power. A chamber of European regional representatives should be established as a complement to the European Parliament.

Personalities

The Party's most prominent personality is its parliamentary leader, Ria Beckers. Its elder statesman is its representative in the First Chamber, Bas de Gaay Fortman.

Pacifistische Socialistische Partij — PSP
(Pacifist Socialist Party)

Headquarters	:	Nieuwe Looierstraat 45 postbus 70, 1000 AS, Amsterdam (tel: 020-267374)
Party leader in Second Chamber	:	Andree van Es
Party leader in First Chamber	:	Dr T. E. M. van Leeuwen
Chair	:	S. Boerlage
Youth group	:	Stichting PSP Jongerengroepen
Women's group	:	PSP Vrouwen
Party institute	:	Stichting Wetenschappelijk Buro PSP
Party newspaper	:	Bevrijding (Liberation)
Membership	:	6,450
Founded	:	1957

History

The PSP was founded on Jan. 26 1957, by left-wing radicals and pacifists opposed to both military blocs and seeking an alternative political party both to the pro-Western Labour Party (PVDA) and the pro-Moscow Dutch Communist Party (CPN). From the beginning it combined campaigning with a strong emphasis on extra-parliamentary activities, and it played an important role in the Ban-the-Bomb and anti-Vietnam war movements of the 1960s. In 1965 it became the first Dutch political party to come out against nuclear energy and in 1968–69 participated in one of the first major environmental campaigns, the successful campaign to prevent the construction of a new factory by the French Progil company in Amsterdam.

In its first national election, in 1959, the PSP gained 1.8 per cent of the votes and two seats in the Second Chamber. It has since had a fluctuating electoral history, gaining four seats in the Second Chamber in 1963 and 1967 (with 3 per cent and 2.9 per cent of the national vote respectively) and steadily declining to only one seat and 0.9 per cent of the vote by the 1977 election, recovering to 2.1 per cent and 2.3 per cent in the 1981 and 1982 elections (with three seats on each occasion) and again collapsing to only 1.2 per cent and one seat in the 1986 elections.

In the 1970s the PSP suffered two schisms. In 1972 the so-called "left proletarians" left the party as did in 1974 the oosterhesselengroep who sought the unity of all left-wing parties. In 1985 there was a further schism, with the party group leader in the Second Chamber, A. G. van der Spek, leaving the party.

Unlike the Radical Party (PPR) the PSP has never participated in government, and has never come to a national electoral agreement with the Labour Party. It has, however, made electoral agreements with other small parties of the left. In 1984 it gained a seat in the European Parliament as part of the wider Groen Progressief Akkoord (PSP, Radicals, Communists and Greens, or Groen Platform) and in the 1987 provincial elections it made a number of pacts with the Communists, and in some provinces with both the Communists and Radicals. In these elections all three parties made a limited recovery from their poor performance in 1986. Apart from its single seats in the Second Chamber and in the European Parliament, the PSP has one seat in the First Chamber and ten in the various provincial assemblies.

Support

In the 1986 national elections the PSP almost halved from 2.3 per cent (1982) to 1.2 per cent. Its strongest province was North Holland with 2.0 per cent, largely because of its vote in Amsterdam (3.4 per cent), although the PSP also has some support in the smaller towns and villages in the province (Wormer 3.5 per cent, Alkmaar 2.3 per cent, Texel 2.3 per cent). Elsewhere the PSP is strongest in the university towns and cities, with its best performances in Nijmegen (3.9 per cent), Utrecht (3.5 per cent) and Groningen (3 per cent). As with the PPR its highest vote in the whole country was in the agricultural college town of Wageningen, where it received 4.3 per cent of the vote.

The PSP's vote has gone up and down sharply and it appears to have enjoyed relatively little voter loyalty. At times it has had a particular appeal to young people, especially in 1971 (when 8 per cent of 21–22 year-olds voted for the PSP compared to 1.4 per cent of all voters).

Organization

The party is divided into branches (with a minimum of 15 members but no more than 200) and *gewesten*. Above these are the party council and the national executive consisting of at least 15 members and elected every two years by the party congress. In 1973 the first PSP women's groups were founded. The party also has its own foundation (*Stichting Wetenschappelijk Buro PSP*). The PSP's member in the European Parliament sits in the Rainbow Group.

Policies

The PSP advocates the replacement of the existing capitalist and western-orientated system by a decentralized Socialist Netherlands truly independent of both superpowers. It claims that the Dutch Labour Party has come too much to terms with the existing system and that both Labour and the Communists have put too much emphasis on purely material gains. The PSP sees itself as more than just an ecological party but rather as a bridge between the "Red" and the "Green" political traditions. Its concept of "Socialism" is not one of state control in the Soviet or Chinese sense but instead of a radical democratization of Dutch society, giving more power to smaller political and economic units. In economic policy it advocates workers' self-management, a universal minimum wage, a 25-hour working week and a flexible retirement age.

The party puts a strong emphasis on choice and individual freedom. Children should be able to choose (at age 12) whether they wish to take their father's or mother's name and from the age of 16 they should be allowed to apply for housing in their own right. Squatting should be permitted, cannabis should be legalized. Abortion should be a matter of a woman's choice and should then be free on the national health service. The rights of all minorities should be strongly protected, including homosexuals, the handicapped and prostitutes. There should be equal rights for Dutch and foreign residents and racism should be combated.

Women's liberation is one of the main policy points of the PSP. The Netherlands should become a less patriarchal society and become more "feminized". Women should not be treated as half of a couple but as individuals. The pornography industry should be curtailed.

The PSP also puts a strong emphasis on environmental policy. Nuclear energy should be abandoned. The cost of public transport should be halved and there should be low speed limites for cars.

The PSP has a radical housing policy including fixed rents and reimbursement for those paying more than 20–25 per cent of their income in rent. In agriculture the hold of agribusiness should be broken and there should be greater self-sufficiency on a regional or national basis where appropriate. It also advocates a reduction in meat consumption.

In media policy the PSP is opposed to commercial television. As the party's name implies pacifism is one of its central tenets. The PSP wants to see the Dutch army abolished and the Netherlands to leave NATO. It advocates non-violent direct action against the stationing of Cruise missiles. At international level all nuclear weapons should be abolished and both NATO and the Warsaw Pact disbanded.

Third world development receives a high emphasis and the PSP advocates the waiving of all debts for the poorest countries. It supports a wide range of liberation movements and advocates a total boycott of South Africa. The PSP is strongly anti-EC and would like to see it abolished, as it perceives it as a capitalist entity with superpower pretensions.

The PSP is in competition on the far left of the Dutch political spectrum with the Radical party and the Communist party, which has gradually moved away from Moscow and more towards the PSP's policy positions. In view of their electoral weakness and their many policies in common, the three parties have forged a number of local, provincial and even national electoral agreements.

Personalities

The party's most prominent public personality is its sole member of the Second Chamber, Andree van Es. Another leading party figure is the former national parliamentarian (and leader of the parliamentary group) and PSP member of the European Parliament, Bram van der Lek.

Communistische Partij van Nederland — CPN

(Dutch Communist Party)

Headquarters	: Hoogte Kadijk 145 – 1018 BH, Amsterdam (tel: 020-239704)
General secretary	: J. Geelen
Chair	: Mevr. E Izeboud
Youth organization	: *Landelijk Jongerenwerkgroep*
Women's organization	: *Landelijk Overleg van CPN - Vrouwen*

Newspaper : *De Waarheid* (daily);
Politiek en Cultuur
(magazine)
Party institute : *Instituut voor
politiek en
sociaal Onderzoek*
Membership : 10,000 (1985)
Founded : 1909

History

The Dutch Communist Party (CPN) was the first to be founded in Western Europe, stemming from a schism within the still relatively small *Social Democratische Arbeiders Partij* between the reformist leadership and those who wanted to take a more active revolutionary path. At the Socialist Party's Deventer congress in 1909 the revolutionary dissidents were expelled and they promptly formed a new party, the *Sociaal Democratische Partij*. Among the party's founders were David Wijnkoop and Van Ravensteijn, and several prominent intellectuals such as Henriette Roland Holst and the poet Herman Gorter.

The party grew slowly and had just over 1,000 members after World War I. At the party's congress in Leiden on 16–17 Nov. 1918, the party changed its name to the Communist Party, and in 1919 it joined the Comintern.

In 1929 the party obtained its first representatives in Parliament and in 1930 Paul de Groot became its general secretary and was to remain so until 1962.

Before World War II the CPN had never gained more than 3.4 per cent of the vote, but it gathered greatly in prestige during the war as a result of its prominent role in the Resistance. In 1945 it was offered, and refused, a place in the first postwar government, and in 1946 it achieved its best-ever electoral result, 10.6 per cent of the national vote and 10 seats in the Second Chamber.

From 1946 to 1959 it lost votes at each consecutive election, falling to 2.4 per cent of the vote by 1959 with only three seats in the Second Chamber. During this period it remained an orthodox pre-Moscow party, and in 1958 it expelled four of its then members in the Second Chamber for "revisionism" in the light of unrest in the party over the invasion of Hungary. After this serious schism, however, the party began to take a more independent line. It strongly criticized the invasion of Czechoslovakia and boycotted several international Communist conferences. It also began a limited electoral recovery which led to its obtaining more votes in four successive elections, rising to 4.5 per cent of the votes and seven seats in the Second Chamber in the 1972 elections. In 1977, however, its electoral support fell away dramatically to only 1.7 per cent of the vote and two seats in the Second Chamber. It reacted by advocating coalition with like-minded left-wing parties and by intensifying its Euro-Communist line. It condemned martial law in Poland, for example, and supported Solidarity. It also began a major revision of its electoral programme. In 1984 it adopted a new programme, which dropped references to democratic centralism and to proletarian internationalism. The party's new course led to considerable internal opposition, and the party's new programme was only adopted by 392 votes to 142 with 200 abstentions. Some of the dissidents subsequently left the CPN and formed a new orthodox party, the *Verband von Communisten in Nederland* (Alliance of Dutch Communists), which gained only 4,683 votes in the whole of the Netherlands in the 1986 elections.

The CPN continued to co-operate with the other two small left-wing parties, the PSP (Pacifist Socialists) and the PPR (Radicals). A common list, the *Groen Progressif Akkoord*, was agreed upon between these three parties and the Green Movement for the 1984 European elections. The list won two seats and an agreement was reached whereby the Radical representative would stand down for a CPN representative in the second half of the five year term. Subsequently, the three parties explored the idea of creating a merged party, but this did not come about.

The CPN held its own in the 1981 and 1982 elections but in 1986 it suffered a further major defeat, being reduced from 1.8 per cent to 0.6 per cent of the vote, and losing all of its three seats, leaving it without parliamentary representation for the first time since 1929. It retains seats, however, at local and provincial level, and in some areas it has made further electoral alliances with the PSP and the PPR.

Support

The collapse of the CPN vote to only 0.6 per cent in the 1986 national elections left it with only two provinces where it obtained over 1 per cent of the vote, Groningen (1.5 per cent) and North Holland (1.4 per cent). These are the two traditional strongholds of the party. It has always been strong among the working class and intellectuals in Amsterdam, the largest city in North Holland, and in the 1945 provincial elections it obtained over 30 per cent of the city's vote. Even in 1982 the CPN still got 8.7 per cent of the Amsterdam vote, but this declined dramatically to only 2.8 per cent in 1986. This decline was mirrored in its other North Holland base of Zaanstad where the party's vote dropped from over 10 per cent in 1981 to 2.7 per cent in 1986.

The other traditional party base has been among labourers in the poorer agricultural regions of Groningen province, notably in certain villages such as Finsterwolde and Beerta close to the German border which have had a long Communist tradition and which were still giving over 40 per cent of their vote to the *Groen Progressif Akkoord* in the 1984 European parliamentary elections. Even in Groningen province however, the party's vote collapsed from 4.2 per cent in 1982 to 1.5 per cent in 1986.

The CPN had also had a certain success among the settlers in the new province of Flevoland created from newly drained polders but here too the vote fell away sharply.

Outside North Holland, Groningen and Flevoland the CPN only got above 1 per cent of the vote in 1986 in certain urban areas like Nijmegen, Delft and Utrecht. Even in working class Rotterdam it could get only 1 per cent. It has made particularly little impact in the Catholic parts of the country.

Organization

The CPN's branches are organized into districts based on geographical areas determined by the party executive. Members of the party can also form work groups, *bedrijfsgroep*. District conferences are held twice a year. Districts are responsible for the choice of candidates for communal and provincial elections.

At national level there is a party executive, a twice-yearly party conference and a biannual party congress. Candidates for national elections are chosen by the party executive in conjunction with the district executives.

One of the key elements in the CPN's reform programme adopted in February 1984 was greater internal democracy within the party. The programme rejected a monolithic way of thinking and acting for the party and laid down that the views of minorities within the party should be allowed and respected, and that differences of opinion should not be dealt with in a disciplinary way. As a result of an agreement with the PPR and PSP (see above), the CPN now have one member of the European Parliament who sits in the Rainbow rather than the Communist group.

Policies

The CPN has, in recent years, taken considerable steps toward becoming an alternative party of the left rather than remaining a traditional Communist party. This is confirmed in the party's 1984 programme "Winning power to achieve Socialism in the Netherlands", as well as in its subsequent policy statements. The party builds on the Marxist tradition but now claims to be open to other movements such as feminism. It is critical of its former sectarian tendencies and open to alliances with the other parties of the left and notably the PPR and PSP as well as other social movements. It recognizes, however, that these should not be subordinated to any one party line. It recognizes the need for a democratic and parliamentary form of government, with a plurality of parties, and the right to political opposition.

On economic policy it still seeks a Socialist economy marked by social ownership of and control over the main means of production and banking, and it supports a mixture of nationalization and "socialization" of major companies. It is opposed to "state socialism" and seeks greater democratization of economic life through the granting of more power to municipal councils and provincial governments and through greater self-government for factories on economic questions. While in favour of economic planning it believes that freedom for independent initiative must be guaranteed within the overall planning context. Independent small businesses, shopkeepers, farmers and co-operatives all have an important and lasting role to play — especially since the traditional working class structure no longer exists in the Netherlands.

The CPN puts a strong emphasis on greater control of multinational enterprises through a mixture of domestic and international actions. It supports a drastic shortening of the working week to 25 hours, but with a transitional 32-hour week at first.

Apart from reduction of economic inequalities CPN now puts a much stronger emphasis on the reduction of other types of inequality as well. The struggle of feminists and homosexuals is of central importance. The dominating family ideology and patriarchal structure of Dutch society must be combated. There must be equal rights for immigrant workers. There must be a much higher priority on environmental protection and the conservation of natural resources. The Netherlands should no longer make use of nuclear energy.

On defence policy the CPN puts the highest priority on the prevention of nuclear war. The USA is the greatest pace-maker in the arms race but the Soviet Union is to blame as well. There should be a move away from sterile bloc politics. All nuclear weapons should be removed from Dutch soil and the Netherlands should withdraw from NATO. Arms production should be stopped and replaced by socially useful industry.

The UN should be strengthened and a high priority given to third world development. There should be a total boycott of South Africa.

The CPN opposes European political integration and seeks fundamental reforms of the EC in it present form, but, unlike the PSP, it does not advocate the dismantling of the Community or Dutch withdrawal.

Finally, on internal constitutional matters the CPN seeks a strengthening of the powers of Parliament, and also the granting of more powers to local and regional authorities, including the eventual direct election of mayors by municipal councils.

Personalities

The most prominent personalities in the party in recent years have been two of its former parliamentarians, Evelien Eshuis and above all its former parliamentary leader, Ina Brouwer.

De Groenen
(The Greens)

Headquarters : Coriovahlumstraat
31, 6411 CA Heerlen

A green platform was established in 1982, including environmentalists, radicals and left-wing alternatives. It was later split over the decision to join in a wider Green Progressive Accord to fight the 1984 European election. A minority of its members who objected, in particular to the presence of the Communist Party within the Accord, broke away and helped to form a new party, the Greens.

The Greens polled 1.3 per cent in the 1984 European elections, but only obtained 18,500 votes in the 1986 national election, and did not secure representation on either occasion.

Groen Progressief Akkoord
(Green Progressive Accord)

Headquarters : Nieuwe Looiersstraat
45–47, NL-1017 VB
Amsterdam
(tel: 31-0-20-235 515)

This is not a fully fledged political party but a mechanism for co-operation between three political parties, the CPN (Communists), PPR (Radicals), PSP (Pacifist Socialists — see separate entries) and a fourth group called the Groen Platform Nederland (Green Platform). The

Groen Progressief Akkoord was put together before the 1984 European Parliament elections, and obtained 5.6 per cent of the vote and two seats. It is linked to extra-parliamentary political movements, and puts a particular emphasis on environmentalism, feminism, equality between all races and third world development.

The address of its Green Platform component is: Groen Platform Nederland, Mauritslaan 3, NL 3851 XC Ermelo (tel; 31-0-3417-544 93 and 31-0-50-157 08).

Fundamentalist Protestant parties

Three such parties are represented in Parliament, the *Staatkundig Gereformeerde Partij* (SGP), the *Gereformeerd Politiek Verband* (GPV) and the *Reformatorische Politieke Federatie* (RPF). A fourth party, the *Evangelische Volkspartij* (EVP) also contests elections at national level but currently has no seats in Parliament.

The combined total national vote for all these parties was under 4 per cent in 1986, but they are a remarkably enduring element in the Dutch political landscape. Moreover, in some provinces they are much stronger, as in Zeeland, where they received almost 11 per cent of the vote. In certain communes, notably Urk and Staphorst, the religious parties still obtain almost 50 per cent of the total vote.

Representing different strands in fundamental Dutch Protestantism they illustrate the Dutch tendency toward political fragmentation. In policy terms, however, they have many features in common. The only firm precept is the Word of God, and the Bible is their compass in all matters. They put a strong emphasis on law and order and preach respect for all authority, unless that authority is used in contradiction to God's law. The government's role, however, in such matters as the economy and education should be severely restricted. They are strongly in favour of self-help and private enterprise. Moral issues are evidently of key importance. They are completely opposed to abortion and euthanasia, want to restrict divorce and are against any changes in traditional relations between men and women. They advocate strict Sunday observance and oppose gambling. In foreign policy they are strongly anti-Communist and pro-NATO and also pro-Israel on biblical grounds. They are also strong nationalists and, while they favour European economic co-operation, oppose European union on nationalist grounds and because of incompatibilities with such ancient adversaries of Protestant Holland as Spain and Rome.

In spite of these many similarities there are certain differences in tone and emphasis between the parties' policies as shown in their recent manifestos. Nevertheless, the parties do co-operate in some elections, in some municipal and provincial elections and for the European Parliament, where they have presented common lists and succeeded in getting an SGP member elected.

(i) Staatkundig Gereformeerdepartij — SGP
(State Reform Party)

Headquarters	:	Laan van Meerdervort 165, 2517, AZ s'Gravenhage (tel: 070-468688 or 070 456226)
Chairman	:	Ds. D. Slagboom
Secretary	:	C. G. Boender
Party leader in Second Chamber	:	Bas van der Vlies
Party leader in First Chamber	:	H. G. Barendregt
Youth group	:	*SGP-Jongeren*
Institute	:	*Stichting Studiecentrum*
Party newspaper	:	*De Banier*
Membership	:	21,500 (1985)
Founded	:	1918

History

The party was founded in Middelburg, in Zeeland, in 1918, to represent the views of those seeking a much more strictly biblical organization of political and social life. In 1922 the party polled 26,700 and its first prominent leader, the Rev. G. H. Kersten, was elected to the Second Chamber. A second seat was won in 1925 and a third in 1929, and in 1933 it won 2.5 per cent of the national vote, its best performance. After a period of internal difficulties it stabilized and since 1945 it has survived with an extraordinary stable national vote of between 1.8 per cent and 2.4 per cent and two seats in the Second Chamber until 1952 and with three seats in every subsequent election. It also has one seat in the First Chamber, 20 provincial councillors, 11 nominated mayors and one seat in the European Parliament, won in co-operation with RPF and GPV.

Support

The SGP is the longest established and strongest of the fundamentalist Protestant parties in the Netherlands, with almost half of their total vote (1.8 per cent out of 3.9 per cent in 1986)

and with three out of their five seats in the Second Chamber. Unlike the GPV the SGP is inter-denominational.

By far its strongest province electorally is Zeeland, where it was founded, and where it still had 7.9 per cent of the vote in 1986. It also has substantial support in South Holland (3.1 per cent), Gelderland (3.0 per cent), Flevoland (2.6 per cent), Utrecht (2.5 per cent) and Overijsel (2.2 per cent). It is very weak in large cities, has a certain strength in some of the medium-sized provincial towns (Goes 7.1 per cent, Middelburg 6.3 per cent, Kampen 5.4 per cent), but its real strength lies in smaller communities in parts of Zeeland, in the area east of Rotterdam, between Amersfoort and Zwolle, and west of Arnhem. Its greatest strongholds are Rijssen (33.5 per cent of the vote in 1986), Urk (30.7 per cent) and Staphorst (31.7 per cent) where traditional costume is still often worn, vaccinations avoided, and the use of cars restricted on Sundays.

Organization

The party has 287 local branches and 34 municipal groups. Above these levels the party is organized within individual provincial electoral districts (19 party groups) and at full provincial level (11 groups). The national executive of the party consists of no more than 15 members, each with a five-year term of office. The party's annual conference is usually convened in February. The party has its own foundation and a publicity and training centre, as well as a network of study centres with their own publication *Ons Contact*. There is also a party newspaper *De Banier*.

The SGP has one MEP, Dr Van der Waal.

Policies

In the party's own words it strives for "our nation to be reigned entirely on the basis of the ordinances of God as revealed in the Holy Scriptures". It adheres to the so-called "Three Forms of Unity", the Heidelberg catechism, the Dutch Confession of Faith (*Confessio Belgica*) and the Five Articles against the Armenians (the Dort Canon of 1618–19, proclaimed at the Synod of Dort where Calvinist orthodoxy was fully confirmed).

The SGP has perhaps the most uncompromising programme of the fundamentalist Protestant parties of the Netherlands, and the one which is most directly coercive. It seeks tougher prison sentences and advocates censorship and punishment for blasphemers. It claims that "idleness is the devil's handmaiden" but that some forms of sport and leisure are obscene. It is opposed to Dutch participation in the Olympic Games. It wants a return to the breadwinner concept and opposes women going out to work. There should be no public transport on Sundays. It wants a stronger army but supports conscientious objection on religious but never on political grounds. The party emphasizes the historical, religious and linguistic links with Dutch Christendom in South Africa, and hopes that South Africa will change from within, but opposes sanctions.

(ii) Gereformeerd Politiek Verbond — GPV (Reformed Political Association)

Headquarters	: Berkenweg 46
	Postbus 439 3800,
	AK Amersfoort
	(tel: 033-16) 13546
Chairman	: Dr J. Blokland
Secretary	: S. J. C. Cnossen
Party leader in	
Second Chamber	: G. J. Schutte
Party leader in	
First Chamber	: J. van der Jagt
Youth group	: *Landelijk Verband*
	van Gereformeerde
	Politieke
	Jeugtstudieclebs
Foundation	: *Groen van*
	Prinsterer Stichting
Newspaper	: *Ons Burgerchap*
Membership	: 13,044 (1985)
Founded	: 1948

History

The GPV was founded in 1948 by dissidents from the Anti-Revolutionary Party (see entry on CDA) who felt the latter was becoming too materialistic and unchristian. A dominant influence was the theologian Prof. Dr K. Schilder (1890–1952) whose teachings had led to a schism within the Reformed Churches. The founder of the GPV came from the Freed Reformed Churches (*Gereformeerde Kerken Vrijgemaakt*).

The GPV began participating in national elections in 1952 when it won 0.7 per cent of the vote and won its first seat in the Second Chamber in 1963. Its best years were 1971 and 1972, when it won two seats in the Second Chamber and 1.6 per cent and 1.8 per cent of the vote respectively.

Its first programme of political guidelines was only drawn up in 1966. This was revised in the period 1979–1982. The party currently has one member of the Second Chamber (G. J. Schutte) and won exactly 1 per cent of the vote in 1986. It also has one member of the First Chamber.

Support

The party's support comes exclusively from members of one religious denomination, the Freed Reformed Churches. Its area of greatest strength is the province of Groningen where it won 3.9 per cent of the vote in 1986. It also has much higher votes in the rest of the north (Drenthe 1.8 per cent, Friesland 1.6 per cent) than the SGP. The GPV also has 2.3 per cent of the vote in Overijsel 1.7 per cent in Flevoland and 1.6 per cent in Utrecht. It is much weaker in South Holland and Zeeland than the SGP.

Among the towns its best votes are in Assen (4.8 per cent), Kampen (4.2 per cent), Groningen (4.0 per cent), Zwolle (3.3 per cent) and Amersfoot (3.2 per cent) where its headquarters are located. Among the smaller communities it has less strongholds than does the SGP but in Bunschoten it received 26 per cent of the vote in 1986.

Organization

The GPV has 213 local branches and 11 provincial groups. It is run at national level by a general association council. Its foundation is called the *Groen van Prinsterer Stichting* and it has a training institute, the *Stichting Mandaat*. It also has its own small labour union and would like its own broadcasting association.

Policies

The GPV is less conservative than the SGP. Its main feature, however, is its exclusiveness in that it seeks to create its own sphere of influence among members of the Freed Reform Churches.

Like the SGP, the GPV subscribes to the Three Forms of Unity of the Reformed Churches. The party's vocation is to summon government and people to give praise and honour to God and it wants this latter objective to be formally inscribed into the Dutch Constitution.

It supports strong government authority in combating lawlessness and materialism. One of its policies is to strengthen the royal prerogative and to give the monarch the power to suspend laws and even to dismiss individual ministers if they stray from the path appointed by God. It wants to limit the government's role in other areas. It seeks to restrict state ownership, wherever possible, and is in favour of privatization. It is also strongly in favour of decentralization. It emphasizes the rights of social groups, and particularly the family, over those of the individual. It is, however, opposed to the right to strike. It puts a strong emphasis on environmental protection. It is in favour of nuclear energy for civilian use. It is extremely anti-Soviet and pro–NATO. It supports "Star Wars" but opposes a purely European nuclear defence. Development aid should be linked to the spread of Protestantism and evangelical activity.

(iii) Reformatorische Politieke Federatie — RPF
(Reformational Political Federation)

Headquarters	:	Postbus 302, Groenelaantje 20, 8070 AH Nunspeet (tel: 03412-56744)
Chairman	:	Dr H. Visser
Secretary	:	F. J. Nieuwenhuis
Party leader in Second Chamber	:	Meendert Leerling
Party leader in First Chamber	:	Dr I. R. E. Schuurman
Institute	:	*Wetenschappelijk Studiecentrum*
Newspaper	:	*Nieuw Nederland* (monthly)
Youth organization	:	*Reformatorische Politieke Jongerenorganisatie* (RPJO)
Membership	:	8400 (1985)
Founded	:	1975

History

The RPF was founded on 15 March 1975 by people from three different groups, members of the National Evangelical Association (a group close to the GPV — see above) but who could not become members of the GPV because they were not in the Free Reformed Churches, members of a group called the *Reformatorische Politieke Jongeren Contact* (RPJC) — breakaway members from the Anti-Revolutionary Party's youth wing, and finally a further group from the Anti-Revolutionary Party dissidents, the *Gespreksgroep van AR-gezinden*, who were unhappy with the drift of their party towards Christian Democratic unity with the Catholics and with other Protestants. They joined up with some independent branches in Gelderland and Overijssel and formed a federation under the name RPF. In 1981 and 1982 they succeeded in electing two representatives to the Second Chamber with 1.5 per cent of the vote but in 1986 they slipped sharply back to 0.9 per cent of the vote and with only their leader, Meendert Leerling, in the Second Chamber. They have one member in the First Chamber. They also have 12 provincial councillors and around 90 municipal councillors.

Support

Unlike the GPV the RPF is not limited to any one church and its members come from different Protestant denominations, including Baptists and Pentecostalists. Its support is more thinly spread than that of its Protestant rivals, and its highest level of support on a provincial level in 1986 was only 1.9 per cent in Flevoland and 1.7 per cent in Overijssel. It won between 1 per cent and 1.5 per cent in seven other provinces. Its highest vote in a sizeable town was 6.5 per cent in Kampen and in smaller communities 13.3 per cent in Urk and 12.4 per cent in Oldebroek.

Organization

The RPF has around 190 branches. There are co-ordinating groups at provincial level (*Provinciale Kontaktraden*). At national level there is a federation council which, in its turn, chooses the members of the federation executive. Within the party there is a youth organization (*Reformatorische Politieke Jongerenorganisatie* — RPJO) for party members of between 14 and 30 years old. The party newspaper *Nieuw Nederland* comes out on a monthly basis.

Policies

The RPF's policies are similar to those of the SGP and the GPV and like them are based on the Bible. Indeed, their 1986 manifesto is sub-titled "A Biblically Responsible Policy" and one of their demands is that a new preamble be inserted in the Dutch Constitution stating that the Dutch Government is subordinated to God. Nevertheless, the tone of its manifesto is both relatively more moderate and more "populist" than those of its rivals. It has many reservations about the movement for equal rights for women, but recognizes that women have been disadvantaged in some areas. The party is less strident about AIDS, and also accepts "in vitro" fertilization, although under stringent conditions. While opposed to European Union and a European independent deterrent, like the SGP and the GPV, it puts much more emphasis than them on European co-operation. While pro-NATO it is also more hesitant about the Strategic Defence Initiative. In one area, however, it goes further than the other parties, in that it advocates the reintroduction of the death penalty, a quite exceptional demand in the Dutch political context.

(iv) Evangelische Volkspartie — EVP
(Evangelical People's Party)

Headquarters	: Postbus 681 2501
	CR's - Gravenhage
	(tel: 070 659289)
Chairman	: C. Ofman
Secretary	: J van den Berg
Foundation	: *Stichting Wetenschappelijk Instituut van de Evangelische Volkspartij* (Chairman: W. Kraan)
Women's organization	: *Emancipatie Komissie* (Chair: Ms M. Kemphuis)
Party newspaper	: *EVP - Info*
Membership	: 2,400 (1985)

History

The EVP was founded in 1981 by left-wing members of the Anti-Revolutionary Party (ARP) (see entry on CDA) who opposed the ARP merger into the CDA, and by members of the *Evangelische Progressieve Volkspartij* (Progressive Evangelical Party), a small already existing party.

In the 1982 election the EVP won 0.7 per cent of the national vote, and got one of its number, C. Ubels-Veen, elected to the Second Chamber. In 1986 the EVP fell back to 0.2 per cent of the national vote and lost its only seat. Its best province was Friesland with 0.5 per cent of the vote, its second best was the other northern Protestant province of Groningen.

Policies

The EVP is the most radical of the small religious parties. In the 1986 general election it opposed the stationing of Cruise missiles as well as civil nuclear energy. It advocated a shortening of the working week to 32 hours, introduction of a sabbatical year every seven years and the inclusion of maximum as well as minimum incomes.

Centrumpartij
(Centre Party)

Headquarters	: Postbus 670, 2501
	CR's Gravenhage
	(tel: 070 469380 or
	(05234) 1244)
Chairman	: N. Konsa
Secretary	: D. H. M. Segers
Party newspaper	: *Middenweg*; *Centrumnieuws*

History

The Centre Party was founded in 1980. In spite of its name it has occupied the extreme right wing of the Dutch political spectrum. Its founders were former members of the *Nederlandse Volksunie* (Dutch People's Union) who set up the National Centre Party in 1979 and then the Centre Party the year after.

In the 1982 national elections the Centre Party obtained over 0.7 per cent of the vote and its leading figure, Dr J. G. H. Janmaat, was elected to the Second Chamber.

In 1984 the Centre Party split with Janmaat leaving the party and setting up a new party the *Centrumdemocraten* (the Centre Democrats). He remained in Parliament as a member for the new party.

In 1988 both parties put up candidates. The Centre Party dropped to 0.4 per cent of the vote and the Centre Democrats only won 0.1 per cent of the vote with neither party winning a seat. In the 1987 provincial elections the Centre Democrats won 0.3 per cent of the vote, and a handful of votes (just over 1,000 in the whole country) were won by candidates on the list *Centrumpartij* 1986.

The Centre Party won most of its support on the basis of its strong stand against immigrants in Holland and it won its highest votes in the larger cities. In 1982 the Centre Party obtained almost 4 per cent of the vote in Rotterdam, and even in 1986 the combined vote of the two far right parties in the city remained at 2 per cent.

Frysk Nasionale Partij
(Frisian National Party)

The province of Friesland is part of the historic Frisian territory which extended along the North Sea coast into Germany. The distinctive Frisian language still survives and is spoken by a large number of people in the province. It enjoys a certain amount of official recognition, and a *Fryske Akademy* exists to help safeguard its welfare. There is no meaningful separatist movement in Friesland. The *Frysk Nasionale Partij* only contests provincial and not national elections. In 1987 it obtained 4.5 per cent of the votes in Friesland, and won two seats in the provincial assembly.

Portugal

Francis Jacobs

The country

Portugal is a country of over 35,500 square miles, with a population of around 10.5 million. It is a unitary state but includes two autonomous regions, the island groups of the Azores and of Madeira. Portugal is a homogeneous country culturally and linguistically, and Catholicism is the dominant religion.

The capital and by far the largest city is Lisbon. The only other large city is Porto, the centre of the most industrialized region of the country. There is a great difference between the northern part of Portugal, densely populated, especially near the coast, and with a large population of small farmers renting or owning land, and much of southern Portugal, notably the Alentejo region, which is much drier and more sparsely populated. Before 1974, in particular, this region contained large agricultural holdings or *latifundia* worked by landless agricultural labourers.

There are over 5 million Portuguese living abroad, both in America and elsewhere in Europe. In partial compensation Portugal had a huge influx of returnees from its former colonies after the 1974 revolution.

Political institutions

Portugal is a republic with a single chamber legislature, the *Assembleia do Republica*.

The Assembly consists of 250 members, elected for a four-year term (with the possibility of earlier dissolution) in 18 electoral districts in continental Portugal, in the two autonomous regions of the Azores and Madeira, and in two constituencies for overseas Portuguese (Europe and the rest of the world). The constituencies are multi-member constituencies, ranging greatly in size from the 50 members elected in the Lisbon district and the 36 in the Porto district, down to the three elected in Portalegre and four in Bragança. While the d'Hondt system of proportional representation is used within each constituency, the effective electoral threshold is much lower in the larger constituencies (notably Lisbon and Porto), than elsewhere.

The Prime Minister, who is drawn from the Assembly, is designated by the President, but since the 1982 constitutional revision, which strengthened the Parliament, his government must have a majority within the Assembly. The government has extensive legislative competence, including the power to pass decree laws. The Assembly has exclusive legislative powers in other areas, and can delegate others to the government.

The political powers represented in the parliament work within parliamentary groups. Parties with few members in the Assembly can form groupings (*Agrupamentos* rather than *Grupos*), enjoying most of the powers of the groups. Even single members have considerable rights. The Assembly is presided over by a president, who is second in the constitutional hierarchy after the President of the Republic.

The President of the Republic is elected for a five year term by direct popular suffrage. Until 1982 the President had much greater powers, including the right to name Prime Ministers from outside the normal party structure, and without a parliamentary majority. The President's powers are now more circumscribed but are still substantial. The President designates the Prime Minister and can dissolve the parliament and name a date for new elections. The President can also veto legislation, although such a veto can be overriden by a majority within the Parliament.

Brief political history of Portugal

1820–1910: constitutional monarchy

Struggle between liberals and absolutists from 1820–34, and between radical liberal Septembrists and moderate liberal Chartists until the 1840s; beginning of two party system in the 1870s with *rotatavismo* or rotation between the *Partido Regenerator* and the *Partido Progressista*; rise of Republican movement from 1870s.

1820   Liberal revolution.
1822   Liberal Constitution (provides for single-chamber Parliament).

Map of Portugal showing 18 electoral districts and number of seats in each, and 2 autonomous regions of Azores and Madeira, as well as geographical areas.

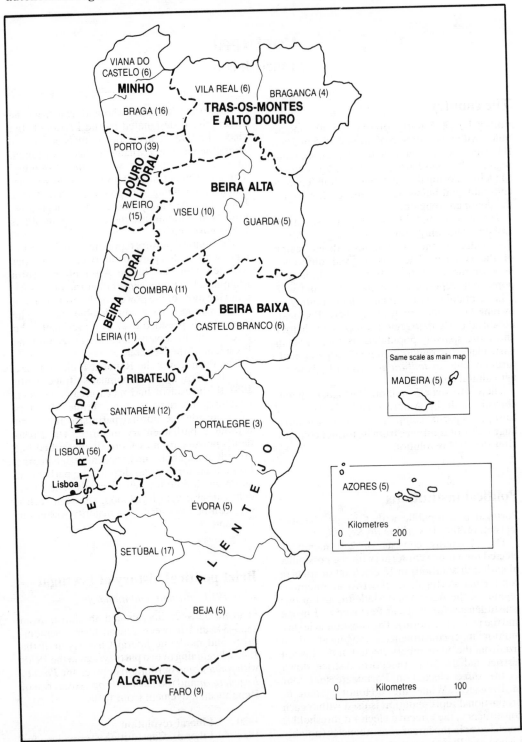

Source: adapted from *World Atlas of Elections*.

1826	*Carta Constitucional* (less radical Constitution which establishes a two-chamber Parliament).
1832	Civil War between liberals and absolutists.
1834	Constitutional monarchy established with liberal regime.
1836	Septembrist revolt.
1838	Third Portuguese Constitution.
1852	Direct elections re-introduced.
1910	Monarchy overthrown.

1910–26: First Republic

First period of republican democracy with 1917–1918 interlude of Sidonio Pais dictatorship; fragmentation of party system.

1911	Republican Constitution. First schism within Republican Party between radicals and moderates.
1926	Republic overthrown by military coup.

1926–74: Estado Novo *regime.*

Almost 50 years of dictatorship with Antonio Salazar Prime Minister and dominant figure of regime from 1932–68; colonial wars begin in 1960s; Marcello Caetano takes over from Salazar, at first attempts to liberalize regime and then again clamps down.

1933	New Constitution establishes *Estado Novo* corporatist state with one party, the National Union.
April 25, 1974:	Armed Forces Movement otherthrows dictatorship.

1974–76: provisional governments

Period of political turmoil with rapid succession of governments, attempted coups and counter-coups, nationalizations and land expropriations, as well as decolonization.

April 1974:	Spinola President, Palma Carlos forms first provisional government.
July 1974:	Vasco Gonçalves communist-influenced Prime Minister in second provisional government.
September 1974:	Failed Spinola coup. Spinola replaced by Costa Gomes as President. Vasco Gonçalves forms third provisional government. Land expropriations begin.
March 1975:	Failed coup. Council of the Revolution established. Vasco Gonçalves

	forms fourth provisional government. Large-scale nationalizations begin.
April 1975:	Constituent Assembly elections. Socialists emerge as largest party.
July 1975:	Socialists and Social Democrats leave government in protest against its actions. Anti-communist riots begin.
August 1975:	Vasco Gonçalves forms short-lived fifth provisional government but is forced to resign.
September 1975:	Sixth provisional government is formed by Admiral Pinheiro de Azevedo.
November 1975:	Attempted coup put down by Ramalho Eanes. Revolutionary period comes to an end, and left-wing influence recedes.
April 1976	New Portuguese Constitution. Elections held in which Socialist Party wins largest number of seats.

1976–77: minority Socialist administration

Mário Soares as Prime Minister.

June 1976:	General Eanes elected President with 60.8 per cent of the vote.

1978–end 1979: governments of presidential inspiration

President Eanes successively chooses Nobre da Costa, Mota Pinto and Maria de Lurdes Pintasilgo to be Prime Minister, none of them with stable parliamentary majorities.

December 1979:	Right-of-centre Democratic Alliance wins a majority in elections.

1979–1983: Democratic Alliance governments

Coalition between Social Democrats and Centre Democrats. Sá Carneiro and Balsemão as Prime Ministers.

October 1980:	Democratic Alliance increases its majority in new elections.
December 1980:	Sá Carneiro killed in plane crash and subsequently replaced as Prime Minister by Balsemão. General Eanes re-elected as President.

July
1981: First Balsemão government collapses. Balsemão forms new government.

1982 Constitution revised, weakens powers of President, reinforces Parliament, reduces military influence.

End
1982: Second Balsemão government collapses. A month later President Eanes dissolves Parliament, and sets date for new election.

April
1983: Socialists emerge as largest party in new elections.

1983–85 Central Block Government

Coalition between Socialists and Social Democrats with socialist Mário Soares as Prime Minister.

June
1983: Central Block Government formed.
June
1985: Central Block Government collapses. New elections convened.
October
1985: Social Democrats emerge as largest party in new elections.

1985–87 Minority Social Democratic Administration

Cavaco Silva as Prime Minister.

January
1986: Portugal enters EC.
February
1986: Mário Soares elected President.
July
1987: Social Democrats win absolute majority in new election.

1987–present: majority Social Democratic administration

Cavaco Silva as Prime Minister.

Main features of the current political system

The main feature of the modern Portuguese political system has been the need for the country to adapt to the massive political and economic changes that have taken place since the overthrow of the 50-year dictatorship on April 25, 1974.

Democracy had to be established without stable ground rules, with the military playing a central role and with new political parties.

Portugal's colonies were granted rapid independence, and the small and overcrowded country was swamped with returnees from those colonies without land and without jobs. There were six provisional governments in under two years, and three attempted coups. A minimum wage was established, large agricultural holdings were occupied and expropriated, and there were large scale nationalizations of all kinds. Since 1970 the political system has grown more stable, but Portugal has had to face an opening up of its protected and often backward economy, especially since Portugal's entry into the European Community in 1986 has begun to alter its traditional geo-political and economic orientation.

The legacy of the two turbulent years of 1974–76 is still a major one, and much of the subsequent political activity has been dedicated to defending or dismantling it. In the left-wing mood of 1974–76 all the parties felt the need to describe themselves as left of centre or at the very least as centrist. This explains the fact that the country's major right-of-centre party (the PSD) still calls itself the Social Democratic party and still has not jettisoned its left-wing socialist programme. Even more significantly Portugal still has western Europe's most left-wing Constitution, adopted in 1976 and describing Portugal as a country in "transition to socialism" and with economic clauses such as one pronouncing the "irreversibility" of any nationalizations. Since 1976 the Constitution has been a continuous battleground with a first major revision in 1982 and a second one currently under way. Moreover, the right-of-centre parties have been attempting to reverse the nationalizations, labour laws and land reform that took place in 1974–76 with the fiercest opposition coming from the Communists and far left.

The Portuguese political system has not yet fully settled down. The constitutional revision of 1982 eliminated the anomalous position of the military, and changed the balance of power between the President and the Parliament in favour of the latter. There are still pressures, however, to remove some constraints from the President or to change other features of the constitutional order, such as the existing electoral system.

The political parties themselves, with the exception of the Communists, are all essentially creations of the 1970s. They have tended to be rather fluid in ideology and even in personnel, with some of the leading figures changing parties, sometimes on several occasions. Individual personalities, such as those of Mário Soares, General Eanes, Francisco Sá Carneiro and Aníbal Cavaco Silva have tended to have greater electoral importance than their parties' policies. Moreover, until 1983 Portugal seemed to be gradually settling down into a more predictable pattern, with four main political parties. The 1985 and 1987 elections, however, have shown swings in electoral support which are quite exceptional by western democratic standards, with the Socialists falling from 36 per cent to 20 per cent between 1983 and 1985; an entirely new party, the PRD, winning 18 per cent only a few months after its formation in 1985, and then falling to only 4.9 per cent in 1987; and the Social Democrats rising from under 30 per cent to over 50 per cent between the 1985 and 1987 elections. The present political pattern, therefore, is of one large and one small party on the right of centre (the PSD and CDS respectively), one focal point of opposition on the left of centre (the Socialists) as well as one much smaller party with an uncertain future (the PRD), and finally one well-entrenched but "outsider" party on the far left (the Communists), Nevertheless, considerable modifications to this pattern are likely in the future.

One further feature of the Portuguese political system that deserves mention is the continued existence, to a lesser extent than before, of substantial regional divisions with a major impact on electoral behaviour. The most important is that between northern and southern Portugal. Northern Portugal, with its small farmers and more widespread but often smaller-scale industry has tended to be much more clerical and conservative and the far left is very weak. Southern Portugal (not the Algarve, but especially the Alentejo), with its agricultural labourers and fewer but larger industrial concentrations, has been a bastion of the Communist Party. The island groups of the Azores and of Madeira have been more like the north, and have been conservative strongholds.

A further, if less marked division, has been the urban-rural one, with the urban areas more responsive to the parties of the left in central-northern Portugal than their rural counterparts. In the Alentejo, on the other hand, the far left has tended to win higher votes in the villages than in the towns. A different type of division has been that between Lisbon and the rest of the country, with the political elite still being largely based in Lisbon.

The main political issues in Portugal are currently the following:

Constitutional reform

The main emphasis in the new round of constitutional reform is on modifying its restrictive economic clauses, such as those on the irreversibility of nationalizations. Another possible change is to the electoral system, with proposals having been made for Portugal to move to a majority-based system, or to one with smaller constituencies. Any attempt to remove proportional representation, however, is highly unlikely to win the two-thirds parliamentary majority required for any constitutional change.

Portuguese election results 1975–present (percentage of vote and seats won)

	1975	1976	1979	1980	1983	1985	1987
Partido Socialdemocrata (PPD/PSD) (Social Democrats)	28.3% (81)	25.2% (73)	with AD	with AD	27.2% (75)	29.8% (88)	50.1% (146)
Partido do Centro Democratico Social (CDS) (Democratic Social Centre Party)	8.2% (16)	16.7% (42)	with AD	with AD	12.9% (30)	9.7% (22)	4.3% (4)
Alianca Democratica (AD) (Democratic Alliance)	—	—	46.3% (128)	48.3% (134)	—	—	—
Partido Socialista (PS) (Socialist Party)	40.7% (116)	36.7% (107)	28.2% (74)	28.7% (74)	36.1% (101) (with allies)	20.8% (57)	22.3% (59)
Partido Comunista Portugues (PCP) (Communist Party)	13.5% (30)	15.3% (40)	with APU	with APU	with APU	with APU	with CDU
Movimento Democratico Portugues (MDP/CDF) (Portuguese Democratic Movement)	4.4% (5)	—	with APU	with APU	with APU	with APU	0.6% (0)
Alianca Pueblo Unido (APU) (United People's Alliance)	—	—	19.5% (47)	17.3% (41)	18.1% (44)	15.5% (38)	—
Coligaçao Democratica Unitaria (CDU) (United Democratic Coalition)	—	—	—	—	—	—	12.2% (30)
Partido Renovador Democratico (PRD) (Party of Democratic Renewal)	—	—	—	—	—	18.4% (45)	4.9% (7)
Others	4.9% (2)	6.0% (1)	5.7% (1)	5.7% (1)	3.7% (0)	6.1% (0)	3.9% (0)

Privatization

Until the Constitution is changed privatization of nationalized enterprises can only be carried out up to 49 per cent. There is great controversy over which, if any, enterprises should be privatized, and under which terms.

Agrarian reform

The issue of what to do about the 1975 legacy of expropriation of the large agricultural holdings in the Alentejo and Ribatejo, and the degree of compensation to the former owners. Should the agrarian reform law be revised?

Labour laws

The left defend the post-revolutionary legacy of protection of workers' rights; the right would like to develop a more flexible system, including greater ease in carrying out dismissals.

Regionalization

The need for administrative decentralization, and the question of the establishment of the proposed new regional entities.

Media policy

The issue of whether the private sector should be allowed into radio and television, and, if so, under what conditions and the extent to which the public sector should also retain a stake in the various media, including newspapers. A further controversial issue is that of the domination of the media by the government of the day.

European Community membership

With the exception of the Communist Party, the major parties all favoured Portugal's EC membership, although not necessarily the ways in which the negotiations were carried out. Portuguese withdrawal is not an issue. The main problem is how the Portuguese economy can adapt to the European market, and in particular to the open market challenge of 1992.

Relations with Spain

EC membership for both Spain and Portugal has brought the issue of their future relations (in particular, the opening up of traditional economic barriers between the two countries) to the fore.

Relations with the Portuguese-speaking world

All parties would like these relations to be further developed. The future of Macau under Chinese rule and the issue of independence for East Timor are important issues. Most controversial in party political terms is the attitude to take towards the Angolan and Mozambique struggles, and the activities within Portugal of Unita and Renamo.

Portugal's NATO membership

Not controversial in itself, but there is disagreement over the role that Portugal should play within NATO, and over the future status of the foreign military bases within Portugal.

The morality of public life

The issue of clientelism and corruption in public life has been emphasized by the PRD.

Partido Social Democrata — PSD
(Social Democratic Party)

Headquarters	: Rua S. Caetano 7–9, P1200 Lisbon (tel:602140 or 602215)
President of National Political Committee	: Aníbal Cavaco Silva
Secretary-general	: Manuel Dias Loureiro
Youth organization	: *Juventude Social Democratica* (tel: 670233, secretary: Carlos Coelho)
Newspaper	: *Povo Livre*
Membership	: 120,000 (1988)
Founded	: May 1974

History

The party was first founded under the name *Partido Popular Democratico* (Popular Democratic Party) on May 6, 1974, only a few days after the revolution of April 25. Its most prominent personalities were Francisco Sá Carneiro, Francisco Balsemão and Joaquim Magalhães Mota, former deputies from the Caetano regime who had unsuccessfully tried to liberalize it. At the PPD's first congress in November 1974 Sá Carneiro was elected secretary-general of the new party.

In the left-wing mood of 1974–75 the PPD proclaimed itself a socialist party, and adopted a programme which was highly critical of the capitalist system. In 1975 it applied to join the Socialist International, but the Portuguese Socialist Party vetoed its entry. Nevertheless, from the start the PPD became the main pole of attraction within the new Portuguese political system for those who were not on the left.

The PPD participated in most of the provisional governments in the years 1974 to 1976.

In the constituent Assembly elections of April 1975, it won 26.4 per cent of the vote and 81 seats.

In December 1975 it suffered its first schism, when 14 deputies on the party's left wing, including Mota Pinto, left the PPD. In 1976 the PPD (unlike the right-of-centre CSD) supported the new left-wing Constitution and also gave its support to the candidacy of General Eanes for President. In the legislative elections of April 1976 the PPD won 24.4 per cent of the vote and 73 seats, confirming its place as the second-largest party.

From 1976 to 1979 the party remained in opposition. In June 1976 it established its electoral dominance in the regional assemblies of Madeira and the Azores. In October 1976 it changed its name from the PPD to the *Partido Social Democrata* (PSD), although the initials PPD continued to remain in use in a subsidiary capacity. In the local elections of December 1976 the PSD showed that it had solid roots by winning 623 seats, and 115 chamber presidencies.

Sá Carneiro remained the dominant personality within the party, but on two occasions stood down briefly from the leadership (and in November 1977 even left the party) as a result of internal party disputes.

In May 1977 the PSD established a pact with the Christian Democrats (CDS), but relations between the two parties worsened, notably after the CDS entered into a coalition government with the Socialists. In late 1978 the choice of Mota Pinto, a dissident Social Democrat, as an independent Prime Minister led to severe divisions within the PSD as to whether to support the new government. In April 1979 there was a new schism within the PSD as a result of disputes over the position that the party should adopt towards Mota Pinto's budget. Thirty-seven deputies left the party, including one of its founders, Magalhães Mota.

In July 1979 the *Aliança Democratica* (Democratic Alliance) was formally created between the PSD, the CDS and the PPM, with agreement on a common candidates' list and programme. In the elections of December 1979 the Alliance won 42.5 per cent of the vote and 128 seats, and was able to form a new coalition government, with Sá Carneiro of the PSD as Prime Minister.

Sá Carneiro proved to be a strong and authoritative Prime Minister. In the elections of Oct. 5, 1980, the Democratic Alliance increased its majority, winning 47.5 per cent of the vote and 134 seats (of which 82 were PSD seats). In the presidential elections later that year, Sá Carneiro, who was now a fierce opponent of President Eanes, supported the unsuccessful candidacy of General Soares Carneiro (no rela-tion). On Dec. 4, 1980 Sá Carneiro died in an air crash.

Francisco Balsemão, a newspaper publisher, became the new president of the PSD, and also Prime Minister. His control over the PSD was much less than that of Sá Carneiro, and factional divisions within the party increased sharply. His relations with the CDS were also less good. Balsemão resigned as Prime Minister in the summer of 1981, but was subsequently able to form a second administration which lasted until December 1982.

In December 1982 the Democratic Alliance suffered only a moderate setback in the local elections (minus 4 per cent), but Balsemão interpreted the results as a loss of confidence in his administration, and resigned. After a month of indecision within the party, President Eanes dissolved Parliament, and called new elections, in which the Democratic Alliance was not renewed, and its component parties fought on their own. The PSD won 27.2 per cent of the vote and 75 seats.

In June 1983 a new coalition government was formed between the Socialist Party and the PSD, with Mário Soares as Prime Minister. The PSD's new leader, Carlos Mota Pinto (the former independent Prime Minister, who had left the PSD in 1975 but returned to it in June 1981) was appointed Deputy Prime Minister. The so-called "Central Block" coalition government lasted from June 1983 to June 1985.

Relations between the Socialists and Social Democrats gradually became more tense. There were disputes over abortion and later over the 1985 budget (which six PSD deputies refused to support). In early 1985, Mota Pinto resigned as leader.

In May 1985 the initial favourite for the leadership, João Salgueiro, was defeated by Aníbal Cavaco Silva. Cavaco Silva won on an anti-socialist ticket, and his election led to the final breakdown of the coalition with the Socialists.

In the 1985 elections the PSD won just under 30 per cent of the vote and 85 seats. Cavaco Silva then formed a minority administration.

In the presidential elections of January 1986, the PSD supported the candidacy of the former CDS leader, Freitas do Amaral, who narrowly lost to Mário Soares. In 1987 the PSD minority government lost a motion of confidence in Parliament and new elections were called.

On July 19, 1987 the PSD won the greatest triumph in Portuguese electoral history, gaining over 50 per cent of the vote on its own, and 148 of the 250 seats in the Parliament. Cavaco Silva was then able to form a new PSD administration with its own parliamentary majority. The PSD also heads the autonomous regions of Madeira and the Azores.

Support

The PSD has become a "catch-all" party, with broad-based support which has been rising steadily since its foundation. In 1987 its support leapt from under 30 per cent to over 50 per cent. Its membership is largely based on the middle classes and on professionals. It has substantial support among clerical workers and the skilled working class, and also in rural areas (in 1983 8.5 per cent of its members were farmers).

Its strength in rural areas and in small towns is shown by the fact that it has traditionally been stronger in local than in national elections. Already by 1979 the PSD had more local mayors than the then larger Socialist Party.

In regional terms its strongest areas have been the islands of Madeira and the Azores, and northern Portugal. In the 1985 national elections the PSD won 56.2 per cent in Madeira (almost double its national average of that year), and this rose to 65.4 per cent in 1987. In some Madeira communes the PSD won over 80 per cent (e.g. Ponta do Sol 83.4 per cent, Santana 81.3 per cent). In the last regional elections in Madeira the PSD won easily.

In 1985 the PSD won 48.1 per cent in the Azores, but this rose sharply to 66.6 per cent in 1987, the highest vote for the PSD in any Portuguese constituency. In the last regional elections the PSD won a majority in the Azores.

In mainland Portugal the PSD has been strongest in the interior regions of the north, and in the two coastal districts of Aveiro and Leiria. Its strongest electoral district has traditionally been Vila Real (62.6 per cent in 1987 and 42.1 per cent in 1985). In 1987 it also won over 60 per cent in Viseu (63.3 per cent, 37.6 per cent in 1985) Aveiro (62.4 per cent, 38.4 per cent in 1985), Leiria (60.8 per cent, 38.4 per cent in 1985) and Bragança (60.8 per cent, 35.1 per cent in 1985). It also won 59.8 per cent in Guarda (33.5 per cent in 1985). In a number of individual municipalities in the districts it won over 70 per cent of the vote in 1987, and in some over 80 per cent (e.g. Vagos in Aveiro 81.2 per cent).

The PSD is slightly less strong in the rest of the central districts and in the interior district of Castelo Branco, but in 1987 it won over 50 per cent in all these districts.

Its weakest northern district is Coimbra (50 per cent in 1987 compared to 29.4 per cent in 1985, but with only 44 per cent in the university town of Coimbra itself), followed by Porto (51

per cent in 1987, 29.3 per cent in 1985), Castelo Branco (52.1 per cent in 1987, 31.2 per cent in 1985), Braga (53.3 per cent in 1987, 32.8 per cent in 1985) and Viana do Castelo (54.4 per cent in 1987, 33.5 per cent in 1985).

Moving south, the PSD is considerably weaker in Santarem (47.9 per cent in 1987, 27.7 per cent in 1985) and in the district of Lisbon, where it won 45.8 per cent in 1987, compared to only 25.6 per cent in 1985. In the city of Lisbon the PSD won 48 per cent in 1987.

The PSD's weakest area is southern and south-central Portugal, and in particular the Alentejo. Its traditionally weakest district is Beja, but even here its vote rose sharply in 1987 (24.5 per cent, compared to only 13.8 per cent in 1985 and only 10.7 per cent in the last local elections). A number of municipalities in Beja still gave the PSD under 20 per cent of the vote in 1987 (e.g. Aljustrel 16.2 per cent). The PSD is also relatively weak in the districts of Evora (32.1 per cent in 1987, 19.1 per cent in 1985), Setubal (32.6 per cent in 1987, 15.4 per cent in 1985) and Portalegre (37.4 per cent in 1987, 20.9 per cent in 1985). The only southern district where the PSD is much stronger is the Algarve (46.7 per cent in 1987, 28.3 per cent in 1985).

Organization

The PSD is a decentralized party, with great local strength. At national level it has often been less cohesive, and at times of weak central leadership (such as the period between the death of Sá Carneiro and the rise of Cavaco Silva) it has been divided into competing factions, with great power remaining with its regional "barons". Its Constitution has been changed on numerous occasions, with even the title of the party leader changing at several congresses (secretary-general, party president and now president of the national political committee). At times the leader has been separately elected, on others as part of a slate of candidates. Sometimes there has only been one list, at others several competing lists. As president of the national political committee, Mota Pinto faced a hostile national council. When Cavaco Silva was first elected leader in 1985 his adversaries managed to win control of the bureau of the party congress.

Under Cavaco Silva's strong leadership and electoral success these party divisions have been greatly reduced.

The PSD currently has around 120,000 membership (of which 2,000 are outside Portugal). The lowest levels of party organization are its "nuclei" (normally based on parishes and which must have a minimum of 20 members) and its "sections", generally based on municipalities and which must have a minimum of 40 members. There are 340 such PSD sections throughout Portugal. Within the 18 districts the party's district organization provides for district assemblies, political committees and district executives (permanent committees).

Within the two autonomous regions of Madeira and the Azores, the PSD has its own organizations with their own separate statutes.

At national level the party's current statute provides for a national congress to be held every two years, but 14 have been held since 1974. 770 of the delegates to the congress are specially elected or designated, 600 by the party's sectional assemblies (including those overseas), 50 from the regions and districts, and 60 each from the labour and youth organizations. The national congress elects the party's representational bodies (e.g. the directly elected members of the national council, and the members of the national jurisdiction council) by a proportional electoral system, and its executive bodies by a majority system.

The congress elects 55 members (and 10 substitutes) of the national council, which also contains 10 members chosen by the youth organization, five by the labour organization, two representatives of the overseas membership (one for Europe and one for the rest of the world) as well as national, regional and district office-holders. The council meets every two or three months, and plays an important party role.

The national political committee consists of 17 members, and meets every 15 days. Among its important tasks are to approve the composition of PSD governments or shadow governments.

The president of the national political committee is the effective leader of the party. The secretary-general has a more administrative role. There is also a permanent national committee of eight members, (consisting of the president of the national political committee, the four to six vice-presidents, the parliamentary group leader, and the secretary-general) which meets at least once a week.

PSD candidates for national elections are approved by the national council on the basis of lists proposed by the district committee and then examined by the national political committee. The latter can also veto local candidates.

Since 1983 the party statutes have permitted the holding of internal party referenda on important strategic questions. In practice this has only been used on one occasion, in 1985, to decide on the party's option for the forthcoming presidential election.

The party's youth group *Juventude Social Democratica* (JSD) has about 41,000 members, and is the largest youth organization in Portugal. It is represented at all levels within the party organization, with 60 members at the national congress, 10 on the national council, six of the 20 members of the parliamentary group executive (including a vice-president) and two designated members of the key national political committee. Nineteen of the PSD Members of Parliament were candidates nominated by the youth organization.

The part has a women's organization, *Mulheres Portuguesas Social Democratas*.

The PSD has its own labour organization, *Trabalhadores Sociais Democratas*, with 30,000 members, and with the right to 60 members at the party congress, five members of the national council and one of the national political committee. It constitutes the Social Democratic tendency within the trade union federation, the UGT. The UGT presidency has traditionally been held by a Social Democrat. The Social Democratic group within UGT was originally called *Tesiresd*, but this clashed with the party leadership over the issue of its independence from the party line. The TSD was set up instead, and eventually became dominant.

The PSD newspaper is called *Povo Livre*. The party has membership dues of 50 Escudos a month. All dues income remains with the local section. The national party gets its income from other sources, including state finance.

The PSD is now a member of the Liberal Group (ELDR) within the European Parliament, of which it is one of the largest components. In order to accommodate the Portuguese Social Democrats the former ELD added the word "Reformist" to its title. The PSD, however, is not a member of the Liberal International.

Policies

As the largest Portuguese party, and as the main alternative to the left, the PSD covers a wide ideological spectrum from outright conservatism to moderate social democracy. The party's 1974 programme, which has still not been superseded, is strongly socialist in tone. Its centre of gravity, however, has gradually shifted to the right. This has been accentuated under the leadership of Aníbal Cavaco Silva, who has put his emphasis on liberal economic policies. The party's leaders continue to claim, however, that it is a pragmatic party, neither socialist nor conservative.

The party's 1985 and 1987 manifestos have put their main emphasis on economic and constitutional reforms. The role of the Portuguese state needs to be sharply cut back, and the primary role needs to be played by the private sector, with much greater emphasis being given to competition and market forces. Sales of state holdings should help to reduce the public deficit. The fiscal system should be reformed. Portuguese public administration should be modernized, with simplified laws and administrative procedures. A strong emphasis is also put on reform of Portugal's existing labour laws, where the PSD seeks more flexibility, including more recourse to part-time and temporary work. It was the PSD's attempts to reform the labour laws which led to the recent general strike, and also led to the PSD's proposals being found to be unconstitutional by the Portuguese Constitutional Tribunal.

Parallel to its attempts to open up the economy, the PSD also strongly advocated constitutional reform, arguing that the 1976 Portuguese Constitution, even after its 1982 reform, still constitutes a socialist strait-jacket for the Portuguese economy and society. The PSD wishes to remove therefore a number of the more ideological economic articles from the Constitution, such as that barring it from selling more than 49 per cent of existing state holdings.

The PSD would like to see the number of Members of Parliament reduced, the introduction of a more specifically constituency-based electoral system, and scope for popular referenda.

Another 1974–75 legacy which the PSD seeks to change is in the field of agrarian reform. The PSD's 1987 manifesto speaks for example, of decollectivizing agriculture, selling state lands, and providing indemnities for proprietors whose land was lost.

Liberalization of the existing media laws is another PSD policy, with an end, for example, to the state monopoly over television, and the introduction of private competition.

As a party strongly implanted in local and regional government the PSD is a firm advocate of decentralization.

At one point it appeared that the PSD might support the use of civil nuclear energy in Portugal, but this is no longer the case.

The PSD has generally enjoyed good relations with the Catholic Church hierarchy. In 1983–84 it was the main party along with the Christian Democrats to oppose the liberalization of abortion.

The PSD is now putting a greater emphasis on meeting the challenge of the 1992 European Internal Market, although it believes that it needs to be complemented by expanded regional and social programmes in order to increase European economic cohesion. It supports the objective of European union.

The PSD supports a complete and active Portuguese participation in the Atlantic Alliance.

Personalities

The dominant figure within the PSD is Aníbal Cavaco Silva, who is the president of its national political committee, as well as being Prime Minister of Portugal. He is a former Minister of Finance who returned to the banking sector and unexpectedly won the leadership contest in May 1985. He has established a hold over the often fractious PSD that none of its leaders have had since Francisco Sá Carneiro. He comes from the Algarve.

The Deputy Prime-Minister and Minister of Defence is Eurico de Melo, the party leader from Braga in the north of Portugal. He is also a vice-president of the party.

Two other powerful ministers who are also party vice-presidents are Fernando Nogueira, minister at the presidency and also Minister of Justice and Antonio Capucho, who is the minister responsible for relations with the Parliament.

The two other party vice-presidents besides de Melo, Nogueira and Capucho are Carlos Brito and Fernando Correia Afonso, who is the PSD parliamentary leader.

The current president of the Parliament (second in the protocol hierarchy after the President of Portugal) is Vitor Crespo, a former party candidate for Prime Minister (in early 1983).

Two former party leaders still have a certain influence within the party, Rui Machete and Francisco Balsemão.

The current secretary-general of the party is Manuel Dias Loureiro.

Of those with independent power bases in the party the two most significant are the leaders of the autonomous regions of Madeira and the Azores. Madeira is ruled by Alberto João Jardim, and the Azores by João Mota Amaral.

Besides these the party's district leaders have an important role within the party, and the majority are on its national council.

Partido Socialista
(Socialist Party)

Headquarters	:	Rua da Emenda 46, 1200 Lisbon (tel: 32 61 71)
Secretary-general	:	Jorge Sampaio

Youth Organization	:	*Juventude Socialista*
Publication	:	*Accao Socialista*
Membership	:	100,000
Founded	:	1875 (Refounded April 1973)

History

A Portuguese Socialist Workers' Party was founded in 1875, but with Portugal's low degree of industrialization and also because of the much greater strength of the Republican movement, it never enjoyed much success. In 1925 the *Seara Nova* ("New Harvest") Group was established, and played a considerable part in developing socialist theory. During the long period of Salazar's rule the socialists only played a very limited role, although sporadic attempts were made at reviving socialist groups (e.g. the Republican and Socialist Alliance of 1932–34 and the Socialist Union of 1950–1954). In 1964 Portuguese Socialist Action was founded, which, in the 1964 election, sponsored an Electoral Committee of Democratic Unity, which only enjoyed very limited success. In 1972, however, Portuguese Socialist Action was admitted to the Socialist International, and in April 1973 it took the name of Socialist Party at a congress held in exile at Bad Munstereifel.

Immediately after the revolution of April 25 the Socialists took part in a Popular Front with the Communists and Social Democrats, but left shortly afterwards. In Spinola's first provisional government there were three Socialist ministers. With recruits from all backgrounds, including progressive Catholics, the Socialists became Portugal's largest party at the Constituent Assembly elections of April, 1975, winning 37.9 per cent of the votes and 115 seats. They also became the main focal point of those who wished to defend democracy and to prevent Portugal from falling under communist domination. Shortly after the elections the Socialist leader, Mário Soares, resigned from the government in protest, and several difficult months followed before the tide turned at the end of 1975.

The Socialists played a key role in the promulgation of the 1976 Constitution. In the 1976 national elections they again became the largest party, with 35 per cent of the vote and 106 seats, and formed a minority Socialist government, with Mário Soares as Prime Minister, which lasted until December, 1977. In the course of 1977, however, the government ran into economic difficulties, and was forced to turn to the IMF. In 1977 two Socialist deputies were expelled from the Socialist Party after voting against the government's budget, and

subsequently formed a new party, the POUS (*Partido Operario de Unidade Socialista* — see separate entry). Mário Soares then sought to broaden the base of his government and formed a new administration with the Centre Democrats (the CDS).

This only lasted for the first half of 1978, and eventually collapsed in June after disputes over such issues as land reform and private medicine. President Eanes then dismissed Mário Soares as Prime Minister, the beginning of a long period of tension between the two men.

The Socialist Party was in opposition during the period of minority governments of "presidential inspiration" in 1978 and 1979. It suffered further schisms, with the departure of Lopes Cardoso to form a new *Unio de Esquerda para a Democracia Social* (UEDS, the Left Union for Social Democracy) and the subsequent departure of two other prominent Socialists — António Barreto and José Medeiros Ferreira. On the other hand it gained new recruits with the arrival of members of the Socialist Intervention Group (SIG). At its March 1979 congress the Socialist Party adopted a more pragmatic and less ideological programme.

In the 1979 national elections the Socialists suffered a considerable electoral setback, winning only 73 seats on 27.1 per cent of the vote, and going into opposition to the new AD coalition government. The development of internal party factions continued, with divisions between the Soares-led "Establishment", the *Historicos* (the party old guard, critical of the unideological way in which the party had developed) and the *Socialistas Novas* (or "New Socialists") of technocratic party reformers, such as Vitor Constancio and António Guterres.

To counteract the right-of-centre government alliance the Socialist secretariat sponsored a new socialist-led alliance, the *Frente Republicana e Socialista* (FRS — Republican and Socialist Front) which included the Socialist Party, the UEDS (see above) and the *Associação Social Democrata Independente* (ASDI, the Independent Social Democratic Association). The FRS contested the 1980 national elections, but with very poor results, winning only 27.1 per cent of the vote and 71 seats.

After the defeat, conflicts between Mário Soares and the majority of the secretariat intensified. Soares was turning against the FRS strategy, and advocating an opening up to the Social Democrats. By 1981 he had successfully re-asserted his control over the party apparatus at the expense of what became known as the "ex-secretariat", although the dispute took much longer to die down.

In the national elections of April 1983 the

Socialists won a considerable victory with 36.1 per cent of the vote and 100 seats. They formed a new coalition with the Social Democrats, the so-called "Central Block" government, with Soares as Prime Minister. The new government lasted from 1983 to 1985, but relations between the two coalition parties got progressively worse with disputes over such issues as abortion and the budget. After Cavaco Silva became the new Social Democrat leader the government finally collapsed. New elections were called in which the Socialist Party's candidate for Prime Minister was Almeida Santos. They suffered a severe defeat, dropping from 36.1 per cent to only 20.8 per cent, with only 56 seats in Parliament, and again returned to opposition.

In June 1986 the Socialist Party elected a new leader, Vítor Constâncio.

In the presidential elections in late 1986 Mário Soares appeared initially to have little chance of success, but managed to win 25.4 per cent in the first round of elections, and to emerge as the standard-bearer for the left. Winning the reluctant support of his old Communist adversaries he narrowly won the second round of elections with 51.5 per cent.

In the 1987 national elections the Socialists only made a limited recovery from the 1985 débacle, winning 22.2 per cent of the vote and 60 seats. In the European elections they won a very similar vote of 22.5 per cent and six seats. Nevertheless the Socialists had the consolation of emerging as the largest party of opposition.

Constâncio resigned as leader in October 1988. Jorge Sampaio became the new party leader in January 1989.

Support

From 1975–79 and in 1983, the Socialist Party was Portugal's largest party, and it is still the second largest party. Along with the Social Democrats it is the only party whose support is truly nationally-based with a substantial presence in every region of the county. In the 1985 elections it lost heavily to the Reformists (PRD) in particular. In the 1987 elections it won back much of the Reformists' vote (as well as a substantial number of Communist votes), but lost votes to the Social Democrats.

There is a marked variation in the pattern of Socialist support in the north and south of the country. In northern Portugal the Socialists win considerable support from the urban and industrial working class, as well as from rural employed workers. In southern Portugal, where employed workers are still largely Communist, the Socialists win more support from rural proprietors and from the middle classes in the towns.

A significant problem for the Socialists has been the softness of their support and their relative lack of electoral strongholds. In 1987 the Socialists did not receive more than 28.7 per cent of the vote in any electoral district, and only got more than 40 per cent in a handful of minor communes. This has led to great variations in their vote from election to election.

The Socialists' highest vote is in the electoral district of Coimbra, where it has received over 28 per cent in the last two elections. In the municipality of Soure it received 40 per cent in 1987, and in the town of Coimbra 30.6 per cent. In the 1987 election the Socialists polled well in north-western Portugal, considerably increasing their vote over 1985 in the electoral district of Porto (26.7 per cent compared to 23.5 per cent), Braga (25.9 per cent compared to 21.8 per cent) and Viana do Castelo (20.2 per cent compared to 18.4 per cent). In the Social Democratic strongholds of north-eastern Portugal, however, the Socialist vote declined from 1985 to 1987 (Bragança 22.7 per cent to 19.1 per cent, Vila Real 22.9 per cent to 20.2 per cent, Guarda 23.1 per cent to 21.8 per cent, Viseu 20 per cent to 18 per cent). In the remaining northern districts of Aveiro and Leiria the vote was relatively stable at around 23 per cent and 19 per cent respectively. While Leiria is a relatively weak area for the Socialists its includes the municipality with the highest Socialist vote in Portugal in 1987, Castenheira de Pera (46.7 per cent).

In central Portugal the Socialist vote rose in 1987. In the electoral district of Lisbon, for example, it went from 19.8 per cent to 21.2 per cent, although this is far short of the 35 per cent that it had won in 1983.

In the Alentejo and southern Portugal the Socialist Party is relatively weak, especially in Evora (its weakest district in 1987 at 15.5 per cent, compared to 14.3 per cent in 1985), and Setubal (17.6 per cent in 1987, 16.5 per cent in 1985). It is stronger in Portalegre (25.2 per cent in 1987, 23.7 per cent in 1985) and in the Algarve electoral district of Faro (25 per cent in 1987, 22.3 per cent in 1985) where it has also had considerable local election success.

In the islands, the Socialist Party is the second party to the overwhelmingly dominant Social Democrats. The Socialists are stronger in the Azores (20 per cent in both 1985 and 1987 with their highest votes in the islands of Pico and Corvo) than in Madeira (16.2 per cent in 1987, 13.2 per cent in 1985 with their only 1987 vote over 30 per cent being on the small neighbouring island of Porto Santo).

Organization

The Socialist Party has a weaker local organizational structure than its largest competitor, the Social Democrats. At its last congress the party reformed its local organizational structure. There are now two major types of local section, those organized on a territorial basis (with a minimum of 50 members) and those on a professional and socio-economic interest group basis. There are still some individual workplace sections, but these have not flourished. In addition new party committees are being established at council level.

At district level, the party is organized in federations, each with a management committee of 15–51 members, and with a secretariat of five to seven members. The federation congress meets every two years, generally in May. There are separate Socialist groups in the autonomous regions of the Azores and Madeira.

At national level the national congress is held every two years. In 1988 the congress was attended by over 1,600 delegates, of whom 1,400 were elected members.

The national committee consists of 201 members directly elected by the congress (on a list basis using the d'Hondt method of proportional representation), 20 members of the Socialist Youth Movement and the 24 co-ordinating secretaries of each federation. It meets three or four times a year. The political committee includes the party's secretary-general, president and leader of the parliamentary group, as well as the party leader in the Azores and Madeira, and two representatives of the youth movement. Its nucleus, however, consists of the 151 members directly elected (by the d'Hondt system of proportional representation) by the national committee. The political committee meets every 20 or 30 days.

The party leader is the secretary-general, whose method of election has varied in recent years. Mário Soares was directly elected, but in 1986 Vítor Constâncio introduced a new system whereby the secretary-general was elected as head of a list for the party secretariat. In 1988 the party congress again introduced the system of separate election of the secretary-general by the members of the congress.

The party's secretariat consists of 15 members, each responsible for a particular sectoral area.

Party candidates for the national assembly are proposed by the federations, and then chosen by the political committee, with the last word going to the national committee in the case of disputes between the federations and the political committee. European Parliament candidates are also chosen by the political committee, but on the basis of proposals from the secretary-general.

The party's youth movement is called *Juventude Socialista*, and has organizational and financial autonomy. It is entitled to 20 places on the national committee, and to two places on the political committee.

There is now no formal women's movement within the Socialist Party, but provisions are made for women's quotas on electoral lists. The 1988 congress decided that 25 per cent of the members of the main party organs (e.g. secretariat, national committee and political committee) must be women.

The Portuguese Socialist Party is independent of the trade union movement. Nevertheless the Socialist trade union group (*Tendencia Sindical Socialista*, or "Socialist Union Tendency") is the largest component within the UGT trade union confederation. The secretary-general of the UGT is always a Socialist. The Tendency's executive has a right (laid down in the party constitution) to be heard by the main party bodies on all economic and social policy questions. Its leader can participate in Socialist secretariat meetings.

The official party organs are the weekly paper *Accao Socialista*, and the monthly review *Portugal Socialista*.

Party finances have been shaky. Minimum membership dues are 100 Escudos a month. In theory members should pay 6 per cent of their monthly salaries, but this rule is not generally respected. Party office-holders have to pay considerable sums to the party. Its MEPs currently pay 300,000 Escudos a month.

The Socialist Party is a member of the Socialist International, and of the Federation of European Socialist Parties, and is in the Socialist Group in the European Parliament.

Policies

The Portuguese Socialist Party is now a moderate reformist social democratic party, whose most recent (1986) programme has eliminated most of the Marxist elements in its original programme. It portrays itself as an inter-class party, providing an alternative both to the liberalism and over-reliance on the market of the ruling Social Democrats, and to the rigid collectivist orthodoxy of the Communist Party. Having attempted both an alliance with small left-wing parties (the FRS) in 1980, and the "Centre Block" alliance with the Social Democrats in 1983, and having seen the near collapse of its most plausible ally (the PRD), it does not currently seek any alliances with other parties. It has been consistently opposed to any alliance with the Communist Party to its left.

The Socialist Party now believes that there should be a less state-centred and centralized economy and that unnecessary tiers of bureaucracy should be removed. There should be an open mixed economy, with a vigorous private sector. On the other hand, the Socialists consider that the state must retain an important catalytic role, in order to influence economic management, and to correct abuses of power. Planning should still play a significant role, although not with the rigid quantitative targets that were popular in the 1960s.

The Socialists also call for a more coherent industrial policy, which should include selective incentives for innovation and improvement of the technological level of Portuguese industry. The party does not oppose privatization per se, and indeed, considers that some would be desirable. There should, however, be a proper timetable for any privatizations, and public sector monopolies should not just become private ones. Public sector holdings are still essential in certain strategic sectors and the Socialists have suggested that they be restructured into three major group.

The Socialists have also advocated a lessening of tax burdens.

They are critical of the present Social Democratic government's attempts to reform Portugal's labour laws. They believe that the government's proposals, in the name of "flexibility", might lead to the firing of industrial workers by management without just cause. The Socialists call for a shortening of the working week to 40 hours. There should also be greater economic and industrial democracy.

The Socialist Party puts a strong emphasis on the need for a better distribution of wealth within Portugal. It defends the Portuguese welfare state, but recognizes that it needs to be reformed.

As regards agrarian reform, there should be a stop to expropriations, and necessary indemnities should be paid. Nevertheless, the PS believes that the current government is going too far in its plans to dismantle what has taken place since 1976.

There should be a new emphasis on consumer and environmental protection. The Socialist Party opposes the possible future use of civil nuclear energy in Portugal.

The Socialists are prepared to negotiate on the controversial economic clauses of the existing Constitution (e.g. those providing for the irreversible nature of nationalizations) on condition that the present government does not try to alter such matters of constitutional principle as the maintenance of proportional representation in national elections. The Socialists would also like to see the introduction of consultative referenda.

The Socialists support the decentralization of the Portuguese administrative system.

It was under Socialist rule that Portugal first applied to join the European Community in 1977. The party supports European union, but considers that great emphasis should be put on economic and social cohesion. The appropriate industrial and structural measures will have to be taken to help Portugal adapt to the challenge of the 1992 internal market. The Socialists voted in favour of the ratification of the Single European Act.

The Socialists fully support an active Portuguese role within NATO, but want the European "pillar" of NATO to be reinforced.

Personalities

Jorge Sampaio took over as the new party leader in January 1989 after the resignation of Vítor Constâncio. Sampaio is a 49-year-old lawyer and a former opponent of Soares. He is also a former leader of the parliamentary group.

One of the most powerful figures within the party is António Guterres, who has a strong control over the party apparatus and organization. Jaime Gama is currently the international secretary of the party. He was Constâncio's opponent for the leadership of the party in 1986.

The historic leader of the party, Mário Soares, was elected President of Portugal in late 1986. His direct supporters currently have relatively little weight within the party. The most well-known such supporter is probably Maldonado Gonelha, a former Labour and Health Minister. The *Carta Aberta* minority group, with which he and others, such as João Soares, were associated at the 1988 congress, only won a few votes.

Partido Renovador Democrata — PRD
(Democratic Renewal Party)

Headquarters	: Travessa do Fala sá ⅜, 1200 Lisbon (tel: 323997 or 361591)
Party President	: Herminio Martinho
Secretary-general	: Pedro Canavarro
Youth organization	: *Juventude Renovadora Democratica*
Members	: 6,000–7,000
Founded	: Feb. 24, 1985.

History

The *Partido Renovador Democratica* (PRD) was formed by supporters of the then President Ramalho Eanes in February 1985. Eanes, a career military officer who had played a decisive role in the events of November 1975, had become a popular President of Portugal in his two terms of office. He had an image as an austere but honest and independent President above the everyday manoeuvres of party politics.

President Eanes did not participate directly in the early activities of the new party, which elected Herminio Martinho as its first President in June 1985. Shortly afterwards the Centre Block government fell, and Parliament was dissolved by President Eanes. On election day in October 1985 the new party won over one million votes (18 per cent of the total) and obtained 45 seats in the Parliament. A large percentage of its votes came from disillusioned socialists, but it also won considerable support from other parties, including the Communists.

The PRD abstained in the voting over the formation of the new minority Social Democratic government.

The autumn of 1985 saw the PRD get into increasing difficulties over its choice of presidential candidate, and over its participation in the local elections; the party suffered from lack of local organization and problems over nomination of candidates. In December 1985 the PRD only won 4.7 per cent in the local chamber elections. Shortly afterwards, the party's presidential nominee, Salgado Zenha, was defeated in the first round of elections. In the final round the PRD's national council recommended a vote for Mário Soares, a choice followed by over two-thirds of its supporters.

In October 1986 Ramalho Eanes, now free of presidential duties, was formally elected as PRD party president at its second convention.

In March 1987 the PRD put down its own censure motion on the Social Democratic government, hoping to be able to form a new coalition with the Socialists, but contacts were broken off when President Soares dissolved the Parliament.

In July 1987, the PRD suffered a severe defeat, its votes dropping from 18 per cent to 4.9 per cent and its Members of Parliament from 45 to seven. In the simultaneous European Parliament elections it won even fewer votes (4.4 per cent) obtaining just one seat, that of Mederros Ferreira, who later abandoned the PRD and joined the Socialist Group. Shortly after the election Eanes withdrew as party leader.

Herminio Martinho, its original president, again took over the day-to-day running of the party. At the party's third convention, in May 1988, Martinho was formally re-elected as party president.

Besides its seven deputies in the National Assembly the PRD has 51 municipal councillors, 276 members of municipal assemblies and 726 members of parish assemblies.

Support

According to the PRD's own survey of its membership, 28.4 per cent of its members in 1988 worked in the services sector (compared to 11.4 per cent of the Portuguese population) and 13.8 per cent were high level technicians and teachers (compared to only 3.4 per cent of the general population), 16.3 per cent of its members were industrial or construction workers, only slightly under the national total of 19.4 per cent. The PRD had a considerable student membership (7.9 per cent compared to their 1.1 per cent share in the Portuguese population) as well as lower, but above average percentages of members from the liberal professions and from industry and commerce. There were very few farmers (1.4 per cent of total membership) and farm labourers and fishermen (1.2 per cent). The PRD membership is a well educated one, with 15.4 per cent with higher educational qualifications compared to only 2.3 per cent of the Portuguese population.

In 1985 the PRD won remarkable electoral support for a new party, obtaining over 10 per cent in all but three of the 20 electoral districts and regions (Bragança 6.9 per cent, Vila Real 18.6 per cent) and Madeira (9.7 per cent), and over 20 per cent in six (24.4 per cent in Eanes' home district of Castelo Branco, 23.8 per cent in Martinho's home district of Santarem, 21.2 per cent in Lisbon, 20.5 per cent in the Algarve (Faro), and 20.4 per cent in both Setubal and Porto). Only in north-eastern Portugal, in the one coastal district of Aveiro, and in the Communist heartland of Beja in the Alentejo was it well below its national average.

In 1987, however, its vote collapsed dramatically everywhere. Its two highest votes were now in the Alentejo (district of Setubal 8.7 per cent and of Evora 7.7 per cent) where its vote more than halved, as it did in the southern Alentejo district of Beja (where it fell from 11.6 per cent to 5.7 per cent). Elsewhere in central and southern Portugal its 1987 vote was only a third or less of its 1985 vote (in Santarem district down from 23.8 per cent to 7.3 per cent, in Lisbon district from 21.2 per cent to 6.9 per cent, in Faro from 20.5 per cent to 6.3 per cent, in Portalegre from 18.7 per cent to 6.3 per cent). In only a few communes was its vote above 10 per cent, with its best 1987 performance in two municipalities in Santarem district, Cartaxo (14.8 per cent) and Galega (14.6 per cent). Its best performance in towns were in Evora (9.6 per cent) and Setubal (9.6 per cent, but where its vote fell from 24.6 per cent in 1985). In the city of Lisbon it polled 6.5 per cent.

In north-central and northern Portugal the PRD's decline was even more severe. In the central districts much of its 1985 support went straight back to the Socialist Party or over to the Social Democrats. Its vote was often around a fifth of what it had been in 1985 (in Porto district 4 per cent compared to 20 per cent, in Coimbra 3.5 per cent to 16.9 per cent, in Braga 3.3 per cent to 16.8 per cent, in Leiria 3.1 per cent to 15.4 per cent and Aveiro 2.7 per cent to 13.3 per cent). In one Porto municipality, Felgueiras, its vote was only one-eighth of what it had been. It generally fared less badly in the towns (Viana do Castelo 8.9 per cent, Coimbra 4.4 per cent) and in a few left-wing strongholds (Marinha Grande 7.7 per cent). In the north-eastern interior the PRD's vote, already relatively weak, fell into insignificance (e.g. Bragança 1.3 per cent and Vila Real 1.3 per cent), in some cases only around one-sixth of its 1985 vote. Even in Eanes' home district, Castelo Branco, the 1987 vote was only 5.9 per cent compared to 24.4 per cent in 1987. The PRD's vote also fell sharply in the islands (from 15.2 per cent to 3 per cent in the Azores, from 9.7 per cent to 3.3 per cent in Madeira).

Organization

The PRD has never built up a strong local organization, as it showed in its weak 1985 local election results not long after its triumph in the national elections of that year. It has never had a large number of members and has not built up effective affiliated organizations.

The other striking feature of the PRD's organization is the greater emphasis on giving freedom of manoeuvre to its members and elected candidates than on rigid party discipline. Its members have a right, for example, to organize themselves into internal party factions, and its elected members cannot be mandated and may vote according to their conscience. Only in a few very limited cases must party discipline apply.

The PRD's local organizations are mainly based on the municipalities concelhos, each of which must have a council convention and a council executive committee. If there are more than 100 members within a commune, the communal organization is encouraged to form smaller residential or workplace sections.

Above the municipalities are the districts, each with their district committees (40 to 250 members, meeting four times a year) and district executive committees of five to 11 members. In the Azores and Madeira there are separate regional organizations, which have their own statutes but which have to be ratified by the PRD's national council.

At national level the PRD's national convention is held every two years, and is chaired by a bureau (Mesa), with a president and four other members. The national council meets every three months. It includes 60 members elected by the national convention by the d'Hondt method of proportional representation. The party's leader, its president, is elected at the head of a single list which he or she has chosen. The winning list then forms the party's national executive committee, currently with 15 members. Day-to-day party management is carried out by an even smaller permanent committee consisting of the president, the secretary-general and two other members.

The national executive committee may choose to establish a national consultative council of five to 15 members to advise on key questions. There is also a party research department (Gabinete de Estudos). The party also has statutory provisions for direct consultation of its members.

Party candidates for the national and European Parliaments are proposed by the national executive committee, and finally designated by the national council.

The party's youth movement Juventude Renovadora Democratica is open to 16–28 year olds, and has only recently been formally constituted. There is no women's movement. There are statutory provisions for the workers' organization, Organização Autonoma dos Trabalhadores do PRD, but this has not yet been properly established.

There is currently no party newspaper, although there was one (O Renovador) just before the 1987 election.

Party membership dues are variable, with a maximum of 50 Escudos per month.

The PRD currently has no formal international links. From 1986 to 1987, when it had four members in the European Parliament they joined the European Progressive Democrats, along with the French RPR, the Irish Fianna Fáil and the Scottish Nationalists.

Policies

After its disastrous election results in July 1987, the resignation of its leader, General Eanes, and the departure of many of its prominent activists, the PRD's continued existence has been in doubt. Nevertheless, the party held its third convention in May 1988, and re-affirmed its programme and objectives. Its future will undoubtedly depend greatly on how it fares in the forthcoming local and European Parliament elections.

The PRD's initial electoral success depended on the prestige of the then President Eanes. Its motivating force was a reaction against the increasing dominance of the political parties at the expense of the presidency, and the clientelism and corruption that was seen to be increasingly characterizing both the political parties and the Portuguese public administration. The PRD put itself forward as an advocate of new moral and ethical standards in Portuguese public life, placing the national interest above narrow partisan benefits — and honesty, efficiency and independence of action as the benchmarks by which to judge public service.

The PRD also attacked what it saw as the subservience of the other parties to outdated ideologies, whether old style socialism or 19th century liberalism or neo-liberalism. The PRD promised to judge each issue on its merits and to be a constructive opposition, supporting Government actions when they were justified.

With its emphasis on social solidarity, and on the fact that economics must not have priority over wider values, the PRD now places itself firmly to the left of centre of the political spectrum, although it initially attracted support from people of all political backgrounds.

The PRD is technocratic in outlook, and puts its main emphasis on the need to modernize Portuguese society. Its supports the market as the basic underpinning of economic life, but also recognises the need for state intervention in a number of areas. There should be overall state planning, although this should not be either bureaucratic or collectivist. Moreover, the state should be involved incertain strategic economic sectors.

It is strongly against the replacement of state monopolies by private oligopolies, but is prepared to accept certain privatization.

The PRD distinguishes itself sharply from the present government on social issues, where it opposes narrow individualism and puts more emphasis on social solidarity and on redistribution of wealth.

Its 1986 programme accepts that civil nuclear energy may have a role to play in the future, but it should only be introduced as part of a coherent national energy plan. For the moment its introduction is unnecessary.

The PRD calls for increased decentralization of the Portuguese administration and for the creation of administrative regions. It believes that the debate over constitutional reforms should not be limited to Parliament, but should be open to wider public debate. The present semi-presidential system of government should be retained, but some of the restrictions imposed on the President during the last constitutional revision in 1982 should be removed. The PRD's 1986 programme also put forward the possibilities of smaller electoral constituencies with a closer link between the electors and elected, combined with an additional national constituency to help compensate for the inevitable loss in proportionality.

The PRD is a strong advocate of a more participative Portuguese system of democracy, introducing both consultative and deliberative referenda, and the right of popular petition. The Portuguese public administration should become less bureaucratic, and much more autonomous from the government of the day. The PRD also wants more independent candidates to stand for public office.

The PRD supported Portuguese accession to the European Community, but was critical of the way in which the negotiations were conducted, and the failure to have a proper debate within Portugal on the final terms of accession. The PRD points out the difficulties involved in Portuguese adaptation to the Community and pledges strong defence of Portuguese interests. It supports the objective of European unity. It voted in favour of ratifying the Single European Act and supports an increase in the powers of the European Parliament.

The PRD supports Portuguese membership of NATO, and wants it to participate in a less passive way than in the past. Its 1986 programme calls for renegotiations over the foreign military bases in Portugal, not to have them removed, but to get more favourable terms. Its main theme on all foreign policy issues is an emphasis on enhanced Portuguese independence and national pride.

Personalities

Now that General Eanes, the original inspiration for the PRD's creation, is no longer an active participant in the party leadership, the leading figure within the party is Herminio Martinho. Martinho comes from Santarem in Central Portugal. He was the first president of the party from 1985 to 1986, and was reconfirmed as president at the party congress in May 1988. He is also the leader of the PRD parliamentary group.

Among the other leading figures within the party, Jorge Figueiredo Dias, a university professor, is the current president of the bureau of the party's national convention and Miguel Galvao Teles, a well-known lawyer and specialist on constitutional issues, is the president of its national jurisdiction committee. The new party secretary-general is Pedro Cana-varro. The other two members of the party's permanent committee (besides Martinho and Canavarro) are Marques Junior and Ivo Pinho. Other prominent members include Carlos Lilaia, a specialist on regionalization, Magalhaes Mota, a former PSD minister, and long-term parliamen-tarian, and José Carlos do Vasconcelos.

Partido do Centro Democrático Social — CDS
(Democratic Social Centre Party)

Headquarters	:	5 Largo Adelino Amaro da Costa, Lisbon (tel: 874632)
President	:	Diogo Freitas do Amaral
Secretary-general	:	Luis Felipe Paes Beiroco
Youth organization	:	*Juventude Centrista* (president: Manuel Monteiro)
Membership	:	22–23,000
Founded	:	July 19, 1974

History

The CDS was founded on July 19, 1974. Although inspired by Christian Democratic principles, it described itself as a centrist party. Its most prominent personality was Diogo Freitas do Amaral, who led the CDS from the outset.

With the discrediting of the far right after the 1974 revolution, the CDS was the most conservative of the major parties in the new Portuguese political order. As such it was in a difficult position in the left-wing climate of 1975. Its meetings were disrupted, and its headquarters were attacked. As a result it lost considerable organizational ground to other parties, and notably to the Social Democrats who were its closest political competitors. In the constituent assembly elections of April 1975, the CDS only won 7.5 per cent of the vote and 16 seats.

The political situation had eased by 1976, and in the National Assembly elections of April 1976 the CDS had a greatly improved result, with 16 per cent of the vote, and 42 seats. The CDS was the only party represented in the Parliament not to support the new Portuguese Constitution.

The CDS was in opposition in 1976 and 1977, but at the end of the latter year it managed to forge an agreement with the Socialist Party, whereby the CDS entered into the second Soares government, with three ministers (including Foreign Affairs) and five secretaries of state. There were wide ideologi-cal and political differences between the two parties, but the Socialists wanted to broaden their governmental basis at a time of difficult economic decisions, and the CDS wished to gain credibility as a party of government.

The Socialist – CDS government lasted for the first half of 1978, but collapsed in August of that year, with agrarian reform and private medicine among the primary issues in dispute.

The CDS was in opposition again for the rest of 1978 and in 1979. In 1979 the party forged a new coalition, *Aliança Democratica* (AD), with the Social Democrats, the PPM and others. The coalition won 125 seats on 45.2 per cent of the national vote. Freitas do Amaral became Depu-ty Prime Minister and Amaro da Costa Defence Minister. The CDS also had a number of other ministers and secretaries of state.

In the 1980 national elections AD increased its majority, with 133 seats on 47.5 per cent of the vote.

The CDS tactician Amaro da Costa died in the December 1980 plane crash that killed Social Democratic Prime Minister, Sá Carneiro. The CDS then participated in a new AD coalition under Balsemão but Freitas do Amaral did not take part. There was resentment within the CDS that the Social Democrats had provided the new AD Prime Minister without sufficient consultation with their allies, and the new AD government worked less well than its predecessor.

Balsemão resigned but later managed to form a new government, in which Freitas do Amaral again returned as Deputy Prime Minister. Rela-tions between the coalition partners became progressively worse, and the government was largely held together in order to achieve the common objective of revising the 1976 Consti-tution.

After the fall of the second Balsemão govern-ment Freitas do Amaral resigned from the party leadership. Basílio Horta acted as interim leader until the next party congress when Lucas Pires of the liberal wing of the CDS forged an alliance with Adriano Moreira, the leader of the party conservatives, to win the party leadership.

Lucas Pires led the CDS from 1983 to 1985. The *Aliança Democratica* was not revived for the 1983 national elections, in which the CDS only won 12.4 per cent of the vote and 30 seats, and subsequently went into opposition to the new "Centre Block" government of Socialists and Social Democrats. After the collapse of the

Centre Block in 1985 the CDS again entered negotiations with the Social Democrats but felt that they were asking too high a price, and the two parties fought the elections separately. The CDS suffered a further setback, with 9.7 per cent of the vote and 22 seats, and Lucas Pires resigned as leader. Adriano Moreira defeated Morais Leitao to become the new party leader. The CDS remained in opposition.

In the presidential elections in late 1986 the CDS candidate, Freitas do Amaral, was easily ahead on the first round with 46.3 per cent of the vote, but narrowly lost to Mário Soares, in the decisive second round, with 48.7 per cent.

In the 1987 national elections the CDS was disastrously defeated, losing most of its support to the Social Democrats, and ending up with 4.4 per cent of the vote, and four seats in the Parliament. On exactly the same day the CDS won 15.4 per cent (and four seats) in the elections to the European Parliament.

At the 1988 party congress Adriano Moreira stood down as leader, and was replaced by the original leader, and former presidential candidate, Freitas do Amaral.

Besides its four Members of Parliament and four MEPs, the CDS has 30 mayors of Portuguese municipalities and 520 parish council presidents.

Support

The CDS has traditionally been strongest among higher professionals and the upper middle classes. Until its 1988 débacle it also had a considerable base among the lower middle class, and in certain farming regions. The electoral strength of the party is overwhelmingly based north of the Tagus river. The party's strongest electoral districts are the northern coastal district of Viana (16.6 per cent in 1985, 7.7 per cent in 1987) and the interior districts of Bragança (17 per cent in 1985, 7.5 per cent in 1987), Viseu (19.8 per cent in 1985, down to only 6.9 per cent in 1987) and Guarda (19.2 per cent in 1985, 6.5 per cent in 1987). The CDS's highest votes in 1987 were in closely adjacent municipalities in eastern Viseu (e.g. Sernancelhe 16.2 per cent and Satao 15.8 per cent) and western Guarda (Aguiar da Beira 15.9 per cent).

Elsewhere on the northern coast the CDS has been strongest in Leira (12.5 per cent in 1985, 6 per cent in 1987), Braga (14 per cent in 1985, 5.9 per cent in 1987) and the prosperous farming district of Aveiro (13.5 per cent in 1985, 5.3 per cent in 1987). The CDS has been weaker in the districts of Coimbra (8.6 per cent in 1985, 4.5 per cent in 1987) and Porto (9.7 per cent in 1985, 4 per cent in 1987), as well as the northern

interior districts of Vila Real (12.5 per cent in 1985, 5 per cent in 1987) and Castelo Branco (9.6 per cent in 1985, 4.7 per cent in 1987).

In the central districts of Lisbon and Santarem the CDS also halved its vote between 1985 and 1987 (in Lisbon from 8 per cent to 3.7 per cent, in Santarem from 7.7 per cent to 3.6 per cent).

The CDS has always been very weak in southern Portugal, and especially in the Alentejo districts (Setubal 3.8 per cent in 1985, 1.9 per cent in 1987; Evora 3.3 per cent in 1985, 2.1 per cent in 1987; Beja 2.2 per cent in 1985, 2.0 per cent in 1987). It has been only slightly stronger in the district of Portalegre (4.9 per cent in 1985, 3.1 per cent in 1987) and in the less left wing Algarve (district of Faro 6 per cent in 1985, 3.1 per cent in 1987).

In the island regions the CDS has been stronger in Madeira (7.8 per cent in 1985, 5.2 per cent in 1987) than in the Azores (6.4 per cent in 1985, 3.3 per cent in 1987).

In the European Parliamentary elections, where the CDS was much more successful, the party's liberal economic message seems to have found greater response in the towns than in the countryside.

The CDS has been traditionally strong in Macau.

Organization

The CDS has not had a very strong organizational structure, with a top-down structure and a generally weak local base.

The lowest tier of party organization consists of its territorial nuclei, which must have a minimum of 15 members. Above these are the communal council groups and the 18 district groups.

At national level the party congress meets every two years. At the 1988 party congress there were slightly over 800 voting members.

The CDS national council includes 25 members elected by proportional representation at the party congress. In 1988 members were elected from three separate lists. The national political committee, which consists of between 40 to 50 members, includes 25 elected on a majority list basis at the party congress. It may create specialized committees, and meets once a month.

Day-to-day political management is carried out by the party's 11-member steering committee, elected on a single list at the party congress on a majority basis. The steering committee is headed by the president, who is the overall party leader, and includes the secretary-general, who is the chief administrator.

Party candidates for national elections are

chosen by the national council on the basis of lists proposed by the regional and district political committees.

The CDS provides scope for internal party referenda. Of the party's flanking organizations the most significant is its youth movement, *Juventude Centrista*. A list headed by its president won eight of the 25 elected seats on the party's national council at the 1988 congress, with 35 per cent of the votes cast.

The CDS has a women's group, *Mujeres Centristas* (MCDS). There is also a small CDS trade union group, the *Federação dos Trabalhadores Democratas Cristãos* which is part of the UOT, and won two of the elected national council seats at the 1988 party congress, with 6 per cent of the votes cast.

At present there is no party newspaper or official organ. Party dues are variable, and there is no minimum membership fee.

The CDS participates in the European People's Party in the European Parliament, and in the European and International Christian Democratic movements.

Policies

The CDS shares the centre-right of the Portuguese political spectrum with the Social Democrats, to whom it lost the majority of its electorate in the 1987 parliamentary elections. It is uncertain to what extent this was due to tactical voting, and whether it will be able to regain these lost votes. It is also uncertain to what extent its much better performance in the simultaneous European Parliament elections reflected its true strength, or merely rewarded an excellent personal campaign by Lucas Pires. In the national election campaign the CDS tried to portray itself as an essential ingredient of a centre-right majority. It is currently trying to distinguish itself from the Social Democratic majority government by attacking it much more aggressively.

The CDS is generally perceived to be the most conservative of the mainstream Portuguese political parties. Practically all within the CDS would describe themselves as Christian Democrats, and emphasize the social teaching of the church as well as market economies. Nevertheless, there are three main tendencies within the party: the conservatives, who advocate traditional economic and social values, and who include many former supporters of the Salazar – Caetano regime; the liberals, who emphasize the need to radically open up the Portuguese economy; and the more cautious centrists, who wish to steer a middle course.

Like the Social Democrats, the CDS campaign in 1987 called strongly for a reduction in the role of the state, and for "less state and more liberty". The CDS advocated the elimination of all unnecessary regulations and administrative practices. It put a strong emphasis on far-reaching privatization of the bloated public sector. It called for a major change in the fiscal system, with lower taxes, incentives for families and a simplified tax structure.

The CDS supports greater flexibility in labour legislation. It is highly critical of much of the post-1974 legacy, including agrarian reform without sufficient compensation for the victims of expropriations. It also seeks compensation for the refugees from the former Portuguese colonies who lost all their belongings when independence was granted.

A centrepiece of the CDS strategy is further constitutional reform. It now seeks to eliminate the Marxist elements in the Constitution, and in particular, those economic clauses which act as a barrier to private enterprise and prevent denationalization. It also seeks a constitutional prohibition of abortion. Among proposed changes have been: a reduction in the number of deputies in Parliament; a clearer delimitation of the legislative competences of Parliament and of the government; and the introduction of popular referenda.

In education policy the CDS seeks greater freedom of choice, and equality of treatment between the public and private sectors. It also wants a greater private role in the health and social security fields.

The CDS claim to have been the first party to have advocated the end of the state's television monopoly, and to call for private television.

On European Community policy the CDS favours European union and has strongly emphasized the need for adaptation to the 1992 internal market.

The CDS supports close Portuguese participation in NATO.

Personalities

The president of the CDS is again Diogo Freitas do Amaral, who was re-elected in 1988 after having previously been the party leader from 1974 to 1983. Freitas do Amaral was the Deputy Prime Minister in both the Sá Carneiro and second Balsemão governments, and was the narrowly unsuccessful presidential candidate in 1986. Freitas do Amaral is a representative of the centrist group within the party, and is cautious as regards ideological liberalism.

The leader of the party's liberal wing is Francisco Lucas Pires, whose position was strengthed by his outstanding performance as leader of the party list in the 1987 European Parliament elections. He was the party leader from 1983 to 1985. He has strongly advocated liberal economic ideas, for example, through the writings of the so-called Group of Ofir, with which he has been closely associated. He believes strongly in Portugal's European vocation and the need for it to fully adapt to this new role.

Among the key figures on the party's steering committee are Nogueira de Brito, Basílio Horta, and Morais Leitao. The party's secretary-general is Luis Beiroco. Antonio Martins Canaverde presides over the bureau of the national council. Manuel Monteiro is the president of the party's youth movement and headed a list which won eight seats on the national council in early 1988.

The leader of the party conservatives has been Adriano Moreira, who stood down as party leader in early 1988, and was Minister for the Overseas Colonies in the Caetano government.

Partido Comunista Português — PCP
(Portuguese Communist Party)

Headquarters	: Avenida Soeiro Pereira Gomes 1, Lisbon (tel: 779142)
Secretary-general	: Alvaro Cunhal
Youth organization	: *Juventude Comunista Portuguesa*
Publication	: *Avante*
Membership	: 200,000 (December 1983)
Founded	: March 6, 1921

History

The Portuguese Communist Party was founded on March 6, 1921, largely by anarcho-syndicalist workers. The PCP is one of the few communist parties which was not founded as a result of a schism within a socialist party.

The PCP's first secretary-general was José Carlos Rates. During its first period of legal existence from 1925 to 1926, it gained few adherents. After the 1926 military coup the party began 48 years of illegal, clandestine existence.

In 1929 Bento Goncalves became the new party's secretary-general, and gave the PCP a tighter new organizational structure, which enabled it to become a more effective focus of resistance to the regime. 1931 saw the first edition of its clandestine newspaper *Avante*. The party helped to organize demonstrations and strikes, and notably an uprising in the town of Marinha Grande in 1934 over the regime's decision to close down existing trade unions. Bento Goncalves was arrested in 1935 and died in prison in 1942.

Many of the party's activists were imprisoned for long periods (Alvaro Cunhal for 12 years until his spectacular escape from Peniche prison in 1960) and considerable numbers were tortured and killed.

The PCP supported a number of electoral campaigns of government-authorized candidates, such as Norton de Matos in 1949, and General Delgado in 1958. In 1961 Alvaro Cunhal became secretary-general. In 1969 the party helped to sponsor a democratic electoral committee (CDE), which contested the election of that year.

The years of clandestine struggle had gained the party considerable prestige, and it began to play an important role immediately after the 1974 revolution. Alvaro Cunhal was Minister without Portfolio in the first provisional government of Palma Carlos. The second provisional government was headed by an officer with Communist leanings, Vasco Goncalves. After Spinola's failed coup in September 1974, Costa Gomes became President, and the Communists became even more influential. Early in 1975 the large agricultural holdings in the Alentejo and Ribatejo began to be occupied and expropriated. After the failed coup of March 11, 1975, large-scale nationalizations were carried out. Communist Party membership, which had been under 3,000 before April 1976, and which had risen to 30,000 by October 1974, reached 100,000 by the time of the constituent elections in April 1975. These were, however, a considerable disappointment for the Communist Party, which only gained 12.5 per cent of the vote and 30 seats. When this was followed by more nationalizations by the Goncalves government, riots broke out, especially in central and northern Portugal. PCP offices were sacked in a number of towns and the Communist Party came under increasing pressure from the gradually reviving centre and right, as well as from the powerful extreme left.

After Vasco Goncalves was forced to resign in August 1975, and especially after the coup and counter-coup of November 1975, the Communist Party's influence began to wane, although they played an important role in the adoption of the new Portuguese Constitution of 1976. In the 1976 elections for the National Assembly, the PCP gained 14.6 per cent and won 40 seats. In spite of this improvement over their 1975 result they went into opposition to the Socialist minority administration, and have never since participated in government.

In June 1976 the PCP candidate in the presidential election, Octavio Pato, only won 7.6 per cent, and was easily beaten by the candidate for the far left, Otelo do Carvalho. The PCP subsequently supported President Eanes.

In September 1976 the PCP established an electoral coalition (the United People's Electoral Front or FEPU) with two other left-wing parties, the MDP (see separate entry) and the FSP.

In September 1979 the FEPU was replaced by a new electoral coalition between the PCP and the MDP entitled *Aliança Povo Unido* (United People's Alliance or APU). APU made a major advance in the December 1979 national election, winning almost 19 per cent of the vote, and 47 seats in Parliament. The PCP and MDP then constituted separate parliamentary groups, although the MDP was never perceived as truly independent by the other political parties.

In the 1980 elections the APU fell back, winning 41 seats on 16.8 per cent of the vote. In the subsequent presidential elections Carlos Brito was put forward as the Communist candidate, but was subsequently withdrawn in favour of President Eanes.

In the 1983 election the APU coalition made a limited recovery, winning 44 seats on 18.1 per cent of the vote, but in subsequent National Assembly elections the Communists have fallen back sharply. In 1985 APU (with an additional party participating, *Os Verdes* — the Greens) only won 38 seats on 15.5 per cent of the vote, although they subsequently won 19.4 per cent in the 1985 local elections. In the 1986 presidential elections the Communists first supported the candidacy of the former socialist Salgado Zenha, but when he was defeated in the first round, they were forced to take the decision of supporting their old adversary, Mário Soares, as the lesser of two evils. The MDP had been growing increasingly unhappy with their subordination to the Communists within the APU, and before the 1987 elections they decided not to renew the APU coalition. The Communists then contested the election in the new coalition called the *Coligação Democratica Unitaria* (the United Democratic Coalition or CDU), their partners being the Ecologist Party *Os Verdes* and a group of dissident MDP members, *Intervenção Democrática*. In the 1987 elections the CDU won 31 seats on 12.2 per cent of the vote. In the simultaneous European Parliament elections the CDU won three seats, with 11.5 per cent of the vote.

The PCP has 1,062 elected members in municipal assemblies and 1,586 parish councillors. It holds power in 46 municipal chambers.

Support

PCP membership is strongest among industrial and agricultural workers, with a considerable percentage among office workers and technical employees. There are very few farmers among its members. There has been a decline in the number of young members.

In regional terms the greatest area of communist strength is Alentejo, a large region of southern Portugal. It was characterized before 1974 by large *latifundia* and landless agricultural labourers, who took part in the occupation and expropriation of these lands after 1974, and who were the main beneficiaries of agrarian reform. The Communist's four strongest electoral districts are in the Alentejo, notably Beja (the CDU won 38.6 per cent of the Beja vote in 1987, down from APU's vote of 44.8 per cent in 1985), Evora (36.1 per cent in 1987, 41.2 per cent in 1985) and Setubal (32.7 per cent in 1987, 38.2 per cent in 1985). In several municipalities in these districts the CDU was still receiving around 50 per cent of the vote in 1987 (e.g. Montemor-o-Novo 50.85 per cent, Alandroal 50.55 per cent). In the 1985 local elections the Communists won over 50 per cent of the vote in all three districts. In the northern Alentejo district of Portalegre the Communists are rather less strong (20.8 per cent in 1987, 25.1 per cent in 1985), although the CDU's highest vote in the whole country in 1987 was in the Portalegre municipality of Avis (52.4 per cent). South of the Alentejo, in the Algarve, the Communists are much weaker (10.9 per cent in the electoral district of Faro in 1987, 15.3 per cent in 1985).

The only other area of substantial Communist strength is the Ribatejo (12.6 per cent in the electoral district of Santarem in 1987, 16.4 per cent in 1985). In the electoral district of Lisbon the Communists won over 32 per cent in the local elections in 1985, but only 20 per cent in the national elections of that year. By 1987 their Lisbon district vote was down to 16.5 per cent. In the City of Lisbon they only won 14.9 per cent in 1987, and their highest votes were in some of the outlying satellite communities — such as Sobral de Monte Agraco (30 per cent), Loures (21.45 per cent) and Amadora (21.1 per cent).

In northern Portugal the Communists have always been weak, and became even weaker in 1987. Their highest votes are in the more industrialized districts, such as Porto (9.4 per cent in 1987, 12 per cent in 1985). In 1987 they won 12.7 per cent in the town of Viana do Castelo and 9.6 per cent in the town of Braga. There are other scattered pockets of Communist strength, such as the municipality of

Marinha Grande (of 1934 uprising fame) (25.85 per cent in 1987), and Covilha (16.1 per cent in 1987).

The Communists' weakest coastal district in northern Portugal is Aveiro (4.4 per cent in 1987, 6.5 per cent in 1985). Its weakest mainland area of all is the highly rural north-eastern interior. In the district of Vila Real it won 4.1 per cent in 1987 (5.9 per cent in 1985), in Bragança and Guarda 3.3 per cent (down from 5.4 per cent and 5.2 per cent respectively in 1985) and in Viseu (2.9 per cent in 1987, 5 per cent in 1985).

The Communists have made minimal impact in the Azores (2.3 per cent in 1987, 4.4 per cent in 1985 with a 1987 high over 8 per cent in the island of Flores) and in Madeira (1.9 per cent in 1987, 3.2 per cent in 1985).

Organization

The PCP's organizational structure was developed to reflect the coalition of clandestine operation under the dictatorship. After April 1974 the party's membership grew rapidly, but until 1988 the organizational structure remained essentially unchanged, still following the orthodox communist pattern of rigid democratic centralism. The party now recognizes that some changes are needed. The concept of democratic centralism, for example, is being re-interpreted in a less rigid sense.

In December 1983 (membership figures are released at each congress) the PCP had 200,000 members, making it the largest Portuguese party in terms of membership. The basic unit of the party are its cells, which are generally organized on a workplace rather than residential basis. Each cell has its assembly and secretariat. The number of cells has been declining in recent years. When a cell is too large it can be sub-divided into nuclei.

The PCP is organized at parish, municipal and district levels.

At national level the party congress is meant to be held every four years. Extraordinary party congresses can also be held: the last such congress was held in February 1986 to ratify the leadership's decision to back Mário Soares in the second round of the presidential election.

The party congress elects the central committee consisting of 91 full members and 74 substitutes, who may not vote but are allowed to speak and to fully participate in other ways. The central committee is meant to have a majority of working-class members.

The central committee elects the political committee of 18 full members and seven substitutes, the secretariat of eight members and two tutes, the secretariat of eight members and two substitutes and the party's secretary-general. Since the party's tenth congress there has been a permanent political secretariat of five members, which has become the organ of day-to-day party management.

The PCP youth movement is called *Juventude Comunista Portuguesa* and has 30,000 members. It was formed in 1979 by a merger between the Communist youth and students' organizations.

There is no mass women's organization, but a representative committee has been established, the *Organisação de Mulheres Comunistas*.

The PCP has no special trade union group, but its members are the dominant force with the *Confederação Geral de Trabalhadores Portugueses* (General Confederation of Portuguese Workers — CGTP-Intersindical), which was the main trade union confederation until the establishment of the Socialist and Social Democratic UGT in 1979.

The party's newspaper is *Avante*, currently with a circulation of around 50,000. There is also an organizational bulletin *O Militante*, as well as a PCP economic journal and a local government review. There is another newspaper *O Diario*, which is closely associated with the party. There are two Communist publishing houses, Caminho, which generally deals with historical and social works, and Avante, which is more concerned with political works.

An important event in the PCP year is the annual *Festa do Avante*, first initiated in 1976. This is a large popular festival held over two or three days in a central site, generally in or near Lisbon. There are also many local and regional festivals.

Elected PCP members are expected to pay the party difference between what they earned before the election and their new parliamentary salary.

The PCP is a member of the Communist Group within the European Parliament.

Policies

The PCP is still a very orthodox Communist party, both in its tone (proclaiming itself as a revolutionary Marxist-Leninist party and denouncing imperialism and monopoly capitalism), and in its actual policies. Within the international communist context it is much closer to the French and orthodox Greek parties than to the Italian or Spanish parties. It has never supported Eurocommunism, and has remained close to the Moscow line.

The party is still dominated by the personality of Alvaro Cunhal who has led the party since 1961, along with a small group of other leaders whose formative experience took place during the hardship and suppression of the Salazar dictatorship. Nevertheless Cunhal is now well into his 70s and there is uncertainty about the party's future direction.

For a while in 1974 and 1975 the PCP was in the mainstream of the Portuguese political spectrum, participating in government, with close links with the armed forces, and with strong political forces to its own left. Since 1976 it has become progressively more isolated, the armed forces movement has become of little significance, and the far left is now very small. The PCP now sees as one of its key roles the defence of the values of the April 25th revolution, which it never ceases to cite as well as defence of the post-1974 gains, agrarian reform, nationalizations, labour laws and the Portuguese Constitution itself. The PCP identifies the Social Democrats and the CDS as potentially counter-revolutionary forces of the right, and calls for the "convergence" of all "democratic" forces to combat their policies. Before the 1987 elections they proposed co-operation between themselves, the Socialists and the PRD. The Socialists in particular have made it clear that they have no wish to ally with the Communists. The only allies of the Communists have been small parties such as the MDP and now the Greens, who have enabled the Communists to show their openness to other political creeds and to try and attract wider support for Communist-led coalitions.

The Communists are strongly opposed to the constitutional changes that are being proposed by the present government. While prepared to accept modifications, they believe that the proposed changes would result in a new Constitution with a different spirit. Moreover, they claim that the negotiations are taking place behind closed doors, and that there must be a much more open and public debate on such an important theme. They are strongly opposed to any attempt to alter the existing system of proportional representation.

The Communists also denounce what they claim to be the government's attempt to achieve constitutional change on a piecemeal basis by introducing legislation on particular issues, such as privatization, agrarian reform and labour law.

The Communists strongly defend the nationalizations that took place after April 1974 and oppose the government's attempts at privatization and deregulation. They maintain that key sectors must remain fully in public hands.

They strongly defend the land expropriation and agrarian reform that took place in 1974–75. They oppose attempts to dismantle these reforms, and to create new *latifundia*.

A third area of special concern for the Communists is labour law reform, which they believe will undercut worker security and lead to large-scale dismissals without due safeguards. In opposition to the government's plans the Communists put forward a number of other proposals, including the elaboration of a national system of professional training, increasing the national minimum wage, and a reduction in the working week to 40 hours.

The Communists put a particular emphasis on greater economic self-sufficiency for Portugal. There should be a proper Portuguese industrial policy, and Portuguese traditional industries should be modernized. The Communists emphasize that they are not against the private sector as such. While opposed to large national and multinational capitalist enterprises, they believe that there should be more assistance to small and medium-sized enterprises and to co-operatives. They also seek fiscal reform with fewer taxes on vital goods and higher ones on luxuries.

Their 1987 election manifesto rejected any attempt to impose civil nuclear energy on Portugal rapidly, while reaffirming the importance of nuclear energy as an energy source of the future. They stress, however, that it must be accompanied by careful scientific, technical and industrial planning.

The Communists seek a more integrated social security system, and a proper national health service. They put a strong emphasis on reducing regional economic disparity. They call for more decentralized administration.

The Communists' foreign policy emphasizes defence of Portuguese national independence, from economic, cultural, political, diplomatic and military interference from outside, and particularly from the imperialist powers and from the great concentrations of economic capital.

They strongly opposed Portuguese entry into the EC, which they believe will have disastrous economic consequences for Portugal, as well as detracting from national sovereignty and weakening the Portuguese revolutionary process. They recognize that Portuguese withdrawal from the EC is no longer a realistic prospect and see their role as helping to maximize any positive EC benefits for Portugal, and minimizing its negative effects.

They voted against ratification of the Single European Act when it was debated in the Portuguese Parliament — and also seek renegotiations of certain features of the Portuguese terms of accession, including those concerning fisheries. They are opposed to the liberalization of capital movements, and believe the 1992 internal market will merely lead to increased penetration of foreign capital in key sections of the Portuguese economy. They would like Portugal to be able to maintain import restrictions in sensitive product areas.

The PCP recognizes that Portuguese withdrawal from NATO is unrealistic. The NATO bases in Portugal, however, should not be reinforced, and the bases should not be used for aggressive action against other countries. They are opposed to nuclear vessels visiting Portugal, and call for an Iberian nuclear-free zone.

Personalities

The PCP's secretary-general, Alvaro Cunhal, still plays a decisive role. He was the leader of its youth movement during the 1930s, spent 12 years in prison and became its secretary-general in 1961. His austere character and orthodox views have left a strong mark on the PCP.

Among the other leadership figures are the other four members of the PCP's permanent political committee: Carlos Brito, the leader of the PCP's parliamentary group; Carlos Costa, who is a key man in running the party machinery; Octavio Pato, the party's presidential candidate in 1976; and Domingo Abrantes.

Partido Ecologista — Os Verdes
(Ecology Party — The Greens)

Headquarters	:	Avda Torre de Belém, 8–A, 1400 Lisbon (tel: 61 70 46)
Youth organization		*Organização de Juventude do Partido Os Verdes*
Membership	:	1,000
Founded	:	1982

History

Portugal has not traditionally had a strong environmental movement, although a number of environmental associations have developed in recent years. The party which put the emphasis on ecological themes was ironically the monarchist party, the PPM (see separate entry). Around 1982, however, a number of pacifists and environmental activists who believed that ecological causes could not be taken out of their wider social context decided to create *Os Verdes*. In the 1985 national elections the small party joined forces with the Communists and the MDP in the alliance known as APU, which gained 15.5 per cent of the vote and 38 seats. One of the seats went to Herculano Pombo, a member of *Os Verdes*. In the 1987 elections the alliance

was renewed, this time without the MDP, under the new name *Coligação Democratica Unitaria* (Unitary Democratic Alliance — CDU), which won 12.2 per cent of the vote and 31 seats. On this occasion two members of *Os Verdes* were elected to Parliament on the CDU list, Herculano Pombo and Maria Santos. They formed a separate parliamentary group from the Communists.

Support

Since they have only contested elections within the wider APU and then CDU framework (see entry on Portuguese Communist Party), a separate analysis of their regional pattern of support is not possible.

Organization

The Greens claim to have around 1,000 members, although they do not know the exact number. The local branches are called *Colectivos de Base*, and have their own assemblies and local executives. There are currently eight regional groups. At national level the party congress is called the National Ecology Convention, and is held every three years with delegates elected by the local and regional assemblies, as well as representatives of the regional executives and the national office holders.

The congress elects 30 members of the national council, which also contains one representative of each regional executive committee. In its turn the national council elects the 15 member national executive committee. There is no formal post of secretary-general, and the leadership is thus collective. Unlike some other Green parties, there is no rigid rule of rotation of party or elected posts.

The party's youth organization is called *Organização de Juventude do Partido Os Verdes*, and is open to 16–21 year olds.

There is no formal party newspaper, but the first edition of a new party magazine *Alternativa Os Verdes* appeared in May 1988.

The party's elected members, like those of the Communist party, are requested to contribute to the party the difference between their previous salary and their salary as parliamentarians.

The Greens are establishing links with the European Green Alternative grouping of political parties, GRAEL. They are also developing a liaison group with the Green parties of the Mediterranean basin, namely those in Spain, France, Italy and Greece.

Policies

Os Verdes is a very small party and its continued parliamentary existence depends on the alliance with the Communists. The party states that its alliance with the Communists within the CDU framework is an electoral rather than organic political alliance, and that its members form their own separate parliamentary group within the National Assembly. The Greens recognize that the alliance is the only way they can obtain parliamentary representation within the existing electoral system and that the Communists were prepared to have them as allies, and are the only large party outside the mainstream Portuguese power structure. The Greens reaffirmed the CDU alliance for the 1988 local elections, but sought more autonomy and weight within the CDU.

The Greens' main emphasis is on protection of the Portuguese environment, but they define this in the widest possible sense. They emphasise that they are not merely conservationists, and that broader economic and social changes are needed.

Economic development should no longer be based on narrow profit motives and on large monopoly enterprises. The Greens reject the concept of zero economic growth, but consider that qualitative growth is required. Small enterprises and co-operatives need to play a far greater role. There should be recycling of resources, and careful urban planning.

An alternative energy plan should be prepared, emphasizing conservation and use of renewables, with a complete renunciation of civil nuclear energy.

The Greens oppose big dam projects and are also very concerned about the spread of "industrial" forests of eucalyptus, which could ultimately lead to the death of Portuguese traditional species, and even to desertification. The Greens defend smaller agricultural units and are opposed to the dismantling of the agrarian reform which took place after April 1974. They do not support privatization.

The Greens favour decentralization and the development of regionalism. They seek a more participative democracy, and defence of the right of minorities, such as sexual minorities and of Africans resident in Portugal. They call for more environmental and nutritional education, and for enhanced consumer protection. They have put down draft legislation for the legalization of naturism.

They are hostile to the European Community, which they believe is a centralized capitalist organization which has little to do with the decentralized Europe of the regions that they seek to foster.

They want a neutral Portugal, and seek a gradual reduction in Portuguese involvement in NATO, leading to its eventual departure. They seek the closing of NATO bases in Portugal, and condemn the entry of Portugal into the Western European Union. They support conscientious objectors.

Partido Popular Monárquico — PPM
(Popular Monarchist Party)

Headquarters	: Largo do Picadeiro 9, 1200 Lisbon (tel: 1–36 65 87 or 37 15 67)
President	: Augusto Ferreira do Amaral
Publication	: *Reipovo*
Founded	: May 1974

History

The Portuguese monarchy was overthrown in October 1910, and there has been no major political pressure to restore it. During the 1960s, however, a group of progressive monarchists emerged, mainly opposed to the Salazar regime. Independent monarchists' lists were presented in 1965 and in 1973. On May 23, 1974, the Popular Monarchist party (PPM) was founded.

Its leader from the outset was Gonçalo Ribeiro Telles, an architect with strong environmental views, who was Environment Minister in all but one of the six provisional governments from 1974–1976. The PPM had only limited electoral strength, however, obtaining 0.6 per cent in the 1975 constituent elections, and 0.5 per cent in the 1976 national elections, not winning a seat on either occasion.

In June 1979 the PPM entered into an election pact with the PSD and CDS known as the *Aliança Democrática*. Although it was very much the junior partner, the PPM managed to win five seats under the AD umbrella in 1979 and six in 1980. In the Sá Carneiro government it had one minister, in the first Balsemão government two, and in the second no less than four.

With the collapse of AD in 1983 PPM again stood on its own, winning 0.5 per cent of the vote and no seats. In 1985 it reached an agreement with the Socialists whereby its leader, Ribeiro Telles, was elected on the Socialist list in Porto. In the 1987 election it again stood separately winning only 0.4 per cent of the vote. In the European elections, however, held on the same day, the PPM managed to win almost 3 per cent of the vote on the strength of an entertaining campaign led by Miguel Esteves Cardoso.

At the party's 12th congress in April 1988, Ribeiro Telles finally stood down as leader and was replaced by Augusto Ferreira do Amaral.

Support

In the 1987 national elections the PPM only won 0.4 per cent of the vote, with its highest votes in the electoral districts of Viano do Castelo (0.8 per cent) and Coimbra (0.7 per cent). In no municipality did it win more than 1.45 per cent. In the local elections in 1985 it won council seats in Lisbon (where it won 2 per cent of the vote) and in Aveiro. Its best ever performance was in the 1987 European elections with nearly 3 per cent.

Organization

The PPM has a national congress and a national council, and is led by its president.

Policies

The PPM still advocates restoration of the Portuguese monarchy, believing that this will help to maintain Portuguese cultural unity and historical continuity. Nevertheless, its strongest present characteristic is its emphasis on environmental policy. It attacks both socialism and liberalism as materialistic ideologies which lead to a squandering of natural resources. The PPM calls for more attention to be paid to Portugal's ecological balance, for control of urban sprawl (Ribeiro Telles was a Lisbon City planner in the 1950s), and for preservation of nature reserves. It has been strongly opposed to the introduction of civil nuclear energy and has led a campaign against the further spread of eucalyptus trees in Portugal. It believes that these damage the Portuguese ecosystem, and lead to desertification.

The PPM is strongly opposed to centralized government, and advocates community politics. It wants the existing districts replaced by more meaningful regions with real powers.

As regards constitutional reform, the PPM seeks a new electoral system which would be less discriminatory against smaller parties. It advocates the introduction of two houses of parliament, an assembly with 150 members elected in one national constituency, and a chamber of regions, with two representatives for each region. It would like much wider use of referenda at local, regional and national levels.

As regards foreign policy, the PPM emphasizes the need for Portugal to maintain its distinct culture and individuality. It believes that Portugal is a Euro-Atlantic country with a maritime vocation rather than being a minor part of the Iberian Peninsula. It believes that the European Community must not go further than inter-government co-operation, and it is totally opposed to the creation of a United States of Europe. On the other hand it would permit free association with Portugal of those territories historically linked with it, such as Timor.

Personalities

The PPM's new leader is Augusto Ferreiro do Amaral. He was a founder of the Monarchist youth movement, and was Minister for the Quality of Life in the first Balsemão government. He is also the brother of the current PSD Minister for Commerce.

The head of the PPM list for the European elections was Miguel Esteves Cardoso, humorist and journalist who is the editor of a new weekly paper, *Independiente*.

Movimento Democrático Português — Comissão Democrática Eleitoral — MDP/CDE
(Portuguese Democratic Movement — Democratic Electoral Committee)

Headquarters	: 27 Rua Coelho da Rocha, Lisbon (tel: 66 23 03)
Secretary-general	: Jose Manuel Tengarrinha
Founded	: November 1974

History

The *Commissão Democrática Eleitoral* (Democratic Electoral Committee) was founded in 1969 in order to contest the elections of that year. It was supported by Communists and left-wing Catholics.

After the revolution of April 25, 1974, it was re-established as the *Movimento Democrática Português* (MDP, Portuguese Democratic Movement, with the CDE label also being retained).

The MDP was initially a broad popular front, including Socialists and Social Democrats, but the latter withdrew in May 1974, and the MDP was left as a Communist-dominated organization. In November 1974 the MDP/CDE took on a new structure as a formally constituted party, close to but separate from the Communist Party.

In the constituent assembly elections of April 1975 the MDP/CDE won 4.1 per cent of the vote and five seats. It did not, however, take part in the April 1976 elections. Later it entered into an electoral coalition with the Communist Party for the local elections held in December 1976. For the December 1979 national elections the MDP/Communist electoral coalition was renewed under the label *Aliança Povo Unido*

(APU). The MDP gained three seats on the APU lists, and then formed its own separate parliamentary group. Despite voting differently from the Communists on several occasions (for example, when it abstained rather than voted against the 1982 constitutional revision), the MDP never succeeded in establishing an image as an independent political force.

In the October 1980 elections the MDP won two seats under the APU label, and won three seats in the April 1983 elections. Between 1983 and 1985 relations between the MDP and the Communists became more tense, with the MDP increasingly trying to assert its independence, especially in northern Portugal (e.g. Braga), where the Communists were particularly weak. The MDP became more critical of the Communists, and tried to seek new links with the Socialists. The 1985 national elections were again fought under the APU label, and the MDP retained three seats.

Before the 1987 elections the majority of the MDP finally broke with the Communist Party, and contested the elections on a fully independent basis. A minority within the MDP took part in the Communist-led CDU coalition, under the name *Intervenção Democrática* (Democratic Intervention).

The mainstream MDP only won 0.5 per cent of the national vote, and failed to win a single seat in Parliament.

Support

The MDP has traditionally been a party of teachers and intellectuals, and of the middle and upper classes, who support the left, but have been more comfortable within the MDP than the Communist Party. On its own its electoral support proved to be very limited in 1987. Its strongest electoral district was the Algarve (Faro), where it won 1.1 per cent of the vote. Elsewhere it was strongest in the Communist areas of Alentejo (Beja 0.9 per cent, Setubal 0.9 per cent, Evora 0.8 per cent, Portalegre 0.7 per cent). It only obtained over 2 per cent in a handful of Alentejo municipalities. In Lisbon District (and in the City itself), it won 0.7 per cent. In northern Portugal it won 0.4 per cent or under every where apart from the electoral districts of Aveiro (0.8 per cent) and Viana do Castelo (0.6 per cent).

Policies

The key issue for the MDP has been whether it can survive on its own or only in close alliance with the Communist Party. Its attempt to assert its independence in 1987 was unsuccessful, and the party's future became highly uncertain.

In the 1987 elections the MDP tried to carve out a niche between the Communist and Socialist Parties. It argued that it represented the continuing values of the revolution of April 25, 1974, supporting participatory democracy and a pluralist political system. It proclaimed that it was a flexible and "open" party — responsive to the new social movements and prepared to co-operate with the Socialists and the Reformists (PRD). It has also expressed its sympathy for the ideas of the dissident French Communist, Pierre Juquin, who has addressed the party.

It considers that Portuguese entry into the European Community was decided upon without a proper evaluation of its effects on the vulnerable Portuguese economy. It was sceptical of the Single European Act, and abstained in the parliamentary vote on its ratification. It now accepts Portuguese membership as inevitable, but wants to minimize its harmful effects on Portugal by reinforcing the community's structural funds, and renegotiating potentially harmful agreements, such as those on Portuguese fisheries.

Personalities

The long serving leader of the party is José Manuel Tengarrinha, a history professor from the Algarve. Another prominent member of the party has been Helena Cidade Moura, a party vice-president.

Small parties of the Left

In the aftermath of the April 25 revolution the extreme left had considerable initial success, and Otelo Saraiva de Carvalho, the army officer who was its candidate in the June 1976 presidential elections, obtained as much as 16 per cent of the vote. Since then it has further fragmented and declined, with only one of the many small parties, the UDP, consistently winning a seat in Parliament. In the 1987 national elections five parties of the far left put up candidates. None of them won a seat, and the combined total of votes was only 2.4 per cent.

Uniao Democrática Popular — UDP
(Popular Democratic Union)

Headquarters	: Rua Alexandre Herculano 55, Lisbon (tel: 68 94 13)
Secretary-general	: Mario Tome
Founded	: October 1974

The UDP has generally been the strongest of the small parties on the far left of the Portuguese political spectrum. It was founded in October 1974 in a merger between three Marxist-Leninist groups, the *Comite de Apoia da Reconstução do Partido — Marxista-Leninista*, the *Comites Comunistas Revolucionários — Marxista-Leninista* and the *União Revolucionário — Marxista-Leninista*.

In the elections for the constituent assembly in 1975 it won 0.79 per cent and in 1976 its vote rose to 1.69 per cent. In 1979 it won 2 per cent, in 1980 1.4 per cent and in 1983 0.5 per cent when it lost the parliamentary seat that it had held since 1975. In 1985 it won 1.3 per cent and in 1987 dropped to 0.9 per cent, not winning a seat. In mainland Portugal its best 1987 performances were in the districts of Setubal (1.5 per cent) and Lisbon (1.4 per cent), where in 1985 it had only been 238 votes away from obtaining a seat. In the City of Lisbon it won 1.5 per cent and in the Lisbon municipality of Azambuja 3.34 per cent, its best performance in a municipality on the mainland. The UDP's strongest area in all Portugal, however, is the island of Madeira where it won 3.1 per cent in 1987 (5 per cent in 1983). In the municipality of Machico it won 8.22 per cent. In the 1985 communal assembly elections the UDP won 6.8 per cent of the Madeira vote.

Partido Socialista Revolucionário — PSR
(Revolutionary Socialist Party)

Headquarters	: Rua Palma 268, Lisbon (tel: 86 46 43)
Leader	: Francisco Louca
Founded	: 1980

The PSR was founded in a merger between two existing parties, the *Partido Revolucionário de Trabalhadores* and the *Liga Comunista Internacionalista*. In the last two elections, in 1985 and 1987, it won 0.6 per cent of the vote on both occasions, but no seats. The only district where it won over 1 per cent of the vote in 1987 was Beja (1.1 per cent). The PSR sees itself as a non-conformist party of the left, and is Trotskyist in orientation.

Partido Comunista de Trabalhadores Portugueses — Movimento Reorganizativo do Partido do Proletariado — PCTP-MRPP
(Communist Party of Portuguese Workers — Reorganized Movement of the Party of the Proletariat)

Headquarters	: Travessa André Valente 7, 1200 Lisbon (tel: 37 19 19)
Leadership	: Arnaldo Matos

The MRPP was founded in 1970, and the party took its new name in 1979. It has contested all general elections since 1976. In the 1987 elections it won 0.4 per cent, compared to 0.3 per cent in 1985, obtaining no seats. Its best performance in 1987 was in the left-wing Alentejo district of Beja (1 per cent). Its 1987 election programme called for a referendum to be held on Portugal's withdrawal from the EC, for Portugal to leave NATO, and the dismantling of existing Portuguese military bases. Portugal's external debt should be repudiated, all foreign enterprises in Portugal should be nationalized, along with all the basic sectors of the economy. There should be a free National Health Service. All members of parliament and public administrators should be paid a worker's average salary.

The PCTP is Marxist in orientation, and has denounced developments in China since Mao's death, and even Albanian attacks on Mao.

Partido Comunista Reconstruido — PC(R)
(Reconstructed Communist Party)

Headquarters	: Alegria 12, Lisbon (tel: 30 27 15)
Leadership	: Eduardo Pires

The PC(R) won 0.3 per cent of the vote in 1987, compared to 0.2 per cent in 1985. In 1987 it won over 1 per cent of the vote in a number of municipalities, performing best in the interior district of Castelo Branco (0.8 per cent), in Beja (0.7 per cent) and Evora (0.7 per cent). It put up no candidates on the islands, or in the district of Lisbon.

It is strongly against the European Community, and believes that the Single European Act is an attack on Portuguese national sovereignty.

Partido Operario de Unidade Socialista — POUS
(Workers' Party for Socialist Unity)

The POUS was founded in September 1979 by dissident socialists, of whom the two most prominent were Carmelinda Pareira and Aires Rodrigues. Rodrigues polled 0.22 per cent of the vote in the 1980 presidential elections.

In the 1987 elections it only polled 0.2 per

cent of the vote, putting up candidates in seven electoral districts. In 1985 it had polled 0.3 per cent of the vote, putting up candidates everywhere.

The POUS calls itself the Portuguese section of the Fourth International, and seeks the creation of a world party of socialist revolution. It is strongly anti-EC.

Small parties of the Right

Partido da Democracia Cristão — PDC
(Christian Democratic Party)

Headquarters	: Rua Passodico 28–2, Lisbon
Secretary-general	: Santos Ferreira
Founded	: 1974

The PDC is a right-wing party, which contests elections under the Christian Democratic banner, although the European and International Christian Democratic groupings recognize the CDS (see separate entry) as their Portuguese component.

The PDC was founded in 1974. In the 1975 constituent assembly election campaign it formed a short-lived alliance with the CDS (the Union of the Christian Democratic Centre) but the alliance broke up and the PDC was forbidden from taking part in the elections, because of the turbulence that it was causing, and because of its alleged involvement in the attempted coup of March 11th.

The PDC took part in the 1976 elections, and gained 0.5 per cent of the vote. In the 1980 elections it allied itself with two parties of the far right, but only won 20,000 votes.

It has continued to contest elections. In 1985 it won 0.7 per cent of the national vote, and also took part in the local elections of that year, obtaining a municipal assembly seat in Aveiro and another in Santarem, where it also obtained a handful of parish assembly seats. In the 1987 national elections it won 0.5 per cent of the vote. Its highest votes were in the north-eastern interior districts (Viseu 1.6 per cent, Bragança 1.2 per cent, Vila Real 1.1 per cent, Castelo Branco 1 per cent, Guarda 0.9 per cent) and to a certain extent in the Azores (1 per cent) and in Santarem (0.8 per cent). Its highest votes in the country were in two municipalities in the district of Viseu, Sernancelhe (4.98 per cent) and Carregal do Sal (3.74 per cent). The PDC has never won a parliamentary seat.

The PDC combines Christian Democratic causes (strong opposition to abortion) with right-wing ones (fierce anti-Marxism, compensation for the returnees from the colonies).

The PDC's long standing leader is Santos Ferreira.

Spain

Francis Jacobs

The country

Spain is a country of 195,000 square miles, with a population of almost 40 million. Besides the mainland it also includes two island groups (the Balearic Islands and the Canary Islands), as well as two enclaves on the Moroccan coast, Ceuta and Melilla. Spain also claims sovereignty over Gibraltar.

It has great regional diversity and there are independence movements in the Basque Country and Catalonia, as well as lesser ones in Galicia and the Canary Islands. Seventeen autonomous regions have recently been created on top of the traditional 52 provinces.

There are three minority languages besides Spanish: Catalan (spoken in Catalonia but also in parts of the Valencian region and the Balearic Islands, as well as adjacent France and Andorra); Basque (spoken in parts of Navarre, as well as in the Basque Country); and Galician, which is akin to Portuguese.

There are a large number of Spanish emigrants living outside Spain, especially in France.

Political institutions

After the re-establishment of democracy a new Constitution was promulgated in 1978, providing for a parliamentary monarchy with a bicameral legislature.

The Congress of Deputies is by far the most powerful of the two Houses, investing the executive and with the power to censure it, initiating legislation and having the last word on it. It currently has 350 members (the Constitution provides for between 300 to 400 members), elected for a maximum term of four years, although Congress can be dissolved before that date. The constituencies are based on the provinces, with a minimum of three deputies per constituency (only one each for Ceuta and Melilla), and with the total rising according to population, so that the largest constituencies, Madrid and Barcelona, have 33 deputies each. The smaller constituencies are over-represented, with approximately one deputy for every 27,000 electors in Soria, for example, compared to only one for every 108,000 in Madrid or Barcelona. Within each constituency deputies are elected by the d'Hondt system of proportional representation, but parties must win at least 3 per cent of the vote in a constituency in order to qualify. The effective electoral threshold is of course much higher than this in the smaller constituencies. Members do not explicitly represent their constituencies but Spanish interests as a whole.

There are no strict rules about forming parliamentary groups. Such a group must have at least 15 members, and 15 per cent of votes in all the constituencies in which it presents candidates, or else have a minimum of five members and over 5 per cent of the entire national vote. *Izquierda Unida*, for example, with nine seats but only 4.6 per cent of the national vote cannot form a parliamentary group. All members not within a parliamentary group are members of the Mixed Group (*Grupo Mixto*).

The Senate has far fewer powers than the Congress, although it can make proposals and put forward amendments. It has 208 members, elected at the same time as the Congress, but on a simple plurality vote basis. There are four senators per constituency, irrespective of constituency size. The only exceptions are: the Balearic Islands with five senators (three for Majorca and one each for Ibiza and Menorca); the constituency of Tenerife with six (three for the Island of Tenerife, and one each for La Palma, Gomera and Hierro); the constituency of Las Palmas with five (Gran Canaria three, Lanzarote one and Fuerteventura one); and Ceuta and Melilla with two each.

The government is invested by the Congress of Deputies, and must have a majority within the Congress. Ministers remain as members of the legislature.

Spain has 60 members of the European Parliament, with the whole of Spain as one constituency. Candidates for the European Parliament cannot be members of the National Parliament. The first Spanish European Parliament elections were held in June 1987 for a special two-year term before the 1989 European election.

Every four years there are also elections to the parliaments of the 17 autonomous regions, from which the regional executives are then drawn. Early dissolution of the regional parliaments is also possible. The elections in the Basque Country, Catalonia, Galicia and Andalusia are held separately, whereas the elections in the other 13 regions are held at the same time (on the last occasion in June 1987). The regional parliaments differ greatly in size, from 33 in La Rioja to 135 in Catalonia. Compared to national elections the participation of purely regional parties is much greater, and they have greater electoral strength.

Map of Spain showing 14 autonomous regions and 52 provinces (which serve as multi-member constituencies for national elections). Number of seats in each constituency also included.

Source: adapted from *World Atlas of Elections*.

Finally, there are also municipal elections, which are held throughout the whole country every four years (on the last occasion in June 1987).

For administrative purposes the provinces are also important. The provincial governments are known as *diputaciones*. In some parts of the country, notably Catalonia, smaller units known as *comarcas* have great historical importance.

Political parties receive state subsidies proportional to their electoral results. The system of state financing of parties was overhauled in 1988.

Brief political history

1833–39 First Carlist War.
1868–74 First Republic (Second Carlist War 1872–76).
1875–98 Alternation of Liberals and Conservatives (*Turno Pacifico*).
1898– Fragmentation of political system.
1923
1923-30 Primo de Rivera dictatorship.
1931–36 Second Republic (Republican Socialist Coalition 1931–33, Conservative Republican/CEDA Coalition 1933–36, Popular Front 1936).
1936–39 Civil War.
1939–75 Franco's regime.
1976 Restoration of monarchy (Juan Carlos).
1977 First democratic elections after fall of Francoism (UCD victory).
1978 New Constitution adopted.
1981 Attempted coup.
1982 Socialists come to power (re-elected 1986).

Main features of the current political system

The two key themes in Spanish politics since the re-establishment of democracy have been the need to consolidate the democratic system without reopening the wounds of the Civil War, and without provoking a new military intervention; and secondly, the need to face up to the demands for autonomy from the historic regions within Spain, notably from Catalonia and the Basque Country. In the latter case the Spanish government has also had to confront one of Europe's most vigorous terrorist movements.

The delicate process of consolidating democracy has led to a number of changes in the Spanish political system. Firstly it has led to the effective removal of one of Spain's former political cleavages, that between monarchists and republicans. The monarchy is now accepted and republicanism is no longer a major force.

A second change has been the reinforcement of the political centre. Spanish politics have been highly polarized in the past and ultimately this led to the Civil War. After Franco's death the emergent democratic parties, including Franco's traditional opponents, the Socialists and Communists, sought a gradual transition, rather than a sudden break, and sought to present themselves in as moderate a light as possible. Extremist parties did not flourish. Spain's formerly powerful anarchist tradition (incorporating a major anarchist trade union, the CNT) did not re-emerge. Extremist parties of the right also fared poorly.

A further important change has been the decline in anti-clericalism, formerly very strong in some parts of Spanish society. The other side of the coin is that the Spanish church, while still powerful, has a less dominant role than in the past. Church attendance is greatly down, and the church has been unable to prevent the enactments of law permitting divorce and abortion. With rapid economic growth Spanish society has also become generally much less traditional. One of the reasons for the Socialists' electoral triumph in 1982 was the feeling that they were the most likely party to carry out the necessary reforms to modernize Spanish society that had been originally initiated by the UCD government.

The most sensitive issue of all has been the reform of the armed forces, which have been successfully reduced in size and modernized in structure. The threat of military intervention now appears much more remote.

The other key theme, however, that of relations between the Spanish centre and the peripheral regions or "nations" has not yet been resolved. Autonomous regions, with their own governments and parliaments, have not only been established in the three regions which negotiated new autonomy statutes during the Second Republic (Catalonia and, belatedly, the Basque Country and Galicia), but in the rest of Spain as well, including artificial regions with little or no regional identity at all. The need to meet essentially political demands for greater autonomy has thus been mixed with the issue of administrative decentralization. A new tier of government has been created between the national government and the provinces, leading, in some cases, to considerable administrative overlaps, and to unnecessary bureaucracy.

At the same time, the historic regions are not fully satisfied with the degree of their autonomy, and the way in which their autonomy statutes have been implemented, especially since the 1981 coup attempt slowed down the process of implementation and led to the enactment of the controversial LOAPA (Institutional Law for the Harmonization of the Devolution Process) in the same year.

In Catalonia and the Basque Country, and to a much lesser extent in Galicia and the Canary Islands, there are calls for much greater autonomy, for a truly federal Spain and even for full independence. At the same time the Basque terrorist group, ETA, has proved a major threat to the Spanish state, which has been uncertain on how to cope with it. These issues are also discussed below in the special sub-sections on the Basque and Catalan political systems.

Besides the two key themes mentioned above, the main political issues in Spain have included the following:

Economic policy: Spanish economic growth has been rapid but uneven with considerable social and regional divisions and often with high environmental costs. The Socialist government's tough austerity programme has kept public deficits and inflation down, but unemployment has risen to among the highest levels in Europe, and Spanish social security is still weak. The Spanish political parties are divided as to which mix of measures are needed to tackle these problems, such as whether the public sector should be reduced, or whether there should be a greater emphasis on reducing unemployment and tackling regional and social disparities.

Spain and the European Community: Spain's membership of the European Community is now a reality and there are few sharp divides between the parties on the ultimate political objectives of Spanish membership (most are in favour of stronger European co-operation and some of full European union), but there is more controversy over the European policies that need to be pursued, and whether Europe should be a third force between the superpowers.

NATO and the American bases: The referendum over Spanish membership of NATO in 1986 led to sharp political divisions. With the "yes" vote and the subsequent negotiations to implement the referendum's conditions (including removal of the American bases) the issue has declined somewhat in importance.

Spanish election results 1977–present (percentages of vote and seats won)

	1977	1979	1982	1986
Union de Centro Democratico (UCD)	34.6%	35.0%	6.8%	—
(Union of the Democratic Centre)	(166)	(168)	(12)	
Centro Democratico y Social (CDS)	—	—	2.9%	9.2%
(Democratic and Social Centre)			(2)	(19)
Coalición Popular (CP)	8.4%	6.0%	26.2%	26.0%
(Popular Coalition)[1]	(16)	(9)	(106)	(105)
Partido Socialista Obrero Español (PSOE)	29.4%	30.5%	48.2%	44.1%
(Spanish Socialist Workers Party)	(118)	(121)	(202)	(184)
Partido Comunista de España (PCE)	9.4%	10.8%	4.1%	see IU
(Spanish Communist Party)	(20)	(23)	(4)	
Izquierda Unida (IU)	—	—	—	4.6%
(United Left)				(7)
Convergencia i Unió (CIU)	3.7%	2.5%	3.7%	5.0%
(Convergence and Union)[2]	(11)	(8)	(12)	(18)
Esquerra Republicana de Catalunya (ERC)	0.8%	0.7%	0.7%	0.4%
(Republican Left of Catalonia)	(1)	(1)	(1)	(0)
Partido Nacionalista Vasco (PNV)	1.7%	1.5%	1.9%	1.5%
(Basque Nationalist Party)	(7)	(7)	(8)	(6)
Herri Batasuna	—	1.0%	1.0%	1.1%
(United People)		(3)	(2)	(5)
Euskadiko Ezkerra	0.4%	0.5%	0.5%	0.5%
(Basque Left)	(1)	(1)	(1)	(2)
Others	11.6%	11.5%	4.0%	7.6%
	(10)	(9)	(0)	(4)

[1]Coalición Popular (of whom the nucleus is now the Partido Popular) stood as Alianza Popular in 1977.
[2]The 1977 figures for Convergencia i Unió refer to the results for the PDC.

Gibraltar: The call for Gibraltar to be returned to Spain is a common theme, rather than one which divides the Spanish parties. There is less unanimity, however, as to whether a link should be made with the issue of Ceuta and Melilla and whether they should be returned to Morocco.

Education: The comparative treatment of the public and private education sections.

Moral issues: The divorce and abortion laws were divisive issues, but with the declining force of traditional Spain moral issues are less important than in the past.

The current Spanish political structure is characterized by the dominance of the Socialist Party, which has a strong hold at both national and regional level, and which is faced by a severely divided opposition. The Socialist dominance of the government apparatus and of many Spanish institutions has become a political issue in its own right, with accusations of clientelism from the opposition.

One final feature has been the continuing significance of strong personalities in Spanish political life, with the decisive roles since Franco's death being played by Adolfo Suárez and Felipe González, and to a lesser extent by Manuel Fraga. This has led to a great fluidity in Spanish political life, with UCD, for example, disintegrating after Suárez's departure.

Partido Socialista Obrero Español — PSOE
(Spanish Socialist Workers' Party)

Headquarters	: Ferraz 70, Madrid 8 (tel: 470–1112)
Secretary-general	: Felipe González
President	: Ramon Rubial
Spokesman of parliamentary group	: Eduardo Martín Toval
Youth group	: *Juventudes Socialistas* (Secretary-general: Javier de Paz)
Newspaper	: *El Socialista*
Membership	: 213,000 (January 1988)
Founded	: 1879

History

The *Partido Socialista Obrero Español* (PSOE) is one of the most powerful political parties in Western Europe today. It has an absolute majority in both Houses of Parliament, with 184 deputies and 124 senators and runs the Spanish government. It has 470 deputies in the regional parliaments and provides the leadership of the majority of regional governments. It has 2,000 mayors and 21,000 councillors.

The PSOE was founded clandestinely in 1879 in Madrid. Its first leader was a Madrid printer, Pablo Iglesias, who provided a disciplined ethos for the new party. He was a strong advocate of class struggle, and opposed any co-operation with the bourgeois parties. From 1881 the party was able to operate legally.

In 1888 the party's associated trade union, the *Unión General de Trabajadores* (UGT — General Union of Workers) was founded, and shortly afterwards the first party congress was held.

In 1891 PSOE won its first local council seats. In 1905 Iglesias was elected to the Madrid council. In 1908 the PSOE opened its first *Casa del Pueblo* ("People's House") in Madrid, and these subsequently sprang up all around the country, serving as local party headquarters, social centres, centres for conferences, congresses and lending libraries.

In 1908 PSOE abandoned its strategy of working on its own, and entered into an electoral alliance with Republican parties, which led to Pablo Iglesias being elected to parliament as PSOE's first deputy in 1910.

In 1917 the party took part in a major national strike, which was crushed by the army, and which underlined the difficulties of a revolutionary path to socialism. In the early 1920s the party was severely divided over the issue as to whether to join the Third International. After three contradictory party congresses the majority decided not to join and the minority left to form the Spanish Communist Party. In 1923 Puerto de la Cruz on the island of Tenerife became the first municipality to have a Socialist majority. The party responded hesitantly to the imposition of Primo de Rivera's dictatorship late in 1923, with some of its leaders, such as Largo Caballero, giving him tactical support.

The establishment of the Second Republic in 1931 gave the Socialist Party a position of real power. It won 115 seats in the constituent *Cortes* and participated both in the provisional government and in that of Manuel Azaña. In the 1934 elections, however, the party lost badly and fell back to only 58 seats.

In 1936 the PSOE played a prominent part in the electoral victory of the Popular Front with Republicans and Communists. It did not participate in the subsequent government, largely at the instance of the party's populist leader, Francisco Largo Caballero, although his main opponent within the party, Indalecio Prieto, was in favour of co-operation with the Republicans.

After the outbreak of the Civil War Largo

Caballero became the Prime Minister on the Republican side. He was subsequently replaced as Prime Minister by another Socialist, Dr Juan Negrín. After the Nationalist victory many of the party leaders went into exile, although many were killed or died in prison, like Julian Besteiro.

In 1944 the PSOE held its first congress in exile, in Toulouse, where it had established its headquarters. Rodolfo Llopis was elected as its secretary-general.

During the 1940s and 50s the Socialists lost considerable ground to the Communists. The internal Socialist leadership was crushed by Franco, and the leadership in exile became increasingly out of touch with developments within Spain, waiting for Franco to die or be overthrown, and doing relatively little to undermine the system from within. Moreover, the rise of the Communist-dominated union, *Comisiones Obreras*, led to the Socialists and UGT losing their grip over the labour movement.

In the 1960s various groups sprang up in Spain in opposition to the exiled leadership. In 1968 Professor Tierno Galván formed a new Socialist party, the *Partido Socialista del Interior* (later the *Partido Socialista Popular* — PSP).

In 1972 younger Socialists active within Spain felt strong enough to challenge the exiled leadership of Rodolfo Llopis. From 1972 to 1974 there were two rival Socialist leaderships, holding separate conferences and both seeking recognition from the Socialist International, but in 1974 at the party's 26th congress at Suresne (the 13th in exile) the old guard was finally ousted. The new leadership was centred especially around groups from Seville in Andalusia (González and Guerra) and from the Basque Country (Redondo, Rubial, Múgica and Benegas). Felipe González was elected as the new secretary-general.

The Socialists set up their own *Plataforma de Convergencia Democrática* with other opposition forces to counter the rival *Junta Democrática* led by the Communists. In March 1976, however, a common opposition front was finally established in the form of *Co-ordinación Democrática* (so-called "*platajunta*").

In February 1977 the PSOE was finally legalized. In the first democratic elections later that year it became the second-largest party, winning 28.5 per cent of the vote, with 118 deputies and 47 senators. The rival Socialist party, the PSP, won 4.5 per cent of the vote and four deputies in the Congress.

By agreeing to the new Spanish Constitution the party accepted the monarchy and abandoned its republican tradition. A big push was also made towards Socialist unity, with the PSOE merging with the PSP and with another group called *Convergencia Socialista* (whose numbers included Enrique Barón, Joaquin Leguina and Jose Barrionuevo). In Catalonia the Socialist Party of Catalonia merged with the Catalan branch of the PSOE.

The 1979 elections, however, were a disappointment for the PSOE, which was hurt, in particular, by a rival party in Andalusia, the *Partido Socialista de Andalusia*. The PSOE won 30 per cent of the national vote and 121 seats, only a small advance from 1977.

González and Guerra then launched a major campaign to modernize the party, by tightening its organization and by presenting it as a moderate reformist party stripped of its Marxist rhetoric. The left within the party (led by Pablo Castellano and Luis Gómez Llorente) resisted strongly the attempt to remove Marxism from the party's programme, and they won a temporary victory at the party's 28th congress in May 1979. Felipe González resigned, but no alternative leader could be put forward. At a special party congress in September 1979 González was re-elected secretary-general and the left was marginalized within the party.

With the fragmentation of the governing UCD and the disarray within the Communist Party the PSOE was increasingly able to present itself as a united, disciplined and moderate party. In May 1982 it performed extremely well in the Andalusian regional elections, winning 52 per cent of the vote, and 66 of the then 94 seats in the regional parliament. Finally on Aug. 28, 1982, it won the national elections, winning 47.3 per cent of the national vote and 202 of the 350 deputies, and was then able to form a government with Felipe González as Prime Minister.

After 1982 the PSOE managed to consolidate its hold on the levers of power. In 1983 it won another victory in the regional elections, gaining control of the majority of regional parliaments and governments.

After the NATO referendum in 1986 there was further disillusionment within the left of the party. Some dissidents joined the left socialist party, PASOC. Another prominent left-winger, Pablo Castellano, was eventually expelled from the party.

In the 1986 elections PSOE fell back from 1982 but managed to retain its absolute majority on 44 per cent of the vote. Felipe González was again able to form a single-party government.

In the 1987 elections PSOE fell back considerably, winning 39.1 per cent of the vote in the European elections (and 28 of the 60 Spanish seats) and 37.2 per cent in the municipal elections (compared to 43 per cent in 1983). It also lost its majority in seven regions and in six of the most important municipalities, although it was able to hold on to power in some cases by making alliances with other parties.

In spite of this fall in popularity (labour unrest has intensified, for example) the opposition is still divided and the PSOE is thus still able to maintain its political dominance.

Support

The PSOE is now a truly national party, winning support in all parts of the country and among all social classes. It is much less working-class and trade union-dominated than it used to be. Studies of its membership have shown that almost 28 per cent come from the new middle classes (teachers, technicians, professionals) and this proportion has risen for those members entering after 1982. Small businessmen and the self-employed provide another 19 per cent. Civil servants are an important component of the party's support, and make up around 10 per cent of the party membership. Only around half the party's members are also members of the Socialist trade union, the UGT. The party's own studies show that 70 per cent of the party's members are salaried workers. Eleven per cent of the members are women. Almost 35 per cent proclaim themselves Catholics.

The heartland of PSOE support is southern Spain. The party's strongest region is undoubtedly Andalusia, from which both González and Guerra come, and which provides over 50,000 of the 213,000 Socialist party members. In the province of Jaén alone the party has over 10,000 members, 2.1 per cent of the electorate, by a long way its highest percentage of membership in the country. In the 1986 regional elections PSOE won 47 per cent of the vote and 60 out of the 109 seats in the Andalusian regional parliament. In the national elections of 1986 it won over 50 per cent in all eight Andalusian provinces, with highs of 62 per cent in Huelva, 61 per cent in Cadiz and 59 per cent in Seville. In some of the smaller Andalusian towns the party did even better, with well over 70 per cent of the vote (e.g. Arcos de la Frontera 78 per cent).

The only other areas where PSOE won over 50 per cent in 1986 were Extremadura (Province of Badajoz 57 per cent, Caceres 54 per cent) and Southern Castilla la Mancha (Province of Ciudad Real 52 per cent, Albacete 51 per cent), where it controls both regional governments.

The País Valenciano has the second-largest number of party members after Andalusia (over 29,000) and PSOE has been the largest party in all elections since 1977 in the provinces of Valencia (47 per cent in 1986) and Alicante

(49 per cent in 1986). In 1986 PSOE also won 49 per cent in Murcia. PSOE controls the governments of both the País Valenciano and Murcia, although its vote slipped badly in the 1987 regional elections.

Outside its southern heartland PSOE's strongest area is the traditional industrial region of Asturias, where it has always been the largest party and still controls the regional government. It won 46 per cent of the Asturian vote in the 1986 national elections.

Madrid is still an important base for the party, and has the third-largest number of PSOE members (over 16,000). The party won 41 per cent of the Madrid vote in the 1986 national elections, and 38.6 per cent in the 1987 regional elections. The mayor of Madrid is Socialist, as is the president of the regional government, although on a minority basis.

In the rest of central and northern Spain PSOE is relatively weaker, although in 1986 it was still the largest party in many provinces and even wider regions, for example in all three provinces in Aragón (e.g. Huesca 44.5 per cent, Zaragoza 43.5 per cent) and even in four of the nine provinces of Castilla y León (e.g. León 45 per cent, Valladolid 42 per cent).

In some parts of Castilla y León, however, PSOE is weakened, not merely by the strength of *Partido Popular* but also of the CDS. Such is the case, for example, in Segovia (32.5 per cent in 1986) and especially in Avila where PSOE came third in 1986 with only 24.5 per cent of the vote.

PSOE is also weak in most of Galicia (e.g. Lugo 29.5 per cent in 1986, Orense 33.5 per cent), although even here it was the largest party in the province of La Coruña (39 per cent in 1986), and has pockets of even greater strength in certain industrial communities (e.g. Rianxo 56 per cent in 1986).

PSOE faces particular problems in the Basque Country and in Catalonia, although it is stronger in these regions than the other Spanish parties.

In the Basque regional elections in 1986 PSOE actually won more seats than any of the regional parties, although it obtained less votes than the PNV, and its good result was almost entirely due to divisions among the Basque parties. PSOE won 33 per cent in the 1986 national elections in the province of Alava, but only 26.5 per cent in Vizcaya (in spite of much higher votes in industrialized areas of long Socialist tradition around Bilbao), and 23 per cent in Guipúzcoa. In some of the smaller Basque towns and rural areas PSOE gets its lowest support in all Spain (e.g. Guernica y Luna 10.85 per cent).

The Socialists are somewhat stronger in

Catalonia (e.g. Barcelona 43 per cent in 1986, Tarragona 38 per cent, although only 31 per cent in Gerona and 30.5 per cent in Lérida). The mayor of Barcelona is Socialist, although the greatest Socialist strength is in the industrial towns outside Barcelona where there are large numbers of immigrant workers from outside Catalonia. In some of these communities the Socialist vote is over 60 per cent (Santa Coloma de Gramenet 66 per cent, Cornella de Llobregat 63 per cent in 1986).

In rural areas of Catalonia the Socialists are much weaker than the main regional grouping, *Convergència i Unió*. The Socialists also do better in national elections than in the elections for the Catalan parliament.

Finally, in the Canary Islands PSOE has lost ground to the main regional party and to the CDS. PSOE is stronger in the constituency of Tenerife than in Las Palmas.

Organization

PSOE is a party with a federal structure but with a strong central organization, tightly controlled by the party leadership, and governed by rules designed to ensure that this control is maintained.

This tradition of strong centralized leadership stems from the party's founder, Pablo Iglesias, and was reinforced during the years of underground activity when Franco ruled. The leadership of González and Guerra who took over in 1974 brought a new professionalism to the party organization, with a new emphasis on electoral research and on careful marketing of the party image. The need for party unity was firmly reasserted, especially after González and Guerra triumphed over the party's left wing at the special congress of autumn 1979.

The party's present constitution specifically forbids the formation of organized "tendencies" within the party, although it does allow the formation of looser "currents of opinion" to stimulate internal party debate.

At present only one such "current", *Izquierda Socialista* (Socialist Left) actually exists, and with little power.

PSOE has over 213,000 members. It has long had a low number of members relative to its electoral strength, and still has less members than *Partido Popular*. Nevertheless, its membership has grown rapidly since it came to power in 1982. The basic units of the party are its local groups, of which there are just under 4,000 (3,962 in late 1987) in the whole of Spain. Minimum membership is three (nine for groups outside Spain), although groups need at least 10 members to be directly represented at higher levels in the party. Maximum membership for a local group is 500. Each local group has an assembly and local committee.

Above the local groups in the municipalities are the provincial groups, with provincial assemblies, committees and executives. In certain places (e.g. Catalonia and the País Valenciano) there are also *comarcal* groups, whereas in the Balearic Islands and the Canaries there are island groups.

Within each autonomous region there is a regional or "national" party, e.g. in Catalonia where the Catalan Socialist Party is referred to as the national party and the PSOE as a whole as the federal party. Nevertheless, the special status of the Catalan Socialist Party is not recognized within PSOE's federal constitution.

PSOE's federal constitution gives regional parties full autonomy to determine their own programmes within their area of competence.

At federal level a congress is normally held every three years. Until 1979 the federal congress was dominated by party militants, with over 1,000 delegates chosen on a local basis. Since 1979 delegates have been chosen by provincial parties, which can also join together to form a single delegation from each autonomous region. These have been generally chosen on a winner-takes-all basis. Thus there have been only around 50 provincial or regional delegations at the federal congress. Key votes at the congress, such as the election of the federal executive committee (including the party leader) and the vote on the management of the party by the previous executive have been cast by the leaders of the delegations, not by individual delegates, and on a majority basis. There is relatively little open dissent at the congress. In 1988, for example, only one report was put forward by a provincial delegation as an alternative to the keynote report of the party leadership.

The federal committee meets every six months, and is a large body with representatives from all tiers of the party, including the secretary-general and electoral representatives from each regional party, as well as 36 members directly elected at the federal congress. There is provision for representation of minority views, in that any current which receives more than 20 per cent of the vote receives 25 per cent of the directly elected seats (e.g. *Izquierda Socialista* recently won 22.57 per cent of the vote and nine of the 36 seats).

The most powerful party body is the federal executive committee, whose 23 members are directly elected by block vote of the delegation leaders at the federal congress (thus ensuring that most of them receive 100 per cent support, as in 1988).

Besides the party president (honorific) and party secretary-general (effective party leader), the federal executive committee consists of the deputy secretary-general, nine secretaries responsible for particular party departments (who are not allowed to occupy other public posts at the same time) and 11 at–large members with no specific responsibilities. The federal executive committee meets once a week, and has a collective responsibility for its decisions.

Party candidates are reviewed by a *Comisión Federal de Listas*.

The PSOE parliamentary group is divided into congress and senate groups, each of whom elects a president who is also the party spokesman in each chamber.

The party's main headquarters is at Ferraz 70 in Madrid, at the site of the home of the party's founder, Pablo Iglesias. PSOE has 250 direct employees, of whom 200 work at the party headquarters. PSOE also has a training centre, "Jaime Vera", named after a prominent 19th century party philosopher.

The party's youth group is entitled *Juventudes Socialistas de España* and has only limited independence. It was founded in 1903.

There is no women's group within the party's federal constitution, though a group exists entitled *Mujeres para el socialismo*. At the 31st federal congress, however, the party took the decision that a minimum of 25 per cent of all party posts should be reserved for women.

PSOE has always had close ties with the *Unión General de Trabajadores* (UGT), one of Spain's two major trade union organizations. PSOE members are encouraged to belong to the UGT and such members can form Socialist union groups within their workplace, but there are no formal links between UGT and PSOE, and their recent relationship has been characterized by considerable tension.

The party's newspaper *El Socialista* was founded by Pablo Iglesias in 1886 and appears every 15 days. There are also a number of more theoretical party magazines, including *Leviatan*.

The current minimum party membership subscription is 250–300 pesetas per person per month, but with an objective of 1 per cent of a member's income. This does not apply to youth members, the unemployed or retired people.

PSOE is a member of the Socialist International, the Federation of European Socialist Parties and of the Socialist Group within the European Parliament, where it has 28 members and a vice-president of the Parliament.

Policies

PSOE is currently a pragmatic and not very ideological governing party. It has changed dramatically since the new leadership took over in 1974. González himself was always conscious of the need for a moderate image if the Socialists were to re-establish themselves after the fall of the dictatorship. Nevertheless, the party's rhetoric was still Marxist, and with a class-based analysis of Spain's problems.

The members of PSOE have come increasingly from the new middle classes and do not share the same historical perspective as many of the old activists. The party's position has adjusted accordingly.

A first important step was the dropping of the party's republicanism with its recognition of the monarchy in the new Spanish Constitution. A second was the dropping of Marxism as the key ideological reference point for the party, at its special conference in autumn 1979.

In the run-up to the 1982 elections PSOE put its emphasis not just on its moderation but also on its unity, in contrast to the fragmenting UCD. Its 1982 election programme was a reformist one, aimed at the consolidation of Spanish society. It did, however, have a few specific promises, the creation of 800,000 new jobs, a reduction in working hours, a non-nuclear Spain and a referendum on Spanish membership of NATO.

Among the Socialist achievements in their 1982–86 term were Spanish entry into the European Community; major reforms of the Spanish education system; the legalization of soft drugs; and the passing of a law on abortion. The government's austere economic policy saw a mixture of success and failure with economic growth increased, and inflation and public deficits down, but with unemployment sharply up, and regional and social inequalities maintained or even increased. Industrial reconversion in problem sectors such as steel and shipbuilding was initiated.

The process of granting regional autonomy was consolidated, with elections in those regions which had not yet held them, but the result was considerable duplication of bureaucracy in Madrid and in the regions and accusations by the regions that the Socialists had too centralist a perspective. A firm line was taken by the government on Basque terrorism.

One particular success was the relationship with the armed forces. The Spanish military structure was modernized and the number of troops reduced. On the other hand the Spanish arms industry was promoted. One of the hardest battles was the turn-around on NATO. As late as June 1983 the party was still in favour of Spain leaving NATO, but by October 1984 González was calling for Spain to remain in NATO subject to certain conditions: no nuclear weapons in Spain; non-involvement in NATO's integrated military structure; and a reduction in the American presence in Spain. This issue caused considerable turmoil within PSOE, with up to a third of the party opposed to the change in position, and with a minority even leaving the party in consequence. In the run-up to the referendum, however, the Socialist union, the UGT, and the Young Socialists were persuaded not to campaign against NATO membership, in spite of their opposition. The "yes" vote of the referendum provided a useful springboard for the subsequent Socialist success at the 1986 elections.

The Socialist government's main foreign emphasis was on integration within the European Community. United States' interference in Nicaragua was condemned, and the Sandinistas recognized although treated with caution. Strong support, however, was given to the Contadora peace process.

Spanish claims to sovereignty over Gibraltar were maintained but the status of Ceuta and Melilla was not questioned. Support was given to the Palestine Liberation Movement, but steps were also taken toward the recognition of Israel, and of its right to exist within secure borders.

PSOE's 1986 election programme put its emphasis on continuity rather than far-reaching reform, and it made no specific promises as in 1982. It defended the government's economic record as necessary for the building of a more competitive Spain, and it put a strong emphasis on the promotion of new technology, on supporting small firms and co-operatives and on increasing social concentration and industrial democracy. Among the changes from 1982 was a greater acceptance of civil nuclear energy, albeit with stronger safeguards. The manifesto also supported the idea of a united Europe, but with greater economic cohesion than at present.

Since 1986 the new Socialist government points to some further achievements, such as the inter-party agreement on Basque terrorism and agreement to reduce the American military presence within Spain. The development of private television is another new project. PSOE has also come under increasing criticism on both policy and other grounds.

Strong criticism has come from the traditional Socialist union, the UGT, and from its leader, Nicolás Redondo, who claims that the government is no longer Socialist but technocratic and neo-liberal, and that its policies have led to more unemployment, and to increased inequalities in income, and between the richer and poorer parts of Spain. He argues that the union's moderation has been one of the central elements in the economic successes that there have been, but that not enough is being given in return. PSOE's 31st congress did not solve the problems between party and union, and it is uncertain how their relations will develop in the future.

Criticism has also come from those concerned about the party's dominance of the government apparatus, civil service and media, and the abuses of power and clientelism that this has led to. Concern even within the Socialist Party on these matters is currently leading to the formulation of a code of conduct for Socialist office-holders.

The party's 31st congress in 1988 put forward no new major policy initiatives, although it accepted an amendment from the Catalan Socialists that the 1978 constitution should be interpreted in a more federal sense than at present. The implications of this are still unclear, although there are likely to be more powers transferred to the autonomous regions. The party also called for local government to be given more powers.

The party's existing economic policy was strongly defended against Redondo's attacks, on the grounds that economic growth and a more competitive economy were prerequisites for any subsequent redistribution.

PSOE is currently preparing a set of longer-term policy objectives, in the so-called "Programme 2000".

Personalities

Felipe González was born in 1942. Trained as a lawyer, he was active in the opposition against Franco under the alias "Isidoro". He has been the party's secretary-general since 1974, and also Prime Minister since 1982. His youthful image and moderation played a decisive role during the period when the party re-established itself after 1977 and won power in 1982. Although his image has now suffered somewhat from familiarity, and his dominance of the party is sometimes criticized ("Felipismo") he is still central to the party's success.

His control of the party is assured through his number two, Alfonso Guerra, who is also Deputy Prime Minister. Born in 1940, Guerra dominates the party machine and its nominating processes. His supporters are in the majority in most of the regional party delegations.

The third man within the party is Jose Maria (Txiki) Benegas, a Basque who has just been re-elected as the party secretary responsible for organization matters. Benegas has also been secretary-general of the Basque Socialists, in which capacity he has been a candidate for Basque president and has had a key role in supporting the current Basque government.

The Minister of Defence, Narcís Serra, a former mayor of Barcelona, has been highly successful at modernizing the Spanish armed forces and reconciling them to democracy.

The Economics Minister, Carlos Solchaga, is one of the technocrats at odds with the party's trade union wing. Other influential ministers include the Foreign Minister, Francisco Fernández Ordóñez, a prominent minister under the UCD government before he left UCD and allied himself with the Socialists; the Justice Minister, Enrique Múgica; and the Minister of Education, Javier Solana.

Besides the party leaders in Madrid there are also a number of regional leaders, the so-called "Caliphs". José Rodríguez de la Barbolla ("Pepote") is the secretary-general of the Andalusian Socialists and is also the president of the Andalusian regional government.

Raimón Obiols is the secretary-general of the Catalan Socialists (see separate entry) a left-of-centre critic of the Madrid leadership and an advocate of a federal party as well as of a federal Spain.

Other major regional figures are Joan Lerma, the president of the Valencian Generalitat (government) and the leader of the second-largest delegation at the party conference; and Joaquin Leguina, the president of the autonomous community of Madrid, and one of the few relatively independent centres of power within the party.

Among the municipal leaders the most prominent are the Mayor of Madrid, Juan Barranco, and the Mayor of Barcelona, Pascual Maragall.

The most significant party critic is the UGT leader, Nicolás Redondo.

Among those who support Redondo within the party is Ricardo García Damborenea, the Socialist leader in the Basque province of Vizcaya.

The party's left-wing current, *Izquierda Socialista* (Socialist Left), has little effective power within PSOE and none of the key leadership posts, although it managed to win 22.5 per cent of the votes and nine out of the 36 federally-elected seats at the recent election for the party's federal committee. One of those elected was Antonio García Santesmases, a young university professor who is a strong opponent of Spanish membership of NATO. The only province in all of Spain where *Izquierda Socialista* has a majority within the

Socialist Party is Cáceres in Extremadura, the former fief of Pablo Castellano.

Enrique Barón Crespo only narrowly lost against Henry Plumb for the presidency of the European Parliament in January 1986. PSOE also has one member of the European Commission, Manuel Marín, a former Spanish negotiator for EC accession.

The party's president is Ramón Rubial, a Basque who was born in 1906 and became a member of PSOE in 1922.

Partido Popular — PP
(People's Party)

Headquarters	: Genova 13, Madrid 28004 (tel: 419–20–27 or 419–40–08)
National president	: Manuel Fraga
Secretary-general	: Francisco Alvárez Cascos
Youth group	: *Nuevas Generaciones* (president: Rafael Hernando)
Membership	: 230,000 (1988)

History

Alianza Popular was founded on Oct. 9, 1976, as a coalition between seven small parties headed by former ministers (known popularly as the *Siete Magníficos*, Manuel Fraga Iribarne, Laureano López Rodó, Gonzalo Fernández de la Mora, Frederico Silva Muñoz, Licinio de la Fuente, Cruz Martínez Esteruelas, Enrique Thomas de Carranza). On Nov. 23, Manuel Fraga Iribarne was elected secretary-general. On March 5, 1977 the first national congress was held: five of the six parties merged to form one party, the *Partido Unido de Alianza Popular*, while the other two (*Acción Democrática Española* and *Unión Nacional Española*) chose to retain their separate identity within a wider Federation of *Alianza Popular*.

In the 1977 elections *Alianza Popular* polled poorly, winning 8.23 per cent of the vote and 16 seats in the Chamber of Deputies (and two senators).

AP eventually accepted the new Constitution but was particularly concerned about the powers given to the autonomous regions and the abolition of the death penalty for terrorist offences. Some of its more conservative supporters, however, left in protest.

In January 1979 AP entered into a federation with two other groupings, *Acción Ciudadana Liberal* of José Maria de Areilza and the *Partido Demócrata Progresista* to form *Coalición Democrática*.

In the second national elections of March 1979 *Coalición Democrática* won only 5.96 per cent of the national vote, with nine seats in the Chamber of Deputies (three senators). In the municipal elections of April 1979 it slumped to its lowest-ever vote, 3.1 per cent.

In November 1979 the federation began to reorganize itself, with Fraga becoming president and Jorge Verstrynge the secretary-general. At the third national congress in December 1979 a couple of parties left the federation, but others joined it instead.

At AP's fourth congress in February 1981 a number of other parties joined up with it in the federation, and it decided to adopt a less conservative stance. It began to win increasing support from those disillusioned with the UCD government, including many Christian Democrats concerned about the legalisation of divorce.

The first major success came in November 1981, when *Alianza Popular* won 26 seats in the Galician regional elections, making it the largest party in the region, and enabling it to take charge of the regional government.

Two more parties joined the federation in February 1982, which again emphasized its pluralistic character as a wide grouping of right-of-centre forces, including Conservatives, Christian Democrats, Liberals and regionalists. In the Andalusian regional elections of May 1982 it came a poor second to the Socialists but succeeded in pushing the governing UCD into third place.

On Sept. 14, 1982 the federation was reconstituted as *Coalición Popular*. Its main components were *Alianza Popular*, the *Partido Demócrata Popular* (Christian Democrats led by Oscar Alzaga who had abandoned UCD) and the *Unión Liberal*. It also included a number of conservative regional parties, notably the *Partido Aragonés Regionalista*, the *Unión Valenciana* and the *Unión del Pueblo Navarro* (See separate entries).

In the national elections held shortly afterwards *Coalición Popular* established itself as the only major opposition to the victorious socialist party winning 25.4 per cent of the national vote, 106 deputies and 54 senators.

Coalición Popular successfully held together during the whole of the 1982–86 legislature. In the 1983 regional and municipal elections it did outstandingly well. It won 33.3 per cent and 273 seats in the regional elections, and was also to form the regional government in both Cantabria and the Balearic Islands. In the municipal elections it polled 25.8 per cent and elected 20,957 councillors (up from only 2,362

in 1979). It provided mayors in 11 provincial capitals.

In the Galician elections it won 41.7 per cent of the vote, and 34 seats, again providing the regional government.

It also strengthened its links internationally, entering the International Democratic Union in June, 1983 and joining up with the British and Danish Conservatives in the European Democratic Group when Spain sent its first delegation to the European Parliament.

Coalición Popular, however, began to run into serious difficulties in the course of 1986. Not all the refugees from the collapse of the centrist UCD felt comfortable within the conservative coalition. The decision to call for abstention rather than for a "yes" vote in the NATO referendum also caused considerable unrest, with a number of prominent figures dissenting strongly.

In June, 1986 *Coalición Popular* polled 26.15 per cent of the national vote, electing 105 deputies and 63 senators. The failure to move forward from 1982, to which the unsuccessful attempt by Miguel Roca to establish a new right-of-centre party (the *Partido Reformista Democratico*) also contributed, brought the underlying tensions within *Coalición Popular* to the fore. In July 1986 the 22 coalition deputies belonging to the *Partido Demócrata* broke with *Coalición Popular* and joined the group of independent members within the *Cortes*. In October 1986 Jorge Verstrynge, who had been replaced as secretary-general the previous month, left *Alianza Popular*, along with three other parliamentarians.

Later on in the autumn of 1986 there was a much publicized conflict between *Alianza* and certain major banks, who had previously supported it but now called for a speedy repayment of campaign debts. There was also a dispute among the *Alianza* members of the Galician regional government. In the November regional elections in the Basque Country *Coalición* support dropped from 9.4 per cent in the previous elections to only 4.8 per cent and from seven seats to two. On Dec. 2, 1986 *Alianza*'s founder and dominant leader, Manuel Fraga, resigned as party leader.

In January 1987 the 11 members of *Unión Liberal* also left the *Coalición*, and joined the independent group in the *Cortes*. *Alianza Popular* was now on its own.

There was then a bitter leadership struggle between the party's provisional leader, Miguel Herrero de Miñón and the 35-year-old Antonio Hernández Mancha, decisively won by the latter at the party's seventh congress in February 1987. Arturo García Tizón became the new secretary-general. A younger generation of *Alianza* politicians came to power.

In the June 1987 elections *Alianza Popular* fell back considerably, winning 20.3 per cent of the municipal vote (down from 25.8 per cent previously) and losing over 7,000 councillors. It also dropped from 273 members of regional parliaments to 231. In the European Parliament elections, with Fraga leading the party list, it fared better, winning 24.6 per cent and 17 seats. Nevertheless, *Alianza* had the satisfaction of seeing its former coalition allies reduced to electoral insignificance, thus showing that most of the coalition vote had been for its *Alianza Popular* component.

After the elections *Alianza Popular* was able to take charge of the regional governments in Castilla y León and in La Rioja. In 1989 Fraga returned as president of the party, which also changed its name to *Partido Popular* (PP). The *Partido Liberal* announced its intention to rejoin the *Partido Popular*, which was also joined by five deputies and one senator from *Democracia Cristiana*, which subsequently took the decision to disband and to join *Partido Popular*.

Partido Popular has around 16,000 local councillors, 2,000 mayors, and 266 deputies in regional parliaments.

Support

PP wins particularly strong support among industrialists and those working in commerce and finance. A 1984 survey of its members also showed that 13 per cent of its members were from farming backgrounds. Nevertheless, easy generalizations about its support pattern cannot be made. In Andalusia it is stronger in the cities than in the rural areas, whereas in Galicia it is the other way round. PP also wins good support in certain industrial towns, such as the highly depressed community of Reinosa where it is the largest party.

In regional terms *Partido Popular*'s strongest fief is Galicia, where it is easily the largest party. In 1985 it won 41.17 per cent in the regional elections in Galicia, and 34 out of the 71 seats in the regional parliament. In the 1986 national elections *Coalición Popular*'s best performance in all of Spain was in the Galician province of Lugo, where it won 47 per cent. In Fraga's home town of Villalba the coalition won over 77 per cent of the vote, but it polled outstandingly in other small Galician towns as well (Lalin 63 per cent, Chantada 55 per cent).

A second region of particular strength is Cantabria where it holds 18 out of 39 seats in the regional parliament, with 45.8 per cent in the regional elections.

In the Balearic Islands *Coalición Popular* actually polled better in 1987 than in 1983, winning 25 of the 59 seats in the regional parliament on 36.7 per cent of the vote. It is particularly strong in Ibiza, where it gained 53 per cent in 1987.

PP is generally strong in the Central Meseta in Castile and in the small region of La Rioja. In the region of Castilla y Leon in 1986 *Coalición Popular* was the largest political grouping in the provinces of Soria (42 per cent), Zamora (40.9 per cent), Burgos (39.4 per cent) and Segovia (36.5 per cent) and a close runner-up to the Socialists in Palencia (39.6 per cent) and in Salamanca (35.9 per cent). It has 32 seats in the regional parliament elected in 1987 and heads the regional government.

In Castilla la Mancha it is less strong at regional parliament level but stronger at municipal level, where it provides the mayor of three provincial capitals, including Toledo. Of the five provinces in the region *Coalición Popular* came first in the 1986 elections in that of Guadalajara (41.9 per cent) and a close second in Cuenca (39 per cent) and to a lesser extent in Toledo (35 per cent).

In La Rioja *Coalición Popular* won 39 per cent in 1986 and *Alianza Popular* won 34.6 per cent in the 1987 regional parliament elections.

Madrid is also an important base for the party. It won 32 per cent of the vote here in 1986, and Alianza 31.4 per cent (and 32 seats) in the Madrid regional elections in 1987.

It has considerable but lesser strength in Aragon and the Canaries (in both of which it was badly affected in 1987 by the success of regional parties), Murcia, Valencia and Asturias. It is a poor second to the Socialists in Extremadura and Andalusia, although in both regions it polls better in the cities (e.g. Granada 34.9 per cent and Cáceres 34.4 per cent in 1986). In some smaller Andalusian towns *Alianza Popular* is very weak (Nerva 8.9 per cent in 1986).

The party's weakest regions are Catalonia and the Basque Country. In Catalonia it polled about 15 per cent in 1986 in Barcelona itself, but often only around 6 per cent in the smaller towns. In the Basque Country *Coalición Popular* also won 15 per cent in 1986 in Bilbao, but was extremely weak outside the cities, especially in the province of Guipuzcoa, where it won 8.6 per cent and was in fifth place. In the town of Bermeo it only won 2.5 per cent.

Organization

The federal structure of *Coalición Popular*, in which *Alianza Popular* was allied with a number of other parties, has now collapsed. *Alianza*

Popular itself has been a centralized party, with a regional tier which has little independence, and which has the same structure throughout Spain, including Catalonia and the Basque Country. The relaunched *Partido Popular*, however, is developing a new set of statutes.

Partido Popular has a larger membership than any other Spanish party. It is organized at six different levels, district, local (within a municipality), *comarcal*, provincial, regional and national. At national level a congress is held on a three–yearly basis, although extraordinary congresses take place more frequently. The congress elects the national president and 30 members of the national executive committee.

A large national directorate (*Junta Directiva Nacional*) with between 200 and 250 members meets once every two months. The national executive committee meets at least once a month and consists of 47 members. In 1986 a new system was introduced whereby 30 of these were elected by the congress on an open list system, with delegates nominating any 30 members of their choice, and the winners being those with the most votes. A closed list was again used at the 1989 congress. There is also a small permanent committee, which meets on a much more regular basis.

The party also has a number of study committees which prepare reports on particular areas of policy for debate by the congress.

Candidates for the Congress of Deputies and for the Senate are first put forward by provincial electoral committees. The appropriate regional electoral committees then give their opinion on these proposals, and the final decisions are then taken by the national electoral committee.

Partido Popular has a large central staff at its headquarters at Calle Genova.

The party's youth wing is called *Nuevas Generaciones* and is open to 18–30 year olds. It has considerable strength in Spanish universities, notably in the law faculties.

There is also a women's organization called the *Asociación Democrática Conservadora*.

The party's newspaper is called *Alianza*. The party has a minimum membership fee of 100 pesetas per month, though many pay more. Public finance has also been an important source of income.

Partido Popular is a member of the European and International Democratic Unions. Its 17 members in the European Parliament sit in the European Democratic Group with the British and Danish Conservatives.

Policies

Partido Popular is currently the largest party on the centre-right of the Spanish political spectrum and also the largest opposition party to the Socialists. Since the last national elections in 1986, however, it has had to confront a number of difficulties. The first was the break-up of *Coalición Popular* with the departure from the coalition of both the PDP (now *Democracia Cristiana*) and the *Partido Liberal*. While neither party fared well in isolation and have now both returned to the fold, their departure contributed to a failure by *Alianza Popular* to seize the initiative in opposition to the Socialists. A second factor has been the electoral growth of regional parties such as those in Aragon, Navarre and Valencia, which are of the centre-right, and have had links with *Partido Popular*, but which have also eaten into its electorate.

The third and perhaps most important factor has been the two changes of leadership from Manuel Fraga to the youthful and untried leadership of Antonio Hernández Mancha, and now again back to Fraga, which has caused uncertainty about the party's direction and image. Moreover, the party has been confronted with a pragmatic Socialist government, and a charismatic and populist opposition rival in Adolfo Suárez of the CDS. *Partido Popular* is thus faced with fundamental decisions as to how best to present itself, and whether to emphasize populist conservatism or economic liberalism.

In 1989 it attempted to relaunch itself under its new name as a broad-based party of the centre-right with Conservative, Christian Democratic and Liberal components, and open to wider coalitions with other national and regionalist parties in opposition to the Socialist government.

The party's main policy theme at present is that the Socialist government has become too powerful, and that it has set up a patronage machine reaching into all areas of Spanish life. *Partido Popular* wants this process to be reversed, and for there to be more freedom for the individual and less state intervention.

In economic policy it attacks the failure of the government to reduce the high levels of unemployment. It believes that the best alternative strategy is to liberalize the economy through a lowering of taxation levels and less public expenditure. The state should spend less but more efficiently and with greater transparency. Competition law should be reinforced and state monopolies should be restricted or eliminated. There should be privatization in certain sectors and more deregulation. The labour market should be made more flexible.

The party advocates a reduction in expenditure on administration of social security, but not on social security payments themselves. In industrial policy it puts its accent on support for new technologies and for small and medium-sized enterprises but also calls for the maintenance and modernization of traditional industries like shipbuilding and steel for economic, regional policy and strategic reasons. It has not opposed civil nuclear energy although it calls for enhanced safety measures.

Partido Popular continues to advocate a tough policy on law and order issues and on fighting terrorism. It has also called for a special anti-drug plan. It puts less emphasis on moral and social conservatism than it used to do. It no longer gives strong emphasis to the death penalty and while many of the party remain opposed to the recent liberalization of abortion, repeal of this law is not a major plank in the party's programme. The party puts more emphasis, instead, on the need to reform the law on adoption and to take all measures possible to discourage women from seeking abortions.

Another area of policy where the party has changed its emphasis is its attitude towards regional autonomy. While it still defends Spanish unity, it no longer calls for a reduction in the power of the autonomous regions. It believes that the regions should have proper financial autonomy and that their diversity should be respected. It does, however, call for government to be at the lowest possible level and it thus strongly defends the powers of local municipalities and of the provinces.

The party has been a consistent supporter of Spanish entry into the European Community. It has called for a European Union which, nevertheless, preserves the historic tradition of its various member states. In the past it has been cautious about any abandonment of the national veto, although it now accepts greater use of qualified majority voting and believes that the European Parliament should become more of a co-legislator. The party supported the Single European Act. The Community should be given new own resources but Spain should not become a net contributor. The party supports the development of a Europe without frontiers, including free movement of capital and a strengthened European monetary system. On the other hand there should also be greater economic cohesion, with more regional expenditure. The Common Agricultural Policy should be reformed to reduce existing surpluses, and to make it more market-oriented. The European Community should not become a "fortress Europe" but be open to the rest of the world.

The party has been strongly in favour of the Atlantic Alliance and of close relations with the United States. In the referendum on Spain's participation in NATO, however, it advocated abstention on the grounds that the terms of the referendum were misguided and that Spain would only become a second class member of NATO. The call for abstention proved difficult to accept even for many of the party's own supporters.

Partido Popular continues to call for the re-establishment of Spanish sovereignty for Gibraltar.

Personalities

In January 1989 Manuel Fraga, the party's leader from 1976 to 1986 was again elected as its president, after a two-year break. Fraga is now 66. He has expressed his wish to be a candidate to lead the regional government of his native Galicia.

Six vice-presidents were elected at the 1989 congress, of whom only Abel Matutes, a member of the EC Commission, was also a vice-president in the former leadership team. Marcelino Oreja is a leading exponent of the Christian Democratic wing of the relaunched party, and was chosen to head its list for the 1989 European elections (with as yet uncertain consequences for the party's subsequent links in the European Parliament). Oreja is a former Spanish Foreign Minister (in the UCD government of Adolfo Suárez); government representative in the Basque Country, and now secretary-general of the Council of Europe.

José María Aznar is the president of the Castilla y León regional government, and has become increasingly powerful within the party. The other three vice–presidents elected at the congress are Miguel Herrero de Miñón (the defeated leadership contender in early 1987), Félix Pastor and Isabel Tocino.

The new party secretary-general is Francisco Alvarez Cascos, and the new deputy secretary-generals are Federico Trillo, Rodrigo Rato and Juan José Lucas.

The party's spokesman in the Chamber of Deputies is Juan Ramon Calero; in the Senate José Miguel Orti Bordas; in the European Parliament, Fernando Suárez. Of the party's other current presidents of regional governments, Gabriel Canellas is the president of the Balearic Islands and Joaquin Espert of La Rioja. Juan Hormaechea, the president of Cantabria, is an independent elected at the head of the party list.

José Antonio Segurado, the former leader of the *Partido Liberal*, has now brought his party back into *Partido Popular*. Among the other prominent recruits of the relaunched party is Rodolfo Martin Villa, the former UCD minister.

Neither the former party president, Antonio Hernández Mancha, nor the former secretary-general, Arturo García Tizón, have specific party roles under the new leadership.

Christian Democracy

Christian Democracy in Spain has had a lengthy history, with well-known personalities such as Manuel Giménez Fernández, José Maria Gil Robles and Joaquin Ruiz Giménez. With the limited exception of the CEDA in the 1930s, however, no party in this tradition has enjoyed much electoral success. Only in the Basque Country (with the *Partido Nacionalista Vasco — PNV*) and to a lesser extent in Catalonia (with the *Unió* component of *Convergencia i Unió*) have such parties prospered.

Since the re-establishment of democracy in 1977 Christian Democracy at Spanish national level has been fragmented. Some were active in *Izquierda Demócrata Cristiana* (Christian Democratic left, the party of Joaquin Ruiz Giménez) and Christian Democrats also formed one of the major components of the governing party, UCD. As UCD collapsed more and more Christian Democrats joined their more conservative brethren in *Coalición Popular*.

The *Partido Demócrata Popular*'s (PDP) leading personality was Oscar Alzaga, and it held its first party congress in 1982. It proclaimed itself a lay party, but in the Christian Democratic tradition. It abandoned the UCD and in the 1982 national elections it joined up with *Alianza Popular* in the broader electoral coalition called *Coalición Popular*. Under this banner it succeeded in electing a considerable number of members of parliament, who then sat in the *Coalición Popular* parliamentary group.

In the 1986 elections the PDP again participated in *Coalición Popular*, and it won 22 out of the Coalition's 105 seats in the Congress and eight of its 65 seats in the Senate. Shortly afterwards, however, Oscar Alzaga and the PDP broke with *Coalición Popular*, and left its parliamentary group on July 14, 1986.

In the 1987 elections the PDP stood for election in its own right, but had disastrous results, only winning 0.9 per cent in the European Parliament elections (obtaining no seats) and 0.8 per cent in the municipal elections. It did only marginally better in certain of the regional elections, winning 1.71 per cent in Castilla la Mancha and 2.51 per cent in Castilla y León. In the latter region it won one seat thanks to its high vote in Segovia. After these elections Oscar Alzaga stood down as leader, and was replaced by Javier Rupérez.

In March 1988 the PDP took on the new name of *Democracia Cristiana*. In 1989 five of its deputies and one senator left the party to join the relaunched *Partido Popular*, whose own Christian Democratic wing had been reinforced by the placing of Marcelino Oreja in a prominent leadership position. Shortly afterwards *Democracia Cristiana* itself decided to disband and to join up with *Partido Popular*.

Centro Democrático y Social — CDS
(Social and Democratic Centre)

Headquarters	: Jorge Juan 30 5º, 28001 Madrid (tel: 431 7200)
President	: Adolfo Suárez
Parliamentary group spokesman	: Agustín Rodríguez Sahagún
Secretary-general	: José Ramón Caso
Youth group	: *Juventudes del CDS* (national secretary: Manuel Alonso)
Newspaper	: *CDS*
Membership	: 50,000 (December 1987)

History

Suárez stood down as Spanish Prime Minister in early 1981 and gave up his party positions within the then ruling party, the UCD. On July 29, 1982, he founded a new party, the *Centro Democrático y Social* (CDS), aimed at being a more homogeneous party of the centre than the very disparate UCD. The CDS held its first congress on Oct. 2–3, 1982 with 600 participants, and Adolfo Suárez was elected as its president.

In the national election of Oct. 28, 1982, in which what was left of the UCD was reduced from 168 to only 11 seats, the new CDS won nearly 2.8 per cent of the vote and two seats in the Congress of Deputies, (including Suárez). In the municipal and regional elections of 1983 the party had only limited success.

Suárez himself, however, retained considerable personal popularity, and the CDS became a new focal point for voters disillusioned with the Socialist government, but not wishing to support Fraga and *Coalición Popular*. The CDS developed populist positions on a number of issues, such as the need for a more independent foreign policy for Spain from that of the United States. CDS supporters were given a free vote in the NATO referendum in early 1986.

In the 1986 national elections the CDS improved its position dramatically, rising from

2.8 per cent of the vote to 9.3 per cent and from two to 19 seats in the Congress of Deputies. It also won three senators for the first time. In the 1987 European elections it won 10.19 per cent of the national vote and seven members of the European Parliament and in the municipal elections it gained 9.77 per cent (up from 1.8 per cent in 1983). It also won a large number of seats in the various regional parliaments, notably 18 of the 84 seats in Castilla y León, 17 of the 96 seats in Madrid and 13 of the 60 seats in the Canary Islands. In a number of cases it held the balance of power. The CDS is now the third-largest political party in Spain, and has won new recruits in Parliament from among former members of the collapsed *Partido Liberal* and *Democracia Cristiana*.

Support

Most of the prominent CDS leaders are former members of the UCD. A large number of its members however, are new in politics. The party's own survey of delegates at its 2nd congress showed that 57 per cent were in this category, 35.6 per cent were former UCD activists and 7.4 per cent came from other parties. Less of its members are practising Catholics than those of *Partido Popular*, but more than those of other Spanish parties. Recently the CDS has been winning a fair number of former Socialist supporters as well.

The party's strongest region is Castilla y León where it won 19.5 per cent of the vote in the 1987 regional parliament elections. Within this region its particular stronghold is the province of Avila, Suárez' native province, where it is by far the largest party with 41.3 per cent of the vote in the 1986 national elections, with one deputy and with three senators out of the four in the province. In Suárez' birthplace of Cebreros it won 64 per cent of the vote in the 1987 local elections.

Elsewhere in Castilla y León the CDS also has considerable strength, winning 23.5 per cent in Segovia, 18.3 per cent in Salamanca and 17 per cent in Valladollid in the 1986 national elections.

A second stronghold of the CDS are the Canary Islands, where it won 19.08 per cent in the 1987 regional elections. Here it is much stronger in the province of Los Palmas (21 per cent and two deputies in the 1986 national elections) than in Santa Cruz de Tenerife (12.3 per cent). The CDS is strong in Lanzarote, Fuerteventura and Gran Canaria. In the western islands it is strongest in La Gomera.

Five of the party's 19 deputies are from Madrid, where the party won 14 per cent of the vote in the 1986 national elections and 16.7 per cent in the 1987 regional elections.

In the 1987 regional elections the CDS also did very well in traditionally left-wing Asturias, where it won 18.5 per cent of the vote (up from 13.2 per cent in the 1986 national elections).

The CDS is especially weak in the Basque Country, in Catalonia and in Andalusia, where its lowest support is in the province of Seville, with only 3.6 per cent of the vote in the 1986 national elections. In 1986 its weakest province in the whole of Spain was Gerona, in Catalonia, with 2.5 per cent.

Organization

The CDS was founded very largely in reaction to developments within the UCD, a loose coalition of disparate elements with little central discipline and with many powerful "barons" whose supporters were loyal only to them. It had a large nominal membership (up to 150,000) which was largely passive, and a cumbersome central bureaucracy. It was primarily a party of government.

In contrast the CDS is a much more homogeneous party with strong central discipline. It has a federal structure, but the party's president has very considerable powers. Compared to the Socialists and *Partido Popular* it still only has a small central bureaucracy.

The party now claims a membership of 50,000 (December 1987) up from only 12,000 in 1986 and 25,000 in June 1987. At municipal level the party has over 3,000 local committees, although the exact number is unclear. Above this the party is organized at provincial and regional level. Each province and region has its own assembly or congress, its own committee, president and secretary-general. There is no separate CDS party in the Basque Country or in Catalonia and the party has the same regional tier there as in the rest of Spain.

At national level a national congress is held every three years, and consists of no more than 1,000 members elected by the provincial assemblies. In between congress the supreme organ of the party is the national convention, which is supposed to be held every six months.

The national committee is the most powerful central body within the party, and consists of the party's president and secretary-general and 19 others elected by the congress. It can, and does, revoke decisions of lower organs within the party and can dissolve provincial parties if necessary. The party president is elected by secret vote at the congress, and is given an exceptional range of powers, presiding both over the parliamentary group and also chairing the national committee. The secretary-general oversees the party's organization. Until recently the party had a headquarters staff of only five but this has risen to 25. The party does not wish to expand this number, if possible. The party is reinforcing its secretariat, however, at local, provincial and regional level.

Candidate selection for the Congress of Deputies and for the Senate, as well as for regional parliaments and a number of other offices, is initially in the hands of the provincial committees. Their proposals must be approved by the national committee, which sets up a national electoral committee for this purpose. The national committee has the right to entirely change the list in national elections, but only to change the head of the list in regional and local elections.

The party has a youth group, *Juventudes del CDS*. This was not established immediately for fear that it would detract from the main task of setting up a basic organizational structure for the new party, but it has since grown rapidly and now has 5,000 members (end 1987). It concentrates on youth matters, and is not encouraged to be an "internal opposition" within the party. The CDS has no separate women's organization.

The party imposes membership dues of 333 pesetas per month, although the unemployed need not pay and students and retired people pay especially low rates. Membership dues are centrally collected, and there is a central membership register. In reaction against the UCD practice of local barons affiliating large numbers of paper supporters, CDS membership dues are paid individually. If payment is not made within six months of being due, membership is suspended, and after one year it is withdrawn. From 1982–86, 1,000 members were forced to leave the party.

The party newspaper, *CDS* is sent out to its members on a monthly basis. Until recently the CDS had no formal international links with parties outside Spain, although it enjoyed good relations with such parties as the PSD of Sá Carneiro and PRD of Eanes in Portugal. In the European Parliament its seven members sit as independents, although they participated in a short-lived technical co-ordination group, with other independents (notably the Italian Radicals). In January 1988, however, the CDS was accepted as a member of the Liberal International.

Policies

The CDS sees itself as a progressive party of the centre, committed to the modernization of the Spanish economy and of Spanish society, and offering a third way between capitalism and Marxism. The CDS claims to fight against the Spanish tendency towards polarization into two opposing camps, and seeks to promote much greater co-operation.

According to the CDS leadership, the former UCD played a very useful role in the period of transition from dictatorship to democracy, but was unable to carry out the necessary reforms to consolidate this democracy. This was because of contradictions between its separate Liberal, Social Democratic and Christian Democratic components, and above all between its "progressive" and its "conservative" wing. The CDS claims not to have these divisions, and to be firmly committed to fundamental economic and social reforms.

According to CDS the Socialists came to power with reforming ambitions, but have failed to properly carry them out when in government. Instead they have themselves become "the establishment" and have created their own clientele. Their rule has been characterized by opportunism and short-term pragmatism without any longer term objectives. On economic policy, for example, the CDS believes that the Socialist Party has been too "liberal" and has failed to tackle injustices and inequalities within Spanish society with sufficient vigour. According to CDS a free market economy is essential but needs to be complemented by corrective public action. In this, as in other fields, the freedom of the individual must be balanced against the overall welfare of society at large.

The CDS wishes to see higher levels of investment within Spain, and greater promotion of new industries and technologies. It wants to greatly increase spending on research.

The party wishes ultimately to replace civil nuclear energy with other sources, but believes that there is no alternative to maintaining it (but, if possible, not increasing dependence upon it) in the short and medium-term. The CDS now puts an increasing emphasis upon consumer and environmental protection.

Ethical problems, like abortion and divorce, were a source of particular division within the UCD because of the continuing Liberal and Christian Democratic ideologies within it. The CDS opposes abortion, but is in favour of a less rigid code than at present, in order to distinguish between the differing circumstances which lead to abortions. The CDS would like to have further delegation of central powers to the autonomous regions but emphasizes the need to avoid duplication of bureaucracy at national and regional levels. The party continues to believe, however, in the indissoluble unity of the Spanish state.

Foreign policy and defence are areas where the CDS adopts a distinctive position. It calls for Spain to be more independent of the United States. In the referendum on Spanish membership of NATO the CDS left its supporters free to vote the way they wished, but it was critical of the referendum taking place without the government spelling out its longer-term strategic and defence objectives for Spain. The CDS accepts the results of the referendum, but insists on its terms being followed to the letter. The CDS calls for much greater defence co-operation within Europe (but on a non-nuclear basis) and for a better balance of power between Europe and the United States within the NATO Alliance. In the longer term the CDS would like to see the disappearance of both military blocs. It is also in favour of reducing the length of Spanish military service.

The CDS is in favour of a united Europe and of reinforcing the powers of the European Community institutions. It wishes to have much closer ties with Latin America.

Personalities

The CDS leader and main electoral asset is Adolfo Suárez, a former secretary-general of Franco's *Movimiento* who successfully led the transition to democracy in his term as Prime Minister from 1977 to 1981.

The party's spokesman in the Congress of Deputies (and on the Madrid council) is Agustín Rodríguez Sahagún, the only other CDS member besides Suárez who was elected in the 1982 elections. He is a former Minister of Industry and Energy, and Defence Minister. In 1981 he was the president of the UCD.

The party's secretary-general is José Ramón Caso, a former UCD official and long-term supporter of Suárez, who is a deputy for Madrid. The party's head of list in the European Parliament elections has been and again is Eduardo Punset, the Minister responsible for Spain's negotiations with the European Community in the period from 1980 to 1981.

Among other leading personalities in the party are Frederico Mayor, for a short while a member of the European Parliament and now the new secretary-general of UNESCO, Rafael Calvo Ortega, who was the former secretary-general of the UCD, Raúl Morodo, who was the former secretary-general of the Popular Socialist Party of Tierno Galván, and Rosa Posada, president of the regional parliament in Madrid.

Izquierda Unida — IU
(United Left)

History

Izquierda Unida is an alliance between a number of separate left-wing Spanish parties and groups, which was first put together on April 24, 1986 in order to contest the 1986 national elections. A leading catalyst for its formation was the broad-based campaign against Spanish membership of NATO in the referendum of March 1986.

The major component of the *Izquierda Unida* was the *Partido Comunista de España* (PCE), and it was immediately joined by the *Partido de Acción Socialista* (PASOC) and the *Federación Progresista*. More controversial was the adherence of the pro-Soviet *Partido Comunista de los Pueblos de España* (PCPE) and later of the *Partido Humanista* and of the *Partido Carlista*. Finally, another party with an historic name, *Izquierda Republicana*, also associated itself with the alliance. In addition there were a number of independents on the list, including Humberto da Cruz of the Spanish Federation of Friends of the Earth. The most notable absentee party on the left was *Unidad Comunista*, the breakaway Communist party led by Santiago Carrillo.

In Catalonia *Izquierda Unida* fought the 1987 elections under a different label, *Unió de la Esquerra Catalana*. Moreover the PCPE's sister party in Catalonia, the *Partit dels Comunistes de Catalunya* (PCC) did not participate, and stood on its own. *Izquierda Unida* also used different names in Galicia, the Basque Country and in the Canary Islands.

In the 1986 national elections, *Izquierda Unida* won 4.66 per cent of the vote and elected seven deputies, four from the PCE, one from the PSUC (the Catalan Communist Party) and also the leaders of the PCPE (Ignacio Gallego) and the *Federación Progresista* (Ramón Tamames). The elected members retained the *Izquierda Unida* label, although they were not able to form a separate parliamentary group and had to sit in the Mixed Group.

The alliance again contested the 1987 municipal, regional and European elections. Its election manifesto was signed by the PCE, PCPE, PASOC, the *Federación Progresista* and by *Izquierda Republicana* but this time not by the *Partido Carlista* and the *Partido Humanista* which were no longer active in the alliance. In Catalonia *Izquierda Unida* stood under a new name, *Iniciativa per Catalunya*. In the European Parliament elections the alliance won 5.24 per cent of the vote and three seats, one each for Fernando Pérez Royo of the PCE, Antoni

Gutiérrez of the PSUC, and Alonso Puerta, the secretary-general of PASOC.

In December 1987 the *Federación Progresista* decided to abandon the alliance and its leader, Ramón Tamames, eventually joined forces with the CDS of Adolfo Suárez.

In 1988 *Iniciativa per Catalunya* won 7.63 per cent of the vote in the Catalan regional elections. This time the PCC as well as PSUC participated in the coalition.

Organization

The governing body of *Izquierda Unida* is its political council, which meets once a month, and which contains a number of representatives of each of the component parties, as well as three or four associated independents. The council seeks to operate by consensus. Below the national level *Izquierda Unida* operates through regional and local assemblies. Until now the president of the alliance has always been the secretary-general of the PCE, by far its largest component party, but there has been recent discussion as to whether the two posts should be separated in the future. The component parties retain their own separate political identities, and indeed do not agree on all political issues (the PCPE in particular, has been more hard-line than the others, and opposed, for example, Spanish membership in the European Community, unlike the majority within the alliance).

The future of *Izquierda Unida* remains uncertain. In the 1986 and 1987 elections it succeeded in reversing the fall in Communist Party fortunes, but it did not do much better than the PCE achieved on its own in the disastrous year of 1982, and far worse than the PCE's results in 1977 and 1979. The degree to which the electoral alliance of *Izquierda Unida* has added to the core vote of the PCE is not at all clear.

On the other hand some of the smaller parties represented within the alliance have resented the dominance of the PCE. This was one of the issues in the departure from the alliance of the *Federación Progresista*, whose leader felt that decisions were being taken by the PCE without his party being consulted. The specific reason for the split was the unilateral signing of an anti-terrorist pact by Gerardo Iglesias, the then president of the *Izquierda Unida*.

A further factor of uncertainty is whether the new PCE leadership put more emphasis on achieving reunification of the three Communist parties (PCE, PCPE and *Unidad Comunista*) or on further consolidating *Izquierda Unida* as a broad left-wing movement with a personality of its own, and reflecting left alternative and Green concerns as well as more traditional Communist ones.

(The component parts of *Izquierda Unida* are described separately below. For the distribution of its national electoral support, and for a description of its policies, see the section on the *Partido Comunista de España — PCE*. Policy differences and major personalities are described under the separate headings.)

Partido Comunista de España — PCE
(Spanish Communist Party)

Headquarters	: Santísima, Trinidad 5, Madrid
Secretary-general	: Julio Anguita
President	: Dolores Ibárruri ("La Pasionaria")
Parliamentary spokesman	: Nicolás Sartorius
Youth group	: *Union de Juventudes* (secretary: Jesús Montero)
Newspapers	: *Mundo Obrero, Nuestra Bandera*
Membership	: 60,000 (1987)

History

The Spanish Communist Party was founded in November 1921, in a merger between the Communist groups who had seceded from the Socialist Party over the issue of whether the latter should become a member of the Third International. It was not until November 1933 that the first Communist deputy was elected in Malaga. In 1934 the Communist and Socialist youth movements merged. The Communist Party began to pursue a Popular Front strategy. In January 1936, such a Front gained power, and 17 Communist deputies were elected.

The Communist Party gained greatly in influence and in membership during the Civil War. Two Communist ministers were included in the Largo Caballero Cabinet in September 1936, and party membership grew from an estimated 40,000 in July 1936 to 250,000 by March 1937. One important reason for its growth was its reputation for discipline and organization in a situation of turmoil. Lasting scars were also left through such incidents as its suppression of the rival Catalan Marxist party, the *Poum*.

After the Civil War many of the top leaders went into exile, but a number remained within Spain to organize resistance. In 1943 Dolores Ibárruri ("La Pasionaria"), became the party's secretary-general. In 1948 the party abandoned its support for guerrilla activities and began to concentrate more on changing the system from within. In 1956 it adopted a policy of national reconciliation and of co-operation between all democratic forces opposed to the regime. It gained considerably in prestige through its effective work within Spain, notably in the workers' commissions, (*Comisiones Obreras —* CCOO), which sprang up throughout Spain after 1958 to improve labour conditions. The workers' commissions steadily overtook the traditional Spanish unions, the Socialist UGT and the Anarchist CNT, which refused to work within the system.

In 1956 Santiago Carrillo became the new secretary-general. Although the party had begun to adopt a rather more independent line it was still a generally orthodox pro-Moscow party. In 1964 two reformist critics, Fernando Claudín and Jorge Semprún were expelled from the party. Only in 1968 did the party begin to distance itself from Moscow after the invasion of Czechoslovakia.

In 1974 the party was the leading force behind the formation of the so-called *Junta Democrática* of certain groups opposed to the regime, and later participated in a broader-based coalition with the Socialists, *Co-ordinacion Democrática*.

In early 1977 the Communist Party accepted the monarchy and the monarchist flag, and in return was legalized on April 2. In the 1977 national elections it won 9.2 per cent of the vote and won 20 seats in the Parliament.

The Communist Party now adopted a strongly Eurocommunist line. In October 1977 it participated in the Moncloa pact. In the 1979 national elections it increased its vote slightly to 10.7 per cent and 23 seats.

In the 1980s, however, the party began to lose ground, partly as a result of the contrast between the party's Eurocommunist principles and Carrillo's rigid centralism and authoritarian style of leadership. In November 1981 some leading party "renovators" were expelled. There was also a clash between the central leadership and party leaders in the Basque Country.

In the 1982 national elections the party dropped from 10.7 per cent to only 4.1 per cent of the vote and from 23 to four seats in the Spanish Parliament. In November 1982 Carrillo stood down as secretary-general and was replaced by Gerardo Iglesias.

In December 1984 the hard-liners led by Ignacio Gallego broke away to form a new party, the *Partido Comunista de los Pueblos de España* (PCPE). At the end of March 1985 Carrillo was replaced as spokesman of the parliamentary group by Fernando Pérez Royo. Carrillo finally left the party to set up (in October 1985) a rival grouping, the *Mesa para la unidad de los Comunistas*. In the Galician regional elections, which followed shortly afterwards, the new grouping almost won as many votes as the official party.

The referendum on Spanish membership of NATO in March 1986 proved to be a catalyst for broad co-operation between a number of left-of-centre parties and groups, and after the referendum this led to the creation of *Izquierda Unida* (see separate entry). Santiago Carrillo's *Mesa* did not join. The hard-liners of PCPE took part, but their Catalan sister party, the PCC, did not.

In the 1986 national elections *Izquierda Unida* received 4.66 per cent of the vote and won seven seats, of which four went to the PCE. Carrillo lost his seat in Madrid, and his *Mesa* ended up with no seats, and just over 1.1 per cent of the vote.

In the 1987 European Parliament elections *Izquierda Unida* won 5.2 per cent of the vote and three seats, of which one went to the PCE.

In 1988 Gerardo Iglesias was replaced as secretary-general by Julio Anguita. In early 1989 some of the leaders of the PCPE, including Ignacio Gallego, rejoined the PCE.

Support

Although *Izquierda Unida* has polled somewhat better than the Communist Party alone in 1982, it has only polled around half the votes that the PCE was able to obtain in the 1977 and 1979 elections.

The strongest region for the Communist Party is Andalusia, where it won seven seats in the 1979 national elections, and where *Izquierda Unida* was still able to win three seats (in the provinces of Córdoba, Málaga and Seville) in the 1986 national elections. In the 1986 Andalusian regional elections *Izquierda Unida* polled even better, winning 18 per cent of the vote and 18 out of the 109 seats in the regional parliament. Its strongest province of all is Córdoba. In the regional elections in 1986 *Izquierda Unida* won almost 33 per cent of the provincial vote, only 3 per cent less than the leading Socialist party. Córdoba is the only substantial Spanish city with a Communist mayor. In some of the smaller Andalusian towns and villages *Izquierda Unida* fares even better and in some places wins the most votes, as in Marinaleda (53.7 per cent in 1986 national elections) and in Torredonjimeno 41 per cent). Besides Córdoba it is strongest in the provinces of Málaga, Seville and Jaén.

The second region with a powerful Communist presence is Asturias, where its vote has not fallen as much as anywhere else. The PCE won 13 per cent of the Asturian vote in 1979 and *Izquierda Unida* won 9 per cent in 1986, holding on to its seat in the national parliament. In several towns in Asturias it won over 20 per cent of the vote (Mueres 20.8 per cent, Lariana 22 per cent). In the latest regional elections it won 12.1 per cent of the vote and four of the 45 seats in the regional parliament.

Izquierda Unida currently has two seats in Madrid, where it won 6 per cent of the vote in 1986. In 1979 the PCE won 13 per cent of the Madrid vote. In the regional assembly *Izquierda Unida* won seven out of the 96 seats on 7.4 per cent of the vote.

The Communist vote has fallen most disastrously in Catalonia. In Barcelona the Catalan Communist Party (the PSUC — see separate entry) had won 20 per cent of the vote in 1977, and 18.8 per cent in 1986. In Catalonia as a whole it only has one seat, compared to nine in 1977.

Another region where there has been a severe loss of support is the País Valenciano, where the PCE had three seats in 1979 (with 13 per cent of the vote in the province of Valencia and 11 per cent in Alicante) and where *Izquierda Unida* in 1986 had only 5 per cent of the vote in Alicante and Valencia and no seats. *Izquierda Unida* won 8 per cent of the vote, however, in the País Valenciano in the 1987 regional elections and six out of 89 seats in the regional parliament.

The alliance also has deputies in the regional parliaments of Estremadura (where it is much stronger in Badajoz than in Cáceres), the Canaries, Murcia (where it won 7.45 per cent in the 1987 regional elections) and Aragon (where it has a certain support in Zaragoza but is very weak in Teruel).

The weakest area for the Communist Party is the Basque Country where in the 1986 national elections *Izquierda Unida* only received 0.8 per cent of the vote in Alava and Guipuzcoa and only 1.5 per cent in Vizcaya. It is also very weak in Navarre (1.5 per cent in 1986) and Ceuta (1.5 per cent in 1986). It is also weak in the Balearic Islands (2.3 per cent in 1986), Castilla y León (between 1.9 per cent in Zamora in 1986 to 3 per cent in Valladolid), Melilla (2.7 per cent in 1986), Cantabria (3 per cent in 1986) and Galicia. It has moderate support in Castilla la Mancha (ranging from 2.5 per cent to 4.5 per cent in 1986).

Organization

The PCE has around 60,000 members, a figure which has been falling steadily since 1977. The party's structure has been strongly influenced by its 40 years of clandestine activity, and is still characterized by democratic centralism, and by tight internal discipline. After the departure of the authoritarian Santiago Carrillo, however, attempts are now being made to involve the membership more actively, through the introduction of a more open party culture, through the possibility of referenda (to be called by the central committee or by 51 per cent of the members), through more regular turnover of party office-holders and wider participation in party decision-making.

The basic unit of the party is the local group or *agrupación*, of which there are around 3,000 throughout Spain. Until now these have been on a territorial basis, but the party wishes to extend them to the workplace as well (e.g. within factories, small firms, etc). The party also wishes them to become smaller units, with a low minimum number of members (five to six) and a maximum of no more than 20 or 30.

There is a separate Communist Party in each Spanish region (only a regional committee in Madrid). Their degree of autonomy, however, is not very great. The main exception is the Communist Party in Catalonia (the PSUC — see separate entry under Catalonia), which is described in the PCE's own constitution as an independent Catalan national party, united fraternally to the PCE. The PCE and the PSUC are represented in each other's meetings and leadership structures, and are in the same parliamentary group unless they decide otherwise by mutual consent.

In the Basque Country the local Communist Party, the EPK, has an insignificant presence, in the aftermath of the events of autumn 1981, when most of the local party abandoned the PCE and merged in *Euskadiko Ezkerra* (see separate entry).

The PCE's national congress is held every three years. At the 12th congress held in February 1988 there were 625 delegates (one representative for each 100 members, half chosen by local groups and the other half by conferences of the regional parties). Once a year, and on special occasions, a party conference is also convened.

The party's central committee meets every two months. The executive committee meets on a monthly basis, and is being reduced in numbers from the previous total of 28 to 15 members and is being renamed as the political committee.

The key leadership position in the party is that of secretary-general. The post of president is an honorary one.

Candidates for the national parliament are put forward by the party's regional committees, after receiving suggested lists from the provincial committees. The central committee then decides on the final list for each constituency.

New rules are now being promulgated which will only allow party office-holders to occupy one function within the party, and for not more than three congresses (nine years).

The party has a youth organization, the *Unión de Juventudes Comunistas* (UJCE). There is no separate women's organization, although there is a women's committee within the party structure. The party now wishes to introduce positive discrimination for women, so that 25 per cent of party posts would be reserved for women.

The PCE's main strength is its close links with Spain's largest trade union organization, *Comisiones Obreros* (CCOO). To work in liaison with it the party has established a trade union committee. The party also has links with farm labourers' organizations.

The PCE has associated itself closely with a number of civic groups, parent-students associations and neighbourhood groups (*asociaciones de vecinos*).

The party's weekly newspaper is *Mundo obrero* which was founded in 1930. Its theoretical journal is *Nuestra Bandera*, which appears every two months.

The PCE is making a strenuous effort to eliminate the major debts still left over from the 1982 national elections, and is making considerable cutbacks in party expenditure. It has also launched a special fund–raising campaign through the sale of party bonds on top of its usual revenue from membership dues, state contributions and contributions from party office-holders, upon which the party has relied heavily in the past (up to 60 per cent of income). In 1988 the party received one-fifth of what it used to receive in 1979 from public officials, and only 40 per cent of its 1979 revenue from membership dues, party bonds and social occasions.

The PCE currently has one member of the European Parliament, who sits with the other *Izquierda Unida* members in the Communist and Allies Group.

Policies

The central question facing the PCE is how and whether it can recover from its current weak position in the Spanish political spectrum.

The two immediate issues facing the new party leadership are how to achieve unification of the divided Communist parties (the PCE, the more hard-line PCPE and the PTE–UC of Santiago Carrillo) and how best to develop the broader left-wing alliance of *Izquierda Unida*, two objectives which are not always compatible.

The 1988 party statutes still refer to the PCE as a political organization at the vanguard of the working class, and based on revolutionary Marxism.

The structure of the PCE, however, is now clearly Eurocommunist, differing on policy detail perhaps, but much closer to the Italian than to the French Communist Party. Moreover, the PCE is attempting to reconcile its character as a tightly structured party of the traditional working class with its aspirations for a broader-based movement of left-wing forces, more closely linked to the new social movements, such as the peace movement, ecologists and feminists. The recent electoral programmes of *Izquierda Unida* are heavily influenced by the need to reflect these new concerns.

On economic policy *Izquierda Unida* (IU) pronounces itself in favour of the mixed economy, with maximum market flexibility, but within a context of democratic planning. It calls for much greater attention to be paid to the objective of full employment within Spain and of better distribution of wealth. It seeks an increase in public investment.

It calls for nationalization of the seven largest private banks in two stages. Within the private sector it emphasizes support for small and medium-sized enterprises, and for co-operatives.

IU is the only Spanish parliamentary grouping to advocate the abandonment of nuclear energy. It also puts a very strong emphasis on environmental policy, which should not only be run by a separate ministry, but should be integrated into all other policies.

IU seeks the establishment of a free national health service, with a strong emphasis on preventive medicine. There should be 100 per cent social security coverage for the unemployed, retirement at 60 and more rights for Spanish migrant workers.

The divorce law should be extended in scope, and a new abortion law introduced. There should be proper family planning and full equality for women. There should be no discrimination against homosexuals.

Spain should become a more participative society. Industrial co-determination, however, in the German sense, is not supported.

IU seeks a much more decentralized Spanish government structure. Spain should become a federal state, with more powers and financial autonomy being devolved to the existing regional governments. The provinces should be less strong, and more powers should be given to local *comarcas* (districts). The Spanish Parliament should be reinforced at the expense of the executive and the Senate reinforced to become a proper territorial chamber. The voting system should be more proportional. The possibilities for holding referenda should be extended, at national and municipal level.

The campaign against NATO membership helped to forge IU, which is still opposed to Spanish membership of NATO, but now puts its main emphasis on strict observance of the terms of the referendum. It seeks the departure of Spain from the military committee of NATO and the declaration of the Iberian Peninsula as a nuclear-free zone. The bilateral military agreement with the United States should be denounced, and the US bases dismantled. There should be no foreign military use of Spanish ports or airports. The Civil Guard should be demilitarized and conscientious objectors should be protected.

The PCE supported Spanish entry into the European Community as early as 1978, and in 1985 it voted in favour of Spanish adhesion. Within IU there are differences of position on this issue, in that the PCPE is much more critical of the European Community than is the PCE. Nevertheless, IU is united in attacking the current form of the European Community, considering it to contain too little "Europe" and too little "Community". IU seeks a strong Europe of the Peoples, independent of either bloc, and much less Atlanticist than at present. It puts a stronger emphasis, for example, on a non-nuclear Europe as a third force than does the Italian Communist Party. It calls for more powers for the European Parliament and Commission at the expense of the Council of Ministers, and it wants the 1989 European Parliament to be given a constituent mandate to draw up a new draft treaty for European union. Community financial resources should also be increased, with much more going to regional and social purposes, and much less proportionately to the Common Agricultural Policy.

On other foreign policy matters the PCE also sees a strong linkage between the problems of the Spanish Sahara, Ceuta and Melilla, and Gibraltar. The Spanish Sahara should have self-determination under Polisario, Ceuta and Melilla should be returned by Spain to Morocco within a 20–25-year time frame, and Gibraltar should return to Spanish sovereignty, but with ample autonomy for the territory and its inhabitants.

IU seeks the establishment of a Palestine state, and does not yet recognize Israel. In development policy it supports Spain reaching the suggested UN aid target of 0.7 per cent of its GNP.

Personalities

The new secretary-general of the party is Julio Anguita, who replaced Gerardo Iglesias at the PCE's congress of February 1988. Anguita is a former mayor of Córdoba, and is often known as the "Red Caliph". He is a schoolmaster by training. As the former president of IU in Andalusia he is also a noted advocate of closer links between the PCE and the other left–wing social movements.

Anguita's predecessor was Gerardo Iglesias, a working-class man from the mining region of Asturias who had been party secretary-general since he was chosen by Santiago Carrillo in November 1982. Although he subsequently broke with Carrillo, and helped to develop the strategy of IU, his leadership was generally felt to be insufficiently forceful to arrest the decline in the PCE's fortunes. He remains influential within the party, however, and won the most votes in the election for the central committee in February 1988, even more than did Dolores Ibárruri, "La Pasionaria", who was re-elected as PCE president. Her post is of symbolic importance only, but "La Pasionaria", born in 1895, remains a powerful link with the past. She was famous for her oratory during the period preceding and during the Civil War, and was secretary-general of the party in exile from 1942 to 1956.

Another key figure within the party is Nicolás Sartorius, a journalist and lawyer who comes from an aristocratic family of distant Polish origin. Sartorius, a deputy from Seville, is one of the main power-brokers within the party, and has been its main parliamentary spokesman.

The weight of *Comisiones Obreros* was increased within the party's general committee at the congress in February 1988, with the number of its representatives going up from 10 to 17. The veteran *Comisiones* leader, Marcelino Camacho, who helped to build the union up to its present strength and who is now its president, remains a vital figure within the party, as is his successor as the union's secretary-general, Antonio Gutiérrez.

Francisco Frutos, who is the party's expert on economic and social matters, and who was the head of its trade union committee, remains an important figure within the party apparatus.

The only PCE member of the European Parliament is Fernando Pérez Royo.

The secretary-general of the Catalan Communist Party (PSUC — see separate entry) is Rafael Ribo.

Anguita's successor as Mayor of Córdoba is his close ally, Herminio Trigo.

Within the party apparatus other important figures include Francisco Palero Gómez, who has been the national secretary responsible for party organization, and Simón Sánchez Montero, one of the old guard within the party, who was its international secretary.

Partido Comunista de los Pueblos de España — PCPE
(Communist Party of the Peoples of Spain)

Headquarters	: Calle Saturnino Calleja 16, 28002 Madrid (tel: 4138131)
Secretary-general	: Juan Ramos
Youth group	: *Colectivos de Jóvenes Comunistas*
Newspaper	: *Nuevo Rumbo*
Membership	: 17,000
Founded	: 1984

History

The PCPE is an orthodox pro-Soviet Communist party founded by Ignacio Gallego, who resigned from the central committee of the *Partido Comunista de España* (PCE) on Oct. 11, 1983 in fundamental disagreement with its Eurocommunist line, and who founded a new *Partido Comunista* on Jan. 19, 1984. The party subsequently took its present name. In December 1984 the party was further reinforced by the arrival of other dissidents from the PCE, notably Jaime Ballesteros.

The split at national level was also mirrored within Catalonia by the creation of the *Partit dels Comunistes de Catalunya* (PCC) as a breakaway from the Catalan Communist Party PSUC (see separate entries). In Andalusia there is also a linked party, the *Partido Comunista del Pueblo Andaluz* (PCPA), founded in October 1985.

In spite of major policy differences with the PCE leadership the PCPE took part in the *Izquierda Unida* coalition in both the 1986 and 1987 elections (the PCC did not initially participate but joined up with the PSUC in the 1988 Catalan regional elections).

The PCPE has had one seat in the Congress of Deputies (that of Ignacio Gallego in Málaga), four deputies in regional parliaments, 10 mayors and 220 local councillors. In early 1989 several of its leading figures, including Ignacio Gallego, left the party and returned to the main PCE.

Support

The PCPE has pockets of strength throughout the country, such as Andalusia, Madrid, Valencia, Castilla la Mancha, the Balearic Islands, and Catalonia.

Organization

As an orthodox Communist party the PCPE sticks rigidly to democratic centralism, and has criticized the PCE for challenging this key Leninist principle of party organization.

In 1988 it claimed to have 800 territorial cells, and about 100 working place cells. Above these it is organized at provincial and regional level. Its national congress is held every three years, and elects a central committee of 108 members, which meets at least every three months. The central committee elects the party's president and secretary-general, its executive committee of 22 members and the inner party's secretariat, which numbers seven members in all.

The PCPE's youth organization consists of its *Colectivos de Jóvenes Comunistas*. Its central newspaper is called *Nueva Rumbo*, and has a circulation of 20,000.

The PCPE is the second-largest party within the coalition of *Izquierda Unida*. It continues to maintain strong relationships with orthodox Communist parties in other countries, and welcomed, for example, the creation of the hard-line New Communist Party of Great Britain.

Policies

The PCPE claims that it is the true guardian of the traditions of the Spanish Communist Party, and emphasizes its continuing loyalty to the Soviet Union, and to the 1917 October Revolution. It is highly critical of Eurocommunism, and maintains that Soviet "Glasnost" and "Perestroika" are not the same thing as Eurocommunism.

A central strategic objective for the PCPE has been reunification of Spanish Communism, but on its own hard-line terms.

In the absence of any immediate alternative, however, the PCPE has participated in the coalition of *Izquierda Unida*. It does not agree with a number of its policies, but supports the principle of a broad left-wing coalition, and *Izquierda Unida*'s core objectives.

The PCPE defines itself as a "class" party, and supports the dictatorship of the proletariat. It does not believe that there is a third way between capitalism and socialism. It advocates widespread nationalizations, including that of the banks and of the whole energy sector. It seeks expropriation of big landholdings, and major agrarian reform.

The PCPE (also influenced by its PCC affiliate) advocates a federal structure for the Spanish state. It would like to see the Senate turned into a chamber of Spanish peoples and nationalities, and also calls for electoral reform.

One of its main differences with the other parties in *Izquierda Unida* lies in its hostility to European integration (seen as merely of interest to capitalists and imperialists) and to Spanish membership of the EC. It calls for the Spanish people to decide in a referendum whether they wish to remain within the European Community, but it has had little influence on *Izquierda Unida* on these issues.

The PCPE is fiercely critical of Spanish membership of NATO, and still wants Spain to leave even after the referendum. It seeks the dismantling of US bases, the establishment of Spanish neutrality and the dissolution of both military blocs.

The PCPE also disagreed with the PCE's decision to sign the anti-terrorist pact in 1987. It believes that this will not lead to peace in the Basque Country, and also calls for closer involvement with the Basque Nationalist Party, *Herri Batasuna*.

Personalities

The secretary-general is Juan Ramos who came from the Catalan sister party, the PCC. Other leading figures include José Seradell, responsible for organization, and Jaime Ballesteros, responsible for international relations.

Partido Acción Socialista — PASOC
(Socialist Action Party)

Headquarters	: Espoz y Mino 5, 1º Izquierda 28012 Madrid (tel: 4737376 or 4737406)
President	: Julián Lara Cavero
Secretary-general	: Alonso Puerta
Newspaper	: *Acción Socialista*
Membership	: 10,000
Founded	: January 1983

History

PASOC is the third-largest party within the coalition of *Izquierda Unida*, and represents a merger between what was left of the old guard who lost out in the battle to control the Socialist party (PSOE) in the early 1970s and dissidents from the Socialist left–wing who left PSOE in the early 1980s.

From 1972–74 a younger generation of socialists, led by Felipe González, wrested control of PSOE from the elderly Rodolfo Llopis, and the others who had led the party in exile in France since the 1940s. The latter did not accept their defeat, and for a while there were two parties claiming to be the PSOE. The former leadership were forced to change the name of their group in 1976 to *PSOE–Histórico*, to emphasize continuity with the past. In the 1977 elections PSOE won 118 seats and PSOE–*Histórico* none, although the latter did obtain a considerable number of votes. They continued their separate existence, with their own congresses. In 1981, however, they became a party without a name when a court ruled that they could not use the name PSOE–*Histórico*. They then unsuccessfully tried the name *Partido Socialista*.

Meanwhile some left–wingers within PSOE were becoming increasingly unhappy at the way in which PSOE was evolving into a moderate reformist Social–Democratic party. They also felt that there was insufficient internal democracy within the party.

In January 1983 the veterans from PSOE–*Histórico*, who had little organizational strength but had a headquarters and a certain amount of money, got together with the more recently departed members of PSOE (mainly members of *Izquierda Socialista* and another group, the *Co-ordinadora Socialista Federal*) to form the *Partido Acción Socialista* (PASOC). There were also participants from another small party, the *Partido Sindicalista*. The septuagenarian, Julián Lara became president, and Modesto Seara became secretary-general.

PASOC subsequently joined the coalition which fought against NATO membership in the 1986 referendum, and it then became a founder member of *Izquierda Unida*, in which it has remained until the present.

It currently has one member in the European Parliament, and one representative in the Andalusian and Madrid regional parliaments.

Support

PASOC is strongest in Andalusia (especially in the provinces of Málaga and Granada) and in Madrid, where over half of its federal committee live. It also has support in the País Valenciano and in Cantabria. It is almost non-existent in some areas, such as Navarre and La Rioja.

Organization

PASOC has around 10,000 members. In reaction to PSOE practice its local groups and delegates have considerable autonomy.

Its local groups must have a minimum of three members. A regional tier is created where appropriate. At national level the party's federal congress is held every two to three years. Delegates of the local groups are chosen proportionately to their membership, and cannot be mandated. The party's federal committee usually meets every three months. The federal executive committee, which is directly elected by the congress, contains 12 members and meets on a weekly basis. It includes the president and secretary-general. PASOC has a very small central staff, and its headquarters are those of the former PSOE–*Histórico*.

Its newspaper is called *Acción Socialista*. Two-thirds of the party's regular income comes from *Izquierda Unida*, and the other third from its own membership dues. Its member in the European Parliament sits in the Communist and Allies Group.

Policies

PASOC is a left–wing Socialist party which maintains that it is the true heir of the Spanish Socialist tradition which is being betrayed by the increasingly conservative PSOE. It has strongly supported the *Izquierda Unida* strategy.

PASOC advocates widespread socialization of the means of production, including nationalization of the energy sector. It calls for a fairer distribution of wealth, and for democratic planning of the economy. It seeks a shortening of the working week to 35 hours, and ultimately to 30 hours. It puts a strong emphasis on ecology and is opposed to the use of civil nuclear energy. It calls for Spain to have a federal structure.

A minority within PASOC are critical of Spain's EC membership. The majority, however, put their emphasis on seeking change within the EC, so that it becomes much more of a Europe of the Peoples, becomes more Socialist and shows more solidarity with the third world.

PASOC respects the result of the NATO referendum, but continues to advocate dissolution of both the Warsaw Pact and NATO. It is opposed to US bases in Spain.

Personalities

The party president, Julián Lara, is now over 80, and is a veteran Socialist personality from the days of civil war and exile. The party's secretary-general, Alonso Puerta is a former PSOE deputy-mayor of Madrid who came into conflict with the PSOE leadership. In 1987 he was elected to the European Parliament. Pablo Castellano, the former leader of the left within PSOE, has recently joined PASOC.

Izquierda Republicana — IR
(Republican Left)

Headquarters	: Calle de Alfonso Cano 93, Bajo 6, Madrid
Other contact point	: C/Montera 19–3ºA, 28013 Madrid (tel: 521 94 67)
President	: Paulino García Partida
Secretary-general	: Isabelo Herreros Martín
Membership	: 1,000–1,500

History

Izquierda Republicana is currently the smallest of the four national parties participating in the coalition of *Izquierda Unida*. It has, however, inherited a famous party name. *Izquierda Republicana* was founded in 1934 and its first president was Manuel Azana. It obtained 88 deputies in the February 1936 elections, and was part of the Republican government from 1936 to 1939.

After the restoration of both democracy and a constitutional monarchy in the 1970s Republicanism had become very weak, and there was a further division between its more moderate and more socialist wings. The former became active in ARDE (*Acción Republicana Democrática Española*) which has had very little influence, while the Socialist wing took control of *Izquierda Republicana*, which was legalized too late to fight the 1977 elections.

Izquierda Republicana joined the coalition of *Izquierda Unida* before the 1986 elections, and has remained in it since, although it has very little weight.

Support

Izquierda Republicana has a very small electoral base. Among its areas of support are the País Valenciano (especially in parts of Alicante), Madrid, the Basque Country, Cantabria and Castilla y León.

Organization

Izquierda Republicana has between 1,000 and 1,500 members and its internal organization is governed by federalist principles. It has local, provincial and regional groups. Its national congress is held every two years, and elects the 17 members of its national executive committee, including the party president and secretary-general. There is also a federal executive committee, consisting of both the national and regional executive, which meets at least three times a year.

The party's youth movement is called *Juventudes de Izquierda Republicana*, and is open to 18–21 year olds. The party has a news bulletin called *Politica*.

It claims links with parties such as the Republican Party in Italy and the MRG in France, as well as with parties in Venezuela, Argentina and Chile.

Policies

Izquierda Republicana still calls for a Republican Spain, although this is not its major policy priority. It also advocates a federal and decentralized Spain.

Its main emphasis is now on the building of Socialism in Spain. It describes itself as a radical anti-capitalist party. It is opposed to the presence of Spain in any military bloc, and advocates neutrality and non-violence.

It wishes to remain within the *Izquierda Unida* coalition, as long as its autonomy and separate character are fully respected.

Personalities

The party's president is Paulino García Partida, a 50-year-old academic. The secretary-general is Isabelo Herreros Martín, a journalist in his mid-30s.

Partido de los Trabajadores de España — Unidad Comunista — PTE–UC
(Workers' Party of Spain–Communist Unity)

Headquarters	: Plaza de Santa Bárbara 10, 2º Izquierda 28004, Madrid
President	: Santiago Carrillo
Secretary-general	: Adolfo Pinedo
Membership	: 14,000

History

The PTE–UC is the party of the breakaway Communist leader Santiago Carrillo. As long-standing leader of the Communist Party (PCPE), Carrillo was doubly controversial, first, because he led the party in a Eurocommunist direction, and secondly (and paradoxically) because he permitted very little internal democracy within the party. He resigned as secretary-general of the PCE in 1982, but came into increasing conflict with the new party leadership, and in 1985 left the party.

He then established a new group, the *Mesa para la Unidad de los Comunistas*, which did not participate in the coalition of *Izquierda Unida*.

In the 1986 national elections it only polled 1.12 per cent of the vote, and failed to win any seats in the Parliament. The party took its present name in early 1987. In the 1987 European elections it obtained 1.15 per cent of the vote, and again failed to win a seat. Attempts at reunification with the other two Communist parties have so far failed.

Organization

At national level there is a party congress, which elects the president, general-secretary and 57-member central committee. The latter then elects an executive committee.

Personalities

The PTE–UC is dominated by the historic Communist leader, Santiago Carrillo, now well into his 70s.

Partido Carlista
(Carlist Party)

History

Carlism is one of the oldest political traditions in Spain, and stems from the attempt to depose King Ferdinand VII in the early 19th century, and replace him by his younger brother, Carlos. This was the beginning of a long-standing dynastic claim by the descendants of Don Carlos, and which provoked two civil wars in Spain in the 1830s and 1870s. The Carlists represented intransigent Catholicism, and defended traditional regional rights. They were opposed to centralization and to liberalism. Their strongest political base was Navarre.

In the 1930s they gave strong support to the Nationalists in the Civil War.

In the later period of Franco's rule the Carlist claimant was Prince Carlos Hugo, who led the traditionally right-wing movement increasingly to the left, and took the Carlists into the opposition *Junta Democrática* led by the Communist party. He eventually renounced his dynastic claims.

The move to the left was contested by the Carlist right led by Carlos Hugo's brother, Sixto de Borbón. There was violence (with fatalities) between the two groups in 1976 at the annual Carlist pilgrimage to Montejurra in Navarre (the site of their greatest 19th century victory). Carlos Hugo no longer resides in Spain.

The Carlist party rather controversially took part in the coalition of *Izquierda Unida* for the 1986 national elections with Juan Francisco Martin Aguilera as its representative. It has not since played a role in the coalition. The Carlist tradition, whether expressed in left or right-wing terms, is now very weak. Its main base is still in Navarre.

Los Verdes
(The Greens)

Headquarters	: Pilar de Zaragoza 83, 28028 Madrid
Membership	: 2,500 (1987)

History

The confederation arose as a result of ecologist conferences in Tenerife in May 1983 and in Málaga in June 1984. It was legally registered in November 1984, and was inaugurated at a congress in February 1985. Green candidates stood in the 1986 national elections in a number of constituencies, but with little success.

In the 1987 European elections there were two Green lists, with *Los Verdes* winning 0.55 per cent of the vote and a separate list of the *Confederación de los Verdes* winning 0.34 per cent. In the simultaneous municipal and regional elections Green candidates obtained more than 1 per cent of the vote, and a few local councillors were elected.

Organization

The confederation is co-ordinated nationally by an executive board (*Mesa Confederal*), consisting of members of the regional Green federations, which remain autonomous as regards their structure and local policies. The bureau designates a commission for various aspects of policy and administration.

Among the major individual Green parties are: *Los Verdes Alternativos* (whose headquarters are at Apartado de Correos, 52135, 28080 Madrid. They were legally registered on Oct. 21, 1986, have about 200 members and a more organized structure than the confederation); *Los Verdes* (Apartado 5085, 28080 Madrid); *Alternativa Verde* (Catalonia); *Alternativa Ecoloxista* (Galicia); and the Ecological Party of Euzkadi.

The confederation has been an observer member of the European Greens since October 1985.

Basque Country (Euskadi)

The current autonomous region of the Basque Country (Euskadi in Basque) has well over two million inhabitants, and consists of the three provinces or "historic" territories of Guipúzcoa (Gipuzcoa), Vizcaya (Bizkaia) and Alava (Araba). Its capital is Vitoria.

The area of Basque culture and language, however, is wider than these three provinces, and includes a considerable part of Navarre (Nabara) and the southern part of the French department of Pyrénées–Atlantique, where there are 250,000 Basques living in the three historic Basque provinces of Soule (Zuberoa), Labourde (Laburdi) and Basse-Navarre (Benabarra).

The Basque Country includes areas of heavy industrialization notably around Bilbao, as well as areas of lighter industry and densely populated farming areas with isolated farmsteads. It also includes large numbers of non-Basque immigrants from other parts of Spain.

The Basques are generally very traditional, and the Catholic Church plays an important role in their society. The Basque language (Euskera) is unlike any other in Europe, but is only spoken by a small percentage (around 20 per cent) of the population, and is a minority language even among native Basques. Its position has been undercut by its repression under Franco, by the industrialization of the Basque Country and the consequent arrival of non-Basques, as well as of movement of the Basques into the cities, and also by the language's intrinsic difficulty. Strenuous attempts, however, are being made to increase its use. It is an official language within Euskadi.

Basque political institutions

The Basque Statute provides for an autonomous community within the Spanish state under the name of Euskadi, and with its own parliament and government in Vitoria.

The Basque Parliament is unicameral with a term of office of four years, but with earlier dissolution possible (as in 1986). There are 75 seats in the parliament, with Vizcaya, Guipúzcoa and Alava equally represented with 25 seats, although they have very different populations (Vizcaya's electorate being over 900,000, compared to 530,000 in Guipúzcoa and only 200,000 in Alava). As a result the Socialists, for example, obtained seven seats in Alava, with under 35,000 votes (1986 election) and six in Vizcaya with nearly 143,000.

The Basque Country has a greater degree of fiscal independence, compared to the other Spanish autonomous regions, collecting its own taxes and then handing over a certain quota to the Spanish state.

The first elections to the new Basque Parliament took place in 1980, and there have been two other elections in 1984 and 1986 (see table).

It takes five deputies to form a group in the Basque Parliament and there are currently five such groups. There is also a system of financing of political parties by the Basque government.

The Basque government is drawn from the Basque Parliament. Its president is called the *Lendakari*, who resides in the government palace of *Ajuria Enea*. The Basque Country has a strong tradition of decentralization and the three Basque provinces retain significant powers. A 1983 agreement between the Basque government and the provincial administrations (the so-called Law of the Historical Territories) provided the latter with considerable fiscal autonomy.

The Basque Country has its own police force (the *Erzaintza*), although it must share its powers with Spanish state police, and also has its own television service, *Euskal Telebista*, which broadcasts in Basque and in Spanish.

Brief political history

19th century	Attacks on the traditional liberties (*fueros*) of the different Basque provinces by Napoleon, by Spanish Liberals in 1820s and in 1841.
1876	Final abolition of the *fueros* of Guipúzcoa, Biscay and Alava (but not of Navarre). Maintenance, however, of a degree of fiscal autonomy (*conciertos económicos* 1876–1937).
1890s	Sabino de Arana, first nationalist leader, defines concept of *Euskadi*; creation of Basque Nationalist Party (PNV) in 1894; first advocates independence, but later a greater degree of autonomy within the Spanish state.
1931–36	Several failed attempts to establish a Basque statute of autonomy (majority of Navarre municipalities reject inclusion of Navarre in such a project — 1932).
October 1936	A Basque statute of autonomy finally approved, after Civil War had already begun. José Antonio Aguirre, president of provisional government; wide coalition between Basque political forces.
1936–39	Civil War. Provisional government supports the Second Republic. Bombing of Guernica (1937). Basque Country captured by Nationalists and loses its privileges. Navarre and Alava support Franco. Alava retains its *conciertos económicos* and Navarre retains its own legislature and government.
1939–79	Francoist repression particularly severe in Basque Country. Basque gov-

ernment in exile in France (José Antonio Aguirre, first president of government in exile until 1960, Jesús Mario de Leizaola, second president). Terrorism begins in Basque Country (1960s).

1970	Burgos trial of 16 Basque militants, including two priests.
1973	Basque commando assassinates Spanish Prime Minister Admiral Carrero Blanco.
1975–77	After death of Franco, fight for amnesty for Basque prisoners and for Basque autonomy.
1978	Spanish Constitution approved, but with over 163,000 Basques voting against it.
1979	Basque Statute of Autonomy (Statute of Guernica) approved in referendum. Navarre excluded, but given option to join.
1980	First Basque parliament elections. Carlos Garaicoetxea of PNV first president or *lendakari* (1980–85).
1985	Legislative pact between PNV and Basque Socialists. José Antonio Ardanza second *lendakari*.
1986	Early elections called. Inconclusive results, with Socialists largest party in terms of seats. Coalition government formed between PNV and Socialists (early 1987) with Ardanza continuing as *lendakari*.
November 1987	Anti-terrorist pact between the main parties in the Spanish *Cortes*, and the Basque parties (with exception of *Herri Batasuna* and *Eusko Alkartasuna*).

Features of Basque political system

Until the Franco period the Basque Country posed fewer difficulties for the Spanish central government than did Catalonia, but since then it has constituted the most intractable Spanish political problem, and has spawned Western Europe's largest terrorist organization.

The Basque Country has never been a unified political entity, and the first problem has been one of definition. Even parts of the generally accepted Basque provinces, such as Western Vizcaya, are outside the Basque linguistic region, and Alava, in particular, has looked rather more to central Spain than the other two provinces. The French Basque Country is undeniably Basque, but Basque parties have had practically no foothold within the French political system. The main problem, however, has been posed by Navarre, whose northern part is Basque-speaking, and which has strong historical links with the Basque Country. It has, however, its own distinctive political character, being a bastion of the Carlists (see separate entry under Spain), retaining its *fueros*, supporting Spanish unity and the Nationalists against the Republic, and rejecting incorporation within an autonomous Basque region.

The political system within the Basque Country is a multi-party system, with a number of major divisions. The first is over support for Basque nationalism. In the 1977 Spanish elections the Spanish state parties were still able to win a majority of the votes in the Basque Country, but since then a large majority of Basques (generally around two-thirds) have voted for the Basque national parties (the *abertzales* or "patriot" parties) instead of for the Basque branches of the Spanish state parties. This has been true of all elections, national as well as regional.

A second division has been over violence and terrorism, with one of the Basque national parties, *Herri Batasuna*, which is close to ETA, adopting an ambiguous attitude on these issues.

A third has been between left and right. The most powerful of the Spanish state parties, the Socialist Party (PSOE) has always been strong among immigrants and in the industrial regions of the Basque Country. In the 1986 regional elections it won more seats than any other party. There are also left–right divisions among the Basque Nationalist parties, with *Herri Batasuna* claiming to be Marxist–Leninist and with *Euskadiko Ezkerra* being a left–Socialist party. In contrast, the main Basque Nationalist Party, the PNV, has been a generally conserva-tive party with strong links to the Catholic Church, which has played a distinctive political role in the Basque Country, and supported calls for Basque autonomy.

Fears of a clerical corporatist Basque Country played a large part in opposition to Basque autonomy in the past, although these fears have largely receded.

Most recently even the conservative Basque Nationalist vote has been divided, with the splitting-off of *Eusko Alkartasuna* from the mainstream PNV, although personality conflicts have played a large role in this schism. This has meant that the PNV, on its own, is no longer the dominant political force in the Basque Country. So politically divided is the Basque Country that, in the 1986 regional elections, the largest party was different in each province, the Socialists in Alava, *Eusko Alkartasuna* in Guipúzcoa and the PNV in Vizcaya.

These political divisions have made the Basque Country very difficult to govern, and have meant, untypically for Spain, that a coalition government has had to be formed. The ruling coalition is between the Basque Socialists and the conservative PNV, with the other Basque Nationalist parties in the opposi-tion. The other Spanish state parties, the CDS and *Partido Popular* especially are electorally insignificant at present, although they have some support in Alava. The Communists are extremely weak everywhere in the region.

The main political issues in the Basque Country are the following:

— The degree to which Basque autonomy and/or "self-determination" should be de-veloped. Can the existing statute of auton-

Basque regional elections 1980–present (number of seats won in the Regional Parliament)

	1980	1984	1986
Partido Nacionalista Vasco (Euzko Alderdi Jeltzalea—PNV/EAJ) (Basque Nationalist Party)	25	32	17
Eusko Alkartasuna (EA) (Basque Solidarity)	—	—	14
Euskadiko Ezkerra (Basque Left)	6	6	9
Herri Batasuna (United People)	11	11	13
Partido Socialista de Euskadi (PSE-PSOE) (Basque Socialist Party)	9	19	18
Coalicion Popular (Popular Coalition)	2	7	2
Union de Centro Democratico (UCD) (Union of the Democratic Centre)	6	—	—
Centro Democratico y Social (CDS) (Democratic and Social Centre)	—	0	2
Partido Comunista de Euskadi—PCE/EPK (Euskadiko Partido Komunista) (Basque Communists)	1	0	0

omy be given fuller implementation? Should there be full independence for the Basque Country?

— The issue of whether and how Navarre could be incorporated within the Basque autonomous region.

— The issue of decentralization within the Basque autonomous region and the degree of autonomy of the individual Basque provinces.

— Terrorism: How best can it be brought to an end? Should there be direct negotiations with ETA? How can former terrorists be "re-inserted" into Basque society?

— Economic policy: What are the best ways of coping with the extremely high levels of unemployment in the Basque Country and the restructuring of its traditional heavy industries which are currently in so much difficulty?

Eusko Alderdi Jeltzalea/Partido Nacionalista Vasco
(Basque Nationalist Party)

Headquarters	: Gran Vía 38–7º, Bilbao 1 (tel: 4434108)
President	: Xabier Arzalluz
Youth group	: *Euzko Gaztedi* (EGI)
Newspaper	: *Deia*
Founded	: 1895

History

The development of Basque nationalism at the end of the 19th century was largely a reaction against the rapid process of industrialization in the Basque Country between 1875 and 1890, and the consequent arrival of non-Basque immigrants in large numbers. Native Basques, especially among the middle classes and in rural areas, felt that their culture and language were threatened by these new developments. A rallying cry was found in the call to re-establish the former Basque liberties, or *fueros*, which had been lost in 1876.

The *Partido Nacionalista Vasco* (PNV) was founded by Sabino Arana (1865–1903) in 1895. The PNV attempted to become a broad-based nationalist party across class divides. It established its own community centres or *Batzokis*. In 1911 it set up an associated trade union, *Solidaridad de Obreros Vascos* which has survived up to the present day in the form of the union ELA/STV.

Its electoral strength was limited, however, by its failure to win wide support among workers and in the industrial areas of the Basque Country, nor to win significant support from the Basque industrial and financial oligarchy. Its image remained one of a conservative anti-immigrant and deeply Catholic party. Its main support came in the province of Vizcaya, with some limited support in Guipúzcoa. It was much weaker in Alava, and especially in Navarre, where the conservative vote was dominated by the Carlist movement (see separate entry). Even in the Basque Country proper the PNV never won more than 30 per cent of the vote.

The PNV's identification as a conservative party was reinforced by occasional electoral alliances with other right-wing parties, and it was this which gave it its first seat in the Spanish parliament, in Navarre in 1918.

With the coming of the Second Republic in 1931 the PNV took the opportunity to push hard for Basque autonomy, and it was the PNV-inspired "movement of Basque mayors" which put forward the proposed Statute of Estella.

In 1933 the PNV won a higher vote than ever before, winning over 44.5 per cent of the vote in Vizcaya, 26 per cent in Guipúzcoa and 20 per cent in Alava.

In 1936 a Basque Statute of Autonomy was finally approved, and the PNV leader, José Antonio Aguirre, became a president of the provisional Basque regional government at the head of a coalition with several other parties. After the recapture of the Basque Country by Franco's Nationalists Aguirre became the president of the Basque government in exile, being succeeded in 1960 by another PNV leader, Jesus María de Leizaola. Another key figure who helped to maintain the PNV during the Franco years was Juan de Ajuriaguerra, who died in 1978. In 1977 Ajuriaguerra took a position in favour of the new Spanish Constitution, but was in a minority in the PNV's executive committee. In the subsequent referenda the PNV campaigned for abstention.

In the 1977 Spanish elections the PNV won more votes than any other party in the Basque Country (28 per cent) and in the first Basque regional elections in 1980 it was easily the largest party with 39.3 per cent of the vote and 25 of the then 60 seats. Carlos Garaicoetxea, of the PNV became the Basque Country's first president or *Lendakari*. The party's leading figure in the Spanish parliament, Xabier Arzalluz, returned to become the party's president.

In 1984 the PNV again won a working majority, on an even higher percentage of the vote (41.7 per cent) and with 32 seats in the Basque Parliament.

The party was subsequently divided, however, by a conflict between the party's two dominant figures, Garaicoetxea and Arzallus (see section on *Eusko Alkartasuna*).

At the beginning of 1985 a supporter of Arzallus, José Antonia Ardanza replaced Garaicoetxea as Basque president and Garaicoetxea subsequently formed his own party, *Eusko Alkartasuna*. The new party inflicted severe electoral damage on the PNV in the regional elections in 1986, when the PNV remained the largest party in votes (23.5 per cent compared to the previous 41.7 per cent) but lost 15 of its former 32 seats, and came second to the Socialist Party in terms of seats.

The PNV subsequently entered into a coalition with the Socialists, and Ardanza remained as Basque president. In the 1987 elections the PNV did poorly in the municipal elections, and failed to win a seat in the European Parliament.

Support

The PNV has been the largest party in all national and regional elections in the Basque Country since 1977, but its electoral strength has been severely harmed by the creation of *Eusko Alkartasuna*.

Even in the disastrous 1986 regional elections, however, the PNV remained the largest party in seats and votes (29 per cent) in its stronghold of Vizcaya, where it had won 43 per cent in 1984 and 40 per cent in 1980. It had also been the largest party in Vizcaya in the national elections in 1986, with 29.3 per cent and three seats in the Spanish Congress of Deputies and three out of the four senators from the province. One of its stronger towns was Guernica, where it won over 44 per cent of the vote. In the 1987 local elections, where the PNV did badly, it resisted best in Vizcaya, and its candidate was again elected mayor of the Basque Country's largest city of Bilbao.

The PNV had been particularly hurt by *Eusko Alkartasuna* in Garaicoetxea's own fief of Guipúzcoa. In the 1980 and 1984 regional elections it had been the largest party with 37 per cent and 40 per cent of the provincial votes respectively and in the 1986 national elections it was also the strongest party with 28.6 per cent of the vote, two seats in the Congress and three of the four senators. In the 1986 regional elections, the PNV slipped to fourth place in Guipúzcoa, with only 16 per cent of the vote.

In Alava where the PNV had gained 30 per cent in the 1980 regional elections and 36 per cent in 1984, it fell back to 20 per cent in 1986, and came second to the Socialist Party. The PNV has always been weaker in national elections in the more Spanish-influenced province of Alava,

where it won 19 per cent in 1986, with one seat in the Congress and one in the Senate.

What little electoral strength the PNV once had in Navarre has been eliminated by the schism with *Eusko Alkartasuna*.

Organization

The PNV describes itself as a confederation of regional organizations, sovereign in their own sphere and united in a confederal pact. It is well implanted in Basque life, especially in the province of Vizcaya, but its organizational structure has been hurt by the schism with *Eusko Alkartasuna*, particularly in Guipúzcoa and Alava.

The party's constitution is expressly governed by the Christian Democrats' principle of "subsidiarity", that decisions should be taken at the lowest level that is appropriate. The lowest basic units within the PNV are its municipal organizations.

Each municipal organization has a municipal assembly (which can be convoked by 15 per cent of the local membership) and municipal executive or *junta*, known in Basque as *Uri Buru Batzarak*, and which has a two-year term of office.

Within each province or "historic region" the sovereign party body is the regional assembly, consisting of representatives elected by the municipal assemblies of the region. Besides its statutory meetings the assembly can be convoked by 15 per cent of the municipal juntas. At regional level there is also a regional council, which is the party executive within the region, and consists of five or more members elected for two-year terms.

The national assembly of the party meets once a year. Among the ways it can be convoked on special occasions is at the request of a fifth of the members within a region, or by 15 per cent of the municipal juntas, or members from the whole of the Basque Country.

The national executive party is called the national council or, in Basque, the *Euzkadi Buru Batzarra* (EBB). This meets at least once a week and consists of three councillors from each region, elected by each regional council for two-year terms. The EBB chooses its president, who is the effective party leader and has a powerful hold over the entire organization.

At national level there is also a supreme tribunal of justice and also the national party secretariat, located in Bilbao.

The party has a tough law of incompatibilities, limiting the terms of office-holders and preventing the simultaneous holding of public and party office, or even party and trade union office. The present EBB president, for example, Xavier Arzalluz, had to leave the Spanish parliament in Madrid to become EBB president in 1980, and had to stand down in 1984 because his two terms of office had elapsed, although he has now been re-elected.

The party's youth wing is called *Eusko Gaztedi* (EGI). A special women's committee has recently been proposed. The party also has an associated trade union, ELA/STV (*Solidaridad de Trabajadores Vascos*), founded in 1911 and well-organized with about a quarter of all trade union representation in the Basque Country.

The party's newspaper is called *Deia* and has a circulation of over 50,000. There is also another newspaper *Gaceta*, and a journal, *Euskadi*. At international level the PNV is associated with the various Christian Democratic organizations, the European Christian Democratic Union and the Christian Democratic International. Although it currently has no members within the European Parliament, it did have members among the first Spanish delegation to the Parliament, who sat in the European People's Party.

Policies

The PNV has traditionally been a conservative nationalist party, advocating much fuller development of the Basque national identity leading eventually to independence. It has been close to the Catholic Church, and conservative on social issues.

In the 1970s there was a clash within the party between its conservative wing (known as the *Sabinianos* after the founder of the party, and led by Anton Ormaza) who sought independence and non-involvement in Madrid politics but who also followed the traditional confessional line, and a more pragmatic group, led by Xabier Arzalluz, who saw the need for the party to participate in Spanish politics and to be more open to the centre–left and to moderate Social Democrats. The party followed the latter course (if only by a narrow majority) and the PNV became more of a catch-all party of the centre–right, non-confessional in character although continuing to emphasize its Christian Democratic roots.

The further schism which led to the creation of *Eusko Alkartasuna* was in large measure a question of personality conflict but policy differences were subsequently emphasized, with the PNV, for example, putting more emphasis on decentralization and the powers of the provinces.

One of the PNV's major challenges is to win back lost support from *Eusko Alkartasuna*,

and to clearly re-establish itself not only as the dominant Basque nationalist party of the centre–right, but as the largest party in all regions of the Basque Country.

The PNV abstained on the new Spanish Constitution of 1977 because the latter failed to give sufficient recognition of the historic rights of the Basque people, but it subsequently accepted the statute of autonomy on the understanding that the historic rights were not being renounced by the party, and would be re-asserted when practicable. The PNV now emphasizes its practical achievements in developing Basque autonomy and institutions. It also calls for devolution as regards administration of justice and for the right to call referenda.

The PNV seeks the re-integration of Navarre within the Basque Country. With full respect for the free will of the people of Navarre, every step should nevertheless be taken to try and achieve this objective. The French Basque Country is considered to be an integral part of the Basque nation, and the PNV calls for the establishment of a statute of autonomy for French Basques on the lines of that conceded in Spain. The PNV signed the anti-terrorist pact of December 1987.

The PNV puts a strong emphasis on federalism and on decentralization. It calls for further development both of Basque national institutions, and of provincial and municipal ones. It strongly defends its law of historic territories in 1983, which gave back a considerable degree of autonomy to the separate Basque provinces with their differing traditions.

The PNV seeks the further enhancement of Basque culture and of the Basque language, and it would like to see certain posts eventually being reserved for Basque speakers. It supports the use of a unified Basque language, but one which does not crush the different Basque dialects.

On economic matters it calls for a greater measure of planning, while retaining the central role for the private sector. There should be increased economic democracy and a stronger social security system.

The PNV advocates a federal and united Europe. It wishes to see the 1989 European Parliament becoming a constituent assembly to draw up a new European Community treaty. Among its objectives would be the creation of a new European Senate of the Nations and Regions, majority voting on all issues within the Council and a more powerful European Commission and Parliament, with the former becoming more of a real executive and the latter more of a real legislature. The Community budget should be increased. There should be a common internal market but also economic cohesion, a European monetary space and co-operation on cultural matters, as well as common European foreign and defence policies.

The Basque Country should be recognized as a nation among other European nations, and there should be direct links between the Basque autonomous community and the EC institutions. The Basque Country should form a separate constituency for European Parliament electoral purposes.

Personalities

The leading personality within the PNV is its president Xabier Arzalluz, a former Jesuit from a humble Carlist family background who has played a dominating role within the party over the last few years. His clash with Carlos Garaicoetxea led to the latter's departure to form a new party.

Another important figure within the party is the current president of the Basque regional government, José Antonio Ardanza, who has been a loyal supporter of Arzalluz.

Eusko Alkartasuna — EA
(Basque Solidarity)

Headquarters	: Sancho ed Sabio 21 (Atzean), San Sebastian (Donostia) 20010
President	: Carlos Garaicoetxea
Newspaper	: *Alkartasuna*
Membership	: 10,000
Founded	: 1986

History

Eusko Alkartasuna (EA) stems from a split within the ranks of the Basque Nationalist Party (PNV).

The party's founder and leading personality, Carlos Garaicoetxea, was a PNV member and the first president of the re-established Basque regional government. He held this post from 1980 to the end of 1984, but from 1982 onwards he came into increasing conflict with Xabier Arzalluz, the president of the party's executive committee. Garaicoetxea felt, as Basque president, that he was made to be too subordinate to the party leadership. He was also opposed to the promulgation of the Law on Historic Territories.

In 1984, the internal conflict came to a head over the expulsion of three PNV deputies in Garaicoetxea's home province of Navarre, who preferred an alliance with local Socialist parties than with the *Coalición Popular*, as the PNV leadership preferred. Garaicoetxea was critical both of the proposed alliance with *Coalición Popular*, and of the lack of internal party democracy within the PNV.

In early 1985 Garaicoetxea was replaced as Basque president by José Antonio Ardanza, a man closer to Arzalluz.

In autumn 1986 Garaicoetxea launched a new party, *Eusko Alkartasuna*. Eleven of the 32 PNV members in the Basque Parliament left the party and joined EA. Early elections for the Basque regional parliament were then convoked by the PNV, at least partly to catch EA before it was properly organized. This strategy was unsuccessful, however, and EA obtained 16 per cent and 14 seats in the regional parliament, an increase of three on those who had defected from the PNV.

In the elections on June 10, 1987, EA enjoyed further success in the municipal elections. Unlike the PNV EA won regional and municipal seats in Navarre, and also a seat in the European Parliament.

In November 1987 EA was the only Basque party apart from *Herri Batasuna* not to sign the Madrid pact against terrorism in the Basque Country. This caused dissatisfaction among some in the party, who have subsequently called for measures of reconciliation with the PNV.

Support

EA's electoral stronghold is the province of Guipúzcoa, where it was the largest party in the 1986 Basque regional elections, with 23 per cent of the vote and seven of the 25 provincial seats. It was the largest party in Guipúzcoa in the 1987 municipal elections. It won over 24 per cent of the vote in San Sebastián (Donostia) and seven councillors. The mayor of the town is now from EA.

EA was only the third largest party in Alava in the 1986 regional elections, with 14.5 per cent of the vote and four of the 25 seats, but it became the largest party in Alava in the 1987 municipal elections. It also won in the town hall of Vitoria, where it gained 32.7 per cent of the vote and 10 councillors.

EA is weaker in the PNV's stronghold of Vizcaya. It was only the fourth largest party in 1986, with 12 per cent and three of the 25 regional members, and it was well behind the PNV in the 1987 municipal elections as well, gaining under 11 per cent in Bilbao. It did well in Guernica, however, where it gained 21.7 per cent of the vote.

EA won also 7 per cent of the votes in the 1987 regional election in Garaicoetxea's home province of Navarre, with three out of the 50 deputies in the regional parliament. It also won two seats on the Pamplona City Council.

Organization

A large percentage of EA's members are former members of the PNV, but the party's constitution differs from that of the PNV in a number of ways. EA gives less power to the municipal and regional tiers and more to the national party, and directly to the membership. The party gives a more public role to its president, who is president of the party rather than of the national executive. The office of secretary-general has been created. Unlike the PNV, there is also to be a regular party congress.

The basic party unit is the local organization, for which a minimum of 10 members is required. Each such organization has a local assembly (*Hiri Batzarra*) and a local executive (*Hiri Batzarde Eragilea*).

At regional level there is a regional assembly (*Lurraldeko Batzarra*) and a regional executive (*Batzarde Eragilea*).

At overall Basque level there is a national congress (*Biltzar Nagusia*), a national assembly (*Batzar Nagusia*) and a national executive (*Euskadiko Batzorde Eragilea*).

The national congress meets every three years. The first such congress in 1987 was attended by 1,000 people, including 20 to 30 representatives of the French Basque Country with speaking and voting rights. It consists of representatives of the local organization chosen in proportion to its membership, members of the national assembly and of the national and regional executives, as well as those who have been elected to public office on behalf of the party. It elects 50 per cent of the members of the national assembly, by a system of open lists and proportional representation; the national executive, again by a system of open lists but using majority voting; and the party's president and secretary-general.

The national assembly meets at least three times a year, and half of its members are chosen by the national congress and half by regional assemblies. Among its tasks are to approve (by a two-thirds majority) any electoral or post-electoral pact that is entered into by the party, and to approve lists of party candidates that are submitted to it by the national executive (for Basque, Spanish and European elections) or by regional executives.

The national executive runs the party on a day-to-day basis and is chaired by the party president.

Members are given a number of direct rights in the party statutes. Fifteen per cent of local members can convoke a local assembly, as can 15 per cent of regional members a regional assembly. Twenty–five per cent of the party's total members can convoke a special national congress (so also can two or more regional assemblies, or two-thirds of the national assembly or of the national executive).

The rules regarding incompatibilities of public and private office are less strictly delineated than in the PNV. The party president Carlos Garaicoetxea (for example) is also a member of the European Parliament.

The party's organ of communication with its members is called *Alkartasuna*.

In the 1987 European elections EA took part in a joint list ("Europe of the Peoples") with two other nationalist parties, *Esquerra Republicana de Catalunya* and the *Partido Nacionalista Gallego*. Carlos Garaicoetxea was the only candidate to be elected. He sits in the Rainbow Group.

Policies

EA is a constitutional nationalist party trying to occupy space between the Christian Democratic nationalists of the PNV and the socialist nationalists of *Euskadiko Ezkerra*. It sees itself as a pragmatic centre–left party, closer to Social Democracy than to Christian Democracy.

Since its split from the PNV it has sought to distinguish itself from the party in a number of ways. It claims to put a greater emphasis on social justice and on combating poverty and inequality. It does not adopt a distinctively Catholic position on moral issues. It also attacks the PNV's rapprochement with the Socialist Party, not because the latter is Socialist but because it is Madrid-dominated. Above all it attacks the PNV's clientelism and alleged dominance over the local government and administrative apparatus of the Basque Country, as well as over the Basque media. It also contests what it sees as the lack of democracy within the PNV with its own greater emphasis on internal party democracy, full participation of its members through proportional representation, protection of minorities, and so on. In contrast to its hostility to the PNV it expresses considerable sympathy with *Euskadiko Ezkerra*.

EA wants self-determination for the whole of the Spanish and French Basque Country in one common entity. It also has the objective of incorporating Navarre within the Basque autonomous region. In the short term it advocates building up Basque consciousness in Navarre, and closer links between the two autonomous regions. As regards the French Basque Country it calls for its separation from the wider department of Pyrénées Atlantiques, and the creation of a separate Basque department.

EA condemns the current restrictive interpretation of the Basque autonomy statute, and seeks further transfers of powers to the Basque region in such fields as social security, official credit, and the administration of justice. The Basque Country should only be policed by the Basque police force.

EA denounces violence and ETA terrorism, and supports the peaceful reintegration of former ETA activists into Basque society. It refused, however, to sign the Madrid anti-terrorist pact of December 1987, on the grounds that it had no practical substance and was imposed by Madrid rather than stemming from within the Basque Country. It opposes anti-terrorist laws as being incompatible with human rights.

EA puts a strong emphasis on the further development of the Basque language. Not only is Basque the official language of the party, but its members are called upon to learn Basque by the party constitution. The party wants Basque public officials to be compelled to learn Basque, and for the administration to be completely Basque-speaking in areas in which Basque is spoken.

The EA's constitution calls for both its president and secretary-general to be Basques. EA also seeks the repeal or modification of those laws (the *Ley de Territorios Históricos* and the *Ley de Bases Reguladoras del Regimen Local*) which it claims fragment the Basque Country and undercut the powers both of the Basque central government and the municipalities to the benefit of the individual Basque provinces and of Madrid.

EA has a non-ideological set of economic policies defending the respective roles of the public and private sectors and opposing sterile arguments over the dividing line between the two.

On moral questions EA is opposed to the death penalty, and to any discrimination against homosexuals. Contraceptives should be made readily available, and the retention of an abortion law is accepted as an unfortunate necessity. Combating drug abuse is a high priority.

EA supports educational pluralism, and does not mind if education is public or private so long as the two sectors are competing on fair terms.

EA is not completely opposed to civil nuclear energy, although it wishes to see its use restricted and carefully controlled. On defence questions, EA proclaims itself to be within the pacifist tradition, and opposed to bloc politics and the division of Europe into two zones. EA also sup-

ports the reduction of military expenditure, and the suppression of compulsory military service.

EA supports the building of a federal Europe, but with the current Europe of the states converted into the Europe of the nations. There should be a special legal statute for nations without a state, and within the European Parliament there should be a Second Chamber providing for regional representation. The European Parliament should be given more powers. Both the Parliament's draft Treaty on European Union and the Single European Act are supported by EA.

Personalities

The party's dominant personality is its president and current European Parliament member, Carlos Garaicoetxea, a lawyer from Navarre who was president of the Basque government when still a member of the PNV. He is a charismatic figure with a strong personal following.

Euskadiko Ezkerra — EE
(Basque Left)

Headquarters	: Jardines 5, 1o, 48005 Bilbao
Secretary-general	: Kepa Aulestia
President	: Juan María Bandrés
Newspaper	: *Hemendik*
Founded	: 1977

History

The origin of *Euskadiko Ezkerra* stems from a split within the radical nationalist movement over whether to fight for first Spanish democratic elections in 1977. One of the political groups within the movement, EIA (*Euskal Iraultzaka Alderdia*— the party of the Basque Revolution), which was close to ETA *Político Militar*, decided to join up with the *Movimiento Comunista de Euskadi* (EMK), to take part in the election under the label *Euskadiko Ezkerra* (Basque left).

The new grouping did well in the elections winning 64,000 votes and gaining a deputy (Francisco Letamendia) and a senator (Juan María Bandres) in the Spanish *Cortes*. *Euskadiko Ezkerra* achieved this result in the face of hostility from the other radical nationalists and from ETA *Militar*, and also managed to win more votes than the Basque section of the national Communist party (PCE — EPK).

Euskadiko Ezkerra failed, however, to survive in its original form. ETA *Político Militar* withdrew its support, as did the *Movimiento*

Comunista de Euskadi. EE's deputy, Leta-mendia, was eventually elected for *Herri Bata-suna* instead. Nevertheless, *Euskadiko Ezkerra* managed to survive under the leadership of Marío Onaindia who like Bandres and other party leaders had been a former member of ETA. *Euskadiko Ezkerra* renounced violence and put its emphasis as much on the class struggle as on achieving self-determination for Euskadi. It gradually evolved from being on the far left of the political spectrum to a more moderate position.

In the 1979 elections EE's vote went up slightly, in spite of the successful participation of the rival radical nationalist grouping, *Herri Batasuna*, and in the first Basque regional elections in 1980, EE won 10 per cent of the vote and six seats in the regional parliament.

In 1981 the party received a further boost when there was a split within the Basque section of the Spanish Communist Party and the majority of its activists left and joined up with EE. Members from a small socialist grouping, ESEI, also joined EE.

In the 1984 regional elections, however, EE actually fell back somewhat in terms of votes. In the 1986 regional elections its vote rose again to 11 per cent and it won nine seats (an advance of three seats). In 1987 EE also won a seat in the regional parliament of Navarre. In the European elections of 1987 it took part in a coalition with other regional Socialist parties entitled *Izquierda de los Pueblos*, which won 1.34 per cent of the vote, but failed to win a seat. EE thus lost the seat (held by Juan María Bandres) that it had held in the nominated delegation to the European Parliament.

Support

Euskadiko Ezkerra has a firm but rather static share of the total Basque vote, fluctuating from around 8 to 11 per cent, but with a tendency towards slow growth. Unlike the other Basque nationalist parties it also has a remarkably even distribution of votes between the three provinces within the Basque Autonomous Region. In the 1986 regional elections, for example, EE won 12 per cent in Guipúzcoa, 10 per cent in Vizcaya and 11 per cent in Alava with three seats in each province. In the 1987 municipal elections its vote was also very even at between 8 per cent and 13 per cent, permitting it to win a few councillors almost everywhere. It has few strongholds anywhere with some of its higher votes at only around 13 per cent.

EE also has a much smaller presence in Navarre, where in 1987 it won its first seat in the regional parliament with 3.4 per cent of the vote.

Organization

EE puts a high emphasis on organizing among the new social movements and in the workplace as well as on a more conventional territorial basis. Each EE group must have a minimum of 10 members. Membership has grown only slowly and by 1985 only 120 groups had been formed.

These groups are run by local committees elected by local assemblies of all members or by delegated representatives when there are more than 300 members in a particular locality.

Above these are zonal and provincial territorial and sectoral groups. Finally at full Basque level there are also national sectoral organizations (socio-economic, education, youth, women) as well as the national territorial units.

The party congress (*Biltzar Nagusia*) meets every two years. Among its main tasks are to elect the party's central committee and to ratify the latter's election of the party president and secretary-general.

In order to deal with policy matters of special importance the central committee can also convene a national conference.

The designation of party candidates for election at Basque or Spanish level is carried out by the central committee. Candidates for election at provincial level are designated within those provinces, but must be ratified by the central committee.

EE has strict rules to try and avoid domination of the party by a narrow clique. At least 20 per cent of the national committee must stand down at each election and those holding national party executive responsibilities cannot normally hold them for more than three periods between ordinary congresses. The party has a newspaper called *Hemendik*.

Before 1987 EE had one member in the European Parliament who sat in the Rainbow Group. EE has also co-operated closely with other regional left-wing parties in Spain.

Policies

Euskadiko Ezkerra is a moderate nationalist party of the left. Although many of its activists were former ETA members it has completely renounced violence as a solution to the Basque Country's problems, and supports a peaceful approach based on democratic pluralism. Moreover, while many of its members are former Communists, it rejects Leninism and believes that decisions cannot be taken by an elite and that there must be full internal democracy. It has good relations with Eurocommunist parties such as the Italian party but sees itself as a left socialist party of an undogmatic nature.

Within the Basque Country EE is an important bridge party, critical of the other Basque parties, but capable of working with any of them. It emphasizes that its nationalism is not exclusive or racial in character, and that social concerns and social justice are as important, if not more so, than nationalism. It rejects the messianic nationalism and commitment to the armed struggle of *Herri Batasuna*, and also the conservative nationalism of the PNV, with its emphasis on provincial and ancient rights rather than on Basque unity and solidarity on social, economic and cultural questions. It is also critical of the Socialists, as having been too restrictive in their interpretation of Basque autonomy, and of having become too conservative on economic policy matters.

EE seeks the fullest application of the existing Statute of Autonomy within the framework of the Spanish state, and without ambiguous references to further "self-determination" and "independence". More progress needs to be made, however, in transferring powers from the central to the autonomous government.

EE calls for political normalization within the Basque Country, with an end to the armed struggle and the re-insertion of former terrorists into the fabric of society without recriminations and reprisals. There must be full respect of human rights, and illiberal anti-terrorist laws should be abandoned. Negotiations between ETA and the government should be initiated on such issues as the return of exiles and the release of political prisoners, but not on the full range of ETA's political demands, which would constitute a surrender to armed blackmail. EE supported the anti-terrorist pact of December 1987.

EE would ideally like to see Navarre integrated into the Basque Autonomous Region, but recognizes the very great differences between Navarre and the three existing Basque provinces. It thus seeks the development of closer relations between the two regions, leading, if possible, to a referendum on integration within Navarre.

EE calls for co-operation between all social groups in order for the Basque Country to emerge from its current economic crisis. The market economy will not achieve this on its own, and the public sector and public planning must play a major role. There will have to be far-reaching industrial reconversion. The highest priority must be given to fighting unemployment. There should be greater economic and industrial democracy and a shorter working week. The social security system should be strengthened, and there should be higher unemployment cover.

EE emphasizes the need to work closely with trade unions and with the new social movements (such as women, youth and environmental groups), but believes that these should keep their autonomy, and not be monopolized by any one political party.

EE is strongly influenced by pacifism. It opposed Spanish participation in NATO in the recent referendum, and is opposed to the stationing of missiles in Europe.

On other foreign policy issues it emphasizes human rights, development aid and the right to self-determination of all peoples. Particular concerns have been the rights of the Saharaoui people, the situation in South Africa and Central America, as well as in Eastern Europe.

EE supported entry into the European Community.

Personalities

The leading figures within *Euskadiko Ezkerra* are its founder, Marío Onaindia (who had been sentenced to death at the Burgos trial of Basque nationalists during the Franco regime), its president Juan María Bandres (who was its member of the European Parliament from 1986 to 1987, and its candidate for Basque president in 1987) and Kepa Aulestia a former member of ETA who renounced the armed struggle, and who is the party's secretary-general).

Herri Batasuna — HB
(Popular Unity)

Headquarters	: Ribera 15–1, Guecho, Vizcaya
Founded	: April 28, 1978

History

Herri Batasuna is a radical Basque nationalist party, or more accurately a political movement consisting of a number of nationalist political groupings in broad support of ETA's armed struggle to liberate the Basque Country (Euskadi).

ETA (*Euskadi ta Askatasuna*) was founded in the late 1950s but it only became an active terrorist movement in the late 1960s. Its most spectacular achievement was the assassination of the Spanish Prime Minister, Admiral Carrero Blanco, in 1973. By the late 1970s ETA was the largest terrorist movement in Europe.

Francoist repression of the Basque Country led to ETA gaining considerable support within the region. After the death of Franco the slowness of the new regime to grant an amnesty to Basque prisoners and to approve a new statute of autonomy, as well as continuing Spanish police brutality in the region, permitted ETA to retain support during the transition to democracy. Meanwhile, a much wider group of Basques were hostile to the new Spanish Constitution. Over half of them abstained in the constitutional referendum, and of those who voted, a quarter voted no. Most then accepted the result, but a considerable number wished to have nothing to do with the new state institutions.

Nevertheless, with the development of a democratic Spain, ETA entered a new and more difficult phase, in which its support base among the Basque people was to become more uncertain.

ETA itself had been subject to internal divisions, and to formal splits almost from its inception, the main issues in question being over whether to continue the violent nationalist struggle or to try to achieve results by more peaceful means, and whether to concentrate on nationalism alone (albeit with a Marxist–Leninist label) or to aim for a wider alliance of the oppressed working class.

In 1966, the first major split occurred when the advocates of a wider class struggle left ETA to form *ETA Berri* (Young ETA) and ultimately the *Movimiento Comunista de Euskadi*. In 1970, ETA further split into the hard-line nationalist ETA Fifth Assembly and the left-wing ETA Sixth Assembly, the latter following a road which led to the *Liga Comunista Revolucionaria* and eventually to the Basque Communist Party, the EPK.

In 1974, ETA began to divide into ETA *Militar*, concentrating entirely on military action and ETA *Político–Militar*, combining both direct action and political actions. A small political group developed that was close to ETA *Militar*, LAIA (*Langile Abertzale Iraultzailen Alderdia* — Patriotic Workers' Revolutionary Party) and another close to ETA *Politica–Militar*, EIA (*Euskal Iraultzako Alderdia* – the Party of the Basque Revolution).

In October 1975 LAIA, EIA and other small revolutionary nationalist groups set up an umbrella co-ordinating group, the KAS (*Koordinadora Abertzale Socialista*), which subsequently put forward a set of nationalist policy demands which became known as the *Alternativa KAS*, and which is still a central point of reference for revolutionary nationalists.

In 1977 the issue as to whether to participate in the first Spanish democratic elections led to sharp divisions within revolutionary nationalism. ETA–*Militar* and LAIA were against participation, while EIA and a large part of ETA

Político–Militar were in favour. EIA joined forces with the *Movimiento Comunista* (the 1966 ETA dissidents) and fought the elections under the label *Euskadiko Ezkerra* (Basque left — see separate entry). The latter then moved into the realm of non-violent politics, and separated themselves from ETA *Político–Militar* as well as ETA–*Militar*.

Dissidents within EIA joined up with other nationalists to form yet another revolutionary group hostile to democracy, HASI (*Herriko Alderdi Sozialisti Iraultzailen* — People's Revolutionary Socialist Party), which is now the most powerful component of *Herri Batasuna*.

HASI joined the loose KAS coalition, which convened a meeting at Alsasua in 1977. This eventually led to the creation of the new movement, *Herri Batasuna* on April 28, 1978, incorporating HASI, LAIA and other small groups as well as a number of Basque political personalities who lent it extra credibility. Perhaps the most well-known of these was Telesforo Monzón, a former member of PNV and of the Basque government in exile.

Herri Batasuna supported the *Alternativa KAS* as the basis of its policy demands, and called for the unification of the French and Spanish Basques within an independent Basque state.

It rejected the authority of the Spanish state and its political institutions. It took part in the 1979 Spanish elections, and performed extremely well, winning several seats including that of Monzón in Guipúzcoa. It refused, however, to take up its seats in the Spanish Parliament.

In the referendum of October 1979 on the new Basque autonomy statute, *Herri Batasuna* campaigned for abstention. In the first elections to the Basque regional parliament in March 1980, it took part and became the second largest party with 17 per cent of the vote and 11 of the 60 seats, but again did not take up its seats in the regional parliament.

Over the years 1981 to 1982 ETA *Político–Militar* split again, and a considerable number gave up violence. The armed struggle remained in the hands of ETA–*Militar*.

In 1984 the Spanish High Court overturned an earlier decision by the government that *Herri Batasuna* could not be permitted to operate as a political party because of its links with ETA.

In the 1984 regional elections, *Herri Batasuna* lost votes if not seats, but in the 1986 regional elections it gained both votes and seats, with 17.5 per cent of the vote and 13 seats in the regional parliament.

It did not sign the Madrid pact against terrorism in November 1987.

Herri Batasuna also has one seat in the European Parliament.

Support

In the 1986 Basque regional elections, *Herri Batasuna* had the third highest number of votes (17.5 per cent) and the fourth-highest number of seats (13). It has consistently polled between 14.5 per cent and 17.5 per cent of the total vote. In the 1987 European Parliament elections, in which the whole of Spain was one electoral constituency, *Herri Batasuna* gained 1.88 per cent of the vote (compared to 1.18 per cent for the mainstream PNV), showing that it won considerable protest votes outside the Basque Country proper. Its vote was 50 per cent higher than in the simultaneous municipal elections where it only put up candidates in the Basque Country and Navarre, and 50 per cent higher than its vote in the 1986 national elections. It has been estimated that it may have won 45 per cent of its vote outside the Basque Country.

Herri Batasuna's strongest electoral province is Guipúzcoa where it won 22 per cent of the vote in the 1986 regional elections and was almost the largest party throughout the province. In certain towns in Guipúzcoa it is clearly the largest party, such as in Pasajes and Hernani (35.26 per cent in the 1986 national elections) in the immediate hinterland of San Sebastian.

Herri Batasuna is also strong in some parts of Vizcaya, where it won 16 per cent in the 1986 regional elections, and was the third-largest party. Among its strongholds are the town of Bermeo (32 per cent in the 1986 national elections) and the historic Basque town of Guernica (26 per cent in the 1986 national elections, and 1987 local elections). It is weaker in Bilbao (13 per cent in the 1986 national elections).

Alava is its weakest Basque province, and it only won 13 per cent of the vote in the 1986 regional elections, although even here it has pockets of strength such as Salvatierra.

A final feature of the *Herri Batasuna* vote is its strength in Navarre, where it is by far the largest of the Basque parties. In the 1987 regional elections, it was the third largest party in Navarre with 13.4 per cent and seven seats. In Navarre's capital city of Pamplona, the party won 17 per cent in the 1986 national elections and in the 1987 municipal elections.

Organization

Herri Batasuna is not a political party in the normal organizational sense, but rather a coalition of political groups, organizations and independents. The most powerful of the groups within the party is HASI (*Herriko*

Alderdi Sozialisti Iraultzailen — The People's Revolutionary Socialist Party), which is also particularly close to ETA. A second political group within *Herri Batasuna* is the much smaller ANV (Basque National Action).

Herri Batasuna has a national bureau (*Mesa Nacional*) of 32 members, including representatives of the political groups, and the provincial organizations. Popular assemblies are frequently convoked.

Herri Batasuna has a youth organization, *Jarrai*. The organ of radical Basque nationalism is the newspaper, *Egin*, with a circulation of 47,000. There is also an associated trade union, LAB (*Langile Abertzale Batzordeak*).

Herri Batasuna has tried to establish contacts with other independence movements within Spain, but has not succeeded in forging a formal coalition with them. It has good contacts with Sinn Féin in Ireland.

It stood on its own in the 1987 European Parliament elections, and its elected member sits as an independent.

Policies

Herri Batasuna represents the most radical and uncompromising strand of the Basque nationalist tradition, and the only one which does not explicitly renounce violence. It has close but publicly undefined links with the terrorist organization ETA, which has a particular hold on the leadership of HASI. The party also proclaims itself a movement of the left, representing the interests of the Basque working class as well as nationalism.

Herri Batasuna has never accepted Spanish state institutions, and considers the Basque autonomy statute to be completely insufficient. From 1980, it boycotted the Basque parliament although its representative "Yoldi" appeared in the parliament in 1987. It has accepted participation, however, in municipal councils, and its elected members in Navarre occasionally attend the Navarre regional parliament.

Its main set of policy demands are still those contained in the so-called *Alternativa KAS*, improved living conditions for Basques, amnesty for all Basque nationalist prisoners, the withdrawal from the Basque Country of the state security forces and the integration of Navarre within the Basque Country. It has sought direct political negotiations on these demands, in which the Spanish government and ETA, the Socialist Party and *Herri Batasuna* would all take part.

Recently, there have been signs of uncertainty, and of divisions between hard-liners and "moderates" over the degree to which the *Alternativa KAS* is negotiable; over the terms of a possible ceasefire; over the attitude to adopt towards former ETA members who had renounced violence and were "reinserted" into society (there was particular controversy over the killing of one such former ETA member, María Dolores Gonzales Catarain, "Yoyes") and over the justification of certain acts of violence (the Hipercor explosion in Barcelona was the subject of particular criticism from some leading figures in the party).

Attempts at direct negotiations between ETA and the Spanish government (the latest were in Algiers in February 1988) have so far proved unsuccessful. As a result of the anti-terrorist pact of late 1987, and the anti-violence accord among other Basque political parties in early 1988 *Herri Batasuna* is in a more isolated position within the Basque political spectrum.

Personalities

Herri Batasuna contains a mix of hard-liners and "moderates", the latter including a group known as the *grupo de los abogados* (the group of lawyers). Among the party moderates are Txema Montero, the *Herri Batasuna* Member of the European Parliament and Inaki Esnaola and Jon Idigoras, party deputies for Guipúzcoa and Vizcaya respectively. Txomin Ziloaga, the other deputy for Vizcaya, was recently deposed as secretary-general of HASI.

Among the hard-liners is the new secretary-general of HASI, Ignacio Ruiz de Pinedo, a young sociologist.

The secretary-general of the ANV group within *Herri Batasuna* is Kepa Bereziartua. The secretary-general of the LAB Trade Union is Joselu Cereceda.

Herri Batasuna's other national parliamentarians are Itziar Aizpurua, deputy for Guipúzcoa, Inaki Aldecoa, deputy for Navarre and José Luis Alvarez Esperantza, its only senator, from Guipúzcoa.

Catalonia

The present autonomous region of Catalonia (Catalunya) has over six million inhabitants and consists of the four provinces of Barcelona, Tarragona, Gerona (Girona in Catalan), Lérida (Lleida). It has its own language, which, unlike Basque, is spoken by the majority of Catalans. The present-day Catalonia is part of a wider region sharing a similar Catalan historical, cultural and linguistic tradition, including part of Valencia, the Balearic Islands, Andorra (where

Catalan is the official language) and the French region of Roussillon (Rossello) and even the City of Alghero (El Alguer) in Sardinia. Due to its early and continued industrialization, Catalonia has had successive waves of migration from other parts of Spain and notably from Murcia and Andalusia. Many of these are still not Catalan-speaking, although many of the earlier arrivals are now assimilated.

Political institutions

Catalonia has its own parliament and government which have strong symbolic value as the embodiment of Catalan identity.

Elections to the re-established Catalan parliament have taken place in 1980, 1984 and 1988 (See table).

The Catalan parliament is unicameral. The parliamentary term is four years, but with the possibility of earlier dissolution. There are 135 members of the parliament, chosen in proportion to the number of inhabitants of the four provinces of Barcelona (85 seats), Tarragona (18 seats), Gerona (17 seats) and Lérida (15 seats).

The government of Catalonia is called the *Generalitat*. The president of the *Generalitat* is drawn from the Catalan parliament.

The most important local units in Catalonia are its 38 historic districts or *comarcas* to which new powers were given in 1988. Catalan parties would like to see the four provinces abolished as they are considered to be superimposed Spanish political bodies. Their own provincial organizations tend to be called inter-comarcal co-ordinating committees in consequence.

Brief Catalan political history

— Catalan cultural renaissance (1850s and 1860s).
— *Bases de Manresa* (promulgation of principles for Catalan self-government) 1892.
— Emergence of *Lliga Regionalista*, conservative-dominated movement for Catalan autonomy (leaders Enrique Prat de la Riba and Francisco Cambo).
— Wider alliance of Catalan political parties (*Solidaritat Catalana*) 1906.
— Establishment of *Mancomunidad* (four Catalan provinces co-ordinating some of their activities within one Catalan unit. First president: Prat de la Riba) 1914.

— *Estat Catala* founded (separatist party under the leadership of Francesc Macía): 1922.

— Dissolution of *Mancomunidad* by Primo de Rivera: 1925.

— Proclamation of Catalan republic within a federation of Spanish republics: April 14, 1931.

— Victory of left-wing Catalan nationalists (*Esquerra Republicana*, led by Francesc Macía and Luis Companys) June 28, 1931.

— Approval of Statute of Nuria (creating new Catalan political institutions) by 75 per cent of Catalan electorate: Aug. 2, 1931.

— More limited statute granted to Catalans by Spanish Republican government: 1932.

— Death of Francesc Macía (first President of Catalan government or *Generalitat*) and replacement by Luis Companys: 1933.

— Proclamation by Companys of independent Catalan state within Spanish federal republic, entire Catalan government arrested and statute suspended: October 1934.

— Left wins elections (*Front Popular, Front d'Esquerres*) and statute of autonomy restored. Companys as president of Catalan government: February 1936. Civil War (1936–39).

— 1938 last meeting of Catalan parliament.

— Companys executed 1940.

— Josep Irla, third president of *Generalitat*, 1940–54 (in exile).

— Josep Tarradellas, fourth president of *Generalitat*, 1955–77 (in exile).

— *Generalitat* restored 1977.

— Josep Tarradellas, provisional president of restored *Generalitat*, 1977–80.

— Statute of Catalan autonomy (statute of Sau) 1978.

— First Catalan parliament elections 1980.

— Jordi Pujol, fifth president of *Generalitat*, 1980–present.

— Second Catalan parliament elections, 1984 (overall majority for *Convergència i Unió*).

— Third Catalan parliament elections, 1988 (*Convergència i Unió* wins new mandate).

Main features of Catalan political system

Of the parties with seats in the Catalan parliament, *Convergència i Unió* and *Esquerra Republicana* only exist in Catalonia. In addition the PSUC (Communists) and PSC (Socialists) are linked to their sister Spanish parties, but

have their own identities and traditions. The local affiliates of the CDS and the *Partido Popular* are of much more recent creation, and enjoy much closer links to their present parties, and are not included in this sub-section.

The two dominant political forces in Catalonia are the centre–right *Convergència i Unió* and the centre–left Socialists. The former is much the strongest party in rural Catalonia, although it is well implanted in the cities as well. The Socialists have greatest strength in the cities, and especially in the individual towns and suburbs on the edge of Barcelona. The non-Catalan immigrant vote is so strong in some of these areas that in 1980 the Andalusian Socialist Party managed to win two seats in the regional parliament. CiU's vote is much stronger in the regional elections than in the national elections.

Of the other parties, the Communists and *Esquerra Republicana* are two parties with great traditions which have become relatively minor parties in electoral terms since the re-establishment of democracy.

The key issue in Catalan politics is undoubtedly the issue of self-determination, and relations with the central government in Madrid. The Catalan parties refer to themselves as national and not regional parties, and are agreed that the present autonomous regions are not working well. They are divided, however, (as much within as between themselves) as to how the situation should be changed, whether there should be full independence within a federal Europe, a federal Spain on West German lines, or something different. Unlike in the Basque Country, however, there is no violent separatist movement of any significance.

Convergència i Unió — CiU
(Convergence and Union)

History

Convergència i Unió is a coalition between two separate parties, *Convergència Democràtica de Catalunya* (CDC — see below) and the much smaller *Unió Democràtica de Catalunya* (see below). In its present form the coalition dates from September 1978.

In its first electoral test under the CiU label in the 1979 national elections the coalition obtained 16.1 per cent of the Catalan vote, eight seats in the Congress of Deputies, and one seat in the Senate. In the 1979 municipal elections it polled 18.9 per cent. Its real breakthrough, however, came in the 1980 Catalan regional elections when it won 27.7 per cent of the vote, and 43 seats in the Catalan parliament.

Jordi Pujol, CDC's leader, was then able to form a government in a coalition between CiU, *Esquerra Republicana de Catalunya* (see separate entry) and the *Centristes de Catalunya* (no longer an active party).

In the 1982 national elections CiU won 22.2 per cent of the Catalan vote and 12 seats in the Congress of Deputies.

In the 1984 regional elections CiU won 46.6 per cent of the vote, and an absolute majority in the Catalan parliament. Pujol would have been able to form his second regional government on his own, but decided to maintain a coalition with *Esquerra Republicana*. This coalition subsequently broke down, and CiU then ruled Catalonia on its own.

In the 1986 national elections CiU obtained 31.7 per cent of the Catalan vote, with 18 members of the Congress of Deputies and eight members of the Senate. In the 1987 European elections, where the whole of Spain was one constituency, CiU polled 4.4 per cent of the vote, and won three seats in the European Parliament. In the 1987 local elections the coalition won 32 per cent of the Catalan vote, obtaining less votes than the Socialists, but far more councillors (4,378 compared to 1,707) and mayors (594 to 142) because of its dominance in rural areas. In Barcelona it won over 35 per cent of the city-wide vote, but failed to wrest control from the Socialists.

In the 1988 regional elections CiU's vote dropped slightly to 46.1 per cent, but it still won an overall majority in the Catalan parliament with 70 out of the 135 seats; Pujol was then able to form a new CiU majority administration.

Support

Convergència i Unió has steadily increased its electoral strength both in elections for the Spanish parliament, where it is the second force in Catalonia behind the Catalan socialists (PSC) and for the Catalan regional parliament, where it is by far the largest political grouping.

It is above all supported by the powerful Catalan middle classes, but it has some support in all social groups, and is competitive everywhere in Catalonia. It is strongest in the small towns and countryside of rural Catalonia, where it has won over 60 per cent of the vote in the last two regional elections in many communities (e.g. Cervera 65 per cent in 1988). In the predominantly rural provinces of Gerona and Lérida it obtained 56.4 per cent and 53.8 per cent respectively in the 1988 regional elections, and 45.5 per cent and 40.4 per cent in the 1986 national elections. CiU's dominance outside Catalonia's industrial regions is shown by the fact that in the 38 *comarcal* (district) councils established in 1988 CiU would have had an absolute majority on 30 of them and a relative majority in four others on the basis of the 1987 local election results.

CiU is relatively less strong in the province of Tarragona (47.6 per cent in the 1988 regional elections) and weakest of all in the province of

---

Catalan regional elections 1980–present (percentages and seats in Regional Parliament)

	1980	1984	1988
Convergencia i Unió (CiU)	27.7%	46.6%	46.1%
(Convergence and Union)	(43)	(72)	(70)
Esquerra Republicana de Catalunya (ERC)	8.9%	4.4%	4.2%
(Republican Left of Catalonia)	(14)	(5)	(6)
Partit dels Socialistes de Catalunya (PSC-PSOE)	22.3%	30.0%	29.5%
(Party of Socialists of Catalonia)	(33)	(41)	(42)
Partit Socialista Unificat de Catalunya (PSUC)	18.7%	5.6%	see IC
(Unified Socialist Party of Catalonia)	(25)	(6)	
Iniciativa per Catalunya (IC)	—	—	7.6%
(Initiative for Catalonia)			(8)
Alianza Popular	—	7.7%	5.4%
(Popular Alliance)		(11)	(6)
Centristas de Catalunya—Unió de Centro Democràtico (CC-UCD)	10.6%	—	—
(Centrists of Catalonia/Union of the Democratic Centre)	(18)		
Centro Democràtico y Social (CDS)	—	—	3.8%
(Democratic and Social Centre)			(3)
Partido Socialista de Andalusia (PSA)	2.6%	—	—
(Andalusian Socialist Party)	(2)		
Others	8.1%	4.9%	3.4%
	(0)	(0)	(0)

Barcelona (43.8 per cent in the 1988 regional elections, 29.6 per cent in the 1986 national elections). CiU is quite strong in the city of Barcelona (48.3 per cent in the 1988 regional elections, with a high of 66 per cent in the district of Sarria–Sant Gervasi and a low of 30.6 per cent in Nou Barris, the only one of the city's 10 districts where it was not the largest grouping), but is much weaker in the so-called "red belt" in the outlying suburbs of Barcelona and in the nearby industrial towns. In the 1986 national elections it got under 10 per cent in a few of these communities (e.g. Santa Coloma de Gramenet, 9 per cent).

Organization

The coalition of *Convergència i Unió* functions as rather more than an electoral alliance, and, although they retain separate identities, the two parties work together at many levels. They form a combined political group in the Catalan regional parliament, and work as a coalition in the Catalan regional government, the *Generalitat*. In the Spanish parliament they form the joint group *Minoría Catalana*, the fourth-largest group in the Chamber of Deputies with 18 seats and the third-largest in the Senate with eight elected seats. Only internationally do they have separate affiliations. In the European Parliament the two parties, while putting up a common list and programme for the elections, sit in separate political groups, CDC with the Liberals and Unió with the European People's Party.

The two parties present common programmes for all elections, whose main features are described below. (The areas where *Unió* has distinctive policies, such as on family policy questions, are pointed out in the separate section on *Unió*).

As a general rule 75 per cent of the coalition's candidates come from *Convergència* and 25 per cent from *Unió*. In the European Parliament elections in 1987, 37 of the 60 candidates were from *Convergència*, 13 from *Unió* and 10 were independents. The order of candidates is decided by a modified D'Hondt system. In the European Parliament elections the second, seventh and 12th candidates, etc., were from *Unió*.

Co-ordination between the two parties on policy matters is ensured by a liaison committee.

Policies

The coalition between CDC and *Unió* enables them to present themselves as a broad-based nationalist grouping of the centre and right, with Conservative, Liberal, Christian Democratic and even moderate Social Democratic elements in their midst. Their image is heavily influenced by the dominant personality of Jordi Pujol, the regional president. Under his leadership CiU has sought to identify itself as the voice of responsible Catalan nationalism, asserting a distinct Catalan national identity through practical measures and through competent management of regional government, and without strident calls for revolutionary change.

Outside Catalonia CiU made one ambitious attempt to extend its influence, by lending support to the 1986 national campaign of the *Partido Reformista Democrático* (PRD). This was a well-financed bid to establish a Liberal–Conservative party throughout the whole of Spain, and its top candidate was Miguel Roca Junyent. PRD ended up winning no seats. CiU has since concentrated on consolidating its own position as the single most powerful regional political grouping within the Spanish state.

CiU's leaders have not made explicit calls for Catalan independence. They accept the framework of the existing Catalan statute of autonomy, as long as it is not restrictively interpreted by the central government in Madrid. Only then will they ask for its revision. They call for changes in the existing financial relations between the central and Catalan government, so that the latter can have much greater financial autonomy. They also seek further transfer of competences to the region.

CiU has also promoted reform of the administrative structure within Catalonia. They have helped to re-activate the historic *comarcas* or districts as a new tier of local government, and are now seeking to fully implement this change, and to decentralize administration where possible.

On the other hand, they would like to create one single Catalan province instead of the existing four. They also call for the reform of the existing Spanish Senate in order to turn it into a proper Chamber for representation of Spanish regions and nationalities.

CiU also seeks to strengthen the identity of the Catalan people in the cultural and linguistic fields, and wants Catalan to be used as a language of the European Community institutions.

CiU's economic policy is a pragmatic one. It emphasizes the central role of the private sector, but recognizes that the public sector must also play an important role in stimulating investment and in ensuring adequate social security. A high priority for CiU is the modernization of Catalan infrastructure, and it seeks to develop rapid rail and other links to the rest of the European Community. CiU has attacked centralizing tendencies on the part of the Socialist government, and called for liberalization of the Spanish economy and for greater flexibility in the labour market.

CiU has also called for severe restraint in the growth of Spanish public expenditure. It has emphasized the need to ensure security in civil nuclear power stations.

CiU is a strong supporter of further European integration. It was in favour of the Single European Act and wants the European Parliament to become a real legislature. It supports measures to strengthen European identity, such as a European flag, and European passport. A united Europe, however, should be a Europe of the peoples and not just of the existing nation states. CiU puts a strong emphasis on promoting co-operation between individual regions in different member states, and in developing a European Council of the Regions. Achievement of the European internal market by 1992 is strongly supported. The Common Agricultural Policy should also be reformed, to make it more market-oriented but also more geared to Mediterranean as well as temperate products. In the context of the European Parliament elections, CiU wants Catalonia to be a separate electoral constituency, and not just to be part of one Spanish national constituency.

CiU supports active Spanish participation in all aspects of the Atlantic Alliance, but Spain must have a non-nuclear status. There should be a stronger European voice within the Atlantic Alliance, and CiU supports the creation of a European Defence Union.

Convergència Democràtica de Catalunya — CDC
(Democratic Convergence of Catalonia)

Headquarters	: València 231, 08007 Barcelona (tel: 2152382)
Secretary-general	: Jordi Pujol i Soley
President	: Ramon Trias i Fargas
Spokesman in Spanish Congress of Deputies	: Miguel Roca i Junyent
Youth group	: Joventut Nacionalista de Catalunya
Newspaper	: Oja Informativa
Membership	: 24,000 (July 1987)
Founded	: 1974

History

Convergència Democràtica de Catalunya (CDC) is the largest component within the coalition of Convergència i Unió. CDC was originally founded in November 1974 not as a proper party but as a federation of different groups and parties including Unió Democràtica, a trade union group called Accio Obrera and groups centred around the personalities of Jordi Pujol and Miguel Roca. In 1975 Pujol's supporters formed a group within the federation entitled Grup d'Accio al Servei de Catalunya (GASC).

On Feb. 18, 1976, CDC was set up as a full political party in its own right, and no longer as a mere federation. Unió, with its longer and distinct Christian Democratic tradition, decided not to join. In the first Spanish national election in 1977 CDC (fighting under the label PDC — Democratic Pact for Catalonia) obtained 16.8 per cent of the Catalan vote, and 11 seats in the Congress of Deputies. In May 1978 another political grouping, Esquerra Democràtica de Catalunya, which had been part of the PDC coalition, and whose most prominent personality was Ramon Trias i Fargas, linked up with Convergència. In September 1978 agreement was reached with Unió so that the two parties would form joint lists in subsequent elections under the label Convergència i Unió.

Support (See section on CiU)

Organization

CDC has around 24,000 members. Its basic territorial unit is the local branch or equip territorial of which there are around 900 around Catalonia. Above these are the district groups (agrupacions), generally organized within each comarca of Catalonia, although there is a different structure within the city of Barcelona. There are five federations, in each of the four electoral areas of Catalonia and in the city of Barcelona. At Catalan level there is a national congress, held at least every two years, and which elects the party's top office holders, including the president, secretary-general and 40 members of the party's national council.

The national council, which meets every three months has 240 members in all. Above this is a smaller national executive committee of 21–25 members which meets at least every 15 days. There is also a smaller permanent secretariat. CDC has a substantial number of full-time workers.

CDC has established a number of sectoral committees to bring together expertise in a number of specialist areas.

The party's youth movement is called Joventut Nacionalista de Catalunya, and is an independent organization with around 4,000 members. It has 10 representatives on the party's national council. Within the movement there is considerable support for Catalan independence.

CDC's news bulletin is called *Oja Informativa* and appears on a monthly basis. CDC's basic membership dues are 350 pesetas monthly, but retired people do not have to pay. The party's elected office holders have to contribute a percentage of their wages to the party.

CDC's two members in the European Parliament sit in the Liberal and Democratic Reformist Group. CDC is also linked with the Liberal International and with ELDR.

Policies

CDC is a catch-all nationalist party of the centre–right. Its detailed policies are described in the section on CiU.

Personalities

The dominant figure within CDC and indeed Catalan politics, is Jordi Pujol, president of the Catalan regional government since 1980. He was imprisoned under the Franco regime and founded CDC in 1974. In his 1984–88 term of office he got into political difficulties over financial problems concerning the Banca Catalana, a bank with which Pujol had previously been closely involved. He was, however, completely cleared and successfully won re-election in 1988. He is a populist politician with a very high public profile. He has been the party's secretary-general, but will now assume the party presidency.

The other most prominent personality within CDC is Miguel Roca Junyent, who has been the CiU spokesman in the Congress of Deputies in Madrid, and led the unsuccessful PRD national campaign in the 1986 elections. Miguel Roca is a lawyer by training and has a more reserved and intellectual style than Pujol. He is now taking over as secretary-general.

The party's president was Ramon Trias i Fargas, who has also been party spokesman in the Spanish Senate. Carles Gasoliba was the head of the CiU list for the 1987 European elections. Josep Maria Cullell was its narrowly defeated candidate to become mayor of Barcelona in 1987.

Unió Democràtica de Catalunya
(Democratic Union of Catalonia)

Headquarters	: València 246
	Pral Barcelona
	(tel: 215 55 66)
President of national council	: Miguel Coll i Alentorn
President of executive council	: Josep Antoni Duran i Lleida
Youth group	: *Unió de Joves*
Women's group	: *Unió de Dones*
Newspaper	: *La Veu d'Unió*
Membership	: 5,500
Founded	: 1931

History

Unió was founded in November 1931 as a Catalan nationalist party of Christian Democratic inspiration. During the Second Republic it was only a small party, but had one member in the constituent assembly of the Catalan parliament, and another in the subsequently elected Catalan parliament. *Unió* had a strong Christian Social component. While it opposed the left–wing majority in the Catalan parliament, and its member was elected in an alliance with the right-of-centre *Lliga*, it supported land reform and opposed the division of Catalonia into competing blocks. It remained loyal to Catalan political institutions up to, and through the Civil War. During this early period *Unió* never had more than one deputy or 2,500 members. In October 1934 it helped to sponsor a trade union of Catalan Christian workers.

During the 36 years of the Franco era *Unió* maintained itself clandestinely, and took part in the co-ordinated opposition to Franco. In 1941 one of its prominent early leaders, Carrasco i Formiguera, was shot by the regime. *Unió* also strengthened its links with Christian Democratic parties elsewhere in Europe.

In 1974 Unió took part in the federation of *Convergència*, but, because of its different historical tradition, did not join the group when it became a single party in 1976. In 1977 *Unió* contested the Spanish general elections, and obtained one seat in the *Cortes*. On Sept 19, 1978 it entered into the electoral pact with *Convergència* that has continued until the present day under the label *Convergència i Unió* (see above).

In the first Catalan parliament elections in 1980 *Unió* won eight of the 43 seats gained by the coalition. In the subsequent Pujol government *Unió* had three ministries, and it also gained the first vice-presidency of the parliament.

In the 1982 national elections *Unió* won three seats in the Congress of Deputies and one senator, and in 1984 *Unió* won 16 of the 72 seats of the coalition in the second Catalan parliamentary elections. It retained three ministers in the new Pujol administration, and Miguel Coll i Alentorn became president of the Catalan parliament.

In the 1986 national elections *Unió* doubled its number of seats in the Congress to six and in the Senate to two. It also had one member in the first nominated Spanish delegation to the European Parliament. In 1987 *Unió* elected a considerable number of councillors (400) in Catalan municipalities, and 50 mayors, as well as one member of the European Parliament.

Support

(See section on *Convergència i Unió*)

Organization

The basic territorial unit of the party is the local delegation, which must have a minimum of 10 members. Above this are comarcal councils and inter-comarcal councils, each with their executive committees. There are six inter-comarcal councils, one for the city of Barcelona, one for the rest of Barcelona province, one each for the provinces of Gerona and Lérida, and two in the province of Tarragona. At Catalan level there is a national congress, which used to meet annually but now meets every two years, and which can consist of all party members or else delegates on the ratio of one for every 10 members. The national council includes the party's elected representatives, as well as delegates from the local and comarcal groups. It meets at least every two months, and elects its own president, who is also that of the whole party. The national council also sets up the party's policy committees, of which there are currently 19.

The national executive committee consists of 15 members elected by the national congress, and with its own president and vice-president. Members of the national executive committee cannot at the same time be members of the bureau of the national council.

The party's candidates are chosen within the appropriate territorial unit (e.g. by inter-comarcal assemblies for national elections). Their decisions can be opposed by the national executive committee, in which case the national council has the final word.

Unió has both a youth organization, the *Unió de Joves* and a women's organization, the *Unió de Dones*. It also has an associated trade union, *Unió de Treballadors*, which is a member of the European Union of Christian Democratic Workers. The party newspaper is called *La Veu d'Unió*.

Unió is a member both of the European Union of Christian Democratic parties and of the European People's Party, with whom its one member sits in the European Parliament.

Policy

Unió fights elections on joint programmes with *Convergència*. Nevertheless its Christian Social tradition ensures that it puts more emphasis than *Convergència* on worker participation and co-determination in industry, and also on family policy. In particular, it is opposed to the depenalization of abortion. It is also opposed to divorce, but accepts the inevitability of some form of divorce law as long as the rights of spouses and children are firmly safeguarded.

Personalities

The president of the national council is Miguel Coll i Alentorn who is now in his 80s, and has been a member of *Unió* since the 1930s. He is also the president of the Catalan parliament, and is a former vice-president of the Catalan government during the Pujol administration.

The president of the national executive committee is Josep Antoni Duran i Lleida, born in 1952, who has been a member of the Spanish Congress of Deputies for the province of Lérida since 1982, and who also represented *Unió* in the European Parliament in the nominated Spanish delegation.

The party's present representative in the European Parliament is Concepcio Ferrer. She is a former vice-president of the Catalan parliament (from 1980 to 1984).

Esquerra Republicana de Catalunya — ERC
(Republican Left of Catalonia)

Headquarters	: c/o Villaroel 45, 08011 Barcelona (tel: 323 44 13)
Secretary-general	: Joan Hortalà
Youth group	: *Joventuts d'Esquerra Republicana*
Newspapers	: *La Humanitat; La Coctelera*
Membership	: 5,000

History

Esquerra Republicana de Catalunya is a Catalan nationalist party, first founded in 1931 in a merger between a number of pre-existing Republican groups. The *Esquerra* contained many different elements from landless peasants in the country to working-class and middle-class supporters in Barcelona and included left–wing social reformers and more conservative politicians.

It became the largest political party in Catalonia in the election of June 1931, displacing the right–wing Catalanist parties from their dominant position.

The Esquerra emphasized support for the national identity of Catalonia as part of a federation of Iberian peoples, and called for a better distribution of wealth. It grew rapidly from 16,000 members in March 1931 to over 68,000 by June 1933. Its leader Francesc Macía became the first president of the Catalan government and on his death was succeeded by Lluis Companys, who formed a coalition led by the *Esquerra*.

In 1933 there was a split within the party, and a minority formed a new party, the *Partit Nacional Republica d'Esquerra* (PNRE). After the attempted declaration of Catalan independence on Oct. 6, Companys was arrested, and in the election of November of that year the Catalan right re-asserted itself at the expense of the *Esquerra*.

In 1936 the *Esquerra*, in coalition with other Republican and left–wing parties (*Front d'Esquerres de Catalunya*) again won power, and Companys became president. After the Civil War Companys went into exile, but was brought back in 1940 and executed.

On the re-establishment of democracy in 1977 *Esquerra Republicana* again began to contest elections.

In both 1977 and 1979 it won one seat in the Spanish Parliament (each time in the constituency of Barcelona) and in 1979 it polled 3.9 per cent of the Catalan vote in the municipal elections. In 1980 it did well in the elections for the Catalan parliament obtaining 8.9 per cent of the Catalan vote, and 14 of the 135 seats. (Eight in Barcelona and two each in Lérida, Gerona and Tarragona.) Its highest percentage was in Lérida with 12.2 per cent.

From 1980 to 1986 *Esquerra* had two posts in a government coalition under Pujol. Its secretary-general, Heribert Barrera, became president of the Catalan parliament.

The party's association with more conservative forces hurt it electorally. It dropped to 2.9 per cent of the Catalan vote in the municipal elections of 1983 and lost nine of its 14 seats in the Catalan parliament elections of 1984, when it only won 4.4 per cent of the vote. In the 1986 Spanish elections it only won 2.6 per cent of the Catalan vote and lost its only member of the Parliament, Francesc Vicens.

At the party's 15th congress it decided to distance itself from the Catalan right and to re-assert itself as an independent political force. It also elected a new leadership under Joan Hortala.

In the 1987 municipal elections it won just over 2 per cent in the city of Barcelona. It won a number of council seats, however, elsewhere in Catalonia. It also participated in the European Parliament elections as part of a coalition with Basque and Galician nationalist parties entitled *Coalicion per l'Europa de les Nacions*. The coalition won 1.7 per cent of the Spanish vote, and claimed one seat in the European Parliament. *Esquerra* has about 230 local councillors and mayors. It won six seats on 4.2 per cent of the vote in the 1988 Catalan regional elections.

Support

The *Esquerra* now only has a low level of support within Catalonia, in spite of its great historical tradition, although predictions that it would decline still further did not prove correct in the 1988 Catalan parliament elections.

In the last Catalan parliament elections it won 4.2 per cent of the vote and its strongest provinces were Gerona (5.5 per cent) and Lérida (5.9 per cent). It won 5.2 per cent in Tarragona and 3.7 per cent in Barcelona. In the 1986 Spanish elections it won 2.6 per cent of the vote with its best performances again in Gerona (3.5 per cent) and Lérida (3.0 per cent). In percentage terms it is weakest in the city of Barcelona, where it only obtained 2.2 per cent of the vote in the 1987 municipal elections. Its best performance in the city was in the district of Gracia with 3.34 per cent. Nevertheless, 1,500 of its 5,000 members are from Barcelona. In the 1986 Spanish elections its highest vote in any substantial community was in Vic with just under 6 per cent.

Organization

The lowest unit within the party is the *Entitat*, which must have a minimum of five members. Above these are the local sections of which there are currently around 150. In each of the 38 districts of Catalonia (*Comarcas*) there is a comarcal federation, apart from in Barcelona where there are three such federations. There are five inter-comarcal federations, one each in the three provinces of Lérida, Gerona and Tarragona and two in the province of Barcelona (one in the city, one in the rest of the province).

At Catalan level there is a national congress which can be attended by all party members, and which meets every two years unless an extraordinary congress is convoked. A national council of around 200 members (which includes the president of each local section with more than 15 members) meets between four and six times a year. Day-to-day leadership is provided by the national executive committee and by its permanent political committee as well as by the party's secretary-general (who is its effective leader) and the six assistant secretary-generals.

The party's candidates for Catalan and Spanish parliament elections, as well as for municipalities of over 50,000 people are initially chosen within each electoral district. Final decisions are taken by the secretary-general and the party's executive committee, which can add a certain number of names to the list both at the initial and at the final stages.

The party's policy-making is helped by its 21 sectoral committees (*Comisiones de Trabajo*).

The party's youth section is called *Joventuts d'Esquerra Republicana* and currently has around 1,000 members. There is no separate women's section.

There are no other affiliated organizations, although in the province of Lérida the party is aligned with the *Juventud Republicana de Lérida* (a local political grouping which has members of all ages and is not just a youth group). There is also a small trade union, the *Confederación Sindical de Catalunya*, which is independent, but supported by the party.

The party's newspaper is called *La Humanitat* which was founded by Lluis Companys. The youth group has its own review entitled *La Coctelera*.

Members of the party must pay a minimum fee which is currently 600 pesetas a month for all but the retired and the unemployed (100 pesetas), and youth members (200 pesetas). In addition, all party office-holders belonging to the party must give 10 per cent of their income to the party.

Esquerra has close links with Basque and Galician nationalist parties. The Basque member who was elected for the *Coalicion per l'Europa de las Nacions* in the 1987 election (Carlos Garaikoetxea) meets regularly with *Esquerra* to report on his activities. He sits in the Rainbow Group in the European Parliament. *Esquerra* supports the European Free Alliance and the Confederation of Western European Nations without a state.

Policies

Esquerra Republicana is currently attempting to recover from a long period of decline. It has ended its coalition with the more right–wing Catalan nationalist grouping, *Convergència i Unió* and is attempting to assert itself as the only distinctively Catalan nationalist party of the left.

Esquerra has been an ageing party but has recently gained a number of new members from certain citizens' associations and pressure groups fighting for the Catalan language and culture (like the *Crida de la Solidaritat per la Defense de la Llengua Catalana*) who have given the party a stronger emphasis on achieving full independence for Catalonia. While all the major Catalan parties have more or less explicit pro-independence wings this element is probably strongest in *Esquerra Republicana*.

Esquerra would like to see a Catalan nation within a confederal Europe, and seeks to extend the role of the Catalan language.

It was the only parliamentary party to oppose the post–Franco Spanish Constitution on republican grounds, but the aspiration to a Catalan republic is not now strongly emphasized.

Pacifism has been an important strand of the *Esquerra* tradition, and it strongly defends the right to conscientious objection. In the 1986 NATO referendum *Esquerra* campaigned against Spanish membership of NATO. It would like to see a neutral, non-aligned Catalonia. It is strongly anti-nuclear.

Esquerra would like to see more responsibility devolved to the districts or *comarcas* both from the provincial tier which should be abolished, and from the central Catalan government. It is a strong supporter of local citizens' initiatives.

Its economic policy is less distinctive, and generally has a progressive Liberal orientation.

Personalities

The party's current leader is Joan Hortalà, a professor of economics at the Free University of Barcelona and formerly responsible for industry policy within the Catalan government. His predecessor as secretary-general, Heribert Barrera, is the president of the *Esquerra* group within the Catalan parliament and was number two on the Europe of the Nations list for the 1987 European Parliament elections.

Its top candidate in Barcelona in the 1987 municipal election was Albert Alay. Of the radical newcomers in the party one of the more influential is Angel Colom, a founder and leader of the *Crida*, who is currently an assistant secretary-general of the party, and who is a supporter of an independent Catalonia and a "green-leaning" *Esquerra*.

Partit dels Socialistes de Catalunya — (PSC–PSOE)

Headquarters	: C. Nicaragua 75–77, 08029 Barcelona
Secretary-general	: Raimon Obiols
Youth group	: *Joventut Socialista de Catalunya*
Membership	: 14,000
Founded	: 1978

History

The *Partit dels Socialistes de Catalunya* (PSC–PSOE) is the most autonomous part of the Spanish Socialist Workers' Party (PSOE).

Socialism has been traditionally weak in Catalonia, especially because of the strength of rival anarcho-syndicalism. In 1923 it was further weakened by a division between a group of Catalan socialist intellectuals who emphasized Catalan autonomy, and founded a party called the *Unió Socialista de Catalunya* and other, generally more working class members who wanted to maintain closer ties with the Spanish Socialist Party. Attempts to forge Socialist unity during the 1930s continued to founder over the issues of support for Catalan autonomy, links with the unions and the degree to which a unified party should be open to the middle class or join in a popular front.

Socialist unity was finally achieved after the re-establishment of democracy when three main groups, the *Partit dels Socialistes de Catalunya* (Congress 1976), the *Partit Socialiste de Catalunya (Reagrupament)* and the Catalan federation of the Spanish Socialist Party (PSOE) joined together in July 1978 to form the PSC–PSOE.

In the 1977 national elections the Catalan Socialists had won 28.4 per cent of the Catalan vote and 15 seats, and in the 1979 national elections the PSC obtained 29.2 per cent and 17 seats in the Spanish Congress of Deputies.

While thus quickly asserting themselves as the strongest Catalan party in national elections, they were less successful in Catalan regional elections. Led by Joan Reventos they only won 22.3 per cent in the 1980 regional elections and 33 seats in the Catalan parliament, well behind *Convergència i Unió* (CiU).

The PSC profited, however, from the later collapse of the Communist vote to win 45.2 per cent of the Catalan vote in the 1982 national elections, and 25 of the seats in the Spanish Congress of Deputies.

In the 1984 regional elections, in which they were now led by Raimon Obiols, their vote rose to 30 per cent (41 seats in the Catalan parliament), but they fell further behind the CiU. In the 1986 national elections the PSC continued to poll better than the CiU with 40.6 per cent of the Catalan vote and 21 seats in the Congress.

In the 1987 municipal elections the PSC lost a few of their municipal bastions, but held on to the biggest prize of all, the city of Barcelona, where they polled 42.4 per cent of the vote.

In the 1988 regional elections they polled 29.5 per cent of the vote, and obtained 42 out of the 135 seats in the Catalan parliament.

Support

The PSC is the largest Catalan party in national elections, but only a poor second in Catalan regional elections. It does particularly well among non-Catalan workers, who provide up to half of its electorate.

The PSC's stronghold is the "red belt" of Barcelona suburbs, and adjacent industrial towns, such as Cornella (over 50 per cent support in the 1988 regional elections) and Badalona. In the city of Barcelona it is strong enough in local elections to hold on to the town hall, but in the 1988 regional elections was ahead of CiU in only one of the city's 10 districts. This was its stronghold, Nou Barris, where it polled 43.7 per cent in 1988 and 61 per cent in the 1987 local elections. Even in the local elections it only polled 19.4 per cent in its weak district of Sarria Sant Gervasi.

The PSC is generally rather weak in much of rural Catalonia, and obtained little over 10 per cent in the 1988 regional elections in small towns such as Cervera and Tremp.

In provincial terms the PSC is strongest in Barcelona (31.2 per cent in the 1988 regional elections) and Tarragona (26.8 per cent in 1988) and weaker in Gerona (23.5 per cent in 1988) and Lérida (23 per cent in 1988).

The PSC does well in the city of Gerona, however, in local elections, largely because of the popularity of its Socialist mayor.

Organization

The PSC sends a large delegation to the congress of the Spanish Socialist Party, PSOE.

Within Catalonia the PSC is organized in municipal groups and in federations, of which there are 21 in individual *comarcas* (districts) or groups of *comarcas*.

At Catalan level a congress is held at least every three years. The party's national council includes 70 members elected at the congress, and meets around once every four months. The national executive committee is elected by the congress and meets in plenary once a month. A smaller secretariat, including the president and first secretary, meets once every 15 days.

Besides the territorial structure there are also sectoral organizations. A distinctive feature of the party's organization is the provision that 15 per cent (to rise to 18 per cent) of the party leadership and of the party's electoral lists must consist of women.

The PSC's youth movement is called the *Joventut Socialista de Catalunya*. The party also has close links with the trade unions, through UGT of Catalonia.

Policies

The most sensitive issue for the PSC is the extent of its independence from the Spanish Socialist Party, PSOE. Its opponents claim that it is not a true Catalan party, and only a branch of PSOE, and the PSC has made vigorous attempts, especially under the current leadership of Raimon Obiols, to assert its Catalan character. It thus describes itself as a national party, and the PSOE as the federal party. It has not, however, managed to have a separate parliamentary group within the Spanish Congress of Deputies, although this would be numerically possible.

In its policies the PSC is inevitably less centralist than PSOE. The PSC recognizes that the Spanish Constitution is not a federal one, but believes that that should not prevent the development of the Spanish autonomous regions in a federalist direction. The competences of the Catalan region should be extended, and Catalan identity should be further strengthened. Catalanism should not remain a conservative monopoly, and the PSC is highly critical of the Pujol government to which it has been in opposition since 1980. It calls for a greater reduction in regional inequalities.

It was particularly critical of the abolition of the Metropolitan Corporation of Barcelona, and seeks to re-establish it. It was also very unenthusiastic about the new powers given to the historic Catalan *comarcas* (districts), which it considered to be a rather unnecessary and anachronistic tier of local government.

The PSC has called for the substitution of civil nuclear energy.

Personalities

The party's leader is Raimon Obiols, who has a less populist style than his CiU counterpart, Pujol, but who has strengthened the PSC's Catalan credentials.

Another important party leader is Pascual Maragall, who was re-elected as mayor of Barcelona in 1987, and under whom Barcelona has obtained the 1992 Olympic Games.

Joaquim Nadal is the popular mayor of Gerona.

Partit Socialista Unificat de Catalunya — PSUC

(Unified Socialist Party of Catalonia)

Headquarters	: Carrer Ciutat 7, 08002 Barcelona (tel: 301612)
Secretary-general	: Rafael Ribó
Youth group	: *Joventut Comunista de Catalunya*
Newspaper	: *Treball*
Membership	: 8,000
Founded	: 1936

History

The *Partit Socialista Unificat de Catalunya* (PSUC) is a Eurocommunist party with different origins from its sister party, the *Partido Comunista de España* (PCE). The PSUC was founded on July 23, 1936, from a merger of both Socialist and Communist parties, its four main components being the *Unió Socialista de Catalunya*, part of the Catalan federation of the Socialist Party (PSOE), the Communist Party of Catalonia, and the *Partit Catala Proletari* (the proletarian Catalan party). It failed, however, in its objective to unify Catalan Marxism, in particular because there remained a second Communist party in Catalonia, the *Partido Obrero de Unificación Marxista* (POUM) which was later brutally eliminated in 1937.

The PSUC, whose first secretary-general was Joan Camorera, grew rapidly to 60,000 members and participated in the Catalan government. At the end of the civil war in 1939 it was made illegal, but was recognized by the Communist movement as the Catalan section of the International.

After being severely repressed under Franco it was legalized in 1976 and took part with two members in the provisional regional government of Catalonia. It contested the Spanish elections in 1977 along with the Spanish Communist Party (PCE), of which the PSUC was one of the most powerful components with 40,000 members. In 1977 the PSUC won 18.2 per cent of the Catalan vote and eight seats in the Spanish Congress of Deputies. In 1979 its vote dropped to 17.1 per cent, but it retained eight seats. In 1980 it obtained 18.7 per cent in the first Catalan regional elections, and 25 seats in the Catalan regional parliament.

At the party's fifth congress, however, in 1981 there was a severe schism between Eurocommunists and pro-Soviet hard-liners within the party. The Eurocommunist leadership of Gregorio López Raimundo and Antoni Gutiérrez were temporarily forced to stand down, but they eventually regained control of the party after a bitter internal struggle in which a number of leading figures were expelled.

In 1982 a new hard-line *Partit dels Communistes de Catalunya* (PCC — see separate entry) was established. The results were disastrous for the PSUC, which by 1982 had only retained around one third of its 1981 membership, with a third having gone to the PCC, and the remainder having abandoned both parties. In the 1982 national elections the PSUC's vote dropped to only 4.6 per cent of the Catalan vote, with only one seat in the Congress of Deputies.

In the Catalan regional elections of 1984 it obtained 5.6 per cent and six seats. In the 1986 national elections it led a Catalan equivalent of the *Izquierda Unida* coalition, the *Unió de la Esquerra* (the Union of the Left), but the PCC did not participate. The coalition obtained 3.9 per cent and only one seat.

In March 1987 the PSUC formed a broader coalition, the *Federacion de Iniciativa per Catalunya* (IC), which still survives, and in which the PCC now participates, along with another party, the *Entesa de Nacionalistes de Esquerra* (ENE). In the 1987 European elections PSUC managed to elect one of its members to the European Parliament.

In the 1988 Catalan regional elections *Iniciativa per Catalunya* made a relative recovery, obtaining 7.6 per cent of the vote, and eight seats in the regional parliament.

Support

The PSUC is strongest in the "red belt" of the Barcelona suburbs, and outlying industrial towns, such as Badalona, Sabadell, Sant Feliu de Llobregat, and Santa Coloma, where it is particularly strong in local government but to a lesser extent in regional and national elections as well. It has less strength in the city of Barcelona itself.

In the other three Catalan provinces PSUC has its highest support in Tarragona, and is weakest in Gerona and Lérida. It has generally very low votes in rural Catalonia.

Organization

The PSUC is the most autonomous of the component parties of the Spanish Communist Party (PCE), at which it had 70 delegates at the last federal congress. The PSUC has been a pioneer in modifying the Communist principle of democratic centralism.

Its territorial structure consists of groups and local committees. At provincial level there are inter-comarcal committees.

The party's congress is held roughly every three years. There is a central committee of around 100 members, an executive committee of around 30, and a political secretariat of 15.

The party's youth movement is called the *Joventut Comunista de Catalunya*. The party's newspaper, *Treball* appears on a weekly basis,

and has a circulation of 10,000. PSUC's member in the European Parliament sits in the Communist and Allies group.

Policies

The PSUC is Eurocommunist in orientation, and has been a strong advocate of more Catalan autonomy. In the 1988 elections the coalition which it led called for the reform of the existing Catalan Statute of Autonomy. It has also sought the creation of a single Catalan province instead of the four existing ones. The coalition has called for the nationalization of the Catalan financial sector.

Personalities

The party's secretary-general is Rafael Ribó, who is also the president of the *Federacion de Iniciativa per Catalunya*.

The party's member of the European Parliament is Antoni Gutiérrez, a former long-serving secretary-general of the PSUC.

Entesa dels Nacionalistes D'Esquerra — ENE
(Accord of the Nationalists of the Left)

This is a small party of the Catalan left, which has put a particular emphasis on Catalan nationalism. Its leader, Jaume Nualart, has advocated Catalan independence.

In the 1987 European elections it took part in an electoral coalition with the Basque party *Euskadiko Ezkerra*, and other regional parties of the left called *Izquierda de los Pueblos* (Left of the Peoples), which won 1.34 per cent of the national vote but no seats in the European Parliament.

ENE is now part of the Catalan left–wing coalition, the *Federacion de Iniciativa per Catalunya*, which won 7.6 per cent of the vote in the 1988 Catalan regional elections. Jaume Nualart, ENE's leader, won one of its six seats.

Partit dels Comunistes de Catalunya — PCC
(Party of Catalan Communists)

Secretary-general : María Pere
Founded   : 1982

The PCC was founded in April 1982 in a breakaway of pro-Soviet hard-liners from the main Catalan Communist party, the *Partit Socialista Unificat de Catalunya* (PSUC), in a precursor of the later split within Spain as a whole which led to the creation of PCC's sister party, the *Partito Comunista de las Pueblas de España* (PCPE).

The PCC won the support of four members of the PSUC group in the Catalan regional parliament. The most prominent figure within the PCC was the veteran Communist leader, Pere Ardiaca. In the 1984 regional elections the PCC only won 2.4 per cent of the vote, and failed to obtain any seats in the Catalan parliament.

In the 1986 national elections, in which its sister party, the PCPE, participated within the coalition of *Izquierda Unida*, the PCC did not join the *Unió de la Esquierda Catalana* (*Izquierda Unida*'s title in Catalonia). It stood on its own, only gaining a very low vote (1.83 per cent in Barcelona, 1.04 per cent in Tarragona, 0.75 per cent in Lérida and 0.61 per cent in Gerona) and no seats.

The PCC has since changed its strategy, and now participates in broad left coalitions. In the 1988 Catalan regional elections it stood on a joint list with the PSUC and the *Entesa dels Nacionalistes d'Esquerra* entitled *Iniciativa per Catalunya*, which obtained 7.6 per cent and eight seats in the parliament. Two members of the PCC, its secretary-general, María Pere, and Celestino Sánchez were thus elected to the regional parliament.

The PCC is very closely linked to the PCPE, and a former PCC leader, Juan Ramos, is now secretary-general of the PCPE.

The PCC has a newspaper called *Avant*, with a print-run of 10,000.

Other Spanish regional parties are listed by region below. It should be noted that a Federation of regional parties has been established.

Federación de Partidos Regionalistas
(Federation of Regional Parties)

This federation includes the following region-alist parties:

Partido Aragonés Regionalista
Unión del Pueblo Navarro
Unión Valenciana
Extremadura Unida
Partido Regionalista de Cantabria
Unión Mallorquina
Partido Riojano Progresista
Unión Melillense

Galicia

Galicia is the only region apart from the Basque Country and Catalonia to have been granted a special statute of autonomy before the Civil War, when the Galicians overwhelmingly approved such a statute in a referendum in 1936. It had no time to function, however, before the Civil War broke out. After the restoration of democracy, however, Galicia was recognized as a historic region. Like the Basque Country and Catalonia it now holds its regional elections at a different time from those of the other regions. The last such elections were held in 1985.

Galicia is an area of marked cultural indi-viduality, consisting of the four provinces of La Coruña, Lugo, Orense and Pontevedra. It has its own language, Galego, akin to Portuguese, and spoken by the large majority of the Galician population.

Galicia has a long tradition of regional and even separatist parties, of which the *Partido Galleguista* (founded in 1931) of Santiago Quiroga and Alfonso Castelao played a decisive role in obtaining the 1936 Statute of Autonomy. In recent years a number of new such parties have developed but although they have had lim-ited successes none of them has had the impact of their Basque and Catalan counterparts. Galician politics are still dominated by the major Spanish national parties, notably *Partido Popular*, for which Galicia is one of its major strongholds.

Coalición Galega — CG
(Galician Coalition)

Leader and
  secretary-general   : Xosé Barreira Rivas

The *Coalición Galega* (also known as the Galician Centrists after one of its components, the *Centristas de Galicia*) was formed mainly by ex-members of the UCD, and of the *Partido Galleguista*, both of which were dissolved in 1983.

Coalición Galega is a moderate nationalist party, which in 1985–86 was closely associated with the centrist politics of Miguel Roca. In the 1985 Galician regional elections *Coalición Galega* had a major success, winning 11 out of the 21 seats, and becoming the third party of Galicia, obtaining 13 per cent of the vote in Galicia as a whole. It was particularly strong in Orense (22.83 per cent and four seats) and Lugo (20.6 per cent and three seats). In the 1986 Spanish elections, however, it slipped back only winning 3.65 per cent in La Coruña (compared to 10 per cent in 1985) and 4.25 per cent in

Pontevedra (9 per cent in 1985). It did win one seat in its stronghold of Orense, where it polled 14 per cent.

Coalición Galega split in 1986–87, with a group of its members leaving to form the *Partido Nacionalista Gallego* (see separate entry).

Later in 1987 *Coalición Galega* formed part of the new Galician government led by Gonzales Laxe of the Socialist Party, and in which the *Partido Nacionalista Gallego* also participated. In the 1987 municipal elections it took part in a coalition with the PDP and the Liberal Party, which was generally unsuccessful.

Coalición Galega has continued to suffer from internal divisions, and is currently low in the polls.

The party's present leader, Xosé Luis Barreiro, was elected almost unanimously to the post in November 1987. He was formerly a member of *Alianza Popular*, and was vice-president of the Galician junta. He has sought to reunite *Coalición Galega* and the *Partido Nacionalista Gallego*.

Partido Nacionalista Gallego — PNG
(Galician Nationalist Party)

This is a new party of the centre–left. It was founded in January 1987 as a result of a split within *Coalición Galega*. The PNG consisted of its "progressive" wing, and was supported on its formation by five members of the regional parliament. In 1987 it became part of the new Galician government led by the Socialists, and also including *Coalición Galega*. The *Partido Nacionalista Galego* recently lost two of its three deputies and its future is highly uncertain.

In 1987 it took part in an electoral coalition with *Eusko Alkartasuna* and *Esquerra Republicana de Catalunya* called *Coalición por la Europa de los Pueblos*, which won 1.7 per cent of the vote in the European Parliament elections. The PNG's leader, Pablo Gonzales Marinas, a former member of UCD and then *Coalición Galega* was in third place on the list, but was not elected. The PNG has a membership of over 1,000, mainly in the provinces of Pontevedra and La Coruña.

Partido Socialista Gallego — Esquerda Galega — PSG–EG
(Galician Socialist Party — Galician Left)

This is a nationalist party which appeals, in particular, to left–wing intellectuals. Within Galicia it occupies a not dissimilar political position to *Euskadiko Ezkerra* in the Basque Country, with whom it participated (along with the Catalan party ENE) in the coalition called *Izquierda de los Pueblos* ("Left of the Peoples") in the 1987 European Parliament elections, which won 1.34 per cent of the Spanish vote, but no seats.

The *Partido Socialista Gallego — Esquerda Galega* won one seat in the Galician parliament in the 1981 regional elections, but increased this to three in the 1985 regional elections, in which it won well over 5 per cent of the Galician vote. Its strongest province was Pontevedra, where it won two seats on 8.87 per cent of the vote. It also won a seat in La Coruña with 5.75 per cent of the provincial vote.

In the 1986 national elections it again polled best in Pontevedra (5.23 per cent), and then in La Coruña (3.68 per cent).

Camilo Nogueira is the leading party figure.

Bloque Nacionalista Gallego — BNG
(Galician Nationalist Bloc)

This is the most radical of the Galician nationalist parties. It won three seats in the 1981 Galician regional elections, but only 4 per cent and one seat in the 1985 regional elections. Its only seat (that of Xosé Manuel Beiras) in the regional parliament was obtained in its strongest province of La Coruña, where it won 5.3 per cent of the vote.

In the 1986 Spanish elections its highest vote was again in the province of La Coruña (2.5 per cent). It stood in the 1987 European elections, but obtained a very low vote.

The *Bloque* opposed the Galician autonomy statute.

Navarre

Navarre has strong historical and cultural links with the Basque Country (and has a substantial minority of Basque speakers in the north of the region), but has had a very different political development. It was still titled a "Kingdom" up to 1839, and succeeded in maintaining its historical *fueros*, a framework of law, traditions and practices. Navarre has been intensely Catholic, conservative and royalist. It was the heartland of the Carlist political tradition. It supported the Nationalists during the Civil War, and was rewarded by being allowed to keep its separate political institutions and privileges and a stronger measure of regional autonomy than anywhere else in Franco's Spain. The main political issues in Navarre have been the defence of the *fueros* or foral traditions, and the claim of nationalists in the Basque Country for Navarre to be incorporated within this region.

Unión del Pueblo Navarro — UPN
(Union of the Navarrese People)

Headquarters	:	Plaza Principe de Viana 1–4º, 31002 Pamplona (tel: 227211 or 227212)
Leader	:	Jesús Aizpún
Founded	:	1979

History and Support

The *Unión del Pueblo Navarro* (UPN) was founded in 1979 by Jesús Aizpún, a former UCD deputy who abandoned the UCD because he felt that its leader and then Spanish Prime Minister, Adolfo Suárez was too sympathetic to Basque claims for the annexation of Navarre.

In the 1979 national elections UPN won 11.2 per cent of the Navarre vote, and it won 16 per cent in the elections, also in 1979, for the Navarre Foral parliament.

UPN received substantial material support from the conservative *Alianza Popular* of Manuel Fraga and in the 1982 national elections, UPN took part in the electoral coalition of *Coalición Popular* which won almost 26 per cent of the Navarre vote. In the 1983 elections for the regional parliament of Navarre UPN ran on its own, and won 23.5 per cent of the vote.

In the 1986 national elections UPN renewed its alliance with the *Coalición Popular* which increased its vote to almost 30 per cent in Navarre. Finally, in the 1987 regional parliament elections UPN won almost 25 per cent standing on its own, and was a close second to the Socialist Party.

Besides the two seats in the Spanish Congress of Deputies which it won in 1986, UPN has 14 members out of the 50 in the Navarre regional parliament, and 138 local mayors throughout Navarre. It also holds the presidency of the Navarre Foral parliament, the presidency of the Navarre Federation of Municipalities and the office of Mayor of Pamplona.

Organization

The UPN has local organization at three different levels, local municipal level, *comarca* or district level, and *merindad* level (a traditional Navarre territorial unit). It has an annual general assembly, a regional council (including 50 members elected at the general assembly for four–year terms of office) which meets once a trimester, and a similar executive committee, whose members are directly elected by the general assembly for four–year terms. The party's leader is its president, and it also has vice-presidents and a secretary-general.

The UPN's youth movement is called the *Juventudes de Unión del Pueblo Navarro*.

The UPN is one of the participants in a recently created *Plataforma de Partidos Regionalistas*, or Platform of Spanish regional parties (now a Federation). It is exploring the possibilities of co-operating in a regionalist alliance in the 1989 European elections.

Policies

The *Unión del Pueblo Navarro* is a conservative regional party, defending the cultural and historical identity of Navarre and its old foral institutions. It believes that Navarre's interests are better defended by a Navarre-based party than by a Spanish party, and it strongly advocates decentralized government. On the other hand it does not support independence for Navarre, and defends the unity of Spain. It is strongly opposed to Basque claims to annex Navarre. In national elections the UPN links itself with the conservative *Partido Popular*, which grants UPN wide freedom of manoeuvre within Navarre, but UPN contests regional elections on its own, although still with backing from local conservatives.

On other issues the UPN's programme is strongly influenced by Christian humanism. It defends the family as the fundamental unit of society, and opposes abortion. It attacks purely materialistic conceptions of society, and calls for a progressive social policy.

Its basic party programme opposes Marxism and dirigistic state planning. It supports the social market economy, and considers private initiative to be the main driving force of economic development. Protection of Navarre's environment receives a high priority as do measures to strengthen Navarre's industrial base and to reduce its high unemployment.

Canary Islands

These have a special statute as regards the EC, but are otherwise an integral part of Spain. A number of regional parties asserting local interests have emerged in particular islands, especially in Fuerteventura, Tenerife and Hierro). A small independence movement has also developed, but with little electoral success. The Canaries have 13 members of the national assembly (elected in two big constituencies), 11 senators (with each island entitled to at least one senator) and 60 deputies in the regional parliament, with each island a separate constituency.

Agrupaciones Independientes de Canarias — AIC
(Canaries Grouping of Independents)

This is an electoral federation of a number of regional parties in individual islands. Its dominant component, however, is a party on Tenerife, the *Agrupación Tinerfena de Independientes* (the Tenerife Group of Independents), whose leader is Manuel Hermoso, mayor of Santa Cruz.

In the 1986 Spanish elections the AIC won 18.45 per cent of the vote and one deputy in the national assembly in the constituency of Tenerife (which also includes the islands of La Palma, Gomera and Hierro). In the second Canaries constituency of Las Palmas (also including Lanzarote and Fuerteventura) it won no seats, and had little strength.

In the 1987 regional elections the AIC won over 21 per cent of the vote and became the third largest party in the Canaries regional parliament, with 11 seats. Its biggest success was on the island of Tenerife, where it won seven seats with almost 42 per cent of the vote.

Asamblea Canaria — AC–INC
(Canarian Assembly)

This is a left-of-centre regional party. It won no seats in the 1986 national elections (with 6 per cent in the constituency of Las Palmas and 5 per cent in the constituency of Tenerife). In the regional parliament, however, it won two seats in the 1987 elections and 7 per cent of the vote, and with 10 per cent on the island of Gran Canaria.

Asamblea Majorera — AM
(Majorera Assembly)

Address : Calle las Ventas,
5/a 35600 Puerto de
Rosario, Islas
Canarias

This is the strongest political party on the island of Fuerteventura (whose inhabitants are known as Majoreros, hence the name of the party). It was founded in 1977, and because of its concentrated support has had considerable success, sending a senator to the Spanish Senate and currently having three of the island's seven representatives in the Canaries regional parliament, and with over 38 per cent of the island vote. In 1983 it has done even better,

winning four of the seven seats with over 46 per cent of the vote. It has been helped by the decision of other left-of-centre Canaries political groupings not to put up candidates on the island, but to support *Asamblea Majorera*. In 1979 AM won control of the *Cabildo Insular* (island government).

In each municipality it has a municipal assembly, with a municipal co-ordinating committee as its executive. At island level there is an island assembly, and an island co-ordinating committee. It has around 100 active members. Up to 300 people take part in its assemblies.

Asamblea Majorera is a left–wing nationalist party, whose main scope is defence of the interests of the island of Fuerteventura. It seeks improvements in the island's standard of living, and is particularly concerned about the island's environment, and the dangers of uncontrolled speculative tourist development.

Within the Canaries parliament it advocates economic planning to reduce economic and social disparity between the islands. It also seeks the neutralization of the Canaries.

Asamblea Herrena Independiente

This party defending the identity of the island of Hierro won 27.6 per cent and one seat in the Hierro constituency in the 1983 regional parliament elections, and this rose to 36.8 per cent and two of the three island seats in the 1987 regional elections, making it the largest party on the island.

Congreso Nacional Canaria

This is a Canarian independence movement led by Antonio Cubillo, who claims that the Canaries are in a colonial situation, and that the Canarians or *guanches* are Africans and not Europeans. Cubillo would like to see the re-establishment of the original Berber language and would welcome a confederation with an independent Sahraoui Republic.

Comunidad Valenciana (Valencian Community)

The Valencian region was once part of the Kingdom of Aragon, and a language closely linked with Catalan is still spoken by a considerable number of people within the region. This linguistic individuality has been one of the main catalysts for the development of regional movements within Valencia.

Unión Valenciana — UV
(Valencian Union)

Headquarters : Avda Giorgeta 16–1º,
46007 Valencia
(tel: 357 62 54 and
357 62 64)
Political leader : Vicente González
Lizondo
Founded : August 1982

History

Unión Valenciana (or *Unió Valenciana* in Valencian) was founded on Aug. 30, 1982, as a conservative regionalist party in defence of Valencian identity and interests.

In the 1982 national elections it took part in the electoral alliance of *Coalición Popular* and one of its founders, Ramon Izquierdo, was elected to the Congress in Madrid. In the 1983 regional elections it again stood as part of *Coalición Popular*.

In the 1986 national elections, however, *Unión Valenciana* ended the alliance with *Coalición Popular*, and narrowly won a seat in the Congress in the Valencia constituency.

In the 1987 elections *Unión Valenciana* again stood on its own, and considerably increased its vote over 1986, largely at the expense of *Alianza Popular*. In the regional parliament elections it won 15 per cent of the vote in the Valencia constituency and won six seats in the regional parliament. In the municipal elections it won 20 per cent of the vote in the city of Valencia (with seven seats on the council) and did well in a number of other municipalities. In the European Parliament elections it also ran on its own, and won 0.84 per cent of the total Spanish vote and did not win a seat.

Support

Within the three provinces of the Valencian region *Unión Valenciana* obtained the vast majority of its vote within the province of Valencia (5 per cent in the national elections in 1986, almost 15 per cent in the regional parliament elections in 1987), and very few votes in the provinces of Castellón (0.53 per cent in 1986) and Alicante (0.29 per cent in 1986).

The party is particularly strong in the city of Valencia where it won over 20 per cent throughout the city in the 1987 municipal elections, but between 23 per cent and 28 per cent in certain parts of the city (such as the old town). Outside the city it had particularly high votes in the municipalities of Catarroja (29.2 per cent) and Almussafes (28.3 per cent).

Organization

Unión Valenciana has established local branches, with their local assemblies and governing councils (*consells*) in a large number of municipalities. It has been attempting to establish a district (*comarcal*) structure between the branches and its three provincial organizations (with their provincial assemblies and provincial executive committees of between 16 and 18 members). At Valencian regional level there is a periodic congress, as well as more frequent assemblies. There is a central executive committee of 24 members which includes the party president.

The party has a youth movement, *Juventudes de Unión Valenciana* (*Joventuts Unió Valenciana*).

There is a regional information bulletin produced by the party called *Una Veu* (A Voice).

Unión Valenciana has established links with other Spanish regional parties of the centre and right, and notably the *Agrupación Independiente Canaria*, the *Partido Aragonés Regionalista* and the *Unión del Pueblo Navarro* (see separate entries). Certain common policy positions have been adopted and the parties are currently exploring the possibility of a common list for the European Parliament elections in 1989 (their combined vote would have entitled them to a seat in 1987).

Policies

Unión Valenciana is a regionalist party of the centre–right which stands for the defence of the cultural, social and economic interests of the Valencian community. It wants the Valencian Statute of Autonomy to be modified to provide for explicit reference to the Kingdom of Valencia (*Reino de Valencia* — its historic name). It also advocates measures to stimulate bilingualism within Valencia (Spanish and Valencian). It calls for wide recognition of a Valencian regional anthem (the *Himno Regional*) and of the traditional Valencian flag (the *Senyera*). It attacks the centralist philosophy of the Madrid government, and seeks the fullest possible transfer of powers within the spirit of the existing Spanish Constitution. It points out the constitutional distinction between "nationalities" and "regions", and claims that Valencia lies within the former category.

On the other hand *Unión Valenciana* emphasizes that it is not a separatist party, and that it considers Valencia to be an essential and inalienable part of the Spanish whole. It is also fiercely opposed to Catalan claims for Valencia to be annexed by Catalonia on the grounds of the historical and linguistic links between the two regions.

On other issues *Unión Valenciana* strongly defends the rights of the family and emphasizes the key role of the private sector. It supports the social market economy.

Spanish integration into NATO is accepted by *Unión Valenciana*, but the party seeks a revision of the defence treaty with the United States. The party also underlines the European vocation of the Valencian community, but has strongly criticized the terms of Spanish adhesion to the EC, which have harmed Valencian agricultural interests.

Personalities

The party's political leader is now Vicente Gonzales Lizondo, its candidate for mayor of Valencia in 1987. Its deputy in the Spanish Congress is Miguel Ramón Izquierdo, who is also the party president. He is a former mayor of Valencia from the Franco era. The party's secretary has been Manuel Campillos.

Unitat del Poble Valencià — UPV
(Unity of the Valencian People)

This is an alliance of two parties, the *Agrupamento del País Valencia* and the *Partit Nacionalista del País Valencia*. In the 1986 national elections it stood on its own, winning 29,000 votes and 2.4 per cent of the vote in the province of Valencia, but only 0.9 per cent of the vote in the province of Alicante.

In the 1987 elections it entered into a coalition with the Communist-led alliance *Izquierda Unida*, and succeeded in winning seats in several municipalities and in the Valencian regional parliament.

The *Unitat del Poble Valencià* is a left–wing regionalist party.

Aragon

Partido Aragonés Regionalista — PAR
(Aragon Regionalist Party)

Headquarters	: Paseo de Sagasta 20, Zaragoza 6 (tel: 76 214127)
President	: José María Mur
Secretary-general	: Emilio Eiroa García

The *Partido Aragonés Regionalista* (PAR) is a centre-right regionalist party. It originally had strong links with the *Alianza Popular* of Manuel Fraga and in the 1982 national elections took part in the electoral alliance of *Coalición Popular*, winning two seats in the Congress of Deputies and two in the Senate. In the 1983 regional and municipal elections PAR stood on its own. It obtained over 20 per cent of the vote for the regional parliament and 13 seats, and also won a considerable number of council seats, including four in the city of Zaragoza.

In the 1986 national elections PAR again stood on its own, obtaining almost 10 per cent of the vote in each of the provinces of Huesca and Teruel and 11.6 per cent of the vote in the province of Zaragoza, where it succeeded in electing its leader, Hipolito Gómez de las Roces to the Chamber of Deputies in Madrid.

In the 1987 elections PAR polled extremely well. In the municipal elections it won 23 per cent of the vote in the city of Zaragoza, and doubled its number of councillors to eight, and it also won 15.5 per cent (and four councillors) in the provincial capital of Huesca. It did less well in the provincial capital of Teruel with 7.65 per cent.

In the regional parliament elections it obtained 28 per cent of the vote and 19 seats, overtaking *Alianza Popular* to become the second-largest party. In the constituency of Teruel it won 17.6 per cent and three seats, in Huesca 25.3 per cent and five seats and in Zaragoza 31 per cent and 11 seats.

Hipolito Gómez de las Roces, PAR's historical leader, subsequently won the presidency of the Aragon regional government, in which PAR's five members share power with three independents, and with external support in the Aragonese parliament from other parties of the centre–right. He was replaced as president by the party's former secretary-general, José María Mur. Emilio Eiroa García became the new party secretary-general. The party's seat in the Spanish Chamber of Deputies was taken up by Isaias Zarazaga.

The PAR has a youth movement called *Rolde*, and a party newspaper called *Alcarze*. Standing on its own for the European Parliament elections in 1987 it only won 0.55 per cent of the vote and no seats in the parliament. It is now exploring the possibility of a wider electoral alliance with other centre or right-of-centre regionalist parties (such as the *Unión de Pueblo Navarro*, and the *Unión Valenciana*) for the 1989 European elections.

Cantabria

Partido Regionalista de Cantabria

This centre–right regionalist party obtained 6.8 per cent in the first regional parliament elections in Cantabria in 1983, winning two seats. It did not stand in the 1986 national elections. In the 1987 regional elections its vote rose to 12.9 per cent and it won five seats in the regional parliament (out of 39). In the 1987 municipal elections it had 8 per cent of the vote in the Cantabrian regional capital of Santander, and two city councillors. In Reinosa it won 8 per cent of the vote and one council seat, in Torrelavega 11 per cent and three seats. Standing on its own in the 1987 European Parliament elections it only won 0.08 per cent of the Spanish national vote.

The party's leader is Miguel Angel Revilla.

Balearic Islands

Unió Mallorquina — UM

This centre–right regionalist party won 15.4 per cent of the vote in the 1983 regional parliament elections and six out of the then 54 seats. In the 1987 regional parliament elections its vote declined to 9 per cent and it only won four seats, all in the constituency of Mallorca. In the 1987 municipal elections it won 6.6 per cent of the votes in Palma, and two council seats. In the small town of Inca in the centre of Mallorca it obtained 45.6 per cent of the vote and 11 council seats. Standing on its own in the 1987 European Parliament elections it only obtained 0.10 per cent of the Spanish vote. UM has no strength in Ibiza, Menorca or Formentera.

The president of the party is Jerónimo Alberti, who stood unsuccessfully as a candidate for the PRD coalition put together by Miguel Roca in the 1986 national elections, when the *Unió Mallorquina* did not put forward candidates in its own right.

PSM —Esquerra Nacionalista

This left–wing regionalist party won 2.2 per cent in the 1986 national elections and no seats. In the 1987 regional elections it won 4.88 per cent and two seats in the regional parliament, both in the constituency of Mallorca.

Extremadura

Extremadura Unida

This is a centre–right regionalist party of Liberal orientation which won 8.5 per cent and six seats in the regional parliament of Extremadura in the 1983 regional elections. In 1985 there was a schism within the party, and in the 1986 national elections it only won 5.23 per cent in the province of Cáceres and under 1 per cent in Badajoz. In the 1987 regional elections it only won 5.65 per cent and four seats in the regional parliament. Its strength is in the province of Cáceres (12.2 per cent and all four seats in 1987, 16.4 per cent in 1983) and it is weak in the province of Badajoz (1.63 per cent in 1987, 3.37 per cent in 1983). The party has advocated the division of Extremadura into five new *comarcas* or districts. Its leader has been Pedro Canada Castillo. In the 1987 European elections it stood alone, and won 0.18 per cent of the total Spanish vote.

La Rioja

Partido Riojana Progresista

This small centre–right regionalist party was founded by former members of the UCD after the latter's collapse. It won 7.5 per cent and two seats in the first regional parliament elections in La Rioja in 1983, as well as 97 local councillors in the 1983 municipal elections. It won 6.4 per cent and retained two seats in the second regional parliament elections in 1987. It also has a council seat in the regional capital of Logroño. Its leading figure has been Javier Rodríguez Moroy, a former president of the Rioja regional government.

Melilla

Unión Melillense

This is a small regionalist party in the Spanish enclave of Melilla on the north coast of Morocco.

Andalusia

Partido Andalucista

Headquarters   : Ramon 1, Cajal
                         1–9a–2 Edificio
                         Sevilla 1, Seville

This Andalusian regional party was formed in the late 1970s as the *Partido Socialista de Andalusia* (Socialist Party of Andalusia). Its leader was Alejandro Rojas Marcos. In spite of its name it was a rival to the Spanish Socialist Workers Party (PSOE), and helped to take away votes from the PSOE in its Andalusian stronghold. In the 1979 national elections the *Partido Socialista de Andalusia* (PSA) took four seats in the Spanish Congress of Deputies, one in Cadiz (where it won 19 per cent of the vote), one in Málaga (12 per cent of the vote) and two in Seville (14 per cent of the vote). It subsequently opposed the Andalusian Statute of Autonomy as not being far-reaching enough.

In the Catalan parliament elections in March 1980 the PSA won 3 per cent of the vote in the province of Barcelona, and two seats in the Catalan parliament on the strength of votes from the large population of Andalusian immigrants.

In the 1982 Andalusian regional elections, however, the PSA only won 5.6 per cent of the Andalusian vote and three seats in the regional parliament. In February the PSA changed its name to *Partido Andalucista*. In the simultaneous national elections and Andalusian regional elections in 1986, the *Partido Andalucista* did much better in the latter than in the former. In its two strongest provinces of Cádiz and Seville for example it won 10.2 per cent and 8.85 per cent respectively in the regional elections compared to 4.2 per cent and 4 per cent in the national elections. Overall it won 5.86 per cent of the Andalusian vote for the regional parliament, and two seats, that of Luis Urunuela Fernández in Seville and Pedro Pacheco in Cádiz.

In the 1987 municipal elections the *Partido Andalucista* had variable success but polled extremely well in certain municipalities. In Jeréz a list headed by Pedro Pacheco won 57 per cent of the vote and 17 council seats, and in Seville a list headed by Alejandro Rojas Marcos won 20.8 per cent of the vote and seven council seats (compared to no seats in the previous municipal elections). Other towns with a high vote for the party included Ecija, San Fernando, Isla Cristina and Ronda.

In the 1987 European elections the *Partido Andalucista* stood in its own right and won 0.98 per cent of the Spanish vote, more than double its vote of 0.47 per cent in the 1986 national elections. Although it won no seats it had the highest vote of any of the Spanish regionalist parties standing on its own outside Catalonia and the Basque Country.

United Kingdom

Francis Jacobs

The country

The United Kingdom of Great Britain and Northern Ireland is a country of 94,000 square miles with a population of over 56 million. The vast majority of these live in England (over 47 million), with over five million in Scotland, under three million in Wales and one-and-a-half million in Northern Ireland. Although the Church of England is the largest in the country, there is also a strong non-conformist tradition, especially in the north of England, Wales and Scotland. There are four million Catholics, particularly strong not just in Northern Ireland but also among the many Irish people resident in Great Britain. There are five different Celtic peoples within the British Isles, the Scots, (subdivided into Highland and Lowland Scots), the Welsh, the Manx, the Cornish and the Irish, with the situation in Northern Ireland being further complicated by the existence of two separate traditions, the majority Ulster Protestants and the minority Catholics. Since the war there has been a large increase in the number of Commonwealth immigrants into the UK, of whom the largest group consisted of Bangladeshis, Indians and Pakistanis and West Indians.

Northern Ireland has a completely different political system from that in the rest of the United Kingdom, and is the subject of a separate sub-section below. There is also a small subsection on the Isle of Man, which has a different status, and where the main British parties do not compete.

Political institutions

The United Kingdom is a hereditary constitutional monarchy. It is a unitary state. Scotland has retained its own legal and judicial system, its own established (Presbyterian) Church and educational system, and there is a Secretary of State for Scotland and a Scottish Office in Edinburgh. Wales also has a Secretary of State and a Welsh Office in Cardiff. Political control, however, is vested in the House of Commons at Westminster and there are no Scottish or Welsh Assemblies. Northern Ireland sends MPs to Westminster but also used to have its own parliament and government. These were suspended in 1972, and Northern Ireland is now run by a UK Secretary of State, although an assembly with very limited powers has since been re-established (see separate section below).

The legislature is bicameral. By far the most powerful is the House of Commons, which has 650 members, directly elected under a simple majority system in single member constituencies (523 in England, 72 in Scotland, 38 in Wales, 17 in Northern Ireland).

Although the composition of these constituencies is periodically modified as a result of Boundary Commission recommendations there are still great differences in the size of their electorates.

Even apart from special cases, such as the Western Isles (23,000) and the Isle of Wight (almost 100,000), seats range from below 50,000 (e.g. Hammersmith) to well over 90,000 (Milton Keynes).

Each candidate must put up an electoral deposit (formerly £150, now £1,000) which is forfeited if the candidate receives less than a certain percentage of the vote (formerly 12 per cent, now only 5 per cent). Candidates' expenses are restricted by law.

Any vacancies are filled through special by-elections.

The House of Commons has a maximum parliamentary term of five years, although the Prime Minister has discretion to dissolve Parliament at any time. The Commons are presided over by a Speaker. Legislation is examined by special standing committees. In 1979 a new structure of select committees was set up to review the work of different government departments.

The House of Lords has over 1,200 members, and consists of a mix of hereditary peers and life peers. Practically all new peers and peeresses are now in the latter category, and are appointed by the monarch at the recommendation of the Prime Minister. There are also 19 law lords and 26 bishops and archbishops of the Church of England. Until 1911 the Lords had, in theory at

Map of England and Wales showing counties and Metropolitan counties.

least, practically equal powers to the Commons, but it now has only delaying powers, although its amendments can be influential. It is presided over by the Lord Chancellor. Only a minority of peers take a regular and active part in its work. Of the over 700 peers who are members of specific political parties an overall majority are Conservatives. Labour is underrepresented as compared to the Commons, while the centre parties have more substantial representation in the Lords than in the Commons.

The British Prime Minister is generally drawn from the leader of the largest party in the Commons (although other arrangements may be made by inter-party agreement as long as they are not defeated in the Commons). The Prime Minister chooses the other ministers, who are generally members of the Commons, but who may also be drawn from the Lords. If the government is defeated in a vote of confidence (an extremely rare event) it is customary for new elections to be called.

Popular referenda can also take place. In 1975 there was one on whether the United Kingdom should remain in the European Community, and referenda on the government's devolution plans were held in Scotland and Wales in 1979.

There is no state funding of political parties in Britain.

Local government in England and Wales consists primarily of county and district councils, with borough councils in London. There are also a larger number of smaller and weaker parish councils. In 1985 the existing Greater London Council and the six metropolitan county councils were abolished.

In Scotland there is a separate local government structure of regional, district and island councils.

Local elections are held on the first Thursday in May. The most important are normally those for the county councils, which are held every four years.

The UK has 81 members of the European Parliament, with 66 seats in England, eight in Scotland, four in Wales, and three in Northern Ireland. The majority "first past the post" system is used for the 78 seats in England, Wales and Scotland, but the single transferable vote system of proportional representation for the three Northern Irish seats.

Brief political history (since 1832)

1832	Great Reform Bill extending the franchise.
1846	Peel's reform of the protectionist Corn Laws splits the Conservative Party, and leads to a restructuring of the British political system.
1859	Whigs Radicals and Peelites combine against Derby. Beginning of modern Liberal Party.

1860s to 1880s	Beginning of Conservative/Liberal two-party system. Era of Disraeli and Gladstone (further extension of franchise 1867).
1886	Liberal Party splits over the issue of Irish Home Rule.
1886– 1906	Era of Conservative dominance under Sailsbury and Balfour (Labour Representation Committee founded in 1900).
1906–15	Period of Liberal dominance under Campbell-Bannerman and Asquith. Major social reforms and direct clash between the Commons and the Lords, after which the latter's powers are reduced in 1911.
1915–18	Wartime coalition under Asquith and then Lloyd George.
1918–22	Coalition between Conservatives and Lloyd George Liberals, Lloyd George as Prime Minister, Representation of People Act gives women over 30 the right to vote. Irish Free State recognized and partition of Ireland becomes definitive 1922.
1922–31	Period of three-party politics, but characterized by Labour advance and Liberal decline.
1931–5	National government formed under MacDonald and later Baldwin.
1935–40	Conservative governments under Baldwin and Neville Chamberlain (1937 abdication crisis, 1938 Munich and era of "appeasement").
1940–5	Wartime coalition under Winston Churchill.
1945–51	First Labour majority government under Attlee (carries out wide range of reforms, introduces free National Health Service, begins decolonization).
1951–64	Conservative rule under Churchill, Eden, MacMillan and Sir Alec Douglas-Home.
1964–70	Labour rule under Harold Wilson.
1970–74	Conservative government under Edward Heath (suspension of Stormont government in Northen Ireland 1972, British entry into EC 1973)
1974–79	Labour government under Harold Wilson and James Callaghan, referendum on EC membership with 67.2 per cent "Yes" vote in June 1975; government defeat in referenda on devolution plans for Wales and Scotland in March 1979.
1979– present	Conservative government under Margaret Thatcher.

Main features of British political system

A first striking feature of the British political system is the way it has gradually evolved over a long period of time without a codified Constitution or a Bill of Rights, and with a great reliance on custom and on practice rather than on formal written rules or laws. It has also been characterized by stability and lack of extremism.

An important determinant of the British political system has been its retention of the majority "first past the post" system in practically all types of election. This system has had a number of advantages and disadvantages. It has enabled a close link to be maintained between an MP and a constituency (although in practice national issues have tended to be more important than local factors in ensuring a candidate's election) and has also permitted long periods of stable majority one party government. On the other hand it has enabled parties to win big majorities on a minority share of the overall vote (the present Conservative government has won three absolute majorities in a row with between 42 per cent and 43 per cent of the vote) and it has ruthlessly penalized parties whose support is evenly spread rather than being concentrated in certain areas (in 1983 the SDP/Liberal Alliance won only 23 of the 633 British seats outside Northern Ireland with 26.4 per cent of the total vote).

The political system has thus normally been characterized by two-party dominance, Liberals and Conservatives until 1920, Conservatives and Labour from 1930 onwards. As a result the dominant parties have tended to be catch-all parties, with smaller groups and tendencies absorbed within them.

The electoral system has worked less well, however, when there have been more than two competitive parties, as in the 1920s and to a considerable extent in the 1980s, with a substantial SDP/Liberal Alliance (and with additional nationalist parties in Wales and Scotland). At the time of writing it is uncertain whether the UK is likely to revert to two-party dominance.

Maintenance of a multi-party system would increase the possibility of "hung" parliaments, with no party having an overall majority. Coalition governments might again become more familiar. While there has not been such a government since the war (although Heath considered one with the Liberals in February 1974, and there was a loose Liberal-Labour Pact in 1977–78) there have been several coalition governments in the past. Besides the wartime coalitions in 1915–18 and 1940–45 there have also been peacetime coalitions from 1918–22 and from 1931–35. There have also been several electoral pacts between different parties.

The main cleavages in British political life are economic and regional in nature. Britain has been a very class conscious society and there have been sharp class differences in voting patterns, although the Conservatives have won considerable support among part of the working class (notably in recent years) and Labour have sometimes had middle class support as well. Class structures have become increasingly fluid, but have still not completely disappeared (and are by no means strictly correlated with relative material success).

Nevertheless, the United Kingdom is in regional terms more sharply divided than ever before, with the main cleavage being between the more prosperous and more disadvantaged regions of Britain. It is often referred to as a North-South divide (although there is poverty in parts of the South, such as inner London, and areas of prosperity and economic development in parts of the North). The Conservative Party now has practically all the seats in the South-East (outside London), South-West and East Anglia and the Labour Party is dominant in Britain's inner cities and in the industrial regions of the North, Wales and Scotland. The Conservatives won the vast majority of rural and suburban seats in England, and Labour those areas with the highest indices of disadvantage, among the unemployed, unskilled working class and ethnic minorities. Housing tenure (in particular owner-occupied housing as against council housing) has been an important determinant of voting patterns.

This polarization has harmed the centre parties with their more even spread of votes (although they have been more successful opponents of the Conservatives in rural and suburban Britain than in opposing Labour in industrial and inner-city Britain).

In Scotland and Wales demands for a greater measure of self-government or even for full independence have developed. The additional nationalist cleavage has led to something more resembling a multi-party system than in England, and has also modified the more traditional economic cleavages as well. While the Conservatives are the largest party in rural England, for example, they have strong competition in rural Scotland and Wales. In the 1987 elections all types of Scottish seat swung sharply against the Conservatives, and Labour won some prosperous Scottish seats which would be solidly Conservative in England.

There also used to be religious cleavages

as well, with the Conservatives being strongly supported by the established Church of England, and with the Liberals and later Labour attracting non-conformists, Jews and Catholics. With the decline in religious observance, in particular, this cleavage is much less significant than it was.

There remain some differences between the major parties on moral and social questions, with the Conservatives putting more emphasis on law and order issues, capital punishment and on restricting Commonwealth immigration.

The major political issues in the United Kingdom at present include the following:

General economic policy

(a) The attitudes towards the shift in economic policy-making that has taken place during the nine years of the present government.

(b) The relative emphasis to be placed on fighting inflation or unemployment.

(c) The extent to which the state should be involved and to which market forces should be extended to sectors where they have been absent or restricted in the past (e.g. through privatizations).

(d) Should there be a major increase in public expenditure on infrastructure and other investments?

(e) The future of manufacturing industry and the degree to which traditional industries should be protected and restructured.

Labour and trade union reforms

(a) Do the trade unions still have too much power or have the changes of the last few years left them with too little? Do Britain's trade union structure and practices need to change, with fewer craft unions and more industry-wide unions, with single union deals, no strike agreements, etc.?

(b) Should there be more statutory industrial democracy on German lines, or should it be left to voluntary agreements?

The future of the welfare state

(a) Has it been weakened over the last few years? How can it best be reinforced?

(b) The future of the National Health Service.

(c) Housing (council house sales are now less controversial, but other issues such as the future of the private rental sector and of mortgage tax relief and above all the costs of rising house prices are coming more to the fore).

(d) Education: Should there be a core curriculum, how can parents' choice be extended, should schools be allowed to opt out of local authority control, the balance between public and private schools, etc.

(e) Integration of the tax and benefit system.

Energy policy

(a) The future of civil nuclear energy, and of nuclear waste disposal.

(b) The amount of investment needed in the coal industry.

(c) The privatization of the water and electricity generating sectors.

Immigration policy

(a) Are further restrictions needed on immigration into the United Kingdom?

(b) How can race relations best be improved, and immigrants better integrated into the United Kingdom?

Moral issues

For example:

(a) Should capital punishment be reintroduced?

(b) Should the existing abortion law be made less liberal?

Environmental and land policy issues

General constitutional issues

(a) Electoral reform (in particular the introduction of proportional representation).

(b) Should the European Convention of Human Rights be incorporated into British law, Bill of Rights?

(c) How should the existing Official Secrets Act be reformed, and to what extent should there be freedom of information?

Devolution

(a) To what extent should there be devolution measures in favour of Scotland and Wales?

(b) The extent of administrative and political devolution and decentralization to regions within England?

Local government issues

(a) The relationship between local and central government, and the degree of independence of the former vis-à-vis the latter.

United Kingdom election results, 1945–present (percentages and seats)

	1945	1950	1951	1955	1959	1964	1966	1970	Feb. 1974	Oct. 1974	1979	1983	1987
Conservatives	39.8% (213)	43.5% (298)	48.0% (321)	49.7% (344)	49.4% (365)	43.4% (304)	41.9% (253)	46.4% (330)	37.9% (297)	35.9% (277)	43.9% (339)	42.4% (397)	42.0% (376)
Labour	47.8% (393)	46.1% (315)	48.8% (295)	46.4% (277)	43.8% (258)	44.1% (317)	48.0% (364)	43.1% (288)	37.2% (301)	39.2% (319)	36.9% (269)	27.6% (209)	30.7% (229)
Liberal Party	9.0% (12)	9.1% (9)	2.6% (6)	2.7% (6)	5.9% (6)	11.2% (9)	8.5% (12)	7.5% (6)	19.3% (14)	18.3% (13)	13.8% (11)	—	—
Liberal/SDP Alliance	—	—	—	—	—	—	—	—	—	—	—	25.4% (23)	22.4% (22)
Communists	0.4% (2)	0.3% (0)	0.1% (0)	0.1% (0)	0.1% (0)	0.2% (0)	0.2% (0)	0.1% (0)	0.1% (0)	0.1% (0)	0.1% (0)	0.0% (0)	0.0% (0)
Scottish Nationalists (SNP)	0.1% (0)	0.0% (0)	0.0% (0)	0.0% (0)	0.1% (0)	0.2% (0)	0.5% (0)	1.1% (1)	2.0% (7)	2.9% (11)	1.6% (2)	1.1% (2)	1.4% (3)
Plaid Cymru	0.1% (0)	0.1% (0)	0.0% (0)	0.2% (0)	0.3% (0)	0.3% (0)	0.2% (0)	0.6% (0)	0.6% (2)	0.6% (3)	0.4% (2)	0.4% (2)	0.4% (3)
Others	2.4% (20)	1.0% (3)	0.6% (3)	1.1% (3)	0.4% (1)	0.6% (0)	0.6% (2)	1.4% (6)	3.0% (14)	3.1% (12)	3.3% (12)	3.0% (17)	3.1% (17)

Notes: – Conservative total includes Ulster Unionists up to and inclusive of 1970 results.

– Labour total includes candidates with Co-operative Party endorsement.

– SDP/Liberal Alliance total for 1983 includes 17 Liberals and 6 SDP, and for 1987 17 Liberals and 5 SDP.

– Others includes Northern Ireland parties. The rise in this category from 1974 reflects the end of the Ulster Unionists' Alliance with the Conservatives.

(b) Local government finance: should the rates system have been replaced by a poll tax, or would local income tax be a better solution?

Northern Ireland

(a) What should be the future of Northern Ireland? Anglo-Irish Agreement, devolution to Northern Irish institutions, judicial system, etc.

Media policy

The European Community

(a) Continued British membership of the EC is much less in question than it was (although some still do not accept it), but there are differing attitudes towards future European integration.

Defence policy

(a) The balance between defence and disarmament measures.

(b) Should the UK retain an independent nuclear deterrent, and if so should it be progressively modernized? (Unilateral or multilateral disarmament).

Conservative Party

Headquarters	: 32 Smith Square, London SW1P 3HH (tel: 01–222 9000)
Leader	: Margaret Thatcher
Chairman	: Peter Brooke
Membership	: 1,500,000

History

The Conservative Party had no formal date of foundation, but a "Tory" conservative political tradition gradually evolved. A more clearly discernible Conservative Party began to emerge during the 1830s after the Reform Act and great Tory defeat of 1832. The dominant party figure was Sir Robert Peel, who after an initial short-lived government in 1834–5 formed a more long lasting government in 1841.

In 1846, however, the Conservative Party was totally split over Peel's repeal of the protectionist Corn Laws, with those who were opposed to repeal (notably rural landowners) forming the core of a new Conservative protectionist party.

Apart from three brief periods of government in 1852, 1858–9 and 1866–68 the Conservatives remained in opposition until 1874. Upon Lord Derby's resignation in 1868 Disraeli took over as leader until his death in 1881.

Disraeli reinforced the role of the National Union (founded in 1867) and in 1870 established a new Conservative Central Office. He also gave the Conservative Party a new profile, as a truly national and "patriotic" party. In his later years he also became strongly imperialist. His personalized political struggle with Gladstone gave firmer shape to the two-party system. Disraeli was Prime Minister from 1874 to 1880.

After 1885 there was a long period of Conservative ascendancy under Lord Salisbury, who was party leader from 1885 to 1902, and Prime Minister in 1885–86, 1886 to 1892 and again from 1895 to 1902. Party organization was also strengthened during this period.

Arthur Balfour was party leader from 1902 to 1911, and Prime Minister from 1902 until his great electoral defeat in 1906. The party became more narrowly conservative, especially on social issues, and also took up the issue of tariff reform (the introduction of some form of imperial preference in place of Free Trade) which was to remain a divisive issue within the Conservative Party until well into the inter-war years.

The Conservative Party remained in opposition from 1906 until World War I. Bonar Law led the party from 1911 until 1921, taking a strong line, in particular in defence of Ulster Unionism.

From 1915 the Conservative Party took part in the Liberal led coalition governments of Asquith and Lloyd George. At the end of the war the Conservatives remained in coalition with the Lloyd George Liberals.

Upon Bonar Law's resignation as party leader in 1921 he was replaced by Austen Chamberlain, a supporter of the coalition. In a meeting, however, in the Carlton Club in late 1922 the Conservative parliamentary party in the Commons rejected their leader's wish to remain within the coalition by a vote of 185 to 88. Austen Chamberlain resigned and the Lloyd George coalition collapsed. After the subsequent election, the Conservatives were able to form a government, with Bonar Law recalled as party leader and Prime Minister. Bonar Law was again forced to retire on health grounds a few months later, and Stanley Baldwin was chosen as his successor. Baldwin, who was skilled in conciliation and compromise, remained as party leader for 14 years until 1937. He was Prime Minister from 1922–23 and 1924–29. In 1931 he brought the Conservatives into a national government under Ramsay MacDonald. The Conservatives were the main beneficiaries of the national government's electoral landslides in 1931 and 1935, and Baldwin was again Prime Minister from 1935–37.

After the royal abdication crisis in 1937 Baldwin retired, and was replaced by Neville Chamberlain, whose premiership was tarnished by the failure to rearm adequately in the face of the increasing threat from Nazi Germany, and his policy of appeasement which culminated in Munich in 1938.

In 1940 Chamberlain was forced to resign after it became apparent that he had lost the confidence of the House. The subsequent wartime coalition government was then led by Winston Churchill (an opponent of appeasement, who had left the Conservative Party to become a Liberal in 1904, and only rejoined it in 1925), whose inspiring oratory and ruthless and single-minded leadership were ideally suited for the circumstances.

In the 1945 election, however, the Conservatives suffered an overwhelming defeat. Churchill remained as leader of the opposition, and the party structure underwent a successful reorganization under the successive party chairmanships of Lords Clitheroe and Woolton.

In the 1950 elections the Conservatives greatly reduced the Labour government's majority, and in 1951 narrowly won the election. Churchill again became Prime Minister. The Conservatives in power changed the emphasis of policy, but did not overturn the legacy of the 1945–51 Labour government, and accepted the new welfare state. They did, however, succeed in loosening existing economic controls, and reducing economic austerity.

In 1955 Churchill was replaced as leader and Prime Minister by Anthony Eden. Shortly afterwards the Conservatives increased their majority at the 1955 general election. Eden's premiership was destroyed by the controversy over the Anglo-French Suez expedition. He resigned in January 1957 and Harold MacMillan won the leadership.

MacMillan was initially a successful Prime Minister, who led the Conservatives to their third successive electoral victory in the 1959 general election.

In his new term MacMillan put in motion the process of African decolonization and applied for UK membership of the EC in 1961. His image suffered, however, from his abrupt dismissal of a third of his Cabinet in July 1961, and de Gaulle's veto of British entry into the EC frustrated one of his key policy objectives. Incidents like the Profumo affair had a further damaging effect. MacMillan resigned as Prime Minister in 1963. Renouncing his peerage, Sir Alec Douglas-Home led the party into the 1964 election, in which the Conservatives lost by only a narrow margin.

When Home resigned as leader in July 1965,

Ted Heath became the first elected Conservative leader, winning 150 votes to 133 for Reginald Maudling and 15 for Enoch Powell.

In 1966 the Conservatives were severely defeated, but in 1970 won an unexpected victory in the general election, and Heath became Prime Minister. He initially promised more of the free market and less state intervention in the economy. In 1972, however, the government reversed its policies, with a revival of incomes policy, tripartite economic management between the government, employers and unions, industrial intervention and an expansionary budget.

In 1973 the government had its greatest success with British entry into the EC, but subsequently had increasing industrial difficulties, ending with an unsuccessful show-down with the miners. The Conservatives narrowly lost the ensuing election in February 1974 and lost again by a slightly wider margin in October 1974.

In 1975 Heath's leadership was challenged and he was unexpectedly outvoted by Margaret Thatcher in the first ballot (119 votes to 130). In the decisive second ballot, Margaret Thatcher with 146 votes defeated Whitelaw (79) and three other candidates to become the first woman to lead a major British political party.

In 1979, the Conservatives were returned to power, and Mrs Thatcher became Prime Minister. In the European Parliament elections shortly afterwards the Conservatives won 60 of the 81 UK seats on 50 per cent of the vote.

Mrs Thatcher's conviction politics polarized public opinion, but the successful Falklands expedition and a neatly divided opposition helped to lead the Conservatives to a huge victory in terms of seats in the 1983 elections.

In the 1984 European Parliament elections the Conservatives won 45 seats on 40.8 per cent of the poll. In the 1987 national election Mrs Thatcher won her third successive term of office with a slightly reduced overall majority (376 seats on 42 per cent of the vote).

Support

The Conservatives have now won three general elections in a row, but not with very high percentages of the total vote. Their major victories in 1983 and 1987 were in fact achieved with a lower percentage of the vote than when the Conservatives lost to Labour in the 1964 elections. The Conservative success in terms of seats is largely attributable to the effects of a majority electoral system at a time of divided opposition and of efficient concentration of the Conservative vote in Southern, rural and suburban England.

Nevertheless, the Conservatives are currently the party with the broadest national support, at least within England if not within Wales or Scotland. Not only are they the first party in most of rural and suburban England (in much of which Labour is only third), but they are the second party in most urban and industrial English seats, where Labour is first. They are the strongest party among managers and the self-employed, but also have had a greatly increased vote among the working class and among trade unionists, notably among skilled workers. This has been particularly true of those who have moved to New Towns (who have not automatically transferred their former, and generally Labour allegiance) and of owner-occupiers. In 1983 the Conservatives had 30 per cent higher support among owner-occupiers than among council house tenants (53 per cent to 23 per cent), and whereas the Conservatives were weaker than Labour among the working class as a whole, they appear to have been stronger than Labour among working class owner-occupiers.

The Conservatives have been traditionally strong among women, although this may have declined in 1987. Several other areas of past Conservative strength are no longer as significant as they were, such as the "landed" vote of squires and landowners (although larger farmers are still generally Conservative) and the Anglican Church ("the Tory party at prayer", as it used to be called).

On the other hand the Conservatives are particularly weak among the most disadvantaged social and economic groups, the unemployed, and among the ethnic minorities (to a greater extent among West Indians than among Asians).

In regional terms there has been surprising continuity in patterns of Conservatives' voting support over time. Even in Peel's time the Conservatives were the party of England in general, and of Southern and South-Eastern England in particular. They were already weak in Northern England and in Scotland.

In 1983 and 1987 this pattern is still true, and if anything, has been reinforced in recent years.

In both 1983 and 1987 the Conservatives won around 46 per cent of the English vote and a large majority of the seats (362 out of 523 in 1983, 357 in 1987).

In South-East England outside London they won 55.6 per cent of the vote in 1987 (an increase over 1983) and 107 out of the 108 parliamentary seats. Their best counties were Surrey (60.6 per cent) and West Sussex (60 per cent). In East Anglia their 1987 vote also increased from 1983, reaching 52.1 per cent and

winning 19 of the 20 seats. In South-Western England the Conservatives lost ground slightly to the Alliance but still won 50.6 per cent of the 1987 vote, with 44 out of the 48 seats. Even in London the Conservative vote increased in 1987 (although not in all constituencies).

The Conservatives gained 45.8 per cent of the Greater London vote and 57 out of the 84 constituencies (50 per cent and 44 out of 55 seats in outer London but still 36.9 per cent and 13 out of 29 seats in inner London).

The Conservatives also did well in the volatile Midlands, with 48.6 per cent of the vote in 1987 in the East Midlands (31 out of the 42 seats) and 45.5 per cent in the West Midlands (36 out of the 58 seats). Even in Birmingham it won 38.8 per cent, and five out of the 11 seats.

In Northern England the Conservatives are generally much weaker. In 1987 they won 37.4 per cent in Yorkshire and Humberside (21 out of the 54 seats), 38 per cent in North-Western England (34 out of 73 seats) and 32.3 per cent in Northern England (eight out of 36 seats).

They are particularly weak in the Metropolitan County of South Yorkshire (24.9 per cent in 1987, down from 28 per cent in 1983, and with only one of the 15 seats), Durham and Northumberland (28 per cent each in 1987) and Merseyside (28.9 per cent). Their weakest cities are Liverpool (17.4 per cent in 1987, down from 29.3 per cent in 1983), Sheffield (24.9 per cent in 1987, down from 29.4 per cent), Manchester (27.5 per cent), Hull (27.7 per cent) and Newcastle (29.9 per cent). In Teesside they had 31.4 per cent in 1987, in Leeds 33.6 per cent and Bradford 39 per cent. They won no seats at all in 1987 out of the 20 in Bradford, Hull, Liverpool, Manchester and Newcastle.

On the other hand the Conservatives did well in many parts of rural and suburban Northern England (county of North Yorkshire 53.1 per cent in 1987), and even in individual urban constituencies (Bolton, Hyndburn), where they held seats against the odds.

The Conservatives had no such consolation in Scotland, where their already weak position in 1983, was greatly eroded in 1987, and where they lost seats not just in inner city and heavy industrial seats, but also in rural constituencies (e.g. Argyll and North-East Fife to the Alliance, Banff, Moray and Angus to the SNP) and prosperous suburban constituencies (e.g. Strathkelvin and Bearsden to Labour). In 1987 they only won 24 per cent of the Scottish vote and 10 of the 72 seats, compared to 28.4 per cent and 21 seats in 1983. In Glasgow they only won 12.6 per cent of the vote (compared to 18.8 per cent in 1983) and none of the 11 seats.

The Conservatives also did badly in Wales

in 1987, arresting a longer term improvement in their vote in an area of traditional weakness. Their vote dropped much less than in Scotland (29.5 per cent in Wales in 1987, compared to 31 per cent in 1983) but they lost six of their seats (holding eight out of 38 Welsh seats in 1987, instead of 14 in 1983).

They still have substantial support in Cardiff (38.9 per cent in 1987), in the non-Welsh speaking areas of rural Wales (e.g. South Glamorgan, Pembrokeshire) and the retirement and holiday towns on the North Welsh coast. They are still weakest in industrial South Wales (Mid-Glamorgan 17.8 per cent in 1987 and none of the seven seats).

Organization

The Conservatives have the highest membership of any British party (around 1.5 million, down from around 2.8 million in 1953), and are also the wealthiest and best organized. It is a direct membership party, but with a three-headed organizational structure consisting of its constituency associations within the National Union, the parliamentary party and the party's administrative apparatus (Central Office) and also with a powerful network of affiliated organizations. Relations between the parliamentary party and the party at large have been much less divisive than within the Labour Party, with much less pressure for extra-parliamentary control and much more emphasis on party unity and discipline. The party leadership has more scope for independent manoeuvre, and the party conference is more stage managed, with motions selected for debate being rarely hostile to the leadership. On the other hand the Conservative Party has been more ruthless in despatching defeated leaders than the Labour Party, and individual constituencies do not take kindly to outsiders being imposed on them by Central Office.

The basic units of Conservative Party organization are its constituency associations. Each association has an executive council of between 30 and 80 members, which elects a smaller finance and general purposes committee. The association officers include a president, a chairman (the effective leader of the association), and an honorary treasurer. The officers are elected annually by the executive council and are not meant to hold office for more than three consecutive years. Many constituencies also have one full time party professional or agent. Although their numbers have declined there were still 280 such agents in 1985, by far the largest number in any British political party.

At local level within the constituencies the party is organized into ward or polling district branches. Where possible the party tries to organize itself at an even more local or "block" level.

Above the constituencies the party is organized within separate areas in England and Wales. The Scottish Conservative Party has a separate organization.

Each area has its area council (consisting of MPs and candidates, representatives of the constituencies, and affiliated organizations), an executive committee, a finance and general purposes committee and area officers elected annually at the area council. Central Office is represented by an area agent and one or more deputies.

At national level the umbrella organization for the constituency associations is the National Union, which has an executive committee of around 200 members meeting around eight or nine times a year, and a smaller (around 60 members) general purposes committee, meeting around five times a year. The party chairman (who may be in the Commons or the Lords) and the deputy chairman and vice-chairman are directly appointed by the party leader and not by the National Union.

The central council of the National Union includes five representatives of each constituency as well as Conservative parliamentarians and representatives of the area and affiliated organizations and meets once a year in the spring. With up to 4,000 members it resembles the party conference on a smaller scale.

The party conference is held annually, over a week in October. Over 5,000 members may attend, including eight representatives from each constituency. Unlike the Labour Party Conference the Conservative Party Conference does not formally make policy, but acts more as a party rally, and also as a sounding board for party opinion.

There are also separate Scottish and Welsh conferences.

The party leader was until 1965 chosen by an informal process of consultation and soundings among influential members of the party, but since that date has been directly elected by the parliamentary party in the Commons. In the first ballot victory can only be obtained by a candidate with an overall majority and, at the same time, 15 per cent ahead of the next candidate in terms of all those entitled to vote. In the second ballot all the candidates may remain, and new ones may enter the contest. An overall majority is required in the third ballot. Only the three highest placed candidates may remain, and the single transferable vote is used to find the winner. When the party is in opposition, the leader must be re-elected every year (although this is generally a formality). The leader chooses the Cabinet and other ministers, when in government, and the shadow spokesmen in the Lords and Commons when in opposition.

Within the parliamentary party in the Commons there is a powerful backbench committee, called the "1922 Committee" (after the meeting of MPs at the Carlton Club which rejected Lloyd George's coalition). Its chairman and executive committee are elected annually by the backbenchers. It meets weekly. When in power ministers do not attend, but the whips are present. There are also party backbench committees, which generally meet weekly. When in opposition, they are normally chaired by the appropriate shadow minister. A special business committee brings together the officers of the 1922 committee and of the backbench committees.

There are also more informal groupings of Conservative members on a more ideological basis. The most well known of these is a grouping on the party right, the "Monday Club".

Conservative Party Central Office co-ordinates the party apparatus and the network of Conservative agents, and consists of a number of departments. Within it is the Conservative Political Centre, the former educational department of the party, which is responsible for organizing courses and policy discussions. The Conservative research department is most influential when the party is in opposition. There is also a party adult education college, Swinton Conservative College.

Conservative Party parliamentary candidates are chosen by the constituency associations. A list of approved parliamentary candidates is kept at the Central Office, with approval now being based on a written and oral selection process on almost civil service lines. The constituency associations, however, need not choose someone on the central list. Shortlists are drawn up by special selection committees and generally no less than three candidates are asked to address the constituency executive committee. These used to take the effective decision, with the candidates' appearance before a general meeting of the association being a formality, but associations are now encouraged to leave the final decision to such a general meeting. The party's central standing advisory committee on candidates has the power to withhold or withdraw approval of a selected candidate.

The Young Conservatives (founded as the Junior Imperial League in 1906) have branches in most constituencies, and an advisory committee at national level. The Conservative student organization is now the Conservative Collegiate Forum after its predecessor, the Federation of Conservative Students was disbanded by Central Office for its right-wing libertarian views and indiscipline. There is also a Conservative Graduates' Association.

There are women's branches in most constituencies. At national level there is a women's national advisory committee and an annual women's conference.

The Conservative Trade Unionists were founded as the central Labour Advisory Committee in 1918. Other advisory committees at national level include that on local government and that of the Conservative political centre.

The Conservative clubs have played an important role in Conservative Party organization, starting from the Carlton Club in the 1830s. The Association of Conservative Clubs, founded in 1894, includes two representatives from each of the Carlton, Junior Carlton, Constitution and St Stephen's Clubs, and representatives of the other 1,500 affiliated and inter-affiliated local Conservative clubs.

In recent years a number of think tanks have had significant influence in the development of conservative policy, although their links with the party have only been informal. The Centre for Policy Studies has been particularly influential.

The Conservative Party's national newsletter to its members is called *Newsline*.

Conservative Party finance depends largely on both fundraising within the constituencies and donations from business. Of the £11.1 million raised in 1985 £7.8 million was raised in the constituencies (of which just under £1 million was contributed to central funds) and £3 million consisted of donations. The party's honorary joint treasurers play a key role in central fund raising. The party has no minimum individual membership subscription, but asks for an average annual donation of at least £6 per member.

The Conservative Party used to have close links with the Unionist party in Northern Ireland, but these have been cut, and relations have grown increasingly distant.

In the European Parliament the 45 Conservative members are the largest component within the European Democratic Group, and have always provided its chairman. The other Conservative international affiliations are with the European and International Democratic Unions.

Policies

The Conservative Party has traditionally been a broad-based party of the centre-right. It has tended to distrust ideology and abstract ideas, and emphasized a few broad themes, the need for gradual change while conserving the best of national traditions and institutions, defence of God, King and Country (and for a time also Empire), the need to maintain the freedom of the individual, and the need for state intervention to be kept within limits. Its liberal economic instincts, and defence of landed (and later middle-class and business interests) have often, however, been counterbalanced by aristocratic paternalism, and "One Nation" conservatism. In its long periods in government it has generally been pragmatic, and has on several occasions been prepared to enter into coalition with other parties. After 1951 the Conservative government did not attempt to reverse the welfare state, accepted a considerable degree of state economic intervention and only denationalized steel.

Margaret Thatcher has created a new, harder and more populist image for the Conservative party, emphasizing law and order and patriotism, the free market and popular capitalism, hostility to big government, to trade unions and to left wing local councils, and even to the "establishment". This image is partly a reflection of Mrs Thatcher's own personal style of leadership, but also of longer-term changes within the Conservative Party, in which landed interests and Tory paternalism are no longer so important, and in which many prominent members are self-made men of middle-class or even skilled working-class origin. The current Conservative Party puts more emphasis on economic liberalism.

In spite of these changes, the Conservative Party still contains a wide spectrum of opinion. A distinction is often made between more socially concerned "wets" and hard-line "drys". While many of the former have been dropped by Mrs Thatcher from her Cabinets, they are still well represented within the party. Moreover the distinction is mainly valid for economic policy matters. Many of those who are "dry" on economic matters are liberal on social and moral matters. True social Conservatives are more common among the constituency activists, and to a lesser extent among the backbenchers than among the members of the government. This particularly emerges in debates on such subjects as pornography, law and order and hanging. Nevertheless, the different strands of the extreme right within the party (whether advocating total reliance on market forces and dismantling of the welfare state, a "moral majority" social programme, or anti-immigrant views) are generally weak.

One of the reasons for the Conservative Party's electoral success has been its continuing capacity to adapt to new circumstances. It is currently going through a particularly successful period, due partly to its policies and image of strong leadership, and partly to the divisions among the opposition parties. It is uncertain how it will adapt when it eventually loses its current political dominance, and whether, for example, it will again adopt a more conciliatory style.

The Conservative government's economic policy has emphasized greater reliance on market forces, reducing the size of the public sector which it has seen as "crowding out" the private sector, and greater concern with fighting against inflation rather than against unemployment.

When they came to power the key economic decision-makers were hostile to traditional Keynesian demand management techniques, and favoured supply side measures instead. They put their reliance on monetarist doctrine, controlling the growth of the money supply, and developing a medium-term financial strategy. They sought to cut government spending, and to reduce the size of the public sector borrowing requirement.

There was also a shift away from direct towards indirect taxation. The top marginal rates of income tax were immediately cut, and the standard rate has also been reduced. On the other hand there was an immediate increase in VAT rates, although the Conservatives have continued to defend the continuation of zero rates on such items as food, fuel and housing.

Other themes have been the removal of exchange-controls, and the reduction of bureaucratic controls in general.

Privatization has progressively gained more and more emphasis. By selling off shares in public companies to the wider public the Conservatives have also favoured their objectives of greatly extending share ownership, and of popular capitalism.

Other sectors (e.g. bus transport) have been deregulated.

The Conservatives have put a strong emphasis on self-employment, on small firms and on the services sector. The need to create an "enterprise culture" has been a repeated theme. Regional policy has received less emphasis. In practice, however, the government has often been pragmatic, and has provided subsidies for companies such as British Leyland.

Another strong theme has been the need for Britain to move away from economic corporatism, and from state planning and tripartite concertation. The Conservatives have argued, in particular, that the trade unions had grown much too powerful by the 1970s and trade union reform has featured in the three successive Conservative governments. They also eventually won a long and bitter confrontation with the miners in the second Thatcher government.

Whereas trade union democracy has been strongly emphasized by the Conservatives, they have opposed statutory workers rights to be informed and consulted on the lines of the EC's Vredeling proposals.

The Conservatives have supported the continued use of civil nuclear energy.

They have recently put an increasing emphasis on the need to reconcile agricultural and environmental objectives.

The Conservatives emphasize that it is not their intention to dismantle the welfare state, and that they have increased spending in crucial areas such as health care. They seek, however, to make it more cost effective.

One of the Conservative's most popular policies has been in the field of housing, with the sale of council houses to their tenants at reduced rates. The Conservatives are also seeking to increase opportunities for private rented accommodation.

In the field of education, the Conservatives have been very critical of the trend towards comprehensive schools at the expense of the grammar schools, and have strongly defended the independent schools. The present government is now trying to develop a national core curriculum for all schools, to increase parental choice, to allow popular schools to expand in size and to allow state schools to opt out of local education authority control.

The need for tough law and order measures and support for the police have been particularly strong themes at Conservative Party conferences. The majority of party activists, Mrs Thatcher and the majority of Conservative backbenchers have been in favour of capital punishment, but a majority of cabinet members have been opposed, in the series of parliamentary votes on its reintroduction.

Leading Conservative spokesmen have attacked the permissiveness of British society, and called for a return to more traditional moral values, but this has not been a major emphasis of government policy. The recent attempt, for example, to modify the British abortion laws in a less liberal direction was supported by many Conservative MPs, but the government did not help the bill's passage.

Immigration has been a sensitive theme within the Conservative Party ever since Enoch Powell's "rivers of blood" speech in 1968, in which he warned of the great dangers of immigration, which caused him to be sacked from Heath's shadow Cabinet. Conservative manifestos have taken care to point out the tough measures that they are taking to restrict further immigration into Britain, while opposing discrimination against ethnic minorities within Britain.

The Conservatives have also been considering alternatives to the existing broadcasting system, including greater reliance on advertising instead of licence fees and liberalizing the transfer of Independent Television licences.

The Conservative government has done little in the field of constitutional reform. They have defended the House of Lords against proposals for its abolition or reform from other parties. Only a minority of Conservatives have supported any change from majority voting to proportional representation. When in opposition Ted Heath's shadow Cabinet had supported the establishment of a Scottish Assembly but no initiative was taken to this effect during his government. The majority of Conservatives have subsequently been opposed to Welsh and Scottish devolution.

The government has also been opposed to enactment of major freedom of information legislation, and has taken a number of well publicized actions to prevent the diffusion of classified information. It has now put forward a restricted reform of the Official Secrets Act.

A vocal minority of Conservatives have been strong defenders of the Ulster Unionist cause in Northern Ireland (a controversial issue within the party since the 19th century), but the Conservatives no longer have close ties with the Unionists. One of the Conservative government's major policy initiatives has been the establishment of the Anglo-Irish Agreement.

The Conservatives have attacked local government overspending, and the actions of left wing Labour councils in particular. They have "rate-capped" a considerable number of councils, and abolished the Greater London Council, and the metropolitan counties. They are now attempting to replace the entire system of local government rates with a community charge or "poll tax".

On defence policy the Conservatives have not suffered the policy divisions of the other British parties. They have argued that a strong defence policy constitutes the most effective peace policy, and in their 1987 manifesto claimed to have increased defence spending by more than 20 per cent in real terms since 1979. They believe in the retention of an independent British nuclear deterrent, and are currently updating it with the introduction of Trident. They claim that their acceptance of Cruise missiles being stationed in Britain was one of the factors bringing the Soviet Union back to the negotiating table.

As regards the European Community, the Conservatives have generally supported British membership, having made the first application to join under MacMillan, and having brought Britain in under Ted Heath.

The Conservatives contrast their support for the Community, but strong defence of British interests, with Labour's hostility and what they see as the SDP and SLD's federalist over-enthusiasm. There is, however, a minority of anti-marketeers and Community minimalists within the Conservative parliamentary party, and another minority of committed federalists, who are better represented among the Conservative MEPs.

The Conservatives have emphasized the need for a Community internal market, especially in such fields as services, and the liberalization of capital movements. Full British membership in the European Monetary System exchange rate mechanism has been a controversial issue within the government, with the Prime Minister opposed and some others now in favour.

A particular emphasis of the Conservative government has been on mitigating the British contributions to the European Community budget, and general EC budgetary discipline. They have been wary about increased Community spending in areas such as research. Liberalization of air transport has been another theme.

The Conservatives have tended to emphasize their practical approach towards European economic integration contrasting with the usual rhetoric on European union which they see as short on substance.

Margaret Thatcher has recently emphasized her preference for cautious step-by-step co-operation, and her hostility to more visionary steps, such as a European Central Bank and European Union. Conservatives in the European Parliament mainly abstained on the Spinelli Draft Treaty on European Union, but were generally in favour of the Single European Act.

The Conservatives have generally supported European political co-operation, and increased European co-operation on defence and security matters.

On other foreign policy issues the Conservatives have continued to emphasize the dangers posed by the Soviet Union, and were highly critical of events in Poland and Afghanistan. Their 1987 manifesto stated that they would not negotiate on the sovereignty of the Falklands. They were flexible, however, in negotiating a final agreement in Zimbabwe (support for Rhodesia had been a rallying call among many on the Tory right in the 1960s and 1970s), and a

new status for Hong Kong. The Prime Minister has opposed trade and economic sanctions on South Africa. The Conservative government also followed the American lead in withdrawing from British membership of UNESCO.

Personalities

Margaret Thatcher has been the leader of the Conservative Party since 1975 and British Prime Minister since 1979. She has a scientific and legal background, and represents Finchley in London. She has been an unusually dominant party leader, and has won three successive general elections. There has been a steady turnover among her ministers, notably among those who appeared most sceptical about the change in policy emphasis, such as Prior, Pym and Soames.

Among the most prominent current ministers are Sir Geoffrey Howe, who was previously Chancellor of the Exchequer, and is now Secretary of State for Foreign Affairs, and the current Chancellor of the Exchequer Nigel Lawson. Douglas Hurd, a former Minister for Northern Ireland is the current Home Secretary. Cecil Parkinson, the current Secretary of State for Energy is a former successful chairman of the party and has been strongly supported by Mrs Thatcher. Among others who have become more prominent in recent years are Kenneth Baker, the Secretary of State for Education and Science and Kenneth Clarke, the newly promoted Health Minister. Nicholas Ridley, the Secretary of State for the Environment, is a prominent "dry". Peter Walker, the Secretary of State for Wales, and who has held several ministerial positions, is a former supporter of Ted Heath, and the only survivor of the original "wets" in the government.

Of leading Conservatives outside the government, Michael Heseltine, a former Secretary of State for the Environment and for Defence, who resigned over the Westland affair, is a possible leadership contender, as was the former minister and party chairman, Norman Tebbit, although this possibility has now receded. Leon Brittan is the Conservative member of the European Commission.

Labour Party

Headquarters	: 144–162 Walworth Road, London SE17 1JT (tel: 01–703 0833)
Leader	: Neil Kinnock
Deputy leader	: Roy Hattersley
General secretary	: Larry Whitty

Membership : 300,000 (1986 – figures for direct membership)

Founded : 1900

History

The Labour Representation Committee was set up in 1900 as a loose alliance between the trade unions and a number of Socialist organizations, the Independent Labour Party (ILP, founded in 1893 by Keir Hardie), the Social Democratic Federation (SDF, a Marxist group founded by H. M. Hyndman in 1883) and the Fabian Society, an intellectual ginger group advocating gradualist Socialism that had been founded in 1884. The new alliance had no direct membership and no one unifying ideology. Its central objective was to secure the election of more "Labour" candidates to Parliament.

In the 1900 election it obtained two MPs, Keir Hardie and Richard Bell. In 1901 it suffered its first schism, with the departure of the SDF Marxists.

After the 1906 election the greatly enlarged parliamentary group of 29 elected Keir Hardie as its first chairman. The alliance also changed its name to the Labour Party, but continued as a federation without direct membership.

In 1914 the ILP initially opposed the war. Eventually, however, Labour members participated in the wartime coalition governments of both Asquith and Lloyd George.

In 1918 Labour left the coalition government and won 59 seats in the general election. It also adopted a new constitution. Direct membership was now allowed for the first time, and local Labour parties were represented on the party executive (as were women's sections), although the majority of executive posts remained in the hands of the affiliated organizations, executive committee members were to be chosen directly by the whole conference instead of on a reserved basis.

The constitution also provided a new Socialist purpose for the party, notably in its celebrated "clause 4–4", which established the objective of the common ownership of the means of production.

Labour later refused the Communist Party's request to affiliate and also decided not to adhere to the Third International. For a while certain Communist candidates were not opposed and even endorsed by Labour, but later the party took a harsher attitude towards Communist party membership.

In the 1922 election Labour made a great advance to 142 seats. Ramsay MacDonald was subsequently elected as parliamentary party chairman and for the first time was now referred to as the party "leader".

In the 1923 elections Labour became the single largest party. Early in 1924 MacDonald became Prime Minister in the first, minority, Labour administration, which was defeated in Parliament after only eight months in office. In the subsequent general election it had a net loss of 40 seats.

In the 1929 election Labour won 288 seats, and formed its second minority government under Ramsay MacDonald. In 1931 proposed austerity measures, including a 10 per cent cut in unemployment benefits, split the Cabinet. MacDonald eventually emerged as leader of national government with the Conservatives and certain Liberals. All those associated with the national government were subsequently expelled by the Labour Party. In the election that followed the party was reduced to only 52 members, and lost most of its prominent parliamentarians. MacDonald's "betrayal" remained a long term sore within the party.

MacDonald was succeeded as leader by Henderson, but as he did not regain a place in Parliament, he was replaced by the elderly pacifist, George Lansbury.

In the years 1931 and 1932 the Labour Party suffered two schisms, the first when Oswald Mosley (whose attempt to get the party to advocate expansionary economic policies had not been supported) left and set up the New Party (subsequently to become Fascist); the second when the increasingly radical and marginal ILP (under the leadership of Jimmy Maxton) finally went its separate way.

After Lansbury's resignation as leader, Clement Attlee became stopgap leader until the 1935 general election when Labour rose to 154 seats. Attlee then defeated Herbert Morrison and Arthur Greenwood to retain the party leadership, a post he was to hold for 20 years until 1955.

In 1937 the party constitution was again revised, to provide for separate election of the trade unions, constituency and socialist society members of the national executive rather than by the whole conference.

In 1939 the Labour Party supported British involvement with less dissent than in 1914. In 1940 Labour joined Churchill's War Cabinet, with Attlee as Deputy Prime Minister. In 1945 they won a massive victory at the polls, and formed their first government with an outright parliamentary majority. The Attlee government carried out a number of major reforms, including the creation of a free National Health Service, as well as large scale nationalizations. In the 1950 election, however, it lost 78 seats, but narrowly held on to power. In 1951 the party was further damaged when three Labour ministers, led by Aneurin Bevan, resigned over the proposal to impose certain charges within the National Health Service. Finally the Labour government lost power in 1951.

Labour now went into opposition for 13 years, losing further general elections in 1955 (after which Attlee finally retired and Hugh Gaitskell became the new party leader) and in 1959.

After the 1959 elections Gaitskell tried unsuccessfully to modernize the party's objectives by eliminating clause 4-4 from the Labour Party constitution. In 1960 the party conference took a decision to support unilateral nuclear disarmament. Gaitskell refused to accept the decision, and had it reversed at the 1961 party conference, winning new authority within the party. In 1963, however, he died suddenly and was succeeded by Harold Wilson.

In 1964 Labour won a narrow victory and Harold Wilson became Prime Minister. In 1966 he called new elections, in which he greatly increased his majority.

After Labour's election defeat in 1970 the party became increasingly divided over the Common Market issue.

In the aftermath of the 1974 miners' strike Labour narrowly regained power and slightly increased its majority in further elections held later the same year. Labour sought to distinguish itself from the Conservatives by intensifying co-operation with the trade unions through the "Social Contract".

In 1976 Wilson unexpectedly resigned, and James Callaghan became the new party leader and Prime Minister.

The government's fragile majority was temporarily bolstered by a pact with the Liberal Party. Labour got into increasing political difficulties over its unsuccessful attempt to introduce devolution in Scotland and Wales, and over a wave of official and unofficial strikes in the winter of 1978–79. In the 1979 elections Labour lost to the Conservatives and in the subsequent European Parliament elections only won 17 seats.

In opposition Labour entered a period of damaging internal disputes, with the party left seeking to assert greater party control over the actions of the parliamentary party and of future Labour governments.

In 1980 Callaghan stood down as leader and in the last election under the old rules of election by the parliamentary party, the candidate of the left, Michael Foot, defeated Denis Healey by 139 votes to 129. Shortly afterwards there was a bitter contest over the party deputy leadership, in which Healey narrowly defeated Benn in the

first test of the new electoral college by 50.4 per cent to 49.6 per cent.

In January 1981 a number of prominent Labour politicians finally broke away from the party, and founded the new Social Democratic Party (see separate entry).

In the 1983 general election, Labour only won 209 seats on 27.6 per cent of the vote, its worst result in seats since 1935 and in percentage of the vote since 1918.

After the election Michael Foot stood down as leader. The electoral college then chose Neil Kinnock as leader, and Roy Hattersley as deputy leader. In the 1984 European Parliament elections Labour made a substantial recovery, winning 32 seats on 39 per cent of the poll. In the 1987 general election, however, Labour suffered another severe defeat, winning 229 seats on 30.8 per cent of the vote.

Support

Since the 1920s Labour has been the dominant party in industrial Britain and among the working class. It has always fared less well in rural areas, especially in England, although in its *annus mirabilis* of 1945 it won a surprising number of predominantly rural seats. In its best periods (notably in 1945 to 1951 and in the 1960s) it has also appealed more widely to middle class voters, and to professionals.

The party's electoral base has been severely eroded in recent years. From a high of 48 per cent as recently as 1966, it only won 27.6 per cent in 1983 and 30.8 per cent in 1987. The working class vote has become less solid for Labour. Its old non-conformist support is no longer a very important determinant. In much of suburban and rural England Labour's support has become extremely weak. While it has become stronger than ever among the most disadvantaged (the urban poor, the unemployed, black people, people living in council houses and the less educated), it has become weaker amongst professionals and business people, those in employment and those owning their own houses. In spite of this narrowing appeal the concentration of Labour's vote has meant that it can still rely on a substantial number of parliamentary seats.

In regional terms Labour is strongest in the cities and industrial areas of the North of England, and of Scotland and Wales. There had already been a long term trend to Labour in many of these areas and this was strongly reinforced in 1987.

In the English metropolitan counties outside London, Labour is the largest party in five out of the six, and there were big swings in

Labour's favour in most of them (e.g. South Yorkshire 48.8 per cent in 1983 to 56 per cent in 1987, Tyne and Wear 45.4 per cent to 53.6 per cent, Merseyside 39.9 per cent to 47.4 per cent). Labour is the largest party in 15 out of 20 of Britain's largest cities, with its highest urban votes in Glasgow (61.8 per cent in 1987), in Liverpool (56.8 per cent), Manchester (54.5 per cent), Hull (53.2 per cent), and Sheffield (50.4 per cent). In all these cities, apart from Sheffield and Manchester (one seat each for the Conservatives), Labour won all the seats. Labour also did very well in all those mining areas, where the miners' strike had been well supported, losing badly, however, in the break-away miners' areas in Nottinghamshire.

Labour did best of all in Scotland, where it won 42.4 per cent of the vote (compared to 35.1 per cent in 1983) and 50 of the 72 seats. It did particularly well in central Scotland, winning prosperous suburban seats (such as Strathkelvin and Bearsden) as well as its traditional inner-city and industrial seats, and even increasing its vote in rural Scotland.

In 1987 Labour also did well in Wales, reversing a slow decline in the Labour vote in many parts of the Principality. Labour won 45.1 per cent of the Welsh vote and 24 of the 38 seats, continuing its old dominance of the South Wales mining area (63.9 per cent of the vote in the county of Mid Glamorgan) and obtaining its highest majority of over 30,000 in the Rhondda seat, but also polling well in the middle-class and professional areas of cities like Cardiff.

In the traditionally volatile areas of the West Midlands and of London Labour fared less well than in other urban areas, although it increased its 1987 vote over 1983. In London, however, Labour had a net loss of three seats to the Conservatives, with good swings in its favour in some seats but severe setbacks in others.

In the non-metropolitan English counties, Labour was third to the Conservatives and the Alliance in 24 out of 39 counties. In the South outside London Labour generally fared very poorly for a national party, winning 16.8 per cent and one out of the 108 seats in South-East England outside London, 15.9 per cent and one out of 48 seats in South-West England and 21.4 per cent and one out of 20 seats in East Anglia, where Labour used to have its main agricultural strength (among the Norfolk farmworkers), which has now practically dis-appeared. Labour's worst counties are in the more prosperous regions of the Home Counties (Surrey 11.4 per cent in 1987, West Sussex 11.8 per cent) and in the South-West (Dorset 11.3 per cent, Somerset 11.8 per cent, Cornwall 12.6 per cent).

Organization

The Labour Party is unusual among European parties in retaining a mix of direct and indirect membership and an organic relationship with the trade union movement. The early 1980s were dominated by constitutional battles which ended up with rules changes favouring the extraparliamentary party. The leadership is now faced with the dilemma of how best to extend intra-party democracy (such as through the introduction of one person, one vote, on such matters as candidate selection and reselection) while retaining a powerful role for the trade unions.

In 1987 the Labour Party claimed just under 300,000 direct members, compared to over one million in 1952.

The basic organizational unit is the constitu-ency party, each of which has a general com-mittee consisting of delegates from the affiliated organizations (trade union branches and trades councils, socialist society and co-operative party branches) as well as from the bodies providing for direct individual participation, the local Labour Party branches, the women's sections or councils, and the Labour Party Young Socialist branches. The constituency's executive commit-tee is then elected on a representative basis at an annual meeting of the constituency party.

A key problem faced by the constituency parties is the decline in the number of party agents. In 1951 there were 296 full-time con-stituency agents, by 1980 this was down to only 100, and the number has further declined since.

The next possible tier above the constituencies are the district Labour parties, in which two or more constituencies may be involved. Above these are the county Labour parties (in Scotland regional parties), with their own management and executive committees.

The Labour Party also has regional councils, which have generally had little power within the party.

At national level the Labour Party Conference takes place on an annual basis. Delegates to the conference are elected by the constituency Labour parties (on the basis of one delegate for up to 5,000 members) as well as by the co-operative societies, the national Socialist societies (like the Fabians) and the national trade unions. Labour MPs and endorsed can-didates participate at the conference on an ex officio basis. Delegates are often mandated.

There are only slightly more trade union delegates than constituency party delegates, since the trade unions do not usually take up their full complement of one delegate for every

5,000 members. The co-operatives and socialist societies only send a handful of members.

In terms of voting power, however, the conference is dominated by the trade unions, whose voting weight has even risen since the decline in the individual membership of the constituency parties. Already by 1970 the unions were casting over 85 per cent of the votes, and the largest unions had more voting weight than all the constituency parties put together.

The most controversial feature of the trade unions' dominance of the conference has been the fact that the individual unions' votes are cast as a block, with no consideration of minority standpoints within the union and with non-party members being able to play a role. Key conference decisions have thus often depended on small majorities within the delegations of the larger unions. The elimination of the block vote is an objective of some party reformers.

Party activists, however, have tended to be more concerned about the non-application of conference decisions by Labour's leadership, a periodic complaint which took particularly intense form after the fall of the last Labour government in 1979.

Two thirds majorities at party conferences are required for a policy to be included in the manifesto.

The party conference also elects the National Executive Committee (NEC), which consists of 12 trade union representatives, seven members of the constituency parties, one of the socialist societies and one youth representative (each elected by their separate organizations), a women's section of five members and the party treasurer (both elected by the whole conference, and hence dominated by the block vote) and the party leader and deputy leader sitting on the NEC on an ex officio basis. The NEC has a powerful role within the party, and its composition is a matter of key importance for the party leadership, with which the NEC has sometimes been at odds.

The NEC also has a number of important sub-committees (e.g. Organization and Home Policy) and a number of advisory committees.

In the early 1980s one proposed reform was to give the NEC full control of the party election manifesto, instead of responsibility being shared by the NEC and the parliamentary party. This proposal was not implemented.

The parliamentary party has its own caucus, and elects its own officers, including its chairman. When the party is in opposition it also holds shadow Cabinet elections, in large measure a popularity test among MPs, but one which the leader must bear carefully in mind in allocating shadow Cabinet positions.

Until the early 1980s the Parliamentary Labour Party also used to have exclusive responsibility for choosing the party leader. After a long period of controversy within the party, the 1981 Wembley conference devised a new method whereby the leader and deputy leader are chosen by an electoral college, 40 per cent for the unions, 30 per cent for the Parliamentary Labour Party and 30 per cent for the constituencies.

The party headquarters are run by its general secretary.

Labour Party parliamentary candidates are chosen by the constituency parties, traditionally by a special selection conference on the basis of a shortlist drawn up by the constituency executive. The National Executive Committee has had the right to intercede. At the 1987 conference the party discussed ways of involving more party members in the choice of candidates. One member one vote was rejected, but the conference voted to widen the franchise for the selection (and reselection) of candidates to an electoral college, composed partly of the rank-and-file membership, and partly of the block votes of the local unions and of the local socialist societies. The precise details still had to be worked out.

One of the main constitutional reforms of the early 1980s was mandatory reselection of MPs during the life-time of each parliament, in order to permit challenges to sitting members and to make them more accountable to their constituencies. Relatively few members have since been de-selected, but many members now have to devote much more time to cultivate their relationships with their local parties.

The Labour Party's youth movement is the Labour Party Young Socialists. Accused of being dominated by the Militant Tendency, it was restructured at the 1987 party conference. Its upper age limit was reduced from 26 to 23 (cutting its 7,000 membership in half), and its regional structure was abolished. The youth representative of the NEC is now also to be chosen by the Labour Students and the Young Trade Unionists as well as by the Young Socialists.

There are women's sections councils throughout the party, and five women representatives on the NEC.

Many black members of the party have sought the introduction of special "black sections", but this has been rejected so far by the party leadership, and by the party conference.

There have been a number of organized groups or factions within the Labour Party, both on the party left ("Keep left", "Victory for Socialism", "Tribune", founded in 1966 and still functioning, the "Campaign for Labour Party Democracy", the "Labour Co-ordinating Committee", "London Labour Briefing", the "Campaign Group", etc.) and on the party right ("Campaign for Democratic Socialism", the "Manifesto Group", "Campaign for Labour Victory"). The most controversial, however, has been the "Militant Tendency", formally only a newspaper with an editorial board, but considered by the Labour leadership to constitute an illegal party within the party. Its leaders have been expelled, but it still has close links with some members of the parliamentary party.

The party used to produce its own newspaper for its members, *Labour Weekly*, but this has recently had to be discontinued.

Labour Party finance is still largely dominated by the contributions from the affiliated trade unions. In 1980 they contributed 80 per cent of the central party funds, and half of its local funds. In 1987 they raised £4 million for the party. Six million trade union members currently pay the political levy.

The current Labour Party membership fee is £10. There has been a recent proposal that those trade union members who already pay the political levy should pay only £2 to enjoy full membership rights.

The Labour Party is a member of the Socialist International, the Confederation of European Socialist parties, and of the Socialist group within the European Parliament (in which it has its own 32 member caucus, the British Labour Group).

Policies

The Labour Party has traditionally been a broad-based party, with its membership spanning the range from cautious Social Democrats to left-wing Socialists and more orthodox Marxists. There has always been a certain tension between Labour's ideals and its generally pragmatic behaviour when in government, and this has tended to come to the fore when the party has returned to opposition. This was particularly the case after the 1979 defeat, when the party's divisions cost it major support which it has failed to regain, although the troubles within the former Alliance have reduced the threat to its status as the leading opposition party.

The party leadership is thus in a difficult position. It would like to update the party's policies and to give it a more unified and outward-looking image. It must also appear to be firmly in charge, without sacrificing party democracy and radicalism. Moreover the party

must not appear to be too closely involved with the unions, while not alienating its historic partners and main financial sponsors. Some of the current leadership's recent difficulties are attributable to the tensions between these differing objectives.

Labour continues to emphasize certain central themes; that Britain must become a less divided society, that unemployment must be reduced, and that there must be greater emphasis on social and community values rather than on just individual freedoms. Specific policies, however, are having to be re-assessed.

The 1983 manifesto, which was heavily influenced by the left's alternative economic strategy, called for greatly increased public spending, economic planning, re-nationalization of public assets, the reintroduction of exchange controls and back-up import controls, with tariffs and quotas.

The 1987 programme referred more cautiously to the need for "social ownership" in certain strategic sectors, while not promising to reverse all privatizations that had taken place. It proposed a shorter and more flexible working week (but without mentioning specifics, unlike the 35-hour-week proposed in 1983). Labour proposed a £6 billion package to combat unemployment through public investment in infrastructure and new jobs in health, education and other caring services. It also called for a £3.6 billion anti-poverty programme, including a statutory national minimum wage. Among the ways Labour's programme would be financed would be through a wealth tax, and by reversing extra tax cuts for the richest 5 per cent in the population.

Labour called for the establishment of a British Industrial Investment Bank, to ensure finance for industry, and for a stronger regulatory framework for the City and for mergers, takeovers and monopolies.

Exchange and import controls were downplayed, as was state planning. Labour sought to replace the present government's legislation on trade unions, but supported union secret ballots on strike decisions, and in election for union executives.

Labour continues to support the introduction of greater industrial democracy, but has insisted that it be carried out through the existing trade unions. Since the experience of the last Labour government, the party has been generally hostile to statutory incomes policies, and has tended to prefer voluntary agreements within the collective bargaining framework.

The 1987 manifesto called for a gradual reduction in British dependence on civil nuclear energy, although there are supporters of nuclear power within the party. Labour has also called for a more vigorous environmental policy than that of the present government.

The Labour Party presents itself as the strongest defender of the welfare state and of the National Health Service.

Whereas the 1983 manifesto called for an end to enforced council house sales, the 1987 manifesto expressed support for the maintenance of council tenants' right to buy, but wanted local authorities to be required to invest the proceeds in constructing new houses for rent. Labour also sought to reverse the drop in public spending on housing. Labour maintains its traditional emphasis on ensuring security of tenure for private tenants.

On education policy Labour has been responsible for the introduction of comprehensive education and used hostile rhetoric against the public schools, but in 1987 did not call for their abolition. Labour has called for cheaper public transport, and opposed bus deregulation.

Labour has accepted the need for immigration controls, but emphasizes the need to combat discrimination and racism within Britain.

Labour has strongly associated itself (especially at local government level) with protection of the rights of the disadvantaged, of women and of ethnic and sexual minorities. Animal rights, and opposition to hunting, have been increasingly emphasized.

Some of its most publicised clashes with the present government have been over issues of local government expenditure. Labour opposes the poll tax, but has not come out strongly in favour of a specific alternative.

Devolution has been a controversial issue within the Labour Party, and helped to bring down the last Labour government. Labour now seeks the introduction of a democratically elected Scottish Assembly, but does not call for a Welsh Assembly. Its current leader was a strong opponent of such an Assembly. Instead it calls for greater powers and funding for the Welsh Development Agency.

A minority within the party have supported militant Irish republicanism. A United Ireland remains Labour's aspiration, but to be achieved peacefully, democratically and only by consent of its population. The Anglo-Irish Agreement is supported.

Labour calls strongly for a Freedom of Information Act. Its 1987 manifesto sought the introduction of state aid for political parties. The Labour left has called for the abolition of the House of Lords, but this has not been a major priority. Minorities on both the left and right of the party have also called for the introduction of proportional representation.

On foreign affairs issues Labour's internationalism has tended to be more oriented towards support of the Commonwealth, English-speaking developing countries and the UN than it has towards the European Community.

Labour's policy towards the latter has fluctuated considerably. In 1962 its leader Hugh Gaitskell opposed the first application to join the EC, but the second British application was made by the Wilson government. After 1970 the party became polarized between supporters and opponents of entry, generally but not exclusively on left-right lines. Wilson himself took a middle line, opposing the terms rather than the principle of entry. In 1971, 69 Labour rebels supported the Conservatives' entry terms. Labour eventually came out in favour of a referendum on EC membership. The Wilson government allowed its members to campaign on either side, although Wilson himself recommended acceptance of the renegotiated terms of membership.

From 1979 onwards Labour took an increasingly hostile view. It campaigned only very feebly in the 1979 European Parliament elections and in 1980 the conference came out in favour of British withdrawal, a request that was reflected in the 1983 manifesto.

By the 1984 European Parliament elections, Labour recognized that British withdrawal was not an immediate practical possibility, and called for Britain to get the best deal out of membership. Labour signed the European Socialist manifesto (unlike in 1979), although expressing reservations about some of its specific policies. The 1987 manifesto made no mention of withdrawal.

The Labour leadership is currently adopting a low-key approach towards European Community issues but the Community is sometimes now seen as an ally against the Conservative government. Party opinion, however, is still volatile.

Labour's strongest emphasis is on reform of the Common Agricultural Policy. It is concerned about the negative impacts of the 1992 internal market. It supports EC-wide reflation, and stronger EC regional, social, research and environmental policies. It is highly sceptical of further European integration, and generally opposed the Single European Act and the European Parliament's proposed Draft Treaty on European Union.

Probably no issue has harmed the Labour Party more electorally than that of defence, both because of divisions over this issue and because of the positions actually taken. The controversial element of the policy has been the move towards opposition to the British nuclear deterrent. The 1960 conference had originally adopted a unilateralist stance, but this was reversed in 1961. After 1979 the party as a whole again turned in favour of unilateral disarmament as Britain's contribution towards wider disarmament. Labour's 1987 manifesto called for the decommissioning of Polaris, the cancellation of Trident and, if necessary, the removal of American Cruise missiles and other nuclear weapons from British soil. Labour has continued to emphasize, however, that it supports British membership of NATO, and the maintenance of strong conventional defence forces. This policy is still supported by the large majority of party members, but a minority would prefer a more multilateral approach.

Other Labour foreign policy positions have included strong defence of human rights and support for much more comprehensive measures against the South African regime. In the past Labour has often been very pro-Israel, but the new Labour left has been more sympathetic to the Palestinian cause.

Personalities

The leader of the Labour Party is Neil Kinnock, first elected in the party conference in October 1983 at the age of 41. He has never been a Minister, but was shadow education spokesman from 1979 to 1983. His background is on the left-of-centre of the party (notably on the issue of unilateral disarmament), but he has been a generally pragmatic leader and on several occasions he has had to stand up to the party left. He is Welsh and represents Islwyn.

The deputy leader is Roy Hattersley, the former Minister for Prices and Consumer Protection from 1976 to 1979. He is associated with the centre-right of the party. He was the shadow home affairs spokesman from 1980 to 1983, shadow chancellor from 1983 to 1987, and since 1987 is again shadowing Home Affairs. He comes from Yorkshire, but represents a Birmingham seat (Sparkbrook).

Of the other shadow spokesmen among the most prominent is John Smith, the shadow chancellor. Bryan Gould, the trade and industry spokesman is a New Zealander who skilfully fronted Labour's election campaign in 1987, and subsequently came top of the shadow Cabinet elections. Gerald Kaufman is the spokesman on foreign and commonwealth affairs, and a former Minister of State for Industry from 1975–79. Dr John Cunningham is the spokesman on the environment, and Robin Cook is the health and social security spokesman. Gordon Brown is a newly prominent figure.

John Prescott, the shadow energy spokesman, unsuccessfully challenged Roy Hattersley for the deputy leadership of the party in 1988.

In 1988 the party left again challenged for the party leadership and deputy leadership, in a campaign designed as much to debate Labour's policy stance as to actually depose Kinnock and Hattersley. The unsuccessful candidate for the leadership was Tony Benn, the highly influential leader of the party left after the 1979 elections. One of the more influential of the soft left is the blind MP David Blunkett, from a local government background in Sheffield. One of the more well-known figures of the hard left is Ken Livingstone, the last leader of the Greater London Council.

Co-operative Party

Headquarters	: 158 Buckingham Palace Road, London SW1W 9UB (tel: 01–730 8187)
Secretary	: David Wise
Founded	: 1917

The first Co-operative was founded by a group in Rochdale in 1844. Co-op stores spread rapidly and in 1863 the Co-operative Wholesale Society was established. In 1869 the Co-operative Union was founded in order to co-ordinate Co-operative activities. It is still based in Manchester, and run by an executive elected by the societies.

In 1917 the congress decided that co-operators should seek direct representation in Parliament and local administrative bodies, and a Co-operative Party was established as a department of the Co-operative Union. From the start it worked closely with the Labour Party, and in 1918 Alfred Waterson was elected as the first Co-operative and Labour Member of Parliament.

It has never affiliated nationally with the Labour Party, but has come to an agreement of mutual co-operation with it. At local level Co-operative Society parties may affiliate to constituency Labour parties. One society, the Royal Arsenal Co-operative Society, has been directly affiliated to the Labour Party. In every election a number of candidates have continued to run as Labour and Co-operative candidates and are committed to join the Parliamentary Labour Party if elected. There has been an agreement whereby Co-operative Party candidates are allocated a certain percentage of safe, marginal and hopeless Labour seats. Difficulties have occasionally emerged as over the de-selection of the Labour and Co-operative MEP, Brian Key, before the 1984 European elections when the Co-operative Party protested without effect. After 1959 it was agreed that there should be up to 30 Co-operative candidates. In the 1987 general elections there were only 20, of whom nine were elected. There were six sponsored candidates in the 1984 European Parliament elections of whom three were elected. There are also a number of Co-operative Party members in the House of Lords.

The Co-operative Party organization is primarily dependent on affiliation by Co-operative Societies. There are over 100 subscribing societies, with the largest number in the Scottish, Midlands and Southern sections of the Co-operative Union. There are also individual members of the party (currently 15,000) and local party branches. An annual conference of the Co-operative Party takes place every spring. The party has a national executive committee, with representatives of the sections, the central executive, the Co-operative Wholesale Society, the Co-operative Presidents, the Co-operative Women's Guild and the parliamentary and European parliamentary Co-operative groups. The Co-operative Parliamentary Group elects a chairman, and appoints group spokesmen.

For its income the party is overwhelmingly dependent on donations from the societies, with individual membership contributions only playing a minor role. The Co-operative Party is affiliated to the International Co-operative Alliance.

In policy matters the Co-operative Party works closely with the Labour Party (the Co-operative, Labour and trade union movements meet in a consultative committee, known as the National Council of Labour). One area of policy difference has been on the European Community, where the Co-operative Party never came out formally against membership of the European Community, and motions supporting withdrawal have been defeated at its conference.

Social and Liberal Democrats (SLD)

Headquarters	: 4 Cowley Street, London SW1P 8NB (tel: 01-222 7999)
Leader	: Paddy Ashdown
President	: Ian Wrigglesworth
Chief executive	: Andrew Ellis
Members	: 85,000 (September 1988)
Founded	: March 1988

History

The Social and Liberal Democrats were formally launched in March 1988, stemming from a merger between the vast majority of Liberals and the majority of Social Democrats. A minority of the latter have decided to maintain a separate Social Democratic party (see separate entry).

The historical background to the SLD's component parties is described separately below.

(i) Liberal Party

The founding date of the Liberal Party is often given as 1859, when the Whigs, Radicals and Peelites joined together, although the greatest catalyst for the development of a Liberal Party had come some time earlier in the form of the anti-Corn Law Free Trade campaign.

William Ewart Gladstone was the Prime Minister in the first Liberal government which lasted from 1868 to 1874. The great rivalry between Gladstone and the Conservative leader Disraeli initiated the long period of a two-party system dominated by the Conservatives and the Liberals.

In 1877 a Liberal National Federation was founded. In 1886, however, the party split over the issue of Home Rule to Ireland. The minority under Joseph Chamberlain left the party and founded the Liberal Unionists, who remained allies of the Conservative Party until they formally merged with them in 1912.

After the split Liberal parliamentary strength immediately dropped and the Conservatives dominated government until 1906, with only short interludes of Liberal government under Gladstone and the Earl of Rosebery.

In 1906 the Liberal Party won its greatest ever election victory, obtaining 400 seats in Parliament. Sir Henry Campbell-Bannerman was Prime Minister from 1906 to 1908, when he was replaced by H.H. Asquith. The 1906 Liberal government was one of the greatest reforming governments in British history. It also clashed with the Conservative dominated House of Lords. The Lords' powers were curtailed after Liberal victories in the 1910 elections.

In 1915 Asquith formed a wartime coalition with members of the Conservative and Labour parties. In 1916 the party split in two after David Lloyd George outmanoeuvred Asquith to take over as Prime Minister, a post he retained until 1922 when he resigned after the majority of Conservative MPs decided to abandon the coalition.

Throughout the 1920s the Liberals remained competitive in the only British decade with a genuine three-party system.

In 1918 and 1922 the Asquith and Lloyd George Liberals fought on separate tickets. In 1923 they reunited over the issue of defence of free trade under Asquith's leadership and won 159 seats. In 1924 they only won 44 seats and Lloyd George returned as leader. In 1929 their vote rose, but they still only gained 59 seats. They remained a creative source of ideas, however, with both Maynard Keynes and William Beveridge contributing to their policy statements.

The creation of the national government in 1931 split the Liberals three ways between Liberal Nationals, mainstream Liberals and independent anti-coalition Liberals.

In Churchill's wartime coalition the Liberals were only given a minor role, with their leader, Sir Archibald Sinclair being made a minister but outside the central war Cabinet.

In the 1945 elections the Liberals only won 9 per cent of the vote and 12 seats. Sir Archibald Sinclair lost his seat and was replaced as leader by Clement Davies. Its vote dropped to only 2.6 per cent by the 1951 elections, with only six seats being won.

In 1956 Jo Grimond became the new leader of the Liberal Party, and succeeded in reviving it. In 1958 Mark Bonham Carter became the first Liberal by-election victor since 1929. In 1962 the party won the Montgomery and Orpington by-elections.

In 1964 the Party's vote almost doubled to 11.2 per cent, but only nine seats were won. In 1967 Jeremy Thorpe succeeded Grimond.

In the 1970 general election the party only won 7.5 per cent and six seats. In the same year it adopted the new strategy of Community politics, which was subsequently to win it great local success.

In mid-1972 the Liberals won two by-elections in Rochdale, and Sutton and Cheam, and this was followed by a period of strong Liberal revival, with three gains in by-elections in 1973 and with the party winning 19.3 per cent and 14 seats in the February 1974 national elections. The Liberals were left holding the balance of power, but rejected an offer by Ted Heath for them to come to an agreement with the Conservatives. In October 1974 they put up more candidates, but only won 18.3 per cent of the vote and 13 seats.

In 1976 Jeremy Thorpe had to resign his leadership after damaging personal and financial allegations had been made against him. The subsequent leadership election, in which David Steel defeated John Pardoe by 12,500 to seven thousand was the first Liberal (and British major party) contest to involve the whole membership.

In 1977–78 David Steel brought the Liberal Party into a pact to support the Labour government. Labour's concessions to the Liberals were relatively minor, but the Liberal Party was given a taste of government responsibilities. In 1979 the Liberal Party's vote dropped to 13.8 per cent, with only 11 seats won.

In 1980 Steel encouraged the Social Democrat's breakaway from the Labour party, and in September 1981 successfully brought the Liberal Party into an alliance with the newly formed SDP, in spite of the hostility of certain Liberals to the new party. The SDP/Liberal Alliance quickly proved popular, and later in 1981 the Liberal Bill Pitt became the Alliance's first by-election victor. In the 1983 general election the Alliance won 25.4 per cent, the best third party performance since the 1920s. The Liberals won 17 of the Alliance's 22 seats.

In the 1983–87 Parliament Alliance support went up and down, two of the Liberal high points being their by-election gains in Brecon and Radnor, and in Ryedale.

In the 1987 general election the Alliance won 22 seats on 22.6 per cent of the vote. The Liberals had 17 of these seats, losing five seats but winning three.

The Liberals were less divided over merger negotiations than the SDP, but a considerable number became increasingly concerned over the possible loss of the Liberal name and identity.

(ii) *Social Democratic Party (SDP)*

The Social Democratic Party (SDP) was founded in early 1981 as a result of a schism within the British Labour Party (separate entry).

There had long been divisions within the Labour Party over such issues as unilateral nuclear disarmament (in Gaitskell's day) and the battle over EC entry in the early 1970s. Many of the Labour pro-Marketeers later joined the SDP.

In 1973 an early portent of the final SDP split was when Dick Taverne resigned his seat at Lincoln after clashing with his left-wing constituency party, and won the subsequent by-election as a Democratic Labour candidate.

In November 1979 Roy Jenkins called for a radical realignment in the centre of British politics. In the course of 1980 prominent members of the Labour Party, notably Shirley Williams, Bill Rodgers and David Owen, began to discuss the possibility of a break with the Labour Party as a result of its increasingly extreme policies and of its proposed constitutional changes.

The final break came after the confused special congress of the Labour Party at Wembley in January 1981 to decide on a new method of electing the Labour leader. Jenkins, Owen, Williams and Rodgers (henceforth known as the "Gang of Four"), meeting at Limehouse issued a Declaration of principles, and established a Council for Social Democracy. By March 5, 13 Labour members had abandoned the party, and were taking the SDP whip. The new SDP was formally launched on March 26, 1981, by which time one Conservative MP, Christopher Brocklebank-Fowler, had also joined the SDP. The new party recruited support from a wide range of people, including many who had not previously been active in party politics.

In July 1981 Roy Jenkins came a close second to the Labour winner in a by-election at Warrington. Labour members continued to join the new party (six in October 1981 alone), and an Alliance was forged with the Liberal Party. In November 1981 Shirley Williams returned to Parliament after a by-election win at Crosby. By the end of 1981 the SDP had 70,000 members, 40 local councillors, 27 MPs and 34 members of the House of Lords.

In 1982 Roy Jenkins narrowly won the Glasgow Hillhead by-election early in the year. The Falkland campaign took the party out of the public eye and few seats were won in the local elections. In July 1982 Roy Jenkins defeated David Owen to become the new party leader, after the initial year of collective leadership. Shirley Williams became party president.

In the 1983 general election the SDP only won six of the Alliance's seats, and the large majority of SDP MPs lost their seats. Shortly afterwards Jenkins resigned as leader and was replaced without a contest by David Owen.

From 1983 to 1987 the Alliance enjoyed varying fortunes, doing poorly in the 1984 European election with 19.5 per cent and no seats, but winning several by-elections and performing well in local elections, notably in the county council elections in 1985, where the Alliance ended up running minority administrations in six councils, and sharing control in three others.

In early 1987 Rosie Barnes of the SDP won a by-election at Greenwich, but in the 1987 general elections the SDP lost three of its eight seats, including Roy Jenkins's seat at Hillhead.

After the election the SDP split over the issue of whether to merge with the Liberal Party.

(iii) *The merger*

The experience of working together within the Social Democratic-Liberal Alliance convinced many activists in both parties that they would be more effective if they merged, in view of the duplication of party bureaucracies, and of the amount of time wasted in negotiating the division of seats. Some Liberals saw an opportunity for their party to modernize its constitution and organizational structure. Finally the 1987 general election campaign convinced many in both parties that for the Alliance to have two separate leaders was an experiment that should never be repeated.

Immediately after the 1987 election the Liberal leader, David Steel, called for a rapid decision on merger. The Social Democratic (SDP) leader, David Owen, was opposed to this, but the party's national committee was split. In a meeting in July it voted by 18 to 13 to preserve the separate identity of the SDP. A decision was also taken to ballot the SDP's 58,000 members. The next few weeks were bitter ones, with the historic founders of the party on opposite sides, Roy Jenkins, Shirley Williams and Bill Rodgers supporting merger and Owen continuing to oppose it. In August 1987, SDP members voted by 57.4 per cent to 42.6 per cent in favour of opening merger negotiations. Owen resigned as leader, and Bob MacLennan replaced him. The SDP's "parliament", its Council for Social Democracy, then voted to support merger negotiations, as did the Liberal Assembly.

Owen and his followers took no part in the subsequent negotiations between the two parties which were concluded in January 1988, although final agreement was held up by the two leaders putting forward an accompanying and very controversial party prospectus without adequate consultations. This had to be withdrawn, and a new and more acceptable statement was drafted.

A special assembly of the Liberal Party then voted in favour of merger by 2099 to 385. The SDP Council for Social Democracy took the same decision with a vote of 273 in favour, 28 against and 49 abstentions. David Owen's supporters did not participate in the vote. In subsequent ballots of the two parties' full membership, 87.9 per cent of Liberals who voted supported merger and 65.3 per cent of the SDP. Turnout, however, was very low at 52.3 per cent and 55.5 per cent respectively.

In July 1988 Paddy Ashdown was elected leader by a vote of 71.9 per cent to the 28.1 per cent of Alan Beath. Ian Wrigglesworth was elected president of the party against Des Wilson and Gwynoro Jones. The party currently has 19 MPs and 3,000 councillors. In September 1988 it voted to adopt the name "Democrats" as the short name of the party.

Support

It is too early to tell whether the SLD support base will be distinct from that of the former SDP/Liberal Alliance, although for the time being it has clearly shrunk as a result of the divisions of the last year.

The only parts of Britain where the Liberal Party was solidly rooted were in the Celtic fringes of Scotland and Wales, and to a much lesser extent in the West Country, the Welsh Marches and in certain areas of Northern England with a non-conformist tradition. There were also pockets of local government strength, such as that developed in the 1970s in Liverpool, but these did not lead to parliamentary success on any scale. Finally, in parts of Southern England the Liberals were still the traditional party of opposition to the dominant Conservatives but were seldom, if ever, strong enough to oust them at national elections. To a considerable extent, especially at by-elections, the Liberal vote was also a protest vote which easily reverted to the two major parties.

The creation of the SDP and its Alliance with the Liberals brought with it the hope that there would be new support in areas where the Liberals had had little impact, such as much of urban and working-class Britain. In the 1983 general election Alliance support did indeed rise in these regions, but not enough to win new seats, and there appeared to be relatively little difference between the respective appeals of Liberal or SDP candidates in either urban or rural seats.

In the 1987 general election Alliance support dropped somewhat from 1983, being squeezed in most areas of tight Labour-Conservative contests, and also in areas of traditional Labour support.

The British electoral system has continued to penalize the Alliance vote because of its lack of any firm social or regional base. In social terms it has a more even spread of support than the Labour or Conservative parties, although it is strongest among the middle classes and weakest among the unskilled working class, the unemployed and immigrants. There appears to be a strong correlation between levels of education and Alliance voting, with its highest vote among university graduates. Among the groups giving it strong support have been academics, clerics of all religions, leaders of voluntary organizations, as well as teachers, lawyers and other successful professionals. It does well among small hill farmers, but poorly among larger farmers.

In regional terms its most consistent support is still in the Celtic fringe. Nine of the 19 SLD seats are in Scotland and three in Wales.

In Scotland it is especially strong in the Borders, where it holds two seats and in the Highlands and Islands, where it holds all the seats in the West and North from Argyll up to Orkney and Shetland with the exception of the Western Isles. The Alliance was much weaker in urban and industrial Scotland, though much stronger in Edinburgh (22.8 per cent in 1987, but 28.6 per cent in 1983) than in Glasgow (14.9 per cent in 1987, 21.2 per cent in 1983). Scotland appears to have been the only part of Britain where there was anti-Conservative tactical voting in 1987, and this may help explain the sharp Alliance drop in support in these areas as well as their two gained seats (Fife North-East and Argyll).

In Wales the three SLD seats are all in rural Central Wales (both Welsh and non-Welsh speaking), but the Alliance is weaker in nationalist Northern Wales, and in industrial Southern Wales (e.g. Mid-Glamorgan 12 per cent in 1987). In 1983 it polled well in the Welsh capital of Cardiff (27.2 per cent) but its vote fell in 1987 (21.7 per cent).

In England it is strongest in rural areas, and to a lesser extent suburban areas, and weakest in industrial areas and the inner cities.

In 1987 the Alliance was second to the Conservatives (even first in rural Northumberland) in 23 out of the 39 non-metropolitan counties. It was strongest in South-West England where it obtained 33 per cent of the vote, but only three out of the 48 seats. Its best county was Cornwall, with 40 per cent of the vote (but only one of the five seats), and in several other counties, such as Somerset (37.9 per cent), Devon (36.6 per cent) and Dorset (30.8 per cent) its vote went up in 1987 over its 1983 figure.

In South-Eastern England outside London it was second almost everywhere in 1987, with 27.2 per cent of the vote, but none of the 108 seats. In East Anglia it was also second with 25.7 per cent. In Greater London it was third with 21.3 per cent in 1987.

In the West and East Midlands and Northern England it was generally in third place (with a few rural exceptions such as Northumberland and North Yorkshire), and with a considerable drop in its 1983 vote. Among its weaker cities were Birmingham (15.9 per cent in 1987), Bradford (15.6 per cent in 1987, down from 25.7 per cent in 1983), Manchester (17.7 per cent) and marginal Tory/Labour Nottingham (13.5 per cent) and Leicester (12.9 per cent), where it was badly squeezed. It did better in a few areas of local government activism, such as parts of East London, Leeds (26.3 per cent in 1987), and Liverpool (25.6 per cent), where its vote rose on the anti-Conservative tide. In most of industrial and urban inner city Britain it was behind the Conservative Party as well as the increasingly dominant Labour Party.

Organization

The new SLD structure is a blend of two very different organizational traditions. Liberal organization had developed in a very ad hoc and decentralized manner over a long period of time, with separate parties in Ulster, Wales and Scotland as well as England. Membership was a matter for the individual constituencies, regional groups and associated bodies, and not for the Liberal Head Office (with total Liberal membership often unknown). It also had a vocal annual assembly and quarterly party council at which not only the constituencies and regional groups but also a variety of recognized groups could take part. Many matters were not regulated by the party's constitution and had to be solved on a case by case basis. The party gave great scope for individual groups of activists, but this also made it very difficult to control. On the other hand the leader, who was only chosen by the parliamentarians until 1976, could singlehandedly veto conference decisions.

The SDP on the other hand had a much more disciplined and centralized structure, with a purpose-made modern constitution. There was no federal structure, a central register of members, only a weak Annual Assembly and a stronger elected Council for Social Democracy, careful checks and balances in policy formation between the Council and the much smaller Policy Committee, and far fewer associated organizations. A number of its organizational features were a direct reaction to Labour Party practice, such as the provision that no member of the Council for Social Democracy could be mandated in any way, or the provisions for secret ballots of all the members. Compared to the Liberal Party the SDP was more of a top-down party, and more susceptible to control by its leadership.

The SLD now has a constitution providing for more central organization than that of the old Liberal Party, but incorporating many features of Liberal practice as well.

The SLD has a federal structure. The Scottish and Welsh state parties have their own conferences and leadership structures governed by their own separate constitutions, which are similar but not identical to those of the federal party. There is also a state party in England, with rather less independence. Unlike the Liberal Party there is no SLD state party in Northern Ireland. The responsibilities of the federal party (e.g. overall strategy and preparation for parliamentary elections) are clearly delineated.

Party membership is more tightly controlled than it was in the Liberal Party. Members may join locally or nationally through the youth or students' organizations, but not through regional groups or through other affiliated organizations (like the women or trade union groups) as in the old Liberal Party. There will be no one central membership register as in the SDP, but each state party will keep a register. In October 1988 total SLD membership was around 85,000.

The basic organizational units of the party are its local parties, which must have a minimum of 50 members. Unlike in the SDP, whose area parties were based on larger groups of constituencies, the SLD local parties are primarily based on individual parliamentary constituencies. Local parties may also be formed in Northern Ireland or outside the United Kingdom. Branches can also be established within a local party. Above the local parties regional parties are being constituted throughout England.

At federal level a federal conference is held twice a year. Participation is lower and more tightly regulated than it was at Liberal Party assemblies, but much higher than at the meetings of the SDP's Council for Social Democracy. The conference includes representatives elected for two-year terms (and who cannot be mandated) by the local parties on a sliding scale according to membership and representatives of the party's student and youth organizations.

The federal executive includes the party's officers, two MPs and one member of the House of Lords, two principal local authority councillors, one representative of each state party and 14 persons elected annually by the federal conference.

The party leader is elected by secret ballot of the entire party membership. When the party is in opposition a leadership election must normally be held within two years after a general election. If 75 local parties request an election or if a motion of no confidence is passed by a majority of the party's MPs, an earlier election may be called.

The party's president chairs its federal executive and is elected for a two-year term by secret ballot of the entire membership. The federal vice-presidents are designated by the state parties in England, Wales and Scotland. The party's federal headquarters is run by a chief executive.

Party policy-making at federal level is the joint concern of the federal conference and of a special federal policy committee of 27 persons, including 13 persons elected annually by the federal conference. The federal policy committee may establish policy working groups including outside members. The policy-making process is more regulated than in the old Liberal Party, with the federal policy committee submitting interim policy proposals (green papers) and definitive policy proposals (white papers) to the federal conference, which then has the final word. The federal policy committee can delay a decision by the federal conference, but has no final power of veto.

Party parliamentary candidates must be on an approved list of candidates held centrally by each state party. Candidates are chosen by all those local party members present at special hustings meetings or who write in to ask for a ballot form, a compromise between the Liberal system of only involving members attending hustings and the SDP system of involving all its local members.

The SLD provides for guaranteed minimum representation for women as local party representatives to the federal conference, as members directly elected by the federal conference onto the federal policy committee and the federal executive, and on parliamentary candidate shortlists.

There are also provisions for consultative ballots of all party members on any fundamental issues where the values and objectives of the party are at stake.

The party has a number of specified associated organizations consisting (except in the case of youth and students) exclusively of party members. The youth organization and the student organization are given more powers than the other specified organizations, which include associations for candidates, councillors, agents, women and trade unionists. There are also other associated organizations which may include non-members.

The SLD newspaper to its members, which appears weekly, is called the *Social and Liberal Democrats News*.

The SLD does not have the financial support provided by the trade unions to the Labour Party or by business donations to the Conservatives, and is heavily dependent on membership dues and donations. There are both minimum and recommended membership fees.

The SLD has now decided to join both the Liberal International and the European Liberals, Democrats and Reformists (ELDR). In Northern Ireland close relations have been established with the Alliance Party.

Policies

Now that the demotivating process of merger is behind it, the SLD still faces a number of difficult political and strategic problems. The first is to blend two different traditions of political philosophy, and organization. The SLD also faces the immediate problem of how to tackle the continuing SDP, which has a much smaller base than the SLD but is more

homogeneous and has an established and charismatic leader. Unless the SDP collapses, and in the absence of electoral or other agreements between the two parties, the centre-ground of British politics will continue to be damagingly divided. Finally the SLD has to decide on the extent to which it wishes to work with other parties and, in particular, whether it aims to replace Labour on the centre-left, or to join with it in an anti-Conservative alliance.

Differences between the Liberal and Social Democratic parties were generally more ones of political culture than of policy content.

The Liberal Party's members shared one central belief in the party's emphasis on individual freedom, but otherwise spanned a wide ideological spectrum from cautious conservatives to libertarian left-wingers. The party's decentralized character and the increasing emphasis on community politics and on local activism encouraged this diversity, but also sometimes led to indiscipline and incoherence. Compared to continental liberalism, however, the British Liberals have generally been more on the centre-left of the political spectrum, and put less emphasis on economic liberalism.

There has also been a more radical minority within its midst, symbolized by the Young Liberals in the 1960s and later by some elements within the Association of Liberal Councillors (ALC), who have been heavily influenced by counter-culture and Green values. The Liberal Party also retained a non-conformist pacifist tradition among a number of its members.

The SDP on the other hand included leaders with extensive recent experience of government, and had a more managerial style than the Liberal Party. It was also more of a top-down party, with an articulate but relatively deferential membership, and greater internal discipline. Its left wing, such as the "Limehouse Group", was smaller and less radical than its equivalent in the Liberal Party. In theory it put a higher emphasis on equality rather than freedom, but in practice there was no great divide between the SDP and Liberal parties on this issue. If there was an initial division within the SDP it was between those (especially those from traditional working-class backgrounds) who sought a more moderate version of the Labour Party, and those who emphasized the "newness" of the SDP, and the opportunity to "break the mould" of the existing British political system. As time went by, however, a gap also opened up within the SDP over the issue of how close relations should be with the Liberal Party.

On many policy areas, there was broad agreement between the SDP and the Liberals and these are now major themes of the SLD. This is especially true of the Alliance's proposed charter of reforms on constitutional matters, where it advocated the replacement of the majority electoral system by the Single Transferable Vote system of proportional representation, which would be both fairer and lead to a more consensual style of government. The Alliance also called for repeal of the restrictive Official Secrets Act and its replacement by freedom of information legislation. Both parties agreed on socially liberal policies with a strong emphasis on protection of human rights, with a new ministry of justice and the incorporation of the European Convention on Human Rights into British law in a Bill of Rights. Both parties were strongly in favour of decentralization of government. The 1987 Alliance manifesto called for the creation of a Scottish legislative Assembly and a Welsh senate (the need for home rule had been a feature of Liberal Party policies since Gladstone's time). There was also considerable support for the development of regional assemblies within England, although this was a more controversial issue, especially within the SDP. Both parties were united, however, in attacking increasing centralization under the Conservative government. The Alliance was opposed to both the existing system of rates, and the Conservatives' proposed poll tax, and advocated their replacement by a system of local income tax.

Among the other Alliance constitutional proposals were the need for fixed term parliaments and reform of the House of Lords, with replacement of hereditary members by representatives of the regions. The Alliance strongly supported the Anglo-Irish Agreement.

Both Alliance parties placed a strong emphasis on the need for a more class-free Britain and one not governed on behalf of specific sectoral interests. The Alliance parties claimed that they were advocating a more market-oriented policy than Labour, and one more concerned about the economic and social divisions of Britain than the Conservatives. Individual freedom and social justice, and "toughness and tenderness" should be carefully balanced. The state had an important role to play, but it should be an "enabling" rather than all dominant state, encouraging active citizenship and individual initiative. There should not be constant switches of economic policy. Privatization should be examined case-by-case on its merits.

The SDP/Liberal Alliance put more emphasis than the Conservatives on fighting unemployment. The Alliance in both 1983 and 1987 advocated programmes of economic expansion, although on a lesser scale than the Labour Party. They called for public investment in such fields as infrastructure, and health and social services.

The expansionary programme would be complemented, however, by a tax based incomes policy, which would help to control inflation (although incomes policy is no longer much emphasized by the SLD). The Alliance called for vigorous industrial and competition policies, and an extension of industrial training.

The Alliance parties were opposed to a harsh attitude to trade unions, but advocated trade union reform, to return the unions more to their membership by making them more democratic and accountable.

A long-standing Liberal theme picked up by the Alliance was the need for more industrial democracy in the workplace, as well as an extension in employee share-ownership.

The Alliance parties strongly defended the welfare state. A centrepiece of the Alliance's 1987 programme was the need to merge the tax and benefits systems in order to create one integrated system, which would be both simpler and more just.

There were divisions in the past over civil nuclear energy (with the SDP more in favour and the Liberals opposed). The SLD is now generally in opposition to its continued development.

The Alliance put a strong emphasis on environmental protection and on sustainable or "Green" economic growth. This is now one of the major policy themes of the SLD, which is launching a "Green Crusade".

Although there was initial hesitation among some activists (especially in the Liberal Party) the Alliance came out in support of council house sales.

The Alliance was very critical of the Conservative government's treatment of the teachers, and what they saw as its neglect of skill training and of Britain's system of further education.

On transport policy the Alliance was critical of the way in which bus deregulation had been carried out, and advocated competitive tendering under local council control in order to safeguard uneconomic but needed routes.

On immigration policy the need for controls was accepted, but the Alliance was pledged to repeal what it saw as the sexist and racist aspects of the 1981 British Nationality Act.

Both Alliance parties (and now the SLD) have supported much closer European integration, less recourse to national vetos within the council and greater powers for the European Parliament, including co-legislative powers between Parliament and council. The Alliance supported the Spinelli Draft Treaty on European Union, and the Single European Act, full British participation in the European Monetary System and the further development of monetary integration. The Alliance was critical both of Labour's opposition to the EC (a key factor in the creation of the SDP) and of the Conservative's grudging attitude towards EC initiatives on joint research programmes, environmental protection, industrial democracy and other social measures.

The Alliance advocated restructuring of the European Community's budget, with less resources devoted to the Common Agricultural Policy, and more to its regional, social, research and other policies. The Alliance also supported greater European co-operation on political and security matters.

Perhaps the most significant area of difference between the Liberals and SDP was on defence policy, although neither party was united on the subject. Although the majority of Liberals accepted NATO membership and the need for adequate defence, the Liberal Assembly in 1981 and 1984 opposed the stationing of Cruise missiles in Britain, and later supported their removal. The 1986 Liberal Assembly at Eastbourne narrowly passed an amendment which was widely interpreted as unilateralist.

The SDP on the other hand, although containing a minority of Campaign for Nuclear Disarmament (CND) activists, was more in favour of the stationing of Cruise missiles, and of the maintenance of a British independent nuclear deterrent. This is one of the key issues on which David Owen has staked the existence of the continuing SDP.

The 1987 Alliance manifesto contrasted Alliance policy with Labour unilateralism and insufficient Conservative emphasis on the need for nuclear disarmament. The manifesto expressed the Alliance's commitment to NATO, but also the need to build up its European pillar, with greater European co-operation on procurement and standardization. It accepted the presence of Allied bases and nuclear weapons on British soil on the basis of clear arrangements for a British veto over their operations, including possible dual key systems. The British minimum independent nuclear deterrent would be maintained until it could be negotiated away as part of a global arms negotiation process, in return for "worthwhile" Soviet concessions. Trident should be cancelled (although this will have to be reviewed by the SLD), and any modernization should freeze British capacity at a level no greater than that of Polaris.

Other Alliance policies included strong support for development policy (with aid up to the United Nations target of 0.7 per cent by the end of a five-year parliament) and economic sanctions on South Africa.

Personalities

The SLD's leader, elected in July 1988, is Paddy Ashdown, who is a former paratrooper and diplomat, and only entered Parliament as a Liberal member for Yeovil in 1983. He defeated Alan Beith, another Liberal MP, but of much longer standing (elected for Berwick in 1973), who had been Liberal chief whip and Steel's deputy leader.

The SLD president is Ian Wrigglesworth, a former Labour and then SDP member for Stockton South.

The leader of the Welsh SLD is Richard Livsey, former Liberal and MP for Brecon and Radnor. The leader of the Scottish state party is Malcolm Bruce, another former Liberal, and MP for Gordon.

The leader of the SLD in the House of Lords is Roy Jenkins, the former Labour minister and President of the European Commission.

Social Democratic Party (SDP)

Headquarters	: 25–28 Buckingham Gate, London SW1E6LD (2nd floor) (tel: 01–821 9661)
Leader	: David Owen
President	: John Cartwright
National secretary	: Fiona Wilson
Membership	: 30,000

History

The continuing Social Democratic Party consists of that substantial minority of party members who opposed merger with the Liberal Party (see entry on the Social and Liberal Democrats) and decided that they wished to remain members of an independent SDP. Led by David Owen, the SDP leader from 1983 until August 1987, and supported by two others (John Cartwright and Rosie Barnes) of the SDP's five MPs, they played no part in the merger negotiations once they had lost the initial SDP members' ballot and the ratifying vote at the 1987 Portsmouth party conference. Almost immediately a support group "Grassroots Uprising" developed throughout the country, and by October 1987 Owen's supporters had established a new headquarters under the name "Campaign for Social Democracy" with six full-time members of staff. The campaign was backed by 15 members of the SDP's national committee, and its supporters included David Sainsbury, who had been the largest single contributor to SDP funds. Increasingly the campaign began to function as a separate party recruiting supporters, and organizing special conferences. Most of its members took no part in the vote on merger at the SDP special conference at Sheffield in January 1988, although a minority participated in both the debate and the final vote. A substantial number also voted "no" in the SDP's members ballot.

On March 8, 1988, the SDP was formally re-established as a separate party, claiming to be supported by 30,000 members. David Owen was elected as leader, and John Cartwright became president. The continuing SDP had three MPs, and 23 (out of a total of 40) SDP working peers in the Lords. A new national committee was also chosen, including 17 members of the old committee, and 21 new members.

In local elections the continuing SDP has only put up a small number of candidates, who have enjoyed little success. In recent by-elections it has polled less well than the SLD. The continuing SDP's first annual conference was held in September 1988.

Support

There is no electoral evidence yet of a distinctive continuing SDP support pattern. In 1983 and 1987 (see section on SLD) differentials between the performance of former Liberal or SDP candidates appeared to be more related to the type of seat fought than to differing appeals of the two parties.

Two of the three SDP MPs, and a considerable percentage of its national committee and party membership are London-based. Many other members come from areas such as certain parts of the North of England where the Liberal Party was weak, or where relations between the two Alliance parties were strained.

Organization

The continuing SDP has retained the former SDP's constitution. Unlike the SLD it has a unitary rather than federal structure.

The basic units of membership are its area parties, based on groups of constituencies rather than a single constituency.

At national level an annual conference is held in September at which any party member can attend, and can participate in conference debates, but which has no decision-making powers. Much more power is vested instead in the party's "parliament" or "Council for Social Democracy" (CSD), which is a much smaller body than the SLD Conference and consists of elected representatives (emphatically not delegates) of the SDP area parties.

The CSD meets three times a year, including one occasion concurrent with the party conference. The SDP's executive body is its national committee, with 38 members. Eight are directly elected by the national party membership (including four men and four women), and the others include representatives of the parliamentary party, the SDP's regional units, three local council representatives and a representative of the Young Social Democrats. The party's leader and president are directly elected by the national membership. The party has a national secretary, who heads a staff of eight. Party policy-making is shared between the CSD and the national committee (which has a powerful policy committee), with the presentation of initial ideas papers ("green papers") followed by definitive or "white papers". The national committee has a more powerful position than its SLD equivalent, and the CSD a less powerful one than the SLD Conference.

Unlike in the SLD parliamentary candidates are chosen by all the members of an area party by secret ballot, irrespective of whether they attended hustings meetings, and without having to apply specially for a ballot form. There are provisions for minimum representation of women on candidates shortlists.

The SDP has a number of associated groups such as the Social Democratic Youth and Student Group (SDYS). Unlike in the SLD, membership of the student and youth groups does not qualify individuals for direct rights within the party, unless they also join an area party.

The party's newspaper is called *New Social Democrat*.

The party has no international affiliations.

Policies

The outlook for the continuing SDP is highly uncertain. Its leader is nationally known and is a formidable parliamentarian, and the party is more homogeneous than the merged Social and Liberal Democrats (SLD). On the other hand it is smaller than the SLD, has fewer MPs and a much smaller base in local government.

At present the two parties are damaging each other by putting up rival candidates. The SDP believes that they will eventually have to come to some kind of electoral agreement, at least not to stand against each other in certain seats. The SLD argues that this would negate one of the main advantages of merger, and appears very reluctant to enter into any kind of agreement, at least at the present moment when the SDP has enjoyed very little electoral success. There is still considerable bitterness between the two parties.

The members of the continuing SDP appear to be motivated by a combination of pride in the party they helped to create in 1981, and suspicion of the Liberal Party on grounds of both organizational style and policy.

They claim that they joined the SDP in 1981 (many after having already changed from another party) with the intention of staying within it and building it up. Some now claim that they were always critical of the rapid decision for the SDP to enter into an alliance with the Liberal Party, and feel betrayed by former SDP leaders, whom, they now believe, always intended the SDP to be a transitional arrangement before full merger with the Liberals. On internal battles within the former SDP's national committee they constituted the group that was most reluctant to extend joint selection of candidates between the SDP and Liberals.

The members of the continuing SDP argue that the merged Social and Liberal Democrats will be dominated by the former Liberal Party elements, and they claim that if they had wished to become Liberals they would have done so before the creation of the SDP. They claim that the Liberal Party was too anarchic and undisciplined in organizational terms, and they also attack the Liberals' policies on defence in particular. They point to the Liberal assembly at Eastbourne in 1986, which appeared to adopt a unilateralist stance on Britain's nuclear deterrent, as an illustration of Liberal Party weakness. Another policy area of difference is on civil nuclear energy. They also believe that such groups as the Young Liberals were far too left wing.

The continuing SDP believes that the "new politics" in Britain will consist of a multiparty system, with a considerable number of parties which will be forced to work with each other, and enter into coalition governments.

The continuing SDP argues that, unlike the old Alliance, which contained a wide spectrum of views from left to right and had to adopt blurred compromise policies, it will be able to put forward clear and radical policies without splitting the difference between left and right wing positions.

The continuing SDP's broad policy stance is closer to that of the Conservative Party than to the Labour Party. It believes that the Labour Party is fundamentally wrong on a large range of issues, its corporatist and "statist" approach to the economy, lack of enthusiasm for the market, and its unilateralist defence position. The Conservatives, on the other hand, have been correct in their anti-corporatist actions and in their emphasis on the market, but they have been too selective in their application of market forces, and have not given enough attention to the distribution of wealth and to the really disadvantaged in society.

The continuing SDP advocates a "social market economy", in which the liberating forces of the market would be applied to a greater extent than at present, but where the compensating social measures are also not neglected. They advocate a stronger competition policy and a flexible labour market. They are hostile to an incomes policy and to a wage freeze as creating unnecessary market rigidities, and believe they should only be used as a last resort. They are also critical of Keynesian demand-management techniques in general. They put more emphasis on indirect rather than high direct taxation. They are generally favourable to privatization.

They advocate full integration of the existing tax and benefits system, and a move towards more selective benefits to help the really disadvantaged. They are opposed to a minimum wage approach, but are exploring the idea of a more comprehensive minimum standard of living guarantee. They have a strong commitment to the National Health Service, and believe that patients should be guaranteed of being treated within a certain time limit.

On defence policy their leadership has clearly expressed a commitment to a strong British defence and to multilateral rather than unilateral disarmament. They point out that the deployment of Cruise and Pershing missiles in Europe helped to bring the Russians to the negotiating table, and they support the retention of an independent British nuclear deterrent. They accept that it should be modernized, and believe that Trident's deployment should not now be stopped. On the other hand they claim to put more emphasis than the Conservatives on the need for reduction of nuclear arsenals, and on the need for enhanced European defence co-operation.

On constitutional issues they strongly advocate proportional representation and freedom of information. They also want a more decentralized Britain (Owen has put forward the idea of example of a decentralized wage fixing structure for local authority employees) but they are sceptical about the need for regional assemblies in Britain. They are strongly in favour of further European Community integration, although Owen is less federalist than some of the SLD leaders.

Personalities

The dominating personality within the continuing SDP is its leader David Owen, who led the former SDP from 1983 to 1987. He is a former Labour Foreign Minister and is the MP for Plymouth-Devonport.

The party's president is John Cartwright, a former Labour MP, who held his Woolwich seat for the SDP in both 1983 and 1987.

Scottish National Party (SNP)

Headquarters	: 6 North Charlotte Street, Edinburgh EH2 4JH (tel: 031–226 3661)
Chairman	: Gordon Wilson
Parliamentary leader	: Margaret Ewing
National secretary	: John Swinney
Founded	: 1934

History

A Scottish Home Rule Movement briefly flourished in the 1850s, and was revived in the 1880s. A "Scottish Home Rule Association" was founded in 1886, and between 1889 and 1914 no less than eight motions or draft laws calling for Home Rule were put forward in the House of Commons. In 1894 one such proposal even won a majority of votes (180 to 170), but no further action was taken.

Map of Scotland showing regional boundaries.

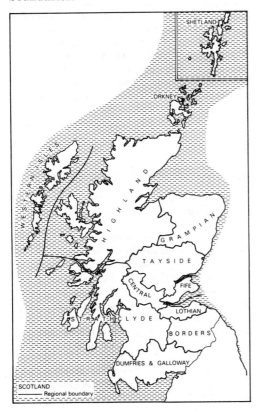

After World War I the Scottish Home Rule Association was revived. Later a "Scots National League" was founded, with a more cultural emphasis, but also calling for complete independence for Scotland. In 1926 a breakaway group from the League formed the "Scottish National Movement". Finally a new party, the "National Party of Scotland" was founded in 1928, also advocating Scottish independence. Its highest vote was the 16.9 per cent it won in Kilmarnock in 1933.

A more moderate party, the "Scottish Party", was founded in 1932, advocating Home Rule rather than full independence.

In February 1934 the two parties merged to form the New Scottish National Party, the beginning of the present SNP.

In 1935 the SNP got good results in certain constituencies, mainly in rural Scotland (Western Isles 28.1 per cent).

In 1940 there was dissent within the party, with a pacifist minority opposed to conscription. In 1942 one of its leading figures, John McCormick, started a breakaway group, the "Scottish Union". He took with him a considerable percentage of party members.

The SNP polled well in wartime by-elections, winning 37 per cent in Argyll in 1940, and finally winning its first parliamentary seat, with Dr Robert McIntyre's narrow win (in the absence of a Conservative candidate) in Motherwell in 1945. In the general election the seat was again lost, and the SNP polled only 1.2 per cent of the Scottish vote.

For the rest of the 1940s and 1950s the SNP had little success. The initiative passed to extra-parliamentary pressure groups like John McCormick's Scottish Covenant Association, which managed to collect a large number of signatures in favour of the creation of a separate Scottish Parliament. There were also more extreme groups like the Scottish Liberation Army. For the rest of the 1950s, however, there was little nationalist activity. In 1959 the SNP put up five candidates, and won 0.8 per cent of the Scottish vote.

The nationalist movement again began to revive in the 1960s. In 1961 the SNP came a good third in the Bridgeton by-election with 18.7 per cent. The number of members and local branches were raised considerably. In the West Lothian by-election in 1962 the SNP's candidate (William Wolfe, a future chairman of the party) came second with 23.3 per cent. In the 1964 elections the SNP won 2.4 per cent of the Scottish vote and by 1966 5.1 percent.

In 1967 SNP Winnie Ewing won the Hamilton by-election, with 46 per cent of the vote in what had always been considered a rock-solid Labour seat.

In the 1970 election the SNP won 11.1 per cent of the Scottish vote, but lost Hamilton. In exchange they gained one new seat (their first ever in a general election) when Donald Stewart won the Western Isles.

The increasingly promising prospect of "Scottish" North Sea oil helped to further revive the SNP.

In November 1973 Margo MacDonald won the Glasgow Govan by-election from Labour. In the February 1974 elections the SNP put up 70 candidates and won 21.9 per cent of the Scottish vote. Govan was lost, but the Western Isles constituency was retained, and six new seats were won, Aberdeenshire East, Argyll, Banffshire, Clackmannan and East Stirlingshire, Dundee East, and Moray and Nairn. In the October 1974 elections the SNP fared even better, becoming the second largest party in Scotland with 30.4 per cent of the vote and winning four new seats (Angus South, Dumbartonshire East, Galloway and Perth and East Perthshire).

The focus in the next few years was on the promised devolution legislation. The final proposals for a Scottish Assembly were generally regarded as unsatisfactory. A referendum was held in which a Scottish Assembly was supported by 51.6 per cent of those who voted, but this only constituted 33 per cent of the total, short of the 40 per cent that the legislation required.

The collapse of the devolution plans seriously hurt the SNP, and in the 1979 elections it only won 17.3 per cent of the Scottish vote, and lost all but two (Western Isles, and Dundee East) of its 11 seats. Shortly afterwards, however, the SNP gained one seat (that of Winnie Ewing in the Highlands and Islands) in the first European Parliament elections).

After 1979 the SNP was joined by members of the Scottish Labour Party (a 1975 breakaway from the Labour Party over the extent of devolution, whose two MPs, Sillars and Robertson, had lost their seats in 1979). The SNP now debated whether it should take a more Socialist course. In 1982 members of the "Socialist 79" group were expelled from the party.

In June 1983 the SNP only won 11.8 per cent of the Scottish vote, although it retained its two seats. In 1984 Winnie Ewing retained her Highlands and Islands constituency in the European elections.

In the June 1987 general election the SNP enjoyed mixed fortunes. It lost its existing two seats, but gained three new ones, polling 14 per cent of the total Scottish vote.

In the 1988 local elections it won a substantial number of new seats. In November 1988 Jim Sillars won the Govan by-election for the SNP.

Support

The SNP has had support across the whole social spectrum, although its activists have mainly been middle class. In its years of greater success it has had particular appeal to younger voters.

The SNP does not have the electoral bastion that Plaid Cymru enjoys in Welsh-speaking North Wales. Although it held the most Gaelic-speaking Scottish constituency, the Western Isles, from 1970 to 1987, this was largely a personal vote, and the SNP does not hold the other Scottish constituencies with considerable numbers of Gaelic speakers. The SNP's greatest strength in national elections is in north-eastern and eastern rural Scotland, where it holds its three seats of Banff and Buchan, Moray and Angus East, and where it was a good second in 1987 in the constituencies of Perth and Kinross, and Tayside North. In the Borders the only constituency where the SNP has shown consistent strength is Galloway and Upper Nithsdale, which it held from 1974 to 1979, and where it came a good second in 1987.

In national elections the SNP has been generally much weaker in urban and central Scotland, although it has benefited from anti-Labour protest votes in by-elections (e.g. Hamilton and Govan) and has also done well in many local elections. The SNP is second to Labour in a number of parliamentary constituencies in central Scotland, but generally far behind.

The SNP has often had higher than average support in the New Towns. It is very weak in Edinburgh (7 per cent in 1987, 5.4 per cent in 1983), slightly stronger in Glasgow (10.2 per cent in 1987, 7.6 per cent in 1983). Its strongest city has been Dundee.

Organization

The SNP has built up a strong grass-roots structure, based primarily on its local branches, of which there were 359 in 1983.

Within each constituency there is an SNP Association, consisting of delegates from the branches, sub-branches and groups.

A national conference is held annually.

The governing body of the party is its national council, which meets around four times a year. It contains over 500 members, including one delegate from each branch, two from each constituency association, and 30 members elected directly at the annual conference.

A national assembly is held at least twice a year, and is particularly concerned with discussion of party policy.

There is also a much smaller National Executive Committee, consisting of the national office holders, 10 ordinary members, three MPs, one MEP and one representative of the Youth Movement.

The national office bearers are elected at the annual conference. The most powerful party posts are those of chairman, and senior vice-chairman. The party president has more honorific duties. An important difference between the SNP party chairman and those of other British parties is that he or she does not necessarily have to be a Member of Parliament.

SNP prospective parliamentary candidates are chosen within the constituencies, but must be approved by the National Executive Committee.

The SNP has a number of affiliated organizations. The Young Scottish Nationalists — "Clann Alba" are entitled to six delegates of the National Assembly, and one member of the National Executive Committee. There is also the Federation of Student Nationalists, the Scottish Nationalist Trade Unionists (founded in 1965) and the Andrew Fletcher Society (a discussion group founded in 1974, and named after Andrew Fletcher of Saltoun, an opponent of the union with England).

The SNP has a monthly newspaper, the *Scots Independent*. Dues from the members are distributed between the branches and the central organizations. The SNP has also received a number of legacies, such as the "Neil Trust", which is used for electoral purposes.

The SNP's one member of the European Parliament was at first an independent, but in 1979 joined the RDE Group, which also includes the French Gaullists (RPR) and Ireland's Fianna Fáil.

Policies

The SNP has won support from a wide variety of sources, from those who positively seek full independence for Scotland (a March 1987 opinion poll indicated that 57 per cent of SNP supporters were in favour of this option), those who seek a greater measure of devolution within the UK, and those who believe that success for the SNP ensures greater British government concern for Scottish interests. There has undoubtedly been a strong protest vote element to SNP support, against economic conditions in Scotland and against the remoteness of government in London. The discovery and development of North Sea oil also gave a great boost to the SNP, in that it appeared to give greater economic credibility to a self-governing Scotland.

The SNP is hard to place within the ideological spectrum. It has tended to have a different tone in Labour voting industrial Scotland than in rural areas, where its members have sometimes been referred to as "Tartan Tories". In the early 1980s it appeared to be turning somewhat to the left, but this trend has now been curtailed. The SNP can now best be seen as a pragmatic party of the centre to centre-left. Unlike Plaid Cymru it has placed relatively little emphasis on cultural and linguistic issues.

Its formal policy statements call for full independence for Scotland, but its strategy has differed over the years. In the mid-1970s it accepted Labour's plan for devolution as an unsatisfactory but necessary half-way house, but after the referendum debacle a more fundamentalist approach prevailed. The SNP's current emphasis is to push for the establishment of a Scottish constitutional convention, at which specially elected Scottish delegates elected by proportional representation could decide on the most acceptable framework for self-government, with the SNP representatives calling for full independence. The SNP believe that a decisive breakthrough can be made when the SNP manage to win over half of the 72 Scottish seats. Until that moment they are prepared to work with any other party (except the Conservatives), which will accept the idea of such a convention. They see their particular allies as the other Scottish pro-devolution members, and Plaid Cymru with whom they have forged an alliance of mutual support.

The SNP seeks adoption of a written constitution for Scotland, providing for the right of the Scottish people to self-determination, and to sovereignty over its territory and natural resources. All those resident in Scotland upon independence or born (or with a parent born) in Scotland would have a right to Scottish citizenship. An independent Scotland would remain within the Commonwealth, and the Queen would remain Head of State. The SNP claims not to want barriers between itself and England, and has argued for an association of states of the British Isles on the lines of the Nordic Council in Scandinavia and which would permit free movement.

The SNP calls for a single-chamber Scottish parliament, elected for fixed term periods by a system of proportional representation. The Scottish prime minister and cabinet would be drawn from the parliament. Referenda would be authorized. There would be a Bill of Rights, guaranteeing fundamental rights and liberties.

The SNP's economic policy is not a very ideological one, with its main emphasis on Scottish control of Scottish resources. Its central premise is that other small European countries, like Austria and Norway, have been far more successful economically than Scotland, in its capacity as a dependent and peripheral region of a larger state.

The SNP supports a mixed economy, with thriving public, private and co-operative sectors. The balance of its policies, however, are social democratic in character. The state must continue to play a major role.

The centrepiece of the SNP's economic policy in 1987 was a jobs plan, that would reduce unemployment by over two-thirds within a period of five years. A Scottish Oil Fund would use oil revenues to finance new investment. The state would provide special support for economic sectors of the future. There would be a major public works programme. Scottish shipbuilding would be maintained. An independent Scotland would have its own steel quota within the EC, rather than its steel industry being a dispensable part of a wider British steel industry.

The SNP puts more emphasis on direct rather than indirect taxation. The SNP also calls for a tripartite economic council, representing unions, employers and government, which would agree on an annual national bargain on pay, prices and dividends. A national minimum wage would be established. The SNP is a strong supporter of industrial democracy, and advocates works councils and employee directors.

The SNP's energy policy has gradually become more anti-nuclear. The 1987 manifesto called for no new nuclear power stations, and a systematic phasing out of existing ones at the end of their working lives. Oil production in the North Sea would be curbed, so as to sustain world oil prices. Non-Scottish nationals and companies should be able to lease, but not own Scottish land.

The SNP seeks reinforcement of the welfare state. The SNP now supports sale of council houses, provided that new houses are built to meet letting demand.

SNP education policy has been critical of the divisiveness caused by private schooling, but does not attack it directly.

The SNP's language policy calls for the recognition of Gaelic, Scots and English as official languages in an independent Scotland. All documents should be bilingual, and there should be spending on Gaelic broadcasting at a level comparable to spending on Welsh language TV. There should be more bilingual road signs, and more funding for Gaelic education.

The SNP seeks the repeal of the "poll tax" and its replacement by local income tax.

The SNP has gradually become more favourable towards the European Community. In 1975 the SNP campaigned against EC membership on a platform of "no voice, no entry". The 1983 election manifesto still stated that the EC's centralist approach was not well suited to Scotland. The SNP called for a referendum on Scottish membership of the EC, at which the SNP would recommend its rejection.

At the 1983 party conference, however, there was a shift of emphasis, with the party considering that it might be willing to recommend membership if renegotiations managed to secure a number of EC guarantees for Scotland on such issues as fisheries, oil and steel. By the 1984 European Parliament elections the tone was an even more favourable one, with the party manifesto stating that the European Parliament had been more sympathetic to Scottish interests than the Parliament at Westminster.

The SNP now points out the advantages of an independent Scotland in Europe. It would chair the EC Council of Ministers, for example, and have its own veto. Scottish representation in the European Parliament could double from eight to 16. Scotland could benefit from direct EC expenditure in Scotland rather than its being channelled through London.

The SNP supports an increase in the powers of the European Parliament, but is opposed to creation of a unitary European state, preferring a reinforced Europe of the Nations. The SNP is critical of the Common Fisheries Policy and seeks establishment of an exclusive 100-mile Scottish zone. The SNP calls for major revision of the Common Agricultural Policy, including more support for disadvantaged farmers.

The SNP's defence policy calls for all nuclear weapons and bases to be removed from Scotland, and for a nuclear-free Europe. Defence expenditure should be used to strengthen Scotland's conventional forces. The SNP has been ambiguous on NATO membership. Its 1983 manifesto expressed support for the Western Alliance, but stated that the SNP would defer judgement on NATO membership as long as NATO sought to use Scotland as a front-line nuclear base. The 1987 manifesto opposed membership of any military alliance possessing nuclear weapons.

Personalities

The party chairman is Dr Gordon Wilson, the former Director of the SNP oil campaign and the MP for Dundee East from 1974 to 1987. He was elected SNP chairman in 1979. The senior vice-chairman is Margaret Ewing (daughter-in-law of Winnie Ewing), who was elected as MP for Moray in June 1987. She is also the parliamentary leader, and, as Margaret

Bain, was formerly MP for East Dumbartonshire from 1974 to 1979. The other three SNP MPs are Andrew Welsh, the provost of Angus since 1986, who was elected MP for Angus East in 1987 after formerly representing Angus South from 1974 to 1979; Alex Salmond, who was elected MP for Banff and Buchan in 1987; and Jim Sillars, who won Govan in 1988.

Winnie Ewing has been SNP member of the European Parliament since 1975, first as a nominated member and then directly elected for the Highlands and Islands in 1979 and in 1984. She had formerly won the Hamilton by-election in 1967, but lost the seat in 1970. She held the Moray seat in Westminster from 1974 to 1979.

Plaid Cymru
(Welsh Nationalist Party)

Headquarters	: 51 Cathedral Road, Cardiff CF1 9HD (tel: 0222–31944)
Party president	: Dafydd Elis Thomas (since 1984)
Party chair	: Dafydd Huws
General secretary	: Dafydd Williams
Founded	: 1925

History

Plaid Cymru stemmed from a merger in 1925 between a Caernarfon-based group of nationalists, and a second group entitled *Mudiad Cymreig* ("Welsh Movement").

Its initial emphasis was on preserving the Welsh language, and on breaking all links with other political parties in Wales and England. The party's meetings were all in Welsh, its newspaper *Y Ddraig Goch* ("Red Dragon") was only in Welsh, and the party also decided that any successful Westminster candidate would not take up his or her seat.

The party was initially heavily influenced by the traditional Christian values of its leader, Saunders Lewis (party president from 1926 to 1939), who converted to Catholicism and was a follower of the ideas of the French Catholic writer, Maurice Barrès and of Maurras and *Action Française*. Lewis also sought the de-industrialization of South Wales and the return of agriculture as the main Welsh economic activity.

In its early years the party remained a middle-class intellectual cultural club, putting forward few candidates even for local elections. In its first electoral test, in Caernarfonshire in 1929, the party got only 1.6 per cent of the vote, although it did very well in one little village, Talysarn. After this setback,

the party abandoned its policy of seeking to boycott Westminster and in 1932 started to bring out a newspaper in English as well (the *Welsh Nationalist*).

The party's first big impact came in 1936 when Saunders Lewis and two of his fellow leaders were put on trial and sent to prison for setting fire to a bombing school which the Royal Air Force was constructing on the Lleyn peninsula in North Wales. The sympathy that it won for this action was later largely forfeited by its attempts to boycott George VI's coronation, the foreign policy stance of some of its leaders (which included neutrality in the Spanish Civil War, and sympathy for Salazar and Mussolini), and its later opposition to World War II conscription.

At the end of the war Gwynfor Evans became the new president of the party, a position which he retained until 1981. Under his leadership the party slowly changed its character, becoming better organized, fighting more elections, and becoming less of a Conservative Christian Democratic party.

In the 1960s a Welsh language society (*Cymdeithas yr Iaith Gymraeg*) was established, which provided a more radical outlet for many younger nationalists. In 1966 Plaid Cymru finally obtained a Westminster seat when its president, Gwynfor Evans, won a by-election at Carmarthen. The party's subsequent increase in support and credibility was shown by its excellent second place to Labour in more unpromising electoral territory in South Wales, in Rhondda West and Caerphilly.

Nationalist opposition to the Prince of Wales' investiture and increasing violence from an extremist fringe cost the party a considerable measure of popular support. In 1970, however, the party put up candidates in 36 seats (up from 20 in 1966) and won 11.5 per cent of the Welsh vote, but lost its only seat in Carmarthen.

In February 1974 the party's share of the Welsh vote dropped slightly to 10.7 per cent, but it won two new seats, that of Dafydd Wigley in Caernarfon and Dafydd Elis Thomas in Merioneth. In October 1974 it obtained a third seat when Gwynfor Evans regained Carmarthen.

During the latter part of the 1974–79 legislature the three Plaid MPs had considerable leverage when there was a hung parliament. The party was later put in an extremely difficult position by the Labour government's proposals for a limited measure of Welsh devolution. The party was uncertain whether to oppose them as completely inadequate or to accept them as a limited first step. When they were comprehensively rejected by the Welsh electorate in the referendum in 1979 Plaid was forced to set up a commission of inquiry to see what had gone wrong, and to make recommendations for a new strategy for the future.

In the 1979 election the party's Welsh vote dropped sharply to 8.1 per cent, and Gwynfor Evans again lost his seat in Carmarthen. In 1981 he finally stood down as president and Dafydd Wigley took over. In 1983 the party's share of the Welsh vote remained at 7.8 per cent. In 1984 Dafydd Elis Thomas became the new party president.

In the 1987 election its overall share of the Welsh vote dropped slightly to 7.3 per cent, but it gained an additional seat in Ynys Mon (Anglesey).

Support

Plaid Cymru has been described in the past as a party of poets, teachers and preachers. It has attracted many intellectuals and artists, from Saunders Lewis to the singer Dafydd Iwan. A disproportionate number of its activists have been university lecturers, school teachers and non-conformist ministers. The party has often had a particular appeal among the very young. The party is weakest among Anglicans, strong among those with no religion, but strongest of all among non-conformists. It is far stronger among Welsh speakers than among those who only speak English. It has found it difficult to expand out of its primarily middle-class activist base to win consistent support among working-class voters, and trade unions.

In Wales as a whole Plaid Cymru is only the fourth political force but this masks its much greater strength in the county of Gwynedd in rural Welsh-speaking North Wales, where it holds three seats, Meirionydd Nant Conwy, Caernarfon and Ynys Mon (Anglesey). In Caernarfon it was not far short of winning 60 per cent of the vote in 1987. The largest party branches are also in Gwynedd. Bethesda, for example, has had over 300 members and Blaenau Ffestiniog around 400. In Caernarfon almost every village has a branch.

In Welsh-speaking Central and Western Wales Plaid Cymru is less successful although it retains a substantial base of support in seats such as Carmarthen and Cardigan.

The Plaid is much weaker in both rural and industrialized South Wales. While it has gained a strong protest vote in by-elections (as in Rhondda West and Caerphilly in the 1960s), and has had a substantial local government presence (for example in Mid-Glamorgan), it has not polled well in general elections in these areas. The only South Wales constituencies where it has had more than minor support have been those where it had had previous by-election support (e.g. Caerphilly), where there are still a substantial number of Welsh speakers (e.g. Llanelli), or both (e.g. Rhondda). In the 1984 European Parliament elections Plaid Cymru only obtained 7 per cent in the South Wales constituency, compared to 17.5 per cent in North Wales.

Organization

In the past Plaid Cymru was rather loosely and informally organized, but a number of organizational changes were made in the period of rapid party expansion after 1966. In 1970, for instance the office of party president and party chairman were formally separated.

The basic organizational unit is the *Cangen* or branch, which must have a minimum membership of 10. Above the branches there are District Committees (a *Pwllgar Ranbarth*), based either on a parliamentary constituency or a district council area (in order to put a greater emphasis on local elections), but in practice still generally based on the former.

The third organizational tier consists of the regional councils (*Cyngar Talaith*), corresponding to the county councils. These are meant to deal with issues at county level, such as the drawing up of county council manifestos, but are the weakest organizational tier within the party.

The Plaid's annual conference (*Y Gynhadledd*) is the highest authority in the party. Branch delegates are chosen on a sliding scale according to branch numbers. The conference is prepared to defy the leadership of the party, as in a recent conference debate on defence when the leadership's unilateralist but pro-NATO line was rejected in favour of an outright withdrawal from NATO.

In between national conferences party business is in the hands of the National Council (*Y Cyngar Cenedlaethol*), which deals primarily with policy-making and implementation, and which meets quarterly, and the smaller (26 member) National Executive Committee (*Y Pwllgar Gwaith Cenedlaethol*), which meets monthly, and which deals with organizational, financial and strategic matters.

The party chairman is elected on a two-yearly basis by the national conference, and deals primarily with matters of internal party organization.

The party's principal spokesman is its president, whose election is on a decentralized branch and district committee basis, so that all members of the party can participate.

There are only two party workers at its headquarters, although there are also full time workers and Plaid organizers in certain key constituencies.

Parliamentary candidates are chosen by the district committees, where these cover the area of a parliamentary constituency or by an ad hoc constituency committee, where the district and the constituency are not the same. The National Executive Committee must then ratify the candidature, although this is normally a formality.

Plaid Cymru has a number of associated organizations. The youth movement (*Mudiad Ieunctid Plaid Cymru*) is open to anyone from the ages of 11 to 25, and is organized in cells. There is also a women's section. Starting from 1982 the national committee of the women's section had the right to elect five representatives to the national executive. This modest measure of affirmative action was controversial within the party, and not renewed when the initial trial period ended in 1986. The national organization of Plaid Trade Unionists has not been very successful so far.

Plaid Cymru has a Welsh-speaking newspaper, *Y Ddraig Goch* ("Red Dragon") as well as an English language one, which is now called *Welsh Nation*. The party also issues a monthly bulletin, *Rhagom*.

Plaid Cymru's current membership dues are £2 for those in work and £1 for the unwaged, which are collected through the branches, which keep half the fee, and pass on the rest to headquarters. Another important source of income is the Annual St David's Day Fund, for which targets are set for each district committee.

On Nov. 8, 1986 Plaid Cymru concluded an agreement with the Scottish Nationalist Party to enter into a parliamentary alliance after the next general election, in which they agreed to fight for a number of joint objectives, as well as to provide mutual support for each other's individual objectives.

While Plaid Cymru has no member at the European Parliament it has joined the group of parties contained within the European Free Alliance, one of the components of the Rainbow Group within the European Parliament.

Policies

Although the party has moved to the left many of the choices facing Plaid Cymru today are similar to those that it had to face before the war; the balance to be struck between defending the language and pushing for independence; the need to develop a coherent economic policy rather than just concentrating on cultural and political goals; and the need not to create too

wide a divide between predominantly rural Welsh-speaking Wales, and the more industrialized English-speaking Wales. The party has also had to decide whether to concentrate on parliamentary elections to conduct single issue campaigns or to embark upon a wider programme of extra-parliamentary activities. In this latter context non-violence against persons has been a fundamental principle of the party since Saunders Lewis's day, although a small minority of more extreme nationalists have given nationalism a more violent name, by setting off bombs to coincide with the investiture, and by destroying English second homes in Wales.

The two main issues for the Plaid have been the protection of the Welsh language and the furthering of Welsh self-government. Saunders Lewis put the primacy on the first goal, and believed that independence, with the language having died in the meantime, was hardly worth achieving. On the other hand too strong an emphasis on the language issue could risk alienating the English-speaking majority. The most recent success of the Plaid on language issues was the creation of the fourth television channel in Wales as a Welsh language station. The Plaid's 1987 election manifesto called for the adoption of a new Welsh language Act to ensure the same status for the Welsh and English languages in all aspects of Welsh national life.

The other key Plaid objective, the attainment of Welsh self-government, was made more difficult by the Welsh electorate's rejection in 1979 of the Labour government's already limited plan for devolution. The party remains committed to independence for Wales and continues to point out the disadvantages of being subject to rule from London. It also claims that other small European nations have achieved better economic results than the UK, and that energy-rich Wales would be able to emulate them. Tactically, however, it recognizes the difficulties of pushing directly for independence.

The party's own commission of inquiry recommended a greater concentration on local government elections than on the less promising Westminster arena, and the further development of Welsh economic enterprises and associations, which would deepen the sense of "Welshness", and create more nationalists.

The Plaid's main campaign at present in this sphere is for the creation of a 100-member Welsh senate which would assume all the powers of the Secretary of State at the Welsh office, and which would be elected by proportional representation (STV) for a fixed term of four years. It would also have the power to initiate legislation to be presented in the Parliament of Westminster, and the power to scrutinize all Westminster and European legislation.

One of the Plaid's long-standing aims is for Wales to become a member of the United Nations. Its general attitude to the European Community, however, has been hostile, but it recognizes that a small nation like Ireland has gained benefits from membership. Its main demand, therefore, has been that Wales must win full national status within the EC. It believes that the Europe of the future will be the Europe of a hundred flags and that the "Red Dragon of Wales" must be among them.

On defence issues the party's old pacifist tradition is still strong. The 1987 manifesto demanded immediate nuclear disarmament by Britain and the removal from Wales of all American military installations. An independent Wales should withdraw from NATO. Military expenditure in general should be cut.

The party has become more republican than it was in the time of Saunders Lewis who supported the monarchy. After the war a number of republicans left Plaid Cymru and founded a new party which collapsed a few years later. Most Plaid members were opposed to the investiture of the Prince of Wales. Republicanism is not, however, a major plank in the party's platform.

The party puts a particularly heavy emphasis on energy issues. One of the catalytic events in Plaid Cymru's development was the campaign on the Tryweryn reservoir issue in the 1950s. The fact that Welsh water rates have often been higher than English rates, although Wales has been producing much of the water, has been used by the Plaid to argue for greater Welsh control over its own resources.

Plaid Cymru is a strong advocate of increased support for the Welsh coal industry, and opposes any further nuclear power stations.

Economic policy in the wider sense has not been the easiest policy for the party in that the interests of rural Wales have often diverged quite strongly from industrial Wales. Those Plaid members particularly concerned with the party expanding into English-speaking industrial Wales, have also pushed for the development of closer links with the trade unions (which have remained weak) and for a more socialist economic policy.

The party's economic policy has instead often been rather generally defined, combining the need to increase investment in Wales, and a measure of Wales-wide planning with rather unspecified support for "decentralized socialism", support for co-operatives (a continuing theme since Saunders Lewis) and for industrial democracy, and the creation of industrial parks in strategic locations. The 1987 manifesto put a strong emphasis on the need to create a single body — Action Wales — that would combine the role of all the public agencies responsible for economic development in Wales. The party also emphasized full employment and the need for a minimum wage.

Personalities

The current president is Dafydd Elis Thomas, MP for Meironydd Nant Conwy, who has been more on the left wing of the party than his predecessor and fellow MP (for Caernarfon), Dafydd Wigley. I.W. Jones is the party's third and newly elected MP for Ynys Mon (Anglesey).

Gwynfor Evans is no longer president or in Parliament but retains considerable influence as an elder statesman.

Green Party

Headquarters	: 36/38 Chapman Road, London SW9 0JQ (tel: 01–735 2485)
Membership	: 7,000 (1988)
Founded	: 1973

History

An ecology party was first founded under the name "People" in 1973, and contested 11 seats in the parliamentary elections of 1974. In 1975 it took the name "Ecology Party". In 1981 it won a seat on the Cornish County Council. At its conference in 1985 it changed its name to the "Green Party" by a vote of 244 to 93. In 1985 it also elected an all-women team of co-chairmen, and 13 women onto its 21-member council. In the 1987 elections it put up 133 candidates, and obtained about 1.3 per cent of the total poll. It currently has around 60 seats on parish councils, and three district councillors.

Support

The Green Party has considerably more electoral support than any of the other small British parties. It put up far more candidates than any small party in the 1987 general elections, and in all types of seats, urban, suburban and rural. It polled over 1,000 votes in 16 constituencies, all in southern England, with a highest vote of 3.7 per cent.

Organization

The Green Party has a conference held in the spring, a 21-member party council, and three co-chairs. It emphasizes participation and consensus in decision-making, and rotation of leadership. It is affiliated to the European Greens.

Policies

The Green Party does not just concentrate on environmental protection objectives, but on a much wider ecological approach to all policy issues, emphasizing conservation of all resources, decentralization and self-sufficiency, opposition to nuclear power in all forms, a proper balance between masculine and feminine values and the growth of spiritual and personal values at the expense of materialism.

The centrepiece of its economic policies is a national income scheme, replacing all existing welfare benefits and tax allowances, and replacing them by a guaranteed and unconditional minimum income for all. To help finance this the Green Party has advocated the development of new taxes, such as a natural resources tax on all imported and home grown raw materials to encourage conservation, a progressive turnover tax and a tax on advertising. It has also mooted a durability tax, with a rate related to the life-span of an article. It believes people should live in more self-sufficient local communities, producing more socially useful products and services, with much more recycling and repair than at present. The Green Party advocates the retention of major public services and strategic industries in public ownership, but where possible these should be broken up into smaller units. The Green Party is highly critical of multinational and large private companies, and has advocated a corporation tax whose levies would be set according to the size of the company. Work flexibility is strongly emphasized, with encouragement to job sharing, part-time work and time off for study or caring for one's family.

The Greens are strongly anti-civil nuclear energy, which should be rapidly phased out.

The Greens have advocated radical transport policies, with less emphasis on the automobile. New motorway construction should be stopped, and there should be no expansion of air travel.

The Greens call for full application of the "polluter pays" principle as well as the creation of an Environmental Protection Agency. A strong emphasis is put on protection of animal rights. The Greens are strongly opposed to battery farming and vivisection, and believe that all hunting and coursing with hounds should be stopped.

The Greens call for a high level of British agricultural self-sufficiency, mixed rotation and organic farming, and much smaller farms.

The Greens advocate proportional representation using the single transferable vote.

They also seek a Bill of Rights, freedom of information and data protection legislation. They call for devolution to Wales and Scotland and regional assemblies throughout England. The most important local tier of government should be district councils. They are strongly opposed to the poll tax.

Their defence policy is uncompromisingly anti-nuclear. They advocate immediate unilateral nuclear disarmament, no American bases in Britain and British withdrawal from NATO. They support conventional defence in the form of a non-nuclear, non-aligned European Alliance. They oppose the arms trade.

The Greens have called for British withdrawal from the EC. They call for increased aid to the third world, aimed at such countries acquiring more self-reliant economies.

Communist Party of Great Britain

Headquarters	:	16 St John Street, London EC1M 4AL (tel: 01–251 4406)
General secretary	:	Gordon McLennan
Party membership	:	10,000 (1987)
Founded	:	1920

History

The Communist Party of Great Britain was founded in 1920 by members of the British Socialist Party, the Communist Unity Group of the Socialist Labour Party, the Guild Communists, and other groups. It affiliated to the Communist International. In its first parliamentary contest, in Caerphilly in 1921, its candidate obtained over 2,500 votes.

The Communist Party's application to affiliate with the Labour Party was rejected. At first, however, Communists were eligible to stand as Labour candidates, and a wealthy Parsee, Shapurji Saklatvala was elected MP for Battersea North on a Labour ticket. He lost his seat in 1923, but regained it in 1924 by 554 votes as a fully fledged Communist candidate. In 1924 the Labour Party decided to exclude individual Communists from membership.

The Communist Party also began to organize within the trade union movement.

In 1929 the party's first general secretary, Albert Inkpin, was succeeded by Harry Pollitt, who was to remain leader until 1956, with only one short interruption.

In the mid-1930s the party (which had gone through a narrow sectarian phase in the late 1920s) began to return to a Popular Front strategy, and again supported Labour candidates in the 1935 election. Labour again refused a Communist request for affiliation. In 1935 Willie Gallacher was elected as Communist MP for West Fife.

The Communists played an active role in the International Brigade in the Spanish Civil War, took part in large scale demonstrations against fascism, and opposed appeasement. They made a significant impact among intellectuals and in universities.

After the German-Soviet pact, the party was divided over whether to support British participation in the war. The executive voted to oppose it, and Harry Pollitt resigned after being put in the minority, only to return as general secretary when the Soviet Union entered the war. 1943 saw the party reach its maximum membership of 55,000 and its third request to affiliate to the Labour Party received the support of 26 per cent of Labour delegates.

In 1945 Willie Gallacher was re-elected in West Fife, Phil Piratin was elected in Mile End in East London and Harry Pollitt was only narrowly defeated in the Rhondda. In 1950, however, the party put up a record total of 100 candidates but all of them lost. Since 1950 there has never been a Communist Member of Parliament.

Khrushchev's criticisms of Stalin in 1956, and the Soviet intervention in Hungary led to a considerable loss of party members. In 1956 John Gollan took over from Harry Pollitt as general secretary.

The party gradually became more critical of the Soviet Union, and in 1968 it opposed the invasion of Czechoslovakia. In 1975 Gordon McLennan took over as general secretary.

In May 1985 the Eurocommunist leadership defeated the pro-Moscow hardliners, but the latter regrouped around Mick Costello, the party's former industrial organizer, and Tony Chater, the editor of the *Morning Star*. Eventually the *Morning Star* group was expelled from the party, and formed a New Communist Party.

By 1987 the Communist Party had around 10,000 members, but in the general election only put up 19 candidates, far less than the Greens. The party has a few local councillors, however, and retains considerable support in the trade union movement.

Support

The Communist Party has never had a mass political following, and apart from 1950 has never fielded more than 58 parliamentary candidates. It has had a few pockets of local support, the mining communities in the Rhondda Valley in South Wales and in the Fife coalfield in Scotland, and in parts of the East End of London. Its handful

of candidates in the 1987 general election (most of whom only won 200 to 300 votes) were, with the exception of the Rhondda and a couple of Scottish industrial constituencies, in inner-city constituencies.

The highest number of votes cast for any of its candidates was 879 in Nottingham North, followed by 869 in the Rhondda.

Organization

The Communist Party still retains the orthodox Communist structure of democratic centralism. Its basic units of membership are its branches. There are both workplace branches and territorially based local branches, each run by a branch committee. Above these are the district committees. District congresses are held every two years. In Scotland and Wales there are separate party structures. At national level the congress is held every two years, in which branch and district delegates participate. The congress elects the party's executive committee, which in its turn elects the party's officers (its leader is called the general secretary) and a political committee. There is also a youth group, and Young Communists' League.

The party leadership has feuded with its longstanding newspaper, the *Morning Star* and has established a weekly paper, *7 Days*. There is also an influential theoretical monthly *Marxism Today*.

Policies

The 1977 party programme, its most recent, made it clear that the party accepted parliamentary democracy in Britain, with freedom for all democratic political parties, including those hostile to socialism. It argued that the Communists should ally with the Labour Party's left wing, along with the new movements such as the black, women's, youth, environmental and peace movements to form a broad democratic alliance. While it rejected revolutionary violence (unless there was a right wing coup against an elected left wing government) its political and economic analysis and proposals were generally orthodox Marxist ones.

The party's general election manifesto in 1987 supported the introduction of the single transferable vote system of proportional representation, the establishment of Scottish and Welsh Assemblies, a new Freedom of Information Act, British withdrawal from Northern Ireland, and unilateral nuclear disarmament (with the scrapping of Trident, removal of Cruise missiles, and closing of American nuclear bases in Britain). It called for the repeal of the racist immigration and nationality laws, and of anti-trade union legislation. It called for the introduction of local income tax. It advocated the ending of civil nuclear energy. It opposed the restrictions and policies of the EC, and called for a public ownership programme with genuine democratic control and the introduction of the 35-hour week. The party has warmly supported *glasnost*.

Personalities

The party's leader is Gordon McLennan. Martin Jacques is the editor of *Marxism Today*.

National Front (NF)

Headquarters : 50 Parsons Road,
Croydon,
Surrey CRO 2QF
(tel: 01–684 0271)
Founded : 1967

History

The National Front was founded in 1967 by leading members of several far-right groups.

The Front's first chairmen were A. K. Chesterton and John O'Brien. John Tyndall took over as chairman in 1972, while Martin Webster became his deputy as national activities organizer. Both had been active in Neo-Nazi fringe parties.

Support for the far right was mainly stimulated by the increasing controversy over Commonwealth immigration into the United Kingdom, especially over the issues of the Kenyan and Ugandan Asians.

In the 1970 elections the NF contested 10 parliamentary constituencies, winning an average of 3.6 per cent of the vote. Its best result came in 1973, when it obtained over 16 per cent in a by-election in West Bromwich. In 1973 the NF also obtained its highest membership of 14,000.

In the February 1974 election its 54 candidates averaged 3.3 per cent of the vote, and in October 1974 it obtained its highest ever vote in an individual constituency in a general election of 9.5 per cent in Hackney South.

In the mid-1970s divisions opened up between certain members with a former Conservative background and the former Neo-Nazi leadership. For a brief time control was wrested from Tyndall by a former Conservative, Kingley Read, but the Conservative element finally left the party and formed a new "National Party", including 2,000 former NF members. In early 1976 Tyndall returned as NF leader.

The NF did extremely well in the 1976 local elections (8.9 per cent of the vote in

the seats contested, with figures in individual wards of up to 27.5 per cent), and in the 1977 GLC elections, spurring the development of an Anti-Nazi League.

In the 1979 election, however, the party contested 303 seats, but polled badly, with an average for its candidates of only 1.3 per cent.

The party now underwent a damaging series of schisms, the first in 1979 giving rise to a more moderate National Front Constitutional Movement (later the Constitutionalist Movement and then the Nationalist Party). In 1980 Tyndall left the party after a dispute with Webster, and at a later date founded the British National Party. Andrew Brons became the NF chairman.

The NF's electoral decline accelerated in the 1980s. By 1984 Martin Webster had been ousted.

In 1984–5 the NF received new publicity as a result of a dispute concerning the registration of an NF supporter, Pat Harrington, as a student at North London Polytechnic.

In 1986–87 there were further divisions within the NF. The NF has continued to contest some local elections and occasional by-elections (Joe Pearce of the National Front Support Group, one of the two main factions, stood in the 1987 Greenwich by-election). In the 1987 national election, however, they no longer put up any parliamentary candidates.

Support

The NF's electoral support and membership has greatly declined from its heyday in the 1970s. The age and class profile of its membership has also been transformed. In its early days it attracted many middle-aged, middle-class right-wing Conservatives, whereas its main current appeal is to the young, white working class, often in their early 20s. Many are unemployed, many are skinheads and there appears to be a considerable correlation with violent football support groups.

In regional terms its main support has come in inner cities with high immigrant populations, such as parts of the West Midlands, other cities of the Midlands and North, such as Leicester and Bradford, and above all the East End of London, which has a long tradition of support for the far right dating from the days of Oswald Mosley and even before.

Organization

The NF's organizational structure has been modified on several occasions, and has recently been weakened by the fall in active members and the damaging schism within the party.

At local level the party is organized in "branches" or smaller "groups". At national level there is a national directorate of 18 members elected by a ballot of all of the voting members of the Front. The national directorate elects on an annual basis the chairman and deputy chairman. A smaller executive council consists of the chairman, deputy chairman, and four other members of the national directorate. The NF's annual general meeting is open to all voting members.

A young National Front was created in 1977. The party's newspaper is called *National Front News*. There is also a members' bulletin, and a review called *Nationalism Today*. Its bookselling operation, *Nationalist Books* began as *Burning Books* in 1986.

Until recently membership was £8 a year. Proposals were recently put forward for a new division between Friends of the Movement, who would continue to pay £8 (£6 if unemployed) and party cadres and candidate cadres who would have to pay £10 a month (£5 a month if unemployed).

The NF has established links with groups in the white Commonwealth and South Africa, as well as far right-wing groups in Europe, notably the Italian extra-parliamentary right.

Policies

The NF is a Radical Nationalist Party, whose main policy plank is Britain for the British and opposition to a multiracial society. It seeks to stop all non-white immigration to the United Kingdom, and to begin a programme of phased repatriation of immigrants already in Britain. It also retains an anti-Semitic and anti-Zionist character, although these are less important themes.

It is strongly opposed to multinationals and to all large private concentrations of capital. No foreign ownership of British industry should be allowed. It is not enthusiastic about state ownership, and greatly prefers producer co-operatives and small private firms. The Stock Exchange should be abolished, and the banks should be nationalized. It believes in a strong trade union movement, but with only one union for each industry, and with no contributions to political parties. It has adopted a generally hostile position to civil nuclear energy.

It supports strong law and order measures, capital punishment and the introduction of national youth service. It has been socially conservative in other areas, such as abortion. It is strongly in favour of the monarchy, but its 1983 manifesto called for abolition of the House of Lords. It has established links with Ulster Loy-alist groups and believes that Northern Ireland should remain part of the United Kingdom for all time.

The NF is strongly opposed to the European Community, and believes that Britain should leave the United Nations. It advocates departure from NATO, and the removal of all foreign bases from British soil. It is firmly anti-Communist, but is unsympathetic to the United States as well, as it is dominated by Zionism and big business. It is in favour of apartheid in South Africa, and regrets its dismantling. It is pro-Palestinian.

In recent times factions within the party have advocated a return to ruralist values, and love of nature and the land. Others have preferred to emphasize more traditional themes.

British National Party

Headquarters	: 52 Westbourne Villas, Hove, Sussex

This is a breakaway organization from the National Front led by John Tyndall. In 1980 Tyndall left the Front and formed the New National Front, which was dissolved and re-grouped as the British National Party in April 1982. It contested 53 constituencies in the 1983 general election, but with negligible success, with its best performance only 1.3 per cent in Walsall South. It contested the Greenwich by-election in early 1987 (winning 0.3 per cent of the vote), but it put up no official candidates in the 1987 general election, although two unofficial candidates won 1.4 per cent and 0.6 per cent in South London suburban constituencies.

The BNP emphasizes British nationalism, repatriation of immigrants, reintroduction of the death penalty, anti-Communism and conservative social measures.

Fellowship Party

Headquarters	: Woolacombe House, 141 Woolacombe Road, Blackheath, London SE3 8QP
President	: Donald Swann
General secretary	: Ronald Mallone
Chairman	: Sidney Hinkes
Founded	: 1955

This is a small pacifist party, which claims to have been the first to present petitions against all governments' nuclear weapons tests. It has opposed military conscription, nuclear power and the European Community. It advocates total world disarmament, and is opposed to both the Warsaw Pact and NATO. It has also supported proportional representation, common ownership of the means of production and distribution, industrial democracy and decentralization.

It has an annual conference, and a national executive, and produces a publication called *Day by Day*. It has links with the Pacifist Socialist Party of the Netherlands.

It has put up parliamentary candidates, but has polled few votes. In 1987 it fielded one candidate who received 59 votes.

Humanist Party

This put up three candidates in the 1987 general election, who polled 134, 98 and 65 votes respectively.

Orkney and Shetland Movement

This movement fielded a candidate in the Orkney and Shetlands constituency in the 1987 general election who polled 3,059 votes.

Workers Revolutionary Party

Headquarters	: 21 B Old Town, London SW4 0JT
General secretary	: Mike Banda

The Workers Revolutionary Party was founded in 1973. In previous forms it can trace its descent from the Militant Group, created by former Communists in the 1930s. In its postwar guise as the Revolutionary Communist Party and later the Socialist Labour League it adopted an "entryist" strategy within the Labour Party, and in particular the Young Socialists, but many of its members were expelled from the Labour Party in 1965.

It began contesting general elections in 1974 and by 1987 had fielded 110 candidates, none of whom had polled many votes. In 1985 it suffered a severe split, when its historic leader, Gerry Healy, was accused of debauchery and expelled from the party, leading to the subsequent expulsion of other Healy supporters on the party's central committee, including its most famous members, Vanessa and Corin Redgrave.

The Workers Revolutionary Party advocates Trotskyist policies. It has called for a revolutionary general strike, the formation of Soviets, the replacement of the police by a workers' militia and the nationalization without compensation of financial institutions and major industries.

It has produced a daily newspaper called *Newsline*.

Red Front

The Red Front fielded 11 candidates in the 1987 general election, mainly in inner-city constituencies. Its highest vote, however, was 538 in Knowsley North. It is the electoral label of the Revolutionary Communist Party which is Trotskyist in orientation.

Socialist Party of Great Britain

Headquarters	: 52 Clapham High Street, London SW4 7UN
Founded	: 1904

This was founded in 1904 by left-wing members of the Social Democratic Federation, which had already abandoned the Labour Representation Committee. It is a small Marxist party of the far left which has consistently rejected all co-operation with other parties.

Applicants for membership are required to undergo an examination in their knowledge of Marxism. Annual conferences attended by instructed delegates from the local branches take binding decisions. It is opposed to any form of leadership — and its general secretary and executive committee, elected annually by postal ballot of the whole membership are answerable to the conference. It has a monthly publication called *Socialist Standard*, and has links with other small sister parties in other countries adhering to the World Socialist Movement.

It put up one parliamentary candidate in 1983 and another in 1987, who polled 85 and 81 votes respectively.

Mebyon Kernow
(Sons of Cornwall)

Headquarters	: 11 West Street, Liskenod, Cornwall (tel: 0579–42314)
Chair	: Loveday Carlyon
Founded	: 1951

Mebyon Kernow was founded in 1951 with the objective of promoting Cornish identity as a Celtic nation. At first it took the form of a movement open to members of other political parties, and several Cornish MPs were in sympathy with its aims. It then became more active politically in its own right and members of Mebyon Kernow are no longer allowed to be members of any other political party active in Cornwall.

By 1968 Mebyon Kernow had won a seat on the Cornish county council, and had a number of urban and rural district council seats. In 1970 Richard Jenkins stood as a Mebyon Kernow candidate in Falmouth and Camborne, winning 960 votes. The party subsequently put up one candidate in both elections of 1974 and also in 1979. In 1983 its two candidates, one in Falmouth and Camborne and one in St Ives, won 582 and 569 votes respectively (1.2 per cent in both cases). In 1987 it did not field any candidates.

Mebyon Kernow has already experienced two schisms. In 1969 a short-lived Cornish national party was founded, and in 1976, a Cornish nationalist party. The latter fielded two parliamentary candidates, once in 1979 and once in 1983.

A number of publications have been produced by or associated with Mebyon Kernow, *New Cornwall* (which ceased publication in 1972), *Cornish Nation* and then the very short-lived *Cornish Voice*, but there is none at present.

In 1986 party membership fees were £3, and £1.50 for the unwaged.

Mebyon Kernow calls for Cornwall to be fully recognized as one of the six Celtic nations, and seeks acknowledgement of that fact by governments in London and throughout the world. It seeks to foster the development of the Cornish language and to spread knowledge about Cornish history and culture. Mebyon Kernow has called for self-government in Cornish domestic affairs, and for a Cornish Assembly, *Cuntelles Kernow*. Mebyon Kernow has links with the Celtic League and with the European Free Alliance.

Northern Ireland

Northern Ireland is a part of the United Kingdom of Great Britain and Northern Ireland, with an area of 5,452 square miles and a population of over 1.5 million. It consists of six of the nine counties in the historic Irish province of Ulster. Its largest city is Belfast.

Northern Ireland is divided into two religious communities, the majority Protestants with around 65 per cent of the population, and the Catholics with around 35 per cent. Besides the Church of Ireland there are a number of other Protestant denominations, of which the largest is the Presbyterian Church of Ireland. The Catholics are particularly numerous in West Belfast, in the city of Londonderry ("Derry" to Nationalists, and where Catholics are in a majority), in the southern part of County Londonderry, Tyrone and southern County Fermanagh, as well as in South Armagh and South Down.

Northern Ireland's history and political system are clearly distinct from those of the rest of the United Kingdom, and have thus been covered in a separate section of this book.

Political institutions

Northern Ireland is entitled to 17 Members of Parliament at Westminster, who are elected by the "first past the post" majority system, and to three members of the European Parliament, who, unlike anywhere else in the United Kingdom, are elected by the single transferable vote (STV) system of proportional representation.

There are also 26 district councils of 566 elected representatives, who have only limited power. Local council elections are held every four years, the most recent being in 1973, 1977, 1981 and 1985.

The Anglo-Irish Agreement of November 1985 established an Intergovernmental Conference concerned with Northern Ireland, which provides a framework for contacts between the British and Irish government over political and security matters in Northern Ireland, the administration of justice in the province, and the promotion of cross-border co-operation.

Brief political history

The Ulster Plantation, beginning in the early 17th century, and consolidated by the victory of the Orange dynasty over the Stuarts at the end of that century, brought an influx of Protestant settlers into the province. There was strong Protestant opposition to Gladstone's Irish Home Rule Bills in 1886 and 1893, and in 1905 an Ulster Unionist Council was established. The most prominent Unionist leader was Sir Edward Carson. Opposition reached a new pitch with the presentation of a third Home Rule Bill in 1912. Unionists organized to prevent Home Rule being enacted, and a paramilitary Ulster Volunteer Force was set up. Home Rule was passed in 1914, but was suspended for the whole of the 1914–18 war.

Lloyd George's imposed Government of Ireland Act of 1920, which provided for the setting up of separate parliaments in the six most strongly Protestant counties of Ulster and in the rest of Ireland was rejected by the latter, but accepted by the former, and the Northern

Map of Northern Ireland showing 6 counties.

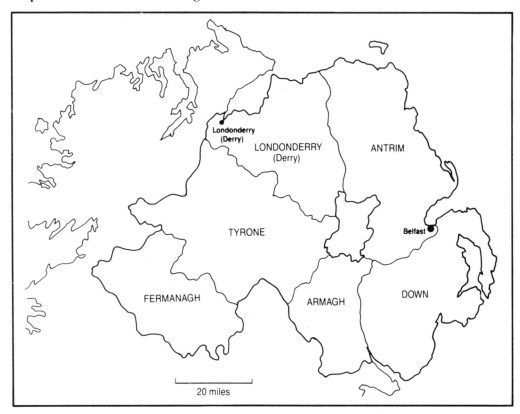

Londonderry
(Derry)

LONDONDERRY
(Derry)

ANTRIM

TYRONE

Belfast

FERMANAGH

ARMAGH

DOWN

20 miles

Ireland Parliament was set up on June 22, 1921. Northern Ireland subsequently opted out of the Anglo-Irish Treaty of December 1921, and retained its separate status. A Boundary Commission, set up as a result of the Treaty, and clearly expected by the South to award it large sections of the North, did not do so, and the status quo was maintained.

The Protestant Unionist majority promptly took control of the institutions of the new state. They dominated the regional parliament at Stormont, which had legislative powers over most local Northern Ireland issues (with Westminster retaining powers over defence and foreign affairs in particular). The Northern Ireland House of Commons had 52 members (elected by proportional representation until 1929, when it was replaced by the first past the post system in all constituencies apart from the University seats), and the Senate had 26 members. Northern Ireland was also entitled to 13 seats at Westminster.

Northern Ireland had six Unionist Prime Ministers, Sir James Craig (Lord Craigavon after 1927) from 1921 to 1940, John Andrews 1940–43, Sir Basil Brooke (Viscount Brookeborough from 1952) 1943–63, Captain Terence O'Neill 1963–69, Major James Chichester-Clark 1969–71 and Brian Faulkner from 1971–72.

The one-third Catholic minority never accepted the legitimacy of Northern Ireland's institutions. They also experienced considerable civil disabilities under the Stormont system, especially in the fields of housing and employment. Even in areas with Catholic majorities most of local government was under Ulster Unionist control.

The Catholic response varied greatly. The mainstream Nationalists, whose most prominent leader in the early years of the state was Joseph Devlin, alternated between boycotting the Northern Ireland Parliament, and taking their seats, and between pushing for Irish unity, and improving the lot of the minority in Northern Ireland. Periodically, however, more extreme republicanism came to the fore, seeking to achieve Irish unity by campaigns of violence north and south of the border.

Finally, and primarily in the city of Belfast, attempts were made to set up political organizations on a class rather than sectarian basis, by emphasizing socialist solutions for both Catholic and Protestant workers. The success of these movements was always temporary and local, and they too were fragmented between groups closer to the British Labour Party and others close to the Irish Labour Party.

In the mid-1960s, under the more conciliatory leadership of Terence O'Neill, who became the first Northern Irish Prime Minister to meet his Southern counterpart when he met Sean Lemass in February 1965, there was initially some hope of progress, but this was short-lived.

In 1968 the Catholic civil rights movement became much more active. After 1969 there was a great intensification of unrest and violence. There were severe riots in many areas of Northern Ireland, and the British Army intervened directly in the province. In August 1971 internment was introduced, there were 22 killed in four days of rioting, and the Catholic minority was further alienated; 13 civilians were killed by the Army in one day in Londonderry in January 1972. Shortly afterwards in March 1972, the British government abolished the entire Stormont system of a separate Northern Ireland Parliament and government, and began to run the province directly under a Northern Ireland Secretary of State.

In 1973 a referendum was held in Northern Ireland, in which 591,820 voted to remain within the UK and 6,463 voted to join the South, with the vast majority of Nationalists abstaining. Later in the year a new attempt was made at establishing a devolved Northern Ireland assembly, with 78 members being elected by proportional representation in multi-member constituencies.

In December 1973 the Sunningdale Conference of British and Irish ministers and representatives of a designated Northern Ireland Executive (consisting of members from the Ulster Unionists, the SDLP and the Alliance Party) agreed to form a Council of Ireland, with a 14-member Council of Ministers and a 60-member Consultative Assembly consisting of elected members from Ireland and Northern Ireland. In January 1974 the power-sharing Northern Ireland Executive was established, with six Ulster Unionist members, four SDLP members and one Alliance member, and with the Unionist Brian Faulkner as chief executive.

Protestant Loyalists were generally opposed both to the Sunningdale Agreement, and to the executive. In May 1974 the latter was brought down by a strike of Protestant workers, and the Sunningdale process of Anglo-Irish co-operation was never implemented.

In 1975 there was a new attempt to break the deadlock with elections to a Northern Ireland constitutional convention, which was meant to put forward new solutions. It too got nowhere and by March 1976 it was abandoned.

In 1981 the IRA got a major publicity boost with a series of prison hunger strikes.

In October 1982 elections were held for yet another Northern Ireland Assembly, with 78 seats, which was meant to provide for "rolling" or step-by-step devolution, and which established six committees to scrutinize the work of the Northern Ireland Office. Sinn Féin and the SDLP refused to take up their seats in the Assembly.

In 1983–84 the SDLP played a prominent role in the work of the New Ireland Forum, which prepared a report on Northern Ireland's problems with the participation of the major parties in the South.

On Nov. 15, 1985 an Anglo-Irish Agreement was reached at Hillsborough, which set up a framework for Anglo-Irish co-operation over the specific problems in Northern Ireland, and which provoked a fierce reaction from the vast majority of Unionists. In January 1986 all the Unionist MPs resigned their seats in Westminster in protest, and fought a series of by-elections intended to act as a demonstration of Unionist solidarity on the issue. The Northern Ireland Assembly was finally dissolved in June 1986.

Features of the Northern Ireland political system

The main political parties present in the rest of the UK are not organized and do not contest elections in Northern Ireland, although individual candidates have very occasionally stood. There is a certain pressure for the main British parties to reverse this stand and organize within the province, but they do not believe this to be a realistic or desirable option. The parties active in Northern Ireland are thus unique to the province (apart from those which also stand in the Republic of Ireland).

The sectarian divide between the Protestant and Catholic communities remains the dominant cleavage in Northern Ireland politics.

Politics among the Protestant community was characterized under the Stormont regime by the dominance of a monolithic Ulster Unionist Party, but Ulster Unionism has fragmented since the introduction of direct British rule, a process which has been accentuated by the use of proportional representation in many elections. Dividing lines between the various Unionist parties have been fluid, but the main cleavages have been over the ways in which the parties have reacted to the various political initiatives affecting the province, and over their degree of loyalist intransigence. At times of particular perceived threat to the Unionist Community (e.g. after Sunningdale and during the power-sharing executive, and especially after the Anglo-Irish Agreement) there has again been greater unity between the Unionist Parties. There are still divisions however, over whether Ulster should again aim for devolution (and in what form), for independence or for full integration with the UK.

There is much less of a cleavage than among Catholics over the issue of violence, although there has been significant support for paramilitary activities among some Protestants. Those parties that have had particularly close ties to the Protestant paramilitaries (e.g. the Vanguard Party of William Craig, or the Volunteer political party of Ken Gibson) have not had enduring success. On the other hand the major Unionist parties have had some links to paramilitary elements.

The two major parties on the Protestant side are the official Unionist Party, and the Democratic Unionists of Ian Paisley, which became an increasingly powerful challenger in the 1970s and 1980s.

On the Catholic side divisions are less over objectives (most Catholics share the aspiration of an ultimately united Ireland) than over means, and especially over the use of violence. The IRA is one of the most powerful terrorist movements in Europe, and its political arm, Sinn Féin, continues to enjoy the support of a considerable proportion of the Catholic population. Sinn Féin is also active, although much less successfully, in the Republic of Ireland.

The standard-bearer of more moderate and non-violent Nationalism is the SDLP, which has been particularly associated with the New Ireland Forum and with encouragement for the Anglo-Irish Agreement. Founded in 1971, it has been more successful in mobilizing Nationalist voters than its predecessors.

Attempts to forge consensus over the sectarian divide have not been very successful. The most enduring has been the Alliance Party, founded in 1970, but its impact has been primarily among a minority of middle-class voters, especially around Belfast.

Certain parties on the left (e.g. the old Northern Ireland Labour Party and the current Workers' Party) have also attempted to appeal to both Catholic and Protestant workers, but with little success. The left has generally been weak in Northern Ireland, especially outside working-class Belfast, and it too has been divided by sectarian factors, and over links with Ireland and the UK.

The main current issues in Northern Ireland politics are still the dispute over the Anglo-Irish Agreement, and how best to react to IRA violence.

Official Ulster Unionist Party (OUP)

Headquarters	: 3 Glengall Street, Belfast BT12 5AE, Northern Ireland (tel: 0232–22 46 01)
Leader	: James (Jim) Molyneaux
Deputy leader	: Harold McCusker
President	: Sir George A. Clark

History

The Official Ulster Unionist Party (OUP) is the largest party in Ulster, and the main, although much weaker, successor of the once dominant Unionist Party which fragmented in the early 1970s. The OUP's central organization is formally called the Ulster Unionist Council, but the party still prefers to describe itself as the Ulster Unionist Party.

The first Ulster Unionist Council was set up in 1905 to support continued Union with Britain, and to oppose any measure of Home Rule. Its first prominent leader was Sir Edward Carson.

After Ireland was partitioned in 1921 and Home Rule introduced in Northern Ireland, the Unionists took control of the new institutions that had been established in the province. There were six successive Unionist Prime Ministers. The Unionist Party was mainly led by members of the landed and industrial establishment, but had a wide social base among the Protestant population. It also had close ties with the mainstream Protestant Churches and with the powerful Orange Order (with its district lodges, its seven county grand lodges and its ruling Grand Lodge of Ireland). The Unionists' abolition of proportional representation helped to prevent the rise of rival Unionist groups, although a Progressive Unionist Party unsuccessfully contested 12 Stormont seats in 1938.

Within Westminster the Ulster Unionist MPs had a close link with the Conservative Party, and voted with them in the House of Commons.

Divisions within the Unionist Party began to intensify during the 1960s over support or opposition to the seemingly conciliatory policy of Captain Terence O'Neill. There was a revival of support for hard-line Protestant groups.

The suspension of Home Rule in 1972 was a severe blow for the prestige and position of the Unionist Party, and it later split into rival groups. By the 1973 Assembly elections there were already three main Unionist groups, a pro-British White Paper Unionist group led by the former Prime Minister Brian Faulkner (which won 12 seats), the DUP of Ian Paisley (see separate entry) which won eight seats, and a hard-line Vanguard Party, led by William Craig, and close to paramilitary elements, which won seven seats.

The 1973 Sunningdale Agreement and the introduction of a Protestant-Catholic power-sharing Executive headed by Brian Faulkner in early 1974 led to further divisions. Anti-Executive Unionists (led by Harry West), Vanguard and DUP got together to form the United Ulster Unionist coalition (UUUC).

In January 1974 the Unionist Party rejected the Sunningdale Agreement and Faulkner was forced to resign as party leader, being succeeded by Harry West. Faulkner remained, however, as head of the Northern Ireland Executive, as leader of a new Unionist group, the Unionist Party of Northern Ireland (UPNI), which supported power-sharing, but opposed the Sunningdale proposal for a Council of Ireland.

The credibility of Faulkner's group was greatly weakened by the results of the February 1974 Westminster elections when it only won 94,000 votes and no seats, compared to 367,000 votes and 11 seats for the component parties of the UUUC. Faulkner's party was further undermined by the success of the Ulster Workers' Council strike in May 1974, and the subsequent collapse of the Executive. In the closely balanced 1974–79 British Parliament the Unionist MPs had an important bargaining position. The Conservatives could no longer rely on their support, and this was finally shown in 1979 when two Unionists supported Callaghan's Labour government in the vote of confidence.

In the 1975 elections for a Northern Ireland Constitutional Convention Harry West's Unionists obtained 19 seats, Vanguard 14, the DUP 12 and Faulkner's UPNI only five seats. After the collapse of UPNI William Craig's Vanguard was the next party to lose support after Craig's reputation as a hard man of Ulster Unionism was fatally weakened by his proposal for voluntary Unionist power-sharing with the SDLP. By 1977 when the UUUC was finally dissolved Harry West's Official Unionists (OUP) and Paisley's DUP were the only major Unionist contenders.

In the 1979 European Parliament elections Harry West came a humiliating third among Unionist candidates, not only behind Paisley but also behind the OUP's John Taylor, who was elected. West later resigned as leader, and was replaced by James Molyneaux.

In the 1982 elections for the new Northern Ireland Assembly the OUP obtained 29.7 per cent of the vote and 26 of the 78 seats.

In the 1983 Westminster elections the OUP won 11 seats on 34 per cent of the vote. In 1984 its candidate in the European elections, the outgoing MEP, John Taylor, was re-elected with 147,000 first preference votes, but only in third place behind Paisley of the DUP and Hume of the SDLP. In the 1985 local government elections it outpolled its main Unionist rival, the DUP, by 29.4 per cent to 24.3 per cent and won 190 council seats.

The OUP totally rejected the Anglo-Irish Agreement in late 1985, and joined forces with the DUP to campaign against it. All its MPs resigned their seats, in order to demonstrate the degree of Unionist hostility to the Agreement in by-elections, and the OUP and DUP did not oppose each other.

The OUP obtained 51.7 per cent of the vote and ten seats, but lost its seat in Newry and Armagh to the SDLP. In the 1987 Westminster elections a similar electoral pact was reached with the DUP, and the two parties fought on a joint manifesto. The OUP obtained 37.8 per cent of the vote and nine seats, losing a further seat when Enoch Powell was finally defeated in South Down by the SDLP.

Support

The OUP still has the broadest support of any Ulster party. It has benefited from the agreement in 1986 and 1987 for neither the OUP or DUP to challenge each other in the seats that they already held. In both European Parliament elections in 1979 and 1984 the OUP has been weaker than the DUP.

Organization

The basic tier of OUP organization are its constituency associations, which may divide into district and branch associations.

The Party's council meets on an annual basis and consists of elected delegates from the constituency associations, representatives of the various organizations affiliated to the party and a number of other ex officio and co-opted members. The council elects its officers, consisting of a president, four vice-presidents, four honorary secretaries and one honorary treasurer, on an annual basis. The council also elects the party leader.

The party has a large executive committee (over 100 members) which must meet four times a year. The executive committee also appoints the secretary to the council, who is the chief executive officer at Unionist headquarters. There is also a party annual conference.

The party has active youth and women's groups, the Ulster Young Unionist Council and the Ulster Women's Unionist Council. Another affiliated organization is the Ulster Unionist Labour Association.

The OUP still has organic links with the Orange Order. Representatives of the county grand lodges of the Loyal Orange Institution are given places on the party council and on its executive committee, as are representatives of the Association of Loyal Orange Women and of the Apprentice Boys of Derry. The Orange organizations produce a monthly paper, the *Orange Standard*.

Another affiliated organization is the Queen's University Ulster Unionist Association. There is also an Ulster Unionist Councillors' Association.

The Ulster Unionists used to vote together with the Conservative Party in Westminster. Links were weakened in the 1970s, although young Unionists were allowed to affiliate to the Federation of Conservative Students until it was dissolved in 1986. The last links between the OUP and the Conservative National Union were cut in the aftermath of the Anglo-Irish Agreement.

From 1979 the OUP member of the European Parliament sat in the European Democratic Group with the British Conservatives, but after the Anglo-Irish Agreement he left them and joined the Group of the European Right led by Jean Marie le Pen, to the disapproval of the OUP leadership.

Policies

The OUP is the party of the Northern Ireland Protestant establishment. The OUP has also tended to adopt a less strident and populist tone than the DUP, although the two parties have formed a common front since the Anglo-Irish Agreement, and policy differences between them do not appear to be very great.

The main policy plank of the OUP is the need to maintain the Union between Great Britain and Northern Ireland under the British Crown. The OUP is totally opposed to a United Ireland. It is critical of the way in which the Republic of Ireland has developed since independence in terms of its conservative Catholic-influenced constitution and lack of pluralism, as well as its economic inefficiency. The OUP also points to the decline of the Protestant minority in the Republic as an indication of what would

happen in a United Ireland. The OUP is also opposed to any kind of institutional or structural Anglo-Irish ties on Northern Irish matters. Within Northern Ireland the OUP is also opposed to institutionalized power-sharing between Protestants and Catholics.

The OUP has been hostile to all the recent British government initiatives on Northern Ireland. Unlike the DUP, which supported the creation of a new Northern Ireland Assembly in 1982, the OUP was critical of the Assembly believing that it would be either a meaningless talking shop, a device to foist unacceptable power-sharing on the Protestant majority, or else some form of Council of Ireland. The OUP finally participated, however, in the scrutiny work of the Assembly.

The OUP totally rejected the Anglo-Irish Agreement (especially on the grounds of interference of a hostile foreign government in domestic UK affairs), and has campaigned for it to be abandoned or suspended. Its joint manifesto with the DUP in 1987 was entitled "to put right a great wrong".

It believes that it received a powerful mandate to oppose the Agreement from the people of Ulster in the special by-elections in early 1986. It has not supported an indefinite strike as used against Sunningdale in 1974, (although it has supported a one-day strike), but it indicated its intention to boycott Westminster on all but a few selected occasions, to withdraw its members from nominated boards in Northern Ireland and to adjourn local council business wherever possible (although this has been challenged by some OUP local councillors). It is uncertain whether alternative strategies will now be adopted in view of the fact that the Anglo-Irish Agreement has now been in place for almost three years. The OUP has been divided as to whether to push for more complete integration within the UK or to again push for devolution.

The option of the fullest possible integration was one put forward by Enoch Powell, in particular, during his 13 years as a Unionist MP. In the 1987 election it was strongly advocated by the OUP Constituency Association in North Down, whose candidate, Bob McCartney, stood as a Real Unionist in a challenge to the sitting MP, Jim Kilfedder, and won over 14,500 votes.

As regards the option of devolution, leading Unionists recognize that the pre-1972 Stormont regime cannot be re-created, but they do not accept 1974 type power-sharing either. There should be no rigged executive. The majority should rule, but there might be certain safeguards for the minority (e.g. in committee chaimanships).

In the past the OUP has called for an end

to direct rule by Britain, and the introduction of much greater local democracy in Ulster. In a Unionist discussion document, *The Way Forward*, it was suggested that the functions and powers transferred from the Northern Ireland county and county borough councils to Stormont just before the latter's abolition should be devolved to a Northern Ireland Assembly. A Bill of Rights for Northern Ireland might also be considered.

The need for the people of Ulster to have the same local government rights as people elsewhere in the UK has been a strong party theme. Another theme has been the need for tough law and order measures, with many of its leaders in favour of reintroducing capital punishment, for example.

The OUP calls for the banning of Sinn Féin, and has adopted a policy of total non-co-operation with any elected Sinn Féin councillors. It has supported an increased role for the RUC and the UDR in ensuring Ulster's security.

The OUP has been generally hostile to the current terms of the UK's membership of the European Community, and believes that it has had negative impacts on Ulster.

Personalities

Jim Molyneaux has been the party's leader since 1979. He used to represent the constituency of South Antrim in Westminster, but in 1983 he made a successful switch to Lagan Valley. He was born in 1920.

Among the other leading figures in the party are the Reverend William Smyth, a former imperial grand master of the Orange Order and the current MP for South Belfast, John David Taylor who has been both a Westminster MP and also a Euro-MP since 1979, and Harold James McCusker, the deputy leader, who is also an MP in Westminster.

Democratic Unionist Party (DUP)

Headquarters	: 296 Albertbridge Road, Belfast BT5 4PY, Northern Ireland (tel: 0232–45 85 97)
Leader	: Reverend Ian Paisley
Deputy leader	: Peter Robinson
Chairman	: James McClure
Founded	: 1971

History

The Democratic Unionist Party (DUP) is the second of the two Unionist parties that are still in contention in Ulster after the fragmentation of the once monolithic Unionist movement. The DUP's main electoral asset has been the Reverend Ian Paisley, its founder and leader, and who has come to symbolize Protestant fundamentalism and Loyalist intransigence.

Paisley's initial support base has been his own Church, the Free Presbyterian Church, which he founded in 1951, and of which he has been the Moderator or leader ever since (with only one short interlude). Paisley was critical of the mainstream Presbyterian and Unionist establishments which he tried to outflank by fierce anti-Catholicism and by strong defence of traditional values.

In 1956 Paisley was associated with the creation of a group called Ulster Protestant Action. In particular it opposed Unionists whom it felt were too ready to make concessions to Catholics.

Terence O'Neill, the Ulster Prime Minister in the 1960s was a particular target for Paisley's criticism, especially after his historic meeting with the Irish Prime Minister (Sean Lemass) in 1965. Paisley was involved in the creation of the Ulster Constitution Defence Committee (UCDC) in 1966, along with its associated divisions of Ulster Protestant Volunteers (UPV). Later in 1966 Paisley was given a short prison sentence, which raised his profile among hard-line Loyalists.

In the 1969 Stormont elections Paisley stood directly against O'Neill in his Bannside constituency, and five of his supporters also stood, this time under the title "Protestant Unionists". None were elected, but Paisley ran O'Neill close with 6,331 votes to O'Neill's 7,745. In April 1970 Paisley was elected to the Stormont Parliament in a by-election, along with another Paisleyite candidate. In the 1970 Westminster elections Paisley won a seat in North Antrim.

In 1971 Paisley got together with several dissident Unionists (of whom the most influential figure was Desmond Boal) to found a new Democratic Unionist Party, a name chosen to appeal to a wider audience than the old title of Protestant Unionism. Its main motivation was opposition to the Unionist Prime Minister, Brian Faulkner, and to any possible sell-out of the Protestant population of Northern Ireland.

In the 1973 local elections the DUP obtained 21 out of the 526 seats, and in the elections for the new Ulster Assembly eight seats (11.6 per cent). Later in 1973 the DUP joined up with William Craig's Vanguard Party and dissident Unionists under Harry West in a United Ulster Unionist Coalition (UUUC), in opposition to the idea of a power-sharing executive between Protestants and Catholics and to the Sunningdale Agreement. In the February 1974 elections the UUUC obtained 11 out of the 12 Westminster seats, humiliating Faulkner and his executive, and providing Paisley with a great personal victory in his North Antrim constituency. Paisley appeared initially to show hesitation at the beginning of the Ulster Workers' Council strike which brought down the power-sharing executive, but later gave it strong support.

In the 1975 elections for the Northern Ireland Constitutional Convention, the DUP obtained 14.7 per cent and 12 seats. In 1977 Paisley supported an unsuccessful Loyalist strike aimed at restoring Stormont and ensuring tougher security measures in the province. Other Unionists did not provide strong support for the strike, and the UUUC was eventually dissolved. In spite of this setback the DUP obtained 74 seats in the 1977 local elections.

The DUP strengthened its position in 1979. It obtained three seats in Westminster and a month later Paisley was elected to the European Parliament with 29.8 per cent of the first preference votes. In 1981 Paisley attempted to further strengthen his image by a series of "Carson Trail" rallies, and by announcing the creation of a "Third Force" of paramilitary volunteers, which never, however, got off the ground. In the 1981 local elections the DUP obtained 142 councillors (16 on Belfast council), and succeeded in outpolling the official Unionists.

In 1982 the DUP strongly supported the re-establishment of a new Northern Ireland Assembly, which it believed would create a new platform for the Unionist cause, and would enable much greater scrutiny of Northern Ireland's administration. In the 1982 Assembly elections the DUP obtained 21 seats on 23 per cent of the vote. It subsequently took a full part in the Assembly, and chaired two of its committees.

In the 1983 Westminster elections the DUP polled 20 per cent and again won three seats.

In the 1984 European Parliament elections Paisley easily topped the poll with 33.6 per cent of the first preference votes in the province. In the 1985 local government elections the DUP obtained 24.3 per cent of the vote.

The DUP came out in strong opposition to the Anglo-Irish Agreement, and joined a United Loyalist Front with the Official Unionist Party. After resigning their seats in early 1986 in protest against the Agreement, the DUP and OUP agreed not to oppose each other, and the DUP's three MPs were re-elected. In the 1987 Westminster elections a similar agreement was reached, and the DUP only stood in the three constituencies they already held and

one additional non-Unionist constituency. All three MPs (Paisley, McCrea and Robinson) were re-elected.

Support

The firmest support base for the DUP has been among members of Paisley's own Free Presbyterian Church, which has around 50 congregations in different parts of Northern Ireland.

The DUP has also attracted a much wider protest vote among Protestants critical of the Unionist and Orange establishment, and among the more uncompromising Loyalists fearful of a sell-out of Ulster interests. Many DUP votes have constituted personal support for Paisley as the most charismatic Unionist leader. The DUP has had particular support among lower middle-class and rural fundamentalists, and among the Protestant working classes.

In 1987, its largest majority was in Paisley's North Antrim constituency, where it won almost 65 per cent of the vote. In Peter Robinson's East Belfast seat it won just over 60 per cent.

Organization

The DUP has a delegates' assembly and a central executive. The Reverend Ian Paisley plays a dominant part in the party organization, having wide discretion as leader over such issues as policy formulation and choice of party candidates. Peter Robinson has had an important role in developing the party's organizational structure.

There is still a strong organizational link between the DUP and the Free Presbyterian Church, which helps out in party election campaigns, and in providing finance.

The DUP has also had ties with the Independent Orange Order.

At times Paisley and the DUP have had links with Protestant paramilitary groups (as in 1974 and 1977, the Third Force Initiative in 1981, Ulster Resistance in 1986), whereas at other times greater distance has been taken between them. From 1966 until 1982 Paisley was associated with a newspaper called the *Protestant Telegraph*, but in 1982 this was replaced by a new paper called *The Voice of Ulster*.

While the Free Presbyterian Church has now expanded outside Northern Ireland (with around 10 congregations in Ireland, England, North America and Australia), the DUP has no formal international links, and Paisley has sat since 1979 as an independent member of the European Parliament.

Policies

Since the disappearance of Vanguard the DUP has consolidated itself as the strongest focal point for hard-line Unionists, and as the main rival to the Official Unionists. The DUP has had a more populist tone than the Official Unionists, and been less close to the Orange Order and the Unionists' establishment.

Paisley has been consistently identified with strong views against Catholicism and the Papacy (e.g. attempting to prevent the Pope from speaking during his visit to the European Parliament in 1988), and has been strongly opposed to any ecumenical initiatives and to the World Council of Churches. He has followed on a long tradition of Protestant fundamentalist preachers in Ulster, but closest philosophical links today are with fundamentalists in the southern United States (notably Bob Jones in South Carolina). In parts of Ulster the DUP's elected councillors have been active in carrying out some fundamentalist policies (e.g. strict Lord's Day observance), whereas in other areas (notably in working-class Belfast) such policies have been less to the fore.

The DUP's specific policy positions on the status of Ulster have varied considerably over the years (e.g. support for integration into the United Kingdom in 1971 and for renewed devolution in 1977 and 1982, as well as switches from caution to daring, and from more conciliatory positions to harder-line stances). Paisley has always been seen, however, as a fierce opponent of a United Ireland, a tough defender of Ulster's historical traditions and constitutional rights, and of firm law and order measures within the province. He has thus appeared to offer greater certainty for Unionists than other leaders in the province at a time of major change.

In a paper submitted to the Northern Ireland Assembly in September 1984, the DUP called for the re-establishment of a devolved Northern Ireland government on a majority rather than power-sharing basis. Such a government should be fully involved in any talks over Northern Ireland's future, and should also be given a direct say in security matters. IRA terrorism should be militarily defeated. There should be no secret talks between the UK and Irish governments. While the minority should not be directly represented in the Executive they should be protected within the Assembly and its committees. The DUP also accepted that existing safeguards and remedies against discrimination on religious or political grounds, as laid down in the 1973 Act, should be maintained. There should be a UK or failing that, Northern Ireland Bill of Rights.

The DUP was prepared to see enhanced co-operation on economic and other matters with the Republic of Ireland, as long as the latter gave de jure recognition of the status of Northern Ireland, and abandoned any claim to sovereignty over it.

The DUP opposed the report of the New Ireland Forum, and has totally rejected the Anglo-Irish Agreement. It fought the 1987 Westminster elections on a joint manifesto with the official Unionists, whose sole objective was to reverse the Anglo-Irish Agreement.

The DUP has opposed membership of the European Community, which it believes is too Catholic dominated, undercuts British sovereignty and has negative economic impacts.

Personalities

The Reverend Ian Paisley has been the party's leader and dominating figure since its foundation, and has represented it in the Northern Ireland Assembly, in the British Parliament at Westminster since 1970, and in the European Parliament since 1979. He is still the Moderator of the Free Presbyterian Church. He has a strong physical presence (the "Big Fellow") and is a forceful orator. He was born in 1926.

The party's deputy leader is the much younger (born in 1948) Peter Robinson, who has been MP for East Belfast since 1979. He comes from a different and more secular background than Paisley (he is not, for example, a Free Presbyterian) and has had links with Protestant paramilitaries. He has been DUP general secretary and played an important role in building up the party structure.

At one stage he appeared to become a rival focus of leadership to Paisley within the DUP, especially at the time of his cross-border raid on Clontibret in County Monaghan, but he subsequently lost prestige by paying the fine that was imposed on him in the Republic of Ireland. He resigned from the deputy leadership in October 1987, but was reappointed in early 1988.

The DUP's third MP at Westminster is the Rev. McCrea, who represents mid-Ulster, and who is also a successful Gospel singer.

Social Democratic and Labour Party (SDLP)

Headquarters	: 38 University Street, Belfast BT7 1F2, Northern Ireland (tel: 0232-32 34 28)
Leader	: John Hume
Deputy leader	: Seamus Mallon
Chairman	: Alban Maginness
General secretary	: Patsy McGlone
Founded	: 1970

History

The Social Democratic and Labour Party (SDLP) is the largest party among the Catholic community in Northern Ireland.

The Nationalist tradition had taken a number of different political forms, the Nationalist Party in the 1920s, and National League of the North in the late 1920s and early 1930s, the Anti-Partition League in the 1940s and fifties, and again the National Party. It had few major leaders (probably the most significant was Joe Devlin until his death in 1934), and was often conservative in tone, and heavily influenced by the Catholic clergy. It also veered from participation to abstentionism. In Belfast, however, there was some support in working-class Catholic areas for socialist ideas, expressed through parties such as the Northern Ireland Labour Party and the Republican Labour Party.

In the 1960s the National Party became rather more structured. In 1965, and under the leadership of Eddie McAteer, they took on the position of official opposition at the Stormont for the first time in their history, and in 1966 they held their first ever annual conference. There was still dissatisfaction, however, with the old-fashioned conservatism of the Nationalists. In 1965 the middle-class reformist National Democratic Party was founded, although without great success. In 1968–69 the intellectual initiative in the Catholic community passed to the Civil Rights movement, which attracted able new recruits, such as John Hume, who defeated Eddie McAteer in Derry in the Stormont elections in 1969.

Finally in August 1970 the Social Democratic and Labour Party (SDLP) was founded in order to provide broader-based and more effective representation for the Catholic community and, if possible, to attract some Protestant support as well. Gerry Fitt, who came from the more Socialist rather than nationalist wing of the party, became its first leader. He was also its only MP at Westminster.

In October 1970 members of the National Democratic Party also decided to join up with the SDLP, which soon completely displaced the Nationalist Party.

In the Assembly elections in 1973 the SDLP emerged as the dominant party within the Catholic community, obtaining almost 160,000 votes and 19 seats, compared to no seats for the old Nationalist Party.

In the power-sharing executive that took office under Brian Faulkner in January 1974 the SDLP had four of the 11 posts. Gerry Fitt was the deputy chief executive, and John Hume, Austin Currie and Paddy Devlin also participated. This has been the SDLP's only experience of government.

In the elections for the Constitutional Convention in 1975, the SDLP obtained 156,000 votes and 17 seats.

In the 1979 Westminster elections Fitt was re-elected as the party's only MP and in the European Parliament elections a month later John Hume obtained over 140,000 first preference votes to be elected in second place after Ian Paisley. Later in 1979 Fitt resigned as leader (he left the SDLP and became an independent Socialist MP at Westminster) and in November Hume was elected as SDLP leader.

In 1981 the SDLP lost prestige when it did not contest the Fermanagh and South Tyrone by-elections against Sinn Féin. In the Assembly elections of 1982 the SDLP obtained 18.8 per cent of the vote and 14 seats but boycotted the work of the Assembly. In the 1983 Westminster elections the SDLP polled 17.9 per cent of the vote, with Hume gaining the SDLP's only seat in the Foyle constituency.

In the 1984 European Parliament election Hume was re-elected with over 151,000 first preference votes (22.1 per cent). In the 1985 local government elections the SDLP polled 17.8 per cent.

The SDLP supported the Anglo-Irish Agreement in late 1985. In the 1986 by-elections caused by the resignation of the Unionist MPs in protest against the Agreement, Seamus Mallon captured the former OUP-held seat of Newry and Armagh.

In the 1987 Westminster elections the SDLP obtained 18.1 per cent. Besides retaining the seats of Hume and Mallon it also won a third seat when Eddie McGrady dislodged Enoch Powell in the constituency of South Down.

Support

The SDLP is the majority party among Catholics, being particularly strong among the Catholic middle classes and weaker in working-class Catholic areas in Belfast and in some traditional Republican areas elsewhere. The SDLP now holds the two majority Catholic border constituencies of Newry and Armagh, and South Down, and also John Hume's fief of Foyle, based on the city of Derry, where he has a large personal majority. The SDLP had a high vote in 1987 in West Belfast which used to be Gerry Fitt's constituency, but still lost by over 2,000 votes to Sinn Féin. In Mid-Ulster and in Fermanagh and South Tyrone the Catholic vote is rather evenly split between the SDLP and Sinn Féin. In spite of the party's original intention to broaden the traditional Catholic Nationalist base the SDLP has practically no Protestant members.

Organization

The SDLP constitution provides for both individual and corporate membership (trade unions affiliated to the Irish Congress of trade unions, co-operative societies, socialist societies, professional associations and cultural organizations being eligible for the latter status).

The basic local tier of SDLP membership are its branches. Above these are the party's constituency councils and district executives, in both of which the branches are represented according to a sliding scale based on the numbers of their membership.

There is an annual conference, consisting of delegates from the branches and from the corporate affiliates (although every delegate must be a fully paid up individual member of the party). The party conference elects the party's officers (the party chairman, two vice-chairmen, international secretary, treasurer and assistant treasurer).

The Executive Committee consists of the party officers, 15 other members directly elected at the party conference, the leader, deputy leader, chief whip and one other member of the Constituency Representatives Group and one member of the association of SDLP district councillors. The executive meets at least 12 times a year.

The Constituency Representatives Group consists of SDLP elected members of the Northern Ireland Assembly (when relevant), the UK Parliament, the European Parliament and also the Irish Parliament (in 1982, for example, the party's current deputy leader, Seamus Mallon, was nominated to the Irish Senate). The Group elects the party leader, but this choice must then be ratified by the party conference.

There is also a Central Council, consisting of the executive, the Constituency Representatives Group and district councillors, as well as representatives of the branches, constituency councils and district executives, which meets at least twice a year.

Besides the Association of SDLP District Councillors there is also a women's policy group.

Party candidates for UK or European elections are chosen by branch delegates at selection conventions. The Executive Committee must ratify the choices made.

The SDLP has a party newsletter called *Newsline*. As regards finance, each branch must pay a minimum annual subscription of £1 for each of its members. Each corporate member must pay 25 pence for each of its members that it wishes to affiliate.

The SDLP has not had formal links with any party elsewhere in the UK. It has had very close ties with the main parties in the Republic of Ireland. The SDLP is a member of the Socialist International, and of the Confederation of European Socialist Parties, and John Hume has an active member of the Socialist Group in the European Parliament.

Policies

The SDLP is the main voice of non-violent nationalism within Northern Ireland. The SDLP was created as a blend between differing political strands, traditional Catholic nationalism, civil rights activism, and urban Socialism. As the SDLP has evolved, the dominant strand has been that of traditional Catholic nationalism, although it has been more outward-looking and better led than the old Nationalist Party. The more Socialist strand, epitomized by such politicians as Paddy Devlin and Gerry Fitt (who significantly both left the party) has been less powerful. The main policy emphasis of the party has been on the National question, although there has been a related emphasis on defence of the economic and social interests of the Catholic community in Northern Ireland.

The SDLP promotes the cause of Irish unity freely negotiated and agreed to by both the people of Northern and Southern Ireland. It believes that the root of the Northern Irish problem is a conflict between two separate national identities, that cannot be resolved within a purely Northern Irish context. The SDLP thus opposes both a return to Home Rule under majority control and also direct British rule, and considers that power-sharing between Unionists and Nationalists is essential. It opposed the restoration of the Northern Ireland Assembly in 1982, and did not take up its seats in the Assembly. It opposed the Assembly gaining control over former local government functions, and has also opposed the devolution of additional powers predominantly Unionist controlled to district councils.

A central theme of the SDLP, and of John Hume in particular, has been the central need to get rid of the "guarantee" by the British government to the Unionists in Northern Ireland that they can remain within the United Kingdom as long as a majority so wishes. The SDLP considers that this guarantee fossilizes political attitudes, and reinforces narrow sectarianism. If it were removed, the Unionists would have to become more flexible and face up to alternative solutions.

On the other hand the SDLP has not called for a commitment by the British to withdraw from Northern Ireland. The SDLP has opposed IRA violence, and considers that this is both unacceptable in its own right and also economically very harmful to Northern Ireland in terms of destruction of economic activities and discouragement to investment within the province.

Instead of a purely Northern Ireland solution, the SDLP has called for the totality of British-Irish relationships to be re-examined. A change in the relationships between the two communities in Northern Ireland needs to be paralleled by changes in North-South as well as Anglo-Irish relations.

To reinforce North-South relations the SDLP actively participated in the New Ireland Forum, along with the three major parties in the Republic of Ireland.

The SDLP has also strongly supported the Anglo-Irish Agreement as a framework for further progress in an evolving relationship between Britain and Ireland. SDLP support for the Agreement has also firmed up support for it in the Republic of Ireland.

The SDLP's economic policy has not been very ideologically based, and has concentrated on practical problems of unemployment, unfair employment practices, uneven distribution of economic activities around the province, and poor housing and social services. The SDLP is critical of the Conservative government's record on economic matters, and calls for more investment in the underprivileged parts of Ireland and for more cross-border economic co-operation. Public spending should be increased to prevent a further deterioration of social services. The SDLP has advocated much stronger support for the Irish language, and the establishment of an Irish cultural Institute.

The SDLP is strongly in favour of the European Community. It supports the establishment of the Single Market by 1992, but considers that this must be accompanied by measures to ensure economic and social cohesion within the Community, and common social standards. It calls for an expanded role for the European Parliament. Its MEP John Hume has supported both the Spinelli Draft Treaty on European Union and the Single European Act.

The SDLP would also like to see the European Community playing a more independent role in world affairs. It has called for the maintenance of Ireland as a nuclear-free zone.

The SDLP has supported the establishment of a New International Economic Order, and called for reinforced development aid. It has also called for comprehensive sanctions against South Africa.

Personalities

The party's leader and dominant personality is John Hume, born in 1934. His political base

has been Derry, where he was a Civil Rights leader in the late 1960s and which he first represented in Stormont in 1969. Since 1983 he has also represented Foyle in Westminster. He has been a member of the European Parliament since 1979, the year when he became the leader of the party (he had been deputy leader since 1970).

The party's deputy leader is Seamus Mallon, who has represented Newry and Armagh in Westminster since 1986. He has been generally regarded as "Greener" than Hume in his attitude on nationalist questions.

Sinn Féin

Headquarters	: 51–55 Falls Road, Belfast, Northern Ireland
President	: Gerry Adams

History

Sinn Féin represents the extreme Republican wing of Northern Irish Catholic politics, of which it constitutes the civilian arm, with the Irish Republican Army (IRA) constituting the military arm. Sinn Féin functions in both the Republic of Ireland (see separate entry on Sinn Féin in the Irish section of this book) and in Northern Ireland.

In Sinn Féin's early manifestations in Northern Ireland politics it had only limited success. In 1921 the original Sinn Féin won six seats in the first elections for the six county parliaments, with more votes than the rival Nationalists. In the October 1924 Westminster elections, however, Sinn Féin's vote dropped sharply, and no seats were won even in Catholic areas. In the 1925 Northern Ireland elections Sinn Féin's vote dropped further, although they hung on to two seats. By the next Stormont elections in 1929 there were no longer Sinn Féin candidates. In 1933 however a Republican was elected to Stormont from South Armagh.

In the 1955 Westminster elections Republican candidates were put up in all 12 constituencies in Northern Ireland (half of them in jail for their role in an IRA raid at Omagh). Their candidates obtained over 150,000 votes and two of them were elected, although both were unseated on the grounds of ineligibility (one of them won the subsequent by-election, but was again unseated), and their seats were awarded to the defeated Unionist candidates.

In 1956 the Northern Ireland government banned Sinn Féin. It subsequently stood in the Westminster elections in 1959, but polled under half the votes that it had won in 1955.

Sinn Féin was inactive electorally in the 1960s, although a number of Republican clubs were organized. The Republican movement began to develop a left wing and in 1969–70 this led to a split within the Republican movement, with the left wing forming "Official Sinn Féin" (see section on Workers' Party in Irish section of book) and the traditionalist advocates of armed struggle and abstentionism forming "Provisional Sinn Féin".

As Northern Ireland's troubles intensified in 1969–72, the Catholic minority was radicalized, and the "Provos" won greatly increased support. In 1972 they obtained greater political recognition when IRA internees were granted special category status (being effectively granted political prisoner status, which they lost in 1976), and direct talks were held in London between the British government and IRA representatives. In 1973 the ban on Sinn Féin in Northern Ireland was lifted.

During the 1970s the Provisionals were opposed to participation in elections, and called for boycotts of the local and Northern Ireland Assembly elections in 1973, the Constitutional Convention elections in 1975, and the first European Parliament elections in 1979.

In 1981 the IRA enjoyed a new wave of popular support after the deaths of Bobby Sands and a number of other IRA prisoners in the H-Bloc hunger strikes. At its *Ard Fheis* (annual conference) in November 1981, Sinn Féin adopted a new strategy of contesting elections at the same time as pursuing the armed struggle.

In the 1982 elections to the new Northern Ireland Assembly, Sinn Féin obtained 10.1 per cent of the total vote and five seats. In the 1983 Westminster elections it put up 14 candidates, who obtained 13.4 per cent of the vote, with Gerry Adams being elected in West Belfast. In the 1984 European Parliament elections Sinn Féin's candidate, Danny Morrison, obtained 13.3 per cent of the first preference votes. In the 1985 local elections Sinn Féin obtained 11.8 per cent of the vote, and in the special 1986 Westminster elections 6.6 per cent.

In the Westminster elections in June 1987 Sinn Féin obtained 81,018 votes (11.2 per cent of the total), with Gerry Adams holding his seat in West Belfast against vigorous opposition from the SDLP.

From January 1988 Sinn Féin had a series of high level meetings with the SDLP. In Autumn 1988 the British government announced restrictive new measures to prevent Sinn Féin media appearances, while still not banning Sinn Féin as a party.

Sinn Féin also has 60 seats on local councils.

Support

Sinn Féin has demonstrated that it has considerable electoral support among the Catholic population of Northern Ireland. It has shown that it can be competitive against the SDLP in contests where both parties are standing, and that it can win even wider Nationalist support in the absence of an SDLP candidate (as in the two Fermanagh and South Tyrone by-elections in 1981).

Sinn Féin is strongest in Catholic communities like those in West Belfast, Newry, Strabane and Londonderry (Derry), especially in areas of high social deprivation and in certain rural areas adjacent to the border.

Sinn Féin's strongest bastion is the Catholic ghetto based around the Falls Road in West Belfast, where Gerry Adams defeated the moderate left wing nationalist Gerry Fitt in the 1983 Westminster elections, and defeated an SDLP rival in 1987.

The other two Westminster constituencies where Sinn Féin has had particular electoral strength have been Fermanagh and South Tyrone (where Phil Clarke was elected in 1955, and Bobby Sands and Owen Carron on hard-line nationalist tickets in 1981) and Mid-Ulster (where Tom Mitchell was elected in 1955 and where Bernadette Devlin was elected as a Nationalist Unity candidate in 1969). Sinn Féin has also had considerable local government success in these areas.

Organization

Sinn Féin is organized north and south of the border and has the same President in Ireland and Northern Ireland. It has a national council and annual congress (*Ard Fheis*). It produces a weekly newspaper, *An Phoblacht* ("Republican News", with a circulation of 42,500), a quarterly called *Iris* (with a circulation of 3,000) and an occasional Irish-language newspaper called *Saoirse* ("Freedom") with a circulation of 2,000).

Sinn Féin has had contacts with far left and national liberation movements in other countries. It has had considerable financial support from sympathizers in other countries, notably from the Irish-American community in the USA.

Policies

Sinn Féin describes itself as an open, democratic and revolutionary political party, dedicated to the unity and independence of Ireland. Its longer term objective is British withdrawal from Northern Ireland and national self-determination for all of Ireland. At the same time it also campaigns in the shorter term for improved economic and social conditions for the Nationalist community in Northern Ireland by winning concessions from what it describes as the "Six County Administration". It also promotes nationalist self-help through the provision of services at local community level.

Sinn Féin has traditionally refused to recognize overall British and specific Northern Irish political institutions. It has continued to have close links with the Irish Republican Army (IRA), and has supported violent, military solutions to the problems of the Nationalist community in Northern Ireland. For much of the time it has not supported participation in elections, and when it has so participated, its candidates have pledged not to take their seats in any Northern Irish Assembly or in Westminster. Since 1981, however, Sinn Féin has more consistently advocated a concurrent electoral and military strategy ("Ballots and Bullets"). In 1984 it signalled that it was prepared to take up a seat in the European Parliament if its candidates were elected, and in 1986 that it would likewise participate in the Irish *Dail*.

Sinn Féin has also tended to move towards the left in recent years. Militant Republicanism has not traditionally been very ideological in economic terms, and in 1969–70, those who put more emphasis on the class struggle and on Socialism went off to create Official Sinn Féin (now the non-violent Workers' Party), while those who remained tended to be anti-Marxist. The national question is still far more important for Sinn Féin than Socialist ideology, but Sinn Féin has nevertheless now positioned itself clearly on the left of the spectrum on both domestic and international issues.

Sinn Féin considers that the partition of Ireland is undemocratic, and that British colonial rule must come to an end. British troops should withdraw, and their support props, the Ulster Defence Regiment (UDR) and the Royal Ulster Constabulary should be disarmed and disbanded. Sinn Féin's strategy is to persist until mainland British opinion turns against a British presence in Northern Ireland. Sinn Féin is opposed to the Anglo-Irish Agreement, which it believes has reinforced the constitutional status quo, and provided false hopes for the Nationalist community.

In 1972 Sinn Féin called for a federal structure for Ireland, with regional assemblies in each of the four historic provinces, including Ulster. By 1981–82, however, it had turned against this option, considering that it was

tactically useless (unacceptable to Unionists) and politically undesirable (the Unionists would dominate any Ulster Assembly). Sinn Féin now calls for a unitary 32-county Socialist Republic in Ireland.

Once the British have withdrawn an all-Ireland Constitutional Conference should be held to draw up a new Irish constitution, and a new Irish system of government. Such a constitution should include written guarantees for the "Loyalist" Protestant Community. Sinn Féin points out that the Loyalists are only a minority in the whole of Ireland. No attempt should be made to dispossess them, but they should nevertheless yield to the decision of the Irish majority.

On economic and social policy Sinn Féin puts a strong emphasis on immediate measures to reduce poverty and deprivation among the Nationalist community in Northern Ireland, and among working-class people and small farmers in particular. Ending Irish partition would help in the longer term but in the shorter term other measures should be taken. There should be affirmative action in favour of Catholics seeking employment, and much tougher legal guarantees against discrimination. Sinn Féin has also called for the introduction of a statutory minimum wage.

Sinn Féin seeks a much stronger emphasis on social welfare provision. It is opposed to spending cuts, and calls for new measures to help the elderly and one-parent families. There should be a massive increase in expenditure on housing, and a rent freeze to apply to all rented accommodation in the six counties. Sinn Féin calls for greater equality for women.

Sinn Féin is opposed to civil nuclear energy, and has called for the closure of Sellafield, and an end to the dumping of nuclear waste in the Irish Sea.

Sinn Féin calls for a greatly reinforced emphasis on promoting the Irish language and culture. There should be compulsory teaching of both Irish and English in schools, and bilingual road signs. Sinn Féin calls for withdrawal from the European Community, claiming that this undermines Irish sovereignty and hurts Northern Ireland's industry and agriculture.

On defence policy Sinn Féin is strongly anti-nuclear, and supports the Campaign for Nuclear Disarmament.

Sinn Féin supports the Algiers Declaration on the Rights and Liberation of Peoples. It supports the creation of a democratic and secular state of Palestine. The ANC should be recognized and there should be total economic sanctions against South Africa.

Sinn Féin opposes what it sees as US imperialist aggression in Central and South America in particular.

Sinn Féin supports the struggle of the Basques, Bretons and Corsicans, but explicitly disassociates itself from non-nationalist terrorist organizations, such as the Red Brigades and Baader-Meinhof.

Sinn Féin supports the establishment of a New International Economic Order, with debt renegotiations for developing countries, and lower industrialized country tariffs against developing country goods.

Personalities

Sinn Féin's president is Gerry Adams, born in 1948. He was elected to the Northern Ireland Assembly in West Belfast in 1982, and to the British House of Commons in 1983 and 1987, not taking up his seat on any of these occasions.

Danny Morrison, who has been editor of the party newspaper, *An Phoblacht*, was the party's European Parliament candidate in 1984.

Alliance Party of Northern Ireland

Headquarters	: 88 University Street, Belfast BT7 1HE (tel: 0232–32 42 74)
Party leader	: John Alderdice
Secretary	: Eileen Bell
Chairman	: Bill Barbour
Party president	: Paddy Bogan
Membership	: 12,000

History

The Alliance Party was founded in April 1970, in an attempt to provide a non-sectarian alternative with an appeal throughout Northern Ireland. Its first leader was Oliver Napier.

It gained 63 seats in the 1973 district council elections. In the Assembly elections of June 1973 it took 9.2 per cent of the vote and won three seats. It was also a useful bridge between Unionists and Nationalists during the period of the power-sharing executive under Brian Faulkner in 1974, when Oliver Napier was one of the 11 ministers. After the executive's fall in May 1974, eight Alliance members were elected in the Northern Ireland constitutional convention elections in 1975 on 9.8 per cent of the vote.

The Alliance Party did not succeed, however, in consolidating its early gains. It has had a certain success at local level (especially in the 1977 local elections when it came third with 14.3 per cent), where it has held the balance of power on some district councils

but it has failed to elect a Westminster MP. It was closest to doing so in East Belfast in 1979, when Oliver Napier finished third but only 900 votes short of the winner. When the new Northern Ireland Assembly was established in 1982, Alliance won 10 out of the 78 seats with 9.3 per cent and unlike the Catholic parties took full part in its deliberations. In the June 1983 Westminster elections it polled 8 per cent. In 1984 Oliver Napier was replaced as leader by John Cushnahan.

In December 1985 the Alliance Party withdrew from the Assembly in criticism of the way it was being used by the Ulster Unionist opponents of the Anglo-Irish Agreement.

In the Westminster elections of June 1987 Alliance put up candidates in every Northern Ireland constituency except West Belfast, and retained about 10 per cent of the vote in the province. In September 1987 John Cushnahan stood down as leader and was replaced by John Alderdice.

Support

The 10 per cent of the vote won by the Alliance Party in June 1987 is unevenly spread around the province. Alliance's greatest strength is in predominantly Unionist constituencies with a large middle-class and professional vote, although it has won some support across the sectarian divide. It is stronger in urban and suburban than in rural Ulster. It won 32 per cent of the vote in East Belfast, and 26 per cent in East Antrim and over 21 per cent in South Belfast. The then party leader, John Cushnahan, got just under 20 per cent in North Down. Where the SDLP vote was maximized, as in Newry and Armagh or South Down, Alliance was squeezed to under 2 per cent of the vote. Finally, Alliance was generally very weak in the West of the province, not winning more than two or 3 per cent of the vote in constituencies like Fermanagh and Mid-Ulster.

Organization

The Alliance Party is divided into 30 associations, one for each of the 26 district councils, and one for each of the four district electoral areas within Belfast. Each association sends six delegates to the party council, which meets three or four times a year.

The party has a monthly publication, called *Alliance* (7,000 copies).

A Young Alliance organization is open to any party member under 30 years of age.

The Alliance Party of Northern Ireland is not formally linked to any British mainland party, but had informal links with the SDP and Liberal Alliance. In 1984 the Alliance

Party became a member of the Federation of European Liberals and Democrats (ELD). The Alliance has recently discussed the possibility of co-operation with the Social and Liberal Democrats, and also with the Progressive Democrats in Ireland.

Policies

Alliance's main aim is to unite the two communities in Northern Ireland. The Alliance Party of Northern Ireland believes that Northern Ireland should remain an integral part of the United Kingdom, but with no discrimination against, and full civic involvement by, the Catholic minority. Alliance continues to believe that there should be devolved government in Northern Ireland but on a power-sharing basis between the Protestant and Catholic communities rather than on the old basis of Unionist dominance.

Alliance is highly critical of the lack of constructive suggestions from the Unionist parties and of their boycott of Westminster in the wake of the Anglo-Irish Agreement. Alliance itself is critical of the secretive way in which the Anglo-Irish Agreement was promulgated, but considers that there is no practical alternative to it. It is opposed to the idea of full Northern Ireland integration within the United Kingdom as running counter to practical realities.

While it has considerable common ground with the SDLP, it is critical of the latter's lack of support for the Northern Ireland security forces. It would also like the government of Ireland to delete the territorial claim to Northern Ireland contained in Articles 2 and 3 of its constitution. Alliance strongly argues for a Bill of Rights in Northern Ireland based on the European Convention of Human Rights and directly enforceable in Northern Ireland courts. Alliance's other policies have no particular ideological basis. It seeks a substantial increase in public expenditure in Northern Ireland, especially on infrastructure projects, in order to increase job opportunities in the public and private sectors.

Alliance is in favour of religious integration in education but believes that this cannot be imposed, and must only come about by consent. Alliance is opposed to both the rating system and the idea of a poll tax, and is in favour of a local income tax. Alliance puts strong emphasis on consumer and environmental protection.

Finally, Alliance is a strong supporter of the European Community and its further development. It points out the assistance that the European Community has given to Northern Ireland and believes it to be an appropriate framework to help solve Northern Ireland's problems. It supports more powers for the European Parliament, and full British entry into the European Monetary System.

Personalities

Alliance's current leader is John Alderdice, who has maintained the party's tradition of having a Catholic leader despite a majority Protestant membership.

Ulster Popular Unionist Party (UPUP)

Headquarters : "Eastonville", Donaghdee Road, Millisle, Co. Down, Northern Ireland

Leader : James (Jim) Kilfedder

This party, which is essentially the personal vehicle of Jim Kilfedder, was founded as the Ulster Progressive Unionist Party in January 1980. Kilfedder has represented North Down in Westminster since 1970, initially as a mainstream Unionist. He survived a strong challenge from a Real Unionist candidate, Bob McCartney, in 1987.

Kilfedder was the Speaker of the Northern Ireland Assembly from 1982 to 1987, and was a candidate for the European Parliament elections in 1979 (when he won over 38,000 first preferences) and in 1984 (when he won slightly over 20,000 first preferences).

In most matters the UPUP is aligned with the Official Unionists, although it takes a more liberal line on social issues.

The Workers Party

Headquarters : 6 Springfield Road, Belfast

This is the semi-autonomous Northern section of the Dublin-based WP, a left-wing Socialist Party which originally stemmed from official Sinn Féin and which now renounces violence. (For fuller details see the section on Ireland.) Its policies are class rather than sectarian based.

The chairman of the WP in Northern Ireland is Seamus Lynch. Its organ is the *Northern People* (weekly). In the 1987 Westminster elections it contested 14 seats. Its highest vote was in Belfast, where it came ahead of the Alliance candidate and polled 3,062 votes.

Isle of Man

The Isle of Man is an island of 227 square miles with a population of 65,000, with new residents coming to outnumber native born Manx. Manx Gaelic is a Celtic language akin to Scots Gaelic and Irish, which had practically died out as a first language by the 1920s, although a number of Manx nationalists and others interested in Manx culture have learnt it as a second language. The Isle of Man has a top income tax of only 20 per cent, no corporation tax and many tax advantages, and has become an important tax haven and financial and services centre.

The Isle of Man is a British Crown Dependency, with an appointed Lieutenant-Governor (who serves a five-year term) acting as the representative of the Crown. The British government looks after its foreign affairs and defence, but otherwise it has very extensive self-government. It has no representatives in Westminster, and is not in the European Community.

The Isle of Man has a distinctive system of government, the *Tynwald*, which is a thousand years old, and dates from the Viking occupation of the island. The High Court of *Tynwald* consists of the Lieutenant-Governor representing the Sovereign, and an Upper and Lower Chamber. The latter is called the House of Keys, and is a 24-member Parliament, with fixed five-year terms. The island is divided into 15 constituencies, two three-seat constituencies, five two-seaters and eight single-member constituencies. Elections used to be by a relative majority system, but in 1985 the single transferable vote was introduced. Voters must express at least two preferences, and candidates must attain an electoral quota. Vacancies are filled in by-elections. The new system was first used in the 1986 elections, although it is still controversial.

The House of Keys elects eight members of the 10-member Legislative Council, or Upper Chamber. These members are usually drawn from the House of Keys (if chosen they must of course resign from the House), but this is not obligatory. The other two members of the Lower Chamber are ex officio members appointed by the Crown. The *Tynwald* also has a number of important Boards or Committees. The full *Tynwald* is presided over by the Lieutenant-Governor, and deals above all with financial matters and taxation. For other matters the two chambers sit separately, and pass bills in three readings. Before becoming law they must have the Lieutenant-Governor's assent.

The Manx system of government has evolved considerably in recent years. One of the most important changes was the replacement of the Lieutenant-Governor's Executive Council by a new Council of Ministers, presided over by a chief minister chosen by the House of Keys, and containing eight cabinet ministers chosen by the chief ministers. On the other hand certain traditional practices remain, such as the proclamation of new laws at an annual open air assembly on Tynwald Hill every July 5.

The main political issues on the island include the nature of its customs links with the United Kingdom, transport links with the mainland, the island's current constitutional status, the extent of new development on the island and the maintenance of its character and culture. One controversial issue (though more outside than within the island) has been its retention of judicial corporal punishment. Its insistence on maintaining birching was eventually condemned by the European Court of Human Rights.

The Isle of Man has never developed a fully fledged party-political system, and has been dominated by individual political personalities standing as "independents". In the 1986 House of Keys elections 21 of the 24 members were "independents". Three of these were former British Conservative councillors from the mainland.

In the 1987 elections only one political party, the "Manx Labour Party" managed to win representation in the House of Keys. One other existing party, the "Manx Democratic Party", put up candidates, and there is one other political organization, "Mec Vennin".

Manx Labour Party

Address : c/o House of Keys,
Douglas,
Isle of Man

The Manx Labour Party was founded in 1918 (although the Independent Labour Party started putting up candidates in 1908). By 1924 the Manx Labour Party managed to elect six members in the House of Keys, a figure it has never since exceeded. In the last three elections, in 1976, 1981 and 1986 it has won three seats on each occasion. In 1986 it provided the President of the Legislative Council, and two other members of the Council. It also has one member in the present Manx Cabinet.

Its main electoral support is in the Isle of Man's largest town, Douglas, and in its suburb of Onchan. Its three elected members in 1986 (out of the seven candidates fielded by the party) represented Douglas and Onchan constituencies.

The party has local branches enjoying a high degree of autonomy, and a not very powerful national executive, which is responsible for the general party manifesto. Elected Manx Labour Party members do not take a party whip in the House of Keys.

Manx Democratic Party

This is a conservative-leaning party, founded in 1985 by a former British Conservative councillor who subsequently left the party, which put up five candidates in the 1986 national elections. None of them were elected, and four lost their deposit.

Mec Vennin
(Sons of Man)

Address	:	4 St Ninian's Road, Douglas, Isle of Man

Mec Vennin was founded in 1961 as a Manx nationalist organization defending Manx culture and identity. Its most prominent founders were Douglas Fargher and Lewis Crellin.

In the 1970s Mec Vennin became more of a proper political party, and in 1976 it fielded 10 candidates in the House of Keys elections of whom one was elected.

In 1978 there was a severe split within the party, when its more conservative members, including its only member of the House of Keys, left to create a more moderate Manx National Party, advocating internal self-government for Man.

In the 1981 House of Keys elections the more radical Mec Vennin only fielded one candidate, and the Manx National Party only two, including its sitting member. None of these candidates were elected.

The Manx National Party has since faded away but Mec Vennin survives as a more culturally based organization. It put up no candidates in the 1986 House of Keys elections.

Gibraltar

Gibraltar is a British Crown Colony of under two-and-a-half square miles located on a peninsula on the South Coast of Spain. It has over 29,000 inhabitants, of Genoese, Maltese, Moroccan, Portuguese, Sephardic Jewish as well as British origin. In 1981 74.5 per cent of the population was Roman Catholic, 8.5 per cent Muslim, 8 per cent Church of England and 2.5 per cent Jewish. The economy is heavily dependent on defence, tourism (chiefly day trips) and financial services. Gibraltarians have the right to become full British citizens without any restrictions.

Political institutions

The city of Gibraltar is part of "Her Majesty's Dominions", but now enjoys a considerable measure of self-government in domestic political matters.

The legislature is the Gibraltar House of Assembly, which is elected for a four-year term (with the possibility of early dissolution). There used to be proportional representation but under the present system voters can vote for any eight candidates, and the winners are those with the most votes. No one party can thus win more than eight seats. There are 15 electoral seats in all, and two additional ex officio members (the Attorney-General, and the Financial and Development Secretary). The latter cannot take part in any votes of confidence. The speaker is appointed by the Governor after consulting the Chief Minister and leader of the opposition. The Mayor of Gibraltar is chosen by the elected members.

The Chief Minister is appointed by the Governor from the party (or coalition of parties) commanding a majority among the elected members of the Gibraltar House of Assembly. The seven other members of the council of Ministers are also appointed by the Governor after consultation with the Chief Minister.

The Governor of Gibraltar (who is also Commander-in-Chief) still retains considerable powers, especially over external relations and defence matters, and questions of internal security.

The third element in the Gibraltar Executive, besides the Governor and the Council of Ministers, is the 10-member Gibraltar Council, consisting of the Governor and four other ex officio members, as well as the Chief Minster and four other members from among the minsters.

Gibraltar is not within the customs union of the European Community.

Brief political history

1704   Capture of Gibraltar by the British under Admiral Sir George Rooke.

1713   Treaty of Utrecht confirms British possession of Gibraltar (borders with Spain subsequently closed until 1807)

1950 First substantive measure of self-government for Gibraltar, with establishment of elected Legislative Council and Executive.

1964 Agreement to strengthen system of self-government (number of elected members on Legislative Council, and on Executive Council to be increased, Executive Council to be known as Gibraltar Council, Chief Member to be known as Chief Minister). New restrictions by Spaniards at Gibraltar border. Gibraltar issue raised by Spain at United Nations.

1967 Referendum held in which 12,138 Gibraltarians vote for continued association with Britain, and 44 in favour of sovereignty by Spain. United Nations passes resolution against British position on Gibraltar by 73 votes to 19 with 22 abstentions. Founding of "Integration with Britain party" by Robert Peliza.

1968 Unrest in Gibraltar over proposals by a small minority of "Doves" that there should be an Anglo-Spanish treaty over Gibraltar's status.

1969 Constitutional changes, establishing 15 elected members to the Gibraltar House of Assembly to replace existing Legislative and City Councils, and setting up the present Gibraltar institutional framework. First elections held under new system in which Integration with Britain party of Robert Peliza wins 5 seats and forms new government along with 3 independents led by Peter Isola, with Peliza as Chief Minster. Gibraltar Labour Party (GLP-AACR) goes into opposition for first and only time until 1988.

In 1969 Spain also closes its land frontier with Gibraltar, inter alia depriving Gibraltar of a third of its normal workforce (the Spanish cross-frontier workers). Gibraltar effectively cut off from Spain.

1972 Fall of Peliza government after dispute with one of its independent members. New elections in which GLP-AACR returns to power under Sir Joshua Hassan. Maurice Xiberas becomes new leader of "Integration with Britain Party".

1976 UK government makes it clear that Gibraltar's integration with Britain is not a practical option. Xiberras subsequently resigns as leader of "Integration with Britain Party", and the party itself folds up. In 1976 elections GLP-AACR government of Sir Joshua Hassan wins re-election, but new Gibraltar Democratic Movement (led by Joe Bossano) wins four seats. After election another new party, the "Democratic Party for British Gibraltar" is established, advocating close ties with Britain.

1977 The Gibraltar Democratic Movement disintegrates after loss of three of its four elected members. Bossano forms new Gibraltar Socialist Labour Party".

1980 GLP-AACR of Joshua Hassan again wins re-election, defeating the Democratic Party for British Gibraltar (now led by Peter Isola, and which wins six seats) and the Gibraltar Socialist Labour Party which only wins one seat (that of Joe Bossano). New "Party for Autonomy of Gibraltar" (whose most well-known figure is José Emmanuel Triay, and which advocates a negotiated settlement with Spain) wins no seats. Agreement in principle between UK and Spain to re-open land frontier with Spain.

1981 Gibraltarians granted right to become full British subjects without any restrictions on their moving to Britain.

1982 Land border with Spain opened to pedestrians only.

1984 GLP-AACR of Sir Joshua Hassan wins re-election in election in which future of British Navy Dockyard is main issue. Gibraltar Socialist Labour Party wins seven seats, and Democratic Party for British Gibraltar loses all its seats (and does not contest the next elections). On Nov. 27, 1984, Brussels Agreement between the UK and Spain, which provides a practical framework for talks and co-operation between Britain and Spain over Gibraltar, including the possibility of discussion over sovereignty (although British government undertakes not to transfer sovereignty against the freely expressed wishes of inhabitants of Gibraltar).

1985 Land frontier between Gibraltar and Spain is fully reopened.

1987 Dispute in June over Gibraltar airport, with Spain objecting to its inclusion in EC agreement on air transport liberalization. The airport is subsequently excluded. In December 1987 there is an Anglo-Spanish agreement over the airport (and over improved sea and land links with Gibraltar). The Gibraltar House of Assembly effectively blocks the agreement (one of whose most controversial provisions is the establishment of a separate Spanish terminal exempt from Gibraltar customs and immigration controls), and also decides to challenge the legality of Gibraltar's exclusion from the EC air transport liberalization directive. Sir Joshua Hassan retires as Chief Minister, and is replaced by Adolfo Canepa. A new "Independent Democratic Party" is established by Joe Pitaluga.

1988   Massive election victory of Gibraltar Socialist Labour Party, which wins 58 per cent of vote. Its leader, Joe Bossano, becomes the new Chief Minister.

Features of Gibraltar political system

Gibraltar has not had a very structured political system, and individual personalities (notably Sir Joshua Hassan, and now Joe Bossano) have played a decisive role. The only enduring party has been the GLP-AACR, which has dominated Gibraltar politics and only been in opposition from 1969 to 1972, and since 1988. The Gibraltar Socialist Labour Party has gradually consolidated itself, however, and won twice as many votes as the GLP-AACR in the 1988 elections.

Gibraltar politics has not been very ideological, and left-right divisions have been less important than differences of opinion over the status of Gibraltar. Some have emphasized the need for full integration with Britain (from 1967 to 1976 there was an Integration with Britain Party), but this option is now seen as unrealistic. Those seeking much closer links with Spain (and especially those calling for full integration) have only been a small minority.

Disagreements are not over these issues or even over broad objectives (most Gibraltarian politicians are agreed over no transfer of sovereignty to Spain, but greater self-determination for Gibraltar) but instead over the practical nature of links between Gibraltar, Spain and the UK. The 1984 Brussels Agreement between Spain and the UK, the 1987 agreement over Gibraltar airport, and the issue of continuing payment of pensions to Spaniards who worked in Gibraltar before the frontier was closed in 1969, have been particularly controversial issues in this context.

Among the other current political issues in Gibraltar are the following:

– the future of Gibrepair, the ship repairing enterprise in the former Royal Navy Dockyard;
– the housing shortage in Gibraltar;
– ways of stimulating tourism, and Gibraltar's future as a financial centre;
– cutbacks in UK troops in Gibraltar.

Gibraltar Socialist Labour Party (GSLP)

Headquarters	: c/o Transport House, 5043 Town Range, Gibraltar (tel: 00 350- 75 617)
Leader	: Joe Bossano
General secretary	: Joe Victory
Founded	: 1977

Recent Gibraltar election results						
	1969	*1972*	*1976*	*1980*	*1984*	*1988*
Gibraltar Labour Party/Association for the Advancement of Civil Rights (GLP/AACR)	7	8	8	8	8	7 (29.3%)
Integration with Britain Party	5	7	—	—	—	—
Gibraltar Democratic Movement	—	—	4	—	—	—
Democratic Party for British Gibraltar	—	—	—	6	0	—
Gibraltar Socialist Labour Party (GSLP)	—	—	—	1	7	8 (58.2%)
Party for Autonomy of Gibraltar	—	—	—	0	—	—
Independent Democratic Party	—	—	—	—	—	0 (12.4%)
Others	3	—	3	0	0	—

History and Support

Joe Bossano founded the GSLP in 1977 after a schism within the former Gibraltar Democratic Movement, which had won four seats in the 1976 elections. In the 1980 elections only Bossano himself was elected for the party.

In the 1984 elections the GSLP, which had totally opposed the closure of the Royal Navy Dockyard, won seven seats in the Gibraltar House of Assembly, and became the main party of opposition. The GSLP managed to retain a high profile after the elections, opposing the 1984 Brussels Agreement between the UK and Spain, and the 1987 Airport Agreement. It was also highly critical of the management of Gibrepair, and generally of the GLP-AACR government's handling of the economy. In the 1988 elections it won a landslide victory, obtaining twice as many votes as the GLP-AACR, and with its lowest elected candidate winning 2,800 more votes than the first candidate of the GLP-AACR. Joe Bossano became the new Chief Minister at the head of the first GSLP administration.

Policies

The GSLP is on the left-of-centre of the Gibraltar political spectrum, but is not a very ideological socialist party. Under Joe Bossano it has had a populist style, emphasizing the need for a stronger identity for Gibraltar and its people, with a move away from the old style colonial deference towards the UK towards greater assertiveness and autonomy for Gibraltar (without confrontation, however). At the same time Gibraltar should not become subordinate to Spain, and there should be no deals between Britain and Spain over Gibraltar's status behind Gibraltar's back. The GSLP has also emphasized the need for a more progressive economic policy, and for a turnover in the people running Gibraltar. Its underlying 1988 campaign theme was that it was time for a change after the long years of GLP-AACR government.

The GSLP calls for Gibraltar to be recognized as a small nation in its own right. The people of Gibraltar and not Britain are the true owners of the "Rock", and have the right to decide on their own future, and not to be absorbed by Spain. The GSLP supports the constitutional status quo as the only practical one in present circumstances. Gibraltar should concentrate on strengthening its economic self-sufficiency. The Gibraltar people have the moral right, however, to self-determination and at a later stage should be allowed to opt for greater powers under a revised constitution.

The GSLP has strongly opposed the various agreements between Spain and the UK and in particular the Brussels Agreement of November 1984, which it believes gave Spain the right to negotiate over Gibraltar's sovereignty without sufficient involvement and safeguards for the people of Gibraltar. It is also completely opposed to the December 1987 Airport Agreement, which it considers would deprive Gibraltar of its most valuable asset. Instead it seeks an expansion of Gibraltar Airport's role as an independent centre for international flights without any special concessions for Spain, and without a separate Spanish terminal.

The GSLP declares that it will not support any agreement affecting Gibraltar's future without an explicit electoral mandate to do so. It does, however, support increased economic co-operation with Spain (as well as with other neighbouring countries such as Morocco) as long as there are no strings attached.

The GSLP's economic policy has emphasized the need for major reforms, and for a greater emphasis on social welfare, in particular providing for better care for the sick and elderly and tackling the serious housing situation (including the creation of genuine low cost housing for those of lower income). The GSLP calls for enhanced economic planning and the creation of a Gibraltar Economic Development Council for tripartite consultations between the government, business and the unions. The GSLP government has already introduced a Gibraltar Investment Fund, to help provide for new public and private capital injection into the economy. Among priority projects are the creation of a Gibraltar National Bank to help individuals and small businesses, and also the establishment of a new building component factory and reclamation company. The GSLP believes that the £28 million granted by the British government after the closing of the Royal Navy Dockyard has been wasted, and it calls for the restructuring of Gibrepair, of whose management it has been very critical (and which it has since replaced).

The GSLP emphasizes its fiscal prudence. It underlines the importance of wealth creation before its fruits can be distributed, and it calls for a balanced budget. In particular it wants to reinforce Gibraltar's position as a financial services centre, and has sought to reassure investors that there will be no changes to the current tax exemption for companies. There will be no new capital gains tax. Reduction in other taxes will be brought in at the earliest possible moment. It has undertaken to tackle the pension problem of former Spanish workers in Gibraltar, which it claims could bankrupt the existing pension fund and put Gibraltar's social security at risk. In the 1988 election it announced its intention of changing the law to prevent this happening.

Personalities

Joe Bossano, who is a fourth generation Gibraltarian of Genoese origin, has been the party's leader since its inception in 1977, and has been the Chief Minister of Gibraltar since 1988. His background is in the Labour Movement as the head of the Transport and General Workers' Union, and he made his name as a skilful negotiator and defender of workers interests.

A second leading personality in the party is Joe Pilcher, the Tourism Minister.

Gibraltar Labour Party — Association for the advancement of civil rights (GLP-AACR)

Headquarters	: 31 Governor's Parade, Gibraltar (tel: (00 350) 73 238)
Leader	: Adolfo Canepa
Founded	: 1942

History and Support

The "Association for the Advancement of Civil Rights" (the name "Gibraltar Labour Party" was added to its title later) was first founded in 1942 and has been the only enduring party in Gibraltar politics since that date. Almost from the beginning its leading personality has been Sir Joshua Hassan, from a Moroccan-Jewish background. The party called for a democratic constitution for Gibraltar, and, after limited self-government was introduced in 1950, became the main party in the Legislative Council, obtaining three out of five seats in 1950 and 1953, four out of seven in 1956, three out of seven in 1959 and five out of 11 in 1964 (with the balance being held by independents in the last two elections).

With the reinforcement of self-government in 1964 Sir Joshua Hassan became Chief Minister of Gibraltar. In the 1969 elections, the first under new constitutional provisions, the GLP-AACR won more seats than any other party (seven), but went into opposition to a coalition government formed by Robert Peliza. This was the party's only period of opposition until 1988.

In the 1972 elections the GLP-AACR regained power with eight out of 15 seats, and managed to repeat this in the 1976, 1980 and 1984 elections, with Sir Joshua Hassan remaining as Chief Minister from 1972 until his resignation in December 1987. He was replaced by Adolfo Canepa. In the 1988 elections the GLP-AACR was severely defeated, obtaining only 29.3 per cent and with Canepa winning far less votes than

the last candidate of the GSLP. It won seven seats, however, and is now the main party of opposition.

Policies

The GLP-AACR has generally been a pragmatic centre party. Its 1988 campaign theme was safety first, emphasizing the need for Gibraltar to consolidate its recent gains in prosperity by trusting those with experience in government rather than embarking on risky adventurism under the GSLP.

The GLP-AACR continues to advocate close co-operation with Britain, which it considers to be Gibraltar's only reliable friend. It prefers Gibraltar to be under British sovereignty, rather than to have autonomy under Spain. In 1988 its manifesto called for a Free Association of Gibraltar with Britain, whereby Gibraltar would have a decolonized status, but would choose to retain British sovereignty with a greater say in the way in which it was governed, working with Britain rather than under Britain.

The GLP-AACR has thus been the strongest supporter within Gibraltar of the 1986 Brussels Agreement between Spain and the UK, which it believes has brought greater economic security for Gibraltar without any political sacrifices having been made. It argues that the preamble to the Agreement provides sufficient safeguards for Gibraltar over the sovereignty question. It believes that opposition to the Brussels Agreement, as shown by the GSLP, will lead to a confrontation with Britain which is not in Gibraltar's interest.

It has been somewhat more cautious over the Airport Agreement of 1987. It points out that this is subject to approval by the people of Gibraltar, and that there is no time limit for such approval. Gibraltar should not immediately reject the agreement, and should not be pushed into hasty, unconsidered decisions. In the meantime, the party has supported a legal challenge to the exclusion of Gibraltar from the European Community air transport liberalization package.

On the controversial issue of pensions to pre-1969 Spanish workers in Gibraltar, the GLP-AACR has pointed out that it was only committed to paying Spaniards who were already pensioners before the closing of the border in 1969. Other Spanish workers should only be paid up to the limit of their contributions by 1969, and Gibraltar should not be expected to shoulder any wider burden.

In other respects the GLP-AACR's 1988 manifesto was a generally conservative one. On economic policy the emphasis was on building on past successes and on avoiding radical changes that might reduce investors confidence in Gibraltar. There should also be reductions in levels of taxation.

The party also called for a tightening up of industrial relations law, with the introduction of secret ballots in trade union disputes, limitations on secondary action, and certain restrictions on industrial action in essential sectors.

The GLP-AACR was also committed not to approve any changes in the law to facilitate abortion.

Personalities

The party's leader is Adolfo Canepa, who was Sir Joshua Hassan's deputy for eight years in government before taking over at the end of 1987 at the age of 46.

Independent Democratic Party (IDP)

Tel	: (00 350) 77 959
Chairman	: Freddie Vasquez
Founded	: 1987

History and Support

The IDP was founded in December 1987 by Joe Pitaluga, a top Gibraltar civil servant who had been Sir Joshua Hassan's chief adviser for many years, and who was worried about political developments after Sir Joshua Hassan's departure from active politics, especially the prospect of encroaching socialism.

In the 1988 elections the IDP's eight candidates obtained 12.4 per cent of the vote, but no seats in the Gibraltar House of Assembly. Not long after the elections Joe Pitaluga died, and the future of the party is thus highly uncertain.

Policies

The IDP is a right-of-centre party. In the 1988 elections it argued that a change from GLP-AACR government was necessary for Gibraltar, but that a change to the GSLP was much too risky. The IDP emphasized that it was a practical party, and played on Joe Pitaluga's long experience of foreign affairs. It criticized the concept of Free Association (as put forward by the GLP-AACR) as politically unrealistic, and considered that it was a waste of time to pursue it. It called for friendship with Britain but with a guarantee by Britain of fuller and early consultation of any matter affecting Gibraltar's external relations. It also sought recognition by Spain of the rights of the people of Gibraltar.

Like the GLP-AACR, but unlike the GSLP, the IDP supported the 1984 Brussels Agreement between Britain and Spain. It objected to the agreement's reference to the question of sovereignty, but considered that the Agreement nevertheless provided a useful platform for Spanish politicians to be informed of the wishes of the Gibraltar people.

On the other hand the IDP considered that the 1987 Airport Agreement between Britain and Spain was unacceptable, and contained concessions that could not be supported by the people of Gibraltar. The IDP was also committed to pursuing the issue of the legality of Gibraltar's exclusion from the EC air transport liberalization package.

The IDP took a strong line on the issue of payments of pensions to pre-1969 Spanish workers, considering that the difficulties had been created by Spain itself, and that the current problem for Gibraltar was financially and morally unacceptable.

One of the 1988 campaign themes of the IDP was the need for open, honest government in Gibraltar. It also called for the creation of an ombudsman, and raised the issue of electoral reform calling for an examination of the possibility of reintroducing proportional representation in Gibraltar elections, which would then have to be ratified in a referendum.

Its economic policy programme was a conservative one, arguing that there was no magic formula for the economy, and that it was best not to tinker with it with risky and untried ideas. There should be the most favourable environment for the continued development of the private sector. The IDP would encourage profit-sharing schemes in the private sector. Industrial relations should be divorced from politics and the IDP would resist any politically motivated or irresponsible industrial unrest. The IDP would do everything it could to contain public expenditure subject to the commitment to spend more public money on tackling Gibraltar's housing crisis, its greatest social evil. The IDP would curtail excessive expenditure at Gibrepair.

West Germany

Dr Roland Sturm

The country

The Federal Republic of Germany (West Germany) has almost 61.1 million inhabitants, a total number which has remained fairly stable over the last 20 years. By far the most populous of the ten *Länder* which form the federation (West Berlin as the 11th *Land* has a special status) is North Rhine-Westphalia, with 16.7 million inhabitants, followed by Bavaria, with 11 million.

Bavaria and, above all, Baden-Württemberg have both seen a remarkable growth in their population in the 1970s and 1980s, whereas

Map of the Federal Republic of Germany showing the 10 *Länder*, their capitals and certain other major cities.

Source: Carpress.

North Rhine-Westphalia has lost about half a million inhabitants over the last twenty years. *Länder* with a medium-sized population are: Lower Saxony (7.2 million), Hesse (5.5 million) and Rhineland-Palatinate (3.6 million). In Schleswig-Holstein there are 2.6 million and in the Saarland only 1.05 million people. Three major towns have been given separate *Land* status, namely Hamburg (1.6 million), Bremen (654,000), and West Berlin (1.9 million).

The Federal Republic does not have a central focal point for national life, as the former capital Berlin is divided into East and West Berlin by the Wall, and is still under allied control. Britain, France, the Soviet Union and the United States constitute the highest authority within their respective sectors of the town. Bonn (291,400 inhabitants), where the government of the Federal Republic has its seat, has grown in importance, but is still not one of the major towns of the country. The "capital" of banking and commerce is Frankfurt; Hamburg dominates trade and industry in the north and Munich is proud of its contribution to cultural and economic development in the south. A very successful new centre for technological and industrial development has been Stuttgart, the capital of Baden-Württemberg.

Foreigners account for 6.8 per cent of the West German population (4.1 million). The largest group of foreigners comes from Turkey (1.48 million), followed by the Yugoslavs (598,000), and the Italians (531,300). Since the mid-1970s the number of people coming as migrant workers has declined. In the 1980s there has been a steady increase in the number of foreigners asking for political asylum and settling down in Germany. The 1980s have also witnessed a growing influx of ethnic Germans who for political or economic reasons have left the East European countries where their families had lived for generations.

Political institutions

The formal head of state of the Federal Republic is its President (*Bundespräsident*), currently Richard von Weizsäcker. The President is elected for five years by a "Federal

Assembly" (*Bundesversammlung*) consisting of the members of the *Bundestag* (the federal parliament), and an equal number of electors from the *Land* assemblies. In contrast to the constitutional provisions for the presidency in the Weimar Republic, the *Bundespräsident* has mainly a ceremonial and representational role. He is above party politics and acts as guardian of the constitutional order.

The most powerful political figure is the Chancellor (*Bundeskanzler*) who is the head of government. Article 65 of the Basic Law (*Grundgesetz*) (the Constitution of the Federal Republic) makes the Chancellor responsible for the general lines of government policy (*Richtlinienkompetenz*). He is backed up by individual departmental Cabinet Ministers. In practice Cabinet decision-making is of secondary importance compared to decision-making in the Chancellor's office or as the result of compromise between the heads of the coalition parties (who do not necessarily have to be Cabinet Ministers at the same time).

The Chancellor's power base is his majority in the federal parliament, which is elected for a fixed four-year term. The *Bundestag* can only express its loss of confidence in the office-holder by electing a successor from its midst ("constructive vote of no confidence"). This provision was made part of the Basic Law (Article 67) to avoid the political instability that would be caused by a long vacancy without a Chancellor. In practice it has turned out to be a hindrance to the speedy dissolution of Parliament. When, for example, the present Chancellor, Helmut Kohl, sought a general election to confirm his election as Chancellor in the *Bundestag* after a vote of no confidence in his predecessor Helmut Schmidt, he had to artificially contrive a loss of confidence vote within the Parliament. He could now profit from the possibility given by Article 68 of the Basic Law, which envisages the dissolution of Parliament if no member of the *Bundestag* finds a majority as candidate for the Chancellorship.

The *Bundestag* has 518 members of which 496 are elected at general elections in the Federal Republic and 22 are — at the same time — delegated by the assembly of Berlin (West) in accordance with the relative strength of the parties there. The electoral system is based on proportional representation with party lists of candidates and an electoral threshold for entrance to the *Bundestag* of 5 per cent of the vote, or alternatively, three constituency seats (since 1957).

The voter expresses his or her preference for a party by a so-called "second vote". There also exists a "first vote". This is used for allowing the voter an additional choice among the candidates within the 248 constituencies in which the country is divided and where candidates are elected by relative majorities. Those candidates who secure victory in an individual constituency through the "first vote" are directly elected to the *Bundestag*. Their number is subtracted from the total number of candidates elected for their respective party. This means that the first vote does not change the relative strength of parties in Parliament, which is determined by the second vote, but only influences the choice of who is elected. After the choice of candidates elected on the first vote, the rest of the seats are then filled by those candidates on the party lists. These lists are not national ones, but separate lists for each *Land*. If more candidates for a certain party are successful in constituencies (first vote) than their *Land* share as determined by the second vote, that party then wins "excess seats" (*Überhangmandate*). As a result of this the membership of the *Bundestag* is quite often one or two seats above the normal number of 518 MPs.

Political parties have a strong and institutionalized position within German politics. Article 21 of the Basic Law stipulates that they "shall participate in forming the political will of the people". This constitutional provision is used as justification for the massive state funding of political parties (further reinforced in 1988) and their political foundations, which are involved in a variety of activities from political research, to the provisions of aid to developing countries, to international support to other parties within their political family. Because of the privileged position given to parties in the Constitution, the Federal Republic has been characterized as a "party state" (*Parteienstaat*).

Law-making is not the sole responsibility of the *Bundestag*. The *Länder* executives participate in political decision-making at the federal level through their own chamber, the *Bundesrat* with 45 members, including four seats for Berlin (West). As is the case for the 22 Berlin seats in the *Bundestag*, the four Berlin members of the *Bundesrat* are only entitled to formal participation because of the special status of Berlin. In the *Bundesrat* every *Land* has at least three seats. *Länder* with more than two million inhabitants have four, and *Länder* with more than six million inhabitants have five seats. There are no elections to the *Bundesrat* whose members are delegated to this chamber by the *Land* governments. They consist of the head of the *Land* government and some cabinet ministers. A *Land* delegation to the *Bundesrat* can only vote *en bloc* and as instructed by its respective government. There is a fixed yearly rotation of the chairmanship of the *Bundesrat* between the

Länder. The president of the *Bundesrat* substitutes for the *Bundespräsident* when necessary.

The *Bundesrat* is involved in the federal legislative process as soon as a bill is initiated (a process which may also begin in the *Bundesrat*). At this stage it comments on the draft. There are two categories of bills. For certain bills the *Bundesrat* is entitled to voice an objection (*Einspruchsgesetze*), whereas for others its consent is needed (*Zustimmungsgesetze*). Bills needing the consent of the *Bundesrat* are those which affect the genuine interests of the *Länder* such as their autonomous powers in the spheres of culture, education, police, some financial matters, and above all, public administration. As most of the German laws are administered by the *Länder*, their consent in the legislative process is quite frequently needed. They are also able to block decisions, whether because they are seen as harmful to the interests of one or the other *Land*, or because of party political reasons uniting the executives of those *Länder* with the same political complexion. Objections raised by the *Bundesrat* can be overruled by the *Bundestag* with the same majorities (relative or two-thirds). In most cases of conflict between *Bundestag* and *Bundesrat*, compromises are usually found after negotiations within a joint committee with an equal number of delegates from both chambers (*Vermittlungsausschuss*).

The fifth of the federal institutions besides the presidency, the government, the parliament and the *Bundesrat*, is the Federal Constitutional Court (*Bundesverfassungsgericht*). If asked, it can adjudicate on any aspect of the Basic Law. It acts as a guardian of basic individual freedoms, as set out in Articles 1 to 19 of the constitution, it can also, in cases of conflict, act as a constitutional arbiter, and can examine whether court decisions or laws are compatible with the Basic Law. The Federal Constitutional Court can be seen as the ultimate expression of the principle of the supremacy of law (*Rechtsstaat*), a principle which, for example, also gives every citizen the possibility to ask for a final ruling by an administrative court on every activity of the state which affects him or her.

Among other influential federal institutions, the Federal Bank (*Bundesbank*) is certainly the most important. It is autonomous of the federal government and is responsible for the country's monetary and exchange rate policies.

Brief political history

The Federal Republic of Germany was founded in 1949 as a result of the decision of the political elite, above all within the already existing *Länder*, to opt for a provisional democratic state in the zone of the former German *Reich* that was under Western occupation. The founding of the new state was strongly influenced by four factors:

(1) The experience of the Nazi Third Reich and the crimes committed under Hitler. Only a minority of the German population regarded the defeat of 1945 as a victory for democratic principles. There was, instead, a general unwillingness to ever get again involved in politics, and a desire to forget what had happened during the Nazi period. One of the most difficult tasks in postwar Germany, therefore, was the spreading of durable and deep-seated democratic convictions.

(2) The frame of reference for the founding fathers of the Federal Republic was the experience of the Weimar Republic and the breakdown of its political system. The lessons drawn from this experience influenced many of the institutional provisions of the Basic Law, such as the reduced role of the president in the political process, the constructive vote of no confidence, or the exclusion of elements of direct democracy, like referenda. The central idea was to remedy the defects of the Weimar Constitution in order to ensure a greater degree of stability.

(3) The influence of the Allied Powers was not only important in guaranteeing the democratic character of the new constitution, but also made itself felt with regard to some of its most important provisions, like federalism and the relative autonomy of the *Länder*. Under the Occupation Statute, issued in 1949, the Western allies retained a number of competences, especially with regard to military matters and foreign policy.

(4) The Cold War not only resulted in the division of Germany (the GDR was founded shortly after the Federal Republic had come into existence), but also defined the internal and external "enemy" of the new state. The postwar period in West German politics gave primacy to Western-style democracy and a close alliance with the West (NATO membership in 1955) over the issue of German unity and neutrality.

The greatest domestic policy success of the first Chancellor, Adenauer, and his Economics Minister, Erhard, was the German "economic miracle" of the fifties and sixties, which led to a rapid increase in living standards, the wiping

1. Chancellors and coalitions* in the Federal Republic

1949	Konrad Adenauer I	CDU/CSU. FDP, DP
1953	Konrad Adenauer II	CDU/CSU, FDP/FVP[1], DP, BHE[2]
1957	Konrad Adenauer III	CDU/CSU, DP[3]
1961	Konrad Adenauer IV	CDU/CSU, FDP[4]
1963	Ludwig Erhard I	CDU/CSU, FDP
1965	Ludwig Erhard II	CDU/CSU, FDP[5]
1966	Kurt-Georg Kiesinger	CDU/CSU, SPD
1969	Willy Brandt I	SPD, FDP
1972	Willy Brandt II	SPD, FDP
1974	Helmut Schmidt I	SPD, FDP
1976	Helmut Schmidt II	SPD, FDP
1980	Helmut Schmidt III	SPD, FDP[6]
1982	Helmut Kohl I	CDU/CSU, FDP
1983	Helmut Kohl II	CDU/CSU, FDP
1987	Helmut Kohl III	CDU/CSU, FDP

*For party abbreviations see table on election results.
[1]The FDP split in February 1956: a splinter group, later the FVP (*Freie Volkspartei* = Free People's Party) stayed in the coalition whilst the FDP went into opposition.
[2]The BHE left the coalition in October 1955, the party's ministers remaining in government.
[3]The DP split in July 1960; the major part of the *Bundestag* party joined the CDU.
[4]Temporary withdrawal of the FDP from coalition in November 1962.
[5]FDP left the coalition in October 1966.
[6]FDP left the coalition in September 1982.

out of unemployment, and the reconstruction of German trade and industry. It also established the country's pattern of extreme dependency on international competitiveness and export-led growth. In 1963 Ludwig Erhard succeeded Adenauer as Chancellor. Though he won the election of 1964, Erhard very soon lost power. This was not only because of his apparent inability to manage the country's first severe postwar economic crisis in 1966–67, but also because he had difficulties in coming to grips with modernizing forces in German society, who demanded a new approach to economic management, education policies and democratic participation.

The Grand Coalition of the CDU and SPD that was established in 1966 under Chancellor Kiesinger and Vice-Chancellor and Foreign Minister Willy Brandt, applied Keynesian demand management techniques to German economic policy. These techniques were institutionalized by major changes in the Basic Law. The two-thirds majority of the coalition parties in both the *Bundestag* and the *Bundesrat* also permitted another controversial change in the Basic Law. The reserved powers of the Allied nations in cases of emergency were replaced by national emergency regulations (*Notstandsgesetze*).

With the opposition in Parliament reduced to the small FDP, protests against this change and against government policies in general were mainly put forward by an opposition movement outside Parliament, the *Ausserparlamentarische Opposition* (APO). The underlying conviction behind APO's grievances was that postwar West Germany had done everything to secure material well-being, but had neglected to develop its democratic system. There was criticism that there had been an insufficient break with the country's Nazi past. (The National Democratic Party, NPD, an extreme right-wing party, won 4.3 per cent of the vote at the general election of 1969, and came close to the 5 per cent needed for getting seats in Parliament. At this time it had MPs in the *Land* assemblies of Baden-Württemberg (9.8 per cent in 1968), Bavaria (7.4 per cent in 1966), Bremen (8.8 per cent in 1967), Hesse (7.9 per cent in 1966), Lower Saxony (7.0 per cent in 1967), Rhineland-Palatinate (6.9 per cent in 1967), and Schleswig-Holstein (5.8 per cent in 1967). The APO also criticized the support given by the West German government for the Vietnam war. In addition there was the feeling that democratic change and sexual and social liberation had not gone far enough. The student movement at the universities, in particular, advocated policies calling first for reform and later revolution.

Reforming policies were taken up by the first social-liberal coalition government, which was established after the election of 1969, with Willy Brandt as chancellor and Walter Scheel (FDP) (later *Bundespräsident* from 1974–79), as Vice-Chancellor and Foreign Minister. In foreign policy the new government successfully furthered *détente* with the East through its *Ostpolitik*, and, with regard to domestic policy, passed a great number of reform laws in the fields of education, social security, public morality and the administration of justice. For a short period planning was also strongly emphasized as a central element of modern public administration.

Willy Brandt resigned in 1974, after it had turned out that Günter Guillaume, one of his closest advisers, was a GDR spy. His resignation signalled the end of costly reforms and of efforts to increase political participation. His successor, Helmut Schmidt, was proud of being a pragmatist rather than a visionary like Brandt. After the oil price shock of 1973–74 his first priority was to overcome the economic crisis. German society under Schmidt rediscovered conservatism (*Tendenzwende*). The protest movement at the universities died down, and was discredited by the terrorism of the left-wing RAF (*Rote Armee Fraktion*), the so-called Baader-Meinhof gang.

The new social movements of the late seventies tended to concentrate on single issues, like the environment, peace or feminism, and were no longer university-based, but broad popular coalitions. The eighties saw a worsening of economic problems in West Germany. The oil price rise of 1979 fuelled inflation which reached a rate of 5.1 per cent in 1982, with unemployment at 7.5 per cent. Helmut Schmidt, supported above all by the FDP Economics Minister Otto Graf Lambsdorff, opted for an austerity economic strategy designed to fight inflation by cuts in public expenditure, and to reduce unemployment by stimulating investments through higher profits for enterprises.

These policies, combined with Helmut Schmidt's support for the siting of Pershing II missiles, resulted in a growing estrangement between the Social Democratic Chancellor and his party. The FDP saw its chance to change coalition partners without having to change its policies, and in 1982 they supported the election of the Christian Democrat Helmut Kohl after a vote of no confidence in Helmut Schmidt. Though the inflation rate was brought down after 1982 the unemployment rate remained fairly constant at 8 per cent. The central theme of the first years of the Kohl government was fighting the budget deficit, and later on a tax reform in two stages, in 1986 and 1990. In the fields of social entitlements and civil liberties a more conservative stance was adopted, whereas Hans-Dietrich Genscher, the long-serving FDP Foreign Minister (in office since 1974), helped to guarantee continuity in German foreign policy.

Main features of the current German political system

West German federalism has developed very distinct features. The co-operation between the federation (the *Bund*) and the *Länder* as, in theory, fairly autonomous units has, since the mid-1960s, been transformed into "interlocking federalism" (*Politikverflechtung*). With regard to decision-making and the implementation of policies, the division of responsibilities between the *Bund* and the *Länder* has become blurred. Decisions may, for example, be initiated at the *Land* level, because of financial incentives from the federal government, which in turn are the result of earlier pressure by the *Länder*. The *Länder* implement such programmes, but may also be restricted in this process if the *Bund* insists on the fixing of guidelines.

The German bureaucracy is dominated by civil servants with a legal training. Law, and conformity with legal provisions, are always two of the first points of reference for policy-makers. German politics is overregulated. It suffers not only from constant rule-making by politicians, but is also affected by the tendency of both German citizens and politicians to use the courts, and especially the Federal Constitutional Court, as *Ersatz* law-makers. Social conflicts are only rarely solved by political compromise, and bureaucracies and judges retain a powerful role.

The mainstream political spectrum in West Germany is narrower than in most other Western democracies. As a result of Weimar, Nazi Germany and the GDR, the message has spread that democracies die when they allow the growth of political extremism. The Federal Republic sees itself as a democracy in self-defence. Parties on the left of the Social Democrats and to the right of the Christian Democrats are regarded as enemies of democracy and extremists are not allowed to hold civil service jobs (*Berufsverbot*). Even Parliament with its majority of FDP, CDU/CSU and SPD has not allowed the Green Party (in Parliament since 1983) the same privileges enjoyed by every other parliamentary party.

Contrary to the fears of the founding fathers that the Federal Republic could develop into a second Weimar, the choice between competing democratic parties became much narrower after the first few elections. In 1961 there were only three parties left in Parliament. It took more than twenty years before a new party, in the form of the Greens in 1983, succeeded in entering Parliament. The relative strength of the parties has forced them to form coalitions in order to command parliamentary majorities.

2. Seats and percentages won by the political parties in the *Bundestag*[1]

	1949	1953	1957	1961	1965	1969	1972	1976	1980	1983	1987
Christlich-demokratische Union (CDU)/ Christlich-soziale Union (CSU) (Christian Democratic Union outside Bavaria/ Christian Social Union in Bavaria)	139 (31.0%)	243 (45.2%)	270 (50.2%)	242 (45.3%)	245 (47.6%)	242 (46.1%)	225 (44.9%)	243 (48.6%)	226 (44.5%)	244 (48.8%)	223 (44.3%)
Sozialdemokratische Partei Deutschlands (SPD) (German Social Democratic Party)	131 (29.2%)	151 (28.8%)	169 (31.8%)	190 (36.2%)	202 (39.3%)	224 (42.7%)	230 (45.8%)	214 (42.6%)	218 (42.9%)	193 (38.2%)	186 (37.0%)
Frei Demokratische Partei (FDP) (Free Democratic Party)	52 (11.9%)	48 (9.5%)	41 (7.7%)	67 (12.8%)	49 (9.5%)	30 (5.8%)	41 (8.4%)	39 (7.9%)	53 (10.6%)	34 (7.0%)	46 (9.1%)
Die Grünen (The Green Party)	—	—	—	—	—	—	—	—	0 (1.5%)	27 (5.6%)	42 (8.3%)
Bayernpartei (BP) (Bavarian Party)	17 (4.2%)	0 (1.7%)	0 (0.9%)	0 (0.2%)	—	—	—	—	—	—	—
Deutsche Partei (DP) (German Party)	17 (4.0%)	15 (3.3%)	17 (3.4%)	0[2] (2.8%)	—	—	—	—	—	—	—
Kommunistische Partei Deutschlands (KPD) (Communist Party of Germany)	15 (5.7%)	0 (2.2%)	—	—	—	—	—	—	—	—	—
Wirtschaftliche Aufbau-Vereinigung (WAV) (Union for Economic Reconstruction)	12 (2.9%)	—	—	—	—	—	—	—	—	—	—
Zentrum (Z) (The Centre Party)	10 (3.1%)	3 (0.8%)	0[3] (0.9%)	—	0[4] (0.1%)	0 (0.0%)	—	—	—	—	0 (0.1%)
Deutsche Konservative Partei—Deutsche Rechtspartei (DKP-DRP) (German Conservative Party— German Right-wing Party)	5 (1.8%)	—	—	—	—	—	—	—	—	—	—
Südschleswigscher Wählerverband (SSW) (South Schleswig Union of Voters)	1 (0.3%)	0 (0.2%)	0 (0.1%)	0 (0.1%)	—	—	—	—	—	—	—
Independents	3	—	0	—	—	—	—	—	—	—	—
Gesamtdeutscher Block/Bund der Heimatvertriebenen und Entrechteten (GB-BHE) (German Unity Bloc/ Federation of those driven out of their home country and who have been denied their human rights)	—	27 (5.9%)	(4.6%)	—	—	—	—	—	—	—	—

[1] Second votes, without Berlin (West)
[2] Gesamtdeutsche Partei (German Unity Party)
[3] Föderalistische Union (Federalist Union)
[4] Christliche Volkspartei (Christian People's Party)

This has given the small FDP a key strategic position, in which it has the power to make or undo coalitions. Political change in West Germany has been less dependent on election results than on coalition arrangements.

The German political system has been characterized by a high degree of stability to which the need for coalition and compromises has contributed. Social cleavages, be they of class, religion, or region still help to explain German voting behaviour, but these cleavages do not lead to open social conflict. The trade union organization is highly centralized and organized on the principle "one industry — one union". There are many legal and procedural barriers against the outbreak of social conflict. The basic stability of the German political system rests on the one hand on the strength of the new German institutions and on the other hand on a fairly high degree of acceptance of the system and pride in the country's economic achievements, although this is sometimes combined with pessimism as to whether this will endure.

Nevertheless the consensus is challenged from certain quarters. Some claim that the system is too rigid and inflexible, and others that German society has been too materialistic. While German's NATO membership and Western orientation is accepted by most Germans, there is also support for neutrality that is linked to the more widespread and persistent desire for German reunification. A degree of pacifism has also been one reaction to Germany's past among some of Germany's young people in particular.

One final important theme that should be mentioned is the importance of the environmental issue in West German politics, spurred, in particular, by the growing concern over acid rain and *Waldsterben* ("forest death"). All the major German parties now support strong environmental measures, though there is still controversy over specific issues, such as over the future of nuclear power (e.g. the recent conflict over the nuclear re-processing plant at Wackersdorf).

Sozialdemokratische Partei Deutschlands —SPD
(German Social Democratic Party)

Headquarters	: Erich-Ollenhauer-Haus, Ollenhauerstr. 1 5300 Bonn (tel: 53 21)
Chairman	: Hans-Jochen Vogel
Vice-chairpersons	: Herta Däubler-Gmelin, Oskar Lafontaine, Johannes Rau
Chief administrator (*Bundesgeschäfts-führerin*)	: Anke Fuchs
Youth group	: *Jungsozialisten*
Women's group	: *Arbeitsgemeinschaft socialdemokratischer Frauen (ASF)*
Workers' group	: *Arbeitsgemeinschaft für Arbeitnehmerfragen (AfA)*
Employers' group	: *Arbeitsgemeinschaft Selbständige*
Members	: 910,063
Founded	: 1863 (*Allgemeiner Deutscher Arbeiterverein*), called SPD since 1891.

History

The SPD is the party with the longest history of all parties in the *Bundestag*. In 1863 Ferdinand Lasalle founded the reformist, state-oriented *Allgemeiner Deutscher Arbeiterverein* (General Workers' Association). Six years later, in 1869, Wilhelm Liebknecht and August Bebel united the Marxist revolutionary tendency within their *Sozialdemokratische Arbeiterpartei* (SD-AP, Social Democratic Workers' Party). In 1875 both groups joined together to form the *Sozialistische Arbeiterpartei Deutschlands* (SAPD, German Socialist Workers Party). Between 1878 and 1890 the party's activities were made illegal by Bismarck's anti-socialist law. When the party was again able to openly take part in political life after 1891, its Erfurt Programme continued to call for socialist revolution. In reality, however, it was already a social reformist party.

The controversy within the party over the SPD's attitude to German participation in World War I resulted in a split, which divided the party into a majority wing (MSPD) who took a "national" position, and a minority, the so-called independent wing (USPD), which was anti-war. This split was later partially mended, but a minority on the party's left broke away in 1918 and founded the Communist Party of Germany (KPD). During the Weimar Republic the SPD was one of the strongest defenders of its Constitution and participated in most of Weimar's coalition governments. This practical involvement in day-to-day politics was still accompanied by a radical criticism of capitalism, which found its expression in the SPD's Heidelberg programme of 1925. In 1933, the SPD, which had been the only parliamentary party to vote against the transfer of unlimited emergency powers to Hitler, was made illegal by the Nazis.

In 1945 the SPD was re-established in all four occupation zones of the defeated *Reich*. In the West of Germany the first party chairman after World War II was Kurt Schumacher (1895–1952), who had been held as a prisoner in concentration camps since 1933, and who led the party until his death. Contrary to his wishes the SPD did not develop into the natural party of government after the war. The economic miracle of the fifties made the social democratic concept of more planning and nationalizations look obsolete. Meanwhile in the East of Germany, and under Soviet pressure, the Social Democrats, led by Otto Grotewohl, had merged with the Communists and had formed the Socialist Unity Party of Germany (SED, *Sozialistische Einheitspartei Deutschlands*) in 1946. Schumacher did not, however, give up the hope that the division of Germany could be reversed, believing that the attractiveness of the Federal Republic compared to the weakness of the GDR would leave the latter no choice but to join the West. This was also of strategic importance for the party, since, without the SPD's traditional strongholds in Thuringia, Saxony and Greater Berlin, all now situated in the GDR, he saw little chance for his party to win electoral majorities.

Acceptance of the division of Germany, which slowly grew in the SPD after Schumacher's death, meant that the party had to find new voters in the Federal Republic outside the disintegrating working-class subculture, if it ever wished to return to government. This necessary change of strategy took, however, a number of years. Schumacher's successor, Erich Ollenhauer (1901–1963), was more of a low key party administrator than a programmatic thinker. In the mid-fifties the membership of the SPD reached its lowest point in postwar history (585,000). In 1955, the SPD tried to gain additional strength by forging a coalition with the trade unions and critical intellectuals, in order to oppose German rearmament. Any positive effect which this alliance might have had in broadening the base of the party's support was wiped out by the Russian invasion of Hungary of 1956 and the effects on public opinion of Adenauer's pension reform of 1957. The election defeat of 1957, in which the Christian Democrats were perceived by the electorate as more competent on the central issues of economic well-being and national security, considerably strengthened those forces within the SPD who wanted to broaden its electoral base. They sought to attract new voters not interested in the old class divisions and to present the party as a potentially responsible party of government, thus freeing it from its image of being the permanent opposition party. Fritz Erler (1913–1967), Herbert Wehner (born 1906), and Carlo Schmit (1896–1980), who assisted Ollenhauer in leading the Parliamentary Party, were the driving forces behind the basic change in its policy programme, which was adopted by the party at a special party congress in Bad Godesberg in 1959.

The Godesberg programme still described the SPD as a party of democratic socialism, but pointed out that this philosophy might have different roots in Christian ethics, humanism, or classical philosophy. The traditional reference to Marxism was notably absent. The SPD now accepted existing commitments in national defence, private property and a free market economy with as much market sovereignty as possible and as much planning as necessary. The party called for the social component of the market economy to be strengthened by an expansion in the welfare state. To achieve more democratic control in the economic sphere, the SPD no longer insisted on nationalizations, but supported the introduction of industrial co-determination (*Mitbestimmung*). An arrangement was also sought with the churches. Godesberg now stands in SPD party history as the symbol for its transition from an ideological *Weltanschauung* party to a pragmatic catch-all-party (*Volkspartei*).

This new strategy also made it necessary for the SPD to seek possible coalition partners to its right. The choice of the popular mayor of West Berlin, Willy Brandt, who had become party chairman in 1958, as its candidate for the Chancellorship in 1961 as well as the party's American style election campaign, signalled the SPD's readiness to promote a new image. In both the elections of 1961 and 1965 the SPD won additional votes. After the break-up of Ludwig Erhard's coalition government, the SPD entered a broad coalition in 1966 with the CDU/CSU, and the SPD was finally in a position to prove that it had, in the words of its 1969 election slogan. "the better team" to govern the country.

Within the government, however, there were certain conflicts between the coalition partners, which culminated in a debate over the revaluation of the German mark, with the CDU/CSU opposing this measure and the SPD, together with the *Bundesbank*, supporting it. Another important area of difference was over policy towards Eastern Europe. In 1969 Gustav Heinemann (1899–1976) became the first Social Democrat to be elected to the office of President of the Federal Republic. His election was only possible, because of additional support from the FDP, thus serving as a test for the feasibility of a future SPD-FDP coalition. After the 1969 election the first Social Democratic-Liberal coalition was formed. Its Chancellor, Willy Brandt, only had a majority of 12 MPs. this majority had withered away by 1972 in a climate of political confrontation which focussed on the new Chancellor's reforms and above all on his *Ostpolitik*. As there was neither a majority for Brandt, nor for his Christian Democratic challenger, Rainer Barzel, within the *Bundestag*, Parliament had to be dissolved. The ensuing election brought the greatest victory for the German Social Democrats in postwar history, and the only time that the SPD became the strongest party in Parliament. Since its all-time low in the mid-fifties the membership of the party had been growing steadily. It was 954,394 in 1972 and reached its record strength in 1976 (1,022,191 individual members).

In 1974 Brandt, whose popularity had seriously declined as a result of his image of indecision, resigned as Chancellor although remaining as party chairman. Helmut Schmidt became Brandt's successor as Chancellor. Herbert Wehner remained as head of the parliamentary party. The *troika* of Schmidt, Brandt and Wehner then led the party until the end of the SPD/FDP coalition in 1982. Schmidt was a self-confessed workaholic who wanted to get things done (*Macher*) with a pragmatic rather than ideological outlook.

A more theoretical debate on the party's future role was also initiated in the 1970s with the report of a programme committee under Helmut Schmidt and the two vice-chairmen Hans Apel (for the right-wing) and Jochen Steffen (for the left), which presented its framework for future party policies in 1973 (*Orientierungsrahmen für die Jahre 1973–1985*). The party left successfully challenged this report, which had very much concentrated on effective development of the market economy and on efficient government, but had lacked any vision for the future of West German society. A new committee under Peter von Oertzen (who is on the left of the party) wrote a second draft of the *Orientierungsrahmen 85*, which was accepted by the SPD's party congress in Mannheim in 1975.

After the party returned to opposition in 1982 and lost the election in 1983 its beaten candidate for this election, Hans-Jochen Vogel, became head of the parliamentary party. The SPD's candidate for the 1987 elections was Johannes Rau, the head of state of North Rhine-Westphalia. In 1987 Willy Brandt resigned as party chairman when his choice of a female, Greek non-party member as press officer for the SPD was not accepted by the party. Vogel was then given the additional responsibility of being party chairman.

Support

Though the SPD has today lost its long-lasting predominance in the major German towns, it is still true to say that the SPD is stronger in towns than in the countryside, and in areas where there is a low percentage of Catholics. Centres of support for the SPD are regions where the working class is concentrated, but after Godesberg, the party has also made considerable progress in winning over the middle classes. Their support, however, has proved relatively volatile.

The SPD today has its main strongholds in the areas of declining industries in the North (Hamburg, Bremen, Schleswig-Holstein), the Saarland and North Rhine-Westphalia, although there has often been a different pattern in

---

3. Social structure of the SPD party membership (in %)

	1930	1952	1956 1957	late 1966	Oct. 1968	June 1973	1977	1984
Workers	59.5	45	40	32	34.5	26.4	28	24.4
Employees	10.0	17	—	19	20.6	21.9	24	22.6
Civil Servants	3.9	5	14	8	9.9	8.9	10	7.4
Self-employed	4.5	12	6	5	5.2	4.8	5	4.9
Farmers	—	2	1	—	—	0.3	—	0.66
Pensioners	4.6	12	25	18	24.2	13.3	10	7.2
Housewives	17.1	7	14	16	4.3	9.9	11	12.5
Students	0.2	—	—	1	0.9	5.8	9	14.7
Others	—	—	—	1	1.5	7.3	—	2.9

Source: Klaus von Beyme: *Das politische System der Bundesrepublik Deutschland*, Munich: Piper, 5th edition 1987, p. 75.

Land elections. The SPD lost, for example, Hesse in 1987, which it had held since 1946, and in the same year, and, in the wake of the Barschel scandal, won Schleswig-Holstein, that had been CDU-governed since 1950. The five constituencies with the best results for the SPD in the most recent national elections were Duisburg II (63.1 per cent), Essen II (62.7 per cent), Dortmund II (60.7 per cent), Herne (60.4 per cent), and Gelsenkirchen I (60.3 per cent).

The social structure of the SPD's membership has become more similar to that of the parties to its right, although the share of workers and employees among SPD party members is higher than in other parties. Half of the members of the SPD (CDU: 19 per cent) are also members of trade unions. It is still difficult for the SPD to recruit support among the self-employed and farmers. (See table 3.)

The change in support for the SPD was also reflected by the changes in social complexion of its Parliamentarians and party workers. Workers and industrial employees had already been under-represented since the re-establishment of the party after the war, but this increased in the 1960s and 1970s, when there was a massive influx of civil servants and other public sector employees into the party.

Organization

There are about 9,000 local party organizations within the SPD (*Ortsvereine*), which together form 250 area parties (*Unterbezirke*). The boundaries of the area parties are often similar to those for the constituencies at *Land* and general elections. The party's most important organizational tier is the district organization (*Bezirke*). There are 22 party districts. The districts decide themselves whether they want to unite to form a party organization at the *Land* level (*Landesverband*).

The highest statutory authority for the party is its biannual national party congress. The 400 delegates to this congress are selected by the *Bezirke* according to the relative strength of their membership. The party congress elects the party executive (*Vorstand*) which has about 40 members, among which are the chairperson of the party, the vice-chairpersons and the treasurer. The task of organizing day-to-day business falls on the party's governing body, the *Präsidium*, which is about a third of the size of the party executive. It is elected by the party executive, which also elects a chief administrator (*Bundesgeschäftsführer*). In order to represent the views of the party organization inside and outside Parliament at the *Land* and regional level there is a party council (*Parteirat*),

with an advisory role. Different social groups and professions (like lawyers, doctors, teachers, local government representatives of the party and others) form special working groups (*Arbeitsgemeinschaften*) who act as pressure groups inside the party to influence its policies. An important means of furthering the party's political aims is through the formally independent Friedrich-Ebert Foundation.

The SPD tolerates "tendencies" or factions inside the party. They have no formal status, but meet as a kind of club or interest group. The membership in these tendencies, like the *Kanalarbeiter*, or the *Godesberger Kreis* on the right, and the *Frankfurter Kreis* or the *Parlamentarische Linke* on the left is not fixed and their boundary lines are not always clear. Some of them are rather short-lived, while others are relatively permanent and have, as the example of the *Kanalarbeiter* has demonstrated, even been able to develop a kind of veto power within the parliamentary party.

The SPD has not, however, tolerated party positions which are too close to Communism. In the early fifties a few hundred members had to leave the party because of their co-operation with the Communist Party. Because of their far left-wing tendencies the SPD forbade first its student association SDS (*Sozialistischer Deutscher Studentenbund*) in the 1960s and then its successor SHB (*Sozialdemokratischer Hochschulbund*) to speak for the party and to use the Social Democratic label. The SDS was dissolved in 1970. In 1977 the chairman of the youth organization *Jungsozialisten* was accused of sharing the GDR's analysis of West German society and had to leave the party. In 1981, when some left-wing critics of Helmut Schmidt's policies sought a policy renewal for the party, one MP, Karl-Heinz Hansen, was thrown out of the party and was joined by another dissenter.

The German trade unions are formally independent from the SPD. They give primacy to organizational unity over party political criteria. They are therefore in theory above parties, although they are closest to the SPD. In practice, many union members and most union leaders are at the same time members of the Social Democrats, sometimes in leading positions. This does not mean, however, that it is easy for a SPD-government to control the unions. There were union protests against the government's policies during the Grand Coalition, as well as during the periods when Willy Brandt and Helmut Schmidt were Chancellor.

Individual candidates for parliamentary constituencies at general elections are chosen within the constituencies on the basis of proposals from the local party organizations and subject to ultimate control by the upper level of the party hierarchy. The ranking of the second vote candidates on a *Land* list is decided upon during a *Land* congress of party delegates. More important than this formal procedure, however, are the compromises on the party list that are hammered out at the level of party elites.

At its Münster party congress in 1988, the SPD decided to introduce a quota for the representation of women both in party functions and seats for the SPD in parliaments. It is planned to give female representatives 40 per cent of party jobs no later than 1994 and 40 per cent of its seats no later than 1998.

The party has its own policy-making apparatus, working through a number of committees which specialize in different fields. In October 1988 a new "super-committee" was founded under the chairmanship of Oscar Lafontaine, with the intention of co-ordinating the party policies on economic, finance, tax, social, environmental and energy matters in order to develop a consistent programme for an ecological and social renewal of industrial society. Representatives of the party at different political levels (Europe, *Bundestag, Land* assemblies) participate in the policy committees. Political reactions to current affairs are mainly formulated by the party's executive and/or the parliamentary party. The party's representatives in the European Parliament sit in the Socialist Group within the European Parliament. Since 1984 the SPD has had an office for European affairs which assists the party executive and is responsible for the coordination of all party initiatives with a European dimension.

The chairperson of the SPD group in the European Parliament and its vice-chairpersons were recently given the right to participate in meetings of the leadership of the SPD parliamentary party in the *Bundestag* to guarantee an adequate exchange of information. Another device for the co-ordination of European and national politics is a service group for European politics under the vice-chairman of the SPD's parliamentary party, to transfer information for parliamentarians from the European level to the national level and vice versa. The SPD is also a member of the Confederation of Socialist parties of the European Community, and of the Socialist International.

Traditionally the SPD has relied considerably for its finances on members' contributions, which used to be much bigger than those of the right-of-centre parties. Today there is a tendency towards greater similarity in the income structure of the two major parties. For 1987, the SPD's total income was DM 225,087 million. Membership fees and regular contributions to the party's central fund made up 49.1 per cent of this income, 1.8 per cent came from dividends on party assets, 2.9 per cent were income from other activities of the party and 9.4 per cent consisted of financial gifts from sources outside the party. The party organization at the subnational level contributed 4.9 per cent of the SPD's budget. The second major source for the income of the party (which will gain importance in the future), is state funding, which already made up 31.9 per cent of the SPD's income in 1987.

The SPD has a newspaper called *Vorwärts*, but its continuation is in doubt.

Policies

Since the Bad Godesberg Conference in 1959 the SPD has been a generally pragmatic and moderate Social Democratic Party. This is still the case on most policy questions, although the party is more radical on certain defence policy and energy issues. It continues to support closer European integration.

When the SPD lost power in 1982 there was a significant shift in the SPD's policy emphasis. Helmut Schmidt had generally adopted a more conservative stance (for example on economic and defence policies), and had also been constrained by its government role and its coalition with the FDP. In opposition, the SPD sought to adopt a more radical image, to win back voters lost to the Green Party in particular. A new emphasis was put on ecology, the dangers of nuclear power and policies of disarmament and strengthened contacts with East Germany.

The feeling that the party needed a new general framework for its policies led to the decision at its 1984 congress in Essen, to draft a modernized version of the Godesberg programme of 1959. This so-called Irsee draft was published in 1986. Meanwhile Oscar Lafontaine and the younger generation of SPD leaders in the *Länder* have sought greater influence within the party, with the result that a decision on the Irsee draft has been delayed.

In the Irsee draft there are general references to the basic values of freedom, justice and equality, and solidarity. In international politics the party stresses the responsibility of the developed countries for furthering third world development. Priority is given to disarmament policies. Defensive weapons should replace offensive ones (*Strukturelle Nichtangriffsfähigkeit*). Another key concept is partnership, because of a mutual interest in international security (*Sicherheitspartnerschaft*). This concept, developed by the party's expert on disarmament questions, Egon Bahr, has allowed the SPD to establish close contacts with the East German ruling party, the SED.

The SPD has taken its own independent foreign policy line in this sphere, accepting the difference in ideology with the SED, but at the same time emphasizing peaceful coexistence and exerting pressure on the East-German government behind the scenes to grant concessions on human rights questions.

A novel feature of the Irsee draft is the prominent role that it gives to ecological questions and to feminist demands for a genuine equality between the sexes. The SPD in opposition has looked for new allies, for example among citizens' action groups, who have no longer been willing to delegate defence of their demands to traditional party organizations.

Industrial production should no longer destroy the environment and the state should intervene to guarantee this principle. Nuclear energy is only accepted as a temporary solution to energy problems. In the long run it should be replaced by alternative sources of energy. The SPD opposes the more advanced breeder reactors and the whole process of energy production from plutonium, such as reprocessing. The party does not oppose technological change, but it wants better controls on new technologies. It should be the task of the state to evaluate not only the financial or organizational consequences of these technologies, but also their effects on society. Human dignity should be given priority over the needs of machines. New tax structures are also being examined whereby contributions to social security would be levied on firms in relation to their intensity of mechanical production.

The party's strategies to combat unemployment include state programmes for training and temporary employment, and shorter hours of work (which should be reduced to 35 hours a week).

The SPD has also been a strongly pro-European Party, advocating common foreign and security policies, and a much closer co-ordinated economic policy. There should be a European Political Community and the powers of the European Parliament should be strengthened. The Single European Act was supported by the SPD, which felt, however, that it did not go far enough. The SPD has been a pro-NATO party in general terms, but has called for a strengthening of the European pillar.

The calls for a shorter working week has led to internal conflicts within the SPD. The majority of the party and the trade unions oppose reductions in income for shorter working hours. A minority group headed by Oscar Lafontaine, on the other hand, thinks that income reductions are necessary. Without those, it is argued, the firms would hesitate to employ new workers. They would either buy new machinery that makes human work superfluous, or they would try to force their employees to work extra hours to make up for the loss of working time. Oscar Lafontaine criticized the majority position for its bias in favour of those in work (who enjoy the full protection of their unions), whereas the unemployed tend to have no comparable lobby. There is a similar confrontation between Lafontaine and the majority of the party on the issue of greater flexibility in working time.

These internal party conflicts have, however, had another dimension. Praise for Lafontaine's position came, above all, from the political right, such as the FDP. After Lafontaine's brief flirtation with the idea of a coalition of Social Democrats and the Green Party after the 1987 election (which came to an end with the coalition between these two parties broke up in Hesse in the same year), he developed a preference for an SPD-FDP coalition. Willy Brandt's earlier vision of an SPD led on the left, is today only favoured by a minority within the party. Johannes Rau's strategy as the party's candidate for the chancellorship in 1987, was to go it alone and to build a "new majority" for the SPD, as has been possible in North Rhine-Westphalia and the Saarland (where the SPD holds absolute majorities). This also failed and is no longer seen as a realistic option. More encouraging for the SPD was the fact that an SPD-FDP coalition government was formed after the 1987 *Land* election in Hamburg, which was seen as a signal that after all the ill-feelings caused by the FDP's change of coalition partners in 1982, political co-operation between the two parties is again possible. In 1989 the Berlin SP agreed on a coalition with the local Green Party (Alternative Liste). This broadened the range for possible coalition.

Personalities

The party chairman and head of the parliamentary party is Hans-Jochen Vogel, born in 1926. From 1960 to 1972 he was mayor of Munich, from 1972 to 1974 he served as Minister for Housing and Regional Planning and from 1974 to 1981 as Minister for Justice. In 1981 he was sent to Berlin by his party to defend the SPD majority, but he was not successful. In 1983 he was the SPD's candidate for the Chancellorship at the general election. Willy Brandt is honorary chairman of the SPD and honorary president of the Socialist International. The party's heads of state governments in the *Länder* are Björn Engholm (Schleswig-

Holstein), Klaus Wedemeier (Bremen), Hartmut Voscherau (Hamburg), Johannes Rau (North Rhine-Westphalia), Walter Momper (Berlin), and Oscar Lafontaine (Saarland). The former Chancellor Helmut Schmidt has retired from politics and is now one of the editors of the Liberal weekly paper *Die Zeit*.

Christlich Demokratische Union Deutschlands — CDU
(German Christian Democratic Union)

Headquarters	:	Konrad-Adenauer-Haus, Friedrick-Ebert-Allee 73-75, 5300 Bonn 1 (tel: 54 41)
Chairman	:	Helmut Kohl
Vice-chairpersons	:	Ernst Albrecht, Norbert Blüm, Hanna-Renate Laurien, Lothar Späth, Gerhard Stoltenberg, Rita Süssmuth, Walter Wallmann
General secretary	:	Heiner Geissler
Chief administrator	:	Peter Radunski
Youth group	:	*Junge Union*
Women's group	:	*Frauenvereinigung*
Workers' group	:	*Sozialausschüsse*
Employer's group	:	*Mittelstandsvereinigung* (small and medium-sized firms) *Wirtschaftsvereinigung*
Group for those exiled after World War II	:	*Union der Vertriebenen und Flüchtlinge*
Senior citizens' group	:	*Seniorenuion*
Members	:	715,637
Founded	:	1945 (1950)

History

The CDU was founded after World War II as a party open to all strata of society. A central purpose of the new "Christian" party was to overcome traditional religious divisions between Catholics and Protestants. The party was assisted in its effort to become the dominant force on the political right by the allied forces' policies as regards the acceptance of new parties in defeated Germany, which favoured the concentration of the party system and the exclusion of the extreme right.

In the first years after the war the CDU was a heterogeneous federation of regional parties. It was usually controlled by community leaders, whose reputation had often been gained outside the field of politics. One major centre for the new party was Berlin, where the CDU was led by prominent ex-members of the Weimar Catholic Centre Party, like Jakob Kaiser, Andreas Hermes and Josef Ersing. Jakob Kaiser became the first chairman of the CDU in the Soviet occupation zone. He and Ernst Lemmer lost their leading position in the party when the Socialist Unity Party (SED) started to exert pressure on the bourgeois parties in 1947 and demanded their support for "socialist transformation". In 1948 the East German CDU with its new chairman Otto Nuschke, joined the "National Front", which accepted the leading political and social role of the Socialist Unity Party.

A second major centre for the party was Cologne, where Konrad Adenauer had his power base. Adenauer was elected acting Chairman of the CDU in the British occupation zone in 1946 and chairman of the Rhineland CDU. There was a marked difference in the outlook of the two centres, one — Berlin — feeling itself more responsible for Germany as a whole, and the other — Cologne — ready to accept the idea of working within the framework of the Western occupation zone.

At the beginning, the heterogeneous party organization was matched by a variety of party ideologies. Central to them was the social teaching of the Catholic Church. The Dominicans were influential, especially within that wing of the party which had not given up the hope of finding common ground with the political left for the rebuilding of Germany. They advocated a brand of Christian socialism as the best organizational principle for society, whereas the Jesuits, who were in a majority in the ideological debate, favoured a reduced role for the state. The leading theoreticians of Christian solidarity, like Oswald Nell-Breuning SJ, wanted the state to step back, whenever individuals were ready to shoulder the responsibility for the provision of needed social services. They also wanted to overcome class divisions by the free association of people of similar social status, so that everybody found his or her place in society and received a fair share of the common good.

Directly after the war, capitalism was discredited within large parts of the CDU, and for a short period it was possible for the smaller left-wing of the party to influence its policy decisions. The *Ahlener Programm* of 1947 expressed certain anticapitalist views. The economy, it said, should be regulated, especially in order to break the power of monopolies, and economic planning should be used as an instrument for guaranteeing adequate production for the needs of the population. At the same time, however, the programme stressed the productive role of the private sector and wanted planning to be self-regulated by chambers of industry along with representatives of both the consumers and local government. It also supported industrial co-determination.

From the start Adenauer fought against Christian Socialist ideas. He believed nationalizations were impractical and inopportune. His aim was to establish a market economy in the West of Germany with a much diminished role for the state. In foreign policy matters he respected the security interests of the Western powers and was convinced of the need for a Western alliance to defend the West against Communism. He saw no secure future for a non-allied Germany, which was the alternative favoured by the left-leaning Jakob Kaiser and the SPD. A German government could only regain some room for manoeuvre when it was governing a country firmly integrated within the West, and he also supported the idea of a new German capital in the Western occupied zone. Germany's heavy industries should also be linked with those elsewhere in Western Europe.

The rapid improvement in the German economy and change in attitudes within West German society after the currency reform of 1948 played an even more decisive role for the CDU. Ludwig Erhard, who had fought successfully for currency reform and had been the leading figure in formulating economic policies in the British-American bizone (but who only became a party member in 1949), became its most influential figure on economic policy and later Adenauer's popular and long serving Economics Minister. The Düsseldorf principles which underpinned the CDU's policies in the preparatory stage of the first *Bundestag* election, stressed the advantages of a "social market economy". In contrast to earlier debates in the party, control of the productive sector of the economy was no longer envisaged. The party opted instead for an *ex post* corrective function of the state, with the necessary social policy measures to complement the market economy.

The CDU was a government party even before it had its first party congress in Goslar in 1950. Government practice thus prevailed over theoretical policy-making. Konrad Adenauer, the party's first Chancellor, was an authoritarian leader whose successes bridged policy conflicts. Ideology was thus played down until the 1960s.

Not until Ludwig Erhard took over the offices of Chancellor in 1963, was a new effort made by the CDU to set out its vision of the society that it wanted. Against an uncontrolled and destructive social pluralism, Erhard set his model of a harmonized society (*formierte Gesellschaft*), whose task it would be to secure the priority of the common good over the wishes of special interest groups.

In 1966 the CDU entered a Grand Coalition with the SPD after Erhard's former coalition with the FDP had fallen apart. The CDU no longer defended Erhard's concept, which was regarded as backward-looking. Pluralism in society was now accepted as a fact of life and Keynesian demand management and its instruments were given preference over Erhard's neo-liberalism in economic policies. The broad debate in West German society over democratic participation in the wake of the student rebellion, also affected the CDU. In 1968 it adopted the Berlin programme, the first party programme that had been debated at all levels of the party organization. Its main aim was to increase the party's profile within the Grand Coalition in discussions over reform of education, health and social policies. The Berlin programme remained uncompromising, however, as regards the Federal Republic's relationship with the GDR (the GDR should not be recognized as a separate state) and in its opposition to a further extension of co-determination arrangements in industry.

Only after the CDU went into opposition after 1969, was the character of the party transformed. Greater stress was now laid on party reorganization and on the reformulation of policies to give the party a sharper profile. Not before the party's 1972 electoral defeat, however, was its leadership prepared to admit that its role as an opposition party might be of a longer lasting nature.

Following a decision at the 1973 Hamburg party congress, a programme committee headed by Richard von Weizsäcker initiated a more thorough debate on the party's basic values. At the Mannheim party congress in 1975 Heiner Geissler (a *Land* minister for social security who in 1977 became the party's general secretary), put forward the problem of the "New Social Conflict" (*Neue Soziale Frage*) as a major concern of the party. This conflict was seen as one between those social groups in German society whose interests were well looked after by organized lobbies, and the forgotten fringe groups (the old, the disabled, foreign workers). The SPD government was accused of having neglected the latter group.

At its Ludwigshafen congress in 1978 the CDU adopted a new programme, which spelt out the basic values and fundamental policies of the party. The prospect of staying out of government for the foreseeable future led to a new debate on strategy. One group, represented by the CSU leader Franz-Josef Strauss, by Alfred Dregger (then party chairman in Hesse) and Hans Filbinger (then head of state in Baden-Württemberg) saw the FDP in long-term alliance with the SPD and they thus sought an all-out confrontation on the issue of freedom (CDU/CSU) against socialist (SPD/FDP), with the strategic aim of eliminating the FDP as a political competitor. This strategy failed in 1980 when Strauss was made the Christian Democratic candidate for the chancellorship, and lost the election.

Helmut Kohl led the second group, whose strategy was to maintain a good relationship with the FDP and to make every effort to win the Liberal Party over as a coalition partner. This strategy finally succeeded in 1982 when the FDP left the coalition with the Social Democrats and elected Helmut Kohl as Chancellor. The new coalition of CDU/CSU and FDP has lasted until the present day.

Support

The CDU still has its largest majorities in rural communities (especially among the self-employed) and in areas with high percentages of Catholics. The CDU is confronted, however, with the withering away of traditional voting patterns, and is increasingly reliant on volatile middle class support. The CDU's greatest strength is in the South of Germany. It has held an absolute majority in Baden-Württemberg since 1972 and is in coalition governments with the FDP in Rhineland-Palatinate, Hesse and Lower Saxony. The CDU won lower Saxony from the SPD in the 1970s and Berlin for a short time in the 1980s. It has fewer strongholds with absolute majorities of up to 65 per cent than the Bavarian

CSU. A particular stronghold for the CDU is Cloppenburg-Vechta (Lower Saxony) where the party gained 66 per cent of the vote in 1987. No less than a quarter of the CDU's membership consists of the self-employed, whereas the party is under-represented among workers. In the party organizations of Schleswig-Holstein, Lower Saxony and Westfalen-Lippe there is a strong over-representation of farmers. One third of the CDU members work in church organizations (SPD: 2 per cent). The party membership includes more Catholics (59 per cent) than Protestants (34 per cent). The party is still generally stronger among the more economically successful. (See table 4.)

Organization

The modernized CDU apparatus is today much better organized than it was in the fifties or the sixties, benefiting, in particular, from a restructuring during its years of opposition. In 1973 the new party chairman Helmut Kohl and its then general secretary Kurt Biedenkopf started to centralize the party organization. The *Land* parties were made responsible to the party headquarters in Bonn, which developed its role as a centre for policy formulation, as a service centre for party activities at lower levels, and for systematic support for, and placing of, party members in vacancies for public offices. The CDU headquarters has more than 200 employees. Annual costs for the headquarters rose by 378.9 per cent between 1968 and 1977 (over the period of intense reorganization).

The party organization was also restructured at the local level. In 1982 the CDU had 251 district organizations (*Kreisverbände*), 2,706 municipal and municipal district organizations (*Stadt- und Gemeindebezirksverbände*), and 6,195 local organizations (*Ortsverbände*). The party reorganization undertaken at the 1975 Mann-

---

4. Social structure of the CDU party membership (in %)

	1955	1956	Dec. 1964	Oct. 1968	Sept. 1973	May 1978	1984
Workers	15	10	14.5	13.1	11	10.7	8.8
Employees	18	} 38	19.8	16.9	26	24.4	26.9
Civil servants	9		10.9	15.8	13	12.3	9.7
Self-employed	38	39	37.1	32.8	38	25.4	21.1
Pensioners	7	5	—	14.2	6	5.2	4.1
Housewives	13	7	—	6.6	8	10.4	12.3
Students	—	—	—	0.5	5	6.6	2.1
Others	—	—	17.5	—	3	2.0	2.0

Source: Klaus von Beyme: *Das politische System der Bundesrepublik Deutschland*, Munich: Piper, 5th edition 1987, p. 73.

heim party congress included the gradual phasing out of the *Ortsverbände* and the strengthening of the role of its municipal organizations. These were to develop into additional service centres to support the work of the district organizations. For its political work at the regional level, the CDU has established its *Landesverbände*. Their shape is in some cases identical with the *Länder* (for example Schleswig-Holstein, Baden-Wüttemberg), but in other cases they are based on older historical traditions (for example Oldenburg, Braunschweig, Westfalen-Lippe). In addition to its 13 *Landesverbände* the CDU also has an organization for the CDU in exile, the Christian Democrats of *Mitteldeutschland*, by which is meant the territory of the GDR.

Decisions of the party at the federal level are made by the biannual party congress consisting of 750 delegates of the regions elected at the municipal, district or regional level, the honorary chairpersons of the CDU and 30 delegates of the CDU in exile. In addition to the congress there is a permanent steering committee (*Bundesausschuss*) of 140 members, often called the "small party congress". It consists of regional delegates (whose number depends on the strength of their respective party membership), eight delegates from the CDU in exile, the party executive, one representative of every working group in the party and the chairpersons of the policy committees of the party executive. Control of the executive is one of the steering committee's key tasks.

The party executive has 32 members. This is still too large a unit to conduct day-to-day business, which is thus entrusted to the governing body of the party, its *Präsidium*. The CDU has specialized working groups (*Bundesvereinigungen*) to work among special social groups, like the old, the young, workers, employers etc. In contrast to similar organizations in the SPD, one does not have to be a member of the party in order to become a member of one of these groups. A new development in the CDU's organizational structure is the party's commercial branch. In 1987 the CDU founded a computer software firm (*Dico-Soft*), which offers services for organizational work.

Candidates for the first and second vote at general elections are selected by the CDU in a similar way to within the SPD. Occasionally a constituency candidate is elected by direct vote of all party members without making use of the delegates' system. The party's European MPs are members of the European People's Party. The links between the national and European parliamentarians are co-ordinated at a number of levels. There is a working group on "European policies", which is part of the parliamentary party's International Politics Group. The chairman of the CDU/CSU group in the European People's Party has the right to participate at meetings of the leadership of the CDU/CSU parliamentary party in the *Bundestag*. Once a year there is a joint meeting of the CDU/CSU group in the European Parliament and the *Bundestag* party. National party specialists in particular policy fields have been named as co-ordinators responsible for the exchange of information with their counterparts of the European Parliament. A European Affairs Office acts as a support structure for policy co-ordination between both groups.

The CDU is also a member of the European Union of Christian Democrats and the Christian Democratic International, as well as of the European and International Democratic Unions.

In the fifties the CDU was mainly dependent on financial contributions from industry. As a result of the party reorganization during the period of opposition, and because of membership drives, membership fees became a more important element of total party income. The party finance scandal of the eighties which exposed several industrialists, made them more careful when giving donations. Today, the CDU and its political foundation, the *Konrad-Adenauer-Stiftung*, rely heavily on state funding. For 1987 the CDU's income was DM198,524 million. Membership fees and regular contributions to the party's central fund made up 44.1 per cent of its income. Three per cent came from dividends for party assets, 4.5 per cent was income from other party activities. Financial donations from sources outside the party made up 15.5 per cent of the CDU budget. The party organization at the subnational level contributed 2.8 per cent of the CDU's income, whereas the lion's share of contributions other than membership fees was provided by state funding which accounted for 30.1 per cent of the party's finances.

Policies

The policies of the Kohl government have their main theoretical basis in the party's *Ludwigshafen* programme of 1978. In this programme, the party defined itself as a catch-all party of Christian inspiration, and including social, liberal and conservative tendencies. The basic values underlined by the party are freedom, solidarity and justice. Important aspects of freedom are individual responsibility (which reduces the state to a back-up role), and its defence against its internal and external enemies. Solidarity means a guaranteed social safety net. Justice means fair chances for all and the responsibility of the state for those who fall too far behind.

The institution of the family has a special place in the CDU's programme, and is seen as the basis on which the whole of society is built. Combined with the state's support for the family is the idea that the state should do its best to stop the decline in birth rates.

Workers and employers should work in partnership. The economic order favoured by the party is the social market economy. The state has the duty to guarantee a healthy mix of small, medium-sized and big enterprises. Private property is one of the cornerstones of the social market economy. The CDU asks the individual citizen to accept his or her responsibility to those external effects of the market economy which are destructive of the environment.

The CDU believes that the state has taken on too many services, thus creating an over-dependency upon it of the individual citizen. It is, therefore, necessary to reduce the social, bureaucratic and financial costs incurred by the state and to extend the scope of the social market economy. Deficits in the state budget should be paid for by economic growth, which is to be promoted by tax reductions.

In the field of international politics, the CDU's *Ludwigshafen* programme accepted *Ost-politik*. The party also stresses, however, that the problem of the division of Germany remains on the political agenda. The CDU wants a united and federalist Europe based on the subsidiarity principle, and has voted to ratify the Single European Act. In defence policies, the party is a strong supporter of the NATO alliance and of a close relationship with the United States.

The CDU in government has tried to for-mulate its policies within the framework of the *Ludwigshafen* party document, but there has also been a considerable degree of independent policy development by the cabinet. In foreign policy a conflict developed between hardliners (*Stahlhelm-Fraktion*) and wets (*Genscheristen*) over the *détente* policies of the liberal Foreign Minister Genscher, a conflict which became less sharp after negotiations between the superpow-ers had begun. That there are two competing concepts of foreign policy within the party was also demonstrated by the party divisions over the public statements of support for the Chilean opposition by Norbert Blüm and Heiner Geissler (respectively, a minister and the general secretary of the party).

One key economic policy aim is the reduc-tion of the growth rate of the budget deficit. The policies of the government have favoured medium-sized and small enterprises and have given general incentives for investments by industry through tax relief. Direct taxes have also been reduced for consumers whereas indi-rect taxes have been increased.

In the field of social policy there have been reforms in state health and social secu-rity provisions in order to cut down costs. The labour market has been given additional flexibility through partial deregulation. State programmes for cheap housing now enjoy a very low priority, but the market was to some degree deregulated here, too, in order to attract new private investment. Privatization has made little headway. The Post Office will be divided in three independent units, but its services (telecommunications, banking, other services), will remain under state control.

With regard to law and order policies the conservative wing in the CDU, supported by the CSU, succeeded in enacting a number of tough measures to fight terrorism and civil dis-obedience. The hardliners in this field have not been successful, however, in making abortion illegal.

In technology policy the CDU supports international space projects and other co-operative efforts at the European level and through bilateral contacts with the United States. Co-operation with the countries of the Third World has been put into a new framework giving priority to contacts with those third world countries which are important for German exports.

During the 1987 general election campaign, divisions opened up over future party strategy. The party's general secretary Heiner Geissler sees the FDP in one political camp with the Christian Democrats, a camp which is in confrontation with the united red and green opposition. To win majorities it is necessary, he believes, to win over the volatile vote in the middle of the political spectrum. Such voters should be offered a liberal, progressive CDU to prevent them from joining the ranks of the opposition. Geissler's opponents do not believe that the political landscape is divided into political camps. They think that a more radical profile (a more conservative one) would attract voters, who would be able to see more clearly what the party really stands for. Such a strategy would also prevent the erosion of the party's right-wing, and perhaps even free the CDU from its dependency upon the FDP. An aggressive strategy against the FDP would, however, be impossible, if Geissler's analysis was correct and the FDP was just another "wing" of the CDU-led political camp.

Personalities

The party chairman and Chancellor is Helmut

Kohl. The CDU/CSU parliamentary party is led by Alfred Dregger. The Speaker of the *Bundestag* is Rita Süssmuth, who became well-known for her campaign against AIDS when she was Health Minister. Another CDU member is Richard von Weizsäcker, who is the Federal President. Current CDU ministers besides these are Wolfgang Schäuble (head of the Chancellor's office), Finance Minister Gerhard Stoltenberg, Dorothee Wilms (Relations with the GDR), Norbert Blüm (Employment and Social Security), Rupert Scholz (Defence), Ursula Lehr (Youth, Family, Health, Women), Klaus Töpfer (Environmental Protection and Security of Atomic Reactors), Christian Schwarz-Schilling (Post Office and Telecommunications), and Heinz Reisenhuber (Research and Technology). The heads of CDU-led *Länder* governments are Lothar Späth (Baden-Württemberg), Carl-Ludwig Wagner (Rhineland-Palatinate), Walter Wallmann (Hesse) Ernst Albrecht (Lower Saxony).

Christlich Soziale Union in Bayern — CSU
(Bavarian Christian Social Union)

Headquarters	: CSU-Landesleitung, Nymphenburger Strasse 64-66, 8000 München 2 (tel: 1 24 31)
Chairman	: Theo Waigel
Vice-chairpersons	: Franz Heubl, Friedrich Zimmermann, Jürgen Warnke, Mathilde Berghofer-Weichner
General secretary	: Erwin Huber
Chief administrator	: Manfred Baumgärtel
Youth group	: *Junge Union Bayern*
Women's group	: *Frauen-Union de CSU*
Workers' group	: *Arbeitnehmer-Union (CSA) der CSU*
Groups for the self-employed	: *Arbeitsgemeinschaft Landwirtschaft der CSU* (farmers)
	: *Arbeitsgemeinschaft Mittelstand der CSU* (small and medium-sized firms)
Group for those exiled after World War II	: *Union der Vertriebenen/Ost- und Mitteldeutsche Vereinigung der CSU*
Newspaper	: *Bayern-Kurier*

Members	: 184,293
Founded	: 1945 (1946)

History

The CSU is a regional party, which competes in elections only in Bavaria, but which also seeks to play a role in federal politics in its own right. The CSU is granted the same access to resources and representation enjoyed by other national parties. It has an agreement with the CDU, who together form a united Parliamentary Party in the *Bundestag*, which does not allow the CDU to compete at general elections in Bavaria and which restricts the CSU activities to Bavaria.

This double role of the party, which is part of the West German Christian Democratic Movement, but has, at the same time, a specific Bavarian character, developed after the war, mainly because of the survival of a distinct Bavarian political identity. When the party was founded in 1945, it could build on the traditions of the Weimar Bavarian People's Party. It sought, nevertheless, to be more than just an interest group for Catholic Bavaria. The party's aim was to unite political Protestantism and political Catholicism. Its programme was inspired by Christian ethics and the need for social justice.

5. Election results for the CSU in Bavaria at Bavarian and general elections

	Election to the Landtag		Election to the Bundestag	
	Votes in %	Seats	Votes in %	Seats
1946	52.3	104*		
1949			29.2	24
1950	27.4	64		
1953			47.8	52
1954	38.0	83		
1957			57.2	53
1958	45.6	101		
1961			54.9	50
1962	47.5	108*		
1965			55.6	49
1966	48.1	110*		
1969			54.4	49
1970	56.4	124*		
1972			55.1	48
1974	62.1	132*		
1976			60.0	53
1978	59.1	129*		
1980			57.6	52
1982	58.3	133*		
1983			59.5	53
1986	55.8	128*		
1987			55.2	49

* = absolute majority in the Landtag

The first party chairman was Josef (Ochsen-sepp) Müller (from May 1946 till May 1949). He led the liberal-conservative wing of the CSU which wanted to develop it as a Christian party with a mass organization. In this he was supported by, among others, Michael Horlacher, Wilhelm Eichhorn, Heinrich Krehle, and Franz Steber. A second group in the party included Fritz Schäffer as one of its most important figures. Schäffer was given the office of Bavarian head of state by the Americans for some months in 1945 and later was Finance Minister (from 1949 to 1957) and Justice Minister (1957–1967) in Konrad Adenauer's Cabinets. He and Alois Hundhammer, Walter von Miller, Josef Baumgartner and Carl Lachbauer wanted to turn the CSU into a regional Bavarian and Catholic party, relying for its success on the control it exerted over the state apparatus. This group also sought a closer identity of the CSU with farming interests, in a *Land* which was still predominantly agrarian in its economic structure.

From the start strong forces within the CSU were opposed to Müller's readiness to co-operate with Christian Democrats in other German regions. The first party congress in 1946 voted against any integration of the CSU within a broader framework of a national Christian party, a position which did not change when the CDU united at the national level in 1950. Within Bavaria itself the CSU had, during its first years, to resist the challenge of its rival Bavarian Party (BP), which was not licensed by the American forces until 1946, but then tried to present itself as the more Bavarian of the two parties. In a way this turned out to be a handicap for its future development as it made no progress outside the Southern Catholic Bavarian core regions. In the Bavarian Protestant North and in Franconia in general the BP was almost non-existent. In 1948 the popular Baumgartner, who had left the CSU, was elected as chairman of the BP, which then strengthened the party's appeal. The CSU was at this time in a deep crisis, as shown by its worst ever election results in 1949 and in 1950. Müller's ideal of a broad-based mass party seemed to promise no success in a *Land* in which political life was still controlled by local factors and personalities.

In 1949 Hans Ehard, the Bavarian head of state, took over as CSU party chairman. He led the party until 1955. Under Ehard the party was closely linked with the Bavarian state administration, which he controlled. His chairmanship strengthened the party and gave it more coherence, but party organization remained loose and it remained a union of locally influential personalities with their own personal followings. Nevertheless the CSU's appeal again became much broader than that of the BP, which had lost much of its momentum after the question of autonomy for Bavaria had finally been settled by West Germany's federal constitution.

Although the BP then participated in Bavarian coalition governments (thus temporarily halting its decline) its final defeat and the integration of its electorate into the ranks of the CSU was accelerated by a scandal, in which the BP ministers of the coalition were involved. They were accused of corrupt practices when, for the first time (and against the opposition of the CSU) casinos were licensed in Bavaria. The CSU's successful campaign against this decision even brought the BP into disrepute among its traditional supporters, the Catholic Church and the farmers' organization.

The short period in which the CSU was in opposition (between 1954 and 1957) was one in which the party was reorganized. After 1955 it was led by Hanns Seidel who wrote a new programme for the party and gave it a new framework for its policies. As Bavarian head of state after 1957 Seidel also promoted the *Land's* industrialization. The CSU ceased to be a party mainly oriented towards safeguarding the Bavarian heritage and accepted the challenges of social change.

The modernization of Bavaria blurred the religious and social differences between the core area in the South and the rest of the *Land*, and allowed the party to become the major political force everywhere in Bavaria. In this process the CSU and the Bavarian state became more and more synonymous. Since 1962 the CSU has had an absolute majority in the Bavarian *Landtag*.

Hanns Seidel's successor as Bavarian head of state was Alfons Goppel, who governed the *Land* from 1962 till 1978. His successor as party chairman was Franz-Josef Strauss, who led the party from March 1961 until his death in October 1988, and became the most important representative of the party in Bonn. He was Minister for Research in Atomic Energy in 1955 and Minister of Defence from 1956–1963 in Adenauer's Cabinets. He had to leave the latter post because of his role in the *Spiegel* affair, in which the news magazine *Der Spiegel* was the victim of a raid by the Ministry of Defence after an article it published on a defence issue, which was interpreted by the Ministry as treasonous. Strauss was back in government in 1966 as Finance Minister within the Grand Coalition. In 1978 he "retired" to the office of head of state in Bavaria. Although he was offered several ministries (though not the FDP-held foreign office which Strauss wanted) after the conservatives' return to power, he did not join Helmut Kohl's government. From his position as Bavarian leader outside the Cabinet he could make optimal use of the CSU's double role in German politics. On the one hand he put pressure on Bonn as the champion of true Bavarian interests and true blue conservatism, and on the other hand was able to directly influence coalition policy agreements, even intervening regularly to correct policy decisions that he disliked.

A moment of particular tension between the CDU and the CSU came in 1976 over the best strategy for a return to power in Bonn. The CSU wanted more confrontation, especially with the FDP and decided at a conference of its inner circle in Wildbad Kreuth to leave the common parliamentary party of the CDU and CSU in the *Bundestag*. This move also implied the threat of an extension of the CSU into other parts of Germany, where friends of the CSU were experimenting with fourth party models (*Aktionsgemeinschaft Vierte Partei*). The CDU

reacted with the counter-threat of a CDU branch in Bavaria. In the end the CSU revoked its decision. Its leadership realized that a national CSU might be in danger of losing its absolute majority in Bavaria, as the CSU membership reacted far less enthusiastically to the plans of the party leadership than had been expected. After the death of Franz-Josef Strauss in 1988 the new leadership of the party definitively ruled out a new Kreuth.

Support

The changes in the party's support structure reflect the extension of the party's role from a mainly Catholic, agrarian and conservative force to the Bavarian state party of the seventies and the eighties. Generally speaking the CSU has its special strength in the same social groups as the CDU. In the seventies it has also increased its membership among those employed in industry and among civil servants.

The CSU has more electoral strongholds than

6. Social structure of the CSU party membership

	31.12.1981 total	in %	21.12.1976 in %
male	151,891	86.6	88.1
female	23,404	13.4	11.9
Catholic	139,141	82.2	84.3
Protestant	29,134	17.2	15.0
under 29	15,292	8.8	11.3
30–44	62,832	35.9	37.0
45–59	58,265	33.3	30.3
60 and older	38,509	22.0	21.3
Years in the party:			
0–10	111,649	64.7	69.3
11–20	42,178	24.5	21.0
21–30	15,545	9.0	7.0
31–35	3,079	1.8	2.7
Workers*	25,681	18.4	17.7
Employees*	38,791	27.8	25.3
Civil servants*	21,872	15.7	15.6
Farmers*	22,516	16.2	19.1
Self-employed and professions*	28,830	20.7	20.5
Family members helping in the family business*	1,692	1.2	1.7
Pensioners	7,979	4.9	6.8
Housewives	8,385	5.1	4.7
Students	7,593	4.6	4.1

*percentages refer to the CSU-membership in employment whereas the other percentages refer to the total membership of the CSU.

Source: Alf Mintzel: *Die Christlich-Soziale Union in Bayern* e.v., in: Richard Stöss (ed.): *Parteienhandbuch*, Vol. 1, Opladen: Westdeutscher Verlag, 1983, (661–718), S. 710.

the CDU. Four of the five best constituency results for the Christian Democrats at the 1987 elections were secured by the CSU, namely Bad-Kissingen (65.4 per cent), Deggendorf (65 per cent), Rottal-Inn (65 per cent) and Straubing (64.4 per cent). (See tables 5 and 6.)

Organization

The CSU has organizational units at local level (*Ortsverbände*), district level (*Kreisverbände*), regional level (*Bezirksverbände*) and *Land* level (*Landesverband*). There are 10 *Bezirksverbände*, more than 100 *Kreisverbände* and almost 3,000 *Ortsverbände*. The organizational structure of the CSU is, in its main features, parallel to the administrative structure of the Bavarian state. Seven of its ten regional organizations are identical with the seven Bavarian regional administrative units: Oberfranken, Mittlefranken, Unterfranken, Schwaben, Oberpfalz, Oberbayern and Niederbayern. In addition there are three *Bezirksverbände* for metropolitan agglomerations: Augsburg, Nürnberg-Fürth and Munich.

Between 1946 and 1968 the only task of the party congress, whose delegates often represented the party without prior elections at the lower level, was to elect a party chairman. The organizational reform, forced on the party by the 1967 Bundestag law that laid down a set of requirements for democratic parties within the Federal Republic, led to changes in the party structure.

The CSU now has a party organization that is similar to that of other German parties. It has working groups with the same function as those in the CSU, with particularly strong organization among farmers, small firms and the self-employed. The CSU's party congress, with its more than 1,020 delegates, decides on the policies and the programme of the party, and elects its executive. Elections to party offices are held biannually. Besides the party congress there is also a smaller party council (*Parteiausschuss*), which controls the work of the CSU-MPs in the *Bundestag* and in the Bavarian parliament. Day-to-day business of the party is assured by the party executive (with no more than 46 members) and the 19-member-strong governing body of the party, the *Präsidium*.

Candidates for European elections are elected by a special conference of delegates selected at all levels of the party organization. Candidates for *Bundestag* elections for the first vote are selected at constituency level by 60 delegates at a district party meeting. Candidates for the second vote are put on a list by a *Land* party conference. The party's European MPs are members of the European People's Party. The CSU is also in the European Christian Democratic Union, Christian Democratic International, and European and International Democratic Unions.

Like the CDU, the CSU used to be seen by industry as its natural ally, with the result that it received financial support from this source in the first decades of its existence. Donations from industry still play a major role for CSU finances. Nevertheless state funding has gained considerably in importance for the party and its political foundation, the *Hanns-Seidel-Stiftung*. In 1987 the CSU's income was DM49,525 million. Membership fees and regular contributions to the party's central fund made up 29 per cent of its income. 1.5 per cent from dividends for party assets, and 3 per cent were income from other party activities. Financial donations from sources outside the party made up 29.2 per cent of the CSU budget (CDU: 15.5 per cent, SPD 9.4 per cent). The party organization at the sub-national level contributed 2.5 per cent to the party's funds. Most of the money for the CSU came from state funding (34.8 per cent).

Policies

The CSU is the most conservative of the parties in the *Bundestag*, and is generally more conservative than its CDU ally. The CSU has adopted four major policy programmes since it was founded, in 1946, 1957, 1968 and 1976. The 1976 programme defines the CSU as a Christian catch-all party; conservative, because it stands for the defence of traditional Christian values, and liberal because it upholds personal liberty. The CSU also describes itself as a social-minded party which cares for the weak and wants a just society.

The CSU favours a strong state in the field of law and order. In general, however, the party seeks a reduced role for the state. The CSU is in favour of privatization and decentralization.

The party's main economic aim is the strengthening of the social market economy. Personal freedom is seen as being logically connected with private property and economic freedom. The CSU warns against the dangers for economic growth posed by an oversized state sector and unreasonable demands by social groups (the unions). The party praises the role of small and medium-sized firms in the economy, and farmers are guaranteed an increase in their incomes in order to keep up with increases of incomes for other social groups.

The idea that the family has to be given priority over all other forms of social organization is also to be found in the CSU's programme, though this has a less prominent place in the programme of the CSU than in that of the CDU. The CSU is in favour of new technological developments, and supports product innovation. Environmental problems should be controlled at the planning stage.

In the field of foreign policy, the CSU warns against blind faith in *détente*. The party believes that this has led to too many concessions to the East, without the East having to make substantial concessions on its own part. Only a strong NATO alliance is able to guarantee the independence and security of Western Europe. In addition, the party stresses that German unity has to remain as a topic on the political agenda.

Like the CDU, the CSU has supported a European Union and voted for the Single European Act, although it has emphasized the need to protect Germany's federal structure.

The policies of the party over the last twelve years were above all those laid down by its late chairman Franz-Josef Strauss. He embodied the party in Bavaria, at the national level and abroad. Though both Christian parties, the CDU and the CSU, have a common world view, there have been several conflicts between the parties. Differences of opinion between the two parties were after 1973 very often differences of opinion between the respective party chairmen.

There was disagreement with the CDU, apart from over questions of party strategy, in a number of policy fields, such as foreign policy. Leading representatives of the CDU were ready to actively campaign against violations of human rights in non-communist countries. Strauss criticized their hostile attitudes towards such regimes as the Botha government in South Africa, or that of Pinochet in Chile. Instead of attacking the heads of state in these countries, which he believed was counterproductive in achieving peaceful political change, he preferred political persuasion.

The CSU's policy sometimes brought the party into conflict with the FDP's Foreign Minister Genscher. Strauss did not succeed in unseating his rival, but he exerted some influence on German foreign policy via the Ministry for Economic Co-operation with the Third World, which was headed by CSU Ministers, first by Jürgen Warnke (from 1982 till 1987), and from then on by Hans Klein, who had become known to a wider public as press representative from the 1972 Munich Olympic Games.

Another area of foreign policy on which there have been occasional differences with the CDU has been *Ostpolitik*. Though Strauss accepted the treaties which were the result of the *Ostpolitik*, he retained what he saw as a realistic perception of the aggressiveness of the Soviet Union and the Eastern bloc. This did not prevent him from meeting the heads of states of Communist countries, and thereby carrying out a form of "private" foreign policy. Some of his u-turns in this respect were even difficult for the CSU to accept. When Strauss helped Helmut Kohl's government in 1983 to improve its relationship with the GDR by facilitating a billion Deutschmarks credit to the GDR , there was widespread protest within the CSU. One consequence of this protest was the founding of a conservative party to the right of the CSU in the autumn of the same year, the Republicans (see separate entry). This party, led by former CSU-members, won 3 per cent of the vote at the 1986 Bavarian election. Strauss's readiness to support economic co-operation with the East was not matched by an equal enthusiasm for disarmament co-operation. The CSU protested publicly against the reduction of atomic missiles in Europe, not only because it was not consulted prior to Helmut Kohl's decision to agree, but also because it could not detect any reduction in Soviet military superiority in Europe.

The CSU is of all German parties the strongest champion of the peaceful use of atomic power. The first German nuclear reprocessing plant is being built at the Bavarian site of Wackersdorf. Frequent protests against this plant are perceived by the Bavarian state as a law and order problem. The CSU is ready to demonstrate that internal security can be guaranteed, no matter what the opposition. It also considers that the existing laws against terrorism are too soft. Though this had led to conflicts with the FDP, the CSU's Interior Minister within the Kohl government succeeded in revising a number of internal security laws, to give the state more possibilities to intervene.

In economic policy, the CSU's general support for the market economy has not hindered the party leadership in its active support for the industrialization of Bavaria, whose growth has had a strong military component. Strauss himself did not shy away from an active involvement in industrial policy, for example when he led the lobby for Airbus industries, whose board of directors he chaired. Another area where the CSU government has intervened is agriculture, in which competition has always been given low priority compared to the need to safeguard the interests of Bavarian farmers against hostile plans from Brussels and elsewhere. Another example came in 1988. When indirect taxes were raised (including petrol tax for cars), in order to offset reductions in direct taxation, Strauss insisted on a tax exemption for the petrol of hobby pilots. Though only a minor sum was involved, the conflict over this demand partially overshadowed Helmut Kohl's tax reform programme.

Personalities

After the death of Franz-Josef Strauss in late 1988, Theo Waigel, the chairman of the CSU group in the CDU/CSU parliamentary party, was elected to the office of party chairman in November 1988. The CSU Ministers in Helmut Kohl's Cabinet are: Friedrich Zimmermann (Interior), Ignaz Kiechle (Agriculture), Jürgen Warnke (Transport), Oscar Schneider (Housing and Urban Planning), and Hans (Johnny) Klein (Economic Co-operation with the Third World). Franz-Josef Strauss's successor as Bavarian prime minister is the former Bavarian Finance Minister Max Streibl.

Freie Demokratische Partei — FDP
(Free Democratic Party)

Headquarters	: Thomas-Dehler-Haus, Baunscheidt-strasse 15, 5300 Bonn 1 (tel: 54 70)
Chairman	: Otto Graf Lambsdorff
Vice-chairpersons	: Irmgard Adam-Schwaetzer, Wolfgang Gerhardt, Gerhart Baum
General secretary	: Cornelia Schmalz-Jacobsen
Chief administrator	: Rolf Berndt
Youth group	: *Junge Liberale*
Members	: 64,565
Founded	: 1945 (1948)

History

The importance of the FDP in the party system of the Federal Republic has primarily stemmed from its role as the junior partner in government coalitions. Though the FDP is a relatively small party, it has been able to make or break governments by deciding on its coalition partner. Apart from a short period in opposition at the end of the fifties and during the Grand Coalition, the FDP has been represented in every West German government by three to five ministers, no matter whether the government was led by Christian Democrats or by Social Democrats.

There were two parties in the liberal tradition during the Weimar Republic, the DSP (*Deutsche Staatspartei*, German State Party) on the left and

the DVP (*Deutsche Volkspartei*, German People's Party) on the right, which helped to provide a focus for the post war party's identity. The DVP, which had been founded under the name of *Volkspartei* at Epiphany 1866 in Württemberg (up to the present day at Baden-Württemberg FDP has continued to hold an annual Epiphany meeting of the party), could build on a genuine tradition of political liberalism in this *Land*. In 1945 the DVP was licensed as a political party. It was led by Reinhold Maier (who became the first head of state of Württemberg-Baden and later Baden-Württemberg's first prime minister, and who also led the FDP between 1957 and 1960), by Wolfgang Haussmann and by Theodor Heuss (the first President of the Federal Republic from 1949 till 1959).

In other German regions left or right of centre liberal parties were also organized: for example in Baden the *Deutsche Partei* (German Party), in Südwürttemberg-Hohenzollern the *Demokratische Volkspartei* (Democratic People's Party), in Hamburg the *Partei Freir Demokraten*, in Bremen the *Bremer Demokratische Volkspartei* (Bremen Democratic People's Party), and in addition, the FDP to its left. A prominent representative of the Bavarian FDP was Thomas Dehler, who between 1954 and 1957 became the party's third chairman after Theodor Heuss (1948–49) and Franz Blücher (1950–54). The party in Hesse called itself the *Liberal-Demokratische Partei* (Liberal-Democratic Party). In Rhineland-Palatinate there were at first two liberal parties which merged in 1947 to form the *Demokratische Partei Rheinland-Pfalz*. Berlin was the centre for the LDP (Liberal Democratic Party) which rapidly spread throughout the Soviet occupation zone.

The attempt in 1947 to establish one liberal party for the whole of Germany under the name *Demokratische Partei Deutschlands* (Democratic Party of Germany) failed because of the pressure that the Socialist Unity Party exerted on the Liberals in East Germany to support socialism. A number of LDP members fled to the West, among them Hans-Dietrich Genscher, the Federal Republic's Foreign Minister, who was chairman of the FDP between 1974 and 1984, and Wolfgang Mischnick, who has led the FDP's parliamentary party in the *Bundestag* since 1968.

In December 1948, in Heppenheim (near Heidelberg) all the regional parties within the Western occupation zones met to merge in a newly founded FDP. Their intention was to bridge the gap between the conservative national wing and the socialist-orientated left wing of the liberal movement, which had in the past frequently given rise to party schisms. The FDP was united by its opposition to the CDU's clericalism and its *Rheinbund* (the option for a German state in the West) mentality on the one hand and to the SDP's preference for socialism and planning on the other. It remained divided, however, on questions of the party's identity.

This division gave rise to scandal when (above all in North Rhine-Westphalia and Lower Saxony) former Nazi officials tried to infiltrate the party (Naumann affair: Naumann was the junior minister in Goebbel's propaganda ministry). The resistance of the FDP's leadership to these developments opened up political careers for young technocrats in the North Rhine-Westphalia party, like Erich Mende (from 1960–68 chairman of the party and Vice-Chancellor and Minister for Relations with the GDR between 1963 and 1966), or Walter Scheel (from 1968–74 chairman of the party, from 1969 till 1974 Vice-Chancellor and Foreign Minister, and from 1974–79 President of the Federal Republic).

The FDP had become one of the coalition partners in Adenauer's first Cabinet. A quarrel over the government's decision on the future of the Saarland (Adenauer preferred a European solution instead of a national one) led in 1956 to a party split, with certain FDP ministers, who later founded the FVP (*Freie Volkspartei*, Free People's Party), supporting Adenauer, and the mainstream party joining the opposition. The FDP's major problem at that time was to avoid the fate of other conservative parties, like the DP or the GB-BHE, which were unable to prevent themselves from being absorbed by the CDU/CSU.

In its Berlin programme of 1957, the FDP positioned itself as the "Third Tendency in German politics", its "liberal middle between the extremes". In the 1961 election the FDP's youngish new party chairman Erich Mende campaigned for a coalition between his party and the Christian Democrats, but under a different Chancellor than Adenauer. This strategy led to the FDP winning its best ever election result (12.8 per cent). A compromise with the CDU/CSU after the election allowed Adenauer, who had threatened the FDP with the alternative of a Grand Coalition, to remain Chancellor, but not for the period of the whole Parliament. Mende did not search for a Cabinet post. The FDP was subsequently seen by many as having lacked the courage of its convictions. After 1963 when Erhard succeeded Adenauer as Chancellor, budget problems led to a new conflict in the coalition. The FDP's determined opposition to tax increases forced it to leave the Cabinet in 1966.

During the period of opposition to the Grand Coalition, the FDP developed a new image. It changed its logo from FDP to F.D.P. and presented itself as a reforming party on the issue of *Ostpolitik*, political participation and educational and economic policies (*Hannoveraner Aktionsprogramm* 1967). In 1968 Walter Scheel succeeded Erich Mende as party chairman. The left liberal wing was also reinforced within the party, which showed its willingness to enter into future co-operation with the Social Democrats, through its support for the presidential candidacy of Gustav Heinemann (SPD) in 1969.

Willy Brandt's social-democratic-liberal coalition, which came into existence in the same year, remained however under the threat of backbench revolt from the conservative wing of the FDP, which was not willing to support the new *Ostpolitik*. In 1971 Erich Mende, Heinz Starke and Siegfried Zoglmann left the FDP and joined the CDU/CSU parliamentary party. The FDP's reform wing was then further strengthened, with the party's adoption of the reform-orientated *Freiburger Thesen* (Freiburg manifesto). Further FDP politicians left the parliamentary party, however, and Willy Brandt had to face an early election in 1972, as he had lost his parliamentary majority. The great election victory of the SPD/FDP coalition rewarded the FDR's new line.

During its coalition with the SPD from 1969 till 1982, the FDP tried to develop further its image as the party of *Ostpolitik*, of liberalization, of criminal laws (for example with regard to abortion), and as a strong defender of the market economy against interventionist tendencies in the SPD. Some in the party even saw the coalition between FDP and SPD as a historic coalition between the modern bourgeoisie and the workers, to end class confrontation in a united effort to modernize society. In the more conservative climate of the late seventies it very soon became clear that this was overstating the coalition's potential.

After the mid-1970s the FDP began to co-operate more with the CDU at individual *Land* level. The FDP began to feel that the Schmidt government was putting insufficient emphasis on market forces in tackling Germany's economic problems. Moreover the threat of the Green Party, which was absorbing some of the FDP's support among left-leaning groups in the middle classes, gave the party chairman, Genscher, further reasons for strengthening his personal ties with the CDU leadership. In September 1982 the coalition's Economics Minister, Count Lambsdorff (FDP), presented a paper on the development of further economic policies, whose stress on market liberalism even on social policy questions proved hard for the Social Democrats to accept. Helmut Schmidt decided to govern without the FDP, and to seek an early election. Parliament, however, elected Helmut Kohl (CDU) as Chancellor, with FDP support.

For a brief period of time, this FDP switch in position from the left to the right of the party political spectrum seemed to threaten its very existence. William Born (the honorary chairman of Berlin FDP), Günter Verheugen (the party's general secretary), Andreas von Schöler (a junior minister), Helga Schuchardt and Ingrid Matthäus-Meier were the most prominent members of the party who left it. Most of these dissenters joined the SPD, but some tried to found a new left-leaning Liberal Party, the *Liberale Demokraten* (Liberal Democrats), who were, however, not very successful in the few elections in which they put up candidates. Their best result was 0.43 per cent in Bremen in September 1983, when the main FDP received 4.59 per cent of the vote.

Though the FDP at first experienced great difficulties in securing representation at the *Land* level, and in 1984 lost all its seats in the European Parliament, it slowly recovered from the setback that it had suffered as a consequence of its decision to change coalitions. It succeeded once again in changing its pattern of support and in becoming a party with a more conservative following. In the process it not only changed its programme and leadership when it replaced its former chairman Genscher by Martin Bangemann in 1985, but also replaced its left-leaning youth organization DJD (*Deutsche Jungdemokraten*, German Young Democrats), in which non-party members were also participants, by the *Junge Liberale* (Young Liberals), an association open only to party members. The party's chairman Bangemann, decided in 1988 to give up his position as Economics Minister in Helmut Kohl's government, which he had held since 1984, and to return to Europe as

EC Commissioner. Though Count Lambsdorff was under a cloud after he had had to retire as Economics Minister in 1984, because he had been convicted of illegal activities in a party financing scandal, he succeeded in defeating (albeit narrowly) Irmgard Adam-Schwaetzer to become the party's new chairman in late 1988.

Support

The support pattern of the FDP has changed considerably after its successive switches in coalition partners. Until the mid-1960s the party was strongest among the non-religious "old" middle classes, above all farmers, artisans, small businessmen, employees, and civil servants. After 1969 a new generation of reform-minded academics, higher paid employees and members of the services sector with decision-making responsibilities (the so-called "new" middle classes) joined the FDP. The FDP now became the party of the more highly educated and those with a certain degree of personal freedom at work. After 1982 the party's former support pattern was revived to some extent. An increased number of self-employed and artisans joined the party and it increased its support among senior managers and top civil servants.

The FDP has always been weak among organized labour. In contrast to the fifties and sixties anti-clericalism is no longer an important factor. (See table 7.)

The FDP has its main strength in urban constituencies, especially in those where the economically successful middle classes are concentrated. The party's greatest regional stronghold is still Baden-Württemberg, though less clearly so than in the fifties and sixties. In this *Land* the FDP had its five best constituency election results at the 1987 general election: Stuttgart I (18.1 per cent), Ludwigsburg (15.6 per cent), Waiblingen (15.3 per cent), Nürtingen (15 per cent), and Schwäbisch-Hall (14.8 per cent).

The FDP has profited more than any other

---

7. Social structure of the FDP party electorate (in % of the groups mentioned, at the last four elections)

	1976	1980	1983	1987
Worker, no training	2	6	3	5
Trained worker	6	11	2	4
Employees and civil servants with an average income or less	10	15	4	9
Top civil servants and top employees	14	10	3	18
Self-employed (small and medium-sized firms)	5	13	11	18
Catholics	4	7	5	7
Non-Catholics	11	16	5	7

Source: Forschungsgruppe Wahlen e.v.: Die Konsolidierung der Wende: Eine Analyse der Bundestagswahl 1987, in: Zeitschrift für Parlamentsfragen 18 (1987), (253–284), p. 267f.

8. The FDP as the party of the second vote (% of first votes for other parties compared to FDP second vote decisions)

First votes for:	Second votes for the FDP in				
	1972	*1976*	*1980*	*1983*	*1987*
CDU/CSU	7.9	8.0	13.3	58.3	43.2
SPD	52.9	29.9	35.5	10.1	13.1
FDP	38.2	60.7	48.5	29.1	38.7
Die Grünen	—	—	2.0	1.7	3.2

Source: Eckhard Jesse: *Die Bundestagswahlen von 1972 bis 1987 im Spiegel der repräsentativen Wahlstatistik*, in: *Zeitschrift für Parlamentsfragen* 18 (1987), (212–242), p. 237.

party from the peculiarities of the German electoral system. The FDP systematically campaigns for the "second" (which in the eyes of many voters seems to be the minor) vote, and the party campaigns for the introduction of the second vote-system in those *Länder*, which do not yet have it for their *Land* elections. Both the SPD and the CDU have also asked their supporters on occasion to give their second vote to the FDP, in order to secure the FDP's survival when it was needed as a coalition partner, as in 1972 or in 1983. As the accompanying table shows, the second vote preferences change completely with changes in coalition agreements. Whereas, of those voting FDP with their second vote in 1972 52.9 per cent voted SPD with their first vote, of those supporting the FDP in 1983 58.3 per cent voted CDU/CSU with their constituency vote. (See table 8.)

Organization

The highest authority within the FDP is its annual party congress of 400 delegates. Like the other parties, the FDP also has a "small party congress", its *Bundeshauptausschuss*, which has 144 members, and a party executive for day-to-day business, consisting of its governing body (*Präsidium*), 24 additional elected members, and those FDP members in government or official positions at the federal, *Land* or EC-level. There are also party policy committees (*Bundesfachausschüsse*). The FDP has 11 *Land* associations parallel to the existing *Länder*. The party also organizes at the area (*Bezirk*), district (*Kreis*) and local level (*Ortsverband*). In 1983 the party had 2,300 local organizations. The party has generally had difficulty in developing a mass membership.

Party candidates for elections are selected in the same way as in the other German parties. Because the FDP has not even the slightest chance of winning a constituency, it is relatively easy to become the party's candidate for the first vote. On the other hand there is tough competition for the top positions on a *Land* list for the second vote. The party has at the moment no European MPs. It has been an active member of the European Liberals and Democrats (ELD) (whose secretary-general is a party member) and of the Liberal International. Since 1975 the FDP has had an Office for European Affairs, which assists both the national and European MPs of the party. German Liberal MEPs have the right to participate in the meetings of the national FDP's parliamentary party. The latter has, in addition, established a separate working group on European policies.

Although inhibited by the party finance scandal of the 1980s donations from industry have traditionally been a major source of income for the FDP. Industry not only supported the conservative FDP of the fifties and sixties, but also saw in the FDP a useful brake against socialist experiments during its coalition with the SDP.

Today, the FDP and its *Friedrich-Naumann-Stiftung* rely heavily on state funding. For 1987 the FDP's income was DM45.570 million. Membership fees and regular contributions to the party's central fund made up 19.1 per cent of its income, 0.6 per cent came from dividends for party assets, and 2.2 per cent was income from other party activities. Financial donations from sources outside the party made up 28.6 per cent of the FDP's budget. The party organization at the sub-national level contributed 1.8 per cent of the FDP's income, whereas the lion's share of the party's finances was covered by the state, namely 47.7 per cent.

Policies

The Liberal manifesto of 1985 provides the framework for FDP policies. Its central organizing idea is that of individual freedom and defence of citizens' rights. Society should be based to a greater extent on self-help, help for neighbours and on personal responsibility. The privacy of the individual should be safeguarded with adequate data protection laws. State regulation of the media should be reduced.

According to the Liberal manifesto, every citizen has a responsibility towards the environment. Citizens' action groups should be given the possibility of taking their cause to administrative courts. Protection of the environment should, in the FDP's view, be integrated into the first part of the constitution guaranteeing basic human rights. New technologies are welcomed by the party, not only for environmental protection purposes, but also for the opportunity that they provide for the development of creativity and individuality at the workplace. In the future, the FDP wants work to be tailored more according to individual needs. The deregulation of labour laws is a pre-condition to achieving this objective.

The manifesto describes the market economy as the only mechanism capable of reducing unemployment. More competition has to be brought to the labour market to control high German wage levels. The state should support private investments by reducing its budget deficit and certain state subsidies, and through privatization and deregulation. The FDP wants more support for small and medium-sized enterprises, and to make it easier for individuals to set up their own businesses.

The manifesto seeks a reduced role for the state, with social problems tackled by private initiative, as well as by the state. In contrast to the Christian parties' attitudes, the FDP has no ideological preference for the institution of the family, and wants to give other social units the same legal status.

With regard to constitutional reform the FDP seeks the extension of direct democracy through referenda or the direct election of local mayors. The manifesto advocates controls of the unions, not only because of liberal criticism of their monopoly on the labour market, but also because of fear that they may have too much power in case of industrial conflict. The FDP therefore seeks clearly defined limits to union power in case of strikes.

The FDP supported the Single European Act, but has called for much bolder steps towards full European Union, and a common security and foreign policy.

In its Wiesbaden declaration of October 1988, the FDP made a new effort to define its relationship with the big parties, the SPD and CDU/CSU. Although now in coalition with the CDU/CSU, the FDP defines itself as being equidistant from both big parties. The FDP sees itself as the party of freedom, whereas it characterizes both the CDU/CSU and the SPD as parties with an authoritarian bias. The SPD is authoritarian because it favours state intervention in the economy, the CDU/CSU because they often emphasize law and order at the expense of individual liberty. The FDP sees itself as the only party which is able to combine policies in defence of both civil liberties and economic freedom. The party defends coalitions as pragmatic co-operation for a limited period of time with the aim of finding majorities for what the citizens really want.

Within Helmut Kohl's cabinet the FDP has always been eager to stress dissent in order to prove that it is again playing an independent role. This was easier until autumn 1988 than it is today, because the FDP could rely on the constant attacks of Franz-Josef Strauss (the CSU leader) against the party, and it could counter-attack. After the death of Strauss the FDP's task is more difficult. There are three fields in which the party has tried to establish a distinctive profile:

(1) *Détente*. The FDP's Foreign Minister Genscher is the driving force behind the government's disarmament policies. In this his policies are often closer to what the SPD wants than to the wishes of the CDU/CSU hard liners.

(2) *The strengthening of the market economy*. Here Count Lambsdorff, in particular, is an outspoken critic of state interventionism and too many social policy commitments by the state. He also defends more competition on the markets in a more far-reaching way than many within the CDU/CSU, because they do not want to enter into conflict with special interest groups. Lambsdorff, however, has not always been successful in these policies. He failed to prevent, for example, tax increases, such as the new tax on natural gas, or the merger of Mercedes and MBB.

(3) *Civil liberties*. This is the main emphasis of the left-leaning minority within the party. The defence of civil liberties is mainly entrusted to Gerhart Baum, the party's former home secretary (from 1978 till 1982) and Burkhard Hirsch. Both find it increasingly difficult to muster resistance against the plans of the CSU-led interior ministry.

Personalities

The party's chairman is Otto Graf Lambsdorff. The FDP's parliamentary party is led by Wolfgang Mischnick. The FDP's Ministers in Helmut Kohl's Cabinet are Hans-Dietrich Genscher (Foreign Office), Hans A. Engelhard

(Justice), Helmut Haussmann (Economics), and Jürgen W. Möllemann (Education and Science). The former Federal President, Walter Scheel, is the party's honorary chairman. The party's former chairman and former Economics Minister, Martin Bangemann, is now a member of the EEC Commission. He is also a former chairman of the Liberal Group in the European Parliament.

Die Grünen
(The Green Party)

Headquarters	: Colmanstrasse 36, 5300 Bonn 1 (tel: 69 20 20)
Leadership	: Ruth Hammerbacher Verena Krieger Alph Fücks
Chief administrator	: Eberhard Walde
Members	: 42,500
Founded	: 1980

History

The Greens first emerged locally in the late 1970s, and then developed a national structure. Early speculation that the new party represented a transient protest vote have proved inaccurate, now that the party has secured representation in the *Bundestag* for the second time and is present in many *Länder* parliaments.

The earliest alliances of opposition groups to form Green parties occurred at *Land* level. This development was furthered by the electoral success of the French ecologists in 1977 and the support given by the SPD/FDP coalition for civil nuclear energy in the same year. Green Party organizations were gradually formed with the aim of competing at elections. The idea that priority should be given to ecological over economic needs, was shared by all regional groups, but there was otherwise a great diversity of views among these groups, with support for "green" ideas ranging from traditional Christian conservatives to new left anti-system forces. As a result, Green groups were at the beginning deeply divided over their attitude towards former Communists. At some of the first elections in which the Greens took part, as at the *Land* level in Hamburg and Hesse, there was competition between Green parties of both the right and left.

Several groups tried to unite the Greens by seeking to establish a centralized organizational network. In Lower Saxony the GLU (*Grüne Liste Umweltschutz*, Green List for Environmental Protection), tried to expand its influence into other *Länder*. Herbert Gruhl, a former CDU-MP, organized in 1978 a conservative national Green Party, which he called GAZ (*Grüne Aktion Zukunft*, Green Action for the Future). The AUD (*Aktionsgemeinschaft Unabhängiger Deutscher*, Action Group of Independent Germans), which under their chairman Haussleitner (since 1966) had moved from right-wing nationalism towards supporting the protest movement against the Grand Coalition and citizens' actions groups, also put itself forward as a possible umbrella organization.

The European elections of 1979 provided an important organizational stimulus for the Green Party. The different Green tendencies (AUD, GAZ, GLU, the SH Greens and others) — supported by prominent personalities, like the author Heinrich Böll, the theologian Hellmut Gollwitzer, and the former APO-leader Rudi Dutschke — united to field more than 110 candidates for *Die Grünen*. Among those candidates were Gruhl, Haussleitner, Petra Kelly (a former EC civil servant), Baldur Springmann (a farmer and a leading member of the Schleswig-Holstein Greens), and the artist Joseph Beuys. The party won 3.2 per cent of the vote and failed to overcome the five per cent hurdle. Though it gained no seats in the European Parliament, the party received a substantial campaign reimbursement of DM4.5 million, which consolidated the party's finances. In October 1979 the *Bremer Grün Liste* (Bremen Green List) succeeded as the first political grouping within the Green movement to win seats in a *Land* parliament (four).

An attempt was then made to forge a broad Green coalition to secure representation in the Bundestag. After a preparatory meeting in Offenbach in November 1979, a first party congress of *Die Grünen* met in Karlsruhe in January 1980. One issue which overshadowed the congress were the public statements by conservative Greens that they were not willing to co-operate with former Communists. In the end, the 1,004 delegates at the party congress succeeded in founding the party, in giving a new limited mandate to the executive of the party (which had been elected for the European election campaign), and in accepting the election manifesto for the European elections as a provisional programme.

At its second party congress in Saarbrücken in March 1980, the Greens voted for Haussleitner, Petra Kelly and Norbert Mann as chairpersons with equal competences. The broad coalition from left to right, which had been secured by far-reaching compromises, broke apart at the party's third congress in Dortmund in June 1980, when Herbert Gruhl was not elected as a successor for Haussleitner on the party executive. In October 1981 the conservative wing of the ecological movement united to found its own *Ökologisch-Demokratische Partei* (ÖDP, Ecological and Democratic Party), whose chairman was Herbert Gruhl until February 1989.

Though the Greens were not a very influential force at the 1980 election, which was above all a contest between Helmut Schmidt and Franz-Josef Strauss, the main environmental issues (forest death or *Waldsterben*, nuclear power stations), and the peace issue (deployment of Euro-missiles) remained on the political agenda and provided rallying points for Green politics. The Green Party also benefited from the estrangement of former SPD voters, as a result of Helmut Schmidt's conservative economic policies. Between the elections of 1980 and 1983, the party worked as a new political force in the *Länder* parliaments of Baden-Württemberg, Berlin (*Alternative Liste*, AL), Bremen, Hamburg (*Grüne Alternative Liste*, GAL), Hesse, and Lower Saxony. The party's success in Baden-Württemberg in 1980 was the first proof that the Greens could also be influential at *Land* and not just individual city level, and in areas with a conservative political tradition.

After the general election of 1983, the Green Party entered the *Bundestag* for the first time. The presence of the party in the Federal parliament ensured that its public image was more dependent on the parliamentary party than on its executive. Being an MP was more attractive for the moderate wing of the party which sought to reform the political system, than to the strong forces on the party left who wanted to replace it. The first speakers for the Green parliamentary party were Petra Kelly, Marieluise Beck-Oberdorf and Otto Schily. Joschka Fischer became the party's first administrator of parliamentary affairs. The Greens' presence in the *Bundestag* was anathema to many MPs of the old parties, not only because of the casual clothes they wore, and the flower pots they brought with them, but also because they were regarded as an unreliable democratic force. As a consequence, an all-party coalition against the Greens prevented them from participation in parliamentary control of the secret services and from obtaining an office of vice-president of the *Bundestag*.

Meetings of the Green parliamentary party were open to the public and often chaotic. The decision of the 1983 party congress at Sindelfingen to confirm rotation of Green MPs every two years caused particular unrest within the parliamentary group. One prominent MP, the former NATO general Gert Bastian, left the parliamentary party (until February 1986) over this decision, whereas others, like Petra Kelly, were not prepared to obey it.

In 1984 the parliamentary group elected a new leadership with exclusively female members (*Feminat*): Antje Vollmer, Waltraud Schoppe, Annemarie Borgmann, Christa Nickels, Erika Hickel, and Heidemarie Dann. In January 1985 the party bought a 19th century estate, the *Haus Wittgenstein*, as a meeting place for the party. The last activities of the *Feminat*, including its attempt to start a dialogue with jailed left-wing terrorists of the Red Army Faction (RAF) were the subject of particular criticism. In March 1985 a new leadership for the parliamentary party was chosen (Hannerget Hönes, Sabine Bard, Christian Schmidt, Eberhard Bueb, Axel Vogel, and Uschi Eid), who put a new emphasis on social and employment policies.

The strategic issue of the party's attitude towards the SDP became of increasing importance for the party.

In December 1985 the first Red-Green coalition was formed in Hesse with Joschka Fischer as the party's first Minister (for the Environment). Fischer, a representative of the reformist wing of the party, was criticized by the purists on the left who argued that the coalition with the SPD had forced the Greens to make unacceptable compromises, such as delaying in closing down all nuclear power stations. Fischer found support however, for his policies within the parliamentary party, which was led after 1986 by Hannegret Hönes, Annemarie Borgmann, Ludger Volmer (later Willi Hoss), Axel Vogel, Hans-Werner Senfft, and Uschi Eid. The party executive (Jutta Ditfurth, Rainer Trampert, and Lukas Bechman), with its purist majority, took a different stance.

By the national elections of 1987 the party had secured representation in every *Land* parliament with the exception of North Rhine-Westphalia, the Saarland and Schleswig-Holstein. In this election, the Green Party won 15 additional seats in the *Bundestag*. The party was now led here by Helmut Lippelt, Regula Schmidt-Bott, Christa Vennegerts, Hubert Kleinert and Charlotte Garbe. Most of the succeeding *Land* elections, however, were disappointments for the Greens. Shortly after the 1987 general election, the SPD-Grünen coalition in Hesse fell apart, because of a production permit for a Hanau plutonium firm (Alkem). In Hamburg, the feminist purists who represented the party in the *Land* parliament turned their back on th idea of a Red-Green coalition. The party also seemed to have lost its momentum in the widest sense. The party was shaken by finance scandals in the North Rhine-Westphalia party organization and in Bonn, concerning construction projects for the Haus Wittgenstein. These developments occurred at a time of heightened tensions within the party between its two main wings. Certain reformist Greens, such as Thea Bock in Hamburg, who were active in areas where the purists dominate, left the party. The conflict escalated between the realists (*Realos*) with their strongholds in the parliamentary party and most *Länder*, and the fundamentalist purists (*Fundis*), who dominated the party executive (Jutta Ditfurth, Christian Schmidt, Regina Michalik). A middle group organized by Antje Vollmer (*Aufbruch 88*, Fresh Start 88) tried unsuccessfully to bridge the gap between the two wings. In December 1988 at the Karlsruhe congress to elect the party's candidates for the European election, the delegates showed their dissatisfaction with the role of the purist minority on the party executive, and withdrew the executive's mandate. Until the next election in March 1989 the party was administered by an emergency executive. In the meantime the *Aufbruch* group has been attempting to organize a grass roots vote on future party strategy, in which all members would be given policy papers from each group in the party, and a general vote would then make clear which of them has majority support.

In January 1989 the Green parliamentary party elected new spokespersons, Antje Vollmer and Helmut Lippelt (both from the *Aufbruch* wing) and the *Fundi*, Jutta Oesterle-Schwerin; Otto Schily, the candidate of the *Realos*, was not elected.

The party congress in March 1989 led to greater party unity. The *Fundi* lost influence. The party is now based on a coalition between the *Realos*, Fresh Start and the independent Left.

Support

The active membership of the Green Party has fluctuated considerably. For a long time the party saw itself not only as the main alternative force within German politics, but also as the party of the young. The party has now not only lost its status as the undisputed champion of the interests of spontaneous social movements, but has also acquired an age problem. The need for a youth organization of the party has been discussed, and the party is in the hands of those between 25 and 45 years of age, with many of the party leaders having become politically active in the late 1960s and early 1970s.

The dominant groups in the Green Party electorate are the more educated, higher level employees and civil servants, professionals, those living in towns with between 20,000 and 100,000 inhabitants, and young voters. They are particularly strong in the education and service sectors. The Green Party is thus mobilizing the new middle classes. Green voters are often not directly involved in the production process, which has probably facilitated their critical stance towards new technologies and economic growth. (See table 9.)

At the 1987 general elections, the Green Party won 20 per cent of the vote of those who voted for the first time. This election also demonstrated the concentration of Green support among highly educated, politically interested and informed young voters. The party had its best results in urban areas, many of which are dominated by a local university. It won 19.2 per cent in München-Mitte, 18.4 per cent in Freiburg, 16.2 per cent in Bremen-Ost, 15.5 per cent in Frankfurt III, and 15.1 per cent in Tübingen. Voters for the Green Party put less stress on economic aims, like fighting unemployment, and more on environmentalism and disarmament policies. On issues there was a greater affinity of Green voters with the SPD than with the other parties. The Green vote has also had a strong tactical component, thus increasing the risk that the party may lose its parliamentary representation in a generally hostile political climate.

---

9. Social structure of the Green Party electorate (in % of the groups mentioned, at the last four elections)

	1976	1980	1983	1987
Worker, no training	—	0	1	3
Trained worker	—	0	3	9
Employees and civil servants with an average income or less	—	2	7	10
Top civil servants and top employees	—	1	17	8
Self-employed (small and medium-sized firms)	—	0	2	5
Catholics	—	2	6	6
Non-Catholics	—	2	7	12

Source: Forschungsgruppe Wahlen e.v.: Die Konsolidierung der Wende. Eine Analyse der Bundestagswahl 1987, in: Zeitschrift für Parlamentsfragen 18 (1987), (253–284), p. 267f.

Organization

The Green Party was founded as an anti-party party, not only with regard to its programme, but also to its organization. The party is organized at local, district, area and *Land* level. The party congress is called *Bundesversammlung* (federal assembly). In between party congresses the *Bundeshauptausschuss*, a kind of small party congress, is its highest authority. The party is led by its executive (*Bundesvorstand*) of 17 members, which has three chairpersons of equal status.

There are a number of distinctive Green organizational criteria which make it stand out from other German parties:

(a) The decision-making process in the party is open to the public, and as decentralized as possible, guaranteeing local autonomy. This rule has occasionally led to chaos, however, and to decision-making in informal groups.

(b) No party functionary is allowed to have a second party office or a seat in a parliament. Re-election is only possible on one occasion.

(c) Party functions and seats for the party are to be shared out equally between both sexes. Here the Green Party has been very successful. In 1987, 25 of its 44 elected MPs were female.

(d) Rotation of the parliamentary representatives of the party has been a central principle and was tried out, for example for the *Bundestag*, between 1983 and 1987. It proved, however, to be impractical and has, therefore, been given up.

(e) Party functionaries and representatives are bound by party decisions, and have to justify their decisions in front of the party. In practice this has not prevented the parliamentary parties of the Greens from becoming relatively autonomous from their respective party organizations.

(f) The income of party representatives in public offices is subject to control. A Green MP should not earn more than a skilled worker. The extra money he or she gets, goes to party funds. This has led to conflicts with a number of MPs who felt that they were being treated unfairly, up to the point where prominent MPs, like Petra Kelly, decided on her own income as an MP according to her own interpretation of her needs. The money that MPs hand over goes to eco-funds, which finance alternative projects, like safe houses for battered

women, shops selling natural food, or firms controlled by their employees.

(g) For a long time, the party hesitated to accept state funding for a political foundation, as do the other parties. Only after the Federal Court (reacting to an initiative of the Green Party to ban state funding) had decided that such funding was not illegal, did the party take the decision, at its 1988 party congress in *Ludwigshafen*, to set up its own political foundation. The *Stiftungsverband Regenbogen* (Rainbow Association of Foundations) will comprise three autonomous foundations with equal rights. One will be the Heinrich Böll-foundation, concentrating on the third world, the second will be a women's foundation, and the third will be an umbrella organization for *Länder* foundations.

The Green Party has seven seats in the European Parliament. Its representatives are members of the Rainbow Group, of which they are the largest component. For the 1989 European election the party, which has always tended to use its European candidatures for symbolic purposes, has decided to field a Polish gipsy as its top candidate, Rudko Kawczynski, who is ineligible for election, because he does not have German citizenship.

The party is a member of the European Greens.

Though the Greens are against excessive state funding of political parties, they have greatly profited from the laws on party finance, made by the other parties against their wishes. The state is the most effective source of party income, be it directly or indirectly through the money which goes to Green MPs in parliaments. For 1987, the income of the Green Party was DM64.622 million. Membership fees and regular contributions to the party's central fund made up only 8.6 per cent of its income. Two per cent came from dividends for party assets, 1.6 per cent were income from other party activities. Financial donations from sources outside the party made up 18.3 per cent of the Greens' budget. The party organization at the sub-national level contributed 31.3 per cent to the party's finances, whereas 38.2 per cent of these were covered by direct state funding.

Policies

There have been numerous explanations for the development of a powerful Green Party in Germany. Respective analysts have seen the Green Party:

(a) As the political arm of the so-called

new social movements, those mobilized groups outside the traditional (working class) social movement which campaign on issues neglected by traditional politics, like women's liberation, nuclear disarmament, the environment, or gay rights. In this perspective, the Green Party is a kind of umbrella organization, which is only able to survive when it is stimulated by the new social movements. These analysts believe that if they fail to keep up their momentum, the party will disintegrate, as there is a latent conflict in the double nature of the party as both party and movement.

(b) As the expression at the level of party politics of a new basic cleavage within society, as important as class, religious, or regional divisions. This new social cleavage is seen as the conflict between a growth and zero-growth society, that is between a society which gives priority to economic imperatives in contrast to one which gives priority to ecological needs. If this analysis is correct, this would mean that the existence of the Green Party, or at least the themes that it emphasizes, will be more permanent, because the structural conflict between economy and ecology will remain a problem for society for a long time.

(c) The advent of the Green Party has less convincingly been explained as a reflection of a silent revolution in society, which has replaced materialist by post-materialist values. In this view there are certain strata of society (which will become increasingly dominant in the future), which no longer have any urgent material needs. As their well-being has been secured, they now seek more political participation and are mainly concerned with policy issues, like the protection of the environment. In its sociological version, this analysis sees the Green Party as a middle class phenomenon, if not a fashion. It wrongly assumed that the Green Party would develop into a single-issue movement, not able to cover the traditional fields of politics.

(d) The least convincing explanation is that which sees the Green Party as the expression of cyclically recurring political protest. Certain conservative politicians have thus even compared the Greens with the Nazis. These Green opponents hope that it will thus disappear sooner or later as an anti-system force and will be integrated either as a party or as a social movement into the traditional political consensus.

The Green Party's basic values are:

(a) Harmony with nature by giving priority to criteria of ecological balance over those of economic growth. To achieve this aim, greater social solidarity is regarded as a necessary pre-condition.

(b) A social orientation which seeks the removal of economic exploitation within society.

(c) Grassroots democracy, which means, above all, more decentralized decision-making and self-organization.

(d) No use of force.

The party calls for peaceful means for bringing about political change, which does not, however, exclude civil disobedience.

The programme of the Green Party emphasizes the need for a fundamental reform of the current economic system with its many externalities which are detrimental to the environment. The party wants to strengthen human control over technological developments and their industrial use, and calls for technological progress to result in an increase in human freedom, for example through longer holidays and shorter working hours. A central part of the Green programme is the demand to end civil nuclear energy and to put resources instead into the further development of alternative energy sources. In agriculture, the party calls for chemical to be replaced by ecological production methods. The party's housing policy emphasizes the need to protect local communities and neighbouring spirit, and the development of better housing with more room for children and green parks. Less priority should be given to the car and more money should be invested in public transport.

The Green Party calls for non-military aid for third world countries according to the needs and preferences of the local population. In international politics the party seeks global cooperation to save the environment. It advocates strong disarmament policies, such as weapon-free zones in Eastern and Western Europe, and the prohibition of chemical and biological weapons.

The Greens oppose existing restrictions on civil liberties. They want better career opportunities for women, a better social situation for elderly women, and greater protection for women from getting raped. Mothers and fathers should have equal opportunities to look after their children without financial loss. The party opposes discrimination against fringe groups in society, like migrant workers, gypsies, or gays.

The Greens have also opposed the European

Community in its present form, calling for a neutral, decentralized and federal or confederal Europe of the regions. They oppose a European security policy, and extensions in the powers of the European Parliament. They were the only *Bundestag* party to vote against the Single European Act.

Disagreement about the party's basic programme has seldom been voiced. There seems to be a major difference of opinion only in the party's women's movement, where a conflict has developed between those pro-life women, who want to stress the role of the women as mother (*Müttermanifest*), and those who have feminist (and this includes pro-abortion) views. A more serious division (with the danger of a party split) has developed between the party's pragmatic wing (*Realos*) and the purists (*Fundis*) over party strategy. The latter, a great majority of whom come from New Left groups, have begun to call themselves the party's socialist left. The differences between both groups are difficult to reconcile:

(a) *Fundis* want to close down nuclear power stations immediately, *Realos* are ready to phase out nuclear power step by step.

(b) *Fundis* accept the use of force against the state as long as it is not directed against human beings, *Realos* only accept peaceful civil disobedience.

(c) *Fundis* want the Federal Republic to leave NATO immediately, *Realos* would be content with more disarmament.

(d) *Fundis* are against coalitions with the SPD, *Realos* want Red-Green coalitions.

Personalities

Prominent representatives of the *Realos* wing are Otto Schily, MP, Joschka Fischer (leader of the parliamentary party in Hesse), and Hubert Kleinert MP. The *Fundis* have their centres in Frankfurt: Jutta Ditfurth (the ex-party chairperson), and Hamburg: Thomas Eberman MP, Rainer Trampert, and Christian Schmidt. A new middle group, Fresh Start 88, is led by Antje Vollmer MP.

Other Parties

Deutsche Kommunistische Partei — DKP
(German Communist Party)

Headquarters	: Prinz George Strasse 79, D-4000 Düsseldorf
Chairman	: Herbert Mies
Secretary	: Karl-Heinz Schroeder
Publication	: *Unsere Zeit* ("Our Time") (daily newspaper)

History

This is the successor party to the former Kommunistische Partei Deutschlands (KPD), founded in 1918 by Karl Liebknecht and others including Rosa Luxemburg and Wilhelm Pieck (who later became GDR President). The KPD was the third strongest party in the Weimar Republic, winning, for example, 17 per cent of the vote and 100 seats in the Reichstag elections of 1932.

After 1945 it was reconstituted in all four occupied zones of Germany, later merging with the Social Democrats in the Soviet controlled zone to form the ruling Socialist Unity Party. In West Germany the KPD gained representation in most *Land* parliaments and rejected the new West German Basic Law. It later won 15 seats in the first *Bundestag* elections in 1949. In 1953 it lost these seats, but still held four seats in the Bremen *Land* parliament and two in that of Lower Saxony in 1956, when the party was banned as unconstitutional.

The DKP was formed in 1968 after undertaking to observe the principles of the Basic Law. From 1972 Communists and other left-wing sympathizers were effectively banned from public service employment under the so-called *Berufsverbot* regulations introduced by the then SPD-led federal government. However, these regulations were overruled by two courts in June 1985, following which Saarland became the first state to revoke them.

Support

The DKP has had minimal electoral support since its refoundation in 1968. It only obtained 0.1 per cent of the vote in 1976, and 0.2 per cent in 1980 and 1983. It did not even contest the 1987 federal elections.

Organization

The party's highest authority is its congress, convened every three years and which elects party officials and a party board, which in turn elects a *Präsidium* and a secretariat. The party has local branches on a territorial and work-place basis, and has district as well as area organizations. It is mainly financed by the GDR government.

Policies

The DKP has closely followed the Soviet and GDR line, but is now experiencing serious internal problems because of Gorbachev's *Perestroika* policies, which have been supported by many in the party's grass roots, but less so among the party leadership, which has continued to follow the more cautious GDR line.

Nationaldemokratische Partei Deutschlands — NPD
(National Democratic Party of Germany)

Headquarters	:	Rötestrasse 4, Postfach 2881, D-7000 Stuttgart 1
Chairman	:	Martin Mussgnug
Publication	:	*Klartext* (monthly, *Deutsche Stimme*)
Founded	:	1964

History

The NPD was founded as a national focus for a variety of extreme right splinter groupings, and included neo-Nazi sympathizers. In the 1965 *Bundestag* elections it polled 2 per cent of the vote and in 1969 it was not far short of federal parliamentary representation with 4.3 per cent. In 1966-67 it had gained seats in several *Land* parliaments (eight in Hesse, 15 in Bavaria, four in Schleswig-Holstein, four in Rhineland-Palatinate, 10 in Lower Saxony and eight in Bremen). In 1968 it had gained 12 seats in Baden-Württemberg. It lost all these *Land* seats in 1971–72.

It has since had no parliamentary representation, winning 0.6 per cent in the 1987 *Bundestag* elections. It obtained 6.6% of the vote in the Frankfurt local elections in 1989.

It has recently agreed to a tactical alliance with another extreme right-wing group, the *Deutsche Volksunion* (DVU—see separate entry). Under the label *Liste D* (List Germany) this coalition won 3.4 per cent of the vote and one seat in the Bremen *Land* Assembly in 1987.

Policies

The NPD is an extreme right-wing party. It has emphasized the need to mobilize against the influx of foreigners in Germany.

Deutsche Volksunion — DVU
(German People's Union)

Headquarters	:	Paosastrasse 2, D-8000 Munich 60
Chairman	:	Gerhard Frey

History

This is an extreme right-wing group, which in 1987 made a tactical alliance with the NPD. The DVU/Liste D movement won 3.4 per cent and one seat in the Bremen *Land* Assembly later in the year.

Die Republikaner — REP
(The Republicans)

Headquarters	:	Sandstrasse 41, D-8000 Munich 40
Founded	:	1983

This is a small but growing right-wing party, which was founded by two former CSU *Bundestag* parliamentarians (Franz Handlos and Ekkehard Voigt) who had opposed Franz-Josef Strauss' role in arranging a major loan for the GDR. It was also joined by members of the former *Bürgerpartei* (Citizens Party), led by Hermann Joseph Fredersdorf. Franz Schönhuber later emerged as its main leader.

The REP obtained 3 per cent in the 1986 Bavarian *Landtag* elections, but did not contest the 1987 federal elections. It polled 7.5 per cent (and obtained 11 seats) in the 1989 Berlin *Abgeordnetenhaus* elections, benefiting in particular from a strong protest vote from former CDU supporters. Their campaign was also largely directed against the influx of foreigners. Their success also means that they will be represented in the *Bundestag* after the 1991 elections.

The party has called for the reunification of Germany, environmental protection, lower business taxes, restrictions on foreigners, referenda to be held on major issues and compulsory youth service.

Its current leaders include Franz Schönhuber, a well-known journalist, and its general secretary, Harold Neubauer.

Ökologisch-Demokratische Partei — ÖDP
(Ecological Democratic Party)

Headquarters	:	Friedrich-Ebert-Allee 120, D-5300 Bonn
Federal chairman	:	Hans-Joachim Ritter
Publication	:	*Ökologie und Politik*

This is the successor party to the *Grüne Aktion Zukunft* (GAZ) founded by Dr Gruhl, a former CDU parliamentarian, and which became one of the components of *Die Grünen* (see separate entry). It opposed the left-wing policies event-

474

ually adopted by the Greens, and Dr Gruhl sub-sequently left the Greens to found a new more conservative and pro-life ecological party. It has had little electoral success, only winning 0.3 per cent of the vote in the last *Bundestag* elections in 1987. In 1989 the party split over the future direction of its policies and the more right-wing minority led by Gruhl left the party.

II NON-EC COUNTRIES

Austria

Francis Jacobs

The country

Austria is a country of just over 32,000 square miles with a population of over 7.6 million. It is a Federal State consisting of nine Länder or provinces — Vorarlberg, Tyrol, Salzburg, Oberösterreich (Upper Austria), Niederösterreich (Lower Austria), Kärnten (Carinthia) Steiermark (Styria), Burgenland and Wien (Vienna). Vienna is the capital, and by far the largest city, with around 20 per cent of Austria's population.

Austria is overwhelmingly Germanic in culture and language, but there are a few ethnic minority groups, notably the Slovenes in Carinthia, and the Croats and Magyars in Burgenland. Most Austrians are Catholics.

Map of Austria showing the 9 _Länder_, their capitals and certain other towns.

Source: Carpress.

Political institutions

Austria is a Federal Republic, with a bicameral legislature consisting of the *Nationalrat* (National Assembly) and the *Bundesrat* (Federal Council).

The National Assembly consists of 183 members — elected by proportional representation for four year terms of office, although there is a possibility of earlier dissolution. Each province is a constituency, and is allocated seats on the basis of its population. Seats won directly in the constituencies (using the Hare quota of proportional representation) are called *Grundmandate* (basic seats). Party votes still left over within the

constituencies are then grouped together within one of the two Unions of elected districts (the first consists of Vienna, Lower Austria and Burgenland, the second the rest of the country) and the so-called *Restmandate* (left over seats) are then allocated. Parties are only eligible to receive seats under this second allocation if they have won at least one basic seat. Voters may also express personal preferences, but this only plays a very limited role.

The National Assembly is by far the most powerful of the two Houses of Parliament, and the Federal Chancellor, who is the head of the government, is drawn from within its ranks.

The *Bundesrat*, or Federal Council, consists of 58 members chosen indirectly as a result of party strength in the provincial parliaments. Intended to reflect the provincial dimension in Austrian political life, the Federal Council's weakness (it has only limited delaying powers) reflects the relative weakness of Austrian Federalism. The chairmanship of the Federal Council rotates between the different provinces.

The Federal President is directly elected every six years. If no candidate wins more than 50 per cent in the first round there is a run-off election between the two best placed candidates. The President can be removed by popular referendum but this can only be authorised by a two-thirds majority in the National Assembly. The President's role is primarily ceremonial. Members of the Habsburg family are explicitly barred from standing for the Presidency.

The nine Länder, or provinces, have more limited powers than their equivalents in many other federal states. In particular they have no revenue raising capacity. Each province has its own *Landtag* or Parliament. Vienna has 100 seats in its *Landtag*, Lower Austria, Upper Austria and Styria have 56 seats each and the others all have 36 seats each. The provincial executive is headed by a *Landeshauptmann* or Provincial President. Beneath the provincial tier are the districts (*Bezirke*) and the communes.

A particular feature of Austrian society is the institutionalisation of the major economic interest groups through the three major Chambers of Commerce, Labour and Agriculture. Federal elections for the first two are held

478

every five years. Elections for the Chamber of Agriculture are held at provincial level only.

Austrian constitutional law provides for the holding of popular initiatives, although these have no binding effect. Five such popular initiatives have been undertaken in recent years. Referenda can also be held. In practice only one has taken place, on nuclear energy, in 1978.

There is public funding for political parties. A law in 1975 greatly extended its scope.

Brief political history of Austria

1918–34 First Republic (dominant coalition of Catholic Conservatives and Nationalist Parties. Socialists mainly in opposition and dominate "Red Vienna).

1918 Collapse of Habsburg Austro-Hungarian Empire, creating of a separate Austrian state.

1920 New Constitution.

1929 Constitutional modification.

1934 Brief civil war, crushing of Socialists, Dolfuss ends Parliamentary democracy.

1934–38 Corporatist dictatorship of Dolfuss and Schuschnigg.

1934 Killing of Dolfuss by Nazis.

1938–45 Austrian union with Germany.

1938 *Anschluss*.

1945 Austria taken over by the Allies and divided into four zones of occupation with the Soviets occupying Lower Austria, some of Upper Austria and Burgenland. Vienna under four power control.

1945–66 "Red-Black" coalition between SPÖ and ÖVP (ÖVP provides all Federal Chancellors. *Proporz* system introduced. Socialists provide all Presidents).

1945 Three-party provisional government (SPÖ, ÖVP, KPÖ).

1947 Last KPÖ (Communist) Minister leaves government.

1949 WDU (Nationalist Liberal Party) authorized to stand in elections.

1955 Signing of State Treaty, Austria passes constitutional law providing for permanent neutrality in exchange for withdrawal of all occupying forces.

1966–70 Period of ÖVP majority rule.

1970–72 Period of SPÖ minority rule.

1970 Reform of electoral system (number of National Assembly seats increased from 165 to 183, number of constituencies reduced from 25 to nine).

1971–83 SPÖ majority rule (Kreisky era).

1975 New law of parties provides for greatly increased public funding for political parties.

1983–86 SPÖ-FPÖ coalition (Sinowatz-Steger government).

1986 Waldheim elected first ÖVP President of Austria. Replacement of Sinowatz by Vranitzky as new Federal Chancellor. New elections called after change of leadership within FPÖ.

1986– New "Red-Black" coalition between Present: SPÖ and ÖVP and Franz Vranitzky as Chancellor.

Main features of the Austrian political system

The main features of the Austrian party system since the creation of an independent Austrian state in 1918 have been the division of Austrian society into competing groupings or *Lager*, and the system of consensus and social partnership that has been developed since 1945 in order to overcome these divisions.

Between the two World Wars the *Lagers* were at their height, with Austria divided between Catholic Conservative, Socialist and Nationalist groupings. This was reinforced by a sharp division between the centre and periphery of the small new Austrian state, with the oversized capital of Vienna controlled by the Socialists and the rival areas by the Catholic Conservatives.

In the meantime many pro-German Nationalists questioned Austria's right to exist at all. In 1934 these conflicts led to a brief civil war and in 1938 the *Anschluss* by Germany was welcomed by many Austrians.

Since 1945 the *Lager* system has been considerably modified. The Nationalist *Lager* was greatly reduced in size and a coalition was forged between the Catholic and Socialist *Lagers*. Changes within Austrian society have subsequently had major effects on the system.

The disparities between Vienna and the rest of the country have lessened, the peripheral areas in the West have become much more prosperous, agriculture has become much less dominant and even manufacturing industry has been overtaken in importance by the services sector. The Catholic Church has had a lesser hold on the population, and the traditional Catholic issues such as abortion have not been at the centre of conflict in postwar Austrian politics.

Nevertheless, the old divisions survive in a number of ways, notably in the high level of identification of many Austrians with one or other of the two main parties. The Socialists still win 60–70 per cent of the vote in many industrial communities and many working class areas and the People's Party wins the same percentages in many rural areas. Even more striking is the high level of membership in the two parties, still not far short of 1.5 million or almost 30 per cent of the Austrian electorate.

Possession of a *Parteibuch* (party membership card) is still perceived to be invaluable in obtaining a job or even housing. Moreover the two main parties are still closely linked to the main economic interest groups, the Socialists with the Austrian Trade Union Federation and with the Chambers of Labour, the People's Party with the employers, and with the Chambers of Agriculture and Commerce. Each party, and in particular the Socialists, have a large number of other affiliated organizations, such as Socialist Friends of Nature, and Socialist Automobile Clubs. Real social differences between *Lager* are being steadily undermined, but the effects of past differences still live on.

Since 1945, however, the two main *Lager* have forged a remarkable system of consensus and social partnership that has led to considerable economic achievements and to very low levels of social and industrial conflict.

From 1945 to 1966 there were 20 years of grand coalition between the two main parties, whose effects were reinforced by the system of *Proporz* — of proportional division of public posts between members of the two parties. The corporatist chambers and the socialist partners in general have institutionalized their co-operation with each other, through such mechanisms as the powerful Parity Commission for Prices and Wages, which agreed on broader economic objectives as well as on prices and incomes policy. A high level of consensus on economic policy was obtained.

Since 1966 the system has been modified, with first four years of the People's Party governing on its own, and then 13 years of the Socialists. Nevertheless, the *Proporz* system and much of the apparatus of co-operation survived practically intact. Legislation was still mainly adopted with cross party agreement and economic objectives were still widely shared. In the 1970s Austria appeared to be weathering the world economic crisis very well, with practically full employment and yet relatively low inflation.

At present the system still survives, and since 1986 there has, indeed, been a new grand coalition. Nevertheless, it has been shaken in several ways, by the development of citizens' initiatives and of a strong new environmental movement, by a number of cases of corruption which have appeared to stem from the inherent nature of the system of clientelism and party privileges and perhaps most fundamentally by a growing feeling that Austrian economic management needs to be modified and liberalised. The success in the 1986 election both of the Greens and to an even greater extent of the Freedom Party reflects public concern with the existing system. Within both main parties a struggle is on between party traditionalists (e.g. the unions in the Socialist Party, the farmers in the People's Party) and the modernists who are seeking to appeal to the same sectors within Austrian society, the managers, professionals and new middle classes in the services and white collar sectors.

The main political issues in Austria at present are the following:

General economic management: The system of economic management has had many successes in the past but Austrian economic growth is now faltering, and even unemployment has risen. Above all there is a massive public debt and an increasing burden of tax service. Among the issues which are having to be tackled are:

- cutting public spending
- reforming the Austrian tax system, for example through lower income tax rates and fewer tax exemptions
- reform of the cumbersome pensions system and the general burden of social security in a country with an exceptional number of elderly people
- cutting the level of subsidies, extending privatization and other ways of tackling the inefficiencies of Austria's large nationalized sector which still employs 17.5 per cent of all those employed in Austrian industry.

Whether or not to join the European Community: Is joining the EEC consistent with Austria's continuing neutrality (which is not in question) and how would the Soviet Union react? What would be the impact on the Austrian economy (would it be more dominated, for example, by West German capital?)? Could Austria align itself more closely with the European internal market short of full membership?

National identity and nationalist issues: The Waldheim question: this has opened up a wound about the Austrian past and led to much unfavourable international publicity about Austria. The Greens and some Socialists have called for Waldheim's resignation, but others, irrespective of how they feel about Waldheim's behaviour, have been forced to defend their elected president.

The South Tyrol issue: the question of the

Austrian election results 1945–present (percentages and seats won)

Date of elections to national council	1945	1949	1953	1956	1959	1962	1966	1970	1971	1975	1979	1983	1986
Österreichische Volkspartei (ÖVP) (Austrian People's Party)	49.8% (85)	44.0% (77)	41.3% (74)	46.0% (82)	44.1% (79)	45.4% (81)	48.3% (85)	44.7% (78)	43.1% (80)	42.95% (80)	41.9% (77)	43.2% (81)	41.3% (77)
Sozialistische Partei Österreichs (SPÖ) (Socialist Party of Austria)	44.6% (76)	38.7% (67)	42.1% (73)	43.0% (74)	44.8% (78)	44.0% (76)	42.6% (74)	48.4% (81)	50.0% (93)	51 % (95)	51 % (95)	47.65% (90)	43.1% (80)
Kommunistische Partei Österreichs (KPÖ) (Communist Party of Austria)	5.4% (4)	5.1% (5)	5.3% (4)	4.4% (3)	3.3% (0)	3.0% (0)	0.4% (0)	1 % (0)	1.4% (0)	1.2% (0)	1 % (0)	0.7% (0)	0.7% (0)
Wahlpartei der Unabhängigen (Electoral Party of Independents)	—	11.7% (16)	10.95% (14) (Linksblok Volksopposition)	—	—	—	—	—	—	—	—	—	—
Freiheitliche Partei Österreichs (FPÖ) (Freedom Party of Austria)	—	—	—	6.5% (6)	7.7% (8)	7.05% (8)	5.4% (6)	5.5% (6)	5.45% (10)	5.4% (10)	6.1% (11)	5.0% (12)	9.7% (18)
Grüne Alternativen (Green Alternatives)	—	—	—	—	—	—	—	—	—	—	—	3.3% separate Green Lists (VGÖ-ALÖ)	4.8% (8)
Others	0.2%	0.5%	0.4%	0.06%	0.05%	0.5%	3.7%	0.45%	0.04%	0.03%	0.05%	0.2%	0.3%

rights of the German-speaking majority in the Italian South Tyrol has gradually become a less important nationalist issue, especially since the adoption of the latest measures in 1988.

The Slovenes in Carinthia: a relatively minor, but persisting issue of conflict over the extent of the Slovenes' rights.

Environmental issues: For a while this was a key political issue, with first the controversy over the opening of the Zwentendorf nuclear energy plant and the whole future of civil nuclear energy in Austria, and later the conflict over the proposed Hainburg power plant in the Danube wetland. Both these issues are now resolved and there is no single key environmental issue at present, although there is a generally higher level of environmental concern, notably on such problems as acid rain. Moreover, an environmental movement has developed that now has representatives in Parliament outside the traditional Austrian *Lager*.

What to do with the Draken aircraft: This is a relatively minor but continuing issue of what to do with the Draken aircraft that were purchased from Sweden for Austria's armed forces, but which no-one in Austria wants to have located in their region.

Electoral reform: Both major parties wish to reform the existing Austrian electoral system, to provide for a greater link between members and their constituencies, by increasing the number of constituencies, and including a minimum national threshold.

Österreichische Volkspartei — ÖVP
(Austrian People's Party)

Headquarters	: Kärntnerstrasse 51, 1010 Wien (tel: 51521)
Party leader	: Josef Riegler
General secretary	: Helmut Kukacka
Women's organization	: *Österreichische Frauenbewegung* (ÖFB) (federal leader: Dr Marilies Flemming)
Youth organization	: *Junge Volkspartei* (JVP) (federal leader: Othmar Karas)
Political Academy	: *Politische Akademie-Vereinigung für politische Bildung* (president: Dr Alfred Maleta)
Newspaper	: *Neues Volkblatt*
Membership	: Around 685,000 (only 3,000 of whom are direct members)
Founded	: 1945

History

The ÖVP in its present form was founded in 1945. The Christian Democratic tradition in Austria, however, is a much older one. Its first prominent figure was Karl von Vogelsang, who tried to forge a united Christian party in the 1870s. From the beginning, however, there was a sharp division between the conservative Catholic establishment and Christian social reformers.

In 1889 a Christian Social Party was founded by Dr Karl Lüger, a populist orator who became the Mayor of Vienna in 1897. Around 1900 the first Christian trade unions were founded and in 1907 the Christian Social Party entered national government for the first time.

After Lüger's death in 1910 the party became increasingly dominated by the conservatives, and, after 1918, it became the leading conservative party in the greatly reduced Austria. With the Socialists now dominant in Vienna the Christian Social support came mainly from rural Austria, from the clergy and from the business community. Its dominant personality was a Catholic priest. Mgr. Ignaz Seipel. The party advocated a corporatist organization of society and was fiercely anti-Marxist.

Although the party generally won less votes and seats than the Socialists it was able to remain in power for most of the 1920s, (initially under Seipel) and early 1930s, through coalitions with the Agrarians and the Pan-Germans.

When Dollfuss ended Austrian democracy in 1933 the party no longer played a direct role. Nevertheless, the Fatherland Front which ruled the country under Dollfuss and his successor, Schuschnigg, was based largely on the old Christian Social Party, as was its corporatist philosophy.

At the end of the war, a number of personalities from different backgrounds, Leopold Figl representing the farmers, Julius Raab representing business interests and Leopold Kunschak and Lois Weinberger representing the Christian trade unions got together to form a new Christian Democratic Party on a different basis from the pre-war party. The ÖVP was to be a People's Party open to all, and no longer to be so closely linked with the Catholic Church. The most important components of the party were to be the three Leagues of Farmers (ÖBB), Workers (ÖAAB) and Employers (ÖWB).

In the first election after the war the new ÖVP achieved 49.8 per cent of votes, a percentage of support which it has never since exceeded. It also became the largest Austrian party, a position which it maintained in seats if not always in votes (e.g. 1953 and 1959) until 1970. Apart from its exceptional performance in 1945 and its poor results in 1953 its support remained remarkably stable at around 44–46 per cent in all the elections until 1966.

In the long "Red-Black" coalition which lasted from 1945 to 1966 the ÖVP always provided the Federal Chancellor. Its first four postwar chairmen all became Chancellors, Leopold Figl from 1945–53, Julius Raab from 1953–61, Alfons Gorbach from 1961–64 and Josef Klaus from 1964–66. These came from the different interest groups within the party, with Figl coming from the Farmers' League, Raab and Klaus from the Employers' League and Gorbach from the Workers.

Party policy became increasingly pragmatic and non-ideological, accepting a considerable role for the state in the national economy and partnership between capital and labour. Under Raab's Finance Minister, Reinhard Kamitz, a "social market economy" policy on the lines promoted by Ludwig Erhard, in West Germany, helped the Austrian economy to enter a period of particularly rapid growth.

The renovation of the party in the 1960s led to the replacement of Alfons Gorbach by Josef Klaus first as party chairman and then as Chancellor, and to a major electoral advance by the party in the 1966 general election when it gained 48.3 per cent of the vote, and an absolute majority of seats.

The coalition ended and from 1966 to 1970 the ÖVP ruled alone with Josef Klaus as Chancellor. In 1970 it suffered an electoral setback and left government for the first time since the war. It became the second largest party to the Socialists, a position which it has retained in all subsequent elections, although it has kept 41–43 per cent of the vote.

The ÖVP entered a long period of opposition which lasted until 1986. None of its successive leaders, Hermann Withalm (1975–79) or Karl Schleinzer (1971–75), Josef Taus (1975–79) or Alois Mock (1979 to 1989) was able to match Bruno Kreisky in popularity and even after his departure the ÖVP was unable to seize the initiative from the Socialists although it did succeed in winning the presidency for the first time when its candidate, Kurt Waldheim, was elected in 1986. After the 1986 elections when both parties lost support the ÖVP returned to government with eight ministers in a new grand coalition with the Socialists, and with its chairman, Alois Mock, as Vice-Chancellor and Foreign Minister. In April 1989 the government coalition was reshuffled after Josef Riegler replaced Alois Mock as party leader and Vice-Chancellor.

At *Land* level the ÖVP has remained more successful in recent years than at federal level and six of the nine *Land* Presidents are members of the party. The ÖVP also dominates communal politics in Austria with over 80 per cent of the communes having ÖVP mayors.

Support

The ÖVP support has retained 41–49 per cent support in all elections since 1945 in spite of the steady decline in the *Lager* mentality of the interwar years and also the decline of one of its major support groups, the peasant farmers whose numbers dropped from over 30 per cent of the Austrian population in 1950 to under 10 per cent by the late 1970s.

The ÖVP has remained the dominant party, however, in rural Austria, in the small villages and farming areas. The Federal Chamber of Agriculture is still dominated by the ÖVP where it still wins over 80 per cent of the vote in chamber elections (84 per cent in 1983).

The ÖVP is also the dominant party among the business community, (84 per cent in Federal Chambers of Commerce elections in 1985). It is the strongest party among the federal bureaucracy (among whom it won over 62 per cent of the vote in 1983).

There also remains a strong correlation between regular church attendance and voting for the ÖVP even in many of the towns. It has been weak generally among blue-collar workers (36 per cent in 1984 in Chamber of Labour elections).

An interesting feature of the 1986 elections is that the ÖVP appears to have lost particularly heavily among middle-class voters, mainly to the Greens and FPÖ, while holding its own and even gaining some support in blue-collar communities.

In regional terms, the ÖVP has won its highest percentage of the vote in Tyrol and in Vorarlberg. In both of these provinces, it has generally won over 50 per cent of the vote and in Vorarlberg over 60 per cent although its support dropped sharply in the province to only 53 per cent in 1986. Another party bastion has traditionally been Lower Austria where it still won 47.3 per cent of the vote in 1986. It is particularly strong in the rural electoral districts between the Danube and the Czech border, where it gets up to 75 per cent of the vote in a number of communes (e.g. Gnadendorf, 78 per cent in 1986).

The ÖVP is also the largest party in the *Land* of Salzburg (40.9 per cent in 1986 down from 46.1 per cent in 1983) and roughly equal to the Socialists in the *Land* of Upper Austria (41.5 per cent). It is behind the Socialists in Styria (41 per cent to 44.1 per cent) and in Burgenland (42.8 per cent to 49.0 per cent).

In Salzburg, Upper Austria and Styria it has a lower than average vote in their main cities (Salzburg city 36.25 per cent, the industrial city of Linz 29.03 per cent and Graz 38.32 per cent). It is especially weak, however, in the small industrial towns (Bischofshofen 25.42 per cent, Steyr 24.38 per cent, Leoben 24.5 per cent, Eisenerz 19.0 per cent). Its weakest town in Austria is Kapfenberg in South Styria where it only received 16.43 per cent of the vote in 1986.

In Burgenland the pattern of electoral support is somewhat different in that the ÖVP is particularly strong in the *Land* capital of Eisenstadt (56.87 per cent in 1986) and the Socialists have a higher than average vote in many rural communities. Burgenland has seen a steady decline in the ÖVP vote from a majority position before 1964 to its present position well behind the Socialists.

The ÖVP is currently particularly weak in Carinthia (27.2 per cent in 1986, down from 32.9 per cent in 1983). It has always been a weak *Land* for the ÖVP but this has been accentuated as a result of local FPÖ strength under Dr Jörg Haider. In no sizeable Austrian town does the ÖVP have a lower vote than in Villach (23.5 per cent).

Finally, the ÖVP has also been traditionally weak in Vienna where it obtained 33.2 per cent in 1986. In the more prosperous suburbs of Vienna it got over 45 per cent of the vote (Josefstadt 47.19 per cent, Währing 48.53 per cent) and it was strongest of all in the city centre (54.75 per cent). In working-class areas it got under 25 per cent of the vote (Donaustadt 24.71 per cent, Semmering 22.69 per cent). In 1986 it lost votes heavily in its former bastions (the party had previously won over 60 per cent in the city centre) but held or even increased its votes in its weakest areas in the city.

Organization

The ÖVP is a much more decentralized party than the SPÖ, consisting of a federation both of its provincial parties and of its six sub-organizations. Each of the latter are organized at provincial level, and there are thus 54 major ÖVP party units around the country. The decentralized nature of the party is evident in numerous ways. Of the ÖVP 1,000 employees only 70 are employed at the national headquarters. Moreover only 10 per cent of all party expenditure is spent at federal level. The ÖVP is considerably more successful at provincial and communal level than it is nationally.

The ÖVP is primarily an indirect membership party. In 1968 the ÖVP had only 3,168 direct members. The vast majority of its members (720,000 in 1968, around 695,000 today), are indirect members through the six sub-organizations, or "Leagues" of which the party is composed. In descending order of size there is the *Österreichischer Bauernbund* (ÖBB or Farmers' League, with over 400,000 members in 1986), the *Österreichischer Arbeiter und Angestelltenbund*, (the ÖAAB or Workers' and Employees' League, with 277,000 members in 1986), the *Österreichischer Wirtschaftsbund* (the ÖWB, or Employers' and Businessmen's League with 138,000 members in 1986), the *Österreichischer Seniorenbund* (the ÖSB, or Senior Citizens' League, with 157,000 members in 1986), the *Junge Volkspartei* (the JVP, or Young People's Party, with 115,000 members in 1986) and finally the *Österreichischer Frauenbewegung* (ÖFB or women's movement, with 78,000 members in 1986).

Each such league is financially autonomous, and is organized at federal, provincial, district and local levels. It is possible to be a member of more than one such league, and also to be a member of a league without being a member of the ÖVP (although this latter is rare). League membership is also increased by the practice of family membership at a cheaper rate for dependents of full members. Exact membership of the ÖVP as a whole is thus very hard to calculate.

The three big economic leagues (ÖBB, ÖAAB and ÖWB) play an extremely important role both within the party and within Austrian society as a whole. Until 1980 their leaders were automatically deputy leaders of the federal party. Moreover ÖVP cabinet members have had to be chosen on a roughly proportional basis from these leagues and party leaders have come from different leagues (Raab, Klaus and Withalm from the ÖWB, Figl and Schleinzer from the ÖBB, and Gorbach, Taus and Mock from the ÖAAB).

Within the national chambers the ÖBB is dominant in the Chamber of Agriculture (84 per cent of the votes in the 1985 chamber elections) the ÖWB in the Chamber of Commerce (84 per cent in 1985) and the ÖAAB (which is a league with a much larger number of white-collar workers and civil servants than manual workers) plays a significant if secondary role in the Chamber of Labour (36.5 per cent in the 1984 chamber elections).

Besides the sectional organizations, the ÖVP is also organized directly on a territorial basis. The exact structure varies from province to province. As a general rule, however, the lowest party unit is the local party organization (*Ortsparteiorganisationen*) of which there are 1,568 in the whole of Austria (of which 1,189 are in the particularly well organized ÖVP province of Lower Austria). Above these are communal parties (*Gemeindeparteiorganisationen*) of which there are 2,296. In Vienna there are separate organizational units, the sections (*Sektionen*) of which there are 179. Above these are the 186 district parties (*Bezirksparteiorganisationen*) of which 38 are major district (*Hauptbezirk*) organizations, and the nine provincial parties.

At federal level the Federal Congress (*Bundesparteitag*) is generally convened every three years, and includes delegates from the geographical and sectoral and affiliated organizations. Among its main tasks are to elect 40 members of the Party Directorate, a party leader and six deputy leaders.

The Party Directorate (*Bundesparteileitung*) meets around once a month, and consists of 50 members and 10 statutory members as well as the 40 elected by the Congress.

The Party Executive (*Bundesparteivorstand*) meets twice a month, and consists of 17 or 18 members, 10 statutory members (including the party leader and the six deputy leaders and the general secretary) and seven or eight elected by the Party Directorate (these generally include the leaders of the six sub-organizations). For certain purposes there is also an enlarged Party Executive (*Erweiterter Bundesparteivorstand*) which also includes all the provincial party leaders who are not already on the Executive.

The ÖVP members in the Parliament are members of the ÖVP *Parlamentsklub*. There are 77 ÖVP members in the National Assembly. There are 33 in the Federal Council.

The ÖVP has a sizeable headquarters staff at 51 Kärntnerstrasse in Vienna, presided over by the general secretary, who is a powerful figure within the party; two general secretaries have gone on immediately to become party leaders (Withalm and Schleinzer).

More power is given to the local organizations in the choice of candidates than in the Socialist party. The Federal party can place only a limited number of persons on party lists. In the past the party has experimented with primaries in most provinces (e.g. in 1975), but these were discontinued in 1979. There are also party rules to prevent cumulation of elective offices.

As regards policy formulation a role in background research is carried out by the party's Political Academy, founded in 1973, which also carries out political training. PR work and media and journalist training is carried out by the Friedrich Funder Institute. The Karl von Vogelsang Institute concentrates on research into party history and into that of Austrian Christian democracy. The party also has a communal umbrella group (*Kommunalpolitische Vereinigung*) to co-ordinate and provide advice for the party at communal level.

The party still has strong informal links with the Catholic Church, and all postwar party leaders apart from Schleinzer have been members of the ÖCV, the Association of Catholic Fraternities.

Within the trade union movement the ÖVP provides a vice-president of the ÖBB, the Austrian Trade Union Federation. Party sympathizers within the ÖBB are organized in the *Fraktion Christlicher Gewerkschafter* (group of Christian trade unions, founded in 1951). The ÖVP has a number of other affiliated organizations besides the six main sub-organizations, although it has far fewer than the Socialist party. Among these are an academic support group (*Österreichischer Akademikerbund* or ÖAKB), a group which provides help after natural disasters (the *Katastrophenhilfe Österreichischer Frauen* or KÖF), a group which looks after single mothers, orphans and other children (*Österreichischer Kinderrettungswerk*, or ÖKRW), a welfare group providing home help for the sick and aged (*Österreichischer Wohlfahrtsdienst* or ÖWO), a group which provides legal and technical help for both landlords and tenants (the *Österreichischer Mieter, Siedler und Wohnungseigentümerbund* or ÖMB) and finally a social support club (the *Kameradschaft Politischer Verfolgter* or KPV).

Party finance is based mainly on the provinces and the leagues. The party newspaper is called *Neues Volkblatt*. The ÖVP is linked both to the Christian Democrat and Conservative movements, being a member of the European Christian Democratic Union and of the Christian Democratic International, as well as the European and International Democratic Union.

Policies

The pre-war Christian Social party was fundamentally a conservative party close to the Catholic church. The postwar People's Party had a quite different character, putting a greater emphasis on the progressive social teaching of the church and accepting a clear division between church and state (and church and party) and that the state had an important role to pay in the economy. The years of coalition with the Socialists and of consensus politics helped to reduce the differences between the two main parties, which, with the exception of a few areas such as family policy, became mainly differences of emphasis rather than of substance.

The long years of opposition in the 1970s and 1980s led to strong rhetorical attacks by the ÖVP against the Socialists, especially over economic policy, where the ÖVP called for greater economic liberalism and a less wasteful state.

Now that the ÖVP is again back in a grand coalition it is helping to carry out some of the policies that it advocated, but is nevertheless facing two particular difficulties to distinguish itself clearly from the increasingly pragmatic socialist leadership of Vranitzky and to overcome its own internal differences of emphasis. The ÖVP is a highly decentralized party, divided into three major interest groups and participating in both the Christian Democratic and Conservative internationals. As with the SPÖ there is an obvious divide between the party traditionalists (notably within the declining Farmers' League) and the party modernists, who wish to compete for the same electorate as their equivalents within the SPÖ. The ÖVP's internal structure, however, may make it difficult to resolve this conflict.

The ÖVP continues to support further liberalization of the Austrian economy and a reduced role for the state. The highest priority is to reduce the existing budget deficit. The economic situation of the nationalized industries needs to be improved, less should be spent on the subsidization of the State Railways, a particular ÖVP target. The coalition's privatization programme should be pursued, and the ÖVP is prepared to go further than the Socialists, who continue to insist on a 51 per cent state holding. Another ÖVP emphasis is on tax reform where the ÖVP has sought a reduction in top tax rates, and a drop in the overall tax burden. The ÖVP also wants greater flexibility in working hours, and in the labour market in general. Within the public sector it advocates less bureaucracy, and greater mobility of the work force. Wastefulness in the social security system should be reduced. The ÖVP also supports employee participation, and employee shareholdings.

There are few sharp differences with the Socialists over energy or environmental policy.

The ÖVP turned against civil nuclear energy during the 1970s, and now puts a strong emphasis on environmental issues.

The church's social thinking continues to pay a considerable role in the party's background programmes (for example the traditional Christian Democratic emphasis on subsidiarity). In 1974 the ÖVP was opposed to liberalization of abortion, but has made little attempt to reverse the law since. Differences between the two main parties are perhaps sharper over family policy. The ÖVP would like to see defence of the family unit placed within the Austrian Constitution. Moreover any tax reform should include more help for families. Unlike the SPÖ, the ÖVP calls for progressively lower taxes on families from the third child onwards.

On constitutional questions the ÖVP has strongly advocated a more personalized electoral system, with more constituencies and a more direct link between an elected member and his or her constituency. It has also called for more effective follow up to current initiatives, so that if parliament rejected an initiative which had received over 500,000 signatures there should automatically be a popular vote on the question. The ÖVP advocates more powers for the Austrian provinces, and also for the currently weak Federal Council. It has also called for an ending of the state media monopoly.

A particularly sensitive issue for the ÖVP has been the position of President Kurt Waldheim, who has been called on to resign by many outside Austria as well as by the Greens and some Socialists within Austria. Waldheim is the first ever ÖVP president and the party has had to strongly defend him. Wider sensitivities over a related issue was shown by the recent resignation of the former ÖVP general secretary, Dr Michael Graff, after remarks interpreted as anti-Semitic.

On foreign policy, the ÖVP is now more united in its support of Austrian entry into the EC than is the SPÖ. The ÖVP believes that participation in the European Internal Market is essential for the modernization of Austria's economy. Austria would also benefit from joint EC research, EC environmental measures and capital liberalization. All this can only be achieved by full Austrian membership. An application should be made by 1989, with a view to membership by the mid–1990s at the latest.

The ÖVP does not believe that EC membership will compromise Austria's neutrality, which it continues to support wholeheartedly. Austria should act as a bridge between East and West.

Personalities

The ÖVP leader is Josef Riegler, who is also the Deputy Chancellor of Austria. He is a former Agriculture Minister. His predecessor Alois Mock is still Foreign Minister. Mock was the party leader from 1979 to 1989, and has been president of the European Democratic Union and the International Democratic Union.

Two of the ÖVP ministers in the present coalition government are the Minister of Economic Affairs, Wolfgang Schüssel, and the Defence Minister, Dr Robert Lichal. The other ÖVP ministers are Dr Marilies Flemming (also the leader of the ÖVP Women's Movement), Dr Erhard Busek and Franz Fischer.

The leaders of the three main economic leagues within the ÖVP are Alois Derfler of the ÖBB, Dr Herbert Kohlmaier of the ÖAAB and Rudolf Sallinger of the ÖWB. The ÖVP leader in the National Assembly is Friedrich König, and the party's general secretary is Helmut Kukacka.

The ÖVP's real power base is the Austrian provinces, and six of the nine provincial presidents are members of the ÖVP — Siegfried Ludwig in Lower Austria, Dr Joseph Krainer in Styria, Alois Partl in Tyrol (who took over from Edward Wallnöfer who had been president for almost 30 years) and Dr Herbert Kessler in Vorarlberg.

Sozialistische Partei Österreichs — SPÖ
(Austrian Socialist Party)

Headquarters	: Löwelstrasse 18, 1014 Wien (tel: 0222/63 27 31)
Party chairman	: Dr Franz Vranitzky
Leader of parliamentary group	: Dr Heinz Fischer
General secretaries	: Heinrich Keller and Günther Sallaberger
Women's organization	: *Bundesfrauenkommittee* (chair: Jolanda Offenbeck)
Youth organization	: *Arbeitsgemeinschaft Junge Generation in der SPO* (chair: Christian Cap)
Research foundation	: Dr Karl Renner Institut (director: Dr Erich Froschl)
Party Newspaper	: *Neue AZ*
Membership	: 680,000 (1988)
Founded	: 1889

History

The Socialist party refounded in 1945 entailed the revival of a socialist movement going back to the 1860s, when the first workers' vocational training association was formed. In the 1870s, however, the emerging movement split into two main wings, "Moderates" and "Radicals", who advocated a more revolutionary path to socialism. At a unity conference at Hainfeld (Lower Austria) on Dec. 30, 1888–Jan. 1, 1889 the two wings were reconciled and the Social Democratic Party was formally established. Its first prominent leader was Victor Adler, of Jewish origin like a number of the subsequent leaders of the party. Later in 1889 the party's newspaper, the *Arbeiterzeitung* was founded, and in 1893 the first Austrian trade union congress was convened.

A number of intellectuals in the party, calling themselves "Austrian Marxists", attempted to develop a distinctive philosophy for the party, reconciling reformist and revolutionary socialism, and putting a strong emphasis on party unity.

In the 1897 elections the party obtained 14 seats in the Parliament, and in the first decade of this century greatly increased its electoral strength. During World War I the party was divided over the attitude to take towards the war, but avoided a damaging split. The Socialist Party became the most powerful party in the new Austria after 1918. In 1918 the Socialist Karl Renner became Chancellor, and from 1918 to 20 the party was in coalition with the Christian Social Party.

The government fell in 1920, and the Socialists went into opposition to the new government of Christian Social Party and pan-Germans. There now followed a period of increased polarization of Austrian political life. The Socialists retreated into their *Lager* in "Red Vienna", particularly, where they dominated local politics with up to 60 per cent of the vote. The Socialist administration in Vienna created a whole Socialist subculture within the city, building kindergartens, libraries, swimming pools, hospitals and other social and cultural facilities for the Viennese working class. Above all they constructed great housing developments (Karl Marx Hof, Engels Hof) to a high standard. The new Communist party was given no room to develop and the Socialists had a mass membership within the city, with 400,000 members (out of 650,000 members in the whole of Austria).

There were increased tensions between the Socialists in Vienna (and in a few other strongholds such as the industrial towns of Styria), the Christian Social Party and the Pan-Germans and Nazis. An armed militia on the right, the *Heimwehr* was matched by a less effective *Schutzbund* on the left. In 1927 there was rioting in Vienna, in which many Socialists lost their lives and a period of "cold civil war" ensued. No general action was taken even after the Parliament was suppressed by Dolfuss in 1933, and in February 1934 the Dolfuss government crushed the Socialist experiment in Vienna, after several days of bitter fighting in the Viennese suburbs. Party leader Otto Bauer and other leading socialists went into exile.

During the years that followed the party (in exile and underground in Austria) split into Socialists and Revolutionary Socialists. In 1945 the party was revived. In an attempt to reconcile the two groups the sub-title "Social Democrats and Revolutionary Socialists" was added to the party's main name.

The new party was very different from its predecessor. Many of the party intellectuals and left wing theoreticians did not return after the war, and the party's leadership was taken up by pragmatists and trade unionists around Karl Renner who were prepared to go into coalition with their old Christian Democratic adversaries. The Revolutionary Socialists had very little impact within the new party.

The grand coalition between the Socialists and Christian Democrats ("ÖVP") lasted from 1945 to 1966. The ÖVP provided all the Chancellors but the Socialists all the Presidents (Karl Renner 1945–50, Theodor Körner 1951–57, Dr Adolf Schärf 1957–65, Franz Jonas 1965–74). Before being elected President Schärf had been the party chairman from 1945 to 1957, as well as Vice-Chancellor in the government. His successor in both roles from 1957 to 1966 was Dr Bruno Pittermann.

In the 1945 elections the Socialists obtained 44.6 per cent. They dropped to 38.71 per cent in 1949, but in all subsequent elections until 1966 they fluctuated between 42 per cent and 45 per cent of the national vote. In two elections, 1953 and 1959, they won more votes than the ÖVP but were always second in terms of seats.

The SPÖ again became a mass membership party, rising from 357,000 in 1945 to a peak of 727,000 in 1960. The distribution of party membership also changed. Whereas over 60 per cent of the prewar Socialist membership had been in Vienna, this was down to 43 per cent in 1945, and the figure has since declined to just over 32 per cent. The compensating rise in other *Länder* was particularly marked in Upper Austria. The provincial organizations gradually gained more influence within the party.

The SPÖ had fewer formal links with the trade union movement than the prewar Socialists. Nevertheless the party dominated the Austrian

Trade Union Federation (ÖGB) and its leaders, Johann Böhm (1945–59), Franz Olah (1959–63) and Anton Benya (1963–) have all been prominent members of the SPÖ.

In keeping with the pragmatism of those who revived the party in 1945 no new party programme was drawn up to replace the Linzer Programme of 1926. Only in 1958, and after intense controversy between traditionalists and reformers, was a new programme adopted. It differentiated democratic socialism from communism and capitalism but accepted the mixed economy and private ownership and limited the scope of nationalization.

In the run-up to the 1966 election the SPÖ was challenged by a breakaway Democratic Progressive Party (DFP) led by the former trade union president and Socialist minister, Franz Olah, who had been expelled from the SPÖ after accusations that he had diverted party funds. The DFP only received 3.3 per cent of the vote, but harmed the SPÖ which lost enough votes to the ÖVP to permit the latter to end the coalition. Dr Bruno Pittermann was then replaced by Dr Bruno Kreisky, who was to lead the party until 1983.

The SPÖ was in opposition from 1966 to 1970 and took the opportunity to renew its policies and organization. In 1970 the largest electoral swing since 1945 brought the SPÖ from 42.6 per cent to 48.42 per cent and enabled it to form a single party minority government with FPÖ parliamentary support. In 1971 the SPÖ became the first Austrian party to win over 50 per cent of the vote. It repeated its achievement in 1975 and in 1979. Bruno Kreisky remained Chancellor from 1970 to 1983 and the Presidency also remained in Socialist hands when Franz Jonas was replaced by Dr Rudolf Kirschlager (1974–86), although he was not formally a party member.

At a time of increased economic instability elsewhere the "Austrian Way" attracted considerable attention as a result of its economic stability and above all high levels of employment that were maintained.

In 1978, a new party programme was adopted. In the early 1980s, however, a number of financial scandals affected the party's image, with prominent SPÖ ministers, Hannes Androsch and Karl Sekanina, being involved. In the 1983 elections the SPÖ lost five seats and its absolute majority. Rejecting a grand coalition with the ÖVP it made a controversial coalition with the much smaller FPÖ. Dr Bruno Kreisky finally stood down as Chancellor and was replaced by Dr Fred Sinowatz.

In 1986 the SPÖ lost the presidency for the first time when its candidate, Dr Kurt Steyrer was defeated by Kurt Waldheim of the ÖVP. Sinowatz stood down as Chancellor and was replaced by Dr Franz Vranitzky. Later the SPÖ/FPÖ coalition was terminated after the FPÖ chose a new and more right-wing leader, Dr Jörg Haider, and new elections were held in which both the SPÖ and the ÖVP lost support. A grand coalition between the two parties was then constituted with Vranitzky remaining as Chancellor and with the Socialists having eight ministers.

In 1988 Vranitzky became party chairman as well as Chancellor. The SPÖ is represented in all provincial governments apart from Vorarlberg, and provides the provincial presidents of Vienna, Burgerland and Carinthia. Besides its 80 members of the National Assembly and 30 members of the Federal Council it has 206 members of the provincial parliaments. There are 543 Socialist mayors.

Support

Even after its 1987 setback the SPÖ is still the largest Austrian party. It has a wider basis of support than in the pre-war years, in that it is no longer so dependent on workers and on Vienna. It is still the best supported party by far among manual workers but has also won considerable support among civil servants and white-collar workers in general. It also does very well among pensioners (in the 1970s it was estimated that over 28 per cent of its members were over 60). On the other hand it has been weaker among professionals and the self-employed and among farmers and forest workers.

In geographical terms the party is still strongest in Vienna, although Vienna only provided 22.4 per cent of the total party vote in 1987, compared to 46 per cent in 1930 and just under 35 per cent in 1949. The SPÖ has always provided the Mayor of Vienna and in *Landtag* elections has only once gone below 50 per cent since the war. It has also polled very strongly in Vienna in national elections, and still gained 52.92 per cent of the vote in its bad result of 1986. The SPÖ is weakest in the inner city of Vienna (28.4 per cent of the vote in 1986) and strongest in traditional working class suburbs like Simmering (65.3 per cent) and Favoriten (64.0 per cent). In 1986 it gained in its weakest area of inner Vienna but lost substantially in its strongholds.

Outside Vienna the only other provinces where the SPÖ has been the dominant party are Burgenland (only since 1964) and Carinthia. In 1986 the SPÖ received 49 per cent of the vote in Burgenland (47 per cent in the recent *Landtag* elections) and just under 48 per cent in Carinthia, where it has been the largest party since the war. It is stronger in Villach (53.5 per cent) than in Klagenfurt (44.4 per cent).

The party's next highest percentage in 1986 was in Styria, where it obtained 44.2 per cent. The party is particularly strong in some of the small industrial towns in this province (Kapfenberg 71.6 per cent, Eisenerz 66.6 per cent, Bruck an der Mur 59 per cent) but weaker in its largest city of Graz (42 per cent).

The SPÖ polls well in Lower Austria (42.5 per cent in 1986) but has almost always been the second party to the ÖVP in both *Landtag* and national elections. In some of the rural communes in this province it polls under 7 per cent (Aderklaa 6.73 per cent).

In Upper Austria the SPÖ has had very varied results. It only had 28.3 per cent in the 1945 *Landtag* elections compared to 59.1 per cent for the ÖVP, but it had overtaken the ÖVP in *Landtag* elections by 1967. In recent years it has again slipped back. It gained 42.3 per cent in the 1986 national elections, polling well in its largest city of Linz (53.8 per cent).

The SPÖ is weaker in Salzburg where it polled 37 per cent in 1986 (just over 36 per cent in the city of Salzburg but over 59 per cent in the industrial town of Bischofshofen).

The SPÖ's weakest provinces are Tyrol and Vorarlberg. In both *Landtag* and national elections the SPÖ has seldom polled much more than 30 per cent in the Tyrol and it obtained 29.3 per cent in 1986. In Vorarlberg it is even weaker, especially in *Landtag* elections. In the 1986 national elections it obtained 25.7 per cent of the vote.

Organization

The SPÖ has the strongest organizational structure of any Austrian party. It is much more centralized than the ÖVP and has a larger number of affiliated organizations. Its level of membership compared to its voters is remarkably high, especially in Vienna where the party has 215,000 members (practically one member for every two party voters, and around 20 per cent of the total Viennese electorate). Almost 70,000 of its members are party *Vertrauenpersonen* (trusted persons) who hold party offices, enjoy special political training and collect the party dues.

The basic units of party membership are the local organizations (*Ortsorganisationen*) of which there are 2,847 throughout Austria, and the sections (*Sektionen*) of which there are 1,061. Above these are the district organizations (*Bezirksorganisationen*) of which there are 115. The nine provincial organizations each have their own provincial congress and provincial executive.

At Federal level the highest party organ is the Federal Congress, which meets every two years. It consists of 500 to 600 delegates from the district and provincial organizations, from the party executive and parliamentary group, as well as from a large number of affiliated organizations. Among its tasks are to elect the party executive and to ratify the latter's choice of the party chairman and party presidium.

The Federal Party Executive consists of 56 full members, of whom 40 are elected in proportion to the strength of the various provincial parties. Each province must have at least one representative. The executive meets around once a month, and chooses the party chairman, the party presidium and also the two central secretaries, one for organizational matters and one for political questions.

The Presidium consists of the party chairman and seven deputy chairmen. The enlarged Presidium includes the leaders of provincial parties as well as two union and one women's representative.

In addition to the Federal Congress, a Federal Party Council can also be convened by the executive. It deals with party and organizational matters, such as nominations for the Federal presidency and for the National Assembly elections.

The Socialist Parliamentarians in the National Assembly and the Federal Council, of which there are 80 in the former and 30 in the latter, are organized in *Klubs*.

Party candidates for national elections are put forward by the party executive, acting on the recommendations of the provincial organizations. They are then ratified by the party council.

The SPÖ has established a long list of incompatibilities between holding different elected public posts at the same time. A party tax is also levied on Socialist office-holders.

The main youth organization within the SPÖ is called the *Arbeitsgemeinschaft Junge Generation in der SPÖ* and is open to all members below the age of 38. There is another organization for 14–20 year olds, the *Sozialistische Jugend Österreichs*, and a students' organization, the *Verband Sozialisticher Studenten Österreichs* which at times has been very radical.

There are a network of women's committees at local, district and provincial level. The Federal Women's Congress then elects the 25-strong Federal women's committee.

The SPÖ has a Federal training committee (the *Bundesbildungsausschuss*) and a party foundation, the *Dr Karl Renner Institute*, which organizes seminars and research.

The SPÖ does not have direct organic links with the Trade Union movement, but the effective links are still very strong. The SPÖ dominates the elections for the Chamber of Labour (winning up to two thirds of the seats), and provides the leadership of the Austrian Trade Union Federation and most of its affiliated unions. The Socialist group within the Federation, the *Fraktion sozialistischer Gewerkschafter* is the dominant political group and is entitled to 50 delegates to the Socialist Federal Congress and two members of the enlarged Presidium.

There are also a large number of other affiliated Socialist organizations, around 30 in all, of which nine are directly entitled to delegates at the Federal Congress. Those entitled to delegates are the Socialist Sports Organization (*Arbeitgemeinschaft für Sport und Körperkultur-Askö*) which has over one million members, a pensioners' organization (the *Pensionistenverband*) with 355,000 members, the Socialist teachers' group (*Sozialistischer Lehrerverein Österreichs*), an organization which looks after children's welfare (*Kinderfreunde*), the Socialist peasants (*SPÖ Bauern*), the Socialist co-operative group (*Fraktion sozialisticher Gewerkschafter im Konsum*), an economic association (*Freier Wirtschaftsverband Österreichs*), an anti-Fascist and anti-racialist group (*Bund sozialistischer Freiheitskämpfer und Opfer des Fascismus*) and an association of Socialist academics, intellectuals and artists (*Bund sozialistischer Akademiker, Intellektueller und Künstler*) which has around 17,500 members and includes professionals of all kinds, such as engineers and lawyers.

Among the other affiliated organizations are the Socialist Friends of Nature, Socialist Esperanto Speakers, Socialist Stamp Collectors, Socialist Motorists and Cyclists (the former Workers' Cycling League), a Socialist anti-alcohol organization, a Christian Socialist group, a Jewish society, singers and musical organizations, a Workers' Fishing Association and even a Socialist association of allotment gardeners and small livestock breeders.

The party's official organ is the daily newspaper, *Neue AZ*. There is also a daily Socialist newspaper in Carinthia, the *Kärntner Tageszeitung*, a Socialist press agency and party newsletter *Sozialistische Korrespondenz*, and a magazine called *Zukunft*.

The SPÖs membership dues are currently 35 Schillings a month, paid for 13 months, with income from the 13th month being used for elections and special party purposes. In 1985 (a more typical year than the election year of 1986) over half the party's income came from membership dues, and around a quarter from the state grant to political parties.

The SPÖ is a prominent member of the

Socialist International and is an observer member of the Confederation of Socialist Parties of the EC.

Policies

The years of postwar coalition and consensus considerably reduced the differences between the two main parties. Nevertheless, during the years of Kreisky's dominance the SPÖ was still putting its emphasis on distinctively Socialist economic policies such as extensive economic planning, maintenance of full employment even at the cost of rising budget deficits and defence of Austria's large nationalized sector.

Franz Vranitzky, however, is confronted with a very different political and economic situation where the SPÖ is again in coalition with the ÖVP and where the costs of the seemingly very successful economic polices of the 1970s have become much more apparent.

Budgetary austerity and privatization are now on the agenda and the future of the nationalized industries is under close review. The SPÖ is now less ideological, and more technocratic, and is directing its appeal more to professionals, managers and the new middle classes. Nevertheless the SPÖ's left wing is still quite strong, and the party still has powerful links with the trade unions. The extent of Vranitzky's room for manoeuvre still has to be defined, and may well be tested over such issues as Austria's possible application to join the EC within the near future.

The difference on economic policy between the coalition partners is mainly now one of degree. The Socialists accept that the public budget deficit will have to be drastically reduced from the present levels of over 5 per cent of GDP to 2.5 per cent by 1992. Restructuring and initial steps towards privatization have been accepted by the SPÖ, who have insisted, nevertheless, on maintaining 51 per cent control by the state.

The Socialists strongly defend Austria's social security system, but are undertaking reform of some of its more costly aspects. Reform of the tax structure is also being tackled.

The SPÖ has supported a reduction in the working week to 35 hours, but this is being downplayed by the current coalition. On agricultural policy the SPÖ recognized that surpluses need to be reduced, and supports a cut-back in certain subsidies.

Until the late 1970s a majority within the party supported the use of civil nuclear energy, but the SPÖ adjusted rapidly to the results of the Zwentendorf referendum and supports alternative energies. The SPÖ puts more emphasis than the ÖVP on the need for a shift of priorities from road to rail.

Another policy difference with the ÖVP is over family policy where the SPÖ, for example, does not advocate giving progressively higher state support per child in larger families. The SPÖ also opposes any trend towards a more elitist educational system. Anti-clericalism, however, is no longer an issue.

The SPÖ advocates the introduction of a new electoral system, based roughly on the German model. The link between voters and candidates would be strengthened and personalized by the introduction of individual constituencies. There would then be a proportional top-up of seats in order to reflect a party's national strength, as long as the party had obtained either one constituency seat or passed a minimum national threshold. The SPÖ also calls for the strengthening of direct democracy.

Elements within the party have called for Waldheim's resignation and at one stage Vranitzky hinted at his own resignation over the issue, but at the moment the SPÖ is adopting a lower profile on this matter.

There is more hesitation within the SPÖ over the issue of Austria's full adhesion to the European Community than in the ÖVP or FPÖ. The SPÖ supports closer relations with the EC, and, in particular, wishes to participate to the fullest extent in the 1992 internal market. There is some opposition within the party, however, to full entry, although Vranitzky is currently exploring the possibility of presenting an Austrian application. At the very least the State Treaty and Austrian neutrality would have to be fully protected.

The SPÖ seeks to restrain Austrian arms production and arms exports, and to reinforce Austrian development aid.

Personalities

The current party leader is Dr Franz Vranitzky who became Federal Chancellor in summer 1986 (replacing Dr Fred Sinowatz) and who was also elected SPÖ party chairman in May 1988. Vranitzky, who is just over 50, is a technocrat with a background in banking. In 1984 he had been appointed Austrian Finance Minister. His youthful image and pragmatic management style have proved to be considerable assets for the SPÖ.

Among the party's other ministers in the current coalition government, two of the most influential have been Karl Blecha, a leading figure from the Kreisky era but who has recently been forced to resign, and the long-standing Social Affairs Minister, Alfred Dallinger, who from 1975 to 1980 was vice-president of the Austrian Trade Union Federation.

Other SPÖ ministers have included Johanna Dohnal, Dr Hilde Hawlicek, Ferdinand Lacina, Dr Franz Loeschnak and Dr Rudolf Streicher.

A very powerful party figure is the leader of the SPÖ parliamentarians in the National Assembly, Dr Heinz Fischer.

The first President of the National Assembly was Leopold Gratz, a former mayor of Vienna and also former Foreign Minister.

Of the SPÖ's provincial leaders the most prominent are Leopold Wagner, who is both party leader and Chief Minister of the province of Carinthia, and Helmut Zilk and Hans Mayr, respectively Mayor and Deputy Mayor of Vienna. Dr Karl Grünner, the party chairman and Deputy Chief Minister of Upper Austria, is another influential party figure. Since May 1988 the two SPÖ central secretaries have been Dr Heinrich Keller and Günther Sallaberger.

Freiheitliche Partei Österreichs — FPÖ
(Austrian Freedom Party)

Headquarters	: Kärntnerstrasse 28, 1010 Wien (tel: 0222 52 35 35)
Party chairman	: Dr Jörg Haider
General secretary	: Dr Norbert Gugenbauer
Newspaper	: *Neue Freie Zeitung*
Youth organization	: *Ring Freiheitlicher Jugend*
Members	: 37,000
Founded	: 1955

History

The Freedom Party (FPÖ) dates in its present form from late 1955, but its origins date from the pre-war nationalist grouping which was the third of Austria's traditional *Lager*. This grouping was strongly pro-German and was also anti-clerical (and at times anti-Semitic as well). Its most prominent spokesman before World War I was Georg von Schönerer (1842–1921), who also advocated extension of the suffrage and social reforms. In 1910 the *Deutscher Nationalverband* (German National Association) was founded, and became the largest political grouping in the 1911 elections.

After World War I there were two main components of the nationalist *Lager*, the *Grossdeutsche Volkspartei* (Pan-German People's Party) and the *Landbund* (Agrarian League). The nationalists were less numerous than the Catholic and Socialist groupings, but by par-ticipating in government in a series of coalitions with the former were instrumental in keeping the Socialists out of power throughout the 1920s. In the 1930s the nationalists fragmented, with some supporting the Austro-Fascist governments of Dolfuss and Schushnigg, and others the National Socialists and later the *Anschluss*.

After the war, the pan-German Nationalists were not licensed to fight the 1945 national elections, and much of the former *Landbund* was absorbed by the Austrian People's Party. In 1949, however, a new nationalist party was founded under the name *Verband der Unabhangigen* (VdU — the Association of Independents). Its two most prominent leaders were Herbert Kraus and Victor Reimann, who put their emphasis more on economic liberalism than on traditional nationalism, and on opposing the carve-up of power between the People's Party and the Socialists. They also called for a halt to postwar recriminations, and the full reintegration of all Austrian citizens, including former Nazis.

In the 1949 elections the new party was licensed to stand under the name *Wahlpartei der Unabhängigen* (Electoral Party of Independents). They polled extremely well, obtaining 11.67 per cent of the vote and 16 seats in the Parliament. They were especially strong in western Austria, where they gained up to 20 per cent of the vote and weak in the Russian occupied zone, where they were nearer 4 per cent. They also won 117 seats in the Chamber of Labour elections. They were not a united force, however, and were divided, in particular, between their liberal and their more stridently nationalist wing.

In 1951 they put up a candidate in the Austrian presidential elections, Dr Burghard Breitner, who won over 15 per cent in the first round of elections, and absolute majorities in the cities of Salzburg and Innsbruck. In the second round the VdU supported the People's Party candidate.

Internal party divisions now came more out into the open. The VdU opened negotiations with dissidents from the People's Party, and Kraus resigned as party leader and was replaced by Max Stendebach. The most extreme nationalist, Stüber, was expelled from the party in November 1953, and subsequently formed his own party.

In the 1953 elections the VdU lost ground slightly, obtaining 10.95 per cent of the vote and 14 seats. In 1954 its shift in a more nationalist direction became clearer with the adoption of its Bad Aussee Programme, which declared that Austria was a German state. In October 1954 the party fared extremely badly in a number of

492

provincial elections, and lost most of its seats in the Chamber of Labour.

In 1955 a new *Freiheitspartei* (Freedom Party) was founded by Anton Reinthaller, who had held prominent posts during the Nazi period. Negotiations between the VdU and the Freedom Party were later successfully concluded and a merged *Freiheitliche Partei Österreichs* came into existence. Anton Reinthaller became the first party leader.

The new party began extremely badly by losing eight of the 14 seats that had been formerly held by the VdU, winning only 6.52 per cent of the vote in the 1956 national elections. Moreover, the VdU founders, Kraus and Reimann, and other members of its more liberal wing, did not get involved in the new party.

In 1957 the FPÖ agreed on a joint Presidential candidate with the People's Party, Wolfgang Denk, who lost, however, to the Socialist candidate. In 1958 Reinthaller died and was replaced by another former Nazi, Friedrich Peter, who was to remain party leader for 20 years.

In 1959 the FPÖ slightly increased its vote to 7.7 per cent and eight seats in parliament, but its vote again dropped in the 1962 and 1966 elections. Between 1966 and 1975 it polled between 5.4 per cent and 5.5 per cent in four successive national elections.

Although it was a tiny third force compared to the two major parties, the FPÖ occasionally played a key balancing role. In 1963 it allied with the SPÖ to prevent the People's Party attempts to allow the return to Austria of the Hapsburg heir, Otto. In 1970–71 it played a supporting role for the SPÖ minority government of Bruno Kreisky. The most important result of this co-operation for the FPÖ was a new electoral law which was more favourable to smaller parties, and enabled the FPÖ to rise from six to 10 seats in parliament on the same percentage of votes. In 1973 the FPÖ had another success when Dr Alexander Götz was elected as mayor of Graz with People's Party support.

On the departure of Peter as party leader in 1978, Götz became his successsor. His leadership was short-lived, however.

In 1980 Dr Norbert Steger, an economic lib-eral, was elected party leader when he defeated Harald Ofner, a more traditional nationalist. In 1980 the FPÖ candidate for president, Willfried Gredler, obtained 17 per cent of the vote.

In the 1983 election the FPÖ slipped to only 4.98 per cent of the vote. Its 12 seats, however, were crucial in view of the failure of any party to win an overall majority, and the FPÖ then entered government for the first time in a coalition with the Socialists. Steger became Deputy Chancellor and Minister of Trade, Ofner became Minister of Justice and Dr Friedhelm Frischenschlager became Minister of Defence. There were also three FPÖ state secretaries. The coalition lasted for three years. One particular controversy was when Frischenschlager person-ally welcomed the Nazi war criminal Reder on his return to Austria from imprisonment in Italy.

In 1986 Steger was overthrown as party leader by the younger and more aggressive Dr Jörg Haider. The Socialist leader, Franz Vranitzky, then ended the coalition and called for new elections. The FPÖ's vigorous campaign under its new leader gained it considerable sup-port and it almost doubled its vote to 9.73 per cent and won 18 seats in the Parliament. In two subsequent elections in late 1987, in Burgenland and in Vienna the FPÖ's vote again increased sharply.

The FPÖ is well represented in the various provincial parliaments (Vienna eight, Carinthia five, Salzburg four, Upper Austria, Burgenland and Vorarlberg three, Styria and Tyrol two); has members of the provincial governments of Carinthia and Vorarlberg, and provides the deputy mayors of Graz and Klagenfurt.

Support

The FPÖ is now at its highest ever level of support (although lower than that won by the VdU in 1949 and 1953). It has a core vote of traditional nationalists, including some supporters and apologists for the Third Reich. Another strong element of its support comes from economic liberals, such as young managers, the self-employed and professionals like doctors and lawyers. A third element is that of general protest voters against the existing Austrian political system.

In 1988 the FPÖ did very well among younger voters. A third of its voters were under 30, and it won 14 per cent of all first time voters.

In provincial terms the FPÖ is strongest in the highly nationalist province of Carinthia, which is also Haider's current political base. The VdU had been strong in Carinthia (winning 20.5 per cent in 1949 and 15.7 per cent in 1953) and the FPÖ vote in 1986 was almost 21 per cent (up from under 11 per cent in 1983). In some communes the FPÖ vote in 1986 was close to 30 per cent (Feldkirchen 29 per cent, Rodenthein 28 per cent).

The FPÖ's other particularly strong province is Salzburg, where it won 16 per cent in 1986 (up from 8 per cent in 1983) and has won over 18 per cent in the past. In the city of Salzburg the FPÖ won over 18 per cent in 1986.

The FPÖ has also polled very well in Vorarlberg though its 1986 vote (12 per cent) rose less sharply than in other parts of Austria (having been 8 per cent in 1983, but 21 per cent in 1969).

In 1986 the FPÖ also got above its national percentage of the vote in Tyrol (11.25 per cent, but higher in certain communes such as Kufstein 21 per cent and Kitzbühl 18 per cent), Upper Austria (11.03 per cent), and Styria (9.89 per cent, where it polled best in the western mountain regions adjacent to Salzburg and Carinthia).

The FPÖ is much weaker in eastern Austria, in the province of Lower Austria (6.07 per cent in 1986), in the city of Vienna (5.68 per cent) and in Burgenland (5.37 per cent), although it has since increased its vote in provincial elections in both Vienna and Burgenland.

Organization

Compared to the two mass parties, the ÖVP and SPÖ, the FPÖ has a small membership of 37,000. The lowest tier of party organization are the local groups, which must have a minimum of 10 members. Each local group is entitled to delegates to the district party congress. There is also a district leadership. Above these are the provincial or *Landesgruppen*.

At federal level the Federal Party Congress must be convened at least every two years, and consists of delegates from the provincial groups. Among the tasks of the Federal Congress are to elect the party leader and his deputy, as well as a number of members of the party leadership council and the party executive.

The party leadership council (*Bundespartei-leitung*) is a relatively large body, consisting of the executive and other members elected at the congress, the national parliamentarians and any FPÖ members of the national and provincial governments. It meets at least four times a year. It also elects the party's general secretary.

The Federal Executive Council consists of the party leader and deputy leader, the parliamentary leaders, the provincial party leaders and four other members. It meets once a month. There must be at least one woman on the executive. A more restricted group of the party leaders and deputy leaders consisting of the two parliamentary leaders and the general secretary forms the Party Presidium.

The FPÖ parliamentarians are organized in the FPÖ *Klubs*. There is also a Federal Party Tribunal for party disputes, which is elected by the Federal Congress, as are the two party auditors.

The FPÖ's youth organization is called the *Ring Freiheitlicher Jugend*. Apart from this the FPÖ has far fewer affiliated organizations than the ÖVP or the SPÖ. Among the organizations that exist are an economic association, the *Ring Freiheitlicher Wirtschaftstreibender* (RFW) and a pensioners' group, the *Osterreichischer Pensionistenring*.

The party's newspaper used to be called *Neue Front* and is now called *Neue Freie Zeitung*.

The party is quite heavily dependent on public financing.

Since 1979 the FPÖ has been a member of the Liberal International. Since 1986 some members of the International have wished to see the FPÖ expelled because of what they see as links with certain right-wing nationalist and anti-semitic elements, but this point of view has not prevailed within the International.

Policies

The two main policy strands within the FPÖ have been nationalism and liberalism. For a long time the nationalist grouping within Austrian society considered that the small Austrian state left over after World War I was neither a viable nor a meaningful political unit, and that Austria's place lay within a wider German framework.

Since 1945 this position has been more difficult to sustain and nationalists have put their emphasis on reconciliation of the German peoples within a wider European union. The existence of Austria as a political unit has been gradually accepted. The more extreme nationalists have tended to go into fringe political parties and movements. Nevertheless nationalism and defence of Germanic identity and culture has remained an important trend within the FPÖ, and former Nazis and Nazi apologists, while present in other Austrian parties, have been more numerous and influential in the FPÖ than in the other mainstream parties.

The other main strand within the FPÖ has been liberalism, with its emphasis on a clear separation of church and state, and on a more open economy, with a fuller role for the private sector and a lesser role for the state. Risk-taking should be better rewarded, and bureaucracy should be reduced.

This is closely related to a third theme that has been successfully exploited within the FPÖ: criticism of the Austrian political and economic establishment.

The FPÖ has continuously attacked the *Proporz* system that has characterized Austria since the war, and the consequent clientelism, political privileges and even corruption. The FPÖ has thus attracted those who have felt excluded by the system, or who have felt that the system is holding back Austria's economic development.

In the 1986 election campaign all three of these themes were skilfully harnessed by the party's attractive young leader, Dr Jörg Haider. Moreover, now that the FPÖ was no longer in government it was able to adopt a more populist tone, contrasting with the more cautious policies of the former Deputy Chancellor and party leader, Norbert Steger. The FPÖ's subsequent success in recent provincial elections has indicated that it will continue to win generalized protest votes against the current "Red-Black" coalition.

The FPÖ believes that there should be more far-reaching privatization than the cautious measures taken by the present coalition. Existing wasteful state industries should be cut back, as should the whole system of state subsidies. There should also be a more liberal tax system, one that is less sharply progressive and provides greater rewards for personal initiative. There should be more flexible working time. The FPÖ puts a strong emphasis on reforming the current pension system. The present network of more than two dozen organizations administering the system should be drastically reduced, if possible, to a single federal organization.

The FPÖ defends the individual family farm, and believes there should be less subsidies to the agrarian bureaucrats, the co-operatives and other large organizations.

The FPÖ advocates an extension of direct democracy and a reduction in the influence of the two big political parties on all aspects of Austrian life. The existing network of leagues and chambers should be loosened. The tax and other privileges of the civil service and of politicians should be abolished. There should be tough measures against corruption.

The party prides itself on having been the first to come out against civil nuclear energy, and against the Zwentendorf plant, although its position on this issue is no longer so distinctive. It now calls for a nuclear-free Europe. The FPÖ puts a strong emphasis on environmental protection in general. On defence issues the FPÖ strongly supports Austrian neutrality.

The FPÖ supports Austrian entry into the European Community.

On development policy it calls for achievement of the UN target of 0.7 per cent GNP in aid to developing countries, but believes in stimulating self-help rather than creating new dependencies.

Personalities

The dominant figure within the party is Dr Jörg Haider who was only 36 when he was elected party leader in September 1986. Origi-

nally from Upper Austria, he is a former chairman of the FPÖ youth movement. His political base is nationalist Carinthia, where he was the provincial party chairman, and a member of the provincial government. Haider is currently both party leader and chairman of the FPÖ parliamentary group in the *Nationalrat*.

The party's secretary-general is Dr Norbert Gugenbauer who was elected in 1986 and is the same age as Haider. He is a specialist on defence questions.

Among the other influential figures within the party are the former Defence Ministers, Dr Friedhelm Frischenschlager and Helmut Krünes, the former Minister of Justice, Harold Ofner and the former State Secretary for Finance, Holger Bauer. Dr Gerulf Stix is the third president of the *Nationalrat*. Dr Tassilo Brösigke has been president of the National Audit office since 1980. Klara Motter is responsible for women's issues within the party.

Die Grüne Alternative
(Green Alternative)

Contact address	:	Millergasse 40, Wien (tel: 5979181)
Party secretaries	:	Johannes Vogenhuber, Pius Strobl
Parliamentary group leader	:	Freda Meissner-Blau
Founded	:	1987

History

The Austrian environmental movement was given its initial impetus by the successful campaign to prevent the Zwentendorf nuclear power station from being put into operation.

In the early 1980s two separate green parties were founded, the *Alternative Liste Österreichs* (ALÖ) and the rather more conservative *Vereinigte Grüne Österreichs* (United Greens of Austria — VGÖ), as well as a number of citizens' initiative groups. The 1983 national elections were separately contested by both parties, with the VGÖ winning 1.9 per cent of the vote and the ALÖ 1.4 per cent. Neither won any seats in the Parliament.

In 1984 there was a further mobilizing of the green vote with increasingly vocal protests against the proposed Hainburg hydroelectric plant in an environmentally highly sensitive part of the Danube Valley. In November 1984 the Greens won a major success in the Vorarlberg provincial elections, obtaining 13 per cent of the vote and gaining four seats in the *Landtag*, the first ever green members in a provincial parliament. Shortly afterwards the Hainburg project was brought to a halt.

In the 1986 presidential election the Greens' most prominent public figure, Freda Meissner-Blau, stood as a candidate and won 5.5 per cent of the vote. In the Styrian provincial elections the Greens won 3.73 per cent and two seats in the *Landtag*.

The sudden national elections called by Franz Vranitzky in late 1986 caught the Green movement unprepared. A concerted attempt was made to create a unified list of the VGÖ, the ALÖ and also a group called the *Burgerinitiative Parlament* (BIP). A unified list was finally reached in most parts of Austria but conflict over the way the list was formulated led to two lists being presented in Vienna and also in Carinthia.

The main Green list ended up with 4.8 per cent of the national vote, and with eight seats in the Parliament. The rival Green alternative list that was put up in Vienna only won 0.66 per cent of the city vote and the rival list in Carinthia fared even worse.

On Feb. 14–15, 1987 a unified Austrian Green Party was finally forged, and took the name *Die Grüne Alternative*. One of the parliamentarians, however, Dr Josef Buchner, was unhappy about the arrangement, and wished to conserve his own independence. More conservative than the other parliamentarians he had taken issue with a number of the policy stands adopted by the group and broke with them entirely along with one other member.

In the Viennese *Landtag* elections in June 1987 the Green vote slipped back to 4.4 per cent (it had been over 6 per cent in 1980) and no seats were won on the city council, although 55 seats were won locally.

Support

The Green vote is predominantly a middle-class one. The Greens are also much stronger in cities than in the countryside. Analysis of their 1986 national vote showed that they had a particular appeal to young voters and to women. Fifty-eight per cent of their vote came from those under 30, and they appear to have won no less than 12 per cent of first-time voters. Sixty per cent of their voters were women. Green voters are also highly educated; 54 per cent had a university entrance qualification or a degree. The fact that the Greens appeal not just to left-wing voters is shown by the considerable percentage of former People's Party voters who appear to have supported them.

In regional terms the Greens have had two main areas of strength, Vienna and Western Austria. The Greens won over 6 per cent in Vienna in the 1986 national elections (nearer 7 per cent if the Green alternative list is also included). The strongest parts of Vienna for the Greens are the inner western suburbs such as Neubau, Mariahilfe and Josefstadt where they got up to 9 per cent of the vote, and where their vote held up well even in the poorer results in the 1987 *Landtag* elections.

In Western Austria the Greens' strongest area is undoubtedly the province of Vorarlberg, where they made their first breakthrough in the *Landtag* elections in 1984, and where they won 8.28 per cent in the national elections in 1986, obtaining around 9 per cent of the vote in the towns of Bregenz and Feldkirch and almost 10 per cent in Dornbirn. The Greens also polled well in 1986 in the Tyrol (5.56 per cent) especially in Innsbruck (just under 9 per cent) and in Salzburg (5.61 per cent). In Salzburg city, the Greens obtained 8.55 per cent of the vote.

They obtained lower votes in Upper Austria (4.58 per cent, but with 6.27 per cent in Linz, and a very high 13.08 per cent in the small community of Steyregg), Styria (3.96 per cent, but over 7 per cent in Graz), and Carinthia (3.35 per cent). Their lowest vote in Austria was in Burgenland (2.32 per cent), a position subsequently confirmed in the Burgenland provincial elections.

Organization

The Greens have a very loose organizational structure. Opposed to the dominant role that party membership plays in Austrian society, they claim not to have a clear idea as to the size of their own membership. Their own 1987 constitution claims that they do not wish to be a party organization in the traditional sense. They see themselves as a co-ordinating group, reinforcing the work of individual citizens' initiatives and movements, with whose autonomy they wish to interfere to the minimum extent.

The Green Alternatives are divided into nine provincial organizations, each fully autonomous on provincial matters. In addition there are Green groups among different Austrian ethnic minorities, notably among the Slovenes of Carinthia.

The federal congress currently consists of 183 members. Each province is automatically entitled to nine delegates, and ethnic minorities are entitled to four delegates in all. The remaining delegates are chosen on the basis of the population of each province. The federal congress meets at least once a year. Among its tasks are to ratify candidates' lists and the federal policy programme, for which two-thirds majorities are required.

The federal committee consists of 20 members (formerly 30 but reduced in 1988), two representatives from each province and two from the ethnic minorities. The committee meets around 10 times a year, and is the highest party organ between federal congresses.

The federal executive, including the party's financial officer, is directly elected by the party congress. It used to consist of eight members as well as a non-voting party secretary. As a result of reform in 1988 it now consists of seven members, including two party secretaries (*Bundesgeschäftsführer*) with full voting rights and generally with reinforced powers compared to that of their predecessor. Members of the federal executive cannot hold any public office apart from in communes of under 50,000 inhabitants.

The Green parliamentarians are organized in a *Grüne Klub*. Green training institutions exist at federal and provincial levels. Forty-four per cent of the public money for training purposes goes to the provinces and 56 per cent to the federal level.

One party principle is that there must be at least 50 per cent women in all elected party posts. Another is defence of minority rights. If one third of party delegates disagree with a party position the minority position must be written into the programme.

Policies

The Green Alternatives contain a wide spectrum of members, from relatively conservative conservationists to those who want a much more radical change in society. The fusion between two separate Green parties as well as of members coming from different citizens' movements and citizens' initiatives has not been an easy one, and there have been several schisms within the party, most recently that led by Josef Büchner. A further problem for the party is that several of its mobilizing issues, such as the battle to stop civil nuclear energy in Austria, and the power station at Hainburg, are now issues of the past.

The Greens' current programme goes beyond narrow conservation objectives and calls for major changes in the organization of the Austrian economy and of Austrian society. There should be a much more decentralized economic system, with small economic units, with more local self-sufficiency, and with less waste, lower energy usage and with less unnecessary transport of goods and people. There should be a shift away from producing unnec-

essary goods such as steel and towards other more "environmentally-friendly" production. The currently wasteful Austrian state industries should not be privatized but should be redirected in more socially useful directions.

The working week should be sharply reduced. In addition everyone should be given a social wage whether they work or not, with a guaranteed basic income. The current tax system should be drastically reformed. There should also be guaranteed housing.

The Greens seek decentralized energy solutions, including energy conservation and use of renewables. Waste should be separated and recycled to a much higher degree than at present. Less public money should be spent on motorways and high speed roads. More should be transported by rail, and public transport should be reinforced.

There should be much greater equality of men and women. Handicapped people should be better integrated rather than being subject to social "apartheid". The rights of Austria's ethnic minorities should be fully protected.

Refugees should have the right to live and work in Austria, rather than just use it as a transit camp.

The Greens wish to see Austrian democracy reinforced. There should be more possibility of binding referenda. Industrial democracy in the workplace should be extended. There should be fewer subsidies for political parties, and special privileges for parties and their members should be removed.

The Greens have been highly critical of President Waldheim, for whose resignation they have called. They also put considerable emphasis on the commemoration of the 50th anniversary of *Anschluss*, and the need for Austrians to accept more responsibility for their past.

As regards defence, the Greens call for a smaller Austrian army, and are opposed to the Draken aircraft that have been purchased from Sweden. As a longer term objective the Austrian army should be abolished. The large Austrian arms industry should be curtailed, and Austrian arms exports should be stopped.

On development policy Austria should meet the 0.7 per cent of GNP UN aid target.

The Greens are generally opposed to Austrian entry into EC, which they consider will bring Austria closer to NATO as well as being potentially harmful for small industry and for small Austrian farmers.

Personalities

By far the most well-known Green personality is Freda Meissner-Blau, who was the Green candidate for president in the 1986 elections and is the leader of the Green parliamentary group. She is a former member of the Socialist party. Another influential member of the parliamentary party is Peter Pilz, who has a particular interest in arms production issues. Manfred Srb is particularly concerned with protection of the handicapped, and is himself a handicapped member of parliament. Another Green parliamentarian, Karel Smolle, is a representative of the Slovene minority in Carinthia.

The two current party secretaries are Johannes Vogenhuber and Pius Strobl. Their predecessor was Werner Haslauer.

Vereinigte Grüne Österreichs (VGÖ)
(United Greens of Austria)

Headquarters	: Goethestrasse 9, A-4020 Linz
Chairman	: Josef Buchner
General secretary	: Wolfgang Pelikan
Membership	: 500

This is the more conservative wing of the Green Movement in Austria. It was founded in 1982, and contested the 1983 elections on a separate basis. In 1986, however, it fought the National Council elections as part of a wider Green alliance, which obtained eight members. In 1987 Josef Buchner of the VGÖ, who disagreed with some of the radical positions of the Green group, broke with the newly established Green Alternatives (see separate entry) and asserted his own independence along with one other of the parliamentarians.

The VGÖ has a publication called *Blatter der VGÖ*. The VGÖ has sections in all nine provinces.

Kommunistische Partei Österreichs — KPÖ
(Austrian Communist Party)

Headquarters	: Höchstadtplatz, A-1026 Wien
Party chairman	: Franz Muhri
Secretaries	: Walter Silbermaier, Hans Kalt
Party newspaper	: *Die Volkstimme*
Members	: 12,000
Founded	: 1918

History

The KPÖ was founded in Vienna on 3 November 1918, thus becoming one of the earliest European Communist parties. In 1919 it launched an unsuccessful uprising in Vienna. It never enjoyed much success during the First Republic, and never won a seat in Parliament. In 1933 it was banned. It also gained a few recruits after the Socialists lost the civil war. Its main growth, however, came after 1938, when it played a considerable role in the resistance to the Germans.

In 1945 it gained 5.4 per cent of the vote and four seats, polling particularly well in Vienna and Carinthia, and to a lesser extent in Lower Austria and Styria. It had participated in the provisional Austrian government, with the portfolios of Interior and Education. After the elections it had one minister, Karl Altmann, at the Ministry of Power. It also participated in a number of provincial governments, including such unlikely *Länder* as Tyrol and Vorarlberg. In 1947 the Communists left national government, never to return.

In spite of being branded as the "Russian party" and the unpopularity of the Russian occupation of eastern Austria, the KPÖ managed to maintain its voting strength well into the 1950s, winning 5.1 per cent and five seats in 1949 and 5.3 per cent and four seats in 1953. In the late 1951 presidential election, its candidate Gottlieb Fiala won 5 per cent of the votes. After the events of 1956, however, it lost a third of its membership and by 1959 its vote had dropped to 3.3 per cent and it lost its last seats in parliament.

In 1965 Franz Muhri took over as leader from Johann Koplenig who had led the party since 1924. The KPÖ tried to modernize itself by adopting a new and more pragmatic programme ("The Theses"), in which the party accepted a peaceful road to socialism, political pluralism, and the maintenance of a private sector. In the 1966 elections the party only contested Vienna, and elsewhere recommended a vote for the SPÖ.

The 1968 Soviet invasion of Czechoslovakia brought tension between the old hardliners and party reformists to the fore. At first the party issued a cautious condemnation of the invasion but neither faction was satisfied. At the 1969 party conference a leading rebel, Ernst Fischer, who had sought a stronger condemnation, was expelled from the party. There were subsequently many departures from the party, and by 1970 the conservative hardliners had again won control, but at considerable political cost. The party has never since won more than 1.4 per cent in national elections, and by 1970 it had lost its last seats in *Land* parliaments such as Vienna (where it had held seven seats in 1949), Carinthia and Styria.

In the 1983 elections it gained 0.66 per cent of the votes, and in 1986 0.72 per cent.

Support

The KPÖ now has minimal electoral support. Even in the working-class areas of Vienna its highest votes in 1986 were 1.46 per cent in Donaustadt and 1.36 per cent in Floridsdorf. Elsewhere in the country by far its best result was in the industrial community of Eisenerz (3.98 per cent). Its second best result was in Knittelfeld (2.81 per cent).

Organization

The KPÖ has around 12,000 members, and its organization is still governed by the principle of democratic centralism. The party congress takes place every three years. 477 delegates attended the 1987 congress. There is also a 69-member central committee (1987 figure) and a politburo of 11.

Among its associated organizations are its youth movement, the *Kommunistische Jugend Österreichs* (KJÖ) (reformed in 1970 after the previous group had had to be disowned as a result of the turmoil in the party), its women's movement, the *Bund Demokratischer Frauen*, and two other associations the *Mieterschutzverband* and the *Zentralverband der Sozial-rentner*. Its trade union group the *Fraktion der Gewerkschaftlichen Einheit* is weak, and the Communists only won 0.8 per cent of the vote in the 1984 Chamber of Labour elections.

The KPÖ is a wealthy party, partly on the strength of its substantial industrial holdings acquired in the decade after the war from the Soviet occupation authorities in eastern Austria, and partly from its control over certain aspects of trade with the Soviet Union (such as imports of Russian vodka). It has a large headquarters staff, and its own publishing house. It produces a weekly newspaper called the *Volkstimme* and a monthly publication *Weg und Ziel*.

Policies

After the defeat of the revisionists in the period of inner party turmoil in 1968–70 the KPÖ has again been an orthodox communist party, loyal to the Soviet Union and rejecting Eurocommunism.

Personalities

The party's leader since 1965 (and only its second since 1924!) has been Franz Muhri from Styria.

Cyprus
Francis Jacobs

The country

Cyprus is the third largest island in the Mediterranean, with an area of 3,572 square miles. It is divided into six districts (Nicosia, Limassol, Larnaca, Paphos, Famagusta and Kyrenia), and its capital is Nicosia. Before the Turkish invasion in 1974, Cyprus had a population of around 650,000, of whom 80 per cent were Greek Cypriots (overwhelmingly Greek Orthodox in religion) and 18 per cent were Turkish Cypriots (Islamic in religion). Before independence, the Greek and Turkish Cypriot communities were intermingled throughout the island with the exception of the predominantly Greek Cypriot area in the Central Troodos Mountains. There were also a small number of minority groups, notably Maronites (Lebanese or Syrian Christians), Armenians and "Latins" (mainly Catholics of Crusader, Venetian or other Italian merchant origin).

The 1974 Turkish invasion divided Cyprus into two zones, a Greek Cypriot zone in the south and a Turkish Cypriot zone in the north. Of the historic districts, Paphos and Limassol are entirely within the Greek Cypriot zone, as is the vast majority of Larnaca district. Nicosia district is divided, with around 62.5 per cent in the Greek Cypriot zone. Famagusta district is mainly within the Turkish Cypriot zone, and Kyrenia district is entirely within it. In all, the occupied Turkish Cypriot zone accounts for around 37 per cent of the entire territory of the island.

Map of Cyprus showing the 6 districts, the boundary of the Turkish military occupied zone, and the number of seats in each constituency.

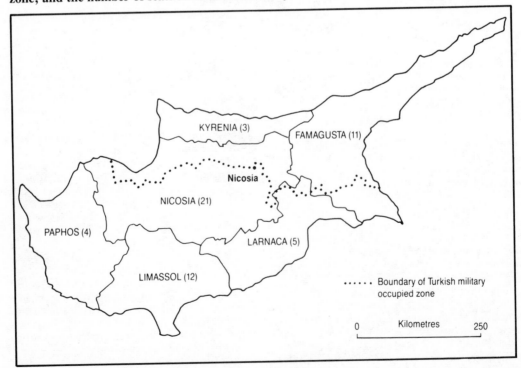

Source: adapted from *World Atlas of Elections*.

The division of the island led to an influx of 200,000 Greek Cypriot refugees from the Turkish zone of the island into the unoccupied area, as well as a large transfer of Turks in the opposite direction. There are now minimal numbers of Turkish Cypriots in the unoccupied zone and vice-versa.

There are, however, still over 1,600 "missing" Greek Cypriots, who are unaccounted for. The demography of the Turkish-controlled zone has now been profoundly modified by an influx of around 30,000 Turkish troops and a large number of settlers from mainland Turkey (estimated by the Greek Cypriots at 60–65,000). There is no freedom of movement between the two zones, and only one crossing point along the whole boundary between them. Nicosia, the capital of the Republic of Cyprus and of the "Turkish Republic of Northern Cyprus" is a divided city like Berlin.

Within the territory of the Greek Cypriot-controlled Republic of Cyprus, there are also two substantial British sovereign base areas, a western one at Akrotiri and an eastern one at Dhekelia.

Political institutions

Cyprus's constitution on its independence in 1960 divided Cyprus into two ethnic communities. Greek and Turkish were both official languages. The President was to be elected only by Greek Cypriots and the Vice-President by Turkish Cypriots, who were to be entitled to three out of 10 ministers in the government. The Turkish Cypriots were also allowed to elect separately 15 out of the total of 50 seats in the House of Representatives (the balance of 35 being elected by Greek Cypriots), and also to have 30 per cent of the civil service and 40 per cent of the police force and army. There were also to be separate Greek and Turkish Community Councils. The Turkish community was also given a number of other important safeguards. The Vice-President had a right of veto on certain fundamental matters, and certain laws required simple majorities among both Greek and Turkish Cypriot members. In the House, for example, there was a theoretical blocking minority of only eight (a simple majority of the 15 Turkish Cypriot members).

The system set up at Independence never functioned well and in December 1963 the Turkish Cypriot members left the Parliament, never to return. The 1974 Turkish invasion finally created two separate political entities, with their own separate political institutions, the Greek Cypriot-controlled Republic of Cyprus

and a Turkish Federated State of Cyprus, which was formally proclaimed in 1983 as the Turkish Republic of Northern Cyprus (whose legitimacy is only recognized by Turkey).

Republic of Cyprus

The political system of the Republic of Cyprus is based on that established at Independence, with continued provision for Turkish Cypriot participation in theory, although there is of course no such participation in practice. The political system provides for a clear separation of powers, more comparable to that in the United States than to any other European system.

The Constitution provides for a powerful presidency. The President is directly elected for a five-year term of office by simple majority. If no candidate wins more than 50 per cent in the first round, then there is a second round between the two leading candidates.

The members of the government (the Council of Ministers) are chosen directly by the President. There is no Prime Minister.

The President does not have to have a majority in the House of Representatives, and his government cannot be brought down by a vote in the House. Members of the government may not be members of the House, and if the latter are chosen to serve, they must resign from the House.

The President may address the House, and individual ministers may make statements in it, but the President and ministers are not constitutionally bound to appear before it or its committees.

The President has veto rights in certain foreign affairs, defence and security questions (as does the Vice-President, although this post does not currently exist in the absence of Turkish Cypriot participation), but only delaying powers in other areas. Legislation may be introduced by both the government and the House of Representatives. The President can send a bill back to the House in case of disagreement, but if the House revotes it, the President cannot further block it unless there are constitutional implications, in which case the President can refer the matter to the supreme Constitutional Court.

The House of Representatives is also elected for a five-year term, with the possibility of new elections before the end of the term, if the House itself so decides by an absolute majority of its members. If the House dissolves itself more than one year before the end of its term, the new House only serves for the unexpired period of the old House, and there are then new elections. If the House dissolves itself less than one year before the end of its term (as happened in 1985) the new House will also serve the period of the unexpired term in addition to the five years.

The House currently has 56 members (the number was increased in 1985 from 35). There are provisions for 80 members in all, with 24 places having been left vacant for the Turkish Cypriots (in 1985 the number was increased from 15).

The electoral constituencies are the six historic districts (including those under Turkish occupation), with the 56 Greek Cypriot seats divided between Nicosia (21 seats), Limassol (12), Famagusta (11), Larnaca (5), Paphos (4) and Kyrenia (3). Refugees from the occupied districts vote for candidates of that district irrespective of where the refugees live in unoccupied Cyprus. A refugee from Kyrenia living in Limassol, for example, will vote for the Kyrenia list of candidates.

Elections are held by proportional representation, with an initial distribution of seats within a constituency according to the Hare quota, and subsequent distribution of seats left over within the constituency to parties polling more than 10 per cent of the vote (or 8 per cent if they have already won a seat in the first round). There are also provisions for by-elections in cases of vacancy.

The House is presided over by a President (who must be a Greek Cypriot). If the Turks participated they would have a right to a Vice-President. There are 11 standing committees, and five new ones have also been established. The House may initiate legislation, but representatives cannot introduce bills which relate to increases in budgetary expenditure.

Besides the Greek Cypriot members of the House, the Armenian, Maronite and Latin religious communities each have one representative in the House, who do not have a right to vote, but have a right to speak on matters affecting their community.

There are also communal chambers which exist to deal with certain matters connected with education and personal and religious status.

Turkish Republic of Northern Cyprus

The Turkish Federal State of Cyprus, which was established in 1975 drew up a new Constitution, which provided for an elected President, a Prime Minister (unlike in the Republic of Cyprus) and a 40-member National Council. The first presidential and council elections were held in 1976.

In 1983 the Turkish Republic of Northern Cyprus was formally declared.

A new Constitution was drawn up in 1984 and ratified in 1985 in a referendum in which 49,447 of those eligible to participate voted in favour and 21,012 voted against. The new Legislative Assembly consists of 50 members. Parties must obtain a minimum of 8 per cent of the vote to be eligible for seats in the Assembly. The first presidential and Legislative Assembly elections under the new Constitution were held in 1985.

Brief political history of Cyprus

1878   Turkey cedes Cyprus to Britain.

1883   Legislative Council (with very limited powers) meets for the first time.

1914   Britain formally annexes Cyprus.

1915   Britain offers Cyprus to Greece if latter prepared to participate in war with Allies against Germans (following previous overtures by Britain).

1923   Turkey renounces its claim to Cyprus. Turkish Cypriots are given two years to opt for Turkish nationality and to move to Turkey. Only 2,500–3,000 leave the island.

1925   Cyprus is declared a Crown Colony.

1931   Severe riots in Cyprus, with demonstators calling for Union with Greece ("Enosis"). Legislative Council and elections are subsequently suspended by the British. Political parties are dissolved.

1941   Political parties are again legalized.

1948   Britain proposes a measure of self-government for Cyprus, but this is considered inadequate by pro-Enosis politicians.

1950   Michael Mouskos is elected as Archbishop Makarios III. A plebiscite shows that 95.7 per cent of Greek Cypriots are in favour of Enosis.

1955   EOKA guerillas, under the leadership of right-wing General Grivas ("Dhigenis"), begin violent campaign for Cyprus to be united with Greece.

1955–59   Continued campaign by EOKA, and rise in conflicts between the Greek and Turkish communities. A violent Turkish Defence organization (TMT) is also founded. Turks push for "taksim" (partition).

1959   Zürich and London agreements reject union of Cyprus with Greece and partition, but provide for the establishment of an independent Cyprus. British are allowed to retain two sovereign base areas by the so-called Treaty of Establishment. A Treaty of Guarantee provides for Greek, Turkish and British guarantees of Cyprus' sovereignty and a Treaty of Alliance provides for defence co-operation between Greece, Turkey and the Republic, and the stationing of Greek and Turkish troops. A provisional government is established. Elections are held in which Archbishop Makarios III obtains 66.8 per cent of the vote against John Clerides of the Democratic Union to become first President of Cyprus (Kutchuk becomes Vice-President).

1960–74 *Independent United Cyprus*

1960   Elections are held in which pro-Makarios Patriotic Front obtains 30 of the 35 Greek Cypriot seats. 15 Turkish seats won by Cyprus Turkish National Union. Cyprus becomes fully independent.

1963   Turkish minority in Parliament block tax laws, Makarios puts forward 13 points to change Constitution (e.g. proposing to abandon veto power of President and Vice-President, and to provide for unified municipal administrations). Intercommunal fighting revives. Turkish Cypriot representatives leave House.

1964   Continued intercommunal violence. Elections postponed. UN peace-keeping force stationed on island. Turkish Cypriot enclaves established. Turks intervene in Kokkina region, but US discourages full-scale Turkish invasion of Cyprus.

1967   Revival of severe intercommunal violence.

1968   Makarios re-elected as President.

1968–74 Intercommunal talks between Greek Cypriots led by Glafcos Clerides and Turkish Cypriots led by Rauf Denktash. Patriotic Front falls apart and three new parties are established (left-of-centre EDEK and right-of-centre Unified Party and Progressive Front). EOKA B is set up by Grivas to push for Enosis with Greece. Makarios is re-elected without opposition in 1973.

1974   Grivas dies. Coup against Makarios on July 15 sponsored by Greek military junta. Makarios escapes and Nikos Sampson becomes new Cypriot President. Turks invade on July 20. New Cypriot regime collapses and Glafcos Clerides becomes Acting President pending return of Makarios. Second and more comprehensive Turkish attack leads to Turks occupying 37 per cent of Cyprus territory.

1974–present: *Divided Cyprus*

1975   Proclamation of Turkish Federated State of Cyprus.

1976   Creation of new parties on the right-of-centre of the Greek Cypriot political spectrum (pro-Makarios, DIKO, and anti-Makarios, DISY). New elections in which DIKO becomes largest party. Denktash elected as President of Turkish zone.

1977   Meeting between Makarios and Denktash, with apparent agreement on four guidelines (including aim of independent, non-aligned, bi-communal Federal Cyprus). Makarios dies in August. Kyprianou becomes Acting President, and then elected unopposed to finish Makarios term.

1978   Kyprianou re-elected unopposed as President of Cyprus.

1979   Meeting between Kyprianou and Denktash concludes with 10 point agreement to relaunch intercommunal negotiations.

1981   New House elections, in which AKEL and DISY emerge as largest parties. In Turkish occupied zone new elections in which Denktash re-elected as President, and his National Unity Party is again largest party.

1982   DIKO and AKEL agree on Minimum Programme of Democratic Co-operation.

1983   DIKO–AKEL agreement leads to easy re-election of President Kyprianou (with 56.5 per cent) over Glafcos Clerides of DIKO (33.9 per cent) and Dr. Lyssarides of EDEK (9.5 per cent). Turkish Republic of Northern Cyprus is proclaimed on Nov. 15.

1984   Security Council of United Nations adopts Resolution 550 on Cyprus calling on all states to respect the sovereignty, independence, territorial integrity, unity and non-alignment of Cyprus, and not to recognize Turkish Republic of Northern Cyprus. Agreement between DIKO and AKEL falls apart over disagreements on "national question" and Kyprianou's handling of negotiations.

1985   Failure of Kyprianou-Denktash talks. AKEL and DISY vote censure on

Kyprianou in the House, and later in the year vote together for early dissolution of House. New elections held, in which DISY becomes largest party. New elections also held in occupied Cyprus in which Denktash wins re-election as President with 70.5 per cent of the vote.

1988   New presidential elections in Republic of Cyprus. In first round Glafcos Clerides of DISY wins 33.3 per cent, Giorgios Vassiliou (independent, but backed by AKEL) obtains 30.1 per cent, outgoing President Kyprianou of DIKO obtains 27.3 per cent and Dr Lyssarides of EDEK obtains 9 per cent. In second round Vassiliou defeats Clerides by 51.6 per cent to 48.4 per cent, to become new President of Cyprus.

Main features of political system

Pre-1974

The main political features of pre-independence Cyprus were the powerful support for Union or "Enosis" with Greece among the Greek Cypriot population, growing intercommunal tensions between Greek and Turkish Cypriots, and fears among the Turkish Cypriot population which led to a growing demand for "Taksim" or partition. There were political divisions between advocates of violent and non-violent solutions on both sides, with the rise of the violent EOKA movement among Greek Cypriots (whose methods, if not final objectives, were resisted by the Communist AKEL Party in particular) and with the corresponding rise of TMT among Turkish Cypriots. Left-right divisions also existed (with the communist AKEL the only properly organized political party), but were not of central importance. An unusual feature of Cyprus politics was the important role of the Church, which gained additional prestige under Archbishop Makarios III by its strong support for Enosis.

Independence in 1964, although it contained limitations, led to a change in the terms of political debate. Demand among Greek Cypriots for Enosis declined, and the ideal of a truly independent non-aligned Cyprus became of greater importance. There was also dissatisfaction over the terms of the new Constitution, which Greek Cypriots found overly restrictive and cumbersome. Divisions between Greek and Turkish Cypriots gradually deepened, and tensions grew between two of the three guarantor powers, Greece and Turkey. From late 1963 onwards,

Turkish Cypriots no longer took a full part in the new state's political institutions.

A fully fledged political system did not really develop during these years. Cyprus politics were dominated by President Makarios, who combined secular and religious authority. On the right and centre of the mainstream political spectrum the dominant force was the shapeless and unideological Patriotic Front, and all major parties (including the Communist AKEL Party) supported President Makarios and his policies. The collapse of the Patriotic Front in 1969 led to the development of new parties (EDEK, the Progressive Front and the Unified Party), but the political system was still not well defined. The only opposition to Makarios came mainly from a minority on the far right, who supported Enosis and the Greek military junta, and who helped to launch the EOKA B terrorist movement.

The Greek-inspired 1974 coup against Makarios, and the consequent Turkish invasion led to the development of two completely separate political systems on the island. It also helped to finally discredit the idea of Enosis with Greece.

Post–1974 in the Greek Cypriot-controlled Republic of Cyprus

The dominating political issue since 1974 has been whether Cyprus can be re-united, Turkish troops and settlers removed, full freedom of movement and property ownership re-established, and a truly independent Federal State of Cyprus constructed, and on what terms.

In the years immediately before Makarios' death, a new division developed between pro- and anti-Makarios forces. The right and centre of the political spectrum divided in 1976, with pro-Makarios politicians helping to launch DIKO and an anti-Makarios leader, Glafcos Clerides, founding DISY.

The Republic of Cyprus now has a basically four-party system. Besides DIKO and DISY on the centre and right of the spectrum, the dominant party on the left is the Communist AKEL. There is also a much smaller Socialist Party, EDEK. A number of other parties have been founded (notably in 1981 when the Pan-Cyprian Renewal Front, the New Democratic Front and the Centre Union were all formed, and in 1986 when a Liberal Party was founded), but these have been of minor significance.

The death of Makarios has led to a greater development of the political system, but the system is still very much dominated by individual personalities (Kyprianou of DIKO, Clerides of DISY, Lyssarides of EDEK, etc.) and the parties are generally not very ideological. Even the seemingly ideological AKEL, and the more pro-Western and pro-free enterprise DISY have been very pragmatic in behaviour, and the difference between the parties has tended to be more one of emphasis than of major substance. What has been of greatest importance has been the parties' roles in providing patronage and service for constituents. The fluidity, however, of the political system is illustrated by the election (although with AKEL support) of an independent non-party businessman, Giorgios Vassiliou, as President of Cyprus in early 1988.

The main political divisions are over the handling of the "national question", and are less over ultimate objectives than over negotiating strategy and tactics, such as whether hard-line or more conciliatory approaches will be more fruitful, and what concessions will have to be made to Turkey and to Turkish Cypriots. At present DIKO and EDEK are rather more hard-line than AKEL and DISY.

There are also differences of emphasis on foreign policy orientation (relations with the Western powers, degree of non-alignment, Cyprus–EC relations and possible adhesion). Differences on domestic issues do not appear to be very sharp.

Post–1974 in the Turkish-controlled Turkish Republic of Northern Cyprus

The dominant Turkish Cypriot party when Cyprus became independent was the *Kibris Milli Türk Birligi* (KMTB – Cyprus Turkish National Union), led by Dr Fazil Kutchuk, who had founded the party in 1955, to defend the interests of the Turkish community, and who was elected Vice-President of Cyprus under Makarios in 1960. In the first House of Representatives election in 1960, the KMTB obtained all 15 of the Turkish Cypriot seats in the House. From 1963 onwards they played no more part in the work of the House, and by 1973 the party had itself disintegrated.

After the 1974 Turkish invasion a new political system was established. There was no longer the same pressure for a single party defence of Turkish Cypriot rights and a multi-party system developed, in which the dominant party was nevertheless the right-of-centre *Ulusal Birlik Partisi* (UBP – National Unity Party) led by Rauf Denktash. Denktash himself was elected President of Cyprus, and the party obtained 30 of the 40 seats in the first National Council elections in 1976.

Since 1976 the UBP has continued to be by far the largest Turkish Cypriot party, although it had lost its overall majority by 1981 and Turkish Cyprus thus entered into an era of

coalition governments. The other two main parties in Turkish Cyprus have been the Social Democratic *Toplumcu Kurtulus Partisi* (TKP — Communal Liberation Party); and the more left-wing *Cumhuriyetci Türk Partisi* (CTP — Republican Turkish Party), which was originally much less successful than the TKP but which outpolled it in the 1985 presidential and parliamentary elections.

There have also been a number of other smaller parties, some of which have been of only short duration and of little electoral significance.

Besides the left–right division in the Turkish Cypriot political spectrum, another has been that between the original Turkish Cypriots and the new Turkish settlers who have come to Cyprus since 1974, and who have often come from culturally conservative and poor Anatolian backgrounds. The *Yeni Dogus Partisi* (YDP – New Dawn Party), for example, which obtained 9 per cent and four seats in the 1985 parliamentary elections, has primarily developed to defend the interests of the settlers. The key political debate, however, has been over the degree to which Turkish Cyprus should attempt reconciliation with the Greek-controlled Republic of Cyprus, retain an entirely separate identity or further integrate with Turkey.

Contested presidential election results in the Republic of Cyprus since Independence

1959   Archbishop Makarios III, 67 per cent; John Clerides (*Demokratiki Enosis Kyprou* — DEK, Democratic Union) 33 per cent.

1968   Makarios 95.5 per cent, Dr Takis Evdokas (*Demokratikon Ethnikon Komma* — DEK, Democratic National Party) 4 per cent.

1983   S. Kyprianou (DIKO) 56.5 per cent, G. Clerides (DISY 33.9 per cent), Dr Lyssarides (EDEK 9.5 per cent).

1988   First round: G. Clerides (DISY) 33.3 per cent, G. Vassiliou (Independent, backed by AKEL) 30.1 per cent, S. Kyprianou (DIKO) 27.3 per cent, Dr Lyssarides (EDEK) 9 per cent.
Second round: G. Vassiliou 51.6 per cent, G. Clerides 48.4 per cent.

Presidential elections in Turkish Cyprus since 1974

1976   Rauf Denktash (UBP) 76 per cent, Ahmed Mihdat Berberoglu (CTP) 24 per cent.

1981   R. Denktash (UBP) 51.8 per cent, Ziya Rizki (TKP) 30.5 per cent, Özker Özgür (CTP) 12.8 per cent,

General Huramettin Tanyar (TAP) 4.8 per cent.

1986   R. Denktash (UBP) 70.2 per cent, Özker Özgür (CTP) 18.3 per cent, Alpay Durdaran (TKP) 9.6 per cent, others 2 per cent.

Anorthotikon Komma Ergazomenou Laou — AKEL
(Progressive Party of the Working People)

Headquarters   : 10 Akamantos Street, Nicosia (tel: 44 11 21)
Secretary-general : Dimitris Christofias
Membership   : 15,000
Founded   : 1941

History

AKEL is a party of Communist orientation and is the only one of the current Cypriot parties to predate independence.

The Communist Party of Cyprus (KKK) was first founded in 1925, and held its first congress in 1926. Among its early leaders were Charalambos Vatyliotis ("Vatis") and Costas Christodoulides ("Skeleas"). It called for a united anti-British front of all Cypriots of all classes.

In 1931 the KKK was forced to go underground, and was formally proscribed in 1933. Its members remained involved, however, in trade union activities, helping to found, for example, a Pancyprian Trade Unions' Conference in 1939.

On April 14 a new party, AKEL, was founded by Communists and other left wing intellectuals. At first it opposed participation in World War II, but later changed its mind.

By 1943 AKEL was already enjoying success in municipal council elections (e.g. winning majorities on the municipal councils of Limassol and Famagusta). In 1945 a youth organization, AON, was founded and some of AKEL's prominent trade union representatives were put on trial and sentenced.

In 1946 AKEL had further success in municipal elections, including those in Nicosia. In 1948 AKEL supported a four-month strike of workers at the Cyprus Mines corporation. In the 1949 local elections, however, AKEL lost support. In 1949 Ezekias Papaioannou became AKEL's secretary-general, a post he was to hold until 1988.

AKEL, which had long called for self-determination for Cyprus, now began to put a greater emphasis on union with Greece. In 1950 it supported "Enosis" in the plebiscite of that year.

In the troubles of the mid-1950s, AKEL was opposed to General Grivas and to EOKA violence. It was not actively involved in EOKA, and some of its members suffered at its hands. Nevertheless AKEL was again banned by the British in 1955 as a subversive organization.

In 1959 AKEL was again legalized. It objected to the terms of independence because of the continuance of the British bases and the limitations on Cyprus' sovereign rights. In 1959 it supported the Democratic Union against Archbishop Makarios, but in the 1960 elections it agreed to co-operate with the pro-Makarios Patriotic Front in exchange for a certain number of seats in the House of Representatives.

AKEL won five seats, and also three seats in the Greek Communal Chamber. It subsequently became strongly supportive of Makarios on both domestic and foreign policy issues, especially his stance in favour of an independent non-aligned Cyprus.

In the 1970 elections, nine AKEL members were elected to the House of Representatives. AKEL was strongly opposed to the rise of EOKA B, and to the Greek junta-sponsored coup in 1974, which led to the Turkish intervention.

In 1976 AKEL took part in an electoral alliance of the three pro-Makarios parties, in which it again obtained nine seats in the House. In 1979 it obtained seats on a large number of rural councils.

After the death of Makarios AKEL was supportive of his successor, President Kyprianou. It withdrew its support from him in 1980, but this was only of brief duration.

In 1981 AKEL stood in its own right without any electoral alliances with other parties, and emerged as the largest party in terms of votes, with 32.8 per cent of the vote and 12 out of 35 seats in the House.

In 1982, AKEL entered into a Minimum Programme of Democratic Co-operation with President Kyprianou's DIKO Party, in which AKEL agreed to support the Government (without formally entering it) in order to achieve a number of key objectives, primarily to help resolve the "national question".

In 1983 AKEL supported the re-election of President Kyprianou.

In December 1984 the agreement between AKEL and DIKO was ended by Kyprianou, after basic disagreements over his negotiating strategy on the national question (especially his handling of a UN-sponsored meeting with Denktash). AKEL accused the President of being too intransigent and missing an important negotiating opportunity, and AKEL was accused in its own turn of being too conciliatory.

In early 1985 AKEL supported its conservative adversary DISY in a censure motion against the President and later in the year voted with DISY in favour in early House elections. In the consequent elections in December 1985, AKEL's vote fell away sharply, and it only polled the third largest number of votes, with 27.4 per cent and 15 out of the 56 seats in the House.

In the 1987 municipal elections AKEL's vote recovered to 32.5 per cent and it managed to elect mayors in nine municipalities, mainly in the sprawling communities around Nicosia and Limassol, but also in the major town of Larnaca.

AKEL continued to oppose President Kyprianou and in 1987 decided to sponsor an independent candidate, Georgios Vassiliou for the 1988 presidential elections. Vassiliou narrowly won against Glafcos Clerides in the second round of the elections.

Shortly afterwards AKEL's long-serving secretary-general, Ezekias Papaioannou died and was replaced by Dimitris Christofias in April 1988. Christofias defeated his rival, Pavlos Diglis by 63 votes to 11.

Support

AKEL is proportionately one of the strongest Communist parties in Europe, and has a much longer tradition and far greater support than the Socialist Party, EDEK. AKEL is strongly rooted in the trade union organization, PEO (the Pancyprian Federation of Labour) and among working class voters in the larger towns and in the satellite communities around them.

In percentage terms its highest vote has been among voters from the district of Famagusta, among whom it was the largest party in 1981 with 39.1 per cent of the vote and second in 1985 with 34.1 per cent. Its second strongest area has been Larnaca, where it won 36.3 per cent in 1981 and 33 per cent in 1985.

In 1981 AKEL was also the largest party in Limassol and among voters from Kyrenia with 35.7 per cent and 34.3 per cent respectively, but it slipped to third in both districts in 1985, with 28.2 per cent in Limassol and 26.3 per cent among Kyrenia voters.

In Nicosia it was only second with 29.4 per cent in 1981, and it fell to third with only 24 per cent in 1985.

AKEL's weakest district by far has been the old Makarios stronghold of Paphos, where the Socialist EDEK Party wins its greatest support (although still below AKEL). AKEL obtained 20.8 per cent in Paphos in 1981 and only 19.2 per cent in 1985.

Organization

AKEL has been a highly structured party, with a more disciplined organization than that of any other Greek Cypriot party. It has depended less on individual personalities than other Cypriot parties, and more of its elected politicians have been full-time party professionals or trade union officials. It continues to be organized on the traditional Communist principle of democratic centralism.

AKEL claims to have around 15,000 members organized in local branches around the country. There are also party branches in London and in Athens.

AKEL has seven district organizations, four on a traditional territorial base in Limassol, Paphos, Larnaca and Nicosia and three among the refugee communities from Nicosia-Morphou, Kyrenia and Famagusta.

At national level a congress is held every four years and elects a central committee of around 100 members (including alternates) which meets up to four times a year.

In its turn the central committee elects a political bureau of 15 members, which meets on a weekly basis, and also the party's secretary-general, who is its political leader.

AKEL has a youth organization called EDON (United Democratic Youth Organization) and a women's organization called POGO (Pancyprian Federation of Women's Organizations). AKEL still has strong links with the Pancyprian Federation of Labour (PEO) and the Union of Cypriot Farmers (EKA).

AKEL has a daily newspaper called *Haravgi* (Dawn), and has also produced a journal of political theory called *New Democrat* and a publication called *World Marxist Review*. It also produces an occasional English-language bulletin called *AKEL Newsletter*.

AKEL has close ties with other world Communist parties. Its closest affinity with any Turkish Cypriot party is with the Republican Party.

Policies

AKEL is the leading Cyprus Party of the Left. Its rhetoric has been orthodox Communist but its actual policies have been cautious and pragmatic. It has earned its success by its solid organization, its implantation in the labour movement and its apparent ability to service constituents' demands. It has never put up an AKEL member as a presidential candidate and has successively backed Presidents Makarios, Kyprianou (until its final break with him in December 1984) and Vassiliou.

AKEL believes that primacy must be given

to the national question of occupation of Cyprus, and Cyprus' failure to achieve true independence. Class struggle, while important, must remain of subordinate importance until the national problems are solved. In this context AKEL has called in the past for governments of national unity in Cyprus. It has also shown itself willing to enter into alliances with "bourgeois" parties to achieve national objectives. While it recognizes that its co-operation with Kyprianou's DIKO was eventually a failure, it continues to believe that the underlying strategy of such an alliance was correct.

AKEL's objective is a fully independent, reunified and Federal Cyprus. AKEL has always put a strong emphasis on the need for common cause between native Greek and Turkish Cypriots.

AKEL strongly supported Makarios's policy of a non-aligned Cyprus, and has consistently called for a demilitarization of Cyprus, with a dismantling of foreign military bases.

While AKEL emphasizes its differences with DISY, which it considers to be the most conservative and pro-NATO Cypriot party, and that with the largest number of ex-EOKA activists, it appears currently closer to DISY in its less intransigent approach to the national question than the more hard-line DIKO and EDEK.

AKEL became very critical of what it saw as Kyprianou's inflexibility in late 1984 when he allowed the chief Turkish negotiator, Denktash, to appear to seize the initiative on the proposed United Nations Draft Framework Agreement, which Kyprianou would not accept. AKEL supported a more positive Greek Cypriot attitude towards this Framework Agreement, which it believes would have underlined a greater readiness to negotiate.

AKEL considers that there should be a close link between international action and intercommunal talks to solve the Cyprus problem. As regards the former an international conference should be convened to provide for the withdrawal of all foreign troops and settlers, the dismantling of all foreign bases and the demilitarization of Cyprus, as well as effective international guarantees for the full independence of Cyprus and territorial integrity. Other matters would have to be dealt with by intercommunal talks, which would aim at a full rapprochement of Greek and Turkish Cypriots.

In general foreign policy questions, AKEL has adopted an Orthodox pro-Soviet position. It was critical of the Chinese Communist stance. It supported the Soviet invasion of Afghanistan.

AKEL has also been highly supportive of the PLO, the ANC and the Sandinistas.

In domestic policy AKEL has generally been a pragmatic reformist party, aiming at raising Cypriot living standards by appropriate economic and social measures. It believes that a high priority should be given to fighting Cyprus public spending and foreign trade deficits, with measures of economic retrenchment, but not at the expense of the less well off. There should be a redistribution of tax burdens. AKEL is opposed to the introduction of VAT.

AKEL supports a strengthening of the role of the state in the economy. Trading in aid products and oil refining should come under state control, and the state should also get involved in the banking and insurance sectors. It considers that there should not be too much of an imbalance between the tertiary and other sectors.

AKEL has supported land reform. It emphasizes equal rights for women, and the concept of equal pay for work of equal value.

AKEL considers that there has been an unacceptable increase in the number of government employees put in place to serve narrow party interests. It calls for an end to what it sees as the scandalous use of state machinery by the government.

AKEL has opposed the EC-Cyprus Customs Agreement, and any idea of Cyprus joining the EC. It considers that Cyprus will lose out economically (Cyprus will become more dependent on Western European economic monopolies, and there will be too great an economic imbalance between Cyprus and other European countries), and also politically, in that Cyprus will lose independence and find it more difficult to keep out of NATO and to maintain its non-aligned foreign policy. AKEL recognized that this was one area where it disagreed with Georgios Vassiliou, but noted that he promised a plebiscite on the Customs Agreement.

Personalities

Dimitris Christofias was elected as AKEL's secretary-general in April 1988. Among the prominent leaders in the party have been Andreas Fantis, the long serving editor of the party newspaper *Haravgi*, and Andreas Ziartides, general secretary of the Pancyprian Federation of Labour (PEO) for over 40 years.

Demokratiki Komma — DIKO
(Democratic Party)

Headquarters : 16 Stassicratous
Street,
P.O. Box 3979,

	Nicosia
	(tel: 47 20 026)
President	: Spyros Kyprianou
Membership	: 15,000
Founded	: 1976

History

The Democratic Party (DIKO) was founded in 1976 by a number of political personalities on the centre and right of the Greek Cypriot political spectrum, who supported Archbishop Makarios and his policies. Many of those who joined the new party came from the former Progressive Front, which had been one of the two main parties on the right-of-centre of Cypriot politics after the demise of the broader-based Patriotic Front and before the events of 1974. DIKO was a new party, however, and even contained elements from the former Unified Party. DIKO's leading figure was, and has remained, Spyros Kyprianou, Makarios' Foreign Minister between 1960 and 1972.

In the 1976 elections DIKO obtained 21 seats, and became the largest party in Parliament. Kyprianou was subsequently elected President of the House of Representatives, and became Acting President of Cyprus on the death of Makarios in 1977. On Aug. 31, 1977 he was chosen to serve for what was left of Makarios' term of office. In 1978 he was elected without opposition for a full five-year term in his own right, after his main rival, Glafcos Clerides withdrew when Kyprianou's son was kidnapped (and subsequently released).

In 1980 DIKO's strength was considerably reduced when AKEL withdrew its support, and a number of DIKO personalities went off to form new parties, the New Democratic Front of Alekos Michaelides, the Centre Union of Tassos Papadopoulos and the Pancyprian Renewal Front of Dr Crysostomos Sofianos, or else to join the Democratic Rally of Glafcos Clerides. In the 1981 elections the much weakened DIKO only came a poor third, with 19.5 per cent of the vote and eight seats in the House of Representatives, although the breakaway parties failed to win any representation at all.

In April 1982 DIKO and AKEL agreed on a minimum programme of co-operation between the two parties, concentrating on the national question and on a policy for an independent non-aligned Cyprus. In the 1983 presidential elections Kyprianou was supported by AKEL as well as by DIKO and was easily re-elected with 56.5 per cent of the vote.

In December 1984 the agreement between DIKO and AKEL was ended over disagreements on the national question, with AKEL critical of Kyprianou's handling of the negotiations, and with DIKO claiming that AKEL was undercutting its position and going back on the terms of the agreement.

In new parliamentary elections in late 1985 DIKO strengthened its position considerably, becoming the second largest party with 27.6 per cent of the vote, and with 16 seats in the House of Representatives.

In the last part of President Kyprianou's term of office relations between him and the majority of the Parliament became increasingly difficult. In the 1988 elections Kyprianou ran for re-election without the support of AKEL. In the first round he polled 27.3 per cent of the vote, coming third behind Clerides and Vassiliou, and thus being eliminated from the second round. DIKO is now adjusting to being a party of opposition.

Support

DIKO has not had very stable support, being based more on support for personalities than for ideology. It was the largest party in 1976, only third in 1981 and second in 1985. Kyprianou obtained 56.5 per cent in the 1983 presidential elections, but only 27.3 per cent in 1988. DIKO also gained considerable support from being a party of government, and the impacts of it now being in opposition are still uncertain.

As a party particularly associated with support for former President Makarios, DIKO has been consistently strongest in Makarios' home district of Paphos, where it has been the largest party in all recent elections, even in its poor year of 1981. DIKO polled 27.4 per cent in Paphos in 1981 and 38.8 per cent in 1985. Kyprianou also polled far ahead of his rivals in Paphos in his unsuccessful bid for re-election as President in 1988, obtaining 37.7 per cent of the constituency vote.

DIKO's uncompromising stand on the national issue also seems to have helped it among voters from the occupied district of Kyrenia, where it was the second party in 1981 with 26.3 per cent of the vote and the largest party in 1985 with 33.6 per cent.

DIKO's third and fourth strongest districts have been Limassol (21.5 per cent in 1981, rising to 30.9 per cent in 1985) and Nicosia (19.1 per cent in 1981, 27.9 per cent in 1985). In both districts it was only third in 1981, but second in 1985.

DIKO has been weakest in the districts of Larnaca (15 per cent in 1981, 22.7 per cent in 1985) and especially Famagusta (14.8 per cent in 1981, 19.9 per cent in 1985). DIKO has been consistently third in both districts, which also gave Kyprianou his lowest share of the poll in the first round of the 1988 presidential elections.

Organization

DIKO claims to have around 15,000 members and to have around 500 local branches in every polling district. The local branches elect delegates to district congresses (which are held every three years) and to the national or pancyprian congress.

DIKO has 11 district committees, one each for Larnaca, Limassol and Paphos; two for Nicosia (one within Nicosia district for those within free and occupied Nicosia and one for refugees from occupied Nicosia in Limassol); two for wholly occupied Kyrenia (one for Kyrenia refugees in Nicosia and one in Limassol); and finally four for Famagusta (one for unoccupied Famagusta, and one each for Famagusta refugees in Nicosia, Larnaca and Limassol).

At national level the pancyprian congress of DIKO is held every three years, and directly elects the party's president and secretary-general.

DIKO's central committee consists of 100 members (to be increased to 140), containing representatives of the districts (elected at district congresses and ratified by the national congress) on the basis of their population. Above this there is a smaller, but still substantial political bureau, which includes the top party officers, the presidents of the district committees, the DIKO members of Parliament and the presidents of its youth, women and research organizations.

DIKO's youth organization is called NEDIK and its women's organization is called GODIK. DIKO also has a policy research organization, its group for studies.

DIKO produces a daily newspaper, *I Eleftherotypia* (Free Press) and also a weekly paper, *Eleftherotypia tis Defteras*.

DIKO has had no formal international links, although it has considered ties with Liberal International.

Policies

DIKO is on the centre-right of the Greek Cypriot political spectrum. It is primarily distinguishable from the other major right-of-centre party, the Democratic Rally (DISY), by its different origins (support for rather than opposition to President Makarios) and by the fact that under former President Kyprianou, it has been a party of government, rather than of opposition. It has not been a very ideological party and has had a generally pragmatic series of policies, prepared to co-operate with the Communist Party, AKEL, for example, when this was seen to be in the national interest.

Now that it is in opposition for the first time, DIKO is in a more difficult strategic position. It has lost important powers of patronage, and relations between Kyprianou and the current President Vassiliou still appear to be distant. DIKO's leaders now consider that it must sharpen its image. DIKO, which was portrayed by its opponents as too inflexible over the national question when in government, is now seeking to distinguish itself from DISY and AKEL (and from President Vassiliou) by adopting a harder line over negotiated solutions to the Cyprus problem. Its future success, therefore, may well be linked to the extent to which the Turks maintain their present position or else are prepared to make concessions.

DIKO considers that the Cyprus problem is one of invasion and occupation and of violation of basic human rights. It is thus opposed to the step by step approach, which it claims is supported by both DISY and AKEL. It believes that this so-called "realism" will merely permit the Turkish occupiers to consolidate their presence in Cyprus. The essential step, therefore, is the removal of Turkish troops (who should not be allowed to remain after the setting up of a transitional government) and also of the new Turkish settlers.

DIKO also emphasizes the need to convene an international conference to deal with the wider aspects of the problem, preferably under the aegis of the UN Secretary-General.

International guarantees should be provided, without the unilateral right of intervention by any one guarantor government.

DIKO calls for a unified Cyprus with a federal structure, providing for full freedom of movement, of settlement and of property ownership.

DIKO has also called for more expenditure on defence. DIKO strongly defends the Makarios foreign policy line of the need for a non-aligned Cyprus, free from any ties of dependence on foreign interests. While differences on this issue are more a question of degree, DIKO considers itself to be less strongly pro-Western than DISY. DIKO does, however, support an EC-Cyprus Customs Union and the eventual entry of Cyprus into the European Community.

On internal matters DIKO has not adopted a dogmatic stance. It supports the mixed economy. While emphasizing the importance of private enterprise, it is not prejudiced against nationalization of certain sectors of the economy if this is considered to be in the national interest. DIKO has supported institutionalized trilateral co-operation between the social partners.

Personalities

DIKO's dominant personality is still Spyros Kyprianou, who was Foreign Minister of Cyprus from 1960 to 1972, and President of Cyprus from 1977 to 1988.

Alexis Galanos is DIKO's political spokesman in the House of Representatives.

Dimokratikos Synagermos — DISY
Democratic Rally

Headquarters	: K. Skopou 2,
	P.O. Box 5305
	Nicosia
	(tel: 44 97 91)
President	: Glafcos Clerides
General secretary	: Alecos Markides
Membership	: 9,000
Founded	: 1976

History

The Democratic Rally (DISY) was founded in 1976 by Glafcos Clerides as a right-of-centre grouping of politicians opposed to President Makarios. Clerides had been a leader of the pro-Makarios Patriotic Front and in 1969 had founded the Unified Party, some of whose members were subsequently supportive of or neutral towards the coup against Makarios in 1974.

From 1975 onwards relations between Clerides and Makarios worsened over the issue of how best to tackle the national question, with Clerides calling for more flexibility and becoming the first Cypriot politician to accept that a new Cypriot state might have a bizonal character. In 1976 Clerides was finally dismissed as the long standing chief negotiator in intercommunal talks. DISY was formed in the same year.

DISY was based to a considerable extent on former members of the collapsed Unified Party, but also included members from the former Conservative Democratic National Party and even some members from the Progressive Front. There were a considerable number of former EOKA activists and sympathisers with the 1974 coup.

In its first electoral outing in 1976 DISY obtained 24 per cent of the vote, but no seats due to an electoral agreement between the three pro-Makarios parties, AKEL, DIKO and EDEK.

In 1978 Clerides did not stand against President Kyprianou after the latter's son was kidnapped in the run-up to the presidential elections. Clerides' relations with Kyprianou subsequently worsened.

In the 1981 parliamentary elections DISY obtained 12 out of 25 seats in the House on 31.9 per cent of the vote, narrowly behind AKEL but well ahead of the President's party DIKO.

In the 1983 presidential elections Clerides came second with 33.9 per cent but far behind Kyprianou, who was supported by both DIKO and AKEL.

In February 1985 Clerides called for the resignation of President Kyprianou over his inflexibility in negotiations over the Cyprus question and his alleged mishandling of the UN-sponsored talks with Denktash in New York. DISY subsequently voted with AKEL to pass a censure motion in the House against Kyprianou. Later in 1985 DISY pushed hard for the premature dissolution of the House. In the new elections in December 1985, DISY's vote rose slightly to 33.6 per cent and it obtained 19 seats in the House, thus becoming the largest party in Cyprus.

In the 1988 presidential elections Clerides came top in the first round of voting with 33.3 per cent but was defeated by Georgios Vassiliou after polling 48.4 per cent in the run-off.

Support

DISY is a broad-based party which has consistently enjoyed over 30 per cent support in the polls in all Greek Cypriot elections in the 1980s. It has been strong among the urban middle class and businessmen, and among farmers. It has also had trade union support as well, notably from among members of the SEK (Confederation of Labour of Cyprus).

DISY has been consistently strongest among voters from Famagusta district, among whom DISY has normally been the largest party. In the 1981 parliamentary elections DISY was narrowly second to AKEL in Famagusta with 38.3 per cent, but was first in 1985 with 39.5 per cent of the vote. In the 1983 presidential elections Clerides polled 46.2 per cent in unoccupied Famagusta. In 1985 he polled 45.2 per cent in the first round and 57.6 per cent in the second.

DISY's second strongest district is Nicosia, where it was the first party in both the 1981 and 1985 elections with 32.8 per cent and 34.4 per cent of the vote respectively. Clerides narrowly defeated Vassiliou in the Nicosia district in the 1988 run-off, with only 50.7 per cent of the vote. DISY is also well supported in Larnaca, where it polled 33.8 per cent in 1981 and 35.2 per cent in 1985. It is slightly weaker in Limassol (30.1 per cent in 1981, 31.4 per cent in 1985), although it was narrowly the largest party in the district on the latter occasion.

DISY has been weaker among voters from

the wholly occupied district of Kyrenia, where it came third in 1981 with only 24.4 per cent and second in 1985 with 27.4 per cent.

DISY has been weakest of all in the Makarios stronghold of Paphos, where it only obtained 20 per cent in 1981 and 23 per cent in 1985. In the 1983 presidential election Clerides only obtained 22.7 per cent in Paphos. In 1988 he obtained 23.1 per cent in the first round and 39.6 per cent in the run-off against Vassiliou, who had his most comfortable margin of victory within Paphos district.

Organization

DISY prides itself on its lack of formal ties with organized interest groups, and also on the extent of its internal democracy, with all its top officials elected by secret ballot among the elected representatives of party members rather than being nominated by party leaders.

DISY has around 9,000 members who are organized in more than 400 local party branches. DISY has organizations in all of the six Cyprus districts, with district executive committees and chairmen, and with district congresses held every three years.

At national level a congress is held every three years, with the last such congress having 400 participants. The congress directly elects the party's president, two vice-presidents and secretary-general, as well as the party head of organization, and the chairman of the party's youth group.

DISY's central council is the parliament of the party and consists of around 100–130 members elected at the respective district congresses, with the number of seats from each district dependent on the number of votes won by the party there at the last parliamentary elections. The top party officers are also members of the council, which meets every three months.

DISY's political committee consists of around 70 people, including the members of the executive committee of each district. It generally meets every month. The political committee's executive is its political bureau which consists of the top party officers (the party head of finance and the president's secretary also attend but without voting rights) and which meets more than once a week. There is also an enlarged political bureau, which also includes the district chairmen and the party's deputies in the House, and which meets around every 15 days.

The party has a youth organization called NEDISY, whose chairman is elected at the party congress but whose vice-chairman is elected only by NEDISY members.

DISY has no separate organization for its women members. At least 15 per cent of all party political posts, however, are reserved for women up to political committee level.

DISY has no formal links with other organizations or interest groups, although it has been close, for example, to the SEK, the Confederation of Labour of Cyprus.

DISY has no party newspaper, but two papers are close to the party, *Simerini* (Today) and *Alithia* (Truth).

DISY is a member both of the European and International Christian Democrats, and also of the European and International Democratic Union. DISY has close links with *Nea Demokratia* in Greece.

Policies

DISY is a right-of-centre party with a broadly conservative free-enterprise orientation. It has also been the most strongly pro-Western Cypriot party on foreign policy matters and has been accused by its opponents of serving the interests of the West and of NATO. The original binding force of the party was opposition to Makarios and his policies, but DISY support continued Cyprus Independence, and does not advocate "Enosis" with Greece.

DISY has remained an opposition party but Clerides now has closer access to President Vassiliou than does former President Kyprianou.

In practice differences between DISY and other parties are often more ones of tone and emphasis than of major substance. In general DISY is fairly close to DIKO on economic policy matters, but on the national question has been closer to the Communist Party AKEL than to either DIKO or EDEK. During the 1988 presidential campaign Clerides announced that he would, if elected, seek to create a government of national unity of all parties.

On the national question DISY has emphasized the need for practical steps and for realism rather than the rigidity which, it believes, characterized the policy of former President Kyprianou. DISY has called for flexibility and for a step by step approach to save what is possible to save by means of negotiations.

DISY calls for Cyprus to become a unitary state with a federal structure and with separate rights for Turks on certain issues, but with full freedom of movement. Some territory should be given back by the Turkish zone, and Turkish troops should be withdrawn. In 1985 Clerides supported the idea that there could be a phased withdrawal of these troops according to a planned timetable. DISY also supports the principle that the post-1974 Turkish settlers should leave Cyprus. There should be broadened guarantees without unilateral intervention rights by any one state.

DISY is not opposed to the summoning of an international conference to help resolve Cyprus problems, but does not believe that this is a very practical suggestion.

DISY supported the Customs Union with the EC, and was also the first party in Cyprus to be in favour of Cyprus becoming a full member of the EC.

Personalities

DISY's president is Glafcos Clerides, born in 1919 as the son of a well-known lawyer and politician John Clerides.

Clerides is himself a lawyer by training and was the Minister of Justice in the 1959–60 transitional government before full independence. In 1960 he was first elected to the House of Representatives, and held the post of President of the House from 1960 to 1976.

He was a member of the Patriotic Front from 1960 to the late 1960s, and he founded the Unified Party in 1969, and DISY in 1976. From 1968 to 1976 he was the chief Greek Cypriot negotiator in talks with the Turkish Cypriot representative, Rauf Denktash. For a short time in 1974 Clerides was Acting President of Cyprus before the return of Makarios. He was an unsuccessful presidential candidate in 1983 and 1988.

The party's general secretary is Alecos Markides, born in 1943 and a lawyer by training. He was first elected as a member of the House in 1985.

DISY's two vice-presidents are Yiannakis Matsis, a former leading member of EOKA in the 1950s and a former party general secretary, and Leontios Ierodiakonou, a former elected member from the Democratic Party who subsequently became an independent and was elected as a member for the Democratic Rally Party in 1981.

Eniaia Demokratiki Enosis Kendrou — EDEK — Sosialistiko Komma Kyprou
(Unified Democratic Centre Union — Socialist Party of Cyprus)

Headquarters	: Stassinos Avenue and Bouboulina Str. 2, P.O. Box 1064, Nicosia (tel: 45 01 21/2 or 45 86 17 19)
President	: Dr Vassos Lyssarides
Secretary-general	: Takis Hadjidemetriou
Membership	: 4,000–5,000
Founded	: February 1969

History

The left of Cyprus politics has been dominated in the past by the Communist AKEL party, and there has been no long-standing Socialist tradition in Cyprus. EDEK was founded in 1969 and has attempted to fill this gap, but is still by far the smallest of the four major parties in the unoccupied part of Cyprus.

EDEK's founders came from the left wing of the broad pro-Makarios Patriotic Front, when the latter was dissolved in 1969. Its dominating personality, Dr Vassos Lyssarides, who has been the president of the party since the outset, had

Parliamentary elections in the Republic of Cyprus since Independence

	1960	1970	1976	1981	1985
Greek Cypriot					
Patriotikon Metopon (Patriotic Front)	30	—	—	—	—
AKEL	5	9	9	12 (32.8%)	15 (27.4%)
Proodeftiki Parataksis (Progressive Front)	—	7	—	—	—
Eniaion Komma (Unified Party)	—	15	—	—	—
EDEK	—	2	4	3 (8.2%)	6 (11.1%)
DIKO	—	—	21	8 (19.5%)	16 (27.6%)
DISY	—	—	0	12 (31.9%)	19 (33.6%)
Others	—	2	1	0 (7.6%)	0 (0.3%)
Turkish Cypriot					
Kibris Milli Türk Birligi (Cyprus Turkish National Union—withdrew in 1963)	15	—	—	—	—

been a Patriotic Front deputy and the personal doctor of Archbishop Makarios.

EDEK sought to provide an alternative to the old polarization between Communism and the right, and to defend the political independence of Cyprus against those (notably the Greek junta) who threatened its continued survival as a separate democratic entity. It also called for the nationalization of mines, and the ending of British bases in Cyprus. It did not originally call itself a Socialist Party (the name EDEK stands for "Unified Democratic Centre Union"), but its general ideology was clearly Socialist.

In its first elections in July 1970 it obtained two seats in the House of Representatives. In 1973 the party's constitution was changed, and the title "Socialist Party of Cyprus" was explicitly added, although the party remained familiarly known as EDEK.

In 1974 EDEK strongly opposed the coup against Makarios, which was sponsored by the Greek military junta, and subsequently called for the return of Makarios from exile. In August 1976 the far right unsuccessfully attempted to assassinate Dr Lyssarides, although Daros Loizou, the organizing secretary of the Socialist Youth Organization was killed.

In 1976 EDEK took part in an electoral alliance with the other two pro-Makarios parties (the Democratic Party and AKEL), and managed to win four seats in the House of Representatives.

In the 1981 elections EDEK stood on its own, and only obtained 8.2 per cent of the vote and three seats in the House. In 1982 Dr Lyssarides obtained 9.5 per cent of the vote in the presidential elections of that year.

In the 1985 elections EDEK's vote rose to 11.1 per cent and it obtained six seats in the enlarged House of Representatives. Dr Lyssarides was subsequently elected President of the House on the votes of EDEK and of the Democratic Party members.

In the first round of the presidential elections in 1988, Dr Lyssarides obtained 9.2 per cent of the vote. In the second round EDEK finally chose to support the independent candidate Georgios Vassiliou.

Support

The strongly clientelist structure of Cyprus politics has made it difficult for the relatively small EDEK to break into the support base of the other main parties, and notably the main party on the left, AKEL, which has been strongly entrenched among working-class voters, and in the trade unions. EDEK has had particular appeal to left-wing intellectuals who are opposed to the Communists.

EDEK's strongest electoral district is Makarios's home area of Paphos, where AKEL is at its weakest. In 1981 EDEK obtained 11.3 per cent of the vote in Paphos district, but this rose to 18.3 per cent in 1985. Dr Lyssarides obtained 14.7 per cent of the Paphos vote in the first round of the presidential elections in 1986.

EDEK's second strongest district is Nicosia (10.6 per cent in 1981, 13.2 per cent in 1985 and 10.9 per cent in the 1988 presidential election). EDEK also has a certain strength among voters from the wholly occupied district of Kyrenia (9.4 per cent in 1981 and 12.8 per cent in 1985).

EDEK has recently become stronger in Limassol than in Larnaca. In 1981 it obtained 6.3 per cent of the Limassol vote, compared to 8.3 per cent in Larnaca, but in 1985 it obtained 9.4 per cent in Limassol and 9 per cent in Larnaca. This trend was confirmed in the 1988 presidential elections, when Dr Lyssarides obtained 7.9 per cent in Limassol and only 5.8 per cent in Larnaca.

EDEK's weakest district is Famagusta, where it obtained 3.7 per cent in 1981, 6.4 per cent in 1985 and 4.2 per cent in the 1988 presidential election.

Organization

EDEK's organizational structure has been based on the traditional Marxist model of democratic centralism, but the party leadership now believes that this should be changed, and that there should be greater scope for internal party democracy. The party's constitution is likely to be modified to this effect.

EDEK currently has 4,000–5,000 members. Its local sections typically meet in plenary sessions every one to two months, and have secretariats which meet weekly. The party has the objective of also forming local groups among the former residents of every occupied village in Cyprus.

At district level there are EDEK district committees of between seven and 25 elected members. District congresses are held every two years.

At national level a congress is held every four years in Nicosia, consisting of representatives from the local party organizations. The congress elects the party president and also the 50 members of the central committee, which must meet three times a year, but which in practice may meet up to eight times a year.

The central committee elects a political bureau of 15 members, which elects the party's secretary-general and organizational secretary, as well as its president. The political bureau is the party's executive organ, and meets at least once a week.

EDEK has its own socialist youth organization (EDEN). There is also a socialist women's movement. Women currently number about 6–7 per cent of party membership and 10 per cent of its central committee. There is one woman on the political bureau.

EDEK has a daily newspaper *Ta Nea* (The News), with a circulation of 6,250 and a weekly paper, *Anexartitos* (Independent), with a circulation of 7,000.

EDEK is a consultative member of the Socialist International, but is exploring the idea of becoming a full member.

Policies

EDEK is a party of Socialist orientation which calls for an independent non-aligned Cyprus. EDEK regards Marxism as a useful instrument, but not as a doctrine which should be rigidly pursued in all circumstances. It does not support, for example, the concept of the dictatorship of the proletariat. Power should not be exercised by a narrow elite.

EDEK has adopted a hard line stance on the national question, and has dissociated itself, in particular, from what it sees as the over-conciliatory line of AKEL and of the Democratic Rally on such issues as a timetable for withdrawal of Turkish troops. It considers that appeasement of and concessions to the Turks have not led anywhere, and that a more uncompromising position is needed to prevent the Turks consolidating their hold over the occupied areas. It believes that the Cyprus problem is not one of intercommunal relations, but one of foreign occupation of the territory of a sovereign member of the United Nations. EDEK calls for application of Resolution 550 of the United Nations Security Council, withdrawal of Turkish occupying forces and of all Turkish settlers since 1974 and the re-establishment of a unified Cypriot State. Fundamental human freedoms should be re-established for all Cypriots. Turkey should not be accepted as a guarantor power, and should have no rights of intervention.

EDEK was strongly opposed to the Greek military junta, but now has much closer ties with the PASOK government, and considers that Greece has an important role to play.

EDEK has been critical of economic developments in Cyprus, and has called for major structural changes. It points out the need for more productive investment, which will create better employment opportunities, and also for a more equitable system of taxation. EDEK is concerned about the dangers of increased economic dependence for Cyprus, and the trend towards importing foreign goods at the expense of local industry. In recent years it has voted against government budgets, but during the presidential elections in 1988, it abstained on the budget debate while approving the sections on defence and on financial support for refugees.

EDEK has come out in support of EC membership for Cyprus. This is primarily for political reasons, and EDEK has been more wary about its economic impacts, and also about the EC-Cyprus Customs Agreement.

EDEK and its president Dr Lyssarides have had close links with the Non-Aligned Movement. It has supported a wide range of liberation movements, including the PLO, the ANC in South Africa and the Polisario. It is critical of the exploitation of developing countries by metropolitan capitalist economies, and has called for the establishment of a new international economic order. It has supported the Peace Movement, and condemned the installation of Cruise missiles in Europe.

Personalities

Dr Vassos Lyssarides has been the president of EDEK since its foundation in 1969. He was born in 1920, and was first elected to Parliament for the Patriotic Front in 1960. He has been a member of the House of Representatives ever since, and has been its President since 1985. He is a medical doctor by profession and is a strong orator.

Takis Hadjidemetriou has been the party's secretary-general since 1974. He was a member of the House of Representatives from 1976 to 1981, lost his seat in 1981, but was re-elected in 1985. He is EDEK's spokesman in the House. He was born in 1934, and is a dentist by profession.

Turkish Cypriot Parties

Ulusal Birlik Partisi — UBP
(National Unity Party)

Headquarters	: 9 Atatürk Meydani, Lefkosa/Nicosia, TRNC
Leadership	: Dervis Eroglu (parliamentary leader), Oglun Pasalar (general secretary)
Publication	: *Birlik*
Founded	: 1975

History

The UBP is the largest political party in

Turkish Cyprus. Its founder and dominant figure has been Rauf Denktash, chief Turkish Cypriot negotiator from 1968 to 1974 in the intercommunal negotiations. In 1970 he founded a movement called *Ulusal Dayanisma* (National Solidarity), and in 1975 the UBP.

Denktash was elected in 1976 with 76 per cent of the vote as the first President of Turkish Cyprus, and the UBP won 30 out of the 40 seats in the Turkish-Cypriot Assembly elections in June 1976. The UBP's then secretary-general, Nejat Konuk, became the first Prime Minister of the Turkish Federated State of Cyprus. The UBP was also the dominant party in the 1976 local elections.

The UBP began to suffer internal problems, and defections from its own ranks. In March 1978 Nejat Konuk resigned as Prime Minister, and was succeeded by Osman Orek. Both Konuk and Orek subsequently left the UBP to found the *Demokratik Halk Partisi* — DHP (Democratic People's Party) — see entry under *Toplumcu Atilim Partisi* — TAP (Social Progress Party).

In the 1980 local elections the UBP's vote dropped considerably. In 1981 Rauf Denktash was re-elected as President, but with a greatly reduced vote of only 51.8 per cent. In concurrent Assembly elections the UBP's strength was reduced to 18 members, losing overall control of the Assembly, although it remained the largest party and formed a new Government in August 1981.

In December 1981, however, the administration fell on an opposition no-confidence motion and in consequence formed a coalition Government with the Democratic People's Party (DHP) and the *Türk Birligi Partisi* — TBP (Turkish Union Party).

Following the proclamation of the Turkish Republic of Northern Cyprus in November 1983, the UBP participated in a Government headed by Nejat Konuk (as an independent) and in the June 1985 elections increased its representation in the Assembly to 24 seats out of 50. Earlier the same month President Denktash was re-elected

for a further term with an increased majority, obtaining 70.5 per cent of the vote.

As it has narrowly failed to obtain an overall majority in the Assembly, the UBP then formed a coalition with the *Toplumcu Kurtulus Partisi* — THP (Communal Liberation Party) with Dervis Eroglu as Prime Minister. However, the TKP withdrew from this alliance in August 1986, whereupon Eroglu formed a new coalition with the *Yeni Dogus Partisi* — YDP (New Dawn Party).

Policies

The UBP has been the major party of the Turkish Cypriot establishment led by Rauf Denktash. It is a party of Conservative nationalist orientation which advocates an independent bizonal federal State of Cyprus, as well as closer economic integration with Turkey.

Toplumcu Kurtulus Partisi — TKP
(Communal Liberation Party)

Headquarters	: 13 Mahmut Pasa Street, Lefkosa/Nicosia, TRNC
Leader	: Mustafa Akinci
General secretary	: Erdal Surech
Publication	: *Ortam*
Founded	: 1976

History

The TKP was founded by Alpay Durdaran, and obtained six seats in the first Turkish Cypriot Assembly elections in 1976. In 1981 it increased the number of its seats in the Assembly to 13, and it became the main party of opposition. In the presidential elections of the same year, its candidate, Ziya Rizki came second with 30.5 per cent of the vote. By 1985 its support had fallen back, and it only obtained 10 seats in the enlarged Legislative Assembly on 16 per cent of the vote. Its presidential candidate, Alpay

Parliamentary elections in Turkish Cyprus since 1974			
	1976	*1981*	*1985*
Ulusal Birlik Partisi (UBP—National Unity Party)	30	18	24 (37%)
Toplumcu Kurtulus Partisi (TKP—Communal Liberation Party)	6	13	10 (16%)
Cumhuriyetci Türk Partisi (CTP—Republican Turkish Party)	2	5	12 (21%)
Demokratik Halk Partisi (DHP—Democratic People's Party)	—	3	—
Halkci Partisi (HP—Populist Party)	2		
Türk Birligi Partisi (TBP—Turkish Unity Party)	—	1	
Yeni Dogus Partisi (YDP—New Dawn Party)	—	—	4 (9%)
Others	—	—	— (17%)

Durdaran, had previously only polled 9.5 per cent and came a poor third.

After the 1985 legislative elections, the TKP nevertheless entered into a coalition government with the UBP. There were three TKP ministers, including its then leader Ismal Bozkurt. In August 1986 the TKP withdrew from the coalition following economic policy differences with the UBP Prime Minister. The TKP was again the second largest party in the municipal and communal elections held in June 1986.

Policies

The TKP is a party of social democratic orientation advocating peaceful coexistence in an independent, bizonal and federal state of Cyprus, based on the political equality of the Greek and Turkish Cypriot communities, and also free of British bases. It supports the maintenance of the Turkish guarantee, and considers that the three freedoms called for by the Greek Cypriots (freedom of movement, settlement and property ownership) can only be implemented at a later stage when intercommunal relations improve.

Personalities

The TKP's leader, Mustafa Akinci, is also the Mayor of Nicosia.

Cumhuriyetci Türk Partisi — CTP
(Republican Turkish Party)

Headquarters	: 99/A Sehit Salahi Street, Lefkosa/Nicosia, TRNC
Chairman	: Özker Özgür
Secretary general	: N. Talat
Publication	: *Yenidüzen* (New Order, daily organ)
Membership	: 2,500
Founded	: December 1970

History

The CTP was founded by Ahmed Mithat Berberoglu in December 1970. In the 1976 presidential elections Berberoglu obtained 24 per cent of the vote. The CTP only won two of the 40 seats in the 1976 National Council elections. In 1976 Özker Özgür became the leader of the party, a position he has retained to the present day.

In the 1981 National Council elections the CTP again came a poor third with five out of 40 seats, and Özker Özgür also came third in the presidential elections of the same year with 12.75 per cent of the vote.

In the 1985 presidential elections, the CTP advanced to second place, with Özker Özgür obtaining 18.4 per cent of the vote. In the Assembly elections it also became the main party of opposition by obtaining 12 of the 50 seats on 21 per cent of the poll. It was, however, third in the municipal and council elections in 1986.

Organization

The party's supreme body is its congress under which there is a general council, while the party is run by its executive committee. Its daily newspaper is called *Yenidüzen* (New Order). The CTP is recognized by the Communist parties of the Soviet bloc countries.

Policies

The CTP is Marxist-Leninist in orientation, and is the furthest left of the major Turkish Cypriot parties. It is also a strong advocate of rapprochement with the Greek Cypriot community.

The CTP supports the objective of the federal bizonal, bicommunal, independent and non-aligned Cyprus Republic. There should be full equality of the Greek and Turkish Cypriot communities. The CTP has supported the idea of a bicameral federal parliament with a 70–30 Greek–Turkish ratio in the Lower House, and equality in the Upper House, with no legislation coming into effect unless and until approved in the Upper House.

The CTP has called for the maintenance of the Turkish guarantee, and believes that Turkish troops should not be prematurely withdrawn. The three freedoms of movement, settlement and property ownership in a reunified Cyprus should not be immediately implemented until mutual trust can be built up. Moreover freedom of movement would effectively mean the end of bizonality.

Among the practical means of achieving rapprochement between the Greek and Turkish Cypriot communities that have been advocated by the CTP, are exchanges of visits between trade unions, professional bodies and political parties, and cross-border co-operation in health, manpower, culture and sport. There could also be co-operation between the respective police forces on such mutual concerns as drug smuggling. Nicosia Airport could also be re-opened and there could be a joint Cypriot University.

The CTP is also opposed to the British bases in Cyprus.

Personalities

The party's leader since 1976 has been Özker Özgür, who has twice stood for President of Turkish Cyprus in 1981 and 1985.

Yeni Dogus Partisi — YDP
(New Dawn Party)

Headquarters	: 1 Ghengis Khan Street, Lefkosa/Nicosia, TRNC
Leader	: Orhan Ucok
Publication	: *Yeni Dogus* (New Dawn)
Founded	: January 1984

History

The four members of the party's founding council had all come from Turkey to settle in Cyprus, and the party has strongly represented the interests of post-1974 Turkish settlers.

In the June 1985 Assembly elections, the YDP won 9 per cent of the vote and four seats, and became the fourth largest party in the Assembly. After the Communal Liberation Party had withdrawn from the UBP-headed coalition Government in August 1986, a UBP–YDP coalition was formed in which Aytac Beseler of the YDP became Minister of Agriculture and Forestry.

Policies

The YDP has called for a bizonal federal republic in Cyprus guaranteed by Turkey. It has a right-of-centre orientation.

Other Parties

Toplumcu Atilim Partisi — TAP
(Social Progress Party)

Headquarters	: 15A Serif Arzik Street, Lefkosa/Nicosia, TRNC
Leadership	: Irsen Küchük, Ismet Kotak
Founded	: March 1986

This party was founded in 1986 in a merger between the Social Progress Party of Irsen Küchük (founded in 1984) and the Democratic People's Party of Ismet Kotak, which had been founded by Nejat Konuk (the first Prime Minis-

ter of the Turkish Federal State of Cyprus) and other UBP dissidents in February 1979.

The TAP is a right-wing party.

Kibris Demokratik Partisi — KDP
(Cyprus Democratic Party)

Headquarters	: 22 Serif Arzik Street, Lefkosa/Nicosia, TRNC
Leader	: Ekrem Ural
Founded	: January 1985

The party was founded in 1985 by Fuat Veziroglu (who had resigned from the Government the previous month). It failed to win representation in the June 1985 Assembly elections. It is social democratic in orientation and calls for equality and bizonality in Cyprus, with a continuation of the Turkish guarantee.

Calisan Halkin Partisi — CHP
(Party of the Working People)

Headquarters	: 2/F Müftü Ziyni Effendi Street, Lefkosa/Nicosia, TRNC

This is a radical leftist party, whose chairman has been Bekir Azgin.

Yeni Türk Birligi Partisi
(New Turkish Unity Party)

Headquarters	: 12/D2 Han Apartment, Ghengis Khan Street, Lefkosa/Nicosia, TRNC
Leader	: Ismail Tezer
Founded	: February 1985

This is a right-wing breakaway from the New Dawn Party. It failed to win representation in the June 1985 Assembly elections. It is a party of the extreme pro-Turkey right. An earlier Turkish Unity Party, also of the pro-Turkey right had been founded in 1978, won one seat in the 1981 Assembly elections, and entered a coalition Government with the National Unity Party in March 1982. It included Turkish settlers in Cyprus in its ranks, and called for Cyprus to become part of Turkey. It had links with the Nationalist Action Party of Colonel Türkes in mainland Turkey.

Kuzey Kibris Sosyalist Partisi — KKSP
(Northern Cyprus Socialist Party)

Headquarters   : 44 Alan Bey Street,
Lefkosa/Nicosia,
TRNC

General-secretary : Dagan Harman
Founded   : August 1985

This is a party of leftist orientation, favouring total independence for the TRNC.

Finland

Francis Jacobs

The country

Finland is a country of 118,000 square miles with a population of 4,850,000. Finland is officially bilingual (Finnish and Swedish). Over 92 per cent of its population is Finnish-speaking and over 7 per cent Swedish-speaking, primarily on Finland's west and south coasts, and in its major cities. The Åland Islands are almost exclusively Swedish-speaking, and have extensive auton-

omy, and their own political system (see separate section below). There are also small Russian and Lapp-speaking minorities.

Over 92 per cent of the population belong to the Evangelical Lutheran Church. There is also a small (1.3 per cent) Orthodox minority, mainly among Karelians.

Finland has a long border of almost 800 miles with the Soviet Union and in World War II had to give up much of Karelia to the Soviet Union, losing 11 per cent of its territory and leading to the resettlement elsewhere in Finland of over 400,000 Karelian refugees. By losing the nickel-mining region of Petsamo as well, Finland lost its outlet to the Arctic Ocean.

There are around 112,000 Finns resident in Sweden. Finland's capital is Helsinki.

Map of Finland showing 15 electoral districts and number of seats in each district.

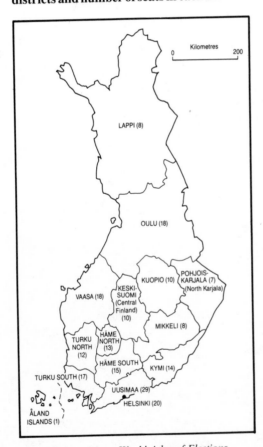

Source: adapted from *World Atlas of Elections*.

Political institutions

Finland is a republic with a unicameral Parliament and one of Europe's most powerful presidencies.

The Parliament (*Eduskunta* in Finnish, *Riksdag* in Swedish) consists of 200 members elected for four-year terms (formerly three years), but with the possibility of earlier dissolution. Parliamentary elections are decided on the basis of the d'Hondt system of proportional representation in 15 electoral districts. There are multi-member constituencies with the number of seats dependent on their population and ranging from seven to 29. The Åland Islands (see separate section) constitute one single-member constituency.

In order to put up candidates, parties must be registered and a list of party supporters containing 5,000 names must be submitted. Electoral alliances between different parties are permitted (even in one or two constituencies only) and can make a significant difference to the results. Associations of voters may also put up candidates, and link up in joint lists. The order of election of candidates is dependent on the number of personal votes that they have received and not because of their place on a list.

The Parliament shares legislative power with the President. An unusual feature of the Parliament is the system of qualified majorities that is required for certain types of decision. Two-thirds majorities are required, for example, for tax increases of more than one year's duration, and five-sixths majorities for constitutional legislation to be declared urgent in order to be passed within the lifetime of one Parliament. Constitutional bills can be held over until the next Parliament by a simple majority, but must then be passed unchanged by a two-thirds majority.

The Finnish President is elected for a six-year term of office. The President used to be chosen by an indirect system of election in an electoral college, but the system was modified before the 1988 presidential election in order to provide for a new element of direct voting. Voters may now cast two simultaneous votes, one directly for an individual presidential candidate (who may be nominated by any registered party which won at least one seat in the most recent parliamentary elections, or else by a group of at least 20,000 enfranchised persons) and a second vote for an electoral college candidate. There are 301 seats in the electoral college, distributed between 15 constituencies with between 11 (N. Karelia) and 43 (Uusimaa) electors.

If any of the presidential candidates wins over half of the total direct vote, he or she is automatically elected. Otherwise the President is selected by the 301 chosen electors, as happened in 1988 when Mauno Koivisto only won 47.9 per cent in the direct popular vote. Electoral college candidates must now be pledged to an individual candidate in advance, although electoral alliances are also possible. If no candidate wins an absolute majority in the first two ballots, only the top two candidates remain in contention in the decisive third round.

Once elected, the Finnish President is expected to be above narrow party politics. There is no limit to the number of times he or she may be re-elected.

The Finnish President has very considerable powers. He may dissolve Parliament and call new elections, appoints members of the Council of State (the government) and presides over the Presidential Council (a weekly meeting of the Council of State). The President may initiate legislation and also has a "suspensive" veto with regard to legislation passed by the Parliament (e.g. if the President vetoes legislation it may only come into force if the Parliament again passes it in unchanged form after new elections). The President also oversees the State administration and appoints senior civil servants. He has exclusive responsibility for Finnish foreign policy. The distinctive Finnish foreign policy line developed after the war, is thus often known as the Paasikivi-Kekkonen line, after the two successive presidents who carried it out.

The Council of State (or Cabinet) consists of the Prime Minister and between 13 and 18 ministers. There is no obligation for ministers to have been members of Parliament, although the majority have been so (around two-thirds of all ministers since 1945). A vote of confidence in the new government is not taken in Parliament when it is first appointed, but there may subsequently be such a vote following a discussion on an interpellation signed by at least 20 members of Parliament.

The Prime Minister presides over the Cabinet, apart from the weekly meeting when the President takes the chair, but has comparatively few formal powers, not just in relation to the President, but even to his or her colleagues. Informally, however, a long serving Prime Minister such as Kalevi Sorsa can enjoy rather greater influence.

In addition to national elections there are also municipal elections, which are held every four years.

Brief political history

Finland under Russian Rule 1808–1917

1808–9	Finland occupied by Russians and subsequently ceded by Sweden. Finland becomes an autonomous Grand Duchy, with the Russian Tsar as Grand Duke. Constitutional system established under Swedish rule is left in force.
1860	Foundation of Finnish Party to defend rights of Finnish-speaking majority. Beginning of period in which main political division is between Finnish and Swedish parties.
1863	Finnish is given equal status with Swedish by language Edict. Finnish Diet (Legislative Assembly consisting of Estates of Clergy, Peasants, Nobility and Burgesses) is convoked for the first time for 50 years. Tsar agrees to other liberal reforms.
1866	Universal education introduced.
1890s	Divisions within Finnish Party leads to creation of Young Finnish Party among its more liberal and socially progressive elements.
1899	Tougher policy of Russification is initiated, which leads to increased repression and to growing tensions between Russians and Finns. First period of oppression lasts until 1905.
1906	Period of renewed liberalization in which major political reforms are en-

acted. The Diet of four Estates is abolished, and replaced by a unicameral Assembly based on equal universal suffrage with proportional representation, and with women obtaining the vote for the first time in Europe. Social Democrats subsequently emerge as the largest political force in the country.
Agrarian League also emerges to represent the interests of the farming population.

1908–14 Renewed period of Russian oppression in which Parliament's powers are curtailed by the Tsar. Divisions develop among Finns as to how to react to the Russians.

1917 Russian provisional government restores Finnish autonomy. Later in year Finnish Parliament formally declares Finnish independence from Russia (which is recognized by Russia on January 4 1918).

Independent Finland

1918 Brief civil war between Finnish "Reds" and "Whites" leads to victory for the latter under General Mannerheim. Many of defeated Reds flee to Moscow where Communist Party is established.

1919 New Finnish Constitution. Finland confirmed as a republic.

1921 Extensive home rule granted to the Swedish-speaking Åland Islands.

1928 Parliament Act.

1929–32 Extreme anti-Communist Lapua Movement becomes active throughout Finland. In 1930 all activities considered to be Communist are banned. Other parties eventually turn against the far right, whose influence is sharply curtailed.

1937 Beginning of series of Red-Green coalitions, with Social Democrats and Agrarians as main government partners.

1939–40 Winter War between Russia and Finland in which Russians are initially blocked. Finland is eventually forced to cede around 11 per cent of its territory (East Karelia).

1941 Finland agains fights against Russia and recaptures lost land.

1944 Cease-fire, in which Finland not only again loses East Karelia but also the Petsamo nickel mines (including Finland's outlet on the Arctic Ocean). The Communist Party is legalized. The Communist-dominated SKDL electoral alliance is established, and participates in government along with other parties.

1946 Paasikivi elected as President (in which post he remains until 1956, and develops Finnish foreign policy line of close relations with the Soviet Union while retaining Finnish independence).

1947 Finland refuses Marshall Aid.

1948 Treaty of Friendship, Co-operation and Mutual Assistance between Finland and the Soviet Union.

1956 Finland joins Nordic Council and United Nations. Beginning of 25 year Presidency of Urho Kekkonen.

1961 Finland joins EFTA as an Associate Member.

1970 Finns reject Nordek (Nordic Customs Union).

1973 Finnish free trade agreement with EC.

Features of the political system

Finnish politics have been characterized by a number of divisions, some of which have persisted up to the present day, while others are no longer of much significance.

A key political divide in the 19th century, that between Swedish and Finnish speakers, is no longer an important one. The rights of the Swedish minority are well protected, and Swedish is a second official language. The Swedish-speaking minority has continued to decline as a percentage of the total population. There is still a party to explicitly defend the interests of the Swedish speakers (the Swedish People's Party), but it is a mainstream rather than outsider party, and it has participated in a large number of government coalitions.

Another division which has declined in importance is that over attitudes towards Communism and the Soviet Union. The 1918 Civil War between "Reds" and "Whites" left long-lasting scars. Communism was banned in the interwar years, and an extreme right-wing movement (the Lapua Movement) also developed. In 1944 the Communist Party was legalized, and the Communist–dominated SKDL entered government. A Treaty of Friendship, Co-operation and Mutual Assistance was signed with the Soviet Union in 1948. Successive long-serving Presidents (Paasikivi and Kekkonen) developed this policy of friendly, but arms-length co-operation with the Soviet Union, which has preserved Finnish neutrality and independence. Certain traditional tensions remained (for example between the Social Democrats and the Soviet Union), but these were much reduced by the mid-1960s, when the Communists again became regular participants in government. There is now a broad consensus on Finnish foreign policy matters, with only limited opposition to the Paasikivi-Kekkonen line, mainly from weak political forces on the right.

On the other hand, more traditional class-based divisions have remained significant in Finnish politics with the Social Democrats and the SKDL and Communists competing for the bulk of the working-class vote; with the National Coalition Party being very strong among the managerial and business classes; and with the survival of parties which are particularly strong among the farming population (the Centre and Rural Parties). These divisions, however, are also becoming rather more blurred.

A very important division in the Finnish political context has been between the centre and the periphery, and notably between more privileged South Finland and poorer and disadvantaged North Finland. The conservative National Coalition Party's support declines steadily from south to north, whereas the north has been a stronghold of the Centre Party and the Communist – dominated SKDL, as well as of protest parties such as the Rural Party.

Divisions over religious and moral issues have been much weaker, and the Christian Democrats, who have made this their distinctive policy plank, have only had very limited support.

Finnish politics remains very much a multi-party system, with no less than 12 registered parties and with nine having representatives in the Parliament. Moreover there is no one dominant party. For a long time after the last war the Social Democrats, the Communist–dominated SKDL and the Agrarian (now Centre) Party had broadly similar strengths, with the National Coalition Party well behind in fourth place. In recent years the Communists have become increasingly divided and have now formally split, with their combined strength greatly declined. The Social Democrats have now become by far the largest party on the left of centre.

On the centre and centre-right the conservative National Coalition Party has now become the party with the second highest level of support in Finland, ahead of the Centre Party.

Of the other traditional Finnish parties, the Swedish People's Party has retained a consistent level of support, whereas the Liberal Party has declined into insignificance, and is no longer represented in Parliament.

The most successful of the new parties which have been formed in recent years has been the populist Rural Party, but it has had greatly fluctuating support. It is no longer a complete outsider party of protest and, unlike the populist Progress Parties in Norway and Denmark, is now participating in government.

A distinctive feature of the Finnish political system has been the strong position of the President, and the comparatively weak position of the Prime Minister and his Cabinet. There have been only three presidents since 1946, whereas there have been a very large number of governments, many of only a few months duration and few of over two years duration. No party has been able to form a majority government on its own since independence, and the usual government pattern has been multi-party coalitions. The current government is a four-party coalition, and some governments have had representatives from six parties.

The Finnish tendency to seek a wide consensus in government is reinforced by the requirement for Parliament to pass certain laws by qualified rather than simple majorities.

Suomen Sosialidemokraattinen Puolue — SSDP
(Finnish Social Democratic Party)

Headquarters	: Saariniemenkatu 6, 00530 Helsinki (tel: 358–0–77 511)
Chairman	: Pertti Paasio
General secretary	: Ulpu Livari
Youth organization	: Central Union of Social Democratic Youth
Publication	: *Demari*
Membership	: 90,000
Founded	: 1899

History

A Finnish Workers' Party was first founded in 1899. In 1903 it adopted its present name, as well as a radical party programme which was heavily influenced by German and Austrian Socialist ideas. Campaigning for an eight hour working day, a unicameral Parliament and universal suffrage, it won strong support from the Finnish industrial working class and from landless labourers and developed the first mass organization of any Finnish party. In the first elections after universal suffrage was introduced, it won 37 per cent of the vote and 80 seats in the Parliament, and was easily the largest party. In subsequent elections it increased its vote until in 1919 it obtained 47.3 per cent and 103 seats, giving it an absolute majority in the Parliament, the only time that this has ever been achieved by any Finnish party.

The Social Democrats subsequently took part in government, but in 1917 new elections were called in which the party's vote fell for the first time (to 44.8 per cent) and it lost its absolute majority.

The Finnish Civil War in 1918 divided the party. The most radical members of the defeated "Reds" fled to Russia where they founded the Finnish Communist Party, whereas the Social Democratic Party was taken over by more moderate reformist members, who had not played an active role in the Civil War. The new chairman, Vainö Tanner, was to remain a dominant figure in the party until 1963. Under Tanner the party embarked on a reformist, rather than revolutionary path.

In the 1919 elections the SSDP still won 38 per cent of the vote and 80 seats, but in 1922 it was hurt by competition from the new radical Socialist Workers' Party, and its vote fell to 25.1 per cent and 53 seats. Radical Socialist competition kept the SSDP below 30 per cent for the rest of the 1920s. For most of the time the party was in opposition, but in 1926–27 the government was briefly formed by an SSDP minority Cabinet.

With the decline of the far left in 1930, the SSDP's vote rose to 34.2 per cent in 1930 and to 37.3 per cent in 1933. The party played a prominent role in the struggle against the hard right anti-Communist Lapua Movement.

In 1937 the SSDP re-entered government in what turned out to be a recurrent formula of Red-Green coalitions between it and the Agrarian Party. In 1939 the party's vote rose to 39.8 per cent. During the war Tanner took an anti-Soviet line. He supported the Winter War against the Soviet Union, and several Parliamentarians who dissented from his line were expelled from the party. The SSDP later declined to take part in the Finnish People's Democratic League (SKDL — see separate entry) when it was founded in 1944, and a considerable number of members and associated organizations on the party's left subsequently joined the SKDL. In the 1945 elections its vote slumped sharply to only 25.1 per cent, although it continued to take part in government with the SKDL and the Agrarians.

From 1946–48 Tanner was imprisoned for his wartime pro-German and anti-Soviet activities. Emil Skog and Vaion Leskinen became new leaders within the party.

After the SKDL was pushed out of government in 1948 a lengthy period ensued when the SSDP was in and out of government. In three successive elections (1948, 1951 and 1954) its vote fluctuated between 26.2 per cent and 26.5 per cent. In 1952 a new party programme was adopted. In 1956 one of the party's leading figures, Karl August Fagerholm (Prime Minister in 1948–50, 56–57 and later in 1958–59) narrowly lost the presidential elections to Urho Kekkonen. In 1957 Fagerholm was defeated by one vote for the SSDP chairmanship by the veteran Vainö Tanner.

The return of Tanner led to a new period of conflict with the party's left, especially over the issue of relationships with the Communists and with the Soviet Union. The Social Democratic opposition won three seats in the 1958 elections and were subsequently joined by 11 other dissident left-wing members of the SSDP Parliamentary Party. In 1959 they formed a new party, the Social Democratic League of Workers and Smallholders, with Skog as chairman.

The Social Democratic League was not a major electoral success. It only won two seats on 4.4 per cent of the vote in the 1962 elections, and although it won seven seats on only 2.6 per cent of the vote in 1966 (as a result of electoral alliances with the SKDL), it had lost all its seats by 1970. In 1973 the majority returned to the SSDP, although a minority under Pare Simonen formed a New Socialist Workers' Party which had minimal success in the 1975 and 1979 elections.

Despite the lack of success of these rival parties, the divisions within the Social-Democratic family cost it dear in the late 1950s and early 1960s. In the 1958 elections the SSDP's vote dropped to 23.2 per cent, and in 1962 it fell to a new low of only 19.5 per cent, the lowest total in the party's history, and which put it in third place among Finnish parties. Moreover the SSDP was continually out of government between 1959 and 1966. In 1961 it joined in an unsuccessful attempt with the Conservatives to find an alternative to President Kekkonen. Relations between the party and the Soviet Union remained at a low point.

In June 1963 the 82-year-old Tanner was finally replaced as chairman by the more conciliatory and left-of-centre Rafael Paasio. In the 1966 elections the SSDP's vote rose sharply to 27.2 per cent, and the party gained 17 seats. The SSDP finally returned to government, this time in conjunction with the Agrarians and the SKDL, who were brought back into government after an 18-year absence.

Since 1966 the SSDP has been almost continually in government and provided the Prime Minister for the vast majority of the time, notably Mauno Koivisto (Prime Minister from 1968–70 and 1979–82) and Kalevi Sorsa (Prime Minister from 1972–75, 1977–79 and 1982–87). In all elections the SSDP has remained the largest party, though with a fluctuating vote of between 23.4 per cent (1970) and 26.7 per cent (1983).

In 1975 Kalevi Sorsa became party chairman. In 1982 Mauno Koivisto became the first ever President of Finland from the ranks of the SSDP.

After the 1987 elections, when the party obtained 56 seats on 24.3 per cent of the vote, the SSDP helped to form a new government coalition, with the Conservatives as their principal coalition partner rather the Centre Party, and they also surrendered the premiership to the Conservatives. In June 1987 Pertti Paasio replaced Kalevi Sorsa as party chairman. In early 1988 Mauno Koivisto was re-elected as President of Finland with 189 votes out of 301 in the electoral college, after he had narrowly failed to win an overall majority in the initial vote.

In the October 1988 local elections the party's vote rose slightly to 25.3 per cent.

Support

Over the last 20 years, the SSDP has consistently been the best–supported party in Finland, although without the electoral strength of certain other Scandinavian Social Democratic parties, notably that of Sweden.

The SSDP has shared the industrial working class vote with the SKDL in particular, but has been more successful than the SKDL among middle class voters. It has been stronger in urban areas and weaker in farming regions.

In regional terms, the SSDP has been stronger in southern, south-eastern and south central Finland than in the peripheral regions of the north and north-west.

In recent years it has done very well in the electoral district of Kymi, and in South Häme, North Karelia and Mikkeli. It has also had a good vote in central Finland, Uusimaa, North Häme, and to a slightly lesser extent in North Turku and Helsinki. It has been somewhat weaker in South Turku.

The SSDP has been weakest in Kuopio, and especially in Vaasa, Oulu and Lapland.

Organization

The SSDP currently has around 90,000 members with local branches both on a territorial basis and in the workplace. Above this, there are 16 district organizations. At national level the party congress meets every three years and elects the party's chairman, the vice-chairman and general-secretary. There is a party council of around 60 members, which generally meets twice a year. Above this is a smaller party executive consisting of chairman,

vice-chairman, general-secretary and nine other members, as well as six substitutes, which meets around once a week. In practice this hardly ever resorts to voting, but if it does, members of the government who are also members of the executive may not vote.

The party's youth organization is the Central Union of Social Democratic Youth. There is a students' organization, the Central Union of Social Democratic Students and children under 15 may participate in the Young Falcons. There is a women's organization, Social Democratic Women.

The SSDP has strong links with the Confederation of Finnish Trade Unions (SAK), and the labour movement in general, but these are of an informal nature.

The SSDP's main organ is called *Demari* (the new name for the former *Suomen Sosialidemokraatti*). It is an independent paper, whose shares are owned mainly by the party, and which appears five times a week. There are papers in other districts as well, such as *Kansan Lehti* in Tampere and *Turun Paivälehti* in Turku.

The SSDP is a member of the Socialist International, and of the Social Democratic Group in the Nordic Council.

Policies

The SSDP is a pragmatic Social Democratic Party which, with the decline and divisions within the Communist-dominated SKDL, has become the dominant force on the left of centre of the Finnish political spectrum. For 20 years after the war it enjoyed uneasy relations with the SKDL, and also with the Soviet government, but these improved under the leadership of Rafael Paasio in the 1960s, when the SKDL re-entered government, and when fences were mended with the Russians.

The SSDP has been a government party "par excellence", and has held the post of Prime Minister for much of the last 20 years. Its most frequent coalition partner has been the Centre Party, and in the past it opposed the entry of the conservative National Coalition Party into the government. Before the 1987 elections, however, it became apparent that relations with the Centre Party had deteriorated. After the elections, the SSDP was opposed to the inclusion of the Centre Party, and preferred to join up with the National Coalition Party and other smaller parties. A minority of politicians, however, on the left wing of the SSDP (the "Red Dozen") would have preferred the party to go into full opposition.

The SSDP considers that economic development should largely be based on market forces, but that the state should provide appropriate framework conditions, and a measure of democratic planning aimed at achieving the collective good. The party approves of private ownership, but also considers that state-run enterprises are an important part of Finland's economic system. Society should control, for example, the operations of banks and insurance companies, and acquire them if the common interest so demands. A strong state is not an end in itself for Finnish Social Democrats, but is a means to rectify the faults inherent in a capitalist economy.

The SSDP puts a strong emphasis on industrial democracy, and on expanded employee rights to participate in decision-making in the workplace. The SSDP considers that there should be increased international co–operation between trade unions as a counterweight to the power of multinational corporations, and has supported the demand within the Nordic trade union movement for corporate group shop stewards. The SSDP also believes that funds jointly administered by employees should be established within companies, and that joint equity participation of employees in the ownership of companies would provide them with a new shared responsibility and with new incentives.

The SSDP considers that a continued increase in material consumption should not be an end in itself, and it puts an increased emphasis on economic development that is respectful of the environment, and of natural resource constraints. Such policies may slow down growth in the short run, but it will be of a more lasting nature.

The SSDP has emphasized defence of the Welfare State, and in its 1987 election campaign promised a major increase in child allowances if it were returned to power.

The SSDP supports enhanced citizens' participation, and has called for the introduction of referenda. Lifelong education and training should be provided, in order to prevent an uneven distribution of knowledge. There should be greater equality between the sexes.

The SSDP strongly supports the Paasikivi-Kekkonen line in foreign policy matters. Finland should remain neutral and co–operate closely with both the Soviet Union and with the other Nordic countries. The primary aim of Finland's peace policy should be nuclear disarmament with immediate elimination of intermediate range ballistic missiles, and plans for the destruction of short range nuclear weapon systems as well. There should be an end to nuclear tests. The SSDP supports the establishment of a Nordic nuclear-free zone, and a nuclear-free Baltic Sea. The SSDP has also called for military

service and civilian service to be developed on an equal footing.

In development policy the SSDP considers that Finland should raise public development aid to the UN target of 0.7 per cent of GDP, and with a longer-term objective of 1 per cent. It also believes that Finland should take a share of the burden in solving the problem of world refugees.

Personalities

Mauno Koivisto, who was elected President in 1982, and re-elected in 1988, is the first Social Democrat to hold the post. He was formerly Prime Minister from 1968 to 1970, and again from 1979–82. From 1968–82 he was Governor of the Bank of Finland. He was born in 1923.

Kalevi Sorsa has been the longest serving Prime Minister of Finland, having held that post from 1972–75, 1977–79 and from 1982–87. From 1975 to 1987 he was also the party chairman. He was born in 1930.

The current party chairman is Pertti Paasio, born in 1939. He is the son of the former party chairman and Prime Minister Rafael Paasio. He is a former chairman of the parliamentary group.

Kansallinen Kokoomus — KOK
(National Coalition Party)

Headquarters	: Kansakoulukuja 3, 00100 Helsinki (tel: 358–0–69 381, fax:358–0–694–6596)
Chairman	: Ilkka Suominen
Secretary-general	: Aarno Kaila
Youth organization	: *Kokoomuksen Nuorten Liitto* (Youth League of the Coalition Party)
Women's organization	: *Kokoomuksen Naisten Liitto* (Women's League of the Coalition Party)
Publication	: *Nyr Kypäivä*
Membership	: 80,000
Founded	: 1918

History

The National Coalition Party (KOK) was founded on Dec. 9, 1918 by pro-monarchy Conservatives, mainly from the Old Finnish Party, but also from a minority of the Young Finnish Party, led by Pehr Eviod Svinhufvud. In the 1919 elections they obtained 15.7 per cent of the vote and 28 seats, but they polled between 17.5 and 19 per cent in subsequent elections through the 1920s. In spite of its defeat on the monarchy issue, KOK was soon associated with government coalitions, and in the interwar years was in office for roughly half the time.

For a while it was associated with the hard anti-Communist right. In 1930 it won 42 seats after calling for anti-Communist legislation, and in 1931 the pro-German Svinhufvud was elected Finnish President, a post he was to retain until 1937. In 1933 KOK took part in electoral alliances with the extreme right IKL (*Isänmaallinen Kansanliike* — Patriotic People's Movement), but party chairman J.K. Paasikivi later dissociated KOK from the right, and helped to bring about the latter's decline. In 1936 KOK's vote dropped to only 10.4 per cent, but it rose to 13.6 per cent in 1939.

From 1939 to 1944 KOK took part in five successive governments, providing the Prime Minister on two occasions in 1943 and 1944 (Linkomies and Hackzell administrations).

After 1945 KOK became primarily a party of opposition, remaining rather more critical of the Soviet Union and of the Finnish foreign policy consensus than other major Finnish parties, although one of the architects of that consensus, J.K. Paasikivi (President of Finland from 1946 to 1956) was a former party chairman.

KOK was out of government from 1944 to 1958. It was generally only the fourth largest Finnish party behind the Social Democrats, SKDL and Agrarians, and its vote fluctuated considerably from a high of 17.3 per cent (33 seats) in 1948 to a low of 12.8 per cent (24 seats) in 1954.

KOK took part with three ministers in the third Fagerholm government from 1958–59, in the first Karjalainen government from 1962–63 and in the Virolainen government from 1964 to 1966. After 1966, however, it again remained in opposition for 21 years, with the pro-Communist SKDL, the Social Democrats and even the Centre Party reluctant to include it in government coalitions.

Under its successive chairmen, Juhta Riht-niemi from 1965 to 1971, and Harri Holkeri from 1971–79, KOK took on a more moderate image, and also indicated its support for the Paasikivi-Kekkonen line on foreign policy issues. In the 1970 elections KOK's vote rose sharply from the 13.8 per cent of 1966 (26 seats) to 18 per cent (37 seats) and it rose from being fourth to being the equal of the SKDL and the Centre Party. KOK had already suffered the loss of a minority of cultural Conservative supporters with the rise of the Finnish Christian Union, and in 1973 lost further Conservative support with

the creation of the Constitutional Party of the Right, but compensated for this by new support from the centre of the political spectrum.

In 1979 its vote again rose to 21.7 per cent (47 seats) and KOK became clearly established as the second largest party after the Social Democrats. In 1982 Harri Holkeri was the runner-up to Mauno Koivisto in the presidential elections, winning 58 electoral college seats.

By 1987, relations between the Social Democrats and their traditional Centre Party coalition partners were becoming increasingly strained, and the Social Democrats began to talk of a coalition with KOK. In the 1987 elections KOK's share of the vote only rose slightly to 23.1 per cent, but it obtained 53 seats, a gain of nine. KOK finally re-entered government with seven of the 18 ministers and for the first time since the 1940s a member of the party, Harri Holkeri, was the Finnish Prime Minister.

In the 1988 presidential elections Harri Holkeri came third in the first round with 63 electoral votes. In the second round he advised his electors to vote for the front-runner Koivisto. Forty–five did so, but 18 again voted for Holkeri.

Support

KOK is now one of the two largest Finnish parties and the largest non-Socialist Party. It has traditionally been an urban professional and middle class party with little support among farmers and in rural areas, but its support base has steadily expanded since the mid-1960s.

There is still a sharp gradient in KOK electoral support from the south of Finland, where the party is strongest and where it competes with the Social Democrats for the white collar vote, to the North, where it is weakest. It is also still stronger in the towns. 37.4 per cent of its voters in the 1987 elections were clerical and administrative employees and 15.2 per cent were executives. 23.2 per cent were workers and only 5.1 per cent were farmers.

KOK has been strongest in the electoral districts of Helsinki, Uusimaa and North and South Häme, but has also won substantial support in North and South Turku, Kymi and Mikkeli.

It has had medium support in Central Finland, Vaasa and North Karelia, and to a lesser extent in Kuopio. KOK has had its lowest support in Oulu, and especially in Lapland.

Organization

KOK currently has a membership of around 80,000. It has around 1,200 local associations linked to the party either directly or indirectly through the party's national member organizations. Above these are 16 district organizations based essentially on Finland's electoral districts.

At national level the party congress meets every two years, and elects a 60 member party council. In its turn the Council elects a 23 member party executive, which is responsible for day-to-day decision-making and also appoints party committees and expert groups. KOK has around 200 full time employees.

The main national member organizations are the *Kokoomuksen Nuorten Liitto* (Youth League of the Coalition Party), *Kokoomuksen Naisten Liitto* (Women's League of the Coalition Party) and *Kokoomuksen Opiskelijaliitto Tuhatkunta* (Student Organization of the Coalition Party, Tuhatkunta). Among the other organizations affiliated to the party are the Paasikivi Institute (in Turku), the National Pensioners' Organization and the Children and Educational Organizations of the Coalition Party.

The KOK produces a weekly members' newspaper called *Nykypäivä*, which has a circulation of 68,000.

KOK became a full member of the European Democratic Union in 1978, and is also a member of the International Democratic Union. It is a member of the Conservative Group in the Nordic Council.

Policies

Although it was once a traditional Conservative Party, the KOK is now a moderate non-Socialist Party, well within the mainstream Finnish political consensus on both domestic and foreign policy questions. Its long exclusion from government by the other main parties was increasingly for tactical, rather than ideological considerations, and by the time of the 1987 elections the Social Democrats were beginning to prefer KOK as a coalition partner rather than the Centre Party.

On economic issues KOK supports the concept of a social market economy, with greater reliance on the market, but maintaining a strong accent on social responsibility. It calls for decentralization and a reduction in bureaucracy. Economic growth should be balanced, and with a greater emphasis on quality of life considerations.

The party has been accused of seeking widespread privatizations but it has rejected attempts to turn basic services provided by society, such as health care, social welfare and education into commercial activities, as this would weaken society's ability to plan and monitor the quality of services. On the other hand it considers that there should be less reliance on central provision of services and more on municipal self-government, and in certain areas private services could usefully complement those offered by the state. State enterprises should be subject to full competition in areas which are outside their basic remit.

A major party emphasis has been on tax reform. Income tax levels should be lowered, and the maximum marginal tax rate, even in the highest income category, should not exceed 40 per cent with regard to national taxes. The party has also called for lower corporate taxation, has opposed wealth taxes, and supported a shift towards indirect taxation and VAT, with basic commodities being free of tax. Before the 1987 elections, the KOK also put forward the idea of integrating the social security and taxation systems within a uniform basic income system, which would guarantee each citizen protection from welfare risks.

The KOK supports a tripartite approach towards labour questions, and an increase in industrial democracy. It calls for more investment in science and research. It has also supported a shift in student aid, away from loans and towards grants. KOK has also called for greater help for families and measures to tackle Finland's housing shortage, including increasing rent controls.

Environmental policy is now given a greater emphasis by the party, which also believes that no new nuclear power projects should be undertaken for the moment, pending greater study on safety aspects.

On agricultural policy KOK has called for a reduction in the current overproduction, but also for the maintenance of self-sufficiency.

KOK advocates more decentralized government, and has supported use of popular referenda and direct popular elections of the president.

KOK is a strong defender of Finnish neutrality and of the Paasikivi-Kekkonen line in foreign affairs, and believes that Finnish foreign policy should be a matter for national consensus and co-operation rather than ideological or narrow party political positions. KOK has also supported work aimed at achieving a Nordic nuclear-free zone.

Personalities

Harri Holkeri is the first KOK Prime Minister of Finland since the early 1940s. He was born in 1937, and was KOK's chairman from 1970–79. He was also on the Governing Board of the Bank of Finland. He was the party's unsuccessful presidential candidate in both 1982 and 1988.

Finnish election results 1945–87 (percentages and seats won)

	1945	1948	1951	1954	1958	1962	1966	1970	1972	1975	1979	1983	1987
SSDP (Social Democrats)	25.1% (50)	26.3% (54)	26.5% (53)	26.2% (54)	23.2% (48)	19.5% (38)	27.2% (55)	23.4% (51)	25.8% (55)	24.9% (54)	23.9% (52)	26.7% (57)	24.1% (56)
KP (Centre Party)	21.4% (49)	24.2% (56)	23.3% (51)	24.1% (53)	23.1% (48)	23.0% (53)	21.2% (49)	17.1% (37)	16.4% (35)	17.6% (39)	17.3% (36)	17.6% (38)	17.6% (40)
KOK (National Coalition Party)	15.0% (28)	17.0% (33)	14.6% (28)	12.8% (24)	15.3% (29)	14.6% (32)	13.8% (26)	18.0% (37)	17.6% (34)	18.4% (35)	21.7% (47)	22.1% (44)	23.1% (53)
SKDL (Finnish People's Democratic League)	23.5% (49)	20.0% (38)	21.6% (43)	21.6% (43)	23.2% (50)	22.0% (47)	21.2% (41)	16.6% (36)	17.0% (37)	18.9% (40)	17.9% (35)	13.8% (27)	9.4% (16)
Deva (Democratic Alternative)	—	—	—	—	—	—	—	—	—	—	—	—	4.2% (4)
SFP (Swedish People's Party)	8.4% (15)	7.7% (14)	7.6% (15)	7.0% (13)	6.7% (14)	6.4% (14)	6.0% (12)	5.7% (12)	5.4% (10)	5.0% (10)	4.6% (10)	4.9% (11)	5.3% (12)
LKP (Liberal People's Party)	5.2% (9)	3.9% (5)	5.7% (10)	7.9% (13)	5.9% (8)	5.9 (13)	6.5% (9)	5.9% (8)	5.2% (7)	4.3% (9)	3.7% (4)	with Centre Party	1.0% (0)
SMP (Rural Party)	—	—	—	—	—	2.2% (0)	1.0% (1)	10.5% (18)	9.2% (18)	3.6% (2)	4.5% (7)	9.7% (17)	6.3% (9)
SKL (Finnish Christian Union)	—	—	—	—	0.2% (0)	0.8% (0)	0.4% (0)	1.1% (1)	2.5% (4)	3.3% (9)	4.8% (9)	3.0% (3)	2.6% (5)
POP (Constitutional Party of the Right)	—	—	—	—	—	—	—	—	—	1.6% (1)	1.2% (0)	0.4% (1)	0.1% (0)
Vihreä Liitto (Greens)	—	—	—	—	—	—	—	—	—	—	—	1.4% (4)	4.0% (0)
VL (Liberal League)	—	—	0.3% (0)	0.3% (0)	0.3% (0)	0.5% (1)	—	—	—	—	(2)	—	—
Social Democratic League	—	—	—	—	1.7% (3)	4.4% (2)	2.6% (7)	1.4% (0)	1.0% (0)	—	—	—	—
Others	1.5% (0)	0.8% (0)	0.6% (0)	0.1% (0)	0.5% (0)	0.7% (0)	0.0% (0)	0.2% (0)	—	2.5% (1)	0.5% (0)	0.2% (0)	1.8% (0)

Ilkka Suominen has been the party's chairman since 1979, and is also the current Minister of Trade and Industry. He has been a vice-chairman of the European Democratic Union. He was born in 1939.

The three party vice-chairmen are Helena Pesola, Vesa Ruoraren and Jouni J. Särkijärvi. Tapani Mörttinen is the parliamentary group chairman. Aarno Kaila has been the party's secretary-general since the beginning of 1988.

Suomen Kansan Demokraatiinen Liitto — SKDL

(Finnish People's Democratic League)

Headquarters	: Kotkankatu 11, 00510 Helsinki (tel: 90–77081)
Chairman	: Reijo Käkelä
General secretary	: Salme Kandolin
Publication	: *Kansan Uutiset* (published by SKDL, together with SKP), *Folktidningen – Ny Tid*
Membership	: 70,000
Founded	: October 29, 1944

History

Shortly after the legalization of the Communist Party (SKP) in 1944 (see below), the Finnish People's Democratic League (SKDL) was founded by Communists and left-wing Socialists as an electoral alliance of the left. It was originally intended as a vehicle for a Popular Front Strategy, but this objective was undercut when the Social Democrats refused to join it, although a number of Social Democratic local branches and associated organizations did do so. It nevertheless became a permanent feature of the Finnish political scene. The Communist Party has never since put up parliamentary election candidates under its own name, but only under the SKDL label. The SKP has remained, however, the largest single element within the SKDL, and has provided the majority of its parliamentarians.

The SKDL obtained 23.5 per cent of the vote and 49 seats in the first postwar election, becoming the second largest party. It took part in the first postwar government coalition from 1944 to 1948, and from 1946 to 1948 provided the prime minister for the only time in its history. Mauna Pekkola was a former Social Democrat, and was one of the non-Communist members of the SKDL. Besides Pekkola, the SKDL had five other ministers in the government.

In 1948 the government collapsed and the SKDL vote lost 13 seats in the elections of that year. It then remained in opposition until 1966. Its vote remained steady at 21–22 per cent in all parliamentary elections from 1951 to 1966, although the number of its seats fluctuated considerably. It remained one of the three major parties of Finland, and in 1958 became the largest Finnish party in terms of seats if not votes.

In 1965 Ele Alenius, a left-wing Socialist, became SKDL secretary-general. In 1967 he became SKDL chairman. The SKDL took on a more moderate image and in 1966 finally returned to government. The SKDL had three ministers in the 1966–69 Paasio government and also in the 1968–70 Koivisto government. The SKDL also updated its basic party programme.

The divisions within the SKP (see below) over the invasion of Czechoslovakia and over the implications of participating in government contributed to a considerable setback for the SKDL in the 1970 elections. Its vote dropped to 16.6 per cent (from 21.2 per cent in 1966) and its number of seats dropped to only 36. It subsequently returned briefly to a coalition government under Karjalainen, from which its three Ministers later resigned to protest against a wage freeze. From 1971–75 it was in opposition, from 1975–76 in government and in 1976–77 back to opposition. It then remained in government from 1977 to 1982. Its vote recovered somewhat from its 1970 low, even reaching 18.9 per cent and 40 seats in 1975.

Since 1982 the SKDL has been in opposition, and has increasingly suffered from the deepening schisms within the SKP.

In the 1983 parliamentary elections its vote fell from the 17.9 per cent (35 seats) it had won in 1979 to only 13.8 per cent (27 seats). Its membership also dropped sharply.

The hard-line minority within the SKP finally left the party in 1985 and subsequently founded a new party which later became SKP-Y (see below). In 1986 they helped to found their own electoral equivalent of the SKDL, the Democratic Alternative (Deva, see below). As a result of these divisions the SKDL lost 10 of its 27 members.

In the 1987 parliamentary elections the SKDL obtained 9.4 per cent of the votes and retained 16 of its 17 seats, performing much better than its rival, Deva, which only obtained four seats on 4.2 per cent of the vote.

In the 1988 presidential elections the SKDL supported the candidacy of its former non-Communist chairman, Kalevi Kivisto (who did not stand under the SKDL label). Kivisto only came fourth in the first round of elections with 26 votes in the electoral college, but coming ahead of Deva's candidate, Jouko Kajanoja.

At the League Congress of the SKDL in May 1988 Reijo Käkelä defeated Claes Andersson to become the new chairman of the SKDL in succession to Esko Helle (who had held the post from 1985 to 1988), and Salme Kandolin became the new general secretary.

Support

Finland has had one of the strongest Communist and far left voting traditions in Western Europe, though the party divisions of recent years have helped to reduce SKDL support from over 20 per cent to the current level of only 13.5 per cent for both SKDL and Deva in the 1987 elections.

SKDL voting strength has been based on two major support bases, a traditional working class and industrial base in southern and south-central Finland, and a more rural base in the peripheral and disadvantaged areas of north and north-east Finland, where it has attracted a social protest vote from economic outsiders such as small farmers and lumberjacks. In the south it has competed especially with the Social Democrats in working-class areas (and has been less successful than the Social Democrats among the middle classes), whereas in the north and north-east it has competed more with the Centre Party.

In the 1983 elections, the last before the split within the SKP and SKDL, far left strength was greatest in the Oulu constituency, in northern Finland, where the SKDL polled 20.1 per cent. In the past the SKDL had polled over 50 per cent in some municipalities within this constituency. The SKDL has also been strong in parts of Lapland where it polled 15.6 per cent in 1983. In Kuopio constituency it received 16.9 per cent and in central Finland 16.5 per cent.

Another particular point of strength was in the constituency of North Häme in south-central Finland, based to a considerable extent on the industrial city of Tampere, and where the SKDL polled 19.9 per cent in 1983. The SKDL also polled well in North Turku and to a lesser extent in South Turku.

It was weaker on the coast of southern Finland. In Helsinki it only obtained 13.1 per cent in 1983, and in Uusimaa 11.7 per cent.

The SKDL had two particular points of weakness in 1983, the Gulf of Bothnia constituency of Vaasa, with its heavily Swedish population (where the SKDL polled 9.1 per cent) and especially the south-eastern constituencies on the Soviet border (North Karelia 8.9 per cent, Mikkeli 7 per cent and Kymi 6.4 per cent).

Organization

The SKDL's statutes provide for both individual and corporate membership. Individuals may join the SKDL directly on a district, enterprise or trade basis. In the early 1980s individual SKDL members accounted for just under 30 per cent of the total.

The corporate members of the SKDL retain their own separate local and district organizations. The most powerful of these has been the *Suomen Kommunistinen Puolue* (the Finnish Communist Party or SKP), which has typically had less than a third of the SKDL members, but the vast majority of the SKDL parliamentarians (e.g. 23 out of 27 in 1983). The other corporate organizations are the *Suomen Naisten Demokraattinen Liitto* (SNDL, Finnish Women's Democratic League), the *Suomen Demokraattinen Nuorisoliitto* (SDNL, Democratic Youth League of Finland) and the *Socialistinen Opiskelijaliitto* (SOL, Socialist Students' League). The Socialists within the SKDL have also formed their own Socialist organization. The SDPL (Democratic Pioneers' League of Finland) also works in close co-operation with the SKDL. Finally there is also a special board to liaise with Swedish-speaking Finns, which is elected by the Swedish-speaking members of the SKDL.

The SKDL's total membership has dropped greatly in recent years. It was 145,000 in 1981, 120,000 in 1985 and is estimated at only 70,000 today.

At national level the SKDL league congress meets every three years, and consists of representatives elected by the SKDL district organizations and also by the corporate member organizations. The congress elects the SKDL chairman (who in the past has sometimes been a non-Communist) and the general secretary. There are also two vice-chairmen).

The SKDL league council meets two to four times a year, and has its own chairman and two vice-chairmen. The smaller league board is the top executive body of the SKDL, which is also elected by the congress. It is assisted by the league secretariat.

The main organ of the SKDL is the *Kansan Uutiset*, which is published by the League in conjunction with the SKP, and which appears five times a week. There is also a weekly Swedish organ, *Folktidningen — Ny Tid*. The SKDL has five main provincial papers, the *Hameen Yhteistyö* (Tampere, five times a week), the *Kansan Tahto* (Oulu, five times a week), the *Kansan Sana* (Kuopio, three times a week), the *Kansan Ääni* (Vaasa, three times a week) and the *Satakunnan Työ* (Pori, three times a week).

The SKDL sits in the Left Socialist Group in the Nordic Council.

Policies

The SKDL has included left-wing Socialists as well as Communists, but the Communist Party has been the dominant force within it and developments within the SKDL have closely paralleled those within the SKP.

In the 1960s the SKDL adopted a new and more moderate party programme emphasizing a Finnish Road to Democratic Socialism and themes such as social justice, the need for a higher minimum wage and greater industrial democracy, as well as state planning and some nationalizations. It also called for greater separation of Church and state. In 1979 a modified programme was adopted, putting less emphasis on nationalization.

The majority within the SKDL has emphasized the need for co–operation between political forces of the left and centre to work for general improvements in Finnish economic and social conditions. It has thus supported SKDL government participation. The SKDL has also been supportive of the Paasikivi-Kekkonen line in Finnish foreign policy. It seeks a nuclear-free zone in Northern Europe. As a result of the schism of the SKP-Y and the creation of a rival electoral alliance, Deva, the SKDL has now lost its hard-line Marxist minority.

Personalities

The SKDL chairman is Reijo Käkelä, who was elected in 1988. He was previously its general secretary and had also been a member of the SKP's politburo. The general secretary is Salme Kandolin.

Kalevi Kivisto was the candidate supported by the SKDL in the 1988 presidential elections. He was born in 1941, and was a former Minister of Culture, Minister of Culture and Science and Minister of Education. He was the chairman of the SKDL from 1979 to 1985, and its presidential candidate in 1982.

Suomen Kommunistinen Puolue — SKP
(Communist Party of Finland)

Headquarters	: Sturenkatu 4/A, 00510 Helsinki
Chairman	: Jarmo Wahlström
General secretary	: Heljä Tammisola
Membership	: 20,000
Founded	: 1918

History

The SKP was founded in Moscow in 1918 by Finnish Reds fleeing after their defeat in the Finnish Civil War. It called for armed revolution and was banned from all activities in Finland, whether of a parliamentary or trade union nature. It remained illegal until 1944, and its headquarters remained in exile. Its most prominent leader was Otto Ville Kuusinen (1881–1964), who was close to Lenin and became a leading Comintern figure, and a member of the Soviet Politburo.

Attempts were also made to organize within Finland, both covertly and openly, under non-Communist labels. A Socialist Workers' Party of Finland was set up in 1920. It enjoyed strong trade union support and in the 1922 elections obtained 14.8 per cent of the vote and 27 seats. In 1923 it again changed its name, but its parliamentarians were tried by the authorities and imprisoned and in 1925 it was finally declared illegal. The party re-emerged in other forms throughout the 1920s and Left Socialists/Communists continued to win 18 to 23 seats in the Parliament up to 1929. In 1930 the extreme right-wing Lapua Movement intimidated voters with Communist leanings, greatly reducing support for the far left, and in 1931 the Communist laws finally banned all activities considered to be Communist. No candidates were put up for the rest of the 1930s. At the beginning of the Winter War between Russia and Finland, a Finnish Communist Government in exile was established at Terijoki in Russian-occupied Karelia, but was only of short duration.

The Communist Party was finally legalized in Finland in 1944. Shortly afterwards the SKP helped to set up a broader electoral alliance of Communist and Left Socialist forces, the SKDL. The SKP has continued to contest national elections under the SKDL umbrella until the present day. In 1944 Yrjo Leino, the son-in-law of Otto Ville Kuusinen, became the Minister of the Interior, and the first Communist minister in a non-Communist country in Europe. It was Leino's removal from the government in 1948 which brought it down, and led to the SKDL (and SKP) going into opposition for a period of 18 years.

For the first two decades after the war the SKP had the same traditional leadership. Aimo Aaltonen was chairman from 1944 to 1966, and Ville Pessi was general secretary from 1944 to 1969. Otto Kuusinen's daughter, Hertta, was leader of the parliamentary group.

Major changes took place in 1966 when Aarne Saarinen became the new chairman of the party, and the SKDL re-entered government. A new generation of "Eurocommunist" reformers began to take over leadership positions in the party, a trend confirmed when Arvo Aalto became the new general secretary in 1969. A more moderate party programme was adopted, calling for a Finnish Road to Socialism.

At the same time a divide began to open up between the reformist majority and the substantial hard-line minority. There were sharp differences over the Soviet invasion of Czechoslovakia in 1968, and also disagreements over SKDL participation in the government. The majority were strongly in favour, but the minority were concerned about the implications for the party's ideology and policies. The minority, whose leader was Taisto Sinisalo, began to build their own separate organization within the party and there might have been an early split without strong Soviet pressure to prevent this occurring.

The divisions within the party continued throughout the 1970s and early 1980s. In 1982 Jouko Kajanoja became chairman in an attempt at reconciliation between the two factions. This failed, and Kajanoja later joined the hard-line minority.

In 1984 the long-serving reformist general secretary Arvo Aalto was elected as chairman in place of Kajanoja and another reformist Aarno Aitamurto was chosen as general secretary. The minority refused to take up places on the central committee or Politburo and in the local elections later in the year presented a number of separate candidates in municipalities such as Helsinki and Espoo. The majority then began to establish their own organizations in those areas where the SKP structure was controlled by the hard-liners.

The final crisis came in 1985. A special party congress boycotted by the minority reconfirmed the reformist leadership (although Aitamurto was replaced as general secretary by Esko Vainionpää) and agreed to changes in the party rules to strengthen the majority's hand. In September 1985 the central committee ordered the minority faction to disband its organization within a month and to close its separate newspaper *Tiedonantaja*. When this ultimatum was rejected, eight minority-controlled district organizations were expelled from the party. In November 1985 the Committee of SKP Organizations, which later became the Communist Party of Finland — Unity (SKP-Y) was founded as a separate party by the hard-liners (see separate entry). In April 1986 they helped to establish the Democratic Alternative (Deva) as a rival electoral alliance to the SKDL. Subsequent attempts at party reunification have proved abortive.

In 1988 Jarmo Wahlström was elected as the new party chairman in succession to Arvo Aalto, and Heljö Tammisola replaced Vainionpää as general secretary.

Support

(See entry on SKDL, as SKP electoral support cannot easily be distinguished from that of the SKDL as a whole).

Organization

The SKP is the most influential component within the SKDL, but its membership has declined greatly. It has been around 50,000 in the past, but by 1983 it was only 33,000. It is now estimated at around 20,000.

The SKP has been governed in theory by the principle of democratic centralism, but in practice this was flouted for years by the minority hard-liners, who set up their own separate organization, and even had their own newspaper.

The SKP has local sections and district federations. The SKP congress elects a 50-member central committee, which elects an 11-member political bureau and the party officers.

The SKP produces a newspaper called *Kansan Uutiset* (People's News) in conjunction with the SKDL, and also a Swedish-language weekly, *Folktidningen* (People's News in Swedish). It also produces a monthly publication *Kommunisti*.

Through the conflict between the party majority and minority the Soviet Communist Party sought to use its influence to avert an outright split, while indicating its support for the minority faction. The Soviet Communist Party has continued to keep open bridges to the majority party, while seeking reconciliation between the two rival groups.

Policies

Since the mid to late 1960s the SKP has been a party with a majority Eurocommunist leadership, calling for an independent Finnish approach to Socialism. Domestically it has been prepared to co-operate in government with other left-of-centre and centre parties and to accept democratic pluralism. It has supported the Paasikivi-Kekkonen line in foreign policy. With the departure of the hard-line minority, the Eurocommunist line is now dominant within the party.

Personalities

The party's chairman is Jarmo Wahlström, who was elected in 1988. He was born in 1938 in Vaasa, and is a former parliamentary group chairman. Aarno Aitamurto is deputy chairman, and is a former general secretary. Heljä Tammisola is the new general secretary, and used to be a party deputy chairman.

Demokraattinen Vaihtoehtoe — Deva
(Democratic Alternative)

Headquarters	: Kornetintie 4, 00380 Helsinki
Chairman	: Kristiina Halkola
General secretary	: Seppo Timenen
Founded	: April 1986

History

After the split between the majority and minority wings of the SKP (see separate entry) and the establishment of the new hard-line Communist Party of Finland — Unity (SKP-Y, see below), the SKP-Y helped to create Deva in April 1986 as their own electoral front equivalent of the SKDL. Ten of the 26 members of the SKDL who had been elected in the 1983 elections joined the new Deva grouping.

In the March 1987 elections Deva lost six of its seats, obtaining 4.2 per cent of the vote and four seats. In the 1988 presidential elections Deva's unsuccessful candidate was Jouko Kajanoja, the general secretary of the SKP-Y.

Organization

The main component of Deva is the SKP-Y, but it also includes a number of other leftist groupings, such as the Socialist Workers' Party, the Communist Youth League and the Socialist Students' League.

Policies

Deva has an orthodox Marxist-Leninist and pro-Soviet orientation.

Personalities

In December 1986 Kristiina Halkola, a singer and actress, was elected to chair Deva. She did not win a seat in the 1987 elections.

Suomen Kommunistinen Puolue — Yhdenälsyys — SKP-Y
(Communist Party of Finland — Unity)

Headquarters	: Kornetintie 4, 00380 Helsinki
Chairman	: Taisto Sinisalo
General secretary	: Jouko Kajanoja
Publication	: *Tiedonuntaja* (daily)
Membership	: 10,000
Founded	: November 1985

History

The orthodox pro-Soviet minority faction of the SKP (see separate entry), which under the leadership of Taisto Sinisalo had been in continuing conflict with the Eurocommunist leadership since the late 1960s, was finally expelled in late 1985. A "Committee of SKP Organizations" was first established, and a new electoral alliance called Deva (see above) was set up in April 1986. The orthodox faction eventually adopted the title "Communist Party of Finland — Unity" (SKP-Y), although the Deva designation continued to be used by the parliamentary group.

Organization

The SKP-Y claims around 10,000 members and has a party congress, central committee and politburo. It has a daily organ called *Tiedontantaja*.

Policies

The SKP-Y stems from those members of the SKP who were most concerned about the implications of SKP participation in coalition governments with parties to its right, and who put less emphasis on an independent Finnish Road to Socialism, and more on closer links with the Soviet Union. In the 1987 elections they advocated increased trade with the Soviet Union. Attempts at reconciliation with the main SKP have so far proved to be unsuccessful.

Personalities

Taisto Sinisalo is the party's chairman. He is a docker from Kotka, and was the leader of the SKP hard-liners from the late 1960s onwards. Jouko Kajanoja is the party's general secretary. He was born in 1942 and was the Minister of Labour from 1981–82 before becoming the SKP chairman in 1982–84. He later joined the minority faction, and was the Deva candidate for president in the 1988 elections. The party's two vice-chairmen are Yrjö Hakanen and Marja Liisa Löyttyjarvi; the latter is one of Deva's four Members of Parliament.

Kommunistiska Arbetarpartiet
(Communist Workers' Party)

Leader	: Markus Kainulainen
Founded	: May 21, 1988

This is a new hard-line Communist Party founded by Markus Kainulainen, who came from the Sinisalo minority party, the SKP-Y (see separate entry), but who believed that it too was making too many ideological concessions.

Keskustapolue — KP
(Centre Party)

Headquarters	: Pursimienenkatu 15, 00150 Helsinki 15 (tel: 358–0–17 03 11)
Chairman	: Paavo Väyrynen
Secretary	: Seppo Kääriäinen
Youth organization	: *Nuoren Keskustan Liitto*
Women's organization	: *Keskustapuolueen Naiset*
Membership	: 300,000
Founded	: 1906

History

The Agrarian Union was founded in 1906 to promote the interests of Finnish farmers. Its most prominent figure was Santeri Alkio (1862–1930), who was the party ideologue and wrote its first party programme. The new party was anti-establishment, defending the rights of the periphery against the centre, of the countryside against the city, of Finnish-speaking peasants against the Swedish-speaking elite. It had links with religious revivalism, and later there was to be much support within party ranks for prohibition.

In its first election in 1907 it obtained nine seats on 5.8 per cent of the vote. Its vote slowly rose over the next decade to 9 per cent (19 seats) by 1916. In the great constitutional debate in 1918–19 it opposed attempts to establish a monarchy in Finland. Between 1916 and 1919 its vote rose sharply, and it obtained 42 seats on 19.7 per cent of the vote in 1919. It now began to participate in government, and from 1917 to the present it has taken part in over three–quarters of all the government coalitions.

Throughout the interwar years the party was generally second after the Social Democrats with over 20 per cent of the vote. In 1929 its vote rose markedly to 26.2 per cent, and although it had fewer votes than the Social Democrats, it had the largest number of seats. In 1930 its vote rose to its interwar peak of 27.3 per cent, but this time with fewer seats than the Social Democrats. In 1933 its vote dropped sharply to only 22.5 per cent, and the party then remained at roughly this level until after World War II.

The KP provided two Presidents of Finland in the interwar years, Lauri Kristian Relander from 1925 to 1932, and Kyösti Kallio from 1937 to 1940. From 1937 there began a long period of red-green coalition between the Agrarians and the Social Democrats.

After the war the Agrarians were led by V.J. Sukselainen from 1945 to 1964. In 1945 they obtained 21.4 per cent (49 seats) and were only the third party after the Social Democrats and the greatly reinforced Communists; but in 1948 they obtained 24.2 per cent and became the largest party in terms of seats if not votes. From 1948 to 1966 their vote remained steady at between 23–24 per cent, with the Agrarians continuing as one of the three main parties.

Between 1950 and 1956 Urho Kekkonen was Prime Minister in five out of the seven administrations and in 1956 he was elected President of Finland. He was to remain as President until 1981, providing enhanced prestige for the Centre Party and being particularly associated with Finland's foreign policy stance of non-alignment but friendly co–operation with the Soviet Union.

The early years of Kekkonen's presidency were a period of particular success for the Agrarians. In 1957 Sukselainen became Prime Minister and from 1959 to 1963 there were three more Agrarian-led governments under Sukselainen, Miettunen and Karjalainen. In 1962 the Agrarian Union became the largest party for the first time, both in terms of votes and seats.

The party did endure, however, a couple of schisms, first with a short-lived Agrarian opposition in 1958. Also in 1958 Veikko Vennamo left the Agrarian's parliamentary group and founded a new Smallholders' Party the following year, which, as the Rural Party, was later to do more considerable electoral damage to the Agrarians.

In 1965 the Agrarian Union changed its name to the Centre Party (KP), in a parallel attempt to other Scandinavian agrarian parties, to broaden its appeal outside the declining farming population. From 1965 to 1980 the KP was led by Johannes Virolainen (who was also Prime Minister from 1964 to 1966).

In 1966 the KP's vote dropped slightly to 21.2 per cent (49 seats), but a much more serious drop took place in 1970, when the Rural Party did very well and the KP's vote fell to 17.1 per cent (37 seats). In 1970–71, however, Karjalainen was again Prime Minister.

The party's vote remained at around 16.5 to 17.5 per cent for the rest of the 1970s. In 1979 it entered an electoral pact with the Liberal People's Party (see separate entry). In 1980 Paavo Väyrynen became the new party leader at the age of 34.

In June 1982 the Liberal People's Party was admitted as a member organization of the KP, keeping an independent structure, but with five reserved seats in the KP's party delegation and two in its party council. In 1983 the joint KP-Liberal Party organization polled 17.6 per cent and obtained 38 seats. In 1986, however, the Liberal People's Party again left the KP to resume its full independence.

In the 1987 national elections, the KP on its own obtained 40 seats on 17.6 per cent of the vote. The Social Democrats, however, indicated that they preferred to form a government with the National Coalition Party and other parties. The KP is thus in the unfamiliar position of being the largest party of opposition.

In the 1988 presidential elections Paavo Väyrynen obtained 68 electoral votes in the first round of voting and was the runner-up to incumbent President Koivisto.

Support

The KP is Europe's most powerful Agrarian Party and is the third largest party in Finland. Half of its members are still farmers. It is particularly strong in rural and small town Finland, and because of its strength in these areas has the largest number of municipal council members of any Finnish party. On the other hand it is weak in Finland's largest cities.

The KP's vote steadily declines from northern to southern Finland. It has been the largest party in the four northern provinces, especially in Lapland and Oulu and to a slightly lesser extent in Kuopio and Vaasa. It has been the second party to the Social Democrats in North Karelia, Mikkeli and Central Finland. It has had fair support in Kymi and North Turku, but has been weaker in South Turku and South Häme and especially North Häme, Uusimaa and Helsinki.

Although it made some progress in south Finland in 1987, it still has no seat at all in the capital, Helsinki, where it is the weakest of the major Finnish parties.

Organization

The KP has around 300,000 members, and has by far the highest membership of any Finnish party. It has around 3,000 local branches in the villages and town districts, 350 municipal organizations and 21 district organizations.

At national level it has a party congress, which is held every two years, and consists of around 3,000 representatives of the local branches and member organizations.

The party congress elects the 130–member party delegation, which holds office for a two–year term and meets twice a year. The party delegation elects the 24 member party

council, which in its turn elects the party's executive board. The party's chairman, three vice-chairmen and secretary-general are directly elected by the party congress.

The KP's youth organization is called the *Nuoren Keskustan Liitto* (NKL, Youth Union of the Centre Party). It was founded in 1945, and has 52,000 members. There is also a student organization (*Keskustan Opiskelijaliitto*, KOL, Students' Union of the Centre Party), which was founded in 1937 and has 3,300 members; and a children's organization of the Centre Party, *Vesaiset*, which was founded in 1956 and has 28,000 members. There is a women's organization, *Keskustapuolueen Naiset* (KN, Women's Organization of the Centre Party), which was founded in 1946 and has 126,000 members.

There are 14 newspapers associated with the party with a total circulation of 455,000 or 16.5 per cent of total newspaper circulation. The main organ of the party is *Suomenmaa*, which is published in Helsinki.

In domestic politics the Centre Party has been the largest party in a centre bloc with the Liberal People's Party, Finnish Christian Union and Swedish People's Party. It co–operates closely with the Centre Parties of Norway and Sweden. In 1976 it hosted in Helsinki the first European Security and Co–operation Conference of Peasant and Centre Parties and Organizations. It sits in the Centre Group in the Nordic Council.

The KP became an observer member of the Liberal International at its Stockholm Congress in 1983.

Since the beginning of the 1970s the KP has had official relations with the Communist Party of the Soviet Union, and claims to have been the first non-Socialist party to have done so. It also has links with the agrarian parties of Bulgaria, Poland and East Germany.

Policies

The KP has had a pivotal position in the Finnish political spectrum, and has taken part in the large majority of Finnish governments, although it is now again in opposition. It has been a non-ideological party of the centre, criticizing both the excesses of socialism and capitalism. Its preferred coalition partner, however, has been the Social Democrats, and it has been reluctant to bring the National Coalition (Conservative) Party into government, although at the 1987 election it supported the idea of a three-party grand coalition with Social Democrats and Conservatives.

The party continues to defend the interests of the farming community, and of the peripheral regions of Finland. A constant party theme is the need for decentralized small production units, which are both good for the environment,and protect local communities. The party calls for balanced regional development, and is opposed to the concentration of production and population in the big cities.

On other economic matters, the KP has been pragmatic, supporting a mixed economy, and state intervention, such as planning and nationalization, when necessary. It now also puts an increasing emphasis on the environment.

The KP defends municipal and regional self-government, and is opposed to trade union corporatism. In the past it has called for use of referenda, and for direct election of government.

The KP is proud of its important role in developing Finland's official foreign policy line of autonomy while maintaining friendly relations with the Soviet Union.

In its development policy, the KP has supported the establishment of the New International Economic Order, and the promotion of agriculture and self-reliance within developing countries. It has called for the sparing use of limited global resources.

Personalities

The party's leader is Paavo Väyrynen, who is still only in his mid 40s. Its floor leader in Parliament is Kauko Juhantalo.

Suomen Maaseudun Puolue — SMP
(Finnish Rural Party)

Headquarters	:	Hämeentie 157, 7th Floor, 00560 Helsinki (tel: 90/790–299, telefax: 90/790 or 299/214)
Chairman	:	Pekka Vennamo
Secretary	:	Aaro Niiranen
Youth organization	:	*Kehittyvän Suomen Nuorten Liitto* (Youth Union of Progressive Finland)
Women's organization	:	*Kehittyvän Suomen Naiset* (Women of Progressive Finland)
Publication	:	*Suomen Uutiset* (News of Finland)
Membership	:	20,000
Founded	:	February 1959

History

The SMP was founded in 1959 (it was originally called the Finnish Smallholders' Party) by Veikko Vennamo, a charismatic populist, who had been a Member of Parliament from the Agrarian (Centre) Party, but had left it in 1958. The new party was anti-establishment in tone, defending the rights of "forgotten Finland", the little man, small farmers concerned with changes on the land (in particular amalgamation of small holdings) and remote and underprivileged regions of the country.

In the 1982 elections it obtained 2.2 per cent of the vote, but lost its only seat, that of Vennamo himself. In 1966 its vote dropped to 1 per cent, but Vennamo regained his seat. The party was then renamed the Finnish Rural Party.

Vennamo was critical of then President Kekkonen, and the SMP made its first major breakthrough in 1968 when Vennamo stood against Kekkonen in the presidential election of that year, and polled 231,000 votes (11.3 per cent of the total). In the 1970 national elections, the SMP polled 10.5 per cent and went up from one to 18 seats in the Parliament, especially at the expense of the Centre Party. In 1972 its vote dropped slightly to 9.2 per cent, but it retained its 18 seats.

Shortly afterwards, however, the party split in two. Thirteen of its Members of Parliament who were critical of Vennamo's authoritarian personality and his willingness to co–operate with parties of the left, in spite of the traditional conservatism of many of his followers, left the party and went off to create a new Finnish People's Unity Party (see entry under League of Civil Power).

In 1973 Vennamo strongly opposed the exceptional law that was passed by Parliament to permit Kekkonen to continue as President without having to face presidential elections.

In the 1975 elections, what was left of the SMP only polled 3.6 per cent, and only two of its seats were retained (this was better, however, than the rival Finnish People's Unity Party, which only held one seat on 1.7 per cent of the vote).

The SMP obtained 4.7 per cent in the 1978 presidential elections. In 1979 it polled 4.5 per cent in the national elections and obtained seven seats in the Parliament. In the course of the same year Veikko Vennamo stood down as leader, and was replaced by his son Pekka Vennamo.

In the 1982 presidential elections the SMP only polled 2.3 per cent but in the 1983 national elections it made a major recovery, polling 9.7 per cent of the vote, and winning 17 seats. It subsequently entered government for the first time by taking part in a four–party coalition with the Social Democrats, Centre Party and Swedish People's Party. In the 1984 municipal elections it obtained over 600 municipal council seats.

In the 1987 national elections its vote again fell sharply to 6.3 per cent and it ended up with only nine seats. It nevertheless entered a new four–party government coalition, with its chairman, Pekka Vennamo as its only minister.

Support

The SMP has made its appeal to small farmers, independent workers and small businessmen, to war veterans and more generally to the disadvantaged and discontented. As a protest party it has had erratic support from one election to the next. It has done best in rural Finland but has had some support everywhere in the country (it has sometimes done better than the much larger Centre Party in Helsinki, for example).

Organization

The SMP has around 20,000 members, organized in local associations throughout the country. Above these there are 16 district organizations. At national level a party convention is held every year in August, which elects the party's national committee. The smaller party board is its executive organ. The party chairman, two vice-chairmen and the party secretary are directly elected at the party convention.

Besides the party's youth organization, the *Kehittyvän Suomen Nuorten Liitto* (Youth Movement of Progressive Finland) there is also a students' organization, the *Kehittyvän Suomen Opiskelijat* (Students of Progressive Finland). There is a women's group, *Kehittyvan Suomen Naiset* (Women of Progressive Finland) and a pensioners' group, *Oikeutta Eläkeläissille* (Justice for Pensioners).

The party has a special Swedish language section, *Finlands Landsbygds Partis Svenska Fraktion*, a trade union section, a Christian work-group and also a Temperance Committee.

The party's newspaper, *Suomen Uutiset* (News of Finland) has a circulation of 40,000 and comes out once a week.

The SMP has no formal international links.

Policies

In the past the SMP has been primarily a protest party, but since 1983 it has had to make the difficult adjustment to becoming a party of government.

Its main emphasis has always been on defence of small farmers, small businessmen, and lower -paid office workers, against the monied and political establishment. It has also supported the periphery against the centre. It is critical of big capitalism and big bureaucracy. The party is against the rigid state control that it believes is advocated by the Socialist parties, and in favour of private enterprise. It has also defended traditional Finnish cultural and religious values. While many of its specific themes are those of the radical right (its closest equivalents in Scandinavia are the Progress Parties of Denmark and Norway), the SMP now sees itself as on the centre-left of the Finnish spectrum.

The party's economic policy has been populist. It opposes bureaucratic red tape. A persisting party theme has been the need for lower taxation of all kinds. In those areas where higher taxes need to be retained for the time being, the burden should shift more onto the rich. A minimum wage should be introduced, and there should be no unfair disparities between manual labour and intellectual work. Insurance rates should be reduced. The value of the Finnish Mark should be strongly defended. There should be a greater emphasis on developing smaller-scale and more diversified industry. The infrastructure of the underdeveloped regions of Finland should be improved.

The SMP has called for strong social security measures, with proper insurance and pension schemes for the old, the disabled and war veterans. There should be a guarantee of work or of further training for every young person. Mothers in the home should be paid appropriate wages. Everyone should be able to obtain their own home, and high rents should be reduced. Small remote schools should be kept open, and large centralized schools should be avoided.

The SMP continues to give strong support to smallholders and to family farmers. It believes that land prices should be kept down. Moreover land should be reserved for Finnish citizens, and should not be bought or rented by foreigners.

"Finland first" has been a recurring party theme, as well as the need for greater self-sufficiency in such fields as energy. The SMP also supports decentralization. It now puts a greater emphasis than before on environmental policy, and on the adverse impacts of uncontrolled economic growth. It is opposed to civil nuclear energy.

The SMP calls for a new constructive spirit founded on honesty, sound morality and Christian ethics. It has been highly critical of the existing party establishment. It has opposed subsidies for political parties, and called for special privileges for parliamentarians to be ended. It attacks patronage and abuses of power.

It has also called for enhanced popular

democracy, through such measures as use of national referenda. It has called for shorter terms of office for Parliament and for municipal councils, and for limitations on the time that the president can serve. Municipal autonomy should be strengthened.

The SMP has not had a particularly distinctive policy in the field of foreign affairs. It has supported official Finnish foreign policy, and the Paasikivi line towards the Soviet Union. It has emphasized the need for disarmament and the need to prohibit the use of force in international relations. It supports the establishment of a New International Economic Order, and has called for economic sanctions on South Africa, in order to hasten a transition to majority rule with minimum bloodshed.

Personalities

The SMP's chairman is Pekka Vennamo, the son of Veikko Vennamo, the party founder and dominant personality for most of its existence. Pekka Vennamo is the Minister for Communications in the present Government.

Suomen Kristilliinen Liitto — SKL
(Finnish Christian Union)

Headquarters	: Töölönkatu 50/D, 00250 Helsinki (tel: 90–40 74 77)
Chairman	: Esko Almgren
Secretary	: Jouko Jääskeläinen
Youth organization	: *SKL — Nuoret*
Women's organization	: *SKL — Naiset*
Newspaper	: *Kristityn Vastuu* (Christian Responsibility)
Membership	: 20,000 (1986)
Founded	: May 1958

History

The SKL is an Evangelical Christian Party, first founded in 1958 to propagate Christian values in politics, and to resist the secularization of Finnish cultural, social and political life. It obtained 0.2 per cent in the 1958 elections. Its continued survival was helped by the law for the public financing of parties in 1967. In 1970 it obtained 1.1 per cent of the vote and its first Member of Parliament, Raino Westerholm (who became the party chairman in 1973).

In 1972 the SKL more than doubled its vote to 2.5 per cent and, assisted by electoral alliances, obtained four seats in the Parliament. In 1975 it won nine seats on 3.3 per cent of the vote in the national election which saw the collapse of the Rural Party's vote.

In the presidential elections of 1978 Raino Westerholm stood as a candidate against President Kekkonen, and obtained a respectable 8.9 per cent of the vote. In the 1979 national elections the SKL retained its nine seats but with an increase in its vote to 4.8 per cent. It subsequently won an extra seat, giving it its highest ever level of 10 seats in the Parliament.

In the 1983 elections its vote dropped to 3 per cent, and it only retained three of its seats. In 1987 its vote dropped further to 2.6 per cent but its number of seats in the Parliament rose to five as a result of alliances in individual electoral districts with the Centre Party and with the Liberals.

Support

The SKL's main political base is among Evangelical Lutherans, especially among members of the National Missionary Society. Those who apply for membership of the party must be Christians by confession.

The Finnish Church has had a traditionally conservative and agrarian background, and the party's greatest strength is in rural south-central and south-eastern Finland. In the 1987 elections its highest percentage of the vote were in the electoral districts of South Häme (3.9 per cent), Mikkeli (3.9 per cent), central Finland (3.6 per cent), North Karelia (3.5 per cent) and Kymi (3.5 per cent).

It obtained its seats in central Finland, Kymi, Helsinki (where it polled 2.8 per cent), Vaasa (2.6 per cent) and South Turku (1.8 per cent). The SKL has been weaker in more radical north Finland. In 1987 it obtained 1.6 per cent in the electoral province of Oulu and only 1.1 per cent in Lappi (Lapland).

Organization

In 1986 the SKL had 20,000 members and 350 local branches. It has a party congress which is held every second year, and which elects a 60–member delegation. In turn this elects a party "government", which elects a seven–member executive committee.

The SKL has women's and youth organizations, and produces a party newspaper called *Kristityn Vastuu*.

The SKL's closest political links are with other Finnish centre parties, such as the Centre Party and Swedish People's Party. It sits in the Centre Group in the Nordic Council.

It has close ties with the other Scandinavian Christian Democratic parties, notably those in Norway and Sweden. The SKL is not a member of the European or International Christian

Democratic organizations, but its youth movement *SKL — Nuoret* is a full member of the Young European Christian Democrats.

Policies

The SKL is a Christian Democratic Party determined to maintain Christian values in Finnish society. Party meetings have begun with Bible readings, prayers and the singing of hymns.

The SKL has always been an opposition party on the centre-right of the political spectrum. It is non-Socialist in orientation, defending freedom for private enterprise, and safeguards for private ownership, but distinguishes itself from Conservatism on the grounds of its greater emphasis on social legislation. It calls for improved measures of social security, especially for children and mothers at home.

It has contributed to the tightening up of the law on abortion, and has also campaigned against free trade in light beer, and helped to abolish this in some counties.

The SKL has also sought to defend religious instruction in state schools. In the 1987 election the SKL objected to the free distribution of condoms in the fight against Aids.

It generally endorses existing Finnish foreign policy, with the exception of relations with Israel, where it considers that Finland has leaned too much towards the Arab States.

Personalities

The party's five Members of Parliament are Esko Almgren, its chairman, Toimi Kankaanniemi, Eeva Liisa Moilonen, Jorma Fred and Sauli Hautala.

Liberaalinen Kansanpuolue — LKP
(Liberal People's Party)

Headquarters	: Fredrikinkatu 58/A/6, 00100 Helsinki 10 (tel: 358–0–44–02–27)
Chairman	: Kyösti Lallukka
Secretary general	: Jari Havia
Newspaper	: *Polttopiste* (monthly)
Membership	: 8,500

History

In its present form the Liberal People's Party was founded in 1965, but it is the most recent party in a much longer Finnish liberal tradition. It stems from divisions within the pre-independence Finnish Party that led to the creation of a more liberal Young Finnish Party in the 1890s.

After independence, the Republican wing of the Young Finns under the leadership of K.J. Stahlberg, helped to found a new party, the *Kansallinen Edistyspuolue* (National Progressive Party). This won 12.8 per cent of the vote and 26 seats in the 1919 elections, the year when Stahlberg was elected as Finnish President, a post he was to retain until 1925.

The National Progressive Party's strength gradually declined during the interwar years, losing most of its support among farmers, for example, to the Agrarian Party. It continued, however, to be supported by the powerful Liberal press. It lost 11 seats in the 1922 elections and by 1939 it was only winning 4.8 per cent of the vote. It nevertheless participated as a coalition partner in the majority of interwar and wartime governments, providing the Prime Minister on several occasions. From 1940–44, R. Ryti was the second Progressive Party President of Finland.

After 1945 the party's vote slumped even further to only 3.9 per cent with five seats in the Parliament in the 1948 elections. In 1951 there was a division within the Liberal family, with the majority founding a new Finnish People's Party (*Suomen Kansanpuolue*) and the Conservative Liberal minority starting a Liberal League (*Vapaamielisten Liitto*).

The Finnish People's Party enjoyed a certain revival, obtaining 7.9 per cent of the vote and 13 seats in 1954, and averaging around 6 per cent through the 1950s and 1960s. It continued to take part in numerous coalition governments. The Liberal League won insignificant support, although it did obtain one seat in Parliament in 1962. In 1965 the two parties again merged to form the Liberal People's Party (LKP).

The LKP obtained 6.5 per cent and nine seats in the 1966 elections, but its support slowly declined in successive elections to 3.7 per cent by 1979, although it was still taking part in government coalitions, as in 1970–71 and in others between July 1972 and May 1977.

In June 1982 the LKP decided to join the Centre Party (see separate entry) as one of its member organizations, with two seats on the Centre Party council and five on its party delegation.

In June 1986 the LKP left the Centre Party to resume its independent status but in the March 1987 parliamentary elections it failed to win a seat.

Support

The LKP is now one of the smallest of Finland's parties, with only 1 per cent support in the 1987 elections. In the past it has had particular support among intellectuals.

Organization

The LKP produces a monthly publication called *Polttopiste*. It is a full member of the Liberal International.

Policies

The LKP is a party of moderate liberal orientation, which has a long tradition of co–operation with parties of the centre and centre-left.

Svenska Folkpartiet/Finland — SFP
(Swedish People's Party of Finland)

Headquarters	: Bulevarden 7/A, P.O. Box 146, 00121 Helsinki 12 (tel: Helsinki 64–03–13)
Party chairman	: Christoffer Taxell
Party secretary	: Peter Stenlund
Youth organization	: *Swedish Youth* (tel: 64–89–74) (chairman: Max Arhippainen)
Women's organization	: *Women's Organization of the Swedish People's Party* (tel: 64–97–43) (chairman: Margareta Pietikäinen)
Publication	: *Medborgarbladet*
Membership	: 56,000
Founded	: 1906

History

The SFP was founded in 1906. It was the successor of the Swedish Party that had developed in the late 19th century in reaction to the creation of the Finnish Party at a time when the division between the Swedish and Finnish-speaking communities was a central feature of political life.

The SFP obtained 24 seats in 1906, and has been a significant party ever since, although its number of votes and seats have gradually dropped along with the decline in the percentage of the Swedish-speaking population as a whole. As a catch-all party among the Swedish community, there has been a wide spectrum of opinion within the SFP. This has occasionally led to divisions, such as over the issue of monarchy against republicanism in 1918, and subsequently over left-right issues, as when a number of its right-wing members left the party in 1973, to help form a new Constitutional Party of the Right (POP, see separate entry).

The SFP has more often been a party of government than of opposition and has taken part in around two–thirds of all Finnish government coalitions. It has often held important government posts and for a short time in 1954 one of its members, R. Törngren, was Prime Minister.

In 1987 the SFP increased its vote to 5.3 per cent, and it obtained 12 seats in the Parliament (13 with its Swedish-speaking ally, the Åland coalition). It subsequently entered a new coalition government with the Conservatives, Social Democrats and Rural Party, in which it holds two Ministries, Education and Science, and Defence.

Support

The SFP has consistently won the support of three out of four Swedish-speaking Finns, who constitute around 6.3 per cent of the Finnish population and are mainly located near the coast of the Gulf of Bothnia, north and south of Vaasa (Vasa in Swedish), and along the south coast from Turku (Åbo), to well beyond Helsinki (Helsingfors). The SFP's vote is thus concentrated in four electoral districts, Vaasa (where it is the strongest party in many areas) and Uusimaa (Nyland in Swedish) in particular, but also Helsinki and South Turku. It does not campaign in the Swedish-speaking Åland Islands which have a separate political system for internal political purposes (see separate entry) and whose national seat is won by the Åland Coalition.

The Swedish-speaking community in Finland is not a homogenous one, and ranges from urban professionals in Helsinki and elsewhere, to farmers in Vaasa. The SFP thus has a wide social base.

The party's vote has been relatively stable at between 4.6 per cent and 6.4 per cent since 1958, following a previous long period of decline (from 10–12 per cent in the interwar years to only 5.7 per cent in 1958). In 1987 its vote actually rose significantly, indicating that it may also have won new support from Finnish speakers as well.

Organization

The SFP has around 56,000 members organized in 140 local branches. It does not organize in the Åland Islands, but is allied with the Åland Coalition.

The SFP has youth and women's groups. Besides its own periodical, *Medborgarbladet*, which appears on a monthly basis and has a circulation of 130,000, the SFP is also supported by 11 independent Swedish-language newspapers, of which the largest are *Hufuudstadsbladet* (with a circulation of 65,000) and the *Vasabladet* (with a circulation of 26,000).

The SFP sits in the Centre Group in the Nordic Council. It joined the Liberal International at its Stockholm Congress in 1983, and is also a permanent observer of the European Democratic Union.

Policies

The SFP's main purpose has been defence of the interests of the Swedish-speaking community in Finland. It has not, however, been separatist or isolationist, and has participated in the mainstream of Finnish political life. There has been a wide spectrum of opinion within the party from centre–left to centre–right, although the party has been non–Socialist in general orientation. It has been non–ideological on economic and social issues. It has supported the Paasikivi-Kekkonen line of active neutrality in Finnish foreign policy. The SFP has also seen itself as playing an important role in Finland's relations with the other Scandinavian countries.

Personalities

The party's chairman is Christoffer Taxell, who was a former Minister of Justice, and who is now the Minister of Education and Science in the present coalition government. The party's other current Minister is Ole Norrback, who has the Defence portfolio.

The party's floor leader in Parliament is Elisabeth Rehn.

Vihreä Liitto
(Green Alliance)

Headquarters	: Eerikinkatu 7/C/1, 00100 Helsinki
Chairman	: Heidi Hautala
Publication	: *Vihreä Lanka*
Founded	: February 1987

History

The Alliance was formed as a co–operative body for various existing local and national organizations, the latter including a political wing (*Vihreä Eduskuntaryhmä*) which in the 1983 elections won two seats on 1.5 per cent of the vote. In the 1987 parliamentary elections it doubled its representation to four seats on 4 per cent of the vote, although doing less well than some had predicted (support being partially undercut by a government decision not to proceed with a new nuclear power station). In the October 1988 local elections Green support

slipped somewhat and they obtained 2.6 per cent of the vote.

Support

The strongest support for the Greens has been in the larger towns and among young people with higher education. Three of its four Members of Parliament come from the electoral districts of Helsinki and of Uusimaa.

Organization

Neither the Alliance nor the political wing were initially registered as political parties, although the electoral impact of the Greens generated pressures for the creation of a properly structured national Green Party. In 1988 a decision was taken by the party's political wing to register as a political party.

Member organizations of the Alliance (local, regional and special interest) have been autonomous with representatives choosing a governing board of 15–25 members at an annual meeting of the Alliance. Membership is around 500 (in 11 member organizations). A weekly publication, *Vihreä Lanka*, has a circulation of 3,000. The Alliance is considering affiliation to the European Greens.

Policies

There is a wide range of views within the Alliance, which also includes a more radical *Linkola* wing.

Personalities

The Green Alliance has been chaired by Heidi Hautala. The political wing's leading figure has been Eero Paloheimo, elected to Parliament in 1987.

Suomen Eläkeläisten Puolue — SEP
(Pensioners' Party of Finland)

Headquarters	: Limingantie 13, 00550 Helsinki
Chairman	: Yrjoe Virtanen
Secretary	: Pauli Kiovula
Founded	: December 1985

In the March 1987 parliamentary elections the SEP obtained 35,298 votes (1.2 per cent) without winning representation. In the October 1988 local elections it polled 0.3 per cent.

The SEP has no particular political ideology, but seeks to represent the special interests of pensioners.

Perustuslaillinen Oikeistopuolue — POP
(Constitutional Party of the Right)

Headquarters	: Mannerheiminti 146/A/3, 00270 Helsinki
Chairman	: Georg C. Ehrnrooth
Secretary	: Panu Toivonen
Founded	: 1973

History

This party was founded in 1973 by Georg Ehrnrooth, who came from the Swedish People's Party. The original motivating force for the party stemmed from opposition to the extension of President Kekkonen's mandate by agreement between the main political parties and without democratic elections. It also attracted more general support from disillusioned Conservatives, especially from the Swedish People's Party and the National Coalition Party (KOK), who did not approve of the latter's move towards the political centre and who also felt that the Finnish foreign policy consensus was too pro-Soviet.

In the 1975 elections the party polled 1.6 per cent of the vote, and Ehrnrooth won a seat in Parliament, but he lost this in 1979 when the party obtained 1.2 per cent of the vote. The party regained a seat in 1983, on only 0.4 per cent of the national vote, but lost this in 1987, when it only won 0.1 per cent of the vote.

The party still claims a membership of 3,000.

Support

The party's support has been declining steadily. In the past its support has been concentrated in Helsinki.

Policies

The party has a Conservative orientation.

Åland Islands

The Åland Islands are an archipelago of around 6,500 islands and skerries located in the Baltic Sea between the Swedish and Finnish mainlands. They have a surface area of 572 square miles, and a population of over 23,000, of which 96 per cent are Swedish-speaking. The capital is Marienhamn, and tourism and shipping are among the main economic activities.

Politically the islands are part of Finland but they enjoy far-reaching autonomy which is currently being further extended. They have, for example, their own flag and postage stamps. They have a separate political system from that of the rest of Finland.

Political institutions

The Åland Islands are unilingual (Swedish only). There is a separate Åland regional citizenship.

They have extensive home rule on all internal matters and even foreign agreements entered into by the Finnish government only apply to Åland with the Åland Parliament's consent, if the agreement deals with a matter within Åland's competence. The President of Finland has a more limited power of veto over Åland legislation than he does over Finnish national legislation, and he may use his veto only if Finnish internal or external security is compromised or if the Åland Parliament has exceeded its legislative competence. Moreover, the Åland Autonomy Act cannot unilaterally be amended by the Finnish Parliament, but only with the consent of the Åland Parliament.

The original Autonomy Act for Åland was revised in 1951, but certain problems still remained over the dividing line between the legislative competence of the Åland and Finnish authorities and the degree of Åland's economic autonomy. In 1987 a special Åland Committee recommended that a number of other legislative and administrative competences be transferred to Åland, and that Åland be given a greater measure of economic autonomy. Åland already had its own small individual budget (and the Åland Parliament has had the power to levy a provincial tax) but the majority of Åland funds have come from an annual allocation from the Finnish budget. Åland will not be given full fiscal autonomy, as some had suggested, but will be given freedom to administer Finnish funds at its own discretion. Åland will also be reimbursed by the Finnish State if the amount of direct state taxes from Åland clearly exceed the average figure in Finland.

The Autonomy Act will finally come into force in the early 1990s.

The Åland Parliament is called the *Landsting*, and consists of 30 members elected every four years by proportional representation. It has a Presidium, consisting of a speaker and two deputy speakers. The right to vote and to stand for the Parliament are confined to those with Åland regional citizenship.

The Åland government is called the Åland Executive Council (*Landskapssryrelse*) and is led by the Åland prime minister (*Lantråd*).

Recent Åland election results (*Landsting*)

	1979	1983	1987
Ålandsk Center (Åland Centre)	42.1% (14)	36.6% (11)	28.5% (9)
Liberalerna Pa Åland (Åland Liberals)	29.7% (9)	28.9% (9)	23.7% (8)
Frisinnad Samverkan (Moderates)	13.9% (4)	16.6% (5)	17.2% (5)
Ålands Socialdemokrater (Åland Social Democrats)	11.9% (3)	16.5% (5)	13.9% (4)
De Gröna (The Greens)	—	—	6.6% (2)
Communists	2% (0)	2.3% (0)	—
Fria Åland (Free Åland)	—	—	2.6% (0)
Others (Independents)	—	—	7.0% (2)

There are also six other members. The Åland Parliament appoints the prime minister and then the other members. Until 1988 the government was chosen on a proportional basis, leading to a permanent coalition of all the major parties in the *Landsting*. A more truly parliamentary system has now been instituted, with the government only needing to have a simple majority in the *Landsting*. Minority governments are not allowed. As a result of the recent changes, there is now a majority and opposition within the *Landsting*. The whole Cabinet or individual members may be dismissed if there is a no-confidence vote within the *Landsting*.

Liaison between Åland and Finland on legislative and fiscal matters (notably apportionment of revenue) is assured by a special Åland Delegation, with two members appointed by the Finnish Cabinet and two by the Åland Parliament, and with its chairman nominated by the Finnish President.

The Åland Islands are also entitled to one representative in the Finnish Parliament (the *Eduskunta*). There is also a County Administrative Board of the Province of Åland to deal with administrative matters for which the Finnish state still retains powers in Åland. The Finnish County Governor (the chief Finnish representative on Åland) is appointed by the Finnish President, following consultations with the speaker of the Åland Parliament.

Since 1970 Åland has had its own representative in the Nordic Council, and this was increased to two in 1984.

The Åland Islands have been demilitarized and neutralized in perpetuity, and Åland citizens do not have to do military service.

Brief political history

1809   Åland Islands ceded by Sweden to Russia along with Finnish Grand Duchy.

1856   At end of Crimean War, in which Åland Islands came under attack from Anglo-French fleet (1854), "Åland servitude" is signed by Britain, France and Russia, in which Russians agree to demilitarization of Åland.

1917   Mass petition signed by 96 per cent of resident Ålanders of legally competent age demanding reunification with Sweden. Newly independent Finland, however, considers Åland to be integral part of Finland.

1918   Unofficial Åland Parliament is elected to seek reunification with Sweden.

1920   Finnish Parliament adopts Åland Autonomy Act, but this does not go far enough for Ålanders. Two Åland leaders, Julius Sundblom and Carl Björkman are imprisoned for high treason.

1921   League of Nations Council awards Finland sovereignty over Åland, but on condition that there are new guarantees for the islanders and that Åland is neutralized. Åland Agreement (treaty between Finland and Sweden) provides for Åland regional citizenship and for guarantees for language and culture of the population of the Åland Islands (e.g. teaching language in Åland Schools is to be Swedish). Guarantees Act subsequently passed by the government of Finland. Under these conditions the Ålanders accept the Autonomy Act for Åland.

June 9, (Åland Autonomy Day)
1922:   First plenary session of popularly elected Åland Parliament.

1951   Revision of Åland Autonomy Act is passed on Dec. 28, 1951. Strengthens Åland's autonomy.

1975   Tough new legislative restrictions on land ownership in Åland for those without Åland regional citizenship.

1987   Åland Committee delivers its report in which it calls for further transfers of power to the Åland Islands.

1988   New more parliamentary form of government comes into operation for first time.

Main features of the current political system

In 1988 the Åland parliamentary system was strengthened with the establishment of a three–party coalition government of the Centre Party, Moderates and Liberals, and with the Social Democrats (their former government partners in an all-party coalition) in the opposition along with the Greens and Independents. It is anticipated that this new division into government parties and opposition will revitalize the political system.

The Åland Islands have had a multiparty political system (six groups are currently represented on the 30-member *Landsting*), but one which has been based on a high degree of consensus and co–operation. Personal differences have appeared to play a greater role than ideology.

One feature of the Åland political system is the weakness of the left, with the only significant party of the left (the Social Democrats) being the fourth largest party.

A further feature of the system is the tradition for the single Åland representative in the Finnish Parliament to be elected not under an individual Åland Party label, but under the umbrella of the Åland Coalition (*Ålandsk Samling*), a broad coalition of all the main Åland parties which represents the islands' interests in the Finnish Parliament. The member from the coalition normally works in the Parliament with the Swedish People's Party (see separate entry under Finland). The coalition is not very active within Åland, but the elected member would typically meet with its representatives once a month. Its current member, Gunnar Jansson, was elected with special support from the Liberals and Social Democrats.

Ålandsk Center
(Åland Centre)

Chairman   : Anders Eriksson
Secretary   : Marianne Grønholm
Founded   : 1976

The Ålandsk Center is the largest party in Åland, although its support has fallen in recent elections. In the current government coalition with the Liberals and Moderates it has three out of the seven members, Göran Bengtz, Ragnar Erlandsson and Magnus Lundberg.

The Ålandsk Center is associated with the Middle Group in the Nordic Council.

Liberalerna På Åland
(Åland Liberals)

Chairman   : Gunnevi Nordman
Secretary   : Lisbeth Eriksson
Founded   : 1977

This is the second–largest party in Åland, although its vote fell sharply in 1987. Its former chairman, the 49–year old Sune Eriksson is the current Åland *Lantråd* (Prime Minister) at the head of a Liberal, Centre and Moderate coalition government. The other Liberal member of the government is Holger Eriksson. Like the Centre Party the Liberals are associated with the Middle Group in the Nordic Council.

Frisinnad Samverkan
(Moderates)

Chairman   : Sven-Olaf Lindfors
Secretary   : Roger Jansson

The Moderates are the third–largest party in Åland, well behind the Centre Party and the Liberals. Their 1987 vote represented a slight increase over that of 1983. They currently have two members in the coalition government with the Centre Party and Liberals, May Flodin and Rune Karlström. The Moderates are associated with the Conservative Group in the Nordic Council.

Ålands Socialdemokrater
(Åland Social Democrats)

Chairman   : Lasse Wiklöf
Founded   : 1968

The Åland Social Democrats are only the fourth largest party in Åland. They almost had the same number of votes as the Moderates in 1983, but their vote dropped in 1987 and they also lost one seat. They were previously in government (represented from 1983–87 by their chairman, Lasse Wiklöf) but they are now the largest party of opposition. They are associated with the Social Democratic Group in the Nordic Council.

De Gröna
(The Greens)

Founded   : 1987

The Greens were founded about six months

before the 1987 elections, in which they obtained 6.6 per cent of the vote and two seats in the *Landsting*. They are currently in the opposition.

Communists

This is an insignificant party in the Åland political context, obtaining 2 per cent in the 1979 elections and 2.3 per cent in 1983, without winning a seat on either occasion. It did not take part in the 1987 elections.

Fria Åland
(Free Åland)

This group advocates the complete independence of the Åland Islands. In the 1987 elections it obtained 280 votes (2.6 per cent) and no seats in the *Landsting*.

Iceland

Francis Jacobs

The country

Iceland is a large island (almost 40,000 square miles) but with only 250,000 inhabitants, well over half of which live in the capital Reykjavik and its immediate surroundings. The only sizeable town outside south-west Iceland is Akureyri on the northern coast. There are no national minorities and few foreign residents apart from the Americans at the Keflavik NATO base. In religion it is almost entirely Lutheran.

Political institutions

Iceland's parliament, the *Althing*, has 63 members. It has a maximum term of four years but it can be dissolved at any time. After it is elected it divides into two Houses with a third of the

Map of Iceland showing 8 constituencies and number of seats in each constituency.

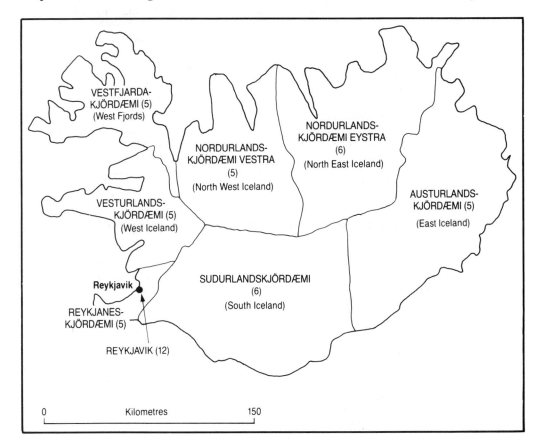

Source: adapted from *World Atlas of Elections*.

members sitting in the Upper Chamber and two-thirds in the Lower Chamber. Both are equal in powers, and bills must pass through both Chambers. Certain matters, such as the Budget, are considered by the two Chambers together (the United *Althing*). Members are allocated to either Chamber by their party leaders. The *Althing* also has a powerful Committee structure. The Prime Minister is responsible to the *Althing*, and is appointed after often lengthy negotiations after national elections. Governments are almost always coalitions of two or more parties and the leaders of the coalition parties normally sit directly in the cabinet. Votes of confidence are not automatically held on the formation of new governments. There is individual rather than collective ministerial responsibility. Ministers are generally *Althing* members.

Iceland's President has mainly ceremonial powers but plays a more important role during the period of cabinet formation. In theory the President can vote a bill and force a popular referendum on the issue, but in practice this has never happened. The President is directly elected for a four-year term. Presidential elections are between personalities rather than between parties. A convention has developed, once presidents are elected, that they are generally not opposed in subsequent elections. The current President is Vigdis Finnbogadottir.

The electoral system used for parliamentary elections is now more fully a proportional system than before and the over-representation of rural areas at the expense of the Reykjavik region has been significantly reduced. Fifty of the 63 *Althing* seats are allocated by the "largest remainder" system of proportional representation in eight multi-member constituencies (Reykjavik 14 seats, Reykjanes nine, West Iceland four, West Fjords four, North-West Iceland four, North-East Iceland six, East Iceland four and South Iceland five). To be entitled to such seats a list must obtain over 7 per cent of the vote in the particular constituency. The remaining 13 seats are "top-up seats", which are allocated between the parties to ensure greater overall proportionality between the votes obtained and seats won. There is a minimum 5 per cent national threshold to obtain these supplementary seats. They are allocated to the best runners-up on the appropriate party list. Subsequent runners-up act as substitutes for the elected members and take their place when they are absent for over two weeks. The order in which members are elected is important in *Althing* protocol (e.g. member is referred to as the Fourth Member for West Fjords, etc.).

Parties may even put up two lists within one constituency. Voters must opt for only one list, but may change the order of that list.

Brief political history

Iceland has one of the longest parliamentary traditions with its Parliament, the *Althing*, being founded as early as the 10th century, shortly after Iceland was first settled. In 1262, however, Icelandic independence was ended and it came under the rule first of Norway and, after 1380, of Denmark. During the period of Danish absolutism the *Althing* continued to wither and it was abolished in 1800. With the growth of a nationalist movement in the mid-19th century the *Althing* was revived in 1845, albeit with a very limited role.

In 1874 Iceland was granted a new Constitution by Denmark which gave a much stronger role to the *Althing*, but executive power rested firmly with Denmark. There now began a period when the issue of home rule from Denmark became the main political issue in Iceland, and contending political forces sprang up offering differing conceptions of how this should be achieved. In 1900 there was the first proper Icelandic election between political parties. In 1904 Home Rule was achieved, with an Icelandic Minister resident in Reykjavik and reporting to the *Althing*.

Differences between contending economic interest groups now began to play a larger role in Icelandic politics. A Farmers' party began to develop from 1912 onwards. In 1916 a Social Democratic Party was also established, with organic links with the emerging trade unions. In 1918 Iceland became independent, but in a personal union with the Danish Crown. Denmark was to represent Iceland in foreign policy matters and the agreement could be abrogated after 25 years. A new Constitution was drawn up in 1920. In 1915 direct elections by secret ballot were introduced and an electoral system established which was mainly a plurality system in single and two member constituencies but with a small proportional element in the form of nationally elected members chosen by the d'Hondt method. Women were also given the vote. In 1934 the system of nationally elected members was abolished but an element of proportional representation still remained with the introduction of 11 supplementary seats. In the interwar period, however, the Icelandic political electoral system was still primarily a constituency-based one.

The electoral system ensured that the Progressive Party, which was strong in the less populated constituencies, was the dominant government party for most of the period before World War II, although the Independence Party was the largest party in terms of votes won.

In the interwar period Iceland had been neutral, and had not joined the League of Nations. During the war, however, Iceland was first occupied by British troops and then after 1941 by the Americans, with the agreement of the then Icelandic government. In 1942 the electoral system was again changed, with the proportional element being further strengthened and in 1944 the personal union with Denmark was ended by Iceland and the country became completely independent of Denmark in all matters.

The political debate after the war was dominated by the issue of Iceland's role in the Western Alliance. Iceland joined the UN but refused the Americans' request for a 99-year lease of the base at Keflavik. In 1946 the government was brought down after it negotiated an agreement with the Americans allowing American civilians to operate the Keflavik base. In 1949 there was a bitter battle over Iceland's proposed membership of NATO, which was finally agreed to by a clear majority in the *Althing* but with all the Communists and even some Social Democrats and Progressive members voting against. Finally, in 1951 a Defence Agreement was negotiated with the United States whereby the Americans were to ensure the defence of Iceland (which has never had armed forces) and the Americans were allowed to station troops at the Keflavik base.

Although this latter agreement encountered lesser opposition in Parliament than the previous issue of NATO membership, it has subsequently been even more controversial. In the early 1950s there were over 5,000 Americans at the military base with 3,000–4,000 Icelanders working for them. Opposition to their presence stemmed, therefore, not just from the Communists but from other nationalists concerned by the overdependence of Iceland on the Americans and on the possible cultural impact.

In 1953 a new political party, the National Preservation Party, won 6 per cent of the vote mainly on the issue of opposition to the Defence Force. In 1956 the *Althing* even voted for the withdrawal of American troops but this was never implemented. In the 1960s there were lengthy disputes about the negative impacts of American services television in Icelandic culture (Iceland did not have its own television until 1966). Gradually however, the disputes became less intense. The number of American troops declined and even when the anti-NATO People's Alliance has had a share in power the issue of NATO membership and the Defence force have not been make-or-break issues.

Another important issue, but which has had much greater external rather than internal impact, has been that of the successive extensions of the Icelandic fishing limits in the 1950s and then the 1970s with the consequent "Cod Wars" with Britain. The extensions were generally supported by all Icelandic parties, and this is now an issue of the past.

The change in the electoral system in 1942 meant that the Independence Party became the largest party in terms of seats as well as votes. The Progressives have generally been the second party, the Communist-influenced People's Alliance the third and the Social Democrats only the fourth. Nevertheless, the longest lasting coalition was that between the Independence Party and the Social Democrats between 1959 and 1971. At other times all forms of coalition have been tried, with the People's Alliance participating in government on several occasions.

The voting system has again twice been changed since the war: in 1959 when the number of members was increased to 60 and the remaining single member constituencies were finally abolished, and before the 1987 elections, when the number of seats was increased to 63 and there was a redistribution of seats away from the rural areas to the more populated constituencies of Reykjavik and Reykjanes.

As in the other Scandinavian countries, Iceland politics have become much more volatile in recent years, with much greater swings in electoral support and with strong electoral performances by entirely new parties. In 1971 the Union of Liberals and Leftists won 8.9 per cent of the vote. In 1978 the two government parties, the Independence and Progressive parties lost 18 per cent of the vote and the Social Democratic party and People's Alliance gained greatly with the former going up from 9.1 per cent to 22.1 per cent of the vote. In 1983 two new parties, the Social Democratic Alliance and the Women's Alliance entered the *Althing*. The former has since disappeared but the latter improved its performance in 1987 when another new party, the Citizen's Party also won over 10 per cent of the national vote.

Main features of the current Icelandic political system

Iceland is a very small country in terms of population and the role of personalities in politics, especially of the party leaders, is very important. Iceland is also a highly political society, with not just very high voter turnouts

Elections in Iceland since 1945 (percentage of vote and seats won)

	1946	1949	1953	1956	1959	Oct. 1959	1963	1967	1971	1974	1978	1979	1983	1987
Independence Party (Sjalfstaedisflokkur)	39.4% (20)	39.5% (19)	37.1% (21)	42.4% (20)	42.5% (20)	39.7% (24)	41.4% (24)	37.5% (23)	36.2% (22)	42.7% (25)	32.7% (20)	35.4% (21)	38.7% (23)	27.2% (18)
Progressive Party (Framsoknarflokkur)	23.1% (13)	24.5% (17)	21.9% (16)	15.6% (17)	27.2% (19)	25.7% (17)	28.2% (19)	28.1% (18)	25.3% (17)	24.9% (17)	16.9% (12)	24.9% (17)	18.5% (14)	18.9% (13)
Social Democratic Party (Althyduflokkur)	17.8% (9)	16.5% (7)	15.6% (6)	18.3% (8)	12.5% (6)	15.2% (9)	14.2% (8)	15.7% (9)	10.5% (6)	9.1% (5)	22.0% (14)	17.5% (10)	11.7% (6)	15.2% (10)
Socialist Party (Socialistaflokkur)	19.5% (10)	19.5% (9)	16.1% (7)	—	—	—	—	—	—	—	—	—	—	—
People's Alliance (Althydubandalag)	—	—	—	19.2% (8)	15.3% (7)	16.0% (10)	16.0% (9)	17.6% (10)	17.1% (10)	18.3% (11)	22.9% (14)	19.7% (11)	17.3% (10)	13.3% (8)
Union of Liberals and Leftists (Samtok frjalslyndra og Vinstri manna)	—	—	—	—	—	—	—	—	8.9% (5)	4.6% (2)	3.3% (0)	—	—	—
Social Democratic Alliance (Bandalagjafnathamanna)	—	—	—	—	—	—	—	—	—	—	—	—	7.3% (4)	0.2% (0)
Women's Alliance (Samtok Um Kvennalista)	—	—	—	—	—	—	—	—	—	—	—	—	5.5% (3)	10.1% (6)
Citizens' Party (Borgaraflokkur)	—	—	—	—	—	—	—	—	—	—	—	—	—	10.9% (7)
Other	0.2% (0)	—	9.3% (2)	4.5% (0)	2.5% (0)	3.4% (0)	0.2% (0)	1.1% (0)	2.0% (0)	0.4% (0)	2.2% (0)	2.5% (1)	0.5% (0)	4.1% (1)

but also very high levels of party membership (almost one in 10 Icelanders is a member of the Independence Party for example). The geographical dispersion of the Icelandic population, however, has also led to Icelandic politics becoming very localized, with great local swings and variations in electoral support for different parties in different constituencies.

The above factors have all contributed to the increasing volatility and fragmentation of Icelandic politics in recent years. Besides the obvious examples of prominent personalities creating new parties (Vilmundur Gylfason leaving the Social Democratic party to create the Social Democratic Alliance in 1953, Albert Gudmundsson leaving the Independence party to create the Citizen's party in 1987) numerous other Icelandic politicians have changed parties. One postwar leader, Hannibal Valdimarsson was the leader of three different parties in succession, and his son, the present leader of the Social Democratic party, only joined the party a few years ago.

Local personality conflicts have also led to a number of breakaway lists in individual constituencies. Sometimes there have been two separate party lists within one constituency. Icelandic parties have also often been remarkably tolerant of such dissidence, as when the Independence party did not expel Gunnar Thoroddson after he and two of his colleagues formed a government with the opposition parties against his own party.

In most respects Iceland is a very homogeneous country, with no national minorities and few immigrants, a common culture and religion and with only limited disparities in classes and between rich and poor. Many of the traditional causes of political cleavage have thus been absent.

The most important cleavage in Icelandic politics is between centre and periphery and especially between the more populated southwest around Reykjavik and the rest of the country. This has accentuated differences between parties (with the Independence Party being the traditionally strongest party in the towns and the Progressive Party in the countryside) but also within each major party as well. Class differences have been too small in Iceland to be a major cause of party conflict. The Independence Party, for example, has won support across class lines.

On the other hand sectoral interests have played a much greater role. The co-operative movement and farmers in general have been the bulwark of Progressive Party support, for example. The trade union movement was originally tied closely to the Social Democratic Party but since 1945 trade union support has been dispersed among the other parties, notably the People's Alliance but also the Independence Party. The top employers and top managers have traditionally supported the Independence Party. Fishermen's votes, on the other hand, have been more evenly divided between the parties. A more recent division has been between the voting pattern of public and private sector workers, with the former, for instance, providing the main basis of support for the People's Alliance and the Women's Alliance. Part of the reason for this has been the difference between the parties on economic issues, over such questions as the role of the state in the economy, the degree to which controls are necessary, the desirability of deregulation and privatization, the future of the welfare state, what to do about agricultural subsidies and how best to fight inflation (Iceland has had 100 per cent inflation at times, the highest in the OECD although this has been mitigated by widespread indexation). Iceland has traditionally been a relatively egalitarian and not very ideological society, where respect for individualism has been balanced by a pragmatic acceptance of the need for state intervention by all parties. This is still largely the case, but divisions on the above issues have grown somewhat in recent years.

Another important set of issues in Icelandic politics have been those linked with Iceland's national and cultural identity. These have been accentuated by the fact that Iceland has a long and rich cultural history but only became independent again very recently. The sharp divisions between the parties on NATO membership and on the impacts of the American base at Keflavik have been closely related to those issues of Icelandic identity. In recent years, however, divisions on NATO and the Defence Agreement have declined somewhat. Nevertheless Icelandic nationalism has been an important source of strength for the People's Alliance and for the Progressive Party in particular.

Religious and moral questions have never played a very major role in Icelandic politics. There has never been a Christian Democratic Party and even the Temperance Movement (which has been strong and has had an impact on all parties) has not been especially associated with any of them. More recently environmental policy has become somewhat more prominent (the Women's Alliance put a considerable emphasis on it, for example) but both it and energy policy are less controversial than in most European countries; Iceland has very little industry and has no need for civil nuclear energy. Divisions on these issues have been very weak.

Sjalfstaedisflokkurinn
(Independence Party)

Headquarters	:	Valholl – Haaleitisbraut 1, Reykjavik (tel: Reykjavik 82900)
Chairman	:	Thorsteinn Palsson
Chairman of parliamentary group	:	Olafur G. Einarsson
Secretary-general	:	Kjartan Gunnarsson
Youth organization	:	SUS (chair: Arni Sigfusson)
Women's organization	:	Landsamband Sjalfstaediskvenna (chair: Thorunn Gestsdottir)
Membership	:	22,000 – 24,000
Founded	:	1929

History

The Independence Party of Iceland has been by far the strongest conservative-leaning party in Scandinavia, and has had a share in government for 37 out of the 58 years since the party was founded.

The party was formally established on May 25, 1929, from a merger of the large Conservative Party and the small Liberal Party, the former, however, only in existence since 1924 and the latter since 1927. Both of them stemmed from another short-lived party, the Citizen's Party, a loose electoral alliance of politicians largely drawn from the two dominant pre-home rule parties. The common strand of these new parties was opposition to the new Social Democrats and Progressive parties, which were based primarily on support from particular sectors of society.

The new Independence Party emphasized its character as a non-ideological party of all the classes, standing for full independence of Iceland from Denmark and for the independence of the individual; in home affairs, its broad philosophy consisted in advocating laissez-faire policies in industry and commerce, with as little state interference as possible in the economy. From its foundation onwards it was consistently the most successful party in terms of percentage of votes cast, but with the electoral system being so heavily weighted in favour of rural areas it generally won less seats than the Progressive Party in the years before World War II and was in opposition for much of that period. In its first election in 1931, for example, it won only 12 seats with 43.8 per cent of the vote, whereas the Progressive Party won 21 seats with only 36.9 per cent. In 1933 the Independence Party obtained its highest ever share of the vote at 48.1 per cent but only three more seats than its rivals, and in 1937 it won only 17 seats with 41.3 per cent compared to the Progressive Party which won 19 with 24.9 per cent.

Changes in the electoral system in 1942, and especially in 1959, helped to strengthen the Independence Party's position in the postwar years, and each of its five chairmen since that date have become Prime Minister, the highly popular Olafur Thors (PM on five occasions: 1942, 1944–56, 1953–56 and 1959–63), Bjarni Benediktsson (1963–70), Johann Harstein (1970–71), Geir Hallgrimsson (1974–79) and Thorsteinn Palsson (1987–88).

In addition, the party has taken part in other governments under Prime Ministers from other parties. Apart from one minority administration, it has always formed coalitions with one or even two other parties as at present. Its most long-lived coalition was with the Social Democratic Party between 1959 and 1971.

Since the war it has always been the largest party, both in terms of votes and seats. Until 1978 it always obtained between 36 per cent to 43 per cent of the national vote but in that year it was heavily sanctioned by the voters after leading an unpopular coalition and only received 32.7 per cent of the vote.

The Independence Party has suffered the loss of two splinter groups to its right. In 1941 a number of its members formed the Commonwealth Party and in 1953 formed the Republican Party. Neither party endured.

In recent years, however, the Independence Party has suffered more severe splits. In 1980 its deputy leader, Gunnar Thoroddson, broke ranks with two other Independence Party colleagues after an inconclusive general election and helped to form a government with the Progressive Party and the People's Alliance, with Thoroddson himself as Prime Minister, and with his own party leader and the vast majority of his former party colleagues in the opposition. Most amazingly of all, however, Thoroddson was not expelled from the Independence Party. The most recent split came in 1987 when the leader of its list in Reykjavik, Albert Gudmundsson, created a new Citizen's Party, which won 10.9 per cent of the national vote and reduced the Independence Party to the lowest vote in its history at only 27.2 per cent. In September 1988 the Independence Party went into opposition.

Support

Even after its severe 1987 electoral setback the Independence Party remains the strongest party in Iceland, and has widespread support among all classes and in all regions of the country. Its strongest support is in the highest income groups and among the university-educated, among employers, managers in the private sector and liberal professionals. (Even in 1987 it is estimated to have won over 50 per cent of the votes of employers and senior managers and administrators and over 40 per cent of the votes of university-educated people.) On the other hand, the Independence Party is unique among Scandinavian conservative parties in the extent of its support among manual workers and trade unionists. It has particularly strong support among workers in trade and commerce at all levels. While only 24 per cent of unskilled manual workers voted for the party in 1987 the Independence Party is still the strongest Icelandic party among that group. Several prominent trade union leaders, including the deputy chairman of the Icelandic Trade Union Confederation, are members of the party.

The Independence Party has strong support in many fishing communities, and is the best supported party among seamen in general, especially among the captains. While much weaker than the Progressive Party in the farming regions of Iceland, it is still the second party in these areas and has particular strength among the less traditional farmers, such as dairy farmers and those engaged in aquaculture.

The party is weaker among the less educated and the lower paid, especially in the public sector and among lower paid civil servants such as health and education workers. The party is also much less well supported by women than by men. In 1987 it is estimated that only 25 per cent of women voted for the party, compared to 34 per cent of the men.

In regional terms the party is strongest in the Reykjavik constituency where it has obtained over 50 per cent of the vote on occasions, most recently in 1974. The party has always controlled the town council of Reykjavik since its foundation, apart from a single four-year period (1978–1982).

The party has also been very strong in the rather more populated areas close to Reykjavik, such as in the Reykjanes constituency (where it, nevertheless, lost 15 per cent of its 1983 vote in 1987) and in the south constituency where it got its highest vote in the country in 1987 at 32.5 per cent.

Further away from Reykjavik the party has a lower level of support, apart from the predominantly fishing constituency of West Fjords, where it is still the largest party. It was only the second party in 1987 in the western and two northern constituencies. Its weakest area of all

has traditionally been the eastern constituency where it has only been the third party since around 1970, and where it only won 16.1 per cent of the vote in 1987.

Organization

The Independence Party has around 22,000 –24,000 members of whom approximately 11,000 are in its stronghold of Reykjavik. A member can join one (or more) of four types of organization, a general association (of which there are 81 around the country), a youth organization (29), a women's association (18), or a labour association (five). All four of these co-exist in the more popular areas. The common organization for these different associations in each township is a council of representatives of which there are 40 throughout Iceland. In each constituency there is a constituency board, elected by the various councils of representatives. In Reykjavik itself there is a different organizational structure, based on neighbourhood councils.

At national level there is a central committee which meets once a month and is the chief decision-making body of the party (consisting of the party chairman and vice-chairman and 11 at large members chosen by the congress, as well as the constituency-chairman, the chairman of its Youth, Women and Labour organizations, five MPs and the chairmen of certain important party committees. In addition an executive committee meets once a week to oversee everyday party work. A party council of around 240 members meets once or twice a year. (It is always consulted, for example on decisions on whether to enter a particular coalition government). Finally, a national congress meets on a biannual basis, and is attended by 1,000–1,100 people.

Parliamentary candidates are chosen at constituency level. Different methods have been chosen by different constituencies, even including open primaries on some occasions when "supporters" and not even formal members of the party have been allowed to take part (this has now been abandoned). Local roots are now more important than in the past, and the influence of the party's national headquarters has diminished. Chosen candidates must be approved centrally, but this is a mere formality. About 30 per cent of the party's funds currently come from a national lottery which is held twice annually, 50 per cent from contributions from individuals, businesses and the rest from miscellaneous sources (such as the renting out of office space at the party headquarters).

The Independence Party does not own any daily newspaper, but has strong links with the biggest daily paper *Morgenbladid* (which supports it editorially). There is also a long-standing magazine produced by the party's youth wing call *Stefnir* and which appears four times a year. The party also produces newspapers at local level and a national newsletter, distributed to around 5,000 party members. Internationally, the Independence Party has affinities with the International Democratic Union (IDU). It is a member of the Conservative Group in the Nordic Council.

Policies

The Independence Party has always been on the right-wing of the Icelandic political spectrum (although within the not very right-wing or ideological Icelandic context). It has generally been the strongest supporter of limited state intervention in the economy, as well as of Icelandic membership in NATO and of the Defence Agreement. Nevertheless, its character as a catch-all party with a broad base of support among all classes and interest groups, as well as its identification as the predominant government party has meant that, in practice, it has been a highly pragmatic rather than ideological party. After the war it downplayed its original laissez-faire policy and became more supportive of the welfare state and of government intervention in the economy. In farming policy, for example, its support among farmers has meant that it has been more cautious about applying market principles to the sector than the Social Democrats have advocated.

Recently, however, it has been perceived by many Icelanders as being more ideologically right-wing, at least in its presentation of policies, if not necessarily in their actual substance. Moreover, whereas in the past it had highly popular leaders on a national basis like Olafur Thors and Bjarni Benediktsson, its current leadership consists primarily of urban professionals with a narrower appeal in the country as a whole. All this has given space for its opponents to attack it, and clearly contributed to the success of the breakaway Citizen's Party in the 1987 elections.

The party's strongest policy plank is to reduce the role of the state wherever possible, to end exchange and other controls and to reduce the state's own business activities (it was the prime mover behind ending the state monopoly on broadcasting). It seeks lower tax levels and a shift from direct to indirect taxation wherever possible. It supports co-operation with foreign industry and the relaxation of rules governing foreign investment in Iceland. It continues to push hard to increase private home ownership,

which is already at a very high level. It accepts, however, a strong degree of government management of fisheries (in spite of pressures from its fishermen supporters in the West Fjords to relax rigid quotas) and is cautious about reducing subsidies to the farming sector.

In foreign policy, in addition to its continuing firm support for NATO and the Defence Agreement, it also rejects the idea of a Nordic nuclear weapon-free zone.

Personalties

The Independence Party's current leader is Thorsteinn Palsson, the Prime Minister from 1987 to 1988 who became party leader in 1983, when only in his thirties and who has a technocratic, rather than populist image. He used to be the editor of an afternoon paper, *Visir*, before becoming the managing director of the Employers' Association. The deputy leader is Fridrik Sophusson, and its two other ministers in the 1987–88 government were Birgir Isleifur Gunnarsson and Matthias A. Mathiesen. Sophusson and Gunnarsson were unsuccessful candidates in the 1983 leadership contest. The most well-known of the other leaders in the party is David Oddsson, who has been a highly forceful Mayor of Reykjavik, to which post he was elected at the age of 34 in 1982.

Framsoknarflokkur
(Progressive Party)

Headquarters	: Noatun 21, 105 Reykjavik
Chairman	: Steingrimur Hermansson
Chariman of parliamentary party	: Pall Petursson
Secretary-general	: Sigurdur Geirdal
Membership	: In range of 10,000–12,000

History

The Progressive Party was founded in December 1916, primarily to defend the interest of farmers and of the co-operative movement. A specific Farmers' Party had first been founded in 1913 but in 1916 there was a split within its ranks and two separate parties (a Farmers' Party and an Independent Farmers' Party) stood, and won seats, in the general election of that year. The founders of the Progressive Party ended the split.

In its first election in 1919 the Progressive Party won 13.3 per cent of the vote and six seats in the *Althing*. It quickly became the dominant party in the rural areas of the country, and the bias of the electoral system toward such areas led to it growing in strength in Parliament disproportionate to its actual electoral support. In 1927 it became the largest party in terms of seats (17) but with only 29.8 per cent of the vote (in contrast the Independence Party gained only 13 seats with 42.5 per cent of the vote). In 1931 it gained 50 per cent of the total seats with 35.9 per cent of the vote (its best ever score), but it still got less votes than the Independence Party. In 1937 and 1942 it again won more seats than any other party, but with far less votes than its major rival.

The Progressive Party provided the three Icelandic Prime Ministers from 1927 to 1942, Trygvi Thorhalisson from 1927 to 1932, Asgeir Asgeirsson from 1932 to 1934, and Hermann Jonasson (the father of the present party leader) from 1934 to 1942. Another key party figure in the interwar years was Jonas Jonsson.

In trying to widen its base into the towns the party alienated some of its more traditional supporters, who broke away and formed a new specifically farming party in 1933. The Farmers' Party survived until 1942, but never won more than around 6 per cent of the vote.

After the war the changes in the electoral system helped to ensure that the Progressives never again won as many seats as the Independence Party, although the disparity between the two parties in seats continued to be much less than that in votes (in 1959, for example, the Progressives won 19 seats with 27.2 per cent of the vote compared to 20 seats for the Independence Party with 42.4 per cent).

The Progressives continued to be the second-largest party in most elections. They have been in government for most of the time, with the notable exception of 1959 to 1971. They have also provided five Prime Ministers, Steingrimur Steinthorsson from 1950 to 1953, Hermann Jonasson again from 1956 to 1958, Olafur Johannesson from 1971 to 1974 and 1978 to 1979 and Steingrimur Hermansson from 1983 to 1987, and again from 1988.

In electoral terms the party did particularly well in its period in opposition in the 1960s when the party moved somewhat to the left, and managed to gain more support in urban areas. In the early 1970s, however, a number of the left-wing nationalists left the party. In 1978 the Progressive Party won only 16.8 per cent of the vote and 12 seats, its lowest number since the early 1920s. The party recovered in 1979, but fell away again in 1983 and 1987 when it gained between 18 per cent and 19 per cent of the vote.

In 1987 the party fared better than some had predicted, very largely as a result of the personal popularity of the outgoing Prime Minister, Steingrimur Hermansson. The party was damaged, however, by more local schisms, with a new National Party taking away some of its traditional electorate in certain constituencies (notably West Fjords) and with one of its long-standing MPs, Stefan Valgeirsson, getting elected in his own right in North-East Iceland (under the label Union for Regional Equality) after the party had discarded him as a candidate.

After the 1987 elections the Progressives joined a three-party coalition, and their leader became Foreign Minister. In September 1988 Hermansson again became Prime Minister at the head of a new coalition of the Progressive Party, Social Democrats and the People's Alliance. The government has to rely for a majority on the single member of the Union for Regional Equality.

Support

The Progressive Party has traditionally been the party of farmers and of the co-operative movement, and its attempts to enlarge its support base have met with only mixed success. Even in 1987 it still had by far the largest regional variations of support of any Icelandic party, ranging from 9.6 per cent in Reykjavik to 38.5 per cent in East Iceland.

Almost half of all Iceland's farmers voted for the Progressives in 1987, even though the party was considerably harmed among farmers by the new National Party and the Union for Regional Equality. The Progressives were also strong in the fishing communities, with over 20 per cent of seafarers voting for the party.

The progressives continue to win good levels of support among skilled and unskilled manual workers, and are markedly stronger in the private sector (19 per cent in 1987) than in the public sector (14 per cent). They are also stronger among those with less education. Only 7 per cent of those with a university education voted for the party.

By far the weakest constituency for the party is Reykjavik. In the past (notably in the 1960s) it has managed to get up to 16 per cent of the vote, but, in 1987 it only won 9.6 per cent. It has also been weak in the neighbouring constituency of Reykjanes but it achieved a spectacular improvement in its vote in 1987 (from 11.9 per cent to 19.8 per cent between 1983 and 1987) as a result of the outgoing Prime Minister standing as a candidate in the constituency instead of his former constituency of West Fjords, where the party's vote slumped in consequence. The

Progressives are generally strong, however, in West Iceland and to a slightly lesser extent, in the West Fjords and South Iceland.

The party is strongest of all in North-West and North-East Iceland and in East Iceland. In this latter constituency it used to gain well over 50 per cent of the vote, and still gained 38.5 per cent in 1987.

Organization

The Progressive Party is the second largest party after the Independence Party, in terms of membership and of organizational strength. The precise number of members is not known, but is estimated at around 10,000 – 12,000. There are approximately 120 branches, although a number of these are inactive. At national level the party has a central committee of 70–80 members and an executive committee of 10–12 members. Every other year there is a general assembly with several hundred participants. The party continues to have strong links with the Icelandic co-operative movement, although these are not of a formal nature.

The Progressives have an active youth wing which developed contacts with overseas liberals at an earlier stage than the parent party. The party's women's organization was only established about five years ago. There is not centrally established membership fee. Collection of membership dues is up to local branches. Membership fees tend to be low or non-existent. One of the important sources of party finance is a lottery in which not just formal members, but party sympathizers in the wider sense participate.

The party's newspaper is called *Timinn*. The party has, at a comparatively recent date, developed formal links with the Liberal International, and its chairman, Steingrimur Hermansson, has been vice-president of the Liberal International. In the Nordic Council the Progressives sit with the Centre parties Group.

Policies

The Progressive Party is in the centre of the Icelandic political spectrum, and on a number of issues it is on the "left" not just of the Independence Party but of the Social Democrats as well. Its key political position has given it a central role in coalition building and it is no coincidence that on four of the last five occasions when the People's Alliance have been in government, it has been under a Progressive Party Prime Minister.

A second important feature of the party has been the continuing tension between being the party primarily of farmers and of rural Iceland and its aspirations to become a truly national party, with the need for a stronger base in Reykjavik and in urban areas. At times it has had considerable success in this latter aim, but occasionally at a cost in rural support, or even to the point of splits within the party.

On economic policy the Progressives support the mixed economy but they are less enthusiastic about privatization and deregulation than either the Independence Party and the Social Democrats. They are generally suspicious of neo-liberalism.

It is no coincidence that they again have the Agriculture and Fisheries portfolios in the present government. They defend agricultural interests, and are polar opposite of the Social Democratic party on these issues. Their emphasis is thus less on cutting subsidies than on agricultural diversification into such new areas as fur farming, agricultural tourism and aquaculture. They have also been the most forceful supporters of a rigid quota system in the fisheries sector, and have prevailed on this matter.

A policy with which the Progressives have been particularly associated is regional policy and the development of a proper infrastructure in the peripheral areas of Iceland.

They pride themselves on being a party of distinctive Icelandic roots without the internationally influenced origins of the Social Democrats or the Communists. They are strongly nationalist on foreign policy and cultural questions.

The Progressives have supported Iceland's membership of NATO (although one Progressive MP voted against NATO entry in 1949, and two abstained) but have had more reservations about the continuing presence of the Americans at Keflavik. At times (generally when in opposition) it has been Progressive Party policy to phase out the American base and Progressive Party supporters have been more opposed to the base than those of the Independence or Social Democratic parties. The party's concern has particularly been over the cultural impacts on Iceland, and the Progressive Party was strongly opposed to the reception of American television in the big controversy over this issue in the early 1960s (the party's current position on media issues is that the state should continue to run one station to ensure quality and impartiality).

Personalities

The party's dominant personality is its chairman, Steingrimur Hermansson, son of a previous Prime Minister. He was a popular and forceful Prime Minister in the 1983–87 government, and was Iceland's Foreign Minister in 1987–88. His

1987 campaign was the first one in Icelandic political history to make use of television advertising. In September 1988 he again became Prime Minister.

His deputy is the current Fisheries and Justice Minister, Halldor Asgrimsson. The party's other Minister in the present Cabinet is Gudmundur Bjarnason (Health and Insurance). The party's parliamentary leader is Pall Petursson. None of these leading figures come from Reykjavik.

Althyduflokkur
(Social Democratic Party)

Headquarters	: Althyduhusinu, Hverfisgotu 8–10, 101 Reykjavik
Chairman	: Jon Baldvin Hannibalsson
Chairman of parliamentary party	: Eidur Gudnason
Secretary-general	: Gudmundur Einarsson
Membership	: est. 3,000–4,000

History

The Social Democratic Party and the Icelandic Labour Federation were founded at the same time in March 1916, as the political and labour arms of the same organization. The two were to remain organically linked until 1940, and members of trade unions were supposed to join the Social Democratic Party.

The Icelandic Social Democratic Party is one of the youngest European Socialist parties. Icelandic politics had been previously dominated by the independence question, there was practically no industrialization, and only a small urban working class. Nevertheless, the new party grew steadily from 6.8 per cent in the 1916 and 1919 elections up to 19.1 per cent by the 1927 election, although it was penalized in terms of seats by the single member constituency system. In 1934 it obtained 21.7 per cent of the vote, its second best performance in its history, and it won 10 seats. Its party newspaper had achieved high circulation and it looked set for further growth.

The party had already experienced, however, the first of the schisms which have consistently weakened it. In 1922 some members left the party in Reykjavik over the issue of whether to join the Socialist or Communist Internationals. In 1930 left-wing dissidents formed a Communist party. The Communists began to pursue a popular front strategy and in 1938 the third and most damaging split in the Social Democratic Party occurred when its left wing joined forces with the Communists to form a new Socialist Party. At the same time tactical alliances between the Independence Party and the Communists managed to loosen the Social Democratic Party's grip on the trade union movement. In 1940 the formal link between the unions and the Social Democrats was broken and in 1942 the new Socialist Party won more votes than the Social Democrats. From 1942 until 1987 Iceland was to be one of the few western European countries where a mainstream Social Democratic party was to remain weaker than its left Socialist/Communist counterpart.

In 1947 Stefan Johann Stefansson became the first Social Democrat Prime Minister of Iceland (the party had first participated in a government in a coalition with the Progressive Party from 1934 to 1938). In the vote over NATO membership in 1949 the majority of the party supported Icelandic entry, although two of its MPs voted against. In 1961, however, the party was unanimous in supporting the Defence Agreement with the Americans.

In the 1950s the party lost its left wing yet again, when Valdirmarsson (who had become party chairman in a coup at the party congress in 1952) and other members joined forces with the Socialist Party to form a new electoral union, the People's Alliance.

From 1949 to 1956 the Social Democrats were in opposition, but in 1956 they joined a three-party coalition with the Progressives and the People's Alliance, and in 1958–59 there was a brief period of Social Democratic minority government under Emil Jonsson. From 1959 to 1971 the party was the junior partner in a coalition with the Independence Party, the longest sustained coalition in modern Icelandic history. During this period the party began to abandon its old emphasis on nationalization and strict control of the economy and became more market-orientated. Indeed, it was a Social Democratic Minister, Gylfi Gislason, who was most responsible for opening up Iceland in freer international trade and leading it into EFTA.

For most of the postwar years the Social Democrats had been only the fourth Icelandic party in strength, generally fluctuating around 14 per cent to 18 per cent of the vote. After the long coalition, however, the party went through a very weak period in the 1970s, when it remained in opposition and its vote dropped to as low as 9.1 per cent (in 1974).

The Social Democrats now went through a period of internal constitutional reform (introduction of open primaries etc.), aimed at modernizing and reviving the party. The chief architect of the new strategy was Vilmundur Gylfason (son of Gylfi Gislason). In 1978 the party was rewarded by its best ever performance in the polls, rising from 9.1 per cent to 22 per cent of the vote. The subsequent coalition government, in which it played a prominent role, was not successful and further elections had to be called in 1979 in which the party slipped back. After a brief period of minority Social Democratic government under Grondal from 1979 and 1980 the party again went into opposition. In 1980 Kjartan Johansson became party chairman. In 1982 Vilmundur Gylfason left the party and formed a new Social Democratic Alliance, whose main programme was one of constitutional reform, including direct elections of the Prime Minister. The Social Democrats were severely hurt by the Alliance in the 1983 elections, winning only 11.7 per cent of the vote to the Alliance's 7.3 per cent. Shortly after the election, however, Gylfason died, the Alliance withered away, and many of its activists, including three of its four MPs, rejoined the Social Democrats.

In 1983 the then party leader, Kjartan Johannson, was defeated at the party congress by Jon Baldvin Hannibalsson. Under his leadership the party revived yet again. It was very successful in the 1986 local elections and had a good, if slightly disappointing, result in the 1987 General Election when it achieved 15.2 per cent of the vote, and overtook the People's Alliance for the first time since the war. The party has been a member of both government coalitions since the elections. It has three ministers in the present government.

Support

Of the traditional Icelandic parties the Social Democratic Party is probably the one with the least firm ties with any particular interest group. It has probably also had the most volatile electoral support (9.1 per cent in 1974, 22.0 per cent in 1978, 11.7 per cent in 1983, 15.2 per cent in 1987). It is the second-strongest party among the working class after the Independence Party, and it is particularly strong among skilled manual workers (estimated at 22 per cent in 1987) and those with technical backgrounds. It is markedly stronger in the private than in the public sector (17 per cent and 13 per cent respectively in 1987). It is also fairly strong among seamen (15 per cent), especially among those in the Western Fjords, where the Social Democrats have been consistently stronger than the People's Alliance.

The Social Democrats are particularly weak among teachers, nurses and public sector employees at a lower level. They are weakest of all among farmers, where their support is also non-existent.

The Social Democrats have enjoyed widely fluctuating levels of support in the city of Reykjavik, and it was here that they recovered best in 1987, rising from 10 per cent in 1983 (the impact of the Social Democratic Alliance at 9.5 per cent was especially strong in Reykjavik) to 16 per cent in 1987.

Their strongest constituency in most elections has been that of Reykjanes, where they have achieved up to 29.4 per cent of the vote (in 1978). Keflavik is one of the towns in Reykjanes where they have been well supported. In 1987 they gained 18.2 per cent of the vote in this constituency. In 1983 and 1987, however, their highest vote has been in the constituency of West Fjords, where they have had strong support from fishermen. In 1987 they obtained 19.1 per cent of the vote.

They have achieved reasonable levels of support in West Iceland (15.2 per cent in 1987) and in North-East Iceland (14.3 per cent) but in North-West Iceland (10.2 per cent) and in South Iceland (10.6 per cent) they have been much weaker. Their vote actually fell in the latter constituency in 1987. Their weakest constituency has always been East Iceland where they have been completely squeezed out by the Progressives and the People's Alliance. They have usually had under 4 per cent in this constituency, although they went up to 6.9 per cent in 1987.

Organization

The Social Democrats probably have the weakest organizational structure of the major Icelandic parties. They are organized throughout the country, but in many areas have few activities and are poorly financed.

Their total membership is uncertain, but is estimated at around 3,000–4,000. They have around 50 branches, and also constituency committees. The party's central committee contains members of the parliamentary party, representatives of the constituency committees and members elected at the party convention.

The party leader cannot always control votes at the party convention. On two occasions, in 1952 and in 1982, party leaders have been replaced by new leaders as a result of votes at the convention.

As part of the campaign for more democracy within the party, the party reformers in the mid-1970s managed to get open primaries written into the party rule book. In practice, parliamentary candidates are not usually chosen by open primaries, although they were used in 1987, for example, to choose candidates in Reykjavik and in Reykjanes.

As far as the making of policy is concerned the parliamentary group and the party chairman are left with very considerable discretion, although wide consultations are made during the preparation of the manifesto at election time.

The party has women and youth groups, but they are only active in a few areas of the country. There are no longer any formal links with the trade unions, but a liaison committee has been established.

Membership fees vary in different parts of the country. The fee in Reykjavik is 500 Kroner. Another source of finance are lotteries.

The party's newspaper is called *Althydublandid*. The party is a member of the Socialist International and of the Social Democratic Group in the Nordic Council.

Policies

The Social Democratic Party is perceived to be in the middle of the Icelandic political spectrum.

It has a distinctive position among Social Democratic parties for a number of reasons. On no less than four occasions it has lost its left wing, which has clearly affected the chances of the party. It has also been less closely tied to the trade unions than most Social Democratic parties. This has reinforced (and reflected) its weak electoral position, but has also perhaps given it greater independence in policy making.

On defence and foreign policy issues it has always been closest to the Independence Party. Although two of its MPs voted against NATO membership in 1949 there was unanimous support among its parliamentarians for the Defence Agreement in 1951. There has been very little neutralist sentiment in the party, which has been staunchly pro-NATO and Defence Agreement (with the limited exception of the party's youth wing).

On its general foreign policy stand the party has indeed probably suffered from being internationalist in its outlook in a newly decolonized country where nationalist sentiments have run deep. The party has certainly lost support to the more nationalist Progressives and People's Alliance on these issues.

On economic policy issues the party has steadily become more market-oriented. In the 1959–71 government it played a considerable role in opening up the Icelandic economy and reducing protectionism. The party has also been generally supportive of recent attempts to deregulate the economy, to privatize, to break with state monopoly on broadcasting, and so on. Its current philosophy is that there should be as free a market as possible in order to pay for the improvements in the welfare state and the better housing, schooling and hospitals that it seeks.

The Social Democrats are certainly the firmest advocates of a freer market in agriculture. They wish to see the current over-production reduced through less subsidies and protection for the sector, and are probably the only Icelandic party to contemplate Iceland being less than fully self-sufficient in agriculture.

The party also advocates trade union reform by greatly reducing the number of unions and having a more coherent industrial union structure.

Personalities

The party's present leader is Jon Baldvin Hannibalsson, the son of a former party leader but who only joined the party himself in 1978 from the Union of Liberal and Leftists. He became a MP in 1982, and party chairman in 1983. After his election he went on a barnstorming tour around the country, and managed to raise the party's morale and level of organization. He is the Minister of Foreign Affairs in the present coalition government, and a former Finance Minister.

The two other Social Democratic Ministers in the government are Jon Sigurdsson, the Minister of Commerce and Industry who has only just entered parliament and who has been one of Iceland's best known economic advisers, and Johanna Sigurdardottir, the Minister of Social Affairs. The current parliamentary leader is Eidur Gudnasson. Another prominent figure in the party is the former leader, Kjartan Johannson.

Althydubandalag
(People's Alliance)

Headquarters	: Grettisgotu 2, 101 Reykjavik
Party Chairman	: Olafur Ragnar Grimsson
Leader of parliamentary party	: Margret Frimannsdottir
General Secretary	: Ottar Proppe
Membership	: 3,000

History

The People's Alliance, one of the strongest parties in the Communist, Left-Socialist tradition in Western Europe, was founded in its present form in 1968, but its historical antecedents stem from much further back.

Both the trade union and Social Democratic movements were late to develop in Iceland, and originally were little influenced by left socialist ideology. In the 1920s, however, left-wing dissidents tried to change the Social Democratic Party from within. They were eventually expelled, and in 1930 formed the new Communist Party.

In its first electoral outing in 1931 it won only 3 per cent of the vote and no seats. It gradually became stronger, however, and in a tactical alliance with the Independence Party, slowly succeeded in loosening the Social Democratic Party's links with the trade unions. In 1937 it won 8.5 per cent of the vote and its first seats in the *Althing*.

Even before the seventh Congress of the Communist International supported popular front strategies the Icelandic Communist Party decided to seek close co-operation with the Social Democrats. This strategy led to a further split among the Social Democrats, with their left wing again leaving to join up with the Communists. The new merged party became known as the "People's Unification Party - Socialist Party". Founded in 1938, it gained over 16 per cent of the vote in its first elections in 1942. It polled more votes than the Social Democratic Party, and from 1942 to 1987 it remained the larger party of the two. It also had a stronger base among the trade unions.

The new Socialist Party was not formally part of the International Communist movement but its leadership consisted mainly of former Communists. Its structure was generally one of democratic centralism, and in foreign policy matters it was generally pro-Soviet.

In 1941 three of its members were the only members of the *Althing* to vote against the agreement for the USA to send American troops to defend Iceland. From 1944 to 1946 the Socialist Party entered government for the first time, in a three-party coalition government, but in 1946 resigned from the government in protest against the Keflavik agreement with the Americans. It strongly opposed Iceland's entry into NATO, and the later Defence Agreement.

In the 1950s it made further soundings to the Social Democratic Party, leading to yet another schism within the latter party, which lost its then chairman, Hannibal Valdirmarsson (father of the present chairman) to the Socialist Party. In 1956, a new electoral union, the People's Alliance, was forged between the Socialist Party, left-wing Social Democrats and the anti-Defence Agreement National Preservation Party. The Socialist Party continued to exist within the new framework, but the differences between the Socialist Party and the People's Alliance became increasingly blurred. In the late 1960s it

was decided to wind up the Socialist Party and in 1968 it became formally known as the People's Alliance (although some of the members of the earlier Alliance, including Valdimarsson, had left to form the new Union of Liberals and Leftists). The party had already become more independent of Moscow. It was sympathetic to Tito's Yugoslavia and criticized the Soviet invasion of Hungary and after the invasion of Czechoslovakia it cut off party political contacts with the invading countries.

Besides its participation in the 1944-46 government, the Socialist Party had also taken part in government between 1956 and 1958. Its successor party, however, the People's Alliance, has been more frequently in government, taking part in coalitions in 1971–74, 1978–79 and 1980–83 and again since 1988. In the 1970s the People's Alliance gained, both in members and in electoral support, and in 1978 it obtained its best ever results with 22.9 per cent of the vote and 14 seats in the *Althing*. Its leader, Ludvik Josefsson, a former Fisheries Minister, was one of Iceland's more prominent and popular politicians.

In the 1980s, however, the People's Alliance has been less successful. The 1980–83 government was an unpopular one, associated in particular with a period of hyper-inflation even by Icelandic standards. In 1983, and even more in 1987, the party lost electoral support. There was also considerable internal conflict within the party. In the 1987 election it obtained only 13.3 per cent of the vote, the far left's worst performance since before World War II. Later in the year Olafur Ragnar Grimsson became the new party chairman. In September 1988 the party re-entered government with three ministers.

Support

The People's Alliance strongest support is currently among public sector employees, such as civil servants, teachers and nurses. According to electoral surveys in 1987, it was almost twice as strong (19 per cent among public sector workers as among those in the private sector (10 per cent).

Traditionally it has also had strong support among intellectuals and artists. Moreover, even after its bad 1987 results, it was still the second strongest party among the university-educated.

In the past it has also had strong support from the trade unions and from working-class voters in the towns, but this has declined considerably. It is still significant (it is estimated that the party got 16 per cent of the vote of unskilled manual workers in 1987) but this is no longer the party's main electoral base.

The People's Alliance is strong among seamen (especially in the fishing towns of Eastern Iceland), among whom it won 21 per cent of support. It is much weaker among farmers (7 per cent), employers and managers (9 per cent) and skilled workers.

In 1987 the party lost significant support to the Women's Alliance, in particular, (it has been estimated that nearly a quarter of the latter's 1987 electorate had voted for the People's Alliance in 1983) but also to some extent to the Progressive Party.

Ever since the war the Socialist Party and later the People's Alliance has been the second-largest party in Reykjavik. In 1987 the party fared particularly badly in Reykjavik, losing over 5 per cent of its vote and slipping to fifth position with only 13.8 per cent of the vote.

Elsewhere in 1987 its support was relatively even at between 10.9 per cent and 13.1 per cent (in the five constituencies of West Iceland, West Fjords — its traditionally weakest area — South Iceland, Reykjanes and North-West Iceland), apart from North-East Iceland (15.7 per cent) and East Iceland, its greatest stronghold, where it got 23 per cent of the vote and was itself the second largest party. In 1971 the People's Alliance overtook the Independence Party to become the second party in East Iceland behind the traditionally dominant Progressive Party and in 1978 it narrowly became the first party in the constituency with 36.5 per cent of the vote. Its strength in the East has been due to a variety of factors, including popular leaders such as Ludvik Josefsson, and its base among fishermen in towns such as Neskaupstadur, its strongest electoral bastion in Iceland, where it has never been out of power at local level since 1946.

Organization

The People's Alliance has around 3,000 members. It has around 60 local branches grouped into constituency parties. The party's central decision-making body is an executive committee of 14 members, 11 elected at the party congress and three by the parliamentary party. The party congress is held every two years and has around 300 to 350 participants (each branch has one representative for every nine members).

A distinctive feature of the party's rules is that there has always been a fixed limit to the terms of office of its leaders. Formerly this was limited to three terms of three years each, but has now been reduced to three terms of only two years each. A more recent party rule (from 1985) provides for positive discrimination for women: women

must now make up no less than 40 per cent of the membership of the party's representative committees at local and national level.

On the other hand, the party has no separate women's organization. Nor did the party have a youth organization, but one has now been established.

The party relies for its financing on membership dues to a greater extent than most other Icelandic parties. At 3,000 Kroner a year its membership dues are the highest of any Icelandic party. These are collected by local branches and a certain percentage (based on the number of members) is then handed over to the centre.

The party's newspaper is called *Thjodviljinn*. The People's Alliance is a member of the Left Socialist group in the Nordic Council but has no other formal international affiliations.

Policies

The People's Alliance is the most left-wing party in the Icelandic political spectrum. It is no longer a traditional Communist party, but nor has it made a formal split with Communism as have the somewhat akin Left Socialist parties in Denmark and in Norway.

Its strength has come from a number of factors, including the opportunities given to it by the weak implantation of its Social Democratic rivals in the Labour movement. Moreover, apart from the support of traditional pro-Moscow Communists, the party has also benefited from the support of intellectuals and others who have been attracted by its strong defence of Icelandic national and cultural identity over such issues as the Defence Agreement with the Americans, and the introduction of television.

The party has gradually evolved in an anti-Moscow direction (See "History" section) and the party hard-liners (such as Einar Olgeirsson) have increasingly been in a minority position. The party's democratic credentials have been fully accepted by the other Icelandic parties, and it has taken part in coalitions with all the major parties. Its performance in office has been pragmatic. While it has never ceased in its opposition to NATO membership and to the Defence Agreement, it has never made these central demands when in government. When it left government in 1983, it appeared to enter a period of uncertainty, especially over the central issue of whether it sought to be a whole-hearted party of government, or of opposition. Its image as a party of government was partially tarnished by its association with the 1980–83 government, and the opposition mantle appeared to be more successfully taken up by the Women's Alliance.

There has thus been considerable internal conflict within the party between the party traditionalists, the so-called "party owners" and those advocating new themes, the self-styled "democratic generation".

In economic policy the party has traditionally advocated public ownership of the larger companies but it has now changed its emphasis. Public or private ownership is no longer seen to be as important an issue as the actual results of that ownership. Nationalization should no longer be a blanket solution, and even privatization is acceptable in certain areas with appropriate safeguards. A greater emphasis is put instead on the right of workers to take part in decision-making and to have a share in ownership. Less reliance should be put on controls, such as price controls and rent controls. The party remains a strong defender, however, of the fabric of Iceland's welfare state and of a strong state role in education and health. The party is beginning to put a stronger emphasis on environmental protection.

On foreign policy and defence matters the People's Alliance would like to see a neutral Iceland, rather than one aligned with the Western bloc. It is insisting less, however, on the issues of NATO and the Defence Agreement, and more on wider questions of disarmament and support for a Nordic nuclear free zone. It recognizes, moreover, that Iceland must be left with some kind of defence.

Its leadership is also considering advocating more widespread use of referenda on contentious political issues.

Personalities

The party's leader is Olafur Ragnar Grimsson, a professor of political science and a former member of the Progressive Party and of the Union of Liberals and Leftists who has few associations with the party's old guard and whose leadership represents a considerable break from the past. He lost his seat in 1983 (after having been first elected in 1979) and did not win it back in 1987. He was, however, elected leader in late 1987 and is the current Minister of Finance.

Svavar Gestsson is the current Minister of Culture and Education, and was the party leader from 1980 to 1987. He is a former Minister of Commerce and Minister for Health and Social Security. The party's third minister is Steingrimur J. Sigfusson, a geologist who has been the party's parliamentary leader. The current parliamentary leader is Margret Frimannsdottir.

Among the other prominent figures in the party are Ragnar Arnalds, a former Chairman of the People's Alliance and of the parliamentary party, as well as Minister of Finance, and of Education and Transportation, and also Asmundur Stefansson, the president of the Icelandic Trade Union Federation, a pragmatist who has ensured generally good relations between the Labour movement and recent governments.

Kvennalisti
(Women's Alliance)

Headquarters	: Hotel Vik, Reykjavik (contact: Gudrun Jonsdottir)
Parliamentary group	: Althing, Reykjavik (tel: Reykjavik 11560, contact: Sigrun Jonsdottir)
Founded	: March 1983

History

The present Women's Alliance was founded in March 1983. This was not the first time, however, that there had been separate women's lists in Iceland. In 1908 four women were elected to the Reykjavik City Council on such a list, and in 1929 a separate list of women candidates were submitted for the parliamentary elections of that year: one woman, Ingibjorg H. Bjarnason, was elected and became Iceland's first female MP. This was an isolated precedent, and only 12 women were elected to Parliament between 1922 and 1979, many less than elsewhere in Scandinavia.

Around 1970 a feminist movement began to develop in Iceland, and on Oct. 24, 1975, helped to mobilize a one day strike of Icelandic women, which won worldwide attention.

In the summer of 1981 the idea of separate lists of women candidates was again mooted, without its proponents being initially aware of the 1908 and 1922 precedents. In 1982 separate lists were put forward for local elections in Reykjavik and in Akureyri in North Iceland, and two councillors were elected in each city.

The Women's Alliance was formally founded in 1983, and put up candidates in three constituencies (Reykjavik, Reykjanes and North-East Iceland) in the general election of that year. They obtained 5.5 per cent of the vote and three seats in the Parliament. In the general election of April 1987 they put up candidates in all eight constituencies, won 10.1 per cent of the national vote, and doubled their number of seats in Parliament to six. They thus became the first new Icelandic party to do better in their second election than in their first. They have remained in opposition, and have since risen considerably higher in the polls.

Support

In April 1987 the Women's Alliance won 10.1 per cent of the vote, but in Reykjavik they did even better with 14 per cent of the vote. They also polled strongly in West Iceland (10.4 per cent) and Reykjanes (9.1 per cent) and obtained between 5.3 per cent and 6.6 per cent in Iceland's other five more rural constituencies.

They were the second party among Icelandic women (with 22 per cent of the vote they were only 3 per cent behind the leading Independent Party) but only the sixth party among men (with 5 per cent of the vote). Moreover, they won much stronger support among public sector employees (20 per cent of the vote) such as teachers and nurses than among private sector employees (8 per cent).

They were also strong among professionals and the better educated. They were weak among farmers, seamen, skilled and manual workers, employers and managers.

They appear to have taken some support from all of Iceland's traditional parties, but most of all from former supporters of the People's Alliance; almost a quarter of those who voted for the Women's Alliance in 1987 appear to have voted for the People's Alliance in 1983.

Organization

The Women's Alliance prefers to think of itself as a movement rather than a party. There are written rules but they are rapidly adapted as a result of experience, and the party's structure is informal and decentralized.

Total membership is hard to calculate but there have been between 1,000 and 1,200 names on its newsletter mailing lists, and there are probably around 200–300 members in Reykjavik. Membership fees vary around the country, and range from nothing in some regions to 1,500 Kroner per year in Reykjavik. Men are entitled to become members of the party, but cannot become candidates on any party list.

The party is organized into local groups which then form regional committees. At national level there is a decision-making committee, which meets on a weekly basis, and consists of representatives from each constituency. Members of the parliamentary group take turns in attending these meetings on a monthly rotation basis. A central principle of the party is that all meetings are open to all members. Attempts are made to reach consensus at these meetings (which are

hence often very lengthy), and formal voting is avoided where at all possible.

A further central principle is rotation of office-holding. Party positions on committees etc. can generally not be held for more than one year at a time, although they can again be held at a later date. Membership of the Parliament (also of the Reykjavik town council) cannot be held for more than six years (the rule was decided as four to eight years, but six years is felt to represent the best compromise between limiting terms of office and providing a minimum of continuity). Two of the party's three 1983 parliamentarians were thus re-elected in 1987, but will be asked to stand down in 1989.

Finally, the Women's Alliance has no formal leader in or outside Parliament, and has a system of rotating spokespersons for parliamentary and other purposes.

Co-ordination is also provided by the two full-time staff members, one working for the parliamentary group and the other for the Women's Alliance as a whole out of its Hotel Vik headquarters.

Policies

The Women's Alliance has two main sets of objectives, first to improve women's position in general and to get better representation of women in decision-making structures (Iceland has lagged behind the other Scandinavian countries in this respect) and secondly to apply women's values to the problems of society. In this context every issue is a women's issue, but each one has a separate women's perspective.

The Women's Alliance seeks to get the work traditionally done by women better recognized by society in both financial and other terms, and also considers that the needs of the family need to be taken much more into account in employment policy. It would like to see the incentive wage system abolished and a raising of lower salaries, a shorter working week, with no loss of pay, and more flexible working hours. There should be a better network of day care centres, and a continuous, not interrupted school day. There should be an increase in maternity leave to six months.

The Women's Alliance is opposed to the development of heavy industry and adopts a cautious approach towards foreign investment in Iceland. Instead it wants more support for the food industry and for small and light industry. In agriculture policy it seeks to keep rural areas populated, and to maintain self-sufficiency.

It puts a stronger emphasis than most other Icelandic parties on environmental issues. A Ministry of the Environment should be established, and there should be more environmental education. The number of tourists should be curtailed in vulnerable areas.

Further education should be strengthened, and an open university system established. There should be an open access third broadcasting channel. Health education should be reinforced and there should be greater emphasis on preventive medicine. The current emphasis on home ownership should be lessened, so that people have a better choice of whether to buy or rent.

The Women's Alliance also seeks greater decentralization in Iceland, with local municipalities gaining in financial independence. The party would like Iceland and the other Noridc countries to be declared nuclear free areas, and would like all military alliances to be broken up. Its 1987 policy statement is not explicitly opposed to Iceland's membership of NATO or the US military presence in Iceland, but it would make both more difficult by seeking to terminate all military projects in Iceland, and by making Iceland financially independent of the military forces located in the country.

The Women's Alliance has gained considerable support as a result of its vigorous opposition stance. Nevertheless, it took part in coalition negotiations after the 1987 elections, although the terms that it suggested were regarded as too expensive by the other parties.

Personalities

The Women's Alliance does not like attention being drawn to individual leaders. Its most prominent representative in the public eye, however, is Gudrun Agnarsdottir who was first elected in 1983 and re-elected in 1987. Its current spokesperson is Danfridur Skarphedinsdottir.

Borgaraflokkur
(Citizens' Party)

Headquarters	: P.O. Box 1303, Reykjavik
Chairman	: Julius Solnes
Chairman of parliamentary group	: Oli Gudbjartsson
Membership	: Estimated at 4,000 (1987)
Founded	: March 25, 1987

History

The Citizens' Party is the newest Icelandic political party. It was founded by Albert Gudmundsson, a leading member of the Independence Party and of the 1983–87 coalition government, who was asked to resign as Minister by his party leader after allegations of tax evasion. He was not, however, asked to resign from the place that he had won as head of the Independence Party ticket for the Reykjavik constituency for the 1987 elections. One March 24, 1987, however, he resigned from the Independence Party in protest at the treatment that he had received, and on March 25 launched his new party. By March 27, the deadline for submitting candidates for the election, he was able to submit lists of candidates in all Iceland's constituencies. Over the following weekend the new party was enjoying 16.6 per cent support in the polls, and on election day on April 25 it won 10.9 per cent of the national vote and seven seats, the best ever performance by a completely new party in Iceland's history. Julius Solnes became the new chairman of the party in December 1988, when Gudmundsson was named as Ambassador to France.

Support

Over 20 per cent of the Citizens' Party support in 1987 came from previous Independence party voters. It did particularly well among skilled manual workers, but also polled well among unskilled manual workers. It got good support in the private sector, especially among small businessmen; it was weakest among those with higher levels of education and among professionals and public sector employees. It was also not very strong among seamen and farmers.

Its highest level of support was in Gudmundsson's own constituency of Reykjavik, where it won 15 per cent of the vote. It won its national average of 10.5 per cent to 11 per cent of the vote in the constituencies closest to Reykjavik, (Reykjanes, West and South Iceland), and it was weaker elsewhere, especially in the North-East (3 per cent), East (3.3 per cent) and West Fjords (only 2.6 per cent).

Organization

The Citizens' Party is estimated to have around 4,000 members, of whom 2,000 are in Reykjavik. It has set up general associations in all constituencies and a youth organization in Reykjavik. It has a membership fee of 500 Kroner, but disadvantaged people can have their fees waived. Anyone who has paid their dues is free to participate in the party's decision-making policies, and to help choose candidates.

Policies

The immediate cause of the Citizens' Party's creation was the personal treatment of

Gudmundsson, rather than a clash over policy. The party's subsequent success in the election, however, indicates that it struck a chord with Independence Party voters in particular.

The Citizens' Party claims that its parent party has moved too far from its roots and is no longer the party of all the people, but is too close to the special interests and big business, rather than to small businessmen and the "little people". It is too ideological in defence of the free market, and not firm enough in defence of the welfare state. Its leaders are urban professionals, who no longer have the popular touch.

The Citizens' Party, in contrast, while on the right of the Icelandic political spectrum, claims to be more to the centre than the Independence Party and to have a softer, more humanitarian tone. While supporting the social market economy it puts more emphasis on the social side, and on defending the disadvantaged in society. It sets out to be pragmatic rather than ideological.

On foreign policy it is strongly in favour of NATO and the Defence Agreement, although revision of the latter may be necessary in the future (e.g. payment for use of the Keflavik base by the Americans).

During the election campaign the party received a certain amount of support from anti-abortion campaigners, although this has not been a major policy plank of the party. The party has recently been divided on the issue of whether to support the Hermansson government, as have some of its members.

Personalities

The party's founder, Albert Gudmundsson, (born in 1923) was Iceland's most celebrated footballer (Nancy, Glasgow Rangers, Arsenal, AC Milan, Nice) before entering politics. He was Minister of Finance (1983–85) and Minister of Industry (1985–87) in the previous government, and was a long-serving member of Reykjavik Council. He was a candidate in the 1980 presidential elections (winning 20 per cent of the vote, and building a national network of followers which stood him in good stead in 1987), and was the Independence Party's leading votegetter in the Reykjavik constituency on several occasions. He stood down as leader in December 1988. The new leader of the party is Julius Solnes, the former leader of the parliamentary group. One of the party's successful candidates was Gudmundsson's son, Ingi Bjorn Albertsson, who had had no previous political experience, like many Citizens' Party candidates. Oli Gudbjartsson is the new leader of the parliamentary group.

Thjodarflokkur
(National Party)

This is a new party which was formed around the issue of more power to regions outside the Reykjavik area, claiming that the wealth being generated by agricultural and fishing villages was being spent in Reykjavik instead. It put up candidates in five of Iceland's eight constituencies in 1987 and won 1.3 per cent of the national vote. In the East and North-West constituencies it won 5.1 per cent and 4.5 per cent of the vote respectively, and in the West Fjords it won 11.1 per cent of the vote. It won votes especially from the Progressive Party, notably in the West Fjords where the Progressives were hurt by the departure of their biggest vote winner and party leader, Steingrimur Hermansson, to another constituency.

The National Party is a grass roots movement, most of whose candidates were inexperienced in politics. Its leader is Petur Valdimarsson.

Flokkur Mannsins
(Humanist Party)

This new party put up candidates in all 8 constituencies in the 1987 elections, and won 1.6 per cent of the national vote, with a highest vote of 2.3 per cent in Reykjavik.

Liechtenstein

Francis Jacobs

The country

Liechtenstein is a small German-speaking country located in the Upper Rhine Valley between Switzerland and Austria. It has a population of 25,000 of whom over 35 per cent are foreigners. Its capital is Vaduz. The southern part of the country is known as the Oberland and contains six of Liechtenstein's 11 communes, as well as the majority of its population. The northern area is called Unterland and contains five communes, but only around 7,500 inhabitants.

Political institutions

Liechtenstein is a constitutional monarchy with government powers shared between the prince and the legislature (or *Landtag*). Foreign representation is looked after by Switzerland with which Liechtenstein also has a customs and currency union. Switzerland also looks after Liechtenstein's posts and telecommunications.

The *Landtag* is a unilateral legislature with only 15 members, nine from the Oberland constituency and six from the Unterland constituency, which is somewhat over-represented in the *Landtag* in terms of its population. In 1988 Liechtenstein's electorate voted by 51.7 per cent to increase the number of deputies to 25. Elections are held every four years and there is a cut-off clause of 8 per cent below which level of support parties cannot be represented in the *Landtag*. Women received the the right to vote at *Landtag* level in 1984 (although women were given the right to vote at communal level in 1976, this was only optional and there were still communes where women could not vote).

The Liechtenstein government is formally chosen by the prince on the basis of nominations from the *Landtag*. It consists of a head of government and three government councillors. Under Liechtenstein's complex division of power between its two main political parties the party with the largest number of seats receives the post of head of government and two other posts on the government council and the second party receives the post of deputy head of government and the remaining post on the government council. The members of the government are not members of the *Landtag*.

An important feature of Liechtenstein politics is the power given to the Liechtenstein people to propose, modify or reject laws through initiatives and referenda. The electors of three communes can request that a law be promulgated, nullified or abrogated. If constitutional questions are involved, the request must come from 900 electors or four communes, who also have the right to request the convening or the dissolution of the *Landtag*. If a law is proposed by popular initiative and is rejected by the *Landtag* it must be submitted to a nationwide vote. The popular vote overrides the vote in the legislature.

Finally, considerable powers are left in the hands of the 11 communes which vary greatly in population, from Vaduz with over 4,650, to Planken with under 300. Each commune has an elected council, presided over by a chairman.

Brief political history

Liechtenstein is named after its princely family, not the other way round. The Liechtenstein family was a distinguished Austrian noble family who bought Schellenberg in the north of the country in 1699 and Vaduz in 1712. In 1719 the new territories of the Liechtenstein family were raised by the Emperor to the status of a principality and from 1815 to 1866 Liechtenstein was one of the numerous states in the German confederation, although it had strong links with Austria which were greatly reinforced in 1852 when it entered into a customs union with Austria-Hungary which lasted until 1919. In 1862 a new Constitution was approved which transformed Liechtenstein from an absolute to a constitutional monarchy with an indirectly elected *Landtag*.

Direct elections to the *Landtag* were introduced in 1918 and modern political parties were founded. A new Constitution was drawn up in 1921 which laid down that the head of the government must be a Liechtensteiner. Until this date not only were the princes themselves absentees (the first prince to visit Liechtenstein only did so in 1842) but the head of government was appointed from Vienna. The judicial authorities were established within Liechtenstein — previously Liechtensteiners had had to have legal recourse to Innsbruck and Vienna. The Constitution also introduced far-reaching provisions for popular initiatives and referenda.

The customs union with Austria was abrogated in 1919, and a new one with Switzerland entered into in 1923.

The 1930s were a time of considerable tension between the two main parties, the *Fortschrittliche Bürgerpartie* (FBP) and the *Volkspartei* (later the *Vaterländische Union* or VU). There was a long battle as to whether proportional representation should be introduced (in 1932 the FBP won 13 seats with 1,200 votes and the *Volkspartei* only two seats with 1,000 votes). A new corporatist movement also sprang up, the Liechtensteiner *Heimatsdienst*, with political and economic ideas similar to those of Dollfuss in Austria. This eventually merged with the *Volkspartei* to form the *Vaterländische Union* in 1936.

The bitter partisan struggle between the government party (FBP) and the opposition (VU) was completely modified as a result of Germany's takeover of Austria in 1938. The two parties were thrown together to defend Liechtenstein's independent status and a system of coalition government was formed between them which has lasted until the present day. In 1939 proportional representation was introduced for the first time. Franz Josef II also came to the throne at this time (1938) and was the first prince to live in Liechtenstein.

The postwar period has seen political stability with the continuation of the two-party coalition and with far less tensions than in the interwar period. One new party, the *Christliche Sozial Partei* was founded but never won any seats, even after the threshold for entry into the *Landtag* was reduced from the extraordinarily high figure of 18 per cent to 8 per cent in 1973.

The main political change took place in 1970 when the *Vaterländische Union* became the leading party in the coalition after 42 years of FBP supremacy. Since then the two parties have alternated, but the VU has had the majority since 1978.

In 1984 Crown Prince Hans Adam took over executive authority from his father, Franz Josef II.

The two main constitutional struggles have been over raising the number of members of the *Landtag*, and over giving women the vote. The parliamentarians have constantly argued that 15 members are too few for the *Landtag*, but in 1919, 1945, 1972 and 1985 they were overruled in the popular votes on this issue. Only in 1988 was the number increased to 25. During the 1980s popular votes also thwarted the *Landtag's* intention to give women the vote. For example the *Landtag's* 1972 initiative on this issue was rejected by 2,126 votes to 1,679. Only in 1984 were women finally given the vote at national level though the law was only ratified by the Liechtenstein electorate by the narrower vote of 2,370 in favour to 2,251 against.

Main features of the Liechtenstein political system

Liechtenstein has been a two-party state and seats in the *Landtag* have never been won by any other party. Moreover, the balance between the two has been extraordinarily close. Even during the years of FBP dominance of the government the difference in the popular vote between the two parties was often no more than around a hundred votes. Since 1945 every election except that in 1958 has seen one or the other party win by an eight-to-seven majority only.

Since the war, Liechtenstein politics have also been characterized by consensus with the two parties working together in a continuing coalition. This has been accentuated by the lack of any parliamentary opposition to the coalition or indeed the lack of any left-wing parties at all.

The main opposition both to the government and to the parliament has come from the Liechtenstein people themselves, in that they have repeatedly rejected proposed laws. The people's powers of initiative and referendum are not merely theoretical, they have also been extensively used, as in the four popular rejections of the parties' attempts to raise the number of members of the *Landtag*. To an extent remarkable even by Swiss standards, direct democracy has been invoked to decide upon a host of controversial issues.

The other side of the coin to this direct democracy has been Liechtenstein's conservatism on the issue of giving women the vote, where it was the last European country to do so at national level. Conservatism on this issue was also shown by the rejection by the Liechtenstein electorate as recently as December 1985 of an equal treatment article to be introduced in the Liechtenstein Constitution.

Vaterländische Union — VU
(Fatherland Union)

Headquarters   : Austrasse 52,
9490 Vaduz
(tel: 075/228 26)

Party chairman   : Dr Otto Hasler
(since 1974)

General secretary : Ernst Hasler
(since 1986)

Party newspaper   : *Liechtensteiner Vaterland*

Youth organization : *Jugend Union*

Women's organization : *Frauenunion*

History

The forerunner of the Vaterländische Union was the *Christlich-Soziale Volkspartei*, founded by Dr Wilhelm Beck at the beginning of World War I and which fought for more democratic rights for Liechtensteiners and for closer links with Switzerland rather than with Austria.

After the introduction of direct democracy in 1918 it gained rapid success with its slogan "Liechtenstein for the Liechtensteiners" (referring to the dominance of Liechtenstein public life by appointed Austrian officials).

It made a particular impact among the working class and was described as a "Red" party by its conservative opponents. Its strength was in the south of the country, the Oberland, and it made relatively little impact in the Unterland. It won 11 out of 15 seats in the 1922 *Landtag* elections, and it headed the Government until 1928, with Prof. Gustav Schaedler as leader. The *Volkspartei* lost power in the 1928 elections. It was to remain completely out of government until 1938 and did not become the majority party in the government again until 1970, 42 years later.

The 1930s were a difficult period for the party. The electoral law was changed by the FBP to make it even more difficult for the *Volkspartei* to regain power, and a new political movement — the Liechtensteiner *Heimatsdienst* — was founded in 1933 which was of corporatist tendencies and opposed to the entire party system.

Eventually the *Volkspartei* and the *Heimatsdienst* decided to merge. On Jan.9, 1936, a new party, the *Vaterländische Union*, was founded in the Hotel Adler in Vaduz.

Most of the programme came from the *Volkspartei* but a small gesture was made towards the corporatist ideas of the *Heimatsdienst*. Relations between the two main parties reached their lowest ebb in 1937 when the FBP government of Dr Josef Hoop confiscated party documents from the former *Heimatsdienst* offices on the grounds that spying was suspected. The takeover of Austria by Hitler, however, alerted both parties to the external danger and in 1938 they went into a grand coalition under FBP leadership. The long battle over the introduction of proportional representation, which had been pushed hard by the VU and opposed by the FBP finally ended with its introduction in 1939. The grand coalition lasted throughout the war and has continued up to the present day. In 1970 the VU won the extra seat that had eluded it since the war, and became the majority party again with Dr Alfred Hilbe as the head of government. Losing its majority in 1974, it regained it in 1978, and has remained the majority party in the two subsequent elections. Since 1978 Hans Brunhart has been head of government.

Support

The *Vaterländische Union* and its predecessor, the *Volkspartei*, traditionally had their main electoral strength in the more populous southern constituency, the Oberland, and were very weak in the northern constituency, the Unterland.

In the 1920 *Landtag* elections for example, the *Volkspartei* won all nine seats in the Oberland and not one of the six seats in the Unterland. In the dark years of the 1930s what few seats it did retain were in the Oberland. By 1945 the VU was again winning more votes than the FBP in the Oberland (972 to 901) but losing the election through its heavy defeat in the Unterland (313 to 652).

Since the war this pattern has gradually changed with the VU becoming stronger in the Unterland and relatively less strong in the Oberland. So, by 1962 the VU ran even with the FBP in the Unterland in holding three seats each but held one less seat than the FBP in the Oberland, a pattern that was repeated in 1974. Electoral differences between the Oberland and the Unterland had thus been greatly reduced.

At communal level the VU is still somewhat weaker than the FBP, holding only four of the 11 commune chairmanships. Both the largest and the smallest communes (Vaduz and Planken respectively), have never been in VU hands since the party was founded in 1936.

As regards the social basis of support for the party there seems to be relatively little difference between the two parties.

Organization

The party is organized into groups based on the 11 communes, which choose delegates to the delegates assembly in proportion to the number of votes won by the party in the commune in the most recent *Landtag* elections. The key is one delegate for every 130 votes in the Oberland constituency and one delegate for every 75 votes in the much less populous Unterland, so that the Unterland is considerably over-represented in the delegate assembly.

The delegates' assembly elects the top party officials and is also responsible for changes in the party statutes and other matters. The party is run by a national executive and by the more select presidium which currently numbers 12 and is responsible for the party's day-to-day reaction to political events.

The party has a youth organization (*Jugend-Union*) and a women's organization (*Frauen-union*), which was founded in 1982. The candidate selection process is the responsibility of the communal assembly for communal posts, of the national executive for certain posts such as magistrates and of the party president for the top posts such as the party's government nominees.

For candidates for the *Landtag* responsibility is shared between the local groups who nominate a candidate from their commune and the party presidium which nominates two candidates from the Oberland and one from the Unterland. The national delegate assembly has to approve the nominations for the *Landtag*, for the government and for some of the other top posts.

Party finances are assured by a combination of membership dues, membership donations and financial assistance from the State (the 1984 law on this subject provides for 180,000 Swiss francs to be divided between the political parties).

Policies

The party's constitution pledges support for "monarchical-democracy", for a Christian world outlook and for the "social market economy".

The party's programme for the 1986 elections further develops these themes. Its Christian Democratic character is shown by its strong emphasis on family policy and both its economic and social policy are characterized by the need to encourage individual responsibility, keep the size of the state administration within strict limits and reduce the number of state forms and minimize state interference in the private sector (the programme also points out the advantage for Liechtenstein in terms of money and jobs of having so many holding companies on its soil and pledges the party's support for "serious" holding companies).

The party puts considerable emphasis on the need to achieve greater equality of treatment between men and women, including equal pay for equal work.

A further important point in the party programme is the need to keep the percentage of foreigners in Liechtenstein within reasonable limits. Perhaps the strongest emphasis in the entire party programme, however, is the need to strengthen environmental protection and to teach this subject in schools. Combating acid rain is a high priority.

Personalities

The leading personalities within the party are Hans Brunhart who is now entering his third term as leader of the Liechtenstein Government, Dr Karl-Heinz Ritter who has been President of the *Landtag* since 1978, and Dr Otto Hasler who has chaired the party since 1974. Two new party vice-chairmen, Oswald Kranz and Franz Schaedler and a new party secretary, Ernst Hasler, were chosen in 1986. The government that was formed in 1986 also included new government councillors from the Vaterländische Union, Rene Ritter and Dr Peter Wolff.

Fortschrittliche Bürgerpartie — FBP
(Progressive Citizens Party)

Headquarters	: Feldkircherstrasse 5, 9494 Schaan
President	: Dr Herbert Batliner
Secretary	: Edgar Nipp
Women's group	: *FBP Kommission für Fraunfragen*
Youth group	: *Jungen FBP*
Newspaper	: *Liechtensteiner Volksblatt*

History

The *Fortschrittliche Bürgerpartei (FBP)* was founded in 1918 and represented the more conservative (the "Blacks") of the two main political groups in Liechtenstein. The party was in opposition until 1928, when it came to power for the first time. It has never been out of government since, governing Liechtenstein alone until 1938, and remaining the majority party in the government coalition until 1970. In the 1930s it dominated elections under the then majority electoral system, winning most of the seats with only a small majority in terms of votes. In 1938 the threatening political situation compelled it to create a grand coalition with its great rival, the *Vaterländische Union*, although the head of government remained a member of the FBP. In 1939 it conceded the principle of proportional representation.

In 1970 the FBP finally lost the leadership of the government to the *Vaterländische Union*, and became the minority party in the government coalition. It had a new period of heading the government from 1974 to 1978, but has again been the minority party in government from 1978 to 1986.

Support

Originally the FBP was the dominant party in Liechtenstein's Unterland constituency, and was weaker although still competitive in the Oberland. Differences in constituency strength between the two main parties have now been greatly reduced, and the Unterland is no longer dominated by the FBP.

In the 1986 *Landtag* elections the party won 42.7 per cent and seven seats in the *Landtag*.

Organization

The FBP has local branches in each of Liechtenstein's 11 communes. The party has an annual congress, consisting of delegates from the local branches depending on the number of votes received by the party at the last elections within the relevant commune. Among the annual congress's tasks is to elect the party president, vice-presidents and the other members of the party presidium.

The FBP has a large National Committee, which meets at least three times a year, a smaller but still substantial party Executive, which meets once a month, and a party presidium consisting of the president, two vice-presidents and two other members (an FBP government representative and the FBP parliamentary group spokesman also participate at its meetings), which meets on a weekly basis. All party officers have a two-year mandate.

The party's youth group is called the *Jungen FBP* and is organized in each of the local communes. There is also a women's group, the *Kommission für Frauenfragen*. The party's newspaper is the *Liechtensteiner Volksblatt*.

Policies

Although originally more conservative than the *Vaterländische Union*, the FBP is now a broad-based party close to its great rival on most major political issues. It supports a free market economy without unnecessary state intervention, but also calls for adequate social security measures, including risk insurance for all workers in enterprises and enhanced care for the elderly. It puts a strong emphasis on family policy.

The FBP campaigned strongly in recent years to give women the vote, and supports further measures to promote equality between men and women. It also points out that women were given the vote in all communes with FBP majorities, unlike some of those with *Vaterländische Union* majorities. The party puts an increasing emphasis on environmental policy and one of its recent proposals has been the suggested introduction of regular car-free Sundays.

The FBP campaigned vigorously in favour of an increase in the number of members of the *Landtag*. (In 1985 it proposed 25 members, compared to 21 suggested by the *Vaterländische Union*). It has also called for a reduction in the 8 per cent electoral threshold.

Personalities

The party's president is Dr Herbert Batliner, a former head of the Liechtenstein government and former president of the *Landtag*.

The deputy head of the Liechtenstein government is Dr Herbert Wille. Emma Eigenmann was the first woman to be elected to the Liechtenstein *Landtag*.

Malta

James Spence

The country

The islands of Malta, Gozo and Comino and their islets making up of the Republic of Malta rise from the Mediterranean 58 miles (93 km) south of the Italian island of Sicily, and 180 miles (290 km) north of the Libyan coast. Its total area of 122 square miles (316 square km) is populated by over 360,000 people (1982), almost all Maltese citizens (343,000 at the December 1986 census), making it one of the most densely populated countries in the world. The population is young — two-thirds 40 years or younger (1983 figures). Its capital, Valletta, is sited at the north-east of the island beside two formidable natural harbours, the Grand and the Marsemxett. Maltese, an old semitic language, has been influenced over the ages by Norman, Sicilian, Italian and English, and is the official language of the country, though English and Italian are widely spoken. The Constitution acknowledges Roman Catholicism as the country's religion and almost all the inhabitants are Roman Catholic.

Political institutions

Malta is a republic with a unicameral Parliament, the House of Representatives, currently of 65 members elected for five-year terms from (currently) 13 multi-member electoral divisions. Early dissolution of the Parliament can be called by the President acting on the advice of the Prime Minister. Members of the House are elected by proportional representation by means of the single transferable vote from an odd number of electoral divisions, not more than 15 and not less than nine, whose boundaries are reviewed from time to time by an Electoral Commission, which is ostensibly independent ("not subject to the direction or control of any other person or authority").

Like elsewhere, electoral boundaries are subject to political dispute. Following the 1981 elections, where the Labour Party won more seats with less votes than the Nationalists, such charges led to the Nationalist Party members boycotting the House. The 1987 elections were held under new constitutional arrangements, whereby the party winning the most votes (over 50 per cent) would automatically also win the most seats; indeed this clause had to come into effect to top up the number of seats won by the Nationalist Party which had gained the majority of votes cast at the June 1987 elections, but had won fewer seats than the Malta Labour Party.

Candidates may stand in more than one electoral division and if elected in each — a not infrequent occurrence, with nine cases in 1987 — counting must recommence in the seat not chosen by the successful candidate.

The powers of Parliament are to make laws and amend the Constitution (with a two-thirds majority of all members of the House). The executive authority is vested in the President, appointed every five years by resolution of the House. He appoints a Prime Minister, a member of the House "who, in his judgement, is the best able to command the support of a majority of the members of that House". Other members of the Cabinet, which has general direction and control of the government and is collectively responsible to Parliament, are appointed by the President, on the Prime Minister's advice. The Prime Minister may be removed from office on a majority vote of no confidence in the House, or if he is defeated at an election or disbarred. The President also appoints the Leader of the Opposition from the next largest party after the governing one(s). He is kept informed of the general conduct of the government. Constitutional proposals to strengthen the presidency are being discussed.

Certain key principles, such as the right to work and free primary education, are fundamental to "the governance of the country" but not subject to judicial arbitration. Fundamental rights and freedoms of the individual including the right to life, protection from arbitrary arrest, freedom of conscience and worship, and protection from discrimination on various grounds are to be enforced through the courts. Political differences on the meaning of these rights led to a series of judicial and other confrontations during the period 1975 to 1987.

The 1987 constitutional reform, besides ensuring the majority of seats to the party with the majority of votes, enshrined Malta's neutral and non-aligned status, and reaffirmed the principle embodied in the 1982 Foreign Interference Act, attempting to reduce foreign intervention in Malta's political life.

Brief political history

Pre-independence (until 1964)

1530   Arrival of the Knights Hospitallers of the Order of St John of Jerusalem, a Roman Catholic Order whose members came from different parts of Europe and had been ousted from Rhodes by the Turks.

1565   Ottoman Siege successfully withstood by the Knights under the Grand Master Jean de la Vallette, after whom the capital is named.

1798–
1802   Napoleon I of France occupies the island. The occupation was resisted by a popular uprising, but left its influence in the subsequent codification of Maltese law (1854–1873).

1802   Treaty of Amiens: British claim to the island upheld against the separate claims of the Knights and the Kingdom of the Two Sicilies, and subject initially to the June 15 Declaration of Rights.

Italian cultural links were also strong. The *risorgimento* was followed closely in Malta, and *italiantià* was a positive quality among many Maltese. While administrative institutions, the *Università* and the *consiglio popolare*, already existed in the 15th century and returned briefly as the French forces were being pushed out, they were not formalized by the incoming British in 1802. A Commission of Inquiry sent out in 1812 concluded that any *consiglio* would be composed of illiterates and fanatics who could turn the population against the British.

1814   Treaty of Paris makes Malta a colony of the British crown.

1835   Constitution set up an advisory council of seven nominated members, but liberties were gradually granted in the next years: the press was "freed" in 1839.

1849   Constitutional revision introduces representative elections, enlarging the Council to 18 members, of whom eight were elected. 88 per cent of

the limited electorate of 3,767 voted, out of a population of 123,000. The Council was nevertheless a disputed (and disputatious) organ, too much in the sway of the British Imperial government for the liking of many islanders.

1878   Committee of Inquiry recommended language reform stimulating political party activity of "anti-reformists" led by Fortunato Mizzi (credited as the founder of the National Party, later to become the Nationalist Party), and others.

1880   This group disputed the Imperial government's attempts to introduce English as the vehicular language in government and in schools. This anglicization offended the Church, whose power was beyond dispute.

Taxation proposed to raise capital for the improvement of the docks was also resisted. Language and taxation disputes had historic consequences for Malta's political party system.

1887–
1902   Constitutional change — the "Knutsford" Constitution ensured that elected Council members were in a majority, and a Senate was formed. Electoral turnout rates rarely exceeded 50 per cent, despite attempts to assure wide representation through the district system introduced in 1891. The language issue continued to dog the elections. A great popular pro-Italian language meeting was held on 11 August 1901, where Fortunato Mizzi was acclaimed leader of the movement.

1903–
1919   The strains over language finally led to the 1903 "Chamberlain" Constitution which reduced the power of the Council. Nationalist and Liberal candidates contested the council elections in 1909 (others having taken place in 1904, and 1907) and the 1917 elections manifesto of the Nationalist Party placed the linguistic issue as the first of three priorities. After a major outbreak of violence on June 17, 1919, in part as a result of the poor postwar economic circumstances, the island was granted full self-government in matters of purely local concern.

1920   On Oct. 15, 1920, twelve people of diverse backgrounds formed the Labour Party Club at a meeting of branch no. 3 of the Workers' Union. Prof. Pier Frendo was invited to be president, Col. William Savona vice-president, and Gianni Bencini as secretary.

1921–
1933
The "Milner-Amery" Constitution of 1921 introduced proportional representation, and encouraged the sudden flowering of the party system for the new National Assembly. The forerunner of the Malta Labour Party of today was one of four parties contesting the 1921 elections. Mgr. Ignazio Panzavecchia led the Maltese Political Union, successor of his popular party, Sir Gerald Strickland the Constitutional Party, and Nerik Mizzi — later to be banished during World War II and interned in Uganda for "subversive activities" — the Nationalist Democratic Party. Each was associated with a newspaper or review.

1921 marks the beginning of the modern era in Maltese politics though the vote was not extended to the majority until 1947. This first election provided a crushing victory for the Maltese Political Union which won 58 per cent of the vote for the Senate and 39 per cent of the vote for the Legislative Assembly, gaining 14 seats of the 32 in the Lower House. The Labour and Constitutional parties tussled for second place, the first gaining this position for the Senate (21.5 per cent of the valid votes), the second for the Legislative Assembly (25.3 per cent of the vote).

The minority MPU formed a coalition government with the Labour Party on April 9, 1922, but the 1924 elections saw an alliance between the MPU and the Nationalist Democratic Party, whose combined strength assured them of 15 seats in the Legislative Assembly with 44.7 per cent of the vote. The Labour Party was beaten into third place. The next elections in 1927 provided no single party with a clear majority of seats; coalitions were the order of the day — this time Strickland's Constitutional Party (15 seats and 41.1 per cent of the vote) allied with the Labour Party (3 seats and 14 per cent of the vote).

1933–40
Constitutional suspension in 1930, due to nationalist riots, restoration in 1931, the "Amery" Constitution in 1933 and restoration in 1947 (with elections in the intervening revocation years) after the massive Luftwaffe onslaught of World War II, suggest the underyling strains for independence that was not achieved until 17 years later in 1964.

1940–43
Successful defence of Italian and German attacks, leading on April 15, 1942, to the award of the George Medal to the island by British monarch George VI.

1944–54
Postwar reconstruction aided by Britain was accompanied by the Malta Labour Party's accession to power in 1947 under Prime Minister Paul Boffa. The young Dom Mintoff, first elected in 1945, and Minister of Public Works and Reconstruction, soon fell out with the old guard on redundancies in the naval dockyard; the Party sided with Dom Mintoff and the Boffa government fell in 1949. The schism let in the Nationalist Party in 1950 with a minority. Dr Enrico Mizzi's death soon after ushered in Dr George Borg Olivier, first elected to the Council in 1939 and whose parliamentary career was to span some 40 years.

1955–63
The 1955 elections were won by Dom Mintoff on the platform of integration with Britain. The Feb. 14, 1956 referendum showed 67,607 voters in favour (75 per cent of those voting); but nearly half the electorate had not voted. The British government awaited confirmation of a general election. Dom Mintoff's government resigned in April 1958, demonstrations occurred, the Constitution was suspended in 1959 and only reintroduced in 1962 when Dr Borg Olivier's Nationalist Party administration was elected in elections that February.

1964
It was natural for Olivier to call for independence on behalf of his party since he belonged to the independence and anti-reformist tradition. This time no insistence on a general election was made; both major parties now supported independence and on Sept. 21, 1964 Malta became a Kingdom within the Commonwealth, with financial assistance from the British for the use of naval and air bases.

Post-independence: 1964 – present

1966
Dr Borg Olivier won the March 1966 elections, but in 1967 Britain began troop withdrawals and his party suffered the electoral fall-out.

1971 The June 1971 elections ushered in the revived Labour Party under Dom Mintoff, who had promised constitutional revision and greater independence. The NATO fleet commander withdrew and at the end of the year Mintoff demanded the closing of the British base and withdrawal of British troops.

1972 New base agreement drawn up with Britain for withdrawal of troops, while Dom Mintoff sought new aid from Beijing (US$17,000,000).

1974 The new Constitution confers republic status on Malta on December 13. Sir Anthony Mamo becomes President.

1976– A new agreement is concluded with
1978 the EC with increased financial aid (26 mecu). Mintoff wins a close election in September that year. Anton Buttigieg becomes the new President in December. In November 1977 Malta agrees a new aid accord with the People's Republic of China, followed in 1978 by aid agreements with Algeria and Libya.

1978 British journalists are expelled and the British Forces Broadcasting Services office closed.

1979 Differences emerge on oil rights on the continental shelf between Malta and Libya. On March 31 the last British troops leave Malta and the British base is closed.

1980 Tensions between Malta and Libya rise; Neutrality agreement concluded with Italy.

1981 USSR recognizes Malta's neutral status. At the December elections Dom Mintoff's Malta Labour Party wins more seats but less votes than the Nationalist Party under its new leader Dr Edward Fenech Adami. NP boycotts parliamentary work.

1982 Agatha Barbara becomes the new state President in February. The Speaker disbars Nationalist MPs from Parliament. Conflict with the Church begins over Church property. Foreign Interference Act comes into force on September 1.

1983 Opposition MPs forbidden contacts with foreign diplomats. In March the 31 NP MPs give up their boycott, but talks between government and opposition break up in July. At the CSCE Conference in Madrid, Malta holds out for a Mediterranean conference and delays conclusion. Nationalization of

Church property law comes into effect in October, but appeal is made to the courts to judge the law unconstitutional.

1984 Contacts with Libya and the GDR reinforced. The Maltese House agrees that private schools (mostly Catholic) cannot charge for schooling. Opposition mounts through the summer and early autumn. In September the first Foreign Ministers' Conference of Non-aligned Nations opens in Valletta. The Catholic schools open their doors once more. In December the Malta-Libya friendship agreement is ratified, and Mintoff declares the Italy-Malta Neutrality agreement dissolved, due to non-compliance of the economic and financial conditions. On Dec. 22, Mintoff resigns as Prime Minister and is replaced by Karmenu (Carmelo) Mifsud Bonnici, and a new Cabinet.

1985 A compromise is reached in April with the Catholic Church on Catholic schools. In June the International Court hands down its judgement on Malta-Libya oil rights. In December Malta and the EC agree new terms for the revised financial protocol for 29.5 mecu (about US$24,000,000) in loans and grants. Visiting Christian Democratic politicians are either turned away or prevented from speaking at public meetings. The Maltese delegation to the Council of Europe's Parliamentary Assembly is turned away as it contains no NP MP.

1986 The Parliamentary Assembly of the Council of Europe receives a new Maltese delegation of Labour and two NP members, and for the first time since 1983 the Maltese take part in the Assembly's work. A parliamentary delegation visits the European Parliament — the first since 1979. In July the constitutional revision package is put before Parliament; negotiations begin. That same month an agreement is reached between the Holy See and the government on financing Catholic schools. In November an aid agreement with Italy is concluded (US$ 120 million between 1987 and 1990).

1987 Constitutional revision is agreed in Parliament in January with one NP vote against. This requires that the party winning more than 50 per cent of the vote should also win the majority of seats. Malta's neutral status is guaranteed and no foreign military presence is permitted. Foreign interference in internal politics is banned.

At the elections in May, the Nationalist Party wins 50.8 per cent of the votes and 35 seats. An NP government was formed. Fenech Adami declares that the Catholic Church has been discriminated against and unjustly provoked in past years. It withdraws a claim against a constitutional judgement, declaring the nationalization of Church property as contrary to the law. In August it was made known that a secret agreement had been concluded in 1982 with North Korea, for the supply of arms and munitions to Malta. Malta's foreign Minister states in Libya that all agreements signed between the two countries will be respected. Links with Egypt are forged. Tabone visits the UK in October and describes Malta's position as being militarily neutral, ideologically attached to the West. Decentralization and encouragement of private enterprise are themes of the budget debate.

1988   Adami visits Libya and both agree to continue investment. Talks continue with the EC on the possibilities of eventual negotiations for Malta's accession to the EC. Constitutional negotiations for the strengthening of the role of the President begin in 1988 and are expected to be concluded in the spring of 1989.

Main features of the current Maltese political system

Malta has an extremely partisan two-party system, with very high turnouts at elections, massive street meetings in the cities and towns at election time, and high levels of political party membership. The two parties have accused each other of bias and corruption, and occasional violence erupts between supporters. A 1985 report prepared by the International Helsinki Federation for Human Rights cited the animosity, verging on hostility, shown by the two political halves of the population towards each other as a severe limitation to resolving the political problems of the islands. Intense partisanship has led to close elections and very little transfer of support from one party to another. This is encouraged by social conservatism shown by the close attachment each citizen has to his street or village, very strong family ties, which

nevertheless can cross party lines — as is the case with the family of former Prime Minister, Karmenu Mifsud Bonnici — and deep-rooted and pervasive religious adherence. The historical antecedents of the current parties and the current political system do help explain this partisanship. The first is the desire for recognition of the nation's independence and of its ability to manage by itself, linked with conception of its nationhood particular to each political party. The Nationalists support less taxation and greater religious influence, and originally a greater role for Italian culture and language, while the Labour Party presses for greater state support, less clericalism and initially a more Anglo-Saxon culture. In the last 40 years these antecedents have also been expressed through tensions between finding allies among the Western industrial countries or among the non-aligned or Soviet bloc states. Malta has searched for a role as a bridge between these groups, and between north and south of the Mediterranean, as a lynchpin for the Mediterranean countries in international fora such as the CSCE, or as the channel of communication for isolated states such as Libya and North Korea. It has shunned a role as naval base or aircraft carrier in favour of neutrality and non-alignment.

This tight-rope walk has led Malta to quarrel with many governments and organizations; from the dispute over Marshall Aid to integration within the UK, from complete independence to aid and outside support for its neutrality, from supranationalism within the CSCE to criticism of supranationality within the Council of Europe or European Community, from succour in the body of the Roman Catholic Church to rejection of the Church's role.

Malta's social conservatism and deep divisions effectively neuter any third party's attempts to establish itself. Since 1947 the two major parties or their offshoots have won 75 per cent of all seats in Parliament — and all of them after 1962. At the 1987 elections, the third and fourth parties combined gained 0.21 per cent of the vote with a 96 per cent turnout.

The current political issues in Malta include the following:

– Accession to the European Community
The Nationalist Party has begun soundings with the EC and its member states on the conditions for Malta's eventual membership, while the MLP had avoided developing Malta's links beyond first stage association.

– Education and schools
While the quarrel between government and Church may have been resolved for primary

and secondary schools, the university reforms under the MLP are being revised.

– Economy and tourism
Malta's search for a greater degree of economic diversity and independence from aid has encouraged tourism to grow and greater emphasis on financial sectors, ship refitting and supply, and textiles and clothing.

– Constitutional arrangements
The Select Committee of the House examining the role of the presidency is drawing up its report and recommendations, which are likely to be published in the spring of 1989. Dom Mintoff is sometimes mentioned as the possible future President under the revamped procedures.

– Law and order
The control of the police force and its politicization came under scrutiny shortly after the 1987 election results were announced; it remains a matter under review.

Partit tal Haddiema — MLP
(Malta Labour Party)

Headquarters	: March 31st Street, Senglea, Malta (tel: 821 023, telex: 1299)
Leader	: Dr Karmenu (Carmelo) Mifsud Bonnici
Vice-leader for party affairs	: Joe Debono Grech
Vice-leader for parliamentary affairs	: Dr Joe Brincat
President	: Vacant
General secretary	: Marie Louise Coleiro
Youth sections	
Young Socialists	: Christopher Agius, president
Labour Brigade	: Joe Zerafa, president
secretary-general	: Effie Mifsud
Women's section	: Maggie Moran, president
Newspaper	: *Il Helsien* and the trade union newspaper *L'Orizzont*
Membership	: about 30,000

History

The MLP's origins predate the founding meeting of the Labour Club at the Workers' Union branch no. 3 on Oct. 15, 1920, and can be traced back to the early Labour Movement formed in the 1880s.

Lt. Col. William Savona, vice-president of the founding group, led the MLP at the 1921 elections and became a senator as representative of the Trade Unions Council. Col. M. Dundon and Prof. Pier Frendo, two other founding fathers, were elected in the IV district to the House and joined five other MLP members there. The key campaign issues for the MLP were compulsory education in Maltese, English as a second language with Italian an option in secondary schools, tax reform and improved living and working conditions. The MLP formed the minority in the coalition government with the Maltese Political Union, whose policies conflicted with those of the MLP.

Dr Paul Boffa, who is often credited with founding the party, did not stand at the first elections in 1921, was elected only in 1924 and became party leader in 1930, leading a victorious MLP into government immediately after World War II.

Under Dr Boffa's leadership pre-war, the MLP began to press for a restructuring of the economy to lessen dependence on British defence spending as a condition for eventual self-government. As labour union membership grew, so did support for the MLP, after having suffered reverses in the 1924 and 1927 elections.

The party's links with the unions were strengthened on the foundation of the General Workers' union in 1943. This union is now the most powerful in Malta with over 30,500 members, and in 1978 was virtually amalgamated with the MLP under Dom Mintoff.

The October 1947 elections swept the MLP into power with 59.5 per cent of the 105,494 valid votes and 24 of the 40 seats, against the Nationalist Party (18 per cent and seven seats), the Democratic Action Party (13.3 per cent and four seats), the Gozo Party (5.2 per cent and three seats), the Jones Party (3.4 per cent and one seat). Dr Boffa became Prime Minister and Minister of Justice, while the young Oxford-educated architect Dominic (Dom) Mintoff took the Ministry of Public Works and Reconstruction, a key post at the time. Income tax, succession tax and old age pensions were introduced. Education to the age of 12 was made compulsory.

In 1949 the party was split, some say over docks redundancies, others say over the issue of Marshall Aid Programme allocations to Malta, which were being denied Malta by Britain. Dom Mintoff triumphed in the internal party struggle, but Boffa left the party and formed his own Malta Workers' Party, which contested the 1950, 1951 and 1953 elections before its dissolution in 1955. It also supported the Nationalists in 1951, after they had a minority government in 1950.

Malta election results 1947–present (percentage of vote and seats won)

	1947	1950	1951	1953	1955	1962	1966	1971	1976	1981	1987
Malta Labour Party	59.9% (24)	28.6% (11)	35.7% (14)	44.6% (19)	56.7% (23)	33.8% (16)	43.1% (22)	50.8% (28)	51.5% (34)	49.1% (34)	48.9% (34)
Malta Workers' Party	—	23.2% (11)	18.7% (7)	11.8% (3)							
Nationalist Party	18.0% (7)	29.8% (12)	35.5% (15)	38.1% (18)	40.2% (17)	42.0% (25)	47.9% (28)	48.0% (27)	48.4% (31)	50.9% (31)	50.9% (35)
Democratic Nationalist	—	—	—	—	—	9.3% (4)	1.3% (0)	—	—	—	—
Christian Workers	—	—	—	—	—	9.5% (4)	6.0% (0)	—	—	—	—
Democratic Party	—	—	—	—	—	—	—	—	—	—	0.2% (0)
Democratic Action Party	13.3% (4)	6.0% (1)	—	—	—	—	—	—	—	—	—
Communist Party	—	—	—	—	—	—	—	—	—	—	0.1% (0)
Constitutional Party	—	9.9% (4)	8.1% (4)								
Gozo Party	5.2% (3)	— (0)	— (0)								
Jones Party	3.4% (2)	— (0)	— (0)								
Others	0.2% (0)	2.5% (1)	2.0% (0)	5.5%[2] (0)	3.1% (0)	5.4%[2] (1)	1.7%[2] (0)	1.2% (0)	– (0)	– (0)	– (0)
Total seats	40	40	40	40	40	50	50	55	65	65	69
Turnout	75.4%	73.9%	74.6%	80.4%	81.2%	90.8%	89.7%	92.9%	95.0%	95.0%	96.0%

Percentages are based on first preference votes cast.

[1] less than 0.05 per cent.

[2] 4.3% for Progressive Constitutional Party in 1953, 3.0% in 1955, 4.8% in 1962 and 1.4% in 1966.

1955 saw the return to power of the MLP under Dom Mintoff and the major campaign to integrate with Britain. Though a round table conference on integration failed, government housing programmes, social insurance and welfare schemes were initiated. Tourist development began to ease dependence on the military bases.

The integration proposals provoked the Catholic Church hierarchy's concern to have guarantees for the interests of the Church in any agreement of this sort. The Church considered that Dom Mintoff's rush to the polls aggravated the sensitive situation and it therefore did not support his campaign. About 41 per cent of the electorate abstained. This high level of abstention, coupled with 13 per cent opposed, helped the British government's argument that integration could only come about with full support shown at a general election. The lead up to these elections was marked by Mintoff's demands for significantly greater assistance from the UK, and by the brief closing down of Malta Rediffusion.

The deal began to unravel. In April 1958 the government resigned. The Labour Party switched policy, and began to support independence.

The Constitution was suspended in 1959 and was not reintroduced until 1962, when the Nationalist Party won at the February elections. Both major parties included calls for independence in their manifestos. The integration debates had roused the Catholic Church's opposition to the MLP. The Church interdicted all MLP periodicals and forbade members of the Church to distribute or read them under penalty of mortal sin. The Party leadership and executive were interdicted too. It was not until well after independence in 1969 that the Church adopted a neutral stance to the MLP.

During the independence negotiations, the MLP advocated since constitutional reform to provide for an independent, secular republic which would consider its links with the Commonwealth at a subsequent referendum. The MLP pressed for neutrality and the elimination of dependence on foreign military expenditure — a policy that had been advocated since before World War II under Boffa's leadership. As a member of the Socialist International, the MLP was able to work on the Labour government in the UK to press for more aid. The 1966 elections were lost to the Nationalists by 48 per cent to 43 per cent (28 seats to 22) with no minor parties represented in the House.

The period was marked by the rundown of the British garrison on Malta, which had numbered about 5,800 in 1966–67 and 2,200 in 1970–71, with a similarly marked reduction in the personnel of the Ministry of Public Buildings and Works.

On its assumption of power in June 1971, after it won the elections by 50.8 per cent to 48 per cent (28 to 27 seats), with no minor party represented, the MLP government under Dom Mintoff renegotiated the base agreement towards its final withdrawal in 1979, brought about constitutional revision — adopted in 1974 — making Malta an independent republic within the British Commonwealth, and developed an actively neutralist policy. It sought new financial support from the People's Republic of China, the USSR, North Korea, the Gulf States, and Libya, while endeavouring to maintain support from Western European countries, in particular France and Italy. Dom Mintoff sought guarantees of Malta's neutrality from the last two and from Algeria and Libya, the last of whom became a substantial source of aid, but this resulted in a loss of support among West Europeans and the USA.

Malta attempted to create a Mediterranean focus in the Conference on Security and Co-operation in Europe, beginning in 1975. Elections in 1976 and 1981 kept the MLP in power — but only just, and with much dispute on the last occasion, when the Nationalists boycotted Parliament until 1983 when an agreement on a constitutional amendment was made. In 1981 a rift developed between Malta and Libya.

In spite of the enemies made by Mintoff, he also ensured a sharper image for Malta.

His battle against the influence of the Roman Catholic Church led to a crisis in education, at university, secondary and primary levels. In December 1984, Dom Mintoff stepped down and was replaced by Dr Karmenu Mifsud Bonnici. An accord was reached on April 27, 1985, between the Maltese government under Dr Bonnici and the Holy See on the principle of free tuition in Church schools and an agreement signed on July 31, 1986 shared the costs of applying the principle for the 1985–86 and 1986–87 scholastic years.

On May 9, 1987, the Nationalist Party won the elections with 50.9 per cent of the vote and took office on May 12. Though that party initially won only 31 of the 65 seats, the constitutional changes introduced in January 1987 assured it of the allocation of a sufficient number of extra seats — 4 in this case — to give it a majority in the House of Representatives. The MLP won 48.9 per cent of the vote and 34 seats. Turnout was at an all time high of 96.1 per cent.

Support

The MLP has claimed a major share of the Maltese electorate throughout the postwar period, although losing support at early elections due to the schism within the left between the radicals and the compromisers. It has drawn its support particularly from the dockworkers and the union movement and though no poll evidence has been published, the geographic distribution of its strength suggests a close correlation between Labour voting and manual workers (and their families), though this may be on the wane.

In geographical terms, the MLP has consistently shown greater strength in the east of the island, in Valletta, Bormla, Marasascala, Marsaxlokk, Zejtun, Tarxien, Santa Lucia, Birzebbugia, Mqabba, Dingli, Qormi and Zebbug, but particularly in the second district in Senglea in which the MLP headquarters (and the original dockyards) are sited, on the east side of the Grand Harbour.

Organization

The decision-making organ of the party is the annual general conference which brings together about 1,000 delegates from 56 localities. These local committees combine in the 13 district committees. The conference selects the party leader and deputy leader, the party spokesmen in the House of Representatives and approves the electoral programme. A 32-member national executive committee meets every one or two months — and its members are also largely elected by conference. This organ has the responsibility of carrying out party policy. The national bureau meets once a week and is dominated by the party leadership, and in practice is the most influential organ of the party. Party membership currently totals about 30,000.

The General Workers' Union collaborates closely, having had in 1986–87 two representatives in the Cabinet of Ministers with voting rights on industrial and social policy. The 1987 election manifesto of the MLP was formulated with the GWU and was approved by the national conferences of both organizations. They share members of their national executives.

The MLP has its own publications, the newspaper *Il Helsien* being the major one. The trade union newspaper *L'Orizzont* also supports the MLP.

The party has a Young Socialist section affiliated to the International Union of Socialist Youth, a women's section and a Labour Brigade, a children's association mainly active in sports and cultural activities, affiliated to the International Falzon Movement.

The MLP is a member of the Socialist International.

Policies

The MLP/GWU electoral programme "for peace and progress" agreed for the June 1987 elections, harked back to the disputes with the Church and with the British, and embraced the principles of Democratic Socialism, the availability to all of access to good and useful education, good medical care, and provision against unemployment, old age and sickness, and justice before the law. It continued to press for social and material improvements, with state participation in some areas of the economy and employee involvement in management of state enterprises. The programme resisted privatization and supported the continuation of its foreign policy — closer links to Arab countries, close ties with the EC (though no application for membership), and independence. The President's powers would be reviewed, provide him/her with new powers concerning the courts, the Electoral Commission, broadcasting and national security. The programme called for parliamentary reform, an ombudsman's office for maladministration claims and laws to regulate collation of information on individuals. It also advocated improvements in the free education system, and in technological education, progress in health, housing (rent subsidy schemes, extension of the Housing Authority powers), culture, protection of the environment, and modernization of Valletta. Workers' consultation by management in private industry would be extended, co-operatives encouraged, and discrimination against women in the workplace outlawed.

Personalities

Dr Karmenu (Carmelo) Mifsud Bonnici, born in Bormla on 17 July 1933, assumed the Prime Ministership in December 1984 on Dom Mintoff's retirement, but bears little similarity to his predecessor. He has a much quieter and less confrontational manner. He began as legal adviser to the Malta Young Christian Workers' Movement, having specialized in industrial and tax law. In 1969 he became legal adviser to the General Workers' Union. He came to Mintoff's notice as the organizer of Labour's election victory in 1981, having had adopted an elaborate series of boundary changes shortly before the elections. He was co-opted into Parliament in 1982 on the resignation of another Labour MP, Paul Xuereb, soon to be acting President on Agatha Barbara's resignation in 1987. He soon became Minister of Labour and Social Services, then senior Deputy Prime Minister and for a time Minister of Education. His style upon ensuring the post of Prime Minister brought about a considerable improvement in relations with the USA and Western Europe, despite his government having apparently warned Col. Gaddhafi of the impending attack from US Airforce fighters in 1986 subsequent to terrorist attacks on American citizens in Europe. One of his brothers is a Nationalist MP and another a Catholic priest.

Dom Mintoff has dominated Maltese politics of the postwar period, and has been the most charismatic of all Maltese Prime Ministers since the war. His leadership of the Malta Labour Party before and after independence in 1964 has been quixotic and deeply concerned to carve an independent niche for Malta. It has wandered from a search for union with the United Kingdom in the 1950s to friendship with Libya's Gaddhafi and then to a stance of independence and non-aligned neutrality in the 1980s.

He was born in Bormla on Aug. 6, 1916, graduated from the University of Malta and went to Oxford as a Rhodes Scholar where he was awarded MA in Science and Engineering. He became secretary-general of the MLP in 1939, and as deputy leader at the 1947 elections assumed the Ministry of Housing and Reconstruction from 1947 to 1949. He is now talked of as Malta's next President.

Partit Nazzjonalista — PN
(Nationalist Party — NP)

Headquarters	: Dar Centrali, PN, Pietà (tel: 623 641, telex: 1941)
Leader	: Edward (Eddie) Fenech Adami
Deputy leader	: Guido De Marco
General secretary	: Dr Austin Gatt
President: general council	: Dr Tonio Borg
President: administrative council	: Dr Joseph Cassar
Treasurer	: Joseph Stellini
Information secretary	: Dr Francis Zammit Demach
Organization secretary	: Salvu Denicoli
President: Youth movement	: Jean-Pierre Farrugia
Women's movement	: Ann Agius Ferranti

History

Paradoxically the earliest champion of independence, the Nationalist Party, has had to sit in opposition during most of post-independent Malta's history. Its foundation owes much to the independence movements in Europe in the latter half of the 19th century, particularly that in nearby Italy. It has a long clerical tradition favouring the Roman Catholic Church.

The "Anti-Reformists", who formed at the 1880 elections to contest the right of the Imperial government to introduce English instead of Italian as the *lingua franca* in schools, and to raise taxation, were the fathers of the modern Nationalist Movement. While Fortunato Mizzi is credited as the first leader of the party, that first election brought other party representatives into the Council. In these early days, the anti-reformists talked of the independence of the Church from the state, and at the end of the century the Bishop's views were opposed to those of the party, which had had its first successes in helping to bring in the 1887 "Knutsford" Constitution which provided for a majority of elected seats on the Council, and for elected members on the Executive Council. Between 1887 and 1901 the party held all executive seats in the Council, and pursued its battle for self-government and independence to the considerable inconvenience of the Imperial government.

After the introduction of the Amery-Milner Constitution in 1921, the Nationalist Party was recreated in that year by Fortunato Mizzi's son, Dr Enrico Mizzi, under the name of the Democratic Nationalist Party. It supported social welfare legislation to add to its demands for the Italian language to be given parity with English. It won 12 per cent of the votes in 1921 and four of the 32 seats and then fought the 1924 elections along with the Maltese Political Union, later forming the government, with Enrico Mizzi becoming Minister of Posts and Telegraphs, Industry and Commerce. In 1926 the two parties merged, bringing together the traditions of the Malta Political Association, founded in 1905 with Francesco Azzopardi, the Comitato Patriotico of Mgr. Panzavecchia founded in 1911, Joseph Howard's Maltese Political Union, and Fortunato Mizzi's Nationalists.

The party became the leading defender of the Catholic faith, of the Italian language and Latin culture against the incursions of Anglo-Saxon culture, English language and Protestant religion. Under Dr Ugo Mifsud and Enrico Mizzi, a vigorous programme of Italianization was undertaken, which brought members of the Nationalist Party into contact with the Fascists in Italy, a contact which was exploited by them briefly and without major effect, particularly after the attacks on Malta during the war.

The suspension of the constitution in 1933 was accompanied by a state of emergency called by the British Colonial Secretary against the further spread of Italian influence. In 1936 Maltese became an official language, at the expense of Italian, and Enrico Mizzi and other leaders were interned in Uganda for alleged activities in conjunction with the Italian Fascists.

The 1947 elections (which saw a dramatic extension of the suffrage to all those 21 years and over), gave the NP 18 per cent of the vote and seven of the 40 seats. The split within the MLP and the subsequent election in September 1950 brought in a minority NP government under Dr Enrico Mizzi. His death on December 20 that year promoted Dr George Borg Olivier to the Prime Ministership. The 1951 elections increased the NP share of the poll to 35.5 per cent (15 seats) and the NP and Paul Boffa's MWP (18.8 per cent and seven seats) formed a coalition government that continued after the 1953 elections.

The NP opposed the MLP plan for integration with Britain arguing that this move would threaten Malta's Catholic culture. It continued to claim self government within the Commonwealth; but its major priority remained postwar reconstruction. When the MLP returned to power in 1955, Dr Borg Olivier and the Catholic Church led by Archbishop Michael Gonzi fought the integration issue, and opposed the referendum.

When the Constitution was restored in 1962, the NP government under Dr Borg Olivier pursued its search for independence which was finally achieved in 1964. The withdrawal of the UK presence east of Suez had reduced Malta's importance as a military base, and the NP government was unable to prevent the reduction of the British garrison and British assistance to the island.

Malta's search for a role was at issue in the 1966 and 1971 elections, the last of which was narrowly lost by the NP by one seat (and about 5,000 votes). The gap between the MLP and NP widened somewhat in 1976, and in 1977 Dr Borg Olivier retired, and was replaced by Dr Edward Fenech Adami as leader of the party. His campaigning style of leadership and organizational ability maintained Nationalist support. At the 1981 elections the NP won a majority of votes but only 31 of the 65 seats; this result prompted him to lead a boycott of Parliament with his party members, which eventually brought about a constitutional amendment to prevent a repetition of the 1981 result.

In 1987 the Nationalists narrowly won the elections (benefiting from the new constitutional provisions stating that a party winning a majority of votes should win a majority of seats), and Dr Edward Fenech Adami subsequently became Prime Minister.

Support

The NP's support is particularly strong in the south-west and west of the main island and on Comino and Gozo, and is probably stronger among white-collar workers and professional people, and among religious adherents. At the 1976 and 1981 elections it achieved the highest share of the vote in Districts X (Sliema),

Malta Nationalist and Labour Party results by District 1976–87						
District	Nationalist Party %			Labour Party %		
	1987	1981	1976	1987	1981	1976
I	48.8	48.5	49.6	51.1	51.4	50.4
II	31.7	30.5	27.8	68.2	69.5	72.2
III	36.2	38.1	34.6	63.7	61.9	65.4
IV	42.0	40.7	38.6	57.9	59.3	61.4
V	44.9	43.2	41.1	55.0	56.8	58.9
VI	46.5	47.2	44.5	53.4	52.8	55.5
VII	47.6	46.9	47.0	52.3	53.0	53.0
VIII	61.3	61.3	58.2	38.3	38.7	41.8
IX	62.8	61.9	54.1	36.8	38.1	45.9
X	64.4	63.2	63.5	35.2	36.8	36.3
XI	61.3	56.9	53.7	38.4	43.1	46.3
XII	59.6	62.7	60.8	41.1	37.3	39.2
XIII	54.2	59.2	56.8	45.8	40.8	43.7

XII (Naxxar, Mosta to St Pauls Bay), VIII (Birkirkara, Tad Dwieli and Ta-raddiena), and IX (St Andrews Barracks, Il Qaliet, Msierah and Msrah, Msida and Pietà, site of its headquarters). In these areas it gained 60 per cent or more of the vote in 1981, and a similar percentage in the (slightly different) districts in 1987. The results in 1981 and 1976 (again slightly different districts) are shown in the table.

Organization

Membership figures in recent years show impressive growth from 4,576 paid-up members in 1977 to 32,706 in 1987 — about 41 per cent of whom were women (1986 figures).

The NP has sectional committees in each of the country's 62 towns and villages. These committees are elected for 12 months during annual general meetings by all paid-up members. There are party clubs or offices in 48 towns and villages and plans to build exist in others. These committees run the local party and elect members annually on to the thirteen district committees and the national general council.

The membership of the sectional committees is drawn from all sections of society — 24 per cent industrial workers, 5 per cent managerial, 10 per cent housewives — and from all age groups (39 per cent 25 years and under, 51 per cent between 36 and 55 years, and 10 per cent over 55).

District committees operate in each electoral district. They co-ordinate the activities organized by the party's section committees and ensure the implementation of decisions taken by the national executive committee, the national administrative council and the general secretariat.

District committees elect each district's representative (who may not be MPs) on to the national executive committee. They meet under the chairmanship of one of the general secretariat's assistants (district managers) and also include two members elected by each sectional committee in the district, the district's NP MPs and a district representative from the Youth Movement and the Women's Movement.

The general council is the party's supreme decision-making body. It discusses and decides on reports and matters presented by the parliamentary group, by the national executive committee or by not less than 50 of its members. It is responsible for approving the electoral programme and the annual report of the national executive committee. Any amendments to the party statutes must be approved by the general council.

The general council elects the party leader and the deputy leader. The leader is elected for an indefinite period but must be confirmed in office within three months of every general election. The deputy leader is elected for a period which expires three months after each general election. It also elects its own president annually.

The general council is made up of 500 councillors. These include 42 members elected by each district, all the members of the parliamentary group and all the members of the national executive committees of the Youth Movement, the Women's Movement and the Workers' Secretariat.

The NP is the only political party on the island to open all its general council sessions to the public and to publish the annual report of its national executive committee.

The national executive committee establishes the party's policies, selects the parliamentary candidates, regulates the management of the party at district and local levels and determines all matters not reserved to other bodies by the party statutes.

It is made up of 51 members including the party leader, the deputy leader, the president of the general council and all former leaders or deputy leaders (ex officio). Ten members are elected annually by the national general council, twelve by the parliamentary group (the other members of the parliamentary group may attend but cannot vote), one by each of the party's 13 district committees and four members by each of the national executive committees of the Youth Movement, the Women's Movement and the Workers' Secretariat.

The national executive annually elects its own president and the party's officials; the secretary-general, the president of the administrative council, the treasurer, the international secretary, the information secretary, the organization secretary and the assistant treasurer.

The day-to-day management of the party is in the hands of the administrative council which is made up of all party officials plus the presidents of the Youth Movement, the Women's Movement and the Workers' Secretariat.

The parliamentary group is made up of all Nationalist MPs. Its meetings are chaired by the party leader.

A shadow cabinet is to serve when the party is in opposition. Its members are to be drawn for a period of one year from the parliamentary group. The members of the shadow cabinet are to be chosen by the party leader, who may call an election within the parliamentary group if he wishes.

The Youth Movement (MZPN) has an independent membership of 5,500 members. It has its own national, district and sectional system with committees in 37 towns and villages. All committees and officials, at local, district and national levels, are elected annually.

The Women's Movement is open to all women who are members of the party. It too has its own national, district and sectional system with committees in 43 towns and villages. All committees and officials, at local, district and national levels, are elected annually.

The NP also has a Workers' Secretariat which is open to all members of the party who are in the labour force. It has its own national organization and has 32 workplace committees, also elected annually.

The NP's Central Office in Pietà, which is staffed by a small team of professionals, houses the leader's office, the general secretariat, the press and information office, the internal office, the library, an audio-visual centre and the party's computer department. There are conference facilities, including a hall which seats 600. The Youth Movement, Women's Movement and Workers' Secretariat also have their main offices there.

The building also houses Independence Press (which publishes a daily and weekly newspaper in Maltese, *In Nazzjon Taghna and 11-Mument* as well as a weekly newspaper in English, *The Democrat*); Independence Print, which is a printing company handling commercial as well as party printing work; and Eurotours, a travel company.

Policies

The NP's electoral programme for the May 1987 elections promoted "work, justice, freedom, as the basis of the future of Malta". It attacked the divisive policies and practices of the MLP, called for reconciliation, the reintroduction of traditional public holidays, the eradication of corruption, the appointment of an ombudsman and the removal of discriminatory measures against the Church, including legislation relating to Church schools and Church property. It defends religious freedom and the Christian values of the vast majority of the people of Malta and Gozo.

The NP also proposed reform of Parliament and of the public services, measures to help youth in work and in the family, to allow the rights of individual petition to the European Court of Human Rights, and the strengthening of constitutional provisions protecting human rights, as well as the depoliticization of the police's functions. Education was a sensitive issue; the plans outlined a policy to allow parents to decide on the type of education they want for their children and to expect good quality education, whatever the type. Proper autonomy of the University was to be restored, with the elimination of the sponsorship system of admission introduced by the MLP. All former facilities of the University would be restored.

As part of family support policy, parental salary would be paid to mothers who dedicate themselves to upbringing of children for a certain time. Legal recourse would be made more effective and care of the elderly improved. Home ownership would be encouraged for all, and state housing would be put up for sale to the occupants.

A National Health Service was to be established "in the light of today's social needs and of the best medical opinion". Devolved health centres would increase the local availability of certain basic health services, and private clinics would be licensed once more. Working conditions would be improved and participation in management would be encouraged in the public and private sectors. There would be sectoral help to re-establish the viability of the dockyards, the grain silos and the foundry. Industrial redevelopment in the Marsaxlokk area would be encouraged and agriculture made more efficient, through extension services. Tourism would be increased in quality to attract higher spending tourists. "The main aim . . . will be work for all." New investment would be needed, better infrastructure created and foreign investment attracted. Malta's heritage would be preserved, its environment protected through land use planning and control.

In foreign affairs, no country would be allowed to achieve undue influence — no foreign bases would be granted, and its neutrality would continue. An agreement would be made for the defence of Maltese territory with free and democratic countries. Strengthened co-operation between Mediterranean countries would be proposed and "in Europe Malta will take her place as part of it by joining the Economic Community under the right conditions . . .".

Personalities

Born in Birkirkara on 7 February 1934, Edward (Eddie) Fenech Adami graduated in law and entered Parliament at a by-election in 1969, having been editor of *Il-Poplu* from 1962 to 1969. He was voted leader in 1977 on the retirement of Dr George Borg Olivier. He reorganised the NP along professional lines, and widened its appeal beyond its traditional support groups. He emphasized Malta's links with the European Community, and played down its traditional links with Britain. Under him, the party advocated close links with NATO, but without a new base, and diversified contacts with the western industrialized countries, but on the basis of full independence.

He relentlessly criticized alleged Labour government excesses — in its use of power, in its campaigns on the courts, on education, on the professional associations (the doctors), on the media, and on gerrymandering electoral boundaries (at the 1981 elections).

He is prepared to negotiate and compromise on issues and his policies are cast in the same mould as those of Christian Democrats in much of the rest of Europe. He has served as vice-president of the European Union of Christian Democrats since 1979.

His predecessor in the post of leader of the party, Dr George Borg Olivier, was born in Bolt on July 5, 1911, and was a member of the Council from 1939 to 1945. He succeeded Enrico Mizzi on his death in 1950 and led the opposition to integration with Britain from 1955 to 1958. While Prime Minister from 1962 to 1971 he presided over Britain's virtual withdrawal from the island, but was unable to attract sufficient industry and investment to replace it and lost the 1971 elections. He died in 1979, having turned over the leadership to Dr Fenech Adami in 1977.

Two other parties contested the May 1987 elections, the Communist Party which received 119 votes, and the Malta Democratic Party which won 380 votes. Both were "squeezed" by the extremely sharp competition between the two major parties which ensured a very high turnout (96 per cent).

Partit Demokratiko Malti — PDM
(Malta Democratic Party)

Headquarters	: Cnr Old Bakery St. and Old Theatre St., Valletta (tel: 384 705)
Leader	: Lino Briguglio

The Malta Democratic Party was formed in 1985 by a number of members of each of the major parties who disliked the deep division of Maltese politics.

The party which had began as the Group of the Political Alternatives under the leadership of Lino Briguglio and Michael Vella (president) espoused Social Democratic principles, called for greater citizen participation in government,

decentralization of power, pluralism and tolerance and protection of the environment and criticized the concentration of power in the hands of the two main parties. It also sought links with the SDP in the UK, though it did not share all their views. The extensive programme of 68 pages covers all sectors of society and politics — and counsels membership of the EC under the right conditions.

Through employee participation, more active consumer groups and unions, the economy would be strengthened. The party's social policy was a caring one based on supplementary income to those in need, human development, compensation for the unemployed and support for the handicapped. Although Malta should not be part of NATO, its defence should nevertheless be aligned with Western Europe. The party was sceptical of the MLP policy of neutrality which it considered was always "up for sale". Since 80 per cent of Malta's trade was with Europe, those links, not those with North Korea and Libya, needed to be strengthened. The workforce needed to become more flexible through training and retraining, to provide "workshop facilities", adaptable light industry and a competitive services industry.

The party only had a small membership, but its aim was to hold the balance of power.

Communist Party

Headquarters	: 135 Melita Street, Valletta (tel: 232 311)
President	: Charles Zammit
General secretary	: Anthony Vassallo
Assistant secretary-general	: Victor Degiovanni
International secretary	: Karmenu Gerada

The Communist Party of Malta was founded in 1969 by former members of the MLP. It did not stand in elections until 1987. The party is "an autonomous political party based on Marxist-Leninist principles". Its electoral programme calling for true socialism under the banner "Politika nadifa u socjalizmu veru", demanded constitutional change to safeguard the interests of each section of the population through countrywide party lists of elections, economic change to increase popular control over economic resources, provision of a uniform public education system, non-membership of the EC, and new ideas for retired people.

It publishes a newssheet Zminijietna.

Norway

Francis Jacobs

The country

Norway is a country of 125,053 square miles, with a lengthy border with Sweden, Finland and the Soviet Union. It has a population of 4,150,000, of whom 95 per cent are Lutherans. Its capital is Oslo. It is ethnically homogeneous, apart from 30,000 Lapps (who call themselves *Same*) who speak a Finno–Ugric language and live mainly in Finnmark, in the extreme North of Norway.

There are two official Norwegian languages, *Bokmål* and *Nynorsk* ("New Norwegian", compiled in the 19th century on the basis of rural Norwegian dialects). Attempts to forge a compromise language (e.g. *Samnorsk*) have been unsuccessful. Some Norwegians' speech is closer to *Bokmål* (especially in the East and North of Norway and in the towns where a classical form of *Bokmål, Riksmål*, is spoken by a minority, especially in Oslo, Bergen and Trondheim) and some to *Nynorsk* (especially in rural areas in Southern and Western Norway).

Political institutions

Norway is a constitutional monarchy. It has a unicameral legislature, the *Storting*, whose number of members was increased from 150 to 155 before the 1973 elections and to its present figure of 157 before the 1985 elections. The *Storting* has a fixed election term of four years, with no possibility of early dissolution whatever the political circumstances. There are 19 multi-member electoral constituencies based on the *fylker* or counties, with the number of seats in each constituency ranging from four in Aust Agder and Finnmark to 15 in Oslo and Hordaland. The number of seats is not strictly proportional to the county's population so that Finnmark, for example, is greatly over-represented and Oslo and Akershus are especially under-represented. Elections are now by the Sainte Laguë system of proportional representation. Voters may delete individual names on party lists, but this has had little or no impact in changing the order of election in practice. Electoral alliances between

Map of Norway showing the 19 counties (*Fylker*), which constitute the electoral constituencies (also shows number of seats per constituency).

Source: adapted from *World Atlas of Elections*.

585

different parties have taken place in individual constituencies in the past (especially between the centre parties), but in 1985 a new electoral law permitted parties to come to agreements to pool votes for their different lists in individual constituencies. This proved especially helpful for the Christian People's Party and Centre Party. The overall effect of the Norwegian electoral system is not strictly proportional, and the existence of constituencies with few members, in particular, has been generally dis-advantageous for the smaller parties. There are no by-elections in Norway, with representatives who leave the Parliament being replaced by their substitutes (*varamenn*).

After the *Storting* is elected it divides into two houses, an Upper House or *Lagting*, with a quarter of the total members, and a Lower House or *Odelsting*, with three-quarters of the members. There is also a powerful committee system linked to the *Storting* as a whole.

Executive power is formally vested in the monarch, but in practice with the Council of State (*Statsråd*), presided over by the Prime Minister (*Statsminister*). Minority governments can be formed (and are common in Norway), but can be brought down if they lose a vote of confidence in the *Storting*. Ministers may or may not be chosen from Members of Parliament (technical experts are sometimes chosen from outside Parliament), but if they are, they must temporarily resign from the *Storting* and be replaced for their term of office by their substitute.

Direct elections to the 19 *fylkestingene* or county councils (there used to be 20, but Bergen is now combined with Hordaland), were first instituted in 1975. Before this date they had been composed of the mayors of all the communes within the county. Elections for the county councils take place every four years (half way between Parliament elections), as do municipal elections in the 454 Norwegian communes.

There is extensive public financial support for Norwegian political parties, provided to their central, county and communal organizations, and for their educational activities.

There are no provisions for referenda within the Norwegian constitution, but consultative referenda have taken place, for example, on the issues of prohibition, and of Norwegian entry into the European Community.

Brief political history

Danish rule over Norway 1387–1814

1814   Denmark forced to cede Norway to Sweden by Treaty of Kiel.

Norwegians declare their independence and adopt Eidsvoll Constitution, which establishes separation of powers and removes privileges of nobility. Indirect elections to *Storting* (Parliament) by means of electoral college, and with relatively liberal franchise (including many farmers).

Norwegians forced to yield to Swedes, but Norway is recognized as a separate Kingdom under the Swedish Crown and allowed to return essential features of Eidsvoll Constitution. Sweden in charge of Norway's foreign affairs, but Norway responsible for its own defence.

Union of Norway and Sweden under Swedish crown, 1814–1905

1869   *Storting* begins to meet on annual rather than three-yearly basis. Political groupings subsequently begin to develop over issues of extension of suffrage, and relationship between Parliament and Executive.

1872   Office of Swedish Viceroy abolished.

1884   Parliamentarism introduced in Norway, with Executive accountable to Parliament. Franchise extended. *Venstre* and *Høyre* become national parties.

1887   Labour party founded.

1898   Universal male suffrage.

1905   Dissolution of Union with Sweden, massively ratified in subsequent referendum. Norway elects to remain a monarchy, with a Danish Prince, Haakon VII as its first King. Indirect system of elections to *Storting* through an electoral college is replaced by direct elections in single-member constituencies, with absolute majority required in first round, and run-off if absolute majority not attained.

Independent Norway: 1905 to present

1907   Limited female suffrage.

1913   Universal female suffrage.

1914–18 Norway neutral in World War I.

1919   Proportional representation (d'Hondt system) introduced in multi-member constituencies.

1928   First short-lived Labour government.

1935   Labour comes to power. Beginning of long period of Labour political dominance.

1940–45 Norway occupied by Germans. All parties dissolved, apart from National Socialist Party led by Vidkun Quisling. Labour-led government in exile.

1945   Brief postwar coalition government followed by Labour majority governments (which lasts until 1961).

1953   D'Hondt system of proportional representation is replaced by modified Sainte Laguë system. Previous distinction between urban and rural constituencies (with one-third of seats allocated to the former and two-thirds to the latter), is also abolished.

1961–63   First Labour minority administration since before World War II.

1963   Kings Bay (Spitzbergen) crisis brings down Labour government. Brief centre–right coalition before Labour returns to power (1963–65).

1965–71   Centre–right coalition government.

1972   Referendum on Norwegian membership of EEC, in which 53.5 per cent of electorate vote No and 46.5 per cent Yes. Labour government resigns and replaced by centre–right minority coalition. Other major effects on political system (*Venstre* Party splits in two, Labour loses many anti-market members, New Socialist Electoral Alliance created).

1973   Election with greatest changes in postwar Norwegian electoral history. Labour Party has worst result since 1930, Liberals lose most of their seats, major successes for Christian People's Party and for two new groups (Socialist Electoral Alliance and Anders Lange party).

1973–81   Minority Labour administration.

1981–83   Minority *Høyre* administration under Kåre Willoch.

1983–86   Coalition government of *Høyre*, Centre Party and Christian People's Party under Kåre Willoch.

1986–   Minority Labour government under
present   Gro Harlem Brundtland.

Main features of the political system

There have been a number of major cleavages within Norway which have been of fundamental importance for the development of its political system (indeed Norway has been the subject of particular interest by political geographers for this very reason).

Firstly there has been a series of economic and class-based divisions between the industrial working class, the small-scale primary producers (farmers, smallholders and fishermen) and the employers and middle-class urban establishment.

Secondly, there has been a set of culturally related divisions over such issues as religious and moral values, prohibition of alcohol, and language conflict (between *Bokmål* and *Nynorsk*).

These two sets of divisions have also led to conflict between the centre and two separate peripheries, the North, which is often disadvantaged and physically very remote, and where economic divisions have been most important, and the South and West, where cultural factors have been more important and which has included strongholds of prohibition, strict religious observance and defence of *Nynorsk*.

These factors have helped to lead to the development of a multi-party system in Norway. During the period of initial constitutional reform in the late 19th century and of the unresolved national question (the desire to dissolve the Union with Sweden), there was essentially only a two-fold political division between Left (*Venstre*) and Right (*Høyre*). At a later date economic issues came more to the fore with the steady rise of the Labour Party. The old Left gradually declined, further undercut in 1920 by the creation of a specifically Agrarian Party (now the Centre Party) and later of a party concerned primarily with moral and religious questions (the Christian People's Party, which has been the strongest Christian Democratic Party in Scandinavia).

From 1935, but especially after the war, the Labour Party became the dominant party within the political system, building a successful coalition between the Labour movement in urban and rural areas and enjoying a hold over government, only equalled in Scandinavia by the Swedish Social Democrats. The Communist Party only had a period of brief success after 1945, and the three parties of the centre–right were evenly divided, with their own separate regional and social bases.

This stable system began to weaken in the 1960s, when Labour first lost its absolute majority and then went into opposition. Socioeconomic changes reduced the importance of some of the old divisions, while new divisions emerged, such as over foreign policy orientation. A limited split over NATO, which led to the creation of a new left–wing Socialist People's Party, but which did not severely weaken the old Norwegian consensus over NATO membership, was followed by a much more serious conflict over whether Norway should join the European Community. This went beyond the old dividing lines of Norwegian politics, with membership of the EC broadly supported by the Labour leadership (but not by all the rank and file membership) and by the Conservatives, and opposed by the far left and the Centre Party,

Norwegian election results showing percentages and seats won by party in the *Storting* 1945–85

	1945	1949	1953	1957	1961	1965	1969	1973	1977	1981[1]	1981[2]	1985
Det Norske Arbeiderparti (Norwegian Labour Party)	41% (76)	45.7% (85)	46.7% (77)	48.3% (78)	46.8% (74)	43.1% (68)	46.5% (74)	35.3% (62)	42.3% (76)	37.1% (65)	37.2% (66)	40.8% (71)
Høyre (Conservative Party)	17% (25)	18.3% (23)	18.6% (27)	19% (29)	20% (29)	21% (31)	19.6% (29)	17.4% (29)	24.8% (41)	31.8% (54)	31.7% (53)	30.4% (50)
Kristelig Folkeparti (Christian People's Party)	7.9% (8)	8.5% (9)	10.5% (14)	10.2% (12)	9.6% (15)	8.1% (13)	9.4% (14)	12.2% (20)	12.4% (22)	9.4% (15)	9.4% (15)	8.3% (16)
Senterpartiet (Centre Party)	8.1% (10)	7.9% (12)	9.1% (14)	9.3% (15)	9.3% (16)	9.9% (18)	10.5% (20)	11% (21)	8.6% (12)	6.6% (11)	6.6% (11)	6.6% (12)
Venstre (Liberal Party)	13.8% (20)	13.1% (21)	10.0% (15)	9.7% (15)	8.8% (14)	10.4% (18)	9.4% (13)	3.5% (2)	3.2% (2)	3.9% (2)	3.9% (2)	3.1% (0)
Det Liberale Folkeparti (Liberal People's Party)	—	—	—	—	—	—	—	3.4% (1)	1.4% (0)	0.6% (0)	0.5% (0)	0.5% (0)
Norges Kommunistiske Parti (Norwegian Communist Party)	11.9% (11)	5.8% (0)	5.1% (3)	3.3% (1)	2.9% (0)	1.4% (0)	1% (0)	—	0.4% (0)	0.3% (0)	0.3% (0)	0.2% (0)
Sosialistisk Folkeparti (Socialist People's Party)	—	—	—	—	2.4% (2)	6% (2)	3.5% (0)	—	—	—	—	—
Sosialistisk Valgforbund (Socialist Electoral Alliance)	—	—	—	—	—	—	—	11.2% (16)	—	—	—	—
Sosialistisk Venstreparti (Socialist Left Party)	—	—	—	—	—	—	—	—	4.2% (2)	5% (4)	4.9% (4)	5.5% (6)
Rød Valgallianse (Red Electoral Alliance)	—	—	—	—	—	—	—	0.4% (0)	0.6% (0)	0.7% (0)	0.7% (0)	0.6% (0)
Fremskrittpartiet (Progress Party)	—	—	—	—	—	—	—	5% (4)	1.9% (0)	4.5% (4)	4.5% (4)	3.7% (2)
Others	0.3%	0.7%	0.0%	0.2%	0.2%	0.0%	0.0%	0.5%	0.2%	0.1%	0.1%	0.4%

[1]Figures include estimated share that individual parties won when they participated in joint lists in some constituencies.

[2]Second results in 1981 are accounted for by a re-run election in the constituencies of Troms and Buskerud. Figures quoted are final corrected figures after the re-run caused by voting irregularities the first time around.

with the Christian People's Party and above all the Liberal *Venstre* Party sharply divided. The 1972 referendum led to a classic division between centre and periphery, and the subsequent 1973 election led to major losses for some traditional parties, with the rise of new anti-establishment groups on the left (the Socialist Electoral Alliance) and on the right (the Anders Lange party, now the Progress Party). This experience in 1973 helps to explain the caution with which many Norwegian politicians are again broaching the issue of possible Norwegian membership.

Since 1973 there has again been less volatility within the political system, although the old pre-1960s Labour dominance has not been re-established. Labour had remained the largest Norwegian Party, and the only one politically capable of providing a majority government on its own. The main alternative to Labour has been the block of centre–right parties, although these have not been homogeneous (e.g. divisions between *Høyre* and the Christian People's Party over the issue of abortion prevented the immediate establishment of a coalition in 1971). The balance of forces between them has been altered by the rapid growth of *Høyre* from the mid-1970s, alongside the weakening socio-economic base of the other Centre parties. Moreover, the two anti-establishment parties of left and right (the Socialist Left Party and the Progress Party) have survived, and the latter is currently enjoying considerable success with its populist liberal economic and conservative law-and-order message.

Of the old cleavages within Norway, the language division is no longer an important determinant of political preference, and the other cultural divisions are less important than they were. The political individuality of the Southern and Western Norwegian periphery is also generally less distinct, although it still shows an overall preference for the centre–right parties. The area around Oslo has shown a marked evolution to the right. The inner East and the North have retained a strong preference for the left.

The old divisions mentioned above should not, however, be exaggerated. In some respects Norway is a rather homogeneous country. Consensus has been an important feature of Norwegian politics (in 1945 the various parties briefly even agreed on a joint political programme), and there are not wide policy differences between the main political parties on such key issues as the role of government, the maintenance of the Welfare State, foreign policy, Norway's membership of NATO and the new emphasis on a high standard of environmental protection. The whole political

spectrum is less conservative than in many other countries. Differences tend to be more over means than ends (although the revived interest in Norwegian membership of the EC could again prove a divisive issue). Minority governments have been very common (at least before 1940 and after 1961), and governments have often had to seek issue-by-issue agreement with opposition parties. Only two governments have been brought down as a result of losing votes of confidence from the other parties. Coalition governments, however, which were once extremely rare, have become more common only since 1963.

A recent feature of the Norwegian political system has been the increasingly strong position of women in political life. In 1965 only 8 per cent of members of the *Storting* were women and the figure is now over a third. The current Prime Minister, and eight of the 18 Ministers in the government, are women.

Høyre
(Conservative Party)

Headquarters	:	Stortingsgt.20, P.O. Box 1536, Vika 0117 Oslo 1 (tel: 02–42 94 20, fax: 02–42 21 41)
Chairman	:	Jan P. Syse
Secretary-general	:	Svein Grønnern
Youth organization	:	*Unge Høyres Landsforbund* (tel: 02–42 78 10)
News bulletin	:	*Høyres Avis*
Membership	:	171,000 (1987)
Founded	:	1884

History

Høyre (literally meaning "The Right") developed in the 1870s as a reaction to the creation of *Venstre*, and to defend a continued separation of powers rather than full parliamentary control. Its main support was among the powerful civil servant elite and the urban establishment in general. *Høyre* was founded as a national party in 1884, with Emil Stang as its first chairman.

With the exception of 1888 when *Høyre* became the largest party in Parliament (largely as a result of a schism within *Venstre*), *Høyre* was normally the second party to *Venstre* in terms of votes and particularly of seats. Its highest percentage of the votes was 49.4 per cent in 1894, but it never won an overall majority of seats. There were, however, *Høyre* Prime Ministers on several occasions, beginning with Emil Stang from 1889–91 and 1893–95 and F. Hagerup from 1895–98 and 1903–5. For a while the Party was known as the *Samlingspartiet* (Union Party) and there were two Prime Ministers with this label, C. Michelsen in 1905–7 and J. Løvland in 1907–8. Before World War II, there were two further *Høyre* Prime Ministers, W. Konow from 1910–12 and J. Bratlie from 1912–13. *Høyre* became increasingly supported by the business community and the urban middle classes.

With the decline of *Venstre* and the divisions within the Labour movement, *Høyre* was briefly the largest Norwegian party in the early 1920s, with around a third of the vote in the 1921 and 1924 elections. Otto Halvorsen was Prime Minister from 1920–21 and in 1923, and A. Berge from 1923–24. Ivar Lykke was Prime Minister from 1926–28, but after he left office, *Høyre* remained in opposition until 1963 (apart from during a brief national coalition in 1945).

In 1927 *Høyre* fell behind the Labour Party. By the 1933 and 1936 elections *Høyre* was still the second party, but with little over 20 per cent of the vote, and far behind Labour. In 1945 it only polled 17 per cent (25 seats).

In the postwar period *Høyre* accepted the basic objectives of the Labour government, while calling for less tight control by the state (notably in the debate about whether to introduce permanent legislation over prices in 1953–54). *Høyre* continued to remain a distant second among Norwegian political parties, although its vote slowly rose to 20 per cent (29 seats) by 1961.

After the Labour government was brought down in 1963 over its handling of safety in the Kings Bay mines in Spitzbergen, John Lyng of *Høyre* briefly became Prime Minister at the head of a four-party coalition of the centre–right, in which *Høyre* had five ministers. Although this government only lasted a month, *Høyre* again returned to government in 1965 with six ministers in another four-party coalition, but in which the Prime Minister, Per Borten, came from the Centre Party. The coalition survived until 1971, when divisions over Norwegian entry into the EC were an important factor in helping to bring it down, with *Høyre* in favour of Norwegian entry, the Centre Party mainly opposed and the other two parties severely divided. *Høyre* campaigned strongly for entry in the run-up to the referendum. After the referendum in 1972 *Høyre* did not join the anti-EC coalition government of the centre, headed by Lars Korvald. In the 1973 elections *Høyre*'s vote slipped back to 17.4 per cent, its lowest percentage since 1945. Its membership also fell.

From 1974 onwards *Høyre* tightened up its organization, and began an impressive electoral advance. In 1977 it agreed a joint programme of action with the two centre parties. Following this *Høyre*'s vote in 1977 rose to 24.8 per cent and 41 seats, an increase of 12 over 1973, and in 1981 rose even further to 31.8 per cent and 54 seats. Membership again grew rapidly.

After the 1981 elections *Høyre* failed to reach agreement with the two centre parties on a new coalition government, largely because of disagreement with the Christian People's Party over the issue of reform of the liberal abortion law. *Høyre* then formed a minority government, with Kåre Willoch as Prime Minister. In 1983 a formal coalition was created between *Høyre*, the Christian People's Party and the Centre Party. Kåre Willoch remained as Prime Minister, and *Høyre* had 11 out of 18 Ministers. In the 1985 elections *Høyre*'s vote dropped slightly to 30.4 per cent and 50 seats, but the coalition continued for another year until May 1986, when it was brought down in Parliament and replaced by a minority Labour government. *Høyre* has since remained in opposition. Willoch was subsequently replaced as party leader by Rolf Presthus. In the 1987 local elections *Høyre*'s vote was badly hurt by the success of the Progress Party, in particular, and its vote slipped to 23.7 per cent. In early 1988 Presthus died and was replaced as chairman by Jan Syse, the head of *Høyre*'s parliamentary group.

Support

Høyre has been the second largest Norwegian party since the late 1920s, and also the largest of the non-socialist parties. It has traditionally been the party of employers and of higher salaried employees, and has been primarily based in urban rather than rural areas. From the mid-1970s it developed a much broader basis of support, winning new voters from the other non-socialist parties and becoming much more of a national party than before. It strengthened its position in regions where it had previously been weak, and in rural Norway it even became the second largest party among the working class. In the 1981 elections it was the first party in six of the 19 constituencies.

In the 1985 elections the party's total vote fell slightly, although it remained the largest party in five constituencies. Its vote actually increased around the capital, but fell off sharply in some of the peripheral regions of Norway. Since 1985 it has appeared to lose support to the right–wing protest party, the Progress Party.

Høyre is still strongest among the self-employed, owners and employers, higher salaried employees in the private sector, the upper middle class in urban Norway and those with the longest education.

Høyre's stronghold has traditionally been the area around Oslo. In both 1981 and 1985 it was the largest party in Oslo (43 per cent in 1985), Akershus (41.3 per cent in 1985) (in both of which its vote rose in 1985) and in Vestfold (40.9 per cent in 1985). It has over 30,000 members in Oslo and over 20,000 in Akershus.

A striking area of advance for *Høyre* in the late 1970s and early 1980s was the West and South of Norway, where it appeared to win a lot of the traditional support of *Venstre*, in particular, but of the other centre parties as well. It is now the first or second party everywhere in the region, whereas it used to be fifth in a constituency like Møre og Romsdal.

Høyre is now narrowly the largest party in Vest Agder (31.2 per cent in 1985) and Rogaland (31.4 per cent), and was first in 1981 in Hordaland (where it polled 35.8 per cent in 1981 and 32.6 per cent in 1985). In 1985 its vote slipped most in this region in Sogn og Fjordane (26.7 per cent in 1981, 22.1 per cent in 1985).

Høyre has remained relatively weak in the inner central and eastern regions of southern Norway. In 1985 it only polled 16.8 per cent in Hedmark and 18.1 per cent in Oppland, although for much of the postwar period it only obtained 8–10 per cent in these regions.

In central Norway *Høyre* has had mixed support. In Sør Trondelag it has been the second party since 1953, and won 27.2 per cent in 1985. In Nørd Trondelag it has been traditionally very weak (4.5 to 7 per cent until 1969) and this was its weakest constituency in 1985 at 15.4 per cent, and the only one where it came third (behind the Centre as well as Labour parties).

Høyre has always had some support in the towns of North Norway. It did well in the region in 1981, but its vote fell away in 1985, especially in Finnmark. In 1985 it obtained 27.2 per cent in Troms, 24.4 per cent in Nordland and 20.7 per cent in Finnmark.

Organization

Høyre greatly strengthened its organizational structure during the 1970s. It also increased its membership from under 100,000 in 1973 to 178,000 by 1983, making it the largest Norwegian party in terms of membership. This figure has since fallen slightly, and was 171,000 in 1987.

Høyre has around 1,000 local branches, and is now organized in almost all of Norway's 454 communes. It has 19 county organizations.

The national assembly (*Landsmøte*) meets every year, but elects the party leadership every other year. The party's central executive (*Sentralstyre*) consists of around 50 representa-tives of the county organizations, the party's flanking organizations, the parliamentary group and the top party office-holders, as well as six directly elected members at the assembly. It meets six to eight times a year. *Høyre* also has a smaller executive committee (*Arbeidsutvalgèt*), which looks after day-to-day business and consists of the party chairman, two deputy chairmen and two other elected members, as well as the leader of the parliamentary group and the chairmen of the women's and youth organizations.

The youth organization is called *Unge Høyres Landsforbund*. It has around 26,000 members (making it the largest Norwegian youth organization) and is entitled to 20 members at the national assembly and three on the central executive. There is also a student group, the *Norges Konservative Studenterforbund*, which has over 1,700 members.

The women's organization is called *Høyre Kvinners Landsforbund*, and has over 18,000 members. The party's central executive has recommended the county and communal organizations to nominate at least 40 per cent women on each list.

The other organizations associated with *Høyre* include its study group (*Høyres Studieforbund*), a pensioners' association (*Fellesrådet for Høyres Pensjonistforeningener*, with over 3,000 members) and the *Norges Borgerlige Organisasjon*, a group to promote wider co-operation between non-socialist forces in Norway. It was founded in 1897 and revived in the 1960s but only has a small membership of around 400.

Høyres' main organ is called *Høyres Avis*. It appears weekly, and has a current circulation of around 11,000. *Høyre* does not directly own its own newspapers, but there are over 35 local and national papers which are close to *Høyre* without being directly owned by the party. The largest of these is *Aftenposten* in Oslo, and another paper with a large circulation is *Addresseavisen* in Trondheim.

Høyre is a member of both the European and International Democratic Unions. It sits in the Conservative Group in the Nordic Council and Council of Europe, and is associated as an observer member with the European Democratic Group in the European Parliament.

Policies

Høyre is the largest non-socialist party in Norway, but cannot realistically aspire to forming a majority government on its own. It is thus more attuned to entering into coalitions than the Labour Party. Since the fall of the Willoch government, however, in May 1986, there has been rather less co-operation between *Høyre* and the other parties of the centre. On economic policy the latter are sometimes closer to the Labour Party than to *Høyre*. On certain moral questions, however, such as abortion, it is *Høyre* which takes a liberal line and is closer to Labour than to the Christian People's Party. The other parties of the centre have also been concerned about being dominated by the much larger *Høyre*. Their future relations are thus uncertain. A further problem for *Høyre* is the revival of a much more thoroughgoing conservative party to its right in the form of the Progress Party.

Høyre itself is a moderate conservative party, whose differences with the ruling Labour Party in the relatively consensual Norwegian political system are more over means than general objectives. It is less Conservative, not just than Margaret Thatcher's Conservatives in the United Kingdom, but also than its equivalent party in Sweden.

It was when *Høyre* was participating in government in 1966 that the welfare state was considerably extended, with the passage of a National Insurance Scheme introducing earnings–related old-age pensions. *Høyre* has called for decentralization, supported strong environmental policies, opposed the use of civil nuclear energy and advocated a boycott of South Africa.

Høyre does consider, however, that there should be more emphasis on the private sector than does the Labour Party, with a better balance of activities between the public and private sector. *Høyre* calls for a more open social market economy, with less bureaucracy and fewer regulations than at present. It supports privatization and deregulation. One of its actions when in government was to help remove the broadcasting monopoly of the Norwegian Broadcasting Company (NRK). It also pursued tax reform, and calls for further cuts in taxation. It has also sought controls on public sector expenditure, while continuing to defend the welfare state. It supports economic democracy, and more flexible working time.

Høyre calls for decentralization in all spheres and enhanced local government autonomy. It has also advocated a fairer electoral system. It has emphasized the need for stronger law-and-order measures.

One of *Høyre*'s most distinctive policies has been its support for Norwegian entry into the European Community, which has been stronger and more consistent than that of any other major party. *Høyre* was united over this issue before the 1972 referendum, and intends to make it a theme in the 1989 election campaign. In the meantime it calls for practical European co-operation in such fields as economic, industrial and shipping policy, and for increased Norwegian participation in European Political Co-operation (EPC).

Høyre has continued to support a strong Norwegian defence posture, and has recently called for a higher increase in defence expenditure than the Labour Party or the centre parties. It believes that NATO membership offers the best guarantee for Norwegian security, but would like to strengthen the European pillar within NATO. It is critical of the idea of nuclear-free zones.

Personalities

Jan Syse was elected as *Høyre*'s new chairman after the sudden death of Rolf Presthus. He is a former chairman of the party's youth organization and former Minister for Industry, and became chairman of the parliamentary party in 1985. He was born in 1940.

The two party vice-chairmen are Wenche Frogn Sellaeg, who has been Minister for Environment and Justice, and Petter Thomassen. Kåre Willoch, *Høyre*'s long-time leader and Prime Minister from 1981 to 1986, remains a highly influential figure within the party. He is the current president of the International Democratic Union. Another influential figure is the party's leading ideologue, Lars Roar Langslet.

Det Norske Arbeiderparti — DNA
(Norwegian Labour Party)

Headquarters	:	Youngstorget 2A, 0181 Oslo 1 (tel: 02–42 91 40)
Chairman	:	Gro Harlem Brundtland
Secretary-general	:	Thorbjørn Jagland
Youth organization	:	*Arbeidernes Ungdomsfylking (AUF)*
News bulletin	:	*Aktuelt Perspektiv*
Membership	:	155,000
Founded	:	1887

History

The Norwegian Labour Party (DNA) was founded in Arendal in 1887. For a while it was both political party and trade union organization, but the two arms of the labour movement were separated with the creation of the *Arbeidernes Faglige Landsorganisasjon* (Norwegian Trade Union Federation) in 1899. The DNA adopted a relatively moderate reformist line. Among its early leading personalities were Christian Haltermann Knudsen and Carl Jeppesen.

In 1903 the first DNA parliamentarians were elected from fishing communities in the North of Norway (Troms county and Bodø, Narvik and Tromsø). In 1906 the party won 16.1 per cent of the vote and 10 seats, and in 1907 DNA won control of its first local communes. The party grew steadily in both votes and membership; by 1915 it was winning 32 per cent of the vote and 19 seats in the *Storting* and by 1919 it had over 100,000 members.

In 1918 a more radical group of leaders, notably Martin Tranmael and Kyrre Grepp, won control of the party, and in 1919 it joined the Communist International (only the second party outside the Soviet Union to do so). In 1921 the party split, and its more moderate members went off to form the *Norges Sosialdemokratiske Arbeiderparti* (Norwegian Social Democratic Labour Party). In the 1921 elections the party's vote dropped to only 21.3 per cent.

In 1923 the DNA finally broke with the Comintern, but this led to the departure of members from its left wing to create the *Norges Kommunistiske Parti* (Norwegian Communist Party — see separate entry). DNA membership was now reduced to only 40,000.

A more moderate leadership now took over the DNA. Oscar Torp became the new chairman, a position he was to retain until 1945. In 1927 the DNA and the Social Democrats reunited, and a number of Communists later also returned to the party. From the low point of 1924, when the party had only won 18.4 per cent of the vote and 24 seats, the DNA advanced to 37.1 per cent and 59 seats in 1927. Early in 1928 Christopher Hornsrud became Prime Minister at the head of the first ever DNA government, but this only lasted for two weeks.

In 1930 the party's share of the vote fell to 31.4 per cent and 47 seats, but it again rose sharply in 1933 to 40.1 per cent and 69 seats, although the party remained in opposition. In 1935, however, the DNA formed a new government with parliamentary support from the Agrarian Party, and Johan Nygaardsvold became Prime Minister. Apart from the wartime years of 1940–45 (and a short period after the war's end in 1945), the DNA was now to remain as the sole party of government until 1963.

In 1945 Einar Gerhardsen became the new party chairman, and he retained his post until 1965. He led a coalition government in 1945, but after the elections of that year, when the DNA won an absolute majority of 76 seats with 41 per cent of the vote, he formed a single-party DNA government. He remained Prime Minister until 1951, when he stood down in favour of Oscar Torp, who was Prime Minister from 1951 to 1955. From 1955 to 1963 Gerhardsen was again Prime Minister. The party retained an absolute majority in the *Storting* until 1961. In 1949 it won 85 seats, and its membership rose to a high of over 200,000. In 1957 it achieved its highest percentage vote of 48.3 per cent.

In 1961 the party was damaged by the creation of the neutralist *Sosialistisk Folkeparti* (Socialist People's Party — see entry under *Sosialistisk Venstreparti*), which included many left wingers from the DNA. It only obtained 74 seats, and lost its absolute majority for the first time since 1936. In 1963 a scandal over the handling of safety measures in a mine in Spitzbergen brought down the government, which was briefly replaced by a four-party coalition of the centre–right. This quickly fell and Gerhardsen returned as Prime Minister for a further two-year period.

In 1965, however, the party only won 68 seats and again returned to opposition, this time for a six-year period. Einar Gerhardsen finally stood down as chairman in 1965 and was replaced by Trygve Bratteli, who held the post until 1975. In 1971 Bratteli became Prime Minister during the period of controversy over Norwegian admission to the EC, an issue which severely divided the DNA. There was a clear majority in favour (three to one at a special party conference), but a substantial minority actively opposed membership. A number of them joined an Information Committee against Membership, which campaigned for a "No" vote in the referendum, and many of whose members subsequently left the DNA. After the referendum the DNA again went into opposition from 1972–3. In the 1973 elections it only won 62 seats on 35.3 per cent of the vote, its worst result since 1930, but it subsequently returned to power with a minority government under Trygve Bratteli as Prime Minister. As a result of a compromise within the party the left-of-centre Reiulf Steen became the new party chairman in 1975, while the more right–wing Odvar Nordli became the party's choice to replace Bratteli as Prime Minister, which he did in 1976.

Nordli remained Prime Minister until 1981. In 1977 the DNA made a major electoral recovery with 76 seats and 42.3 per cent of the vote. In early 1981 Nordli stood down and was replaced by Gro Harlem Brundtland, who then also became party chairman. In the 1981 elections the DNA fell sharply back to 66 seats on 37.2 per cent of the vote, and returned into opposition. In 1976, however, Gro Harlem Brundtland again became Prime Minister at the head of a minority DNA government, which has subsequently been dependent on issue by issue co-operation with other parties. In the 1987 local elections the DNA polled 36 per cent.

Support

Although the DNA now has much lower and more fluctuating support than it did from the 1940s to the 1960s, it is still by some degree the largest Norwegian party. It was the first party in 14 out of the 19 constituencies in 1985, and had an absolute majority over all the other parties in four of them.

Its support base has been a very broad one, in both urban and rural areas, and extending beyond the industrial working class to white-collar workers in the towns, and to forestry workers, fishermen and farmers and agricultural workers in the country areas.

In regional terms its strongest area of support has been the Central and Eastern part of Southern Norway. Hedmark, with its tradition of rural radicalism, has been particularly strong for the party. It has polled over 60 per cent here in the past and its vote has hardly dropped (58.4 per cent in 1985). In neighbouring Oppland its 1985 vote of 56.7 per cent was as high as it has ever polled. Hedmark and Oppland have also had the highest figures for individual membership of the party. The DNA has also been strong in Telemark (50.6 per cent in 1985), Østfold (48.9 per cent) and Buskerud (46.3 per cent).

The other area of particular strength for the party has been North Norway, especially the most northerly constituency of Finnmark, where the party polled 62.1 per cent in 1957, and where it also had its highest 1985 vote of 59 per cent. In Troms the party polled 47.7 per cent in 1985, in Nørd Trondelag 47.1 per cent and in Nordland (where the party has also had a very high individual membership) 45.8 per cent.

The region where the party's electorate has declined most sharply is that around Oslo. In 1957 the party was receiving 50.3 per cent of the vote in Akershus, 47.8 per cent in Vestfold and 46.5 per cent in Oslo, but by 1985 its vote in these districts was down to 34.6 per cent, 35.4 per cent and 34 per cent respectively, and in all three of them it came second to *Høyre*.

On the other hand the party's vote has declined very little in its traditionally weakest region of West and South-West Norway. In Sogn og Fjordane the party has never exceeded its 1985 figure of 36.9 per cent, and it has only declined by a few points elsewhere. In Møre og Romsdal it polled 34.4 per cent in 1985, in Hordaland 33.5 per cent, in Vest Agder 31 per cent and in Rogaland 30.9 per cent, coming second to *Høyre* only in the last two districts.

Organization

With its close links with the rest of the labour movement and with its various "side organizations", the DNA has traditionally had a powerful structure. The party has both individual and collective membership, the latter provided by local branches of trade unions which decide whether they wish to affiliate to their local DNA party group. At present, only the total number of affiliated members is disclosed to the local party rather than their actual names, but this system, and its possible reform, is currently under discussion within the DNA.

In the past, up to two-thirds of the membership has been collective, but this figure has greatly declined in recent years. Collective membership has tended to be highest in Oslo and Østfold and in some parts of the country (notably the North) most members are individual. The DNA currently has 155,000 members, of whom around 33,000 are collective members.

DNA now has around 1,600 local branches, and above these, local parties in practically all of Norway's communes. It has 19 county organizations, each with their own executives of seven to 11 members (with five deputies).

The national assembly meets every other year, and consists of 300 members from the county parties, 200 chosen on the basis of their membership total, and 100 on the basis of votes in parliamentary elections.

The national executive (*Landsstyret*) meets two or three times a year, and comprises the party's top office-holders and 23 other members elected at the assembly. Each of the 19 counties must be represented. The central executive (*Sentralstyret*) is elected by the assembly and consists of the party chairman, vice-chairman and party secretary, as well as 12 other members, including a representative from the youth and women's organizations.

The party's youth organization was originally founded in 1903 and is called the *Arbeidernes Ungdomsfylking*. It has over 18,000 members. There is also a student organization (*Socialdemokratisk Studentforbund*) and a children's group (*Framfylkingen*).

The women's association, the *Arbeiderpartiets Kvinnebevegelse* was founded in 1901 and includes all women members of the party, who are not far short of half of the membership. The association is run by a secretariat, and has its own annual conference. In 1983 the DNA implemented a decision that it had taken in principle in 1981, that each sex was entitled to a minimum of 40 per cent of party candidacies and nominations, including members of the government. Forty three per cent of the DNA's members of Parliament are now women, as are eight out of the 18 cabinet ministers.

Other flanking organizations within the Labour movement include the *Arbeidernes Opplysningsforbund* (Workers' Educational Association), *Norsk Folkehjelp* (a humanitarian group), and the *Kristne Arbeideres Forbund* (an organization for Christian workers).

The DNA still has very strong links with the trade union movement, going beyond union collective membership of the party at local level. The top leaders of the DNA and the LO (Norwegian Trade Union Federation) meet up to once a week in the *Samarbeidskomiteen* (Co-operation Committee) to discuss current political questions, and there are also regular meetings between union and party leaders within the *Faglig Politisk Utvalg*. There are also joint committees at regional and local level. The party receives major financial contributions from the unions (e.g. 1,500,000 crowns from the LO for the 1985 election campaign).

The party has its own weekly subscription news bulletin for its members, *Aktuelt Perspektiv*. The Labour movement still has a substantial local and national press, with a total circulation of around 540,000. There are 30 newspapers, one which comes out four times a week, and seven which come out three times a week. The largest of these papers is *Arbeiderbladet AS*, which is both a national and Oslo local paper.

The DNA receives considerable public funds. This amounted to 35,000,000 crowns in 1986, of which over half went to the national party and the rest to its county and communal parties. The party's finances are also helped by a lottery.

The DNA is a member of the Socialist International, of which its current chairman has been a vice-president. It is also an observer at the Confederation of Socialist Parties of the European Community, and participates in Scandilux, the group for co-operation between parties in small NATO lands. The DNA takes part in SAMAK, the co-operation group between Scandinavian Social Democratic parties and trade unions, and sits in the Social Democratic Group in the Nordic Council. The party has its own Labour Movement International Support Committee (AIS).

Policies

The DNA has generally been a gradualist and reformist Social Democratic Party, and it only had a more radical orientation for a short period after 1918. It has traditionally been suspicious of ideology and intellectualism. It has

also maintained exceptionally close relations with the trade unions. The DNA has been the dominant Norwegian party of government and has only been in opposition (not counting the war) for 12 out of the last 53 years.

For many years after the last war it was able to govern with an absolute majority, but in recent years its governments have been on a minority basis. It has never, however, entered into a coalition with another party or parties in peacetime conditions. The current government of Gro Harlem Brundtland, which has 71 of the 157 seats, has had to rely on ad hoc agreements with other parties, notably with the Christian People's and Centre Parties, to get approval for such matters as the annual budget.

In its economic policy the Labour Party has put little emphasis on nationalization. It has also traditionally emphasized full employment, and is thus particularly concerned with recent rises in unemployment, of which it was very critical when in opposition. In 1985 it called for a job creation programme to provide 150,000 jobs. It has advocated reduced dependence on oil and gas, and better investment of oil and gas revenues. It has also called for more investment in research and in modernization of the public sector, which it also wishes to see more decentralized. Since it has come to power, however, it has also had to implement a number of austerity measures, including devaluation of the crown, tighter control of credit, increased duties and increases in national insurance contributions.

A major emphasis of the party when in opposition was that Norway's welfare state was being weakened in such fields as housing, health care and hospital provision, kindergartens and care for the elderly and the disadvantaged. In the 1985 election campaign it called for increased investment in these fields.

One theme that it is likely to emphasize in 1989 is the need to keep children at school for longer hours at lower levels of education. It also now seeks an extension in paid maternity leave from 26 weeks to one year. The DNA has had a long-standing concern with the length of working life, and has called for a shorter working week and for earlier retirement.

At the time when a Labour government was in power, a liberal abortion law was passed in the late 1970s.

Like other Norwegian parties, the DNA now has an enhanced concern about environmental policy, which will be a major feature of its 1989 campaign. It is beginning to emphasize, for instance, the environmental costs of the private car and the need for increased investment in public transport.

Before the 1972 referendum a majority of

the party leadership and the parliamentary group were in favour of Norwegian entry into the European Community, although 11 of the 14 members of the Parliament and a larger percentage of party supporters were opposed. The defeat in the referendum and its aftermath had such a traumatic effect on the DNA that the issue of Norwegian membership has not been seriously raised again until recently. It is recognized that reopening the debate might again be divisive for the DNA, and there is consensus within the party that an application to join should not be made at present and at least not until after 1992. Norway should co-operate closely with other European countries on such issues as research, technology, energy and environmental policy and should also seek to realign its economy to that of the European Community internal market. The issue of possible adhesion could then be reviewed after 1992.

It was under a Labour government that Norway joined NATO, and it has continued to emphasize the need for Norway to have a strong conventional defence based on general conscription and on Norwegian participation within NATO. There should, however, be full Norwegian political control at all times of military assistance by Norway's allies. There should be no stationing in Norway of foreign armed forces in peacetime, and the assumption continues to be made that foreign naval vessels calling on Norwegian ports respect Norway's policy of not carrying nuclear weapons.

The DNA has also supported the establishment of a nuclear-free zone in the Nordic region, implying the conclusion of an agreement prohibiting the use of nuclear weapons within or against such a zone. It believes that this would help to reduce tensions in the area, and in Europe as a whole.

The DNA has called for greater European co-operation within NATO and has also called for a no first strike nuclear strategy by NATO. It has attacked SDI, and called for the Conference on Disarmament in Europe (CDE) to be made a permanent institution.

The DNA has advocated the strengthening of the role of the United Nations, and the establishment of a UN High Commission for Human Rights. It calls for the implementation of the New International Economic Order (NIEO), for the liberalization of Norway's import policy as regards developing countries, and for the establishment of privileged relations (a mini-NIEO) between Norway and the developing countries of Southern Africa, to make them less dependent on the Republic of South Africa.

Personalities

Gro Harlem Brundtland has been the leader of the DNA since 1981. She is a qualified doctor of medicine, and was elected to the *Storting* in 1977. She was Norwegian Prime Minister for eight months in 1981 and has been continuously since May 1986. She is also a former Minister of the Environment (being appointed at the age of 35), and, when chosen as party leader, was identified with the Labour left wing in matters of economic and social policy. She has also chaired the World Commission on Environment and Development, which was set up in 1983. She was born in 1939.

Einar Førde has been the party's vice-chairman, and also the leader of its parliamentary group. He has been in the *Storting* since 1969, is a former minister, and was born in 1946.

The Foreign Minister is Thorvald Stoltenberg. The leader of the DNA's women's association is Sissel Rømbeck, who is also the current Minister of the Environment and who was the youngest Cabinet member in Norwegian history in 1979, when she was appointed Minister for Consumer Affairs and Government Administration at the age of 29.

Sosialistisk Venstreparti — SV
(Socialist Left Party)

Headquarters	: Storgt. 45.0182, Oslo 1 (tel: 02–20 69 79, fax: 02–20 09 73)
Chairman	: Erik Solheim
Party secretary	: Hilde Vogt
Youth organization	: *Sosialistisk Ungdom*
Newspaper	: *Ny Tid*
Membership	: 13,000
Founded	: 1975

History

The party dates in its present form from 1975, but its origins go back to 1961, when a *Sosialistisk Folkeparti* (Socialist People's Party) was established by left-wing dissidents from the Labour Party and by independent Socialists who were critical of Norway's membership of NATO. Unlike the Socialist People's Party in Denmark it did not stem from a schism within the Communist Party.

In its first election in 1961 it obtained 2.4 per cent of the vote and two seats (one in Oslo and the other in Nordland), whereas the Communist Party lost its last seats in Parliament. The new party held the balance of power in the *Storting*, and helped to bring down the Labour minority government in 1963 over the Spitzbergen mining affair. In 1965 it held its two seats, but with an increase in its vote to 6 per cent. In 1968–69 its youth movement left the party. In 1969 its vote slipped to 3.5 per cent, and its two seats were lost.

The party was revived by its campaign against Norwegian membership of the EC. After the successful result in the 1972 referendum it joined forces with the then Eurocommunist leadership of the Norwegian Communist Party (NKP — see separate entry), a group called *Demokratiske Sosialister* — AIK (the now autonomous successor to the Labour Movement Information Committee, which had worked against EC membership from within the Labour Party before finally leaving it) and a group of independent Socialists. The new electoral coalition (which initially left untouched the autonomy of its participating groups) was called the *Sosialistisk Valgforbund* (Socialist Electoral Alliance). It had a radical economic policy and was anti-EC and anti-NATO, and reaped the benefit of the anti-EC mood in many parts of the country to obtain 11.2 per cent of the vote and 16 seats in the 1973 national elections. It polled no less than 19.1 per cent in Finnmark, and 16.8 per cent in Telemark.

In 1974 a decision was taken in principle to turn the alliance into a proper party, and this was ratified at a Unification Congress in Trondheim on March 14–16, 1975. The new party was to be called the *Sosialistisk Venstreparti* (SV — Socialist Left Party). Its first chairman was Berit Aas of the AIK, and its first parliamentary leader, Finn Gustavsen, the former leader of the Socialist People's Party.

The original component parties had been given until the end of 1976 to dissolve themselves, but the Communist Party (NKP) became increasingly divided over the issue. The NKP had already abstained at the Unification Congress on a resolution critical of certain aspects of the Soviet Union, and later refused to close down its separate party newspaper. In the autumn of 1975 a pro-Moscow hardliner, Gunnar Martin Knudsen was elected leader in the place of Reidar Larsen, and the NKP voted by 117 to 30 to retain its separate identity. A large number, led by Reidar Larsen, then left the NKP to join up with SV.

In 1976 Berge Furre became the chairman of SV, and Reidar Larsen the new parliamentary leader. In the 1977 elections SV's vote collapsed to 4.2 per cent and it only retained two of its 16 seats. The independent NKP was reduced to 0.4 per cent.

In 1981 SV obtained 5 per cent of the vote,

and doubled its number of seats to four. In 1983 Theo Koritzinsky became the new party chairman. In 1985 the party advanced further to 5.5 per cent and six seats in the *Storting*. Erik Solheim became the new party chairman in April 1987. SV polled 5.7 per cent in the 1987 local elections, and has around 670 members in local and regional assemblies.

Support

In recent years SV has had relatively stable if slowly rising support of around 5–6 per cent of the electorate. Its greatest support has been among students and intellectuals with higher education and middle-class backgrounds. It has tended to be well supported among the young and among civil servants. SV has also put a strong emphasis on winning the support of third world immigrants to Norway.

SV has had certain support among workers. It has been extremely weak, however, among the self-employed, and among farmers, smallholders and fishermen in rural Norway.

By far its strongest district in 1985 was Nordland, where it polled 12.1 per cent. It has also had a substantial vote elsewhere in Northern Norway (7.4 per cent in Finnmark in 1985, 6.6 per cent in Troms). Its second strongest district has been Hedmark (8.2 per cent in 1985), with its long Socialist tradition. SV has also had a higher than average vote in Oslo (7 per cent in 1985), and Sør Trondelag (6.9 per cent). SV has been weakest in Southern and Western Norway: its highest votes in this region in 1985 were 5.5 per cent in Telemark and 5 per cent in Hordaland, but it polled under 4 per cent elsewhere. It was weakest of all in Vest and Aust Agder, in both of which it polled only 2.5 per cent.

Organization

SV currently has around 13,000 members in about 350 local branches and 19 county organizations. Its national assembly takes place every second year. SV's national executive (*Landsstyre*) consists of representatives of the 19 county organizations and the top party office holders. The executive committee (*Hovedstyre*) is a smaller body, consisting of the chairman, two vice-chairmen, the secretary-general and five other members. The number of vice chairmen may be reduced to one at the 1989 national assembly.

SV's youth organization is called *Sosialistisk Ungdom*. There is no separate women's organization, although there is a women's committee within the party. From the beginning SV has had a high percentage of women among its leadership. SV's study organization is called the *Sosialistisk Opplysningsforbund*. The party newspaper is called *Ny Tid* ("New Era"), and has a current circulation of around 10,000.

SV sits in the Left Socialist Group in the Nordic Council, although it has no other formal international affiliation. It has, however, held joint meetings with the SF in Denmark, the German Greens and the Pacifist Socialist Party (PSP) from the Netherlands.

Policies

SV is a party of left socialist orientation, and is the furthest left of the parties represented within the Norwegian Parliament. Over the years it has put progressively less emphasis on Marxist dogma and more on the need for decentralized socialism, with increased political, economic and industrial democracy. It is critical of both traditional social democracy, which it believes is too protective of the status quo and of Soviet and Eastern European communism which has been undemocratic, bureaucratic and has trampled on human rights. In the past it has thus spoken of seeking a third way. SV has had close links with the peace and feminist movements, and with third world liberation movements. It has gradually begun to put more emphasis on environmental issues (initially somewhat neglected in favour of socialist industrial objectives), and now seeks to reconcile "red" and "green" themes.

SV is very sensitive about being seen as a mere support party for the Labour Party (DNA), and is critical of what it sees as a technocratic DNA, with a working-class support base, but conservative policies. SV considers that it is too small to be able to go into a coalition with the DNA, and sees its main role as putting forward socialist policies and trying to push the DNA more to the left.

One of the major SV policy themes is the need to fight unemployment and to have a radical redistribution of wealth within Norway, with a more progressive tax policy (with VAT removed, higher direct taxation of the rich, and a closing of tax loopholes), establishment of a high minimum wage, price controls, jobs for all (with redistribution of work based on a six-hour working day) and unemployment insurance at levels based on previous wages.

A second key theme is defence of social welfare, and opposition to any cuts in this area. There needs to be more low-cost housing, more help for families with young children (e.g. more kindergartens) and more help for the old and disadvantaged.

SV has called for nationalizations (e.g. of oil, banking, credit and insurance activities) but points out that public control is not sufficient in itself and needs to be complemented by greater internal democracy at all levels. The public sector needs to become more efficient.

Decentralization, and the need to strengthen local communities, is heavily emphasized, as is the fight to halt depopulation of the countryside.

Women's liberation has been another important party theme. It has called for the establishment of quotas for women when new jobs are created with public money. SV has also strongly defended the maintenance of Norway's liberal abortion law.

SV was active in the campaign to prevent the Alta hydroelectric scheme in Northern Norway, for environmental reasons, and also to protect the rights of the Lappish people; SV has also called for the establishment of a Lappish Parliament. It defends the rights of immigrants to Norway, calls for the removal of immigration controls, and for immigrants to be given the vote in all elections. SV is generally critical of the existing Norwegian electoral system, and wants it to become more truly proportional.

SV remains strongly opposed to a possible Norwegian entry into the European Community. It is also the only party in Parliament to call for Norway to leave NATO. It seeks a Nordic nuclear-free zone and a neutral Scandinavia, independent of all military blocks. It has advocated a decentralized defence system for Norway, with conscription maintained, and with preparation for extensive military and civilian resistance to any aggressor. There should be a special force for contributing to UN peacekeeping efforts.

SV puts a major emphasis on help for developing countries and all national liberation struggles.

Personalities

The party's leader is Erik Solheim, who was 32 when he was elected to the chairmanship in 1987. He is a former party secretary, and former leader of SV's youth organization.

The two deputy leaders are Kjellbjørg Lunde and Per Eggum Mauseth, who are both members of the party's parliamentary group.

Hanna Kvanmo, who is the party's longest serving member of Parliament (in Nordland since 1973), has been its parliamentary leader.

Norges Kommunistiske Parti — NKP
(Norwegian Communist Party)

Headquarters : Grønlandsleiret 39,
P.O. Box 3634,
Oslo 1

Chairman : Kåre André Nilsen
Secretary : Bjørn Naustvik
Newspaper : *Friheten* ("Freedom")
Membership : 500
Founded : November 1923

History

The Norwegian Communist Party (NKP) was founded in 1923 by members of the left wing of the Labour Party, when the latter finally broke with the Comintern. In its first election in 1924 it obtained 4 per cent of the vote and six seats in Parliament. In 1927, however, its vote dropped to 2 per cent (three seats) and from 1930 to 1945 it was unrepresented in the Parliament.

By 1945 it had gained new prestige as a result of its role in the Resistance and won 11 seats in Parliament on its highest ever vote of 11.9 per cent. It polled as high as 25 per cent in Bergen and 22.9 per cent in war-ravaged Finnmark. In 1949 its vote again slipped to 5.8 per cent and it lost all its seats. In 1953 it returned to the *Storting* with three seats on 5.1 per cent of the vote but this fell to one seat on 3.4 per cent of the vote in 1957. In 1961, with a new rival on the far left of the political spectrum (the Socialist People's Party) it lost its only seat and its vote continued to slump to only 1 per cent by the 1969 election.

It campaigned against Norwegian membership of the EC and in 1973 took part in the Socialist Electoral Alliance (see entry under *Sosialistisk Venstreparti*), which obtained 11.2 per cent of the vote and 16 seats. One of the Communist candidates was elected, its Eurocommunist chairman, Reidar Larsen.

The NKP initially agreed in 1974–5 to give up its separate identity and to merge into the proposed new Socialist Left Party, but subsequently changed its mind in late 1975, when it elected a hardline pro-Moscow supporter, Martin G. Knudsen, as its new chairman in place of the Eurocommunist Reider Larsen, who left the party and joined the *Sosialistisk Venstreparti* along with a substantial number of party supporters.

In the 1977 election, what was left of the NKP only polled 0.4 per cent of the vote. In 1981 its support fell to 0.3 per cent and in 1985 to 0.2 per cent.

Support

The NKP is now of marginal political importance, with its support level not only far behind the Socialist People's Party, but even well behind the Workers' Communist Party. It only received 4,245 votes in 1985, with its highest vote the 1.1 per cent that it obtained in Finnmark.

Organization

The NKP has a 35-member central committee, a 15-member political bureau and a secretariat of six members. Its congress meets every third year. It has a newspaper called *Friheten*, which is a semi-weekly, and has a circulation of 8,000.

Policies

The NKP has been an orthodox pro-Soviet party since its Eurocommunist supporters joined up with the *Sosialistisk Venstreparti*.

Personalities

Kåre André Nilsen, a journalist, was elected as the party's leader in 1987, replacing Hans. I. Kleven. A former leader, Martin G. Knudsen, is still active as the head of the party's control committee. Arne Jørgensen has been the editor of *Friheten*.

Arbeidernes Kommunistiske Parti — AKP
(Workers Communist Party)

This is a party of independent Maoist orientation, which was created in 1973. Its main component was the former youth organization of the Socialist People's Party (see Socialist Left Party). It has fought elections as part of a *Rød Valgalliance* (Red Electoral Alliance). This obtained 0.4 per cent of the vote in 1973, 0.6 per cent in 1977, 0.75 per cent in 1981 and 0.6 per cent in 1985, never winning a parliamentary seat on any occasion, although it has won representation at county and communal level. It is much stronger electorally than the orthodox pro-Soviet Communist Party. In 1985 it obtained its highest vote of 1.7 per cent in Oslo. Elsewhere it was strongest in the far North of Norway (1 per cent in Troms, 0.8 per cent in Finnmark) and in Sør Trondelag (0.9 per cent). The AKP has a paper called *Klassekampen* ("Class Struggle").

The AKP leader was Paul Stygan. In 1987 the Red Electoral Alliance elected Aksel Nærstad as its new leader.

Senterpartiet
(Centre Party)

Headquarters : Peder Claussøns gt. 2,
P.O. Box 6890,
St. Olavs Pl.,
0130 Oslo 1
(tel: 02–20 67 20)
Chairman : Johan J. Jakobsen
Secretary-general : John Dale
Youth organization : *Senterungdommens Landforbund*

News bulletin   : *Sentrum*
Membership   : 50,000
Founded   : 1920

History

The party was founded as the *Bondepartiet* (Agrarian Party) at a meeting in Kristiansand in 1920, at the instigation of the *Norsk Landmands-forbund* (Norwegian Farmers Union). This had put forward individual candidates in a number of constituencies in previous elections, but had come to believe that Norwegian farming interests would be best represented by a separate farmers party. The new party's first chairman was Johann Mellbye.

In its first election in 1921 the party polled 13.1 per cent and obtained 17 seats. Its vote continued to rise in subsequent elections, until in 1930 it had 15.9 per cent and 25 seats. In 1931 Peder Kolstad became the party's first Prime Minister, and after his death in 1932 he was succeeded by Jens Hundseid, who remained Prime Minister until 1933 and was the Agrarian Party chairman from 1930 to 1938. In 1933 the party lost support for the first time and in 1935 it lent parliamentary support to the Labour government of Nygaardsvold.

In the first postwar election in 1945, the party's support was at a new low of 8.1 per cent, and it only obtained 10 seats in the *Storting*. Its vote then stabilized, and even slowly increased in successive elections until the early 1970s. In 1959 it changed its name to the *Senterpartiet* (SP — Centre Party) in order to widen its appeal further beyond the declining farming population.

In 1963 SP took part (with four ministers) in the four-party coalition government of John Lyng. In 1965 Per Borten, who had been SP's chairman since 1955, became Prime Minister at the head of a four-party coalition of SP, *Høyre, Venstre* and the Christian People's Party. Besides Borten there were two other SP ministers in the government. After the 1969 elections the government was renewed, but finally fell in 1971. Disagreements over EC membership played a vital role, with the Centre Party opposed to Norwegian adhesion, whereas *Høyre* were in favour and the other two coalition parties were divided. SP subsequently took a considerable part in the ultimately successful campaign against EC membership.

In the aftermath of the EC referendum SP entered the minority coalition government led by Lars Korvald of the Christian People's Party, and in which SP had six ministers. In the 1973 elections SP support rose to its postwar high of 11 per cent and 21 seats, although the party subsequently went into opposition.

With the EC issue less to the forefront, SP's support fell to 8.6 per cent in 1977 and it only obtained 12 seats. The party also switched chairmen in quick succession, with Gunnar Stålsett taking over from Dagfinn Vårvik in 1977, but himself being replaced by Johan Jakobsen in 1979. In 1981 SP's support slipped further to only 6.6 per cent.

In 1983 SP returned to government in a four-party coalition under Kaare Willoch of *Høyre* in which SP had three ministers. In the 1985 elections its support remained stable at 6.6 per cent, with 12 seats in the *Storting*. In the 1985–86 coalition government, SP had four ministers. In 1986 it again went back into opposition. In the 1987 local elections it polled 6.8 per cent.

Support

In recent elections SP was Norway's fourth largest party with a lower level of support than the Christian People's Party and far behind the Labour Party and *Høyre*. In the 1987 local elections it fell behind the Progress Party as well. Its main support base is still farmers and their families, while traditionally it has had low support among industrial workers and white-collar workers.

In regional terms SP has been strongest in Central Norway. Its best constituency has been Nørd Trondelag, the only district where it elected two members of Parliament in 1985 (one of them the party leader). In 1969 it polled 26 per cent in Nørd Trondelag, and it obtained 18.3 per cent in 1985, and was still the second party. Its second constituency has been Sogn og Fjordane, where it obtained 17.3 per cent in 1985, and where it had previously won 23.6 per cent in 1949 and 23 per cent in 1973. Another traditionally strong area is Oppland where it once received 25.9 per cent (in 1949), and where it obtained 12.2 per cent in 1985 and was still the third party. SP was also the third party in 1985 in Hedmark, with 9.6 per cent. In other constituencies in Central Norway it obtained 9.1 per cent in Møre og Romsdal and 8.2 per cent in Sør Trondelag.

SP has been weaker, even in rural areas, in South-West Norway, where the Christian People's Party, and to a lesser extent *Venstre* have been strong competitors for the centre vote. In 1985 SP's highest votes in this area were in Vest Agder (8 per cent) and Rogaland (7.4 per cent), but were only 6.7 per cent in Buskerud, 5.8 per cent in Aust Agder, 5.3 per cent in Hordaland and 4.2 per cent in Telemark. In the Oslo region SP is even weaker, with 4.8 per cent in 1985 in Akershus and only 0.8 per cent in the city of

Oslo, by far its lowest vote in all of Norway. SP has progressively lower support in Northern Norway with 6.1 per cent in 1985 in Nordland, 5 per cent in Troms and only 2.2 per cent in Finnmark.

Organization

SP currently has around 50,000 members in around 480 local branches within the 19 county organizations. The national assembly meets every two years and elects the party's top office-holders and its central executive. This includes the party chairman and two vice-chairmen, the national studies leader, and leaders of the youth and women's organizations, as well as six other members and five deputies. There is also a larger national executive, which includes the 19 leaders of the county organizations as well as the national office-holders.

The party's youth organization is called *Senterungdommens Landforbund* (SUL) and currently has around 3,500 members. It publishes a periodical called *Ungt Sentrum*, which has a circulation of 10,000 and normally appears every three months. SUL was first founded in 1949.

The SP's women's organization is called *Senterkvinnene*. It was founded in 1962, and all women members of the party are automatically members of it. There is also a party study group, *Senterpartiets Studieforbund* (SPJ).

SP produces a publication called *Sentrum*, which has a circulation of 4,300 and which appears around 10 times a year. About 11 local newspapers have been linked to the party, with around a 4.5 per cent share of the total market in the mid-1980s.

SP is a member of the Middle Group within the Nordic Council, but does not have other international affiliations.

Policies

SP is a non-socialist party in the middle of the Norwegian political spectrum, pragmatic in its economic policy and on the role of the state. Although the coalition governments in which it has taken part have all been of the centre–right, it has also co-operated at times with the Labour Party, as on certain budgetary matters during the present Labour government. A particular concern of the party is the need to ensure decentralization and balanced regional development throughout Norway. It believes that it is important not to overconcentrate economic activities in a few urbanized areas, and it opposes what it sees as the centralizing tendencies of both left and right. It wants to maintain regional aid, and to ensure good com-munications and transport for peripheral areas. It is also a strong defender of small economic units.

SP now puts a strong emphasis on environmental policy and on a better use of energy and resources. Alternative energies should be developed. A distinctive position of the party has been its continuing hostility to Norwegian membership of the European Community, to which it was opposed in the early 1970s and still is today. It considers that Community membership would undercut Norwegian sovereignty, encourage the centralization process which it opposes, harm the Norwegian farming interests with which it is still closely associated and also lower Norway's high environmental standards. On the other hand it argues that there should be intensified co-operation within EFTA.

A theme which it emphasized in its 1985 election campaign was the need to provide a wage for those who cared for people (the elderly or ill or handicapped people) in their homes.

SP supports a strong Norwegian defence within NATO. In the past the party's youth wing has been critical of Norway's defence posture, but this is no longer a matter of controversy within the youth organization or the party as a whole.

In its policy towards developing countries SP emphasizes the need for encouragement of self-help.

Personalities

Johan J. Jakobsen has been the party chairman since 1979. He has represented Nord Trøndelag in the *Storting* since 1973, and was also chairman of the party's parliamentary group from 1977 to 1983. He was Minister for Transport and Communications from 1983–6. He was born in 1937.

The two party vice-chairmen are Anne Enger Lahnstein, who is a representative from Akershus in the *Storting*, and Kristin Hille Valla. Johan Buttedahl has been the chairman of the parliamentary group since 1983, and is a representative from Buskerud.

John Dale, the current secretary-general, chaired the party's youth organization in 1966–70.

Kristelig Folkeparti — KrF
(Christian People's Party)

Headquarters	: Rosenkrantzgt. 13, P.O. Box 1477 Vika, 00116 Oslo 1 (tel: 02–20 00 30)
Chairman	: Kjell Magne Bondevik

Secretary-general	:	Odd Holten
Youth organization	:	*Kristeleg Folkepartis Ungdom*
Newspaper	:	*Folkets Framtid*
Membership	:	58,000 (1988)
Founded	:	1933

History

The *Kristelig Folkeparti* (KrF) is the largest Christian Democratic Party in Scandinavia. It was founded by people, many from the *Venstre* Party, who were disillusioned with the existing parties, and who sought a vehicle for putting forward explicitly Christian points of view in Norwegian political life. It put up its first list of candidates in 1933 in the single electoral district of Hordaland. It obtained 10,000 votes, and succeeded in electing one of its members (Nils Lavik) to the *Storting*. In 1936 a second seat was also won and in 1939 a national party organization was established. Nils Lavik became the first national chairman, a post he was to retain until 1951.

In 1945 the KrF stood for the first time in most Norwegian constituencies, having been additionally strengthened by the affiliation of middle-class revivalists from the Oxford Group movement. Its vote went up to 7.9 per cent and it obtained eight seats in the *Storting*. It improved this slightly in 1949, and considerably in 1953 when it obtained 14 seats on 10.5 per cent of the vote. Its vote then remained roughly even in the two subsequent elections. The party remained in opposition for all of this period. Erling Wikberg was the party chairman from 1951 to 1955, and Einar Hareide from 1955 to 1967.

In 1963 the KrF entered government for the first time with three ministers in the short-lived four-party centre–right coalition led by John Lyng. In 1965 its vote fell to only 8.1 per cent, but it then entered a new four-party centre–right coalition led by Per Borten. The KrF again had three ministers. In 1967 Lars Korvald became chairman, a post he was to hold until 1975, and again from 1977 to 1979.

The debate on the EC divided the party between supporters and opponents of Norwegian adhesion, with the latter in a majority. Among them was Lars Korvald who advocated a trade agreement with the EC rather than full membership. After the "No" vote in the referendum Lars Korvald became the first and so far only KrF Prime Minister at the head of a three-party minority coalition of the KrF (which had two other ministers in the government), the Centre Party and the anti-EC members of *Venstre*. In the 1973 elections the KrF's vote went up sharply to 12.2 per cent, and it won 20

seats in the *Storting*. It subsequently returned, however, into opposition.

The key issue for the KrF in the next few years was that of the liberalization of abortion, to which the KrF was strongly opposed. In 1978 an abortion law was finally adopted. In 1981, when the party's vote dropped from its 1977 high of 12.4 per cent and 22 seats to only 9.4 per cent and 15 seats, abortion proved the main stumbling block which prevented the creation of a three-party centre–right coalition, with the KrF refusing to compromise on its insistence that the law be changed.

In 1983 Kjell Magne Bondevik took over as party chairman from Kaare Kristiansen, who had held the post from 1975–77 and from 1979–83. The KrF also re-entered government in 1983 when they took part with four ministers in a three-party coalition led by Kaare Willoch of *Høyre*. A compromise was reached over the abortion issue, KrF agreeing to participate in government without prejudice to its independent position aimed at changing the abortion law.

In the 1985 elections the KrF's vote dropped to 8.3 per cent, but its number of seats rose to 16 as a result of local electoral alliances. In 1986 the coalition was defeated, and the KrF again returned into opposition. In the 1987 local elections the party polled 8 per cent.

Support

The KrF has received its main support from active churchgoers, and members of religious lay organizations, as well as from supporters of the temperance movement.

In its strongholds in South and West Norway it has received both urban and rural support, whereas in other parts of Norway it has tended to have more urban support. During the controversy over EC membership in the early 1970s the party also did particularly well in certain fishing communities.

The party's highest level of support is in South and West Norway, where the religious and temperance counterculture has had its strongest hold. It has been particularly strong in Møre og Romsdal, where it has been the largest party in the past (notably in 1949 when it polled 35.1 per cent) and where at times it has had over 9,000 members. In 1985 it polled 16.4 per cent in the constituency. Its highest percentage in 1985, however, was in Vest Agder, where it polled 17.9 per cent, and where the party had obtained 24.9 per cent in 1977. Other constituencies with high KrF support have included Aust Agder (14.7 per cent in 1985), Rogaland (14.7 per cent in 1985, 21.2 per cent in 1977, and where the party has had 8–9,000 members in recent years), Sogn og Fjordane (13.3 per cent in 1985) and Hordaland, where the party was founded and where it obtained 12.3 per cent in 1985, but 26.8 per cent in 1945. In recent years the party has averaged 7–8,000 members in Hordaland.

Areas of moderate strength for the party have included Telemark (9.2 per cent in 1985) and Østfold (8.8 per cent in 1985), where the party has had pockets of considerable strength on the Swedish border. The KrF has been less strong in Northern Norway (Troms 7 per cent in 1985, Nordland 6.2 per cent, Nord Trondelag 5.1 per cent and Finnmark 4.9 per cent), although even here it has had pockets of stronger support. The KrF has been weakest in the remaining Central and Eastern parts of Southern Norway. In 1985 it obtained 5.2 per cent in Oppland, 4.7 per cent in Buskerud and 4 per cent in both Oslo and Akershus. It was weakest of all in Hedmark (3.1 per cent).

Organization

The KrF currently has around 58,000 members (1988), a decline from a figure of over 69,000 in 1980. It has around 500 local branches and 19 county organizations. At national level the national assembly meets every two years, and includes representatives chosen on the basis of the number of members and of votes won in the last parliamentary election.

The national executive (*Landsstyret*) includes the members of the central executive, the chairmen of the 19 county organizations, three representatives of the parliamentary group and representatives from the youth and women's organizations.

The central executive (*Sentralstyret*) is a smaller body consisting of eight members elected at the assembly (the chairman, two vice-chairmen and five other members), as well as the chairmen of the women and youth organizations, and one representative of the parliamentary group. There are also seven deputy members. There is an even smaller executive group (*Arbeitsutvalget*), which prepares central executive business, and deals with urgent matters.

The party's youth organization, the *Kristeleg Folkepartis Ungdom* was founded in December 1946 and currently has around 6,300 members (early 1989). It is a member of the European Union of Young Christian Democrats, and produces a paper called *Ny Veg*.

The party's women's organization is called *Kristeleg Folkepartis Kvinner*, and has around 4,000 members (mid-1988 figures). The first women's section was founded in 1937, and the national organization in 1947. The KrF also has a study group, the *Kristeleg Folkepartis Studieforbund*.

The party's main publication is called *Folkets Framtid*. It now comes out only once a week (formerly twice), and has a circulation of around 9,600. There is also a periodical, *Idé*, which is produced by people close to the party, and which comes out around four times a year.

The KrF is a member of the European Union of Christian Democrats, and of the Christian Democratic International. It sits with the Middle Group in the Nordic Council, and also co-operates closely with the other Scandinavian Christian Democratic parties, with whom it holds regular joint meetings.

Policies

The KrF is a Christian Democratic party in the centre of the Norwegian political spectrum which has seen its main task as the defence of Christian ethical values in an increasingly materialistic age. It has been closely associated with religious groups and with the temperance movement, and its most distinctive policies have been on family and socio-cultural questions.

In the 1970s it fought hard to prevent passage of a liberal abortion law and did not help form a coalition government in 1981 because of disagreements with other parties over this issue, although it did enter government in 1983. It subsequently pushed unsuccessfully to alter the law. It is nevertheless still committed to changing the abortion law, and this will undoubtedly feature in its 1989 election campaign.

The KrF emphasizes family policy in general, calling for improvements in the economic situation of families, more possibilities for one parent to stay at home, increased support for kindergartens, and so on. It continues to put a strong emphasis on the fight against drug and alcohol abuse, and on their costs for the social budget. It would like more restrictions on alcohol supply, and supports the development of alcohol-free hotels and restaurants. The party has also been concerned with the issue of pornography, and the need for controls over videos.

Another set of issues to which the KrF has attached particular importance are those concerned with development policy and North–South relations. The KrF has called for a Norwegian aid target of 1.7 per cent of GDP. The KrF has also called for economic and other support for church and other private schools.

On economic policy the party tends to be in the middle of the spectrum between the Conservative and Labour parties, putting rather less emphasis than the former on the free market, and rather less than the latter on the role of the state, although these differences are primarily of degree. The KrF has supported strong social welfare measures, and an increase in resources to help the old and handicapped as well as the disadvantaged in society. As in other Norwegian parties, environmental policy is now receiving a higher priority.

In the past the KrF has been divided on the issue of whether Norway should join the European Community. The party has not yet taken a strong stand in the renewed debate on this question, and is likely to take a nuanced position, neither completely in favour nor hostile.

The KrF strongly supports Norwegian membership of NATO. It has recently advocated a slightly higher real increase in the defence budget than the Labour Party, but slightly less than the Conservatives. Its leaders do not believe that the idea of a Nordic nuclear-free zone is a realistic one.

Personalities

Kjell Magne Bondevik has been the party chairman since 1983, and also the parliamentary leader (a position he also held from 1981–3) since 1986. He is a former State Secretary and later minister. He is also a former chairman of the party's youth movement. He was born in 1947. His uncle, Kjell Bondevik, was also a former minister and leader of the KrF parliamentary group.

The two party vice-chairmen are Solveig Sollie (who has chaired the KrF's women's organization, and has been a member of the *Storting* since 1985) and Jon Lilletun. The secretary-general is Odd Holten.

Fremskrittspartiet
(Progress Party)

Headquarters	:	P.O. Box 815 Sentrum 0104, Oslo 1 (tel: 02–41 21 52)
Chairman	:	Carl Hagen
Secretary-general	:	Hans Andreas Limi
Youth organization	:	*Fremskrittspartiets Ungdom* (FPU)
Newspaper	:	*Fremskritt*
Membership	:	10,000
Founded	:	April 1973

History

The original name of the party was Anders Lange Party for a Strong Reduction in Taxation and Public Intervention. Lange was a well-known dog-kennel owner who had become a national celebrity as a result of his political comments in a dog-breeding magazine, which he edited. He founded his new party in April 1973. As its name implied, it was a populist protest party against high taxes and state interference in people's lives, and it had links with the Progress Party which had previously been founded by Mogen Glistrup in Denmark.

In its first election in 1973 the Anders Lange Party polled five per cent, and obtained four seats in the *Storting*. In 1974 Anders Lange died. It was not, however, until 1977 that the party changed its name to its present title of the Progress Party. In the 1977 elections its vote dropped to 1.9 per cent and it lost all its Parliamentary seats.

The party was then completely restructured. In 1978, Carl Hagen became its chairman. In the 1981 elections its vote again rose to 4.5 per cent, and it regained four seats in Parliament. In 1985, however, its vote slipped to 3.7 per cent, and it only retained two of its seats. It held, however, the balance of power in the new *Storting*, and helped to bring down the Willoch government in April 1986.

Since then the party has again revived. In the 1987 local elections the party's vote rose to 12.2 per cent and it won 123 communal seats, making it the third party in support behind Labour and the Conservatives. In subsequent opinion polls its support appears to have risen even further.

Support

The Progress Party has had its highest electoral support in the most densely populated part of Norway: the cities and the districts surrounding them. It claims to have had particular support among young voters, and also to have done well among industrial workers. It has also taken considerable support from the Conservatives, and now appears to be attracting a wider protest vote. It has done well in the region around Oslo; in 1985 it obtained 5.1 per cent in Oslo (6.4 per cent in its first election in 1973 and no less than 19 per cent in the 1987 local elections); 5.2 per cent in Akershus (6.9 per cent in 1973) and 4.8 per cent in Vestfold (6.6 per cent in 1973). It won one of its two seats in 1985 in Oslo.

It won its other *Storting* seat in 1985 in the district of Hordaland (which includes Bergen, and where the party polled 4.8 per cent in 1985, and 6.5 per cent in 1973). The party obtained 19 per cent in Bergen in the 1987 local elections. In percentage terms the party has been even stronger in Rogaland (which includes Stavanger, and where it obtained its highest votes in both 1985 at 6.0 per cent and in its first election in 1973 at 7.9 per cent).

The party has had substantial support in Vest Agder (where it did particularly well in 1973), Aust Agder, Buskerud, Møre og Romsdal and Sør Trøndelag (notably around Trondheim). It has generally been weaker in rural, inland and North and East Norway. Its weakest district is Finnmark (1.4 per cent in 1985), and in 1985 it polled under 2 per cent in Sogn og Fjordane (1.5 per cent), Nordland (1.7 per cent), Hedmark (1.7 per cent), Oppland (1.8 per cent) and Nord Trøndelag (1.9 per cent).

Organization

Although the party has no central registration of its members it estimates that its current membership is around 10,000. It has around 250 local branches and 19 county organizations. At national level it has an assembly which meets every year. The party has a national executive which consists of the 19 chairmen of the county organizations as well as the members of the smaller central executive. The national executive is chaired by a president. The central executive consists of the party chairman, two vice-chairmen and six other members, all elected for two-year terms by the national assembly. Elections take place in alternate years, one year for the chairman and three other members, the next year for the two vice-chairmen and three remaining members.

The party has a youth organization, *Fremskrittspartiets Ungdom* but no women's organization at national level. There is now also a Progress Party Research Institute (*Fremskrittspartiets Utredninginstitutt*), which has links with think tanks in other countries. The party newspaper is called *Fremskritt* ("Progress"). It appears on a weekly basis, and has a current circulation of over 3,800.

The Progress Party has no formal international links with parties in other countries, not even with the Progress Party in Denmark.

Policies

The Progress Party has a populist libertarian orientation, and advocates the strengthening of market forces, less state bureaucracy and a reduction in taxes and state interference in general. It also calls for tough law and order measures, and a strong defence posture by Norway. It is anti-socialist, but has distinguished itself from the other Norwegian parties of the centre and right. Since the 1985 election it has had a key role in the politically balanced *Storting* and has helped to maintain the minority Labour Party government in office since 1986 rather than to bring back the three party centre–right coalition.

The party currently emphasizes three particular policy themes. The first is the need to reduce the overall level of taxation, to simplify the tax system and to shift the balance away from direct to indirect taxation.

A second theme is the need for stronger policies on law and order, with more resources given to the police, and a greater emphasis on protecting the victims of crime. There should be more severe measures against drug pushers, and harder penalties against criminals.

The third is health policy, where the party calls for an increase in resources devoted to health and to protection of the elderly, the sick and the handicapped. The party also calls for greater freedom for patients to decide whether they wish to be treated in public or private hospitals, and to be reimbursed irrespective of the place of treatment.

The party also advocates a bigger role for private enterprise in the education sector, where it wants to permit greater choice as to which school to attend, and whether it is public or private.

The Progress Party believes that the private sector can complement or replace the public sector in other fields as well. The party leader, for example, has suggested selling off the majority public stake in Statoil. The party also considers that state subsidies and handouts should be reduced, and that farming should become more entrepreneurial.

The Progress Party has taken a tough stand against unrestricted immigration into Norway, and seeks a more tightly circumscribed policy on admission of refugees, who should be those recommended by the UN High Commissioner for Refugees, and come directly to Norway rather than drifting in through other states.

The Progress Party has not taken a firm stand either for or against eventual Norwegian adhesion to the European Community, and recognizes that its members are probably divided on the issue. It considers that there should be another referendum on the matter before any final decision is taken.

The Progress Party is a supporter of a strong Norwegian defence commitment within NATO, and calls for greater increases in Norwegian defence expenditure than other Norwegian parties.

Personalities

A considerable measure of the Progress Party's recent increase in popularity is due to the impact of its forceful chairman, Carl Hagen. He was born in 1944 and has a business background. He was secretary of the Anders Lange Party in 1973–74, and has been the chairman of the Progress Party since 1978. He represents Oslo in the *Storting*. The party's other member of Parliament is Hans J. Røsjorde, who represents Hordaland.

The Progress Party's first vice-chairman is Pål Atle Skjervengen, and the president of its national executive is Lodve Solholm.

Venstre
(Liberal Party)

Headquarters	: Møllergata 16, 0179 Oslo 1 (tel: 02–42 73 20)
Chairman	: Arne Fjørtoft
Secretary-general	: Knut-Erik Høyby
Youth organization	: *Unge Venstre*
Newspaper	: *Var Framtid*
Membership	: 13,000

History

Venstre (literally "the Left") is a party in the liberal tradition which was one of the first two parties to be founded in Norway, and which was uninterruptedly represented in Parliament for over 100 years from the 1880s until it lost its last seats in the 1985 election.

Venstre developed around and after 1870 in opposition to the dominant civil service establishment, which later was to regroup itself politically within *Høyre* (the Right). *Venstre* was supported by farmers as well as the emerging middle classes and urban intellectuals, and called for widespread political reforms, including an extension of the suffrage.

After fuller parliamentarism was introduced in 1884 *Venstre* became the largest Norwegian political party, and was in power for much of the period up to 1918 (e.g. Johan Sverdrup 1884–89, J. Steen 1889–93, 1898–1902, O. Blehr 1902–3 and Gunnar Knudsen 1908–10 and 1913–20). In the 1885 elections it obtained 63.4 per cent of the vote, and continued to win over 50 per cent of the vote in all elections from 1891 to 1900. From early on, however, it suffered from internal divisions.

In 1888 conservative members of *Venstre* departed to set up *Moderate Venstre*, which moved closer to *Høyre* and finally lost its separate identity after 1900. After 1905 *Venstre* changed its policy away from more traditional economic liberalism, and again lost a considerable number of members. While some joined *Høyre*, others subsequently established another Liberal Party. *Frisinnede Venstre* (National Liberals), which contested elections from 1909 to 1936 (after 1931 under the name *Frisinnede Folkeparti* or Liberal People's Party). In spite of these schisms *Venstre* continued to have an absolute majority in the *Storting* in all elections up to the end of World War I, although its percentage of the vote steadily declined.

By 1918 its vote was down to 28.3 per cent and in 1921 it was damaged further by the rise of a specifically Agrarian Party, which took away more of its support among farmers and helped to reduce it to only 20.1 per cent. By 1927 its vote was only 17.3 per cent, although it continued to play a governmental role. After Gunnar Knudsen's long premiership there were two other *Venstre* Prime Ministers, O. Blehr (1921–23) and Johan L. Mowinckel (1924–26, 1928–31, 1933–35). Its vote then stabilized until 1940 (with particular support from supporters of *Nynorsk*, and to a considerable extent from pro-temperance and religious groups) but by now it was clearly only the third party.

In 1945 its vote dropped further to 13.8 per cent, with the party losing new ground to the Christian People's Party. In the 1950s and 1960s its level of support remained around or under 10 per cent. It was in the opposition until 1963, when it provided three ministers in the short-lived four-party non-socialist coalition under John Lyng of *Høyre*. From 1965 to 1971 it participated (again with three ministers) in a new non-socialist coalition under Per Borten of the Centre Party.

The issue of Norway's EC membership led to a split within the party, with the majority of the party's parliamentarians in favour of adhesion, but a majority of the party against. The issue came to a head over the decision of anti-market forces within the party to join in the minority coalition government led by Lars Korvald of the Christian People's Party. The pro-marketeers then left *Venstre*, and on Dec. 9, 1972, established a new Liberal Party under the name *Det Nye Folkeparti* (the New People's Party). Its first leader was Helge Seip (a former *Venstre* minister) and it included nine of *Venstre*'s former total of 13 parliamentarians.

The 1973 national elections were disastrous for both Liberal parties. In 1969 *Venstre* had won 9.4 per cent of the vote and 13 seats. In 1973 *Venstre* only obtained 3.5 per cent of the vote and two seats and *Det Nye Folkeparti* 3.4 per cent and one seat. Neither party took part in any subsequent government.

In 1977, *Venstre* retained its two seats on 3.2 per cent of the vote, but *Det Nye Folkeparti* only won 1 per cent of the vote and lost its only seat. In 1980 it changed its name to *Det Liberale Folkepartiet* (DLF — The Liberal People's Party). In 1981 *Venstre* held on to its two seats, but the DLF's support fell to 0.5 per cent, and it did not regain a seat.

Before the 1985 election, *Venstre*, which had gradually put an increased emphasis on environmental issues, indicated that it was prepared to support a socialist government. *Venstre* then fought the 1985 election without any of its former electoral alliances with parties of the centre. It polled 3.1 per cent of the vote, but lost its seats in Parliament for the first time in his history. DLF support remained at only 0.5 per cent.

In 1986 the idea of reunification of the two Liberal parties was again mooted, and in the 1987 local elections there were some local electoral lists between the two parties. In 1988 merger talks were initiated on a serious basis, and the two parties were finally reunified in June 1988. Among the party posts given to former members of the DLF were one of the merged party's vice-chairmanships, and three places in its central executive.

Support

In the postwar years *Venstre* has not had the close links with organized interest groups such as those enjoyed by the Centre Party or the Christian People's Party. It has had a rather diverse support base, ranging from inter-class support in its areas of traditional strength in the South and West of the country, to more middle-class support elsewhere. It had a particular appeal to supporters of the new Norwegian language (*Nynorsk*).

In the past *Venstre* had its highest vote in the South and West of Norway, where it was still the largest party in some electoral districts in the 1940s (e.g. 37.2 per cent in Vest Agder and 31.1 per cent in Sogn og Fjordane in 1945). After the 1972 split, which led to a major loss of support for Norwegian liberalism, *Det Nye Folkeparti* outpolled *Venstre* in such areas of traditional strength as Vest Agder (8 per cent to 4.7 per cent), Hordaland (6.8 per cent to 3.9 per cent) and Rogaland (6.1 per cent to 3.3 per cent) in the 1973 elections. It was also ahead in urban areas like Akershus and Oslo. From Sogn og Fjordane northwards, however, *Venstre* was ahead.

By the 1985 elections, *Venstre* was ahead of its DLF rival throughout the country. *Venstre*'s highest 1985 votes were all in West and Central Norway (Møre og Ramsdal 5.4 per cent, Rogaland 5.2 per cent, Nord Trøndelag 5.0 per cent, Sogn og Fjordane 4.5 per cent, Hordaland 4.5 per cent). It was weakest in East Norway (e.g. Hedmark 1.3 per cent, Østfold 1.8 per cent). The DLF's highest support, on the other hand, was only 1 per cent in Hordaland, 0.9 per cent in Vest Agder and 0.8 per cent in Oslo.

It is currently uncertain how much support will be regained as a result of the recent reunification of the two Liberal Parties. *Venstre* now appears, however, to be attracting rather more urban-based members in Oslo and Akershus.

Organization

The merged party currently has around 13,000 members organised in 400 local branches. Above this it has an organizational structure in each of Norway's 19 counties. At national level there is a national assembly, which is held on an annual basis, and which elects the party leadership. *Venstre* has a national executive, on which all counties are represented, as well as the party's youth and women's organizations. It also includes the members of the smaller central executive. The party has a chairman, three vice-chairmen (the number was increased from two after the merger) and a secretary-general.

The party's youth organization *Unge Venstre* (Young *Venstre*) has around 3,500 members. The women's organization is called *Norges Venstre Kvinnelag* (Norwegian Women's League).

Venstre's newspaper is called *Var Framtid* ("Our Future"). It used to come out once a week, but now only once a month for financial reasons. It has a circulation of around 5,000. There are also local newspapers associated with *Venstre* with under 5 per cent of local paper circulation.

Both Norwegian Liberal Parties were members of the Liberal International, and the reunified party remains an active member.

Policies

Venstre is a liberal party in the centre of the Norwegian political spectrum. It prides itself on its independence from special interests. In recent years it has put a much greater emphasis on "Green" and environmental issues. It used to have a strong temperance and culturally conservative wing, but this is no longer important within the party, which is less traditional on these issues than the Centre and Christian People's Parties.

Differences between the two Liberal parties were no longer so sharp at the time of merger. One potential point of conflict, however, was over the EC, where *Venstre* remained opposed to Norwegian membership, whereas the DLF was in favour of Norway's joining. While the mainstream *Venstre* has not altered its stance of opposition, the reunified party has agreed to carry out a wide-ranging and open review of Norway's links with the EC, to be completed at the party congress in 1991.

On other issues *Venstre* calls for tax reform, with no change in overall tax levels, but with a shift in the burden from direct towards indirect taxes. It seeks more support for regional policy to ensure balanced regional development, and more jobs in the districts.

It also argues that there should also be new jobs created in the energy and environmental sectors and that Norway should develop a more modern industrial structure. *Venstre* now takes a more liberal line on social issues; on abortion, for example, it supports a woman's right to decide.

Venstre supports Norwegian membership of NATO.

Personalities

Venstre's chairman is Arne Fjørtoft, who was the chairman of *Venstre* before the merger. Of the three vice-chairmen Marit Bjorvatn is a former member of the DLF. She had succeeded Alice Ruud as chairman of the DLF shortly before the merger. The other two vice-chairmen of the reunified *Venstre* are Inger Takle and Hovard Alstadheim.

San Marino

Francis Jacobs

The country

San Marino is a microstate of 23 square miles, existing as an enclave between the Italian regions of Emilia–Romagna and the Marches. It is located on and around the slopes of Monte Titano, on whose summit is the city of San Marino. Besides the capital there are eight other communes or *castelli* (castles); Borgo Maggiore, Serravalle, Acquaviva, Chiesanuova, Domagnano, Faetano, Fiorentino and Montegiardino. San Marino has a resident population of around 22,000 and there are almost the same number resident abroad, mainly in Italy but also in France and elsewhere in Western Europe and North and South America. The electorate for the 1984 local elections was thus only 14,000 but well over 21,000 for the 1983 national elections. In 1988 300 voters came from the USA and 60 from Argentina.

Political institutions

San Marino is an independent and neutral state, but this is heavily circumscribed by its position as a tiny enclave very heavily dependent on surrounding Italy. It is neither within the European Community, nor is it a member of the UN, although it has been admitted, for example, into the International Telecommunications Union.

It still retains its medieval political institutions, although the old oligarchy gave way to a much more democratic regime from 1906 onwards. The legislative body or "parliament" is the Grand and General Council, consisting of 60 members elected by proportional representation every five years. The nominal heads of state are the two captains-regent, who are replaced every six months. They are assisted by two secretaries of state, one for foreign affairs and one for finance. The executive, or "congress of state" consists of the two captains-regent, the two secretaries of state and eight other ministers chosen from the parliament. In addition there is also a "council of 12" with certain administrative and judicial powers.

Women were only given the vote in 1958 and the right to stand for office in 1973. Referenda can be held. A highly controversial referendum was held in 1982 on the citizenship rights of San Marino women who married foreigners. There is also a measure of public financing for political parties. Local elections for the *Giunte di Castello* (Castle Juntas) are held every four years. In 1988 San Marino became a member of the Council of Europe.

Brief political history

1815	Congress of Vienna guarantees San Marino independence (interrupted for only two interludes of less than six months since the Middle Ages).
1862	Basic Treaty with Kingdom of Italy.
1906	*Arringo* public assembly of San Marino population which replaces the old oligarchy by a democratic regime.
1914–1918	San Marino neutral in World War I.
Inter-war years	San Marino comes under pro-Fascist regime.
1939–1945	San Marino again neutral (1943 Liberty Committee established as coalition between Communists, Socialists and other left-of-centre forces).
1945	Liberty Committee wins 66 per cent of vote in first postwar elections against rival right-of-centre Democratic Union (dominated by Christian Democrats).
1945–1951	Liberty Committee of Communists and Socialists rule San Marino (1949–51, *Kursaal* crisis with San Marino/Italian frontier being subjected to increasingly severe blockade by Italian government which is opposed to San Marino gaming house).
1951	Brief grand coalition including Christian Democrats. Resolves *Kursaal* crisis. Gaming house is closed, Liberty Committee is dissolved, new elections are held in which the Communists and Socialists are again victorious.
1951–57	Communist/Socialist coalition government.

1957   Communist/Socialist government loses its majority after defection of six members. For a month there is deadlock between a Communist/Socialist government in San Marino and a provisional Christian Democrat, Social Democrat and Independent Socialist government in Rovereta on the San Marino/Italian border. Provisional government comes to full power in October 1957 with Italian assistance.

1957–73   Coalition government between Christian Democrats and Independent San Marino Social Democratic party (1958 former Socialist and Communist leaders put on trial, 1966 government crisis over issue of postal votes, when Social Democrats vote with the left-wing opposition to abolish such votes).

1973–77   Coalition government between Christian Democrats and Socialist party of San Marino.

1978–86   Left-wing coalition government between Communists, Socialists and Socialist Unity Party, Christian Democrats in the opposition (1982 referendum on whether law preventing San Marino women who marry foreigners from retaining their citizenship should be repealed; 57 per cent vote to retain law).

1986– present   "Historic compromise" coalition government between Christian Democrats and Communists, two main Socialist parties in the opposition.

San Marino political system

For such a small country San Marino has a large number of political parties. The 1988 elections were contested by four major and two minor parties. The Christian Democrats are the largest party, followed by the Communists. The Socialists have been severely split, divided in the past between Socialists and Social Democrats, and now between three parties, the sizeable Socialist and Socialist Unity parties and the smaller Social Democrats. San Marino is now the testing ground for an unusual political experiment, a coalition between the Christian Democrat and Communist parties.

The main political issue in San Marino has been over the degree of its independence, and over its relations with Italy in particular. Italy has twice directly interfered in San Marino politics since the war, over a two-year period from 1949 to 1951 when the frontier was blocked over the

Kursaal crisis, and in 1957 when Italy intervened to assist the Christian Democrats and their allies to wrest power from the left. Among the main issues in San Marino politics are the following:

- San Marino and the UN; can it become a full member?
- Relations between San Marino and the European Community (the problems posed by San Marino being in the EC customs territory but not within the Community);
- San Marino radio and television network and how they will develop;
- The possible creation of a San Marino university;
- Possible reform of the San Marino citizenship laws.

Partito Democratico Cristiano Sammarinese
(San Marino Christian Democratic Party)

Headquarters	: Piazzetta Bramante Lazzari — 1 47031 Repubblica di San Marino (tel: 0541-991193/ 992694)
Secretary-general	: Pier Marino Menicucci (elected 1987)
Women's movement	: *Movimento Femminile*
Youth movement	: *Movimento Giovanile*
Newspaper	: *San Marino*
Founded	: April 1948

History

A Christian Democratic party, the *Partito Popolare Sammarinese* was founded in 1920 and won 29 out of 60 seats in its first national elections. In 1923 it went down to 20 seats and in 1926 to 12. For the rest of the inter-war years San Marino was dominated by Fascism.

The 1945 national elections were contested by a centre-right alliance called the Democratic Union, which lost to the rival left-wing Liberty Committee. In 1947 local Christian Democratic groups were founded, and on April 9, 1948 the San Marino Christian Democratic party was formally established. In 1949 the Christian Democrats contested the elections as part of the Democratic Union alliance, and Christian Democratic candidates won 14 out of the Union's 25 seats. The Christian Democrats continued in opposition, apart from a brief

San Marino election results 1945–88 (percentages and seats)

	1945	1949	1951	1955	1959	1964	1969	1974	1978	1983	1988
Comitato Della Libertà (Liberty Committee)	65.9% (40)	57.6% (35)	—	—	—	—	—	—	—	—	—
Unione Democratica (Democratic Union)	34.0% (20)	42.3% (25)	—	—	—	—	—	—	—	—	—
Democrazia Cristiana (Christian Democrats)	—	—	43.0% (26)	38.2% (23)	44.2% (27)	46.8% (29)	44.0% (27)	39.6% (25)	42.3% (26)	42.0% (26)	44.1% (27)
Partito Comunista Sammarinese (Communists)	—	—	29.2% (18)	31.5% (19)	25.9% (16)	24.1% (14)	22.7% (14)	23.6% (15)	25.1% (16)	24.3% (15)	28.8% (18)
Partito Socialista Sammarinese (Socialists)	—	—	22.1% (13)	25.5% (16)	13.8% (8)	10.6% (6)	11.9% (7)	13.9% (8)	13.7% (8)	14.8% (9)	11.1% (7)
Partito Socialista Democratico Sammarinese (Social Democrats)	—	—	—	4.6% (2)	—	—	—	—	4.1% (2)	2.9% (1)	1.1% (0)
Partito Socialista Dem Indep. Sammarinese (Independent Social Democrats)	—	—	—	—	15.9% (9)	16.1% (10)	17.9% (11)	15.4% (9)	—	—	—
Partito Socialista Unitario (Unitary Socialist Party)	—	—	—	—	—	—	—	—	11.1% (7)	13.8% (8)	13.6% (8)
Others	—	—	5.5% (3)	—	—	2.2% (1)	3.3% (1)	7.2% (3)	3.4% (1)	1.9% (1)	1.4% (0)

period in the summer of 1951 in which they took part in a broad coalition government during the crisis with Italy over the San Marino gaming house. Later in 1951 the Christian Democrats took part in elections under their own name — and emerged as the largest single party, although remaining in opposition.

In September 1957 the 23 Christian Democrats and two Social Democrats were joined by five dissident socialists and later by one Independent who had been elected on the Communist list to overturn the long-standing left-wing majority in San Marino. The left-wing government refused to budge, and for a while there were two governments in San Marino, with the Christian Democrats leading a provisional government from a village on the Italy-San Marino border, which was recognized by a number of states, including Italy and the USA. In October 1957 a Christian Democrat-dominated coalition government came to power with Italian assistance.

The Christian Democrats were in power from 1957 to 1978, until 1973 in coalition with the Independent Social Democrats (surviving a serious government crisis in 1966) and from 1973 to 1978 with the Socialists.

The Christian Democrats were in opposition from 1978 to 1986, but in 1986 returned to power with one captain-regent and five of the 10 ministers in a "historic compromise" coalition with the Communist Party.

In May 1988 the Christian Democratic vote rose by almost 2 per cent to 44.1 per cent and the party won 27 of the 60 seats in the Parliament. The Christian Democratic Party also rules five of San Marino's nine communes.

Support

Since it first started contesting elections under its own name the Christian Democratic Party has been by far the largest single political party in San Marino, with its vote never going below 38.2 per cent (1955) and rising to 46.8 per cent (1964). Its share of the 60 seats has varied between 23 and 29. It has thus never won an overall majority on its own. Its 1988 result of 44 per cent was its best since 1964. It has not shared the voting decline of its Italian sister party.

In local elections the Christian Democratic Party is the largest party in all but one commune (Fiorentino, where it only won 24.47 per cent in the 1984 local elections) and it has an absolute majority in three communes (Borgo Maggiore, Domagnano and Chiesanuova). In 1984 its highest local vote was in Chiesanuova (56.88 per cent). In San Marino city its vote was 47.31 per cent.

Organization

The party is organized into 14 sections, each with an assembly, executive and secretary. The party's general congress meets every three years, with the sections represented proportional to their membership. The congress elects the party's central council (currently 46 elected members), which meets every four months and in its turn elects its own president, the party's general executive (nine elected members who meet at least once a month) and the party's general secretary.

The party's parliamentary contingent meets in a council group, which elects its own president.

The party has a women's movement, consisting of local women's groups, an assembly and a 15 person executive. It is led by a central delegate. The youth movement for 14- to 27-year-olds has local sections, an assembly and a 16-person executive. It is also chaired by a central delegate. Both movements have autonomous status.

The party's newspaper is called *San Marino*. Since 1955 the party has been a member of the European Union of Christian Democrats.

Policies

In 1986 the party made the historic decision to go into a coalition with the Communists, an experiment which has been watched with interest in neighbouring Italy. The Christian Democrats have advocated a modernization of San Marino's institutional structure, and diversification of its economy. In 1984 they opposed the introduction of income tax.

In economic policy they oppose both Marxist collectivism and capitalism without a social dimension. They advocate greater individual responsibility and less bureaucracy.

Family policy is strongly emphasized.

The party has called for a more active presence of San Marino in international organizations — and for intensified co-operation with the UN and EC.

Personalities

The party's current secretary-general is Pier Marino Menucucci, elected at its 11th congress in November 1987. The president of its central council is Rosalino Martelli.

San Marino's Foreign Minister is Gabriele Gatti, who is a previous party secretary-general and who helped to engineer the historic compromise with the Communists. San Marino's Finance Minister is Clara Boscaglia, the first woman ever to have government responsibilities in San Marino. Gatti and Boscaglia won the most votes in the party's elections for its central council at the 1987 congress.

Partito Comunista Sammarinese
(San Marino Communist Party)

Headquarters	: Via Sentier Rosso 1, Citta 47031, Republica di San Marino (tel: 0541-991199/ 992375)
Secretary-general	: Gilberto Ghiotti
Membership	: 1,100
Youth organization	: *Federazione Giovanile Comunista Sammarinese*
Newspaper	: *La Scintilla*
Founded	: July 1941

History

A Communist branch was first founded in 1921. In its present form the San Marino Communist party dates from July 1941. In 1945 it won power as part of a Popular Front with the Socialists, called the Liberty Committee, which won 65.9 per cent of the vote and 40 of the 60 seats in the Parliament.

The Communist Party remained in power with the Socialists (apart from the summer of 1951 when it participated in a grand "crisis" coalition including the Christian Democrats) until 1957. From 1951 onwards it took part in elections in its own right rather than as part of a Popular Front. In September 1957 the left-wing coalition lost its majority but tried to hold on to power. In October 1957 it was finally removed with Italian assistance, and the Communist Party went into opposition, where it remained until 1978.

In 1978 it again entered government in a coalition with the two socialist parties. The Communists held four ministries. In 1986 it entered into a "historic compromise", whereby it shared power with the Christian Democrats for the first time. The Communists won five ministries (Interior, Posts and Transports, Tourism and Commerce, Industry, and Education). One of the two captains-regent was also a Communist.

In 1988 the Communists were rewarded for their coalition with the Christian Democrats by becoming the biggest single winners of the national elections, rising from 24.3 per cent to 28.8 per cent of the vote and from 15 to 18 seats in the Parliament. The Communists also provide the mayors in two of San Marino's nine communes.

Support

Ever since they contested elections in their own right rather than as part of a Popular Front, the Communists have been the second largest party in San Marino. Their best-ever result was in 1955 when they won 31.5 per cent of the vote and 19 seats. They then declined to 22.7 per cent and 14 seats by 1969, but they have again risen to their present figure of 28.8 per cent (18 seats), their second best-ever percentage.

In local elections the Communists' strongest commune is Fiorentino, where they won almost 36 per cent of the vote in the 1984 local elections and were easily the largest party. Everywhere else they are the second party to the Christian Democrats (in 1984 they were particularly strong in Serravalle (27 per cent) and Acquaviva (26 per cent) apart from Montegiardino where they are behind the Socialist party as well and in Domagnano where they are also behind the Socialist Unity party. Domagnano is their weakest commune (under 16 per cent in 1984) and they are also relatively weak in San Marino city (18 per cent in 1984).

Organization

The Communist Party has 1,100 members. The lowest organizational tier is the "cell" which must have a minimum of five members and can be organized on a territorial or workplace basis or else on the basis of a cultural or other association. There are 17 such cells within San Marino. Above these there are six sections, generally organized within individual communes. The party's general congress meets every four years, and consists of delegates from the sections. The central committee meets every two months, and consists of 37 members, of whom 35 are elected by the general congress. The congress also elects a control committee (currently with seven members), which deals with the internal workings of the party, including disciplinary actions. The party executive (currently with 12 members) and its secretary-general are elected by the central committee and the control committee meeting in joint session. A party president can also be elected.

The Communists within the Parliament meet in a Communist Council Group which elects its own president. Party conferences are periodically held between congresses to discuss organization or policy matters. The party's youth group is called the *Federazione Giovanile Comunista Sammarinese*. The party also has close links with the *Confederazione Sammarinese del Lavaro* (the San Marino Confederation of Labour), the secretary-general and president of which are members of the central committee.

The Communist Party is still governed by the principle of democratic centralism, with a strong emphasis on party unity and discipline. The formation of party sub-groups is not allowed. The list of party candidates is ratified by the central committee and control committee meeting in joint sitting.

The party newspaper is called *La Scintilla*, of which 10,000 copies are published monthly.

Policies

The San Marino Communist Party has been a party of government for longer than any other Western European communist party, having shared power for exactly half of the postwar years. In character it is not dissimilar to the Italian Communist Party, recognizing that there are many different routes to socialism and fully accepting a democratic pluralistic system of government. It has been open to dialogue with progressive Catholics, and since 1986 has been in coalition with the Christian Democrats. Like the Italian Communists it is trying to forge stronger links with the new social movements, such as the women's and ecological movements.

In economic policy it recognizes the value of the free market, but criticizes the excesses of consumerism. It supports economic planning, greater attention to ecological matters, shorter working hours and enhanced worker participation.

In the 1982 referendum the Communist Party supported the rights of women to retain their citizenship when they married foreigners.

In foreign affairs the Communists support San Marino neutrality, and seek a greater integration of San Marino into the international community, including full entry into the UN.

Personalities

The party's secretary is Gilberto Ghiotti, and its honorary president is Gildo Gasperoni. Giuseppe Renzi is the president of the central committee, and Umberto Barulli the president of the parliamentary ("Conciliar") group. A prominent figure among the five Communist ministers in the current San Marino government is Alvaro Selva, who is the Internal Affairs Minister and one of the architects of the historic compromise with the Christian Democrats.

Partito Socialista Sammarinese
(San Marino Socialist Party)

Headquarters	:	Via Gino Giacomini, 47031 Republica di San Marino (tel: 0541-991184)
President	:	Remy Giacomini
Secretary-general	:	Antonio Volpinari
Youth organization	:	*Movimento Giovanile Socialista*
Women's organization	:	*Movimento Femminile*
Newspaper	:	*Il Nuovo Titano*
Founded	:	1892

History

The San Marino Socialist Party was founded in 1892. One of its first great battles was to fight for the establishment of democratic rights, which were introduced in 1906. The two major figures in San Marino Socialism were Pietro Franciosi, and above all Gino Giacomini (1878–1962).

After the period of Fascist rule the reconstituted Socialist Party took part in the Liberty Committee, which won the 1945 elections. From 1945 to 1957 the party was in power in a coalition government with the Communists (apart from the summer of 1951 when there was a broader-based government). In 1957 the government collapsed when five dissident Socialists and one Communist left their parliamentary parties and allied with the small Social Democratic party and with the Christian Democrats. The remaining Socialists and Communists refused to surrender power, but were eventually forced to back down. Later, some prominent Socialists, including their historic leader Gino Giacomini, were brought to trial for their role in the events of 1957.

The Socialist Party never recovered its former strength after the Social Democratic schism of 1957 and it remained in opposition until 1973 when it returned to power in a coalition with the Christian Democrats. The new coalition fell in late 1977 over the issue of Communist participation in the government, which was advocated by the Socialists. After the 1978 elections a new left-wing coalition was formed in which the Socialists took part in government with the Communists and with the Socialist Unity party.

In 1986 there was another internal schism and the party was again forced to go into opposition when the Communist Party formed a new coalition with the Christian Democrats. In 1987 the Socialist Party initiated attempts at reunification with the small San Marino Social Democratic Party. In the 1988 elections the Socialist Party fell sharply in support from 14.8 per cent in 1983 to only 11.1 per cent and lost two of its seats in the parliament. It now has seven seats.

Support

In the 1950s the Socialist Party was in a respectable third place among San Marino political parties behind the Christian Democrats and Communists, with 22.1 per cent in 1951 (13 seats) and 25.5 per cent (16 seats) in 1955. Since the events of 1957 its vote has fluctuated between the much lower levels of 10.6 per cent (1964) and 14.8 per cent (1983) and on several occasions it has only been in fourth place, as in 1988, its second worst result since the war.

In the 1984 local elections it won 14.67 per cent. Its strongest commune was Montegiardino, where it won 27.1 per cent and was the second largest party. It also polled well in Faetano (21.8 per cent) and Fiorentino (20 per cent). Its lowest vote was in the city of San Marino itself, where it only polled 10.3 per cent and was much weaker than the rival Socialist Unity party.

Organization

The local territorial units of the party are its sections, of which there are 10 around San Marino.

At national level the party congress is held every three years, and consists of delegates from the different sections in proportion to their membership. The congress elects the 35 member central committee, which meets every month and which, in its turn, elects the 15-member party executive, the party president (who presides at the meetings of the central committee) and the party's secretary-general (who presides at the meetings of the executive, and who cannot be a member of the San Marino government or chair the Socialist parliamentary group). The central committee also ratifies lists of candidates for parliament.

Besides the secretary-general there are also three deputy secretaries (two elected and one nominated), who are chosen by the party executive. The Socialist Conciliar or parliamentary group nominates its own group leader.

The party's youth movement is called the *Movimento Giovanile Socialista* and is open to all 14–30-year-olds. The women's group is called the *Movimento Femminile*. The party's newspaper is called *Il Nuovo Titano* and is the successor of the original Socialist paper *Il Titano*, which was founded in 1903.

Policies

The Socialist Party is currently in the opposition, and is particularly bitter at the role played by the Communist Party in breaking up the previous left-wing coalition and allying itself with the Christian Democrats. As part of an effort of party modernization the party recently (1987) changed its symbol by dropping the hammer and sickle and introducing a red carnation and two oak leaves against the background of the three peaks of San Marino.

The Socialist Party is proud of its role in helping to construct San Marino's social security system, and it seeks to consolidate this by making it more efficient and productive. It advocates economic planning, but on an indicative and not imposed basis. In the 1982 referendum it supported the rights of San Marino women to retain their citizenship in cases where they married foreigners.

The Socialists seek institutional reform within San Marino, through abolishing the anachronistic Council of 12, and providing for a clearer separation of the roles of parliament and of the government. They also seek codification of civil rights.

The Socialists wish to extend San Marino's international role.

Personalities

The party's secretary-general is Antonio Volpinari, a former San Marino minister of public works. The party's president is Remy Giacomini, who was party secretary-general for over 20 years and was also the first San Marino ambassador in Rome. The two elected deputy secretaries are Alberto Cecchetti and Marino Zanotti.

A prominent party figure is Giordano Bruno Reffi, another former secretary-general who used to be the San Marino Foreign Minister.

Partito Socialista Unitario
(Socialist Unity Party)

Headquarters	: Via della Tana 117, Republica de San Marino (tel: 0541-991210)
President	: Emilio Della Balda
Secretary-general	: Patrizia Busignani
Newspaper	: *Riscossa Socialista*
Founded	: December 1975

History

In the 1955 national elections a new San Marino Social Democratic Party won 4.6 per cent of the vote and two seats. In 1957 five Socialist Members of Parliament left their party and created an Independent Socialist Party of San Marino. They joined up with the two Social Democrats and the Christian Democrats to form a provisional government existing in parallel with the existing Socialist/Communist government. After a month of stalemate the provisional government came to full power with Italian help in October 1957. In January 1958 the Independent Socialists and the Social Democrats merged to form a new party, the Independent Social Democratic Party of San Marino (PSDIS). The new party was recognized as an observer by the Socialist International in 1958 and as a full member in 1969. Their most prominent personalities were Dr Alvaro Casali, and his successor as secretary, Dr Emilio Della Balda.

The PSDIS remained in a coalition government with the Christian Democrats until 1973 in spite of a crisis in 1966 when it voted with the other left-wing parties over the issue of abolishing postal votes. In 1973, however, they went into opposition, being replaced by the Socialist Party as the Christian Democrats' coalition partner.

In opposition the PSDIS began to reassess its position with regard to the other parties of the left, and in particular toward the Communist Party. This opening up to the Communists was contested by the Social Democratic right within the party, and in late 1979 there was a split within the PSDIS. The majority confirmed the opening to the left, and decided to change the name of the party to the Socialist Unity Party. The minority left to form a new Social Democratic Party.

In the 1978 elections the Socialist Unity Party (PSU) won 11 per cent of the vote, and seven seats, whereas the Social Democrats only gained 4.1 per cent and two seats. The PSU then entered government in a left-wing coalition with the Communists and the Socialists, which lasted until 1986. In the latter year the PSU went back into opposition. In the 1988 elections the PSU maintained its vote far better than the Socialist Party, only losing 0.2 per cent of its vote (from 13.8 per cent to 13.6 per cent) and retaining eight seats in the parliament.

Support

In the three elections it has contested the PSU has had a lower vote than the old PSDIS, but in the 1988 elections it, nevertheless, established itself as the larger of the two San Marino Socialist parties, and as the third party of San Marino. In the 1984 local elections it polled 14.57 per cent, with its highest vote in the left-wing stronghold of Fiorentino (19.7 per cent). It was much stronger than the Socialist Party in the city of San Marino, where it won 17 per cent of the vote. It was weakest in Chiesanuova (7.4 per cent) and in Faetano (6.85 per cent).

Organization

The basic territorial units of the party are the sections. Where there is more than one such section within a commune a co-ordinating committee can be established (a *Comitato di Castello*). The party's general congress is held every three or four years. The congress elects the 35-person central committee, which meets at least every two months, and elects the party president and the 12 person party executive. The executive meets twice a month and nominates the party secretary and one or two deputy secretaries. The post of secretary is incompatible with holding a position in the government. Each member of the executive apart from the president and the secretary is responsible for a specific organizational or policy sector, such as liaison with the communes or economic policy. Besides the party congresses there are also members' consultative assemblies at least every six months.

Candidates for national elections are chosen by the assemblies of the sections in liaison with the party executive, which can reserve to itself the nomination of one-sixth of the candidates. There used to be both women's and youth sections of the party but the former were abolished in 1979 and the latter in 1983, on the grounds that it was better if they were fully integrated into the party. The party has established a study centre (*Centro Studio*). The party newspaper is called *Riscossa Socialista*. The PSU is a member of the Socialist International.

Policies

The PSU sees itself as a libertarian socialist party, putting its emphasis on decentralized decision-making and on greater citizens' participation in economic and political life. The PSU opposes rigid ideologies and is critical both of old style capitalism and of bureaucratic communism. It supports the market economy and calls for more labour flexibility and greater reliance on small and medium-sized enterprises, but considers that the public authorities have an important corrective role to play, in particular through an extended system of forward planning. Environmental planning should be given a high emphasis.

As regards institutional reform the San Marino Parliament needs to be strengthened so that it can have better control over the government. The powers of the captain-regents and of the Council of 12 need to be redefined. The powers of the local communes should be reinforced. The problems posed by San Marino citizenship should again be tackled. The PSU defends a policy of "active" neutrality for San

Marino. It should enjoy all the attributes of a sovereign state (including full recognition of all its trademarks and patents) and should become a full member of the UN.

Personalities

The PSU secretary-general is the young Patrizia Busignani who was first elected in 1983. The party's president is Emilio Della Balda, who is a former secretary-general of the party and a former San Marino Finance Minister.

Partito Socialista Democratico Sammarinese
(San Marino Social Democratic Party)

When the Social Democratic right within the Independent Social Democratic Party (PSDIS) refused to accept the party's opening to the Communists in 1975 (see entry on Socialist Unity Party) they went off to form a new party, including three of the nine PSDIS members of parliament. The 1978 elections were contested under the name *Democrazia Socialista*. The party won 4.1 per cent of the vote and two seats and went into opposition against the new left-wing coalition government. In the 1980s they briefly gave support to the government, but were later divided over whether to support to oppose it. The 1983 elections were contested under the new name *Partito Socialista Democratico Sammarinese* (San Marino Social Democratic Party). The party's vote dropped to 2.9 per cent and they only retained one seat, that of Simone Rossini.

In the next legislature, in which they were in opposition, they reopened dialogue with the San Marino Socialist Party. In the 1988 elections what was left of the party only won 1.1 per cent of the vote and its last parliamentary seat was lost.

Partito Repubblicano Sammarinese
(San Marino Republican Party)

Parties with links to the Italian Republican Party, which is strong in the region of Italy adjacent to San Marino, have had a limited success in San Marino. From 1964 to 1974 a *Movimento per le Liberta Statuarie* (Movement for Statutory Liberties) gained one seat in the parliament in three successive elections. In 1983 a party called *Intesa Democratica — Partito Repubblicano* won 1.9 per cent of the vote and one seat in the parliament. Fighting under the title "Republican Party" in 1988 it only gained 1.4 per cent of the vote and lost its only seat.

Sweden

Doosie Foldal

The Kingdom of Sweden (*Konungariket Sverige*) has a land area of 170,250 square miles, with a population of over 8,450,000. 91.5 per cent of these are native Swedes. Half of the immigrants are Finns (there were 200,000 in 1986), and of the others a high percentage are Yugoslavs, Greeks and Turks. In Stockholm 10 per cent of the inhabitants are of non-Swedish origin.

The native language is Swedish, although there is a small minority of around 15,000 Lapps (*Same*), who live in Sweden's northernmost province (*Norrbotten*) and speak their own language.

Sweden's state religion is Lutheranism.

The capital city is Stockholm. Over 83 per cent of the total Swedish population lives in urbanized areas (1976).

Political institutions

Sweden is a constitutional monarchy under King Carl XVI Gustaf. The King's functions are of a ceremonial and representative nature only. The Act of Succession was amended in 1979 to ensure that the firstborn royal child would accede to the throne, irrespective of gender.

Sweden's unicameral Parliament, the *Riksdag*, has 349 members (the number was lowered in 1975 from 350 after a series of tied votes in the Parliament which had to be resolved by lottery). Parliament has a three-year term of office (with voting day always falling on the third Sunday of September).

Members are elected by the St Lague method of proportional representation. There are 310 members directly elected in 28 multi-member constituencies, which mainly correspond to the 24 provinces, with just a few exceptions: Stockholm and Göteborg are constituencies in their own right, the densely populated area of Lund, Landskrona, Malmö and Helsingborg (*Fyrstadskretsen*) has been separated from the surrounding province, and the province of Älvsborg has been divided into a northern and a southern constituency.

The number of members per constituency (which depends on their number of eligible voters) ranges from two (*Gotland*) up to 36 (Stockholms *Län*) Each constituency is divided into several election districts (with from 10 up to several thousand voters). There are 6,500 such districts in Sweden.

Besides the 310 seats, there are 39 supplementary seats which are distributed between the parties to ensure greater proportionality of the final result. For this purpose the whole country is treated as one constituency. To be eligible for this further distribution of seats, a party must have overcome the four per cent national minimum vote threshold necessary for representation in the *Riksdag*. A party may also win a seat if it has won 12 per cent of the vote in an individual constituency.

Voters not only have the option of voting for party lists, but also of expressing personal preferences within them by crossing out candidates' names or adding new ones. Even totally new lists can be created. The current workings of this system are now being reconsidered by a special committee.

There were 6,329,533 eligible voters in the 1988 elections. This figure not only includes Swedes living abroad, but also immigrants from other Nordic countries. Swedish voters are also given the means of registering their dissatisfaction by casting a blank vote. In 1988 100,000 did so. Voters may also vote by post, an option used by nearly two million voters in 1988. A special election tradition is "little election Sunday", a week before the normal election, in which hospitals, old people's homes and prisons all participate. Forty-two thousand people cast their vote in this fashion in 1988.

The members of the *Riksdag* are not seated in the chamber in their parliamentary groups, but according to the constituencies that they represent, and in an order based on their length of service. The *Riksdag* elects a speaker and three deputy speakers on the basis of an agreement between the parties.

There are 16 parliamentary committees. To be represented on all of these, a parliamentary group must have at least 21 members.

The *Riksdag* has the primary legislative power. However, changes in Sweden's organic laws, (its Constitution, the Law of the Succession to the Throne and the Law on Freedom

Map of Sweden showing 28 multi-member constituencies and number of seats in each constituency.

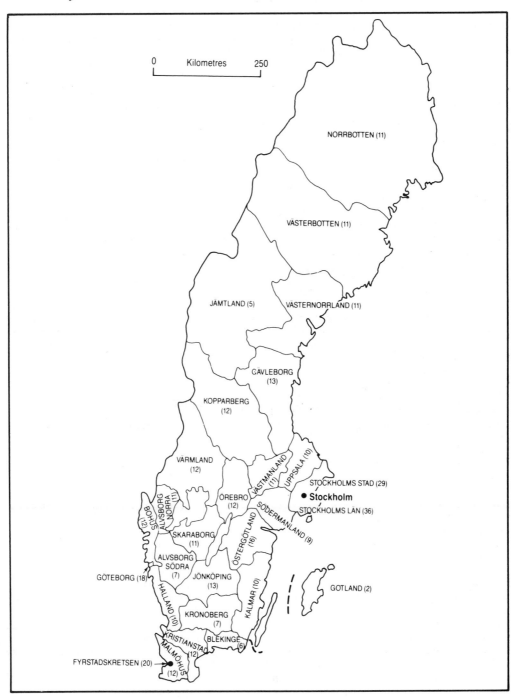

0 Kilometres 250

NORRBOTTEN (11)

VÄSTERBOTTEN (11)

JÄMTLAND (5)

VÄSTERNORRLAND (11)

GÄVLEBORG (13)

KOPPARBERG (12)

VÄRMLAND (12)

VÄSTMANLAND (11)

UPPSALA (10)

STOCKHOLMS STAD (29)

● **Stockholm**

ÖREBRO (12)

STOCKHOLMS LÄN (36)

ÄLVSBORG NORRA (11)

BOHUS (12)

SKARABORG (11)

ÖSTERGÖTLAND (16)

SÖDERMANLAND (9)

ÄLVSBORG SÖDRA (7)

GÖTEBORG (18)

JÖNKÖPING (13)

KALMAR (10)

GOTLAND (2)

HALLAND (10)

KRONOBERG (7)

KRISTIANSTAD (12)

BLEKINGE (6)

FYRSTADSKRETSEN (20)

MALMÖHUS (12)

Source: adapted from *World Atlas of Elections*.

of the Press) may only be adopted if passed by two successive Parliaments after an intervening election.

The Swedish government (*Regering*), led by the Prime Minister (*Statsminister*), is accountable to the *Riksdag*. The speaker nominates a candidate for the post of *Statsminister* and this is approved if not more than half of the total membership of the *Riksdag* vote against. Minority governments are thus possible (as in the case of the Liberal minority government of Ola Ullsten in 1978).

A government may also be brought down by a vote of no confidence requested by 10 per cent of the *Riksdag* and supported by over half of its membership. Individual ministers may be dismissed by the *Statsminister* or as the result of a censure vote by the *Riksdag*, adopted by a majority of its members.

Members of the government must give up their seats in the *Riksdag* for the duration of their term of office, and are replaced during this time by their substitute. A minister may, however, speak in the *Riksdag*.

The Supreme Court (*Högsta Domstolen*) is given the task of examining whether *Regerings* and *Riksdag* legislation can be enforced or whether it is in breach of the Constitution.

Sweden is divided into 24 provinces (*Län*), in which the national government is represented by a *Landshövding* (governor), normally a former politician appointed for a six-year term. The administration of the *Län* is taken care of by the *Länsstyrelsen* (provincial executive). The provincial assembly (*Landsting*) is elected every three years on the same day as the national elections.

Below these are the local councils, which cover the territory of the municipalities (*Kommun*), of which there are 284. Municipal elections also take place on the same day every three years. Since 1976 all foreign citizens who have been in Sweden for at least three years have been entitled to vote in local elections. Foreigners comprised 5 per cent of the voters at the local elections in 1988.

In recent years local government has had increased responsibilities as a result of devolution of central government tasks. Local government finance is ensured by both local income tax and transfers from central government.

There are provisions for referenda within the Swedish political system. In 1922 there was one on prohibition (the introduction of which was narrowly rejected), in 1955 one on switching from the left to the right side of the road (massively rejected), in 1957 one on pensions systems (which was approved) and in 1980 one on the future of nuclear reactors (whose

continuation was approved). The referenda are consultative only. Parliament subsequently introduced driving on the right, for example, in spite of the result of the referendum.

Sweden has an extensive system of state subsidies to political parties. This is mainly linked to a party's number of representatives in the *Riksdag*, with a grant paid at the rate of 239,000 Swedish Kroner (about US$40,000) per seat per annum. There is also a certain contribution to any party which passes a 2.5 per cent national threshold at one of the last two elections. There is also a secretarial grant (at a higher rate to opposition parties than to parties in government). The parties represented in the *Riksdag* received a total of 110.5 million Swedish Kroner in 1987.

State support is also provided to the political youth organizations. Town councils and provinces may also give economic support to parties represented in these bodies, with the size of the grant varying from council to council. Town council support is estimated to be at a level of around 230 million Swedish Kroner in the country as a whole.

Sweden is a member of the Nordic Union and of EFTA, but is not a member of any defence alliance. After its neutrality in World War I and World War II this has become an integral part of Sweden's foreign policy.

Brief political history

1809	New Swedish Constitution (shared legislative power between King and *Riksdag*).
1814	The Swedish-Norwegian union begins with Carl XIII as joint King.
1840s	A period of liberal reform begins.
1866	The *Riksdag* is reformed. A two chamber system is introduced with direct elections to the second chamber. Limited electorate. Free trade and social liberalism. Industrialization.
1901	General military service for men after a long debate on defence policy.
1905	The union with Norway is dissolved.
1909	*Riksdag* reform. Almost universal voting rights for men. Proportional representation.
1911	Social Democrats make a major impact on elections.
1914	Political crisis after King Gustaf V expresses his disapproval of the government's defence policy. Sweden declares its neutrality in World War I.

1917	Principle of government responsibility to the *Riksdag* is fully established.
1921	Universal suffrage for men and women. Sweden tries to gain sovereignty over the Åland islands. The League of Nations turns down this request.
1920s	Period of rapidly changing governments.
1932	Beginning of 44-year period with Social Democrats constantly in government (only three months' break in 1936), either on their own or in coalition. The Swedish welfare society gradually emerges.
1938	*Saltsjöbaden* agreement for "Labour peace" between trade unions and employers.
1939	Sweden declares its neutrality in World War II, but is forced to give major concessions to Germany after Germany has invaded Norway.
1949	Sweden reasserts its neutrality after breakdown of defence negotiations with Norway and Denmark.
1959	Introduction of a national pension plan after intense period of political controversy.
1971	Introduction of a unicameral *Riksdag*.
1973	The international oil crisis leads to Sweden's first major economic depression with high unemployment.
1974	New Swedish Constitution.
1976	The first non-socialist government since 1932 (coalition between Centre, Moderate Unity and People's parties).
1978–79	The government falls on nuclear energy issue. New non-socialist government.
1980	The economic crisis leads to major strikes and lockouts.
1982	Socialists return to government in the first of three consecutive minority Social Democratic governments supported by the Communists.
1984	Major protest against the introduction of asset formation funds.
1986	Prime Minister Palme is assassinated. Ingvar Carlsson becomes new Prime Minister.

Features of the Swedish political system

The most striking feature of the Swedish political system is its stability. The basic shape of the party system has hardly changed since the 1920s and 1930s, and until 1988 there were only five parties consistently represented in the *Riksdag*. There has been one dominant Social Democratic Party (in government for all but six of the last 57 years, and which has lost less support than its sister parties elsewhere in Scandinavia), one small left Communist party and three non-socialist parties of the Centre and Right, whose respective strengths have fluctuated (sometimes very markedly), but often at each other's expense rather than at that of the Left. However, there has been relatively little switching of votes between the left and right blocks.

Moreover, Sweden has not experienced the sort of upheaval elections such as those seen in Norway and Denmark in the early 1970s, nor has there developed a populist protest party on the lines of the Progress parties in Denmark or Norway, or the Rural Party in Finland. Until the rise of the Ecology Party at least, Swedish protest has tended to be expressed through already existing parties.

There are a number of reasons for this stability. A first one is the absence of many sharp cleavages. There have been no significant ethnic, religious or cultural differences (the small Christian Democratic Party which has developed on religious and cultural grounds has never won more than 3 per cent of the vote). Centre-periphery and urban-rural divisions, while helping to explain differences in party political support, are not as sharp as they have been in other Scandinavian countries, such as Norway and Finland. The main divisions, therefore, have been on class and economic lines.

A second reason is an electoral system, which has been extremely harsh on small parties, notably through the 4 per cent electoral threshold.

A more general explanation for stability has been the Swedish preference for consensus solutions, pragmatism and moderation, combined with considerable respect for authority and dislike of extremism of any type. Co-operation between unions and employers has been a strong feature, notably since the *Saltsjöbaden* "Labour peace" agreement of 1938. There has also been widespread consensus on certain public policy objectives, the need for a welfare state (combined with high levels of taxation, but only with a low degree of nationalization), neutrality in foreign policy and so on. The style of decision-making has also reinforced this. Special committees, for example, may spend up to two or three years consulting widely on an issue, before a formal bill on the matter is tabled in the *Riksdag*.

For a long time there were relatively few

Swedish election results, 1944–present (percentage of vote and seats won)

	1944	1948	1952	1956	1958	1960	1964	1968	1970	1973	1976	1979	1982	1985	1988
Turnout (total votes)	71.9%	82.7%	79.1%	79.6%	77.4%	85.9%	83.9%	89.3%	88.3%	90.8%	91.8%	90.7%	91.4%	89.9%	83.3%
Sveriges Socialdemokratiska Arbetareparti (SAP) (Swedish Social Democratic Labour Party)	46.5% (115)	46.1% (112)	46.0% (110)	44.6% (106)	46.2% (111)	47.8% (114)	47.3% (113)	50.1% (125)	45.3% (163)	43.6% (156)	42.7% (152)	43.2% (154)	45.6% (166)	44.7% (159)	43.6% (156)
Vansterpartiet Kommunisterna (VPK) (Left Party—Communists)	10.3% (15)	6.3% (8)	4.3% (5)	5.0% (6)	3.4% (5)	4.5% (5)	5.2% (8)	3.0% (3)	4.8% (17)	5.3% (19)	4.8% (17)	5.6% (20)	5.6% (20)	5.4% (19)	5.9% (21)
Moderata Samlingspartiet (Moderate Party)	15.8% (39)	12.3% (23)	14.4% (31)	17.1% (42)	19.5% (45)	16.6% (39)	13.7% (32)	12.9% (29)	11.5% (41)	14.3% (51)	15.6% (55)	20.3% (73)	23.6% (86)	21.3% (76)	18.3% (66)
Folkpartiet (Liberal Party)	12.9% (26)	22.7% (57)	24.4% (58)	23.8% (58)	18.2% (38)	17.5% (40)	17.0% (42)	14.3% (32)	16.2% (58)	9.4% (34)	11.1% (39)	10.6% (38)	5.9% (21)	14.2% (51)	12.2% (44)
Centerpartiet (Centre Party)	13.6% (35)	12.4% (30)	10.7% (26)	9.5% (19)	12.7% (32)	13.6% (34)	13.2% (33)	15.7% (37)	19.9% (71)	25.1% (90)	24.1% (86)	18.1% (64)	15.5% (56)	9.9% (43)	11.4% (42)
Kristdemokratiska Samhällspartiet (KdS) (Christian Democratic Community Party)	—	—	—	—	—	—	1.8% (0)	1.5% (0)	1.8% (0)	1.8% (0)	1.4% (0)	1.4% (0)	1.9% (0)	(2.5%) (1)	3.0% (0)
Miljöpartiet de Gröna (Green Ecology Party)	—	—	—	—	—	—	—	—	—	—	—	—	1.7% (0)	1.5% (0)	5.5% (20)
Others	0.7% (0)	0.1% (0)	0.1% (0)	0.0% (0)	0.1% (0)	0.0% (0)	1.8% (5)	2.6% (7)	0.4% (0)	0.6% (0)	0.4% (0)	0.8% (0)	0.3% (0)	0.5% (0)	0.1% (0)

Note (1985): Electoral Alliance between Centre Party and KdS

sharp breaches in this consensus, although one was on the issue of pension reform in the late 1950s. Since the late 1970s, however, these have become more frequent.

The future of Sweden's civil nuclear energy programme brought down the first Fälldin coalition in 1978, and caused considerable political tensions for some time afterwards.

There have also been divisions on economic policy, with increased labour unrest and also with sharp polarization over the trade union initiated idea ("Fund Socialism" to its right-wing block adversaries) for a percentage of company profits to be channelled into central funds controlled by the trade unions. These would enable them to take shares in companies over a certain size, and to gradually gain control over them. A more restricted version of the original scheme was enacted in 1983. This issue also led to a wider debate over the future of economic democracy.

Other divisions have opened up on the broad issue of the Swedish welfare state, and over whether Swedish society is over-regulated and over-taxed.

Another lesser, but recently prominent issue is that of immigration. In a widely publicized vote in 1988 one Swedish commune voted not to accept any refugees in its territory.

In spite of these divisions, there have still been no major upheavals in Swedish politics. The Ecology Party, however, was able to enter Parliament in the 1988 elections, and the block of centre and right parties all lost ground. Moreover there was a sharp drop in electoral turnout in 1988, from the usual figure of around 90 per cent to only 83.3 per cent. Sweden still remains a country, however, with a high level of popular involvement in political parties and organizations.

Sweden's Prime Ministers from 1932

1932–36	Per Albin Hansson	(S)
1936	Axel Pehrsson-Bramstorp	(C)
1936–39	Per Albin Hansson	(S)
1939–45	Per Albin Hansson	(National)
1945–46	Per Albin Hansson	(S)
1946–51	Tage Erlander	(S)
1951–57	Tage Erlander	(S, C)
1957–69	Tage Erlander	(S)
1969–76	Olof Palme	(S)
1976–78	Thorbjörn Fälldin	(C, M, FP)
1978–79	Ola Ullsten	(FP)
1979–81	Thorbjörn Fälldin	(C, M, FP)
1981–82	Thorbjörn Fälldin	(C, FP)
1982–86	Olof Palme	(S)
1986–88	Ingvar Carlsson	(S)
1988–	Ingvar Carlsson	(S)

Sveriges Socialdemokratiska Arbetareparti — SAP
(The Swedish Social Democratic Labour Party)

Headquarters	:	Sveavagen 68, S-105 60 Stockholm (tel. 08-14 03 00)
Chairman	:	Ingvar Carlsson
Secretary general	:	Bo Toresson
Spokesperson/chair of parliamentary group	:	Jan Bergqvist
Membership	:	1,200,000
Founded	:	1889

History

The Social Democratic Labour Party (SAP) was founded in 1889. Hjalmar Branting became the first party leader and retained this position until 1925. He also became the first SAP member to be elected to the *Riksdag*, but on the Liberal Party list, with which the SAP co-operated both on the objective of electoral reform and against the conservatives. In 1898 the Labour movement established a separate trade union arm, the *Landsorganisation* (LO — Confederation of Trade Unions) and the first collective agreement with the employers' organization, SAF, was reached in 1905. The party based its policy on Marxist theory, but modified it to suit national circumstances.

The party's total of elected representatives rose steadily, and by September 1914 it had the largest number of seats in the *Andra Kammaren* (the Second Chamber). By 1917 it was substantially the largest party, and entered into a coalition government for the first time, in conjunction with the Liberal Party. In 1920 Branting became the first Social Democratic Prime Minister. Although his government was only of short duration, there were further SAP governments in 1921–3 and 1924–5. In 1925 Branting was replaced as leader by Per Albin Hansson, who retained the leadership until 1946.

By the 1930s the SAP was established as the dominant party in Swedish politics, and from 1932 to 1976 it was continuously in power, apart from a short period in 1936. For 29 of these years it ruled on its own. Its percentage of votes in national elections never dropped below 40 per cent after 1932, and on two occasions (in 1940 and 1968) it won an absolute majority of over 50 per cent of the vote. The series of Social Democratic-led governments initiated expansionist economic policies and established the framework of the

Swedish welfare state. Although a high level of taxation was imposed, the SAP did not seek to undermine the private sector, and put little emphasis on nationalization.

The SAP ruled alone from 1932 to 1936, was in opposition for three months in 1936, and was then in a coalition with the Agrarians (now the Centre Party) from 1936 to 1939. From 1939 to 1944 the SAP led a four-party war-time coalition. From 1945 to 1951 the SAP again ruled on its own. In 1946 Tage Erlander became the party leader, holding the post until 1969.

From 1951 to 1957 the SAP was again in coalition with the Agrarians, but the government eventually fell after a dispute between the two parties over the controversial new SAP proposals for a compulsory supplementary pension system. This was eventually adopted in 1959. From 1957 to 1976 the SAP again governed on its own. In 1969 Tage Erlander was replaced as party leader and Prime Minister by Olof Palme.

In 1976 the SAP finally went into opposition, although remaining easily the largest single party. After six years out of government. The party returned to power in 1982 with a minority government led again by Olof Palme.

In 1985 it retained power. In 1986 Olof Palme was assassinated in a Stockholm street. His successor was Ingvar Carlsson, who remained Prime Minister after the 1988 elections, in which the Social Democrats won 156 *Riksdag* seats (a drop of three since 1985, with losses in all electoral districts) on 43.7 per cent of the vote. As on several previous occasions, they continue to rely on Communist (VPK) support in Parliament.

The SAP is also totally dominant in eight of the Swedish provinces (mainly in the centre and north of the country) and seven more provinces are under SAP rule by virtue of VPK support. At local council level the party has 5,834 seats, down 151 seats from 1985. In 1988 they took power in eight new councils, but lost in six others.

Support

The SAP is still by far the largest Swedish party, and in 1988 won more votes than the three main non-opposition parties put together. The SAP has lost less support than other Scandinavian Social Democratic parties.

The SAP has been the traditional party of Swedish blue collar workers and trade union members. Apart from its strength among workers in industry and agricultural labourers it has also done very well among white-collar workers such as shop assistants. A large proportion of civil servants have also supported the party. The party has been strong among women, but currently has a problem with the youth vote. Compared to the last election in 1985, in 1988 the SAP was able to count on a very high party loyalty of 84 per cent of its voters.

As a rule, the SAP does best in the small and medium sized industrial towns of the north and central regions of the country. It is strongest of all in the northernmost province of Norrbotten, where its vote has been close to 60 per cent and it has won around or over 50 per cent in most other northern and central provinces. It is weaker in the larger cities and neighbouring areas such as Stockholm city and province, Uppsala and Göteborg. In the Fyrstadkretsen around Malmö the Social Democrats are slightly stronger, and in 1988 the party recaptured power from the Centre-right on the Malmö city council.

The SAP is correspondingly also weaker in southern and in particular south-central and south-western Sweden, where their vote has generally been around 40 per cent. The party has been particularly weak in the province of Halland, although even here it is by far the largest party. Moreover the party also has pockets of strength in the south, such as the province of Blekinge, where it traditionally wins over 50 per cent of the vote.

In provincial elections the SAP is sometimes dependent on Communist support to win a majority, as in Östergötland in 1988. They have been hurt in 1988 by the environmentalist vote in the provincial council elections, as in Uppsala and Kalmar.

Organization

Membership of the SAP is very high by European standards, at over one million (or about 47 per cent of the total votes cast for the party at the last election). This high figure, however, is attributable in large measure to the practice of collective affiliation of many trade union members to the party a practice which the 1987 SAP congress decided to discontinue by the end of 1990.

The SAP is organized on the basis of local social democratic clubs, and with "labour communes" in all 284 municipalities. There are also a large number of city and district branches. The party districts have their own annual congresses. There are also workplace branches.

The national congress is held every three years, and includes delegates elected in constituencies within the party districts. The supreme policy-making body between congresses is the party Executive. The party has a large youth organization (the SSU) and a women's organization, which both participate actively in the policy-making procedures of the party.

The party co-operates closely with the Swedish trade union confederation (*Landsorganisationen* — LO) and regular meetings are held between the two organizations. The LO's Secretary-general has often been a SAP member of Parliament. The party also has close contacts with the co-operative movement (*Kooperativa Förbundet* — KF).

The party's policy programme is adopted after being prepared by a specially nominated programme committee. Amendments can be put by all local and provincial party organizations. The party's list for *Riksdag* elections is proposed centrally after having been through a rather lengthy nomination procedure.

The party produces a newspaper called *Aktuellt*, with a circulation of 140,000, and a monthly publication called *Tiden*. There are a number of newspapers associated with the party and one of the country's largest newspapers, *Aftonbladet* is owned by Landsorganisationen — LO. The party lacks a morning newspaper, however, in Stockholm and Gøteborg. The youth organization produces a publication, called *Frihet*, and the women's organization one called *Morgonbris*.

The SAP is a member of the Socialist International (of which Olaf Palme was one of the leading personalities), and is an observer at the Confederation of Socialist Parties of the European Community. It is a member of the Social Democratic group in the Nordic Council.

Policies

The SAP has been a pragmatic party of government. The secret of its success lies in its great ability to adapt to new circumstances. The party has never been convulsed by ideological conflict over economic and social questions. Marxism has always played a minor role and the party has never been obsessed with who owns the means of production, distribution and exchange. Instead of trying to nationalize the economy, the Swedish Social Democrats have worked in close alliance with the powerful trade union movement to create an internationally minded capitalism and a paternalistic welfare socialism based on individual freedom and social citizenship.

The Social Democrats have also in the postwar period tended to become an umbrella organization with close links to different interest groups, ranging from the trade unions (LO) to the Workers' Peace Forum. The party's political

decisions have often emerged as a result of compromises between these groups' demands. In 1982, for example, Palme negotiated with these organizations the contents of the party election programme.

The Social Democrats have worked steadily to create a guaranteed basic minimum income for the individual Swede (cradle to grave), and introduced free child care and old age pension schemes. Unemployment has been kept to a bare minimum and there has been positive discrimination for women on the labour market.

In the last few years the SAP has also put a greater emphasis on measures to achieve economic democracy. In the early 1970s it pushed hard to introduce co-determination, which was enacted on a trial basis in 1972 and on a permanent basis in 1976. The most controversial measure advocated by the party, however, was that of collective capital formation, first put forward by a trade union economist, Rudolf Meidner. This envisaged a certain percentage of annual company profits being transferred to a central fund controlled by the trade unions who would use part of the proceeds to buy shares in Swedish companies, and thus enable eventual trade-union control of Swedish industry. The SAP supported the concept if not the details of the original plan, but called for a lengthy period of review as to how it might work. It proved intensely controversial, and was strongly criticized from within the non-socialist parties. It was eventually enacted in 1983, but in a more restrictive form.

In recent years, the SAP has also had to put a greater emphasis on wage restraint, and on limits in public expenditure. The Carlsson government has also accepted the need for tax reform for those on high wages, and the need to open up local and state monopolies to competition, in order to offer consumers a wider choice.

For economic reasons, the Social Democrats have generally been in favour of civil nuclear energy.

The SAP continues to defend a strong welfare state. In its 1988 election campaign it ran advertisements implying that good Swedish citizens should abandon the egotism of the 1980s and accept that freedom of choice should not be possible in every area, (such as proposed private alternatives to state-run health and child-care services).

The Social Democratic party has always supported and reinforced Swedish neutrality, building up one of the most powerful defence systems and defence industries in Western Europe. Through the Swedish foreign policy developed by the Social Democratic Party, Sweden has taken a very active role in debates concerned with north/south relations, armaments control and international co-operation. The Carlsson government has also pushed for closer contacts with the European Community.

Personalities

The party leader is Ingvar Carlsson, a former political secretary to Tage Erlander, and former chairman of the party's youth organization. When he took over from Olaf Palme after the latter's assassination in 1986, Carlsson became only the fifth leader in the party's history. He was born in 1934.

Moderata Samlingspartiet
(Moderate Unity Party)

Headquarters	: Lilla Nygatan 13, Box 1243, S-11182 Stockholm (tel. 08-23 61 80)
Chairman	: Carl Bildt
Secretary-general	: Per Unckel
Membership	: 180,000
Founded	: 1904

History

The present Moderate Party is the heir to the Swedish Conservative tradition. The Conservatives started up as a parliamentary caucus in the late 19th century. They defended protectionism, high military expenditure and limited suffrage. In 1904 a national campaigning organization (*Allmänna Valmansförbundet*) was established, within which right-wing forces (known generically as *Högern*, the Right) were able to mobilize.

Conservatives and Liberals dominated elections in the first decade of the 20th century, and A. Lindman was Prime Minister from 1906–1911. In spite of the subsequent rise of the Social Democrats, the Conservatives continued to provide a number of Prime Ministers over the next two decade as well, H. Hammerskiöld from 1914 to 1917, C. Swartz in 1917 (a caretaker government only), E. Trygger from 1923 to 1924 and A. Lindman from 1928 to 1930, in what turned out to be Sweden's last Conservative-led government. The combined Conservative vote remained at around 25–30 per cent from 1917 to 1932, when it fell to 23.5 per cent.

In 1935 there was a merger between the two major Conservative groupings, the *Nationella Partiet* (National Party), led by E. Trygger, and the *Lantmanna och Borgare Partiet* (Yeomen and Burghers' Party). Gösta Bagge was chairman of the Right from 1935 to 1944, during which time the party's vote continued to slip to only 15.8 per cent. From 1939 to 1945 the Right took part in a wartime coalition government led by the Social Democrats, but it then returned to opposition from 1945 to 1976 under the successive chairmanships of Fritjof Domö (1944–50), Jarl Hjalmarsson (1950–61), Gunnar Heckscher (1961–65), Yngve Holmberg (1965–70) and Gösta Bohman (1970–81).

The party's vote at first fell to only 12.3 per cent (1948), but then slowly rose in three successive elections to 19.5 per cent (1958). The trend was then again reversed, and its vote fell in four successive elections to only 11.5 per cent by 1970. In the 1968 and 1970 elections it was only the fourth largest party. In 1969 it abandoned the title of the Right Party and renamed itself as the Moderate Unity Party in an attempt to break with its former image of the party of large landowners and businessmen.

In the 1970s it again revived electorally, and in 1976 entered a non-socialist coalition government led by Fälldin of the Centre Party. From 1978 to 1979 it was out of power, but it took part in a new coalition government led by Fälldin from 1979 to 1981 when it left government in protest over the issue of tax reform. It has since remained in the opposition.

Ulf Adelsohn replaced Gösta Bohman as party leader in 1981, and in 1982 took the party to 23.6 per cent of the vote, its best electoral result since the 1920s, which made it by far the largest of the non-socialist parties. In the 1985 elections its vote fell to 21.3 per cent. Adelsohn later resigned, and was replaced by Carl Bildt.

In 1988 the Moderates had a further setback, only winning 18.3 per cent of the vote. It lost 10 seats in the *Riksdag*, ending up with 66. The party has also lost support since 1982 in the local and provincial elections.

Support

Although the Moderates' vote has now dropped in two successive national elections, it is still the largest of the three major non-socialist parties in Sweden. It had previously been successful in winning supporters from the Centre and Liberal parties, but some of these returned to their former allegiance in 1988. The party also lost a number of votes to the Ecologists.

The Moderates have traditionally attracted higher income voters. They have done well among owners of small enterprises (14 per cent of their support in 1982) and middle and higher white-collar workers (48 per cent of their 1982 support). They were weaker among industrial workers and farmers. They used to be especially well supported among women, but this is now changing.

In regional terms the Moderates are strongest in urban areas and in the more prosperous parts of Sweden.

Their strongest constituencies have been Stockholm city and county (where the party obtained almost 34 per cent in its best year of 1982), the constituencies around Malmö in south-western Sweden and Göteborg.

The Moderates generally have a higher level of support in southern Sweden, and are much weaker in northern Sweden, where they have less votes than the Centre Party as well as than the Social Democrats.

Organization

The Moderates' 180,000 members are grouped in around 850 local associations, which belong to *Länsförbund*, or provincial federations. These mainly correspond with *Riksdag* constituencies.

The party congress (*Rikstämma*) takes place every third year, and includes delegates from the local associations. In between councils, a party council (*Partiråd*) also meets. There is a party executive of 19 members.

The Moderates have a women's organization and a youth organization (MU), both of which are linked to the party. A student organization (SKSF) is independent of the party and includes Liberals, Centre Party and independent members as well as Conservatives. The Moderates also have an educational and training facility for party members (*Medborgarskolan*, or the Citizen School), and the party has been closely associated with the Swedish industrial associations.

The party produces a monthly publication for members, which is called *Medborgaren* ("The Citizen"). The youth organization has a publication called *Moderat Debatt*. The student organization publishes a journal called *Svensk Linje*.

The Moderates had traditionally been heavily supported by industry, but in 1976 decided to try and lose their image of being a front organization for industry by deciding not to accept further financial contributions from firms or their organizations. State subsidies are now their major source of revenue. The 1988 election result was thus a severe blow for the party, which risked losing between 3.5 and five million Swedish Kroner in government subsidies.

The Moderates are members of the European and International Democratic Unions. The Youth organization, MU, is a member of DEMYC (The Democratic Youth Community of Europe) and SKSF is a member of EDS (European Democratic Students). The party co-operates closely with the other Scandinavian Conservative parties with whom it sits in the Nordic Council.

Policies

The Moderates are the most conservative major party within the Swedish political spectrum. They have remained in opposition for all of the postwar periods, apart from a short time in 1976–78 and 1979–81, and even then they did not provide the Prime Minister. They have retained, therefore, an opposition image and this, combined with the fact that they tend to be more conservative than their Norwegian and Danish sister parties, has helped to prevent the rise of any populist protest parties to their right (like the Progress parties of Norway and Denmark).

In the 1982 elections, the party strongly attacked the Social Democrats in a campaign run under the slogan "An open society", which won them their highest ever level of support. In 1985 there was again sharp polarization between their leader Adelsohn and the Social Democrats' Olof Palme. In 1988, however, the party's themes were less to the forefront in an election dominated by environmental and other issues.

The party programme is based on both conservative and liberal themes. The party supports the Swedish welfare state, but has led the attack on wasteful expenditure in the public sector and on excessive government involvement in the economy and in people's lives.

The Moderates have called for a free market economy, built on a property owning democracy. They have called for tax reform (and, in particular, lower top marginal tax rates), and for privatization of parts of the public sector. They also took the lead in attacking a compulsory employee profit-sharing scheme that brought 100,000 businessmen out on the street in a demonstration organized by the Swedish Federation of Industry. In the 1985 elections, they continued to campaign for the abolition of the wage earner funds. They also called for cuts in sickness benefits and grants to local government.

The Moderates have also come out in favour of the Swedish programme of civil nuclear energy (on which they clashed with the Centre Party in particular) and of Swedish membership of the European Community. They support a strong defence policy, and are the only Swedish party to be against a trade boycott of South Africa.

Personalities

The party's leader is Carl Bildt, who was born

in 1949, and has been a member of the *Riksdag* since 1979. The party's spokesperson is Cecilia Stegö.

Folkpartiet
(Liberal Party)

Headquarters	: Luntmakargatan 66, S-11383 Stockholm (tel. 08-15 10 30)
Chairman	: Bengt Westerberg
Secretary-general	: Peter Ørn
Chair of parliamentary group	: Ingemar Eliasson
Membership	: 50,000
Founded	: 1902

History

Liberal groups were active in Sweden as early as the 1860s. In the 1890s a Liberal Parliamentary organization was developed and in 1902 a national organization (*Frisinnade Landsföreningen*) was established.

The Liberals called for a reformist programme, including an extension of the suffrage and reinforced parliamentarism. They co-operated with the new Social Democratic Party, whose first member of Parliament, Hjalmar Branting, was elected on a liberal list. They supported free trade, and also included a number of prohibitionists.

The Liberal party was one of the two dominant parties, along with the Conservatives, in the first decade of the 20th century, winning between 45 and 50 per cent of the vote. K. Staaf was the Liberal Prime Minister from 1905 to 1906 and again from 1911 to 1914.

With the rise of the Social Democrats, the Liberal vote declined to only 26.9 per cent by 1914. From 1917 to 1920 the Liberals were in a coalition government with the Social Democrats, with the Liberal, N. Eden, as Prime Minister. By 1921 the Liberal vote was around 19 per cent.

In 1923 the Liberals split over the issue of prohibition. The rural areas supported nationwide prohibition while the more reform-minded urban membership found this to be in contradiction with basic liberal principles.

The rural, teetotal and free church segment went off to form the *Frisinnade Folkpartiet* (Liberal People's Party) and the reform-minded international and economically *laissez-faire* group established the *Sveriges Liberale Parti* (Swedish Liberal Party). Both parties remained electorally weaker than the old Liberal Party, although the *Frisinnade Folkpartiet* remained much the stronger of the two (winning 10–13 per cent of the vote compared to 2–4 per cent for the *Sveriges Liberale Parti*). The *Frissinade Folkpartiet* also led the government on several occasions with C. G. Ekman as Prime Minister from 1926 to 1928 and again from 1930 to 1932 and F. Hamrin in 1932. After 1932 the Liberals remained in opposition.

In 1934 the two parties finally reunited within a new *Folkepartiet*. Gustaf Andersson Rasjön was the party leader from 1935 to 1944. From 1939 to 1945 the Liberals took part in an all-party government under Social Democratic leadership. The party remained electorally weak at around 12–13 per cent of the vote in the elections of 1936, 1940 and 1944.

After 1944, the party revived under the leadership of Bertil Ohlin, who remained party chairman until 1967. The party put less emphasis on *laissez-faire* economic policies and more on social liberalism. Its vote rose by 10 per cent in the 1948 election to 22.8 per cent and went up to 24.2 per cent in 1952. It was thus easily the largest non-socialist party, but remained in opposition.

From 1956, its vote slowly declined again to only 15 per cent by 1968. Although there was a slight revival in 1970, there was a sharp drop to only 9.4 per cent in 1973, by which time it was only a weak third among the non-socialist parties. The party was chaired by Sven Weden from 1967 to 1969 and Gunnar Helen from 1969 to 1975 and Per Ahlmark from 1975 to 1978.

In 1976 the Liberals re-entered government in a three-party coalition led by Fälldin of the Centre Party. In 1978 Ola Ullsten became the new party leader, and after the fall of the Fälldin government Ullsten became the first Liberal Prime Minister since 1932. His one party minority government lasted until 1979. The Liberals were subsequently in a new three-party coalition government led by Fälldin from 1979 to 1981 and a two-party coalition under Fälldin from 1981 to 1982. Their six years in government from 1976 to 1982 made them the longest serving non-socialist party in government after the war.

In 1982, the party's vote fell from 10.6 per cent to only 5.6 per cent and it returned into opposition. In 1983 Bengt Westerberg became the new party leader.

Benefiting from a new image in opposition to the Palme government, the Liberals' vote rose dramatically to 14.2 per cent in 1985 (with their number of seats rising from 21 to 51).

In the 1988 election their vote again dropped to 12.2 per cent, with the party holding 44 seats. They also have 1,410 local council seats, losing 115 seats in 1988. They are generally weaker in local than in national elections.

Support

The party's old base among the rural population and also among urban intellectuals has largely disappeared, as has its support among members of the free churches.

The Liberals now have no firm basis of support and enjoy a low degree of party loyalty, as the volatility of their election results has demonstrated. In the 1988 elections they only retained 66 per cent of their 1985 voters. They appear to have suffered significant losses to the Ecologists.

The Liberals have support, however, in both rural and urban areas. White-collar workers, professionals and people in small and medium-sized industry, have been among the groups supporting the party.

The Liberals have had a generally uneven pattern of regional support. A very strong area has been around Göteborg and in other provinces on and behind the west coast (Bohuslän, Älvsborg Norra). In 1985 the party polled 20.7 per cent in Göteborg and 19.7 per cent in Bohuslan, and its highest percentage in 1988 was also in Göteborg (17.2 per cent), although the party lost a significant number of votes in this region. A second area of strength has been around Stockholm (where the party won over 17 per cent in Stockholm county in 1985) and where it did relatively well in 1988.

The Liberals have also done well in some provinces in south-central Sweden such as Jönköping. By far their best province in northern Sweden has been Västerbotten. Among the provinces where the party has been weaker in southern Sweden are Kalmar and the island of Gotland. Its weakest province in all of Sweden, however, is the northernmost province of Norrbotten (where it only obtained 3.1 per cent in 1982 and 7.6 per cent in 1988).

Organization

The Liberals have fewer members and a weaker organizational structure than other major Swedish political parties. Their 50,000 members are organized in 700 local associations which form 26 regional associations.

The national congress takes place annually except in election -years. There is also a 28-member national executive, 23 of whom are elected by the congress.

The Liberals have a youth organization but no students group, although many Liberal students are associated with the SKSF, which is independent but has close ties with the Moderate Party.

The party's official organ is called *Utsikt*. The Party also has links with some of Sweden's largest newspapers, such as *Dagens Nyheter*.

The Liberals are members of the Liberal International and sit in the Middle Group in the Nordic Council.

Policies

The Liberals have sought to place themselves in the middle of the Swedish political spectrum, calling for a reduction in the role of the state, but in a less strident way than the Moderate Party. The party continues to emphasize the themes of social liberalism that were first introduced by Bertil Ohlin after the war. It rejects *laissez-faire* economic policies (although these were again briefly re-emphasized in the mid 1970s after being first reintroduced by its youth organization). It believes that individualism must be tempered by a sense of social responsibility and the negative aspects of a pure market economy should be brought under control through partnership between private industry and the state.

The Liberals have always, however, opposed the high level of personal and company taxation in Sweden. They opposed the Social Democrat proposals for a centralized wage earner fund.

The party has put a distinctive emphasis on issues of civil and human rights, equality between the sexes and aid for developing countries. It has been a strong supporter of closer links with the European Community, and if possible, of a future Swedish membership. Swedish neutrality should, however, be maintained.

The Liberal Party has sometimes suffered in the past because it has not always had a clear identity for Swedish voters, and because it has allied with different parties on different issues. Its more radical members, for example, have sometimes allied with the socialist block. It is also typical that one of the Ecology Party's leaders was a former Liberal members of the *Riksdag*.

Personalities

The party's leader is Bengt Westerberg who was born in 1943 and is only a recent member of the *Riksdag*. He made a major impact in the 1985 election campaign.

Centerpartiet
(Centre Party)

Headquarters	: Scheelegatan 8, S-10422 Stockholm (tel. 08-54 07 30)
Chairman	: Olof Johansson
Secretary-general	: Ake Pettersson

Founded   : 1910
Membership   : 120,000

History

In 1910 the *Bondeförbundet* (Agrarian Party) was established to represent the small farmers at a national level. It grew out of farmers' organizations already in existence in local communities. The larger farmers also got together in 1915 to create a political party, the *Jordbrukarnas Riksförbund* (Farmers' Union). In 1917 both parties managed to gain seats in the *Riksdag*. In 1920 both increased their number of seats. Working together in the *Riksdag* led to a fusion of the two parties in 1921, using the name *Bondeförbundet*. During the twenties, thirties and forties the *Bondeförbundet* remained a constant factor in Swedish politics. In elections the party averaged 11 to 14 per cent of the total vote, based primarily on agricultural interests. During the depression they came to an agreement with the Social Democrats. In 1936 there was a short-lived minority Agrarian Party government, with A. Pehrsson-Bramstorp as Prime Minister. From 1936 to 1939 they participated in a coalition with the Social Democrats as the minority party but managing to hold the Ministry of Agriculture. As a result of their participation in the coalition, their position became rather unclear to the voters and their vote dropped in the 1940 election.

From 1939 to 1945 they took part in a wider war-time coalition under Social Democratic leadership. From 1945 to 1951 they were in the opposition, but from 1951 to 1957 again participated in a coalition with the Social Democrats under Tage Erlander, again holding the Ministry of Agriculture. In 1957 they broke with the government over the issue of pension reform.

From 1944 to 1956 the party's vote declined in 4 successive elections from 13.6 per cent to 9.4 per cent. This coincided with the reduction in farms and the farming population, which was taking place all across Europe after the war. It also paralleled the development away from special interest parties towards more ideological and broader-based parties. The Agrarian Party tried to adapt to these trends by changing its name to the Centre Party in 1957 as well as revising its strategy, adopting a new programme in 1959 in order to appeal to a wider cross-section of the population. It was a successful move which led to the party's vote rising to its highest ever level of 25.1 per cent in 1973. The party gained a new electorate and new policy themes. It became a caring non-socialist and non-ideological party, one of whose central themes was environmental

protection. From 1968 to 1979 it remained the largest of the three major non-socialist parties.

The Centre Party has led three non-socialist coalitions under Thorbjörn Fälldin as Prime Minister. In 1976 Mr Fälldin (party leader since 1971, when he took over from Gunnar Hedlund, who had led the party since 1949) captured the imagination of the people when his coalition won the elections from the Social Democrats, ending a 44 year long tradition. The first Fälldin cabinet included representatives of the *Moderaterna* and the Liberals. Due to internal disagreements in the coalition, the government fell in 1978, mainly over the Centre Party's strong anti-nuclear stance. After a brief Liberal minority government, a second Fälldin government was established (1979–1981), which had the same coalition members, but in which the coalition government programme left out the issue of nuclear energy and agreed that this issue should be decided upon by referendum.

After a disagreement over proposed tax reform, the Moderates left the coalition in 1981, and from 1981 to 1982 there was a third Fälldin government in which the Centre Party's only coalition allies were the Liberals. Since 1982 the Centre Party has again been in opposition.

After 1976 the Centre Party's vote dropped steadily from 24.1 per cent to only 9.9 per cent in the 1985 election, which it fought in an electoral alliance with the Christian Democratic Party, which only gained 12.4 per cent in all. Fälldin resigned as party leader later in 1985, and was replaced by Karin Söder, the first woman to lead a Swedish political party. In January 1987, however, she had to resign for health reasons, and Olof Johansson became the new party leader. In the 1988 elections the party benefited from a revival of voter interest in environmental themes, and its vote again rose to 11.4 per cent. The electoral alliance with the Christian Democrats was not renewed.

The Centre Party traditionally polls better in local elections than in national ones. In 1988 it obtained 2,250 representatives on local councils with 16.1 per cent of the vote, a gain of 74 seats and 0.5 per cent (a slightly lower rise than in the national elections).

Support

When the Centre Party changed its name from that of the Agrarian Party, part of its new strategy was to broaden its support from the agricultural sector to other parts of the electorate. In this it has had considerable success. Farmers remain loyal to the party (with almost two-thirds of them still supporting it) but the party is no longer so dependent upon them. The Centre Party has successfully recruited salaried employees. A third of its support now comes from white-collar workers, and more than a third from blue-collar workers. Support is also strong among the small business community, of whom almost one in five vote for the Centre Party. The party is still, however, much stronger in rural Sweden and weaker in the large urban areas, and its urban support still often consists of former farmers who have moved to the cities. Its rural support also means that the Centre Party has greater local election than national election strength.

During the 1988 elections, the party leader, Olof Johansson managed to arrest the Centre Party's recent electoral decline throughout Sweden. In 1988 it also enjoyed a high degree of voter loyalty from 86 per cent of its 1985 electorate, even accounting for the fact that the Centre Party had co-operated with the Christian Democrats in 1985 and had severed this relationship in 1988.

The Centre Party's strongest province is the island of Gotland, where it obtained 25.1 per cent of the vote in 1988. Among its stronger provinces in southern Sweden have been Kronaborg, Kalmar, Halland, Skaraborg, Jönköping and the two Älvsborg constituencies, where it has received around or over 20 per cent in the past.

The Centre Party is also the strongest of the non-socialist parties in northern Sweden, especially in Jämtland (22.6 per cent in 1982), Västernorrland, Västerbotten and Kopparberg. It is weaker in Gävleborg, and especially in the northernmost and very left-wing province of Norrbotten. Generally less strong in the provinces of central Sweden, the party is weakest of all in the urban constituencies of the Fyrstadskretsen, Göteborg, and Stockholm county and city (only 4.2 per cent in the Stockholm electoral district in 1988). In the 1988 local elections, however, the Centre Party had a somewhat better result than usual in the town council elections in Stockholm and Malmö. Women and younger voters, in particular, appear to have been drawn more to the Centre Party because of its stand on environmental issues and its opposition to civil nuclear power.

Organization

The party has a direct membership of around 100,000. It is organized in 4,900 sections and 29 districts. The party conference is held annually. There is also a party executive. There are a number of specialized working groups to give advice to the members of Parliament.

The Centre Party has a youth organization, CUF, which produces a publication called *Ung Center*, and a women's organization, whose publication is called *Budkavle*, and has traditionally had close contacts with the *Lantbrukarnas Riksförbund* (the national farmers' organization).

Party publications also include *Fokus*, *Svensk Politik* and *Politisk Tidskrift*. The party has links with a number of other newspapers, mainly of a regional character. The largest is *Skonska Dagbladet*.

The Centre Party has had limited international contacts, but has co-operated with other parties on an international level, for example with its sister party in Norway. It is a member of the Middle Group within the Nordic Council.

Policies

The Centre Party is in the middle of the Swedish political spectrum. Starting off as a party to defend the special interests of farmers it has also gradually developed a strong concern with environmental questions. It also became an early and powerful opponent of the Swedish civil nuclear energy programme, and entered into dispute with the Moderate Party, in particular, over this issue during the first non-socialist coalition government after 1976. It later entered into conflict with the Moderate Party over the issue of tax reform as well.

As other parties took up environmental causes, the nuclear issue lost importance after the referendum and the subsequent framework agreement for phasing out the nuclear programme, and as other economic issues came more to the fore in the early 1980s, the Centre Party lost a great deal of support. It regained some of this support in 1988, when environmental issues were again more prominent. It will be interesting to see how the Centre party co-operates with the Ecology Party in the *Riksdag* during the present legislature.

As a party which still has its roots in rural districts, the Centre Party has also been a strong advocate of decentralization of political decision-making. It seeks to channel more resources to peripheral areas of Sweden and to strengthen political participation at the local level. It tends to propagate the philosophy of "small is beautiful" and advocates support measures for small and medium-sized companies. It also supports a certain measure of worker participation in enterprises. Quality of life is an important party theme.

The Centre Party has been critical of the idea of possible Swedish membership of the European Community, which is overcentralized and would jeopardize Swedish neutrality. The party has agreed along with other Swedish parties that there should be intensified trade negotiations with the European Community, but even this has been criticized by some within the party, notably its youth organization. The party has argued that Sweden should not be obsessed with the European Community and should further develop its links with North America, Eastern Europe, Asia and Third World countries. Co-operation should also be furthered with the Nordic Council and with EFTA.

Personalities

Olof Johansson became the party leader in 1987. He was born in 1937 and has been a member of the *Riksdag* since 1971.

Vänsterpartiet Kommunisterna — VPK
(Left Party — Communists)

Headquarters	: Kungsgatan 84,
	S-11227 Stockholm
	(tel. 08-54 08 20)
Chairman	: Lars Werner
Secretary general	: Kenneth Kvist
Membership	: 16,000
Founded	: 1917

History

In 1917 a number of members from the Social Democratic Labour Party broke away and created a more radical party, the *Vänster-socialister* (Left Socialists), which gained 8 per cent of the vote and 11 seats in the 1917 elections. It subsequently joined the Third International and renamed itself the *Sveriges Kommunistiska Parti* (Swedish Communist Party) in 1921. A minority decided not to follow the majority line, and continued under the Left Socialist label until they eventually joined up again with the Social Democrats in 1924.

In the 1924 elections the Communist movement was again divided, with the main party winning four seats on 3.6 per cent of the vote and a breakaway *Socialistiksa Vänsterparti* (Socialist Left Party) led by Zeth Höglund winning one seat on 1.5 per cent of the vote. The latter party was again of short duration (being wound up in 1926) and in the 1928 elections the Communist Party won eight seats on 6.4 per cent of the vote.

In 1929, however, the Communists suffered a further schism between pro- and anti-Comintern factions, with the former led by Hugo Sillen and the latter by Karl Kilbom. The Kilbom Communists outpolled the pro-Comintern group by 5.3 per cent to 3.0 per cent (and by six seats

to two) in the 1921 elections. They turned themselves into the Socialist Party in 1936 (still winning more votes than the orthodox group) before they finally faded in the 1940s.

The mainstream Communists only polled between 3 to 3.5 per cent in the elections from 1932 to 1940, but they advanced to 10.3 per cent and 15 seats in 1944. After again dropping to 4.3 per cent by 1952 they then contained their losses, and have since managed to survive with a number of reprsentatives in the *Riksdag*.

By the party congress in 1967, the party was moving in a Eurocommunist direction, and it changed its name to its current title. There was a break with Moscow and a total revision of the party programme. As a result, a group of pro-Chinese Communists broke away from the party in the schism which eventually gave rise to the *Sveriges Kommunistiska Parti* (see separate entry).

In 1977 there was a further schism when an orthodox pro-Moscow group left the party to establish the *Sveriges Arbetarepartiet Kommunisterna* (see separate entry).

The VPK's postwar chairmen have been Sven Linderot (1936–51), Hilding Hagberg (1951–64), C. H. Hermansson (1964–75) and Lars Werner. Besides its 21 members in the *Riksdag* the VPK has 631 local councillors (an increase of 27 from 1985).

Support

Since the change to a unicameral *Riksdag*, the VPK has managed to remain a little above the 4 per cent threshold. Its 1988 result of 5.9 per cent was its highest since 1944. It has had a high degree of party loyalty, with 80 per cent of its 1985 voters voting for it in 1988. It has also benefited from a certain degree of tactical voting from Social Democrats who have wished to keep their allies from disappearing from the *Riksdag*. In 1988, however, they appeared to gain more from the non-socialist parties than from the Socialists, and lost slightly to the Ecology Party.

A considerable number of their voters still come from the working class, but these are now in the minority. Since 1968, in particular, they have made gains among white-collar workers, lower civil servants and students, and also women. They have done well among Finnish immigrants. They have low support among small businessmen, and practically none among farmers.

In today's *Riksdag* only three of its members can properly be classified as blue-collar workers. The average age of their *Riksdag* members is 51 and only three are women, the lowest percentage of any party.

In the 1988 elections the VPK gained representation in 15 of the 28 constitutencies, winning their largest number of seats in the Stockholm (seven) and Göteborg (two) areas. Another stronghold was the province of Norrbotten in the extreme north of Sweden, where they obtained 10.4 per cent. They are generally strongest in northern and north-central Sweden, and weakest in the south of the country (notably in Malmö province).

Organization

The VPK has 339 "base" organizations, above which are the district (currently 22) and constituency organizations. The party congress meets once every three years, with delegates from the district and constituency organizations. The congress elects the party chairman and up to 34 other members of the Central Committee (also comprising up to 15 candidate members), which then elects a smaller Executive. A national conference is also held in years when there is no congress.

The VPK's youth organization is called *Kommunistisk Ungdom* (KU — Communist Youth).

The party's main newspaper is *Arbetartidningen Ny Dag*. There is also a theoretical journal, *Socialistisk Debatt*, which comes out six times a year. KU produces a publication called *Stormklockan*.

The majority of the party's funds have come from state support, with a much smaller amount coming from membership fees and from the trade unions.

Policies

The VPK has always considered itself a part of the Swedish labour movement and continues to believe that the way to socialism is through the class struggle. On the other hand they accept pluralistic parliamentary democracy and have become independent of Moscow. They have publicly condemned incursions into Swedish waters by Soviet submarines. They believe that classic socialist theory must be adapted to the realities of the Swedish situation, and to the need for national self-determination.

The VPK has traditionally supported the Social Democratic administrations.

The VPK has also put an increasing emphasis on environmental protection measures, and may co-operate with the Centre and Ecology parties on these issues in the current legislature. They supported the Centre Party's campaign to end Swedish reliance on civil nuclear energy. In their 1988 campaign, they also called for strong action to stop chemical discharges, for a better working environment, and for a lower limit for radon.

The VPK has also advocated shorter working hours, increased taxation on those with high incomes and lower taxes on foodstuffs. It has been critical of the European Community, and called for reductions in military expenditure.

Personalities

The party's leader is Lars Werner, who has been party leader since 1975, and was re-elected for a further three-year term in 1987.

Miljöpartiet de Gröna
(Green Ecology Party)

Headquarters	: c/o Riksdag, S-10312 Stockholm (Tel. 08-786 40 00)
Spokespersons	: Anders Nordin and Fiona Björling
Secretary-general	: Kjell Dahlström
Founded	: 1981
Membership	: 8,600

History

The party was founded on Sept. 20, 1981. One of its key figures was Per Gahrton, a former *Riksdag* member for the Liberal Party.

In its first elections in 1982 it polled 1.7 per cent in the *Riksdag* elections, but did well at provincial and local level. Its 1985 *Riksdag* campaign suffered from lack of funds and its vote fell to 1.5 per cent. In 1988, however, it benefited from a general protest vote against the Swedish political system and renewed concern about the environment, in the light of Chernobyl and the pollution-related death of a large number of fish off the Swedish coast in the summer of that year. It polled 5.5 per cent and 20 seats, becoming the first new party to make a major breakthrough into the *Riksdag* since before World War II.

The party also entered 260 out of Sweden's 284 town councils, and in at least 23 of them did not have enough people to fill the seats they had won. The party now has around 700 representatives on local councils and 81 on provincial councils.

Support

The party appears to have taken far more support from the non-socialist parties in 1988 (especially from the Liberals and Moderates) than from the Left. Most of its *Riksdag* members are also former non-socialists.

The party has been strongest among first time voters and women (who constituted two thirds of its voters in 1985). In regional terms it is strongest in the largest cities; five of its 1988 *Riksdag* members come from Stockholm and its region, two from Göteborg town and province, and two from the Fyrstadskretsen around Malmö in south-western Sweden. It has been weak in the middle-sized industrial towns in central Sweden.

Organization

The *Miljöpartiet* has around 8,600 members. An annual congress elects a political, an administrative, a constitutional and a newspaper board. There are 20 regional and about 200 local branches. The party does not, however, have a formal party leader nor a parliamentary leader. It currently has two spokespersons, one man and one woman.

One of its organizational principles is that a party representative to the *Riksdag* must be nominated in his or her home province.

The party has produced a publication called *Alternativet I Svensk Politik*.

The *Miljöpartiet* currently has four fulltime employees. Very little money has been available to them since their start in 1982, and the party has had to borrow money extensively from its own members. It will now be receiving, however, considerable state subsidies.

The party is affiliated to the European Greens.

Policies

The *Miljöpartiet* put forward a 17-point political programme for the 1988 elections. Environmental protection and pollution control are high priorities. Economic growth should be subordinated to environmental considerations.

The party has called for the abandonment of civil nuclear power within three years, to be financed by a rise in energy taxes. They have also advocated a phasing out of oil and coal. There should be a more environmentally conscious agricultural policy (which should also ensure self-sufficiency in basic foodstuffs), and more investment in the railways to ease road traffic and reduce pollution. They began their 1988 campaign with 10 days by rail around Sweden. They advocated the reduction of the four per cent electoral threshold for entry into the *Riksdag* to only 1 per cent.

There is also concern about closer Swedish relations with the European Community, which the *Miljöpartiet* believes would lead to a loss of national independence in decision-making and to lower Swedish environmental standards.

They have also called for more flexible working patterns for the individual citizen, including flexible retirement age. There should

be a six-hour day. There should be less discrimination against immigrants.

The *Miljöpartiet* supports the peace movement and the creation of nuclear free zones in Scandinavia and Europe.

They have made it clear that they will not support either the Socialists or the non-socialists in the *Riksdag*, but will make their decisions on an issue by issue basis. There has also been some consideration given to forming a "green block" in the *Riksdag*, consisting of the *Miljöpartiet*, the Communists and the Centre Party.

Kristdemokratiska Samhällspartiet — KdS
(Christian Democratic Community Party)

Headquarters	: Målargatan 7, S-10126 Stockholm
Chairman	: Alf Svensson
Secretary	: Dan Ericsson
Membership	: 24,000
Founded	: 1964

History

The party was founded as the *Kristen Demokratisk Samling* (Christian Democratic Assembly) in 1964. Its leading figures included Birger Ekstedt, a pastor who remained the party president from 1964 to 1973 and Lewi Pethrus of the Pentecostal movement.

In its first election in 1964 it obtained 1.8 per cent. Its vote then fluctuated between a low of 1.4 per cent (in 1976 and 1979) and a high of 1.9 per cent (1982); never winning a seat in the *Riksdag*.

In 1985 it entered into an electoral alliance with the Centre Party. Its share of the alliance's total vote of 12.4 per cent was 2.5 per cent, and its chairman, Alf Svensson, became its first representative in the *Riksdag*.

In 1987 the party changed its name to that of the *Kristdemokratiska Samhällspartiet*, and also adopted a new programme. The alliance with the Centre Party was not maintained for the 1988 elections and the KdS lost its only seat in the *Riksdag*, although Alf Svensson was close to the 12 per cent threshold for direct election in a constituency in Jönköping, and the party had its highest ever vote of 3.1 per cent.

The KdS has 40 representatives at provincial level, and over 350 seats at local level.

Support

The KdS improved its vote in almost every *Riksdag* constituency in 1988. Its highest vote was in its chairman's constituency of Jönköping, where it received 10.6 per cent, and where it had already obtained 6.8 per cent in 1982. It also did particularly well in Västerbotten (5.2 per cent) and Skaraborg (4.3 per cent). There is a very high party loyalty among its voters, and it is well supported by religious groups.

Organization

The KdS has around 24,000 members. It has a youth organization (Christian Democratic Youth) with 6,000 members in 130 local groups, and a women's organization (KdS-K) with 3,000 members. It produces a weekly newspaper, *Samhällsgemenskap*. It is a member of the European Union of Christian Democrats, and of the Christian Democratic International.

Policies

The KdS emphasizes that it is not a narrowly confessional party, but defends Christian values in Swedish political life. It opposes current developments in Sweden towards a more permissive society. It calls for a review of the existing abortion law. It emphasizes family policy and calls for firm action to combat drug and alcohol abuse.

The party has also described itself as the third alternative between socialistic and nonsocialistic parties. It has called for a halt to the building of nuclear power stations.

Personalities

Alf Svensson has led the party for 15 years. From 1985 to 1988 he represented the Jönköping constituency in the *Riksdag*.

Sveriges Kommunistiska Parti — SKP
(Swedish Communist Party)

Headquarters	: Box 3144, S-10362 Stockholm
Chairman	: Roland Pettersson
Secretary	: Jan-Olaf Norell
Membership	: 2,000
Founded	: 1967

History

The party was founded as the *Kommunistiska Förbundet Marxist-Leninisterna* (Communist League of Marxist-Leninists) by pro-Chinese dissidents from the mainstream Communist Party after the latter had changed its name (see *Vänsterpartiet Kommunisterna*). The Communist League itself suffered a schism, and later changed its name to its present title. Its national electoral impact has been minimal (e.g. 0.2 per cent in the 1979 general elections). It has a certain local government presence.

Organization

It claims some 120 local branches, and produces a weekly publication called *Gnistan* (the Spark) and a quarterly, *Marxist Forum*.

Sveriges Arbetarepartiet Kommunisterna — SAK
(Communist Workers' Party of Sweden)

Headquarters	: PO Box 307, S-10124 Stockholm
Chairman	: Rolf Hagel
Membership	: 5,000 (1985 claim)
Founded	: 1977

History

The party was formed by three local sections of the *Vänsterpartiet Kommunisterna* (VPK — see separate entry) who were critical of the latter's Eurocommunist orientation and who sought closer links with the Soviet Union. The new party was joined by two of the VPK's *Riksdag* members, but these were not re-elected in the 1979 elections. It has had only very low votes in national elections, but has won some local seats. It has produced a daily publication called *Norrskenflamman* (Northern Lights).

Other small parties

During the 1988 elections, the small parties increased their total representation on local town councils by 23 seats to 235 in all.

In 23 of the town councils on which small parties are represented, they hold the balance of power between Right and Left.

Small extreme parties are not unknown to Sweden. Radical undertones do occur in small parties of this nature, especially in the larger cities. There has been no significant growth in their support during the last elections.

Small parties represented circa 1.3 per cent of the total votes cast in 1985, and in the 1988 elections circa 2 per cent. These figures are somewhat modified due to the fact that the Swedish voter has the right to vote blank, and such votes are registered under the heading "others" with the small parties.

Some of these small parties are only based on one issue, i.e. *Aksjonsgruppen mot fly pa F18* (Action Group against Airplanes on F18), which campaigned against a new major airport. A recurring phenomenon is the *Kalle Anka* party (Donald Duck) which makes fun of the election procedure.

Voters in Sweden are known to elect differently at council, provincial and national level.

Switzerland

Francis Jacobs

The country

Switzerland is a country of around 6.5 million inhabitants. It is a confederation of 20 full cantons and six half-cantons; of these 17 are German-speaking (Zürich, Luzern, Uri, Schwyz, Obwalden, Nidwalden, Glarus, Zug, Solothurn, Basel Stadt, Basel Land, Schaffhausen, Appenzell-Ausser-Rhoden, Appenzell-Inner-Rhoden, St. Gallen, Aargau and Thurgau), four French-speaking (Geneva, Vaud, Neuchatel and Jura), two bilingual with a French-speaking majority (Fribourg and Valais), one bilingual with a German-speaking majority (Berne), one Italian-speaking (Ticino) and one tri-lingual with German, Italian and Romansch speakers (Graubünden).

In religious terms Switzerland is fairly evenly divided between Catholics and Protestants, with the latter in a small majority. Zürich, Basel, Neuchatel, Vaud and Berne are among the predominantly Protestant cantons, while the German-speaking mountain cantons of central Switzerland, as well as Ticino, Fribourg and Valais are overwhelmingly Catholic. A number of other cantons are more evenly divided, including Geneva which, in spite of its Calvinist traditions, has almost as many Catholics as Protestants.

Switzerland has a very high foreign resident population of over 900,000. The canton of Zürich alone has almost 200,000 resident foreigners, and there are major foreign populations in the cantons of Geneva and Vaud (over 100,000 in each) Berne, Aargau and Ticino.

Political institutions

The powers of the Swiss federal institutions are severely limited, both by the powers retained by the cantons (and even communes) and by the regular use of referenda and initiatives (see below). The Swiss Parliament, the Federal Assembly, consists of two chambers with equal powers. The National Council has 200 members elected in the cantons by proportional representation (Hagenbach-Bischoff) on the basis of their populations. The smaller cantons, however, are guaranteed at least one representative, who is then elected on a simple majority basis. The Council of States consists of 46 members, in which each canton, irrespective of size, is represented by two members (half-cantons by one) generally elected by a majority system. A parliamentary mandate lasts four years. Being a Federal Member of Parliament is not a full-time job in itself. The Parliament only meets in plenary session for three weeks each season, although additional committee meetings prolong the time a member must spend in the federal capital, Berne.

The Federal Council is a collegiate body of seven members, each of whom runs one of the Federal Departments of State (Foreign Affairs, Finance, Public Economy, Military, Interior, Justice and Police, and Transport, Communications and Energy). Federal councillors are elected or re-elected every four years (except in cases of resignation or death) by the two chambers of the Federal Assembly meeting in joint session. Since 1959 the Federal Council has always consisted of two Socialists, two Christian Democrats, two Radicals and one representative of the Swiss People's Party. The need for balance between different cantons (e.g. never more than one councillor from any one canton, almost always one from Zürich, Vaud and Berne) and language groups, as well as the personalities of the candidates, all play a role in their election. The official nominees of the government parties are not always elected, and may be beaten by other members of their own party, as happened in 1973 and 1983.

The presidency of the Confederation alternates on a yearly basis between the members of the Federal Council (the annual elections by parliament are only a formality), and a long-serving member of the Federal Council can end up being president on four or five occasions.

The minimum voting age in federal elections is 20. Women were only given the vote at federal level in 1971. Turnouts in federal elections are low by European standards (under 50 per cent in the 1983 National Council elections), although this varies greatly from canton to canton.

Map of Switzerland showing the cantons and half-cantons together with the number of National Council seats in each.

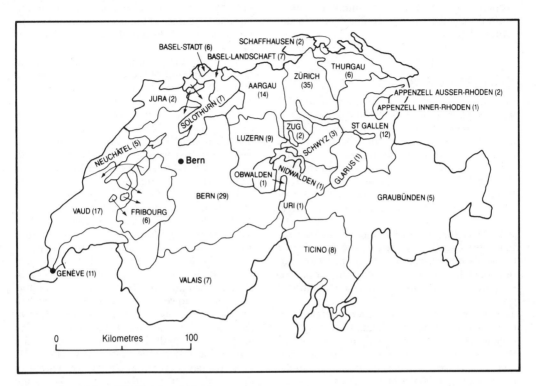

Source: adapted from *World Atlas of Elections*.

Each canton has a unicameral legislature and a cantonal government but the variety of political forms and structures within the cantons is very great.

Voting eligibilities are very different (women have still not got the vote, for example, in the two half-cantons of Appenzell, and the initial voting age varies from 18 up to as high as 27 in some elections in some cantons). Most cantons have introduced the secret ballot but a few German-speaking cantons (Obwalden, Nidwalden, the two Appenzells and Glarus) have still retained direct democracy in the forms of annual town square meetings or *Landsgemeinde*.

Besides participation in a bewildering variety of different referenda and initiatives, voters in some cantons can elect the judiciary, demand the dissolution of the cantonal parliament or the recall of the executive.

The duration of the cantonal parliament's mandates varies from two to five years. Most are elected by proportional representation but four cantons have retained majority voting. In one canton, Appenzell-Inner-Rhoden, there is

still no formal separation of the legislature and the executive.

The cantonal governments normally consist of between five and nine members directly elected by the people and not by the cantonal parliament. Majority voting is used in all but two cantons (Ticino and Zug) but, as at federal level, agreement between the parties often ensures that there is a stable coalition of the same group of parties running the cantonal government. Being a member of a cantonal government is usually, but not invariably, a full-time job.

The lowest, but nevertheless still powerful, tier of Swiss government are the communes. In some cantons they have great autonomy (as in Graubünden which is a confederation of very independent communes, rather like a Switzerland in miniature), in others, especially French-speaking Switzerland, their powers are much more circumscribed. In Vaud, for example, the communes are very weak, and the prefects nominated by the cantonal government play a vital role.

Almost all communes have either a communal assembly with direct democracy or a communal parliament elected by a majority or proportional system. The communal executive is always elected by the people, except in the canton of Neuchatel.

Brief political history

Modern Swiss political history began in 1789 when Napoleon swept away the patchwork system of the existing cantons with their differing privileges, traditions and subject territories and replaced them with a unitary centralized state with the cantons reduced to mere administrative departments. In 1803, however, he was forced to recognise Swiss realities and in the Act of Mediation of that year he reintroduced a federal state.

In 1815 the old order was re-established, but with several differences. The Napoleonic changes were not completely swept away and, in particular, the existence of a number of new cantons was recognised and some additional ones created.

In the ensuing period, however, liberal movements began to develop in a number of cantons, seeking greater democratic rights, freedom of the press and other reforms. Conflict between conservative forces, in particular in the Catholic cantons and the increasingly radical Protestant or anti-clerical reform movements became more widespread and culminated in a brief civil war in 1847 when the conservative Catholic cantons allied in the *Sonderbund* were crushed by federal forces. The 1848 Federal Constitution, however, in spite of being the product of the victorious Radicals, represented a compromise between central and cantonal powers.

Based partly on American experience, a bicameral legislature was established, reflecting actual population patterns in one chamber and equality between cantons in the other. A strong central executive was rejected in favour of a collegiate Federal Council of seven members.

1848 saw the beginning of a long period of Radical dominance of the Swiss federal institutions. In 1874 a new Constitution was introduced. Less centralizing than the would-be Constitution of 1872, it introduced the optional legislative referendum at federal level, and introduced anti-Catholic clauses in the Constitution which have only recently been finally removed.

Throughout this period the former *Sonderbund* cantons remained in a Catholic conservative ghetto, whereas in certain other cantons there were similar conflicts to the German *Kulturkampf* between Church and State. These were short-lived, however, and in 1891 an important breakthrough was made in reducing Catholic isolation when a Catholic became a member of the Federal Council for the first time, thus breaking the Radical monopoly of power.

In spite of the dominance of the Radicals at federal level, and of the Catholic conservatives in the *Sonderbund* cantons, fully organized political parties in the modern sense were only gradually established at federal level, the Socialists in 1888, the Radicals in 1894, the Catholic Conservatives not until 1912. The latter two were particularly fragmented, with the Catholics split between Conservatives and emerging Christian Social movements, and with the liberal/radical forces split between the mainstream Radicals, the old Liberals on the right, and the new Democratic parties to their left. Just before World War I peasant parties began to develop in certain cantons as well.

In 1891 a further important constitutional change had been made with the introduction of the popular initiative. Perhaps the most important change, however, was adopted in 1918 when proportional representation was introduced at federal level and led immediately to a decline in Radical strength from 111 to 60 seats and a rise in Socialist representation from 19 to 41. Proportional representation was introduced in the aftermath of the 1918 general strike. While it was put down, it did also lead to a reduction in the working week to 48 hours. In 1937 a landmark agreement was reached between the workers' and employers' representatives whereby the former effectively renounced the strike weapon, in exchange for union recognition and abandonment of such practices as lockouts by the latter.

Non-Radical participation in the Federal Council was gradually extended. In 1929 a member of the Peasants' Party joined the Federal Council, followed in 1943 by the first Socialist. Several of the newly formed cantonal Communist parties, however, were treated harshly and were banned in certain cantons. After World War II, in which Switzerland managed to maintain its neutrality and avoid invasion, it refused to join the UN, although it had previously been a rather reluctant member of the League of Nations. This decision was recently confirmed in a 1986 federal referendum.

1947 saw the introduction of an important federal social welfare measure, the AVS, an old age and survivors' insurance scheme. The trend toward widening participation in the Federal Council was temporarily interrupted when the Socialists withdrew from government between

1953 and 1959. In 1959 the present government formula was adopted and has survived irrespective of election results, although the latter have been remarkably stable over the last 50 years. Among the non-governmental parties there has been greater volatility. The *Landesring* was established in the 1950s by the founder of the Migros firm to defend consumer interests and has survived with fluctuating fortunes ever since. In the late 1960s a number of new left–wing parties were founded which have established themselves in certain cantons. A number of new right–wing parties have also enjoyed a certain success, because of fears about the increasing number of immigrants in Switzerland. Most recently of all, ecological parties have been enjoying levels of support higher than in most other European countries.

Main features of the current Swiss political system

Swiss politics are highly distinctive, characterized both by intense localism and diversity of political forms and structures, and also by certain strong common features such as stability, co-operation and compromise, and the prevalence of direct democracy.

Swiss diversity is accentuated by a number of linguistic and religious splits. Linguistic differences are probably the least important in explaining Switzerland's current political structure. While some of the smaller parties are based in one linguistic area or the other, the three biggest parties are represented in French, German or Italian Switzerland (and for that matter Romansch Switzerland as well). Moreover, Switzerland has developed on a multi-lingual basis, and the rights of linguistic minorities are well protected. The Jura problem, created when a new French-speaking canton Jura was carved out of predominantly German-speaking canton Berne, was a partial exception, but other reasons (historical and religious) were also important.

If there are differences between the linguistic zones, they are mostly of a cultural nature. Direct democratic forms are more characteristic of the German-speaking cantons, for example. There is sometimes differential voting; compulsory wearing of seat belts received strong support in German Switzerland but much less in French and Italian Switzerland. More recently, opposition to nuclear energy is stronger in German Switzerland.

A second and surprisingly resistant cleavage is that of religion. Unlike its German counterpart, the Christian Democratic Party has remained overwhelmingly Catholic. On the other hand,

parties such as the Evangelicals, the Liberals, the *Landesring* and the Swiss People's Party are overwhelmingly Protestant in their membership. The Radicals have a Protestant tradition but also represent the formerly anti-clerical forces in Catholic cantons such as Ticino or Solothurn. In a canton such as Luzern the old clerical/anti-clerical divide still exists to a considerable degree and political differences are largely due to the persisting "pillarisation" of society.

Class differences, on the other hand, have been of less significance. There is little heavy industry in Switzerland and the parties of the left have always had to look outside the few industrial areas such as Basel to get an adequate level of support. Urban/rural differences have been more significant, and the small farmers have remained influential, especially in the Catholic mountain cantons and in Berne. Switzerland is the only Western European country outside Scandinavia where a Peasants' Party has developed and survived.

Besides these general divisions, Switzerland is characterized by more localized differences, with each canton and many communes having their own specific traditions, and personalities. Some, such as Vaud, are centralized, others, such as Graubünden, very decentralized, some such as Berne, have a tradition of deference to authority, others have no such tradition. As a result, Swiss political parties at federal level are rather weak and normally consist of a loose confederation of very different cantonal parties. Any examination of Swiss political parties has had to bear this strongly in mind. On the other hand there are many common features in Swiss political life. One is the tradition of co-operation and partnership, evident in relationships between the political parties, as in other areas of Swiss life, such as labour relations.

Not only is there a permanent government coalition of four parties at federal level, but there are different but often equally stable governing coalitions at cantonal level. Moreover, this tradition of co-operation extends across ideological divides. The Socialists are outnumbered by the "bourgeois" parties within the Federal governing coalition, but are not excluded. At cantonal level, parties which profess themselves to be against the whole system take part in cantonal government, such as the Communists in Geneva, or the Autonomous Socialists in Ticino. Another remarkable feature is that dominant parties normally do not try to rule on their own but voluntarily give up a share in power to smaller parties. A strong desire to achieve compromise is another distinctive element of Swiss political life. The victors of the Swiss Civil War, those

Swiss election results, 1945 to the present (percentages and seats won in the National Council)

	1947	1951	1955	1959	1963	1967	1971	1975	1979	1983	1987
CVP/PDC (Christian Democrats)	21.2% (44)	22.5% (48)	23.2% (47)	23.3% (47)	23.4% (48)	22.1% (45)	20.6% (44)	21.1% (46)	21.5% (44)	20.6% (42)	20.0% (42)
FDP/PRD (Radicals)	23.0% (52)	24.0% (51)	23.3% (50)	23.7% (51)	24.0% (51)	23.2% (49)	21.7% (49)	22.2% (47)	24.1% (51)	23.4% (54)	22.9% (51)
SPS/PSS (Socialists)	26.2% (48)	26.0% (49)	27.0% (53)	26.4% (51)	26.6% (53)	23.5% (51)	22.9% (46)	24.9% (55)	24.6% (51)	22.8% (47)	18.4% (41)
SVP/UDC (Swiss People's Party)	12.1% (21)	12.6% (23)	12.1% (22)	11.6% (23)	11.4% (22)	11.0% (21)	10.2% (23)	9.9% (21)	11.6% (23)	11.1% (23)	11.0% (25)
Landesring (Party of Independents)	4.4% (8)	5.1% (10)	5.5% (10)	5.5% (10)	5.0% (10)	9.1% (16)	7.6% (13)	6.1% (11)	4.1% (8)	4.0% (9)	4.2% (9)
Parti Suisse du Travail (Communists)	5.1% (7)	2.7% (5)	2.6% (4)	2.7% (3)	2.2% (4)	2.9% (5)	2.6% (5)	2.4% (4)	2.1% (3)	0.9% (1)	0.8% (1)
Parti Libéral Suisse (Liberals)	3.2% (7)	2.6% (5)	2.2% (5)	2.3% (5)	2.2% (6)	2.3% (6)	2.2% (6)	2.4% (6)	2.8% (8)	2.8% (8)	2.7% (9)
EVP (Evangelical People's Party)	0.9% (1)	1.0% (1)	1.1% (1)	1.4% (2)	1.6% (2)	1.6% (3)	2.1% (3)	2.0% (3)	2.2% (3)	2.1% (3)	1.9% (3)
NA (National Action)	—	—	—	—	—	0.6% (1)	3.2% (4)	2.4% (2)	1.3% (2)	3.5% (5)	2.9% (3)
GPS/PES (Green Party)	—	—	—	—	—	—	—	—	—	2.9% (4)	4.8% (9)
POCH (Progressive Organizations)	—	—	—	—	—	—	—	1.0% (0)	1.7% (3)	3.5% (4)	3.5% (5)
Others	3.9% (6)	3.6% (4)	3.2% (4)	3.2% (4)	3.6% (4)	3.7% (3)	6.0% (7)	5.6% (5)	4.2% (4)	2.5% (0)	6.8% (2)

who put down the 1918 general strike and more recently the politicians dealing with the Jura dispute, have all aimed at compromise solutions, taking into account both majority and minority interests.

The most well-known feature of all, however, is the extent to which direct democratic forms are used, such as the meeting of citizens in the annual *Landsgemeinde* which still exist in certain cantons, and the widespread use of referenda and initiatives at both cantonal and federal level, both to challenge laws and constitutional amendments, and to propose new ones.

This has had several effects on the Swiss political system. Firstly, it has undoubtedly weakened the political parties (whose membership tends to be rather low) and strengthened instead the sectoral associations and interest groups. Secondly, it has enabled parties such as the Socialists to be both governing and opposition parties at the same time, participating in government decisions, but also being able to challenge them through referenda and initiatives.

A third effect is the number of occasions on which citizens are called upon to vote and which has led, in certain cantons, and at federal level especially, to among the lowest voter turnouts in any European country. It has also partly reflected, but also reinforced, the conservative nature of Swiss society. Numerous proposals which the main political parties have supported have been rejected by the voters, such as Swiss adherence to the UN. Attempts to give women the vote began as early as 1918 but only came to fruition at federal level in 1971, after several rejections by male voters.

Direct popular control and the part-time and localized nature of much of Swiss politics have not contributed to the emergence of many dominant political figures. Switzerland is unique in Western Europe in having a collegiate leadership rather than a prime minister or president. Very few Swiss politicians have made a reputation outside Switzerland, not even those who have held federal office for exceptionally long periods, such as Giuseppe Motta, Philipp Etter or Max Petitpierre.

On the political agenda there are a number of distinctive Swiss issues. One is the issue of constitutional revision and in particular, the nature of the balance between federal and cantonal power; another is the role of the Swiss militia army (the extent to which it should be supported financially and otherwise and whether civilian alternatives should be provided for conscientious objectors). A third concerns how the numbers of foreigners in Switzerland can be stabilized or reduced, and the extent of their rights. However, environmental protection is probably the most intensely debated political issue of all, especially in the aftermath of Chernobyl and the Rhine chemical disaster at Schwyzerhalle. The further development of public transport, tough new controls on car emissions and even on car use and the future of nuclear energy are all receiving even more attention in Switzerland than elsewhere.

Sozialdemokratische Partei der Schweiz —SPS Parti Socialiste Suisse
Partito Socialista Svizzero
(Swiss Social Democratic Party)

Headquarters	: Pavilionweg 3, Postfach 4084, CH–3001, Berne (tel: 031–241115)
President	: Helmut Hubacher
President of parliamentary group:	Ursula Mauch
Secretary-general	: Andre Daguet
Youth organization	: Socialist Youth
Founded	: 1888

History

The Swiss Social Democratic Party was first founded on an enduring basis in 1888, although there had been Socialist parties at cantonal level previously.

Its first programme put emphasis on extending democracy and the role of central government. The new party was envisaged as one to improve the lot of all Swiss people rather than just the interests of the working class.

In 1890 the party gained its first representative in the National Assembly, Jakob Vogelsanger of Zürich. By 1902 it had seven representatives.

From 1900 until World War I the party took a more radical direction under the combined forces of industrialization and urbanization and a great increase in the number of foreign workers in Switzerland. The 1904 party programme put a much stronger emphasis on the class nature of the party, although it was still relatively moderate. In 1911 its 18 members of the National Council founded a parliamentary group for the first time.

During the tense period of World War I the left faction within the party became more assertive. In 1918 the Olten Action Committee was established under the leadership of the militant socialist, Robert Grimm, and in November a general strike took place which was quickly crushed by the army. The subsequent introduction of proportional representation at federal level, however, led to a massive increase in the number of Socialist seats from 19 to 41 at the next national elections.

The years 1920–21 saw internal strife in the party, and its adoption of a radical socialist programme was not enough to prevent the creation of a new Communist Party in 1921. Nevertheless the Socialist Party continued to gain in strength and by 1928 it was winning more votes in national elections than any other Swiss party, a position it managed to maintain until 1983. In 1931 it attained its highest ever percentage of the national vote, 28.7 per cent.

In the mid-1930s, faced with the rise of Fascism in neighbouring countries, the party began to modify its policies again. In 1935 it reversed its position of opposing national defence efforts and ceased calling for a dictatorship of the proletariat. In 1937 any tendencies towards class conflict were further reduced by the adoption of the so-called *Arbeitsfrieden* between workers and employers in the metal working sector. Not all elements of the party were satisfied with its more pragmatic line. A left–wing group in Geneva, for example, whose leader was Leon Nicole, left the party in 1939.

After its success in the 1943 elections, the SPS finally gained a place on the seven-member Federal Council. Its first councillor, Ernst Nobs, remained on the governing Federal Council for eight years, and was replaced in 1951 by Max Weber. In 1953, however, the finance programme he introduced was rejected by the Swiss electorate and the Socialists then withdrew from the Federal Council for six years.

In 1959 the party's transition towards establishment status in the Swiss political system reached a high-water mark; the party's new programme was more moderate than any of its predecessors, paralleling similar decisions taken by the German Social Democrats at their Bad Godesburg conference of the same year. Moreover, a new government formula was agreed upon by the main Swiss parties (see general introduction) in which the Socialists finally got as many Federal Council places (two) as the Radicals and the Christian Democrats.

From the late 1960s onwards, however, there were increasing tensions within the party, as younger members were increasingly influenced by ecological, peace and women's groups. In 1969 there was a schism within the Ticino cantonal party leading to the foundation of a rival socialist party, the *Partito Socialista Autonomo* (see section on *Partito Socialista Unitario*).

In the early 1980s conflicts between left and right within the party became more intense, especially in certain cantons, such as Basel and Zürich. In 1982 there was a breakaway by the right wing of the Basel Socialist Party, leading to the creation and initial electoral success of a new Social Democratic Party (*Demokratisch–Soziale Partei*) within the canton.

In 1983 the Socialist Party put forward Lilian Uchtenhagen (who would have been the first ever woman member of the federal government) as their official nominee for the Federal Council, but another Socialist, Otto Stich, was elected in her place. There was a long debate within the Socialist Party on whether to withdraw from government in protest but in 1984 a special party congress finally decided against the central committee's recommendation to withdraw by 773 votes to 511.

Support

From 1919 to the early 1980s the socialist vote had remained a stable one at federal level, fluctuating between a high of 28.7 per cent (1931 to a low of 22.8 per cent (1971 and 1983). In 1987, however, the party's vote fell to only 18.4 per cent, and its number of seats in the Council of States from six to five. This represented its biggest single fall in support between successive elections. The SPS is now the smallest of the big three Swiss parties.

The SPS appears to have lost considerable support among its traditional working-class electorate as a result of its internal divisions and "greener" image. This is particularly true in some of the more densely populated and industrial cantons such as Zürich and Basel. The SPS lacks support in the countryside and in the small towns. It is generally stronger in Protestant areas and cantons than in Catholic ones. In 1987 its vote slumped particularly badly in German-speaking Switzerland, whereas the party held its vote (and in some cases even improved it) in French-speaking Switzerland. The SPS has remained relatively weak and divided in the Italian-speaking Ticino.

In 1987 the SPS was strongest in the small industrialized canton of Schaffhausen, where its vote actually rose from 35.3 per cent to 39.2 per cent. The only other canton where it still has over 30 per cent in national elections is Neuchatel (30.8 per cent in 1987): here the Socialist strength is based on the watch-making towns and villages in the Jura. The SPS also had a big rise in support in 1987 in the new canton of Jura (17.8 per cent to 25.5 per cent), and slightly increased its support in Vaud (21.9 per cent to 22.5 per cent), making it one of its stronger cantons.

The SPS is still the largest party in the two half-cantons of Basel (although with a drop of almost 10 per cent in support in 1987 in Basel-Land and a 5 per cent drop in the city of Basel), and also in the canton of Geneva (but with only 18.6 per cent support), where the party has been harmed by the continuing strength of the Communist Party.

The SPS has traditionally been strong in the canton of Berne, despite its relative lack of industrialization, and this is probably explained by the Bernese preference for a strong state role. SPS strength in Berne has declined recently, and in 1987 it fell sharply from its 1983 figure of 28.3 per cent to only 22.3 per cent.

The SPS also used to be the major force in Zürich (reaching 40 per cent of the vote in 1931), but this is now one of its weaker cantons. The party's vote also fell back in 1987 in Graubünden (where the party had previously gained considerably in the postwar period), and also in Solothurn, which has produced two of its recent Federal Councillors.

The SPS has remained weakest of all in the Catholic mountain cantons. In Luzern, for example, the party had only 9 per cent in 1987, barely more than the green–alternative vote in the canton. In two half-cantons, Obwald and Appenzell-Inner-Rhoden there are no organized socialist parties at all.

Organization

The SPS is the most centralized of the major Swiss political parties, with a stronger parliamentary party voting discipline and with a generally stronger federal party.

In terms of membership the SPS is only the fourth largest Swiss party, and it has been steadily declining in numbers since the mid-1960s. In 1986 it had under 42,000 officially paid-up members, although its actual membership is higher than this. Berne has the highest membership (over 12,500 in 1986), with Zürich (over 6,000) a distant second.

The SPS has around 1,100 branches around the country. There are 26 parties at cantonal level. Although there are no cantonal parties in Obwald and Appenzell-Inner-Rhoden there are two cantonal parties in both Berne and Valais, with separate parties for their German- and French-speaking areas.

The party's federal congress is generally held on an annual basis, and consists of up to 1,500 delegates, mainly from the party branches. Among its powers are the election of party officers and final decisions on key matters, such as the launching of federal initiatives. The Congress can be highly independent. In 1984, for example, it rejected the central committee's recommendation for an SPS withdrawal from the federal government.

The SPS central committee, which meets around eight times a year, consists of around 110 members, including representatives of the cantonal parties, the parliamentarians, members elected directly by the Congress and representatives of the youth and women's groups within the party. There is also a representative of the organization of workers' cultural and sporting associations, but no direct trade union representatives. Among other tasks, the central committee has to decide on the party's recommendations in federal referenda, and to launch a referendum against a federal law.

There is also a smaller (18 member) executive committee which deals with more urgent issues and meets on average once a month. Day-to-day matters are looked after by the executive committee's bureau, led by the party's president and vice-presidents. There is a special co-ordinating committee for the party in French-speaking Switzerland, which meets once a month.

The party's statutes provide for representation of Swiss linguistic minorities in certain party bodies, such as its arbitration committee.

The party's youth group (*Jungsozialisten/ Jeunesse Socialiste*) has around 20 branches.

There are around 200 women's groups in the party, and 12 cantonal organizations. At federal level there is a central women's committee (*Zentrale Frauenkommission*), which meets every two or three months, and has around 25 members. A newspaper called *Rote Heft* is produced on a monthly basis. A women's conference is also held. Since 1986 the party has established a minimum quota, whereby at least a third of the party office-holders and candidates on party electoral lists must be women.

There are no formal party links with the trade union movement. There is no national socialist newspaper, but a number of local newspapers are recognized as official press outlets of the party, although they are independent in terms of finance and editorial content. Among the better-known ones are the *Tagwacht,* the *Basler AZ* and the *Volksrecht*. A number have fallen into severe financial difficulties, and some have ceased publication. In French-speaking Switzerland there are no daily socialist newspapers, but the cantonal socialist parties produce their own newspapers on a more irregular basis. The party also produces a journal called *Roten Revue* and a members' bulletin *Sp–Intern*.

The party's income comes mainly from membership dues (over 80 per cent of income in the party's 1988 budget), which are paid monthly and are on a differentiated basis, according to a member's means. Party office holders also pay a contribution. There are special dues for members of the party holding high functions within the confederation, such as federal councillors, judges of the federal tribunal, and even ambassadors. About 10 per cent of party funds are used for training purposes.

The SPS is a member of the Socialist International and is also an observer at the Confederation of Socialist Parties of the European Community.

Policies

Ever since the late 1960s the SPS has been slowly changing its character from being a traditional moderate social democratic party towards one which puts a far greater emphasis on ecological themes, and it is now probably one of the most "green" of the European socialist parties.

This process of transition has led to considerable tensions and conflicts within the party, notably between its older and younger members, and between its more conservative trade union wing and the supporters of ecological, peace and feminist groups. In some cases this has even led to schisms within individual cantonal parties. In the shorter term at least it has weakened the party electorally, as losses among its traditional and trade union supporters have not been fully compensated by gains among younger and green voters who have also had other parties to turn to.

Another consequence of this change has been to widen the gap between the Socialists and the centre–right parties in the federal government. The SPS is now in the awkward position of being both a government and an opposition party at the same time. It has had two of the seven posts on the governing federal council since 1959 yet it has been often placed in a minority position with regard to its government partners. Moreover, there has sometimes been tension between its representatives in government and the party at large, as when the party came out against civil nuclear energy in 1978, thus embarrassing the Socialist head of the Department of Energy, Willi Ritschard.

The Socialists' activities as an opposition party have come out most clearly in their regular support for popular referenda and initiatives; these have acted as a valuable safety-valve for the party's more radical members, although they have sometimes caused internal difficulties within the SPS.

The SPS is still faced with the longer-term question of whether it wishes to remain in the federal government, or to eventually return to opposition. The party was placed in particular difficulty in 1983–84 when (for the third time) its official nominee for federal government responsibilities was rejected by the other parties in favour of a more acceptable Socialist candidate. It decided to remain and in 1987 the parliamentary party itself chose an uncontroversial candidate, thus confirming its decision to continue in government at a moment of party electoral weakness.

The party's two major policy themes in the 1987 federal elections were the need to greatly strengthen environmental policy, and the need to defend and consolidate social welfare policy.

The SPS has expressed its concern about the negative aspects of economic growth. It puts a strong emphasis on the need to reconcile ecology with technical progress and to create "ecological employment". It has argued that "green and red go very well together". By far the largest category of recent actions by the SPS parliamentary group have come in the related environmental and transport fields.

The SPS has been one of the leading supporters of the initiative for a progressive abandonment of civil nuclear energy in Switzerland, calling for a halt to construction of new plants, and a gradual de-commissioning of existing ones.

The SPS seeks to greatly strengthen public transport at the expense of the car. It has supported lower public transport fares and cut-price rail season tickets, as well as new investment in rail transport. It has sought to stop the construction of major new roads, to lower speed limits, and to apply "the polluter pays" principle to motorists as well.

The SPS seeks to tackle air pollution through reinforced emission standards, and the use of appropriate fiscal incentives. The party has called for statistics to be published on the average life span of different consumer goods.

The SPS wants a much higher priority given to environmental protection in agriculture, more natural products with less use of chemicals, and a greater emphasis on quality rather than quantity. The SPS has also encouraged an initiative to protect farming land, and to stop speculation. A new issue of concern for the SPS is genetic manipulation and the need for proper controls and adequate public information and consultation on this subject.

The other major policy emphasis of the SPS in 1987 was on the need to reinforce social welfare measures. The SPS has been proud of its role in developing Swiss social policy, and seeks to prevent it being weakened. A recent issue has been the need to strengthen the legal regime concerning maternity leave. It is also keen to see that equality between men and women is more effectively implemented, and seeks improvements to the divorce law.

In its general economic policy the SPS supports the mixed economy, with the state continuing to play an important role, but also with heavy reliance on a properly functioning market, which in some fields should play a greater role than at present. The SPS has been highly critical of the power of big business and of multinationals in particular.

The SPS does not advocate any new nationalizations, and points out that a change in ownership is not in itself sufficient to improve an enterprise. In the past the SPS has been the strongest advocate of central against cantonal power, but it now calls for more decentralised economic development. An important party theme has been the need for greater economic and industrial democracy within Swiss industry. More far-reaching ideas for worker self-management, popular on the left of the party in the 1970s and 1980s, have not been accepted by the majority of the SPS.

The SPS has also called for a shorter working week, and a better distribution of available work, with more part-time work and job-sharing.

It recognizes that the public budget needs to be balanced in the medium term, but believes that economic austerity and tax cuts and a lesser role for the state should not become objectives for their own sake.

One area where the SPS believes that economies can be made, and where it has come into conflict with the parties of the centre–right, is defence policy. The SPS does not attack the Swiss system of defence (although in 1981 the Young Socialists did sponsor a popular initiative for the suppression of the army, which won minimal support) but it calls for increases in military expenditure (e.g. the costly purchase of Leopard II tanks) to be brought under greater control. It put forward an unsuccessful initiative for military expenditure to be subjected to possible public referenda. The SPS seeks to improve the position of conscientious objectors, and has called for the creation of an alternative civilian service. It also wants Switzerland to be better integrated into the European disarmament process.

The SPS supported Swiss entry into the UN. It calls for a Swiss development aid policy which puts more emphasis on environmental impact. It is critical of existing links with South Africa.

The SPS has adopted a dual stance of tough controls to prevent any new wave of immigration into Switzerland, but also stronger rights for those foreigners already on Swiss soil. The SPS has been critical of recent developments in asylum policy, and has called for it to be kept as liberal and open as possible.

The SPS has called for a strengthening of the National Council at the expense of the Council of States, which, it believes, gives too much power at federal level to small and relatively unpopulated cantons.

Personalities

Helmut Hubacher has been the party president since 1975. The two federal councillors are Otto Stich, first elected in 1983 at the expense of the official party nominee, Lilian Uchtenhagen, and René Felber who was elected in late 1987 at the successor to Pierre Aubert. He was chosen by the SPS parliamentary group in preference to Christian Grobet, who had been the central committee's nominee.

The president of the SPS parliamentary group is Ursula Mauch and the leader of the party's women's organization, the ZFK, is Lucie Husler. The two party vice-presidents are Peter Vollmer and Heidi Beneys. André Daguet has been the party's central secretary since 1986.

Freisinnig Demokratische Partei der Schweiz—FDP
Parti Radical–Démocratique Suisse—PRD
Partito Liberale Radicale—PLR

(Radical Democratic Party of Switzerland)

Headquarters	: Bahnhofplatz 10, CH–3001 Berne C.P. 2642 Berne (tel: 031–223438/39)
President	: Dr Bruno Hunziker
Secretary-general	: Christian Kanter
Youth organization	: *Jungliberale Bewegung der Schweiz/Jeunesse Radicale Suisse* (president: Isabelle Vogt)
Women's group	: *Union Suisse des Femmes Radicales-Démocratiques/ Schweizerische Vereinigung Freisinnig-Demokratischer Frauen* (SVFF) (president Dr Regula Frei-Stolba)
Newspapers	: *Der Freisinn* (70,000) *Politische Rundschau/Revue Politique* (12,000) *Information* (5,000)
Membership	: 150,000

History

The Radical Party has had the longest continuous participation in government of any party in the world, not having been in opposition since 1848. It created the present Swiss federal structure and for a long time was the dominant political force in Switzerland, monopolizing power until 1891, and only losing its overall majority on the Federal Council in 1943. Since 1848, 64 out of the 97 federal councillors have been Radicals. After a period when it won fewer votes then the Socialist Party it is again the largest Swiss party in terms of both votes and seats in parliament

The Radical tradition in Swiss politics stems from divisions within the liberal movement between conservatives and radicals in the early 19th century. In the 1830s and 1840s, Radicals, often supporting federalist and anti-clerical policies, came to power in a number of cantons. By 1847 they had won control of a majority of Swiss cantons, and came into direct conflict with the Catholic Conservative, *Sonderbund* cantons, whom they defeated in a brief civil war. The 1848 Federal Constitution, which created a proper central government while maintaining a strong measure of cantonal autonomy, was essentially a Radical one.

The Radical movement remained a broad-based one, including both classic economic liberals and others advocating a more interventionist role for the state, such as Stämpfli, who fought hard for a unified publicly-owned Swiss railway network. Radicals also helped to institute the federal constitutional revisions of 1874, which introduced measures of semi-direct democracy, such as referenda and initiatives. Radicals continued to be associated with defence of strong federal institutions.

There was still no formally constituted Radical Party at federal level, but in 1878 a Radical Democratic group was established within the Federal Assembly. In 1891 the Radicals finally conceded a place to a Catholic Conservative in the Federal Council, thus ending their complete control over the Council. In 1894 a Swiss Radical Democratic Party was founded. During the late 19th century a number of members on the Radical left wing broke away in several German-speaking cantons to form new "Democratic" parties (see section on Swiss People's Party – SVP).

The Radical Party remained the largest party in terms of votes until as late as 1928. After 1919 its position was considerably weakened after the introduction of proportional representation. In 1914 the Radicals had 111 out of the 189 seats, but in 1919 held only 60. In the same year they also conceded a second seat to the Catholic

Conservative Party in the Federal Council. The Radicals also suffered from a serious schism with the creation of a more exclusively farmers' party, the Farmers', Traders' and Citizens' Party (see Swiss People's Party — SVP). This had a particularly adverse electoral effect on the Radicals in the canton of Berne, where, in 1922, the party lost three-quarters of its seats in the cantonal parliament. In 1929 the Radicals also conceded a Federal Council seat to the Farmers' Party.

In 1928 the Radicals lost their position as the party with the largest number of votes nationally to the Socialist Party (by only six votes), and only regained the lead in 1983. During the 1930s and 1940s their vote gradually slipped until in 1943 they only gained 22.5 per cent. In 1943 they finally lost their overall majority on the Federal Council, when a government post was given to the Socialist Party.

Since then, however, the Radicals' national vote has been extremely stable, never falling below 21.7 per cent and never rising above 24.1 per cent. Since 1959 the Radical Party has had the same number of seats on the Federal Council as the Socialist and Christian People's Parties.

In the 1987 national elections the Radical Party won 22.9 per cent of the national vote, and was the largest party in the National Assembly with 51 seats, and the second party in the Council of States with 14 seats. It has the largest number of members of cantonal parliaments (825) of any Swiss party, and is represented in all except Appenzell–Inner–Rhoden. The Radical Party is represented in all cantonal governments except Berne and Appenzell–Inner–Rhoden, and has 50 out of the 168 members of cantonal governments.

Support

The Radical Party has support in all parts of Switzerland, in Protestant and Catholic, and in German, French and Italian-speaking cantons, in the city and in the countryside. The Radical Party is strongly supported by economic liberals, business interests and the Swiss Protestant establishment, but at cantonal level its support base varies greatly. In some cantons like Zürich it is the party of the *haute bourgeoisie* whereas in others like Geneva and Vaud, this position has been taken instead by the old Liberal Party. In Berne its position among small farmers has been taken by the Swiss People's Party, whereas in certain other cantons, such as Vaud, Thurgau and St. Gallen the Radical Party has remained strongly implanted among the small farmers. As a general rule the Radicals are weakest in the Catholic cantons of central Switzerland (although even here they are almost always in second place to the Catholic People's Party, and in some cantons, like Luzern, have benefited from the anti-clerical vote in the past), but they have often been the largest party in overwhelmingly Catholic Ticino, and almost invariably in majority Catholic Solothurn, where many of their leaders came from old Catholic families. The Radical Party thus has the most heterogeneous support base of any Swiss party.

In the 1987 federal elections the Radicals were the largest party in two major cantons, Vaud (27.4 per cent), and Zürich (20 per cent). Vaud has been one of the party's key strongholds. It is easily the largest party at cantonal level (70 out of 200 seats in the cantonal parliament in the 1986 elections). The party did not surrender its absolute majority over the Vaud cantonal government until 1955, and the party has traditionally controlled the nomination of the powerful cantonal prefects.

In Zürich the Radicals have in the past been weaker than the Socialists but have again become the largest party, at cantonal (46 out of 180 seats in the 1987 cantonal elections) as well as federal level. The other canton where the Radical Party had the most votes in 1987 was Solothurn, where it won 36.3 per cent of the vote, and where it still dominates the cantonal parliament (66 out of the 144 seats in the 1986 cantonal elections).

Other cantons where the Radical Party is in a strong position include the Ticino (where it was second to the Christian People's Party with 34.9 per cent in the 1987 federal elections, but the largest party with 33 out of the 90 seats in the 1987 cantonal elections); Basel-Land (where it was narrowly second to the socialists with 22 per cent in the 1987 federal elections, but narrowly first with 23 out of 84 seats in the 1987 cantonal elections); Aargau (where it was the largest party with 20.3 per cent in the 1987 federal elections); and Schaffhausen, where it won 34.3 per cent in the 1987 federal elections, and was second to the Socialist Party. In the canton of Jura it was second to the Christian People's Party with 33.4 per cent in 1987. In Thurgau and in Geneva the Radicals were only the third party in the 1987 federal elections with 18.5 per cent and 18 per cent respectively, but were only narrowly behind the first party in both cantons.

In a number of other cantons the Radicals have been further behind the leading parties. In Berne their position has been eroded by the SVP, and the Radicals are only the third political force in the canton in both federal (16.1 per cent in 1987) and cantonal elections (40 out of 200 seats in 1986). In Neuchatel, where the primacy on the right is still with the old Liberals, the Radicals are also a poor third (20.5 per cent in 1987). In Graubünden they are only in fourth position (18.3 per cent in the 1987 federal elections), and they have a particularly low vote in the fragmented party politics of the city of Basel (11.2 per cent in the 1987 Federal elections).

In the Catholic mountain cantons dominated by the Christian People's Party the Radicals are generally in a poor second place. They have done well in rapidly developing Zug (almost equal with the CVP in 1987 with 34.1 per cent of the vote), but are well behind the CVP in such cantons as Schwyz, Luzern, Obwalden and Nidwalden. Recently they have done very poorly in Fribourg (a distant third with 16.7 per cent in 1987). They have always been very weak in the Valais (24.5 per cent in 1987, compared to 58.7 per cent for the CVP), where they have a few pockets of support in the lower Rhone Valley like Martigny, but are almost non-existent in the German-speaking upper Rhone Valley (Oberwallis). In Appenzell-Inner-Rhoden there are no candidates under a Radical Party label.

Organization

The Radical Party has the largest membership of any Swiss party at around 150,000 (the party's own estimate at the end of 1987). It is organized in all cantons except Appenzell-Inner-Rhoden, with its name varying from canton to canton (e.g. the *Parti Radical-Démocratique* in Vaud, Valais and Fribourg, the *Parti Radical* in Neuchatel, Geneva and the Bernese Jura, and the *Parti Liberal Radicale* in the Jura). Below these it has 1,400 local sections.

At federal level a Delegates' Assembly meets at least once a year. It includes 300 representatives of the cantonal parties (each canton has a right to a minimum of four delegates and supplementary delegates according to the party's electoral results in the canton), who are elected for four-year terms. A Party Congress is also held at which all members can participate, and which, in practice, tends to be combined with a normal meeting of the Delegates' Assembly.

There is also a 50-member Council of Delegates, which is elected by the Delegates' Assembly, and must include at least one member from each canton. It also has a four-year term, and meets every two months. Among its tasks is the election of the party secretary-general.

Above this is a 9–11 member Executive Committee, elected by the Delegates' Assembly, which also elects the party president and the three vice-presidents (who must come from the three main linguistic regions of Switzerland).

The Radical Youth Group (*Jeunesse Radicale*

Suisse/Jungliberale Bewegung der Schweiz) has 24 cantonal sections. There is an active women's group, the SVFF. Besides these there is also a Radical construction industry association (*Verband Liberaler Baugenossenshaften*) and a Radical press association (*Schweizerischer Freisinnig-Demokratischer Presseverband*).

The Radical Party produces a monthly newspaper called *Der Freisinn*. Special versions of this, with additional local information, are produced in the individual cantons. The party's other publications include *Information*, and a regular political review (*Politische Rundschau/Revue Politique*). It is also well supported in the non-party Swiss press.

The Radical Party is a member of the Liberal International.

Policies

The Radical Party has gradually evolved from constituting the left wing of the liberal movement to being a more conservative party. Its most celebrated slogan in recent years has been "more liberty and responsibility and less state", and it has become the leading advocate among the major Swiss parties of reducing state involvement in the economy. It is still, however, very heterogeneous, with a considerable difference in its character and policy emphasis from canton to canton and with a broad range of views within the party. While not advocating, for example, such far-reaching changes on environmental policy as most other Swiss parties, it has a number of strong environmentalists in its midst.

The Radical Party has always had a lay emphasis, and in some cantons has had an anti-clerical tone, although this is now of much less significance. What does often remain is a strong attachment to the Radical Party for historical and cultural reasons. In those few cantons, for instance, where it is still in competition with the old Liberal Party, tradition and family background tends to play a greater role in explaining whether someone will join one or the other party than policy differences, which are now often rather slight.

Two important themes constantly emphasized by the Radical Party are its historical role as the creator of the present Swiss confederation and its institutions, and the length of its experience in helping to run those institutions. It prides itself as a party of government, and of managerial competence, especially in running the Swiss economy. It considers itself to be a pragmatic party, which rejects utopian ideas and fashionable new solutions, but concentrates instead on realistic and steady adaptation to new circumstances.

The Radical Party puts its faith in greater freedom for the individual, and in the social market economy. The state's tasks should be transferred to a lower level where possible. One of the party's recent slogans has been "one law more, one liberty less".

The share of the state in total expenditure should not increase, and in the longer term should be reduced, and the total tax burden should also be lowered. There should be fewer subsidies, and privatizations where appropriate.

An important party theme has been the need for more reliance on decentralized bargaining between the social partners than on centrally established legislative prescriptions. The Radical Party does not call, for example, for generalised reductions in working hours, but instead for agreements at individual enterprise level linked to individual circumstances and to such factors as rises in productivity.

The Radical Party believes that managers should be left the freedom to manage and that laws against firing employees should not be to strict. It supports, however, schemes whereby employees are encouraged to take shares in their own enterprises, and employee participation in decisions at workplace level.

The Radical Party defends the basic elements of Swiss social welfare policy, and points out its historical role in developing state pension schemes and health and unemployment insurance. It notes the increasing economic constraints on state-funded social welfare, and believes that other solutions, such as agreements negotiated between the social partners, and private schemes, will have to play a greater role.

It now places a greater emphasis on environmental protection than in the past, but it is more cautious on this theme than almost all other Swiss parties. It believes that environmental policies must be vigorously pursued, but must be realistic, and technically and financially appropriate. The Radicals do not believe in doomsday scenarios, and consider that there should not be panic reactions to serious but not insoluble problems.

Environmental policies should be properly integrated with other policies and should not be seen as a pretext for overthrowing the existing market economy. There should be a greater emphasis on qualitative growth, and on what the party describes as an ecological market economy.

The Radical Party believes that civil nuclear energy should not be abandoned until a solution is found that is both better from the environmental point of view and economically justified. Minorities within the party have supported either a moratorium on nuclear energy, or else the option of holding referenda to ratify the opening of new nuclear plants.

In transport policy it is less hostile to road transport and less pro-rail than most other Swiss parties. The construction of new national roads should be subject to tight federal criteria, but should not be completely halted. The Radical Party also seeks an agricultural policy that is more respectful of the environment, and uses more biological methods.

The party puts considerable emphasis on implementing greater equality between men and women, such as equal pay for equal work. The Radicals have also supported a lowering of the age of civil majority to 18. On other moral and ethical issues Radical policy positions have included support for the liberalization of abortion, and calls to ban surrogate motherhood and transactions in human embryos.

On the issue of immigration into Switzerland the Radicals believe that this must be strictly controlled. Their policy on asylum calls for solidarity with genuine victims of persecution, but for a crackdown on abuses. A more restrictive law on asylum has recently been steered through by a Radical member of the Federal Council.

The Radicals are firm supporters of permanent armed neutrality for Switzerland and consequently of a strong Swiss army, which must be given the necessary financial means. The party opposed the proposal for optional referenda on increases in military expenditure. The Radicals believe that people should not be able to opt out of military service, and that women too should be encouraged to volunteer for the army. There should, however, be the possibility of substitute civilian service for genuine conscientious objectors on ethical or religious grounds.

The Radical Party supported Swiss entry into the UN. It believes Switzerland should play a full role in specialized UN organizations, and should fight for the maintenance of a liberal trading system at world level.

The party's leaders consider that Swiss entry into the European Community is inconceivable in present circumstances, but that Switzerland should avoid being isolated by the achievement of the 1992 European internal market. Switzerland should work within EFTA for stronger links with the European Community, should work for Europe-wide liberalization in such fields as economic services (e.g insurance, tourism and the liberal professions), and should join to the fullest practicable degree in European harmonization of standards, and mutual recognition of tests. Switzerland should participate more fully in European research and technology ventures, such as EUREKA projects, and even in RACE and ESPRIT.

Personalities

The party's president is Bruno Hunziker from Aargau. The party's two members of the Federal Council have been the Head of the Department of Justice and Police, Elisabeth Kopp from Zürich (who was the first ever woman member of the federal government when she was elected in 1984 but who was forced to resign in January 1989); and Jean-Pascal Delamuraz from Vaud, who is in charge of the Department of Economics. Kaspar Villiger replaced Kopp in February 1989. The party's current secretary-general is only the fourth since 1919.

Christlichdemokratische Volkspartei Parti Démocrate Chrétien Suisse/ Partito Democratico Cristiano Popolare Svizzero

(Swiss Christian Democratic People's Party)

Headquarters	: Klaraweg 6, POB 1759, CH-3001, Berne (tel: 031-442364)
President	: Eva Segmuller
President of parliamentary group	: Paul Zbinden
Secretary-general	: Hans-Peter Fagagnini
Youth organization	: *Jeunes Démocrats-Chrétiens*

History

After the Swiss Civil War in 1848, when the Catholic cantons of the *Sonderbund* were defeated and a new federal structure instituted, the Catholics were reduced to controlling only four cantons and to having only nine out of the 111 members of the new National Assembly. The next few years were thus devoted to building up Catholic strength in their old strongholds.

In the 1870s the moves towards establishing a more centralized state and the prevailing *Kulturkampf* between Catholics and anti-clericals helped to strengthen Catholic organizations. Nevertheless, the creation of an enduring Catholic political party proved hard to achieve. Swiss Catholics were divided between Conservatives in the central Swiss cantons (who wished above all to maintain cantonal powers and to keep bridges open to non-Catholic Conservatives); the exclusively Catholic authoritarians of Fribourg and the

Valais; the more socially-minded Catholics who had migrated to the primarily Protestant cities ("diaspora Catholics"); and a final group whose main aim was to see Catholics fully integrated into the existing Swiss federal structure. Several attempts to create a Catholic party were thus unsuccessful. In 1891, however, Joseph Zemp of Luzern became the first Catholic politician to break the Radical monopoly of power on the Federal Council.

In 1899 the first Christian Social Workers' Organization was established in St. Gallen, and was followed by the first such organization at national level in 1903. In the same year 12,000 Catholics from all over Switzerland attended *Katholikentag* (Catholic day) in Luzern, the first national gathering of Swiss Catholics and a powerful stimulus toward further Catholic unity. On April 22, 1912 a new party was finally founded. By a vote of 145 to 37 it took the name "Swiss Conservative People's Party", rejecting the exclusively Catholic party sought by the minority, mainly from Fribourg.

Despite the new party's avowed openness to non-Catholics, almost all of its support in practice came from Catholics. The party became more influential after the introduction of proportional representation in 1919, when the Radicals lost their former dominance. In 1919 the KK as it was popularly known (Catholic Conservative Party) gained a second seat on the Federal Council and the Catholic corporatist Jean-Marie Musy from Fribourg joined the existing KK Federal Councillor, Giuseppe Motta, who held his post for the entire interwar period and was one of the dominant political personalities in 20th century Switzerland.

In 1929 the party adopted a programme heavily influenced by corporatist principles, and in 1951 the new programme adopted at Schwyz was still imbued with this spirit. The party remained strongly anti-Communist. Motta, as Foreign Minister, strongly opposed Soviet entry into the League of Nations, and as late as 1949 the party was pushing for penal sanctions against "traitors" in the Swiss Communist party.

Nevertheless, divisions remained between conservatives and social Christians, and in some cantons (Oberwallis 1917, Luzern 1919 and later Fribourg in 1966) separate social Christian party organizations were established. In 1957 the party tried to better encompass both traditions by changing its name to the Swiss Christian Social Conservative Party. The party's electoral support remained remarkably stable. From 1919 onwards the party has fluctuated between 41 and 48 seats in the National Council and between 17 and 19 seats in the Council of States, never winning more than 23.5 per cent of the National

Council vote, and never less than 20 per cent (with the one exception of 1939). It has generally been only the third party in the National Council but easily the strongest in the Council of States, reflecting its strength in the Alpine cantons with small populations. In 1951, with its combined strength of 66 seats in both houses it became, for the first time, the largest party in the Federal Assembly.

In 1967, however, it endured a relative electoral setback, and subsequently sought to modernize itself. In 1970 it adopted new statutes giving more strength to the national party organization, and also changed its name once more to its present name of the "Swiss Christian Democratic People's Party". In 1971 it adopted a new electoral programme. In 1973 one of the party's long-standing objectives was realized when the discriminatory Articles 51 and 52 of the Federal Constitution (anti-Jesuit and anti-new Catholic orders) were finally removed.

In 1987 it won 20 per cent of the vote in the National Council elections, only a slight drop since 1983 but still its lowest vote since 1919. It retained, however, its 42 seats in the National Council, and obtained an extra seat in the Council of State to give it 19 seats, five more than its nearest rival, the Radical Party.

Support

The Christian Democratic People's Party (CVP) is still an overwhelmingly Catholic party. Unlike the CDU in Germany it has attracted few Protestant voters. While many Catholics do not vote for it, 93 per cent of its voters are Catholic and 43 per cent still go to church every week, by far the highest figure in any Swiss party.

Its continuing association with Catholicism has meant that it has a very faithful electorate, but one that is not growing. It is strong among women but weak among the young, strong in many of the poorer mountain areas and weaker in the big cities.

The party prides itself on bridging social classes and in Catholic Switzerland it does appear to have achieved this aim. At national level, therefore, the party is second only to the Socialists in support among workers and public sector employees, and second only to the Farmers' Party among farmers.

The party is still extremely strong in the mountain cantons in Catholic German-speaking central Switzerland. It is the dominant party in the small cantons of Uri, Schwyz, Zug and the two half-cantons of Obwald and Nidwald. It is the largest party in Luzern, (47 per cent in the National Council elections of 1987) where the old clerical/anti-clerical divide has been a long time dying, and where society is still divided between Catholic and Radical "pillars". Further east the CVP is the largest party in St. Gallen (39.4 per cent in 1987) and, to a lesser extent, in Graubünden (28.4 per cent in 1987) where the party has a long social-Christian tradition and has been supported by many of the less powerful people in society. Finally, in Appenzell-Inner-Rhoden the CVP monopolizes political representation of the canton (although the tiny canton is still in the era of direct personalized rather than party politics).

The CVP is not dominant but reasonably strong (the second party) in a number of other German-speaking cantons such as Thurgau, Aargau and above all Solothurn, where it is still the second party in a vigorously contested three party struggle. It is, however much weaker in the heavily populated cantons of Zürich (sixth with 7.1 per cent, behind the Greens in the National Council elections of 1987), Basel City, and especially in Berne, where its support is insignificant (3.3 per cent in 1987). The party is also generally weak in the main centres of French Switzerland and in French Protestant cantons. It has around 12–15 per cent support in Geneva (14.6 per cent in 1987) but only 3–4 per cent in the largest French-speaking canton, Vaud, and hardly exists in Neuchatel. It has a stronger position in the Catholic cantons, such as the new canton of Jura (the largest party at 41.6 per cent in the 1987 National Council elections). Fribourg has long been a centre of uncompromising Catholicism with a strong influence of corporatist and *Action Française* ideas, but more recently there has been a split between Conservative Catholic and Conservative Social elements and the party's strength has declined from 54.1 per cent in 1963 to only 38 per cent in 1983. In 1987, however, it won 44.6 per cent of the vote in the National Council elections. Finally, the Valais is the most Catholic of all cantons (over 95 per cent) and the CVP still gets around 57–58 per cent of the total vote (58.7 per cent in 1987). The party is divided, however, with separate organizations in the French- and German-speaking parts of the canton. In the latter the main political competition is between the "black" Catholic Conservatives and the "yellow" Social Christians, which together have 38 out of the 41 seats in Oberwallis and over 90 per cent of the vote. As for Italian Switzerland, the canton of Ticino is overwhelmingly Catholic but while four of the 17 CVP federal councillors have come from Ticino, the party is generally only in second place to the Radicals, although it was the largest party in the canton in the 1987 National Council elections at 38.2 per cent.

Organization

The party's new Constitution, introduced in 1970, strengthened its national organization but the cantonal parties still retain a high degree of independence. Their representatives in Parliament often adopt differing positions and there is relatively little exchange of ideas between cantons.

The national party has little influence in the drawing up of lists of candidates at cantonal level for federal elections, or on how they subsequently conduct their campaign. The cantonal parties are entitled to have their own statutes adapted "to their own conditions", although their principles, especially on matters of political philosophy, must "correspond" with those of the national party.

On matters of interest to several cantons or of national interest they are asked to "consult" the national party, and must liaise with it when they take positions on federal votes. On the other hand, on important federal questions the national party is also obliged to consult with the cantons. The whole tone is one of negotiation rather than command.

This is reinforced by the fact that the national party lacks effective disciplinary powers over the cantons, besides the drastic measure of expelling them. One small example is that the Constitution provides for a central register of party members but this does not exist as the party has not been able to remedy the lack of membership figures in individual cantons.

A second feature of the party's constitution is that Article 20 calls for an equitable representation of regions, languages, religions, age groups and sexes within the party.

Below cantonal level local parties with a minimum of five members can be established within individual communes. In larger communes they can be further subdivided. They can also group together with neighbouring parties (even across cantonal borders) to form regional parties.

At national level the party's organs are: an annual delegates' assembly (including delegates from the cantonal parties elected in proportion to their strength in votes received and in membership); a national committee of around 50 members; and an executive committee consisting of the party president (elected by the delegates' assembly), the chairman of the parliamentary group and nine other members. The secretary-general co-ordinates the whole of the party's activities.

Youth and women's groups have been established. There are Christian trade unions but it is a matter of concern for the CVP that there are fewer interest groups with close links to the party than is the case for its Radical and Socialist rivals.

The party is also concerned about its diminishing strength in the media. In 12 cantons, especially in urban Switzerland, there are no papers affiliated to the party, and in others the party's presence is weak. There are, however, still a few prominent papers close to the party such as the *Vaterland* in Luzern and the *Nouvelliste* and *Wallister Bote* in Valais.

The CVP is a member of the European Union of Christian Democratic Parties and of the Christian Democratic International.

Policy

Both in its change of name in 1970, and the longer-term policy programmes that it has put forward since 1971, the CVP has been trying to get away from its old image of a Catholic Conservative party.

The party continues to point out that the ethics and doctrines of Christianity are the central basis for its policies, but emphasizes that it is not institutionally linked to any Church. It recognizes that too few Protestants are voting for the party, or participating in its leadership, and that this situation should be changed.

As regards its position in the political spectrum, it likes to see itself as a "dynamic centre" party, above the class struggle and opposed both to the collectivism of the left and to the over-emphasis on individual freedom and materialism of the classic liberal parties.

The CVP is a strong supporter of the cantons' rights against the centre, and of the rights of the less favoured mountain regions.

The two great principles which it believes must accompany individual liberty, are "solidarity" and "subsidiarity". Society must support the weak and less favoured. The urban and rural regions of Switzerland must recognize their reciprocal dependence; there should be some financial equalization between cantons and a vigorous regional policy to ensure that the poorer cantons are not left behind. Subsidiarity means that decisions must be taken at the lowest possible level, starting with the individual and the family, and going up to the commune, the canton and only as a last resort to the federal government. The CVP is thus a strong opponent of centralization.

As in most Christian Democratic parties the CVP's most persistent demand is the need to fully protect the family unit. It seeks a fiscal policy geared to the family's needs with special children's and family allowances, more flexible working time to help families and 16 week maternity leaves, as well as a better co-ordination of family and professional life. It calls for greater equality between men and women, notably at cantonal level where a number of legal inequalities still exist. It is opposed to euthanasia and the death penalty, and puts a new emphasis on opposition to genetic manipulation.

The necessity for some measure of divorce is recognized. As regards the rest of its social policy, it recognises that there are still great gaps in the Swiss social security system which need to be filled. Foreign workers must also be better integrated into Swiss society. The numbers entering should be stabilized. There should be a humane policy towards genuine refugees, but the party has supported measures to reduce Switzerland's attractiveness as a country for asylum.

On general economic policy the party supports a social market economy. Private enterprise is primordial but the State must intervene where necessary. The activities of larger firms must become more transparent and there must be strong cartel laws. Small and medium-sized enterprises should be given special encouragement. Harmonious relations between the social partners are vital and employee-participation should be enhanced. There should be reductions in working time, but greater mobility of the workforce as well. Solutions reached in negotiations between the social partners are preferred to legal remedies.

On the specific Swiss issue of banking secrecy the party points out that this should be maintained, as within the private sphere of the individual, but that there should be no abuses.

As regards state finances the expenditure of the Confederation should not increase more rapidly than the gross social product.

In agricultural policy its main objectives are the maintenance of a sufficient rural population and the defence of the least favoured agricultural regions, with a strong bias in favour of small family farms.

The CVP puts a major new emphasis on environmental protection, on which it had a lower profile in the past. It calls for ecology and economic policy considerations to be carefully balanced. The "polluter pays" principle should be introduced and there should be tough new emission standards. It has supported new speed limits of 80 km per hour outside towns, and 100 km per hour on motorways. There should be a more co-ordinated federal transport policy, with encouragement of public transport and a halt to major new road construction.

The problem of toxic waste should be more vigorously tackled. The party has supported a new system of smog alarms, a ban on aluminium cans and on potentially dangerous sprays, protection of the ozone layer and the fight against acid rain. There should be control of urban sprawl, and strict planning controls.

In 1985 the CVP was still in favour of the construction of Kaiseraugst nuclear power station, but it is now opposed to the construction of new nuclear plants although it does not seek to close down existing ones.

The CVP supports the maintenance of a strong Swiss defence. It opposed the popular initiative to provide for direct democratic scrutiny of military expenditure. The party majority is opposed to civilian service as an alternative to military service but there have been calls within the party for sympathetic treatment of genuine conscientious objectors.

The CVP supported Swiss entry into the UN. It seeks closer co–operation with the European Community particularly with a view to the 1992 European internal market, and Swiss participation in European scientific and technological co-operative ventures.

The party has called for more assistance to third world countries.

Personalities

The CVP's two members of the Federal Council are Arnold Koller from Appenzell-Inner-Rhoden and Flavio Cotti from the Ticino. Both were elected in 1987.

Hans-Peter Fagagnini has been secretary-general since 1974, and Paul Zbinden has been president of the parliamentary group since 1984. Eva Segmuller is the party's president.

Schweizerische Volkspartei—SVP
Union Démocratique du Centre—UDC
Unione Democratica di Centro
(Swiss People's Party/Democratic Union of the Centre)

Headquarters	: Ahornweg 2, Postfach 238, CH–3000 Berne 9 (tel: 031-245858)
President	: Hans Uhlmann
President of parliamentary group	: Hans Rudolf Nebiker
Secretary-general	: Dr Max Friedli
Membership	: 83,000

History

The present party, with its two quite different names in German and French, stems from a merger which took place on Sept. 22, 1971 between two separate parties, the Party of Peasants, Artisans and Bourgeois (*Bauern,*

Gewerbe und Bürgerpartei or BGB) and the Swiss Democratic Party (*Demokratischen Partei der Schweiz*).

By far the larger of these two was the BGB. After World War I a number of peasant parties sprang up in different cantons. A central reason was the belief that the peasants, whose vital role had been underlined during wartime conditions, would have more power with their own political organizations than within the Radical Party. A second motivation was strong anti-socialism and anti-communism. The introduction of proportional representation also offered the possibility of political representation. A Peasants' Party was thus established in Zürich in 1917.

The Berne party, established in 1918 and led by a peasant called Rudolf Minger, had astonishing success, winning half of the seats in the Berne cantonal council only a year after its foundation, and already having 52,000 members. Even at its outset it was not just a peasants' party, but attracted wider support from teachers, civil servants and others. In 1921 it added the name Artisan to its title, to become *Bauern, Gewerbe und Bürgerpartei* or BGB. Although it later lost a number of members and its status as largest party in Berne politics to the Socialists, it retained an enormous influence within the canton.

In 1929 Rudolf Minger became a Federal Councillor, the first peasant to achieve such a position, and starting a tradition that one of the seven Federal Council positions always goes to a Peasants' Party representative from Berne.

In the 1930s the Berne party even survived a damaging split when a more populist and radical young farmers' movement, led by Dr Hans Muller, split away from the parent party and achieved considerable initial success with a mix of socialist and fascist ideas. It did not finally disappear until the mid-1940s.

In other cantons, however, the party took a very different form from the party in Berne. In Thurgau, where it was also very successful, it nevertheless remained in close alliance with the Radicals. In Schaffhausen it remained a purely peasant party and co-operated with the left wing parties, including the Communists. Other cantonal parties too did not expand from their peasant base, and several did not call themselves by the full BGB title until after 1945 (in the case of Schaffhausen only in 1956).

Co–ordination of these various parties at Swiss level was thus rather loose and, although a national parliamentary group existed after 1919, the BGB was only formally founded at Swiss level on Dec. 23, 1936. After the war the party's electoral support slowly declined but at the time of the merger in 1971 it still had 10 per cent of the national vote, 21 national councillors and three councillors of state.

The other political tradition within the new SVP is that of the Swiss Democratic Party. Cantonal Democratic parties were established as early as the 19th century as left-wing break-aways from within the Radical political family, advocating, in particular, more far-reaching measures of direct democracy.

In Zürich they formed a separate group, but did not break away from the Radical family until 1941. In Glarus the separate Democratic and Labour Party became very influential and acted as a mediating force between the socialists and the bourgeois parties. The most powerful Democratic Party of all, however, was in Graubünden (Grisons) where during the post–World War I recession (which particularly hit the canton's tourist industry), they spearheaded a revolt of the less powerful in society against the old Radical establishment. From 1919 to 1943 the Democratic party of Graubünden rose from 10 per cent to 40 per cent of the cantonal vote. Their dominant personality was Andreas Gadient.

In 1942 a Swiss Democratic Party was first established at the federal level. From 1951 onwards it worked together in the National Council with the Evangelical Party. It was, however, represented in few cantons, and at the time of the merger had only a small share of the total vote, two national councillors and two councillors of state.

When the BGB and the Democratic Party merged in 1971 the Zürich Democrats did not join the new party, but rejoined the Radicals. For this and other reasons the first electoral outing of the new party in 1975 led to it getting a lower share of the national vote than the BGB alone had achieved in 1971. A working party was set up to examine the structures and image of the party, and how to reconcile the more conservative BGB with the more progressive Democratic Party traditions. A new party programme was drawn up in 1978. In 1979 its vote rose from 9.9 per cent (1975) to 11.6 per cent.

In the 1983 national elections the party won 11.1 per cent of the total vote. In 1987 it won 11 per cent holding its vote better than any of the other parties in the Federal Council. It obtained 25 seats in the National Council, an increase of two over 1983, but only four seats in the Council of States, a loss of one from 1983.

The SVP has one member of the federal government, inheriting the seat held since 1959 by the BGB.

Support

The SVP is predominantly a party of Protestant German-speaking Switzerland. Over 90 per cent of its electorate is Protestant, and in many Catholic cantons and in most of French Switzerland it does not put up candidates. In the 1987 national elections it only stood in 12 of the 26 cantons and half-cantons.

Farmers still form a strong element of its support in the Protestant German-speaking cantons of Berne, Schaffhausen and Zürich.

The power-base of the party is still the canton of Berne, where it consistently obtains up to a third of the total votes and is the largest party. In the 1987 national elections it won 27.8 per cent of the vote in Berne, and obtained nine seats on the National Council, and one on the Council of States. Berne also provides its one member of the Federal Council.

The party also has a strong presence in the populous canton of Zürich where it is the third party. In the 1987 cantonal elections it received 15.7 per cent of the total vote, but only 6.8 per cent in the city and over 20 per cent in the countryside (winning up to 35 per cent of the vote in the vineyards and farming country in the north of the canton). In the 1987 national elections the SVP won 15 per cent in Zürich and six members of the National Council.

Another canton where it is particularly successful is Thurgau, where it still works closely with the Radical Party, and where its broad-based support makes it the largest party. In the 1987 national elections it obtained 21.7 per cent in the canton, two seats on the National Council and one on the Council of States.

While it has declined from the old position of predominance once enjoyed by the Democratic Party, the SVP still gets a high vote in Graubünden where it was the second political force in the 1987 National Council elections with 20 per cent of the vote.

In the other former Democratic Party stronghold of Glarus the other major parties gave the SVP a clear run in the National Council elections and it thus provides the only National Council representative from the canton.

The SVP also has a significant vote in Schaffhausen (23.5 per cent in 1987) and Aargau (15.6 per cent in 1987), and to a lesser extent in Basel-Land (10 per cent in 1987) and Fribourg 18.9 per cent.

The only completely French-speaking canton where the SVP puts up national candidates is Vaud, where the local party is only loosely affiliated with the SVP and where it has a certain support in rural areas (6.2 per cent in 1987).

The SVP has minimal support in Italian-speaking Switzerland. In the 1987 national elections it only won 1.2 per cent in Ticino.

Organization

The SVP has 15 cantonal parties (in Aargau, Appenzell-Ausser-Rhoden, Basel-Land, Berne, Fribourg, Glarus, Graubünden, Jura, Schaffhausen, St. Gallen, Schwyz, Ticino, Thurgau, Vaud and Zürich). The most powerful of these is the Berne party. At national level the party's highest organ is a delegates' assembly, which meets three or four times a year, and which includes a minimum of 15 delegates per canton. Among its tasks is the election of party president and a number of members of the party's central executive. There is also a regular conference to discuss policy matters (the *Programmparteitag*).

The party's central executive typically meets four times a year. Besides directly-elected national members, and a number of other party leaders, it includes at least one representative of each cantonal party. A large canton like Berne has up to 10 members. In 1976 there were 76 members of the central executive, among whose tasks are the election of the party's secretary-general and members of the executive committee.

The executive committee is a smaller body of between 15 and 19 members which typically meets eight or nine times a year. There is a small central secretariat, currently with a staff of seven. There is also a programme committee, which meets around four times a year, and a number of special party committees in specific policy areas. Party offices are held for a duration of two years, and cannot be held for more than eight years in all.

There is an independent party youth organization, the *Schweizerische Junge SVP*. There is a special party commission to deal with women's questions, with 25–30 members, and a national Women's Conference, which meets at least once a year. There ar also periodic conferences of the president and secretaries of all cantonal parties. The SVP has strong links with farmers' organizations.

The SVP produces a number of cantonal bulletins, such as *Der Zürcher Bote*, and *Le Pays Vaudois*. There is no central party organ.

The SVP has different membership dues in each canton. Its parliamentary group and party office-holders also contribute to the party's finances.

The SVP has no formal links with any political parties outside Switzerland.

Policies

The SVP is the smallest of the four parties in the Swiss Federal Government. It represents a merger between a farmers' party (the BGB) and a progressive liberal party (the Democratic Party), and its character still varies considerably from canton to canton. In Zürich, for example, the party is generally more conservative than in the old Democratic stronghold of Graubünden. At national level, however, the SVP is a pragmatic right of centre party, with one of its recent slogans being "action instead of theories".

The SVP supports a liberal market economy. It is opposed to dirigism, and believes that the state should only take on new tasks when these cannot be better carried out by private enterprise, the cantons or the communes. Reductions in federal expenditure should have a higher priority than an increase in federal income. The party believes that federal direct taxation, in particular, has reached its upper admissible limit. If any increases are needed the burden should fall on indirect taxation. There should be more freedom for heads of enterprises, but also a vigorous competition policy.

The SVP supports flexible working hours, and such measures as job-sharing, but is opposed to any statutory general reduction in working hours. Employee co-responsibility should be encouraged, but primarily through agreements between employers and employees. Employee involvement in decision-making in a firm's management is, however, not supported.

Family policy has a high priority.

The SVP puts a major new emphasis on environmental policy, which is recognized as an area where the Federal Government must play an important role. It seeks to strengthen public transport and believes that there should be no extension in the capacity of the national highway network.

The SVP has become more cautious than it was a few years ago about civil nuclear energy, on which it considers that Switzerland must continue to rely in the short term. It recognizes, however, that Switzerland may need to turn away from nuclear power in the medium to longer term.

The SVP continues to put a high emphasis on agricultural policy, where it strongly defends the small family farm. Agriculture should take on new tasks as well, such as the protection of the rural environment and landscape, as well as maintaining economic activities in peripheral regions of the country.

The SVP is in favour of the revision of the Swiss asylum law in a more restrictive direction. Genuine political refugees should be helped, but those fleeing poor social or economic conditions should not be given the status of refugees. In the short term there should be no increase in the number of foreigners in the country, and in the medium term there should be an actual reduction.

The SVP seeks enhanced powers for the cantons and the communes and would like to see a reinforcement of the system of financial equalization between the cantons. It strongly defends the existing Swiss system of defence, and believes that the Swiss army should be given the necessary resources. It opposed the initiative to introduce an alternative civilian service. A distinctive feature of SVP foreign policy is that it was the only party in the Federal Government to come out in opposition to Switzerland joining the UN.

Personalities

The party's one member of the Federal Council is Adolf Ogi, who replaced Dr. Leon Schlumpf in this post. Ogi is a former party president, former trainer of the Swiss ski team and comes from Berne. The current party president is Hans Uhlmann. Hans Rudolf Nebiker has been president of the SVP National Council Group. One of the leading party conservatives is Dr Cristoph Blocher, the president of the SVP in Zürich.

Landesring der Unabhängigen — LdU
Alliance des Indépendants
(Alliance of Independents)

Headquarters	:	Laupenstrasse 3, Postfach 4080, CH–3001 Berne (tel: 031-26-1636)
President	:	Franz Jaeger
Secretary-general	:	Peter Aebi
Membership	:	5,000
Founded	:	1936

History

The *Landesring der Unabhängigen* (LdU) has been a persisting force in Swiss politics since its foundation in 1936. The name *Ring* alludes to the inner circle in the *Landesgemeinde*, the direct democratic assemblies which still take place in some cantons, and was chosen to symbolize attachment to the traditional forms of direct Swiss democracy.

It has often been the fifth largest Swiss party, and the largest of the smaller parties.

Its founder, and dominating personality for its first 25 years of existence, was Gottlieb Duttweiler, who had founded the Migros food

retailing group in 1925. Migros undercut the prices of its competitors and used innovative sales techniques such as mobile shops, but ran into fierce resistance from cantonal and federal politicians, and from rival commercial interests. Duttweiler eventually decided to counter-attack at a political as well as commercial level. In 1935 independent lists were put forward in the National Council elections, and won five seats in Zürich, one in Berne and one in St. Gallen. On Dec. 30, 1936 the LdU was formally established. Its initial policy planks were the need for a truly free economy and enhanced measures of consumer protection, in order to combat unfair competition from the vested economic interests and to dismantle state-supported corporatism. It also called for the state to re-establish social justice and to fight growing unemployment. It quickly consolidated its support as a party of protest. The party was backed up by a weekly newspaper, *Die Tat*. It put great reliance on direct popular initiatives.

In the 1939 elections it won nine seats in the Swiss National Council on 7.1 per cent of the vote. In 1940–41 Duttweiler began the process of turning the Migros firm into a network of co-operatives. In 1943 sharp divisions opened up within the party, with a number of its parliamentarians critical of Duttweiler's dominant personality and of his unilateral overtures to left-wing politicians.

Eventually certain members on the party's right wing left the LdU. Duttweiler's line prevailed, but at considerable cost to the party, which lost four of its nine seats in the 1943 national elections.

In 1947 its vote further dropped to 4.4 per cent, but it regained three seats, and in 1951 it won 10 seats in the National Council on 5.1 per cent of the vote. In 1952 Duttweiler finally stood down as president of the party (he had briefly stood aside in 1948–49), although he continued to lead the Migros firm.

Throughout the 1950s and early 1960s the LdU's vote remained remarkably stable at 5–5.5 per cent of the vote, and with 10 seats in the National Council in four successive elections from 1951 to 1963. In 1962 Duttweiler died, but the party adjusted successfully to the loss of its founder.

In the 1967 elections, its vote rose to its highest-ever figure of 9.1 per cent, with the LdU winning 16 seats in the National Council, and one in the Council of States. In 1971 its vote dropped to 7.6 per cent (13 seats in the National Council). In the two successive national elections in 1975 and 1979 its vote continued to drop. In 1979 it only gained eight seats in the National Council on 4.2 per cent of the vote.

It subsequently formed a parliamentary group with the *Evangelische Volkspartei* (EVP — see separate entry).

In the 1980s the LdU's support has again stabilized. In 1983 it obtained eight seats on 4 per cent of the vote and in 1987 nine seats in the National Council on 4.2 per cent of the vote. In 1987 it also obtained a seat in the Council of States (where it had previously been represented by Duttweiler from 1949 to 1951, and by Albin Heimann from 1967 to 1979). At the end of 1987 the LdU also had 45 representatives in cantonal parliaments. It also has one representative in the Zürich cantonal government, who was re-elected in 1987.

Support

The LdU has only won support in a limited number of cantons, primarily in Protestant German-speaking Switzerland. It has had only very limited support in French-speaking Switzerland, and has not established itself in Italian Switzerland. It has traditionally been strongest in the larger cities. It has been well supported by those with higher education, and among groups such as teachers.

Its main political base has been the canton of Zürich, the initial base both of Duttweiler and of the Migros firm, and where the LdU was the second party in the canton from 1935 to 1963. In the 1987 elections it was only the fourth largest party in the canton, with 11.4 per cent, and its highest support in parts of the city of Zürich (e.g. 15.8 per cent in Zürich's 11th District). Its only 1987 member of the Council of States, Monika Weber, was also elected in Zürich, where she came top of the poll. Zürich is also the only canton where the party has an elected member of the cantonal government.

The party's second highest vote in 1987 of 10 per cent was in the canton of St. Gallen, where the party has always been strong, and which is also the political base of its current president, Franz Jaeger. The LdU did very well in the last St. Gallen cantonal elections.

The LdU's third stronghold is the city of Basel, where it won 9.4 per cent in 1987. The LdU also has some support in Aargau (4.7 per cent in 1987), Berne (3.6 per cent), Solothurn (3.5 per cent), Basel-Land (2.7 per cent) and Thurgau (2.6 per cent).

In French Switzerland the LdU has had a little support in Neuchatel (but not in 1987) and in the Jura Bernois. In the canton of Vaud its only pocket of support is the commune of Rolle, where it has eight seats in the communal parliament.

Organization

In 1987 the LdU had 5,000 paid up members, and around 5,000 non-paying sympathizers on its mailing list. It has around 181 groups at local, district and regional level within its 15 cantonal parties. At federal level it has a National Congress which is responsible for electing the party's president and four vice-presidents. There is also a smaller Delegates' Council, which meets several times a year, and whose national and cantonal delegates have two-year mandates. The even smaller Party Executive consists of the party's top office-holders, and 10 members elected by the Delegates' Council.

The LdU has a youth movement (*Jungen Landesring/Jeunes Indépendants*) and also a central women's committee of 15 members elected by the Delegates' Council. The LdU's cantonal newspapers are called *Klar* in German-speaking Switzerland, and *Voici les Indépendants* in French Switzerland.

The LdU has a minimum membership fee of Swiss F 50. Its main financial support, however, has come from the Migros firm, which is still closely associated with the party.

The LdU has no formal links with any parties outside Switzerland. Within the Swiss Parliament it established a joint parliamentary group with the EVP in 1979.

Policies

The LdU describes itself as a "social", "liberal" and "green" party. Throughout its existence it has emphasised the need for free competition but has also considered that capitalism must take its responsibilities and consumer protection seriously, and that the state must intervene to defend the weak and disadvantaged. Recently, however, it has put a strong new emphasis on ecological themes, a change contested by some party conservatives who still prefer to put their accent on economic liberalism.

The LdU has traditionally been an "outsider" party, which has never participated in government and has attacked economic and political concentrations of power, and the cosy consensus of the Swiss political system. It has made frequent use of the mechanisms of semi-direct democracy, such as initiatives and referenda, to put forward its specific causes. The LdU has always been, however, a centrist rather than extremist party, although it has sometimes formed ad hoc alliances with politicians of both the left and right, and has been accused of unpredictability (especially under the individualistic leadership of Duttweiler) by its opponents.

The most controversial feature of the LdU

has been its continuing financial and other links with the Migros commercial empire. A considerable number of its parliamentarians have been Migros employees. Duttweiler was both president of the LdU and head of Migros, and although the two posts were separated in 1952, the LdU's 1979–84 president, Walter Biel, was also a Migros director. Both the party and Migros are aware of the need for an arms-length relationship, and party leaders insist that they are left policy-making freedom on specific issues. It is also uncertain how Migros will respond to the LdU's new emphasis on green themes.

On economic policy the LdU supports the establishment of a functioning social market economy. It calls for a vigorous competition policy against private monopolies and cartels, and for the "jungle" of unnecessary state subsidies to be cut back. The power of the Swiss economic establishment should be restrained, and there should be surveillance of consumer prices.

The state should retain an important role as an arbiter, but it should not become over-bureaucratic. There should be greater economic and industrial democracy in the workplace, and a shorter working week. The LdU believes that economic policy should increasingly take account of environmental constraints and there should be greater emphasis on qualitative growth. The "polluter pays" principle should be fully implemented, there should be fiscal incentives for environmental protection and there should be more recycling. Public transport should be made more attractive, and more goods should be transported by rail rather than by road. There should be tougher vehicle emission standards. People should live nearer their work. There should be a moratorium on the extension of the national highway network for 10 years.

The adverse effects of tourism have been heavily emphasized by the party, which has called for a 15-year moratorium on the construction of new funiculars as well as assessment of the need for new mountain railways and new skiing facilities.

In energy policy the LdU has called for the progressive abandonment of civil nuclear energy, with no new plants and no replacement of existing ones. Fossil fuels should not take their place. There should be greater reliance on renewable energy sources and energy conservation.

Agricultural policy should put more emphasis on conserving the environment and on consumer needs. There should be direct payments to farmers protecting the environment. The LdU has traditionally opposed excessive subsidies to agriculture. It supports external protection for Swiss agriculture, but not at too great a cost to the consumer, and with favourable treatment given to imports from third-world countries.

The LdU has supported the suppression of vivisection.

The LdU was an early advocate of women getting the vote in Switzerland, and calls for more far-reaching measures to ensure equality between men and women in all fields. Within the family there should be a new distribution of tasks, and more possibilities for either men or women to take up part-time work.

One of Duttweiler's traditional themes was the campaign against alcohol abuse.

The LdU calls for the strengthening of Swiss semi-direct democracy, and has supportd the establishment of an independent ombudsman to combat maladministration and with fuller disclosure of legislators' economic interests

Swiss federalism should be reinforced, with decisions taken at the lowest possible level. There should be strong measures for data protection. There should be a humane asylum policy, and guest workers in Switzerland should be better assimilated.

The LdU has strongly supported Swiss neutrality, and the maintenance of the Swiss militia system of defence. Swiss arms exports should be limited, however, and there should be the possibility of alternative civilian service for conscientious objectors.

The LdU believes that Switzerland should participate actively in the process of world disarmament, and also supports the establishment of de-nuclearized zones.

The LdU supported Swiss entry into the UN (unlike its parliamentary group allies, the EVP). It has called for stronger support for developing countries.

Personalities

Franz Jaeger has been the party's president since 1985. He is a National Councillor from St. Gallen, and has been a strong advocate of the party putting a greater emphasis on green themes.

Monika Weber has a background as a consumer leader, and is now the LdU's only representative in the Swiss Council of States. She comes from Zürich, and is a former member of the National Council.

Hans Jürg Weder, from Basel, was an early opponent of the Kaiseraugst nuclear power station.

Among the representatives of the less green and more traditional wing of the LdU are three leading personalities from the canton of Zürich: Alfred Gilgen, the party's member on the Zürich cantonal government; Walter Biel, who was party president from 1978 to 1984 and is still a National Councillor; and Sigmund Widmer, another long-standing member of the National Council, who has been the president of the LdU's parliamentary group.

Peter Aebi, the LdU's secretary-general, is a former president of the party's youth organization.

Grüne Partei der Schweiz — GPS
Parti Ecologiste Suisse
Partito Ecologista della Svizzera
(Green Party of Switzerland)

Headquarters	: 1441, CH-3001, Berne (tel: 031-61 99 59)
President	: Dr Peter Schmid
Secretary	: Bernhard Pulver
President of parliamentary group	: Laurent Rebeaud
Founded	: 1983

History

The first cantonal ecologist party, the *Mouvement Populaire pour l'Environnement* (MPE), was founded in Neuchatel in December 1971, initially to protest against a proposed new motorway along Lake Neuchatel. In the 1972 communal elections it obtained 17.8 per cent of the vote in the City of Neuchatel, and eight out of the 41 seats on the Council. In 1976 it won a seat for its president, Jacques Knoepfler, on the city executive.

A number of other ecologist parties were later founded in other cantons. The one with most success was the *Groupement pour la Protection de l'Environnement* (GPE) in Vaud. In 1977 one of its members, Jean-Claude Rochet, was elected onto the Lausanne Municipal Executive. In 1978 it won four seats on the cantonal Grand Council and in 1979 it elected Daniel Brelaz as the first green member of the Swiss Parliament, when he won a seat on the National Council with 6.4 per cent of the Vaud vote.

In 1983 several meetings of ecologist and left-wing alternative parties were convened to examine the possibilities of putting together a Swiss Green Federation. Severe differences emerged between the more moderate ecology parties and the more anarchic and radical alternative parties, both over policy (the ecologists wanted to present the proposed Federation as being above left-right divisions rather than being clearly on the left, and wanted to avoid

the adoption of specific policies, such as the abolition of the Swiss army, that would prove totally unacceptable to the electorate) and over the way in which the meetings were conduced (the ecology parties wanted more business-like and structured meetings). Although there was agreement on certain issues (e.g. the decision to exclude existing national parties, such as the left-wing POCH — see separate entry — from participating in the Federation), the differences finally proved irreconcilable and two separate federations were established.

On May 28, 1983 the more moderate ecologist parties founded the Federation of Green Parties of Switzerland, with five participating parties, the MPE in Neuchatel, the GPE in Vaud, the *Parti Ecologiste Genevois*, the *Grüne Partei des Kantons Zürich* and the Green Party of North-West Switzerland (a small group in Basel, Solothurn and Aargau, which no longer exists under its original title). The Federation's first president was Laurent Rebeaud from Geneva. Meanwhile the left-alternative parties put together a rival federation, The Swiss Green Alternative, which had minimal success and later collapsed.

In Zürich the Green Party won four seats in 1983 on the cantonal Grand Council. In the 1983 federal elections the Federation won three seats on the Swiss National Council, one in Vaud (Daniel Brelaz), one in Geneva (Laurent Rebeaud) and one in Zürich (Arnold Müller). A newly formed *Freie Liste* in Berne led by dissident members of the Radical Party, also won a seat (Leni Robert), and subsequently associated themselves with the Federation, being admitted as full members in October 1984. Also in 1984 existing green groups in Neuchâtel regrouped in a new *Parti Ecologique et Liberté* which took the place of the former MPE in the Federation. A Green Party from the canton of Thurgau was also admitted as a member of the Federation (and subsequently won six seats in the Thurgau cantonal elections).

In 1985 the Federation elected Monica Zingg from Berne as the first woman president of a party at Swiss national level. The *Movimento Ecologista Ticinese* was also admitted to the Federation. In May 1986 the Federation changed its name to The Swiss Green Party.

In 1986 the *Freie Liste* in Berne won 11 seats on the Grand Council of the canton, and two of its members, Leni Robert and Benjamin Hofstetter, were subsequently elected as the first Green members of a cantonal executive. Subsequently one of the Green Party's four members in the parliament, Arnold Müller, left it to join the *Landesring* (see separate entry).

In October 1986 a second group in the canton of Berne, the *Demokratische Alternative*, was admitted to the Green Party after considerable controversy as to whether such an alternative party would fit in with other ecologist parties. Its admission was a factor leading to the resignation of Monica Zingg as the Green Party's president. In the aftermath of Chernobyl and the chemical disaster at Basel the Greens did exceptionally well in elections in Zürich and Geneva.

In the 1987 federal elections, the Green Party's candidates won nine seats in the National Council and were subsequently able to form a parliamentary group for the first time.

Support

The Green Party's support rose considerably in 1987 from its previous level of 2.9 per cent in 1983 to 4.8 per cent in 1987, although this was not as high as many had expected. The Green Party only stood in 11 cantons. It has strong support in both German- and French-speaking Switzerland, primarily in the more densely populated cantons. It is also generally much stronger in Protestant than in Catholic cantons. Past surveys of its electorate have shown that its support is generally strongest among younger voters and those with higher education. It has also been stronger among women than men.

In the 1987 federal elections its highest support in any canton was 11.5 per cent in Geneva, where it won a seat on the National Council. The Geneva ecologists had previously won 8 per cent of the vote and eight seats in the 1985 cantonal elections, and 13 per cent and 11 out of 80 seats in the 1987 Geneva municipal elections. The Greens' other seat in the National Council from French-speaking Switzerland was obtained in Vaud, where the party won 8.4 per cent in 1987. It has held this seat since 1979. In the last cantonal elections in Vaud in 1986, the party won five seats. In the 1985 communal elections it won 65 seats in six communes. It has done well in Lausanne (11.4 per cent in the communal elections in 1985), but is particularly strong in Montreux, where it won 22.1 per cent in 1985 (23 seats on the communal council). Elsewhere in French-speaking Switzerland in the 1987 federal elections it won 7 per cent in Neuchatel and 4.2 per cent in Fribourg (where it also won one seat on the Fribourg Grand Council in the 1986 cantonal elections). In the Valais the local green party (which is only an observer, and not a full member of the Green Party), won 1.6 per cent.

In German-speaking Switzerland the party's highest vote was 10.8 per cent in Thurgau, where it won a seat on the National Council and also had considerable success at cantonal level. In Berne its two local groups won 9.2 per cent

and three seats in the National Council between them (of which almost 7.2 per cent went to the *Freie Liste*), and they also have 14 out of the 200 seats in the cantonal parliament and two posts on the cantonal executive. In Zürich the party won 8 per cent in 1987 and also won three seats on the National Council, following on its vote of over 10 per cent in the 1987 cantonal elections (22 out of 180 seats), where it was slightly stronger in the rest of the canton than in the city of Zürich (with a highest vote of 17.1 per cent in Andelfingen).

The party also won 6.9 per cent in Basel-Land but only 1.1 per cent in Basel Stadt, where a rival green coalition (which is also an observer member) won 2.7 per cent. Another party which is an observer and not a full member, *Grüne Aargau*, won 6.9 per cent of the Aargau vote in 1987, and one seat on the National Council.

The party won 1.9 per cent of the 1987 vote in the Ticino, where in the same year it won 1.7 per cent of the vote and two seats in the Ticino cantonal elections.

Organization

The Green Party of Switzerland currently includes 10 cantonal parties and groups in Zürich, Berne, Fribourg, Basel, Thurgau, Ticino, Vaud, Neuchatel and Geneva. The party's statues permit more than one associated group within the same canton (but they must demonstrate that they are compatible), and there are thus two associated parties within the canton of Berne. There are also five observer parties (two in Basel, one in Valais, one in Aargau and one in Glarus).

At federal level there is a Delegates' Council, which meets twice a year and which is the federal party's "legislature" and a smaller Executive, which meets once a month. The party's president is elected for a two-year term.

In 1983 it was decided that each delegate would pay F 80 to the federal party at the expense of their cantonal party. In 1986 it was decided that the party's deputies in the Swiss parliament would pay 10 per cent of their salaries to the federal party.

The party produces *GPS–Info* with a circulation of 2,000. It is affiliated internationally with the Federation of European Green Parties (since October 1987).

Policies

The Green Party of Switzerland is an ecology party rather than a left-alternative party. Its leaders have a moderate style, and seek to modify Swiss policies in an evolutionary manner rather than advocating revolutionary changes for which the country is not yet ready. The party rejects traditional left-right divisions. It does not find it easy to work with the parties of the far left, nor does the party have the same internal divisions between realists and fundamentalists that are characteristic of the more heterogeneous German Greens.

The Greens do not see themselves as a one issue party, as they believe that ecological principles must be applied in all areas of policy. They have put forward five key principles, the need to take decisions in a longer term perspective, an emphasis on quality rather than quantity, humanism, opposition to technocracy (by which they do not mean rejection of scientific and technical progress, but rigorous questioning of so-called "expert" judgments), and political and economic decentralization. (One of their slogans is that they prefer "the risks of diversity, rather than the fatal risks of uniformity".)

They are highly critical of the current over-emphasis on economic growth, and on the criterion of GDP. There should be more durable and non-polluting products. There should be greater reliance on smaller enterprises and on co-operatives.

There should be less reliance on fossil fuels, and civil nuclear energy should be abolished by the year 2000.

The social and ecological costs of cars should be taken fully into account, and no new national roads or motorways should be built. Public transport should receive a much higher emphasis.

Agriculture should use more biological methods. Existing agricultural land should be protected, and land speculation curtailed. The Greens are also opposed to battery farming techniques and to vivisection.

The Greens have strongly defended the rights of asylum seekers in Switzerland.

The party supports the continued existence of the Swiss militia army (being much more moderate than the Swiss left-alternative parties on this issue), but they call for the creation of a parallel civilian service, and also for a legal statute for conscientious objectors. They also seek the dissolution of all military alliances at world level, and far-reaching disarmament.

They seek controls on the activities of multinationals and call for greater solidarity with the third world.

Personalities

One of the party's most prominent personalities is Laurent Rebeaud, who was one of the party's founders, and the leading personality in the cantonal party in Geneva. He has been a member of the Swiss National Council since 1983, and in 1987 was elected as president of the parliamentary group for a two-year term.

The party's president for the period 1987–89 is Peter Schmid, the founder of the cantonal party in Thurgau, and who is now also a member of the Swiss National Council for Thurgau.

Rudolf Hafner, one of the party's National Councillors from Berne, became well known for revealing financial abuses in the Berne cantonal government. Leni Robert and Benjamin Hofstetter are now Green members of the Berne cantonal executive.

Daniel Brelaz is the longest serving Green member of the Swiss National Council, having been first elected in Vaud in 1979.

Left Alternative groups

The 1968 student and new left movement led to the creation of a number of political groups. The *Partito Socialista Autonomo* (see separate entry under *Partito Socialista Unitario*) became an enduring feature of the Ticino political landscape. In 1971 the Progressive Organizations of Switzerland (POCH — see below) was established, and became the largest force on the far left.

Later a number of Alternative parties were founded in different cantons, primarily in German-speaking Switzerland. In 1983 an attempt was made to group together these parties along with more moderate Green parties within a Swiss Green Federation on the lines of the German Green party. The POCH was excluded on the grounds that it might dominate the smaller parties, but the attempt finally failed because of fundamental differences in policy and style between the left-wing Greens and Alternatives, and the more moderate Greens (see Green Party of Switzerland). A Green Alternative Federation was later created, without much success.

In the 1987 federal elections a number of cantonal alliances were made between various Green, Alternative and left-wing parties. In Luzern, for example, a *Grünes Bündnis* (Green Alliance) was created which incorporated the old POCH organization. In Berne a Green Alliance was created between the POCH, the Socialist Workers' Party, the Communist Party and group of Autonomists. In Zürich another alliance was made between the POCH, a group of Green Alternatives, two other groups, *Frauen macht Politik* (Women make Politics) and a *Stadtliste* (city list). In both Basel-Land and Basel City electoral alliances were forged, in the former *Grüne Baselland* (an alliance between the POCH, left-wing Greens and non-party personalities), in the latter an alliance between the Progressive Organizations of Basel and left-wing Greens. In some cantons electoral alliances were made with the local Socialists (as, for example, in Schwyz where a seat was won).

The left-wing Alternatives have been strongest in the cantons of Zürich (3.8 per cent in the 1987 federal elections, with 17.9 per cent in the fifth district of the city of Zurich), Luzern (see POCH), Ticino (see PSU), and in both half-cantons of Basel, especially within the city of Basel (12.7 per cent in 1987). In the 1987 federal elections there were setbacks in several cantons.

Their political views have been very heterogeneous. Left wing ecological views and the need for massive changes in Swiss society are common features. An "active peace policy" and the need for the eventual abolition of the Swiss army have been other demands.

Progressive Organisationen der Schweiz Organisations Progressistes-Suisses POCH
(Progressive Organizations of Switzerland)

Headquarters : Postfach 1461,
　　　　　　　　　Aarauerstrasse 84,
　　　　　　　　　CH-4600, Olten.
　　　　　　　　　(tel: 062-266707)
Central secretary : Georg Degen
Membership : 10,000
Publication : *Positionen*
Founded : 1971

History

This has been the largest of the far left Swiss Alternative parties. It has entered into alliances with other parties, such as the *Partito Socialista Autonoma*, and in 1987 with a variety of left-wing Green and Alternative groups. It won two seats in the 1979 federal elections and three seats in 1983. In 1987 the POCH and its various alliance partners in the different cantons (see Left Alternative groups above) won 3.5 per cent of the vote, and four seats in the National Council.

Support

The POCH has been strongest in Zürich (where it won 16 per cent on its own in Zürich City's 4th and 5th Districts in the 1987 cantonal elections); the city of Basel (which has had a long left-wing tradition, and where the POCH is now much stronger than the Communist Party); and Luzern where POCH first made a breakthrough in 1983 when it won 6.5 per cent of the vote in

the cantonal elections (and 14.5 per cent in the city of Luzern). In both the 1987 cantonal and federal elections the POCH and its allies polled strongly in Luzern.

Organization

The POCH has sections in seven German-speaking cantons and informal groups elsewhere. There is a national convention which elects a party committee of about 50 members and a 20-member managing committee.

Policy

The POCH is an independent left-wing party which has emphasized both scientific socialism and ecological principles.

Partito Socialista Unitario
(Unified Socialist Party)

Headquarters : Viale Stazione 10,
　　　　　　　　　C.P.2245-CH 6501,
　　　　　　　　　Bellinzona, Ticino
　　　　　　　　　(tel: 092-259462)
President : Dario Robbiani
Secretary : Werner Carobbio
Newspaper : *Politica Nuova*

History

The *Partito Socialista Unitario* (PSU), which operates only in the canton of Ticino, was founded on Jan. 24, 1988 in a merger between the former *Partito Socialista Autonomo* (PSA — Autonomous Socialist Party) led by Werner Carobbio, and the pro-merger minority which had left the Ticino branch of the Swiss Socialist Party, the *Comunita dei Socialisti Ticinesi*, led by Dario Robbiani.

The PSA had been founded in 1969 as a result of a schism within the Ticino branch of the Swiss Socialist Party, when a group of left-wingers, influenced by the 1968 youth movement, were expelled from the cantonal party and formed a new left-wing socialist party. The PSA supported class struggle, and sought to overthrow the capitalist system. It gave priority to extra-parliamentary activities. Opposing a social democracy which had come to terms with capitalism, it co-operated with the Ticino Communist Party. It later also established links with other left-wing Alternative parties in Switzerland, notably the Progressive Organizations of Switzerland (POCH).

In 1975 the PSA won one seat on the Swiss National Council, in a joint list with the POCH, an electoral alliance which was subsequently renewed. The PSA has retained a seat in the National Council until the present day. A parliamentary group was later formed between the PSA, the POCH and the Swiss labour party (the Communists).

In the course of the 1970s and 1980s the PSA gradually moved in a reformist direction. In 1981 the Ticino Communists put forward a proposal for a unified party with the PSA, but this was later rejected by the latter, which began instead to examine the possibility of reunification with the mainstream Socialist Party.

In 1986 a two-year association agreement was negotiated between the PSA and the Swiss Socialist Party, and this was ratified by the latter's Central Committee in May 1986. There was considerable resistance within the Ticino branch of the Swiss Socialist Party to full merger with the PSA. The pro-merger wing formed a working group within the cantonal party (the *Comunita di Lavoro*) under the leadership of Dario Robbiani (the parliamentary group leader of the Swiss Socialist Party), but was placed in a minority position. On Dec. 20, 1986 the *Comunita di Lavoro* came to its own agreement with the PSA, whereby it would present its own lists separate form the Ticino Socialist Party, and in electoral alliance with the PSA. Dario Robbiani, who was still the federal group leader, was then expelled from his own local branch. The *Comunita di Lavoro* became an independent group under the name *Comunita dei Socialisti Ticinesi* (CST).

In the 1987 Ticino cantonal elections the PSA won 7.3 per cent of the vote and seven seats in the Ticino cantonal parliament (the *Gran Consiglio*) and the CST 3.4 per cent and three seats. In the simultaneous elections for the Ticino cantonal government the PSA obtained 10.1 per cent and, due to a quirk in the Ticino electoral system, won a place on the executive for the first time in the party's history.

In the 1987 Federal elections the PSA and CST fought on a joint list, obtaining 10.9 per cent (more than the mainstream Ticino Socialist Party), and one seat on the Swiss National Council.

In January 1988 the PSA and CST formally merged to create the PSU. The new party subsequently applied to the Swiss Socialist Party to renew the association agreement that had previously been negotiated with the PSA. This request is still under review by the Swiss Socialist Party.

Support

The PSU is contesting with the Ticino branch of the Swiss Socialist Party for the third place in the Ticino political spectrum, but far behind the dominant Christian Democrats and Radicals.

Organization

The structure that the PSU has inherited from the PSA consisted of territorial groups (which had to have a minimum of five members) and local nuclei in the workplace or in residential blocks. Above these were the party's regional sections, with their regional assemblies and regional committees. At cantonal level there was the cantonal congress, held every three years and which all members could attend. The congress chose the party's cantonal committee of 20–41 members, whose meetings took place once a month, and which chose the five member political executive as well as the party secretary.

The PSU has inherited the PSA weekly newspaper, *Politica Nuova*.

Policies

The PSA gradually evolved from being an opposition party of the left, with both new left/alternative and communist strands (it based its own structure on democratic centralism, for example) to being a more pragmatic reformist party, closer to the Swiss Socialists than to the Communists. A key objective is still the unification of all Socialists in the Ticino, an objective which has been only partially achieved with the creation of the PSU. The party believes that the old distinctions between Communists and Socialists are no longer useful, and that what is needed is a wider unity on the left to meet new economic, social and political challenges. Clientelist social democracy, rigid communism and even the new left are not up to the task, and a new synthesis will have to be found.

The PSU is now represented on the Ticino cantonal government (an option which it had initially rejected). The party has supported strict controls over cantonal finances. It has called for enhanced measures of social security and emphasizes the fight against unemployment. It has supported increased worker-participation. There should be a greater emphasis on protecting the cantonal environment, and use of civil nuclear power should be given up over a reasonable time period. The PSU was opposed to the revision of the laws affecting foreigners in Switzerland and to the more restrictive law on asylum. It supported the unsuccessful referendum calling for public scrutiny of increases in military expenditure. It believes that its longer term economic and political objectives, such as environmental protection, the transformation of capitalism, the promotion of full employment and peace and disarmament can only be resolved in a united Europe.

Personalities

The party's secretary is Werner Carobbio, the former leader of the PSA. Carobbio is also the party's only representative on the Swiss National Council.

The party's president is Dario Robbiani, the leader of the breakaway pro-merger CST faction of the Ticino Socialist Party, and the former parliamentary group leader of the Swiss Socialist Party. He was the runner-up to Carobbio in the 1987 national elections and thus lost his seat in the Swiss Parliament

Pietro Martinelli is the party's one member of the Ticino cantonal government.

Nationale Aktion für Volk und Heimat Action Nationale Azione Nazionale Acziun Naziunala

(National Action for People and Home-land)

Headquarters	: Ankegässli 1,
	Postfach 59, CH–8956
	Killwangen AG
	(tel: 056-71 19 74)
President	: Rudolf Keller
Secretary	: Anita Wilhelm
Newspapers	: *Volk und Heimat,*
	Peuple et Patrie
Membership	: 5,000

History

National Action developed primarily as a reaction to the great increase in the number of foreigners living and working in Switzerland, with their share of the total population rising from 6 per cent in 1950 to over 17 per cent by the early 1970s.

An action group, the *Nationale Aktion gegen die Überfremdung von Volk und Heimat*, was first founded in the canton of Zürich in 1961, to campaign for restrictions on the number of foreigners in Switzerland. It stood for the first time in national elections in 1969, and its most prominent leader, James Schwarzenbach, was elected to the National Council.

It gained a much higher profile after its near success in a referendum in 1970 on its initiative to reduce the number of foreigners in Switzerland by a third, and with a limitation of 10 per cent on the number of foreigners in any individual canton (apart from Geneva, which would have been permitted 25 per cent). The initiative was supported by 46 per cent of Swiss voters and won a majority in six full and two half-cantons, primarily, but not exclusively, the central mountain cantons.

James Schwarzenbach subsequently left National Action, and founded his own Republican Movement. Valentin Öhn later became National Action president. In the national elections in the autumn of 1971 both groups stood separately, with National Action winning four seats in the National Council (in Zürich, Berne, Basel and Vaud), and the Republicans no less than seven. The two groups then forged a parliamentary alliance.

In 1972 they opposed the Swiss treaty with the EC. They also launched a new petition to reduce the number of foreigners in Switzerland to only 500,000 by 1977. This led to a division within their own ranks as Schwarzenbach opposed this initiative as being too extreme. In the 1974 referendum on the proposals they only won the support of one-third of Swiss voters, and failed to win a majority in any canton. In 1975 the parliamentary alliance between National Action and the Republicans broke up, and later in 1975 both parties suffered badly at the polls. National Action was reduced to only two seats.

In 1977 National Action's proposed initiative on the need to submit future treaties with foreign countries to popular referendum was defeated, but led to a successful federal initiative on the same subject.

Another party initiative, on limitations on Swiss naturalizations, was also defeated. Later in 1977, the party adopted its present name of *Nationale Aktion für Volk und Heimat*. In 1978 Schwarzenbach left active politics, and the Republicans were greatly weakened. In 1979 National Action retained its two seats in Berne and Zürich in the National Council.

In 1982 a bill relaxing some of the existing restrictions on foreign workers was defeated in a referendum, by 690,000 to 680,000, a major success for National Action which had been the only party in the National Council (along with its Geneva sister party, Vigilance) to call for its rejection.

In the 1983 National Council elections National Action gained four seats on a joint list with the Republican movement. It again contested a law to facilitate naturalization for young foreigners, refugees and stateless persons, and, later in 1983, this law was rejected in a referendum by 793,000 to 644,000.

In 1985 it did well in a number of areas in the municipal elections, notably in Lausanne where it gained 11 seats, and became the third largest party. In 1986 its former president, Valentin Öhn, left the party and founded a new Swiss Ecological Liberal Party. In the 1987 Zürich cantonal elections National Action went up from two to six seats.

In October 1987, however, National Action

polled relatively poorly in the national elections, obtaining 2.9 per cent of the vote and three seats in the National Council. Its Geneva ally, Vigilance, lost its only seat.

Support

In the 1987 national elections National Action stood in 10 full cantons and two half-cantons. In percentage terms the party's programme still has its highest appeal in the canton of Geneva (see section on Vigilance for more details), where the right won 8.6 per cent of the vote (14.3 per cent in 1983). In Zürich, National Action won 5.6 per cent of the cantonal vote and two seats in the National Council, obtaining up to 9.5 per cent of the vote in parts of the city of Zürich (e.g. in its 4th District). In the 1987 Zürich cantonal elections National Action obtained between 10–12 per cent of the vote in some parts of the cities of Zürich and of Winterthur.

National Action won its other seat in the 1987 national elections in the canton of Berne, where it obtained 3.2 per cent. Elsewhere it polled best in percentage terms in Basel-Land (6.2 per cent), Basel Stadt (4.5 per cent) and Aargau (4.5 per cent). In French Switzerland in addition to Geneva it also stood in Neuchatel (3.4 per cent) and Vaud (2.8 per cent). It had negligible support in Italian Switzerland (0.9 per cent in Ticino).

Organization

National Action has local, district, regional and cantonal branches. At federal level it has a delegates' assembly, which elects the party's president and vice-president. There is also a central committee of 35 members and an executive committee of nine members.

The party has a youth organization, the ANJ, which has the right to a representative on the party's central committee. In return the parent party has a representative on the ANJ's own committee.

National Action has a German language newspaper, *Volk und Heimat*, which appears 17 times a year (and has a circulation of 7,000) and a French language newspaper, *Peuple et Patrie*, which appears monthly (and has a circulation of 1,000).

Party membership dues are variable according to canton, ranging from Swiss F 12 to 35.

Policies

National Action is a populist party of the right, which emphasizes the need to restrict the number of foreigners in Switzerland, to maintain the maximum degree of Swiss political and economic independence and self-sufficiency, and to preserve the Swiss environment. In recent years some of the objectives that it has promoted (e.g. restrictive policies on refugees and on asylum, Switzerland remaining outside the UN) have been successfully achieved, but its own support-base has been partly recaptured by the government parties, and partly by new protest movements, such as the Greens.

Its most distinctive policy plan continues to be that of the need to keep Switzerland for the Swiss. It believes that Switzerland is over-populated, that there should be restrictions on new immigration and that much of the existing foreign population should leave Switzerland. Swiss nationality should be extremely hard to obtain. The party is also proposed to the sale of Swiss land and property. Swiss workers should have preferential status.

The party's economic policy emphasizes the need to achieve a national market economy, with a more self-sufficient, and less internationalized economy. The party is very critical of economic growth for growth's sake and of materialism, and calls for an economic system putting more emphasis on quality and more respectful of energy and natural resources constraints. Satisfaction of vital needs and cultural objectives should have priority over mere consumption of luxury goods. The party is critical of multinationals and concentrations of economic power, and advocates tough anti-cartel laws. There should be a balanced budget and a stable monetary system. The party supports decentralization of the economy, and people living and working in small communities on a human scale. Traditional crafts should be encouraged.

Environmental policy is a major element in the party's programme. There should be greater use of non-polluting "soft" technologies, and more recycling. There should be more use of renewable sources of energy, and less dependence on fossil fuels. There should be no new nuclear plants. There should be limitations on the amount of land dedicated to industry and to traffic. Public transport should have a much higher priority. There should also be restrictions on animal experimentation.

The party believes that Switzerland should have an agricultural system which is as self-sufficient as possible with encouragement for small peasant farmers, and greater use of natural production methods.

National Action calls for the strictest possible respect of Swiss neutrality. It opposed Swiss entry into the UN. It also believes that Europe should remain the Europe of Nation States. The party believes that there should be increased expenditure on defence.

Personalities

Rudolf Keller has been the party's president since 1986. The party's three members in the National Council are Fritz Meier (one of the movement's original founders in 1961), Hans Steffen from Zürich, and Markus Ruf from Berne.

Vigilance

Headquarters	: place Longemalle 7, CH-1204 Geneva
Leader	: Arnold Schlaepfer

History

Vigilance is a right-wing anti-immigrant party active only in the canton of Geneva (and to a small extent in the neighbouring canton of Vaud), where occasional tensions between the large international community and native Genevans have given Vigilance considerable electoral support. It first won sizeable representation on the Geneva city council in 1967. It also had one member of the Swiss National Council from 1975 to 1987, where the party was allied with the National Action Party (see separate entry).

In 1985 Vigilance had its greatest ever success in the cantonal parliament elections obtaining 19 seats with 10 per cent of the vote (more than any other party). Schlaepfer was not, however, elected to the cantonal executive.

In the 1987 municipal elections Vigilance's vote fell, and it only won nine seats on the council. Its candidate, Jean Cristophe Matt, was not elected to the municipal executive. In the 1987 national elections Vigilance's vote was practically halved compared to 1983, and its 74-year-old member of the National Council, Mario Soldini, who had enjoyed considerable personal popularity, was not re-elected.

Policies

Vigilance is a populist protest party of the right, whose main policy themes have been hostility to foreign influences in Switzerland, and Geneva in particular, and the need to protect the Geneva environment and way of life.

Vigilance has campaigned against the admission of foreigners to Switzerland, and in favour of much more restrictive laws on asylum and refugees. It strongly opposed Swiss entry into the UN. It believes that Geneva must be left for the Genevans.

It has linked this with the need for environmental protection. It has called for the preservation of the Geneva green belt, and for a halt to new housing projects.

Vigilance has been generally hostile to increases in government expenditure, and has called for more rigorous controls on public subsidies. It is opposed to any increases in development aid. It has also called for the abolition of life-time employment for civil servants.

Support for Vigilance appears to have been considerably undercut by recent popular votes for Switzerland not to join the UN and to enact more restrictive legislation on asylum and refugees. It has also lost environmental protest votes to the Greens.

Evangelische Volkspartei der Schweiz — EVP
Parti Evangelique Suisse
(Evangelical People's Party of Switzerland)

Headquarters	: Josefstrasse 32, Postfach 7334, CH–8023 Zürich (tel: 01-44 71 00)
President	: Max Dünki
Secretary	: Hans Schoch
Youth movement	: *Junge EVP*
Women's group	: *EVP Frauen*
Newspaper	: *Evangelische Woche* (fortnightly)
Founded	: 1919

History

A *Protestantisch-Christliche-Partei* (Protestant Christian Party) was first founded in the canton of Zürich in 1917, and soon won two seats on the cantonal council. Similar groups were later founded in other cantons, with the name *Evangelische Volkspartei* (EVP). The party denied that it was narrowly confessional. It emphasized economic rather than religious priorities, with opposition to increasing polarization between Marxism and capitalism as an important theme.

Although it quickly won a seat on the Swiss National Council its growth was slow. For a long time it only retained one seat on the National Council. It subsequently won a second seat, and in 1967 a third seat.

In the 1987 national elections it retained its three seats on the National Council, and obtained 1.9 per cent of the vote in the six cantons in which it put up candidates. There are now eight EVP cantonal parties. There are around 51 EVP members of cantonal parliaments (1987 figure) and 170 members of communal parliaments (1986 figure).

Support

The EVP claims that it is an ecumenical party but it is primarily supported by members of the Evangelical Reformed National Church, who formed 90 per cent of its members in 1986, with the balance of members coming from other Evangelical groups. According to a recent party survey only 0.55 per cent of its members are Catholics. The EVP is also almost exclusively a party of German-speaking Switzerland, with minimal support even in the Protestant cantons of French-speaking Switzerland (although the party has explored the idea of starting a cantonal party in Neuchatel).

The EVP's members come from all backgrounds, although few are self-employed. The average age of members is currently 54.6, and in 1986 24 per cent of its supporters were over 60. 41 per cent of its supporters were pensioners. Around one-third were women.

The EVP's support fell slightly between the 1983 to 1987 elections from 2.1 per cent to 1.9 per cent. It lost support, however, in three out of the four cantons where it put up candidates in both 1983 and 1987 (in Zürich and Aargau quite substantially), and its losses were masked by the fact that it stood in six rather than five cantons in 1987.

The EVP's main political base has been the canton of Zürich, which still accounts for 40 per cent of its membership. In the 1987 national elections it obtained 4.4 per cent in Zürich (5.4 per cent in 1983) and two of its three seats on the National Council. In the 1987 Zürich national elections the EVP won 6.2 per cent (2.5 per cent in 1983), and it obtained 11 seats in the cantonal parliament. It generally polls higher in the country than in the city of Zürich, and its highest vote is in Hinwil (9.6 per cent in the 1987 cantonal elections).

The EVP's other seat in the National Council was obtained in the canton of Berne, where it won 3.4 per cent in 1987 (3.3 per cent in 1983).

In 1987 its highest national vote was in the half-canton of Basel Stadt, where it won 4.5 per cent (4.8 per cent in 1983). In Basel-Land it won 3.4 per cent. In Aargau it also won 3.4 per cent (down from 5 per cent in 1983). In St. Gallen it obtained 2.3 per cent. In 1987 it did not stand in Thurgau, where it had obtained 5.3 per cent in 1983.

Organization

The EVP currently has around 27,000 members, sympathizers and well-wishers. There are eight cantonal parties in Aargau, Basel-Land, Basel Stadt, Berne, Schaffhausen, St. Gallen, Thurgau and Zürich, which are themselves subdivided into local and district parties (there are 12 district parties, for example, in the canton of Zürich). Local parties can also be established even when there is no cantonal party.

At federal level there is an annual delegates' assembly. Every two years the assembly elects the party's president and two vice-presidents, and the other members of the party's central board (*Zentralvorstand*), which consists of at least 13 members. The party's enlarged central board also includes the president of the cantonal parties and the EVP national and cantonal parliamentarians, and elects the party's central secretary. There is also a smaller party executive (*Geschäftsleitung*) of seven members

The EVP has associated youth and women's movements, the *Junge EVP* and the *EVP Frauen*. There is also a linked news agency, the *Protestantischen Pressgenossenschaft* or PPG, which produces the party's fortnightly subscription newspaper, *Evangelische Woche*, which has a circulation of around 6,000. The cantonal parties also produce newspapers (e.g. *EVP-Brief* in Berne and *EVP Info* in Zürich).

In 1986 the federal party had a budget of Swiss F 320,000. Ninety per cent of its income comes from its members' contributions.

In the National Council the EVP has formed a parliamentary group with the *Landesring der Unabhängigen* (see separate entry), although the two parties do not agree on all issues.

Policies

The EVP is a non-confessional centrist party inspired by Christian principles. It emphasizes its independence from all organized interest groups, including individual churches. It rejects dogma and left-right divisions, and claims to judge issues on a case by case basis on their individual merits. It points out that it is progressive on some issues (such as environmental and social questions) and more conservative on others (such as ethical questions, and the protection of the family). It accepts the fundamental underpinnings of the Swiss system, such as neutrality and the free market economy, but also rejects the idea of leaving existing structures unchanged.

In its economic policy the EVP emphasizes the need for healthy state finances and for a social market economy, with strengthened social partnership. It calls for limits to the power of the state, but also of private economic and other interest groups.

It attaches increased importance to environmental policy. It seeks more conservation of energy and other natural resources, and more recycling of waste. No new nuclear plants should be built. The "polluter pays" principle should be firmly established, and fiscal incentives to clean up the environment should be introduced. There should be more support for public transport, and less encouragement to motorists. In agricultural policy the EVP calls for protection of Switzerland's "green capital". It supports more natural farming methods with less reliance on chemicals, and the maintenance of the small family farm rather than increased reliance on factory farming.

The EVP calls for a strengthening of family policy, and of equality between men and women. It also wants stronger support for socially disadvantaged groups in society. It was divided on whether to support the recent proposals for new restrictions in Swiss asylum law, but a narrow majority came out in opposition to such restrictions. The EVP is also increasingly concerned about such ethical issues as genetic manipulation.

On defence policies one of the party's slogans has been "neither red nor dead". It points out that pacifism is not the only possible option for Christians, and has supported the maintenance of adequate Swiss defence. It opposed the initiative for Swiss defence expenditure to be subjected to popular referenda. On the other hand, the EVP puts a strong emphasis on the need for disarmament. It also supports the introduction of a substitute civilian service for conscientious objectors.

The EVP supports Swiss neutrality, and (unlike its parliamentary group partners, the *Landesring*) opposed Swiss entry into the UN.

The EVP also calls for a stronger Swiss development policy to help reduce dangerous north-south divisions. More must be done to make developing countries more self-sufficient, and Switzerland should be more prepared to open its market to their processed goods.

Personalities

Max Dünki has been the EVP president since 1984. He was born in 1932, and has been a National Councillor from Zürich since 1983. The other member of the National Council from Zürich is Hans Öster. The party's National Councillor from Berne is Zwygart Otto. Hans Schoch, from Schaffhausen, is the federal secretary.

Parti Suisse du Travail
Partei der Arbeit der Schweiz
Partito Svizzero del Lavoro

(At cantonal level the party is known as the *Parti Ouvrier et Populaire* in Jura, Neuchatel, Valais and Vaud)
(Swiss Labour Party)

Headquarters	: rue du Vieux-Billard 25, case postale 232, CH–1211 Geneva 8 (tel: 022-281140)
Secretary-general	: Jean Spielmann
Newspaper	: *Vo Realités* (French Switzerland), *Vorwärts* (German Switzerland), *Il lavoratore* (Italian Switzerland)
Membership	: 4,500 (1985 estimate)
Founded	: 1921, refounded 1944

History

The Swiss Communist Party was founded in 1921. Many of its members came from the Social Democratic Party, others were former anarcho-syndicalists. At first it took up a position of independence from other Swiss parties. Later in the 1930s it adopted a popular front strategy of co-operation with other left-wing parties. Until World War II its strength was primarily in German Switzerland, especially in the cantons of Basel, Zürich and Schaffhausen. In Schaffhausen almost the entire Socialist Party defected to the Communists on their foundation. In 1930 the Schaffhausen party broke with Moscow (partly because it insisted on publishing the hours of religious services in the local party newspaper) and later succeeded in having their leader, Walter Bringolf, elected as mayor.

In French Switzerland the party was much weaker and it was here that the individual cantons began to ban the party from 1937 onwards. In 1940 the Swiss Communist Party was finally banned at national level. A Swiss Socialist Federation of former Communists and dissident Socialists was then formed and was now banned in its turn. Finally the Swiss Labour Party was founded on Oct. 14, 1944. Its first president was Léon Nicole, the former leader of the left-wing Socialists in Geneva, who had eventually been expelled from the Socialist Party.

The newly formed party enjoyed considerable success in the immediate postwar period, with almost 200,000 members and gaining 5.1 per cent of the vote and seven seats in the 1947 election for the Federal Council. Unlike the pre-war period its greatest successes were in French Switzerland. The party then began a long decline. Léon Nicole, its most prominent figure, left in 1952, and the party was hurt by its pro-Moscow line over the Communists' seizure of power in Czechoslovakia and the break with Tito. While it has subsequently taken a more independent line on such issues as the invasion of Czechoslovakia it has not succeeded in arresting its long-term decline, in spite of short-term recoveries at cantonal level. It nevertheless always managed to stay above 2 per cent until the 1983 national elections when it slipped sharply to 0.9 per cent and was left with only one seat in the National Council. It has been outflanked by newer parties of the left, more responsive to the alternative politics which sprang up after 1968. In the 1987 national elections it won 0.8 per cent and retained its one seat in the National Council.

Support

The party is strongest among industrial workers and it has only limited success among left-wing intellectuals, who have been more attached to new political parties.

The Swiss Labour Party is now at its lowest-ever level of support. In the postwar period most of its support has come from French Switzerland. In Geneva 36 out of 100 deputies on the Cantonal Council in 1945 came from the party and it was still the largest cantonal party as recently as 1971 although it has now gone under 10 per cent. In 1987 it won its one National Council seat in Geneva and polled 8.7 per cent. In Vaud a number of well-known local notables have been party members and Popular Fronts were once formed in cities such as Lausanne. It polled 3.5 per cent in the 1987 National Council elections. In Neuchatel the party has received most of its support in the Jura mountain areas away from the lake. It got 19 per cent of the vote in 1967 but, as in the Vaud, its support has since declined sharply. In 1987 it obtained 3.8 per cent in the National Council elections. Immediately after the war the party was represented in nine of the cantonal parliaments in German Switzerland including such unlikely places as Appenzell-Ausser-Rhoden. Since then it has been electorally insignificant in most of German Switzerland with the exception of Zürich and the city of Basel, where the party has been strongly supported by the workers in the port and in the chemical factories. In 1947 it was the second largest party in Basel and had a coalition with the Socialists, but it has now lost its support even in the red suburb of Bläsi. In 1987 in the National Council elections it won 1.9 per cent in Basel Stadt. In Italian Switzerland the party is far weaker than the left-wing Autonomous Socialist Party.

Organization

The party's current membership is around 4,500.

By Swiss standards, the Swiss Labour Party is highly centralized. The cantonal parties are only "sections" of the federal party, have autonomy only on cantonal and communal issues and must adhere to the general programme of the federal party. The principle of "democratic centralism" is written into the party Constitution and no separate "tendencies" or "currents" within the party are allowed. Any person resident in Switzerland can join the party, irrespective of nationality (recognizing the fact that most of the underprivileged in Switzerland are non-nationals). The National Congress meets ordinarily every four years.

The Central Committee consists of 40–50 titular members and a varying number of substitutes. Among its tasks are the determination of the party line in all federal votes (if, however a two-to-three majority is not attained the decision is left at cantonal level).

The Central Committee elects the political Bureau (of no more than 17 members), the secretary-general and the members of the national secretariat, who are responsible for the day-to-day running of the party. The party's revenue stems from regular and special levies on members, from collections and gifts and from contributions from elected party members. Levies on individual members are passed to the central party organization by the cantonal sections.

Policies

The Swiss Labour Party remains a relatively orthodox Communist party although it has changed somewhat in recent years. One of the key objectives in its constitution is the abandonment of capitalism and its replacement, first by Socialism and then by Communism. Its analysis is still based on "scientific socialism" and it accuses the Socialist party of class collaboration.

Nevertheless it no longer uses the language of revolution, nor of the dictatorship of the proletariat, and the means that it advocates to change Swiss society are gradualist and democratic. In economic policy it advocates the strengthening of the social security system, a reduction in the working week, and longer paid holidays. It wants greater planning of public investment, defends public sector employment and resists the calls of other parties for a reduced role for the state. It attacks fiscal fraud and the "parasitic" financial sector which is too dominant in the Swiss economy. It criticizes xenophobic attacks on foreign workers. They must be given more rights, although their numbers must be controlled.

The party has shifted its stand from one of being in favour, towards one of opposition to the construction of new nuclear power stations. Environmental protection, in general, gets a higher priority than it did in the past, and one of the key objectives in the party's constitution is to achieve "a harmonious relationship between man, production and nature". The party advocates a strict policy of neutrality for Switzerland. It has supported the principle of Switzerland joining the UN. It supports the Swiss Army as a purely defensive force, but wishes to see a lower percentage of military expenditure and the creation of alternative civilian service for those who do not wish to enter the army.

On foreign policy issues its criticism is mainly directed at the USA and it is still fundamentally protective of the Soviet Union but it has been cautiously critical of events in Afghanistan and Poland. The party has clearly been discomfited by the greater success in recent years of the new political parties on the left more in tune with alternative and green movements. The party is still critical of them, though more guardedly so than in the past, but nevertheless advocates close co-operation with them wherever possible.

Personalities

The party's secretary-general is Jean Spielmann, its one member of the National Council.

Parti Libéral Suisse
Liberale Partei der Schweiz
(Swiss Liberal Party)

Headquarters	: Case postale 625, 3018 Berne (tel: 031-560137/ 031-619961)
President	: Gilbert Coutau (Geneva)
Secretary-general	: Philipe Boillod
President of the Liberal parliamentary group	: Claude Bonnard

History

The Liberal Party evolved out of the reforming movements of the 1820s and 1830s which sought the introduction of more democratic cantonal constitutions. In the post-1848 period, however, the liberal family divided, with the traditional liberals (then known as the *Zentrum* or Centre Party) defending more conservative positions and cantonal rights, and the radicals a stronger central state.

By 1890 the Liberals had only 22 seats in the National Council compared to 83 for the Radicals. They were subsequently not represented on the Federal Council (although there was to be a Liberal federal councillor, Gustave Ador in 1917).

The Liberals were only loosely organized for most of the 19th century but in 1893 they established a Liberal Democratic parliamentary group. In 1913 the Liberal Democratic Party was formally founded. It has since twice changed its name, in 1961 to the Liberal Democratic Union and in 1977 to the Liberal Party of Switzerland.

The Liberal Party is only organized in seven cantons, Geneva, Vaud, Neuchatel, Fribourg, Berne, Basel-Land and Basel Stadt. In this latter canton it has still retained its former name of the Liberal Democratic Party. The Liberals received 2.7 per cent of the national vote in 1987. They have nine seats in the National Council (three from Geneva, three from Vaud, two from Neuchatel and one in Basel Stadt) and three in the Council of States (one each from Geneva, Vaud and Neuchatel). Their concentration of support thus gives them more influence (especially in the Council of States, where in the past they have sometimes had as many representatives as the far larger Socialist Party), than their small numbers would warrant.

A further distinguishing feature of the party has been its link with three of the traditionally great newspapers of Switzerland, the *Journal de Génève*, the *Gazette de Lausanne* and the *Basler Nachrichten* — although only the first survives in its old form.

Support

The Liberal Party is predominantly a party of the French Swiss Protestant establishment. Proportionately the party is most powerful in the canton of Neuchatel where it won 38 out of 115 seats in the 1985 cantonal election. In Neuchatel the party has inherited some of the old royalist support (Neuchatel was linked with the Prussian monarchy until the middle of the 19th century) and its main strength is in the more conservative areas of the canton around the Lac de Neuchatel and in the Val de Ruz. In the 1987 National Council elections it won 30 per cent of the Neuchatel vote.

The Liberals are also very powerful in Geneva where they are the traditional right-wing party and represent the old financial and social "establishment". In 1985 they won 19 out of 100 seats in the cantonal parliament and in 1987, 17 out of 80 in the Geneva municipal elections, leaving them as the largest party in the town for the third consecutive time. In the 1987 National Council elections they won 18 per cent in Geneva. The Liberals also have a significant presence in Vaud, where they are the third largest party behind the Radicals and the Socialists with 45 out of 200 seats in the 1986 cantonal elections. The Liberals in Vaud are particularly strong among the old urban families, the heads of companies, the big farmers and among the wine aristocracy of Lavaux on the shores of Lake Geneva. In the 1987 National Council elections they won 17.4 per cent of the cantonal vote.

The only German-speaking canton where the Liberals have been a major force is the city of Basel where they have been the party of the non-Catholic conservative establishment. In 1984 they won 15 out of 130 seats in the cantonal parliament. In 1987 their vote increased in the National Council elections in Basel Stadt to 12.3 per cent, and they regained a seat on the National Council. The Liberals also have a small presence in Basel-Land. In Fribourg and in Berne, where there are also Liberal parties, they are unrepresented in the cantonal parliament.

Organization

The Liberal Party is still loosely organized at the federal level. Its federal Constitution is minimalist in scope, and there is little co-ordination between the cantonal parties. No national electoral programme is drawn up, for example.

Membership of the national party is reserved for the cantonal parties, groups of at least 30 persons wishing to promote liberal policies in cantons without separate liberal parties, or individual members in cantons without either parties or groups of the necessary size.

The party's organs are a delegate assembly, a central committee and a small central executive. A congress is also held once or twice a year, to examine and pronounce upon policy questions. This congress is open to all party members but cannot take any decisions if a majority of the elected delegates are opposed. The party is a member of the Liberal International (along with the Swiss Radical Party).

Policies

The Swiss Liberal Party is now on the conservative side of the Swiss political spectrum. While in the 19th century it could be located between the Catholic conservatives on its right and the Radicals on its left, it is now quite close in its policies to the latter. The differences between these two branches of the Liberal family are now quite difficult to define, related more to social factors (in some milieux you are born into a Liberal rather than Radical tradition) and to the fact that the Radicals are a party of government and the Liberals are not, than to any substantial difference in policy.

The party makes much of the fact that it is consequently free to speak its mind. These policies are uncompromisingly liberal, in the economic sense at least. A common thread of almost all of its policies is the need to protect the individual and to reduce the role of the state to the necessary minimum. The state should not force social changes by legislation and should let changes take place at their own speed. The current "legislative inflation" should be kept in check. The increase in federal expenditure should not exceed the rate of increase of the federal GNP, the number of civil servants should be restricted, there should be a ceiling for any subsidies. Issues like reductions in working time and industrial democracy should be left to negotiations between the social partners and not made the subject of legislation. A "welfare mentality" should be discouraged. More reliance should be put on indirect rather than direct taxation. Environmental policy objectives should be balanced against the need for economic growth and against individual freedoms. The party has been in favour of the further development of civil nuclear energy.

The party's transport policy emphasises free competition between different types of transport and is thus more pro-road and less pro-rail than most other Swiss parties. The Swiss Liberal Party puts a strong emphasis on defence issues and believes that military expenditure should have a high priority. It is opposed to the establishment of an alternative civilian service.

In foreign policy issues it believes that Switzerland should not let moral judgements about other regimes affect its actions. Unlike most other Swiss parties it did not explicitly advocate Swiss entry into the UN. In domestic policy, however, the Liberals have been strongly anti-communist and before the war pushed for the banning of the Communist Party at cantonal level.

The Swiss Liberal Party is a strong defender of cantonal rights against the federal government and argues that there should be a redistribution of tasks between the two with more responsibilities being given to the cantons.

Personalities

The Swiss Liberal Party has been a party of strong individual personalities, who do not fit any easy stereotypes. Among its leading personalities have been for example, Jean François Aubert of Neuchatel who has been popular even among Greens for his strong environmental stand and Monique Bauer-Lagier of Geneva who, like Aubert, was a member of the Federal Council of States.

Jean Cavadini is its current member of the Council of States from Neuchatel, and André Gautier is its Council of States member from Geneva. Gilbert Coutau, its president, is a member of the National Council.

Jura

The only political violence that Switzerland has experienced in recent years has come as a result of the long-lasting conflict in the Jura region. A separatist movement had gradually developed among the French-speaking inhabitants of the Jura region of the otherwise German-speaking majority canton of Berne. This movement called for the creation of a separate French-speaking canton of Jura. The situation was further complicated by the fact that the French-speaking region was divided into Catholic and Protestant areas whereas the German-speaking majority in the canton of Berne was predominantly Protestant. The separatists were mainly supported by Catholics, although their most well-known leader, Roland Béguelin, was himself Protestant.

After a long and sometimes violent struggle which divided the people of the Jura into separatists and anti-separatists (including some who wished to set up a separate Jura unit within the framework of the canton of Berne), Berne finally conceded the principle that the Jura people should vote on their destiny. In 1974 a narrow majority within the Jura voted to establish a new canton. This was followed by further debate as to which communes should enter the new canton, and which should remain with Berne, as many of the Protestant communes in the southern part of the Jura wished. There was more violent conflict, especially between the separatist *Beliers* (*Rams,* the youth movement of the *Rassemblement Jurassien* — see below) and the pro-Berne *Sangliers* (*Wild Boars*). The worst flash-point of violence has been the severely divided commune of Moutier.

A new canton of Jura was finally established on Jan. 1, 1979. This has not completely solved the Jura problem, however, as there is still pressure for the French-speaking areas which have remained within the canton of Berne to be re-united with the other French-speaking areas within the new canton of Jura.

Rassemblement Jurassien
(Jura Rally)

Address : rue du l'Écluse 10, CH-2800 Delémont

This was founded in the 1950s to fight for the canton of Jura. It is a movement rather than a political party (its members are in different political parties: the main national parties are now well established within the new canton of Jura) which now stands for the creation of "one canton of all six francophone districts" of Jura, and for the "liberation" of francophone territory which is not yet part of the canton.

The *Rassemblement Jurassien* (RJ) has had a powerful organization which existed in parallel (and initially in tension) with those of the main political parties. At the creation of the canton of Jura in 1979 the RJ had 13,000 members with local branches and district federations. It was supported indirectly by two newspapers, the *Jura Libre* and the *Feuille d'Avis du Jura,* and had an active youth movement (the *Beliers* or *Rams*). It had other affiliated organizations, such as *le Mouvement Universitaire Jurassien* and *l'Association Féminine pour la Défence du Jura*.

Two of its better known figures have been Roland Béguelin, who was elected for the Socialist Party in 1979, and Roger Schaffter, who has been active in the Christian Democratic Party (although he was recently defeated in the 1987 elections for the Jura representative to the Swiss Council of States).

Unité Jurassienne
(Jura Unity)

Address : Hotel de la Gare, CH-2740 Moutier

This is a movement rather than a party, with members from different political parties.

Since the incorporation of the predominantly Protestant southern part of the Jura within the canton of Berne in 1979 this group has campaigned for the inclusion of this region in the canton of Jura. In the 1979 general election, Jean-Claude Crevoisier, a former social democratic deputy and then leader of an *Entente Jurassienne* group, won a seat in the National Council, but the movement did not retain the seat in 1983. In municipal elections held in 1986, the *Unité Jurassienne* gained a majority in Moutier.

Its president is Jean-Claude Crevoisier, and its secretary-general is Alain Steullet.

Parti Ouvrier Socialiste
Sozialistische Arbeiterpartei — SAP
(Socialist Workers' Party)

History

The SAP was founded in 1969. It derives from the Revolutionary Marxist League, which had been set up in 1969 by some 100 French-speaking intellectuals who defected from the Swiss (Communist) Party of Labour. It has been particularly active in trade unions and in the anti-nuclear movement. Among the cantons where it has operated are Vaud, Fribourg, Zug and Ticino. It currently has deputies in four cantonal parliaments, but no representative in the National Parliament.

Organization

The SAP's membership is estimated at around 1,000. It has applied the principle of democratic centralism to its internal organization. It has a national congress (there were around 150 delegates at its most recent congress) which elects a 34 member committee, which in turn elects its political bureau. The party produces a periodical called *La Brèche*. The party is the Swiss section of the Fourth (Trotskyist) International.

Policies

The SAP is a party of Trotskyist orientation. At its 7th congress in 1987 it expressed its willingness to wind itself up in its present form in order to achieve its objective of a wider pluralist, left opposition movement in Switzerland, bringing together Green Alternatives, the Swiss Progressive Organizations (POCH — see separate entry), feminism and trade union groups, solidarity movements with the third world, and even Christian groups.

At its 7th congress the SAP decided to put forward a popular initiative on the issue of exploitation and discrimination against women. It is strongly anti-nuclear. It defends strong social welfare and environmental protection measures.

Auto Partei
Parti Automobiliste
(Swiss Car Party)

Headquarters	: Fähnlibrunner-strasse 5, CH-8700 Küssnacht
President	: Michael E. Dreher

Publication	: *Tacho*
Membership	: 6,000
Founded	: March 1, 1985

History and Support

This party was founded in 1985, and was unexpectedly successful in the 1987 federal elections when it stood in 10 cantons and won 2.6 per cent of the total Swiss vote, with two seats in the National Council. One of its seats was obtained in Zürich (where the party polled 3.8 per cent, with a highest vote of 5.9 per cent in the commune of Diesdorf), and the other in Berne (on a vote of 3.2 per cent). The party's highest percentage of the vote was in the canton of Thurgau (6.3 per cent), and the party was also particularly successful in Aargau (5.4 per cent), St. Gallen (5 per cent), Solothurn (4.9 per cent) and Schwyz (4.9 per cent). In Luzern it obtained 3.4 per cent, in Basel-Land 2.6 per cent and in Uri 1.7 per cent.

Policies

The party's success has stemmed primarily from a reaction among certain Swiss voters (especially car commuters) to what they have seen as exaggerated attention to environmental concerns among Swiss politicians, and a strong prejudice against private transport in favour of public transport.

The party's aims are thus to represent motorists' rights, to support the construction of motorways (now opposed by several Swiss parties) and of parking facilities in towns, and to oppose increases in car tax or a levy on vehicles using motorways, as well as all limitations on the freedom of car drivers. In 1987 the party in Zürich attempted unsuccessfully to launch a popular initiative in favour of a 30 per cent drop in vehicle tax within the canton.

In other matters the party generally shares the free enterprise orientation of the conservative wing of the Radical Party.

Personalities

The party's president and current national councillor from Zürich is Michael Dreher, who has been a member of the Radical Party. Its national councillor from Berne is Jürg Scherrer.

Turkey

Francis Jacobs

The country

Turkey is a country of 296,000 square miles, mainly in Asia Minor, but with a small section in Europe. It is a country of great regional diversity, and borders on no less than six other countries: Greece, Bulgaria, Soviet Union, Iran, Iraq and Syria.

Turkey has a fast-growing population, estimated at over 52 million. There has been great rural migration into the cities. Istanbul, the largest city, has over 5 million inhabitants and the other major cities, Ankara (the capital), Izmir, Adana and Bursa have all grown rapidly.

The vast majority are Turks, but there is a significant Kurdish minority possibly up to between seven and eight million, in south-eastern Anatolia. There is also a small Arab minority, around 1.7 per cent near the border with Syria. Only a small number of Armenians still live within Turkey. There are a few other small minority groups, including Georgians and Lazes.

Outside Turkey there are Turkish minorities in Greece and Bulgaria in particular. There are also a large number of Turkish migrants in Western Europe. In 1985 there were 1.48 million Turks in West Germany alone, with 115,000 in West Berlin.

Turkey is 99 per cent Moslem. The large majority of these are Sunnis, but there is also a minority of Alevis (estimated at between 10 to 20 per cent of the total), who are linked to the Syrian Alawis and the Shi'ites. In addition there are a number of traditional Dervish orders (formally outlawed, but still with some influence), as well as several new religious orders, such as the Nurculuk.

Political institutions

Turkey is a unitary republic. Since the fall of the Ottoman Empire it has had three different constitutions, in 1924, 1961 and 1982, each providing for a different balance between Turkey's political institutions.

Turkey's most recent Constitution (as sub-

Map of Turkey showing 67 provinces, also showing number of members of parliament (in brackets) per province, and number of constituencies in provinces with more than one constituency.

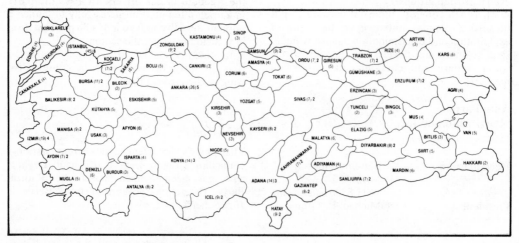

Source: adapted from *Turkish Daily News*.

sequently modified in certain respects) now provides for a Unicameral Parliament (as in the 1924 constitution, but not as in that of 1961, which also provided for a Senate). The present version of the Grand National Assembly consists of 450 members, elected for a maximum term of five years. Until 1961 elections were fought on a majority system, but the 1961 Constitution provided for the introduction of proportional representation, in order to prevent any one party dominating the Parliament. The present Constitution retains a system of proportional representation but with a number of highly restrictive measures again aimed at limiting the number of parties in Parliament.

Turkey is divided into 104 constituencies, based primarily on the 67 provinces, but with 24 of the larger provinces being divided up into separate constituencies. Each constituency has between three and six deputies (with only one exception, Tunceli with only two seats). There is a national threshold of 10 per cent with any party winning less than this total not being eligible for any seats even if it has high support in individual constituencies. In addition, there are provincial thresholds. The total number of valid votes cast in each constituency is divided by its number of seats to obtain a provincial electoral quota which must be exceeded if a party is to win a seat in that constituency. Once these hurdles are overcome distribution of seats within each constituency is by the d'Hondt system of proportional representation.

There is one additional feature which favours the larger parties. This is the system of "contingency seats", allocated to single constituency provinces when they contain five seats (thus giving them a sixth seat), or to separate constituencies within one province when they contain four or more seats. There are 46 such contingency seats which are awarded to the party which wins the largest number of votes in the constituency. Moreover, they are not counted for the purpose of calculating the provincial threshold, thus raising it, and making it more difficult for small parties to win.

The law governing the creation and operation of political parties, as laid down in the 1982 Constitution and in the Political Parties Law of 1983, contains numerous restrictions. Parties' constitutions, for example, may not challenge Turkey's nature as a unitary and secular republic, and Marxist, Fascist, Federalist or religious or ethnically-based parties are, at the very least, severely discouraged. Moreover, parties may be dissolved by the Constitutional Court.

Parties' internal operations are also subject to considerable state supervision. There is a prescribed structure for parties' national, provincial and district organizations and parties are not permitted to form separate youth or women's movements, party foundations or overseas party groups. There are also rules concerning the holding of internal party primaries for choice of party candidates in which all their registered members may take part, and their central organs are only given limited possibilities to directly nominate a certain number of candidates besides those chosen in the primaries. All internal party elections, and delegate and candidate selection are subject to external judicial control.

Within the Grand National Assembly larger parties are also favoured, in that it takes 20 members to form a political group, which have several advantages over independents. There are new strict rules preventing members from changing party in mid-legislature.

Ataturk's 1924 Constitution introduced a presidential system of government, with a powerful president choosing a weaker Prime Minister, and with a parliament with limited powers. The 1961 Constitution weakened the presidency, and gave more power to the Prime Minister and parliament. The 1982 Constitution partially reverses this, and again strengthens the president, although to a degree as yet not fully tested by the new political system.

The President is to be elected for a seven-year term by the Grand National Assembly (although the current president received a direct popular mandate in the 1982 referendum to approve the new Constitution). The President's very considerable powers include designation of the Prime Minister, appointing members of the Constitutional Court, presiding over and even convening Cabinet meetings, and when necessary, imposing martial law. The President also has considerable powers to challenge constitutional changes, and may also dismiss individual ministers at the proposal of the Prime Minister. During the present transitional period, the President is advised by a President's Council, consisting of the members of the former ruling military council (the National Security Council).

The Prime Minister is chosen by the President (so far the leader of the largest party in the Assembly has been chosen), and then chooses his own ministers, who are accountable to the Assembly.

Turkey has a highly centralized administration, based on 67 *vilayets* or provinces, each with their own governor, who is both representative of the central administration and the chief executive of the provincial local government. Below these are the districts, which also form the electoral districts for elections to the provincial general assemblies. Proportional representation is used, but parties must win 10 per cent of the vote to be represented. There is a similar 10 per cent threshold in municipal council elections.

There has also been one special region with a "supergovernor" to cover the areas in which there has been unrest in south-eastern Turkey.

Brief political history

1876

New Constitution provides basis for election of first Ottoman Parliamentary Assembly (1877–78).

1878

Sultan Abdulhamid II suspends Assembly and re-asserts absolutist regime.

1908–18 — second constitutionalist period (fragmentation of Ottoman Empire)

Young Turks help to re-establish Parliamentary Assembly provided for by 1876 Constitution (1908); war in Libya (1911–12); Balkan War (1912–13); Turkey enters World War I as an ally of Germany (1914).

1918–19

Occupation and invasion of Turkey.

1919–23

War of Independence
Mustafa Kemal — "Ataturk" — leads a national campaign to drive out Greek invaders, and to re-assert Turkish national independence.

Sultanate loses direct political powers and relegated to caliphate (1922); establishment of Turkish Republic (1923), with Ankara as new capital.

1923–38

Era of Ataturk
Secularization of government and education, abolition of caliphate and Moslem religious courts, introduction of new civil codes of civil, criminal and commercial law, prohibition of Dervish orders, abolition of fez and turban for men and discouragement of veil for women, replacement of Arabic script by Latin alphabet, replacement of Moslem lunar calendar by solar calendar, purification of Turkish language with removal of many Arabic and Persian influences, increasing direction of economy by state — "étatisme".

1924 Constitution establishes parliament (Grand National Assembly), strong presidential system of government, and universal male franchise; opposition party briefly authorized before return to single-party regime of Ataturk's Republican People's Party (1924–5); opposition party again authorized, and again collapses (1930); women enfranchised (1934).

1938–50

Presidency of Ismet Inönü
Turkey kept neutral during World War II, period of strict étatisme in economic policy and also of gradual transition from single party state to a multi-party democracy.

Inönü decision to permit opposition parties to ruling Republican People's Party (1945); creation of Democratic Party (1946): wins support of rising entrepreneurs and middle classes, modern farmers and urban poor, supports increased role for private enterprise and the lifting of state controls, as well as increased religious freedom.

First parliamentary elections in republican Turkey, Republican People's Party wins 85 per cent of votes (July 1946); creation of Conservative Islamic "Nation Party" (1948).

Second parliamentary elections; Republican People's Party loses power in huge swing to Democratic Party, which wins 408 out of 488 seats on 53.3 per cent of vote. Former President Inönü goes into opposition.

1950–60

Democratic Party government under Celal Bayar as President and Adnan Menderes as Prime Minister
1924 Constitution left formally unchanged but power shifts to considerable degree away from President to Prime Minister; economic policy places more emphasis on the role of private sector and on agricultural development; increasing accusations of government authoritarianism.

Turkey enters NATO (1952); Nation Party closed down (1953); Democratic Party wins re-election (1954); New Freedom Party created by liberal dissidents from Democratic Party (1955); Democratic Party wins re-election but with reduced majority (1957); military intervenes and overthrows Menderes regime (May 27, 1960).

1960–61

Military rule under General Cemal Gursel
Committee of National Unity runs country,

Menderes and two other senior Democratic Party ministers tried and executed. Democratic Party wound up, new Constitution prepared, extreme nationalist minority within military government seek longer period of military rule, but majority decide on quick return to parliamentary democracy.

1961–80

Period of rapidly alternating governments under new multi-party system created by 1961 Constitution

Number of parties increases rapidly with dominant left-of-centre party being joined by substantial Islamic conservative and later extreme nationalist parties on the right, and smaller Turkish Labour Party on the left, as well as other breakaway parties from their own ranks, military again intervenes for a brief period after 1971, followed by increasingly uncertain period of caretaker and non-partisan governments and coalitions, economic problems and rise in terrorism and violence from both the left and the right.

Republican People's Party – Justice Party coalition, with Ismet Inönü as Prime Minister (1961–62); Cemal Gursel as President of the Republic.

Schism within Republican Peasants' Nation Party: New Nation Party created (1962).

Republican People's Party coalition with New Turkey Party (right-of-centre) and Republican Peasants' Nation Party (Islamic conservative), with Ismet Inönü as Prime Minister (1962-63).

Republican People's Party minority government under Ismet Inönü (1963–65).

Non-partisan pre-election cabinet (1965).

Justice Party under Süleyman Demirel (who won leadership contest after death of previous party leader Gumuspala in 1964) wins overall majority in new general elections (1965).

Justice Party majority government under Süleyman Demirel (1965–71) (only period of single party majority rule under 1961 constitutional regime).

Bulent Ecevit becomes secretary-general of Republican People's Party. Inönü remains party chairman, but party begins to move to the left (1966).

Cerdet Sunay elected as President of the Republic (1966).

A number of members of the Republican People's Party's right wing break away to form a new Reliance Party under Turhan Feyzioglu (1969).

Alparslan Türkes (who has been leader of Republican Peasants' Nation Party since 1965) creates new ultra-nationalist Nationalist Action Party (1969).

Justice Party wins new majority in 1969 elections, and Demirel reconstitutes government.

Budget crisis, 41 members of Justice Party defect and create new Democratic Party, emphasizing more liberal economic policies than Justice Party (1970).

Turkish military intervene indirectly (so-called "coup by memorandum"), by giving ultimatum to political parties (1971).

New non-partisan government installed under Nihat Erim (1971–72).

Ismet Inönü finally resigns as leader of Republican People's Party, and Bulent Ecevit becomes new leader with more left-wing stance than Inönü. Some Inönü supporters join Reliance Party (1972).

National Salvation Party (Islamic conservative) formed by Necmettin Erbakan (1972).

Non-partisan governments under Ferit Melen (1972–3) and Naim Talu (1973–4) (Republican People's Party emerges as largest party, but with only 33.3 per cent of the poll in 1973 elections in which eight parties win seats in the Parliament; deadlock follows.)

Fahri Kohrrutürk elected President (1973).

Republican People's Party forms coalition with National Salvation Party, with Bulent Ecevit as Prime Minister (1974).

Cyprus crisis, and Turkish invasion (1974).

Caretaker government after Ecevit resigns in unsuccessful attempt to provoke new elections (1974–5).

Four-party coalition including Justice Party, Nationalist Action Party and National Salvation Party, with Süleyman Demirel as Prime Minister, only enjoys a small majority (1975–77).

General election in which two largest parties advance (with Republican People's Party in the lead), and smaller parties decline (1977).

Short-lived government of Bulent Ecevit's Republican People's Party (June 1977).

Three-party coalition of Justice Party, Nationalist Action Party and National Salvation Party, under Süleyman Demirel. Eventually falls after defections from within Justice Party (1977).

Government of Republican People's Party, Justice Party defectors and minor parties under Bulent Ecevit, political climate becomes increasingly tense and polarized (1978–79).

Minority Justice Party government under Süleyman Demirel (December 1979 to September 1980). (Government puts forward austerity economic programme in January 1980, but terrorism of left and right continues to intensify. Failure to agree on name of new President.)

Military coup on Sept. 12, 1980.

1980–83

Military rule under General Evren and his National Security Council
Admiral Bulend Ulusu appointed as Prime Minister and Turgut Özal as Deputy Prime Minister responsible for economic policy; existing parties wound up; all politicians of former regime barred from political activities until 1988, and party leaders until 1992; clampdown on terrorism, and on activities of the far left, far right and Islamic fundamentalists; martial law and press censorship; new Constitution prepared.

New Constitution strengthens presidency, somewhat weakens prime minister and parliament, and introduces new system of proportional representation favouring largest parties (1982).

Turgut Özal resigns as Deputy Prime Minister (1982).

New Constitution approved in referendum by 91 per cent of voters, and General Evren elected unopposed as President for seven-year term (November 1982).

Political Parties Law sets down conditions for registration of new parties (April 1983).

Registration of new parties begins, new Grand Turk Party held to be too close to old Justice Party and banned (May 1983).

Only three parties allowed to contest November 1983 elections. Motherland Party of Turgut Özal wins 45 per cent of vote and 211 seats, and defeats left-of-centre Populist Party (30 per cent and 117 seats) and military-supported Nationalist Democracy Party (23 per cent and 71 seats).

Turgut Özal designated by President Evren as Prime Minister and creates majority Motherland Party government (December 1983).

1983–present

Re-establishment of democratic regime (Turgut Özal as Prime Minister)

Local elections in which Motherland Party wins control of 55 of Turkey's 67 provinces. Newly authorized Social Democratic Party comes second and wins 10 provinces and new right-of-centre True Path Party third. Populist Party and Nationalist Democracy Party come poor fourth and fifth (March 1984).

Martial law dropped in major cities and in much of Turkey (1985).

Modification of Constitution as regards political parties and electoral law (1986).

Turkey applies to join European Community (April 14, 1987).

Referendum on whether former political leaders can make early return to active leadership decides in favour of their return by narrow margin of 11,723,309 to 11,641,961 (September 1987).

New elections in which seven parties participate, Motherland Party wins majority and Özal is subsequently reconfirmed as Prime Minister (November 1987).

Greek–Turkish summit between Papandreou and Özal (January 1988).

Özal loses referendum on his attempt to convene early local elections (September 1988).

Main features of the current political system

The Turkish political system was given its main ideological underpinnings by Kemal Ataturk, whose emphasis on Turkish national identity, and on a unitary modern, Western-oriented and secular state, have remained central poles of reference ever since. While they have often been challenged they have also been continually reaffirmed, not least by the Turkish armed forces, who have generally seen one of their key roles as being guardians of the Ataturk tradition.

There are a number of cleavages potentially leading to considerable divisions within Turkish politics and society, especially between Westernized and traditional and between urban and rural Turkey, between the more prosperous coastal and western regions and the poorest areas of eastern Anatolia, between secularism and Islamic values, and between Turkey's separate European and Middle Eastern vocations. Particular pressures have stemmed from the rapid migration from the countryside of the cities, with their increasingly large shanty towns. Moreover, the worldwide Islamic revival has not left Turkey untouched, although religious fundamentalism is still much less strong in predominantly Sunni Turkey than in some neighbouring countries. There is even a split, however, within Turkish Islam in that a minority (estimated at between 10–20 per cent) are Shi'ite Alevis, who in the past have even had their own political party (the left-of-centre and not fundamentalist Unity Party).

Another division has been ethnic. While there

are few Armenians left in Turkey (although Armenian terrorists have continued to attack Turkish diplomats in retaliation for the massive death toll among Armenians at Turkish hands in 1915 and before), there are still a large number of Kurds (possibly up to 7–8 million) straddling the Turkish borders with Iran and Iraq, a minority of whom have been fighting for an independent Kurdish state.

In spite of these divisions, and in spite of having had three separate constitutional regimes since the foundation of the Republic in 1923 (1924–61, 1961–82, 1982 to the present), the Turkish political system has had some remarkably constant features since the introduction of a multi-party democracy by President Inönü in the late 1940s.

The first feature has been the tendency towards two dominant catch-all parties of the centre left and centre right (the Republican People's Party on the one hand, and the Democratic and later Justice parties on the other). This was perhaps an inevitable result of the majority electoral system before 1960 and almost certainly of the modified proportional representation system introduced in 1982. Even with the more fully proportional system between 1961 and 1980 (in which no less than eight parties won seats in the 1969 elections), the share of the two largest parties continued to average over 70 per cent in the five elections held over that period.

A second continuing feature has been the presence of an Islamic Conservative Party defending both Islamic cultural values and the interests of small business. Parties in this tradition have run far behind the two main parties, with support ranging from under 3 per cent to highs of 14 per cent in 1961 and 11.8 per cent in 1973.

The more extreme nationalist right and the far left helped to spur violence in the 1970s, but have never been important forces in electoral terms, with the former never winning more than 6.4 per cent (1977) and the latter never more than 3 per cent). Their average support has been even lower. There have been no regional or ethnically-based parties set up to contest national elections.

Another constant has been the ever-present possibility of military intervention. Turkey has a sensitive strategic position — and a long military tradition — and its armed forces are the largest in NATO outside those of the United States. On two occasions, in 1960 and 1980, the military have directly intervened to overthrow elected governments, and to impose new constitutional structures. On a third occasion, in 1971, they intervened indirectly without actually taking power themselves or changing the Constitution. On the other hand direct military rule has not

been of long duration, one year in 1960–61 and three years in 1980–83.

In spite of these constants the actual functioning of the political system has varied considerably. The 1924 Constitution led to long periods of single-party rule by the Republican People's Party from 1924 to 1950, and by the Democratic Party from 1950 to 1960. Nevertheless, it permitted a certain institutional flexibility, in that the strongly presidential regime from 1924 to 1950 gave way to much greater parity between President and Prime Minister during the decade of Democratic Party rule after 1950, reflecting the powerful personality of Adnan Menderes.

The 1961 Constitution, which introduced proportional representation and strengthened the Prime Minister at the expense of the President, weakened the major parties and strengthened the minor ones. The latter were able to win substantial representation in Parliament. Even under these circumstances, the Justice Party was able to hold a stable one-party majority from 1965 to 1970. From 1970 to 1980, however, the system led to a proliferation of governments, with multi-party coalitions, and frequent government crises, and with the Islamic National Salvation Party and extreme right wing Nationalist Action Party, in particular, having an influence well beyond their actual electoral strength.

The 1982 Constitution, with its stringent political and organizational conditions which new parties have to meet to contest elections, and with its unprecedentedly severe national and provincial electoral thresholds, restored a strong advantage to the largest parties. Although based on proportional representation once the thresholds have been exceeded, the electoral system's effects are anything but proportional. In 1987 the Motherland Party won almost 65 per cent of the seats on little over 36 per cent of the vote. With as little as 25 per cent of the vote some parties in 1987 won all the seats within a given constituency. In theory at least, one party could win all the seats with under 30 per cent of the vote, and an overall working majority with 10 per cent.

The 1982 Constitution also restored a considerable degree of power to the presidency. Turkey is still in a period of transition, with the current President being a non-party military man whose term of office was ratified by referendum rather than by being chosen by the Parliament as laid down in the Constitution. It is still too early, therefore, to evaluate the balance of power between the President and Prime Minister when both are party political figures. This could become clearer after the next President is chosen in 1989.

In terms of Turkey's political structure the last few years have also been a period of transition before a new party political balance emerges. Of the three parties registered to contest the 1983 elections only one is still in existence. Numerous parties have come and gone, and there have been major defections from one party to another. At present there are still two claimants to the right-of-centre catch-all party tradition (the Motherland Party and the True Path Party), and a more unequal contest between the two claimants on the left-of-centre (the Social Democratic Populist Party and the Democratic Left Party). The Islamic Conservative and right-wing nationalist traditions have again taken shape in the form of two new parties (the Welfare Party and the Nationalist Work Party), and the former, in particular, appears to have a substantial, if clearly minority, electoral base. No party on the far left has yet been legalized. The future shape of the political system is thus uncertain.

There has been considerable controversy over the extent of democracy in Turkey, especially within the European Community now that Turkey has posed its candidature for full membership. There have undoubtedly been certain human rights abuses, and Turkey's current Constitution is an authoritarian one in a number of respects. The parliament is rather weak compared to the executive, and trade unions are restricted to their operation (and the left-wing confederation DISK is still illegal). Moreover, certain views or activities, such as challenges to Turkish secularism, Armenian allegations of genocide, and Kurdish separatism are reacted to with a harshness which reflects persistent deep feelings on these issues within Turkish society. Nevertheless, Turkey does now appear to have a competitive party political system, in which no one party is assured of long term dominance. It is obviously hoped that linking Turkey to the European Community will help to reinforce Turkish democracy.

Among the issues facing Turkey at the present are the following:

Economic policy

Liberalism versus étatisme, the role of the state in the economy, the extent of privatization and in which sectors, ways in which Turkey's high inflation can be tackled, what should happen to wages and labour conditions, should welfare state measures be developed?

Political party and trade union restrictions

Should the Communist Party be legalized, should trade unions be less restricted as regards strikes, collective bargaining and other activities? The future of the many political detainees.

Entry into the European Community

Turkey became an associate member of the EC in 1963, and applied for full membership on April 14, 1987. Only the Islamic fundamentalists are strongly opposed, although the right in general are unenthusiastic, but whether Turkey is admitted and if so, on what terms will be an important issue in the future.

Cyprus

Turkish troops are still in Cyprus, and Turkish Cyprus has not won international recognition. What solutions can be found?

Relations with Greece

These have long been tense, and have especially focused on differences over Cyprus, continental shelf rights in the Aegean, and rights of overflight. What follow-up will there be to the summit meeting between the Greek and Turkish leaders in Switzerland in late January 1988, and Mr Özal's visit to Greece?

Relations with the Middle Eastern countries

Turkey joined the Islamic conference in the late 1970s, and the Özal government has tried to strengthen relations with a number of Middle Eastern countries. How far should these be developed, and with what countries?

Relations with the United States and NATO

Until the 1940s, Turkey was a neutral country, but joined NATO in 1952. How far should its obligations extend? Bilateral relations with the United States have fluctuated in quality. The United States has recognized Turkey's strategic importance, but the US Congress, in particular, has sometimes clashed with Turkey over such issues as Cyprus. What will be the future of the defence and co-operation agreement between the two countries, and of US installations in Turkey?

Relations with the Soviet Union

How far will these be developed?

Bulgarian treatment of its Turkish minority

How can the latter's rights be protected?

Western Europe

The rights of Turkish "guest" workers in Western Europe.

Armenian terrorism

Kurdish separatism

What to do about the Workers' Party of Kurdistan — PKK — and its aspirations to set up a separate Kurdish state? The problem of the many Kurdish refugees from neighbouring countries.

Islamic fundamentalism, and the role of Islam within Turkish society

Fundamentalism is not as strong as in many Moslem countries, but is present, and occasionally flares up over such issues as female students being allowed to wear traditional Islamic headscarves. What balance should be struck between allowing freedom for the development of Islam within Turkey and maintaining the fundamental principle of secular control established by Ataturk?

Anavatan Partisi (ANAP)
(Motherland Party)

Headquarters	: Necatibey Caddesi 11, Sihhiye, Ankara
Chairman	: Turgut Özal
Secretary-general	: Mustafa Tasar
Founded	: May 1983

History

The Motherland Party (ANAP) is the current governing party in Turkey. It was founded on May 20, 1983 by Turgut Özal, who was the author of the 1980 economic austerity plan during the Demirel-led government. In the military regime which followed he was Deputy Prime Minister responsible for the economy until his resignation in 1982.

ANAP was authorized to contest the 1983 general election. Özal campaigned on a platform of economic liberalism and removal of bureaucratic restrictions. When it became apparent that he was going to do well against the rival right-of-centre Nationalist Democracy Party which was backed by the military regime, President Evren spoke out against him just before the elections, but this intervention appeared to have been counterproductive. As a right-of-centre party not too closely associated with the military, ANAP won the elections with 45 per cent of the vote and 211 out of the 400 seats in the Parliament, putting the Nationalist Democracy Party into third place. President Evren had no option but to appoint Özal as Prime Minister.

Özal began his programme of economic liber-alization. In the 1984 local elections ANAP won 41.4 per cent of the vote, and gained control of 54 of Turkey's 67 provinces, a strong performance in view of the fact that several new parties had been authorized to contest the elections.

ANAP received a number of recruits from other political parties. Fifteen Nationalist Democracy Party deputies joined the ANAP parliamentary group, after their own party collapsed.

In the by-elections of September 1986, ANAP had a relative setback, only winning 31.1 per cent, although obtaining six of the 11 seats at stake. In December 1986 the leadership of the Free Democratic Party decided that it should merge with ANAP. Fourteen of its members joined ANAP, and subsequently its leader Mehmet Yazar.

After the narrow vote in favour of removing the ban on former political leaders in September 1987, Özal called early elections for November 1987. In these ANAP won 292 out of the 450 seats but on only 36.2 per cent of the poll. Özal was then reconfirmed as Prime Minister.

Özal survived an assassination attempt at the ANAP congress in June 1988. He subsequently lost a referendum on his attempt to convene early local elections.

Support

ANAP has currently got the broadest range of support of any Turkish party, from free market businessmen in the cities to Islamic and nationalist conservatives in rural Anatolia. In 1987, it was the best supported party in Turkey's major cities. In Istanbul, where Turgut Özal was a candidate, the party polled 48 per cent; in Ankara around 40 per cent; in Izmir and Bursa around 40 per cent. It also polled well in Adana.

In 1987 ANAP was very strong on much of the Anatolian plateau. Its highest vote of all was in Özal's home province of Malatya, where it received 58.7 per cent of the vote. It received over 40 per cent of the vote in the eastern, Black Sea coast and in north-eastern Turkey, with a high of almost 50 per cent in Gumushane, with other high votes in Sivas, Erzurum, Giresun, and parts of Ordu and Trabzon.

In Central Anatolia it was strongest in the first constituency of Kayseri, and in the right-wing province of Yozgat. It also had a higher than average vote in the provinces around Ankara, Kirsehir, Cankiri, Eskisehir, and especially Bolu. In the religious city of Konya, where the leading Islamic conservative in ANAP, Mehmet Kececiler, was standing, ANAP polled 44 per cent. Further west ANAP polled well in Aydin and Canakkale in particular. In total,

ANAP won all the seats in no less than 30 constituencies, although in some cases this was more a reflection of the divided opposition and the vagaries of the electoral system than of inherent ANAP strength.

ANAP was weakest in the provinces of south-eastern Turkey, with their mix of traditional left-wing constituencies (e.g. Tunceli) rival right-wing constituencies (e.g. Bingöl) and predominantly Kurdish constituencies (e.g. Diyarbakir, Tunceli again, Mardin and Siirt). Even here, however, it did well in Bitlis and to a lesser extent in Hakkari.

ANAP also had lower than average votes in the Democratic Left stronghold of Zonguldak, the True Path stronghold of Isparta and in much of European Turkey, especially Edirne. Practically nowhere, however, did it poll significantly under 20 per cent.

Organization

ANAP has a 50-member national executive committee. It is a member of the European Democratic Union and of the International Democratic Union.

Policies

ANAP is a broad-based party of the centre and right of the Turkish political spectrum. It has clearly won a lot of support from former Justice Party supporters in particular, but also from other political traditions as well. Mahil Silvgan, for example, ANAP's deputy party chairman before 1986, was active in the far-right-wing Nationalist Action Party before 1980, and Turgut Özal himself had been a candidate for the Islamic National Salvation Party as recently as 1977. The main division within the party, however, is between its economic liberals, concerned above all with Turkey's modernization, and its Islamic traditionalists, who wish Islam to have a greater role (although generally not in the fundamentalist sense of certain other Moslem countries).

Özal himself combines elements of both traditions. He is associated above all with economic liberalization and the opening up of Turkey towards Europe while at the same time he is personally very pious, tolerant on the issue of students' wearing religious dress (an issue on which he has taken a different stance from the secularist position of President Evren) and concerned about strengthening relations between Turkey and the Islamic world. Recently the traditionalists have strengthened their position within ANAP, although not within the government.

An issue of particular uncertainty is that of the future relations between ANAP and the True Path Party, since it is unlikely that there can continue to be two broad-based aspirants to the right-of-centre mantle of the former Democratic and Justice parties.

In economic policy ANAP's most distinctive stance has been its break with Kemalist étatisme and its commitment to the free market economy to an extent greater than that of previous Turkish political parties. It has believed that private initiative should play a much greater role, and that state intervention and bureaucratic red tape should be greatly reduced. When it came to power it liberalized foreign exchange and other controls, put more emphasis on increasing exports than on the old policies of import substitution, and developed a generally favourable stance to foreign capital investments in Turkey.

In 1984, it decided to sell bonds for the first Bosphorus bridge, and is now planning to extend policies of privatization and the selling off of a number of Turkey's state economic enterprises. ANAP also claims that it applies the rules of the market to agriculture to a greater extent than in most other countries.

The state's role in the economy has been concentrated above all on massive infrastructure investments, notably housing, roads, telecommunications and electrification projects, especially in the poorer regions of eastern Anatolia. Programmes to assist the less developed regions have been given a high priority. ANAP's critics claim that it has pushed for economic growth at the cost of all other objectives, including not just social policies but also inflation, which has remained at a high level. Moreover, ANAP has retained the military regime's restrictive trade union policies.

ANAP has supported NATO and in 1987, the Özal government made a formal application for Turkey to join the European Community, which it believes will strengthen the process of modernization of the Turkish economy. At the same time, it has also strengthened Turkish links and increased Turkish investments in the Middle East and Moslem countries. On other foreign policy issues it has maintained traditional Turkish foreign policy objectives. Recently it has made an effort to improve bilateral relations with Greece, with the summit conference between Özal and Papandreou in Switzerland in January 1988.

In religious matters it has eased certain restrictions, and encouraged the creation of new mosques and Islamic centres in Turkey's universities and new clerical schools.

Personalities

The party's founder and leader, the Prime

Minister since 1983, is Turgut Özal. He is an economist, who worked for a while at the World Bank and was responsible for the economic austerity programme in January 1980. He became the military regime's chief economic planner as Deputy Prime Minister from 1980 to 1982, before he resigned and began putting distance between himself and the military. He is a devout Moslem, and in 1977 stood unsuccessfully for the National Salvation Party of Islamic Conservatives (if he had been elected he would have been ineligible for an active political role after 1980). He has had health problems (a triple by-pass operation in February 1987) and in June 1988 survived an assassination attempt.

ANAP's most prominent Islamic traditionalist is Mehmet Kececiler, who represents the religious centre of Konya. Other traditionalists include Vehbi Dincerler. An alliance has also been made between the Islamic wing of the party, and the right wing, one of whose most prominent figures is Mustafa Tasar.

In 1988 Islamic Conservatives won 60 per cent of the votes in local party elections before the national congress, and 35 out of the 50 seats on its executive committee.

A rising member within ANAP is Hasan Celal Guzel, whose electoral base is Gaziantep.

Dogru Yol Partisi (DYP)
(True Path Party)

Headquarters : Akay Caddesi 16,
Kucukesat, Ankara
Chairman : Süleyman Demirel
President of
parliamentary
group : Koksal Toptan
Founded : June 1983

History

The True Path Party is in the centre-right tradition of Turkish politics, and contains many supporters of the former Justice Party (1961–80), itself the successor of the Democratic Party of Bayar and Menderes (1946–60).

When new parties were allowed to be registered in May 1983, a Grand Turkey Party was founded on 20 May, but was banned by the military on 31 May as being too close to the former Justice Party.

On 23 June, 1983, the True Path Party was founded instead. In the absence of the former Justice Party leader, Süleyman Demirel, banned from active political involvement for 10 years, its first chairman was E. Yilderim Avci. It was not permitted to contest the first general election in November 1983, and lost valuable ground to the Motherland Party.

The first elections that it was allowed to contest were the 1984 local elections, when it won 13.3 per cent of the vote, coming a poor third but polling more votes than the two runners up in the 1983 general election. In September 1984 an attempt by the State Prosecutor to close down the party as being unconstitutional was rejected by the Constitutional Court.

In May 1985 Husamettin Cindoruk became the new party leader. One of his rivals, Mehmet Yazar subsequently left the party and helped to form yet another party of the right, the short-lived Free Democratic Party.

A number of deputies from other parties joined the True Path Party and by May 1986 it was the fourth largest party in the Parliament with 20 deputies. It polled strongly in the by-elections held in September 1986, with 23.7 per cent of the total vote (coming second to the Motherland Party), and winning four of the 11 seats at stake.

In December 1986, the founding council of the Small Citizens' Party voted to disband the party and to merge with the True Path Party, and in 1987, five former members of the now dissolved Free Democratic Party also joined the party. In June 1987 the True Path Party won 17 posts of mayor out of the 84 at stake in the municipal elections.

After the 1987 referendum narrowly permitted the banned former political leaders to return to full political activity, Süleyman Demirel (who had in fact continued to play an active public role) took over as the formal leader of the party. In the 1987 national elections the True Path Party came third, with 19.5 per cent of the vote, and 59 seats in the Grand National Assembly.

Support

The True Path Party still has a much less broad basis of support than its conservative predecessors, the Democratic and Justice parties, and clearly has lost a lot of its natural support to the Motherland Party. It depends heavily on the name of Süleyman Demirel, and polls most strongly among rural conservatives. It has some support from Islamic groups, notably the Nurcus and Suleymanci brotherhoods.

In the 1987 elections it only had one absolute stronghold, Süleyman Demirel's home constituency of Isparta on the south-western Anatolian plateau, where it polled almost 60 per cent of the vote and won all four constituencies.

It was generally strongest in western and south-western Turkey, being particularly successful in the two Antalya constituencies (over 36 per cent in the second constituency). In most of this region it polled between 20 and 30 per cent.

It also did well along much of the Black Sea coast, notably the second constituency of Samsun where it won 33 per cent of the vote and all three seats. In the first constituency of Zonguldak it profited from the elimination of the Democratic Left Party to win three out of the six seats on only 24 per cent of the vote.

A final pocket of stronger support was in a group of provinces in eastern Turkey, Bingöl, Elazig, the first constituency of Erzurum and Artvin, in an area where it otherwise did rather badly.

The True Path Party was weakest in Central Anatolia, notably the provinces of Kirsehir, Yozgat and Sivas, where it polled under 10 per cent, and especially Malatya (Özal's home province) and Tunceli (a traditionally left-wing area) where it obtained under 5 per cent. The party also polled badly in the far east of Anatolia, and notably in Kars and Hakkari.

A second weakness was that the True Path Party was not very successful in the fast growing major cities, and especially in Istanbul, Izmir and Ankara. Its strongest major city was Bursa.

Organization

The True Path Party has a general administration board of 40 members.

Policies

The True Path Party is the main rival of the Motherland Party in the right-of-centre of the Turkish political spectrum. In the 1987 elections it emphasized the need for fuller democracy in Turkey, and attacked abuses of power by the Motherland Party administration. It was highly critical of the persisting high rate of inflation in Turkey, as well as its rising foreign indebtedness and chaotic banking system.

On the other hand it also criticized the poor distribution of wealth within Turkey, and pledged a new net minimum wage if it won power. It promised full freedom for trade unions, and did not want the state to interfere in collective bargaining.

It called for religious and moral values to be taught at every level of education.

Personalities

The True Path's leader is the pragmatically conservative Süleyman Demirel, one of the elder statesmen of Turkish politics, an engineer by training with a paternalist style. He became the leader of the Justice Party in 1964, and retained this position until 1980. He was Prime Minister from 1965 to 1971, 1975 to 1977, 1977 again and from 1979 to 1980. On two occasions, he has been returned as Prime Minister by military intervention. After being banned from active politics from 1980 to 1986 (and running into trouble on several occasions for defying the ban) he became formal leader of the True Path Party in September 1986.

Sosyal Demokrat Halkci Partisi (SHP)
(Social Democratic Populist Party)

Headquarters	:	Necatibey Caddesi 15, Sihhiye, Ankara
Chairman	:	Professor Erdal Inönü
Secretary-general	:	Deniz Baykal
President of parliamentary group:	:	Hikmet Cetin
Founded	:	November 1985

History

The Social Democratic Populist Party is now the only left-of-centre party represented in the Turkish Parliament, and the main inheritor of the former Republican People's Party tradition. The Republican People's Party was founded by Ataturk, was the only Turkish party until 1946 and the major party of the left until 1980 when it was wound up by the military regime.

Two claimants to the Republican People's Party tradition were founded before the 1983 elections, the Populist Party under the leadership of Necdet Calp on 20 May, 1983, and the Social Democratic Party under Cezmi Kartay on 6 June, 1983. Only the former, however, was permitted to contest the 1983 elections, at which it was the runner up to the Motherland Party with 30.5 per cent of the vote and 117 seats.

In December 1983, Professor Erdal Inönü, son of the famous Turkish politician, Ismet Inönü, became the leader of the Social Democratic Party. It was allowed to participate in the 1984 local elections, winning 23.4 per cent of the vote and 10 municipal councils. In contrast the Populist Party's vote slumped to only 8.8 per cent.

In June 1985, Professor Güven Gürkan defeated Necdet Calp to become the new leader of the Populist Party. Finally in November 1985, the Populist Party and the Social Democrats decided to merge into a new Social Democratic Populist Party, with Professor Güven Gürkan as president. In June 1986, Erdal Inönü became the leader of the merged party.

In the by-elections in the autumn of 1986, the merged party polled rather disappointingly with 22 per cent but Inönü defeated the rival left wing leader, Mrs Ecevit, to win a constituency in Izmir.

In December 1986, however, the Social Democratic Populist Party suffered a serious loss when 20 of its deputies left it, of whom 18 joined the rival Democratic Left Party of Mrs Ecevit.

In the 1987 elections, with the left still divided between the two parties, the SDPP emerged as an easy winner of the contest on the left, but only as distant runner-up (especially in seats) to the Motherland Party. The SDPP obtained 99 seats with 24.7 per cent of the vote.

Support

The SDPP is a broadly-based party, with support among professionals, industrial workers and rural labourers. In the 1987 elections the SDPP had very uneven strength around the country. It generally did well in the cities, winning around 35 per cent in Izmir and 25–35 per cent in the various Istanbul constituencies, and 28–35 per cent in Ankara. The SDPP polled over 30 per cent in European Turkey, and it won six out of the 11 seats in the constituencies of Kirklareli (where it won over 35 per cent), Tekirdag and Erdine. Other areas of strength included much of the Aegean coast (in the third constituency of Izmir province, where the party leader Inönü stood, it won over 37 per cent) and the south coast, where it won over 40 per cent and four out of the six seats at stake in the first constituencies of both Icel and Hatay.

On the Anatolian plateau constituencies with SDPP strength alternated with others of weakness. The SDPP's best constituency in the whole country was the left wing and Kurdish province of Tunceli, where it won almost 50 per cent of the vote and both seats in Parliament. In eastern Turkey, it also did well in Erzincan, Kars and the second constituency in Sivas, and to a lesser extent in Mardin, Malatya and Artvin. In central and western Anatolia, its strongest areas were the provinces of Ankara and Usak.

The SDPP was generally weak on the Black Sea coast where the Democratic Left Party was stronger than average, notably in the province of Zonguldak. The SDPP was very weak in some of the more conservative provinces of eastern Anatolia (such as Gumushane, Bingöl and especially the first constituency of Erzurum, where it obtained its lowest vote in the whole country at well under 10 per cent), and in parts of south-eastern Turkey. In central Anatolia it was weakest in Cankiri, Kayseri and Yozgat. Further west its worst results were in the religious centre of Konya and in the True Path Party stronghold of Isparta. The SDPP's lowest vote in a major city was in Bursa at under 20 per cent.

Organization

The SDPP has an Executive Committee of 44 members. The party is a consultative member of the Socialist International.

Policies

The SDPP is a catch-all left-of-centre party, with its activists ranging from moderate social democrats to others from far left backgrounds. Its most important current challenge is to achieve unity on the left, which by some calculations would have given it 173 seats at the last elections instead of the 99 it won in competition against the Democratic Left Party.

The SDPP calls for a democratic, secular and socially-minded Turkey. It seeks to consolidate Turkish democracy by ensuring full freedom of expression, the protection of basic rights, the right to strike and ending of lockouts, and stronger trade unions. It also seeks the return of the confiscated property of the disbanded confederation of Revolutionary Turkish Workers Trade Unions (DISK), and of the disbanded political parties. It calls for the abolition of film censorship. It believes that religious education should be carried out under the supervision and control of the state.

In economic policy, it has advocated less reliance on economic liberalism and more on democratic state planning. It is highly critical of the present government's record on inflation.

It has called for a minimum wage calculated according to the number of members in each worker's family, and for the sale of shares in state economic enterprises to the workers.

It has supported Turkish membership of NATO, and the application to join the European Community, which it believes will reinforce Turkish democracy. It has called for reform of the Constitution, and penal reform.

Personalities

The SDPP leader is Professor Erdal Inönü, with a previous academic career as a theoretical physicist. He is the son of Ismet Inönü, Ataturk's closest colleague and first Prime Minister, Ataturk's successor as President, and later again both leader of the opposition and Prime Minister as head of the Republican People's Party from 1938 to 1972. Professor Inönü has a quiet and deliberative style of leadership. He was re-elected chairman at the party congress in June 1988 with 72 per cent of the vote.

The other powerful figure within the party is its new secretary-general Deniz Baykal, a highly pragmatic politician and former Republican People's Party activist, who was Finance Minister in the 1974 Ecevit government and later also Energy Minister. His social democratic-leaning list took 27 of the 44 places on the party executive in June 1988, compared to 16 for the party left.

Ismail Cem was nominated in 1988 as an alternative candidate to Erdal Inönü for the party leadership. He is a former head of Turkish television and radio, but only polled 15 per cent in the leadership vote at the June 1988 party congress.

Demokratik Sol Partisi (DSP)
(Democratic Left Party)

Headquarters	: Maresal Fevzi Cakmak Caddesi 17, Besevler, Ankara
Chairman	: Necdet Karababa
Secretary-general	: Nuri Korkmas
Founded	: November 1985

History

The Democratic Left Party was formally founded on Nov. 14, 1985 by the social democratic supporters of Bulent Ecevit, the former leader of the disbanded Republican People's Party who had led the party to the left in the 1960s and 1970s, and who had been Prime Minister on three occasions during the 1970s. As Ecevit was banned from taking part in active politics until 1992 (he spent a total of nine months in prison for defying the banning order, but was finally acquitted in September 1986), his wife, Mrs Rahsan Ecevit, was elected as the party's first leader.

The party was immediately critical of its main rival on the centre-left, the Social Democratic People's Party (SDPP). It took part in the by-elections in November 1986, polling 8.5 per cent, but with Mrs Ecevit losing in a head-to-head contest with the SDPP leader, Professor Inönü, in an Izmir constituency. In December 1986, however, 20 SDPP deputies left the party, and after creating a very short-lived People's Party (seen as a device to get around the restrictions on party defections) 18 of them subsequently joined the Democratic Left Party.

After the September 1987 referendum authorized an immediate return to politics by the former party leaders, Bulent Ecevit took over as Democratic Left leader from Mrs Ecevit. In the general elections in November 1987, the Democratic Left Party polled 8.5 per cent of the votes, but fell short of the 10 per cent national threshold, and won no seats in the Parliament. Bulent Ecevit subsequently stood down as leader. He was subsequently replaced by Necdet Karababa, who announced his intention of keeping the party going.

The DSP is a consultative member of the Socialist International.

Support

In the 1987 elections, the Democratic Left Party received very variable support, with no one consistent area of support, with the partial exception of European Turkey and the Black Sea coast where it polled over 10 per cent in a majority of constituencies. None of its success in individual constituencies was to any avail, as it fell short of the 10 per cent national threshold.

Its strongest support was in Bulent Ecevit's own constituency in the coal mining area of Zonguldak on the Black Sea coast, where it polled over 29 per cent. It also polled over 20 per cent in the second constituency in Zonguldak province. The only other constituencies where it polled around or over 20 per cent were in the diametrically opposite corners of Turkey, Edirne on European Turkey's border with Bulgaria and Greece, and Hakkari in the predominantly Kurdish region on the Iran-Iraq border (the party did not do very well, however, in the other Kurdish provinces).

Other constituencies where the Democratic Left Party had above average support were in Agri and the left wing constituency of Tunceli in eastern Anatolia. In the cities it polled well in Adana, and around 10 per cent in certain Istanbul and Izmir constituencies.

The Democratic Left Party was particularly weak in much of eastern and south-eastern Anatolia (apart from the pockets of support mentioned above), in Demirel's stronghold of Isparta and the religious centre of Konya, and in some of the constituencies on the south coast of Turkey.

Policies

The Democratic Left Party is a social democratic party which faces an uncertain future after it was outdistanced in the 1987 elections by its main rival on the centre-left of the political spectrum, the Social Democratic Populist Party, and the subsequent resignation of the Democratic Left's leader and main inspiration, Bulent Ecevit.

In the run-up to the 1987 elections the Democratic Left Party was highly critical of the SDPP, accusing it of having the old left-wing intellectual elitism, and also of having been infiltrated by the far left. The Democratic Left Party also made it clear that, while it was in favour of the legalization of a separate Turkish Communist Party, it did not itself wish to be part of the Marxist left tradition.

On the other hand, the DLP was also very critical of the Motherland Party government of Turgut Özal, claiming that it had undermined the role of Parliament, and had not introduced full democratic freedom in other areas.

The DLP's main call was for the full democratization of Turkey. Labour rights should be fully restored, with restrictions on the trade unions, on collective bargaining and on the right to strike being completely removed. The concept of "crimes of opinion" was fully rejected, and the DLP called for amnesty for those who had committed minor political offences, or at least a reduction in their sentences to symbolic levels. Private radio and television should be permitted, and censorship of television films should be abolished. The DLP also emphasized respect for religious belief, and that there should be religious teaching covering all religions and sects, but in accordance with a child's own beliefs.

As regards economic policy, the DLP emphasized the need for more social justice. The state should continue to play an important role, but the actual size of the public sector was less important than whether the state could continue to direct the economy for the benefits of society. There should be greater economic democracy. The DLP also put a strong emphasis on regional developments, and called for the creation of a special ministry to deal with the problems of the poorer Anatolian regions with its headquarters in south-east Turkey.

The DLP also called for the creation of a second new ministry to cope with the problems of Turkish refugees (primarily from Greece and Bulgaria) and also of Turkish migrant workers in Western Europe.

Ecevit was Prime Minister in the 1970s, during the Turkish intervention in Cyprus. He later also advocated greater independence and non-alignment in Turkey's foreign policy.

In 1987, the DLP leadership called for good links with the West, but also the need for friendly relations and co-operation with all countries in the region, irrespective of their foreign policy or domestic stance. The DLP supported Turkish membership of the European Community, but pointed out the political and economic adaptations that Turkey would have to make before entry could take place.

Refah Partisi
(Welfare Party)

Headquarters	: Gazi Mustafa Kemal Boulevard 88, Maltepe, Ankara
Leader	: Necmettin Erbakan
Founded	: 1983

History

The Welfare Party is an Islamic conservative party in the same tradition (and with the same leader) as the National Salvation Party which existed from 1972 to 1980, and took part in three coalition governments in 1974, 1975 to 1977 and 1977 to 1978. The refusal of National Salvation Party supporters to sing the national anthem at a rally in Konya was the immediate pretext for the military coup on Sept. 12, 1980. The party was banned, and its leader Necmettin Erbakan, was put on trial, but subsequently acquitted. The party was looked on with considerable harshness by the ruling military government as its religious fundamentalism clashed with the central constitutional principle of secularism that had been established by Ataturk.

A successor party, the "Refah" or Welfare Party was founded in 1983, but was not allowed to contest the national elections of that year. In 1984, it was permitted to take part in the local elections, polling poorly, but winning control of one province.

In 1987, Necmettin Erbakan again became the leader of the party after the lifting of the ban against the former party leaders. In the 1987 national elections it did very well in a few traditional constituencies, but failed to win any seats in Parliament because its 7 per cent of the national poll was well under the 10 per cent threshold established by the electoral system. The National Salvation Party had polled 11.8 per cent in 1973 and 8.6 per cent in 1977.

Support

As demonstrated in the 1987 elections, the Welfare Party's support is strongly concentrated in the south-eastern Anatolian interior. It won over 20 per cent in the two constituencies of Diyarbakir, in Siirt, Bitlis and Bingöl and over 15 per cent in the adjacent constituencies of Elazig, Mardin, Van and Agri. Its highest vote of nearly 29 per cent was in the constituency of Bingöl. Outside this region, its only votes of over 15 per cent were in the first constituency of Kahramanmaras, the second constituency of Trabzon (its only high vote in a coastal region) and in the first constituency of Konya, where it obtained around 19 per cent. This constituency includes the city of Konya, which was the centre of the Whirling Dervishes, and is still a fundamentalist Islamic centre.

On the other hand, the Welfare Party was extremely weak in European Turkey (Thrace) on the Aegean Coast and in much of western and south-western Turkey. In many of these areas it won under 3 per cent of the vote.

The Welfare Party had mixed fortunes in Turkey's cities. In Istanbul it was weak in some areas, but achieved substantial votes in areas of high migration from rural Anatolia. It also had moderate strength in the former Ottoman capital of Bursa, but had a lower vote in Ankara, and was very weak in Izmir.

Policies

The Welfare Party is an Islamic conservative party like its National Salvation Party predecessor. Turkey's Moslems are mainly Sunni, and their fundamentalists are less extreme than, for example, in neighbouring Shi'ite Iran. Turkey's own Alevis, who are close to the Shi'ites, have supported the Unity Party in the past. The Unity Party was active from 1966–1980 and was non-denominational and social democratic in character.

Necmettin Erbakan, as leader of the National Salvation Party, had been prepared to enter coalition governments with both the left-of-centre and traditionally secularist Republican People's Party as well as with the right-of-centre Justice Party.

The Welfare Party has called for a return to traditional Islamic moral and cultural values, and attacked what it sees as the excessively secular legacy of Ataturk. Erbakan himself has also seen a role in defending the interests of small merchants and artisans against big business and the Istanbul corporations. Its 1987 programme called for assistance to small farmers and businessmen, and increased protectionism.

The Welfare Party has emphasized the need to strengthen ties with other Islamic nations, and has strongly criticized Turkey's application to join the European Community. In the 1987 elections some of its candidates also attacked NATO, and called for the withdrawal of up to 15,000 US troops.

Personalities

Many of the party's leaders, and notably the party chairman, Necmettin Erbakan, are former leaders of the National Salvation Party. Erbakan, who helped to found the National Salvation Party in 1972, led it into three coalition governments during the 1970s. He is an engineer by training.

MCP
(Nationalist Work Party)

Headquarters	: Necatibey Caddesi 20, Sihhiye, Ankara
Leader	: Alparslan Turkes

History

The Nationalist Work Party is a right wing nationalist party, and is the successor of the Nationalist Action Party which was active from 1969 to 1980.

The leader of the nationalist far right is Alparslan Turkes, who first came to prominence as leader of the minority of the 1960–61 military junta which wished to hold on to power rather than return Turkey to parliamentary democracy. In 1965 he became leader of the conservative Republican Peasants' National Party, and in 1969 he remodelled it into a new party, the Nationalist Action Party. It advocated a strong role for the state and assertive Turkish nationalism, including concern for the wider Turkish community in Soviet and Chinese central Asia and elsewhere. It was strongly anti-communist. In its internal organization, it emphasized military discipline, and was linked with a parliamentary youth movement, the "Grey Wolves". In the 1969 elections it won one seat with 3 per cent of the vote, and in 1973 three seats with 3.4 per cent. From 1975 to 1977, however, it took part in a four-party government coalition under Süleyman Demirel, which brought it more within the political mainstream, and in the 1977 elections, it won 16 seats with 6.4 per cent of the vote. It participated in a second coalition government under Demirel later in 1977. Its members also entered the state apparatus.

However, Turkes was seen as a neo-Fascist by his opponents, and some of his followers were associated with right-wing violence. After the military coup in 1980 the far right was suppressed with considerable severity, and Turkes and other party leaders were put on trial, although most of the leaders were eventually acquitted.

After the ban on former party leaders was repealed, Turkes again became leader of a new party, the Nationalist Work Party, which contested the 1987 general elections but only won 2.8 per cent of the total vote, and was far from winning a seat.

Support

In the 1987 general elections the Nationalist

Work Party won close to the level of support that its predecessor had won in the 1969 and 1973 elections, although far short of its one real success in 1977.

Its 1987 support was strongly concentrated on the Anatolian plateau, especially north and east of Ankara, Central Anatolia and the northern part of Eastern Anatolia. In all these regions it obtained 5 per cent or more of the vote. Its three strongest constituencies, where it won over 10 per cent of the vote, were the second constituency of Kahramanmaras, Yozgat and the second constituency of Erzurum.

Its support was naturally lowest of all in the constituencies with a high Kurdish population, in south-eastern Turkey, where it won under 1 per cent in the second Urfa constituency, Diyarbakir, Mardin, Siirt and Hakkari. The other area where it was particularly weak was in European Turkey (Thrace). It also won under its national average levels of support around much of Turkey's coastline, and in western Turkey in general. The only major city where it appeared to have considerable support was Ankara, and it was very weak in Istanbul, Izmir and Bursa.

Policies

A strong state and Turkish nationalism are the party's main policy themes.

Personalities

The now ageing Colonel Turkes is the historic leader of the Turkish nationalist right, and is still the chairman of the Nationalist Work Party.

Islahatci Demokrasi Partisi (IDP)
(Reformist Democracy Party)

Headquarters : Menekse Sokak
Nergis Apt
10–A/7–9, Kizilay,
Ankara

Chairman : Aykut Edibali
Secretary-general : Selahattin Yerer

This party leans towards conservatism and was founded in 1984. It contested the 1987 national elections, but only won 0.81 per cent of the vote. Most of what little support it won was in certain constituencies on the Anatolian plateau, and especially Afyon, Yozgat and the second constituency of Erzurum. Its leader is Aykut Edibali. Before the 1987 elections, he advocated an electoral alliance of the right-wing parties, his own party along with the Nationalist Work and Welfare parties.

The party claims a membership of 40,000, and produces a monthly publication called *Islahat*.

Far left parties

The former Turkish Labour Party (the only left-wing Marxist party which has won representation in the Turkish Parliament, whose best performance was 15 seats on 3 per cent of the vote in 1965, but which declined in the 1970s) has not been formally reconstituted after the 1980 military intervention.

The former general secretaries of the Turkish Labour Party (Nihat Sargin) and of the Turkish Communist Party (Haydar Kutlu) were arrested when they returned to Turkey in November 1987. The two parties have now merged to form a new Turkish United Communist Party (TBKP) which is still illegal. Sargin and Kutlu are now on trial.

A party called the Socialist Party was formed in February 1988, but attempts were immediately made to close it down as being unconstitutional. The founders of this party have also been put on trial; however, the party was allowed to operate in the 1987 referendum campaign.

111 WESTERN EUROPEAN POLITICAL GROUPINGS

Francis Jacobs

European People's Party — EPP
European Union of Christian Democrats — EUCD

Headquarters	:	16 rue de la Victoire, B-1060 Brussels (tel: 02-537 25 89)
EPP chairman	:	Jacques Santer
EUCD chairman	:	Emilio Colombo
EPP/EUCD secretary-general	:	Thomas Jansen

The European People's Party is the federation of Christian Democratic Parties in the European Community (see list below). It comprises 14 parties from 10 member states (There is no UK or Danish party).

The EPP member parties are also members of the European Union of Christian Democrats (see list below). The European Union of Christian Democrats forms the European wing of the Christian Democrat International.

The history of the EUCD/EPP goes back to the immediate postwar period. In 1947, the first meeting of the leaders of the Christian Democrat parties of France, Italy, Belgium, Luxembourg, Netherlands, Austria and Switzerland took place in Lucerne. The following May, in Chaudfontaine in Belgium, the constitutive congress of the "Nouvelles Equipes Internationales" took place. The next meeting, in January 1948, invited the German CDU to take part.

In 1965, the NEI became the European Union of Christian Democrats, with Mariano Rumor and Leo Tindemans as President and Secretary General respectively. In 1970, a "permanent conference" of the EUCD member parties and the Christian Democrat Parliamentary Group was set up.

Preparations were made for direct elections to the European parliament in 1975, and in 1976 the European People's Party — Federation of the Christian Democrat parties of the European Community was set up. Leo Tindemans was elected President. Its first political programme was adopted at a congress in April 1978.

Since that time, the EPP has adopted comprehensive joint political programmes for each of the elections to the European Parliament, in 1979 and 1984. The programme for the 1989 elections was put to a congress in Luxembourg in November 1988. The draft covers not just issues where the Community has a direct legislative responsibility, but is a statement of common political purpose. It was drawn up by a committee on which each party was represented.

The secretariat of the EPP is based in Brussels. It is merged with the secretariat of the EUCD and the two organizations have one general secretary. It employs eight full-time staff.

The main organs of the party are the president, elected every two years, the political bureau and the congress. The secretary-general and deputy secretaries-general are also elected every two years, as with the president, by the political bureau.

In addition, there is an informal grouping called the presidium, which consists of the president, the vice-presidents and office holders. There is a vice president from each member party and the chairperson of the parliamentary group is also a vice-president. The president of the EUCD is also a vice-president of the EPP. It normally convenes to prepare meetings of the political bureau which meets approximately eight times per year. The Congress meets every two years.

In addition to member parties, the EPP also has as members the parliamentary group in the European Parliament and a series of associations:

Women's Section
Young European Christian Democrats
European Association for Christian Democrat Local Government Representatives
European Association of the Middle Classes
European Union of Christian Democratic Workers

The income of the European People's Party is made up from subscriptions from member parties and the parliamentary group. The parliamentary group also makes a significant contribution in kind (facilities for meetings etc.).

Following Spanish and Portuguese accession to the Community, a difficulty has arisen in seeing a clear future role for the EUCD. It has member parties in countries which are unlikely to become members of the EEC, in the near future at any rate. The size of the parties vary considerably also as do their attitude to international relations. Therefore a review is now taking place of relations between the EPP and the EUCD, with the working group under instructions to report back to the political bureau both of the EPP and the EUCD, by autumn 1989.

The European People's Party sees itself as a supranational party. It has always been unequivocally committed to the principle of European unification.

Member parties of the EPP

Belgium:
Christelijke Volkspartij (CVP)
Parti Social Chrétien (PSC)
West Germany:
Christlich Demokratische Union (CDU)
Christlich Soziale Union (CSU)
France:
Centre des Démocrates Sociaux
Italy:
Democrazia Cristiana (DC)
Ireland
Fine Gael
Luxembourg:
Christlich Soziale Volkspartei (CSV)
Netherlands:
Christen Demokratisch Appel
Spain:
Democracia Cristiana
Catalonia: Uniò Democratica de Catalunya
Basque Country: Partido Nacionalista Vasco
Portugal:
Centro Democratico Social
Greece:
Nea Dimokratia

Member parties of the EUCD

Austria:
Österreichische Volkspartei
Cyprus:
Democraticos Synagermos
Malta:
Partit Nazzionalista
Norway:
Kristelig Folkeparti
San Marino:
Partito Democratico Cristiano Sammarinese
Sweden:
Kristen Demokratisk Samling
Switzerland:
Christlich-demokratische Volkspartei der Schweiz
Lebanon:
Union Chrétienne Démocrate Libanaise

The Christian Democrat Parliamentary Group in the Council of Europe is also represented as such in the EUCD.

Federation of Liberal, Democratic and Reformist Parties of the European Community — ELDR

Headquarters	: 97 rue Belliard, B-1040 Brussels (tel: 02-234 22 07)
President	: Colette Flesch
Secretary-general	: Mechtild von Alemann

The ELDR is the liaison mechanism of the Liberal and allied parties of the European Community. Its three central objectives are to seek a common position on all important matters affecting the European Community, to inform the public and involve it in the construction of a united and Liberal European Democracy and to support and co-ordinate the member parties in elections to the European Parliament. Its member parties undertake to fight such elections on a common platform.

The Federation of Liberal Parties of the European Community was established on March 26–27, 1976, at a constituent congress in Stuttgart, after four years of preparatory work. Fourteen parties attended from eight member states, of whom nine joined immediately and five later. The Stuttgart Declaration, which was adopted at the Congress, supported the concept of a European Union and set out a number of key political principles. At its congress in the Hague, later in 1976, the new grouping lengthened its name to that of Federation of Liberal and Democratic Parties.

In November 1976 one of the parties that had joined, the Mouvement des Radicaux de Gauche (MRG), suspended its membership. In 1979 one of the two Danish parties in the Federation, Radikale Venstre, decided to leave.

The Federation adopted a political programme and binding manifesto for its 1979 European Parliament election campaign, in which it used the short title ELD/LDE. The further enlargement of the Community subsequently led to new parties joining the Federation, the Hellenic Liberal Party from Greece in 1983, the Partido Reformista Democrático from Spain in 1985 and the Partido Social Democrata from Portugal in 1986. As a result of the latter's entry the grouping again changed its name to Federation of Liberal, Democratic and Reformist Parties of the European Community. In May 1988 the Progressive Democrats from Ireland were accepted as the latest member of the Federation. The Federation adopted its 1989 European election programme at a congress in Luxembourg in December 1988.

ELDR has an annual congress. Those attending include six representatives from each member state, and additional representatives from the national parties according to the number of votes that they won at their last national general election.

ELDR has an executive committee, which includes at least two members appointed by each ELDR party (larger parties may have more members, but there can never be more than four from any on party), six members directly elected at the congress, the chairman of the group in the European Parliament, ELDR members of the European Commission and one member appointed by the Liberal and Radical Youth Movement of the European Community. The executive committee meets at least four times a year, and provides for majority decision-making.

There is also a smaller bureau, consisting of the ELDR president (elected by the congress for a two-year term of office, and eligible for re-election up to a maximum of six years), three vice-presidents, the secretary-general and the treasurer.

Article 14 of the ELDR statutes provides that the federation is represented in the European Parliament by the Liberal, Democratic and Reformist Group.

There are also regular meetings of Liberal leaders in the European Community.

ELDR members

Belgium:
Parti Reformateur Libéral (PRL)
Partij voor Vrijheid en Vooruitgang (PVV)
Denmark:
Venstre
France:
Parti Républicain, Parti Radical
Federal Republic of Germany:
Freie Demokratische Partei (FDP)
Greece:
Hellenic Liberal Party
Ireland:
Progressive Democrats
Italy:
Partito Liberale Italiano (PLI)
Partito Repubblicano Italiano (PRI)
Luxembourg:
Demokratesch Partei (DP)
Netherlands:
Volkspartij voor Vrijheid en Democratie (VVD)
Portugal:
Partido Social-Democrata (PSD)
Spain:
Partido Reformista Democratico (PRD), which is linked to the much more powerful Catalan party, Convergencia Democrática de Catalunya
United Kingdom:
Social and Liberal Democrats
Alliance Party of Northern Ireland

Confederation of the Socialist Parties of the European Community

Headquarters : 89 rue Belliard,
B-1040 Brussels,
Belgium

(tel: 02-231 04 45,
230 44 00, 231 04 58)
Chairman : Guy Spitaels
Secretary-general : Mauro Giallombardo

The Confederation has 14 full members and six with observer status, and serves as a mechanism for co-operation between the Socialist parties of the European Community, the Socialist Group within the European Parliament and Socialist parties in neighbouring countries. It also works closely with the Socialist International.

Co-operation between European Socialist parties gradually intensified after the creation of the European Coal and Steel Community in 1951. In January 1957 a Liaison Bureau was established by Socialist parties from the six founding member states of the European Economic Community. On April 5, 1974, the bureau was turned into the current confederation. The British Labour Party did not become active in the confederation until 1976.

Disagreements between its member parties prevented the creation of a full-length electoral programme for the first direct elections to the European Parliament in 1979, but the Confederation did issue a political declaration and an appeal to the electorate. In 1984, however, a common manifesto was signed by all the member parties, although the British Labour Party did not subscribe to the sections on monetary integration and new Community financial resources, and neither it nor the Danish Social Democrats to the section calling for reinforcement of the powers of the European Parliament. In addition, the two Italian member parties made a special declaration of their support for the European Parliament's Draft Treaty on European Unity.

The Confederation's highest authority is its congress, which is normally held every two years, and must also be held at least six months before each European Parliament election. Those attending the Congress include delegates with voting rights and those with consultative status. The former include 15 delegates from each of the Federal Republic of Germany, France, Italy, and the United Kingdom, 12 from Spain and seven from each of Belgium, Netherlands and Portugal, five from each of Denmark and Ireland and three from Luxembourg. Individual parties are also entitled to additional delegates equivalent to half the number of their members in the European Parliament.

The delegates with consultative status include the members of the Socialist Group in the European Parliament, three representatives of each observer party, two representatives of recognized Socialist associations and representatives from Socialist International member parties or organizations.

One of the tasks of the congress is to elect the Confederation's chairman for a two-year term.

The full members of the Confederation's bureau consist of its chairman, two representatives of each member party and the chairman of the Socialist Group in the European Parliament. Participants with consultative status include one representative of each observer party and each recognized Socialist association, the members of the Bureau of the Socialist Group in the European Parliament, the Socialist members of the European Commission, a representative of the Socialist International and the chairman of the Socialist Group of the Parliamentary Assembly of the Council of Europe. The bureau meets at least four times a year and among its tasks are to elect four vice-chairmen and to appoint the confederation's secretary-general.

A party leaders' conference may also be convened.

The Confederation does not see itself as a supranational party. Article 7 of its statutes calls for its political decisions to be taken on the basis of consensus. It is much more divided than the EPP or the ELDR on the issue of European integration, with some of its members in favour of full European Union and others of continued co-operation between sovereign member states.

Members of the Confederation

Belgium:
Parti Socialiste, Socialistische Partij
Denmark:
Socialdemokratiet
Federal Republic of Germany:
Sozialdemokratische Partei Deutschlands
France:
Parti Socialiste
Greece:
PASOK
Ireland:
The Labour Party
Italy:
Partito Socialista Italiano
Partito Socialista Democrático Italiano
Luxembourg:
Letzeburger Sozialistesch Arbechter Partei (LSAP)
Netherlands:
Partij van de Arbeid
Portugal:
Partido Socialista
Spain:
Partido Socialista Obrero Español (PSOE)
United Kingdom:
Labour Party

Social Democratic and Labour Party (SDLP)

Parties with observer status of the Confederation

Austria:
Sozialistische Partei Österreichs
Israel:
Israel Labour Party
Malta:
Malta Labour Party
Norway:
Det Norske Arbeiderparti
Sweden:
Sveriges Socialdemokratiska Arbetareparti
Switzerland:
Sozialdemokratische Partei der Schweiz

European Democratic Union — EDU

Headquarters	: Tivoligasse 73, A-1120 Vienna, Austria (tel: 43-222-87 16 79 or 87 16 84)
Chairman	: Alois Mock
Executive secretary	: Dr Andreas Khol

The EDU is a working association of European right-of-centre parties which meet to exchange ideas and establish common positions on important policy problems. Its full members and permanent observers include representatives of several political families, but especially Conservatives and Christian Democrats (who are normally also members of the EPP and EUCD). It has a much looser structure than, for example, the EPP and ELDR, and the decisions at its annual leaders' conference are taken by unanimity.

The EDU was found on April 24, 1978, at Klessheim, near Salzburg, and the Klessheim Declaration was its first statement of principles. It was chaired by Josef Taus of the Austrian ÖVP from 1978–79, and since then has be chaired by Alois Mock, also of the ÖVP.

The EDU party leaders' conference is held on an annual basis. It elects the EDU chairman for a two-year renewable term of office. The EDU's steering committee prepares the conference and also runs the EDU between conferences. It meets at least three times a year and comprises the chairman, vice-chairman and treasurer of the EDU (also elected by the conference), the executive secretary (chosen by the chairman) and the secretary-generals of the member parties. It may also establish working committees and expert groups consisting of parliamentarians and specialists and charged with examining specific problems.

The first EDU parliamentarians' conference was held in 1986, and these are now planned to be held on a biannual basis. There is also an EDU finance ministers conference.

The EDU also establishes fact-finding missions, and produces a considerable number of publications.

The organizations which have permanent observer status with the EDU include the European Youth Community of Europe (DEMYC), the European Democratic Students (EDS), the European Medium and Small Business Union (EMSU), the European Union of Women and the European Democratic Groups (the conservative grouping in the European Parliament).

EDU member parties

Austria:
Österreichische Volkspartei (ÖVP)
Cyprus:
Dimokratikos Synagermos (DISY)
Denmark:
Det Konservative Folkeparti
Denmark (Faroes):
Folkaflokkurin
Finland:
Kansallinen Kokoomus
France:
Rassemblement pour la République
Centre National des Indépendants et Paysans
Federal Republic of Germany:
Christlich Demokratische Union (CDU)
Christlich-Soziale Union (CSU)
Greece:
Nea Dimokratia
Italy:
Tiroler Trentino Volkspartei — Europäische Union (TTVP-EU)
Liechtenstein:
Vaterländische Union (VU)
Fortschrittliche Bürgerpartei (FBP)
Norway:
Høyre
Portugal:
Partido do Centro Democratico e Social (CDS)
Spain:
Partido Popular
Sweden:
Moderata Samlingspartiet
Turkey:
Anavatan Partisi (ANAP)
United Kingdom:
Conservative Party

Parties with EDU permanent observer status

Finland:
Svenska Folkepartiet

France:
Union pour la Démocratie Française (UDF)
Italy:
Südtiroler Volkspartei (SVP)
Luxembourg:
Parti Chrétien Social (PCS)
Malta:
Partit Nazzjonalista
Switzerland:
Christlich-Demokratische Volkspartei (CVP)

The European Greens

Address   : c/o Agalev,
                  Tweekerkenstraat
                  78, B-1050 Brussels,
                  Belgium
Co-secretaries : Willy de Backer
                  (Belgium)
                  Per Gahrton
                  (Sweden)
                  Sara Parkin
                  (United Kingdom)

A Federation of European Greens was launched in Brussels in January 1984 on the basis of an earlier Co-ordination Bureau, which had included the Dutch and Italian Radicals as well as a number of emerging Green parties.

The Radicals were, however, excluded from the new Federation, and there were further disputes in March 1984 over the status of the Dutch Green Progressive Accord, to which various Green parties objected because of the Dutch Communist Party's participation. The European Parliament elections have been an important catalyst for Green party co-operation, and in 1984 a programme of common principles was adopted.

Member parties

Austria:
"Grüne Alternativen
Belgium:
Ecolo
Agalev
Denmark:
De Grønne
Finland:
Vihrea Liitto
France:
Les Verts (Confédération Ecologiste - parti Ecologiste)
Federal Republic of Germany:
Die Grünen
Ireland:
Green Alliance (Comhaontas Glas)

Italy:
Lista Verde
Luxembourg:
Dei Grëng Alternativ
Netherlands:
De Groenen

European Free Alliance

The European Free Alliance is a mechanism for co-operation between European regionalist and nationalist parties who seek greater autonomy or independence outside the existing framework of European nation states. They advocate a federal Europe of the peoples, with a second European Chamber to represent ethnic and regional communities in addition to the first chamber of directly elected members. They call for protection and propagation of minority languages and cultures. They believe in decentralization and in strong regional and social policies.

Three members from parties associated with the European Free Alliance were elected to the European Parliament in 1984 (two from the Flemish Volksunie and one from the Partito Sardo d'Azione), and they were subsequently joined after the 1987 Spanish election to the European Parliament by a member from the Basque party, Eusko Alkartasuna.

The Bureau of the European Free Alliance also includes five other members, and a secretary.

The parties and groups which have participated in the European Free Alliance include:

Belgium:
Volksunie
Partei der deutschsprachigen Belgier
France:
(i) Brittany: Union Démocratique Bretonne; Parti pour l'organization d'une Bretagne libre
(ii) Corsica: Unione di U populu Corsu
(iii) Other regions: Elsass-Lothringischer Volksbund; Vlaams Federalistische Partij (French Flanders); Volem Viure al Pais (occitania)
Italy:
Union Valdôtaine
Partito Sardo d'Azione
Movimento Friuli
Slovenska Skupnost
Movimento Autonomista Occitano
Netherlands:
Fryske Nasjonale Partij
Spain:
(i) Basque Country: Partido Nacional Vasco PNV); Eusko Alkartasuna
(ii) Catalonia: Convergencia Democrática de Catalunya (CDC)

United Kingdom:
(i) Scotland: Scottish National Party (SNP)
(ii) Wales: Plaid Cymru
(iii) Cornwall: Mebyon Kernow

Political groupings within the European Parliament

The European Parliament is the successor to the Common Assembly of the Coal and Steel Community, which was in existence from 1952 to 1957 and included 78 members from six member states (all nominated from national parliaments).

After the establishment of the European Economic Community and of the European Atomic Energy Community in 1958 a European Parliament was set up with 142 members, again nominated from six member states' parliaments. With enlargement of the Community in 1973 its membership increased to 198.

Since 1979 the European Parliament has been directly elected. The elections are held over a four-day period in June every five years. A uniform electoral system has not yet been established, and national provisions still prevail. The dual mandate (members who sit both in the European Parliament and in their national parliaments) has become increasingly rare.

Elections for the presidency of the European Parliament are held every two-and-a-half years. The elected vice-presidents of the parliament form its bureau. The enlarged bureau consists of the bureau and the chairmen of the political groups. The parliament also has a series of permanent committees. The plenary sessions are currently held in Strasbourg and the committee meetings mainly in Brussels. The majority of parliament's staff are based in Luxembourg.

The European Parliament's powers have gradually increased. It gradually came to be more systematically consulted on most European Community legislation, and also gained considerable budgetary powers. Its powers were further extended after the adoption of the Single European Act, which reinforced its legislative role in particular.

After the first direct elections in 1979 its membership was increased from 198 to 410, a figure which rose to 434 after Greek entry in the community in 1981. After Spain and Portugal joined the Community, the number of members increased to its present figure of 518; France, Federal Republic of Germany, Italy and United Kingdom 81 each (of which three for Northern Ireland); Spain 60; Netherlands 25; Greece, Portugal and Belgium 24 each; Denmark 16; Ireland 15 and Luxembourg 6.

The Common Assembly first authorized the creation of political groups in 1953, and ever since then they have played a central role. From 1953 to 1958 the minimum number to form such a groups was nine. This was increased to 17 from 1958 to 1965, when it was again reduced to 14. After 1973 the minimum necessary was only 10 if a group had members from at least three countries. After 1979 an attempt to raise the minimum threshold was successfully resisted. A group can now be formed by 21 members from one member state, 15 from two or 10 from three. The groups have not yet become fully fledged European political parties as some had predicted, and are often internally divided on national or other lines, although some groups are more cohesive than others.

The current groups in the European Parliament are the Socialist Group, the Group of European People's Party, the European Democratic Groups, the Communist and Allies Group, the Liberal Democratic and Reformists Group, the Group of European Democratic Alliance, the Rainbow Groups and the Groups of the European Right. The remaining members are non-attached. A Technical Co-ordination Groups was briefly established in 1987 (a successor to a similar group which existed in the 1979–84 parliament), but it soon collapsed.

Socialist Group

Secretary-general : Paolo Falcone
Current membership : 166

The Socialist Group was first founded in June 1953 with 23 members. It was the second largest group behind the Christian Democrats until 1976 (apart from the years 1959–62 when it was also behind the Liberals). Since 1976 it has always been the largest group in the parliament, if only by a narrow margin until Spanish accession to the Community gave it a large number of new recruits. Its last three chairmen have been Ludwig Fellermeier (German SPD, 1975–79), Ernest Glinne (Parti Socialiste of Belgium, 1979–84) and Rudi Arndt (German SPD, 1984–89). There was one Socialist president of the Common Assembly, Paul Henri Spaak (Belgian Socialist 1953–54) and there have been three Socialist presidents of the European Parliament, Walter Behrendt (German SPD, 1971–73), Georges Spénale (French Socialist, 1975–77) and Piet Dankert (PvdA, Netherlands, 1982–84).

Member parties (1984–89 parliament)
Belgium:
Parti Socialiste, Socialistische Partij

Denmark:
Socialdemokratiet
France:
Parti Socialiste
Federal Republic of Germany:
Sozialdemokratische Partei Deutschlands (SPD)
Greece:
PASOK
Italy:
Partito Socialista Italian (PSI)
Partito Socialist Democrático Italiano (PSDI)
Luxembourg:
Letzeburger Sozialistesch Arbechterpartei (LSAP)
Netherlands:
Partij van de Arbeid (PvdA)
Portugal:
Partido Socialista
Spain:
Partido Socialista Obrero Español (PSOE)
United Kingdom:
Labour Party
Social Democratic and Labour Party (SDLP)

Group of the European People's Party

Secretary-general : Sergio Guccione
Current membership : 115

The Christian Democratic Group was founded in June 1953 with 38 members, and remained the largest group until 1976 when it was overtaken by the Socialists. In July 1979 it changed its name to the Group of the European People's Party. Its most recent chairmen have been Egon Klepsch (German CDU, 1977–82 and 1984–present) and Paolo Barbi (Italian DC, 1982–84).

Over half of the presidents of the common assembly and later of the parliament have been members of the group; Alcide de Gasperi (Italian DC, 1954), Giuseppe Pella (Italian DC, 1954–56), Hans Furler (German CDU, 1956–58 and 1960–62), Robert Schuman (MRP, France, 1958–60), Jean Duvieusart (PSC, Belgium, 1964–65), Victor Leemans (CVP Belgium, 1965–66), Alain Poher (MRP, France 1966–69), Mario Scelba (DC, Italy, 1969–71), Emilio Colombo (DC, Italy, 1977–79) and Pierre Pflimlin (MRP, France, 1984–86).

Member parties (1984–89 parliament)
Belgium:
Christleijke Volkspartij (CVP)
Parti Social Chrétien (PSC)
Denmark:
Centrum-Demokraterne
France:
Centre des Démocrates Sociaux; some other

members from the list of the Union pour la Démocratie Française (UDF)
Federal Republic of Germany:
Christlich Demokratische Union (CDU)
Christlich Soziale Union (CSU)
Greece:
Nea Dimokratia (ND)
Ireland:
Fine Gael
Italy:
Democrazia Cristiana (DC)
Südtiroler Volkspartei (SVP)
Luxembourg:
Christlich Soziale Volkspartei (CSV)
Netherlands:
Christen Demokratisch Appel (CDA)
Portugal:
Centro Democratico Social (CDS)
Spain:
Unio Democrática de Catalunya

European Democratic Group

Secretary-general   : Harald Rømer
Current membership : 66

The European Conservative Group was founded in January 1973 with 20 members. In July 1979 it changed its name to the European Democratic Group. When Spain joined the Community, the group was reinforced by members from Alianza Popular (now Partido Popular). Its only member from the official Unionist Party of Northern Ireland (John Taylor) left the group in protest at the Anglo-Irish Agreement.

The group has had five chairmen since its foundation, all from the British Conservative Party (Sir Peter Kirk, 1973–77, Sir Geoffrey Rippon, 1977–79, Sir James Scott-Hopkins 1979–82, Sir Henry Plumb, 1982–86 and Christopher Prout, 1986–present). It has had one president of the European Parliament, Sir Henry (now Lord) Plumb, from 1986–89.

Member parties (1984–89 parliament)

United Kingdom:
Conservative Party
Spain:
Partido Popular
Denmark:
Det Konservative Folkparti

Communist and Allies Group

Secretary-general   : Gérard Laprat
Current membership : 48

The group was founded in October 1973

with 14 members. Its three chairmen (Giorgio Amendola, 1973–80, Guido Fanti 1980–84 and Gianni Cervetti 1984–89) have all come from the Italian PCI. The group is the least cohesive of the major groups in that it does not issue common electoral manifestos, and practically never holds joint group meetings (being divided between Orthodox Communists, Eurocommunists and left Socialists, and between those broadly in favour of the European Community and those opposed).

Member parties (1984–89 parliament)

France:
Parti Communiste Français (PCF)
Italy:
Partito Comunista Italiano (PCI) (including independents elected on Communist list)
Greece:
Kommounistiko Komma Ellados (KKE)
Eliniki Aristera (EAR)
Denmark:
Socialistisk Folkeparti (SF)
Portugal:
Partido Comunista Portugues (PCP)
Spain:
Izquierda Unida (one member from Partido Comunista de España, one from the Partido Acción Socialista and one from the Partit Socialista Unificat de Catalunya)

Liberal, Democratic and Reformist Group

Secretary-general   : Dominique Cattet
Current membership : 44

The Liberal and Allies Group was founded with 11 members in June 1953. It was generally the third largest grouping until direct elections in 1979, with the exception of the period 1960–62 when it had the second largest number of members (in 1961–62 43 out of the then total of 140 members, compared to 44 out of 518 today). The group included the French Gaullists until 1965, when they founded their own separate European Democratic Union.

The group changed its name to the Liberal and Democratic Group in November 1976. In 1986 the name was again extended to its current one after the arrival within the group of the Portuguese Social Democrats. Two of the major ELDR parties are not represented in the parliament, the Liberals (now the Social and Liberal Democrats) in the United Kingdom, and the FDP in Germany.

The last two chairmen of the Liberal Group have been Martin Bangemann (FDP, Germany, 1979–84) and Simone Veil (UDF, France,

1984–present). There have been three Liberal presidents of the European Parliament; Gaetano Martino (PLI, Italy, 1962–64), Cornelis Berkhouwer (VVD, Netherlands, 1973–75) and Simone Veil (UDF, France, 1979–82).

Member parties (1984–89 parliament)

Belgium:
Parti des Reformes et de la Liberté (PRL)
Partij voor Vrijheid en Vooruitgang (PVV)
Denmark:
Venstre (Danmarks Liberale Parti)
France:
Union pour la Démocratie Française (UDF)
Parti Républicain
Parti Radical
Parti Social Democrate
Ireland:
Independent MEP (T. J. Maher)
Italy:
Partito Liberale Italiano (PLI)
Partito Repubblicano Italiano (PRI)
Luxembourg:
Demokratesch Partei (DP)
Netherlands:
Volkspartij voor Vrijheid en Democratie (VVD)
Portugal
Partido Social Democrata (PSD)
Spain:
Convergencia Democrática de Catalunya (CDC)

Group of the European Democratic Alliance (RDE)

Secretary-general   : Thomas Earlie
Current membership : 29

The French Gaullists were originally in the Liberal and Allies group, but left it in January 1965, when they founded the European Democratic Union with 15 members. In 1973 five members of the Fianna Fáil Party from Ireland joined the group, which changed its name to the European Progressive Democrats. After 1979 the group was joined by Winnie Ewing of the Scottish National Party and by a member from the Danish Progress Party. The group subsequently changed its name to its present title. The group has been chaired by Christian de la Malène (French RPR) since 1975.

Member parties (1984–89 parliament)

France:
Rassemblement pour la République (RPR)
Greece:
Independent member (Ioannis Boutos)

Ireland
Fianna Fáil
United Kingdom:
Scottish National Party

Rainbow Group

This group was founded after the 1984 European elections. As its name implies it is a loose coalition of heterogeneous parties and political groupings, although it is more structured than its predecessor in the 1979–84 parliament (the Group for the Technical Co-ordination and Defence of Independent Groups and Members).

The Rainbow Group's main components are the members of the European Free Alliance (a coalition of regionalist and nationalist parties — see separate entry), the Green Alternative European Link (GRAEL — a coalition of green and left radical parties) and the four members of the People's Movement against the EEC in Denmark.

The spokespersons for the Rainbow Group rotate every three months.

Members (1984–89 parliament)

(i) *European Free Alliance*
Belgium: Volksunie (Flanders)
Italy: Partito Sardo d'Azione (whose representative was meant to cede his seat to a member of the Union Valdôtaine)
Spain: Eusko Alkartasuna (Basque country)

(ii) *Green Alternative European Link (GRAEL)*
Belgium: Agalev (The Walloon Green Party, Ecolo is also a member of GRAEL, but its former representative Roelant du Vivier has left the party and sits outside GRAEL within the Rainbow Group)
Federal Republic of Germany: Die Grünen
Italy:Democrazia Proletaria
Netherlands: Groen Progressief Akkoord (coalition of PPR, PSP, CPN and Green platform Nederland)
(iii) Denmark - Volkebevaegelsen mod EF.

Group of the European Right

Secretary-general   : Jean Marc Brissaud
Current membership : 16

This group was founded after the 1984 European elections. Jean Marie Le Pen has been its only chairman. It lost one member when Olivier d'Ormesson left the group, but it was joined by John Taylor of the Official Unionist Party, who had quit the EDG in protest at the Anglo–Irish Agreement.

Member parties (1984–89 parliament)

France:
Front National
Greece:
Ethniki Politiki Enosis (EPEN)
Italy:
Movimento Sociale Italiano-Destra Nazionale (MSI-DN)
United Kingdom:
John Taylor of Official Unionist Party.

Independents

In early 1989 there were 14 such members, of whom six were from the Spanish CDS and three from Italian Radicals.

Belgium:
Jef Ulburghs (elected on Socialist Party list)
France:
Olivier d'Ormesson (formerly of Group of the European Right)
Italy
Partito Radicale
Netherlands:
Staatkundig Gereformeerde Partij (SGP)
Spain:
Centro Democrático y Social (CDS)
Herri Batasuna (Basque Country)
United Kingdom:
Ian Paisley (Democratic Unionist Party)

Political groupings within the Nordic Council

Headquarters : P. O. Box 19506,
S-10432 Stockholm
(tel: 46 10 78 -
14 34 20)

The Nordic Council was established in 1952 as a body for co-operation between the parliaments of Denmark, Iceland, Norway and Sweden, and was subsequently joined by Finland (in 1955). The Faroes and Greenland have their own separate delegations within that of Denmark, and the Åland Islands within that of Finland. In the early 1970s a Nordic Council of Ministers was also established.

The 87 members of the Nordic Council are nominated from national parliaments on the following numerical basis, Danish *Folketing* 16, Faroese *Logting* two, Greenland's *Landsting* two, Finnish *Eduskunta* 18, Ålands *Landsting*

two, Icelandic *Althing* seven, Norwegian *Storting* 20 and Swedish *Riksdag* 20. The Council has plenary meetings, and has also established a number of committees. It has a Bureau of 10 members.

There are four political groupings within the Nordic Council.

Conservative Group
(contact number Stockholm 08-23 61 80)

Denmark:
Det Konservative Folkeparti
Finland:
Kansallinen Kokoomus (KOK)
Åland:
Frisinnad Samverkan
Iceland:
Sjálfstaedisflokkurinn
Norway:
Høyre
Sweden:
Moderata Samlingspartiet

Centre Group
(contact number Stockholm 08-786 44 60)

Denmark:
Det Radikale Venstre
Centrum-Demokraterne
Kristeligt Folkeparti
Venstre
Finland:
Keskustapuolue
Suomen Kristilliinen Liitto
Svenska Folkpartiet i Finland
Åland:
Ålandsk Center
Liberalerna på Åland
Iceland:
Framsóknarflokkurrinn
Norway:
Senterpartiet
Kristelig Folkeparti
Sweden:
Centerpartiet
Folkpartiet
Faroes:
Sambandsflokurinn
Greenland:
Atassut

Social Democratic Group
(contact number Stockholm 08-786 48 58)

Denmark:
Socialdemokratiet
Finland:
Suomen Sosialidemokraattinen Puolue (SSDP)
Åland:
Ålands Socialdemokrater

Iceland:
Althyduflokkurinn
Norway
Det Norske Arbeiderparti
Sweden
Sveriges Socialdemokratiska Arbetareparti

The Siumut party from Greenland also has links with this Group.

Left Socialist Group
(contact number Helsinki 90-77 08 404)

Denmark:
Socialistisk Folkeparti
Faroes:
Tjódveldisflokkurin
Finland:
Suomen Kansan Demokraattinen Liitto (SKDL)
Iceland:
Althydubandalag
Norway:
Sosialistisk Venstreparti
Sweden:
Vänsterpartiet Kommunisterna

Political groupings within the Council of Europe

Address : B. P. 431 RG, F-67006 Strasbourg Cedex (tel: 88 61 49 61)

There are currently 172 members of the Parliamentary Assembly of the Council of Europe, 124 from European Community countries and 48 from other European countries. There are also 172 substitutes. The representatives and substitutes are nominated from among members of national parliaments. Regular plenary sessions are held in Strasbourg (in the same chamber as that where the European Parliament holds its plenaries).

The distribution of members and substitutes is as follows:

European Community countries

- France, Federal Republic of Germany, Italy, United Kingdom (each entitled to 18 representatives and 18 substitutes);
- Spain (12 representatives and 12 substitutes);
- Belgium, Greece, Netherlands and Portugal (each entitled to seven representatives and seven substitutes);
- Denmark (five representatives and five substitutes);
- Ireland (four representatives and four substitutes);
- Luxembourg (three representatives and three substitutes).

Other European countries

- Turkey (12 representatives and 12 substitutes);
- Austria, Sweden and Switzerland (each entitled to six representatives and six substitutes);
- Norway (five representatives and five substitutes);
- Iceland, Malta and Cyprus (each entitled to three representatives and three substitutes. Cyprus currently only sends one representative and one substitute);
- Liechtenstein and San Marino (each entitled to two representatives and two substitutes).

The rules of procedure of the Parliamentary Assembly permit the formation of political groups, which must consist of not less than 15 representatives or substitutes of at least three different nationalities. There are currently five such groups.

Socialist Group

Secretariat : Mme Albanese, Council of Europe, Office 4150, Strasbourg (tel: 88 61 49 61, extension 3322)

There are currently 112 representatives and substitutes in this group. Of the 60 full representatives 45 come from European Community countries and 15 from others. The chairman (1988) is Karl Ahrens of the German SPD.

Christian Democratic Union

Secretariat : M. Manfred-Christian Stricker, Council of Europe, Office 6147, Strasbourg (tel: 99 61 49 61, extension 3529)

There are currently 82 representatives and substitutes in this group. Of the 44 full representatives 33 come from European Community countries and 11 from others. The chairman (1988) is Adolfo Sarti of the Italian DC. One feature of this group is that it includes the representatives of both Liechtenstein political parties.

European Democratic Group

Secretariat   : Mme E. B. Nord,
          Council of Europe,
          Office 4055,
          Strasbourg
          (tel: 88 61 49,
          extension 3703)

This group is not parallel to that in the European Parliament and is more linked instead to EDU membership (apart from Christian Democratic members of the EDU). The French RPR, for example, is a member of the European Democratic Group in the Council of Europe. There are currently 63 representatives and substitutes in this group. Of the 32 full representatives 20 are from European Community countries and 12 from others. The chairman (1988) is Anders Björck of the Swedish Moderate (Conservative) Party.

Liberal, Democratic and Reformers' Group

Secretariat   : Peter Kallenberger,
          Council of Europe,
          Office 4117,
          Strasbourg
          (tel: 88 61 49 61,
          extension 2503)

Besides the ELDR parties, this group also includes representatives of the Centre Parties in Scandinavia (and the Progressive Party in Iceland). Unlike in the European Parliament, it also includes the Fianna Fáil members from Ireland. The group has 50 representatives and substitutes. Of its 24 full representatives 18 are from European Community countries and six from others. The Chairman (1988) is Björn Elmquist of the Danish Venstre Party.

Group of Communist and Allied

Secretariat   : Giuseppe Cannata,
          Council of Europe,
          Office 4154,

          Strasbourg
          (tel: 88 61 49 61,
          extension 3324)

As in the European Parliament, this group includes representatives of the Danish Socialist People's Party. The group has 17 representatives and substitutes. Of its eight representatives seven come from European Community countries and one (the new San Marino representative) comes from others. The Chairman (1988) is Carlos Carvalhas of the Portuguese Communist Party.

Others

There are also a number of representatives and substitutes (around 10 in 1989) who are not affiliated to any one political group. Only two, however, are full representatives (one from the German Grünen and one from the Turkish True Path Party).

Political groupings within the Western European Union

Tel: Paris 47 23 54 32

Representatives to the Parliamentary Assembly of Western European Union are nominated from among parliamentarians of the participating member countries (18 representatives and 18 substitutes from each of France, West Germany, Italy and the United Kingdom, seven representatives and seven substitutes from each of the Netherlands and Belgium and three representatives and three substitutes from Luxembourg). There are, however, only four groups, the Federated Group of Christian Democrats and European Democrats (this merged group is the largest in the Assembly with 42 full members), the Socialist Group (30 full members), the Liberal Group (nine full members) and the Communist Group (six full members, all Italians, with no French participants). There are also two non-attached members.

Index